CARAVAGGIO
and Pictorial Narrative

Dislocating the *Istoria*
in Early Modern Painting

HARVEY MILLER PUBLISHERS
An Imprint of Brepols Publishers
London/Turnhout

British Library Cataloguing in Publication Data
A catalogue record for this book
is available from the British Library
ISBN 978-1-905375-48-6

Printing and binding
by Grafikon, Oostkamp, Belgium

CARAVAGGIO
and
Pictorial Narrative

Dislocating the *Istoria*
in Early Modern Painting

Lorenzo Pericolo

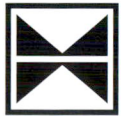

HARVEY MILLER PUBLISHERS

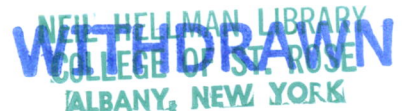

For Elizabeth Cropper
and Salvatore Settis

Table of Contents

ACKNOWLEDGMENTS   1

FOREWORD
Caravaggio and the *Istoria*   3

PART ONE

A Matter of Optics and Rhetoric: The Aporia of Pictorial Narrative Before,
During, and After Caravaggio's Time
Caravaggio's Nonsense   15

Chapter 1
The Glitches in Alberti's *Istoria*: The Human Figure Between Beauty and Reality . .   35

Chapter 2
The Glitches in Alberti's *Istoria*: Time and Action   67

Chapter 3
The False Dichotomy Between Telling and Showing: Beyond Alberti's *Istoria*   93

PART TWO

Blending Genres: Lyrical and Comical Interactions in Caravaggio's Early Paintings
Comedy of Errors   121

Chapter 4
Money and Seduction: Narrative Patterns in Caravaggio's Two Versions of
The Fortune Teller   135

Chapter 5
Behind the Comical Trick: Caravaggio's *The Cardsharps* and Giovan
Battista Marino's "Gioco di Primera"   157

Chapter 6
Love in the Mirror: A Comparative Reading of Titian's *Woman at Her Toilet*
and Caravaggio's *Conversion of Mary Magdalene*   177

PART THREE

The Misplaced Hero: The Challenge of the Istoria *in Caravaggio's Early
Religious Narratives*
Truth in Painting 199

Chapter 7
The Calling of Saint Matthew in Retrospective: Experimenting with Narrative
Disconnections 211

Chapter 8
"Completely Bereft of Action": Narrative Blindness and the Heroic Horse
in the Cerasi *Conversion of Saint Paul* 243

Chapter 9
Visualizing Appearance and Disappearance: Caravaggio's Two Versions
of *The Supper at Emmaus* 265

PART FOUR

*"With the Mind's Eye": Self-Representation and Self-Referentiality in
Caravaggio's Pictorial Narratives*
The Shaman Painter or The Metaphysics of Pictorial Invention 297

Chapter 10
Zuccari's Lantern: The Blind Spot of Painting in Caravaggio's *The Taking of Christ* . . 311

Chapter 11
The Other Michelangelo: The Weight of Composition and Artistic *Paragone* in
Caravaggio's *Entombment* 343

Chapter 12
The Impossible Banality of Representing Christ: Self-Parody and
Tragicomedy in Caravaggio's *Ecce Homo* 375

PART FIVE

*The Work of Memory: Variations on Themes and Telescopic Parallels in
Caravaggio's Late Pictorial Narratives*
Artistic Memory and the Invention of the *Istoria* 403

Chapter 13
Narratives of the *Non-Finito*: On Caravaggio's *Denial of Saint Peter, The Burial of
Saint Lucy,* and *The Resurrection of Lazarus* 415

Chapter 14
Piercing the Canvas: Painting and Meta-Narrative in Caravaggio's
The Incredulity of Saint Thomas and *The Martyrdom of Saint Ursula* 447

PART SIX

Reaction to Change: The Afterlife of Caravaggio's Poetics of Dislocation
The Black Tide of Caravaggio's Painting 481

Chapter 15
Blind and Deaf Actions: Cecco del Caravaggio's Chicago *Resurrection* 495

Chapter 16
The Antichrist of Spanish Painting: Diego Velázquez's *Supper at Emmaus*
and the Two Versions of *La Mulata* 517

Chapter 17
Without a Plot: Valentin de Boulogne's Liechtenstein *Merry Company with*
Fortune Teller 539

EPILOGUE

The End of Narrative? Afterthoughts on the Definition and Function of the *Istoria*
in an Age of Subjectivity 559

TABLE OF ILLUSTRATIONS 573

BIBLIOGRAPHY 589

INDEX 645

Acknowledgments

It makes sense that this project comes to an end where it first started five years ago, in Washington DC. I first arrived in the capital of the United States at the end of August 2005, and when I look back at the scholar I was, fresh from a very long experience of teaching and research in France, it feels as if a century has elapsed. It is extremely difficult for me to put into words how much friends and colleagues in North America have stimulated and reshaped my scholarship. In a sense, this book, better than any preliminary statement, proves their essential contribution to my intellectual interests, methodology, and personality. In these five years, I was awarded three prestigious grants to support and develop my Caravaggio project: in 2005-2006, I was Ailsa Mellon Bruce Senior Fellow at the Center for Advanced Study in the Visual Arts, Washington DC; in 2007-2008, I was Scholar in Residence at the Getty Research Institute, Los Angeles; and in 2007, I received a triennial fund from the Social Sciences and Humanities Research Council of Canada. Needless to say, without the generosity of these institutions the present volume could not have been finished within such a relatively short period. In 2008-2010, I was Visiting Scholar at the University of Toronto, where I wrote an essential part of this monograph: the warm comfort of my office at the University College's neo-Norman building made my sojourn a peaceful, thriving experience. Among the colleagues whose presence and example have constantly inspired or stimulated my work during this time, I would like to single out Charles Dempsey—a paradigm of rigorous and ever-vigorous scholarship; Alexander Nagel—a great interlocutor and bold thinker; and Philip Sohm—a real gentleman, both genuinely humble and intellectually stalwart. I am particularly grateful to Laurence Kanter and Larry Silver for their encouragement and sympathy. I could not send out this manuscript without gratefully mentioning the valuable advice or exquisite friendship of Carmen Bambach, Andaleeb Banta, Emanuele Cafagna, Faya Causey, the late Philip Conisbee, Nicola Courtright, Thomas Cummins, Lamia Doumato, Stephanie Dickey, Marzia Faietti, Gail Feigenbaum, Sarah Fraser, Daniela Gallo, Barbara Gaetghens, Thomas Gaetghens, Jack Greenstein, Michael Ann Holly, Étienne Jollet, Seadin Kolar, Bob La France, Karen Lang, Annick Lemoine, Peter Lukehart, Louis Marchesano, John Marciari, Theresa O'Malley, James Meyer, Greg Most, Keith Moxey, Alessandro Nova, Peter Parshall, Anna Maria Petrioli Tofani, Emily Pugh, Jessica Richardson, Philippe Sénéchal, Richard Spear, Victor Stoichita, David Stone, Mickaël Szanto, Naoko Takahatake, Helen Tangires, Devin Therien, Nancy Troy, Neal Turtell, and Christopher Wood. Aside from scrutinizing my English prose, Jennifer Ng has been an eager reader of this book in its multiple stages of production. Susan Wharton's editing has proved to be extremely helpful; I alone am responsible for any lapses that may remain. The diligent and perceptive eye of Alexandra Hoare has helped me detect potential sources of ambiguity and equivocation in the final proofs. My students at the University of Montreal have discussed with me many of the topics I deal with in this volume, making intriguing observations on Caravaggio's painting. Mickaël Bouffard and Sebastian Ferrero, my outstanding Ph.D. students, have followed the unfolding of my research with exceptional interest and enthusiasm. Since it has only recently been published, I have been unable properly to read, and value the originality of, Michael Fried's *The Moment of Caravaggio*, which I sincerely regret. I cannot thank enough Johan Van der Beke who, upon presentation of my Caravaggio project, was immediately convinced of its quality and agreed to have it published. In 2011, Salvatore Settis will be retiring from the Scuola Normale Superiore, Pisa, where he has served as director for eleven years. To stress Settis's outstanding scholarship in the domain of Greek, Roman, and Renaissance art is superfluous, his work being well known to scholars throughout the world. To mention his firm engagement in defending Italy's artistic patrimony is a necessary token of profound gratitude from any Italian citizen and, generally, from any lover of the arts. To say how much I learned from Settis as a young scholar at the Scuola Normale Superiore, and how much I continue to learn from him is nothing but a due act of acknowledgment. This book is therefore dedicated to him as well as to Elizabeth Cropper, an incomparable paragon of acumen, open-mindedness, and not least, morality. Throughout this monograph, but undoubtedly not enough, I have pointed out the importance to my research of Cropper's groundbreaking insights into early modern art. To a certain degree, this book results from an uninterrupted, sometimes tacit dialogue with her ideas of "novelty, imitation, and theft" in seventeenth-century Italian art. Most important, Cropper has provided a "globetrotter" like myself with invaluable gifts: those of friendship, trust, respect, and hospitality. I hope that the homage of this volume will express the extent of my gratitude, though I am afraid that nothing could satisfactorily do so. During all this time, I was able to count on the distant yet unflinching support and affection of my mother, Maria, my sister, Carmen, my brother-in-law, Pino, and my nephew and niece, Biagio and Roberta. They have been and still are the radiant sunshine of my days and the powerful lantern of my nights. The memory of my beloved father, Roberto, has all along emboldened, enlightened and occasionally comforted me.

Washington DC, August 2010

Foreword

Caravaggio and the *Istoria**

It does not seem that early modern pictorial narrative—the *istoria* as first expounded in Leon Battista Alberti's 1435 *De Pictura*—represents a topic of interest to contemporary scholarship. I find this indifference rather puzzling because painting is paradigmatically assimilated to narration by artists and art theorists from the fifteenth century onward: it is no overstatement to posit that the *istoria* is both the most earnestly reflected-upon pictorial institution of the early modern period, and the theoretical core that configures the notion and finality of art during the Renaissance and the seventeenth century.

That many early modern paintings are designed to narrate is either taken for granted or deemed irrelevant by scholars for one single reason: the structures and mechanisms of pictorial narrative do not appear to offer enough ground for analysis and interpretation. That is, examining the means by which an artist narrates through an image does not seem to affect the exegesis of the artwork's "content," the only element that lends itself to being easily decoded in terms of ideology, culture, society, and history. Moreover, the investigation of the narrative devices employed in the *istoria* demands not only a rigorous study of the image that many would liken to a formalist approach, but also an exploration of the visual tradition that, for many, would resemble an iconographical procedure. But formalism and iconography have lost much of their appeal among art historians. On the one hand, there is a widespread, albeit tacit, mistrust of images insofar as their interpretation is considered subjective and arbitrary: an attitude fully understandable in a culture, like ours, in which words through their propositional functionalities are the privileged tools of hermeneutical explanation. If dissecting and interpreting an image results in an oral or written discourse, then the discourse, and not the image, is the real factor of meaning: a paradox, since the discourse is perceived as unsuitable to "represent" the very image that has begotten it. In this light, the image becomes a distant and unreachable pre-text for an exegetical discourse regarded as the exclusive object of scholarly validation and criticism. Therefore, analyzing the image at best ranks as description: a piece of rhetorical—and not interpretive—*ekphrasis*.

On the other hand, the search for visual sources has been downgraded to a useless exercise of the eye: something that only connoisseurs—those hunters of styles and attributions!—and iconographers—the "outdated" Panofskian sect so fond of visual symbols!—continue to practice. In a sense, the disinterest for visual sources is intrinsically germane to the mistrust of images as "texts" of interpretation. In both cases, everything revolves around making the image serve as a criterion of clarification and exegesis in the scrutiny of the image itself and of other images. However, by renouncing a structural analysis of the image and the quest for its antecedents and analogs, art historians risk delegitimizing and de-historicizing the object of their own research. If the investigation of the image's structure is conceived as inefficient or unreliable in producing information with regard to an artistic discourse, then the history of images necessarily turns into an appendix of some other history: cultural, social, and so forth. By the same token, if the identification of the image's sources and parallels is discredited, mishandled or dismissed altogether, it follows

---

* All translations in this volume are mine unless otherwise indicated. All quotations from the Bible are taken from *The* *Catholic Study Bible: New American Bible*, eds. Donald Senior and John J. Collins (Oxford: Oxford University Press, 2006).

that the image has no history and ought to be observed and interrogated as an absolute: as if artists were harvested in isolation, without visual memory and outside iconic communication. In art as in physics, though, Lavoisier's principle rules: nothing is created or destroyed, but everything is transformed.

Given these premises, it is perhaps elementary that art historians have not concerned themselves with the study and interpretation of both the early modern *istoria* and its uses and elaborations by artists. It is indeed impossible to assess time and action, eurythmy and verisimilitude, causality and duration as evoked in pictorial narratives without tackling the specific structures and iconographical interrelations of images. The *istoria* has not mattered to scholars so far because its evaluation and exegesis, besides appearing to be pointless, have felt hermeneutically problematic.

Even less have Caravaggio's pictorial narratives mattered to art historians. This negligence is undoubtedly a major fault of contemporary scholarship. From Giovanni Baglione to Giovan Pietro Bellori, from Giulio Mancini to Francesco Albani, countless testimonies denounce Caravaggio's inability to execute an *istoria* worthy of the name. Obsessively and systematically, seventeenth-century artists and art theorists pour out their intolerance of, and revulsion at, Caravaggio's half-figures: these segments of bodies that, in their opinion, because they are blown out of proportion in a close-up view through vehement lighting, are fated to be disconnected or ill-coordinated in regard to pictorial action. Once again, while blaming Caravaggio's half-figures, all his detractors note that by no means can these aberrant, impaired, and truncated bodies adapt to an *istoria*, the noblest and paramount genre of painting or, more properly, the quintessence of painting itself. Yet, despite the impressive coherence of all these voices in condemning Caravaggio's misuse and misinterpretation of the *istoria*, scholars have underestimated, overlooked or disregarded the reasons for this criticism.

To my knowledge, only sporadically has Caravaggio's *istoria* drawn the attention of scholars.[1] In particular, two paintings by Caravaggio have raised questions about their narrative coherence: the 1599-1600 *Calling of Saint Matthew* and the 1601 Cerasi *Conversion of Saint Paul*. In the first case, a huge number of essays have been written about the nagging question of who is Matthew in the picture: for the most part, art historians have downplayed the scope of this issue by focusing on the saint's iconography in order to ascertain his true identity as depicted by Caravaggio. The second case is much more relevant from the viewpoint of art history; taking as a departure point Bellori's censure of *The Conversion of Saint Paul*—a picture "completely bereft of action"—Svetlana Alpers argued that Caravaggio's painting foreshadows the "art of describing" specific, in her view, to Dutch artists of the Golden Age: a pictorial model allegedly opposed to Alberti's *istoria*. In connection with Caravaggio's 1601 *Crucifixion of Saint Peter*, Alpers accordingly states:

> The stilled or arrested quality of these works [such as *The Crucifixion of Saint Peter*] is a symptom of a certain tension between the narrative assumptions of the art and an attentiveness to descriptive presence. There seems to be an inverse proportion between attentive description and action: attention to the surface of the world described is achieved at the expense of the representation of narrative action.[2]

---

1 In spite of dealing with the issue of dramatic action in Caravaggio's painting, Lechner 2006 argues naively and summarily, so that this essay does not truly represent an antecedent to the topic of this book.

2 Alpers 1983, xxi. Among the many reviews devoted to Alpers' book, I would like to single out, besides that of Louis Marin mentioned below: De Jongh 1984; Glynne 1984; Veltman 1984; Stumpel 1984; Marmer 1984; Gaskell 1984; Martin 1985;

Bialostocki 1985; Bruyn 1985; and Schneider 1988. Particularly relevant to the topic of this monograph are Ferdinando Bologna's insights into Alpers' book. See Bologna 1992, 172-90. An excellent series of discussions about the concept of realism in seventeenth-century Dutch art, especially with regard to Alpers' viewpoints, is to be found in Franits 1997.

Based upon the dichotomy of the descriptive and the narrative, Alpers' hermeneutics proves to be disputable on several accounts. As construed by Alpers, the "art of describing" is the domain of optical reproduction: the outside world with its minutest details imprints itself on the canvas as if impersonally and with the sole purpose of being discerned as it is. In other words, pictorial descriptiveness tends to cancel out composition in its broadest sense: the artist does not arrange, but exclusively frames figures and objects within the canvas. I seriously doubt that Caravaggio, Velázquez or Vermeer have ever reproduced a piece of reality as they saw it and merely with the intention to copy it: the pictorial image, by definition, is the product of a visual montage that necessarily, and ever so imperceptibly, severs the umbilical cord linking reality to fiction. More important, as is well known to narratologists in the fields of literature and cinema studies, the descriptive may well qualify as a mode of the narrative. Through descriptions, for instance, narrators modify, among other things, the duration of the story. In his 1972 *Discours du récit*, Gérard Genette brilliantly analyzes the ways in which Marcel Proust, in *À la recherche du temps perdu*, stretches the descriptive elements of his "detailed scenes" in order to create narrative foci fraught with dramatic and temporal allusions in constant dialogue with the mainstream story.[3] With its emphasis on the human body, Caravaggio's "descriptiveness" vigorously interfaces with action by manipulating the viewer's perception of the painted narrative. To put it more clearly, pictorial description does not annul narrative: among its effects, it brings about the stillness or arrestedness remarked upon by Alpers, which contributes to an impression of diluted duration within the momentum of the represented action.

As far as I am concerned, the only scholar who has fully understood the importance of the *istoria* in Caravaggio's painting is Louis Marin.[4] Perhaps because he was well acquainted with seventeenth-century French Academic doctrines, Marin was particularly attuned to the great difference embodied by Nicolas Poussin's model of the *istoria* when compared to Caravaggio's pictorial narratives. In his 1977 *Détruire la peinture*, Marin indeed contrasts Poussin's "prospect" with Caravaggio's "aspect": that is, painting as "theory" as opposed to painting as optical mimesis. In conformity with Alberti's concept of the *istoria*, Poussin interprets the painting as the legitimate space of an enunciative representation. Here is Marin's definition of Poussin's pictorial narrative:

> The painting is—must legitimately be—the text of a story whose "characters," or writing, are signs both formal and expressive: formal signs or disposition—the figures' arrangement within the space of the representation scene; expressive signs, which are the expressions, gestures, gazes, movements, and attitudes that exactly signify the affects and passions of the soul. (…) If marshaled in the picture's space, formal signs and expressive signs constitute a legible text; they obey syntactic rules that are not those of the narrative syntax specific to the story represented in the painting, but that are properly figurative. It is therefore necessary to elucidate the rules of this syntax but, as we already know, although the rules are different, the final product will be the same: the representation appropriates its story, and the story strictly governs its representation. Read the painting as the text of the story in representation or as the representation of the story's text: they are at once different yet interchangeable.[5]

3   See Genette 2007, esp. 95 ff. For description in narrative, see also Bal 1997, 36-43.

4   For Louis Marin's aesthetics and theory, see the numerous essays contained in Beyer et al. 2006.

5   Marin 1977, 44: "Le tableau est—c'est-à-dire doit être légitimement—le texte d'une histoire dont les "caractères," l'écriture, sont des signes à la fois formels et expressifs: signes formels ou la disposition—distribution des figures dans l'espace de la scène représentative; signes expressifs, il s'agit des "expressions," gestes, regards, mouvements, attitudes qui sont les signes exacts des affects, des passions de l'âme. (…) Si donc distribués dans l'espace d'un tableau, signes formels et signes expressifs constituent un texte lisible, cela signifie qu'ils obéissent à des règles syntaxiques qui ne sont pas celles de la syntaxe narrative du récit que le tableau représente mais qui sont proprement figuratives. Il faut donc essayer d'élucider les règles de cette syntaxe mais, nous le savons déjà, quoique différentes, leur produit final sera identique: la représentation s'approprie *son* histoire; l'histoire contraint rigoureusement *sa*

Relying on Charles Le Brun's analysis of Poussin's *The Israelites Gathering the Manna in the Desert*—a text that does not entirely reflect Poussin's theory, but glosses it—Marin concludes that, as a pictorial narrative, the *istoria* must represent an action unfolding over time but contained within the strictures of the "pictorial instant":

> The iconic narrative is the representation of the moment–instant of narration configured into a model of atemporal intelligibility. The disposition of the bodies– figures within a plane schematically parallel to the pictorial screen is the fundamental device through which to construct this narrative model, the atemporal present of the instant of representation, the only means available to the classical painter to represent, in its topographic circumstances, a potential narrative transforming the description of the logical relations of space inside the picture into a reading procedure, actively performed [by the viewer], along an axis before/after.[6]

Although Marin's is a rather reductive and not entirely accurate interpretation of the *istoria*'s temporality and of the techniques through which painters enforce it—as I will explain in Part One of this volume—it is noteworthy that he intuits a fact essential to the topic of this book: that Poussin's model of pictorial narrative responds to Caravaggio's by asserting itself as its antithesis. If, according to Marin, Poussin's "representation" separates the referent from its sign, the model from its copy, thereby fostering a detached, spiritual, and intellectual reception of the artwork, Caravaggio's "reproduction" achieves the exact opposite:

> By suppressing the distance between the model and the copy, the *trompe-l'oeil* ensnares the sensitive gaze into the appearance–essence, coaxes the body–eye into fascination with the double and the simulacrum, into stupefaction and, accordingly, the effect it determines is not one of contemplation, of "theory," but of surreality: an impure mixture of angst and petrifaction.[7]

In other words—and at the cost of simplifying the complexity and subtlety of Marin's thoughts—it is evident, upon these assumptions, that Caravaggio's painting collapses temporality by reducing it to the petrifying instant of the ineffable representation: the tremendous yet wonderful unveiling of fiction's fictiveness as it dawns upon the viewer's astonished mind. In Marin's own terms, "in the representation, the instant of vision, the moment of the pulsing color whose effect results in stupefaction and the petrifaction of the narrative representation, explodes."[8] By perfecting the mimetic functionalities of painting, Caravaggio's color technique channels art's prodigious capacity

représentation. Lisez le tableau comme le texte de l'histoire en représentation mais aussi comme la représentation du texte de l'histoire, à la fois *différents* et *substituables*: maîtrise du plus savant des peintres." Besides being interested in seventeenth-century narrative art, Marin consecrated many studies, gathered in a single volume, to the notion and practice of representation in the Italian quattrocento. See Marin 1989.

6   Marin 1977, 70: "Le récit iconique est la représentation d'un moment-instant narratif disposé en forme de modèle d'intelligibilité a-chronique. La disposition des corps-figures dans un plan schématiquement parallèle au plan de l'écran plastique est le moyen fondamental de la construction de ce modèle narratif, du présent intemporel de l'instant de représentation, le seul qui soit laissé au peintre classique de représenter, et de ses circonstances topographiques, un récit potentiel convertissant la description des relations spatiales

logiques dans le tableau, en une succession de lecture selon l'avant et l'après dans sa réception active."

7   Ibidem, 121: "L'imitation en effet garde la distance de la copie au modèle et propose à l'inspection de l'esprit, à la théorie, la loi de maîtrise de la mimésis. Le trompe-l'oeil en supprimant la distance du modèle à la copie, piège l'oeil sensible dans l'apparence-essence, livre le corps-oeil à la fascination du double, du simulacre, à la stupéfaction et du même coup l'effet n'est pas de contemplation, de théorie, mais de surréalité: un mixte—impur—d'angoisse et de sidération. "

8   Ibidem, 127-8: "Reprendre ici le modèle établi pour le tableau d'histoire 'classique' (...) et montrer comment dans la représentation éclate l'instant de vision, le moment de la pulsion colorée dont l'effet est de stupéfaction ou de sidération de la représentation narrative."

to reproduce itself as fiction. More important, "stupefaction" and "petrifaction" do not solely involve the viewers' perception of the image, but also impact upon their capacity for processing "the narrative representation." According to Marin, Caravaggio's *istoria* has the power of freezing time and action: of turning the instant of narration into the revelation of the story's incommensurability in terms of temporality through art's mimetic incantation. Like the mythological Medusa, art immobilizes the viewer's perception of narrative time: Caravaggio's temporality is in fact sheer "instantaneity." In this regard, it is appropriate to read Marin's interpretation of Caravaggio's c.1598 *Judith Beheading Holofernes*:

> Caravaggio presents the beholder with this "central" instant, as the sword's blow is "about to be" accomplished, the blade cleaves halfway through the neck, the head begins to separate from the body, the hair is pulled back by Judith's left hand, and three spurts of blood splash onto the pillow and the sheet. No before, and no after: this one moment, decisive, lethal, of infinitesimal duration. But there is a change of scenario—probably not as surprising as one would expect—the instant of the act is immobilized through the very representation of its instantaneity. The blow is halted midway through its course. Judith will never finish, will never have cut off Holofernes' head and, with her sword stopped, the story of her feat also comes to a stop, without past or future, atemporal. A permanence that is not repetition or obsessive compulsion manifests itself: the immobile "now" of the phantasm.[9]

It is amazing how intensely Marin's prose conveys the impression of a petrifying instantaneity: of a sword never to complete its trajectory, trapped as it is in the figment's illusion, the picture's "phantasm." The exceptional quality of the description makes us forget that the representation of the "central" act was one of the canonical ways through which early modern artists endowed the image with temporality, thereby suggesting a "before"—Holofernes asleep and hence vulnerable to the woman's onslaught—and an "after"—his decapitation and his head carried about in the very sack that the old servant in the painting eagerly prepares for Judith. From this point of view, any *istoria* is the representation of more or less frozen acts, so that if by "instantaneity" Marin means the visual enhancement of an ongoing action in its imminence—what Pomponio Gaurico defines as "enargeia" in his 1504 *De sculptura*—then "instantaneity" might well be the hallmark of works by numerous painters other than Caravaggio. In this last sentence, I do not imply that Caravaggio's *Judith Beheading Holofernes* does not constitute an exception in its timing, duration, and dramatic coherence (or lack thereof): I am rather stating that the effect of instantaneity stems from, and is pre-determined by, a set of pictorial devices that Marin does not take into account at all, and the efficiency of which is historically contingent upon visual conventions (of both painters and viewers) irrelevant for Marin. Like Alpers—whose 1983 *The Art of Describing* came out just a few years after *Détruire la peinture*[10]—Marin envisions Alberti's *istoria* as a monolith: as an unchanged and unchallenged model of defining and making painting, which it truly never was. Furthermore, Marin's dual paradigm of interpretation—the opposition between the enunciative and the mimetic *istoria*—is definitely too large to register the specificity of Caravaggio's or Poussin's pictorial narratives. (Incidentally, Poussin

9   Ibidem, 166-7: "Le Caravage montre au spectateur cet instant 'central,' le coup d'épée est "en train" d'être donné, la lame est à mi-parcours, au milieu du cou, la tête commence à se séparer du corps tirée par la chevelure en arrière par la main gauche de Judith, trois flots de sang giclent sur l'oreiller et le drap. Pas d'avant, pas d'après: ce moment unique, décisif, mortel, un infinitésimal de durée. Mais changement—peut-être n'est-ce pas aussi surprenant qu'on pourrait le croire—l'instant de l'acte s'immobilise par la représentation même de son instantanéité. Le coup se bloque à mi-chemin de son accomplissement. Judith n'en finira pas, n'en finira jamais de couper la tête d'Holopherne et avec son épée arrêtée, le récit de son exploit s'arrête là, sans passé et sans avenir, comme intemporel. Une permanence se manifeste qui n'est point répétition ou compulsion obsessionnelle: le maintenant immobile du fantasme." The same passage, with some noticeable variants, reappears in Marin 1994, 287-8.

is not free of hesitancies and shortcomings in his multiple experimentations with the *istoria*). It is no coincidence that Marin centers his analysis of these two masters around two paintings, Caravaggio's *Medusa* and Poussin's Louvre *Et in Arcadia Ego*,[11] which, in accordance with seventeenth-century aesthetics and taxonomy, do not connote as pictorial narratives. The former indeed is the ornament of a parade shield and the latter a moral allegory in the form of a pastoral. The very fact that, in both cases, the painters resort to the schemes and formulas of the *istoria*—with their implications of action and temporality—indicates how pervasive this pictorial institution was at the time.

Marin's hermeneutical limits and occasional arbitrariness in weighing the specific import of Caravaggio's pictorial narratives become transparent in his interpretation of the 1609 *Resurrection of Lazarus*. The frieze-like disposition of the main actors in the foreground as displayed by Caravaggio in this late painting represented a challenge to the theories of Marin, who associates this type of pictorial configuration with Poussin's *istoria*. As he asserted in the final section of his essay, Marin intended to demonstrate that an "ordered succession of figures parallel to the picture's plane develops and deploys plastically and structurally a syntagmatics which is not narrative and diachronic, but compositional and organizational ["*de composition, de distribution*"]."[12] First of all, unless I am hopelessly wrong, I do not see how a syntagmatics can be other than "compositional and organizational," so that Marin's statement relies on a blatant truism. To avoid this conundrum, I venture to propose that, in Marin's opinion, Poussin's *istoria*, apart from being "compositional and organizational," is also "narrative and diachronic." But since pictorial narration and temporality are functions of the painting's composition and organization, the assumption that the structure of Caravaggio's *Resurrection of Lazarus* is preeminently "compositional and organizational" entails that, virtually, the picture is susceptible to relaying causality and diachrony. Be that as it may, Marin deciphers the configuration of Caravaggio's painting in the following manner:

> An arc of a circle, a quarter of a circle, or rather an ellipse, of which Christ's figure at the left—his body and head—represents the perpendicular radius; the uplifted slab of the sepulcher and Lazarus' body—without his head—the radiuses, which are oblique to the bisector of the right angle (Christ's body–the ground); and the ground the picture's platform, punctuated by the feet—the horizontal radius. The circumference of this elliptical arc is, in turn, modulated by the heads with the remarkable exception of Lazarus'—the last bead of a rosary of three faces (Martha, Mary) along a quasi-vertical line: a compositional and organizational syntagma for my itinerant gaze, which I am obliged to follow. Its departure point is Christ's head high on the left—indeed, at mid-height of the picture's left side; its destination, the skull at the right, lying down upon the ground. Christ's face in the shadow, night, dark; the skull struck by a flash of light. The syntagmatics of the "figurative text" is not the diachrony of the story, nor the temporality of the referential history.[13]

10 Predictably enough, Marin very positively reviewed Alpers' *The Art of Describing*. See Marin 1986, republished with corrections and additions in Marin 1994, 235-50.

11 Marin specifically returned to his interpretations of Poussin's *Et in Arcadia Ego* in Marin 1988.

12 Marin 1977, 195: "Démontrer ceci: une succession ordonnée de figures parallèles au plan du tableau développe et déploie plastiquement, structurellement, une syntagmatique non pas narrative, diachronique, mais de composition, de distribution."

13 Ibidem: "Un arc de cercle, un quart de cercle ou plutôt d'ellipse dont la figure du Christ à gauche—corps et tête— constitue le rayon perpendiculaire, la dalle du tombeau soulevée, le corps de Lazare—moins la tête—les rayons obliques à la bissectrice de l'angle droit (corps du Christ— sol), le sol enfin, la 'première' ligne du tableau, ponctué par les pieds, le rayon horizontal. La circonférence de cet arc d'ellipse rythmée de son côté par les têtes avec l'exception de la tête de Lazare, dernière boule d'un chapelet de trois visages (Marthe, Marie) à la quasi-verticale: syntagme de composition et de distribution pour mon regard-parcours; je lui obéis nécessairement. Son point de départ, la tête du Christ à gauche en haut—en fait le milieu gauche de la toile—; son point d'arrivée, la tête de mort à droite, en bas, sur le sol: la tête du Christ dans l'ombre, la nuit, le noir; le crâne frappé d'un éclat de lumière. La syntagmatique du 'texte figurative' n'est pas la diachronie du récit, la temporalité de l'histoire référentielle."

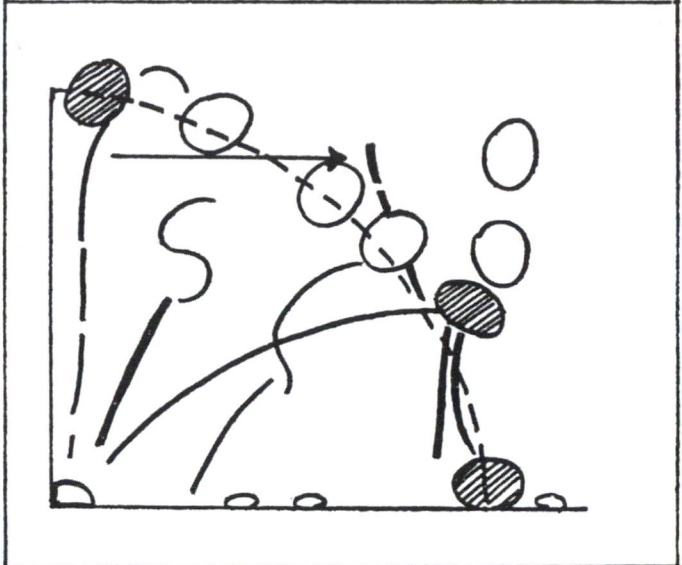

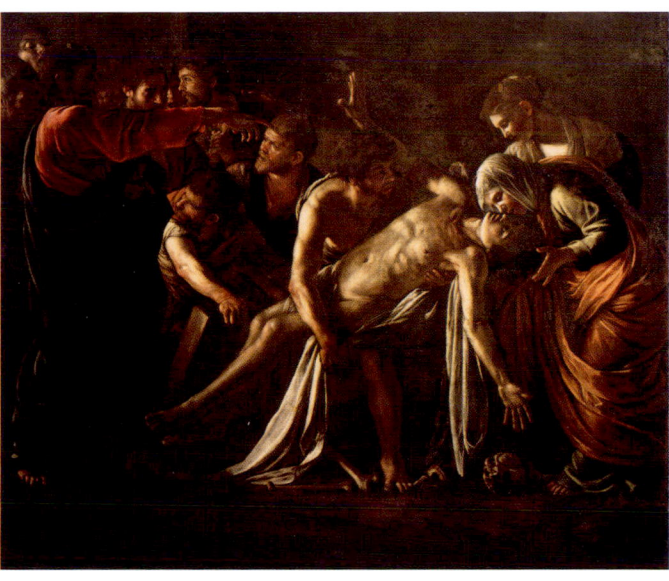

Fig. 1
Louis Marin, Diagram of Caravaggio's *Resurrection of Lazarus*,
reproduced from Louis Marin, *Détruire la peinture*, 1977.

Fig. 2
Michelangelo Merisi da Caravaggio, *The Resurrection of Lazarus*,
Museo Regionale, Messina, oil on canvas, 320 x 275 cm., detail.

To facilitate the task of the reader, Marin opportunely inserts in his volume a hand-made diagram of what he considers to be the main components of Caravaggio's syntagmatics as modulated in *The Resurrection of Lazarus* (Figs. 1, 2). It is interesting that, although Marin positively designates the picture's main configuration as frieze-like, he presupposes instead that a section of ellipse is the principal vector of attention—or syntagma, as he puts it—in the beholder's perception and reading of the painting. In other words, our gaze, in Marin's opinion, is forced to follow an itinerary that begins with Christ's shaded face and ends with the skull at Martha's feet. Even though Marin's sense of geometry must not be judged with rigor—as he admits a little further, the picture's alignments are not perfectly delineated—I must admit that the alleged ellipse connecting Christ's head with the skull is, to a great extent, if not imaginary, overly secondary: as seventeenth-century critics noticed, it is the oblique of Lazarus' resurrecting body that first catches the eye and guides the viewer's gaze within the canvas. I shall give a fuller interpretation of Caravaggio's *Resurrection of Lazarus* in Chapter 13.

For the time being, what intrigues me most is why Marin bases his exegesis of the painting upon an unnoticeable arc of a circle and a rather discreetly introduced skull lying reversed in the right foreground—Marin even compares it with the anamorphic skull of Hans Holbein's *The Ambassadors* and makes it the viewer's counterpart in the picture. I hazard this educated guess: to recognize that a series of orthogonal and diagonal lines form a scaffold for the "ordered succession" of figures in *The Resurrection of Lazarus* is tantamount to asserting that a structural configuration deemed specific to Poussin's *istoria* might be operative in Caravaggio's picture—that some sort of diachrony and narration might be suggested by the Italian master's work. But this possibility contradicts Marin's own tenets about Caravaggio's "instantaneity." Therefore, Marin rids himself of this contradiction by proposing a trajectory of reading that reaffirms Caravaggio's attraction for the "moment–instant" of representation. Yet the opposition between Christ's head and the skull operates on a symbolic level and, if true, does not suggest any form of narrative temporality or causality. Indeed, this dialectic of signs does not encompass any form of "instantaneity." To force the "instantaneous" back into Caravaggio's picture, Marin thus postulates the existence of another figurative syntagma, one binding Christ's pointing hand to Lazarus' hands, of which the right is depicted in profile, the other wide open. In his diagram, Marin goes as far as to outline a direct link between Jesus' and Lazarus' right hands as if they were almost touching one another, whereas on the canvas they are clearly misaligned and at a distance (curiously, Christ's index finger illusorily points toward an adjacent porter's forehead in the painting). Only on these grounds, and at the expense of dismissing several other structural elements, is Marin able to restore the omnipresence of an instantaneous narrative in Caravaggio's picture: the dialogue between the Savior's pointing hand bringing Lazarus back to life, and the reaction to it of the dead man's hovering hand—that is, "*the indication and its response* in the same instant, *instantaneous.*"[14]

For the sake of brevity, I shall not pursue Marin's analysis of *The Resurrection of Lazarus*, especially as it grows more and more self-referential and contradictory as it progresses. Instead, I will draw a lesson from this extremely acute scholar's insights into Caravaggio's narrative. It is a fact that, however fascinating his reading of Caravaggio's pictures might be, Marin does not succeed in assessing and proving the specificity of the master's supposed anti-paradigm of the *istoria*. Even worse, his epistemological method and exegesis greatly flatten the various and sophisticated intricacies of Caravaggio's pictorial narratives.

As this volume seeks to demonstrate, every single painting by Caravaggio must be appreciated and examined in its uniqueness, because none re-proposes and reiterates the same questions or, if so, rarely to the same degree. In a sense, Caravaggio did not devise a new model of pictorial narrative if, by "model," one means a well-delimited system of concepts and procedures. There is something profoundly a-systematic and genuinely extemporaneous in Caravaggio's assaults on the *istoria*: something that prevents the interpreter from pigeonholing his inventions within rigid categories; at best, one can isolate discontinuous trends of a poetics that crop up, unspool, subside, go underground, and resurface in his narratives, always in a different form, and always along a different perspective.

Before I explain how I have come to these conclusions and with what methodology, I need to return to Marin's idea that Poussin's *istoria* shaped itself into the contrariness of Caravaggio's painting. There is no doubt that Poussin, along with many other seventeenth-century artists and art theorists, fiercely reacted to a notion of painting that they sensed as ruinous and destructive of the *istoria*. But once one acknowledges this phenomenon, it becomes perilous to appraise Caravaggio's art retrospectively, that is, in the light of principles and practices developed—so to speak—"posthumously." Moreover, as I have already stressed, early modern artists and art theorists unceasingly and increasingly subjected the concept of the *istoria* inaugurated by Alberti to scrutiny and improvement. To comprehend not only how early modern artists conceived of, among other things, temporality, causality, and verisimilitude, but also how they proceeded in bringing these principles to fruition, technically and practically, it is imperative to reassess the entire problematic of the *istoria*.

In the beginning, when I started working on the material that would comprise this volume, I had not planned on inquiring into the history and evolution of the *istoria* before, during, and after Caravaggio's time. But, as I began to draft the first chapters and expose the results of my research to friends and colleagues, I came to realize that without an extensive introduction, elucidation and critique of the early modern *istoria*, I would not be able to explain precisely of what Caravaggio's dislocations consist. By what means did paintings express action and temporality? And what is time in the *istoria*? How did other structural elements of composition such as disposition, lighting, and chiaroscuro interact in the assemblage of a pictorial narrative? The more I pondered these

---

14 Ibidem, 196: "Sur cet ensemble ainsi distribué, la 'corde' supérieure de l'arc de l'ellipse: le bras du Christ, sa main, le geste d'indication, la pointe de l'index sur la circonférence de l'ellipse; et une tangente à la circonférence: le bras droit de Lazare et sa main, paume ouverte face à la pointe de l'index, frappée par la lumière (la main est face à l'index, mais de profil pour moi). *L'indication et sa réponse* dans le même instant, *instantanées.*"

questions, the clearer it became to me that Alberti's model of the *istoria* was intrinsically flawed: that, on a theoretical and practical level, its glitches could not be emended without refashioning and even compromising its foundations. More surprising, I could eventually discern a pattern in the ways in which Caravaggio dislocated the canonical principles of the *istoria*: that is, by pushing to the fore the inherent contradictions of this pictorial model. At once, I discovered that Caravaggio's dislocations of the *istoria* functioned on multiple levels, but without a consistent pattern: at will, the master overturns some rules, respects others, or manipulates them subtly, too subtly, each time with diverse results—a portent of pictorial inventiveness! Imagine that the *istoria's* principles are the multiple threads with which the painting as a text must be interwoven, and that Caravaggio, instead of intertwining them homogeneously, decides to remove this thread, to thicken or thin that thread in order to enhance or camouflage its impact, or even to leave parts of his work with no threads, as blanks immediately recognizable as such by the viewer. Not only do these "textual" dislocations—or "texture disparities," to keep the simile—generate very different compositions; they also concur to transmit very different meanings and values.

As my research advanced, I understood that I could present the polyvalent material and results of my study only by organizing them in sections, or Parts, each predominantly, but not exclusively, devoted to particular types of dislocations. More to the point, the Parts into which this volume is divided should rather be construed as thematic containers, and their chapters as critical samples, of "tendencies" specific to Caravaggio's handling of the *istoria* in the course of his whole career. In most cases, it turned out that formulas and themes evolved in Caravaggio's pictorial narratives could be presented in some kind of chronological order, as if relating to temporal portions of a pictorial evolution. On further reflection, I concluded that four thematic kernels sufficed to articulate my thoughts and arguments on Caravaggio's poetics of dislocation. Thus, after Part One, which serves as a general introduction to the concept and practice of the *istoria* and its fallacies, and in which I attempt to summarize the scope and characteristics of a discipline to come, pictorial narratology, Part Two centers on Caravaggio's early experimentations with pictorial narratives and with his dislocations of the comedic and the lyrical. In Part Three, I examine Caravaggio's elaborations on, and manipulations of, the Counter-Reformation *istoria* with its claim to replace and underlie universal truths: in the paintings I study here, Caravaggio manages to dismantle and relativize the centrality of the Christian hero. A persistent theme in Caravaggio's painting concerns the identity, role, and function of the painter and his interrelations with the *istoria*: Part Four is entirely consecrated to this topic and the ways in which Caravaggio subverts the principles of pictorial authorship and authority. Part Five was certainly the most complex section of this volume to write: I now see it as a poly-thematic, multi-layered apparatus of reflections about Caravaggio's late pictorial narratives. Not that this Part is deprived of coherence: Caravaggio's re-instantiations of subjects and topics he had previously treated offer a theoretical network in light of which I could afford to interpret some of his most radical creations. Besides dealing with Caravaggio's re-elaborations on his own oeuvre through the work of memory, Part Five also analyzes what I have defined as Caravaggio's devices of meta-narrative.

Early on during the course of my research, I became dissatisfied with this division into five Parts. I feared that a link was missing in the historical and interpretive architecture that I was constructing—a link that would project Caravaggio's enterprise into the future of art's developments. If, as I was persuaded from the outset, the emergence of seventeenth-century academic theories on the *istoria* was triggered, among other circumstances, by Caravaggio's uses and misuses of pictorial narrative, then what determined the defeat and eclipse of the experimental models inaugurated by Caravaggio and expanded by his followers? The prospect of navigating in uncharted seas, outlining the evolution of an aborted pictorial project, and verifying that in a sense history is far from being linear and progressive, simultaneously thrilled and frightened me. Of course, I felt unable to account for an artistic evolution—or counter-evolution—in which so many artists of the first rank were involved, and I am deeply reluctant to explain historical phenomena without having gathered enough evidence to confirm my hypotheses. And yet, I needed a Part Six, an epistemological avenue in which to contemplate the dynamics of Caravaggio's newness, its collisions and ramifications over time. I resolved that I should incur the risk of not being as exhaustive as I wished, and thereby present a "summary" exegesis of the pictorial experimentations and relative failures marking the end of Caravaggism in the 1630s. This is why Part Six grapples with the reaction and counter-reaction to Caravaggio's unsettling originality in the domain of pictorial narrative. Because each Part of this volume is preceded by a substantial introduction, I invite the reader to seek more detailed definitions and elucidations of the numerous concepts and issues considered by this monograph in those preliminary surveys. I have planned each Part as an independent unit, and each chapter, usually devoted to the close reading of a single artwork, can comfortably be perused, and hopefully enjoyed, in isolation.

As much as possible, I have endeavored not to repeat myself and not to dwell more than necessary upon my own conclusions: in this regard, I am fairly satisfied with the variety of hermeneutical approaches and angles secured by my editorial layout. Indeed, even if I was perfectly aware that Caravaggio's dislocations of the *istoria*'s lofty machine constitute a pervasive phenomenology in his oeuvre, I embarked upon my study without any prejudgment or grand thesis to corroborate, letting the single works guide me in my search, question and perplex me, and finally provide me with clues about how to address them. As a result, each case study in this volume opens up a different perspective on Caravaggio's inventiveness and imagery by constantly upgrading and enriching the theme of the Part to which it pertains, and by exalting the unparalleled singularity of each picture. Like Aby Warburg, I in fact believe in the epistemological substantiality and indispensability of details, of any detail that might voice the artwork's distinctiveness. This observation ineluctably leads me to disclose the main lines of my methodology.

Caravaggio's treatments of pictorial narratives are by no means an exercise in style and aesthetics: by exploiting and stretching the possibilities of the *istoria*, he literally criticizes and reassesses the most effective and the subtlest organ of visual hermeneutics and propaganda of his own time. Therefore, nothing is less innocent or fortuitous than Caravaggio's disruptions of this pictorial "monument." By asserting a correlation between the painter and a social, cultural, and religious institution, I necessarily assume that Caravaggio's work engages in a dialectical relationship with history's forces and historical circumstances. Nevertheless, as much as I have made any effort to study Caravaggio's paintings as historical artifacts, placing them within the purview of late sixteenth- and early seventeenth-century art theory, practice, and spectatorship, I do not resign myself to deeming his works mere mirrors of a time period, as if figurative texts were able merely either to describe an art historian's conception of an age in history or to serve as documents of an historical evolution. Artistic creation follows its own logic: it is inscribed within history, interfaces with history, yet transcends history. Artistic creation does not measure up to history, not because it is ahistorical—far, far from this—but insofar as it incarnates a creator's individuality. Although I am sure this must be clear to all scholars and critics, nothing truly compares with Caravaggio's paintings. Their high degree of originality renders them both antecedents of an artistic development and exceptions that defy the normativeness of art production in late sixteenth- and early seventeenth-century art. For this reason, I have implemented and, when necessary, honed my philological aptitudes in interpreting Caravaggio's pictures. As a philologist, I have analyzed his works as aesthetic structures in order to grasp their multiple significances. Philology teaches us that a text always presupposes inter-textuality: that it entertains relations with previous texts, and hence with tradition and conventions, so that its meaning must be extracted on comparative grounds. This philological approach to Caravaggio's pictorial narratives was meant to keep at bay as much as possible a certain arbitrariness inherent in many contemporary interpretations of the master's paintings. I therefore tried to establish the significance and function of expressions, gestures, and attitudes as performed by Caravaggio's figures by regarding them as codes typical of the narrative genre, and in general of early modern image-making. As Marin suggested, there is indeed a lexicon and syntax of figurative narration insofar as any *istoria*, and any image for that matter, is a representation, and not simply a reproduction (I shall clarify this point in Part One).

I shall have achieved my ambition if, at the end of this book, the reader feels not only that his or her understanding of Caravaggio's painting and of an important period in art history has been broadened, but also that much more remains to be said about the painter and his period. I never intended to exhaust the "Caravaggio file"— obviously an impossible enterprise—and on that account, I decided from the start to leave aside many open questions that nevertheless continue to intrigue me. For instance, I seldom mention facts and vicissitudes of Caravaggio's life in this volume,[15] not because I consider them unnecessary, but because our knowledge of them is both scant and biased. When Caravaggio depicted his assistant, Cecco, as a Cupid[16] or an angel, he was blending together biography and artistic creation. If only we could recognize the identity of his models, and the precise nature of their connections to the master! If only we could have the slightest testimony of Caravaggio's sentiments in regard to his murder of Ranuccio Tomassoni, his exile in Naples and Sicily, his triumphs and misfortunes in Malta! Then we would be able to explore the biographical layers of Caravaggio's pictorial narratives with more precision and legitimacy. Also, I have deliberately neglected another path of investigation that, in my opinion, has been too frequently trodden by Caravaggio scholars. That is, I have not further inquired into the relationships between the painter and his principal patrons and protectors. Indeed, innumerable essays have been consecrated to crucial figures in Caravaggio's life and career, such as Cardinal Francesco Maria Del Monte and Marchese Vincenzo Giustiniani.[17] And yet, with the exception of Lothar Sickel's *Caravaggios Rom* (2003), most of these studies rely heavily on prejudice and speculation when it comes to defining the influence exerted upon Caravaggio not only by single patrons, but also by the cultural and religious milieus of early seventeenth-century Rome. In my view, this topic has been squeezed to the point that, in default of new documentation, not much can be added to the knowledge and interpretation of Caravaggio's painting from this historical perspective. If I do not scrutinize many other works by Caravaggio in this book, it is not only because the genre of some of them does not designate them as narratives, but also purely for lack of time and opportunity. In conclusion, I sincerely hope that my contribution will achieve at least one of its objectives: to liberate Caravaggio's immense output from the critical prison of dull commonplaces and unsubstantiated exegeses in which its historical comprehension has languished so long and so regrettably.

---

15 A peculiar attempt at blending biography and artistic production with regard to Caravaggio is represented by Bassani and Bellini 1994.

16 As is well known, Richard Symonds, an English aristocrat in exile, while visiting Rome, noted in his journal (1649-51) with regard to the Giustiniani *Cupid*, now in Berlin: "(...) Checco del Caravaggio 'tis call'd among the painters, 'twas his boy. (...) 'Twas the body & face of his owne boy or servant that laid with him." For Symond's journal and its reference to Caravaggio's *Cupid*, see Wiemers 1986; and Gash 1998, 41. See also Papi 2001, 9-10, who identifies Cecco with Francesco Boneri, and argues, correctly in my opinion, that Cecco is

the "Francesco garzone" living with "Caravaggio pittore" in a house in Vicolo San Biagio, Rome, as attested by a Roman census of 1605. See Ibidem, 7, 51.

17 Here are a few titles that corroborate my point: Frommel 1971; Waźbiński 1994; Gilbert 1995; Danesi Squarzina 1996; König 2001. Sickel 2003 compellingly refutes the claim, made by many scholars (from Friedlaender 1969 to Calvesi 1990), that religious networks such as that of the Roman Oratorio actively supported and influenced Caravaggio's painting. See the Introduction to Part Three for a more detailed criticism of Caravaggio's adherence to Counter-Reformation tenets in the matter of art.

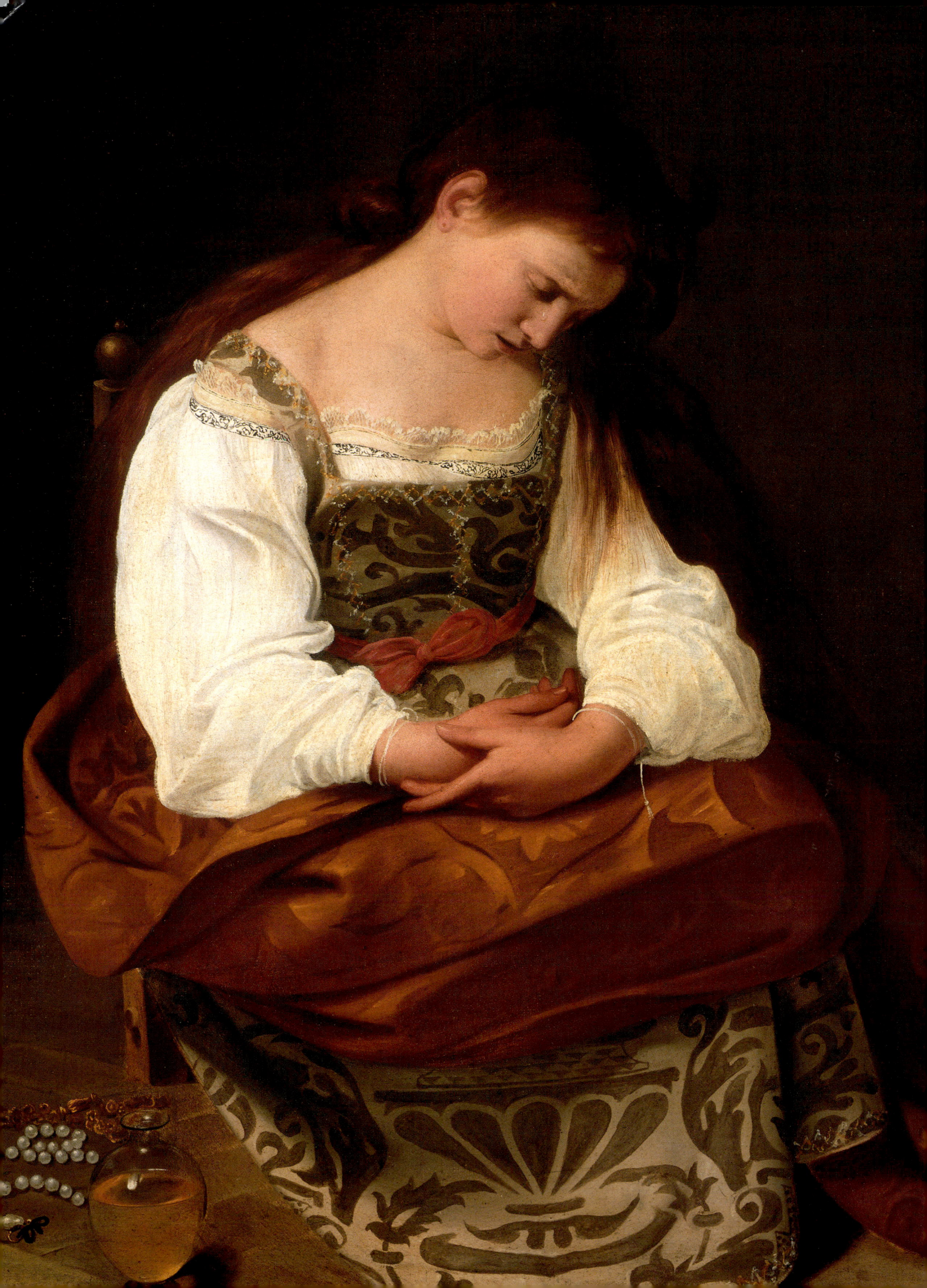

PART ONE

A Matter of Optics and Rhetoric: The Aporia of Pictorial Narrative Before, During, and After Caravaggio's Time

Caravaggio's Nonsense

Some time after 1633, the Bolognese painter Francesco Albani, celebrating the four mythological paintings that he had executed for Cardinal Scipione Borghese around 1621, remarked upon the "twofold delight," both sensuous and moral, that beholders experienced through his "inventions."[1] Without modesty—the text I quote was not intended to be published as such and could be described as autobiographical notes strewn with didactic maxims—the master explained the excellence of his so-called Borghese cycle through his longtime fidelity to "Raphael's path": a seminal path that had been recently "abandoned" by most painters and was now "almost entirely infested with thorns." Developing this metaphor, Albani stated bitterly: "now they set out to follow Caravaggio's path, which is entirely about still objects, and not lively motions conceived by the intellect and painted with mastery of drawing." Albani's statement is surprising on two counts. First, at the time he wrote it, Caravaggio's star had already declined and the movement he had inspired was certainly near extinction. But of course Albani might well be expressing ideas from his formative sojourn in Rome (1601-1617), and from that standpoint his critique would definitely be understandable. I shall come back to this shortly. Furthermore, Albani in this passage seems to allude specifically to still lifes with "melons, watermelons, and other fruits: any weak mind, unable to go farther in composing, focuses on these inanimate objects, in which they easily succeed."[2] In reality, by following the threads of Albani's inchoate theory of art, it can be ascertained that the Bolognese master more ambitiously targeted Caravaggio's method of composing a story. In Caravaggio's painting Albani not only identified "the abyss and total ruin of the most noble and accomplished virtue of painting,"[3] but he also considered it the antithesis of any pictorial excellence, whether it be that of Raphael, Michelangelo, Correggio, or Titian, Albani's almost unconditional idols.

---

1 Malvasia 2:245: "opera nella quale si cava moralità e che pasce gl'animi di duplicato diletto." For the paintings, their dating and replicas, see Puglisi 1999, 135-6, no. 48.

2 Malvasia 2:245: "Ora per apunto, essendosi posto in abandono quella strada, quasi come un nuovo Colombo aperta e battuta da esso Raffaelle e dal suo grand'allievo Giulio Romano, ed ora quasi tutta inspinata, e posto in abbandono quello che divinamente insegnò Raffaelle, ora si sono posti a seguitare la strada del Caravaggio, che tutta è intenta ad oggetti di ferma, non di moti vivaci che vengano dall'intelletto, e che si eseguiscono col possesso del disegno.

Poiché i meloni, cucumeri, frutti diversi ogni debole cervello che non è capace di più passare avanti a i componimenti si ferma nelle cose insensate, le quali facilmente le consegue, e sono capaci e cogniti solo dagl'uomini di poco giudizio etc."

3 Ibidem, 2:244: "Non poté mai tollerare [Albani] che si seguitasse il Caravaggio, scorgendo essere quel modo il precipizio e la totale ruina della nobilissima e compitissima virtù della pittura, poiché, se bene era da laudare in parte la semplice imitazione, era nondimeno per partorire tutto quello che ne è seguito in progresso di quarant'anni."

◄ Plate I: Michelangelo Merisi da Caravaggio, *The Penitent Magdalene*, Galleria Doria-Pamphilj, Rome, oil on canvas, 123 x 98.3 cm., detail.

To be sure, Caravaggio's ability for "simply imitating" was commendable in and of itself. Yet he perverted painters by inspiring them to represent half-figures smuggled as independent works:

> But I will say that as it only appears from the waist up, [the figure] is disconnected from the thighs, rid of the legs and the ground it stands on, bereft of perspective, concepts, and expression, and this is what I need to say initially about invention.[4]

In another passage, Albani elaborates on the equation between the number of figures to be introduced in an *istoria* and the excellence of invention. I translate it with its anacolutha, without amending its logical discrepancies, confident that readers will appreciate its author's apparent flow of consciousness and be able to reconstruct its theoretical associations:

> Since I don't believe that by simply coloring a head along with two hands (and which is worse, motionless) … the weakness of a painter more suited to painting senseless fruits than to representing stories etc. Quite another thing is to devote oneself to a subject that requires a multiplicity of figures and this is why one must elucidate concepts in the same manner as the poet, because concepts are necessary in reading poetical compositions, and without this nobody will excuse skilful hands for their weakness in composing.[5]

Albani goes on to distinguish two types of readings, shallow and in-depth, which can be associated respectively with glimpsing and scanning:

> Many people ignorant of painting (I mean, stupid people) look at pictures as if they were in libraries, their eyes being (usually) drawn to those beautiful books with golden laces and buckles, and they are lured by this external appearance, and leave saying: "I've seen so many beautiful books," adding: "how beautiful they are!" But since they are unable to read, they are also unable to know them from the inside as knowledgeable people do, who actually read within and extol the most beautiful compositions.[6]

On these premises, Albani's reaction to stories with half-figures is highly predictable: "Come on! Since half-figures have no thighs, no legs, no draperies to reveal the painter's quality, how much he knows of perspective, who executed it, they are very disconnected." The next and final sentence, though a corollary, must instead be considered crucial to Albani's art theory: "and then, there is the strict obligation not to represent idle acts, just as poets do not introduce words without a purpose, which on the contrary are signifying, intelligible and appropriate."[7]

To understand Albani's assimilation of half-figures to lavishly bound books, it is necessary to interpolate the elements missing in the comparison: half-figures, as reproduced by Caravaggio

---

4 Ibidem: "Ma che più? essendosi introdotto una mezza figura in scena, si fa passare per un'opra intiera, io dirò che questa viene disubligata (mentre è sola del mezzo in su) dalle cosce, libera è dalle gambe, dal piano ove posa, libera dalla prospettiva, da i concetti e dall'espressioni, e quello dovevo dire prima dall'invenzioni."

5 Ibidem, 2:246: "Poiché a me non mi pare che il semplice ben colorire d'una testa con due mani (col farle ferme) la debolezza del pittore più atto a dipingere frutti insensati, che rappresentare istorie etc. Altro è a obligarsi ad un soggetto che porti numerosità di figure, e conseguentemente bisogna spiegare sempre concetti in quella guisa che fa il poeta, perché in legendo composizioni di poesie ci vuole necessariamente concetti, ché senza questo veruno crederebbe alli intelligenti di mano la debolezza delle composizioni."

6 Ibidem: "Moltissimi ignoranti della pittura riguardano le pitture (dico li molti sciocchi) come [f]anno le pitture delle librarie, e con l'occhio (per ordinario) sono tirati da quei belli libri, che hanno laci e fibie d'oro, e si pescano con questa apparenza di fuori, poi partendosi col dire: ho veduto molti libri bellissimi, giungendovi con questo dire: Oh come son belli! Ma questi non sapendo legere, non hanno né anco capacità di conoscerli per entro come fanno li sapienti, che legono il di dentro e laudano le bellissime composizioni."

7 Ibidem: "Ma dico io! Non vi essendo nelle mezze figure né cosce, né gambe, né i piani che dano a conoscere qual sia il pittore, come ei s'intenda di prospettiva, chi ha operato, sono molto disobligati. Poi vi è l'obligo stretto di non fare atto che sia ozioso così come il poeta non mette parole indarno, anzi significanti, intelligibili e proprie."

and his followers, are prodigies of imitation, and therefore amaze people "ignorant of painting" through their deceptive graphicness.[8] Needless to say, in Albani's view, this "path" of composing is to be condemned. For him, Painting—a prosopopoeia, this time—is like Poetry: she might be compared

> to a beautiful young lady appearing on stage well clad, who captivates [the public's] benevolence at first glance; if she starts to speak and talks nonsense, she'll only conquer the ignorant who solely revel in external appearance, but who don't understand the interior, as if they're shown a well-bound Aristotle with golden buckles: they'll be dazzled by its glowing binding and certainly not by probing its interior, which is like seeing in the dark of night.[9]

This metaphoric blindness, to which Albani often returns, affects both ignorant viewers and uninventive painters. To restore sight, figures must talk:

> I won't speak of certain figures that don't know what they're doing; if any of them was asked about their doings, and if let's say they were animated and able to answer questions, they'd say for sure: "I'm a figure idling like that, and still I know that Raphael would have represented me in another attitude, and I wouldn't ever be idling."[10]

According to Albani, idleness embodies a pure lack of meaning:

> It is certain that painters, just like poets, must account for what they do and represent; suppose that one opens Torquato Tasso's poem and reads any octave; one will learn that nothing is without purpose, every word is significant, and everything acts and is appropriate to the subject; painting should be like this—that is, executed with appropriate and signifying actions pertaining to the subject and hence intelligible.[11]

Despite the obscurity of the syntax and the compulsive rhythm of the argumentation, Albani's thoughts become coherent if studied in relation to one another. As I will show, many of his tenets hark back directly or indirectly to Leon Battista Alberti's 1435 *De Pictura* and do not actually innovate in any respect. As a whole, though, they undeniably break some ground, and this is far from being

8 In this and in other passages, Albani seems to rely on Giovan Battista Agucchi's so-called *Trattato della pittura*, a text first published in 1646 as an excerpt in Giovanni Antonio Massani's *Diverse figure di Annibale Carracci*. Agucchi's *Trattato* probably dates to c.1607-1615. See Agucchi, 147-8: "Da che intenderassi agevolmente quanto meritino di lode li pittori che imitano solamente le cose come nella natura le truovano, e si debba farne la stima che ne fa il volgo. Perché essi, non arrivando a conoscer quella bellezza che esprimer vorrebbe la natura, si fermano su quel che veggono espresso, ancorché lo truovino oltremodo imperfetto. Da questo ancora nasce che le cose dipinte ed imitate dal naturale piacciono al popolo, perché egli è solito a vederne di sì fatte, e l'imitazione di quel che a pieno conosce li diletta."

9 Malvasia, 2:248: "Dunque, signor Raffaelle, le pare che la prima parte del pittore sia l'invenzione? certamente lo dico e l'antepongo, poiché senza quella il poeta non si sostentarebbe, così la pittura, che è suora e compagna si sostenta, se ben dico con più vantaggio della poesia, essendo (come io dissi) come una bella giovane comparsa in palio ben vestita, che a primo comparire cattiva benevolenza, ma nel cominciare a favellare, se dasse in spropositi, si

trovarebbe aver preso solo gl'ignoranti che non si pascono se non di quell'apparenza esteriore, ma l'interiore, che non se n'intendono, come se le mostrasse un Aristotele ben legato, con fibie dorate, questo esteriore come rilucente le abbigliaria la vista, non l'aprire che facessero quello di dentro, che è come un guardar di notte in una oscurità."

10 Ibidem, 2:253: "Io non parlo poi di certe figure che non si sa che cosa si faccino, e a chi li addimandasse a ciascheduna che cosa fanno, e che fossero come dire annimate, e che avessero facoltà di dare risposta a chi le interrogasse, certo potriano dire: io sono una figura che me ne sto così in darno, e so ancor io che Raffaelle m'avrebbe per avventura disposta meglio e non mai oziosa."

11 Ibidem, 2:253-4: "Certo è che il pittore, così come il poeta, deve render conto di quello che fa e rappresenta; poniam caso che s'aprisse il poema di Torquato Tasso e si legesse qualsivoglia ottava. Si ritrovaria che nulla è in darno, ogni parola è significante ed ogni cosa opera, è propria conforme il soggetto etc. Così vorebbe essere la pittura, cioè fatta con atti propri significanti, indirizzati come ho detto al soggetto ed intelligibili."

an overstatement. To my knowledge, Albani's is the first documented attempt to demonstrate articulately the inefficacy of Caravaggio's narratives, well before Giovan Pietro Bellori's (1672). It is true that the doctor and amateur Giulio Mancini in his 1617-1621 *Considerazioni della pittura* had already tackled this issue, but—as we shall see—his analysis of Caravaggio's shortcomings is condensed into a single, albeit diffuse, sentence. It is also known that in his 1633 *Diálogos de la pintura*, the Spanish painter Vincencio Carducho had likewise singled out and vehemently scoffed at Caravaggio's ignorance and incongruousness in composing an *istoria*. I shall expand on this point in Chapter 16. However, Albani's criticism, albeit couched in a set of notes and precepts a few years after Carducho, undeniably echoes opinions and biases nurtured during Caravaggio's lifetime, or at least within the decade after his death in 1610. It is no coincidence that some years before Caravaggio's death, another Bolognese master, Guido Reni—a former

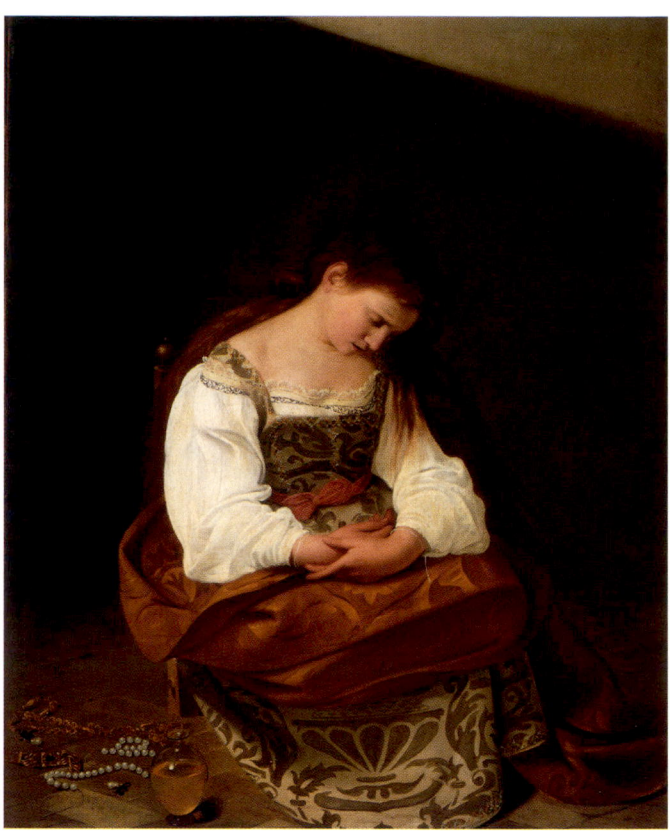

Fig. 3
Michelangelo Merisi da Caravaggio, *The Penitent Magdalene*, Galleria Doria-Pamphilj, Rome, oil on canvas, 123 x 98.3 cm.

friend of Albani's soon to become his arch-enemy—while complaining about the allegedly low fees he received from his paintings, reportedly argued:

> Why do people complain about my delays and the excessiveness of my prices? Does anyone get a half-figure from Caravaggio so fast and so easily? Does it cost less than mine? Doesn't he request double the price? Didn't I only get seventy miserable *scudi* for the Crucifixion of Saint Peter at the Tre Fontane, when Cardinal Scipione [Borghese] had offered him one hundred and fifty?[12]

It is worth emphasizing that Guido had obtained that commission thanks to his capability of "transforming himself into Caravaggio," which he did unequivocally by both imitating the master's style and evoking his 1601 *Crucifixion of Saint Peter* in Santa Maria del Popolo, Rome. It is noteworthy that neither Caravaggio's nor Guido's *Crucifixions* include half-figures. Yet Guido seemingly ranks Caravaggio's work indistinctly under that category, as if Caravaggio produced nothing but half-figures. Of the same opinion, however, was Giovanni Baglione, a notorious enemy of Caravaggio and his rival in Rome. In his 1649 *Vite de' pittori*, he records that because of Caravaggio's fame, "his heads were purchased for more than others' *istorie*."[13] Here, Baglione

12 Ibidem, 2:21: "Che strilli ogn'ora delle mie longhezze, dell'esorbitanza ne' prezzi? Si ha così presto e così facilmente una mezza figura del Caravaggio? Si paga ella meno di una mia, quando ben il doppio ne vuole? Del San Pietro crocefisso alle Tre Fontane, che ho fatto per settanta scudi fecciosi, non ne dava a lui cento cinquanta il cardinal Scipione?" For this passage, and Guido's collection of ancient masters, see Spear 1997, 211, 220.

13 Baglione, 139: "Nondimeno acquistò gran credito, e più si pagavano le sue teste che l'altrui istorie, tanto importa l'aura popolare che non giudica con gli occhi, ma guarda con l'orecchie."

implies that Caravaggio did not even go beyond the figure's head, narrowing down the scope of his ex-rival's talent to even less than half-figures. Not surprisingly, Caravaggio's path, according to Baglione, has been the ruin of young artists who, following the master's example, "devote themselves to representing a head from life, and abandoning the study of drawing's rudiments and art's profundities, revel exclusively in coloring." For this reason, "they do not know how to put two figures together, let alone how to weave an *istoria*, since they do not understand the worth of such noble art."[14]

These testimonies convince me that by persistently denigrating the dullness of half-figures, Albani sought overall to oppose "Caravaggio's path," so that Albani's art theory tends to configure itself as an alternative to Caravaggio's painting. Assuredly, Albani also responded to Caravaggio's revival through the works of Bartolomeo Manfredi, Jusepe de Ribera, Valentin de Boulogne, and others in the 1610s. Thus, Albani's insistence on the danger, clumsiness and pointlessness of half-figures also points to what the German painter and theorist Joachim von Sandrart described as "Manfredi's manner" in his 1675 *Academie der Bau-, Bild- und Mahlerey-Künste*:

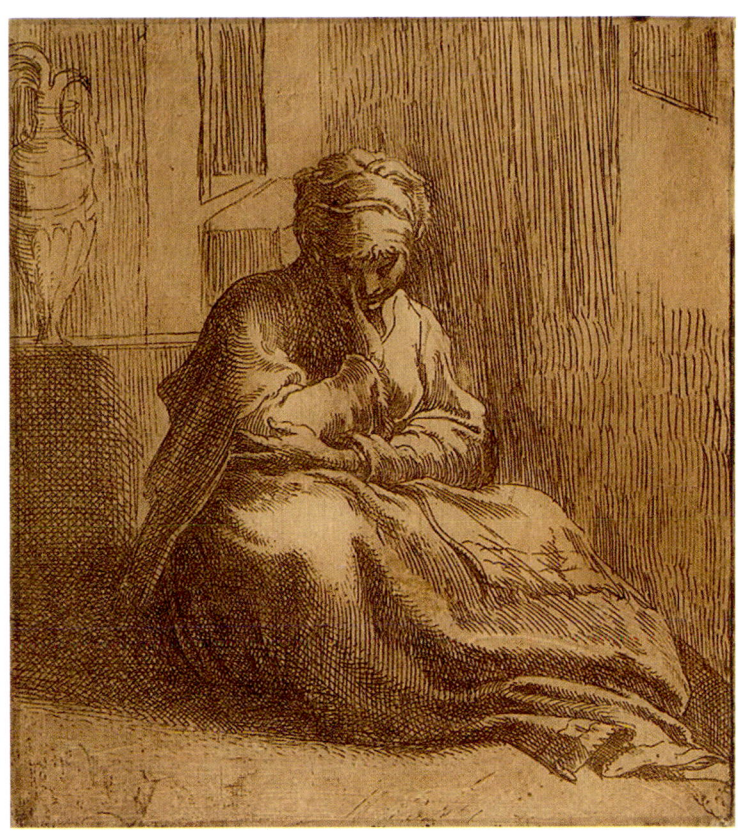

Fig. 4
Parmigianino (Francesco Mazzola), *Saint Thaïs*, etching, 13 x 11.2 cm.

> He [Manfredi] imitated life with great truth and mostly depicted half-figures life-size; he also devoted himself particularly to representing conversations, card-players, banquets, soldiers, and similarly accomplished works.[15]

All of these themes obviously originated in Caravaggio's painting. In his *Vite*, Bellori went even farther by characterizing Manfredi as Caravaggio's changeling:

> [Manfredi] was not a simple imitator of Caravaggio; he transformed himself into Caravaggio, and in painting he seemed to look at nature through Caravaggio's eyes; he followed his methods and his palette was dark, though his technique was more diligent and fresh, and he also prevailed in representing half-figures, which he used to compose his *istorie*.[16]

---

14 Ibidem, 138: "Anzi presso alcuni si stima aver esso rovinato la pittura, poiché molti giovani ad essempio di lui si danno ad imitare una testa del naturale, e non studiando ne' fondamenti del disegno e della profondità dell'arte, solamente del colorito appagansi, onde non sanno mettere due figure insieme né tessere istoria veruna per non comprendere la bontà di sì nobil arte."

15 Sandrart, 277: "Er imitierte das Leben mit großer Wahrheit und mahlte meist halbe Figuren in Lebensgröße, begabe sich auch absonderlich auf Ausbildungen der Conversationen, Spielen, Gastungen, Soldaten und dergleichen volkommenen Werken."

16 Bellori, 234: "Bartolomeo Manfredi mantovano non fu semplice imitatore, ma si trasformò nel Caravaggio, e nel dipingere parve che con gli occhi di esso riguardasse il naturale. Usò li modi stessi e fu tinto di oscuri, ma con qualche diligenza e freschezza maggiore, e prevalse anch'egli nelle mezze figure, con le quali soleva comporre l'istorie."

In other words, by disregarding—and invalidating the utility of—half-figures, Albani intended to attack both Caravaggio and his followers. The main goal of his offensive was to establish the inadequacy of half-figures in building up an *istoria*, the supreme category of painting in his (and Caravaggio's) time.

But in the end, what is wrong with half-figures? Why are they doomed to remain speechless and inert? Are they truly fragments of bodies miraculously duplicated on the canvas? And if so, why are they censured as lifeless counterfeits of otherwise alive pictorial figures? Before approaching Albani's ideas once again, it is opportune to remember that the deadness of Caravaggio's figures must have rapidly become a widespread commonplace. In comparing Caravaggio's *Repentant Magdalene*, now in the Galleria Doria-Pamphilj, Rome (Fig. 3),[17] with Correggio's figure of the Magdalene in the *Lamentation* for the Del Bono Chapel in San Giovanni Evangelista (Parma),[18] Francesco Scannelli noted in his 1657 *Microcosmo della pittura* that Caravaggio "in imitating the truest works of nature seems to be a match for anyone." However, his imitations systematically fail to convey the impression of life. Whereas Caravaggio's Magdalene "shows her naturalness only in the surface's sheer appearance, which is not enough to animate her" so that "she ends up being deprived of spirit, grace and congruous expression, and it can be said that she is dead in every part," Correggio's figure, depicted indeed with "the most beautiful truth," appears "to be crying gracefully (...) expressing with excellence the truest and most appropriate effects of an inner pain," and therefore "enlivened" with the most vivid breath of nature.[19] Similarly, Bellori celebrated Caravaggio's *Repentant Magdalene* for its naturalness and the power of its imitation, "able with a few pigments to render the truth of colors." That said, he clearly belittled the work by insinuating that it does not represent a Magdalene:

> He painted a girl sitting on a chair with her arms in her lap while drying her hair; he represented her in a room and by putting on the ground a small vase of ointment with jewels and gems, he pretended she was a Magdalene.[20]

Undoubtedly, in Bellori's view Caravaggio's figure does not suggest the penitent demeanor of a saint; the Magdalene is nothing but an anonymous girl in a room, wrapped in a shimmering white

17 Apart from Scannelli and Bellori quoted in the text, Mancini, 1:224, also mentions the picture in the seventeenth century. For the painting see Toesca 1961; Friedlaender 1969, 94-6; Moir 1982, 78; Cinotti 1983, 510-2, no. 53; Hibbard 1983, 50-3; Calvesi 1990, 339 ff.; Puglisi 1998, 69-71; Longhi 1999-2000, 1: 254 [1968]; Krüger 1999; Varriano 1999b, 192-203; Sickel 2003, 55-64 [on paintings related to Girolamo Vittrici, who might have possessed the Doria-Pamphilj picture]; Marini 2005, 404-6, no. 20; Colantuono 2006, 64; Varriano 2006, 94-5, 118; Ebert-Schifferer 2009, 65-70; Von Rosen 2009, 97-101; Schütze 2009, 250, no. 10.

18 For the painting, see Gould 1976, 81-3, 266-7; and more recently Fornari Schianchi 2008, 314, no. III.19.

19 Scannelli, 277-8: "Molti al certo hanno dipinto l'opere d'espressa naturalezza, e fra gli altri Michelangelo da Carravaggio nell'imitazione dell'opere più vere della natura pare che non riuscisse a nessuno inferiore. Nientedimeno, se verremo ad osservare la figura della Maddalena citata nel primo libro del medesimo da Carravaggio nella galleria del principe Pamfilio in paragone di questa espressa nel medesimo quadro della pietà di Correggio, la quale oltre alla più bella verità si ritrova in atto addolorato e proprio, e l'altra del Carravaggio non dimostra la naturalezza che nella pura apparente superficie, perché non valendo in fatti per animarla, si ritruova priva dello spirito, grazia e debita espressione che si può dire per ogni parte morta. Ma il divino da Correggio,

come quello che ottenne sopra il talento di più fina maniera anco accoppiato il sodo fondamento dell'arte, lo dimostrò all'occasione co' rari effetti delle proprie più eccellenti operazioni; benché il Vasari mostri sentire altrimenti contra l'esperienza del senso, dando egli continuamente a conoscere aver espresso co' colori mediante la sufficienza di ben regolati contorni non solo l'apparenza dell'esterna naturalezza, ma in ordine all'espressione dell'atto più convenevole. Si vede questa mirabile figura fra l'altre maraviglie star graziosamente piangente che una tal bellezza, così ben espressa non può essere rimirata senza stupore e compassione come quella che dimostra in eccellenza gli effetti più veri e propri dell'interno dolore: figura composta di tutta sufficienza e veramente animata di quel più vivo spirito che possa mai la natura gravemente offesa con saggio di grand'affetto dimostrare."

20 Bellori, 215: "Dipinse una fanciulla a sedere sopra una seggiola con le mani in seno in atto di asciugarsi li capelli; la ritrasse in una camera, ed aggiungendovi in terra un vasello d'unguenti, con monili e gemme, la finse per Maddalena. Posa alquanto da un lato la faccia e s'imprime la guancia, il collo e 'l petto in una tinta pura, facile e vera, accompagnata dalla semplicità di tutta la figura, con le braccia in camicia e la veste gialla ritirata alle ginocchia dalla sottana bianca di damasco fiorato. Quella figura abbiamo descritto particolarmente per indicare li suoi modi naturali e l'imitazione in poche tinte sino alla verità del colore."

20

chemise, brocaded green gown and orange mantle, wholly stripped of expression and significance. Both Scannelli and Bellori instinctively blind themselves to the detail of the tear dripping down the Magdalene's nose, her half-parted lips uttering the hint of a sigh, her disheveled hair clumped atop her forehead or cascading in a disorderly fashion along her shoulders. Like Albani's "ignorant beholders," they deliberately entangle themselves with the surface of Caravaggio's picture, refusing to "read" its profundity. Paradoxically, their description and appraisal of the painting, albeit occasionally thorough, betray the shallowness of a cursory glance. Scannelli and Bellori are even unable to identify Caravaggio's main source and acknowledge his subtle elaboration on it: Parmigianino's etching of *Saint Thais*, another penitent and example of female contemplation[21] (Fig. 4). In fact, Caravaggio rotated Parmigianino's figure approximately 45 degrees, opting for a diving viewpoint, laying Thais' right arm across her lap and tilting her head sideways to free the sinuous curve of the Magdalene's neck. When scrutinized attentively, Caravaggio's treatment of the subject proves neither inexpressive, nor indecorous or ungraceful. It is canonically legitimate in many aspects, although I admit that because of its elusiveness, it might be unsettling with regard to the Counter-Reformation's predilection for the image's legibility. In spite of this, as is also the case for his half-figures, Caravaggio's *Magdalene* is downgraded by Scannelli and Bellori to the equivalent of a torpid, if sumptuous, still life. Worse, the complex process of elaboration that the figure had undergone—from a canonic template by a first-rank master like Parmigianino to its new life in the painting—is ignored to the point that, rather than a religious image, Caravaggio's composition is construed as a genre-scene or, at best, a low-life portrayal.

In the course of this book, I will unveil many other misconstructions of Caravaggio's works. What matters here is to highlight not only the critical myopia of Scannelli, Bellori, Albani and others, but to verify that, while misreading, critics and painters resorted to explanations that are frankly untenable, not to say preposterous. Put otherwise, Caravaggio's pictures disoriented even the most sensitive interpreters of the seventeenth century, generating an irrational repulsion that was mixed with uncontrollable fascination. This persistent phenomenon, which I will call the *Caravaggio syndrome,* deserves further scrutiny. It indeed has created a critical smokescreen that prevents scholars from comprehending many of the most radical innovations introduced by Caravaggio in pictorial narrative and, generally, in painting.

As I have already said, Bellori and Scannelli are not the only ones to deem Caravaggio's figures unfit to carry an *istoria*. Even if he did not refer specifically to half-figures, Mancini[22] blamed Caravaggio and his followers equally for their inability to create a narrative. His opinion, though, relies on a technical argument. According to Mancini, Caravaggio's school

> adheres very much to the truth, which they always keep in front of their eyes while working; they execute single figures well, but I do not believe that they really succeed in composing an *istoria* and showing the affects—which depend upon the imagination, and not upon the observation of things—since they reproduce the truth that they always keep in front of them; it is impossible to gather in a room a multitude of men who represent an *istoria* under the light of a window, having one smiling or crying or pretending to walk while staying put so that one can be copied, and thus these artists' figures, albeit powerfully rendered, lack motion, affects, and grace.[23]

21 Toesca 1961 was the first to suggest this parallel. Convincingly, in my opinion, Ebert-Schifferer 2009, 65, has suggested that a Roman bas-relief representing *Weeping Dacia* also inspired Caravaggio for his *Repentant Magdalene*. Curiously enough, Posèq 1998, 66-8, had already singled out this antique work as a source for Caravaggio, but in relation to *The Death of the Virgin*. For Parmigianino's print, see Zerner 1979, 16-7, nos. 10-I (12) and 10-II (12); Fornari Schianchi and Ferino-Pagden 2003, 333, no. 2.4.5; and Franklin 2003, 1987.

22 For Mancini, his personality and taste for the arts, and his interest in the painting of Caravaggio and his followers, see Salerno 1950; Maccherini 1997; Maccherini 1999; Maccherini 2002; Bury 2003; Maccherini 2004; De Benedictis and Roani 2005; Sparti 2008; Gage 2008; and Gage 2009.

23 Mancini, 1:108-9: "Questa schola in questo modo d'operare è molto osservante del vero, che sempre lo tien davanti mentre ch'opera; fa bene una figura sola, ma nella

Compared to Bellori's or Scannelli's judgment, Mancini's insight into Caravaggio's procedure appears more pertinent, although it, too, is perilously captious. To begin with the last argument, Mancini asserts that it is impossible to force a model to summon up a smile, a cry, or any other emotion indefinitely before the canvas. But what were painters advised in order to grasp and glean "real" expressions?

In his 1678 *Felsina Pittrice*, Carlo Cesare Malvasia relates that another Bolognese painter, Domenichino, during the years of his apprenticeship in the Carracci studio (around 1595), was already acutely aware of this issue. According to Malvasia, Domenichino believed that

> one ought to study those lively expressions of the spirit that, although they can sometimes be observed when a person is moved by an emotion, nonetheless disappear in a flash—not to mention those passions of the mind and inner affects that can alone give life and speech to dead and mute images.[24]

To remedy this, not only did Domenichino read stories and "fables"—that is, mythological writings—thus awakening his imagination, but he also used a technique that would provide his pictures with the required accuracy:

> He would go to places where people most frequently gather and conduct their affairs in order to observe the simplicity of the children, the frailty of the elderly, the compassion of women, the dealings of men, and there, concealed by his cloak, he would as if secretly execute a quick sketch with his pencil to serve as a reminder, or he would hurry home immediately to make a simple sketch.[25]

In other words, a momentary smile or cry, soon to fade away, could imprint itself in Domenichino's mind and be subsequently transferred into a summary sketch. If this was effective for Domenichino, why should it not also be viable for Caravaggio and his followers? Applying a previously studied smile or grin to the model in front of the canvas would have sufficed to ensure the exactitude of an expression. Or did Domenichino's men and women in the street differ significantly from the people whom Caravaggio claimed to use as his models? In the end, is it not the artist's imagination and memory that operate in both circumstances? Or perhaps a smile can reproduce itself in a painting without the intervention of any intellectual faculty? I will not discuss here how much the presence of the model-actor must have interfered in the creative process of Caravaggio and his followers, but I cannot bring myself to believe that their pictures are random segments of reality. First and foremost they are compositions. By this I mean that they are fictive systems of visual signs and as such their configuration springs from an act of artistic invention, and not of mechanical reproduction. This contention brings me to Mancini's first argument: the number of figures.

I will shortly elucidate why the quantity of actors in the *istoria* constitutes a constant theoretical

compositione dell'historia et esplicar affetto, pendendo questo dall'immagination e non dall'osservanza della cosa, per ritrar il vero che tengon sempre avanti, non mi par che vi vagliano, essendo impossibil di mettere in una stanza una moltitudine d'huomini che rappresentin l'historia con quel lume d'una fenestra sola, et haver un che rida o pianga o faccia atto di camminare e stia fermo per lasciarsi copiare, e così poi le lor figure, ancorché habbin forza, mancano di moto e d'affetti, di gratia, che sta in quell'atto d'operare come si dirà."

24 Malvasia, 2:311: "Onde a ciò che più si doveva men si pensasse: a que' primi moti per avventura di che mancan poi sempre quelle pese attitudini del nudo e quelle inette posature de' torsi; a quelle spiritose vivezze che, se pur talvolta nelle

persone commosse si osservano, come baleni spariscono; a quelle passioni dell'animo, a quegl'interni affetti che puon solo dar vita e discorso alle morte anco e mute immagini." I follow Anne Summerscale's translation here, to be published as part of the Malvasia Project, Center for Advanced Study in the Visual Arts, Washington DC.

25 Ibidem: "Là dove più frequenti fossero le radunanze e i commerci, riducendosi ad osservare le simplicità de' fanciulli, le languidezze de' vecchi, le compassioni delle donne e i maneggi de gli uomini, o chiuso nel mantello ricavavane allora, come d'ascoso, con la matite breve memoria, o portandos[']egli fretolosamente a casa di peso, formavane un po' d'ischizzo."

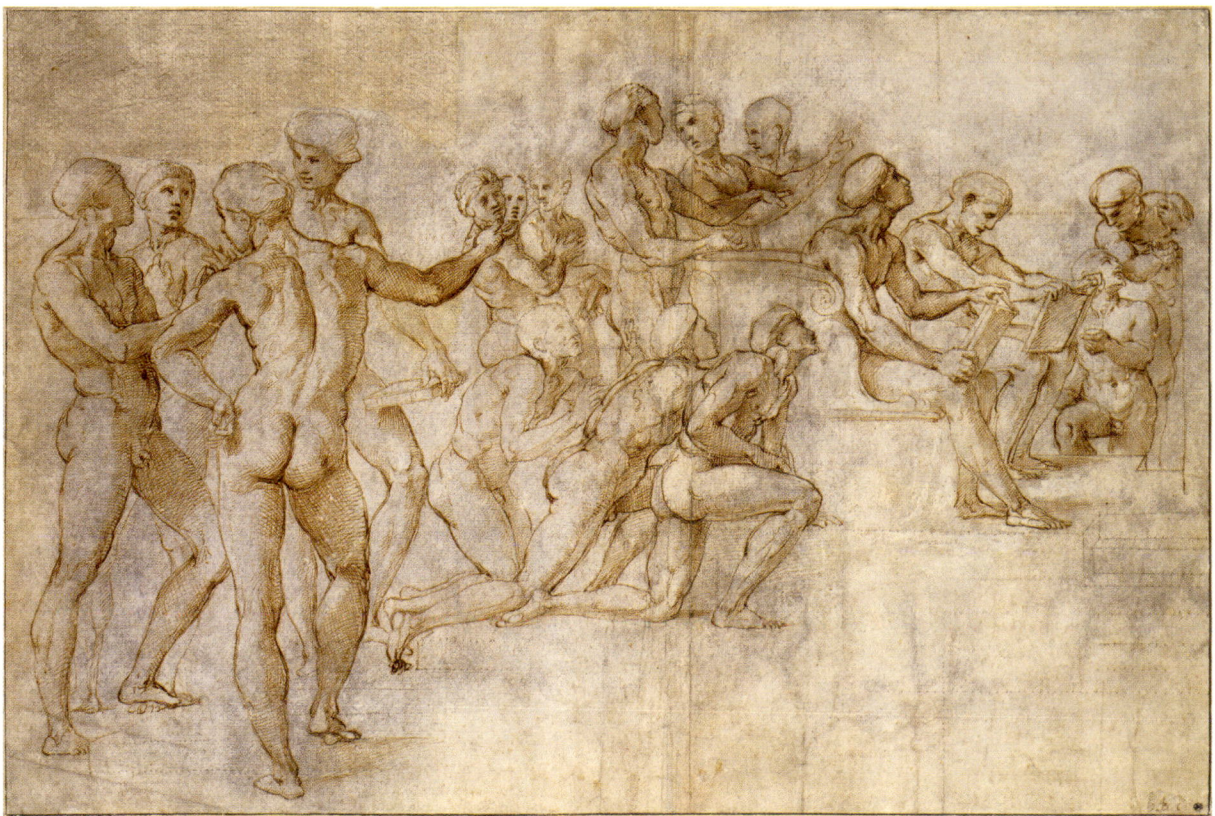

Fig. 5
Raphael (Raffaello Santi), *Nude Figure Study for the Left Foreground Group in the Disputa*, Städelsches Institut, Frankfurt,
pen and ink over black chalk and stylus underdrawing, 28 x 41.6 cm.

problem from the early Renaissance onward. For the time being, I will counter Mancini's point
by simply observing that the multitude of figures never deterred Caravaggio or his followers.
When necessary, all of them were able to compose multi-figure *istorie*. Moreover, the very notion
that in order to execute multiple actions Caravaggio or any of his followers needed to keep all
the figures in place before the canvas is both naïve and absurd. Even if not much is known about
Caravaggio's studio practices,[26] it is quite safe to postulate that, like any other painter, he proceeded
through montage on the basis of a pre-fixed—albeit probably evolving—visual scenario. The fact
that he did not use preparatory drawings does not contradict this assumption. In a sense, one
must conceive of Caravaggio's canvas as an ongoing, to-scale sketch unfolding toward the final
composition through numerous steps. Each of the posing sessions therefore corresponds to a
new partial version soon to replace, modify or fuse into the previous ones in accordance with
the master-scenario. Caravaggio's pictures would most likely appear as impressive palimpsests
in X-rays, were it not for the fact that his painting techniques did not leave enough vestiges of
the work in progress beneath the pictorial surface. In addition, it can be assumed that his lucidity
of vision moved Caravaggio to concentrate on a compositional layout once he had made up his
mind: he would exploit the possibilities of his option, but would not steer away from it in any
noticeable way. At any rate, as compositions, Caravaggio's paintings demanded a solid procedure
of montage, regardless of whether they were intended to represent a single figure or a multiple

26 Of course, Caravaggio's working methods and studio
practices have been the object of study and debate. The
most relevant contributions in this regard are: Christiansen

1986; Gregori 1991; Kroschewski 2002, esp. 37-57, 76-88; and
Varriano 2006, 7-18. For the use of live models by Caravaggio's
followers, see Serres 2003.

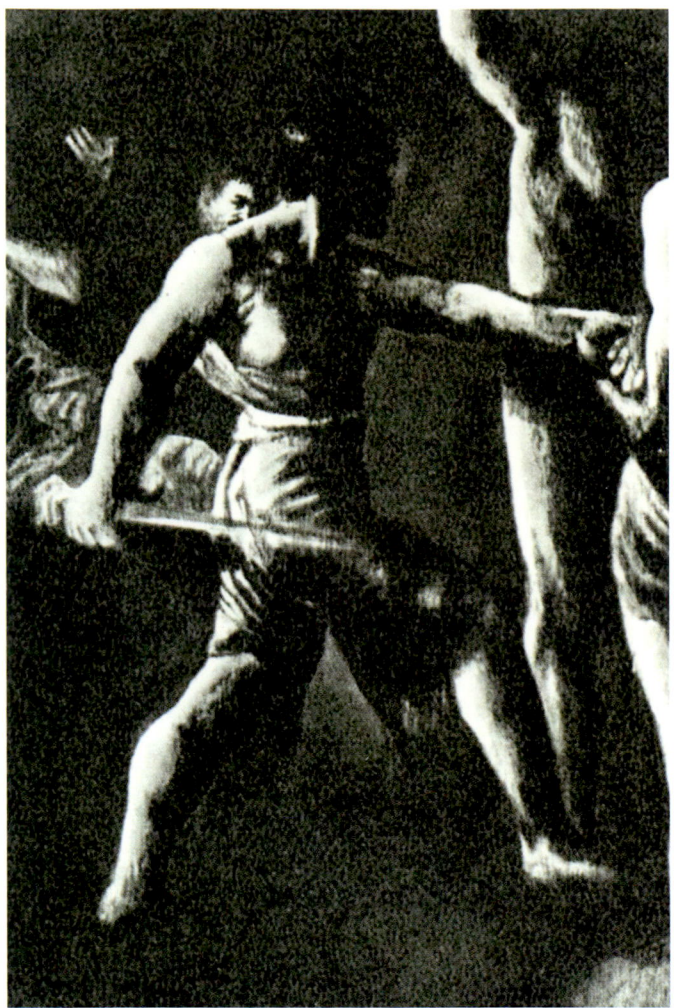

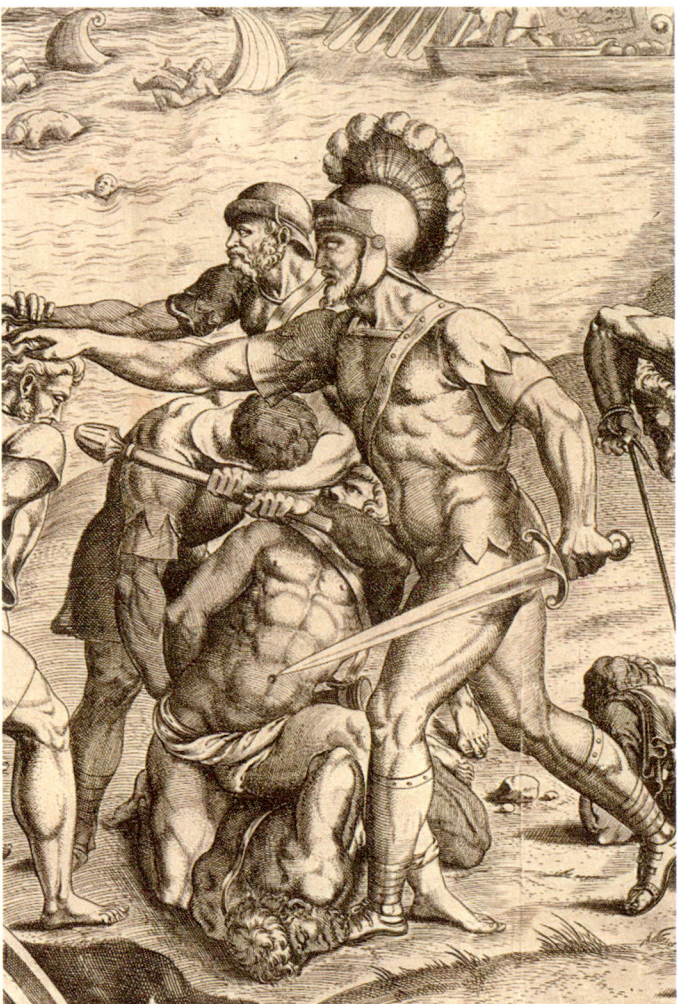

Fig. 6
Reconstruction Diagram of the X-Rays of Caravaggio's *The Martyrdom of Saint Matthew*, detail, reproduced from Leonello Venturi, *Caravaggio*, 1963.

Fig. 7
Anonymous engraver after Raphael (Raffaello Santi), *The Battle of Ostia*, engraving, 37.9 x 52.4 cm., detail.

action. More to the point, one must regard Caravaggio's technique of composing an *istoria* as an abridged and "telescoped" variant of Raphael's practice of *garzone*-studies.[27]

In this regard, consider Raphael's preparatory drawing for the left foreground group of the *Disputa*, now in the Städelsches Institut, Frankfurt (Fig. 5).[28] Francis Ames-Lewis has justly posited that Raphael advanced gradually from the left to the right of the sheet, prompting his apprentices to pose in specific attitudes by forming clusters of figures. He would quickly draw the contours of the posing models with black chalk or a stylus, reinforcing the silhouettes with pen while building up the volumes through parallel- or cross-hatching. After fixing a group in this way, he would repeat the procedure as many times as necessary, arranging his *garzoni* closer to or farther from the foreground while progressively heading toward the sheet's right margin. In examining the Frankfurt drawing attentively, I am inclined to think that even for single groups of figures Raphael might have used only one nude, who would revolve and modify his posture at the master's instigation, staying in place for as long as his attitude was absorbed and immortalized on paper. To prove this, it is sufficient to observe the uniqueness and similarity of the figures' proportions and complexions. In one case, a figure is obviously shifted from a point to another of the visual

27   For this topic, see in particular the excellent Ames Lewis 1986.

28   For the drawing, see Knab et al. 1983, 607-8, no. 290; and Ames Lewis 1986, 76 ff.

field, with almost no variation: I refer to the model on the left margin who rematerializes directly behind the chair, at the upper center of the drawing. In addition, the group of three figures below and next to the chair might well have been obtained by making a single model kneel on both legs or, alternatively, stretch one leg or the other while kneeling, thereby creating a rhythmic effect of *contrapposto*. It is not impossible that the much-praised fluidity of Raphael's groups rested upon, and was tested by, this elaborate "kinematics" of the models during studio sessions. Of course, to stage his actors in a predetermined sequence, Raphael relied on a scenario that he had mulled over repeatedly in many sketches. Arguably, the Frankfurt drawing precedes others in which drapery and chiaroscuro would also be analyzed. From this viewpoint, Caravaggio's practice might appear as the opposite of Raphael's, and this is exactly what Caravaggio himself wanted the public to fathom by asserting his total disengagement from drawing practice.

Yet giving up drawing does not imply that the procedure of inventing and composing is skipped wholesale or could fast-forward to the work's definitive execution. Let us consider Caravaggio's *Martyrdom of Saint Matthew* in San Luigi dei Francesi, Rome. As X-ray photographs have showed,[29] one or more versions of the composition lie below the surface; they dramatically differ from the picture as delivered by Caravaggio in 1600. I will not embark here on a reconstruction of the painting's first drafts, since this is irrelevant in this context, besides being a particularly slippery endeavor. Rather, I will focus on one figure easily identifiable in the X-rays: an assassin wielding a sword (Fig. 6). It is evident that the figure derives from Raphael's *The Battle of Ostia*, as has been correctly argued (Fig. 7).[30] How should one envision the method followed by Caravaggio in painting this figure? Did he proceed like Raphael, by placing the model in a pre-determined posture, outlining his contours on the canvas—not on paper—and bringing out the volume with the brush, rather than with a pen? Is one to suppose that Caravaggio could achieve a figure in just one session? Or is it not more probable that the master completed his figures in several phases, so that they gained definition over time by taking on relief, color, and accessories on their way to completion? In this respect, it has been proposed that the famous incisions often left by Caravaggio on his pictures served as reminders to indicate a model's position at the end of a session.[31] If these factors are true, it must be admitted that Caravaggio discovered a pictorial shortcut enabling him to pass from the pristine stages of invention to the final product by squeezing the studio-related practice of drawing models into the very process of the execution. In other words, Caravaggio did not renounce composition: his method of executing a picture is probably swifter and more spontaneous, but surely no less strenuous, than Raphael's, especially if one bears in mind that, unlike Raphael, Caravaggio could not entrust his apprentices with the task of sketching and advancing his pictures.

To the readers who may doubt the viability of this method, I respond with an observation by Annibale Carracci. In one of his glosses on Vasari's life of Titian, he criticizes the author's persuasion that "it is necessary for him who wants to arrange his compositions well and adjust his inventions (…) to put them first in different manners on paper, seeing how everything pans out." Annibale expresses his disagreement in an amazingly straightforward way: "It isn't as if painters cannot put [inventions] in different manners on the canvas, effacing and remaking them in the same way as on paper! But I don't have the room to prove the bullshit of that idiot Vasari."[32] Unfortunately, Annibale does not supply us with further elucidations, but his direct experience of painting allows him to debunk the theorem on which Vasari founds the supremacy of drawing and the advantages

---

29   See in particular Venturi 1952.

30   See for instance Friedlaender 1969, 112. For the print by an anonymous engraver from the circle of Marcantonio Raimondi representing Raphael's *Battle of Ostia* in reverse, see Boorsch and Spike 1985, 45, no. 7 (34); Cirillo Archer 1995, 32, no. 036.

31   See more recently Cardinali et al. 2005.

32   Benati and Riccomini 2006, 462: "Quasi che non si possono porre in più modi differenti su la tavola, e da quella cassarle e rifarle, come sulla carta, ma mi manca il loco di provar la coglioneria di questo goffo del Vasari."

of the Florentine method of composing an *istoria*. Of course, it comes as no surprise that to discredit Caravaggio's pictorial narratives, Mancini, Albani, Bellori, and others reiterated the arguments used by Vasari against Giorgione and Titian a century or so earlier. Perhaps Caravaggio himself intended to attract this kind of criticism by identifying himself with Giorgione at the beginning of his career. But it is somewhat disconcerting to realize that if Caravaggio's painting was censured on this basis, this occurred with a view toward evincing the superiority of Annibale's art. I will come back to this point later. Returning to Mancini's argument, it is now evident that Caravaggio's method engages the imagination and the memory as much as Raphael's. Or can one truly believe that the sophisticated attitude of the torturer in the first version of the *Martyrdom* happened unintentionally and at a whim? On the contrary, it is obvious to me that if Caravaggio positioned his model in that way, it is because he was heeding a visual scenario: the analog of a preliminary sketch. However, I would like to make it clear that by comparing Raphael to Caravaggio I do not intend to diminish the charge of innovation and provocation inherent in "Caravaggio's path." Nor am I as candid as to dismiss the many disparities that these diverse procedures of composing bring about in terms of the artifact's invention and reception. So far, my intention has been primarily to demonstrate the fragility of Mancini's argumentation with regard to Caravaggio's technique of carrying out an *istoria*.

As for Albani, his criticism of half-figures can hardly be taken seriously. He writes:

> The beginner in the profession of painting who sets out to learn and achieve everything by toiling to imitate nature in making a single half-figure from the waist up, should take care not to wallow in the pleasure he takes in the process, especially if he sticks to it over the years. Indeed, should he want to satisfy the commissions he will receive of putting together many figures, he will be at pains to join one piece to another, for he will not be accustomed at all to taking into account neither the thighs nor the legs of the figures, so that linking them together will prove difficult for him.[33]

Not surprisingly, by limiting himself to half-figures, this unfortunate artist will be "a painter without spirit," unlike Raphael who instead "had the intelligence to socialize with the most prominent literati of Leo X's court."[34] How familiarity with Baldassare Castiglione and Pietro Bembo would have helped Raphael to graft legs and thighs correctly onto his figures remains a mystery. But of course, one would miss Albani's point by focusing on this detail: the gist of his warning is that no excellent painter of an *istoria* would waste too much time toying with half-figures. More pertinently, he also contends that the practice of exclusively depicting half-figures hampers the painter's ability to visualize a multiple action, to wit, the connection of different figures to one another. This conclusion, of course, is acceptable and legitimate, but as I have already said, Caravaggio and his followers used to depict multiple actions as well. Yet Albani disregards the evidence, and with disdain lumps together every painter working with "still objects": flowers, fruits, and—curiously enough—half-figures. In his opinion, even the imitative skills of Zeuxis and Parrhasios are not truly marvelous:

---

33 Malvasia, 2:258: "Quel principiante nella professione della pittura che si propone impararla e conseguire il tutto mediante l'affaticarsi nell'imitazione della natura col fare una sola meza figura dal mezo in su, guardissi dalla dillettazione che in quella prende, massime fermandovicisi per continuazione di anni, poiché, quando vorà eseguire li comandi che le verano di pore di molte figure, durerà poi fatica nell'unire pezzi con pezzi, non essendo (massime egli) avezzo a considerare né le cosce, e né le gambe su le figure, la quale unione le parerà poi dura."

34 Ibidem: "...si lascerà conoscere per pittore molto differente da Raffaelle da Urbino, il quale seppe unire il tutto ne' serviggi in Roma da i pontefici in Vaticano, e ardirò dire che ebbe del miracoloso, benché fu umano, poiché ebbe grand'ingegno nell'accostarsi co' i primi letterati della gran corte di Leone Decimo."

> Sometimes I consider the wonders written about those painters who deceived birds with their well-feigned grapes, and I say to myself that it is one thing to deceive them, and another to deceive people with judgment who know the sense of things, like for instance the inner passions that are much more difficult [to represent] than the external ones: grapes, figs, and melons are much easier [to represent] than those passions.[35]

Although it cannot be proved, it is evident to me that Albani is criticizing here Caravaggio's famous precept as quoted by Marchese Vincenzo Giustiniani: "it is as much toil to depict a good picture of flowers as one of figures."[36] In any case, for Albani, the supposed ease of painting still lifes and half-figures had led painters to relinquish the habit of reading and drawing: "and because they don't read, a desperation arises that makes them veer toward depicting and devoting themselves to flowers, or fruits, or at best to disconnected portraits."[37] All of these objects are "imitations in the image of truth, and not of verisimilitude."[38]

It is now time to recapitulate and evaluate the main points of Albani's criticism against "Caravaggio's path." In the first place, Albani denounces the ineffectiveness of a technical device adopted by Caravaggio in many of his pictorial narratives: the dramatic close-up. Although Albani only mentions isolated "half-figures," the notions of affects, inner passion, grace, expression, worth, legibility, propriety, verisimilitude, and perspective are more specific to the category of the *istoria*. Therefore, one would not be incorrect in maintaining that the half-figure, as the primary constituent of the dramatic close-up re-inaugurated by Caravaggio since his first Roman pictures, not only soared to the status of the master's trademark, but also epitomized all the failures intrinsic to his new paradigm of pictorial narrative, a paradigm so deeply rejected by Albani. Because it is nothing but the empty shell of a body, the half-figure can be equated with melons, figs, watermelons, and flowers: it is motionless, senseless, spatially and physically "disconnected"—that is, inherently unfit to encapsulate and channel the facet of an action worthy of the name. More importantly, Albani argues that by drawing attention obsessively toward the half-figure, Caravaggio and his followers inhibited the viewer's capacity of "reading" the painting. Hence the pictorial narrative, the equivalent of an episode of a book, loses its literality: no longer "poems," the half-figures at best resemble "a couple of verses devoid of concept."[39] In its rigidity, Albani's theoretical system outlines a grid of binomial criteria opposite to, and incompatible with, one another, in which Caravaggio's art represents the negative pole: appearance vs. essence, nonsense vs. meaning, stillness vs. motion, deadness vs. liveliness, (crude) truth vs. verisimilitude, etc. This critical condemnation of Caravaggio's painting is of course largely unsubstantiated. Albani's reaction is an epiphenomenon of what I have already called the *Caravaggio syndrome*, and on this account it needs to be examined within the broader purview of seventeenth-century art history. Along with the criticisms of Mancini, Scannelli, and Bellori, Albani's sentiments attest to the uncomfortable disorientation that

---

35 Ibidem: "Io tal ora esamino le meraviglie che si leggono di quei pittori, che con le bene finte uve inganarono gl'ucelli, e dico altro è ingannare questi, ed altro è ingannare le persone di giudicio che conoscono le cose sensate, come le passioni interne più dificili assai che le esterne, l'uve, i fichi e melloni molto più sono facili che le sudette passioni…"

36 Giustiniani, 42: "Ed il Caravaggio disse che tanta manifattura gli era a fare un quadro di fiori come di figure."

37 Malvasia, 2:258: "in pochi anni, questi abbandonano lo studiare de' libri e la viva voce de' letterati, si credono addottorarsi sopra le opere di pitture o panni razzi, lasciano indietro la cognizione della prospettiva, il legere (frammeggiatamente al dissegnare) libri sempre d'ogni sorte; poiché con questo si acquista l'ingegno, e si resta (non legendo) nell'ignoranza, e

ne segue che dall'ignoranza mai può nascere un vero pittore, e per questo non leggere ne segue una disperazione che li fa voltare per la strada di dipingere, e darsi tutto a' fiori o a' frutti, o alla più al fare ritratti disubligati etc."

38 Ibidem, 2:244: "Si vedono bensì imitazioni a simiglianza del vero, ma non già del verisimile…"

39 Ibidem: "…I tre Carracci, e il più conforme a Raffaelle di Annibale, questi che io sublimo non attesero alle meze figure se non in sua fanciulezza, ma in gioventù e per tutto il corso di sua vita attesero a fare operone, né mai più di Paolo o di Annibale si videro mezze figure, ma spieghi numerosi in Paolo, e gallerie in Annibale furono poemi, in luogo di fare solo duoi semplici versi liberi sciolti da concetto."

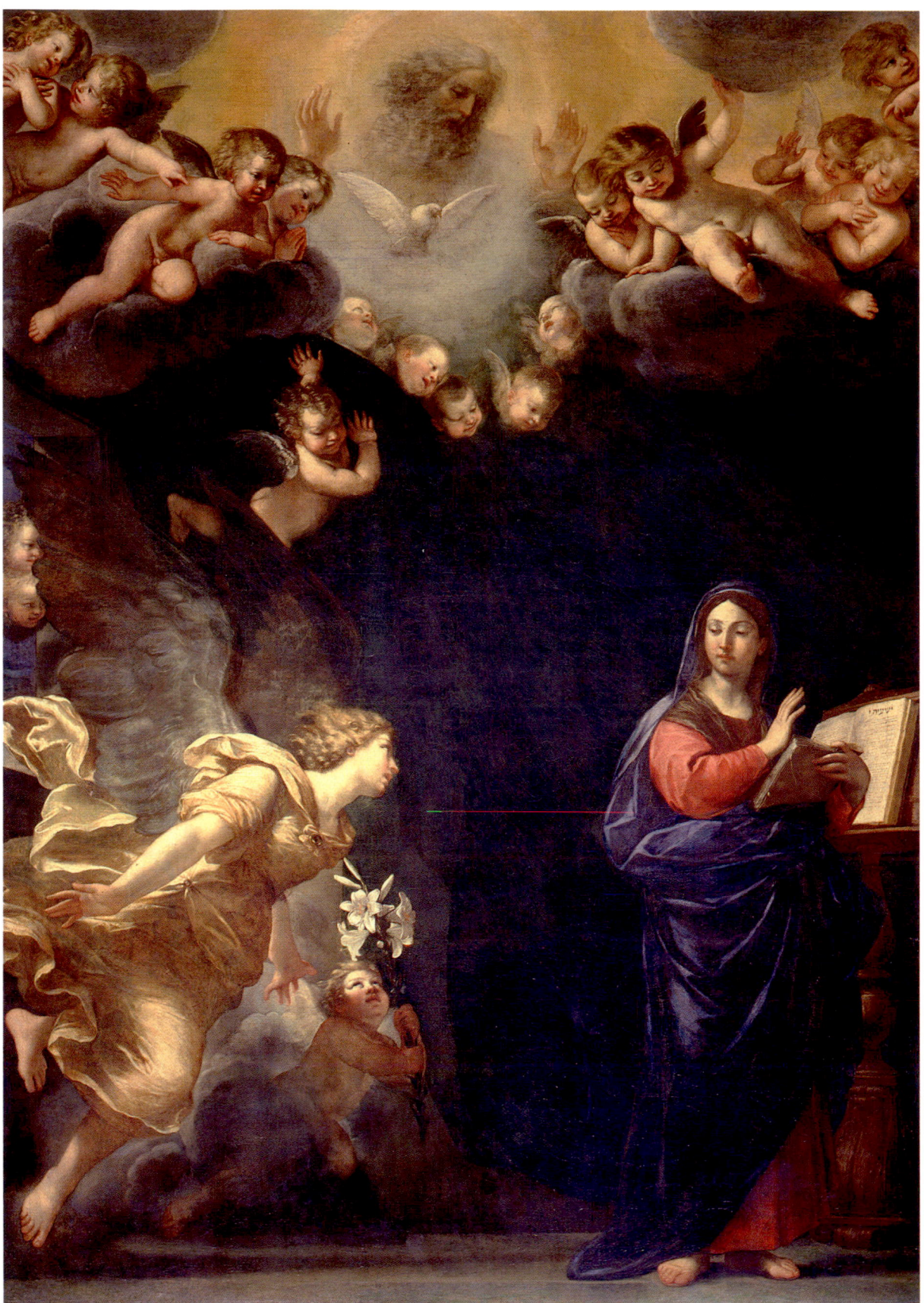

Fig. 8
Francesco Albani, *The Annunciation*, San Bartolomeo di Porta Ravegnana, Bologna, oil on canvas, 365 x 295 cm.

Caravaggio's rendering of the human figure—not merely the half-figure—aroused in artists and theorists alike. Had Caravaggio avoided the *istoria* altogether, his treatment of the human figure and half-figure would have been easily classified as the extravagance of a "comic" painter (I shall explore the concept of pictorial comedy in Part Two). But Caravaggio extended his method of composition to the highest and noblest genre of painting, the *istoria*, and especially to its main sub-category, the sacred story. By doing so, he questioned, undermined, and subverted many principles of pictorial narrative that, taken for granted or viewed as virtually unproblematic, would instead turn out to be intricate and disruptive—for one thing, the relationship between truth and image, and the dialectics of the true and the verisimilar in painting.

In this monograph, I intend to prove that Caravaggio's unprecedented interpretation of pictorial narrative triggered a chain reaction that forced painters and theorists to clarify their ideas of the *istoria*, of action and composition. This chain reaction gave rise to one of the most flourishing seasons of reflection and debate on art and painting: seventeenth-century academism, particularly in France. In this perspective, Albani's critical positions play an eminent role. As a disciple of the Carracci and a colleague of Guido Reni and Domenichino, Albani belongs to a generation that experienced first-hand the repercussions of Caravaggio's painting. The struggle he put up against "Caravaggio's path" is the tip of a larger iceberg, an iceberg that, because of the scarce documentation at our disposal, has gone almost unnoticed. Through Albani we can observe the process of reconfiguration and reorientation to which the *istoria* was submitted by many members of the Bolognese network: not only Guido and Domenichino, but, via Domenichino and not unexpectedly, Nicolas Poussin, whose allegiance to "the Carracci's path" would be instrumental in sealing Caravaggio's defeat in the 1640s and 1650s. It is no coincidence that many decades after Caravaggio's death Bellori, Scannelli, Malvasia, and others kept denigrating Caravaggio's painting in such harsh terms and with arguments as repetitive as refrains: if this occurred, it is because painters like Albani, Domenichino, and Poussin succeeded in creating a consensus on their ideas about the *istoria*. Caravaggio and his followers were the scapegoats of the seventeenth-century classicist movement. Conversely, Caravaggio also contributed—unwillingly, perhaps—to strengthening his rivals' historical and ideological identity.

Nevertheless, the opinions of Albani, Scannelli, Bellori, and others, as I have already noted, do not allow us to grasp the actual scope of Caravaggio's rebellious novelty: there is no doubt that his artistic revolution—the term is not inappropriate—overwhelmed the critical aptitudes of all these artists and interpreters, so much so that they ran short of arguments, resorting sometimes to slander and prejudice, or more often to blaming Caravaggio's lack of decorum. To explain why "Caravaggio's path" was so difficult to pin down, it is necessary to deal with the question of pictorial narrative in its entirety from the Renaissance onward. The ambivalent concept of the *istoria* as both an optical and a rhetorical device of narration is the major cause of the theoretical embarrassment in which Albani and many others were inexorably entrapped. Only in this manner can I lay the groundwork for clarifying the extent of Caravaggio's poetics of dislocation.

Before embarking on this enterprise, it may be useful to dwell a little longer on Albani, since in a letter of 1637 he himself describes the merits and virtues of an exemplary religious image: his 1632 *Annunciation* for San Bartolomeo, Bologna (Fig. 8).[40] Albeit in a specific way, this painting constitutes a complex model of "Albani's path."

Addressed to the Bolognese amateur Orazio Zamboni, whom Albani wanted to engage as the co-author of his soon-to-be-abandoned treatise on painting, the letter begins by grappling with a theoretical question: Michelangelo's excellence in representing the human figure. Shortly afterward, Albani sketches out the points that he intends to develop in the treatise: first of all, the

---

40   For the painting, see Puglisi 1999, 155, no. 69.

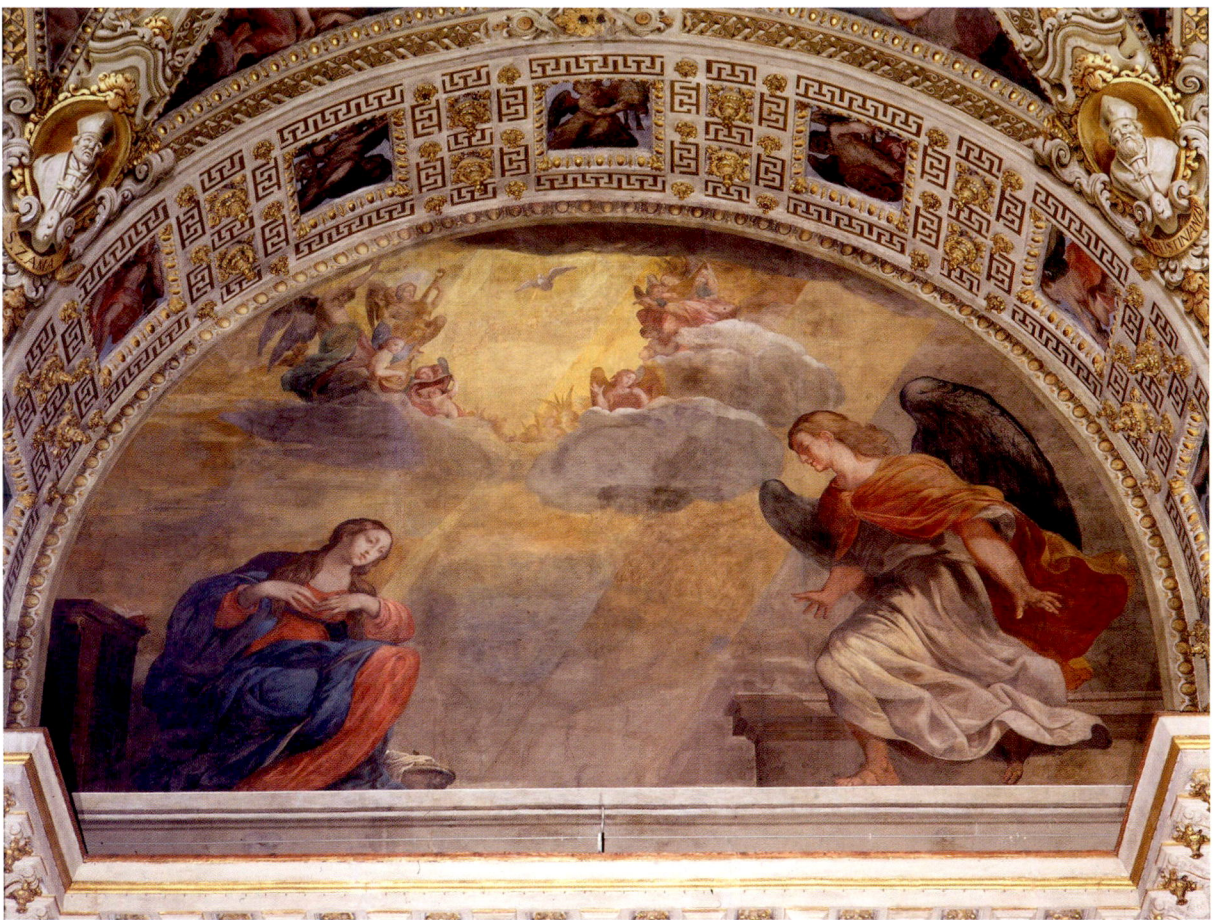

Fig. 9
Ludovico Carracci, *The Annunciation*, San Pietro Cathedral, Bologna, fresco.

supremacy of invention among the other "parts" of painting. In Albani's opinion, "the other parts are subordinate to this [invention], and although each in itself is beautiful, nonetheless they are not as relevant as [invention], and do not shine without beautiful invention, with most beautiful concepts well ordered, and with all figures acting appropriately, and none without a purpose."[41] At this point, almost out of the blue, Albani starts pouring out his bile: people are spreading rumors about his San Bartolomeo *Annunciation*, pretending that it is defective because "the Virgin [keeps] her eyes too low." To absolve himself of the accusation, Albani declares: "I wish to learn first where the criticism comes from, and [the observation] that the angel hovers in the air so much below the holy Virgin that it is a blunder."[42] However, as Albani continues,

> to acknowledge his great mistress the angel ought to humiliate himself [bending] down to earth; I didn't make this angel at random, for his is an act of entering, and greeting, and of a profound reverence, so I showed him lingering on his wings, since he was sent supernaturally by God the Father as his ambassador.

41 Malvasia, 2:255: "...so che si pigliarà animo e si darà principio, frameggiando sempre documenti, col sostentare che l'invenzione è la prima, e le altre parti sono servitrici di quella, e se bene ad una ad una sono belle, non vagliono tanto né risplendono se non in compagnia d'una bella invenzione, con bellissimi concetti ben disposti, e che tutte le figure operino a proposito, ma nulla in darno etc."

42 Ibidem: "Mi fu detto in casa mia domenica sera passata che io, avendo fatta un'Annonziata in San Bartolomeo, e che la Madonna teneva troppo bassi gl'occhi; si è sempre usata la detrazione e il malignare, anzi io ho per buon segno, quando l'opre sono guardate e censurate, ma questa censura non va a proposito, o se si usasse il dare licenza, si direbbe cose vere, e se le darebbe eccezzioni calzanti; io tacqui, e mi partii la mattina seguente per il Medola; ho prima voglia d'informarmi di dove viene l'eccezione, e che l'angelo stava in aria tanto basso più della Beata Vergine che era sproposito."

In the same manner,

> it is necessary in an invention to show many things in a single action, whereas painters nowadays are barely able to show but one expression (…); one must visualize the figures acting so that it is possible to know what they are doing, what they have just done, and are about to do.[43]

This is why the posture of Gabriel's wings indicates that he has just landed and glided into the Virgin's room. Similarly, Mary, "who must have been reading Isaiah at that moment of the unfolding Incarnation," appears to be reading, and turning "upon seeing an angel aloft in human form entering the room, is upset, and sets out to protect the virginal purity she has determined to preserve forever."[44] Proudly, Albani reminds Zamboni that the great Carracci and Raphael taught him how to invent, implying that the objections to his *Annunciation* were inconclusive and gratuitous. Malvasia certainly shared his view, as he also extols the multiplicity of actions that Gabriel performs in the picture, moreover expounding on how chronologically felicitous Mary's attitude in the painting proves to be. Here is the rhetorical question through which Malvasia brings to the fore Albani's good sense of timing:

> Is it not possible that Mary, upon the celestial messenger's unexpected arrival in her secluded room, stood up swiftly, especially since she is depicted standing, holding the open book with one hand, while she uplifts the other with admiration, listening to the angel's words?[45]

Most of the difficulties perceived by alert beholders in appraising the San Bartolomeo *Annunciation* derive from the intricacy of the stylistic, narrative, and allegorical implications Albani intended to weave into the composition. It is a fact that the *Annunciation* is among the most hackneyed iconographic themes in seventeenth-century painting. To make a difference, Albani needed to offer a completely innovative approach to the theme, one that at the same time could display his outstanding knowledge and rare imagination.

Many things can be said about this painting, but I will only stress a few elements. The depiction of Gabriel represented an immense pictorial challenge to Albani: through this angel, he intended to manifest his excellence over, or at least his equivalence to, both Ludovico Carracci, his master, and Correggio. In 1618, Ludovico had executed one of his last paintings, an enormous fresco representing the *Annunciation* in Bologna Cathedral, San Pietro (Fig. 9).[46] According to Malvasia, the old Ludovico, "deceived by the immense height and width of the vault and the narrowness of the scaffolding," committed a memorable mistake: he botched the receding foot of the gliding angel.[47] Albani, who was in Bologna in 1618, must have known about the figure and Ludovico's

---

43 Ibidem: "L'angelo poi per riconoscere la sua gran padrona doveva apunto umiliarsi sino a terra; il detto angelo da me non fu fatto a caso, perché è atto d'ingresso e di salutazione, e riverenza profonda, mostrandolo librato su l'ali, che come cosa sopranaturale è mandato dal Padre Eterno per ambasciatore, così appunto nell'invenzione bisognarebbe mostrare più cose in un sol atto, ché oggidì non ne mostrano malamente una solo espressione e la vera invenzione; bisognarebbe formare le figure operanti, che si conoscesse in fare quello che fa, quello che anco ha fatto e che sono per fare."

44 Ibidem: "E Maria, che doveva leggere d'Isaia in quel punto dell'Incarnazione futura, lo dimostra col mostrare che legeva, e poi si volge avendo veduto sopra arrivare in camera un angelo in forma umana, e si turba, e si mette guardinga della sua propostasi in eterno purità virginale etc."

45 Ibidem, 2:263: "Perché non può darsi ch'ella, all'improviso arrivo del celeste paraninfo nella chiusa camera, sorta ben presto in piedi fosse, tanto più che così ritta figurata, ritenendo anche in una delle mani l'aperto libro, alza l'altra in modo di ammirazione ad ascoltar ciò che favelli?"

46 For the fresco, see Perini 1997; and Brogi 2001, 1:237-9, no. 128.

47 Malvasia, 1:448: "Nella Nonziata solo, nel gran lunettone della stessa catedrale, stranamente incagliossi, ingannato dall'immensa altezza e larghezza di quel vasto volto e angustia del ponte, non potendo scostarsi a rimirarne l'effetto, onde nel pié che, per inchinar la Vergine, ritira l'angelo scorresse lo storpio manifesto e che non si può difendere."

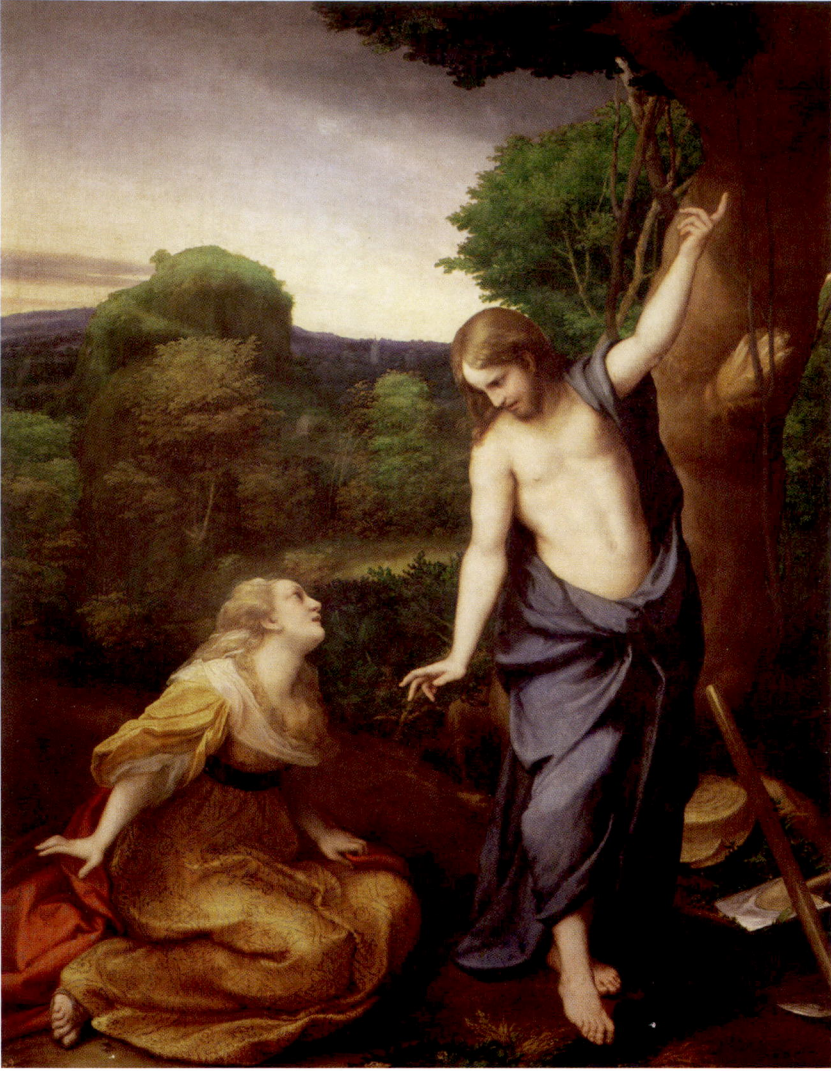

Fig. 10
Correggio (Antonio Allegri), *Noli Me Tangere*, Museo del Prado, Madrid, oil on canvas, 130 x 103 cm.

disappointment with himself. More than a decade later, he resolved to improve upon Ludovico's Gabriel and took up the figure in the San Bartolomeo *Annunciation*: apart from the foreshortened foot, the orientations of the two angels' bodies mirror one another in a striking manner. To adjust the figure to the new context, and to justify the excessive momentum with which Ludovico had endowed his prototype, Albani imagined the angel both in the middle and at the end of his flight: a glowing comet at once slowing and halting in the Virgin's presence. To magnify his beauty, he resorted to another canonical model with which he was well acquainted: Correggio's figure of the kneeling Magdalene in the *Noli Me Tangere* (now in the Museo del Prado, Madrid; Fig. 10).[48] In this painting, the lovely sinner, in profile, her lips slightly parted, stares raptly at the Savior. Albani borrowed her expression and facial traits—the lithe outline of the forehead, nose, chin and throat—while preserving Correggio's chromatic choice: the blond of the hair enhances the yellow-orange of the robe, which in turn plays with the whiteness of the flesh. By intensifying Gabriel's radiance through Correggio's palette, Albani not only showed off his talent as a colorist, but he also created a chromatic pole of attention funneling both climactic motion and allegory into the composition. As a matter of fact, the angel's brilliance simultaneously acts as a sign of divine epiphany and as the trigger of the pictorial action; his bursting-in "sheds light" on the Virgin's attitude of surprise, demureness, determination, and even majesty. Without further parsing Albani's *Annunciation*, it is now clear that the image results from the subtle mechanics of multiple factors, all of them previously over-determined and loaded with a plurality of meanings. The figure, along with its "canonicity," attitude, lighting, connectivity, and position in time and space is meticulously crafted, thereby partaking in the "sense" of the overall story. What characterizes Albani's take on the concept of the *istoria* is the conviction that "sense"— that is, theological, ontological, aesthetical and moral significance in its multi-sidedness—cannot be achieved beyond the optical and physical boundaries of verisimilitude. In other words, his *Annunciation* fails to persuade the viewers not because it lacks sense, but because its excess of sense collides with the temporal and spatial framing of verisimilitude. By charging the figure with a plurality of actions unspooling over time, yet frozen in an unsurpassable instant, Albani

48   For the painting, see Gould 1976, 92-3, 224-6.

ineluctably ends up obscuring the intelligibility and readability of the story. In a certain sense, the issue that Albani raises with his *Annunciation* leads to a theoretical and visual conundrum. At the core of this issue lies a substantial question: how does the figure make—that is, produce—sense in a pictorial narrative? And, equally important to us, why did Caravaggio's treatment of the figure cease to make sense—if it ever did—in the eyes of his contemporaries? In what ways and to what extent did Caravaggio's narratives disturb the sixteenth- and early seventeenth-century concept of the *istoria*? Discovering the answers will take us on a very long journey.

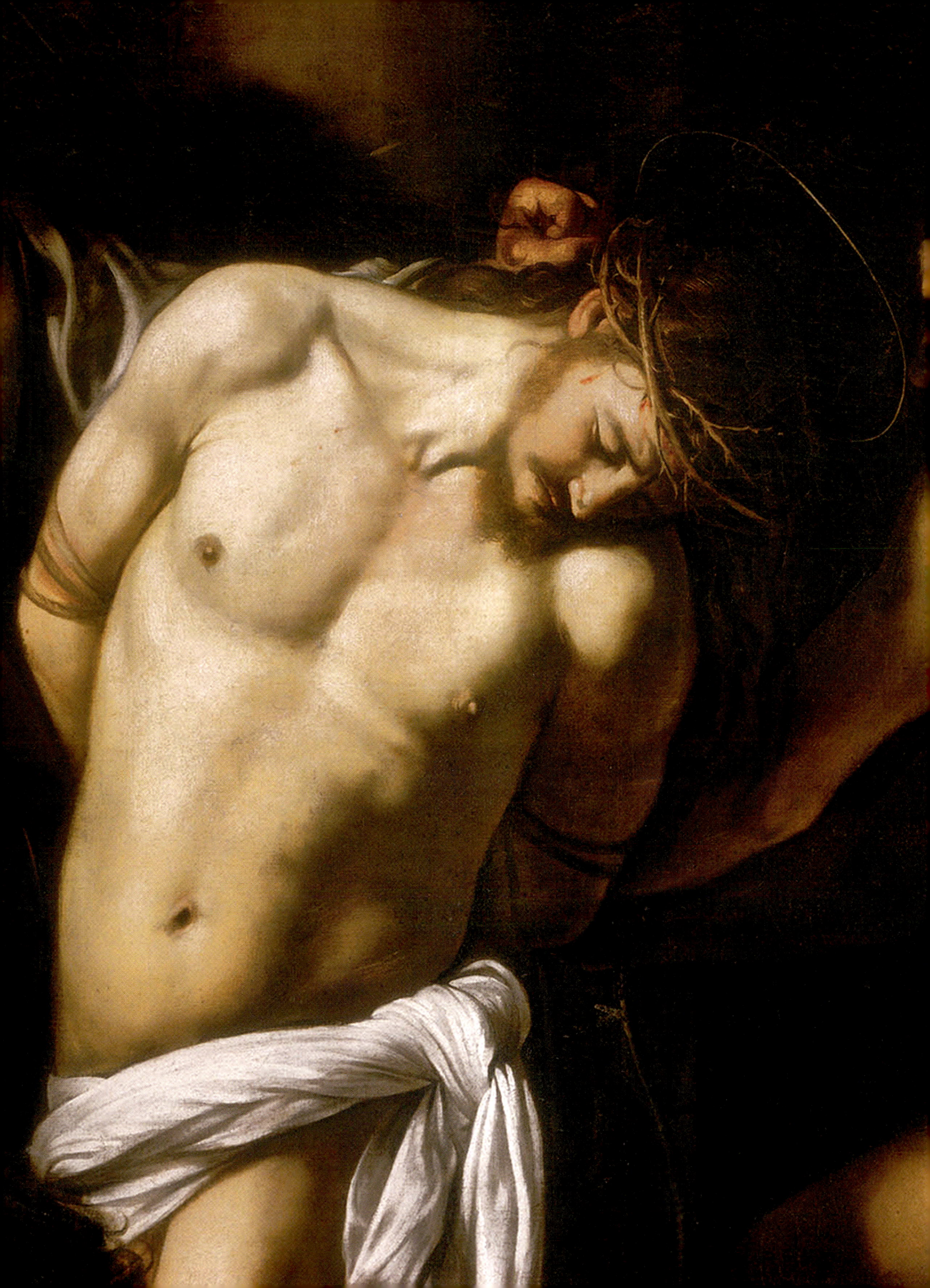

CHAPTER 1

The Glitches in Alberti's *Istoria*: The Human Figure Between Beauty and Reality*

"In all forms there must be their ideas—that is, their perfection—and reason ought to make this manifest to the good painter. There is even an idea of the ugly."[1]

At the dawn of the Italian Renaissance, painting was not conceived of as a half-artisanal, half-scientific device able to reproduce human vision as processed by the eyes and the mind in a definite space and time. Nor was the canvas or panel the surface onto which the painter's sight was metaphorically projected and meant to be imprinted wishfully forever. By and large, the notion of painting as a mechanical art dominated even as Leon Battista Alberti published his fundamental *De pictura* in 1435.[2] In this treatise, Alberti offered painters an interpretation of their manual activity that many, especially outside Florence, must have found simply unsettling:

> [Painters] should know that when they circumscribe the surface with lines, filling these areas with colors, they seek nothing but to represent the multiple forms of surfaces on this surface only, as if the surface they work on with colors were of an extremely transparent glass so that the visual pyramid pierces through it at a determinate distance and position of the central ray and light (…).[3]

The entire first book of Alberti's treatise is dedicated to demonstrating scientifically that a bi-dimensional medium—whether a canvas, a panel or a portion of a wall—can artistically transform itself into a screen reproducing with exactitude and in relief the painter's vision as if it were real, a section of the artist's visual pyramid. Painting, now an unprecedented technological device, not only imitates nature, but also mirrors the external world just as it appears to man's sight. Unknowingly,

---

* All the quotations from Leon Battista Alberti's *De Pictura* are translated from the original Latin version. Nonetheless, in the footnotes, I quote *in extenso* both the Latin and Italian versions in the interest of greater clarity.

1 Testa, 224: "Che in tutte le forme ci debbe essere la sua idea, cioè il suo perfetto, e questo al buon pittore debbe essere manifesto dalla ragione; etiandio del brutto si fa l'idea."

2 For Alberti's artistic theory, see Mühlmann 1981; Poeschke 1985; Grayson 1993; Panza 1994; Bätschmann 1997; Bätschmann 1998; Forster and Locher 1999; Barbieri 2000; Di Stefano 2000; Bätschmann 2002; Krohn 2002; Cieri Via 2007; Passarelli 2007; Di Stefano 2007; Ambrosini 2009. It goes without saying that Alberti's definition of perspective in his *De Pictura* has been submitted to intense scrutiny. For the historical and theoretical implications of Alberti's perspective, see Panofsky 1924-1925; and Damisch 1987.

3 Alberti, 26-9: "E sappiano che quando con sue linee circuiscono la superficie, e quando empiono di colori e' luoghi descritti, niun'altra cosa cercarsi se non che in questa superficia si ripresentino le forme delle cose vedute, non altrimenti che se essa fusse di vetro tralucente tale che la pirramide visiva indi trapasasse, posto una certa distanza, con certi lumi e certa posizione di centro in aere e ne' suoi luoghi altrove. [Ac discant quidem dum lineis circumeunt superficiem, dumque descriptos locos implent coloribus, nihil magis queri quam ut in hac una superficie plures superficierum formae repraesententur, non secus ac si superficies haec, quam coloribus operiunt, esset admodum vitrea et perlucida huiusmodi ut per eam tota pyramis visiva permearet certo intervallo certaque centrici radii et luminis positione cominus in aere suis locis constitutis]."

◀ Plate II: Michelangelo Merisi da Caravaggio, *The Flagellation*, Museo di Capodimonte, Naples, oil on canvas, 266 x 213 cm., detail.

Alberti transcends the Aristotelian notion of mimesis or imitation, which rests on the very idea of representing reality through the conventional signs of language, mimicry, and figurative schemes. In other words, Aristotle's mimesis encompasses artifice and therefore spawns mediated—that is, fictive—realities. On the contrary, Alberti's painting virtually supersedes reality by duplicating it. As an optical implement, the pictorial surface is not meant to decode, exemplify or idealize the external world: at least, not *a priori*. Indeed, in Alberti's view the primary artifice of painting substantially resides in recreating appearance, and appearance in and of itself does not make "sense"; it is utterly meaningless. In Aristotle's *Poetics*, imitation instead aims at and incorporates meaning. Put otherwise, mimesis manipulates reality by recasting it into a novel configuration, and this manipulation constantly tends to a—moral—purpose. Imitation thus extracts meaning from reality. Of course, Alberti does embrace Aristotle's idea of mimesis, and for him painting—first and foremost in the form of the *istoria*—is also a powerful means to convey a teleological and moral outlook. Nevertheless, by likening imitation to optical reproduction, Alberti inadvertently creates a theoretical ambivalence—irrelevant to his contemporaries, as I will show further on—that was to complicate and cripple the concept of narrative painting for centuries to come.

On the one hand, painters assuredly handle the most sophisticated kind of imitation, one that potentially erases the boundaries between fiction and reality. No other art performs as well: certainly not poetry, since words evoke and represent, but are not able to reproduce the external world. On the other hand, pictorial imitation cannot reduce itself to reality at the risk of losing meaning and purpose. Albeit an optical device, painting is also an artificial mechanism, that is, a fictive visual language.

To assess how radical Alberti's conception was at the time it was first enunciated, it is useful to compare it with the alternative though contemporaneous notion of painting specific to late Byzantine culture. Even if all the Byzantine sources I am about to record exclusively refer to sacred images, mostly figures of saints but also biblical stories, Alberti's *istoria*, the quintessence of painting, generally and traditionally includes religious subjects, and on this ground it roughly corresponds to—yet largely exceeds—the Byzantine sacred narratives of this period. In his *Vera Historia*, Sylvester Syropoulos relates Gregory Melissenus' opinion about Italian religious images (a delegate of the Byzantine mission, Melissenus had been dispatched to the Council of Ferrara and Florence in 1438-1439):

> When I enter a Latin church, I do not revere any of the [images of] saints there because I do not recognize any of them. At the most, I may recognize Christ, but I do not revere him either, since I do not know in what terms he is inscribed (οὐκ οἶδα πῶς ἐπιγράφεται). So I make the sign of the cross and I revere it. Yes, I revere the cross that I have made myself, and not anything that I see there.[4]

In his *Contra haereses* (before 1430), Symeon of Thessalonika also inveighs against the use of images in Western churches:

> What else have they [the neo-Latin nations] innovated in opposition to the ecclesiastical custom? The sacred and venerable icons have been piously established to honor their divine prototypes, and to be worshipped by the faithful on account of their holy

---

4 Syropoulos, 250: "Ἐγώ ὅτε εἰς ναὸν εἰσέλθω Λατίνων, οὐ προσκυνῶ τινα τῶν ἐκεῖσε ἁγίων, ἐπεὶ οὐδὲ γνωρίζω τινα· τὸν Χριστὸν ἴσως μόνον γνωρίζω, ἀλλ᾽οὐδ᾽ἐκεῖνον προσκυνῶ. διότι οὐκ οἶδα πῶς ἐπιγράφεται, ἀλλὰ ποιῶ τὸν σταυρόν μου καί προσκυνῶ. Τὸν σταυρὸν οὖν, ὃν αὐτός ποιῶ, προσκυνῶ καί οὐχ ἕτερόν τι τῶν ἐκεῖσε θεωρουμένων μοι." Laurent,

51, translates the phrase that I quote in Greek in the text as follows: "car j'ignore le contenu de l'épigraphe." Here I rely on Mango 1986, 254, who clearly does not accept Laurent's translation. I have modified Mango's translation slightly. For the meaning of the verb επιγραφω, see Lampe 1961, 519-20, s.v.

likenesses, and they show the truth symbolically. Indeed, they represent the Word incarnate for our sake, and all the divine actions, sufferings, miracles, and mysteries [he carried out] for us, as well as the most sacred image of his ever-virgin Mother, and of his saints, and whatever the Gospels and the other divine scriptures (θεῖαι γραφαί) relate, and therefore they symbolically instruct with colors and other materials as if with different letters (ὡς γράμμασιν ἄλλοις). But, as I have said, these men innovate everything, and often depict sacred images diversely in contempt of the established law, since instead of using fictive hair and garments, they embellish them with human hair and drapes, which is not the image of hair and garment, but the hair and garment of a particular man, and which is by no means the image and symbol of a prototype.[5]

Before investigating the implications of this backlash against Western images, it is important to clarify the equivalence of word and painting specific to Byzantium. In the previous passages, I have deliberately reported the instances in which γράφω (grapho) and its derivates are present. In both ancient and Byzantine Greek, this verb means at the same time "to write" and "to draw," so that on a conceptual level word and line function analogously as "signs" through which reality— in its transcendental sense, to wit, the essence of divinity—is expressed. In his c.780 Antirrheticus, Nikephoros of Constantinople defines this equivalence clearly:

> γραφή (graphe) [that is, writing] (…) is of two kinds. The former is delineated in a series and order with the characters of these very letters; it proceeds in syllables, and is elicited by writers. The latter, by imitating the paradigm, is endued with form and impressed through likenesses.[6]

Aware of the divergent functions of word and image, Nikephoros underscores their equal authority, yet underlines the supremacy of painting over writing: images directly access the viewer's mind, thereby transmitting incontrovertible knowledge to it. For this reason, sacred pictures prove to be an authoritative language, thus immutable and strictly codified:

> As the Gospel text (συγγραφή) draws from itself its authority among Christians, and does not need any other text or discourse to support or authenticate it, as it is in and of itself venerable and trustful, so too does the delineation (γραφή) of divine depictions— since it proves to be the same as the Gospel text—derive its veracity from itself, and because it does not require extrinsic proof, it signifies the same facts as the Gospel, and calls for the same honor.[7]

5   Symeon of Thessalonika, 111, Chapter XXIII: "Τί δέ καί ἄλλο αὐτοῖς παρά τὴν ἐκκλησιαστικὴν ἐκαινοτομήθη παράδοσιν; τῶν ἁγίων καί σεπτῶν εἰκόνων εὐσεβῶς παραδεδομένων εἰς τιμὴν τῶν θείων πρωτοτύπων καί τὴν κατά σχέσιν αὐτῶν τῶν ἁγίων εἰκονισμάτων προσκύνησιν τοῖς πιστοῖς, καί τὴν ἀλήθειαν ἐμφαινόντων εἰκονικῶς. Τὸν γάρ σαρκωθέντα Λόγον δι᾽ἡμᾶς εἰκονίζουσι, καί πάντα τά ὑπέρ ἡμῶν αὐτοῦ θεῖα ἔργα καί πάθη καί θαύματα καί μυστήρια, καί ἔτι τό πανάγιον εἶδος τῆς ἁγίας αὐτοῦ ἀειπαρθένου μητρός, καί τῶν ἁγίων αὐτοῦ, καί ἅπερ ἡ εὐαγγελικὴ ἱστορία καί αἱ λοιπαί θεῖαι γραφαί λέγουσιν, ὡς γράμμασιν ἄλλοις, τῇ χρωματουργίᾳ καί λοιπῇ ὕλῃ εἰκονικῶς ἐκδιδάσκουσιν, οὗτοι πάντα καινοτομοῦντες, ὡς εἴρηται, καί τάς ἱεράς εἰκόνας παρά τό νενομισμένον ἑτέρῳ τρόπῳ πολλάκις ἀνιστοροῦσιν, ἀντί εἰκονικῶν ἐνδυμάτων τε καί τριχῶν, ἀνθρωπείαις θριξί καί στολαῖς καλλωπίζοντες, ὅπερ οὐκ εἰκών τριχός καί ἐνδύματος, ἀλλ᾽ἀνθρώπου τινός εἰσι θρίξ καί ἔνδυμα, καί οὐχί εἰκών τε τῶν πρωτοτύπων καί τύπος." See also the partial translation of Mango 1986, 253-4.

For an interpretation of this passage, see also Nagel 2004; and more recently Nagel and Wood 2010, 85-95.

6   Nikephoros, 356: "Γραφή μέν γάρ (…) διττῶς λέγεται· ἡ μέν γάρ τοῖς χαρακτῆρσι τουτωνί τῶν στοιχείων ἐν εἱρμῷ καί τάξει χαρασσομένη, καί συλλαβικῶς προϊοῦσα διά τῶν λογογραφουμένων ἐκφέρεται· ἡ δέ διά τῶν ὁμοιωμάτων μιμήσει τῇ πρός τό παράδειγμα εἰδοποιουμένη καί τυπουμένη." For this topic, see the excellent book by Barber 2002, esp.125-37.

7   Nikephoros, 384: "Ὡς οὖν τοῦ Εὐαγγελίου ἡ συγγραφή αὐτόθεν ἔχει παρά Χριστιανοῖς τό ἀξιόπιστον, οὐ προσδεομένη ἑτέρας συγγραφῆς ἢ λόγου συνηγορήσοντος ἢ προσμαρτυρήσοντος, πρός τό εἶναι αὐτὴν σεβασμίαν καί ἔνδοξον· οὕτω καί ἡ τῶν θείων ἀπεικ[ονι]σμάτων γραφή, ἡ αὐτῇ τῇ εὐαγγελικῇ τυγχάνουσα, οἰκόθεν τό πιστὸν ἐπάγεται, καί οὐκ ἂν δεηθείη τῆς τῶν ἔξωθεν ἀποδείξεως, σημᾶναί τε τά τοῦ Εὐαγγελίου, καί τὴν αὐτὴν ἐκείνῳ τιμὴν ἀπενέγκασθαι."

On this basis, it is now possible to interpret Melissenus' argument, especially the passage in which he confesses to recognize Christ in Western contemporary images, although he cannot adore his effigy since he does not know under which terms his figure is "inscribed." As the words in the Gospel cannot be modified, so too should the system of graphic and figurative signs representing divinity in the ecclesiastical custom remain the same as it had been since the beginning and over the centuries. Hence, it cannot and must not be subverted. Evidently, the depictions of Christ observed by Melissenus during his Italian journey do not conform to this paradigmatic encryption.[8] As a result, they do not "inscribe" or "circumscribe" Christ's eternal essence, nor can they represent the Savior in any conceivable way. In Melissenus's eyes, the style practiced by fifteenth-century Italian artists to execute their pictures is undecipherable. Deprived of the protocol of figurative calligraphy, Christ's images do not represent Christ, but reproduce a man. It would not be rash to conclude that the "naturalism" of the Italian images sincerely shocked Melissenus: as I have said, reproduction is not necessarily representation. The adjustments through which Christ's figure was artistically manipulated in order to conform with man's vision and to appear "real" compromise the status of the image. For this reason, in Melissenus' view Christ's figure embodies painting without signs, and is therefore meaningless.

Not that viewers in Byzantium disregarded imitation altogether: lest one misinterpret, for instance, Symeon's aversion to human hair, it must be remembered that Byzantine pictorial "delineation" is likewise grounded on imitation. The difference is that, although it relies on mimesis, Byzantine painting configures itself as a referential rather than a mimetic system of signs: a semiotics parallel to that of words, and equally fictitious. Perhaps as a consequence of the iconoclastic conflicts, Byzantium soon came to preserve the legitimacy of images by severing them from the perceptive world, and transfiguring line and contour into logography. In a certain sense, the cultural and metaphysical value of icons tended to inhibit and delay the emergence of any sort of naturalism. By naturalistically enhancing the effect of presence (*enargeia*) in their figures and accessories, Western artists of the fifteenth century unhinged the legitimacy of images as practiced by Byzantine painters and, to a certain degree, by their own predecessors in the thirteenth and fourteenth centuries.

Above all, the passages from Byzantine authors quoted here allow us to understand that fifteenth-century Italian images—which seem so natural, almost innate, to our culture—are also conventional networks of figurative signs. What theoretically distinguishes them from their counterparts in Byzantium is in the first place the multiplicity of strategies through which they can render the impression of human vision—as opposed to a figurative "script" tending to operate as a unique canon, and therefore favoring typology over specificity. Furthermore, as a technical and scientific device, painting is inherently and virtually deconstructible into "parts"; it is, thus, a multi-articulated system of separable elements, whereas "delineation" tends to constitute a univocal system of signs. To prove this point, I quote Alberti's famous definition of the *istoria*: "a painter's greatest endeavor is the *istoria*; parts of the *istoria* are the bodies; parts of the bodies are the members; parts of the members are the surfaces."[9] As Michael Baxandall points out,[10] Alberti's divisions and subdivisions of painting were modeled on those of ancient grammar and rhetoric. In another passage, Alberti stresses the affinities between grammar and painting:

> I want the youths who set out now to [learn] painting to proceed as I see those who learn
> to write do. They are first taught separately the characters of letters, which the ancients

8 For this concept, see in particular Maguire 1996.

9 Alberti, 58-9: "Grandissima opera del pittore sarà l'istoria: parte della istoria sono i corpi; parte de' corpi sono i membri; parte de' membri sono le superficie [Amplissimum pictoris opus historia, historiae partes corpora, corporis pars membrum est, membri pars est superficies]."

10 Baxandall 1971, 130.

called the elements; then they learn the syllables, and afterward how to compose all the words. Our apprentices must follow the same principles. They should learn to draw the surfaces' borders correctly, and they need to practice them as if they were painting's first elements; then they should learn how to join the surfaces together, and thereafter the distinct forms of every member by memorizing any kind of difference in each member.[11]

In these ways, apprentices advance step by step, until they are able to reproduce any aspect of nature as if in three dimensions. If one compares Nikephoros' definition of pictorial delineation (γραφή) with Alberti's partition of painting, one will notice that both are molded in analogy to grammar, its components (characters–syllables–words), and its syntax. However, whereas Nikephoros envisages images as graphic units and transcriptions of prototypes—homologous to transcendental ideas, in the neo-platonic sense—Alberti dismembers them into primary, geometrical, and therefore abstract elements: lines, surfaces, members, and bodies. By crossing, overlapping or merging with each other, contours and planes build volumes and reproduce nature, perhaps ideally but never in a "logographic" form. The representation of the *istoria* hence results from the composition of primordial constituents, arranged in accordance with the subject matter. In addition, since painting is above all the imitation of human actions, Alberti adopts the principles of ancient rhetoric by distinguishing in a picture disposition, expression, attitudes, and so on. Basically, these are functions of painting essentially geared to relay and release action. Together, each according to its function and scope, these elements or "parts" contribute to inform and define painting in its highest form: the *istoria*.[12]

Although Alberti's theories have been frequently examined and interpreted, the momentous impact of painting's deconstruction on its foundational components remains, to my knowledge, as yet unexplored. Alberti's brand-new conception of art not only interferes, but also clashes, with the practices and conventions of late medieval artists. If contours cease to be a mechanical, workshop-related script, and turn instead into lines to be inflected at the artist's will and to qualify as stylistic "signatures"; if surfaces, from cursory containers, become through perspective a vector of organization and a factor of meaning; if iconographic schemes and formulas are tested and dissolved into a more sensitive lexicon of expressions and attitudes; if colors begin to lose their magical and symbolic contents, and start to interface with the *istoria*; then artificers can maneuver any single aspect of their artifacts separately. They can harmonize these elements—as art theorists unanimously recommend—but they can also, consciously or unconsciously, shuffle and misalign them in endless combinations. Since lines, surfaces, members, and bodies are not only components of painting but are also innervations of dramatic force, they might or might not support, or partially heed, a subject matter.

To avoid any sort of misalignment and disjunction in the multi-layered structure of the *istoria*, Alberti systematically highlights the importance of respecting a full gamut of principles, all related to congruousness: grace and beautiful symmetry (*concinnitas*), propriety, and decorum:

11 Alberti, 94-5: "Voglio che i giovani, quali ora nuovi si danno a dipignere, così facciano quanto veggo di chi impara a scrivere. Questi in prima separato insegnano tutte le forme delle lettere, quali gli antiqui chiamano elementi; poi insegnano le sillabe; poi apresso insegnano componere tutte le dizioni. Con questa ragione ancora seguitino i nostri a dipingere. In prima imparino ben disegnare gli orli delle superficie, e qui si essercitino quasi come ne' primi elementi della pittura; poi imparino ciascuna forma distinta di ciascun membro, e mandino a mente qualunque possa essere differenza in ciascun membro. [Velim quidem eos qui pingendi artem ingrediuntur, id agere quod apud scribendi instructores observari video. Nam illi quidem prius omnes elementorum characteres separatim edocent, postea vero syllabas atque perinde dictiones componere instruunt. Hanc ergo rationem et nostri in pingendo sequantur. Primo ambitum superficierum quasi picturae elementa, tum et superficierum connexus, dehinc membrorum omnium formas distincte ediscant, omnesque quae in membris possint esse differentias memoriae commendent.]"

12 For Alberti's *istoria* specifically, see Krüger P. 2002; and Grafton 2003. An interesting discussion related to Alberti's notion of the *istoria* is to be found in Puttfarken 2000, 45-68.

In composing the members, it is important that they accord with one another in a beautiful way (*pulchre*). They accord with one another in a beautiful way when relative to proportion, function, form, color, and similar things they correspond to beauty and gracefulness.[13]

In a previous passage, Alberti had already expounded the concept of beauty with regard to the surfaces of the human face. It goes without saying that the same precepts extend to members, bodies, and the overall composition:

From the combination of surfaces pours forth the elegant symmetry and grace that we call beauty (…). The face whose surfaces dovetail with one another so that delicate lights flow into soft shades, the sharpness of the edges being thus suppressed, that face we deservedly define beautiful and graceful.[14]

Besides beauty, grace, and symmetry, functionality is strictly demanded in painting:

Then it is necessary that all the limbs fulfill their function in the action. If the figure is running, it must thrust its feet no less than its hand. But I want every limb of a discoursing philosopher to show more modesty than vigor (…). In Rome, people commend an *istoria* in which the dead Meleager is carried, and those who support the weight seem to suffer and endure pain with all their limbs. Yet in the figure of the dead, there is no limb that does not appear lifeless: everything dangles; hands, fingers, head, all droop inertly, and accordingly all the limbs converge to express the lifelessness of the body.[15]

Consistency of expression, attitude, and motion could engender monotony, especially if painters insist on single aspects of the *istoria*. Variety is therefore desirable, even mandatory, provided that it does not degenerate into chaos and inanity:

But I would like this abundance [of characters and accessories] not only to be ornate with variety, but also grave and temperate with dignity and discretion. I blame those painters, indeed, that to appear abundant, and not to leave anything empty, do not follow any composition, but scatter everything confusedly and inarticulately, so that

13 Alberti, 62-3: "Conviensi in prima dare opera che tutti i membri bene convengano. Converranno quando e di grandezza e d'offizio e di spezie e di colore e d'altre simili cose corrisponderanno ad una bellezza. [In membrorum compositione danda in primis opera est ut quaequae inter se membra pulchre convenient. Ea quidem tum convenire pulchre dicuntur cum et magnitudine et officio et specie et coloribus et caeteris siquae sunt huiusmodi rebus ad venustatem et pulchritudinem correspondeant]."

14 Ibidem: "Nasce della composizione delle superficie quella grazia ne' corpi quale dicono bellezza. (…) Ma quelli visi s'aranno le superficie giunte in modo che piglino ombre e lumi ameni e suavi, né abbino asperitate alcuna di rilevati canti, certo diremo questi essere formosi e dilicati visi. [Ex superficierum compositione illa elegans in corporibus concinnitas et gratia extat quam pulchritudinem dicunt. (…) In qua vero facie ita iunctae aderunt superficies ut amena lumina in umbras suaves defluant, nullaeque angulorum asperitates extent, hanc merito formosam et venustam faciem dicemus]."

15 Ibidem, 64-5: "Poi si provegga che ciascuno membro segua a quello che ivi si fa, al suo officio. Sta bene a chi corre non meno gittare le mani che i piedi; ma voglio un filosofo, mentre che favella, dimostri molto più modestia che arte di schermire. Lodasi una storia in Roma nella quale Meleagro morto, portato, aggrava quelli che portano il peso, e in sé pare in ogni suo membro ben morto: ogni cosa pende, mani, dito e capo; ogni cosa cade languido; ciò che ve si dà ad espriemere uno corpo morto, qual cosa certo è difficilissima, però che in uno corpo chi saprà fingere ciascuno membro ozioso, sarà ottimo artefice. [Tum providendum est ut omnia membra suum ad id de quo agitur officium exequantur. At philosophum orantem malo in omni membro sui modestiam quam palaestram ostentet. (…) Laudatur in Roma historia in qua Meleager defunctus asportatur, quod qui oneri subsunt angi et omnibus membris laborare videantur; in eo vero qui mortuus sit, nullum adsit membrum quod non demortuum appareat, omnia pendent, manus, digiti, cervix, omnia languida decidunt, denique omnia ad exprimendam corporis mortem congruent]."

the *istoria* does not display an event, but tumbles tumultuously (…). As in every *istoria* variety is agreeable, so too is a painting particularly enjoyable when the bodies' positions and movements greatly differ from one another. Thus, let some stand with their faces visible, hands lifted and fingers fidgeting; let others be seated, or kneeling on one knee, or even be lying. If appropriate, some will be naked, and others will attend half-clothed and half-nude, in a mixed manner. However, modesty and discretion must always be honored (…). I therefore wish modesty and discretion to be observed, so that the body's vile parts ought either to be omitted or corrected. Finally, as I have said, I want efforts to be made to avoid [multiple] figures that express exactly the same gesture or posture.[16]

It is no exaggeration to affirm that for Alberti the human figure is the *sine qua non* of painting. Without figures, there is no action; hence the figure bears the burden of the story on its own shoulders. But before entering the fictitious realm of the *istoria*, the figure must undergo a composite procedure of filtering and purification. Proportions must obey a canon; expression and gestures must exactly and intelligibly transliterate the script prompted by the subject matter; eurythmy and propriety dictate attitudes and postures, which in turn do not act independently, but in mutual relation. This transfiguration of the human figure held and increased its validity in Caravaggio's time. In his *Felsina Pittrice*, Malvasia relates the polemics that the first larger altarpieces by the Carracci brothers, Agostino and Annibale, unleashed upon their unveiling. The paramount target of this criticism was Annibale's 1585 *Baptism of Christ* in Santi Gregorio e Siro, Bologna (Fig. 11),[17] to which the following observations might particularly pertain:

The result was that these works were criticized and denigrated by these other painters [Denys Calvaert, Bartolomeo Passerotti, etc.], for—they said—their making was too trivial, and thus an easy undertaking for any inexperienced painter who, feeling himself to lack both the rudiments of art and invention, might just reproduce directly on the canvas some porter in a piece of drapery that he had made to pose naked, thereby gaining much acclaim among those of little understanding with a small investment of ingeniousness.[18]

16 Ibidem, 68-71: "Ma vorrei io questa copia essere ornata di certa varietà, ancora moderata e grave di dignità e verecundia. Biasimo io quelli pittori, dove vogliono parere copiosi nulla lassando vacuo, ivi non composizione, ma dissoluta confusione disseminano; pertanto non pare la storia facci qualche cosa degna, ma sia in tumulto aviluppata. (…) Ma in ogni storia la varietà sempre fu ioconda, e in prima sempre fu grata quella pittura in quale sieno i corpi con suoi posari molto dissimili. Ivi adunque stieno alcuni ritti e mostrino tutti la faccia, con le mani in alto e con le dita liete, fermi in su un pié. E così a ciascuno sia suo atto e flessione di membra: altri segga, altri si posi su un ginocchio, altri giacciano. E se così ivi sia licito, sievi alcuno ignudo, e alcune parti nudi e parti vestiti, ma sempre si serva alla vergogna e alla pudicizia. Le parti brutte a vedere del corpo, e l'altri simili quali porgono poca grazia, si cuoprano col panno, con qualche fronde o con la mano. (…) Così adunque desidero in ogni storia servarsi quanto dissi modestia e verecundia, e così sforzarsi che in niuno sia un medesimo gesto o posamento che nell'altro. [Sed hanc copiam velim cum varietate quadam esse ornatam, tum dignitate et verecundia gravem atque moderatam. Improbo quidem eos pictores qui, quo videri copiosi, quove nihil vacuum relictum volunt, eo nullam sequuntur compositionem sed confuse et dissolute omnia disseminant, ex quo non rem agere sed tumultuare historia videtur. (…) Sed in omni historia cum varietas iocunda est, tamen in primis omnibus grata est pictura, in qua corporum status atque motus inter se multo dissimiles sint. Stent igitur alii toto vultu conspicui, manibus supinis et digitis micantibus, alterum in pedem innixi, aliis adversa sit facies et demissa brachia, pedesque iniuncti, singulisque singuli flexus et actus extent; alii consideant, aut in flexo genu morentur, aut prope incumbant. Sintque nudi, si ita deceat, aliqui, nonnulli mixta ex utrisque arte partim velati partim nudi assistant. Sed pudori semper et verecundiae inserviamus. (…) Hanc ergo modestiam et verecundiam in universa historia observari cupio ut foeda aut praetereantur aut emendentur. Denique, ut dixi, studendum censeo ut in nullo ferme idem gestus aut status conspiciatur]."

17 For the painting, see Posner 1971a, 2:11-2, no. 21; and Benati and Riccomini 2006, 166, no. III.17.

18 Malvasia, 1:363: "Quindi poi fu che da' sudetti vennero tareggiate quell'opere ed avvilite, come di un modo triviale troppo, dicevano, e in conseguenza facile ad ogni imperito che, sentendosi senza fondamento e povero di partiti, ben poteva, nudato un facchino o postogli un panno indosso, copiarlo di peso sul quadro e presso a' poco intendenti farsi un grand'onore con poco capitale d'ingegno." See also Summerscale 2000, 91-2, esp. note 27.

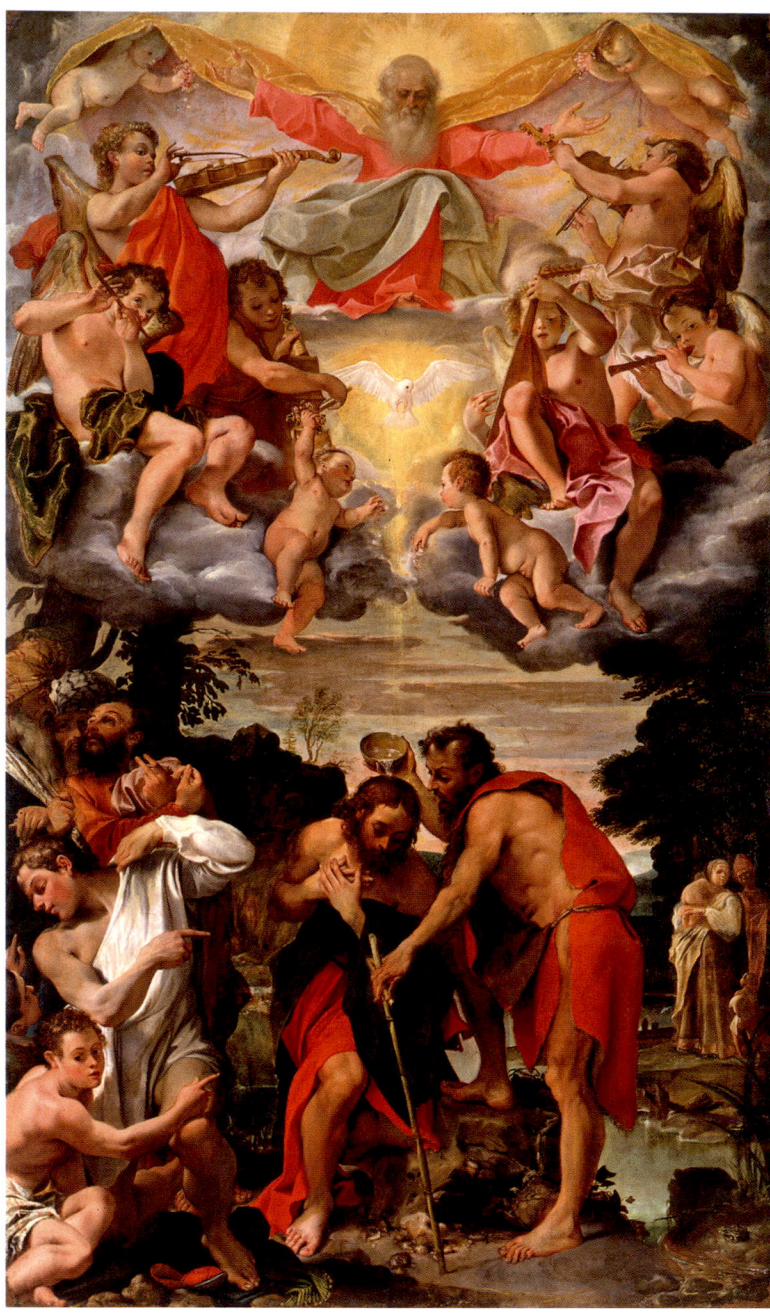

Fig. 11
Annibale Carracci, *The Baptism of Christ*, Santi Gregorio e Siro, Bologna, oil on canvas, 383 x 225 cm.

A vigorous drawing in red chalk by Annibale, now at the Louvre, Paris (Fig. 12), seemingly represents one of these humble "porters," most probably a studio apprentice, half-naked, posing for the *Baptism*.[19] Kneeling on one knee, the boy removes his shirt while turning his head leftward, keeping his eyes closed as if he has just awoken and readied himself for his morning toilet. With bold outlines, Annibale rapidly grasps the entire posture, focusing on the unfolding of the shirt into a reversed parabola framing the boy's profile: an elegant idea that he would omit in the painting. Actually, Annibale did not transpose his model wholesale onto the canvas: he radically modified the model's attitude according to the painting's narrative context. There, the boy—now a neophyte—is about to strip naked, his shirt veiling his body down to his thighs; turning to the left, he talks to a fellow character while pointing out the principal episode: Christ being baptized by John. Annibale thus did hone and adapt his original idea. But even if this was not true, it cannot be said that he sketched his "porter" randomly: the fluency of the shirt's folds and contours in the Louvre drawing confirms that an aesthetic selection has already been deployed, and a segment of composition probed as Annibale's chalk rushes across the paper.[20] Nevertheless, Annibale's detractors would have found both the sketch and the adjustment process still insufficient. Like Michelangelo in Lodovico Dolce's *Aretino* (1557), Annibale "painted porters," contrary to Raphael who depicted "gentlemen."[21] Worse, from figures in the *Baptism* like the one in the Louvre drawing, Annibale's enemies even inferred that no invention whatsoever had intervened to turn Annibale's image into a composition. They in fact claimed that

this was a style to use in a live model class, not in an altarpiece; that the good and the beautiful in art does not reside in setting out to study and examine the figures one

19 For the drawing see Benati and DeGrazia 1999, 67, no. 8; and Benati and Riccomini 2006, 168, no. III. 18.

20 For the practice of drawing from life as practiced by the Carracci, see Goldstein 1988, 89-106; and Feigenbaum 1993. On the limits of Goldstein's interpretation, see Perini 1991.

21 Dolce 172: "Io vi dico che Rafaello sapeva far bene ogni sorte di nudi, e Michel Agnolo riesce eccellente in una sola, ed i nudi di Rafaello han questo di più, che dilettano maggiormente. Né dirò, come già disse un bello ingegno, che Michel Agnolo ha dipinto i facchini e Rafaello i gentiluomini."

by one directly on the canvas, groping along while proceeding and working haphazardly, but rather in producing the entire bulk of the invention purposefully, and in availing oneself of the things seen and studied in the past, so that through the ease and resolution of the execution the results of the difficulties surmounted and their recollection should transpire.[22]

In other words, the figure is only a derivative product of reality. Through a kind of artistic anamnesis, the human body frees itself of contingency, and configures itself in harmonious symmetry through a comparison with pre-stocked schemes and formulas present in the artist's mind. Implicit in Malvasia's text is the conviction that the painter's memory is also supplied with templates inherited from other artists through the copying of canonical compositions, be they prints, drawings, paintings, or ancient sculptures. Therefore, figures are innately rooted in tradition and canon. Not all attitudes are permitted, but only those that hint at, and are enshrined within, a noble repertoire. Abiding by the model does not reinforce the optical impression of reality. On the contrary, it vilifies art:

> It was no wonder (…) that the Carracci ended up producing low, plebeian works, because these were derived and extracted from nature, which is always imperfect, rather than from art, which tames and corrects nature.[23]

It has already become obvious that the censures inflicted on the Carracci at the beginning of their career were to resurface,

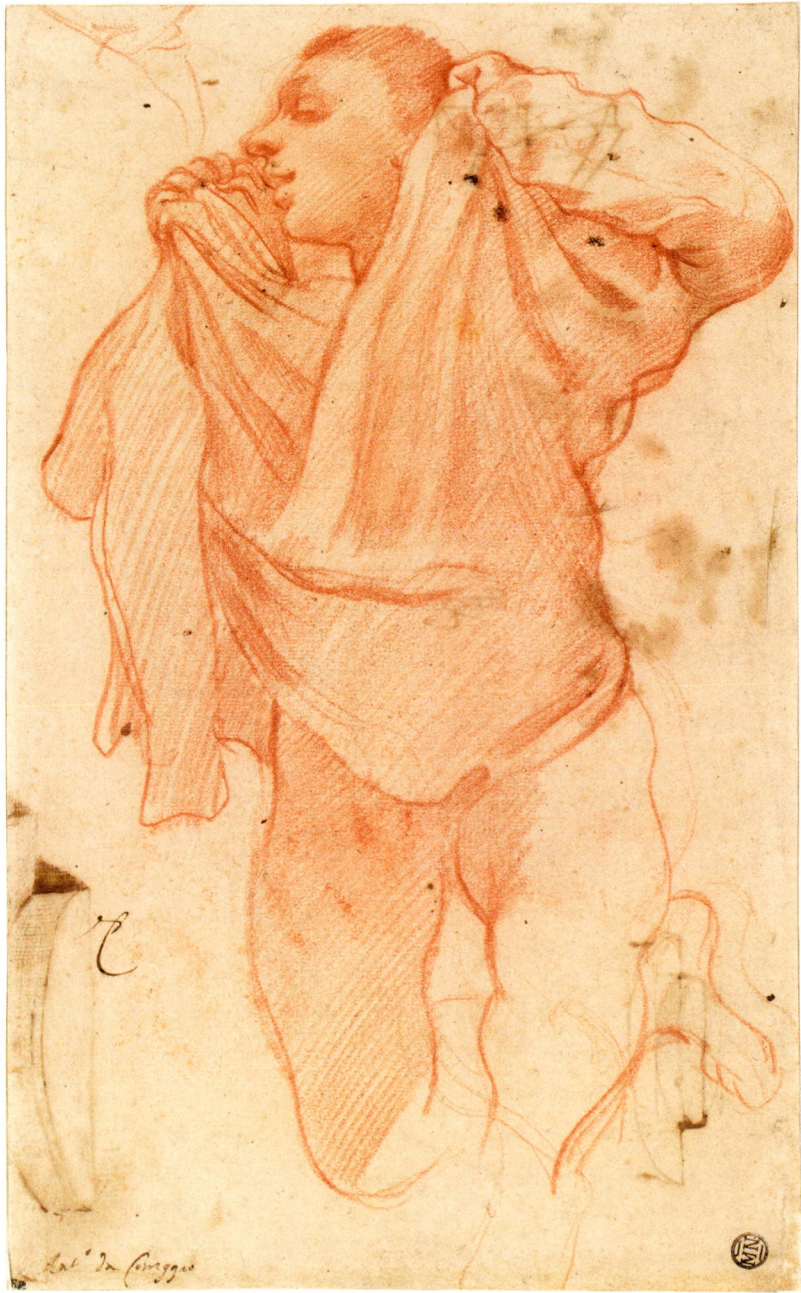

Fig. 12
Annibale Carracci, *Study of a Boy Taking Off his Shirt*, Musée du Louvre, Paris, red chalk, 35.9 x 22.1 cm.

22 Malvasia, 1:363: "esser quello uno stile da praticarsi nell'Accademia del nudo, non da servirsene in un quadro d'altare; che il buono e il bello dell'arte non consisteva nel porsi sull'opra medesima ad istudiare e vedere figura per figura, camminando in tal guisa a tentone ed oprando a caso, ma scaricar di proposito tutta la massa e, valendosi delle cose già viste e studiate, mostrar nella risoluzione di esse il frutto delle fatiche già superate e della memoria serbatane ubbidiente."

23 Ibidem: "non esser poi maraviglia se riuscivan loro quelle operazioni basse e plebee, come che dalla natura sempre imperfetta più tosto che dall'arte, che quella addimestica e corregge, dedotte e cavate, non potessero non restar prive di quel decoro e nobiltà che solo può esprimere un ingegno pratico e ben sicuro."

in nearly identical terms, decades later in connection with Caravaggio. As I have already observed, the idea that working from live models forces the artist to a sort of collage procedure from which invention is excluded also underlies Mancini's criticism of Caravaggio's studio practice. In their attacks, Mancini and Annibale's antagonists cling on to Alberti's learning as interpreted by many art theorists during the Renaissance. Dolce[24] in this respect states that "one must choose the most perfect form by imitating nature in part":[25] in other words, porters are not allowed within the picture unless adequately embellished. Dolce obviously alludes to the renowned examples of Apelles' and Praxiteles' *Venus*, and Zeuxis' *Helen*—artworks inspired by real women, but resembling no specific model in their paradigmatic beauty.[26]

Returning to Alberti, his concept of the figure accentuates the fictitious aspect of mimesis foreshadowed, but never explicitly articulated, by Aristotle. In Alberti's system, the figure does not result from simple imitation: it is the product of a selective process through which it preserves its optical appearance, but definitely loses its immediate link to the external world. In other terms, the figure ceases to reproduce nature; it becomes a compound of fictive signs whose organization is the matter of rhetoric and aesthetics, and not exclusively of optics. Reality does not necessarily compose things; composition dislodges then recomposes reality in accordance with the artist's purpose and the principles of art. Needless to say, Alberti was unaware of the enormous implications of his theoretical tenets. By anchoring composition to perspective, and by placing expression and attitudes under the aegis of natural observation, he strove to tie reality and fiction together inextricably, so much so that the latter could not reclaim its independence without detriment to the former. In sum, the order and eurythmics of a composition, though indispensable, must not be pursued for their own sake, by disregarding reality altogether. Figures cannot trespass the framework of verisimilitude. Truth be told, the balance between reality and fiction is even more precarious than Alberti could ever have imagined. The strong criticism leveled at Michelangelo's figures in the 1550s and 1560s largely proves this point.

It is well known that Giorgio Vasari in both his 1550 and 1568 *Vite* sang the praises of Michelangelo's *Last Judgment*, which he considered the greatest achievement in the recent history of the arts, especially owing to the unrivaled perfection of its figures.[27] The great complexity of poses and attitudes deployed in Michelangelo's monumental fresco, along with the over-refined, at times syncopated harmony of their interrelations, pushes to climactic extremes the concept of variety as formulated by Alberti and developed by late fifteenth-century Florentine masters, from Antonio del Pollaiuolo to Sandro Botticelli. In the *Last Judgment*, the figures determine the pictorial space, substitute for perspective, set off and condense action to an unfathomable extent. It is still rare to come across a sixteenth-century *istoria* in which figures truly absorb the composition in a symbiotic manner to the same degree as Michelangelo's fresco does. Predictably, Vasari's praise immediately stirred strong criticism. It is not surprising that the kernel of these critiques preliminarily concerns the notion of variety. In his *Aretino*, Dolce appreciates this essential component of the *istoria*, but with suspect caution:

> If [painters] represent a man with his back turned, they forthwith depict another one frontally and always continue this order. I do not object to this variety. I rather say that, since it is the painter's duty to imitate nature, it is necessary that variety not appear

---

24   For Dolce's artistic theories, see Puttfarken 1991; Rogers 1992; Sciolla 2000; Rhein 2008. A survey of Dolce as an historical personality is to be found in Terpening 1997.

25   Dolce, 138: "Devesi adunque eleger la forma più perfetta, imitando parte la Natura."

26   See Ibidem, 130.

27   Vasari, 6:69: "Basta che si vede che l'intenzione di questo uomo singulare non ha voluto entrare in dipignere altro che la perfetta e proporzionatissima composizione del corpo umano et in diversissime attitudini (…); e finalmente ha aperto la via alla facilità di questa arte nel principale suo intento, che è il corpo umano."

strenuously contrived, but fortuitous. This is why he must discontinue that order and represent two or three [figures] of the same age, and sex, and with the same attitude, provided that he varies the faces, postures, and draperies.[28]

The same applies to figures in motion:

> It remains to speak of movement, a part that is most necessary, enjoyable, and the source of astonishment. For it is indeed agreeable and marvelous to the viewer's eyes to see in stone, on canvas or on panel an inanimate object that seems to be in motion. But these movements ought not to be continuous, and in every figure, since men do not always move. Nor should they be so fierce that they look frantic: rather, they should be moderate, and varied, and must be even dismissed according to the diversity and circumstances of the figures.[29]

Only in appearance does Dolce follow Alberti's precepts. Not that he contradicts his predecessor, but he certainly pinpoints a virtual fallacy in Alberti's system by indicating that variety might oppose nature to the point of proving "unnatural"—that is, artificial. This tension between fiction and reality might well require a good dose of *sprezzatura*[30] (ease and resolution in Baldassar Castiglione's terms) in order to be concealed, but even in the best case tension persists in every artwork as an unfiltered scoria of the process through which art smelts vision. The paradox of Dolce's statement lies in his suggestion that variety could be disregarded on occasion for a work to be successful, though it is unclear whether the composition itself can tolerate such license. In other words, as a harmonious, and self-regulated compound, the artwork cannot afford to lose even the smallest part of what determines its harmony and governs its structure. That is, unless the composition becomes deliberately defective, which is inconceivable in a theoretical system devised to achieve perfection. By the same token, it is extremely debatable whether artists should or should not discontinue monotonous, yet utterly natural motions of figures on account of the potential "ungracefulness" of these arrangements. If the configuration in which this chain of motion results is undeniably unharmonious, should the story nevertheless be rejected as "un-pictorial"? And what exactly is the point at which art annihilates nature, and fiction overrules reality? As long as the question lingers on an aesthetic level—variety versus monotony—the condemnation of Michelangelo's figures is destined to remain a matter of bias, and not of reason or even common sense. Similarly, by accusing Michelangelo of indecency in his *Last Judgment*, detractors could easily have objected that a most noble theological motive had prescribed the fresco's overwhelming nudity. Nevertheless, Michelangelo's figures were assuredly more vulnerable to another kind of criticism: their inadequacy with regard to action. Giovanni Andrea Gilio forged ahead along these lines: in my view, his are the most compelling and innovative opinions about the relation between figure and the *istoria*, fiction and reality.[31] In his 1564 *Degli errori e degli abusi de' pittori circa l'istorie*,

---

28 Dolce, 146: "Se averanno appresso fatto un uomo volto in ischiena, ne faranno subito un altro che dimostri le parti dinanzi, e vanno sempre continuando un tale ordine. Questa varietà io non riprendo, ma dico che, essendo l'ufficio del pittore d'imitar la Natura, non bisogna che la varietà appaia studiosamente ricercata, ma fatta a caso. Però dee uscir dell'ordine, ed alle volte far due o tre d'una età, d'un sesso e d'un'attitudine, pur che si dimostri vario ne' volti, e varii le attitudine e i panni."

29 Ibidem: "Resta a dire delle movenzie, parte ancora ella necessarissima ed aggradevole e di stupore, ché aggradevole è nel vero e fa stupir gli occhi de' risguardanti vedere in sasso, in tela o in legno una cosa inanimata che par che si mova. Ma queste movenzie non debbono esser continue e in tutte le figure, perché gli uomini sempre non si muovono, né fiere sì che paiano da disperati; ma bisogna temperarle, variarle ed anco da parte lasciarle, secondo la diversità e condizion de' soggetti."

30 For the concept of *sprezzatura* in painting, see Sohm 1985; and Sohm 1991, 11-2, 51-2.

31 For Gilio, see more recently Caputo 2008.

Gilio decries Michelangelo's obsession with the human figure, particularly manifest in the *Last Judgment*:

> He deliberately paid less attention to the truth of the subject and indulged more in his art, eager to show its abundance and excellence, and thereby acted like a lover who, to satisfy his favorite, esteems everything to be fine and legitimate. And I believe this occurred for no other reason than because he saw there [in the Sistine Chapel] a place vast enough to demonstrate, through the great multitude of figures, all the beautiful actions that the human body can achieve by straining or generally posing, and therefore did not want to miss the opportunity to leave the memory of his wondrous ingenuity to posterity. And here is the marvel: not a single figure seen in this representation does the same thing as another; nor does one resemble another. And to this end he banished devotion, reverence, the truth of the *istoria* and the honor due to this most important and great mystery [the End of Days] (…).[32]

Among the mistakes committed by Michelangelo relative to verisimilitude is the disproportion between the overstrain of his figures—in other words, the master's memorable *sforzi*—and the action they are called upon to accomplish. For this reason, in Gilio's view the angels at the upper register of the *Last Judgment*, like "jesters and jugglers," toil absurdly to transport a column and a cross, while they could "support the entire earth effortlessly."[33] I will not inquire here into the concept of the *figura sforzata*, to which excellent studies have already been devoted.[34] Rather, I will insist on the theoretical hiatus between beauty and propriety of action as expressed through the figures in the *istoria*. Gilio in fact would not balk at tipping the balance of art and vision, fiction and reality, in order to withhold the supremacy of "truth." To be sure Gilio, like many other theorists at the time, affirms that beauty as a criterion of measure and conformity is absolutely crucial to the composition, although an unjustified excess of it engenders deformity and results in nonsense:

> I do not want them [painters] to imitate that painter who, to make a saint exhibit a tiny muscle in a knee or in the instep, twisted the figure's leg in such a way that nature could only achieve that by dint of a winch, and not through natural force.[35]

Nevertheless, he acknowledges the necessity of technical *tours de force* such as Michelangelo's *sforzi*, provided that artists "strain" the figure in an "appropriate, graceful, and natural way." Despite this condition, Gilio concedes that sometimes painters must give up on beauty altogether, yielding to truth's hegemony. To prove the point, Gilio surprisingly criticizes the "much praised" 1524 *Flagellation* by Sebastiano del Piombo in San Pietro in Montorio, Rome, notoriously based on a drawing by Michelangelo, who might also have contoured the figure of Christ in the final

---

32 Gilio, 858-9: "Perché egli più s'è voluto compiacere de l'arte, per mostrare quale e quanta sia, che de la verità del soggetto, ed ha fatto come l'innamorato il quale, per sodisfare a la sua favorita, ogni cosa stima lecita e bella; e ciò penso che da altro proceduto non sia che, vedendosi innanzi sì largo campo da mostrare, in tanta moltitudine di figure, tutto quello che vagamente può fare un corpo umano per via di sforzi e d'altri posamenti, non ha voluto perdere l'occasione di non lasciare a' posteri memoria del suo mirabil ingegno. E questa è la maraviglia: che nissuna figura che in questo ritratto vedete fa quello che fa l'altra, e niuna rassimiglia a l'altra; e per questo fare ha messa da banda la devozione, la riverenza, la verità istorica e l'onore che si deve a questo importantissimo e gran mistero, che nissuno lo doverebbe pensare, non che vedere, senza grandissimo spavento."

33 Ibidem, 850: "Per questo io non lodo gli sforzi che fanno gli angeli nel Giudizio di Michelagnolo, dico di quelli che sostengono la croce, la colonna e gli altri sacrati misteri, i quali più tosto rappresentano mattaccini e giocolieri che angeli: conciossia che l'angelo sosterrebbe senza fatica tutto 'l globo de la terra, non che una croce o una colonna o simili."

34 See Cole 2001.

35 Gilio, 852: "Né vorrei che facesse ancora come fece un pittore, il quale, per far mostrare ad un santo un musculetto in un ginocchio o nel collo del piede, gli torse la gamba di maniera che la natura l'arebbe fatto per via d'argani, non per naturale ordine."

composition, at least according to Vasari.[36] From Gilio's text it can be assumed that Sebastiano's Christ was considered a canonical example of male beauty. To paraphrase the author, Sebastiano expressed "all the muscles and limbs of that body beautifully composed, the most beautiful ever in its perfection" in an excellent way, thereby demonstrating the "force of his art."[37] However, Sebastiano's beauty conflicts dramatically with truth:

> The painter would have better shown the force of art in representing [Christ] afflicted, bleeding, covered with spittle, his hair torn out, wounded, deformed, pale and ugly— in brief, bereft of human form. This would have been ingenuity! This is the force and virtue of art, and the artist's perfection! But Sebastiano's Christ seems to have been flagellated and beaten with cotton whips for fun, and certainly not with large and knotty cords, or with something even worse.[38]

With indignation, Gilio ridicules the painter who refuses to depict any sort of ugliness and deformity under the pretext that "painting does not permit it, for this is against art's decorum":

> Oh vanity of man, who makes whatever is appropriate and essential vain, while indulging in insignificant fictions! If art is the ape of nature, why should one not imitate her in this? If nature parades her flaws and jokes in making a man lame, crippled or blind, then why should the painter not represent this mystery [the Flagellation] as it must be? This is why I believe that their vanity weighs more than the principles of art. I see Stephen lapidated without stones; Blaise intact and pretty on the trestle, without blood; James the Apostle without any rods in his head; Sebastian without arrows; Lawrence on the grill unburned and uncooked, but white, and this merely because painting does not admit it, and in order to show muscles and veins! Oh futile vanity! Oh endless error, to value more that which does not act than that which gives the figures form and perfection and which only deserves to be seen and contemplated, and this on the pretext that painting does not permit it![39]

Needless to say, Gilio argues that the cruelty and rawness of these and other images strengthen the viewer's faith and devotion. I shall deal with this argument later. At stake here, apart from religion and piety, is also the status of painting and particularly of the *istoria*. Like Nikephoros many centuries before him, Gilio establishes that pictorial narratives own the same authority as

36 Vasari, 5:89-90: "Né tacerò che molti credono Michelagnolo avere non solo fatto il picciol disegno di quest'opera, ma che il Cristo detto che è battuto alla colonna fusse contornato da lui, per esser grandissima differenza fra la bontà di questa e quella dell'altre figure." For Sebastiano's *Flagellation*, see Hirst 1981, 49-65; and Strinati and Lindemann 2008, 172-6, no. 33. A reduced version on panel of this famous fresco executed by Sebastiano himself exists at the Museo Civico, Viterbo. See Strinati and Lindemann 2008, 204, no. 44.

37 Gilio, 842: "Penso che ciò faccino per mostrare la forza de l'arte, il che sempre è stato l'intento de l'artefice; per poter bene isprimere tutti i muscoli e tutte le membra di quel ben composto corpo, del quale penso che non fusse mai trovato il più bello. Per questo è tanto lodato il Battuto di frate Bastiano in San Pietro Montorio."

38 Ibidem: "Molto più mostrerebbe il pittore la forza de l'arte in farlo afflitto, sanguinoso, pieno di sputi, depelato, piagato, difformato, livido e brutto di maniera che non avesse forma d'uomo. Questo sarebbe l'ingegno, questo il decoro, questa la perfezzion de l'artefice; conciossia che 'l Battuto di frate Bastiano mostra che i flagelli e le battiture fussero fatte con le sferze di bambagio e per ischerzo, e non con grosse ed annodate funi, o con altra cosa peggiore."

39 Ibidem, 844: "Molte volte ho di questo ragionato con pittori; i quali tutti per una bocca m'hanno risposto: 'Nol comporta la pittura, sarebbe contra il decoro de l'arte.' Oh vanità de l'uomo, in far vano quello che è vero e proprio e principale, per dar luogo a le finzioni che non pesano una paglia. Se l'arte è scimia de la natura, perché non deve in questo imitarla? Se ella va dimostrando i scappucci e gli scherzi suoi nel fare un zoppo, uno stroppio, un cieco, perché non deve far anco il pittore questo mistero come esser deve? Però io fo maggior la vanità di questi tali che le regole de la pittura. Veggo Stefano lapidato senza pietre; Biagio intiero e bello ne l'eculeo, senza sangue; Giacopo Apostolo senza pertiche in capo; Sebastiano senza frezze; Lorenzo ne la graticola non arso ed incotto, ma bianco; non per altro che l'arte nol comporta, e per mostrare i muscoli e le vene. Oh vanità vana, oh errore senza fine, stimar più quello che nulla opera che quello che dà la forma e la perfezione a le figure e che solo merita esser veduto e contemplato, con pretesto che la pittura nol richiede!"

the (sacred) texts they draw on, but only on one condition: that painters adhere to the truth with abnegation. (It is no coincidence that Counter-Reformation theorists turned to Byzantine sources in order to regulate sacred images). Here is Gilio's assessment:

> I therefore say that the painter of *istorie*, as he resembles the writer in every respect, should show with his brush that which the other shows with his pen. On this account, both must be trustful and staunch demonstrators of the truth, without slipping into the work anything dissimulated, adulterated or imperfect.[40]

Lest one be misled by the similarities between Nikephoros' and Gilio's interpretation of religious narratives, it must absolutely be born in mind that Gilio's truth manifests itself in the image through optical accuracy, and not only symbolically. Although he never clarifies this point—which by the way is enunciated with ambiguity and in partial contradiction with the criterion of decorum he cares so much about—it is certain that Gilio wanted blood, spit, bruises, lacerations, and charred and burned flesh to look real; that is, rendered with optical precision:

> In fact, it would be a beautiful and novel thing to see Christ on the cross transformed by wounds, spit, torture, and blood; saint Blaise scarred and excoriated by the iron combs; Sebastian pierced with so many arrows that he resembles a porcupine; Lawrence on the grill burned, cooked, blasted, lacerated, and deformed.[41]

The blood-and-gore aesthetics showcased by Gilio, although justified in very specific subject matter, would be unacceptable in late Byzantine culture. Symeon of Thessalonika, whose disgust for human hair and garments has already been verified, in another passage peremptorily condemns the usage of blood—animal blood representing that of the crucified Christ—as displayed in Italian sacred representations of the quattrocento.[42] For Symeon the blood in the image must obey a figurative convention and cannot be "naturalistic." However, this kind of fictitious or symbolical representation of the blood would leave Gilio irremediably unsatisfied. Put bluntly, for Gilio the truth of painting parallels the reality of man's vision, so that without optical verisimilitude the image is inefficient. How the reproduction of figures "divested of human figure," like that of a tortured Christ, can coexist with the requisite beauty and decorum is difficult to understand, and contradictory in many regards. Be that as it may, Gilio obviously states that the idealizing filter through which reality is purified in picture should be disabled when the story's truth so requires: the vileness and ugliness of reality must then seep into the image to fortify its efficacy and coax viewers into believing.

Gilio's opinion is particularly relevant here because it heralds some of the positions espoused by

---

40 Ibidem, 859: "Dico dunque che 'l pittore istorico, essendo in ogni cosa simile a lo scrittore, quello che l'uno mostra con la penna, l'altro mostrar doverebbe col pennello: l'uno e l'altro però deve essere fedele ed intiero demostratore del vero, non intromettendo ne l'opera cosa mascherata, adulterata ed imperfetta."

41 Ibidem, 845: "Certo sarebbe cosa nova e bella vedere un Cristo in croce per le piaghe, per i sputi, per i scherni e per il sangue trasformato; san Biagio dai pettini lacero e scarnato; Sebastiano pieno di frezze rassimigliare un estrice; Lorenzo ne la graticola arso, incotto, crepato, lacero e difformato."

42 Symeon of Thessalonika, 113, Chapter XXIII: "Τί δέ παρ'αὐτοῖς τυπούμενα χάριν Χριστοῦ τῆς σταυρώσεως; Αἷμα ζῴων ἀλόγων ἐν χολάσι ζῴων εἰσάγοντες, ἀντί τοῦ δεσποτικοῦ ῥέειν κατασκευάζουσιν αἵματος ἀπὸ τῶν τοῦ δῆθεν ἐστουρωμένου ἀνθρώπου τινός χειρῶν καί ποδῶν τε καί τῆς πλευρᾶς. Τίς ἄρα ἐκεῖνός ἐστιν ὁ σταυρούμενος; τί δέ τὸ αἷμα; ἀλήθεια ἢ εἰκών; Καί εἰ μέν εἰκὼν, πῶς ἄνθρωπος καί αἷμα; οὐ γάρ ἡ εἰκών ἄνθρωπος. Εἰ δ' ἀληθείᾳ ἄνθρωπος καί αἷμα, οὐκ ἄρα εἰκών." [What else do they represent in place of Christ's crucifixion? They bring [on stage] the blood of irrational beasts inside the bowels of animals and make it pour from the hands and feet and side of whatever crucified man as though it were our Lord's blood. But who is this crucified man? And what blood is this? Is it true or representation? If representation, how can it be man and blood? Man indeed is no representation. And if true man and blood, it is certainly no representation].

Counter-Reformation art theory, especially in Jesuit circles.[43] In its simplest terms, this emphasis on the image's truth underpins the idea that through spiritual and optical reconstruction of a biblical event, believers will bring themselves to experience scripture as if in "flesh and blood," so as to access its innermost learning as a linchpin to embracing faith wholly.

Many scholars have construed Caravaggio's usage of "base" elements of reality as an adherence to the aesthetic principles of the Counter-Reformation. More importantly, they tend to read Caravaggio's realism as irrefutable evidence of the master's deep and sincere religiosity. As a corollary, paintings by Caravaggio that were rejected and strongly censured in his time seem to acquire a strange canonicity in the eyes of modern scholarship: these works end up truly embodying the radical tenets of the Counter-Reformation.[44] By examining the concepts of beauty and reality in connection with the human figure, I intend not only to lay bare the multiple ambivalences and inconsistencies that these notions entail when reshaped by critics and artists following in Alberti's footsteps, but also to demonstrate that an approach to Caravaggio's painting based on the assumption that the master somehow obeyed the principles of Counter-Reformation art proves utterly naïve, let alone ungrounded.

In criticizing the tendency of Caravaggio and his followers to exalt the vileness of nature, Bellori wrote what would become a set piece of his *Vite*:

> Then the imitation of base things started, and [painters] sought out foulness and deformity, as some of them tend to do eagerly. If they are to depict armor, they pick the rustiest option; if a vase, they do not make it intact, but broken and with a cracked spout. Their draperies are stockings, breeches, and large caps, and similarly in imitating the bodies they studiously focus on the wrinkles and flaws of the skin and adjacent parts; they represent knotty fingers and limbs altered by disease.[45]

In Bellori's view, this aesthetics of the vile and the ugly is already symptomatic of, and even compulsive in, Caravaggio's paintings:

> Because of these habits, Caravaggio endured many vexations, since his paintings were removed from the churches, as I have already mentioned with regard to San Luigi dei Francesi. The same happened to *The Death of the Virgin* in Santa Maria della Scala, which was removed because he had imitated to excess a dead woman, swollen. Another picture with Saint Anne was taken out from one of the minor altars at Saint Peter's, because he had portrayed in it the Virgin with the infant Jesus naked in a base manner. In Sant'Agostino, the dirtiness of a pilgrim's foot is put on display, and in Naples, among the [figures] of the Seven Acts of Mercy, there is a man who lifts a bottle and drinks with his mouth open, the wine spilling onto him unabashedly.[46]

---

43   For a definition of Jesuit art in late sixteenth- and early seventeenth-century Italy, see Bailey 1999; and Bailey 2003, 3-30.

44   A long tradition of critical studies on Caravaggio is devoted to the master's alleged deep spirituality and adherence to the principles of Counter-Reformation painting. I will mention only the more relevant of them, from Friedlaender 1969, 117-35, to Calvesi 1990 (a real panegyric to Caravaggio's all-pervasive Catholicism), and more recently Jones 2008, 75-136. Perhaps an extreme example of this hermeneutical trend is represented by Gallo 1996 and Olson 2002. A sharp criticism of Calvesi's views, and in general of the interpretation of Caravaggio's art as reflecting Counter-Reformation principles, is to be found in Bologna 1992, 11-92.

45   Bellori, 230: "Allora cominciò l'imitazione delle cose vili, ricercandosi le sozzure e le deformità, come sogliono fare alcuni ansiosamente: se essi hanno a dipingere un'armatura, eleggono la più rugginosa; se un vaso, non lo fanno intiero, ma sboccato e rotto. Sono gli abiti loro calze, brache e berrettoni, e così nell'imitare li corpi si fermano con tutto lo studio sopra le rughe e i difetti della pelle e dintorni, formano le dita nodose, le membra alterate da morbi."

46   Bellori, 230-1: "Per li quali modi il Caravaggio incontrò dispiaceri, essendogli tolti li quadri da gli altari, come in San Luigi abbiamo raccontato. La medesima sorte ebbe il Transito della Madonna nella chiesa della Scala, rimosso per avervi troppo imitato una donna morta gonfia. L'altro quadro di Sant'Anna fu tolto ancora da uno de' minori altari della Basilica

All these examples have deservedly attracted the attention of scholars. I will only consider here the case of *The Death of the Virgin*, now at the Louvre, Paris (Fig. 13), executed in 1605-1606, rejected and then purchased in 1607 by Pieter Paul Rubens for the Duke of Mantua, Vincenzo Gonzaga.[47] In his *Vite*, Baglione reports that apart from being "swollen," the Virgin in the Louvre picture shows "her legs."[48] More interestingly, Mancini avails himself of Caravaggio's *The Death of the Virgin* to denounce the errors of contemporary artists in handling congruousness and decorum:

> It is necessary to consider the countenance of the figures, which ought adequately to possess those appearances, expressions, and attitudes with which one must depict a person in a determinate action. In this regard, one can see how mistakenly some of the modern painters proceed who, to represent a Virgin and Our Lady, portray some dirty prostitute from the filthy [Roman] courtyards, as Michelangelo Caravaggio did in the painting of Santa Maria della Scala, which on that account was rejected by the good priests, and this is perhaps why poor Michelangelo went through so many torments in his lifetime.[49]

Unfortunately, it is impossible to ascertain whether Caravaggio actually represented a prostitute. However, the swollenness of the Virgin in the Louvre picture is undeniable: her feet, heels, stomach, and neck are almost unequivocally those of a cadaver, so that it can be safely postulated that the depiction of this dead figure derives from a sort of "morgue study." Hypothetically, the reproduction of a corpse with even the most morbid features of death could be forgiven as excessive naturalism: similar to and more than Alberti's *Meleager*, the Virgin here truly impersonates the inertia of a deadly condition. Probably even Gilio would have appreciated this evocation of deadness as a necessary form of visual accuracy, only if—and this is the crucial point—it corresponded to the *istoria*. But the Louvre painting does not evoke a martyrdom or a violent death; technically and theologically speaking, the Virgin never died, but fell into a deadly lethargy, the *dormition*, from which she emerged by ascending to heaven. No swollenness is demanded here. However, Caravaggio resorts to deformity without theological reason. By no means does his representation of the Virgin aim to inculcate a religious orthodoxy through a shocking effect of reality.

In this volume, I will not analyze *The Death of the Virgin*, nor investigate why Caravaggio likened Mary's dead body to a woman's (or a prostitute's) swollen cadaver. I will merely note that by changing a "slumbering" divinity into a human corpse, Caravaggio makes the religious subject shift toward a broader theme: that of man's death and its inexorability. I would nonetheless add that, because of the absence of any allusion to divine transcendence, the Louvre painting falls into a rare pictorial category, that of tragedy, of which it certainly is one of the most sublime examples in seventeenth-century art. In any case, I contend here that to comprehend Caravaggio's alleged excesses of naturalism—which can fairly connote as realistic effects in this context, as I will argue

Vaticana, ritratti in esso vilmente la Vergine con Gesù fanciullo ignudo, come si vede nella Villa Borghese. In Sant'Agostino si offeriscono le sozzure de' piedi del pellegrino; ed in Napoli fra le sette Opere della Misericordia vi è uno che, alzando il fiasco, beve con la bocca aperta, lasciandovi cadere sconciamente il vino."

47   An extensive bibliography on the painting until 1990 is to be found in Askew 1990. An interesting review of Askew's monograph is to be found in Bologna 1992, 587-9. For more recent bibliography, see Marini 2005, 493-6, no. 69; and Schütze 2009, 270-1, no. 40. For the theme of the *dormition* in Caravaggio's painting, see in particular Dempsey 1990.

48   Baglione, 138: "Per la Madonna della Scala in Trastevere

dipinse il Transito di Nostra Donna, ma perché avea fatto con poco decoro la Madonna gonfia, e con gambe scoperte, fu levata via."

49   Mancini, 1:120: "Et avanti che si vada più oltre, si deve considerar il costume delle figure che habbin quell'esser proprio in effigie, affetto et operatione, con la quale vogliamo esprimere una persona che facci quella tal operatione. E di qui si puol vedere quanto che alcuni di moderni faccin male, quali, per descriver una Vergine e Nostra Donna, vanno retrahendo qualche meretrice sozza delli ortacci, come faceva Michelangelo da Caravaggio e fece nel Transito di Nostra Donna, in quel quadro della Madonna della Scala, che per tal rispetto quei buoni padri non lo volsero, e forsi quel poverello patì tanti travagli di sua vita."

shortly—one must first keep in sight that realism[50] is likewise a fictitious device, a complex strategy of visualizing the external world through selection of the low and the base. Neither realism nor idealization are univocal categories, but they comprise an array of interrelated criteria that are in constant rapport with their homologues: beauty, propriety and decorum; asymmetry, inappropriateness and vileness. All of these criteria operate in synchrony in early modern artworks, their charge and meaning changing in mutual interaction. When Caravaggio rigs an aspect of his figure or story by enhancing its baseness, he basically modifies a variant in a system provided with multi-layered significances. Even if in appearance this manipulation persistently qualifies as realism, its function, range and meaning could—and indeed do—greatly differ from case to case. This is why Caravaggio's realism cannot be disentangled from the network of other elements to which it is conceptually bound: to its virtual opposite, idealism, but also to beauty and ugliness, propriety and inappropriateness in dramatic action, decorum and lack thereof. What characterizes Caravaggio's usage of realistic effects is, in my view, the fact that it generates systemic dislocation. To put it differently, the realistic features employed by Caravaggio may or

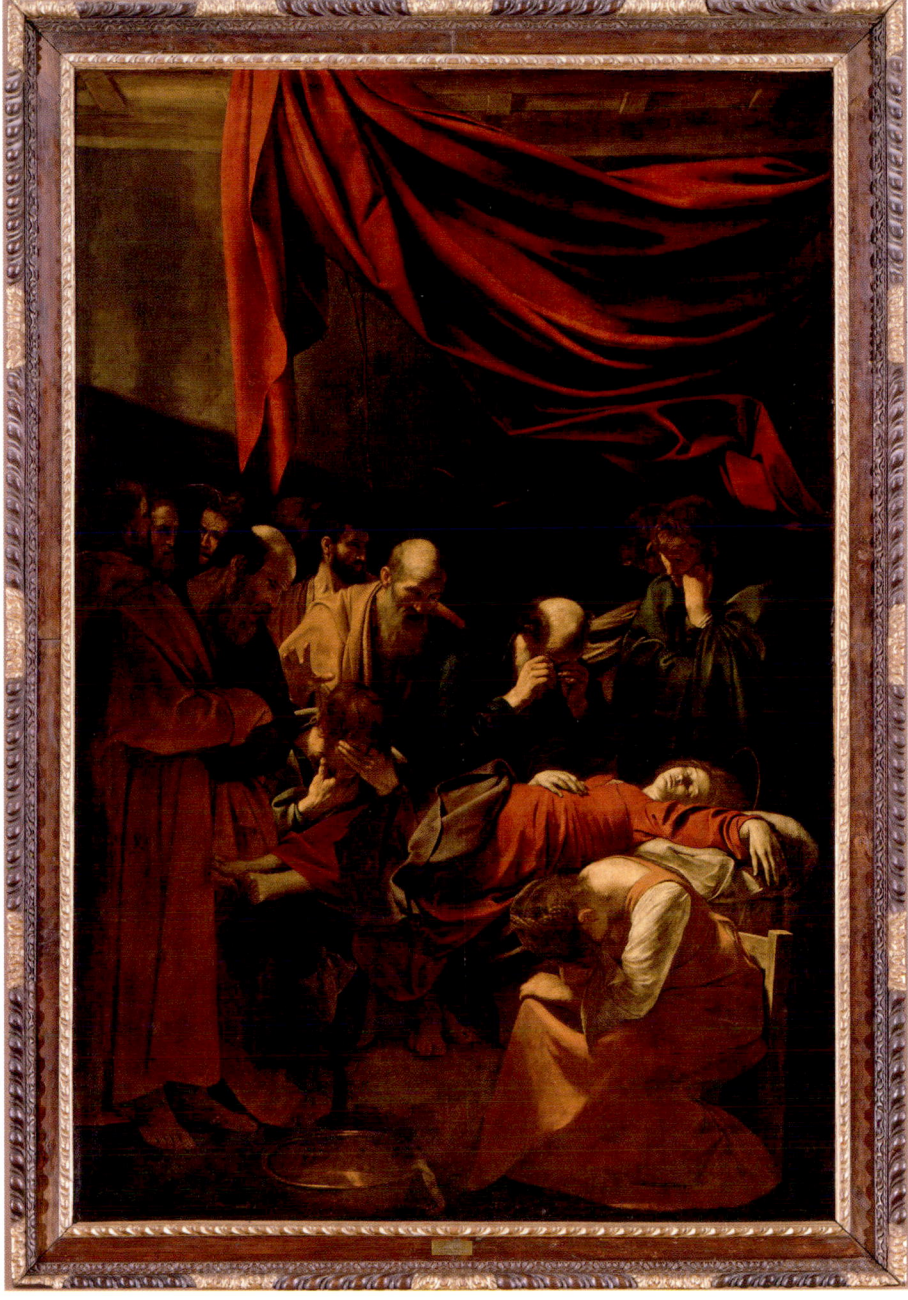

Fig. 13
Michelangelo Merisi da Caravaggio, *The Death of the Virgin*, Musée du Louvre, Paris, oil on canvas, 369 x 245 cm.

may not match, or match only partially, or even contrast with the other elements equally present in his works to which realism is traditionally associated or opposed in the early modern practice and theory of art. For instance, in *The Death of the Virgin*, Mary's "swollen body," perhaps that of a "dirty prostitute from the filthy courtyards," is juxtaposed, among others, to the curled-up figure of Mary Magdalene in the foreground inspired by Roman coins and bas-reliefs. In addition, like Timanthe's

50   For a different interpretation of realism in literature, it is always essential to peruse Auerbach 2003.

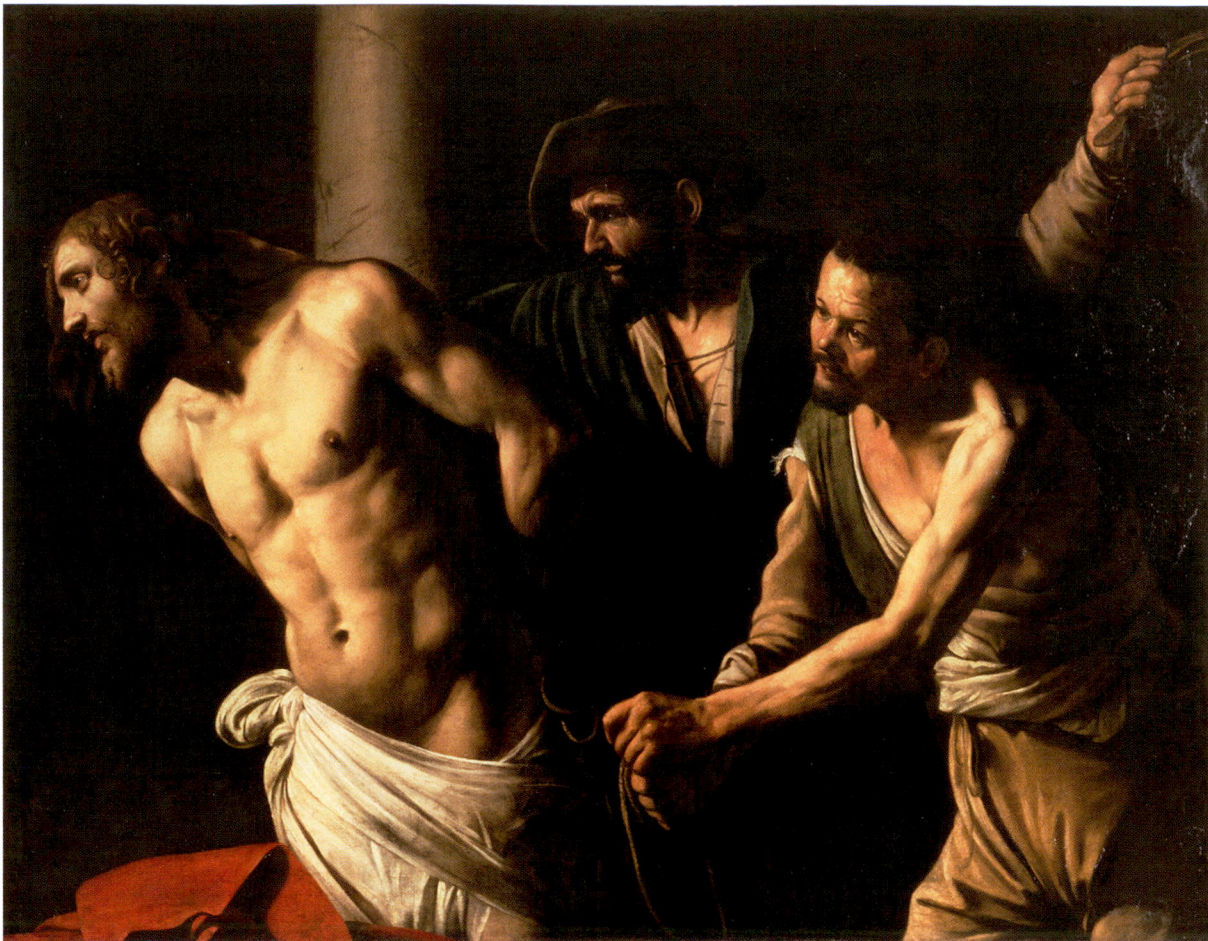

Fig. 14
Michelangelo Merisi da Caravaggio, *The Flagellation*, Musée des Beaux-Arts, Rouen, oil on canvas, 134.5 x 174.5 cm.

celebrated Agamemnon, Caravaggio's Magdalene covers her face to induce viewers into imagining the depth of her inconceivable pain. In other words, Caravaggio's pictorial narrative coordinates—and does not stitch together—the supposedly repulsive body of the dead Virgin and the refined, classically poised figure of the Magdalene, a paradigm of legitimate decorum as a reminder of Timanthe's pictorial feat in ancient times.[51] So canonically beautiful was it, I am led to believe, that Poussin probably took it up and developed it in his 1627 *Death of Germanicus* (Minneapolis Institute of Arts), more specifically in the figure of the mourning Agrippina.[52]

There is no doubt that Caravaggio was perfectly aware of the sophisticated relation between the human figure and the notions of beauty, propriety, and pertinence as requested of the *istoria*. Deliberately, he dislocates their delicate interconnections in ways that bypass and disturb the strict cultural parameters of viewers and critics of his time. Some other examples will elucidate this

51 Timanthes' pictorial feat was well known in the Renaissance and beyond. Among others, it is related by Dolce, 122: "Ecco Timante, uno de' lodati pittori antichi, il quale dipinse Ifigenia, figliuola di Agamennone (…): la dipinse dico inanzi all'altare ove essa aspettava di essere uccisa in sacrificio a Diana, ed avendo il pittore nelle facce de' circostanti espressa diversamente ogni imagine di dolore, non si assicurando di poterla dimostrar maggiore nel volto del dolente padre, fece che egli se lo copriva con un panno di lino, overo col limbo della vesta, senza che Timante ancora serbò in ciò molto bene la convenevolezza, perché essendo Agamennone padre, pareva ch'e' non dovesse poter sofferire con gli occhi propri amazzar la figliuola." I mention a few essays on this topos in Chapter 8, with regard to Caravaggio's Odescalchi *Conversion of Saint Paul*.

52 For the painting, see Rosenberg 1973. A similar claim is made by Fried 2010, 176.

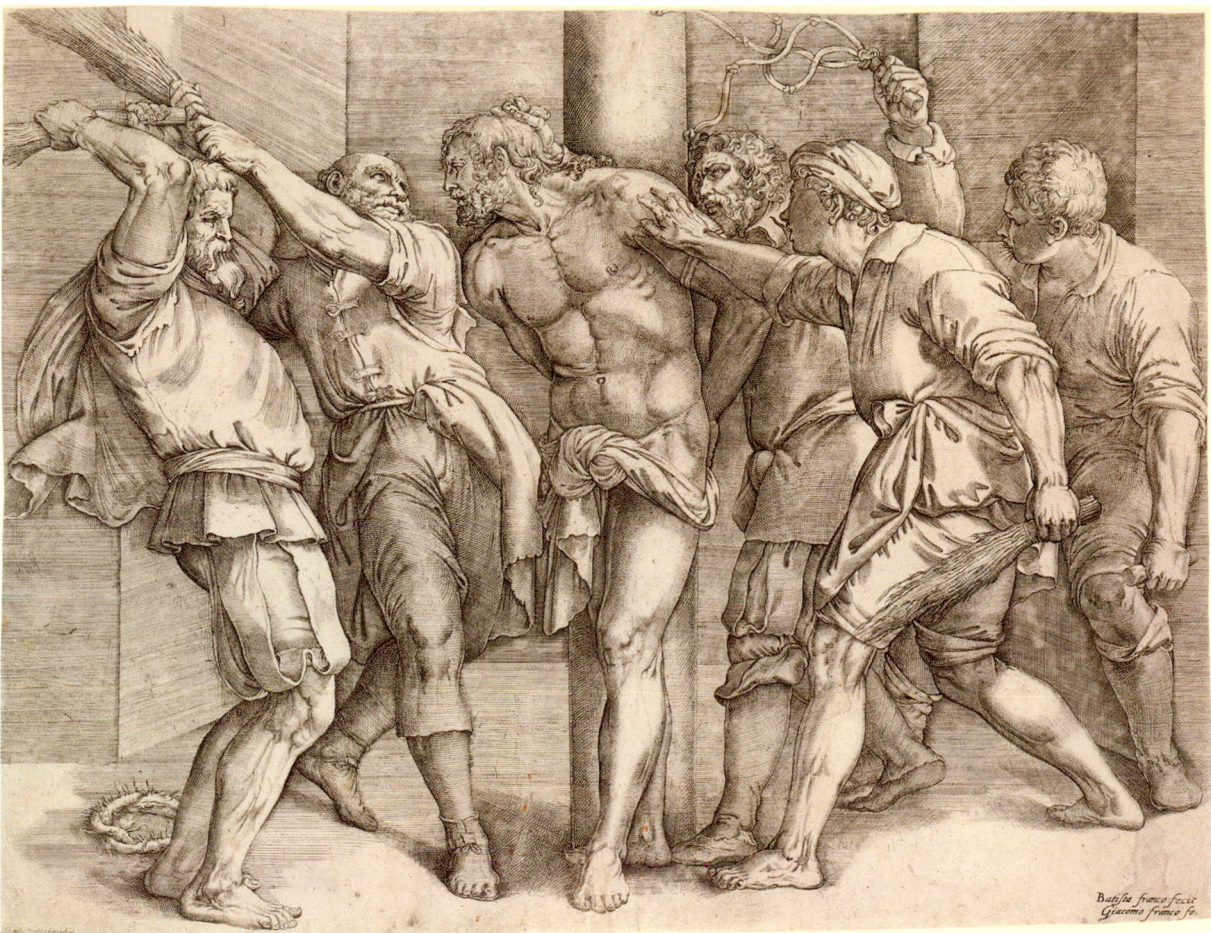

Fig. 15
Battista Franco, *The Flagellation*, engraving, 42 x 54.7 cm.

essential point. On two separate occasions Caravaggio elaborates on Sebastiano del Piombo's figure of Christ in the San Pietro in Montorio *Flagellation*, the very one that Gilio had so fiercely criticized in his 1564 treatise. As Paola Caretta has rightly pointed out,[53] in the 1607 Rouen *Flagellation* (Fig. 14)[54] Caravaggio literally reframes in close-up the figure of Christ at the center of Battista Franco's *Flagellation* (Fig. 15),[55] an engraving assuredly inspired by Sebastiano's picture. It is possible to compare the print with one of Michelangelo's preparatory studies for the San Pietro in Montorio's *Flagellation*, a design now lost but faithfully reproduced by Giulio Clovio in a drawing at Windsor Castle (Fig. 16).[56] Note that in Clovio's composition the torturer at the left flings his arms out to beat Christ, a detail—emended in Sebastiano's painting and greatly attenuated in Franco's engraving—that Caravaggio might have picked up in the figure at the right of the Rouen painting, unless, as I am also willing to believe, the master borrowed this motif from a woodcut by Lucas Cranach representing *The Flagellation* (Fig. 17).[57] Be that as it may, despite the elaborate process of synthesizing

53   Caretta 2008, 20.

54   For the painting, see Rosenberg 1966, 174, no. 194; Spear 1971, 76-7, no. 18; Cinotti 1983, 544-6, no. 65; Hibbard 1983, 325-6 [as uncertain]; Christiansen 1985, 319-22, no. 91 [catalogue entry by Mina Gregori]; Gregori 1991, 300-9, no. 18; Pacelli 1994, 54-62; Finaldi 1998; Puglisi 1998, 270-1; Longhi 1999-2000, 2:243-54 [1960]; Marini 2005, 520-1, no. 80; Schütze 2009, 276-7, no. 50.

55   See Zerner 1979, 166, no. 10-I.

56   For Michelangelo's drawings in connection with Sebastiano's *Flagellation*, see De Tolnay 1975-1980, 1:73-4.

57   See Jahn 1975, 216-7, and esp. 228.

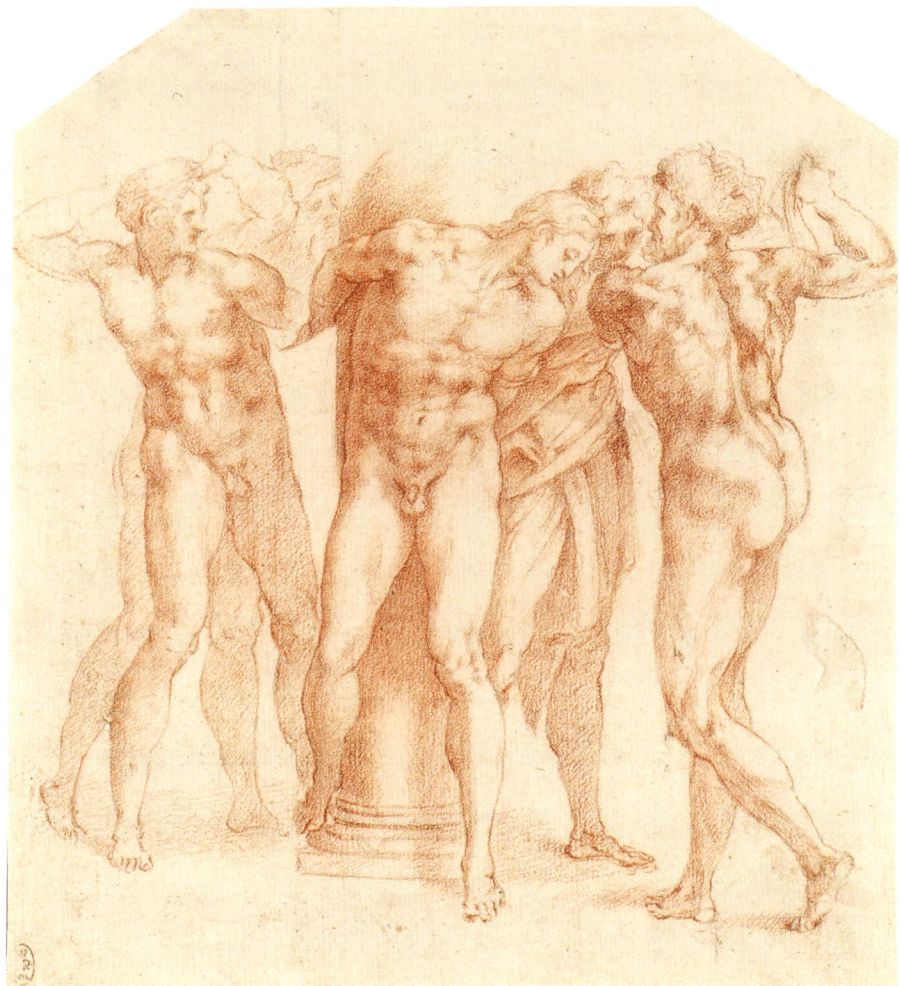

Fig. 16
Giulio Clovio after Michelangelo Buonarroti, *The Flagellation*, Royal Library, Windsor
Castle, red chalk and stylus on white paper, 23.5 x 23.6 cm.

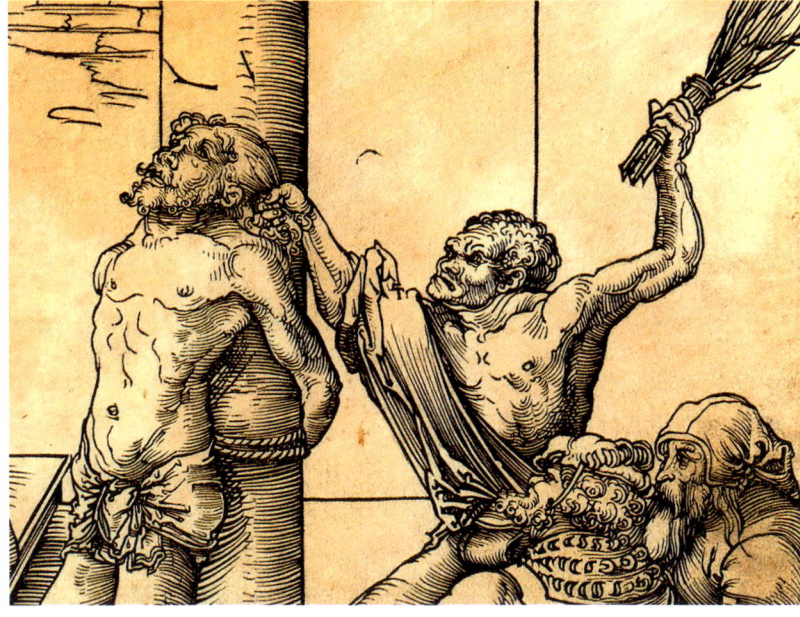

Fig. 17
Lucas Cranach, *The Flagellation*,
woodcut, 24.5 x 17.1 cm., detail.

sources betrayed by the Rouen picture, Caravaggio's attempt to compete with a figurative pattern notoriously linked to Michelangelo is beyond question. The second *Flagellation*, now in Naples, Museo di Capodimonte (Fig. 18),[58] also executed in 1607, because of its life-size format, reminds the viewer of Sebastiano's picture in a most lively manner, even if Caravaggio took every precaution to differentiate it from its prototype. Although I cannot corroborate my suspicions, it is not unlikely that Caravaggio knew Michelangelo's preparatory study for the figure of Christ, now at the British Museum, London (Fig. 19), or at least seen a copy of it.[59] In any event, it is extremely tempting to put Caravaggio's and Michelangelo's figures of Christ side by side; the comparison proves most instructive. Indeed, Caravaggio reiterated Michelangelo's original idea of portraying Christ's head bent over his left shoulder, but he intensified the contrast between the profile of the face and the frontal view of the torso. As a result, Caravaggio reshapes the chest into a trapeze, circumscribed laterally by the symmetrical brackets of the arms, and tilted in response to the arching of the torso, whose spotlighted left contour prolongs itself into the curve of Christ's receding leg (the position of the body's lower part is also indebted to a *Flagellation* by Romanino).[60] By modifying the figure's posture, Caravaggio manages to smooth Michelangelo's anatomical effects and contours: the body's members now detach themselves from the dim background tensely and powerfully, but are also compactly sinuous, thereby relinquishing the graphic sharpness specific to the prototype. Conversely, when compared to Sebastiano's Christ, Caravaggio's is sheer relief and presence: the equivalent of sculpture in painting. It is noteworthy that Caravaggio, instead of accentuating the episode's dramatic tone—it would have been a great opportunity to depict lacerations and excoriations, or any deformity of the human body—decided to exalt the legendary perfection of Christ's body, concentrating on lines and contours, on lighting and relief, on symmetry and eurythmy. More importantly, the action that he represents in the Naples *Flagellation* unequivocally conforms to Christ's attitude. From the point of view of narrative temporality, Caravaggio does not properly depict the act of flogging, but rather its immediate antecedents. To the left, a crouching thug is still binding branches together, while to the right a torturer is solidly attaching the prisoner to the column. Only the third thug, standing at the left of Christ, is about to flog him, therefore yanking at his hair. In other words, through the torturers Caravaggio represents three different chronological steps of the action, all of them ingeniously interconnected and in accord with Christ's posture. Observe that the Savior's deceptively elegant yet forced stride results from the convergence of three diverse forces: he is pulled both rightward (by the pressure of a foot on his calf and the traction of two arms tying him to the column), and leftward (by the hand grasping a lock of his hair). By rewinding the action by a few seconds, Caravaggio avoids making Michelangelo's "error": Christ can preserve his beauty not because of the cotton-made whips that Gilio ironically mocks, but because the torture, technically speaking, has not yet started.

However, in spite of Caravaggio's attempts at improving upon Michelangelo's figure by simultaneously "making sense" of Christ's strained attitude, painters and critics of his time would

58 The painting is mentioned in the seventeenth and eighteenth centuries by Bellori, 225; Celano, 3:121; and De Dominici, 1, I: 275-6: "ma il quadro del maggior altare della chiesa della Misericordia è opera lodata de' suoi pennelli (…), e più il gran quadro della Flagellazione alla colonna del Signore nella chiesa di San Domenico Maggiore nella cappella della famiglia Franco. Quest'opera esposta al pubblico trasse a sé tutti gli occhi de' riguardanti, e benché la figura del Cristo sia presa da un naturale ignobile e non gentile, com'era necessario per rappresentare la figura d'un Dio per noi fatto uomo, ad ogni modo la nuova maniera di quel terribile modo di ombreggiare, la verità di que' nudi, il risentito lumeggiare senza molti riflessi fece rimaner sorpresi non solo i dilettanti, ma i professori medesimi in buona parte." For the painting, see Pacelli 1977; Moir 1982, 140; Cinotti 1983, 468-71, no.

35; Hibbard 1983, 223-5; Christiansen 1985, 322-7, no. 93 [catalogue entry by Mina Gregori]; Bologna 1992, 225-8, 436-8; Pacelli 1994, 41-8; Puglisi 1998, 268-70; Longhi 1999-2000, 1: 197; 220 [1952]; Pagano 2004; Cassani and Sapio 2005, 112, no. 6 [catalogue entry by Ferdinando Bologna]; Pagano 2005, 61-5; Marini 2005, 529-32, no. 86; Schütze 2009, 276, no. 49.

59 For the drawing, see De Tolnay 1975-1980, 1:74, no. 74. At least one ancient copy after Michelangelo's drawing at the British Museum is mentioned as belonging to the collections of the Louvre, Paris; see Joannides 2003, 244-5, no. 97, who suggests that the author of the sheet might be Federico Zuccari.

60 For Romanino's painting, now at the Metropolitan Museum of Art, New York, see Nova 1994, 308-9, no. 79.

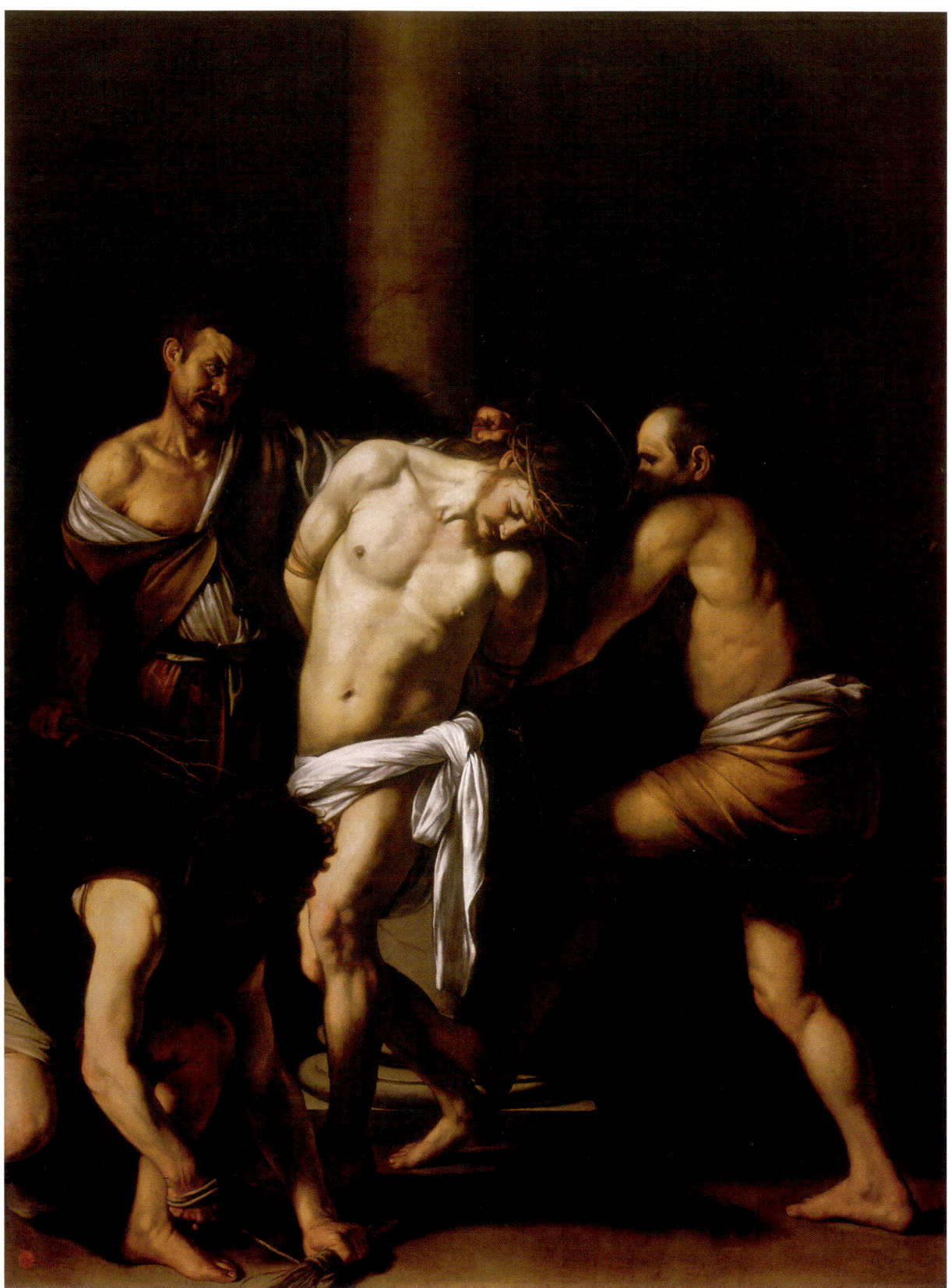

Fig. 18
Michelangelo Merisi da Caravaggio, *The Flagellation*, Museo di Capodimonte, Naples, oil on canvas, 266 x 213 cm.

have never recognized this or similar achievements. It is possible that on an unconscious level the parallel between Michelangelo's and Caravaggio's figures circulated even during the master's lifetime—I will look at this question more closely in Chapter 11. In a passage passed over by scholars, Albani alludes to this while praising the excellence of Michelangelo's *Last Judgment*, especially the figure of Christ, notwithstanding the fresco's shortcomings in perspective:

> Painters cannot equally excel in all the parts [of painting]. If Caravaggio had possessed these talents, he would have been a painter I would call divine. But he did not have knowledge of supernatural things, for he was too attached to the natural. But in the Creation of Adam and Eve Michelangelo aimed to represent the majesty of God, served and carried by thrones and angels, a work that altogether surpassed every other by soaring so high that it lowers the work of any other painter, however celebrated.[61]

In Albani's mouth, the admission of Caravaggio's quasi-divinity comes unexpectedly. For decades, admirers of Michelangelo had defined both the master and his art as "divine."[62] The very idea that Caravaggio would have equaled Michelangelo had he not stuck to nature is sincerely baffling. If I understand correctly, it means that in representing the human body Caravaggio could have actually challenged Michelangelo's supremacy. Considering the Naples *Flagellation*, the question then arises: what would have refrained a painter like Albani from deeming Caravaggio's Christ as "divine" as Michelangelo's Savior in the *Last Judgment*? In what measure and to what extent does Caravaggio's figure adhere more to nature than Michelangelo's? On the contrary, I have already enumerated the many improvements Caravaggio operated on Michelangelo's prototype in matters of

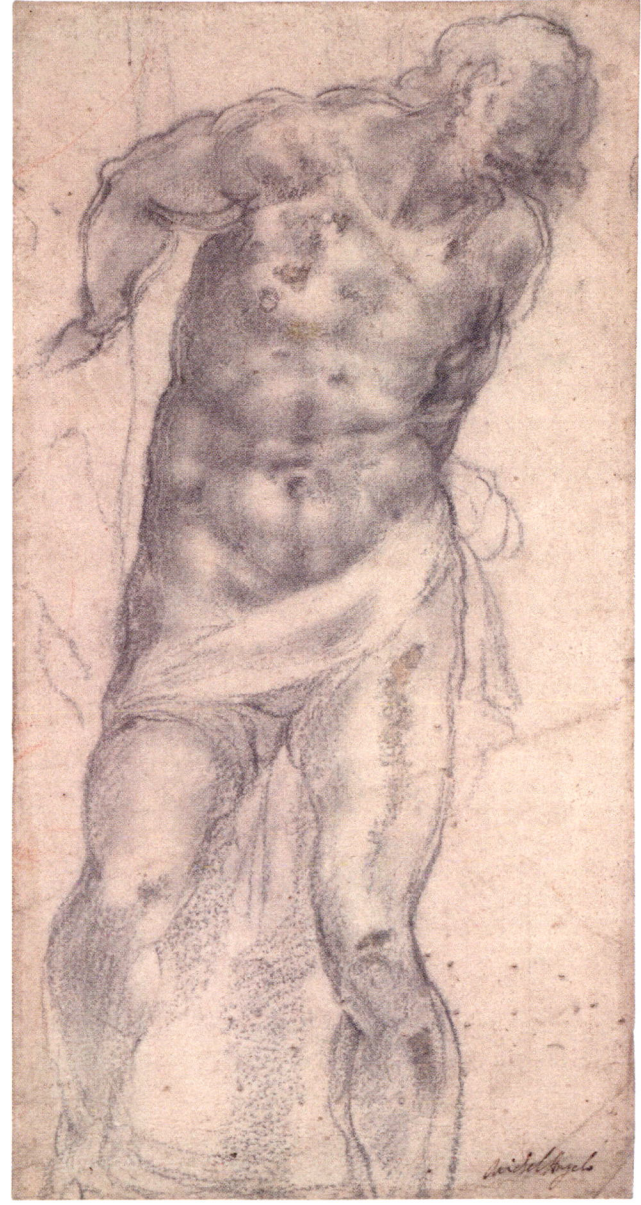

Fig. 19
Michelangelo Buonarroti, *Christ at the Column*, British Museum, London, black chalk on white paper, 27.5 x 14.3 cm

symmetry and eurythmy. Then is Albani's stubborn condemnation another symptom of the *Caravaggio syndrome*? Yes and no. No, because the technique of coloring, lighting, and bringing up relief used by Caravaggio still subverts the principles of harmony, beauty and appropriateness embraced by Albani and many others before him. I have already quoted a passage from Alberti's *De pictura* in which the concept of beauty was clearly associated with the nuance and gradation

---

61   Malvasia, 2:253: "Non possono essere i pittori egualmente eccellenti in tutte le parti. Se il Caravaggio avesse avuto questi requisiti, saria stato pittore dirò divino, questo; non aveva cognizione nelle cose sopranaturali, ma stava troppo attaccato al naturale. Ma il Buonaroti ebbe mira, nella Creazione d'Adamo e di Eva, a rappresentare la maestà del grand'Iddio, servito e portato da i Troni e angeli, opera che tutta insieme

trapassò tant'oltre e tanto alto che fa restar basso ogn'opera d'altro pittore, per celeberimo che sia stato."

62   For Michelangelo's "divinity," see more recently Campbell 2002. For the special status of artists in the sixteenth century, see Emison 2004.

necessary in joining the face's surfaces together, and I emphasized that this principle applies to the body in its entirety, and to the composition in general. In his *Aretino*, Dolce declares in this regard:

> Now it is necessary that the blend of colors be gradated and united so as to represent the natural, and nothing must remain that may offend the eyes, such as the lines of the contours, which must be omitted since they do not occur in nature, and the blackness of fierce and disconnected shades, as I call them. Light and shade when laid out with judgment and skill make the figures rounded, and lend them the relief required.[63]

Dolce was not alone in his bias against abrupt transitions of chiaroscuro. Many other critics commended Correggio solely because of his subtle gradations in coloring and shading figures (his legendary *morbidezza*). Caravaggio certainly knew about this artistic rule—so beloved of Annibale Carracci in his exaltation of Correggio and the Lombard color technique—but he voluntarily transgressed it from a certain point onward in his career. It is no coincidence that Bellori still appreciated Caravaggio's first manner inspired by Giorgione, and therefore characterized by a milder chiaroscuro close to Correggio's. Since the beginning of the 1600s, though, Caravaggio intensified the effects of contrasted lighting, introducing "fierce and disconnected shades" increasingly into his paintings. Paradoxically, it was this new technique of coloring and shading that enabled Caravaggio to grant optical relief and tactility to figures and objects alike in a measure frankly unpredictable at the time.[64] The photographic quality we attribute to Caravaggio's pictures strongly depends on his intense or "harsh" chiaroscuro. Yet it must have been a dilemma for Caravaggio as to whether he should go the distance by flouting proportion and gradation of coloring in order to achieve a magnified illusion of optical accuracy. In the end, all of this came down to a win-lose bargain: a strategic choice that by the same token doomed Caravaggio's painting forthwith to blind censorship. Also, as an inescapable corollary to his new color technique, the intense chiaroscuro of Caravaggio's compositions was to increase the "un-connectedness" of his pictorial narratives: a "defect" already imputed to the master's work, though on other grounds, as proven by Albani's criticism. As I shall demonstrate later, Caravaggio took this issue into serious consideration and exploited instead the various potentialities of pictorial darkness in paintings such as the Brera *Supper at Emmaus*.

It should be clear by now that any rigorous dichotomy between realism and idealization is unfit to fully explain Caravaggio's novelty. I am in no doubt that Caravaggio consciously plays with aesthetic criteria and categories in a way that provokes contradiction. In any case, he undoubtedly juggles with the realistic components of his own pictures by pleasingly uncovering their intrinsic fictitiousness. As a side effect, Caravaggio's realism betrays itself not only as a technical device designed to mirror the outside world with wondrous precision, but especially as a pictorial tactic through which the viewer is both absorbed into, and estranged from, reality: an artful machinery wherein vision and artifice, by fusing together, belie painting's pretense to truth or veracity.

An early example of Caravaggio's realistic tricks is offered by his *c.*1602 *Saint John the Baptist* in the Pinacoteca Capitolina, Rome (Fig. 20).[65] Critics have often remarked upon the similarities

---

63 Dolce, 154: "Ora bisogna che la mescolanza de' colori sia sfumata ed unita di modo che rappresenti il naturale e non resti cosa che offenda gli occhi: come sono le linee de' contorni, le quali si debbono fuggire (ché la Natura non le fa) e la negrezza, ch'io dico dell'ombre fiere e disunite. Questi lumi ed ombre posti con giudicio ed arte fanno tondeggiar le figure e danno loro il rilievo che si ricerca."

64 For the theoretical implications of Caravaggio's chiaroscuro, see Prater 1992.

65 The painting is mentioned in the seventeenth century by Celio, 134; Baglione, 137; Scannelli, 199; Bellori a, 45; Bellori, 217. The *Saint John the Baptist* was commissioned by Ciriaco Mattei and most probably paid for in 1602. In this context see Cappelletti and Testa 1990a; and Cappelletti and Testa 1994, 39-42, 105-6, 139. For the painting see Friedlaender 1969, 89-91; Moir 1982, 114; Cinotti 1983, 521-3, no. 59; Hibbard 1983, 151-5; Calvesi 1990, 242-7; Correale 1990; Bologna 1992, 317-8; Gilbert 1995, 1-61; Barroero 1997; Bersani and Dutoit 1998, 79-83; Puglisi 1998, 205-7; Longhi 1999-2000, 1: 265 [1968, and

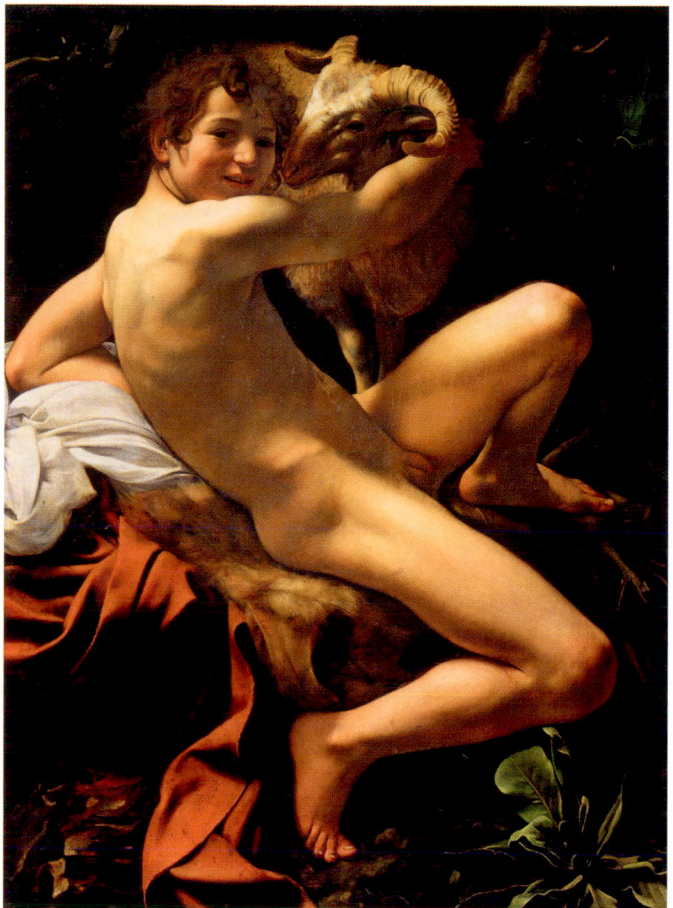

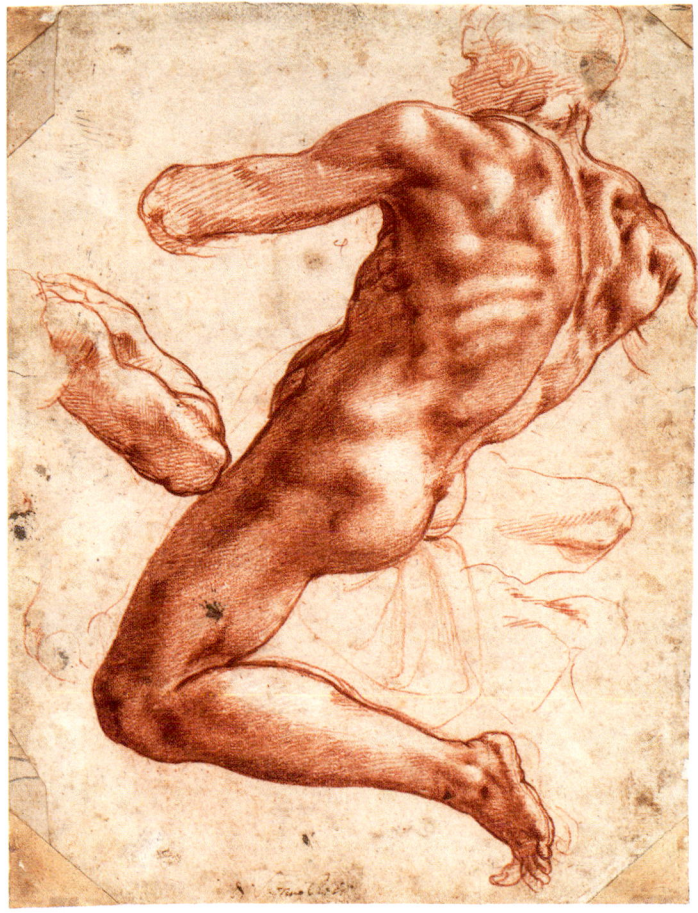

Fig. 20
Michelangelo Merisi da Caravaggio, *Saint John the Baptist*,
Pinacoteca Capitolina, Rome, oil on canvas, 129 x 95 cm.

Fig. 21
Michelangelo Buonarroti, *Study for an Ignudo*, Teylers Museum,
Haarlem, red chalk, 27.9 x 21.4 cm.

between the boy in the painting and one of Michelangelo's *ignudi* in the Sistine Chapel.[66] The affinity of their poses is undeniable. It is instructive to juxtapose Caravaggio's picture to a preparatory drawing in red chalk from the Teylers Museum, Haarlem (Fig. 21),[67] in which Michelangelo studies the posture of this *ignudo* from life. Michelangelo's figure in itself is an eloquent case of strained *contrapposto*: pivoting on his buttocks, the model rotates his torso inward while steadily planting his visible leg on the ground. In reality, the pose conveys an impression of instantaneous and unstable motion, since the entire leg, despite its solid position, seemingly rests on a single toe. Caravaggio did not vary the posture of this leg, although he mitigated the gracious unfurling of his model's toes. More generally, he contented himself with diminishing the strain of the torso with relation to the legs: then, only the boy's shoulders twist in recollection of Michelangelo's *contrapposto*. By making these adjustments, Caravaggio was also able to visually reconstruct the dynamics of the motion of his figure: the second leg, invisible in Michelangelo's prototype, now powerfully allows

with regard to the copy at the Galleria Doria Pamphilj]; Lavin 2000, 8-15; Rudolph and Ostrow 2001; Marini 2005, 475-8, no. 58; Lechner 2006, 98-111; Varriano 2006, 110-1; Kliemann 2007, 192-3; Whitfield 2007; Von Rosen 2007; Von Rosen 2009, 172-86; Schütze 2009, 265, no. 30; Ebert-Schifferer 2009, 148-51.

66 See for instance Longhi 1999-2000, 1: 265: "La polemica fu poi al colmo nella interpretazione del 'San Giovanni Battista' di casa Doria, dove uno dei nudi di Michelangelo nella volta Sistina, visto in controparte, è bensì vitale, prensile come nell'originale, quasi il Caravaggio ammettesse che così talvolta ci appare anche il vero; ma decidesse che, per immergerlo nella realtà naturale, occorre 'macinarne la carne' e interromperlo con i traversoni macchiati dell'ombra. E può essere che la motivazione antinomica rimanga troppo palese."

67 For the drawing, see De Tolnay 1975-80, 1:107, no. 136.

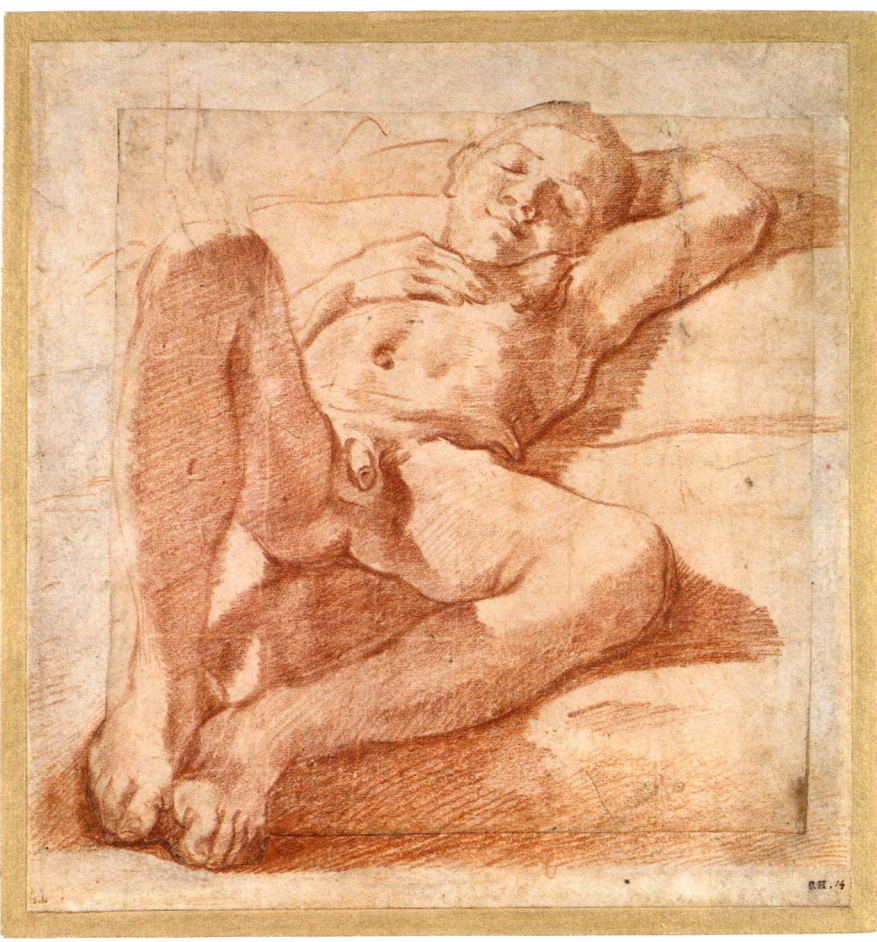

Fig. 22
Ludovico Carracci, *Nude Figure of a Sleeping Boy*, Ashmolean Museum, Oxford, red chalk,
23.7 x 22.3 cm.

the body to hang in place. Once again, Caravaggio's modification of Michelangelo's prototype succeeds in softening the contours and evening up the volumes: evidence of the former is the flexuous outline linking the boy's back, buttocks and thighs; the latter is proven by the flat modeling of his abdomen. This process of beautifying the prototype also aims at recovering a surrogate congruousness of action. Whereas Michelangelo's *ignudo* spins and nearly spirals with no external reason, hence under the pressure of inner energy, Caravaggio's boy purposefully revolves to hug a nearby ram while smiling at the viewer. At first glance, Caravaggio seems to heed the principles of symmetry, eurythmy, and propriety repeatedly recommended by art theorists of his time. In a certain sense, he gives "meaning" to Michelangelo's gratuitous *sforzo*. Yet he does not undertake to improve on his predecessor's idea in a simple view of emulation; rather, he creates a hall of mirrors wherein Michelangelo's artifact, by dint of pictorial artifice, is passed off as a live model that in turn enacts a religious role (if this is indeed Saint John the Baptist). To grasp satisfactorily the boldness of Caravaggio's enterprise, it must be said that the Capitolina painting does not compare to anything created at the time. To be sure, life studies of naked apprentices were not unheard-of: for example, Ludovico Carracci's drawing in red chalk now at the Ashmolean Museum, Oxford (Fig. 22), dated to the 1580s, where a sleeping nude boy is portrayed in felicitous foreshortening, the triangle composed by his spread legs and joined feet serving as a chiaroscuro foil to his sex left carelessly in view.[68] But Ludovico never transferred anything like this onto canvas.

Before proceeding further, I need to clarify my argument: to my knowledge, Caravaggio is not the only painter of the time to test canonical attitudes from artists like Michelangelo with the aid of models.[69] A beautiful drawing in red chalk by Annibale Carracci now at the Uffizi, Florence (Fig. 23), shows on its recto and verso two studies of a boy's foreshortened head.[70] The drawing relates to a *Saint Sebastian* now in a private collection and dated to c.1590. In my opinion, Annibale's

68   See Bohm 2004, 154, no. 52.

69   In his notes on painting, written in the 1640s, Pietro Testa seems to evoke a similar procedure of testing canonical figures. See Testa, 242: "Nel quinto, come si copia nella natura quelle cose che si è osservato nei gran maestri e come a quelle si paragonano..."

70   For this drawing, a preparatory study for the entire figure of Saint Sebastian, and the painting in a private collection, see Benati and Riccomini 2006, 214-8, nos. IV.15, IV.16, and IV.17-18 [catalogue entries by Alessandro Brogi].

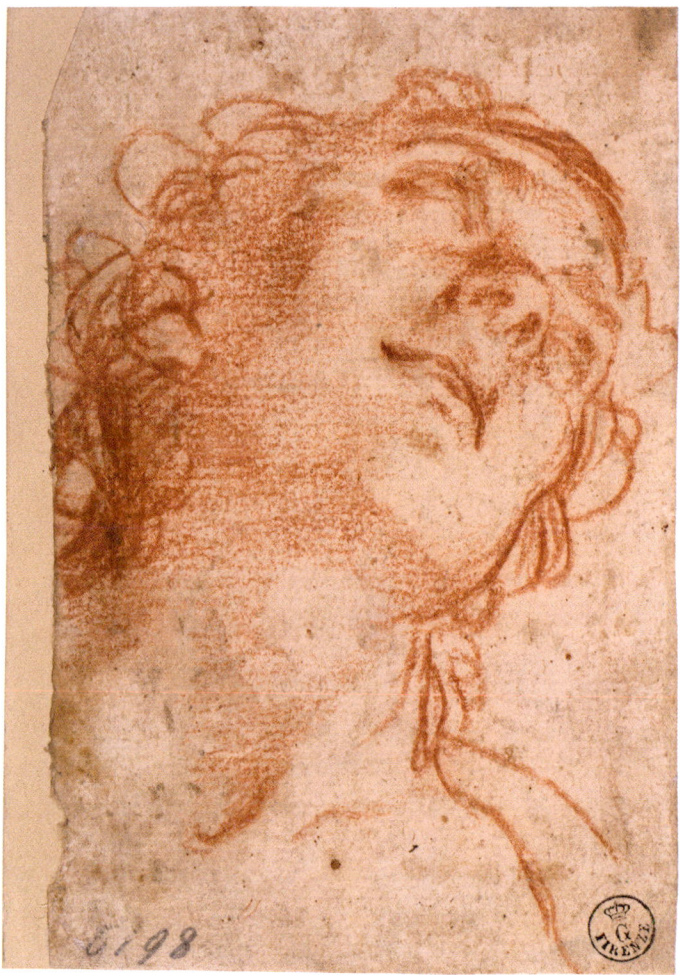

Fig. 23
Annibale Carracci, *Study of a Foreshortened Head*, Galleria degli Uffizi, Florence, red chalk, 12.2 x 85 cm.

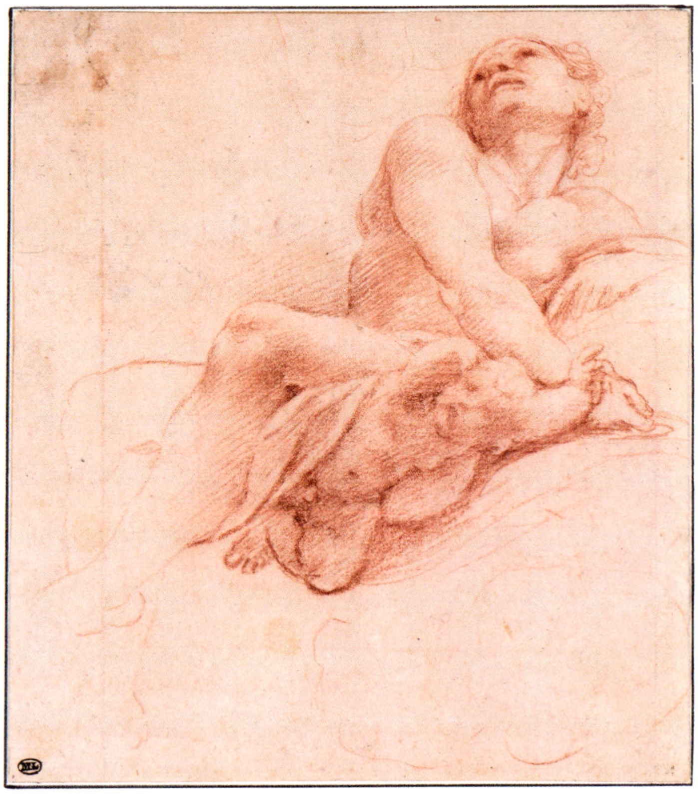

Fig. 24
Correggio (Antonio Allegri), *Nude Man with Supporting Putto*, Musée du Louvre, Paris, red chalk, 16.9 x 14.8 cm.

drawing mimics the technique, and partially imitates the figure, of one of Correggio's preparatory studies for the *Vision of Saint John* (San Giovanni Evangelista, Parma).[71] In this drawing, now at the Louvre, Paris (Fig. 24), also executed in red chalk, Correggio grasps the contours of his model's body while fixing the figure's audacious foreshortening and succinctly envisioning its chiaroscuro effects. The similarities between the foreshortened heads of Annibale's and Correggio's figures is perceptible in two details: the figure's parted lips—forming a sort of tenuous and wide gap—and its towering nose pasted directly onto the forehead. Of course, because he is meant to perch on clouds, Correggio's figure presents a more accentuated foreshortening than Annibale's model, which was destined to appear almost in the foreground. From this comparison, it is obvious that Annibale tries to "naturalize" Correggio's pose, as much as Caravaggio would "materialize" Michelangelo's. However, one would be wrong to consider Annibale's and Caravaggio's procedures identical. In imitating Correggio's draftsmanship and typical foreshortening, Annibale counterfeits his predecessor in an extemporaneous artwork earmarked for connoisseurs. In a painting, Annibale would most likely have dissimulated his borrowing, as prescribed by many an

71 See Popham 1957, 151, no. 12; and Di Giampaolo and Muzzi 1990, no. 16.

art theorist of that time. By contrast, Caravaggio defies viewers immediately to identify his source in a life-size, aggrandized format, prompting them to compare the prototype with the derivate. He extracts Michelangelo's figure from a decorative, architectural context, by framing his *ignudo* within the canvas in a close-up view, the boy's limbs virtually pushing against the picture's borders as if clueing viewers in to the easel's physical limits. In other words, Caravaggio wants beholders to realize that Michelangelo's *ignudo*, initially a motif of beautiful motion unfit to take part in coherent action, is comfortably ensconced within his painting. The frame stages and canonizes Michelangelo's figure, albeit corrected, making of it a work of art in its own right, and not as a part of a ceiling's fictive architecture. Transformed as he is into a smiling boy, Michelangelo's *ignudo* now acts coherently by ironically accomplishing a trivial action—accepting the nudge of an affectionate ram—and assuming the pristine appearance of a studio "porter."[72] If one bears in mind Malvasia's testimony relative to the reception of Annibale's *Baptism*, one can easily make out Caravaggio's intention in the Capitolina painting. He boldly and truly transposes his model wholesale onto the canvas, but in doing so blurs the distinction between idea and nature to a point of no return. Indeed, Caravaggio's boy, albeit the reproduction of a live model (most probably the pubescent Cecco, then an apprentice in the master's workshop), has already been beautified on Michelangelo's example, so that crude reality coalesces into fictitious beauty, or vice versa, at will. Vileness and beauty, banality and dignity of action can no longer be told apart here.

Rather than an improvement on Michelangelo's canonical figure, the ironic conceit deployed by Caravaggio in the Capitolina painting is a vibrant defense of his great predecessor. It nullifies every argument against Michelangelo, by reducing the core of the old and new criticism to joyous relativity. At this point, though, I should warn the reader not to dismiss Caravaggio's irony as a visual prank.[73] The relativism of pictorial modes specific to the Capitolina picture extends to every aspect of the composition. First of all: what is its genre? Is this a religious subject? But if so, which one? Halo and reed cross are patently missing here, and the only attribute present, a ram, cannot be mistaken for the lamb prefiguring Christ that traditionally accompanies the depiction of Saint John. Could it be Isaac, as some scholars have recently advanced?[74] Even in this case, essential attributes would be absent, beginning with Abraham, his knife, and the rudimentary altar on which the young Isaac was to be immolated. And why should Isaac be smiling at the viewer? Or perhaps this is a new genre, the portrait of a life nude, vaguely reminiscent of a Gospel or Bible hero, and through this allusion visually magnified. A similar procedure would be followed by Rembrandt when transfiguring his first wife, Saskia, or the mistress of his mature age, Hendrickje, into mythological or religious heroines, at times lacking most (but not all) of the epithets required by the subject that these female models summon up.[75] However, regardless of his magnification through a biblical aura and the monumental posture bestowed on him, the boy represented in the Capitolina painting is also the focus of sensual, even homoerotic attention. How would this factor fit in with the picture's religious patina? And how is eroticism here compatible with the boy's careless, childish smile? I do not have answers to these questions, but I believe that the issue deserves attention because it clarifies that at stake here is the entire apparatus of rules and conventions through which painting, as a manual practice and an intellectual activity, was perceived in Caravaggio's time. More to the point, the beautified realism I have shown to be operating in the Capitolina picture is not simply a matter of style, pictorial technique, and self-referential reflection on painting's status. Above all, it is the powerful means by which Caravaggio put to the test the whole notion of painting: its *modus*

---

72 Campbell 2004, 106, refers to a similar case with regard to Bronzino's *Martyrdom of Saint Lawrence* (San Lorenzo, Florence), in which one can find "the imitation of 'real' bodies in the form of live studio models."

73 Friedlaender 1969, 91: "one is startled by a most curious mixture of sculptural stylization, mocking Michelangelo, and

the boy's extremely sensuous expression and gesture, which conveys a sharp and testy spirit of persiflage and equivocal mockery."

74 See Barroero 1997; and Rudolph and Ostrow 2001.

75 In this regard, see Pericolo 2010.

operandi, its goals and, as I will repeatedly point out in the course of this book, its role as a vehicle of social order, secular knowledge, and religious orthodoxy.

I have therefore come to the conclusion that realism should be construed in a twofold manner when it comes to evaluating Caravaggio's painting. In a narrower sense, but certainly more common, realism is the depiction of elements—figures, objects, etc.—viewed by a community as intellectually unacceptable, religiously inappropriate, and visually degrading. To be sure, Caravaggio's manipulation of realistic effects might have a social, or even a devotional connotation— one generally associated with pauperism and its various currents in early seventeenth-century Italy—as put forth by many scholars. In his *Vite*, Baglione maliciously notes that the two pilgrims in Caravaggio's Sant'Agostino *Madonna dei Pellegrini* (*c*.1603-1606),[76] "one with muddy feet, and the other with a bonnet worn-out and dirty," were "much acclaimed by the populace," despite the image's "flaws with regard to the parts [of painting] necessary in a grand picture."[77] Nonetheless, despite what Caravaggio's exegetes have claimed so often, the representation of the poor's extreme shabbiness at the beginning of the seventeenth century does not bespeak profound devotion, but rather connotes as a pictorial inappropriateness that, in accordance with Cardinal Federico Borromeo's sentiments, should be—and ordinarily was—dodged even by practitioners of the comic genre. Here are Borromeo's exact words, which I quote from his *c*.1624 *Della pittura sacra*:[78]

> As I have said earlier, it is not enough to avoid the nude, but it is also necessary to avail oneself of clothes suitable for those persons for whom they are employed, since no one is so ignorant as not to understand that honorable citizens must not wear peasants' costumes, and it is a rule of comedy and tragedy that clothes vary in conformity with the status of the people represented: even if these are vile in and of themselves, they never appear as such on stage, and are not acknowledged as such; therefore it is appalling that, whereas comedians like to heed decorum in their costumes, this quality is instead flouted in the field of holy and sacred things.[79]

In other words, representing the poor—the "base" role by definition, which is specific to comedy, as I will explain in the Introduction to Part Two—is also a matter of "encoding." When Borromeo asserts that the vile is neither present on stage nor acknowledged by spectators, he simply distinguishes between the referents—the real-world people that fall into the social and aesthetic category of "vileness"—and their mimetic counterparts—the characters that stand for, but by no means reproduce, their referents: actors that do not need to wear the actual costume of the vile, but don their own conventional mask of "stylized poverty" in order to be correctly identified by the audience. In religious painting, the role of the poor results indeed from a pictorial code; accordingly, the depiction of a "real" poor would not only contravene the principle of decorum, but

76   One can find extensive bibliography on this painting in Cinotti 1983, 524-5, no. 60; Marini 2005, 487-90, no. 65; and Schütze 2009, 268, no. 36.

77   Baglione, 137: "Nella prima cappella della chiesa di Sant'Agostino alla man manca fece una Madonna di Loreto ritratta dal naturale con due pellegrini, uno co' piedi fangosi e l'altra con una cuffia sdrucita e sudicia, e per queste leggerezze in riguardo delle parti che una gran pittura aver dee, da' popolani ne fu fatto estremo schiamazzo."

78   Federico Borromeo's *De pictura sacra libri duo* were first published in 1624. As noted by Barbara Agosti in Borromeo, 3, Borromeo's *Della pittura sacra*, never published during the author's lifetime, must be understood as the Italian translation of the Latin treatise "enriched" with supplementary observations. Agosti also remarks that the ideas expressed

in the *De pictura* are very likely to hark back to Borromeo's sojourn in Rome in 1586-1595. For this reason, I frequently use Borromeo's Italian text as an important source for the concept of the sacred *istoria* at the time of Caravaggio.

79   Borromeo, 26: "E perché, come poco innanzi detto abbiamo, non basta fuggire l'ignudo, ma conviene valersi dei vestimenti i quali siano fatti a proposito della persona per cui s'adoprano, poiché non ritrovasi alcuno così ignorante che non veda l'abito contadinesco non doversi adoperare dagl'onorevoli cittadini, e esser proprio eziandio delle commedie e delle tragedie il vestire secondo la diversità degl'offici e delle persone rappresentate, e che se bene son vili in se stesse, non compariscono però come tali nella scena, né per tali sono riconosciuti; perciò è brutta cosa che per insino dai comici si ami di osservare il decoro nelle vestimenta, e che poi questo si disprezzi nelle cose sacre e sante."

also undermine the circuitry of visual conventions upon which the *istoria, in quo* pictorial mimesis, relies. To put it more abruptly, an edulcorated poor, such as those sweet creatures represented by Federico Barocci in his religious pictures, suffices both to represent the humble and to arouse devotion:[80] thus, Caravaggio's "muddy feet" and "dirty bonnet" exceed the devotional finality that many scholars have lent them as their exclusive motive. At any rate, even if one regards the pictorial shabbiness of some humble figures in Caravaggio's painting as a sign of his religiosity, the fact remains that these "realistic" elements prove too sporadic to be symptomatic of a coherent, intentional, and systemic "poetics of humility." In fact—to pick up a few examples among those previously examined—how could the Virgin's swollen body, the enticing nudity of a porter-like, undefined Saint John, or Christ's flawless anatomy shining through the "blackness of disconnected shades" correlate with a devotion oriented toward the humble and the poor? Rather, I think that these effects of reality pertain to a sub-class of a more ample realism, and therefore ought to be assessed within the purview of the whole category.

Keeping in mind Alberti's concept of painting, I propose that the second, broader category of realism be defined as the extreme application of any technical and compositional practice integral to implement, enhance, and dramatize the functions of images as optical devices, in order not only to evoke the outside world in the picture as true to life, but above all to momentarily abolish the fictitious divide between representation and actuality. In other words, Caravaggio's pictures, especially his pictorial narratives, tend to defuse the images' aura of fictiveness through optical actualization. Moreover, by zooming in on the figures through dramatic close-up, Caravaggio focalizes action around man's inner motivations and external motions. In this way, the image lends itself to being perceived as an immediate extension of the viewer's world. To fulfill actualization, the sort of corporal hyperbolism so vigorously criticized by Albani and Bellori is required: etched wrinkles, disproportionate limbs, and slowed-down acts are, among many others, the tools with which Caravaggio orients the beholder's gaze to pictorial action and its bodily components, thereby putting aside those erudite accessories, rhetorical embellishments, and mulled-over symbolisms required of early seventeenth-century painting, and especially of the *istoria*. When clothes and objects appear in Caravaggio's pictures, they accordingly exhibit their "existential" fragility, as if their being well-traveled could demystify their fictiveness: their being stock-props in an *istoria*.

Focus on action therefore actualizes images, beguiling viewers into drawing immediate parallels between the fiction represented and their own experiences. More to the point, Caravaggio's realism enforces empathy. From this point of view, and not paradoxically, Caravaggio's style, particularly the one he adopted as his trademark from 1600 until his flight to southern Italy in 1606, presents itself as an anti-style in its pretension to render images as if reflected in a mirror. Mirrors indeed reproduce, and do not represent, the world outside. Theoretically speaking, there is no place in the mirror for Correggio and Titian's chromatic harmonies, or for Michelangelo's gracefully strained contours, which instead stem from those painters' capacity for purifying vision. For this reason, pictorial stylization, however it might be enacted, seems to be suppressed by Caravaggio's brush, as it *merely* mirrors things and figures. Although itself the product of a selective stylization, the apparent elimination of any historical style set up by Caravaggio once again shortens the distance between the image and the viewer's world. In the course of this monograph, I will have the opportunity to demonstrate that Caravaggio's mirror-painting is often a deforming device; although apparently a segment of man's natural vision, what transpires on his canvases does not obey the principles of physics, but of invention. On a preliminary basis, Caravaggio's realism nevertheless tends to nullify all the historical accretions associated with style in early modern Italy.

---

80   On Barocci's "maniera devota," see Lingo 2008; Dempsey 2010.

As Charles Dempsey has convincingly argued, Annibale Carracci's eclecticism instead subsumes all the most canonical pictorial languages of Renaissance Italy by generating a super-temporal style.[81] From this point of view, Caravaggio's realism configures itself as a ground-zero style. One can speculate about the reasons behind Caravaggio's stylistic options. At any rate, by invalidating the notion of style, Caravaggio also intended to disarm the charge of fictiveness specific to early modern pictorial representations.

Unfettered by the stylistic filters through which the Carracci, Federico Zuccari, the Cavalier d'Arpino and other masters of early seventeenth-century Rome allude to their great predecessors' achievements, Caravaggio's pictures reach out immediately to the viewer. For an audience haunted by artistic rules and protocols, attuned to styles and eager to judge and discriminate between and against them, Caravaggio's anti-style must have appeared deeply perturbing. If an erudite and knowledgeable gaze is no longer demanded in order to enter the realm of pictorial fiction, and if artistic vision makes itself accessible without specific preparation on the viewer's part, then art ceases to exist, and representation is downgraded to reproduction. This was the instinctive, understandable reaction of painters and critics to Caravaggio's realism, a reaction that, however predictable, contradicts the very tenets on which rules and artistic conventions of Counter-Reformation painting relied, in particular its claim to immediate and unsophisticated accessibility. In fact, there would be another way to interpret the apparent dearth of refinement and aesthetic filters specific to Caravaggio's art. Should realistic effects not facilitate the legibility and intelligibility of images? And if they do, should legibility and intelligibility not be particularly welcome, for through them even the most illiterate of beholders can access sacred images and their religious truth? On these premises, Caravaggio's art might have been defensible, but instead it laid itself bare to even harsher censorship. Why did this happen? I believe that Caravaggio's realism purely and simply does not serve the cause of legibility and intelligibility as promoted by his contemporaries. Even if Caravaggio's technically advanced procedure of rendering reality as present and tangible seems to make his pictures immediately accessible to viewers, in fact this accessibility and proximity more often than not complicate the reading and comprehension of the image. On this count, Caravaggio's realism through its innumerable stratagems is rather a masterly device designed to mar, dismantle or even broaden the concept of the *istoria* as first enunciated by Alberti. By the same token, Caravaggio's realism targets the notion of pictorial truth so crucial to Italian art after the Council of Trent. Through optical accuracy, dramatic immediacy, and perceptual impression of proximity, Caravaggio reveals the contradictory foundations of his culture's innermost order: an order notoriously based on religious orthodoxy. I shall dwell on many aspects of pictorial truth from diverse perspectives in the course of this volume, and especially in Part Three: the complexity of this issue indeed demands a step-by-step procedure of analysis.

81   See in particular, Dempsey 2000. Of paramount interest
with regard to Caravaggio's "style" and its specificity in
comparison with that of Annibale Carracci is Dempsey 2006.

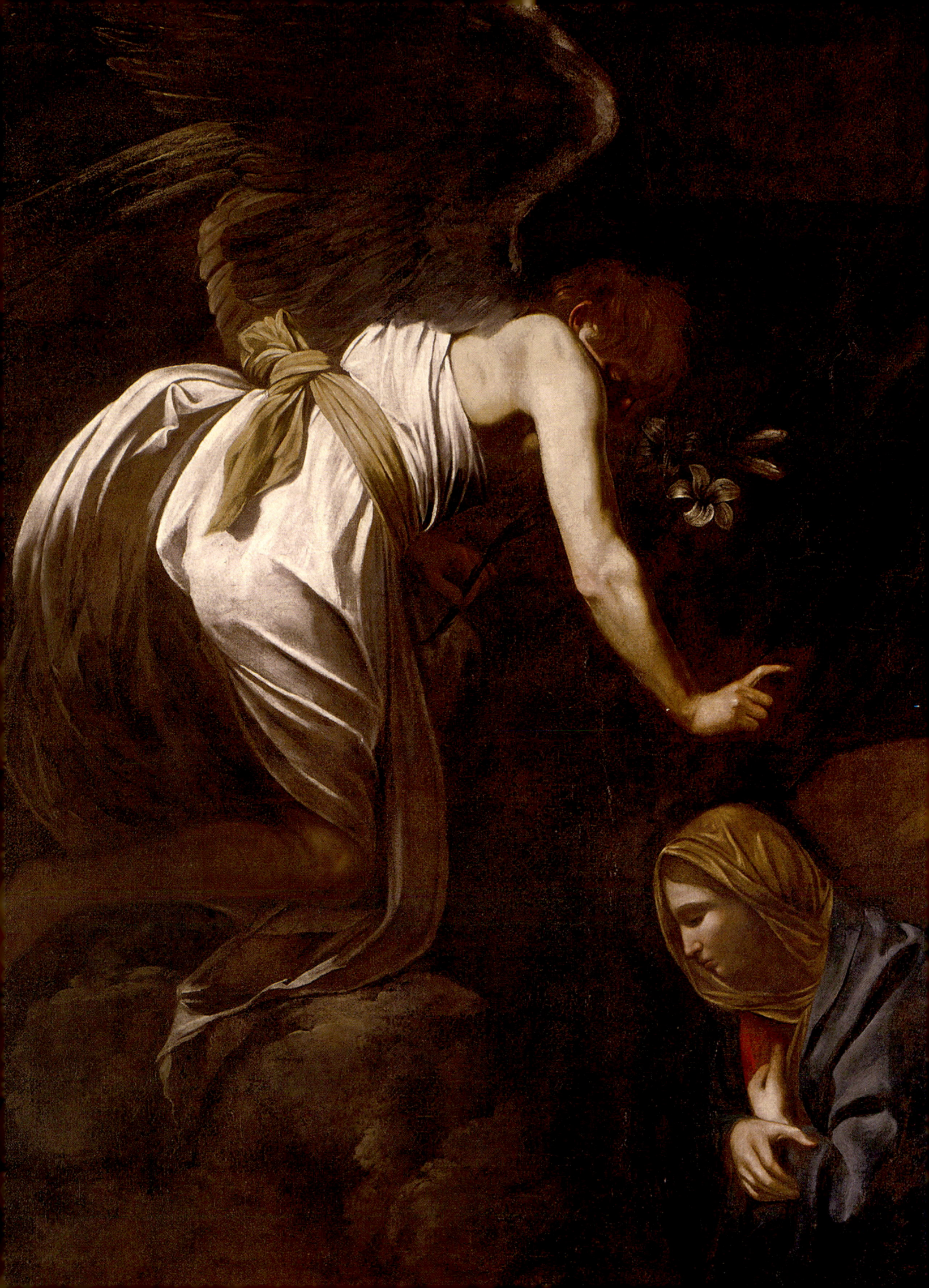

CHAPTER 2

The Glitches in Alberti's *Istoria*: Time and Action

Thus far I have concentrated almost exclusively on the human figure in its singularity, thereby deliberately neglecting the fact that Alberti's *istoria* is centered on human action, and thus demands that many figures be coordinated together in accordance with variety and congruousness. As I have already explained, Alberti himself explicitly recommends the staging of multiple actions as long as multiplicity is limited within reasonable boundaries: "this is why I strongly approve of what I see is observed by tragic and comic poets alike; they invent a story with as few actors as possible, for nine or ten men cannot act together in an appropriate way (...)."[1] I have already pointed out that Mancini criticized Caravaggio's method of composing on account of the impossibility for the painter and his followers to put together a sufficient number of actors on stage in the *istoria*. On similar grounds, Albani disregarded Caravaggio's half-figures as unsuitable to compose a pictorial narrative. Although Alberti warns painters about the risk of chaos and confusion when binding many actions together, he would definitely have agreed with Mancini and Albani, and shared their perplexity about Caravaggio's take on figures and half-figures. Indeed, the concept of variety discourages painters from representing figures partially or in isolation as the focus of an *istoria*. The reason is almost self-evident: half-figures restrict the opportunities of creating subtle variations in gesture and attitude. Harmonious *contrapposti* or elaborate *chiasms*, in this light, could not be felicitously marshaled. Single figures, on the other hand, represent but a limited segment of action. Yet the *istoria*, as a visual device laden with purpose and meaning, calls out for systemic completeness. Beholders must be able to decode and reconstruct the story in its multiple elements: the more information it provides, the more significant and far-reaching its reception becomes. Without ever admitting it, Alberti envisions the *istoria* as the virtual equivalent of a whole rhetorical piece: it is more than an episode or a single action. I will return shortly to this point.

There is another reason why Caravaggio's emphasis on the human figure is potentially at odds with Alberti's thought. From the outset, Alberti conceived of the *istoria* as a rhetorical device capable of incorporating as much data as possible: a visual machinery in which not only figures, but also other paraphernalia, if cleverly subordinate to action, should bespeak the painter's ample erudition and inventiveness in competition with—or in emulation of—poets:

> I therefore advise the diligent painter to be acquainted and on good terms with poets, orators, and other sorts of literati: he indeed will profit from the outstanding ornaments supplied by these learned minds, and certainly will improve his inventions, which in painting meet the greatest praise. The excellent painter Phidias avowed that he himself had learned from Homer how to depict Zeus in all his divine majesty.[2]

1   Alberti, 71: "Atque in historia id vehementer approbo quod a poetis tragicis atque comicis observatum video, ut quam possint paucis personates fabulam doceant. Meo quidem iudicio nulla erit usque adeo tanta rerum varietate referta historia quam novem aut decem homines non possint condigne agere." This sentence does not have its equivalent in the Italian version of Alberti's treatise.

2   Ibidem, 94-5: "Pertanto consiglio ciascuno pittore molto si faccia famigliare ad i poeti, retorici e agli altri simili dotti di lettere, già che costoro doneranno nuove invenzioni, o certo aiuteranno a bello componere sua storia, per quali certo acquisteranno in sua pittura molta lode e nome. Fidias, più che gli altri pittori famoso, confessava avere imparato da Omero poeta dipignere Iove con molta divina maestà. [Idcirco sic

◀ Plate III: Michelangelo Merisi da Caravaggio, *The Annunciation*, Musée des Beaux-Arts, Nancy, oil on canvas, 285 x 205 cm., detail.

In his *Aretino*, Dolce expands on Alberti's notion of congruousness, which according to him should also encompass historical verisimilitude. In analyzing the implications of invention, Dolce states:

> Hence [the painter] must always take into consideration his characters' status, as well as nationality, costumes, locations, and circumstances. Should he depict a combat of Caesar or Alexander the Great, he must not dress the soldiers in today's fashion, and must represent the weapons of the Macedonians in a different manner from those of the Romans. And if he is charged with the depiction of a modern battle, he must not make it in the fashion of the Ancients.[3]

Elsewhere, I have already examined to what extent the visualization of ancient armor and weapons, when recreated with historical plausibility, arouses intellectual pleasure by appealing to the beholder's literary culture.[4] The taste for this kind of setting grew in intensity during the seventeenth century, but it became a substantial component of the *istoria* even earlier. In Dolce's view, Raphael's *Manna* as engraved by Agostino Veneziano (Fig. 25) set the example for other painters in this field. Here is how Dolce justifies his opinion:

> One must make the entire scope of a story involving many figures like a single body devoid of any discordance. If for instance I have to depict the manna pouring over the desert, I must make the Jews, who are represented in such action, gather this celestial food with different attitudes, expressing happiness and the most intense desire, so that none of them will appear to idle, in the same way that Raphael's engraving shows them. Furthermore, Raphael also imagined a real desert with wooden huts consistent with the place and the historical circumstance, giving Moses an austere aspect by cladding him in long drapery, and representing him tall and majestic. He even depicted those embroidered costumes that Jewish women wore at the time.[5]

I shall not dwell here on Caravaggio's total disrespect for historical "place and circumstance." I have already elucidated how Caravaggio tends to actualize the *istoria*, this actualization being strictly related to his realism. In the following chapters, I will enumerate some cases in which, on the contrary, Caravaggio graphically describes costumes that, without being of his time, hark back to historical periods totally unconnected with the subject matter at hand. For the time being, I prefer to emphasize that Dolce's interpretation of historical congruousness, albeit inspired by the *De Pictura*, is never proposed by Alberti himself. Nor is the notion of time in pictorial narratives the

---

consulo poetis atque rhetoribus caeterisque doctis litterarum sese pictor studiosus familiarem atque benivolum dedat, nam ab eiusmodi eruditis ingeniis cum ornamenta accipiet optima, tum in his profecto inventionibus iuvabitur, quae in pictura non ultimam sibi laudem vendicent. Phidias egregius pictor fatebatur se ab Homero didicisse qua potissimum maiestate Iovem pingeret]."

3 Dolce, 118: "Di qui terrà sempre riguardo alla qualità delle persone, né meno alle genti, a' costumi, a' luoghi ed a' tempi, tal che, se depingerà un fatto d'arme di Cesare o di Alessandro Magno, non conviene che armi i soldati nel modo che si costuma oggidì, ed ad altra guisa farà le armature a' macedoni, ad altra a' romani; e se gli verrà imposto carico di rappresentare una battaglia moderna, non si ricerca che la divisi all'antica."

4 See Pericolo 1998.

5 Dolce, 124: "E questo al mio parere dinota che in tutto il contenimento della istoria, la quale abbracci molte figure, si faccia un corpo che non discordi; come sarebbe se io avessi a dipingere il piover della manna nel deserto, dovrei fare che tutti gli ebrei, che in tal cosa si vanno rappresentando, con varie attitudini raccogliessero questo cibo celeste, dimostrando allegrezza e disiderio grandissimo, in guisa che non paresse che alcuno si stesse in darno, come si vede nella carta di Rafaello, il quale oltre a ciò si ha imaginato un deserto vero con casamenti di legnami convenienti al tempo ed al luogo, e dato a Mosé effigie grave, vestendolo di abito lungo, ed hallo fatto di statura grande ed augusta, dando insino alle giudee vesti con raccami, sì come elle usavano." On Agostino Veneziano's print, catalogued as a work by Marcantonio Raimondi, see Oberhuber 1978, 1:17, no. 8 (10).

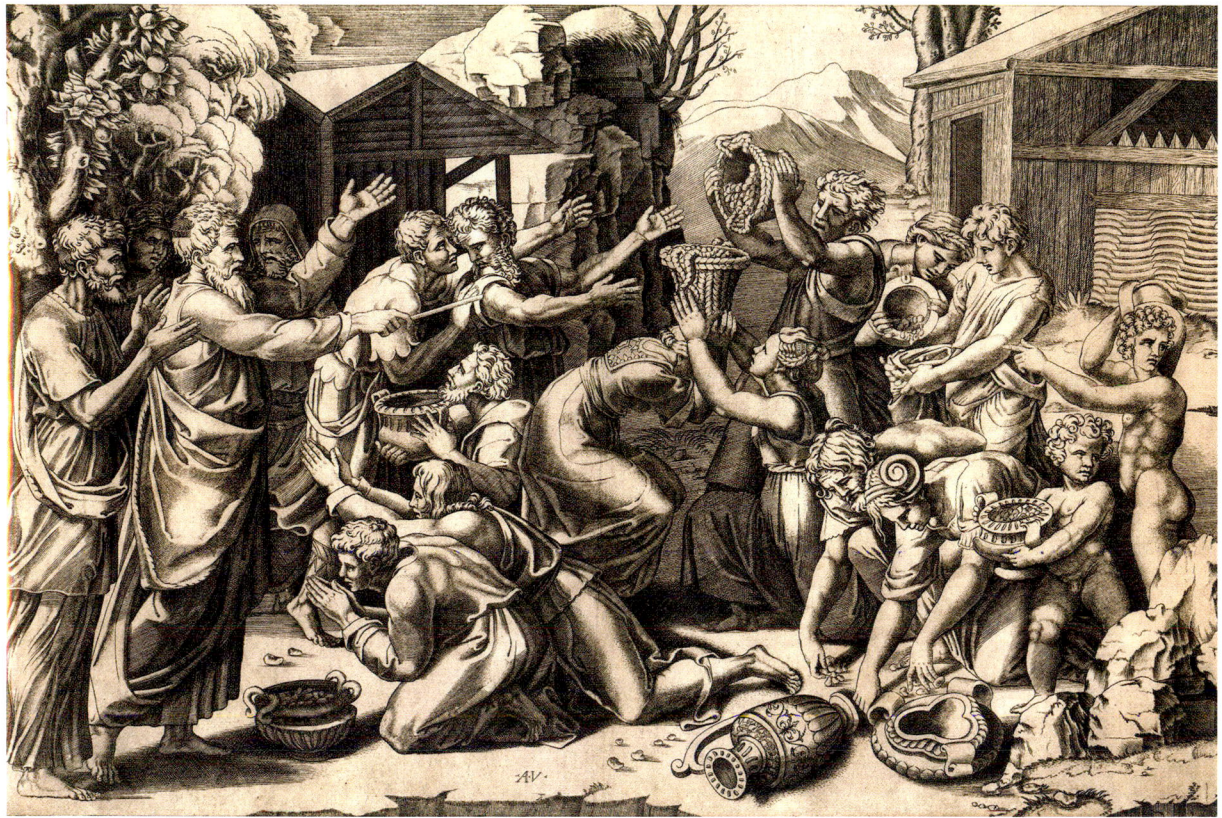

Fig. 25
Agostino Veneziano (Agostino Musi) after Raphael (Raffaello Santi), *The Israelites Gathering the Manna in the Desert*, engraving, 27.8 x 40.8 cm.

object of Alberti's reflection. To my knowledge, Alberti introduces the idea of temporality only in relation with the painter's creative process:

> Moreover, before we set out to depict an *istoria*, we must ponder at some length the order and the means by which we might achieve it in the most beautiful manner. By sketching some templates on paper, we will assess now the whole story, now its individual parts, and will consult with all our friends on this matter.[6]

In creating the composition, painters deconstruct the story and work out its single components separately, one by one and in various steps. It is likely that these distinct parts correspond to groups of figures. However, Alberti does not clarify whether each group must embody a different temporal aspect of the *istoria*. His silence in this regard is rich in implications. It suggests that for Alberti pictorial narratives may also represent more than one moment of a single set of events. Evidently, the Aristotelian unity of place and time is not essential to the *istoria*. Lest I be misunderstood, I contend here that the concepts of congruousness and variety do not rule out the possibility of depicting continuous narratives: that is, stories that simultaneously represent two or several actions occurring

6 Alberti, 102-3: "E quando aremo a dipignere storia, prima fra noi molto penseremo qual modo e quale ordine in quella sia bellissima, e faremo nostri concetti e modelli di tutta la storia e di ciascuna sua parte prima, e chiameremo tutti gli amici a consigliarci sopra a ciò. [Caeterum cum historiam picturi sumus, prius diutius excogitabimus quonam ordine et quibus modis eam componere pulcherrimum sit. Modulosque in chartis conicientes, tum totam historiam, tum singulas eiusdem historiae partes commentabimur, amicosque omnes in ea re consulemus]."

at different times.[7] Conversely, the brand new device of perspective enables painters not only to arrange diverse actions in a single space without engendering disorder, but also to display them in accordance with their importance and meaning relative to the sequence of their unfolding. From this prospect, pictorial space as built through perspective serves as a vector and organizer of time. As the orator gives more or less relevance to an argument through figures of speech and tropes, so too does the painter allot more or less space and visual relief to an episode from an ongoing action. Like the rhetorical discourse, the *istoria* is the fictive container within which all the parts of the composition, whether relevant or less so, no matter if preceding or subsequent, coexist together in harmonious symbiosis. As Lew Andrews has compellingly demonstrated, the "rebirth of continuous narrative" took place at the same time as Alberti circumscribed the notion of the *istoria*. Composed of many episodes occurring at different times, Masaccio's *Tribute Money* in Santa Maria del Carmine, Florence (before 1427), or Lorenzo Ghiberti's *Isaac and Esau* from the east door of Florence Baptistery, the famous Gates of Paradise (1425-1452), offer themselves as an open book showing their entire content, simultaneously inviting viewers both to look at the whole and to browse through its sections in a specific order. Unlike the reader of a book, the beholder can choose his or her own path through the story. Needless to say, the very concept of composition dictates that the paths through which the viewer "peruses" the *istoria* be predetermined and intuitively identifiable by the gaze, so that whatever the itinerary within the story might be, temporality, sequence, and meaning can be easily restored. Further on, I shall deal with the definition of "reconstruction" or "reconfiguration" extensively.

Nevertheless, apart from configuring itself as a fictive compound on the model of poetry and rhetoric, Alberti's *istoria* is likewise construed as an optical device: Masaccio's fresco or Ghiberti's bronze panel should act as the transparent diaphragm of a visual pyramid. Conspicuously, these works are the analogs of the artists' natural vision. Yet, properly speaking, natural vision occurs in a single shot of time, or in an instant. It follows that by deploying the same action at different times, the *istoria* belies its constitutive function as an optical device. Once again, neither Alberti nor the painters and sculptors of fifteenth-century Florence seem to acknowledge the pitfalls of the vicious circle within which their notion of the *istoria* remains entrapped. But by the middle of the sixteenth century, the question of time in the pictorial narrative became central.[8] The first to voice this concern is Dolce in 1557:

> As for the disposition [of the *istoria*], it is necessary that the painter assemble one by one the events of the story he endeavors to depict with propriety so viewers believe that the facts could not have happened in any other way than in the manner he represented them. Nor will the painter put what must go before after, or what must go after before, but he must arrange all things in the very order in which they unfolded. This is what Aristotle in his Poetics and the writers of comedies and tragedies teach.[9]

As in English, the Italian words used by Dolce to define the "before" and the "after" (*inanzi, dapoi*) of a temporal sequence can equally refer to a position in pictorial space: "in front of" and "behind." I

---

7 In this specific regard, I entirely agree with the conclusions reached by Andrews 1995. See also Tomasi Velli 2007, 65-88. There are only scarce studies devoted to the problem of narrative during the Renaissance. Lubbock 2006 is exquisitely descriptive, and therefore hardly useful; Greenstein 1992 investigates the concept of the *istoria* in relation to Mantegna's pictorial narrative; his essay, albeit extremely well informed and interesting, focuses much more on theological issues than on narrative ones. White 1987 remains an essential introduction to the usage of space in connection with narrative in the Italian Renaissance and before. For a different interpretation of the concept of time and temporality in Italian early Renaissance painting, see Bonnefoy 1988.

8 This point has already been established by Tomasi Velli 2007, esp. 43-9.

9 Dolce, 120: "Quanto all'ordine, è mistiero che 'l pittore vada di parte in parte rassembrando il successo della istoria che ha presa a dipingere, così propriamente che i riguardanti stimino che quel fatto non debba esser avenuto altrimenti di quello che da lui è dipinto. Né ponga quello che ha ad essere inanzi dapoi, né quello c'ha ad esser dapoi inanzi, disponendo ordinatamente le cose nel modo che elle seguirono. Questo istesso insegna Aristotele nella sua Poetica a gli scrittori di tragedie e di commedie."

point out the ambivalence of these terms because nowhere in Dolce's *Aretino* is the painter told how to express temporality visually. Even worse, the text is so laconic that it is impossible to ascertain whether Dolce actually exhorts artists to represent an action by also depicting its antecedents and outcome. Should the painter put a preceding action "in front" of the next one, so that its position in space determines if the episode precedes or follows? Or is Dolce just implying that no episode in the action must disrupt the impression of simultaneity, so that painters must not accommodate any fact inconsistent with the chronological framework they opt for from the outset? In either case, it is quite obvious to me that Dolce does not realize how difficult it is to render the impression of temporality in a painting that intends or pretends to narrate the chronological sequence of an event. Nor do mid sixteenth-century artists care about this issue in Dolce's exact terms. In Chapter 9, I shall demonstrate that painters rather resort to what I would define as symbolic narration. Therefore, inconsistency in temporality is very common at the time, and yet it is seldom criticized: Dolce himself would exalt Titian's narratives by ignoring their chronological short-circuits. And, as I will soon explain, he is not the only one to overvalue Titian's involvement with temporality.

Indeed, the problem of temporality is complicated by the understandable difficulty of early modern painters and theorists in distinguishing between the viewer's perception of time and the structure of time as configured by painters through images. To shed light on this crucial and controversial point, I will first rely on Leonardo's testimony.[10] His is the most lucid attempt at grasping the nature of time in painting, especially in opposition to poetry. Unfortunately, his arguments are also tainted by his conviction that painting outshines poetry, and thus they are not immune to sophisms. I begin with one of Leonardo's best-known observations in this regard:

> Painting presents its essence to you in an instant through the act of seeing, and by the very means through which the *impressiva* [sensitive mind] receives the natural objects, [therefore] at the same time as the harmonious proportionality of the parts that compose the whole and pleases the senses is composed. Poetry does the same but with a means less worthy than the eye, since it [the ear] brings to the *impressiva* the figures of the things named with greater confusion and more delay than the eye does, which is the direct channel between the object and the *impressiva*. The eye [indeed] reports with extreme trustfulness the true surfaces and figures of that which rests in front of it; from these [surfaces and figures] springs the proportionality known as harmony that delights the senses with sweet conformity.[11]

In another passage, Leonardo expands *ad infinitum* the process through which the human mind reconstructs the "essence" and "harmony" of poetry upon reading or hearing. He addresses his criticism directly to poets, as if prodding them into recognizing their inferiority:

> Do you not know that our soul is composed of harmony, and that harmony is achieved only in instants in which the objects' proportionalities make themselves visible and audible? Do you not see that in [poetry] there is no proportionality engendered in a single instant, but on the contrary one part is created from the other successively, and

10 Andrews 1995, 61-71, reaches conclusions very different from mine in his analysis of Leonardo's concept of temporality in painting. For Leonardo's famous paragone, besides the English edition and commentary by Kemp 1989 and Farago 1992, see Winternitz 1970; and Azzolini 2005.

11 Leonardo, 13: "La pittura ti rappresenta in un subito la sua essenza nella virtù visiva, e per il proprio mezzo, d'onde la impressiva riceve gli obietti naturali, ed ancora nel medesimo tempo nel quale si compone l'armonica proporzionalità delle parti che compongono il tutto, che contenta il senso; e la poesia riferisce il medesimo, ma con mezzo meno degno dell'occhio, il quale porta nella impressiva più confusamente e con più tardità le figurazioni delle cose nominate che non fa l'occhio, vero mezzo infra l'obietto e l'impressiva, il quale immediate conferisce con somma verità le vere superficie e figure di quel che dinanzi se gli appresenta, dalle quali ne nasce la proporzionalità detta armonia che con dolce concento contenta il senso."

the subsequent part does not emerge if the precedent does not die? This is why I esteem your invention much inferior to that of the painter, because [yours] does not generate a harmonious proportionality. It does not satisfy the beholder's or the hearer's mind as does the proportion of the most beautiful elements that compose this [painted] face in front of me, since they, all together and at the same time, instill such pleasure in me with their divine proportionality that I believe nothing else made by man on this earth could provide me with a greater one.[12]

First of all, it is noteworthy that Leonardo avails himself of a twist of logic that is typical of the aporetic discourse. In fact, he demolishes the unity of a poem by dissecting it progressively into paragraphs, verses, words, and syllables, alienating each part from the others relentlessly. Even as they are pronounced or spelled out, words vanish, the trace of a harmony sought by the poet, but unattainable in its wholeness by listeners, trailing away with them. On the other hand, images and their constitutive proportionalities access the mind forthwith, so that beholders intuitively penetrate their essence and absorb the harmony of both the whole and its parts. To demonstrate painting's primacy, Leonardo induces the reader into believing that time can actually dissolve the entirety of the poem, so that whatever a single book binds together or a page contains on its surface is newly and irrevocably fragmented every time that the literary artwork is reenacted. It should not be necessary to explain why Leonardo's argumentation is in many respects a piece of devilish sophistry; regardless of the time dedicated to reading or hearing a poem, readers and audiences are able to perceive and reassemble the structure and harmony of the whole literary piece with the assistance of their short-term or long-term memory. However, what is perversely misleading in Leonardo's arguments is less their fallacious brilliance than their implication that time in painting radically differs from time in poetry. Thus, for Leonardo there is the short time of gazing and the long time of reading, or hearing. The conundrum of this tenet resides in the assumption that the time necessary for an artwork's perception is identical to the time needed for its reception and processing. On these premises, the fictive time involved in, and structured through, the narration would also correspond to the empirical or physical time during which viewers and readers take in the artwork: a blatant paradox. According to Leonardo's provocative statement, by the time readers leaf through the entire *Divine Comedy*, for instance, they might have forgotten what the poem is about. Of course, this inference is sheer nonsense, as I will clarify at length in Chapter 3. In the meantime, it is important to note that Leonardo's interpretation of time, albeit directed to granting painting a long-wished-for supremacy, is unacceptable to painters as well. Before explaining this, I would like to consider again Leonardo's point of view:

Although the poet's works are read over a long span of time, nonetheless it often happens that they are not understood, so that it is necessary to write comments upon them, in which the commentators seldom understand the poet's idea. And readers often read but a small portion of their works for lack of time; but viewers immediately comprehend the painter's works.[13]

12 Ibidem, 17: "Non sai tu che la nostra anima è composta di armonia, ed armonia non s'ingenera se non in instanti, ne' quali le proporzionalità degli obietti si fan vedere o udire? Non vedi che nella tua scienza non è proporzionalità creata in instante, anzi, l'una parte nasce dall'altra successivamente, e non nasce la succedente se l'antecedente non muore? Per questo giudico la tua invenzione essere assai inferiore a quella del pittore, solo perché da quella non componesi proporzionalità armonica. Essa non contenta la mente dell'uditore o veditore, come fa la proporzionalità delle bellissime membra componitrici delle divine bellezze di questo viso che m'è dinanzi, le quali in uno medesimo tempo tutte insieme giunte mi danno tanto piacere, con la divina loro proporzione, che nulla altra cosa giudico esser sopra la terra fatta dall'uomo che dar lo possa maggiore."

13 Ibidem, 13: "Ed ancorché le cose de' poeti sieno con lungo intervallo di tempo lette, spesse sono le volte che le non sono intese, e bisogna farvi sopra diversi comenti, ne' quali rarissime volte tali comentatori intendono qual fosse la mente del poeta; e molte volte i lettori non leggono se non piccola parte delle loro opere per disagio di tempo. Ma l'opera del pittore immediate è compresa da' suoi risguardatori."

It sounds uncanny that the author of the *Last Supper* or the *Virgin of the Rocks*—pictures about which so much ink has been spilled because of their visual complexities—might assert that paintings do not embed any ambiguity since beholders experience and decipher them instantaneously. If one returns to Albani's criticism of half-figures, one will remember that, on the contrary, Albani likens paintings to poems because of their common readability over a long period of time. Hence, Albani strongly condemns those pictures—including Caravaggio's—that are immediately enjoyable but do not contain matter for extensive scrutiny owing to their dearth of narrative density. In other words, Albani claims the exact opposite of Leonardo: paintings must not only attract, but also indefinitely capture, the viewer's attention. Without a longer span of time, pictures become simply illegible and therefore meaningless. Paradoxically, Albani prides himself not only on having his pictorial narratives and allegories commented by literati, but also on being himself able to gloss them with erudition.

In retrospect, Leonardo's analysis of temporality in painting leads to an impasse. By lending themselves to immediate comprehension, pictures no longer compete with poems: they end up reproducing events that do not necessitate interpretation; they are attractive to the eye but not to the mind. As Albani puts it, they might as well be beautiful books with golden buckles whose contents hide from the viewer's gaze and whose harmonies linger solely on the surface. Needless to say, both Leonardo and Albani embrace Alberti's concept of the *istoria* as a harmonious, meaningful compound. Yet they come to antithetical conclusions when they examine the function of temporality in painting. As has already become evident, it is Albani's position that will prevail in the aftermath of Caravaggio's death and long afterward. Ever since, painters have tried with ever more impatience stealthily to extort from the viewer a prolonged, curious, charmed yet articulate gaze: a gaze that dwells both on the whole and its parts not only to cull details and nuances, but also to meander across space and action. But if this is the painters' objective, what are the compositional and visual strategies able to produce and infuse time into painting? What aspect of temporality are painters interested in developing? Is it the narrative's time, or the beholder's seeing and reconfiguring time? And more importantly, is it possible to achieve this goal without compromising the effect of reality—or the optical verisimilitude requested—of the *istoria*?

I have already quoted a passage from Albani's 1637 letter in which he elucidated how the Virgin in his San Bartolomeo *Annunciation* is caught mid-action in such a way that beholders can piece together a significantly large chronological segment of the unfolding event.[14] It is irrelevant here that the figure of the Virgin, when looked at carefully, hardly seems to express as many facets of the story as those singled out by Albani in his letter. Rather, I will highlight the fact that Albani is concerned with representing an action whose temporality is compressed into, not reduced to, a single moment. The figure's attitude, gesture, expression and disposition are designed to encapsulate time; all these figural devices must also enable viewers to reassemble the threads of temporality that the figure contains in order to visualize the action's temporal sequence: in this case Mary is reading/ turning/ scared and stunned/ while looking at/ and listening to Gabriel. As I have already said, Albani failed to make the Virgin's figure legible enough in its chronological polysemy. Nevertheless, there is no doubt that he was aware that temporality in painting pertains to at least two different functions: one intrinsic to the composition as a fictive structure, the other related to the viewer's ability to mentally restructure narratives. Even if Albani's statement on the figure's chronological polyvalence actually represents a major innovation in seventeenth-century art theory, his remarks are not entirely unprecedented. As Julian Kliemann has pointed out,[15]

14 Malvasia, 2: 255.   15 Kliemann 2001, 22.

Pomponio Gaurico in his 1504 *De Sculptura*[16] had already underlined the importance of temporality in relation to motion in sculpture:

> As for movements, (…) some are primary, when for instance we start moving; others median, when they are midway between the beginning and the end; and others final, when they are close to an end, but have not quite stopped. If they were stopped, they would be defined as states of rest, and not motions. This is why one praises those states of rest that seem to be caused by motion or [in turn] bring about motion.[17]

According to Gaurico, not only do beholders appreciate the large variety of motions summoned by artists in their works; they also enjoy those depictions of movement that are given particular relevance through a rhetorical device of aggrandizement: that is, εὐκρίνεια (*eukrineia* or good discernment). In accordance with rhetoric, Gaurico distinguishes three categories of *eukrineia*: ἐνάργεια (*enargeia* or evidence), ἔμφασις (*emphasis* or anticipation) and ἀμφιβολία (*amphiboly* or ambiguity). These modes of representation are defined as follows:

> *Enargeia*, that is when in an event one represents with utmost evidence that which has preceded and is currently occurring; (…) *emphasis* when in this very event one shows what is imminently going to happen; (…) and *amphiboly* every time that it is doubtful whether the event positioned in the middle ought to be referred to this or that [temporal point].[18]

Gaurico clarifies his three categories in more concrete terms:

> It is obvious that [*amphiboly*] is the middle term between the two others. *Enargeia* indeed makes the event that is not yet accomplished more evident, whereas *emphasis* shows the event to be accomplished; amphiboly therefore presents an event suspended between two [possibilities]. Many greatly commended Polygnotus of Thassos on his amphibolies. It is said that he depicted a soldier in such a way that it was impossible by any means to understand whether "the soldier wanted to climb upon the horse or slide off of it."[19]

It can be assumed that these diverse modes of configuring action bear on viewers in very different ways: they engender certainty (*enargeia*), expectation (*emphasis*), and uncertainty (*amphiboly*). Consequently, artists can maneuver the modes of action in order to activate various states of mind in the viewer. Albeit remarkably pithy, Gaurico's considerations address temporality to a much

16 Besides the edition of Gaurico's treatise by Chastel and Klein 1969, reviewed by Pallucchini 1970, and the more recent critical edition on which I have relied (Gaurico), there are few studies devoted to Gaurico. See Daniele 2001; Blake McHam 2006; and Varotto 2006.

17 Gaurico, 214: "Motuum vero (…) quidam sunt primi, ut quum incipimus moveri, quidam medii, quum intra initium finemque versantur, quidam ultimi, quum ad finem fere pervenerint, necdum firmantur. Si enim firmarentur, status quidem dicendi essent, non motus. Quare et illi status laudantur qui vel a motibus facti videbuntur vel in motus transierint."

18 Ibidem, 216: "ἐνάργεια, quando scilicet ex ea re quodque praecesserit quodque fit evidentissime repraesentatur (…) ἔμφασις, quum quid ex ea ipsa re futurum iam sit

commostratur (…) ἀμφιβολία, quoties dubium fit quae medio locata res huc potius an illuc referri oporteat." In his *Institutio oratoria* (8.3.83), Quintilian defines emphasis as follows: "Vicina praedictae [brachylogy] sed amplior virtus est ἔμφασις, altiorem praebens intellectum quam quem verba per se ipsa declarant. [Similar to brachylogy, but with a greater scope, emphasis conveys a meaning deeper than that expressed by the words in and of themselves]." It is in light of this and Gaurico's definition that emphasis designates "anticipation" or "insinuation."

19 Ibidem, 218: "Scilicet inter illas media: ut enim altera manifestiorem quae nondum acta est rem facit, altera futuram ostendit, ita et haec rem utrinque dubiam proponit. Quod in Polignoto Thasio pellaudarunt. Fertur is militem ita pinxisse, ut diiudicari haud ullo sane pacto potuerit, '…conscendere mallet/ miles equum, an mallet equo descendere miles,' (…)."

lesser degree than they grapple with the viewer's reception of artworks. Therefore, it comes as no surprise that sixteenth- and seventeenth-century theorists generally overlook Gaurico's assessments in connection with time in painting. More importantly, even when the timing of action would become essential to critics, amphiboly as a third category of temporality would go systematically unacknowledged. Obviously, ambiguous actions are not viewed as fit to the *istoria*: perspicuity in temporality is rather the highest ideal in this field. Not surprisingly, Caravaggio instead very often plays with temporal amphibolies. I will come back to this point shortly.

By downplaying the historical influence of Gaurico's categories of *eukrineia*, I am far from asserting that the issue of temporality in its multivalence and with regard to motion was not discovered until Albani's time. In his *Discorso in materia di pittura*, written *c.*1564 and never published until relatively recently, the Neapolitan doctor Bartolomeo Maranta set out to defend Titian's *Annunciation* formerly in San Domenico Maggiore, Naples (Fig. 26),[20] from the attacks it had received since its installation there around 1557.[21] Some of the criticism directed at Titian's picture may now appear hilarious: for one thing, Maranta pedantically accounts for Gabriel's alleged fatness in the *Annunciation*; he also parses the figure's anatomy bone by bone and muscle by muscle in a view to corroborating Titian's anatomical accuracy. Yet Maranta's closer analysis of the painting attests to the thoroughness with

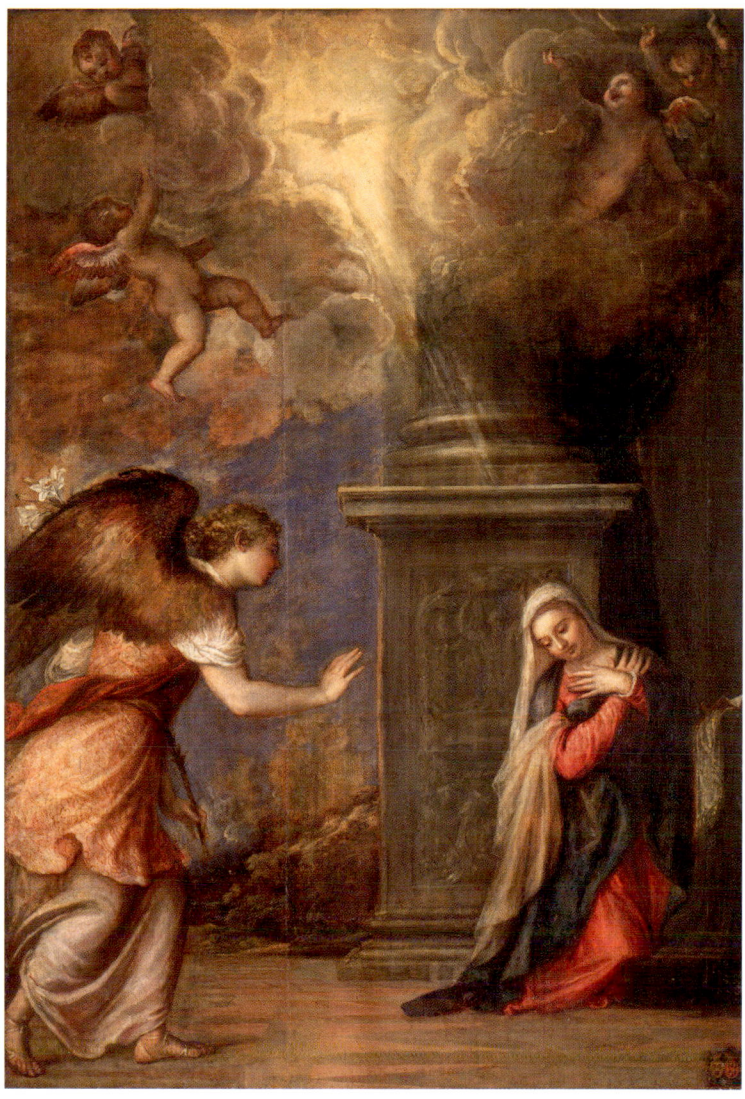

Fig. 26
Titian (Tiziano Vecelli), *The Annunciation*, Museo di Capodimonte, Naples, oil on canvas, 280 x 193.5 cm.

which artworks started to be scanned in the years following the Council of Trent. Noticeably, the representation and perception of temporality are among Maranta's main concerns.

In objecting to the reasoning of those detractors who disliked the angel's profile in Titian's *Annunciation*, Maranta praises the master's ability to evoke so much expressivity through the face's partial view:

> To display the greatness of his ingenuity, Titian did not want to show more than half of the angel's face, but in such a beautiful way that he managed to depict the mouth in the act of speaking, so that in seeing but the half of it [the face] one seems also to see whatever remains hidden.[22]

20   For the painting, see Wethey 1969-1975, 1:72-4, no. 12; and more recently Ferino-Pagden 2007, 254-6, no. 3.3 [catalogue entry by Marsel Grosso].

21   For Maranta's interpretation of Titian's *Annunciation* in San Domenico, Naples, see Freedman 1985. For Maranta, see Solimene 1952.

22   Maranta, 871: "Perciochè, avendo Tiziano voluto mostrar la grandezza del suo ingegno, non volle mostrar dell'angelo se non mezzo il volto, ma di sì bel modo fe' spiccar la bocca in atto di parlare che in vederne quel mezzo solo vi par vedere anco tutto quello che si nasconde."

Of course, Gabriel's half-concealed face expresses much more than what the figure's "act of speaking" suggests. In a subsequent passage, Maranta notes:

> [His] face expresses not only the greatest obedience in executing God's decree, but also no less reverence while delivering the message. In addition, if one observes attentively, one will notice [the angel's] great concentration so as not to forget or vary in any way what he had to say, and along with this concentration the confidence and certainty that he cannot afford stumbling over his words, and this is uttered by both his slightly puckered forehead and his eye that pains to open countering the movement of the eyebrow that, by pulling down, would make it half shut: a common feature in those who meditate on things of paramount importance.[23]

The polyvalence of the angel's facial expression—in my opinion an exaggeration on Maranta's part—obeys the supposedly complex temporality of the story:

> And while he is saying *Spiritus Sanctus superveniet in te* ["the Holy Spirit will come upon you"] and the rest [of the sentence] (since Titian represented him proffering these words, as I will show), he seems to ponder whether something remains to be added. Furthermore, his allure betrays a certain divinity, which one cannot express with words, but only the eye of those who carefully consider him grasps it and in a somewhat obscure way forwards it to the mind.[24]

Besides the face, Gabriel's body also translates multiple facets of the narrative staged by Titian. At least, this is Maranta's conviction:

> It remains now to discern the artifice that Titian used in the angel's disposition (...). He depicted him with his left foot ahead, in the attitude of a man who walks with his right hand thrown forward to accompany his speech with gesture, his waist slightly bent and his head slightly cocked backward. He seems to proceed further since it is likely that he comes in from the side toward which the Virgin had her back turned, and [therefore] he is heading to the place to which her face was turned.[25]

Much of Maranta's description may seem redundant. However, the redundancy of this and other passages reveals the intensity with which Maranta as a learned viewer inspects every aspect of the *istoria* in search of meaning and coherence. If on the one hand the abundance of information he extracts from the picture frequently exceeds the scope of Titian's *Annunciation*, on the other hand it confirms that by the mid-sixteenth century beholders were attuned to, and reveled in,

23 Ibidem, 886: "Mostrasi in quel volto non solo ubbidienza grandissima di eseguire il mandato di Dio, ma eziandio non piccola riverenza mentre fa l'imbasciata. Anzi, a chi ben mira, vi vedrà una attenzione grande per far che non si dimentichi e varii in qualche modo quello che aveva da dire, ed insieme con la attenzione una sicurezza ed un esser certo di non potere in parlando inciampare, e questo vuol significare quella fronte alquanto corrugata e l'occhio renitente a bene aprirsi contra el moto del ciglio che, calando giù, il faceva mezzo serrare; motivo commune di tutti coloro che di cosa di gran momento ragionano."

24 Ibidem: "E mentre sta in atto di dire *Spiritus Sanctus superveniet in te* e quel che segue (percioché in dire queste parole lo ha dipinto, come diremo), par che pensi se altro

gli restarà da sopragiungere. Ha oltre queste cose un certo che di divinità nell'aspetto, la quale non si può bene con le parole esprimere, ma l'occhio solo di chi attentamente il considera lo conosce ed in un certo modo oscuro lo comunica al pensiero."

25 Ibidem, 887: "Ora resta a veder l'artificio che nella disposizione dell'angelo ha Tiziano usato (...). Egli l'ha fatto col pié manco avanti, in forma di uom che camini con la mano dritta cacciata in fuori per accompagnar con questo atto il suo parlare, con la vita alquanto piegata e con la testa che mostra di rilevarsi un poco indietro. Sta in atto di caminare più avanti, percioché è verisimile che, essendo egli giunto da quella parte dove tenea la Madonna rivolte le spalle, era per andare a incontrarla dalla parte dove avea il viso rivolto."

the polyvalence of the figures' expressions and attitudes. To sum up, Titian's Gabriel plays out: obedience /humility/ zeal/ confidence/ meditation/ majesty/ and even a subconscious fear of botching his mission, while he looks at/ and talks to the Virgin. But even more important, the polysemy of the figure—either Mary or Gabriel—encompasses multiple aspects of the episode's temporality: its past, present and future. To return to Maranta's last passage:

> But she [the Virgin], upon hearing the noise, quit her prayers and turned to the place from where the angel was coming. Facing her now and staying in the same position as he had then happened to stop, he greeted her, and after expecting and hearing her answer, which was *Quomodo fiet istud* ["How can this be?"] and the rest [of the sentence], he is now saying *Spiritus Sanctus superveniet in te* ["the Holy Spirit will come upon you"] and the rest [of the sentence]. Even as the angel enunciated these words, the Virgin took on that attitude of humility suited to her saying *Ecce ancilla Domini* ["Behold, I am the handmaid of the Lord"] and the rest [of the sentence], and in this way, her arms in the form of a cross, bowing as much as she could considering that she had been caught [off guard] so suddenly, and almost in a rush, she waits for the angel to finish. Accordingly, in this picture Mary does not speak and therefore her mouth is shut. The angel has his mouth open and, as I have already expounded, from the gesture of his hand and from Mary's posture as well as from their faces' appearances it is easy to understand that he is saying: *Spiritus Sanctus superveniet in te*, etc.[26]

At this point, before continuing with Maranta's exegesis of Titian's *Annunciation*, it is necessary to explain why temporality seems to matter so much in this context. Although Maranta never confesses it, he is desperately trying to convince his readers that Titian's picture is consistent with Aristotle's unity of time, the general premise of his discourse being that the Virgin "can express but one single action." Nonetheless, however slightly one studies the painting's narrative, it immediately becomes evident that Titian tramples upon temporality and verisimilitude with great ease: Gabriel indeed has hardly glided into the room when Mary is already performing the act of humility that ends the Gospel's episode. Put otherwise, Titian depicts in a single shot the action's preamble and outcome. No wonder then that Maranta pulls out all the stops to reconcile the angel's motion with the Virgin's immobility, the "before" and the "after" with the "in-between." To this end, he points out that Gabriel's uplifted arm does not correspond to a gesture of salutation, and that Mary's posture cannot be mistaken for surprise. Even if one accepts this argument—and it frankly does not hold water—it still remains to elucidate why Gabriel keeps marching while delivering the last part of his message. At any rate, Maranta's blind eulogy of Titian makes of the Naples *Annunciation* something it was never supposed to be: a paradigm of perfection in the rendering of narrative temporality. Consequently, in Maranta's opinion, the picture not only alludes to the action's antecedents, but also to its imminent outcome:

> But the greatness of Titian's ingenuity—absolutely wondrous in this regard— manifests itself once again in the fact that, although the Virgin stays silent, it is possible

26   Ibidem, 887-8: "Ma ella, sentito il rumore, lasciò l'orazione e rivoltossi verso quella parte donde l'angelo veniva. Il quale, vedendosi già da faccia a faccia con lei in quel modo che in quel punto si ritrovò fermandosi, la salutò, ed aspettata ed intesa già la risposta, che fu *Quomodo fiet istud* e quel che segue, sta in atto di dire *Spiritus Sanctus superveniet in te* con quel che viene appresso; e mentre questo diceva l'angelo, la Madonna, postasi in quell'atto di umiltà che conveniva per avere a dire *Ecce ancilla Domini* con el rimanente, aspettava con le braccia in forma di croce, e con quel maggior inchino che in quella positura, così all'improvviso e quasi in fretta presa, le fu lecito a poter fare, che l'angelo finisse. In maniera che Maria in quella pittura non parla e per questa cagione è fatta con la bocca serrata. L'angelo sta con la bocca aperta, e dal segno della mano sua e dalla disposizione in che sta Maria ed anco dall'aria del volto d'amendue detta di sopra, si può agevolmente comprendere che egli stia dicendo *Spiritus Sanctus superveniet in te*, etc."

to understand from her attitude not only that she is about to reply, but also what the tenor of her reply would be as soon as the angel falls silent.[27]

Once and for all, I would like to emphasize that Maranta applies to a contemporary painting—that is, the Naples *Annunciation*—an array of hermeneutical criteria that are intrinsically extraneous to Titian's practice. In my view, this is irrefutable evidence of two interconnected historical phenomena. Firstly, the obsession with narrative temporality, spurred by an increasing interest in Aristotle's aesthetics as formulated in the *Poetics*, erupted suddenly in the middle of the sixteenth century; it is highly plausible that the Church's renewed reflection on religious images in the aftermath of the Protestant Reformation strongly contributed to this neo-Aristotelian wave. Secondly, neither painters nor beholders seemed to be satisfactorily equipped to handle the problem of temporality in painting. Historically speaking, Albani's 1637 letter about his San Bartolomeo *Annunciation* is the first exhaustive testimony of a painter's concern with multiple temporalities within the purview of the Aristotelian unity of action, which means that by then the question of time in images had already come to maturation. To be sure, other elements permit us to establish that about the time of Caravaggio's death, or shortly afterward, serious attempts to comprehend the mechanisms through which beholders reconstruct temporality from a pictorial narrative had already been made. I am referring here not only to paintings in which the problem of temporality is definitely at stake (like Domenichino's 1616-1617 *Hunt of Diana*, now at the Galleria Borghese, Rome),[28] but also to a crucial source, as revealed by Silvia Tomasi Velli: Giulio Mancini's 1617-1621 *Considerazioni sulla pittura*.[29] In discussing the concept of motion as interpreted by Giovan Paolo Lomazzo in his 1584 *Trattato della pittura*, Mancini affirms:

> Moreover he [Lomazzo] says that painting demonstrates the motion of the material things it imitates. In this regard, it seems to me that either he does not understand the nature of motion or he does not consider the time in which the painter narrates through the thing the painter envisions. By motion one means the continuity of time, since by nature motion is continuous over time, but the painter represents things in the indivisible moment in which there is neither motion nor time, but only stillness. Yet, were we to adjust this observation to good sense, we could say that, through the disposition of the parts, it is possible to represent an attitude enabling the viewer's imagination and intellect to abstract and infer that the figure, although it is seen at rest, is moving. Similarly, we keep imagining that the figure in Saint Peter's Fall of Simon Magus by the Cavalier Vanni, although we see it staying stationary, is moving and falling head-first because of the head's downward orientation, the fearful gaze, the mouth open as if screaming, with the demons nearby chased by Simon.[30]

---

27 Ibidem, 889: "Ma la grandezza dell'ingegno di Tiziano, in questa particolarità senza dubio veruno meravigliosa, fe' che ancor che la Vergine stesse cheta, non di meno si comprendesse dall'atto in che ella stava non solo che già le restava a rispondere, ma eziandio che cosa, subito che l'angelo tacesse, a rispondere avesse."

28 See Kliemann 2001.

29 Tomasi Velli 2007, 129-35.

30 Mancini, 1:159: "Di più dice che con la pittura viene dimostrato il moto delle cose corporee che va immitando: nel che a me pare o che non intenda la natura del moto o che non avvertischi il tempo nel quale il pittore va esplicando per la sua cosa vista perché, dicendo moto, si dice continuità di tempo, essendo di natura di moto l'esser continuo in tempo, et il pittore immita le cose in quello istante indivisibile nel quale non vi è tempo né moto, ma sol quiete. Pur, se noi volessimo ridur a buon senso questo suo detto, si potrebbe dir che, con positioni di parte, si descrivesse una tal attitudine dalla quale l'immaginatione et intelletto dei riguardanti astraesse et facesse sunnotione che quella tal figura, ancorché la vedi star ferma, si muova, come in San Pietro nella Caduta di Simon Mago condotta dal cavalier Vanni, ancorché si veda star ferma, nondimeno, per la position del capo all'in giù, con occhi spaventati, bocca aperta da gridare, con i diavoli appresso allontanati da Simone, ci andiamo imaginando che così si muova et caschi all'in giù; talché veramente non si dipinge il moto, ma si figuran talmente le parti per le quali ci andiam immaginando che si movano e caminino. Et questa tal positione nelle figure non si deve propriamente dir moto, ma affetto e spirito che, concepito e fattone sonnittione et astrattione, si dice moto e movenza."

Mancini mentions a painting by Francesco Vanni executed in 1602, which was famous enough to be engraved by Jacques Callot around 1608-1611.[31] Incidentally, Mancini in another passage commends Vanni's *Fall of Simon Magus* because of the accuracy of its historical setting, so that it is safe to believe that to Mancini's eyes the picture incarnates the idea of excellence in the domain of the *istoria*. Be that as it may, Mancini clearly states that the material nature of painting forecloses the possibility of truly reproducing time and motion. What we perceive as motion in a painting is nothing but the representation of a figure or object perfectly motionless, forever frozen in its pose or configuration. In his 1582 *Discorso intorno alle imagini sacre e profane*, Gabriele Paleotti had already come to a similar conclusion:

> By operation [in painting], we mean any kind of action of whatever thing; in fact, although it seems that only permanent things pertain to the painter's art, and not subsequent things that are determined by motion, the painter is able to make permanent things appear in such a way that, whoever sees them, will distinguish their actions; for instance, if he represents many ships sinking into the sea, although the represented things—to wit, the ships—are permanent, we nevertheless learn the subsequent action—that is, the shipwreck—from their positionings.[32]

Despite the limits of their craft, painters can create the impression of motion in two interrelated ways: through disposition of the body's limbs and the object's parts, and by coordinating the painting's components in perfect synchrony. In other words, by isolating a still-shot of an object or figure in motion, and by arranging the composition so that all the other elements respond to, and match, the action's temporal and spatial framework, artists induce beholders into the illusion of movement. As Paleotti and especially Mancini state, perceiving motion is a matter of abstraction and deduction on the viewer's part. However, to activate the mental functions capable of re-enacting motion, it is necessary that figures and objects be endowed with coherent, univocal and smoothly interacting facets or modes of temporality. Only on this condition can beholders experience the impression of instantaneous movement, and visualize the action's preamble and denouement. Here is Mancini's valuable observation in this regard:

> Just as the instant reduces itself to time by linking the past with the future, so too does the instant of vision join together the preceding and subsequent configurations of the parts that compose the motion, and this is called depicting the motion. Therefore, one defines [the instant of vision] as motion because it forces us to bring to mind the past [configurations] that have determined the motion, as well as the future ones that will continue it; hence, motion consists in all of this flux.[33]

I do not believe that Mancini's interpretation of temporality in painting has ever been valued as much as it deserves. Perhaps on account of his training as a physician, Mancini is able to bend the terminology of Aristotle's *Physics*—that is, the definition of time and motion—to describe a

---

31   See Choné 1992, 137, no. 14.

32   Paleotti, 107: "Per operazione pigliamo ogni sorte di azzione di qual si voglia cosa, perciò che, se bene pare che le cose permanenti solamente cadano sotto l'arte del pittore, e non le successive che si causano da i moti, può nondimeno il pittore dipingere le cose permanenti in apparenza tale che chi le vede distinguerà le loro azzioni, come dipingendo molte navi nel mare in atto di somergersi, se bene le cose dipinte che sono le navi sono permanenti, nondimeno da gli atti loro impariamo la azzione successiva, cioè il naufragio."

33   Mancini, 2:XIX (from Ms. Vat. Barb. Lat. 4315 f. 206r and f. 206v): "Ma come che l'istante si riduce al tempo perché congiunge il passato con il futuro, così questo istante di visione che congiunge le positioni passate delle parti con le future che fanno il moto intanto si dice dipingere il moto in quanto che fa impositione che ne reduchiamo in mente le passate che han fatto il moto, e le future che lo faranno, che in tutta questa flussione consiste il moto."

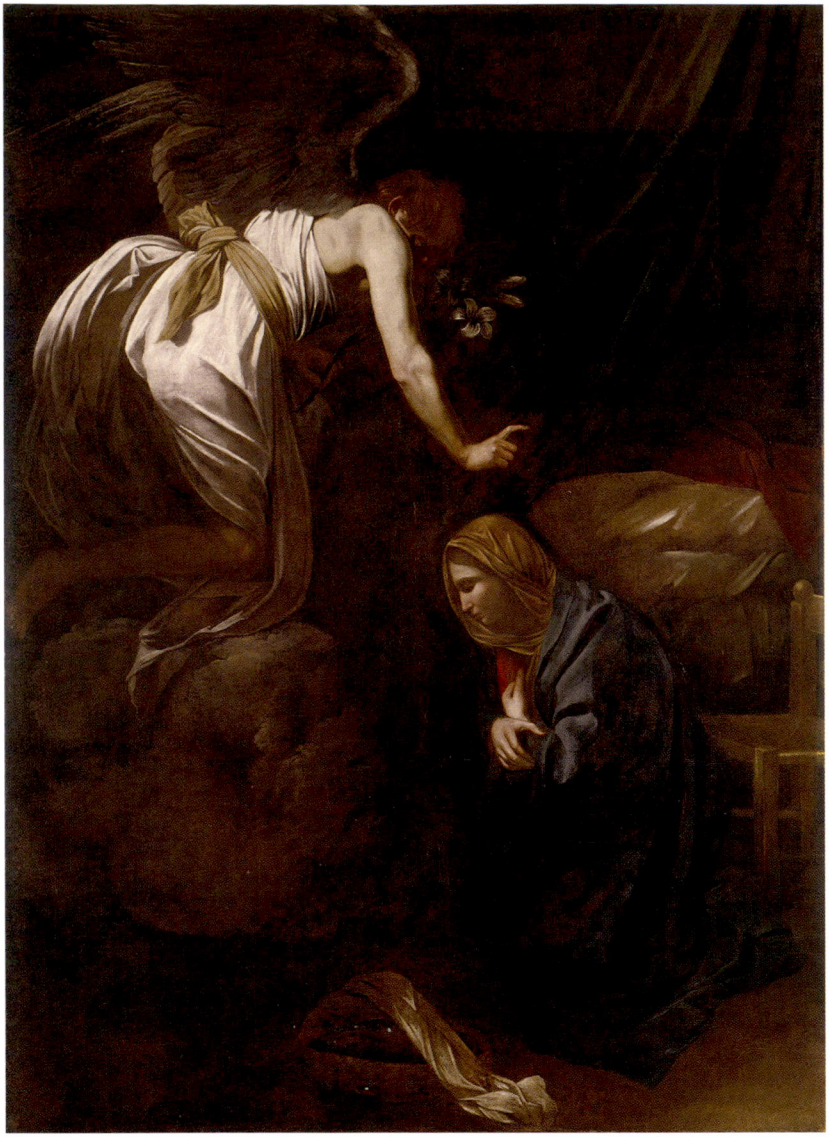

Fig. 27
Michelangelo Merisi da Caravaggio, *The Annunciation*, Musée des Beaux-Arts, Nancy, oil on canvas, 285 x 205 cm.

phenomenon that pertains both to man's physiology—imagination and intellect—and to poetic mimesis. More importantly, he establishes that painters can actually represent time. They do indeed possess the ability to form figures and objects loaded with temporality, and thereby are able to trigger the process through which the image is set in motion by the viewer's mind. In other words, even if paintings depict but a single instant, that instant is nothing but a climactic epitome of time in flux. No matter how long it takes the viewer to go through the story, whether he or she just glances at it or repeatedly scans it, the painting does not lose its temporality: time is built into the composition. The painting's temporal structure is therefore independent from the beholder's time. *Pace* Leonardo, the concept of time has nothing to do with the image's perception and reception, although to be sure the time configured by the painter preordains and controls both the actual time beholders might be willing to spend on the painting and the fictive time within which the story is mentally reconstructed and re-enacted. As a corollary, it must also be clear that neither the painting's time nor the beholder's reconfiguring time correspond to a third category of time: the time pre-figured by the subject matter, from which painters develop the temporal framework of their stories. I shall illustrate this point in Chapter 3.

If viewers are able to sense motion in the painting's stillness, this is also because attitudes and gestures, conventionally codified, through gradual variations constitute a web of interfacing motions. As, according to the early modern practice of painting, painters can adapt a figure's canonical scheme to a new context by partially modifying it, so too do attitudes and gestures allude by force of habit to a whole set of analogous narrative situations visually encoded by the pictorial tradition. Put otherwise, the viewer's faculty of re-ordering the story is set off and supported by his or her visual memory: in a flash, a figure's attitude automatically summons up a gamut of iconographic analogs that converge as one to complete the impression of motion. Hence, these analogs help the beholder insert the figure within the kinetic context of an ongoing action: to paraphrase Mancini, they form the "preceding and future configurations" of the figure's motion. Aside from this aptitude, early modern viewers equally rely on their literary culture to mentally reconstruct pictorial narratives. It is evident that, for example, Maranta's reading of Titian's *Annunciation* is radically biased by his familiarity not only with the Gospel text, but also with the theological doctrine that this biblical episode foreshadows. The dependence of images on written sources is not only essential to comprehend fully the early modern association of painting and poetry; it presupposes above all a network of expectations on the beholder's part that is difficult for a twenty-first-century spectator to grasp. By this, I mean among other things that the temporal structure of every single *istoria* is measured against the temporality specific to its subject matter: the former may conform to, or—and this should be powerfully stressed—diverge from the latter. In this connection, it must be said that beholders too seem to be cognizant of the dialectics between the written text and its painted counterpart in roughly the same terms as I have just described it. Consider Maranta's opinion with regard to Titian's *Annunciation*:

> As a poet cannot alter or vary the plot [*favola*] accepted by everyone (…), although he can vary the episodes (…), so too can the painter not depict the angel in any other way than the one accepted by all. But he can vary the modes, which compare to the episodes in poetry. Therefore, he can purposely represent the announcing angel still hovering aloft, or touching the chamber floor with his feet; he can also modify the figure, making it voluptuous or meager or of an average complexion; because of their variety, these [modifications] make the difference between painter and painter, as the episodes do between poet and poet.[34]

Of course, behind Maranta's ideas lies the concept of pictorial novelty that would become so crucial to seventeenth-century artists. If the script of an Annunciation is already fixed, painters then do not seem to have much latitude in inventing new insights into the episode. Unless, as suggested by Maranta, they tweak out the story's "modes" of narration: among other elements, the action's chronological aspects.

It is fortunate that there exists an *Annunciation* by Caravaggio at the Musée des Beaux-Arts, Nancy (Fig. 27)[35] on which I propose to test the various principles of temporality in painting that I have examined so far. This picture, executed around 1609, was most probably destined for Nancy's primatial church. Even though it has suffered greatly, the painting was never a perfectly accomplished work, for it was obviously executed in Caravaggio's last manner: that is, using the priming as a half-tone and bringing out figures and objects mostly in flat relief through relatively flimsy layers of color. I will return to the specificity of this technique in Chapter 13. The oblique linking the angel to the Virgin dominates the composition. Indeed, the angel's body angles into a square bracket directed toward Mary's kneeling figure. To counterbalance this diagonal, Caravaggio depicted a bed curtain curving askew in Gabriel's direction. The bed and wicker chair further supply the horizontals necessary to anchor the composition to the pictorial space. Along with the basket in the foreground, these are the only elements to stretch the pictorial space toward and away from the beholder. That said, the action's dramatic focus revolves around the axis composed by the bodies of the Virgin and Gabriel, so that space and distance matter only in connection with the reciprocal positions of these two figures. The idea of representing the angel with his back turned—a very unusual one indeed—is probably indebted to Albrecht Altdorfer's 1513 *Annunciation* (Fig. 28).[36] In this woodcut, Gabriel leans forward while skulking in Mary's chamber, his face entirely concealed

34 Maranta, 870: "E come un poeta non può alterare né variare la favola già così accettata da tutti (…) ma ben può variare gli episodi, (…) così il pittore non può dipignere l'angelo in altro modo che in quello che è stato accettato da tutti. Ma il modo il può variare, ché ha proporzione con gli episodi della poesia. Imperoché può a sua posta far che l'angelo mentre annunzia stia ancor sospeso in aria, può farlo toccare il suolo della camera co' piedi, può variar la sua figura di farla piena o scarna o mediocre ed altre cose simili, le quali per la varietà loro fanno differenza da pittor a pittore, come gli episodi da poeta a poeta."

35 For the painting, see Pariset 1948, 108-11; Cinotti 1983, 466-8, no. 34; Hibbard 1983, 338, note 190; Calvesi 1990, 375-6; Macioce 1994, 209-10; Pacelli 1994, 80-3; Marini 2005, 557-8, no. 101; Cassani and Sapio 2005, 134, no. 15; Sciberras and Stone 2006, 95-8; Schütze 2009, 282, no. 61.

36 See Mielke 1988, 160, no. 77.

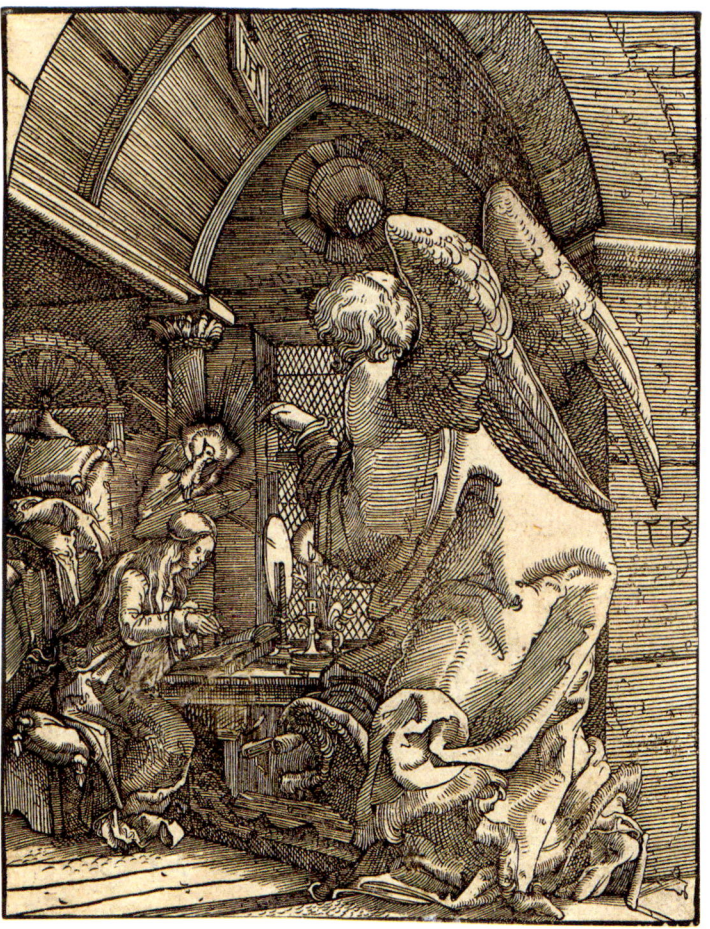

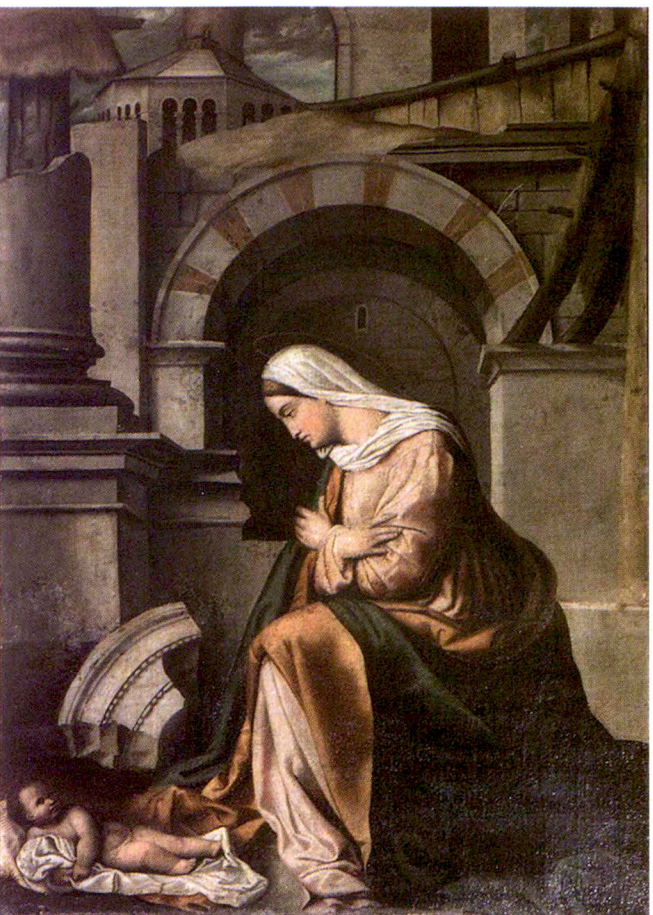

Fig. 28
Albrecht Altdorfer, *The Annunciation*, woodcut, 12.1 x 9.4 cm.

Fig. 29
Moretto da Brescia (Alessandro Bonvicino), *The Virgin Adoring the Infant Christ*, Sant'Alessandro in Colonna, Bergamo, 129 x 92 cm.

by his hair and framed by the vast curves of both his bent sleeved arm and left wing. Light invests his figure from behind, acting as a gust of wind that pushes his tunic against his legs, making the drapery's hems swirl in motion. At the farthest point of the room, the Virgin, sitting at her desk, prays as she meditates on Isaiah's text, the dove of the Holy Spirit perched almost atop her out-of-scale aureole. In the background, a bed—sheets and cushions piled up over it—is barely discernable. The arched vault above Gabriel and the Virgin emphasizes the descending diagonal connecting the two figures. Between them lingers Gabriel's hand, his index finger pointing down toward Mary. Like Altdorfer, Caravaggio shows the angel from behind, the light streaming from above as if splashing his back and making his tunic-like clothing—nothing but an ordinary bed sheet—stick to his body. On the left, a large piece of drapery swells like a parachute on the brink of landing, a subtle counterpoint to the oblique posture of Gabriel's back, which simultaneously responds to the large fold gushing down along the angel's thigh. Unlike Altdorfer, Caravaggio moves the Virgin to the foreground, at the angel's feet. By doing so, Gabriel's suspended hand and pointed finger cease to aim at Mary. Deployed above the Virgin's head, the angel's gesture now indicates the off-scene: a portion of the chamber opposite to the incoming light. I will come back to this detail shortly.

It is not surprising that, in depicting his Annunciate, Caravaggio borrowed the motif of the Virgin in profile, her face tilting downward, her arms crossed over her breast, from Moretto's 1520-1525 *Madonna Adoring the Infant Christ* in Sant'Alessandro in Colonna, Bergamo (Fig. 29).[37]

37   See Begni Redona 1988, 130, no. 18.

It is superfluous here to prove Moretto's influence on the young Caravaggio; many essays have been devoted to this topic.[38] In any event, the attitude of Caravaggio's Mary echoes that of Moretto's except for one single detail: in the Nancy *Annunciation*, the Virgin kneels on both knees. Curiously enough, the linen cloth covering the Virgin's empty basket in Caravaggio's picture subtly evokes the white drapery on which the infant Jesus lies in Moretto's painting. In a sense, the empty basket serves as a visual prolepsis of the predestined and heralded Nativity. It is however true that Mary's position in both paintings does not necessarily imply an act of adoration, since it allows for other meanings. If one explores the iconographic tradition one would discover many examples of this visual formula: they basically fall within three categories according to their narrative function. More to the point, they represent the Virgin praying, pledging humility or adoring her divine Son. Needless to say, in the context of an Annunciation these attitudes relate respectively to the preamble and outcome of the biblical episode, as well as to its

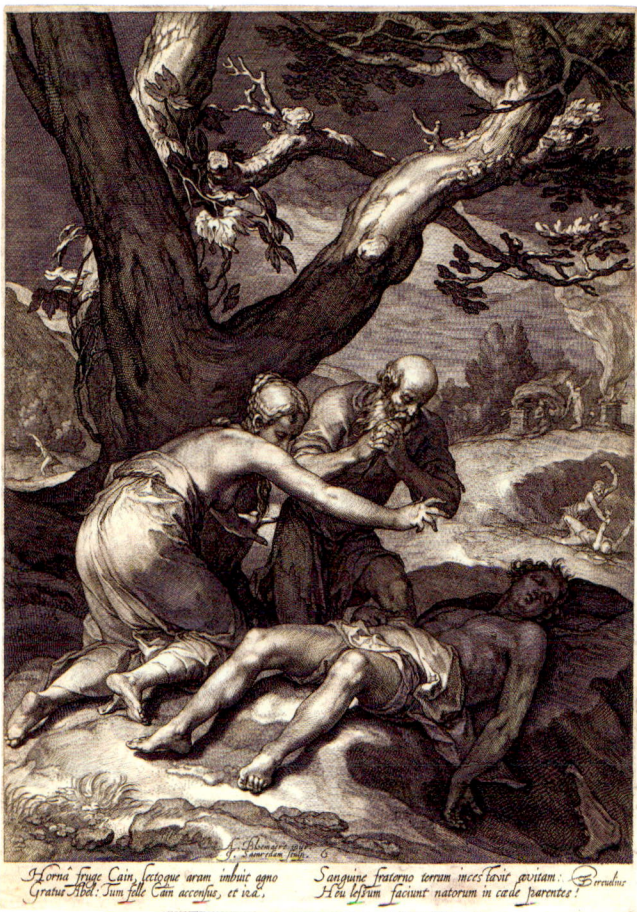

Fig. 30
Jan Saenredam after Abraham Bloemaert, *Adam and Eve Mourning the Death of Abel*, engraving, 25.6 x 19.1 cm.

symbolic aftermath: the Savior's birth and the accomplishment of the Incarnation. Should one establish the specific narrative and temporal value of the Virgin's attitude in the Nancy *Annunciation*, one would seriously be at a loss. As Maranta's interpretation of Titian's Naples *Annunciation* has already made clear, in such ambiguous cases only the angel's action would allow viewers to pick out the exact moment depicted by the painter. But Gabriel's attitude in Caravaggio's painting constitutes in and of itself an iconographic quagmire. Indeed, what is the angel meant to be doing there? I have given the question some thought, and looked for precedents that might shed light on this unconventional attitude. During my research, I came across an engraving by Jan Saenredam after Abraham Bloemart: the 1604 *Adam and Eve Mourning the Slain Abel* (Fig. 30).[39] In the print, Abel's dead body lies askew over a sloping bulk of rock, his legs oriented toward the foreground, his torso and head, which recede toward the landscape at the right, resting in the shade of a mighty tree that flings its split trunk heavenward as if amplifying the bereavement of the youth's parents. Adam hunches over his son's cadaver, fists clutched together in an act of desperation. Eve—and this is the important point—seems suddenly to have burst onto the scene: she angles her body into a square bracket, thrusting her arms forward over Abel's body. At the same time, she kneels against the sloping foreground with her back turned and intensely modeled by the light coming from behind, her bare shoulder and visible arm emphatically jutting out like a spotlighted branch of the adjacent tree. More importantly, her right arm bars her downcast face, foreshortened almost

---

38 Here, I single out Christiansen 1996.

39 For the print, see Strauss 1980, 327, no. 18 (226); Roethlisberger 1993, 1:1256, no. 77.

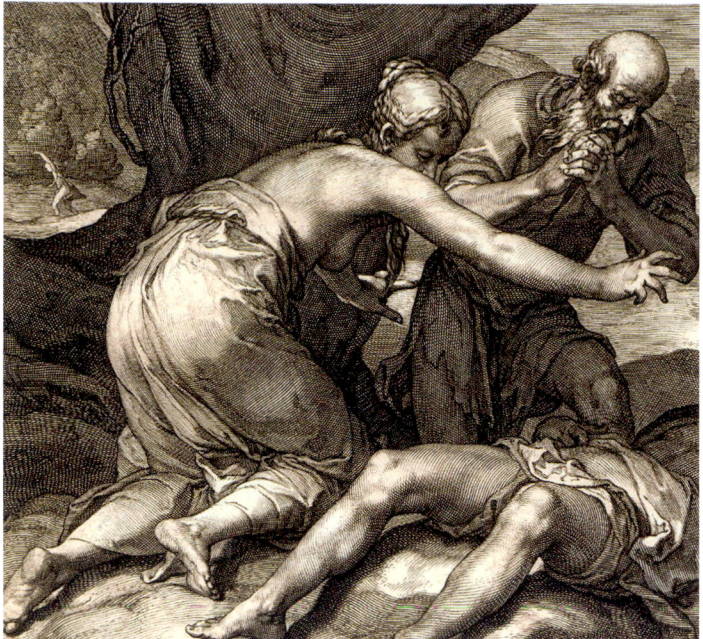

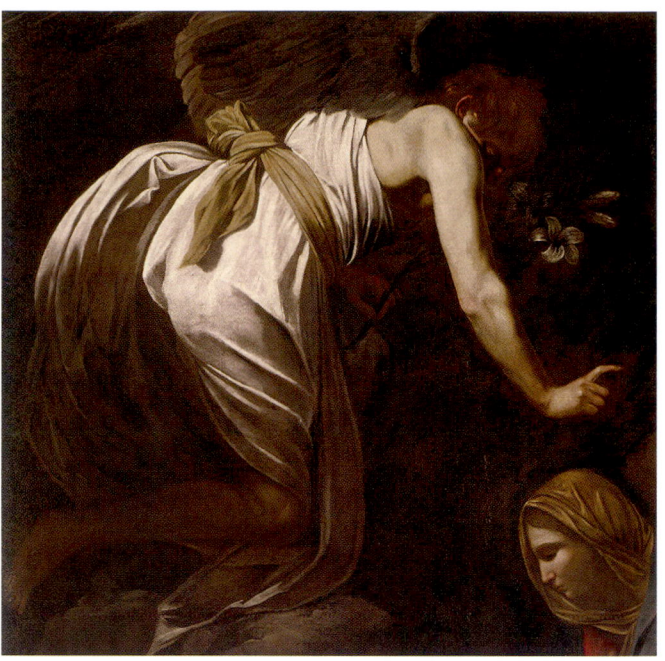

Fig. 31
Jan Saenredam after Abraham Bloemaert, *Adam and Eve Mourning the Death of Abel*, engraving, 25.6 x 19.1 cm., detail.

Fig. 32
Michelangelo Merisi da Caravaggio, *The Annunciation*, Musée des Beaux-Arts, Nancy, oil on canvas, 285 x 205 cm., detail.

in profile, thereby preventing viewers from seeing her expression (Fig. 31). Rhetorically speaking, Eve's attitude connotes as a visual litotes: it blocks out expression to intensify the resonance of the figure's sorrow in the viewer's mind. Once again, Timanthes' *Sacrifice of Iphigenia* sets the example for this visual trope. At this point, I do not deem it necessary to show Caravaggio's debt to Saenredam's print. In spite of a few, comprehensible variations, Caravaggio's Gabriel substantially mirrors Eve's attitude in the engraving. It is fair to assume that since this iconographic scheme channels the impression of a sudden bursting-in motion, Caravaggio might have adopted it in his *Annunciation* for this specific reason (Fig. 32). But then again, how does this attitude square with the painting's temporal and spatial context? Whatever the answer to this question might be, at first glance Gabriel's whole pose seems to embody a visual litotes in its own right. Not only is the angel's expression undecipherable because of the barring arm, but the entire figure overall refuses to be matched with a coherent aspect of motion and temporality. To paraphrase Gaurico, Gabriel's attitude is certainly not a case of *enargeia*: it is difficult to say whether he has just come in, as signaled by the landing drapery, or if he has delivered a part of his message, as indicated by his kneeling position. Nor is this a case of *emphasis*: if the angel is about to perform a climactic action, what should this be? Is he perhaps telling the Virgin that "the Holy Spirit will come upon" her? If so, why is he not then pointing his index finger upward, but inexplicably to the right margin of the canvas? It would probably be more appropriate to define this attitude as an *amphiboly*. I would endorse this definition, but not without previously stressing that amphiboly qualifies as an intermediate state of motion. Yet, in the Nancy *Annunciation*, it is the whole motion that eschews comprehension, as if Caravaggio had intentionally depicted an action potentially without meaning, a posture potentially without referents. Like Michelangelo but on a micro-scale, he strains the anatomy beyond congruousness: observe Gabriel's shoulder mysteriously pressed against his cheek, making the clavicle jut slightly upward. Or consider the right wrist, incomprehensibly bent down to support the thrust of the pointing finger. However, counter to Michelangelo's pictorial habits, these corporal strains—not found in Saenredam's Eve either—are not devised to enhance harmony and symmetry. Rather, they blur the actual scope of the motion represented, thereby belying its verisimilitude. In sum, the angel's posture here is a visual formula exceeding its narrative content and function. It is the metaphor of an announcing act that eludes visualization and dismisses temporality. The most compelling evidence of this contention is Gabriel's hovering hand, faking the gesture of pointing so specific to the Annunciation theme, but in reality substituting for the hackneyed dove conventionally sweeping over Mary's head. In other words, Caravaggio dislocates the traditional motifs of an Annunciation by turning a symbol—the dove—into a gesture, and by reducing a canonical gesture—the pointing of the hand—to a visual sign without an apparent or logical signified. Nonetheless, as I will explain in Chapter 9, Caravaggio's narratives cannot be defined as symbolic: in the Nancy *Annunciation*, the angel's posture does not render a paradigmatic facet of the story. Motion and temporality matter there insofar as it is through their manipulation that the composition acquires its originality. By juxtaposing a multi-temporal formula of praying and adoration with an indefinite scheme of both rest and motion, Caravaggio short-circuits the concept of action as traditionally conveyed by the *istoria*.

As a general rule, Caravaggio tends to lay bare the underlying structures of pictorial motion and temporality not only to unveil their fictiveness, but also to create new vectors of action and time in painting. By concealing Gabriel's face partially and his mouth totally, and by shaping his body into a visual hieroglyph, Caravaggio does not discard the impression of motion: he rather expresses the ineffability of God's decree through the amphiboly of Gabriel's heralding action. On the other hand, by representing Mary in a posture that intersects three different moments of the Incarnation saga, Caravaggio legitimately activates a visual function specific to the fictive time of narrative: by resorting to a multi-temporal and polyvalent iconographic scheme, he makes the temporality of action telescope into the instant of vision. In the Virgin of the Nancy *Annunciation*, therefore, the sacred mystery of the Incarnation is evoked under the simultaneous forms of pre-figuration, immanence, and fulfillment. Yet Caravaggio's Mary, carved out of the canvas's background with force and delicacy, is far from being a supra-temporal emblem of the Incarnation. The stillness of her contemplative posture enlivens the gesture of her hands, not merely crossed over her breast, but grasping her body as though in that moment she were truly feeling the inexpressible pleasure of the ongoing mystery.

In the course of this monograph, I shall examine many other dislocations of temporality in Caravaggio's painting. For the time being, it is tempting to imagine how painters and theorists might have reacted to Caravaggio's transgressions of the principles governing the figures' movements in the *istoria*. A term frequently used by Albani in his criticism of Caravaggio comes inevitably to mind: "idling." As I have already shown, according to Albani, Caravaggio's half-figures do not act the action, but rather "idle" without knowing what their exact role is—if they happen to have any—in the pictorial script. Put otherwise, Caravaggio's figures would be unfit to compose a pictorial narrative appropriately and meaningfully. It is understandable that Caravaggio's tricks on action and temporality, especially because they dismantle the legibility and intelligibility required of images at the time, baffled and irritated artists like Albani who, in contrast, strove to resuscitate and extend the tenets of Alberti's *istoria*. Instead of penetrating Caravaggio's poetics of dislocation, they judged its newness with severity and, even worse, undervalued its importance. Even if the polysemy of Albani's figures proves also to be a subtle attempt at enlarging the temporal boundaries of Alberti's *istoria*, the refinements of Albani's solutions do not live up to the radical ingenuity of Caravaggio's experimentations. Properly speaking, Caravaggio's figures are not multi-taskers—no irony involved, of course: they do not perform various segments of action at once like Albani's Virgin in the San Bartolomeo *Annunciation*. On the contrary, Caravaggio unleashes temporality by grafting motifs, formulas, and schemes traditionally associated with a narrative situation onto

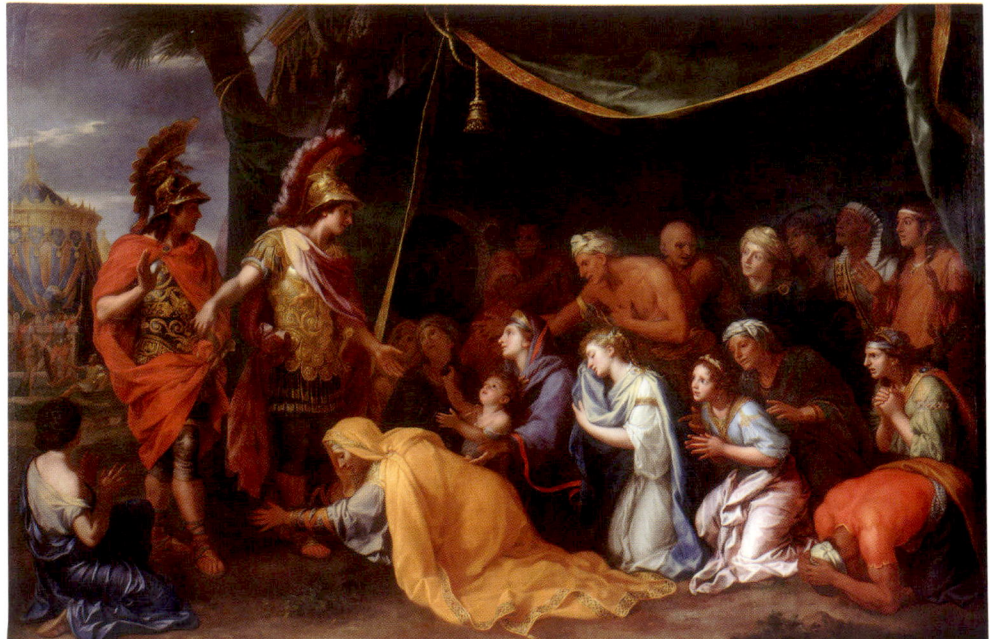

Fig. 33
Charles Le Brun, *The Family of Darius at the Feet of Alexander* or *The Tent of Darius*, Châteaux de Versailles
et Trianon, Versailles, oil on canvas, 298 x 453 cm.

new contexts. Rather than seeking legibility or intelligibility, Caravaggio tends to stimulate—even bombard—the viewer's visual memory with allusions to multiple codes and iconographies at the risk of miscomprehension and in contempt of verisimilitude. Paradoxically, Caravaggio's pictures appear immediately understandable and fairly enjoyable. Except for a few cases, his subjects and stories can be easily identified, yet betray the extent of their complexity only upon closer reading. As much as Albani's pictorial narratives, Caravaggio's pictures demand the attention and expertise of an alert gaze. Because of the far-reaching array of their novel solutions, Caravaggio's stories necessarily exerted a strong, albeit indirect and misleading, influence on artists and critics. As I have already stressed, I am convinced that the vast reflection on pictorial narrative characteristic to seventeenth-century Italy, France, the Spanish Low-Countries, and even Spain and Holland is not unrelated to Caravaggio's mishandlings of Alberti's *istoria*. Of course, this cannot be the only factor accounting for the renewed interest in pictorial narration. But, once again, the shock of Caravaggio's unorthodox poetics in this field certainly contributed to the enormous enterprise of regulating, redefining, restraining, and questioning the principles of the *istoria*, an enterprise that inspired artists from the 1610s on and informed the activities of many Academies in Western Europe from the 1640s onward.

Before I pass to another topic, I should first offer a rapid survey of how painters and theorists construed narrative temporality in the immediate aftermath of Caravaggio's critical misfortune. It is evident to me that, in spite of its acceptability, the monomial equation through which a figure simultaneously performs several actions with a view toward increasing the effects of temporality in the *istoria* would soon appear unviable. By loading single figures with too many signifiers, artists ended up compromising intelligibility. A good example of this overabundance is Albani's San Bartolomeo *Annunciation*, where the Virgin's simultaneous actions impede one another from attaining visual evidence. The same applies later to Charles Le Brun's depiction of Alexander the Great in his 1660-1661 celebrated *Tent of Darius* (Château de Versailles; Fig. 33).[40] In his 1663

40   For the painting, see Pericolo 2001a.

description of the painting, André Félibien[41] remarks on the polyvalence of Alexander's attitude, extolling Le Brun's ability to visualize at once so many aspects of the literary episode he was representing, Alexander's visit to the Persian princesses after defeating Darius, the King of Persia. As Alexander enters the tent where all the princesses are gathered, Darius' wife and her court prostrate themselves before Hephestion, Alexander's favorite, mistaking him for the Macedonian King. Instead of seething with indignation for the unfortunate misrecognition, Alexander forgives the Persian princesses by explaining to them that Hephestion was indeed another himself. According to Félibien, the figure of the Macedonian King is an admirable masterpiece of expression and attitude:

> The painter did not content himself with representing on Alexander's face his youth, the sweetness of his temperament, his valor, and all the other qualities that history relates about this great prince, of whom [the painter] makes a faithful image; one also discerns four diverse types of actions in Alexander's attitude. The compassion he feels for the princesses is visible both in his gaze and expression. His open hand shows his mercy and perfectly voices the grace he bestows upon this court. The other hand leaning on Hephestion clearly reveals that this is his favorite, or another himself; and the left leg that he retracts is a sign of the courtesy he uses with these princesses. The painter did not make him bend further, because he represented him at the moment when he addresses these ladies, because this was not a Greek custom, and because, moreover, he could not lower himself further since his thigh had been wounded during his last combat.[42]

Félibien's enumeration of Alexander's fourfold action would not be complete without Claude Nivelon's additions to it. In his *c.1698 Vie de Charles Le Brun*, Nivelon relates that, besides dealing with Darius' wife and mother, as well as with Hephestion, Alexander also interacts with his enemy's young son and, last but not least, with his beautiful daughter, Princess Statira, whom he would marry soon afterward.[43] Félibien's and Nivelon's enthusiasm should not fool anybody: behind their praises hides the intention of defending Le Brun's picture from its detractors. It should not go unnoticed that Félibien bizarrely excuses Alexander's lack of anatomical flexibility before the harem of the Persian princesses on account of different factors, including the King's recent war wounds. However erudite and subtle, Félibien's evocation of Alexander's mishap during a previous combat not only betokens an obsession with historical accuracy, but also reveals that the figure's posture must have appeared mistimed, mismatched, and obscure, which it undoubtedly is, at least in some respects. The point of all these considerations is that once again, by overstretching the figure's polysemy, the painter does not enhance the impression of motion and temporality in the *istoria*, but rather eclipses the intelligibility of the action.

Although I cannot prove it, I believe that the difficulties involved in exploiting the figure's polyvalence discouraged painters from using this device often, and even then, only with precaution

---

41 For Félibien's personality and his artistic theory, see Germer 1997.

42 Félibien b, 36-7: "Le peintre ne s'est pas contenté de représenter sur le visage d'Alexandre sa jeunesse, la douceur de son temperament, sa valeur et toutes les autres qualités que l'histoire nous apprend de ce grand prince, et dont il fait une fidèle image, mais on voit encore dans ses mouvements quatre sortes d'actions différentes. La compassion qu'il a des princesses paraît visiblement et par ses regards et par sa contenance. Sa main ouverte montre sa clémence et exprime parfaitement la grâce qu'il a fait à toute cette cour. Son autre main qu'il appuie sur Éphestion dit assez qu'il est son favori, ou plutôt un autre lui-même, et sa jambe gauche qu'il retire en arrière est une marque de la civilité qu'il rend à ces princesses. Le peintre ne l'a pas fait incliner davantage parce qu'il le représente dans le moment qu'il aborde ces dames, que ce n'était pas l'usage des grecs, et de plus qu'il ne pouvait pas se baisser beaucoup à cause que dans le dernier combat il avait été blessé à la cuisse."

43 Nivelon, 275-6.

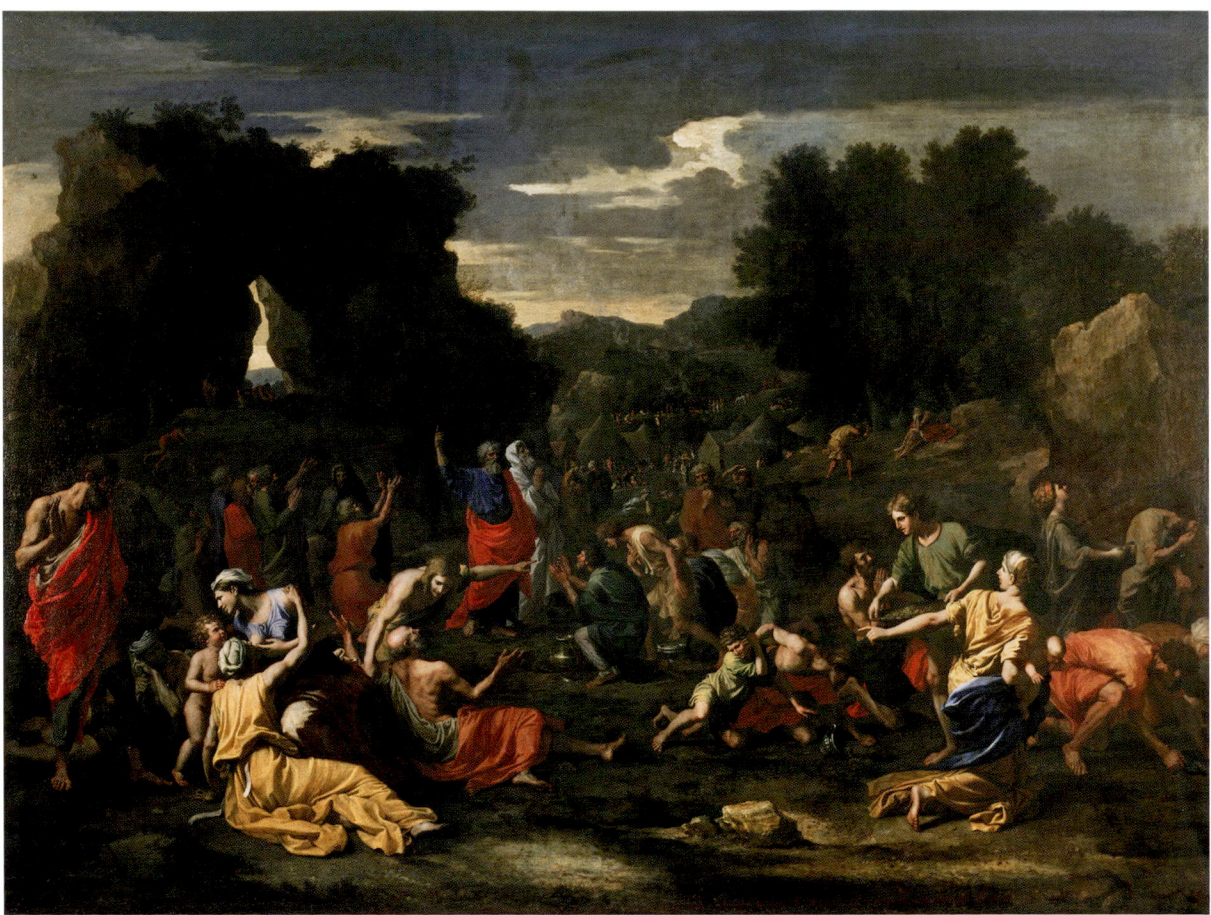

Fig. 34
Nicolas Poussin, *The Israelites Gathering the Manna in the Desert*, Musée du Louvre, Paris, oil on canvas, 149 x 200 cm.

and parsimony.[44] The only clue I can adduce in this regard is the silence of art theorists in respect of the single figure's many-sidedness. In any event, to expand the narrative's temporality, painters resorted instead to a polynomial model of composition: one based upon a relatively large number of figures, each of them encompassing a diverse temporal aspect of the story. As is well known, Nicolas Poussin wholeheartedly embraced this model, as evidenced by his 1639 *Manna* now in the Louvre, Paris (Fig. 34).[45] In a letter to the French painter Jacques Stella, dated to *c.*1637—probably the same year as Albani's letter to Zamboni about the San Bartolomeo *Annunciation*—Poussin writes:

> I have worked out a certain disposition for Monsieur de Chantelou's painting [the *Manna*], as well as certain natural attitudes that show the misery and starvation to which the Jews had been reduced, [but also] the joy and happiness that they experience,

44 An interesting example of a figure's polyvalence is represented by a Christ sculpted by Gianlorenzo Bernini according to Lelio Guidiccioni. In a letter of 4 June 1633 to Bernini, Guidiccioni writes: "Ma Vostra Signoria ha felicemente introdotto pluralità non solo esprimendo più azioni successive in una opera o per dir meglio in una operazione, ma anco accennando quelle che non può esprimere et cavandone spesso significato. Perché per esempio il sudetto ritratto di Nostro Signore che non ha braccia, con un poco di motivo di

spalla destra et alzato di mozzetta aggiunto alla pendentia della testa, che serve a più cose, come ancho il chinar della fronte, dimostra chiara l'attione di accennar col braccio ad alcuno che si levi in piedi…" The letter is published, with mistakes, by Zitzlsperger 2002, 179 ff., esp. 180.

45 For the painting, see Rosenberg and Pratt 1994, 262-4, no. 78.

the wonder that comes over them, and the respect and reverence for their legislator [Moses], with a mix of women, children, and men of diverse temperaments and ages. As I believe, these are aspects that those who know how to read them will not dislike.[46]

It is no coincidence, in my view, that Poussin developed his ideas of temporality in a narrative like the *Manna*;[47] as I have already pointed out, according to Dolce, Raphael's excellence in composing an *istoria* was embodied in his treatment of this very subject. By improving upon it, Poussin thus declared himself as both the legitimate heir of Raphael's perfection and an original yet trustworthy interpreter of Alberti's *istoria*. In another letter addressed to his patron, Paul Fréart de Chantelou, and dated 28 April 1639, Poussin makes even more explicit his intention to transform the picture into the equivalent of an epic episode, perhaps as grand as Raphael's story, and hence able to be read and understood in its amplitude:

> I think that you will easily recognize which [figures] languish, which admire, those that feel compassion, those that perform acts of charity, or are in great misery, or want to feed themselves, or console others and so forth, since the first seven figures on the left will tell you what I have written here, and the rest is of the same tenor. Read the story and the painting in order to know if everything is appropriate to the subject.[48]

As can be observed, Poussin supplies each figure with no more than one relevant action. As a prism, the story is broken into multiple facets, one linked to another in a harmonious and coherent manner, but most importantly, each one reflecting a specific aspect of the action—joy, misery, hunger, compassion, etc.—and of temporality—misery and hunger mirror the desolation of the Jews wandering in the desert; joy and admiration highlight the sudden pouring of the divine food over the Jewish population; respect and reverence project the action into the future, since they confirm both the chosen people's renewed trust of Moses and God's benevolence upon Israel. At first glance, the principles of Alberti's *istoria*—its variety, proportionality, and congruousness—are respected in Poussin's *Manna*, and do not seem to conflict with the unity of action and time so strenuously sought by painters since the mid sixteenth century. Indeed, the rhetorical complexity of Poussin's picture is attained, apparently at least, without sacrificing the instant of vision: in Poussin's view, what is represented in the *Manna* might actually occur in a single moment, even if viewers need to dwell much longer on the composition to take in the event's entire unfolding. The time of seeing is therefore equated with that of reading. In a certain sense, Poussin seems here to square the circle of temporality in painting. Yet what he truly succeeded in doing was to make clear that time in pictorial narratives is a matter of rhetoric, and not of optics. In fact, to deploy temporality on the surface of the canvas, the painter inexorably erodes, and even deletes the impression of instantaneity specific to the natural vision. At any rate, this is the conclusion that the audience of the Académie Royale de Peinture reached at the end of a lecture devoted to Poussin's

---

46   Poussin, 37: "J'ai trouvé une certaine distribution pour le tableau de monsieur de Chantelou, et certaines attitudes naturelles qui font voir dans le people juif la misère et la faim où il était réduit, et aussi la joie et l'allégresse où il se trouve, l'admiration dont il est touché, le respect et la révérence qu'il a pour son législateur, avec un mélange de femmes, d'enfants et d'hommes d'âge et de tempéraments différents: choses, comme je crois, qui ne déplairont pas à ceux qui les sauront bien lire."

47   For Poussin's theory of art and the importance of the *istoria* in it, see Lee 1967; Thuillier 1967; Fumaroli 1982; Imdahl 1985;

Bätschmann 1990, 111-8; Thürlemann 1990, 111-37; Puttfarken 2000, 229-62 [a general survey of French seventeenth-century theories on the *istoria*, also in relation to Poussin]; Careri 2005, esp. 157 ff.; Unglaub 2006; and Stumpfhaus 2007.

48   Poussin, 45: "Je pense que vous reconnaîtrez aisément celles qui languissent, qui admirent, celles qui ont pitié, qui font acte de charité, de grande nécessité, de désir de se repaître, de consolation et autres, car les sept premières figures à main gauche vous diront tout ce qui est ici écrit et tout le reste est de la même étoffe. Lisez l'histoire et le tableau afin de connaître si chaque chose est appropriée au sujet."

Manna given by Charles Le Brun on 5 November 1667.[49] I will not expand here upon the reasons why Poussin was politely accused of tampering with the biblical text; suffice it to know that the painter had depicted the episode of the manna in a different way and order from those of scripture. It seems to me that this point of the discussion is a mere pretext to attack not only Poussin, but also his supporters, by unveiling how vulnerable the polynomial model of composition proves to be with regard to temporality. Indeed, Poussin's narrative only works out on one condition: the viewer's eye must advance through the episode one figure at a time, then group by group. If considered in its entirety, the picture loses its verisimilitude: the simultaneous presence of joy and misery, hope and gratitude becomes unlikely, or even impossible. To defend Poussin from these substantial accusations, an anonymous person attending the 1667 lecture argued:

> If the principles of theater allow poets to join together several events occurring in different times in order to form a single action, provided that nothing is contradictory and that verisimilitude is properly heeded, then it is even more understandable that painters take this license since, without it, their works would be devoid of that which makes the composition more admirable and reveals the beauty of their author's ingenuity.[50]

In the first place, this interpretation of the Aristotelian unity of action is, in my opinion, most similar to the one that underpins Alberti's definition of the *istoria*. I have already elucidated this point while dealing with the problem of continuous narrative. However, the clever interlocutor who introduced this argument failed to notice that, if hypothetically one were to lay out all the episodes of a theatrical piece in a single space one after another, then actors would appear more than once at the same time, and sometimes the same figures would materialize side by side on stage. This phenomenon, if I understand correctly, negates the principle of the visual or optical verisimilitude integral to Alberti's concept of imitation. Therefore it is inherently impossible for a painting to operate as a tragedy or a drama. From the outset, and because of the medium with which they work, painters are condemned to focus on short segments of action, and to extricate from this abridged raw material as many facts, motions, and situations as they are able to evoke without infringing verisimilitude. Even in this case, though, if artists want to compose their stories by limiting themselves to a single act of a theatrical piece, they risk crossing the temporal boundaries set by the instant of vision:

> To depict perfectly the story that he represented, [Poussin] required the parts of a poem that are necessary to pass from the catastrophe to the happy ending. One sees that these groups of different people playing out diverse actions are the equivalents of the episodes that compose what we call vicissitudes, and the means to make known the change that occurred to the Jews when they step out of extreme misery and enter a happier condition.[51]

---

49 An essential survey of the Academic debates in France is still Teyssèdre 1957, 76 ff. See also Duro 1997.

50 *Conférences*, 1:173: "Quelqu'un ajouta à ce que Monsieur Le Brun venait de dire que, si par les règles du théâtre, il est permis aux poètes de joindre ensemble plusieurs événements arrivés en divers temps pour en faire une seule action, pourvu qu'il n'y ait rien qui se contrarie et que la vraisemblance y soit exactement observée, il est encore bien plus juste que les peintres prennent cette licence, puisque sans cela leurs ouvrages demeureraient privés de ce qui en rend la

composition plus admirable et fait connaître davantage la beauté du genie de leur auteur."

51 Ibidem, 174: "Car, pour représenter parfaitement l'histoire qu'il traite, il avait besoin des parties nécessaires à un poème, afin de passer de l'infortune au bonheur. C'est pourquoi l'on voit que ces groupes de figures, qui font diverses actions, sont comme autant d'épisodes qui servent à ce que l'on nomme péripéties et de moyens pour faire connaître le changement arrivé aux israélites quand ils sortent d'une extrême misère et qu'ils rentrent dans un état plus heureux."

For the sake of completeness and intelligibility, the story thus demands that pictorial action reflect as much as possible the initial, intermediate, and final vicissitudes of the event to be represented. Painters can find a way chronologically to stagger these facts by stitching them together into a harmonious and coherent composition. To this end, they imagine attitudes, gestures and expressions appropriate and convincing enough that the unfolding action becomes self-evident to viewers, even transparent in its implications. This kind of verisimilitude is a rhetorical one, for as an artifact or compositional device, it relates to congruousness, variety, and proportionality. Yet to achieve this goal painters should not dismiss visual or optical verisimilitude: whether initial, intermediate or final, actions must occur concomitantly in the instant of vision, a fictive unity of time that substantially differs from the physical instant. I bring up this distinction because, if one measures the instant of vision against the parameters of physical time, this instant would not tolerate the simultaneity of initial, intermediate, and final actions. Thus the instant in painting is a convention, a felicitous point in time in which action prodigiously extends beyond the present, metabolizing within itself the permanence of the immediate past and the imminence of the near future. Even if the fictive instant of vision is accepted as a pictorial license to engender temporality, its fictiveness implies that in the end the verisimilitude involved in the *istoria* cannot by any means be classified as optical. A pictorial narrative once again is not a vision reproduced, but the selective representation of meaningful events arrayed so as to imitate, and sometimes merely summon up, the unfolding of an action. By enlarging the scope of Alberti's *istoria*, Poussin also anticipated its end. Lessing's famous statement about painting as the art of space as opposed to poetry as the art of time does not mean that temporality is excluded from the visual arts, as many tend to believe. Lessing overall stresses the fact that time is always a fictitious device in painting, unrelated to natural vision and to a certain degree independent from its mechanisms.[52]

Its intrinsic contradictions notwithstanding, the theoretical system of norms and practices inaugurated by Domenichino, Albani, Poussin, and other masters in the first half of the seventeenth century with their pictorial narratives, and refined by the French Academy from the 1660s onward, would long prevail. Since it is rooted in a polynomial model of composition, the "academic" *istoria* configures itself as almost the opposite of Caravaggio's pictorial narratives: close-up views, a segmentation of the human body through framing or chiaroscuro, a limited number of figures, the quasi-suppression of perspective and spatial depth, a scarcity of, or indifference to, historical circumstances and accessories, and the misalignments of actions and temporalities; all of these qualities are exactly what Albani, Domenichino, Poussin, and others tried so hard to eradicate from the practice of the *istoria*. They were certainly successful in their task. However, their success must not make us forget that, sometime between 1595 and 1630, Caravaggio and his many followers invented an alternative way of composing pictorial narratives. This is what I shall endeavor to demonstrate in the course of this volume.

52 In this regard, see Mitchell 1984, esp. 101-4. For Lessing's *Laokoon* and his discussion of time and space in art, see also McClain 1985; Lagny 1998; Barner 2003; Geimer 2003; Schrader 2005, 51-84; and Wallenstein 2010.

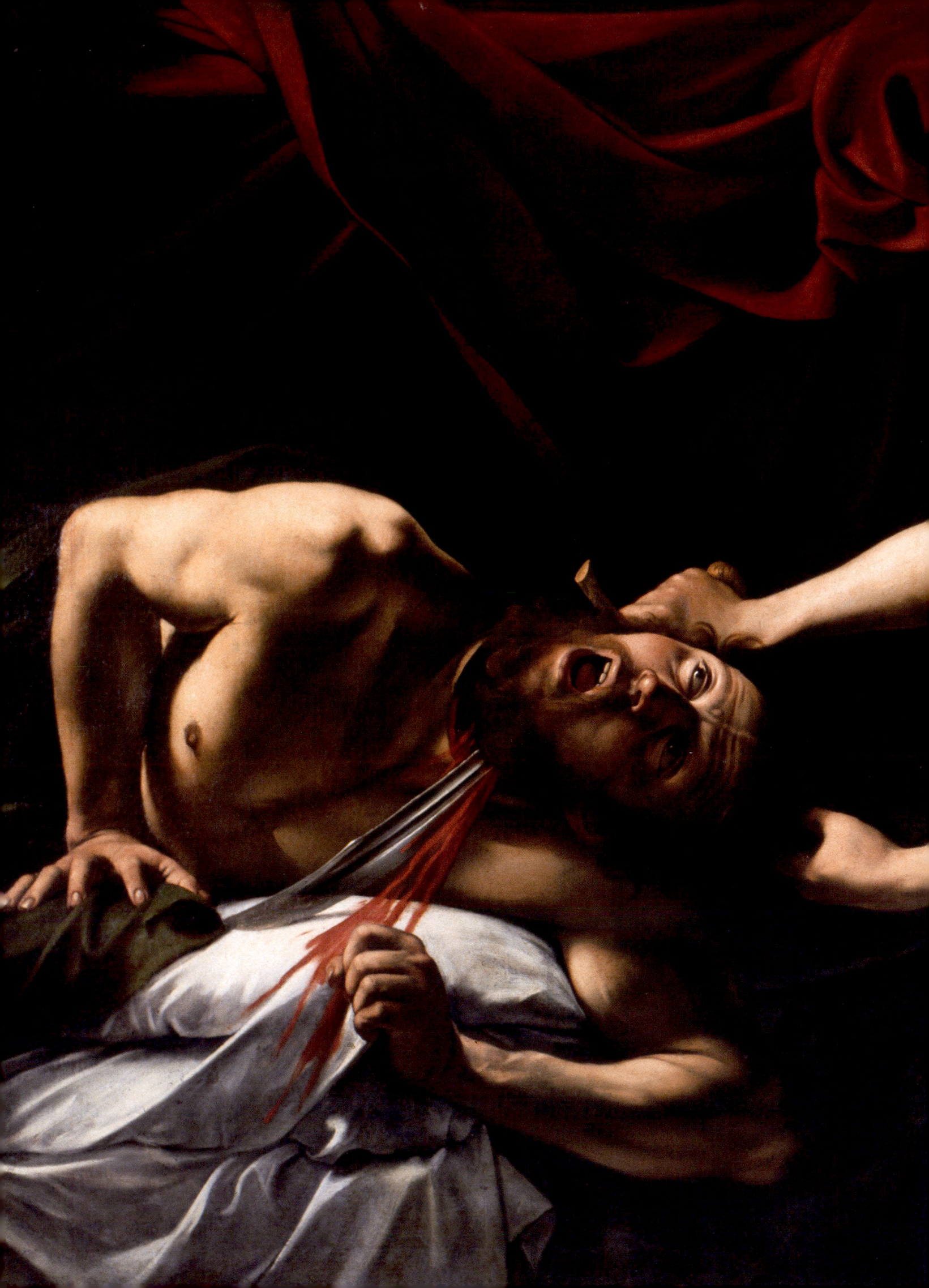

CHAPTER 3

The False Dichotomy Between Telling and Showing: Beyond Alberti's *Istoria*

"The fictive, then, might be called a transitional object, always hovering between the real and the imaginary, linking the two together. As such it exists, for it houses all the processes of interchange. Yet, in another sense, it does not exist as a discrete entity, for it consists of nothing but these transformational processes."[1]

In spite of their extraordinary acuteness—unmatched, to my knowledge, in the kindred field of contemporary literary theory—seventeenth-century art critics and painters did not possess the theoretical equipment to assess and correctly evaluate what I have defined as Caravaggio's poetics of dislocation. In the Introduction to Part One, I isolated an artistic phenomenon that I called the *Caravaggio syndrome*: to wit, the obvious embarrassment of authors such as Baglione, Mancini, Albani, Bellori, Malvasia, and Scannelli in gauging Caravaggio's paintings. Not only are they driven by an unflinching bias against the master, but they also misread and misinterpret his pictures by overlooking, vaguely recalling, or deliberately ignoring essential elements of the composition. Their exegetical inadequacy is to some extent the result of ill will; it mostly depends on an aesthetics by which they all, directly or indirectly, abide and which basically shuns and condemns any sort of discrepancy, disparity, and incongruence between the subject matter and its visual translation, or broadly speaking between content and form.[2] As I have already shown and shall demonstrate later, the system of dislocations activated by Caravaggio in his narratives varies in scope, intensity, and intentionality. It is a diabolical mechanism in which the painter tampers with some basic tenets of the *istoria* while inhibiting, preserving or enforcing others, each time uniquely, so that pinpointing his fallacies with regard to the principles of the then-canonical pictorial narrative would have required much more than scathing, snide remarks, and to a certain extent generic accusations. Caravaggio's painting was disturbingly fascinating; it transcended understanding because it played with different levels and categories of dislocation. Most importantly, his pictorial narratives tended not to work out as a conventional *istoria*. In other words, the means by which Caravaggio built action and temporality through figures and objects should have rewarded an exegetical procedure in contrast with the theoretical tenets of early modern art: a hermeneutics capable of encompassing dissonance, inconsistency, obscurity, and ambivalence. Needless to say, this sort of hermeneutics did not exist at the time. Furthermore, Caravaggio transgresses genre-based codes in ways that are almost imperceptible, in some cases subliminal. His manipulations are even more pervasive in that they do not impose themselves upon the viewer at once; on the contrary, they act latently by ensnaring beholders into images that feel all too "natural," but whose interpretation is punctuated by subtle twists and wondrous indeterminacy, by visual sleights of hand and shifts of narrative logic.

1   Iser 1993, 20.

2   For a definition of subject in early modern art, see Nagel and Pericolo 2010, 1-15.

Of course, Caravaggio's innovations in the domain of pictorial narrative deserve to be studied and clarified in detail, but to this end it is necessary to rely on a hermeneutical method that has not yet been developed for the visual arts. In other fields of the humanities such as literature, theater or cinema, scholars have formulated complex theories capable of construing narratives, whether in the literary tradition—epic poems, tragedies, comedies, and especially novels—or more recently for movies, television series, and even video games.[3] In art history, though, there is no narratology worthy of the name. It might sound absurd that a humanistic discipline like art history, which has mostly emerged from the early modern debates about the *istoria*, has stubbornly continued to appraise visual narratives with criteria that are frankly obsolete. In a certain sense, art historians have never surmounted the impervious yet comfortable barrier constituted by the fifteenth-century equivalence of poetry and painting: Horace's *ut pictura poësis* as embraced by Alberti and the subsequent cohort of early modern art theorists. At this point, I do not need to demonstrate why this equivalence—albeit so important from a historical prospect—fails to explain unorthodox models of visual narration like those of Caravaggio and his followers. Although I cannot spend much time defining pictorial narrative and its principles on a novel basis, I shall attempt briefly to set out some guidelines essential to analyzing Caravaggio's stories without stumbling into the miscomprehensions deriving from Alberti's concept of the *istoria*. These guidelines will merely be sketched out—I shall elaborate upon them as the book proceeds and as the topic requires—and they cannot replace a study entirely consecrated to a branch of our discipline that hopefully will be initiated soon: pictorial narratology.

In keeping with Alberti's definition, the *istoria*—of which the term "pictorial narrative" is a synonym, in my view—must be construed as the representation of human action either in painting or sculpture. In other words, it is the visualization of an account—traditionally termed "subject matter"—involving human events in a temporal sequence. Even if it is often identified with a written text, the account or subject matter does not truly pertain to any specific medium, and is generally characterized as the mental record of an event or sequel of facts, whether real or otherwise. As such, the account precedes its embodiment in an oral, written, visual or multi-media form of communication. In conformity with Aristotle's notion of mimesis or imitation as set out in the *Poetics*, Wayne C. Booth, followed and only partially corrected by many other narratologists, distinguishes between two modalities of narration: telling and showing.[4] If the account is related by a narrative voice (the narrator), then the story configures itself as a description of events: a description that could in no way "imitate"—or physically re-enact—human actions, even if it can evoke them with utmost liveliness and minuteness. This sort of descriptive, or indirect, narrative constitutes the category of "telling." Conversely, if the account is enacted in a dialogical form, as if unfolding in front of the audience, in this case the narrative falls into the category of "showing." In this sort of narration the narrative voice vanishes, and every character introduces his or her point of view without the filter of the narrator. At first glance, then, pictorial narrative should rank as a sub-category of the "showing" modality. In reality, the differentiation between "showing" and "telling," though most suitable for explaining literary artworks, when applied to images allows for great misconstructions. First, it underpins the incorrect premise that a dialogical (or direct) form of narrative is closer to imitation than a diegetic (or indirect) one.[5] In this regard, it is noteworthy

---

3 In this regard, I will mention only the "classics": Booth 1961; Barthes et al. 1977; Ricœur 1983; Branigan 1992; Bal 1997; Gaudreault 1999; Genette 2007 [published originally in 1972 and 1983]. Altman 2008, which intends to delineate an all-comprehensive theory of narrative valid for any media, is in my opinion theoretically confused and over-ambitious. For narrative in television series, commercials, and video games, see Ryan 2003; Allrath and Gymnich 2006; Carr D. et al. 2006; and Huisman et al. 2006.

4 See Booth 1961, 211-40. For a recent interpretation of the concept of mimesis, see Halliwell 2002. A beautiful interpretation of the Aristotelian mimesis is in Ricœur 1983, 66-104.

5 But see Genette 2007, 166: "Du point de vue purement analytique qui est le nôtre, il faut ajouter (ce que l'argumentation de Booth ne manque pas de faire apparaître au passage) que la notion même du 'showing,' comme celle d'imitation ou

that Lodovico Castelvetro in his 1570 commentary on Aristotle's *Poetics* asserts that painting, like poetry, can operate in both a "narrative" (*narrativo*) and a "representative" (*rappresentativo*) mode. That is, "showing" is not the only modality of a pictorial narrative:

> And yet, without abandoning the example of painting, Aristotle in a sense might have expounded this point through a better similitude, by saying: because poetry avails itself of two modes of representing a possible action—that is, through words and things or only through words—of which one resembles the represented thing more and the other less, (…) in this sense, one can demonstrate painting's conformity, as painting may represent the variety of colored things through a variety of colors, or may represent the variety of colored things not through a variety of colors, but through chiaroscuro, which I said ancient Greeks called μονόχρωμα [*monochrome*]. This second mode of coloring is similar to that of narrative poetry, which uses but words in representing things and words, and the first mode of coloring is similar to that of the representative poetry, which employs words in place of words and things in place of things.[6]

In emending Aristotle's simile, Castelvetro refers to a passage in the *Poetics* in which the representative mode is assimilated to painting and the narrative to sculpture in the round, thereby implying that painting was by definition the art of non-mediate mimesis. Through the example of the monochrome, Castelvetro not only redefines Aristotle's doctrine, but uncovers and emphasizes the codified nature of painting: in a representation, even the usage of colors becomes a mimetic cipher, or a pictorial sign. Once again, "showing" is by no means a synonym of "reproducing" or "mirroring" reality. To understand fully Castelvetro's point of view, one can compare black-and-white movies to color ones. Would one affirm that color movies "show" the essence and significance of a narrative better than the old black-and-whites? To be sure, color may increase the movie's effect of adherence to the spectator's visual reality, but this phenomenon does not transform color movies into candid shots of reality as opposed to the "fictiveness" of black and white films. Nevertheless, as ingeniously brilliant as it is, Castelvetro's statement that, in painting, monochromes are the equivalent of the "telling mode" of representation on account of their lack of colors indicates that, to a certain extent, he is still caught up in the conviction that "showing" is closer to reality—that is, the world of referents to which narratives allude—than "telling." But the grounds of this assessment are unsubstantiated. Whether a dialogue between two or more characters in a novel or the representation of a theatrical piece, the dialogical narrative also depends on a codified language (whether oral, verbal or corporal) that, on account of its codification, necessarily issues into fiction. However true to life the speech, attitude, and expression of an actor may appear, even as they obey a script they become codes of expression, as fictive as the narrator's indirect account of a story. I emphasize this fact since some forms of dialogical narratives relying

---

de représentation narrative (et davantage encore, à cause de son caractère naïvement visuel) est parfaitement illusoire: contrairement à la représentation dramatique, aucun récit ne peut 'montrer' ou 'imiter' l'histoire qu'il raconte. Il ne peut que la raconter de façon détaillée, 'vivante,' et donner par là plus ou moins l'*illusion de mimésis* qui est la seule mimésis narrative, pour cette raison unique et suffisante que la narration, orale et écrite, est un fait de langage, et que le langage signifie sans imiter." Although I entirely agree with Genette's remark, I believe that he "misinterprets" or "misuses" the terms *imitate* and *imitation*. Even if drama imitates "reality," this imitation, as I will explain soon in the text, corresponds to a "language," albeit a visual one, and therefore does not connote as sheer reproduction.

6 Castelvetro, 1:29: "E pure poteva Aristotele, non si partendo dall'essempio della pittura, mostrare in certo modo questo modo con cosa più simile, e dire così: poiché la poesia usa due modi in rappresentare l'azzione possibile, cioè parole e cose o parole sole, l'uno de' quali modi è più simile alla cosa rappresentata e l'altro meno (…), si può in ciò mostrare la conformità nella pittura, la quale rappresenta con varietà di colori la varietà delle cose colorate, o rappresenta pur la varietà delle cose colorate non con varietà di colori ma con lo chiaro e lo scuro, che dicemmo chiamarsi appo i greci μονόχρωμα. E questo secondo modo di colorare è simile al modo della poesia narrativo, che non usa se non parole in rappresentare parole e cose; e quel primo modo di colorare è simile al modo della poesia rappresentativo, che usa parole in luogo di parole e cose in luogo di cose."

95

on imitation do not actually reproduce standard—that is, everyday—attitudes and gestures: ancient Greek comedy and tragedy—on which Aristotle based his conception of mimesis—resort to dancing and mimicry, besides using a poetic language that—according to Roman Jakobson and Russian structuralism[7]—because of its extraneousness to normative language is far from being "reproductive" of reality. Secondly, the distinction between "showing" and "telling" may—and often does—imply that dialogical forms of narrative lack authorial voice. In this light, the events performed by characters would appear to take place independently from an author's viewpoint, whereas those related by a narrator—whether in the first or the third person—would be filtered through a stricter authorial focus. Technically speaking, this assessment might sound pertinent and valid. Theoretically, it is preposterous on several counts. Is it necessary to recall that the figure of the narrator not only differs from that of the author, but that it is as fictitious a character as any other featured in a narrative? The "I" or "he" or "she" who tells a story must of course be distinguished from the other actors insofar as "it"—the figure of the narrator—carries within itself the specific, sometimes omnipresent lens through which the story is perceived and processed by the audience.[8] That the narrator is a "multiple entity" was already evident to Lodovico Castelvetro, who in his commentary on Aristotle's *Poetics* makes a very clear distinction:

> I am not quite sure whether Aristotle is of the opinion that has ordinarily prevailed in men's minds, which is that there are three modes [of representation]: the narrative, which operates δι'ἀπαγγελίας [through a messenger's speech]; the representative, which is enacted δραματικῶς [theatrically]; and a third one that is mixed and composed of the other two (…); unless Aristotle instead believes that there are two modes, the narrative and the representative, the narrative being nonetheless divided into two [sub-modes]: the full narrative and the simple [*scemo*] narrative. I define the full narrative mode as the one in which the speaker speaks on his behalf or [by impersonating] someone else—since it is possible for anyone to do so without muting one's own persona—and the simple narrative mode the one in which one speaks on behalf of oneself: which seems to me likelier and comes closer to the truth.[9]

In mentioning the Greek poet Homer, who either narrates the events of his *Iliad* or impersonates some of its characters by recounting their vicissitudes in the first person, Castelvetro certainly intuits the fictive nature of the narrator figure and his ambiguous relation to the author. In the reader's mind, the passage from the narrating author to the narrating character occurs almost naturally, insofar as neither the narrator nor the actor loses his own identity: that is, his fictive identity. In other words, one would not mistake Hector for Homer when the latter speaks in the first person, although it is self-evident to the reader that Hector's voice is an extension of Homer's. Be that as it may, the narrator's absence from a dialogical form of narrative does not render the story less authorial. It is not difficult to bear this assumption out. A dialogue, an act of a comedy or a tragedy, or the cut of a movie does not produce itself *ex nihilo* or by dint of parthenogenesis: as

---

7   See for instance Jakobson 1990.

8   For the concept of narrator and narrative foci, see Booth 1961, 169-209; Branigan 1992, 100-7; Bal 1997, 19-31, 142-61; Gaudreault 1999, 81-108; and, though only in regard to Marcel Proust, the excellent Genette 2007, 163-218 [*mode*], 219-74 [*voix*].

9   Castelvetro, 1:72: "Io non so ben certo se Aristotele abbia quella opinione che communemente ha occupate le menti di tutti gli uomini, cioè che tre sieno i modi: l'uno narrativo, che si fa δι'ἀπαγγελίας, e l'altro rappresentativo, che si fa

δραματικῶς, e 'l terzo mescolato e composto dell'uno e dell'altro, (…), o se pure abbia opinione che non sieno se non due modi, l'uno narrativo e l'altro rappresentativo, ma che il narrativo si divida in due, cioè nel narrativo pieno e nel narrativo scemo. Io chiamo modo narrativo pieno quello per lo quale il parlatore parla in sua persona e in persona altrui, percioché altri può fare l'una cosa e l'altra senza trasformare la sua persona, e modo narrativo scemo per lo quale altri parla in sua persona sola: il che mi pare assai più verosimile e s'accosta più alla verità."

artworks, they are compositional structures created by an author or a centralized group of authors, be it playwrights, novelists, or movie directors with their staff. Therefore, narratives originally and inherently contain an authorial focus. Whatever one sees or hears or reads in a dialogue, in a theatrical piece or in a movie sequence, is not raw matter of an account, shapeless and polycentric—that is, non-mediated by a comprehensive viewpoint—but the refined and formalized product of a story's artistic crafting and remastering. The artwork's unity results from a concerted intention or in a minority of cases from a compromise between conflicting views on the authors' part. The author is already within the narrative, regardless of the form under which the story is staged. Needless to say, the author can duplicate him- or herself into the narrator, using his or her fictive avatar for whatever purpose he or she fancies: mostly, to create a direct link to the audience or to graduate the effects of fictiveness. At any rate, the fictitious essence of a narrative—any narrative—remains intact.

Obviously these arguments will greatly influence the interpretation of pictorial narrative that I am about to delineate. In the first place, I contend that, once one has rid oneself of the fallacious distinction between "showing" and "telling," it becomes evident that the *istoria*, no more than the diegesis and on the same basis as the dialogical narrative, incorporates an authorial focus: the painter visualizes the story in a way that signifies his or her take on it: it is the product of his invention, regardless of the account's authorship; I will explain this shortly. Like the reader or the spectator, the beholder enters the pictorial narrative through the author's lens: the beholder sees through the painter's eyes. One could object that, by annulling the difference between "showing" and "telling," I disregard a crucial fact: pictorial narratives do not have the equivalent of the narrator—that is, the privileged character that interposes him- or herself between the author and the spectator, showing the story re-enacted with his or her own words—as opposed to the author. Of course, this is not entirely correct, as I will demonstrate shortly. More important, the fact that pictorial narrative very often presents itself as the visual transposition of the author's unique viewpoint does not rule out the possibility for the artist to create and arrange multiple narrative foci. In fact, the early modern *istoria* envisions, and avails itself of, devices of focalization through which the viewer is induced into mentally reconfiguring the narrative from the viewpoint of a designated feature, in principle—but not exclusively—the story's hero or heroine. It comes as little surprise that early modern art theorists were intimately, albeit unknowingly, acquainted with the notion of narrative focus. In his 1584 *Trattato dell'arte della pittura*, Giovan Paolo Lomazzo compares the story's main character to the point in geometry: it is "the principal cause and the principal subject from which all the other parts stem." For this reason, "the main figures must be placed in the middle and all the other parts must be placed around them."[10] Giovan Battista Armenini, in his 1586 *De' veri precetti della pittura*, strongly recommends that the main figure literally shine above the others, which in turn should gradually fade into darkness as they distance themselves from the center of the action:

> Therefore, the main figures should be composed with colors that are naturally more beautiful, attractive and brighter, these [figures] being of more importance than the others for they practically serve as the ground [*campo*] for the entire work (…), and since

10 Lomazzo, 2:246-7: "Conviene principalmente avvertire al punto dal quale derivano tutte le linee, che vanno dai suoi luochi della circonferenza; sì come nel triangolo, nel quadrato, nel circolo ed in tutte le altre forme. Ed il punto propriamente è la figura principale che si pone in mezzo delle sopradette forme. Adunque egli si vuole rappresentare solo in una figura che sia in sé ritirata. Ed in una linea che ha due punti nelle sue estremità, le figure postevi sopra vogliono guardarsi l'una verso l'altra terminando nel punto che è in mezzo. Nel triangolo, che ha tre parte, le figure poste sopra ciascuna d'esse parti hanno da guardare parimente al punto, così nel quadrato che ha quattro canti, così finalmente nel circolo, quante figure si gli vogliono fare d'intorno, tutte hanno da riguardare al punto, sì come a causa principale e principal sogetto dal quale derivano tutte le altri parti. Adunque, le principali figure vogliono essere collocate nel mezzo e tutte le altre parti vogliono essere collocate intorno."

it is necessary to make the other figures on their sides of a lesser size, in accordance with the configuration of the pictorial plane, they [also] ought to lose their colors and dim little by little.[11]

It is noteworthy that Armenini here uses the technical term *campo* that usually denotes the background against which a figure is viewed: in this case, though, it is the figure that acts as a foil for the story by reverberating its sense upon the other actors in a condensed yet paradigmatic manner. Later, according to Charles Le Brun, Nicolas Poussin would compare the story's main figure to a glowing torch, radiating its luminosity over the adjacent figures—which accordingly will gleam by refraction—until its brightness ceases to reach the remotest sections of the canvas. In my opinion, the principle of the "burning torch" is a metaphor by which Poussin refers to the narrative focus in the *istoria*.[12] Hence, by directing the gaze to the story's hero or heroine, the painter employs a technical device whose function resembles that of the narrator: it invites the viewer to approach the narrative from a definite angle. Unlike the narrator—and this should be also highlighted—the technique of visual focalization is exactly that: a technique, and certainly not a feature with its own autonomy, at times almost analogous to the author. Apart from this, the pictorial focus in the *istoria*, as compelling and effective as it may be, does not "coerce" the beholder into entering the narrative solely through the main figure—or through whatever figure is given visual prominence by the artist. Put otherwise, readers of a novel or spectators of a narrative movie are generally forced to follow an order in accessing the story. Although the narrative foci can change in the course of the action, the sequence of these variations is predetermined and unlikely to be altered by readers or spectators—unless one jumps to a chapter or fast-forwards to the next scene, which not surprisingly would compromise the comprehension of the narrative. In the *istoria*, by contrast, beholders can start from a secondary actor or group (a minor narrative focus) or a detail, by restoring the action's unfolding in whatever sequence they choose to follow. Nonetheless, painters see to it that the viewer's gaze is guided toward reconstructing the narrative in its pre-ordained configuration. By order and sequence, I thus mean two different things: there is the order and sequence of an event as configured by the author—and these are not modifiable—and the order and sequence through which readers, spectators or beholders experience the story—and these are variable in the "browsing" of the *istoria*.[13] However, it must be clear that this variability, which is specific to the experience of pictorial narrative, does not vitiate the order and sequence fixed by the painter in the composition.

If the narrative focus of the *istoria* cannot be wholly assimilated to the figure and function of the narrator, what is the objection to attenuating or even abandoning the distinction between "telling" and "showing"? A discussion of this theoretical differentiation is significant for many reasons. I have already elucidated the principal reason, while demonstrating that the indirect narration (or diegesis) is not closer to reality as evoked through imitation than the dialogical or direct one. For

11 Armenini, 162: "Così quei colori si pongano nelle principali figure, i quali siano di sua natura più belli, più vaghi e più vivaci, per essere queste di maggior considerazione tra l'altre, perché servono quasi come per campo dell'opera, le quali bisogna che siano lavorate di color più chiari (…) perciò che, dovendosi far l'altre che gli sono appresso di minor statura, secondo che porge l'ordine del piano, quelle debbono a poco a poco perdere di colore ed oscurarsi."

12 Nivelon, 120: "Car un jour dans Rome, quelques particuliers conversant avec lui le prièrent de lui enseigner une règle sûre et dont on pût se servir pour rendre le héros d'un sujet considérable, tel qu'un très vaillant homme, les armes à la main, au milieu d'autres vaillants hommes combattants. Il leur enseigna ce moyen par la comparaison d'un flambeau allumé à vue d'une distance raisonnablement eloignée pour juger des couleurs, formant une masse blanchâtre mêlée d'une rougeur tendre et dorée tirant sur la chair, cette masse, environnée d'un jaune doré, mariée à l'entour d'un violet tendre participant dans sa circonférence d'un rouge dégradant en brun, se mariant insensiblement aux ténèbres, passant ainsi de ce centre lumineux à ce qui lui est le plus opposé."

13 For the concept of order in narrative, see Branigan 1992, 39-44; Bal 1997, 80-99; Genette 2007, 21-80.

now I will add that the narrative focus conveyed through the *istoria*'s main figure might introduce a point of view seemingly at odds with the author's. Imbued by the aesthetics of the congruous and the harmonious, Armenini and Lomazzo claim that the principal character should stay in the center, brilliantly displayed in order to catch the beholder's eye: its centrality also makes it the focus of the painter's visual field. But the central position of the story's hero or heroine is neither a dogma nor a requisite. Rather, it is a recommended option, for late sixteenth- and early seventeenth-century artists usually disliked any restrictive or excessive symmetry in their compositions. In some cases, painters emphasize a decentered figure, that is, a figure at a certain distance from the composition's median axis, and therefore from the beholder's standpoint. Since the beholder is assumed to see through the author's eyes, it follows that decentered figures can create the impression of a narrative focus alternative to the author's and the viewer's. Also, artists can imagine concomitant or complementary foci of narration, or through secondary characters or groups, intersperse the action with minor narrative foci. Leon Battista Alberti even requires that an intermediate character clarify or enhance the meaning of the *istoria* represented:

> Therefore I like the fact that in the *istoria* somebody leads beholders into what is happening, and either beckons them with his hand to look, or pretends that there is a secret dealing by warning them with a ferocious expression and threatening eyes not to come closer, or points to some danger or some other thing worth admiring, or incites you with his gestures to laugh with him or to lament with him. It is then necessary that all the actions accomplished by the characters depicted either in relation with the viewers or among themselves concur to enact and explain the *istoria*.[14]

Properly speaking, Alberti's "commentator" roughly corresponds to the figure of the narrator, for he or she generates an intermediate narrative focus through which viewers are clued and introduced into the story. I say roughly, because this character is not fully developed in early modern painting, so it does not attain the status of a quasi-authorial focus. More often than not, the pictorial "commentator" in fact lacks the roundness and completeness of an independent character, and therefore acts especially as a vector of emphasis in the story. To be sure, this phenomenon is understandable if one considers that the instant of vision specific to the *istoria* brings about formal restrictions that the long-term span of a novel, a play or a narrative movie can easily bypass: painters indeed have less latitude to transform the "commentator" into the equivalent of the narrator. Yet, on a hypothetical level, the "commentator" has the potential to evolve beyond his or her role as action-monger, by participating in the story without being a satellite of some other character, and by distinguishing him- or herself through his or her awareness of the viewer's gaze. Accordingly, his or her depiction in the *istoria* fulfills a meta-pictorial function. In any event, the "commentator" is only one of the possibilities painters have at their disposal to engender meta-pictorial effects or foster the notion of self-referentiality in the *istoria*. In the composition, in fact, the painter cannot only represent himself as a walk-on, an onlooker or a pictorial "commentator," but he may also portray himself—or for that matter, any other artist—as a figure playing out a role in the pictorial narrative. I stress this point since, as I will show in Chapters 10 and 12, Caravaggio

---

14   Alberti, 72-5: "E piacemi sia nella storia chi ammonisca e insegni a noi quello che ivi si facci, o chiami con la mano a vedere, o con viso cruccioso e con gli occhi turbati minacci che niuno verso loro vada, o dimostri qualche pericolo o cosa ivi maravigliosa, o te inviti a piagnere con loro insieme o a ridere. E così qualunque cosa fra loro o teco facciano i dipinti, tutto appartenga a ornare o a insegnarti la storia. [Tum placet in historia adesse quempiam qui earum quae gerantur rerum spectatores admoneat, aut manu ad visendum advocet, aut quasi id negotium secretum esse velit, vultu ne eo proficiscare truci et torvis oculis minitetur, aut periculum remve aliquam illic admirandam demonstret, aut ut una adrideas aut ut simul deplores suis te gestibus invitet. Denique et quae illi cum spectantibus et quae inter se picti exequentur, omnia ad agendam et docendam historiam congruant necesse est.]"

deeply innovated the role of the "commentator" and expanded the scope of the self-referential portrait in the *istoria*. Even more frequently, he dislocated the narrative foci of the pictorial story to an extent that no other master had previously attempted.

The final reason why I am inclined to downplay the importance of the distinction between "telling" and "showing" is a cultural one. Art historians tend to appreciate, evaluate, and judge pictorial narratives as mere translations of written texts or sources; the analysis of an *istoria* not rarely begins with texts and finishes with other texts: the ones we write to express our appraisal and interpretation of the picture or sculpture. There is certainly no other way for interpreters to make a critical discourse on artworks: we all are destined, fortunately perhaps, ultimately to put our thoughts into a verbal statement. However, we can also stop examining early modern artworks as visual appendixes of writing. I do not deny that early modern art theorists insist that artists, before creating, peruse and ponder written texts: all of these authors claim that pictorial invention is a matter of "reading." But this obsession with literacy—comprehensible among artists who struggle to have their intellectual status recognized as the equivalent of poets—should not lead us to forget that the account to be visualized—that is, the subject matter—is not necessarily a literary one. I do not allude here to allegory and other pictorial conceits and *capricci* that by definition are the painter's work. I mean rather that the sources of an *istoria*—its raw material, so to speak—first and foremost hark back to the pictorial tradition itself. More to the point, artists elaborate upon other artists' inventions in visualizing an *istoria*. As I will argue in the course of this volume, many religious stories are transmitted by scripture in terms too vague to permit the visualization of complex narratives in accordance with the criteria of variety and intelligibility. The pictorial tradition, instead, supplies painters with a repertoire of motifs, visual patterns, formulas, and schemes from which they initially learn to draw and invent, and which later offer templates of narration to be followed, interpreted, challenged or disregarded. Being familiar with Panofsky's hermeneutics, art historians mostly overlook the fact that iconography not only revolves around conceptual or cultural meanings; it should deal especially with the conventions of a non-verbal language, the language of images. As philologists and scholars of literature ground their textual analysis on words and their transmission along and down the paths of literary tradition, so too should art historians recognize the paramount importance of visual matrices in the genesis and structure of images without being blamed for witch-hunting visual sources. For the sake of concision, I will limit myself to the specific case of single figures. It is evident that gestures, expressions, attitudes, and postures form a visual lexicon in which narrative functions are deeply embedded. By modifying them, painters consequently decode and encode segments of action: that is, they decode visual signifiers provided by the canonical tradition and stored in their memory through copying and imitating; and they arrange these signifiers in a novel configuration, an encryption that both viewers and artists are able to decipher and comprehend. This particular form of pictorial elaboration represents the core of invention, and it was understood as such by early modern art theorists. I quote Armenini, in which the most obvious, albeit implicit, formulation of this practice is to be found:

> Through ever so slight variations of some limbs, one takes away much pristine configuration from any figure; by reversing it, or changing the head a little bit or lifting an arm, suppressing a drapery or putting one in a different way or somewhere else, or even by reversing the drawing (…) or simply by imagining it in full relief, the figure seems not to be the same, so that if one well considers these modifications, [one will understand] in how many and diverse manners it is possible to vary a single act of a single figure.[15]

15 Armenini, 95: "Conciosiacosaché qualunque figura, per poca mutazione d'alcuni membri, si leva assai della sua prima forma, perciò che, col rivoltarle o con mutarli un poco la testa o alzarli un braccio, torli via un panno o giungerne in altra parte

Lest Armenini's passage be misunderstood, it is appropriate to recall its context. After sorting out the various techniques used by artists to spark invention, Armenini turns to those ill-talented painters who are barely able to create new compositions. Rather than condemning them, Armenini illustrates a convenient practice to invent the *istoria* by appropriating other masters' ideas: a mechanism of selection and re-combination that, on a smaller scale and in a mechanistic manner, imitates the creative process of skilled artists without attaining their degree of novelty and congruence. Varying figures therefore entails not only simple adjustments to new narrative contexts, but sometimes also manipulations of temporal aspects implicit in visual formulas and schemes. I would like to highlight this point because through such vectors of temporality artists can generate visual prolepses and analepses—flashbacks and flash-forwards—that are commonly considered impossible or unlikely to render in painting or sculpture. As I have already explained, Caravaggio's Virgin in the Nancy *Annunciation* is a good example of this practice, and many other similar or more elaborate cases will be dealt with in the course of this monograph.

Evidently artists, unlike novelists or movie directors, are unable to create chronological correspondences—reiterative actions and temporalities destined to punctuate the evolution of characters or events—within the *istoria*, unless the latter unfolds over several compositions, as might be the case in a pictorial cycle. However, one cannot rule out the possibility of painters reiterating narrative situations by alluding to specific facts and figures treated in former pictures, even when their subject matter differs from the one represented in the latter painting. More particularly, I refer here to what I would define as the work's "internal eye" or "internal memory": visual self-referential connections pointing back to the author's previous inventions.[16] These self-references do not necessarily take on a narrative validity, but some do, and therefore convey notions of temporality in a twofold manner. First of all, they reveal the artist's developments over time. Secondly, as they are vectors of action, their parallelism across the artist's oeuvre sparks a dialectical tension of narrative temporalities. I insist on this point since Caravaggio's late production is densely interspersed with visual reiterations. They bespeak the master's persistent reflection on certain themes as deepened and revisited by his memory. As a consequence, by hinting at narrative contexts of the past, these self-references carry with them, sometimes in a conflicting way, temporal values and implications that load the *istoria* developed in the present with multiple resonances. I will expand on Caravaggio's telescopic concordances in Part Five. For the time being, let me underline one more time that the introduction of proleptic and analeptic effects—an ordinary device through which authors refashion a story's chronological order—is but one of the innumerable strategies artists can adopt in configuring a narrative with originality.

The concept of originality, so essential in early modern discourses on the *istoria*, must be interpreted in a more radical way.[17] In fact, the pre-existing subject matter on which artists usually draw in imagining a pictorial narrative literally dissolves into a sort of blank slate during the creative process. In other terms, the acts of ideating and inventing retransform the account into raw matter, a nebula of narrative motifs in abeyance awaiting the artist's tentative touch to regain form. Although for early modern theorists originality resides solely in the invention—and not in

---

o in altro modo, o rivoltar quel dissegno overo ungerlo per minor fatica o pur con l'imaginarselo che sia di tondo rilievo, pare che non sia più quello, che considerando bene così fatte mutazioni con quali e con quanti modi di una sol figura un solo atto variar si possa." Deliberately, I have not translated the phrase "ungerlo per minor fatica" in the text. In his life of Domenichino, Malvasia, 2:340, relates that the master used to draw the portrait of his sister-in-law, remarkable for her beauty, "on sheets of oiled paper." I have not found any explanation of this technique, but I imagine that the paper was steeped in oil to make it transparent. In this manner, it could be used to make the impression of figures and motifs from other drawings, canvases or prints. By the same token, by working directly on an oiled paper, the artist could transfer his drawing onto some other surface and medium.

16　For this concept, see the groundbreaking monograph of Conte 1974.

17　For the concept of novelty, see in particular Cropper 2005.

the re-appropriation—of a story, they are all familiar with the dissolution process through which pictorial narratives are brought to life. Consider Armenini's assessment in this connection:

> After hearing or reading the argument of the matter, one must reflect well with one's own mind and soul upon what exactly one intends to represent and which means are more appropriate and apt to express it with greatest truth and in accordance with the text's articulation and meaning. In this way, upon long imagining, one comes to form and visualize many parts of that [subject] and easily sets about sketching with a stylus or pen whatever the mind has conceived at its best, until one finally achieves the whole composition, or story, or whatever other matter.[18]

According to Armenini, it is not humanly possible to create a composition all at once:

> The intellect that dwells in our mind and produces inventions avails itself of different ways to find them [these inventions], for because of its natural imperfection it is always unable fully to form the entire composition; one thus must try the matter out several times, I mean now one part, now two, now the whole thing, depending on its extension and specificity, and this occurs in the frenzy of ideating and is forthwith expressed in the form of a blotch, which we call a sketch or draft, so that one sketches diverse attitudes of figures or other things very quickly, as they come to mind confusedly, and in this [artists] resemble poets who, meditating on their improvisations, modify them variously, or suppress them totally or partially, and they hone them until they become unparalleled on account of their beauty and perfection.[19]

To begin, let us uncover an oversimplification in Armenini's take on the process of invention. The ideation of a pictorial narrative cannot be reduced to a sheer translation from the literary to the visual. Even in the case that artists elaborate upon a single text—say, the account of the Annunciation as related by Luke—the act of visualization both exceeds and disfigures the original script. To prove this assumption, suffice it to note that pictorial invention sets facts and action into continuous motion. Supposing that artists limit themselves to the story's letter, and do not interpolate anything alien to it—which nevertheless seldom occurs—the continuity of the imaginative flow automatically fills in gaps and breaks in the literary text, however detailed the latter might be. If the literary source offers scarce graphic data—which is often the case—the expansion and enrichment of the narration grows exponentially. Moreover, on a practical level, the visualization of a story systematically involves the mediation of visual sources. The very method of composition espoused by Armenini demands that artists heed the pictorial tradition by borrowing from it as many elements as possible in a view of elaboration. Images thus serve as catalysts for the

18 Armenini, 89: "Il quale sarà che prima ciascun ben consideri con la mente e con l'animo, udito o letto ch'egli avrà il trattato di quella materia, cioè che cosa sia quella ch'egli ha in animo di rappresentare apunto e qual sia l'effetto più vero, più proprio e più atto a esprimere, secondo che n'addita il discorso ed il lume della scrittura predetta, di modo che, imaginando lungamente, si venga a formar nell'idea più parti di quella ed indi poi leggermente si disponga, sì che con lo stile o con la penna si accenni tutto ciò che si ha conceputo nell'animo con quel miglior modo che per esso si puote, finché si arrivi al fine di tutto l'intiero componimento, o sia istoria o altro che dir vogliamo."

19 Ibidem, 89-90: "Conciosiacosaché quello intelletto, che alberga nell'animo nostro e che crea l'invenzioni, usa diversi modi a trovarle, attesoché per la sua naturale imperfezzione mal può formar sempre il componimento di quelle apieno, e perciò gli è forza che la materia si esprima in più volte, io dico quando una parte e quando due over tutta ancora, secondo le qualità e grandezza sua, e ciò si vien facendo sul furor di quel concetto che subito si espone a guisa di macchia, che da noi schizzo o bozza si dice; conciosiacosaché si accenna diverse attitudini di figure e di altre materie in un tempo brevissimo, secondo che confusamente ne soviene, accadendo ad essi sì come a' buoni poeti accade nelle sue composizioni improvise, alle quali dipoi, più volte discorrendovi sopra con diverse mutazioni, o tutto o parte ne rimovono, e così da loro si limano che come incomparabili restano e di perfezzione e di bellezza insieme."

visualization of a literary text, and substitute for it whenever this is devoid of graphic definition. In imagining an Annunciation, an artist therefore does not rely uniquely on the Gospel: the pictorial tradition lends figures, attitudes, and motifs to the imagination as prospects of inventions upon which to construct a novel composition. In other terms, the subject matter to which Armenini alludes is a hybrid compound, an amalgam of literary suggestions and visual templates bound to a narrative theme. For this reason, I posited from the outset that the matter of narration is neither literary nor pictorial: it is originally intellectual. Once one admits the veracity of this phenomenon, it becomes evident that in processing the narration and selecting the segment of it more suitable for visualization, artists smash the original aggregate of action, fragmenting its elements in order to dislocate them into new arrangements. This process momentarily annuls the narrative and visual coherence of the story, which is indeed "smudged," that is, obliterated in an apparent chaos of lines, contours, and blots. To create, artists are thus forced to make mincemeat of narrative matter. By doing so, they re-create the story at its core and re-appropriate its authorship.

In reality, the dissolution and re-composition process through which a story transforms itself into an image characterizes the modality of narrative consumption altogether. It is always true, in my opinion, that narratives are inherently volatile: to exist and communicate they need to be consumed, that is, smashed and re-processed by artists as well as by the audience.[20] This becomes even more obvious when one examines the diverse types of temporality that operate in the generation, configuration, and consumption of narratives. Encapsulated in the raw matter of the story to be visualized, time is fleshed out of its original consistency, and then re-ordered into new narratives by artists. In experiencing the painting or sculpture, viewers dissolve, then reconfigure, the temporal layout of the action represented, undoing what artists have provided for them.[21] Although the narrative that beholders reconstitute and forge is heavily indebted to that preordained in the painting or sculpture, it is never a mirror image of it. The beholder's lens in fact reappropriates the story once again: it now inheres in his or her personal experience, and therefore it is subjectified through it. It ensues that the perception and recollection of the pictorial narrative's fictive temporality also evolve over time. Even after the direct experience of the artwork is finished, viewers can return to the image—whatever their memory has preserved of it—and reassess its temporal layout and meaning. I do not believe it is heresy to sustain that in many cases our recollection of an artwork proves inaccurate once we manage to re-observe the painting or sculpture from which it stemmed. Nonetheless, despite the risk of inaccuracy, our mind does not stop reflecting and interpreting the story in the artwork's absence. At that point, the story indeed belongs in, and is nourished by, our subjectivity. By this, I do not imply that any exegesis of an artwork is necessarily subjective. I rather argue that, at times unbeknownst to us, stories—whether they be visual or otherwise—persist in and mutate with us, merging into the many others that we have stored in our memory or continue to experience; they pile up as sources of available knowledge and meaning, and on this basis modify our perception of other narratives. The art historian's task, in my opinion, consists in taking a step away from his or her unavoidable subjectivity: to discern whatever artists destined in their pictorial narratives to be matters of reflection for the historical collectivity with which they interacted.

As for the question of temporality, it must be clear by now that, aside from the physical manifestation of time, there is also a fictive time. This in turn is tripartite: there is the time of the account-source: prefigured time; that re-arranged by artists in their artworks: configured time; and that de-constructed and re-constructed by viewers: re-configured time. This is exactly the distinction of fictive temporalities masterfully established by Paul Ricœur in his monumental

---

20   For the concept of reception, see in particular Jauss 1982; and Eco 1979.

21   In this regard, see in particular the definition of "triple mimesis" as developed by Ricœur 1983, 105-62.

1983 *Temps et récit*. Needless to say, Ricœur does not investigate pictorial artworks at all, and his analysis concentrates on the twofold domain of history writing and novels. Also, I must add that re-configured time is of two sorts: that of the artwork's perception—the process through which beholders restore and put to the test the temporal layout of a story in the artwork's presence and during its experience—and that of the recollection of the artwork—the process through which beholders recall and make sense of the story in the artwork's absence. Because of the specific nature of narrative, temporality is strongly linked to spatiality, causality, and eventually to meaning. Hence, de-constructing, re-ordering, restoring, and recalling the story's temporal structure are basic and general acts of, and attempts at, interpretation.

At this point, an ineludible question arises: how do artists orient the beholder's gaze and mind toward the composition's structural and chronological axes? What pushes viewers to follow determinate itineraries in the perception and experience of a pictorial narrative? As I have already determined, the order and sequence through which a novel or a movie are perceived and experienced cannot be modified or, if so, only to the detriment of comprehension. Artists are compelled instead to ideate and trace a network of accesses and routes for viewers in order to ensure the story's understanding. Thanks to this orientation system, beholders manage to rediscover pre-ordained paths of temporality. As banal as it may appear, geometry plays an eminent role in this regard.[22]

In his *c.1679 Verità Pittoresca*, the painter Giovan Battista Volpato distinguishes two different methods of structuring an invention: natural and artificial. Whereas Volpato does not actually shed light on the natural method of invention, claiming merely that it was specific to Albrecht Dürer, Lucas van Leyden, Mantegna, Raphael, Giulio Romano, and Michelangelo, he discusses at length the artificial method practiced by Tintoretto, Barocci, Taddeo and Federico Zuccari, Veronese, Bassano, and Titian. According to Volpato, this method is indeed much simpler to be learned and adopted by young painters since it only includes three patterns of disposition: "triangular, circular and square."[23] For instance, in Bassano's *Nativities*, figures are disposed on the surface within "two triangles intersecting one another," yet, when looked at with regard to their common plane, they form a circular pattern. In Volpato's opinion, the same applies to the "central group" of Tintoretto's *Crucifixion* at the Scuola Grande di San Rocco, Venice.[24] Volpato moreover seems to believe that alignments underpin geometrical patterns regardless of these being triangular, circular or square. Consequently, in whichever of these configurations, "two, three or four heads, in accordance with the circumstance" will be aligned to each other, as showed by Agostino Carracci's print of Veronese's *Mystic Marriage of Saint Catherine*.[25] However, "[an] infinite [number of] examples" of this practice can be seen in Tintoretto, Barocci, and the Zuccari brothers. More interesting, Volpato apparently extends the principle of figurative alignments to "hands, feet or other [parts] which engender the most beautiful harmony by pleasing the eye with a well-disposed and adjusted proportion."[26]

22　Albeit specifically focused on perspective, Kemp 1990, esp. 9-162, demonstrates the importance of geometry as a principle of composition in early modern painting.

23　Bordignon Favero 1994, 408: "E questo componimento artificiale è di gran lunga più facile del primo, perché riduce l'inventioni sotto tre figure, cioè triangolare, circolare e quadrata."

24　Ibidem: "Come chiaramente si può vedere nelle natività del Bassano, che superficialmente esprime doi triangoli intersecati tra di loro, e nel piano è costituita in dispositione circolare, come anco si vede nel groppo di mezzo nelle figure della passione di Tintoretto (...)." For Tintoretto's most famous *Crucifixion* at the Scuola Grande di San Rocco, see Pallucchini and Rossi 1982, 1:189-90, no. 283. Volpato's intimate

knowledge of this composition seems to rely on Agostino Carracci's engraving that reproduces it. See DeGrazia 1979, 254-5, no. 147.

25　For Agostino's print, see DeGrazia 1979, 202, no. 104. For Veronese's painting, see Pignatti and Pedrocco 1995, 2:329-30, no. 203.

26　Bordignon Favero 1994, 408: "Quest'artificio poi è regolato tanto dall'universale, essendo così disposto in tutto, come dal particolare, incontrando sempre a retta linea doi, tre o quattro teste secondo porta l'accidente, e di ciò ne dà l'essempio lo Sposalitio di Santa Caterina di Paulo tagliato dai Carazzi, e l'istesso groppo di sopra accenato del Tintoretto, con altri infiniti essempi così del Barotio, Zucari, Carazzi et molti oltramontani, et in mancanza di quelle altra

Immediately afterward, Volpato explains how to interweave figures: they must dovetail with each other like the insets of an inlay, as exemplified by Tintoretto's *Massacre of the Innocents* at the Scuola Grande di San Rocco, Venice.[27] Noteworthy in this respect, in Volpato's view, is Bassano's method: in his paintings, "if one figure comes forward, another goes backward; if one appears to the left, the other will show to the right; if one has his or her back turned, the other will be frontal."[28]

In spite of Volpato's coarse prose and precarious syntax, it can be assumed that these kinds of symmetries stretch beyond the interconnections between two figures; they likewise govern the ways in which groups are reciprocally interrelated and movements intercept one another. Since most of the artists ranking in the second category are either Venetians or chronologically closer to Volpato, it appears that the artificial method of invention qualifies as historically modern, and therefore is endowed with a sort of reified canonicity. Yet Volpato contradicts himself by commending Michelangelo's *figura serpentinata*, which he mentions among the artificial practices, although his inventor is considered a practitioner of the natural method.[29] Of course, I am not concerned here with Volpato's theoretical coherence, but rather with the casuistry of the figurative patterns that he sketches out in his *Verità Pittoresca*. Whether triangular, circular or otherwise, these visual configurations usher beholders into the image, allowing for an analytical perception and reading of it. By the same token, through them narrative foci and their hierarchies are concomitantly visualized. It is superfluous to say that, counter to Volpato's opinion, these geometrical structures hark back well beyond Titian's age. From a conceptual viewpoint, they become universally acknowledged, albeit rarely parsed, strategies of disposition after Alberti's *De pictura* (1435), and it is no coincidence that, along with perspective, these structural devices of pictorial organization are grounded in geometry. When deployed in a story, alignments, symmetries, and figurative patterns act as vectors of directionality: they punctuate temporality, build spatiality, and account for causality. This concept is also applicable to Caravaggio's stories, even if—as remarked upon and persistently criticized by art theorists—these consist of but a few figures or, worse, half-figures. I emphasize this point since I am convinced that Caravaggio's close-ups and tight framings, instead of diminishing the scope and potentiality of geometrical structures, charge the figures' bodies and their parts with an almost magnetic power of attraction and repulsion: in the overcharged field of interrelations represented by actors in his images, even the slightest symmetry or asymmetry, alignment and misalignment, correspondence or discrepancy of members spawn action and significance, and as such they warrant careful analysis. For this reason, bodies absorb, or literally swallow up, the story's essence; through their visual magnification, they morph into forces through which time, space, and meaning interface or conflict with one another. In Caravaggio's painting, bodies therefore ground the *istoria*. This is certainly not true—or not quite to the same degree—of many other painters of Caravaggio's generation.

Returning to Volpato, it is extremely important that geometrical patterns are not only integral to the story's order or arrangement; they also inflect modes of narration, modulate narrative momentum and ultimately incorporate duration. A crucial passage of the *Verità Pittoresca* is particularly relevant in this context:

---

magnitudine rilevante come di mano, piede, o altro quale forma un bellissimo concerto, apagando l'occhio d'una ben disposta et agiustata magnitudine."

27 For Tintoretto's *Massacre of the Innocents* at the Scuola Grande di San Rocco, see Pallucchini and Rossi 1992, 226, no. 438.

28 Bordignon Favero 1994, 408: "Et osservate che tutte le più belle compositioni sono disposte con questo ordine, e ciò si fa intersiando anco le positure de' corpi, come della stragge dell'Innocenti del Tintoretto ne potette trar l'essempio, e ciò ha usato il Bassano ancora nel suo stille, che se una figura viene avanti, l'altra indietro, e l'una alla destra l'altra alla sinistra, se l'una è in schena, l'altra in faccia, e così le positure e moti intersicati."

29 Ibidem: Queste osservationi sono in oltre li groppi delle figure, in figura triangolare; di tal figura sono anco le figure per sé secondo il preceto di Michiel Angelo, di figura piramidale serpentinata o dritta o rovescia."

Joined with curved lines, acute angles form lively and agile movements, expressed with a certain grace and bizarreness; joined with straight lines, they give rise to violent, impetuous, and fierce motions, as can be seen in Tintoretto. Straight lines convey gravitas and nobility; so too do curves directed backward, as can be seen in Veronese; curves oriented forward [express] sluggishness, humility, and devotion, as in Bassano; on the other hand, curves, not single-handedly but rather in their multiplicity, convey grace, beauty, charm, affection, and devotion, as exemplified by Parmigianino. These principles can be bent to ill use, but he who knows how to practice them will have his task facilitated.[30]

Unfortunately, Volpato's text grows murkier as he follows the many streams of his thoughts. Nonetheless, it is quite evident that he regards lines, curves, and angles as visual markers codified over time by the pictorial tradition, available to artists for variation and elaboration, and malleable enough to grant originality through ingenious and thoughtful selection and combination. Artists therefore—and here Volpato, perhaps unintentionally, echoes Armenini—must use the repertoire of geometrical devices that canonical masters have turned into personal styles, provided that in varying them, appropriateness and congruousness are respected. Also, lines, curves, and angles make up the figures' attitudes and dispositions.

More important, Volpato apparently considers geometric patterns as functional to invention as lighting is. In other words, the axes of orientation by means of which beholders enter and browse through a story are not only structured geometrically, but they are also pre-determined by the chiaroscuro system. Lighting is necessary both to highlight figures, objects, and facts of an action—which I have previously defined as narrative foci—and to connect them to each other. Thus, geometric patterns and lighting ensure the story's articulation and interconnectedness by isolating and linking narrative foci. Not surprisingly, light obeys the same aesthetic principles as lines and curves, so that both the natural and artificial methods of invention are not only rendered "by contours," but also by "shading and lighting." Once again, Volpato divides the art of chiaroscuro in two subtypes, natural and artificial:

...it is quite obvious that under reason's guidance and through nature's example [masters] have determined and expressed their artifices, and you can experience this for yourself while drawing from any relief by candlelight; you'll see that this light brings about the fiercest brightness and shades, sharply contrasting each other, while causing a strong reflection on the opposite side. But if you put a piece of white paper in front of the light, you'll see a completely different way of lighting, producing innumerable half-tones, softer brightness and shades without reflections, and more rounded. Of these two [ways of] lighting, the open [light] one connotes Tintoretto's practice, the shielded [light] one often with interposed paper characterizes Titian's, who brings out the muscles with dark tones without reflections in the parts devoid of light, and this lends more harmony to the whole, whereas the other [practice] proves to be more artificial. If you place a bright reflection opposite to the light produced by a paper or any other white object, you'll obtain more allure, but brightness also gives ever more strength, and what nature does can be used by art. Always heed your inclination (…)

---

30 Ibidem, 408-9: "Gli angoli acuti congionti con le linee curve formano li moti spiritosi, agili, espressi con qualche gratia e bizarria, e con le linee rette congionti danno l'essere a motti violenti, impettuosi e fieri, il che si vede nel Tintoretto; le linee rette danno gravità, nobiltà, ed anco le curve all'indietro, come si vede in Paulo; le curve piegate avanti pigritia, humiltà, devotione, come nel Bassano; le curve poi più tosto moltiplicate che semplice danno gratia, leggiadria, vezzo, affetto e divotione ancora, come da Parmegiano se ne può trar l'essempio, e queste regole si posono retorcere anco in mala parte; ma chi intende il modo di pratticarle rendono facilità, osservando sempre la proprietà de' giesti…"

since in this way you will have more pleasure, but you'd be better off following the bright [practice], by putting for instance the light source in a paper lantern, for one thus creates a threefold disposition, hindering shadows and lights from cutting and opposing one another, and Bassano has been particularly good at this.[31]

By threefold disposition, Volpato specifically refers to a figure deftly composed by shadows and lights imperceptibly separated through half-tones. However, this "triple gradation"—another term coined by the author—must be present everywhere in the *istoria*. Half-tones, indeed, generate soft nuances in the entire composition, and take away "any rawness or barbarism from the whole." Volpato goes as far as to suggest that parts of the figures deprived of light could be rendered with half-tones, including those acute angles of the anatomy that Titian used systematically to color in dark tints, and on which "no brightness is to be seen."[32] In another passage, Volpato seems to imply that Titian pursued this strategy of darkening acute angles by intensifying lighting on the figures' obtuse angles.[33] The same rule applies to drapes, which can be depicted either with angles and straight lines or with curves. Raphael, Michelangelo, and Parmigianino "delicately wrapped the nude" within curvilinear drapes, showing "grace, softness and beauty." In Tintoretto's works, instead, crisp and razor-edged folds, imitating the folding of the limbs, hew to the nude "with bizarre capriciousness," expressing not only the configuration of the drapes, but also that of the muscles.[34] According to Volpato, in fact, angles are specific to musculature, and not to drapes. Although Volpato explicitly endorses stylistic eclecticism, it is clear from his text that only balanced harmony between opposites and appropriateness achieve perfection. Accordingly, any sort of harsh contrast in lighting or excess in devising and opposing geometric patterns are not considered signs of stylistic vigor or "strength," but rather a significant reduction of this quality, as exemplified in Tintoretto's hyperbolic chiaroscuro, which Volpato deems weaker than Titian's color technique.

31 Ibidem, 421: "È cosa chiarissima che con la scorta della ragione ed esempio della natura hanno regolato ed espresso i loro artificii, e di ciò ne potrete da voi stesso far l'esperienza mentre disegnate da qualche rilievo al lume di candela; vedete che detto lume produce lumi ed ombre fiere assai terminate tra di loro, e nella parte oposta produr un evidente riflesso; ma se porrete avanti il lume un pezzo di carta bianca, vedrete un effetto d'allumar tutto diverso, causando assai mezze tinte, lumi ed ombre più soavi prive di riflessi con più tondeggiamento, e di queste due lumi lo scoperto esprime la pratica del Tintoretto, il serrato o con la carta frapposta esprime la pratica del Tiziano, facendo risaltar i muscoli con oscuri senza riflessi nelle parti prive di lume, e questo dà più accordato nel tutto, e l'altro riesce più artificiale, e ponendovi un riflesso chiaro opposto al lume prodotto da carta o altra cosa bianca dà maggior vaghezza, ma il chiaro dona sempre più forza, e ciò che fa la natura si può usare nell'arte. Seguite sempre il genio vostro, come v'ho detto, perché in tal guisa ne prenderete diletto maggiore; ma se potete seguir il chiaro, come posto il lume in un feral di carta, sarà il meglio, per cui si dispone triplicamente, non permettendo che l'ombre e lumi sieno tra di loro terminati o taglienti, ed in ciò è stato artificiosissimo il Bassano."

32 Ibidem: "Mi sovviene ancora un'altra avvertenza circa a questa degradazione di tinte, che non solo si pratica nelle cose particolari, ma nelle universali ancora, disponendo così nelle storie questa triplicata degradazione, che se farà una figura o altra magnitudine chiara ed una oscura, frapporvi una mezza tinta per produrvi soavità in tutto il composto, ché questa disposizione serve per un componimento che leva ogni crudezza e barbarismo nell'accordato, ed in caso che non si

faccia nelle figure frapposto di mezza tinta, s'introduce nelle stesse prive figure, come hanno usato il Bassano ed i Carracci, per la ragione che non può esser veduto chiaro nell'angolo acuto, ché Tiziano se ne esercitò anco particolarmente cercando tutte quelle artificiose acutezze che si potevano penetrare per la forza, in cui è stato il maestro della scuola veneziana."

33 Ibidem, 427: "Gli eccellenti hanno usato aggiustar l'arte con l'arte, come nell'accrescer e diminuir a tempo e luogo le proporzioni nel moto, dar più o meno spirito e grazia, gravità e bizzarria, aggiustando alle volte la natura come il loro ingegno, come nelle costruzioni de' muscoli e disposizione di superficie hanno fatto gli scultori, ed il Goltzio, Muler, Sprangher e simili; nel lume Tiziano, per produr l'effetto desiderato osservando l'angolo acuto nella privazione de' lumi, servendosi solo, come veramente si deve, d'allumar l'angolo ottuso, essendo così il retto come l'acuto incapaci di veduta."

34 Ibidem, 410: "Due son le maniere di far panni; l'una si esprime con linea curva, l'altra con tutti gli angoli e linee rette; (…) quelle di linee curve si veggono nelle opere di Raffaello, Michelangelo, Parmegiano ed altri, che gentilmente circondano il nudo, dimostrano grazia, soavità e leggiadria. Quelli con angoli si veggono nelle opere del Tintoretto, ove formate dalle piegature de' membri, le falde in forma di angoli acuti vanno ricercando il nudo con bizzarro capriccio, ed esprimono non solo la disposizione della superficie, che è il fondamento de' panni nelle figure, ma ancora il più delle volte la costruzion de' muscoli in universale, perché in particolare è solo del nudo, intendo gli angoli più o meno tra di loro."

Along with many other early modern art theorists, Volpato finds artistic excellence in the middle, discouraging artists from tapping into the extremes, and reproving incongruousness, asymmetry, and inappropriateness. Assuredly, Volpato would not have appreciated Caravaggio's painting and, in fact, nowhere in his treatise is the master's name evoked. Caravaggio is no longer a reference point, neither negative nor positive. However, Volpato's theoretical and technical tenets, insofar as they register precepts and practices rooted in the pictorial tradition of Renaissance Venice, from Titian to Bassano, from Tintoretto to Veronese, were assuredly not unfamiliar to Caravaggio. It is often forgotten that Caravaggio's master, Simone Peterzano, was trained in Titian's studio in the late 1560s, and that he was clearly influenced by Veronese, Tintoretto, and Bassano upon his return to Milan.[35] It is quite plausible that discourses on geometrical patterns and dispositions, on lighting and chiaroscuro, were held and exchanged in Venetian workshops, practiced in artworks, and developed by recently trained artists even after their apprenticeship was finished. Many of the Venetian works Volpato proposes as examples were accessible to Caravaggio, and he must have seen and studied them if, as I firmly believe, he spent some time in Venice before proceeding to Rome: Bellori, unjustly discredited in this regard, mentions this sojourn in any case. Despite their roughness and occasional vagueness, Volpato's insights teach us a great deal about invention, disposition, and their functions in pictorial narrative. He outlines a theoretical grid of binary correspondences in which concepts are dialectically opposed to one another: brightness to darkness; straightness to roundness; open to closed; acuteness to obtuseness; backward to forward, and so forth. To be sure, he incites artists to synthetize the extremes, but he also recognizes the overall validity of these elements individually taken, inasmuch as they fulfill diverse missions and comply with diverse modes: liveliness and sluggishness, violence and humility, strength and grace are articulated through them. To attain a specific effect—and Volpato is explicit in this regard—artists can manipulate geometric patterns and lighting at will. Not only does their harmonious assemblage bestow a certain character upon the composition, but their combination, by creating directionality, also impresses velocity and rhythm in the story. In other words, straight lines and curves, obtuse or acute angles in conjunction with brightness and darkness, speed up or slow down narrative duration.

In order to be perfectly clear, narrative duration cannot be measured by, and does not depend upon, physical time. Rather, it pertains especially to the fictive time of reconfiguration—the beholder's process of experiencing and perceiving a story—and translates the pace or speed through which viewers connect the various narrative segments of the *istoria* represented. Inherent in perception, duration qualifies not as a process, but as a modality of a process. Through lines and curves, lights and shadows, artists therefore inhibit or facilitate the synaptic and synesthetic process through which figures, objects, and motions establish a reciprocal connection in the viewer's perception. It goes without saying that, albeit related to the fictive time of reconfiguration, duration is a function of configuring: it is the author who pre-ordains the rhythm and interconnectedness of the *istoria*. Even if Volpato never alludes to duration, it can be easily inferred that, since he includes motion among the elements subjected to artistic manipulation, violence or fierceness, usually rendered through straight lines and acute angles, tend for instance to accelerate the process through which beholders link figures with one another, as well as the velocity with which the gaze shifts or circulates across the painting's surface. By contrast, it is apparent from Volpato's text that each subject matter, or more broadly genre, demands a different mode of painting and therefore diverse durations. It is thus imperative that, once the overall mode of the subject matter is defined, geometric patterns and lighting accord with it.

35 Unfortunately, there is no basic study on Peterzano, his work, and his relation with Caravaggio. Here is the bibliography I could cull in connection with this interesting painter: Fiorio 1974; Valsecchi 1978; Fiorio 1989; Gregori 1992; Colli 1994; Di Giampaolo 2000; Miller 2000; Bora 2002; Miller 2002; and Fiorio 2003.

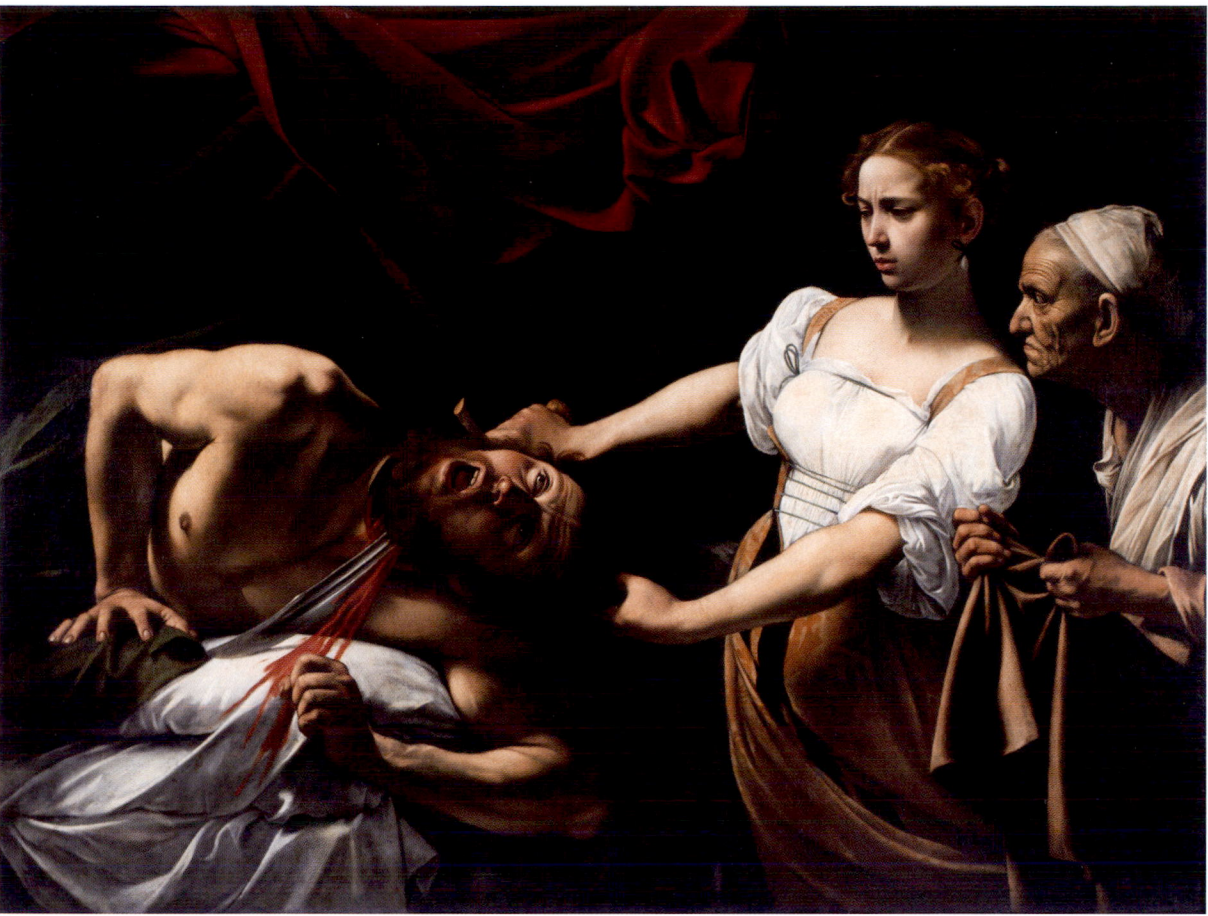

Fig. 35
Michelangelo Merisi da Caravaggio, *Judith Beheading Holofernes*, Galleria Nazionale d'Arte Antica, Palazzo Barberini, Rome, oil on canvas, 145 x 195 cm.

But what if artists decide to disjoin the system of correspondences upon which, according to Volpato and the majority of early modern art theorists, the story's pertinence and propriety rely? And what if artists adopt divergent durations within the same narrative? Would this change the perception of the story? And why would it be necessary for art historians to detect and discuss these divergences and disjunctions, even if the subject matter is wholly comprehensible? To be sure, the last question is a rhetorical one, even if for many scholars duration does not constitute an issue, nor is it even theorized as an essential component of pictorial narrative.

For the sake of the experiment, and as an epilogue to Part One, I will proceed to examine Caravaggio's *c.*1599 *Judith Beheading Holofernes* in the Galleria Nazionale di Palazzo Barberini, Rome (Fig. 35)[36] in light of Volpato's criteria of pictorial modes and compositional rhythms. In his 1982 monograph on Caravaggio, Alfred Moir suggested that a fresco from the rear façade of Palazzo Massimo alle Colonne, Rome, probably executed by a painter of Daniele da Volterra's workshop in the second half of the sixteenth century, might be the main source of the Barberini painting.[37] Although I am convinced that Caravaggio knew this fresco and was inspired by it, I also believe that a *Judith*

36 Only Baglione, 138, and Malvasia, 1:480-1, mention the picture in the seventeenth century. For the painting, see Friedlaender 1969, 158-9; Spezzaferro 1974; Marin 1977, 166-7; Moir 1982, 90; Cinotti 1983, 515-7, no. 55; Hibbard 1983, 65-7; Christiansen 1985, 256-62, no. 55 [catalogue entry by Mina Gregori]; Calvesi 1990, 83-95; Gregori 1991, 188-99, no. 8;

Bologna 1992, 308; Puglisi 1998, 135-8; Bal 1999, 99-105; Longhi 1999-2000, 2:79-85 [1951]; Costa Restagno 2004, 58-69; Marini 2005, 424-6, no. 31; Varriano 2006, 80-1; Schütze 2009, 257, no. 23; Ebert-Schifferer 2009, 108-12.

37 See Moir 1982, 19, 31 [reproduction of the fresco].

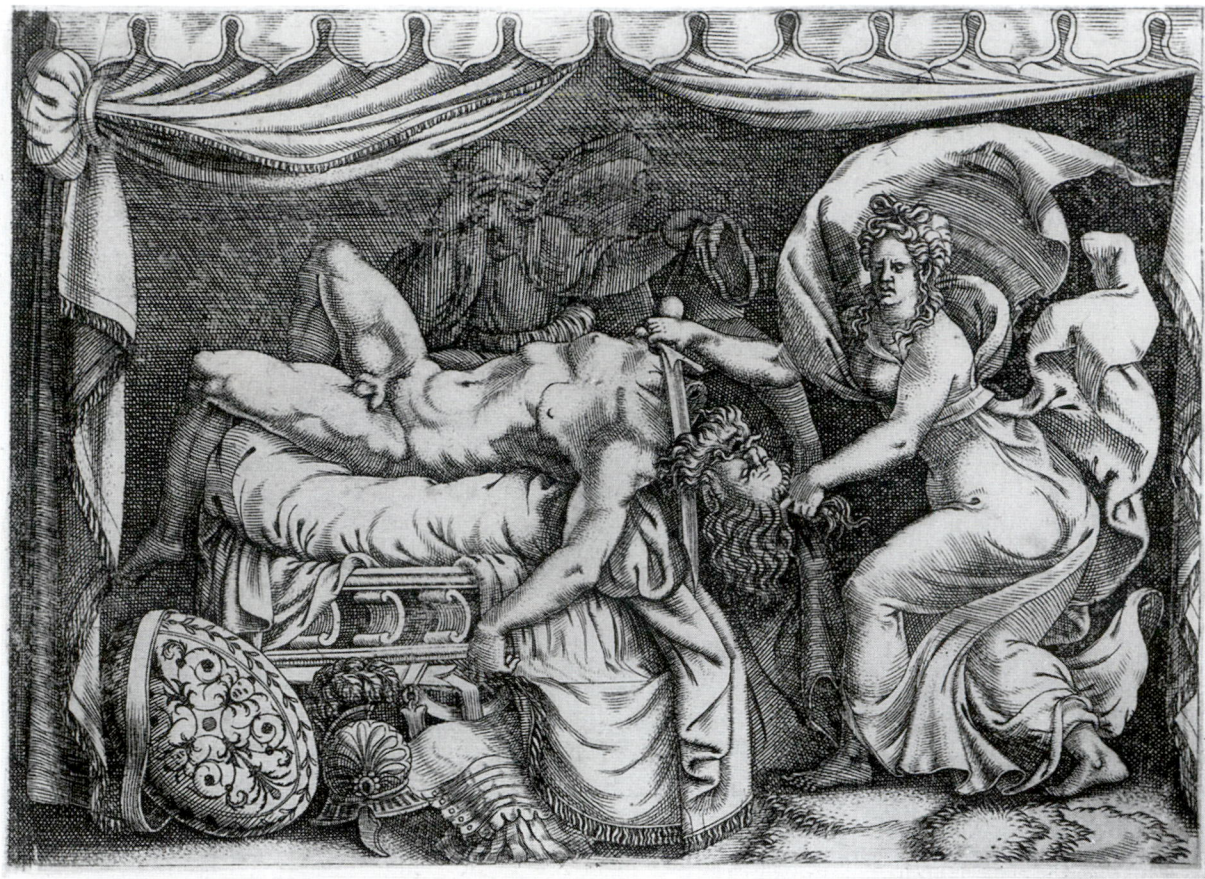

Fig. 36
Anonymous engraver after Giulio Romano, *Judith Beheading Holofernes*, engraving, 15.5 x 21.8 cm.

Beheading Holofernes (Fig. 36), printed by a sixteenth-century anonymous engraver close to Giulio Romano and his circle, compares more compellingly with the picture.[38] In the print, Holofernes lies to the left, naked, his lifted right thigh contributing to the zigzagged outer contours of his figure. His right arm bent downward while the left dangles in the nearer foreground, Holofernes writhes in agony even as his head has been just severed from his body, his eyes shut, his mouth open in a silent shriek. Yanking at his head by grabbing a thick lock of hair, Judith finishes her task, her huge sword flung through the empty space between her victim's neck and beard. Undoubtedly inspired by an antique bas-relief, Judith's figure twists her body with ardor, her two arms almost paralleling one another in a manner most similar to that of her counterpart in Caravaggio's painting. Squeezed forward, Judith's bare and voluptuous breast elicits the intensity of her effort in the print, her eyebrows creased in strenuous concentration while her lips, turning up in the middle then down at their ends, utter a mix of determination and disgust. Judging from the painting's X-rays photographs, Caravaggio was extremely sensitive to the motif of the swelling breast, which he took up and then mitigated in accordance with the motion of his Judith's torso. However, he kept and developed the focused expression of Judith's face as suggested by the engraving. Despite the close-up view, it is obvious that Caravaggio also borrowed the motif of the horizontal mattress, thereby

38   For the print, see Boorsch and Spike 1986, 236, no. 1 (430); Bellini 1991, 151-2, no. 154. This engraving was formerly ascribed to Adamo Scultori. A *c.*1596 drawing by the Cavalier d'Arpino now at the Kupferstichkabinett in Berlin represents a naked male figure on a bed that is certainly inspired by the print with *Judith Beheading Holofernes* at hand. Since Caravaggio worked at the time in the Cavalier d'Arpino's workshop, he must have known both the Berlin drawing and the engraving. For the drawing, see Röttgen 2002, 306, no. 67m.

making Holofernes' head and arm lean beyond its border. Unlike the engraver, he shifted the elderly servant to the right. In the print, she appears behind Holofernes' bed, partially concealed by the baldachin's shade, covering her face in horror as she prematurely hands Judith the sack that is to hold the victim's head. With pictorial wit, Caravaggio reversed this figure's function in the Barberini picture: the old hag now instead of recoiling from the bloody spectacle fixes her eyes on it with an unflinching and almost morbid curiosity. I will comment more extensively upon this figure shortly. Predictably enough, Caravaggio did not limit himself to elaborate upon and reframe the print's composition. Notwithstanding its apparent simplicity, the Barberini painting is the product of a sophisticated pondering of motifs, schemes, and visual solutions only partially exploited in the pictorial tradition. Because of this complexity, I cannot hope here to enumerate exhaustively Caravaggio's sources for the picture.

Albeit very dissimilar in appearance, a print by the Master LPH of *Judith Beheading Holofernes* (Fig. 37)[39] might also have exerted some influence on Caravaggio who, apart from probably liking the curvilinear unrolling of the folds on Judith's gown as well as the conical taping of her bodice, might have appreciated the almost hypnotic expression of the young servant to the right, her face in profile transfixed upon Holofernes' unconscious head on the bed. This latter motif bears some affinity with the servant's attitude and expression in the Barberini picture. Perhaps Caravaggio knew—though I do not know how—a drawing by Rosso Fiorentino, now in the Los Angeles County Museum (Fig. 38),[40] in which Judith and her elderly maid, naked and in front of one another, appear to discuss the sack or its contents. In the drawing, the hag's profile, direct gaze, and strained neck recall that of Caravaggio's old woman. Notice, though, that Rosso's angular contours are absent from Caravaggio's servant, whose profile instead results from the intersections of large convexities and concavities. Even if Caravaggio never saw the Los Angeles drawing, it is important to observe that Rosso opposes the old woman's angularness and meagerness to the young lady's roundness and delicacy: an effect that Caravaggio also aims to obtain by juxtaposing on two different yet contiguous planes the faces of Judith and her servant. Be that as it may, the hag's physiognomy is absolutely not indebted to Rosso's ascendancy. As recently proposed by Paola Caretta, Michelangelo's Sybil of Cumae on the Sistine Chapel ceiling most probably inspired

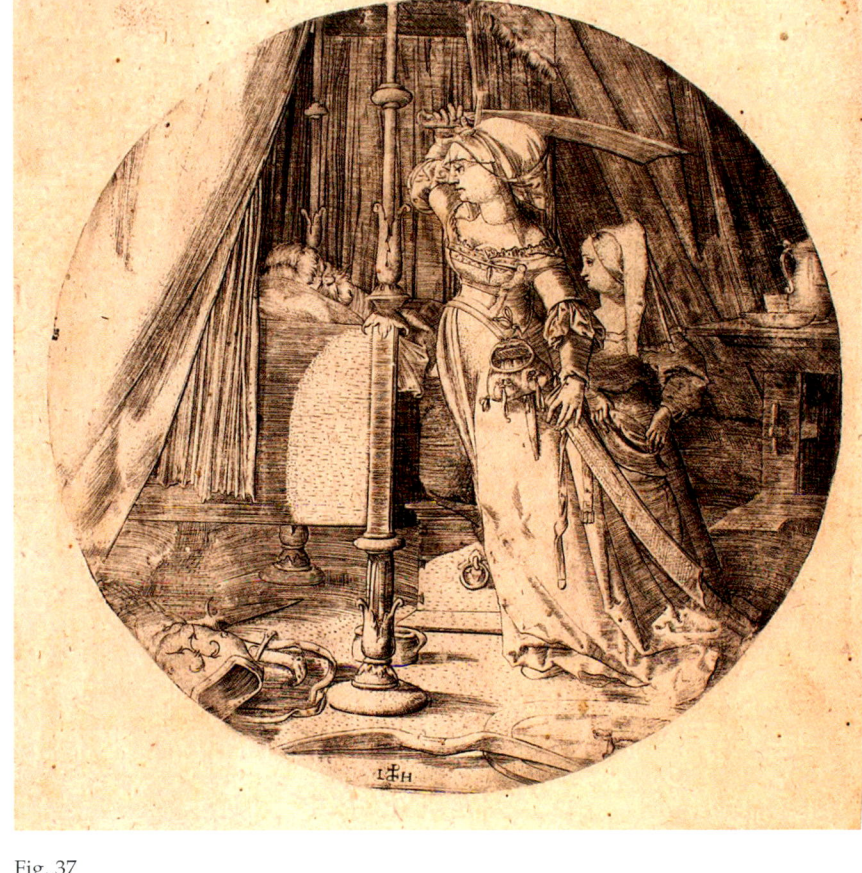

Fig. 37
Master LPH, *Judith Beheading Holofernes*, engraving, 14.2 cm. (diameter).

39   For the print, see Hollstein 1956, 73; Strauss 1981, 312, no. 1 (542).

40   For the drawing, see Carroll 1987, 364-6, no. 116; Franklin 1994, 82.

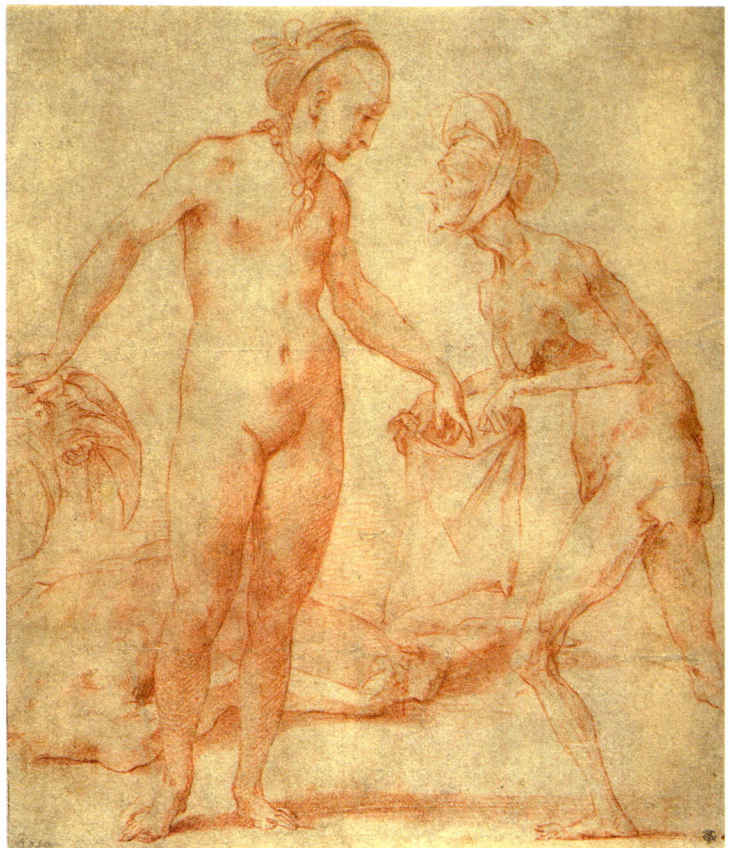

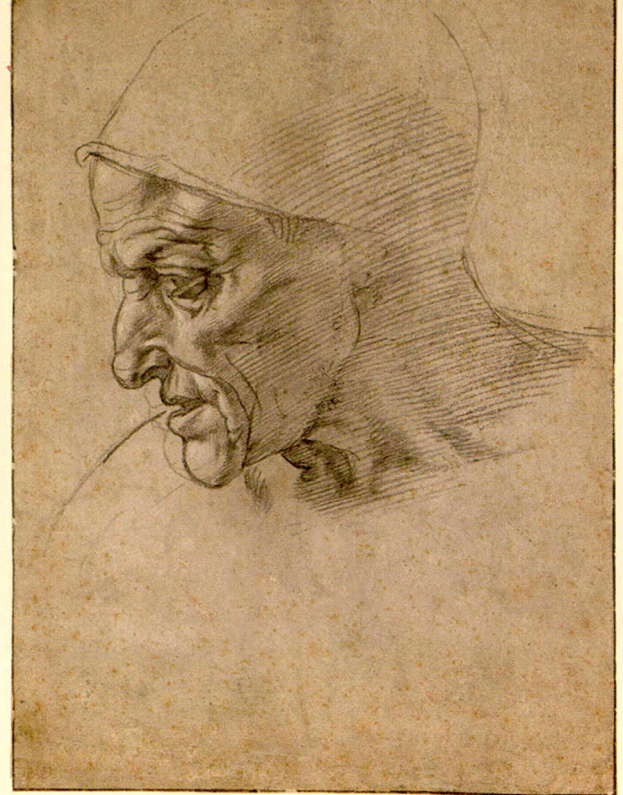

Fig. 38
Rosso Fiorentino (Giovan Battista di Jacopo), *Judith and Her Servant*, Los Angeles County Museum, Los Angeles, red chalk on gray buff paper, 23.2 x 19.69 cm.

Fig. 39
Michelangelo Buonarroti, *Study of the Head of the Cumaean Sybil*, Biblioteca Reale, Turin, black chalk, 23 x 31.5 cm.

Caravaggio for the old servant's figure.[41] A preparatory drawing by Michelangelo at the Biblioteca Reale, Turin, is suitable for comparison (Fig. 39). If one concentrates on the upper outline of the Sybil's profile—that part of it spanning the forehead and nose—the affinity will forthwith emerge into view. Notice also the scar-like oblique furrows irregularly etched on the two figures' cheeks. It must be said, however, that Caravaggio modifies the canon of Michelangelo's head by softening its angles through a curvature, whose pattern is accentuated by the dense array of wrinkles rippling across his old woman's forehead. More important, Caravaggio's variations of Michelangelo's Sybil are pursued on the model of Leonardo's caricatural heads: the servant's chin, now edgeless in the Barberini picture, enhances and responds to the outcrop formed by the pursed lips, which in turn contrasts with and tends toward the nose's down-bent tip. On the other hand, the nose's hooked bridge engenders dissonance and false symmetry in connection with the slightly out-of-scale crescent of the ear's fleshy lobe. It is of paramount importance to remark upon these physiognomic details since they inflect the severity of Michelangelo's Sybil with imperceptible comic overtones, without nevertheless transforming Caravaggio's servant into sheer laughable caricature. I will return to this point later.

It is undeniable that Judith's figure in the Barberini painting is the pivot of the entire action: she is literally in the spotlight; her white bodice and orange dress are, chromatically speaking, the brightest hues of the picture; through her action, she binds the two halves of the composition, left

41 See Caretta 2008, 21. For the drawing, see De Tolnay 1975-1980, 1:115, no. 155.

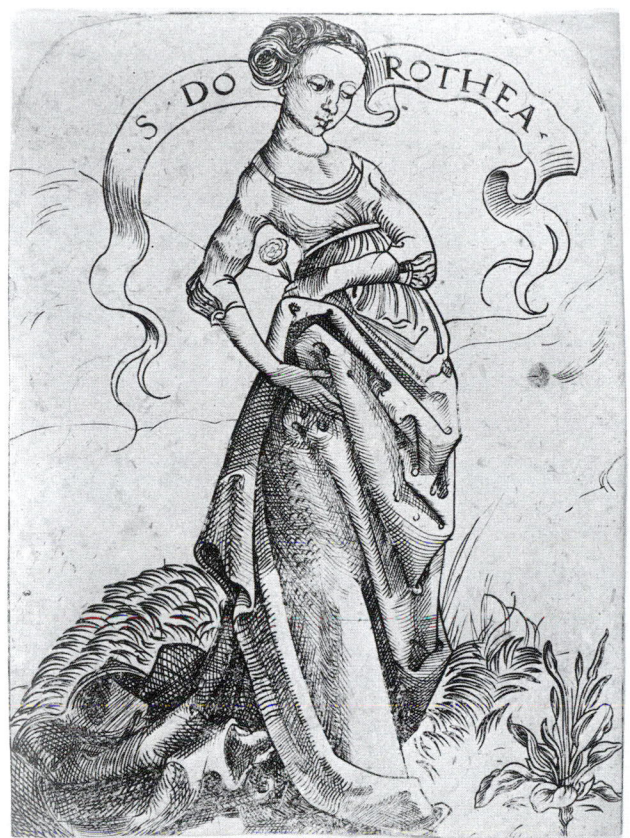

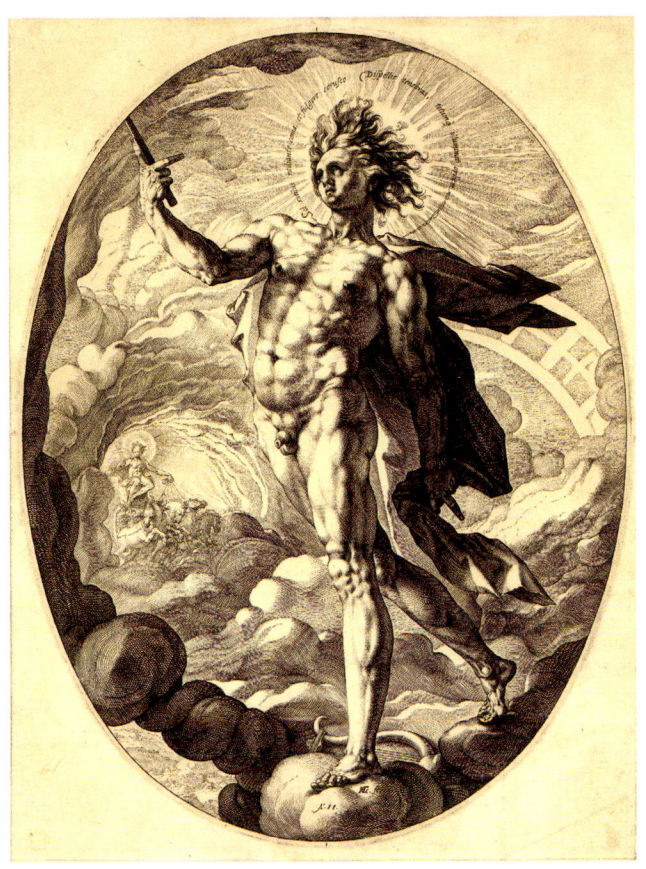

Fig. 40
Master I E, *Saint Dorothy*, engraving, 10.8 x 8.1.

Fig. 41
Hendrick Goltzius, *Apollo*, engraving, 26.4 x 34.9 cm.

and right, together. Her posture is in and of itself a masterpiece of pictorial disposition. Perhaps because she is deeply enthralled by her heroic act, or probably because only the upper part of her figure is visible, her body's elegant torsion might go unnoticed by viewers. Yet its ascending, elliptical motion, splendidly magnified by the grand waves of folds disengaged through the twisting of her orange robe, is surely a felicitous example of *figura serpentinata* as theorized by Michelangelo. The upward and rightward thrust of her torso is masterfully counterbalanced by the downward and rightward pull of her arms. As peculiar as it may be, an early sixteenth-century engraving by the Master I E, a *Saint Dorothy* very much in the manner of Martin Schongauer (Fig. 40), seemingly served as a starting point for Caravaggio's Judith.[42] When reversed, the slender figure of the striding saint forms with its outmost contour an elliptical, graceful arch that resembles that of Judith in the Barberini painting. Observe how Dorothy's three-quarter face bends over her neck and toward her chest with vigorous flexibility in a manner also characteristic of Caravaggio's heroine. Interesting enough, the swirling bun of Dorothy's headdress—so essential in re-calibrating the face's downward motion by liberating the saint's spacious forehead—is echoed not only by the hair knotted behind Judith's head, but also by her half-lit ear. Of course, if Caravaggio was indeed inspired by this figure, he needed to adjust her attitude to a different context, morphing a

42 For the print, see Hutchison 1996, 308, no. 017. Although Hutchison points out that this might be a unique, and therefore very rare, impression, it must be noted that the *Saint Dorothy* now at the Rothschild Collection, Louvre, Paris, belonged to a group of prints donated by Pope Benedict XIV to the Istituto delle Scienze di Bologna in 1755-1756, and was originally attributed to "Bel Martino": that is, Martin Schongauer. In other words, it cannot be ruled out that the *Saint Dorothy* was already in a Bolognese collection in the seventeenth century. In this regard, see Faietti 1993, 21, 26.

contemplative, quasi-allegorical Dorothy into an absorbed, allegedly heroic Judith. In this regard, Caravaggio might also have taken a cue from a more modern composition, Hendrick Goltzius' 1588 print representing Apollo (Fig. 41).[43] There, the Greek god steps forward by confidently arching his torso; his right leg, receding backward, intensifies the ellipsis of his body's outmost contour. More important, his chest and shoulders tend toward the foreground, as is the case in Judith's figure.

It would be inappropriate, let alone useless, to ascertain which of these examples, if any, triggered Caravaggio's imagination. In my opinion, at this level of invention and craftsmanship, any figure in the master's oeuvre results from a complex synthesis of sources, and thereby is laden with multiple references. Put otherwise, the prints of the Master I E or Goltzius are but a sample—significant enough, I hope—of figurative schemes on which Caravaggio might have relied. What matters most in this connection is the particular valence of these templates and their possible uses. In spite of the intense rendering of his muscles, and in contrast with it, the lithe curve of Apollo's external contour and the sinuousness of his attitude are structural elements in common with Dorothy's figure: a certain touch of femininity in an over-muscular male deity. From a rhetorical point of view, the sophistication, decorativeness, and lightness of these figurative schemes perfectly suit an allegorical context; in terms of gender, they rather bespeak female grace. At first glance, these attitudes do not adapt easily to a heroic, even violent action. But then again, the protagonist of this religious yet murderous act is a woman, so curves and ellipses might well be appropriate here. But are they? In other words, does Judith's graceful and serpentine motion fit within the painting's action? Before answering this question, Holofernes' figure must be placed under scrutiny.

If Caravaggio deploys a network of flowing curves in depicting Judith's feat, he on the contrary resorts to straight lines and acute angles in showing Holofernes' last throes. The tyrant's bent arms neatly, though to an unusual extent, bracket the trunk of his torso, a gigantic trapezoid edged by the green blanket. The right arm flexed ninety degrees, the left forming an acute angle, they both circumscribe Holofernes' torso within a lozenge. At its open ends, a clutched fist and a spider-like extended hand epitomize the tyrant's immense pain and his desperate, vain attempt to break free by jerking upward. The paroxysm of excruciating torment and ultimate rebellion that this figure incarnates makes it the analog of a struggling and screaming Laocoön, and it is definitely no coincidence that Caravaggio's Holofernes quotes this ancient sculptural group, now as then located at the Belvedere Court, Vatican Palace.[44] By quotation, I do not mean a one-to-one correspondence of limbs, but something more allusive and in a certain sense more elusive. From the Belvedere *Laocoön* Caravaggio solely imitates the mighty motif of the bent arm and clutched hand seizing and pulling away the serpent, as well as the evocative, up-tilted head with the bellowing mouth. One can verify these borrowings by comparing Caravaggio's figure to the engraved reproduction of the *Laocoön* executed by Marco Dente in the mid sixteenth century (Fig. 42).[45] It is noteworthy that by adjusting the ancient sculpture to the Judith story, Caravaggio not only avails himself of scattered elements from the original—as if the very act of quotation entailed dismembering and foreshadowed the figure's severing—but he also smoothed Laocoön's exuberant deployment of muscles, veins, and tendons. In a sense, Caravaggio regularizes the antique's tormented anatomic relief by inscribing Holofernes' torso within a grid of angles and orthogonal lines. Even the clenched fist, through the relevance of the knuckles, and the open hand, a kind of tripod displaying its many acute angles, prove the point. Nevertheless, Caravaggio preserves the original's vehement motion by transferring it from anatomy to lighting. The painting's light, streaming from the left upper corner, by strongly illuminating Holofernes' arms and torso engenders various sets of shades and

43   See Strauss 1977, 2:456, no. 263.

44   See for instance in this regard Ebert-Schifferer 2009, 108-9: "So natürlich, wie sie auf den ersten Blick aussieht, ist diese

Szene nicht, denn hinter der Mimik und verrenkten Pose des Holofernes verbirgt sich eine Anspielung auf den Laokoon."

45   For the print, see Oberhuber 1978, 2:50, no. 353 (268).

dark spots that segment the integrity of the tyrant's body.

If one now considers Volpato's precepts, it should be clear that the proliferation of acute angles and the contrasted fragmentation of brightness and shades fulfill a double task. First of all, the conjunction of straight lines and acute angles orients the viewer's gaze toward the right half of the picture, while deterring it from proceeding in the opposite direction: Holofernes' raised forearm resembles a visual bar that blocks the eyes from browsing on the canvas's left margin. In other words, the rectilinear disposition of the figure's limbs acts as a vector of directionality by conferring a solemn yet fiery pace to action. The abrupt and shattered lighting of Holofernes' body greatly adds to this effect. Secondly, the square configuration of the tyrant's anatomy excellently expresses the mechanics of the action in its particular temporality. All at once, Holofernes emerges from his drunken lethargy and senses the woman's sword cutting through his neck. With his right hand, he tries to break free by hoisting his torso, to no avail. His left arm instead reacts to the excruciating pain, the fist contracted in hopeless resistance. A bundle of straight lines accompany the suddenness and vehemence of the action, the sword and the blood spurts creating a network of divergent acute angles. Confined within the lozenge of the arms, these straight lines speed up the narrative's pace. Of course, both the sword

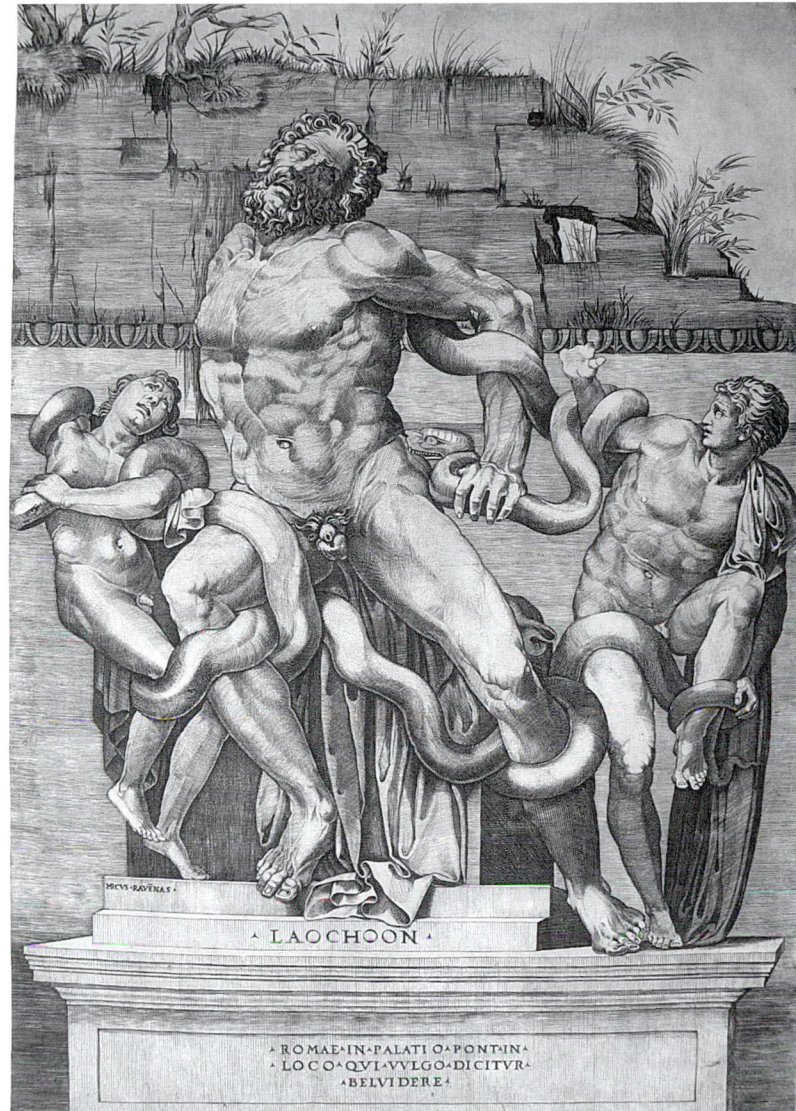

Fig. 42
Marco Dente, *Laocoön*, engraving, 47.2 x 32.4 cm.

and the blood, because of their inflection and position, convey a specific aspect of temporality: that the beheading is almost complete is evinced by the bare rims of the nearly severed neck.

Given the magnitude and vehemence of Holofernes' counteraction and convulsion, so thoroughly designed by Caravaggio, it is at least surprising that Judith's attitude—technically speaking, the focus, center, and cause of the action represented—is instead characterized by a curvilinear rhythm and mode that Volpato would liken rather to "grace, beauty, charm, affection, and devotion." Even if one does not accept Volpato's pictorial system and its implications, it is absolutely clear that Judith's dance-like posture, her torso and hip arching as her shoulders recoil and her head rises, does not conform to Holofernes' Laocoön-like struggle. Aside from the lack of narrative verisimilitude that the combination of these two figures brings about, it is evident that a twofold tempo underlies the unfolding of the action, from Holofernes' *con brio* to Judith's *andante*, not to mention the servant's vibrant stasis. As a result, the narrative temporality accelerates through the immediacy of the tyrant's mortal spasms and slows with the heroine's contemplative awareness and surgical precision in slicing, rather than snapping off, the man's head.

115

To grasp fully the modal discrepancy of these two actions, it is instructive to examine an analogous depiction: Ludovico Carracci's 1584 fresco at the Palazzo Fava, Bologna, representing *Medea Rejuvenating Aeson* (Fig. 43), which Caravaggio might well have seen if he stopped in Bologna during his trip to Rome around 1592-1594.[46] In the fresco, the infamous magician, wholly naked, slits the old man's throat while intently regarding her operation: by bleeding him to death, she will resuscitate him as a young man. Standing near the bed, Medea deploys her nudity unabashedly: Ludovico conceived of her body's contours as a network of sinuous ascending lines, thus translating the slow-paced, phantasmagoric unfolding of the ritual in plain conformity with the subject matter.

It goes without saying that the same conformity does not apply to the Barberini picture, where in addition the servant's protracted stare and almost manic fixity make time come to a halt while increasing the temporal oddities of the episode. By eagerly riveting her gaze on Holofernes, she creates suspense and projects action onto the future: soon, she will be able to enfold the tyrant's head inside her sack. However, if this is her task in delineating the story's temporality, her attitude disrupts narrative duration by not only decelerating, but rather freezing the flow of time: that is, the impression of flowing time in the viewer as determined by the painting's compositional structure. Not surprisingly, the servant's profile might appear to have been pasted onto the painting's surface.

That the intensity and duration of each action remarkably vary from one figure to another is a fault that early modern art theorists consistently note. This is Giovan Paolo Lomazzo's opinion:

> The passions of the soul also modify the body, on account of the human soul's faculty to transform the body under the impulse of passion, and this faculty is moved by a vehement imagination, as it occurs when one is struck by great awe upon seeing or hearing something. In this connection, one must be careful to make the motion of the main passion represented in the figure especially proportionate to the others that depend upon it, in keeping with the force with which passion animates those figures. In this manner, one can avoid so many discordances [*tante discordanze*] that are to be seen in numerous pictures in which, since there is no proportion and correspondence [*proporzione e corrispondenza*] between the motions and the principal action [*effetto principale*] to be represented in the figure as prescribed by the *istoria*, things truly appear to be done as if in a dream: randomly, without consideration, rather than [being] demonstrations of the true *istoria* [*veridica istoria*], representations thought over with proper reasoning and figures introduced with proportionate reason.[47]

It may be objected that modal and temporal disparities can be found in many paintings by other great masters. Depicting a beheading in a consistent manner is certainly an anti-pictorial task. Decapitation indeed must be effected with speed, accuracy, and an incredible force in order to crush the vertebral bones and separate the head from the body. Artists therefore tended to allude to the act of beheading, renouncing its actual representation. Yet, this objection does not hold in regard to Caravaggio's painting. The uncanny and most unusual idea of showing the spurting blood compels beholders to perceive the story and event in its concreteness. Concretely, though, swords do not

---

46   For the fresco, see Emiliani 1993, 8-12, no. 5; and Brogi 2001, 1:110-4, no. 9 [the entire cycle of frescoes at the Palazzo Fava].

47   Lomazzo, 2:106: "Le passioni dell'animo mutano ancora il corpo per la virtù c'ha l'animo umano appassionato di trasmutare il corpo, la qual virtù è mossa dalla veemente imaginazione, sì come avviene in un gran stupore per qualche cosa veduta o udita. Nel che si ha da avvertire, sopratutto, di far proporzionati al moto della principal passione che si finge nella figura gl'altri che gli vengono in conseguenza, secondo la forza con ch'ella gli commove, ché così non si vedranno tante discordanze, come in molti luoghi dipinti si veggono, dove, non essendo questa proporzione e corrispondenza de i moti e dell'effetto principale che si ha da rappresentar nella figura, secondo il prescritto dell'istoria, si può dire veramente che paiono più tosto in sogni e cose fatte a caso, senza considerazione, che dimostrazioni di veridica istoria, o di rappresentazione imaginate con debite ragioni e figure introdotte con proporzionata ragione."

cut through bones as knives do through butter. The point of this entire discussion is that the insertion of a reality effect as radical as the jets of blood greatly bears on the viewer's expectation. This means that the whole composition is expected to match the level of realism brought out by such a paramount element of the narration. But Judith's almost effortless action, and even more her rhythmic gait, belies the beholder's expectation, as well as the impact of the scene's narrative momentum. I concede that Caravaggio joins these disjointed paces and modes— the tyrant's and the hero- ine's—with immense subtlety. Disruption here is anything but ostentatious, and continuity is ensured throughout the paint- ing with utter artistry. Suffice it to observe the wavy chain link- ing Holofernes' right arm and shoulder, his head and Judith's left arm; the drooping curtain and its flowing folds playing with the beheading below and

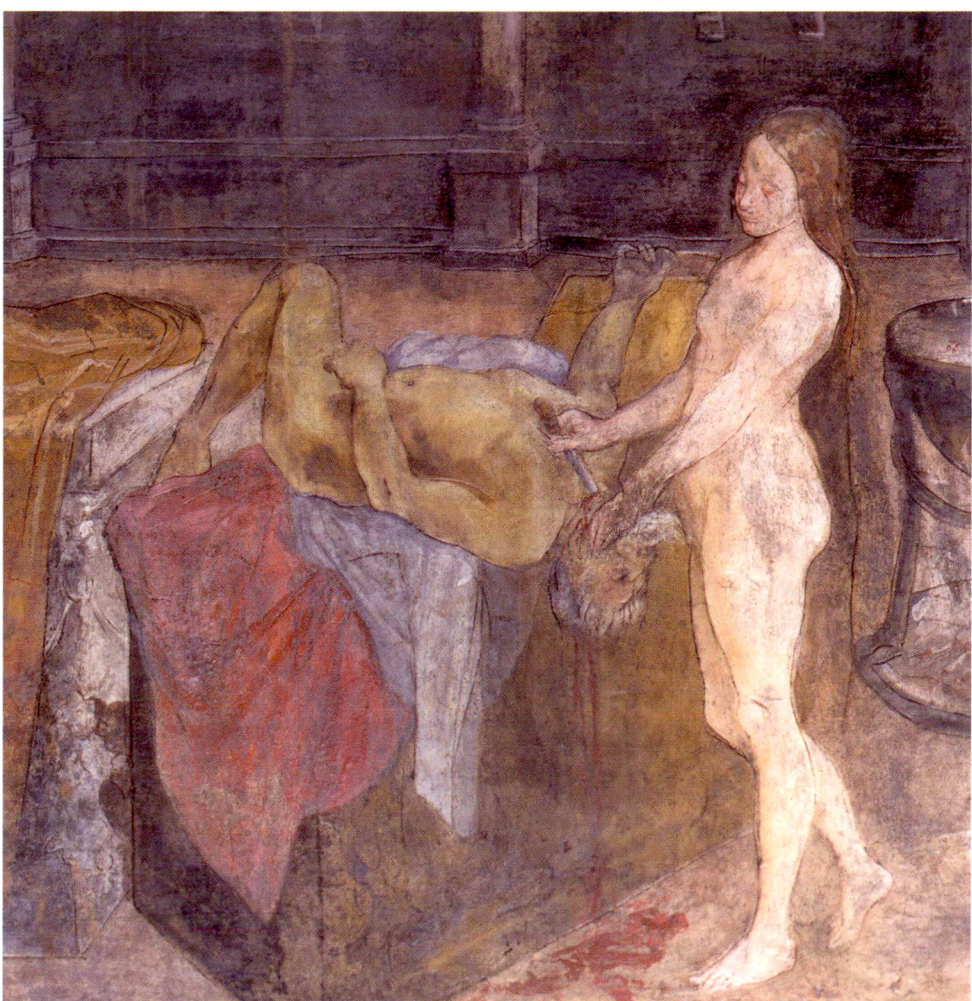

Fig. 43
Ludovico Carracci, *Medea Rejuvenating Aeson*, Palazzo Fava, Bologna, fresco, detail.

thereby reverberating the throes of the tyrant's agony; the curtain's shriveled knot, aloft at the center, making the action culminate by serving as a counterpoint to Judith's head and as a foil to her eloquent absorption. Undoubtedly, these geometric patterns keep together the composition as if within a single movement. Therefore, continuous motion and discontinuous mode and pace coexist in the same composition. But why does Caravaggio concomitantly unsettle and enforce the image's coherence? The refinement of such operation definitely implies artistic intentionality: the Barberini painting is clearly not the work of an inexperienced or fumbling artist.

I contend that these dislocations are the means by which Caravaggio uncovers the intrinsic, insurmountable fictiveness of pictorial narrative. In the case of the Barberini picture, the spurting blood, a visual component absent from the previous iconographic tradition, reveals— as if in retrospect—not only that the visualization of the biblical episode is above all a matter of coding—and hence of conventions—but also that, as encoded texts, images do not mirror reality. By simultaneously enhancing and mitigating the impact of realistic effects, and by manipulating the cause-and-effect connectedness of the story,[48] Caravaggio unequivocally opens the door to the marvelous. In his 1594 *Discorsi del poema eroico*, the Italian poet Torquato Tasso construed the

48   On the concept of "causality" in painting, see Jollet 2002.

117

marvelous as the representation of the Christian prodigious or supernatural,[49] that is, the evocation of events that transcend nature's laws and that would be inexplicable without divine intervention. From this point of view, the depiction of the graceful Judith decapitating the mighty Holofernes with incredible ease constitutes a clear example of the Christian marvelous. The heroine's focused expression, along with her gaze sunk in her oppressor's, as if wondering whether death is truly to be accomplished through her own doing, translates the ineffable actuality of the naturally impossible. The figure of the old servant, inserted as an accessorial attribute to Judith because of her narrative inertness, draws attention to the prodigy's impossibility as it becomes possible through fiction's intervention. Her half-comic, half-serious fixity—does she express avid fixation like Danae's traditional servant who, in competition with her mistress, tries to gather Zeus' golden coins with her stretched apron? Or does she rather express overzealous determination like an enrapt Sibyl on Michelangelo's model?—is as ambivalent as the viewer's response to the picture's evocation of the marvelous. Should one take the episode seriously? Is this the staged product of fiction or the true-to-life representation of a heroic deed? In this perspective, Caravaggio's marvelous deeply differs from Tasso's: his is the insidious insinuation that the heroic, too, is a matter of point of view, since the artist is able to subject it to even a comic angle.

However, there is another kind of marvelous in which only Caravaggio excels. Through his craftsmanship and inventiveness, his pictorial fiction renders the naturally impossible with the evidence and trustfulness of a mirror. Here lies the paradox that underpins Caravaggio's marvelous: images—and more specifically pictorial narratives—do not mirror reality, yet exhibit their fictiveness as a mirrored reality. If Caravaggio imperceptibly disrupts the *istoria*'s visual coherence without compromising it, this is because he conceives of the painting as an intermediate dimension between fiction and reality, between the normative causality of pictorial narrative and the inevitable license of artistic inventiveness. By doing so, he ensnares the viewer into the process of redoubling through which reality turns into fiction. As rhetorical tropes of artistic eulogy stated at the time,[50] Caravaggio's art truly and not metaphorically imprisons the beholder within the illusion that fiction has a reality of its own, since it manifests itself under the master's brush with the consistency of natural vision. To be sure, Caravaggio's marvelous—an important component of his poetics of dislocation—cannot be interpreted exclusively as a conceptual play with art's fictiveness. As I have already mentioned, pictorial narratives and sacred stories in the late sixteenth and early seventeenth centuries are the domain of organized knowledge, cultural mediation, and religious propaganda. As I shall demonstrate in the course of this volume, Caravaggio's poetics of dislocation dismantles epistemic, institutional, and cultural tenets as posited by the Church and agreed upon by societies and governments. For instance, the modal and rhythmic misalignments between figures and actions in the Barberini painting certainly target, among other things, the concept of pictorial truth, on which I will dwell in Part Three of this monograph. For the time being, I will merely stress that Judith's and Holofernes' attitudes and interactions not only concern the narrative congruence of the painting, but also translate role models operative at Caravaggio's time: the heroine incarnated the ideal of strong and virtuous womanhood; the tyrant personified passive and impious manhood resulting from lust and inebriation.[51] By endowing Judith's murderous

---

49   See for instance Tasso c, 1:161: "Non tante maraviglie le quali nel teatro sarebbono per aventura sconvenevoli, e ne l'epopeia sono lette volentieri, sì perché sono sue proprie, sì perché il lettore consente a molte cose a le quali nega il consentimento colui che risguarda. Laonde le machine rade volte si lodano nella tragedia; ma ne l'epopeia spesso scendono dal cielo gl'iddii e gli angeli, e s'interpongono ne l'operazioni degli uomini (…). Laonde tutti questi poemi paiono quasi fatti e condotti a fine da la providenza, a la quale a pena si lascia luogo ne la tragedia."

50   In this regard, see Salerno et al. 1966.

51   There is a vast literature, originating especially in gender studies, consecrated to the theme of Judith and Holofernes in the visual arts and its meaning. See more recently Reineke 2003; Uppenkamp 2004; Warncke 2005. Garrard 1998 has become a classical reference in this context.

action with charming grace and Holofernes' punishment with energetic vehemence, Caravaggio revitalizes cultural and gender-rooted concepts. Judith's action ceases to be a commonplace of unwavering heroism and betrays the woman's incredulity. By fighting back hopelessly like an Old Testament Laocoön, Holofernes lays claim to heroism, a virtue previously foreign to his character. I would not go as far as to say that Caravaggio with his Barberini painting turned upside down the conventional significance attached to the episode of Judith and Holofernes as interpreted by his contemporaries. But I would certainly go so far as to say that, thanks to Caravaggio's dislocations, Judith and Holofernes, from actors of social, cultural, and religious principles become agents of human events. In my opinion, the dismantling of pictorial roles and identities is already an act of incommensurable originality and rebellion in early modern painting.

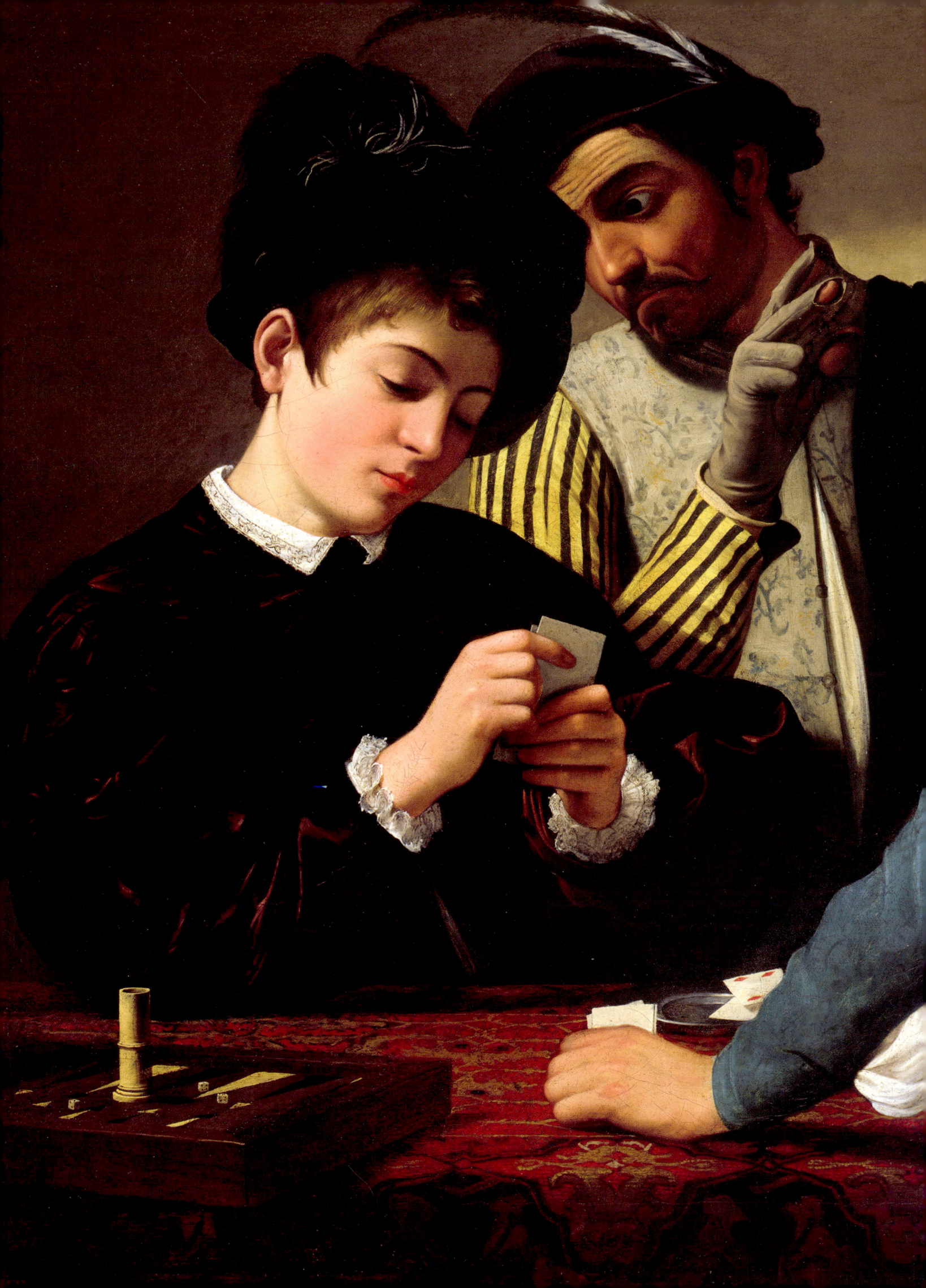

PART TWO

Blending Genres:
Lyrical and Comic Interactions in
Caravaggio's Early Paintings

Comedy of Errors

Symmetry, eurythmy, proportion, propriety, and decorum are the structural components of the *istoria*. As I have already suggested in Part One, no derogation is admitted, although *sprezzatura* (nonchalant license) is welcome as long as it increases the composition's overall harmony by instilling variety. Norms and rules change in accordance with genres. In his 1591 *Figino*,[1] Gregorio Comanini neatly distinguishes the lyrical and the heroic canons by equating figures in painting with verses in poetry:

> Just as heroic poems demand certain kinds of verses, and lyrical poems others, so too is it necessary to use a different set of proportions if one represents a hero in a painting than if one sets out to depict a vile man. Indeed, the representation of the former requires a greater stature than that of the latter. And just as verses are woven with proportionate feet, so too are figures shaped with proportionate heads. I shall clarify my idea with an example. If the poet intends to compose an epic, he will use hexameters, which are composed of six feet; if the painter wants to depict a hero, his figure will consist of ten heads.[2]

Comanini's system of proportions based on heads as units of measurement is irrelevant here, but the conclusion of his argument is noteworthy:

> Here, then, is how symmetry in the art of painting corresponds to the measure of feet in the art of verses. By representing figures of nine, eight, and seven heads, or even of five and four in the case of children, is painting not simply amusing itself in conformity with poetry, which augments or diminishes the number and measure of feet in accordance with the nobility or baseness of the subjects it treats?[3]

1 Very little has been written on Comanini's *Figino*. See Pupillo Ferrari-Bravo 1972; and Maiorino 2001.

2 Comanini, 229-30: "Ché sì come altra sorte di versi conviene a poema eroico, altra sorte a poema lirico si richiede, così a rappresentare con la pittura un eroe un'altra proporzione d'imagine fa di mestiere serbare che se si volesse effigiare un uomo vile. Perciochè maggior grandezza converrebbe dare all'immagine del primo che del secondo. Et come i versi sono tessuti con proporzione di piedi, così le figure sono formate con proporzione di facce. Discopro il concetto della mia mente con questo essempio. Se 'l poeta vuole comporre un poema

eroico, adopera il verso essametro, il quale ha sei piedi. E 'l pittore se vuol figurare un eroe, farà l'imagine di dieci facce con l'ordine che dirò."

3 Ibidem, 232: "Ecco adunque come la simmetria nell'arte della pittura corrisponde alla misura de' piedi nell'arte del verseggiare. Quel formar poscia figure di nove, d'otto, di sette facce, e di cinque e di quattro ancora nella rappresentazione de' fanciulli, che altro non è se non uno scherzo della pittura con la medesima poesia, la quale cresce e scema ne' versi il numero e la misura de' piedi conforme all'altezza overo alla bassezza di quei soggetti ch'ella canta?"

121

◄ Plate V: Michelangelo Merisi da Caravaggio, *The Cardsharps*, Kimbell Museum of Art, Fort Worth, oil on canvas, 91.5 x 128.2 cm., detail.

To paraphrase Comanini, the stylistic amusements through which painters fancy themselves as poets are not limited to rhythm and proportion:

> As poets play with antitheses, that is, with *contrapposti*, so too do painters contrast in the same picture women to men, children to the elderly, (…) and other similar oppositions from which, in painting, springs a charming grace [*vaghezza*] no less than that engendered in good poems by the [juxtaposition of] opposites. [4]

However felicitous antitheses might be, poets and painters should never abuse them lest the gravity of their styles be irremediably marred:

> Nevertheless, it is true that in matters of stylistic dignity and magnificence, the excessive insistence of metaphors and antitheses greatly lessens an oration's or poem's grandeur and majesty, whereas a judicious contempt of these ornaments embellishes and aggrandizes them. If the painter puts an old man near every depiction of a child, or places a man close to a woman, or a dwarf with a giant, or a beautiful young girl with an ugly hag, or a white-skinned Scythian near a dark Moor, it is equally true that his work will be a disgrace and overwrought in every respect. Instead, he must manage to vary his figures and endeavor to display in his pictures a noble negligence rather than a base diligence.[5]

Howard Hibbard[6] has evoked this passage with regard to Caravaggio's *Judith Beheading Holofernes*, which I have extensively analyzed in Chapter 3. In the painting, the visual antithesis of the beautiful heroine and her ugly servant might be construed, if one heeds Comanini's statement, as a masterly signature of the noblest style in painting; that is, unless this rhetorical figure instead denotes stylistic heaviness and a lack of magnificence, since the close-up framing amplifies its effect with overwhelming insistence. In my view, these interpretations of Caravaggio's visual antitheses are alternative only in appearance. As Comanini suggests, the appropriateness of an antithesis, or for that matter of any other rhetorical figure, is to be judged from the figurative network in which it operates. Caravaggio's antithetical juxtaposition of Judith and her servant might well pertain to the highest category of painting, the *istoria*, but before labeling it in such terms other elements ought to be taken into account. In commenting on the hag's profile, I have already noted that, albeit inspired by Michelangelo's Sybil of Cumae, it was visually rigged latently to relay a comic charge. I wish now to expand upon this ambivalence and introduce a drawing by Bartolomeo Passerotti: his 1575-1580 *Head of a Laughing Old Woman in Profile* at the Galleria Estense, Modena (Fig. 44).[7] Observe the irregularity of this face's right contour, culminating in the abyss hollowed out by the collapsing mouth and in the pointed chin's hairy outcrop. Not surprisingly, the interplay of lines constructing her profile and the degree to which their asymmetry is pushed induces ridicule and laughter. Of

---

4 Ibidem, 232-3: "Et come il poeta scherza con gli antiteti, overo co' i contrapposti, così dal pittore sono contraposte dentro una stessa tavola le figure delle donne alle figure de gli uomini; quelle de' fanciulli a quelle de' vecchi; i seni del mare alla terra; le valli a i monti, et altre simili contraposizioni son fatte dalle quali non nasce minor vaghezza nella pittura di quello che da' contrari veggiam nascere ne' buoni poemi."

5 Ibidem, 235-6: "Vero tuttavia è che nella forma della dignità e di magnificenza di stilo, la troppa spessezza delle metafore e de gli antiteti molto scema all'orazione overo al poema di grandezza e di maestà, sì come un giudicioso disprezzo di questi ornamenti gli orna et innalza. Parimente è vero che se 'l pittore, sempre che avrà dipinta l'imagine di un fanciullo,

vorrà porle appresso quella d'un vecchio, overo al fianco d'un uomo vorrà formare una donna, et appo un gigante un nano, et appo una bella donna una brutta vecchia, e a lato d'un bianco scita un negro moro, farà cosa sconcia e affettatissima per ogni capo, dovendo egli destreggiare nella variazione delle figure et ingegnarsi di scoprire nelle sue opere una nobile negligenza anzi che una vil diligenza."

6 See Hibbard 1983, 67. The same passage is mentioned by Gregori in Christiansen 1985, 257.

7 See Ghirardi 1990, 70, for a discussion of Paleotti's interpretation of comic paintings.

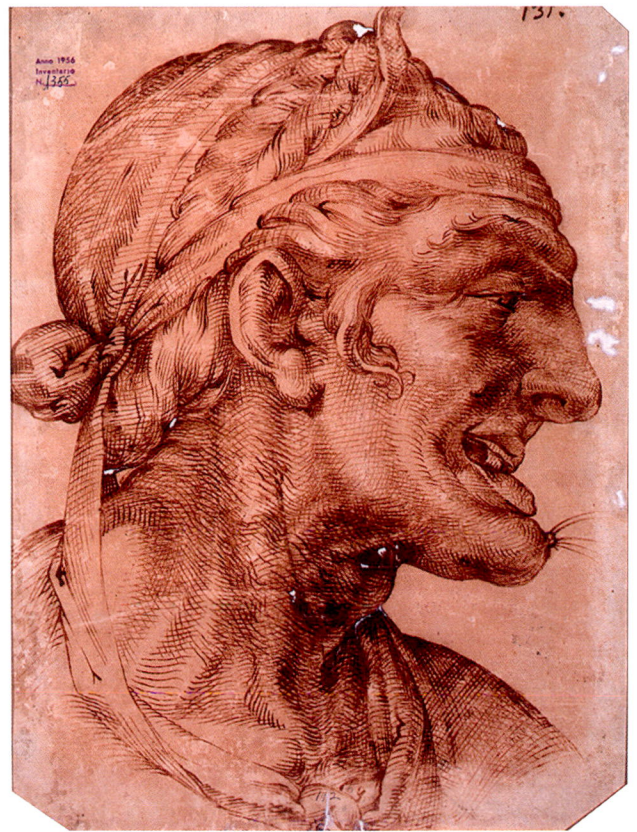

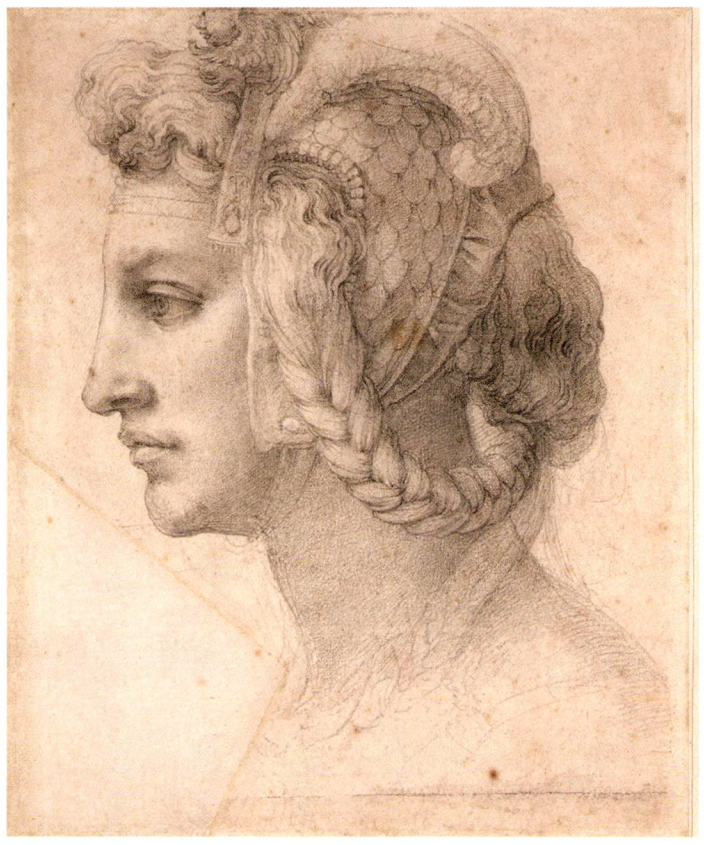

Fig. 44
Bartolomeo Passerotti, *Head of a Laughing Old Woman in Profile*,
Galleria Estense, Modena, ink and pen, 47 x 36 cm.

Fig. 45
Michelangelo Buonarroti, *Head of an Ideal Female Beauty*, British
Museum, London, black chalk, 28.7 x 23.5 cm.

course, the hag's braided hair, bound together by ribbons and gauze, both recalls and parodies
Michelangelo's studies of ideal female heads, like the one now at the British Museum, London
(Fig. 45).[8] In other words, the old woman's elaborate headdress as well as the numismatic format
of her profile are deftly manipulated by Passerotti and turned into laughable props. Needless to
say, Caravaggio's servant is neither a parody of, nor a copy after, Michelangelo. Caught in a quasi-
standby mode of expression, the old woman combines seriousness and comicality in indefinite
tension. I emphasize this point since it epitomizes the difficulties of studying Caravaggio's comedic
narratives.

In the course of this introduction, I hope to demonstrate that comedy in early modern painting
and literature differs noticeably from our current notion of the genre. Yet, despite these historical
differences, even if one is conscientious of the concept and implications of comedy operative at the
time, it is difficult to map out the core of Caravaggio's comedic style. There are at least two reasons
for this difficulty. First of all, as I will demonstrate with examples from Comanini and Lomazzo,
there is no clear definition of pictorial comedy in the early modern period. There is no doubt that
Caravaggio's contemporaries considered his early paintings, for instance the two versions of *The
Fortune Teller* or *The Cardsharps*, utterly comic in spirit and genre, as we shall see in the following
chapters. But whereas art theorists developed a panoply of tedious precepts and complex practices
so that painters could achieve excellence in the *istoria*, there existed only bits and pieces of laconic
observations regarding pictorial comedy. Moreover, its status as an analog, albeit of a lower alloy,
of the *istoria* is never established. It is thus unclear whether even the depiction of a comic episode

8   See De Tolnay 1975-1980, 2:94-5, no. 316.

would have ranked as a narrative in Caravaggio's time, although the term *istoria* was certainly used in connection with pictorial "comedies."

If the definition and role of comedy is, to say the least, indistinct in early modern art treatises, nothing is ever said about the lyrical genre in painting. Love, desire, attraction, longing, bereavement, and jealousy were nonetheless familiar topics to painters. But these sentiments are not usually represented independently. When they appear, love and its kindred passions are either summoned allegorically or take part in epic or religious action. Not that early modern painters conceived of lyrical subjects as exclusively subservient to the *istoria*. My interpretation of Titian's *Woman at Her Toilet* in comparison with Caravaggio's *Conversion of Mary Magdalene* in Detroit will suggest the contrary. However, it seems that the transfer from poetry to painting of the lyrical genre entails practical and theoretical obstacles that are almost insurmountable. In the first place, the lyrical "I," an intimate entity by definition, to a great extent eschews pictorial representation. Since it tends to incorporate the poet's viewpoint, the lyrical "I" in painting should be identified with the painter's gaze, and his lyrical feelings and biases should therefore transpire through the beloved's depiction. If this is true, it ensues that the equivalent of a lyric poem in image should be either a portrait or—if the beloved is contemplated in a specific activity, as for example while at her toilet—a genre scene. Neither of these representations, though, can match the magnificence of the *istoria*. Moreover, the nature of lyrical love—intermediate between divine rapture and eroticism—is predictably regarded with suspicion, if not with disdain, by early modern art theorists. This must have discouraged artists to represent "earthly" love without an allegorical or epic framework to justify its treatment. One should bear in mind all of these factors to understand fully why Caravaggio, in summoning attraction and sensuality in his first paintings, resorted to visual patterns current in northern Europe but seldom employed in Renaissance Italy. Important in this respect is the fact that the lyrical component in Caravaggio's early painting is never divorced from the comic.[9] For this reason, and because documentation regarding comedy is much more copious and accessible, I set out here to examine the concept of the comic in early modern art. Only after grasping the precise scope and significance of this genre will it be possible to approach and clarify the specificity of Caravaggio's visual comedies.

In his 1594 *Trattato della pittura, scoltura et architettura*, Giovan Paolo Lomazzo declares that many of the subjects traditionally linked to comedy should stay in view only in places where "low" people meet:

> In inns and taverns, where everything revolves around eating, drinking, trading, and playing, it is appropriate to depict drunkards, as some Germans and Flemings usually do, pimps bringing harlots, gaming, robberies, scenes of folly, histrionics, jokes and, finally, all sorts of debaucheries.[10]

It is noteworthy that Lomazzo does not explicitly classify these figurative themes among the subjects he qualifies as "ridiculous."[11] Here is instead how he defines this pictorial sub-genre:

> Among the numerous elements necessary to compose an *istoria* of merry and laughable things, the most essential is to indicate the cause generating joy, laughing, and bustle,

---

9 For a different interpretation of the "lyrical" in Caravaggio's painting, see Cropper 2006.

10 Lomazzo, 2:304: "Ne gli alberghi ed ostarie, dove d'altro non si ragiona che di mangiare, bevere, giuocare, si ricercano ubriachi, come fanno tra loro certi todeschi e fiamenghi, ruffiani che conducano fanciulle di partito, giochi, furti,

pazzie, istrionerie, scherzamenti e, finalmente, se non effetti dissoluti."

11 For a recent discussion of the "ridiculous" in Milanese painting of the late sixteenth century, see DaCosta Kaufmann 2009, 102-9.

as for instance in a story of lovers [it would be] their amusements, insistent touching and caresses, and in a ridiculous *istoria* those things that may provoke viewers into laughing.[12]

Even if the ridiculous enters into the realm of figurative excess, Lomazzo prompts painters to treat it with much care and propriety, thoroughly pondering the image's compositional layout and narrative consistency:

> It is then necessary that the cause [of laughter] be introduced appropriately, for if somebody appears to have fun and laugh without reason, it would certainly be preposterously silly. This is why one must show the primary cause of laughing by expressing it in such a way that viewers would laugh upon seeing it, even when no figure in the painting appears to laugh because of the painter's negligence, as is often the case. But if this [the cause of laughing] were to be depicted, beholders would roar with laughter, seeing those thoughtless faces, some turned upward, others tilted sideward, while others instead, facing each other, laugh and split their sides, showing their teeth, opening their mouths uncouthly in diverse acts of laughing, widening their nostrils, their eyes sunk within their heads; the figures will blush, fidget, grow fickle and reckless and move randomly, as it occurs in those circumstances; they will furthermore clap their hands, lift and lower them in different ways, slide sideward, bend backward while facing one another, lean forward with their hands over each other's shoulders, and so forth.[13]

Although the ridiculous implies the exaggeration of expression, attitudes, and postures, to the degree that through their movements figures become the polar opposites of the *istoria*'s heroes and heroines, the inappropriateness of ridiculous characters must be always proportionate and appropriately regulated. To be objects of mockery, comic actors ought to adhere perfectly to their comic essence. Like their counterparts in the *istoria*, they are trapped within their role and strictly fettered by the script they enact. If the laughable does not manifest itself immediately, then the painter is deemed negligent and the picture ineffective. To be sure, I am using the term "comic" in spite of the fact that Lomazzo never mentions it. Moreover, as I have pointed out, inn and tavern scenes also belong to the category of comedy, but Lomazzo neither links them to the ridiculous subjects he describes nor explains how to represent them. Would pimps and harlots, cheaters and drunkards, act and move out of proportion like any other ridiculous actor? Should they therefore betray their comic identity by stirring laughing and merriness? And if not, what kind of reaction must they arouse in beholders? It is obvious only that inn and tavern scenes are meant to be fictive prolongations of the locales in which they figure. But to what end? The issue becomes even thornier

12 Lomazzo, 2:314: "Fra tutte le parte che si ricercano per ben comporre una istoria di cose allegre e di riso, la principale è che si vegga la causa per cui l'allegrezza e lo schiamazzo s'introduce, la quale sarebbe, per essempio, in una istoria d'amore lo scherzare, lo stucicare e simili altri vezzi amorosi; ed in una istoria ridicolosa certe cose atte per sua natura a muovere il riso a chiunque le guarda."

13 Ibidem, 314-5: "Secondariamente, è necessario che simili cause s'introducono a proposito; imperoché se si vedesse alcuno far festa e ridere senza causa, certo che sarebbe una pazzia da bastonate; e però bisogna ponere le cause principalmente del riso ed esprimerle in modo tale che i riguardanti si muovano a riso guardandola, ancora che non si vedesse nella pittura per negligenzia dell'artefice alcuno ridere, come spesso aviene. Il che, se si esprimesse, indurebe all'estremo del riso, facendo vedere quei volti spensierati, rivolti chi all'in su e chi per fianco ed altri in altre maniere che, di rincontro guardandosi, ridano e smascellino, mostrando i denti, aprendo sconciamente la bocca in nuovo e diverso atto di ridere, allargando le narici e nascondendo gli occhi nel capo, onde si veggano rossi, inconstanti, volubili, inconsiderati e posti a caso, come aviene in tali occorrenze; battendo oltre ciò le mani insieme, alzandole ed abbassandole in diversi modi, lasciandosi andare per fianco, riversandosi indietro e ponendosi a fronte, inchinati avanti con le mani sopra le spalle scambievolmente e simili."

when one turns to Comanini's precepts. Since the comic is a pictorial genre, evidently its actors cannot exhibit the same great stature of heroes and heroines; therefore, they should be shorter and perhaps less visible. But is this the only difference between the nobility of the *istoria* and the baseness of comedy? In light of early modern norms and strictures in matters of conformity, it is on the contrary perfectly conceivable that the composition of a comic painting should require diverse and particular formats and layouts. Yet not a single word is proffered in this regard.

To comprehend what the notion of comic represented in Caravaggio's time, one must resort to contemporary literary theory. Lodovico Castelvetro's[14] 1570 careful exegesis of Aristotle's *Poetics* will help us elucidate the question. It should be recalled that Castelvetro does not systematically heed Aristotle's opinion; although he rarely dissents from it in an explicit manner, his interpretation of the *Poetics* leads him to embrace and formulate positions that drastically stray from, or altogether transcend, those of Aristotle. For instance, Castelvetro firmly believes that morality—good and evil in the broadest sense—does not determine the divisions and articulations through which the mimetic arts—tragedy, epic, poetry, and so forth—are practiced and classified. Rather, he strives to demonstrate that the social status of the main characters, whether they be kings, citizens or peasants, governs the specificity of each genre:

> Poetry is divided into different species due not to the good or ill customs of the subjects chosen by the poets for imitation, but rather because of the subjects' status, whether royalty, citizenry or peasantry. In accordance with these qualities, [poets] primarily settle on stories appropriate to the subjects' condition, which are actions that have never taken place, but are likely to occur, not in order to reveal [the subjects'] customs, whether good or evil, but to delight the populace as much as possible with the novelty of the events.[15]

As a general rule, Castelvetro tends to surpass the dichotomy between the high—the aristocracy—and the low—the peasants—by strengthening the importance of the "middle" class he characterizes as citizens. By doing so, he disrupts the traditional associations of nobility with good and peasantry with evil. More importantly, he strips the mimetic arts of their moral function by asserting that aesthetic pleasure, triggered by novelty, is the only goal of mimesis. Of course, many theorists would not follow Castelvetro's opinion in this respect, and numerous art treatises of the late sixteenth and seventeenth centuries would continue to insist on the ethical and religious tasks of images and the *istoria*. Castelvetro nevertheless dilutes the relevance of morality by proposing that other concomitant factors are at play in the conception and unfolding of a poetic fiction: mind, election, chance, condition, and action. The first two concern man's inner qualities; the other three depend on external circumstances. Mind in men acts as either prudence or stupidity; choice results in either good or evil. Chance leads either to happiness or misery. Man's condition is either noble or private (note that the lowest class does not count any longer here, or is assimilated wholesale to the citizenry), and action can be philosophical or civic. However, according to Castelvetro, poetry does not adjust itself to philosophy, and therefore all poetic actions are civic. Mixed together in diverse proportions, these factors—prudence and stupidity, good and evil, misery and happiness, nobility

---

14 For Castelvetro, see more recently Roncaccia 2006; and Firpo and Mongini 2008.

15 Castelvetro, 1:53: "La qual poesia si distingue in diverse spezie non per bontà o per malvagità de' costumi delle persone che sono elette dal poeta da rassomigliare, ma per gli stati delle persone, o reali o cittadine o contadine; e avendo rispetto a quelle, s'eleggono principalmente le favole convenevoli alla loro condizione, che non sono altro che azzioni non avenute ma possibili ad avenire, non per iscoprire i costumi o la bontà o la malvagità, ma per dilettare con la novità del caso quanto si può il più il commune popolo, il quale n'è capace e ne prende maggior diletto che non fa della dottrina o dello scoprimento de' costumi o d'insegnamento appertenente ad arte o scienza o di cose usitate ad avenire sempre ad una guisa."

and citizenry—fashion the specificity of any poetic work. This does not mean that Castelvetro is indifferent to the cultural and moral superiority of the aristocracy as was universally accepted at his time. He indeed admits that although nobility can accompany evil and peasantry good, in most cases positive values inspire the attitudes of the noblest:

> It is true that [social status] does not always carry with it one feature or another indifferently, for citizenry, if it inclines toward peasantry or plebs, will carry with it stupidity rather than prudence, and royalty will instead carry with it prudence. Tragedy, since it imitates royalty, will content itself with good rather than evil, although it does not renounce evil altogether and seems to indulge in misery rather than happiness, even if sometimes happiness is also envisioned.[16]

In my view, the flexibility of Castelvetro's casuistry is absolutely astounding in the context of the standards of his time. Even more surprising is his lack of interest in moral meaning as conveyed by poetry. There follows a passage in which he further clarifies the point:

> Thus, it is evident (...) that nobility, or royalty, and vileness, or citizenry, determine the difference in poetry with regard to the subject matter. One discerns nobility and vileness not through good and evil, but through behavior. If informed by propriety, behavior reveals nobility; if informed by impropriety, it reveals baseness. By propriety and impropriety I do not mean those attitudes and customs that attest to the good or evil of an actor's soul, but those that elicit the kindness or crudeness of an actor, and that rely on the mind, that is, on prudence or stupidity.[17]

In other words, the kindness of nobility is the product of prudence, not of goodness. Castelvetro even chastises Aristotle for dividing humankind on the basis of good and evil, although in the end he concedes that the fault of this division lies with the Stoics and not with Aristotle: they "do not consider anyone noble but the virtuous, and vile but the vicious. [Yet], this [philosophical] sect has no authority in poetry, which follows the common opinion of the populace, according to which there are good and evil among noble men as well as among vile men."[18] Paradoxically, Castelvetro envisages the possibility for a nobleman to be evil, but not to act improperly:

> The nobleman must endeavor to avoid vile men's customs as much as possible, since these are not worthy of the preeminence and nobility by which he seeks to abide, whereas the vile man lives as his appetites urge him, and does not care if others judge him for whom he is not.[19]

---

16 Ibidem, 1:54: "Egli è vero che non si tirano dietro indifferentemente o l'una o l'altra parte sempre, percioché lo stato privato, se dichinerà al contadino e al plebeo, si tirerà dietro più volontieri la sciocchezza che l'accorgimento, e lo stato reale si tirerà dietro l'accorgimento. E la tragedia che rassomiglia lo stato reale si contenterà più della bontà che della malvagità, quantunque non rifiuti ancora la malvagità e paia che si compiaccia più nella miseria che nella felicità, benché riceva ancora la felicità."

17 Ibidem: "Adunque per le cose dette di sopra appare che la nobiltà, o lo stato reale, e la viltà, o lo stato privato, constituiscono la differenza della poesia per cagione della materia; la quale nobiltà o viltà non si discerne per portamenti; i quali portamenti se sono informati di convenevolezza scoprono la nobiltà, e se sono informati di sconvenevolezza scoprono la viltà. E per convenevolezza e sconvenevolezza io intendo modi e costumi che non testimonino della bontà o della malvagità dell'animo dell'operante, ma facciano fede della gentilezza o della rusticità dell'operante, e procedano dallo 'ngegno, cioè dall'accorgimento o dalla sciocchezza."

18 Ibidem, 1:54-55: "E per vero dire, Aristotele in questo luogo, avendo nominati i migliori avendo rispetto alla bontà dell'animo, e i piggiori alla malvagità, s'è accostato troppo agli stoici, li quali non reputano nobile se non il virtuoso, e vile se non il vizioso; la qual setta non ha luogo nella poesia, che seguita il commune parere del popolo, secondo il quale sono de' nobili buoni e malvagi, e parimente de' vili buoni e malvagi."

19 Ibidem, 1:55: "Conciosia cosa che il nobile si guardi a tutto suo potere da' costumi simili a que' del vile, e per conseguente indegni della maggioranza e della nobiltà nella quale si sforza di mantenersi; là dove il vile vive secondo che l'appetito tira, non curandosi che altri il reputi quello che non è."

At first glance, Castelvetro appears to illustrate and perhaps sponsor an elitist culture of appearances, but it would be wrong to evaluate his assessments by this token. In reality, Castelvetro tries to separate the notion of aesthetic pleasure from that of moral utility, and as a consequence, seemingly dismantles the entire system of ethical values on which the definition of mimesis and poetry traditionally relied. What matters to us in this discussion is the fact that genres and characters are not variants, operating independently from social institutions and cultural principles. In Caravaggio's time, representing a gypsy, a naïve youth, a cheater or a woman at her toilet anticipated and appeased certain expectations for viewers who belonged mostly to the elite and would have balked at the idea of being assimilated to the populace. These viewers must have approached the depictions of "vile" actors such as Caravaggio's with prejudice: that is, armed with moral judgments, a sense of superiority, ironic detachment and, perhaps, condescension. To be successful, these images needed not only to translate action with propriety and in a "comic" way, but also to support and confirm the prejudicial standpoint of this audience. Needless to say, Castelvetro's disjunction of the moral and the social would not have applied in this circumstance. It is doubtful, indeed, that beholders of Caravaggio's early "comedies" would have then been able to disassociate moral values from social status. In stating this, I also realize that Castelvetro's theory might give rise to another type of paradox. If, as I have posited, painters must meet their audience's expectations, how much latitude do they have for novel expression? Put otherwise, does novelty not risk interfering with expectation? Remember that the former rests on marvel and presupposes change, whereas the latter feeds on certainties and deep-rooted convictions. I shall return to this question, since I believe it is paramount for an understanding of Caravaggio's novelty in pictorial comedy.

Following in Aristotle's footsteps, Castelvetro recognizes Homer as the inventor of epic in its twofold form, serious and comic, the former resulting in tragedy, the latter in comedy. This distinction is essential to understanding the early modern notion of poetry, from tragedy to comedy. Indeed, the two original kinds of poetry not only mirror the twofold nature of humankind—for some are inclined to magnificence and austerity, others to pleasure and lightheartedness—but they also diverge with regard to their technical configuration: epic is rendered in hexameters, comedy in iambics. Furthermore, epic appeals to nobility, comedy to the populace down to the plebs and peasantry:

> Thus emerged the two qualities that ordinarily accompany the two types of poetry mentioned above, originating in their high and low conditions [respectively], since severity is unlikely to be separated without blame and impropriety from the actions of gods and kings, and pleasantness usually follows the actions of private citizens and servants.[20]

It follows that comedy, in Aristotle's own terms, is the fictional realm wherein the worst and vilest natures are represented:

> As we have said, comedy is the imitation of the worst, but not on account of every vice. The risible partakes of ugliness. Therefore, the risible is a certain defect or deformation, involving neither pain nor damage. For instance, an ugly and distorted face without pain is risible.[21]

20   Ibidem, 1:109: "O più tosto si formarono due qualità che per lo più accompagnano le due sopradette maniere di poesia, nate dalle condizioni alta e bassa, perciochè non pare che la severità si possa scostare senza biasimo di sconvenevolezza dall'azzioni divine e reali, e la piacevolezza per lo più seguita l'azzioni private e servili."

21   Ibidem, 1:126: "Ἡ δὲ κωμῳδία ἐστίν, ὥσπερ εἴπομεν, μίμησις φαυλοτέρων μέν, οὐ μέντοι κατὰ πᾶσαν κακίαν, ἀλλὰ τοῦ αἰσχροῦ ἐστι τὸ γελοῖον μόριον. Τὸ γάρ γελοῖόν ἐστιν ἁμάρτημά τι καί αἶσχος ἀνώδυνον καί οὐ φθαρτικόν, οἷον εὐθὺς τὸ γελοῖον πρόσωπον αἰσχρόν τι καί διεστραμμένον ἄνευ ὀδύνης. Ora la comedia è, come dicemmo, rassomiglianza

Because of its succinctness, Aristotle's definition of comedy does not satisfy Castelvetro, who instead believes that "Aristotle's learning does not allow for laughter through stupidity, but astonishes people owing to its subtlety."[22] To justify Aristotle's position, Castelvetro thus identifies diverse sources of hilarity, of which one in particular provides appropriate matter for comedy:

> The second kind of pleasant things likely to arouse laughter in us is the deception of others. I mean those deceptions on account of which others say, do or endure things that they would never say, do or endure should they not be deceived. Hence, we like and enjoy other people's deception extremely, as it moves us to laugh out of hilarity (…). Indeed, those who are not deceived, upon seeing others being deceived, feel better and superior especially in that feature through which they come closer to God and far surpass the other animals—that is, in reason.[23]

Nevertheless, Castelvetro would not approve of representing any sort of deception in poetry:

> Now, these sorts of deceptions, whether carried out through tricks purposefully hatched by people or arisen by chance, which we have said do not cause any damage to the person deceived, make us laugh and offer a subject matter appropriate to new comedy, and are certainly more decent than those deriving from stupidity or originating in corporal deformities, which seem to be particularly recommended by Aristotle as subject matters for comedy.[24]

It is noteworthy that Castelvetro not only disapproves of Aristotle's definition, but also condemns poetic imitations in which ignorance, stupidity, and physical defects are lampooned. By

de' piggiori, non già secondo ogni vizio. Ma il ridevole è particella della turpitudine. Percioché il ridevole è un certo difetto e turpitudine, senza dolore e senza guastamento, come per non andare lontano, per essempio, ridevole è alcuna faccia turpe e storta senza dolore." It is noteworthy that Aristotle's definition of comedy is generally accepted and upheld by Renaissance literary theorists. In his 1528 *Libro del Cortegiano*, Castiglione, 134, notes: "Il loco adunque e quasi il fonte onde nascono gli ridiculi consiste in una certa bruttezza e deformità, perché solamente o almen più che de l'altre cose si ride di quelle che hanno in sé disconvenienza e pare che stiano male senza però star male. (…) Però conveniente è ridersi degli vicii collocati in persone né misere tanto che movino compassione, né tanto scelerate che il mertino esser condenate a pena capitale." In his 1550 *De ridiculis*, Maggi, 302, asserts: "Ridiculum igitur peccatum et turpitudinem quondam esse sine dolore, ut deformis ac distorta facies absque dolore, auctor est Aristoteles (…) quod etiam Cicero significare videtur cum inquit: haec enim ridentur vel sola vel maxime quae notant et designant turpitudinem aliquam non turpiter." Of a quite different opinion was Annibale Carracci, according to Giovanni Antonio Massani (alias Giovanni Atanasio Mosini) in his 1646 *Diverse figure di Annibale Carracci.* See Agucchi, 157: "(…) la Natura nell'alterare alcun oggetto, facendo un grosso naso, una gran bocca o la gobba, o in altra maniera alcuna parte deformando, ella n'accenna un modo di lei prendersi piacere e scherzo intorno a quell'oggetto, e di sì fatta deformità o sproporzione ridersi ancor essa per la sua ricreazione. E così piacevolmente soggiungeva Annibale che, quando l'artefice questi tali oggetti imita, non può far di meno di non compiacersene ancor esso e darne egualmente diletto ad altri; poiché le cose in tale maniera prodotte, avendo per se stesse del ridicolo, riescono poi, quando sono ben imitate, doppiamente dilettevoli: perché il riguardante gran piacere si prende dalla qualità che muove a riso, e gode dell'imitazione che per se stessa è cosa dilettevolissima." If this is the principle that inspired Annibale's comic representations, and in particular caricatures, it is evident that it diverges noticeably from Caravaggio's "comedy."

22 Castelvetro, 1:157: "Conciosia che gli 'nsegnamenti d'Aristotele per isciocchezza non dieno da ridere, ma per sottilità rendano altrui stupefatto."

23 Ibidem, 1:128: "La seconda maniera delle cose piacentici, potenti a destare il riso in noi, sono gli 'nganni d'altrui: io dico quelli inganni per cagione de' quali altri dice o fa o patisce cose, le quali cose né direbbe né farebbe né patirebbe se non fosse ingannato. Gli 'nganni altrui, adunque, ci piacciono oltre a modo e ci dilettano e ci costringono per l'alegrezza a ridere, essendo cagione la natura nostra corrotta per lo peccato de' nostri primi parenti, la quale si ralegra del male altrui come del proprio suo bene; e spezialmente del male che procede da quella parte che è propria dell'uomo, cioè dal senno naturale, parendo a coloro che non sono ingannati, veggendo gli altri ingannarsi, d'essere da più di loro e di soperchiargli in quella cosa massimamente, cioè nella ragione, per che eglino s'avvicinano a Dio e trapassano di gran lunga tutti gli altri animali."

24 Ibidem, 1:132-3: "Ora gli uni inganni e gli altri, cioè i nati per insidie a posta tesi dagli uomini e i nati a caso, che dicemmo non essere molto dannosi allo 'ngannato, danno da ridere e possono essere soggetto convenevole della comedia nuova, e più convenevole che non sono gli 'nganni procedenti da sciocchezza o da alcuna turpitudine corporale, li quali parevano esser commendati spezialmente da Aristotele per soggetto comico."

distancing himself from Aristotle, he proudly reminds us that the genre of comedy he delineates is unprecedented: modern comedy as opposed to that of ancient Greece and Rome. More importantly, Castelvetro's comedy embraces deception as the source of the risible, and as such it thrives on the audience's reaction to, and complicity with, the act and play of deceiving. In a certain sense, Castelvetro unknowingly or indirectly recognizes the deceptive charge of comedy. More than its opposite, tragedy, comedy implies and requires the beholder's awareness and connivance. In and of itself, the comic fosters the meta-comic by beguiling the spectator into plots structured as deception pieces. However, despite its "political correctness," new comedy does not renounce bawdiness altogether:

> The fourth and last type of pleasant things that move us to laugh are those that pertain to carnal pleasure, such as the [representation of] shameful body parts and lascivious intercourse, as well as the accounts of, and allusions to, [such things]. However, one must be aware that these things do not make us laugh when they are overtly exhibited to the eyes and proposed to the mind in the presence of others, but rather cause us to be ashamed and blush.[25]

Hence, to avoid embarrassment and suspicion, salacity must be presented "under some veil, through which we can pretend to laugh not at the dishonesty, but at something else."[26] Put otherwise, comedy entails but does not contain bawdiness, which is alluded to yet never fully disclosed. Lasciviousness thus operates through innuendo, as demonstrated by a passage from a trecento novella that Castelvetro records in his treatise: "one day, a man endowed with a huge nature went to a whore; when they were in the bedroom and he showed it, the woman laughed out of great contentment."[27] I should emphasize that neither Castelvetro nor Lomazzo envisions love or attraction as an appropriate subject matter for comedy, which consequently remains the domain of "allusive" flesh. As I shall demonstrate in the following chapters, this is far from being the case in Caravaggio's pictorial comedies.

It is no coincidence that two of Caravaggio's major early narrative paintings, *The Fortune Teller* and *The Cardsharps*, hinge on deception: a gypsy charming a young man in order to snatch his ring; a swindler extracting a false card from his belt in order to defeat an innocent boy at a card game. Many scholars have rightly associated the deception theme in these works to the notion of painting as interpreted by Caravaggio. The image itself is perceived and constructed as a joyous, deceptive mechanism in which beholders remain entrapped. Caravaggio's portentous illusionism—his capability to engender reality effects—is a deception act in its own right. While I agree with this interpretation, I do not think it tells the whole story. The paintings I set out to examine not only perform deception, but also encapsulate and convey it. Viewers are caught in the middle of a comedic play they believe they understand, only to discover that it is beyond their comprehension. In the end, they are helplessly deceived by the painter and his pictorial swindle. For one thing, the actors Caravaggio depicts in these pictures—actors that some scholars tend erroneously to pigeonhole as masks of the *commedia dell'arte*—do not obey their comic role. By and large, they do not conform to their comic essence. Therefore, they act unpredictably by

---

25 Ibidem, 1:134: "La quarta e ultima maniera delle cose piacentici che ci muovono a riso sono tutte le cose che pertengono a diletto carnale, come le membra vergognose, i congiugnimenti lascivi, le memorie e le similitudini di quelli. Ma è da por mente che le predette cose non ci fanno ridere quando ci sono proposte aperte avanti agli occhi della fronte o della mente in presenza di persone, anzi ci confondono di vergogna e ci fanno arrossare."

26 Ibidem, 1:135: "Adunque le cose predette piacentici ci fanno ridere quando ci sono in presenza altrui presentate sotto alcuno velame, per mezzo del quale possiamo fare vista di non ridere della disonestà, ma d'altro."

27 Ibidem: "Ecco n'è uno essempio nelle novelle antiche: 'Avenne che un giorno un che avea gran naturale si trovò con una putta; quando furo in camera, e elli lo mostrò e per grande alegrezza la donna rise'."

simultaneously prodding and stifling the cathartic laughter of comedy. To laugh, as Lomazzo suggests, the cause of laughter must be obvious, and the figures utterly ridiculous. Caravaggio instead suspends the swindle in mid-air, omitting its outcome, and misleading the viewer toward a lyrical subtext. More relevantly, his figures do not incorporate the ridiculous canons that, like iambic meters in ancient comedy, would characterize them as comedians. As I shall demonstrate, Caravaggio depicts his comic characters with visual patterns that belong to higher genres: the epic, the lyric, and the martial. To paraphrase Comanini, he employs hexameters or hendecasyllables in evoking the vilest. From the outset, the nature of Caravaggio's comic actors is blurred and, to a certain extent, compromised. As a general rule, their actions are neither excessive nor scurrilous or lascivious, with the sole exception of the cheater's accomplice in *The Cardsharps*. Instead seduction, attraction, contemplation, and wonder dominate. In this way, both the base and low substance of comedy and the social and cultural order it reflects are called into question. Caravaggio's comic figures have lost their identities. In this regard, they are the opposite of masks, although their status remains indeterminate and escapes interpretation. It comes as little surprise that Caravaggio, rather than stating his dissension from the order comedy traditionally incarnates, disrupts his work by dint of suspension. Visual and conceptual uncertainty indeed nourishes the excitement of gaming, increases the effect of deception intrinsic in playing, and sharpens the beholder's curiosity. As such, suspension is a rhetorical device that pertains wholly to both art and gaming.

In his 1582 *Il Gonzaga secondo, overo del giuoco*, Torquato Tasso defines gaming as an "imitation of contests,"[28] and as such assimilates it to the mimetic arts, to poetry overall: "it is thus no wonder that poetry is the profession of poets and a game for spectators."[29] Unlike poetry, though, gaming does not seem to qualify as an art or profession, since fortune and probability—which Tasso brilliantly distinguishes—contribute to its unfolding. Yet Tasso places gaming among the "conjectural arts" like those of "captains and sailors": men who use their experience to establish rules and observations on which they rest in order to remedy the mishaps of fortune and chance.[30] But what kinds of norms and statistics could a player follow? In a card game,

> one [player] makes his observations from the timing in calling the bet, or in accepting it, and from what usually happens to him who calls the bet; or from the adversaries' mood and resolution in escaping or parrying; or from the way of playing, whether bolder or more cautious, whether more or less generous, and from what these moves allow one to do, whether easily or with difficulty. In addition, the player gauges the rest of his own cards and those of his adversaries, keeps in mind those he discards and those still in the deck, anticipates which cards his adversaries hold in their hands, and makes a judgment from their expressions and faces in which fear, hope, greed, and happiness can hardly be faked. On all these observations one will ground what you call the art of gaming.[31]

28 Tasso b, 6v: "Dunque sin'ora, oh signore Annibale, abbiam ritrovato ch'una sorte di giuochi si ritrova, la quale è imitazione delle contese, non vera contesa."

29 Ibidem, 7r: "Niuna meraviglia è dunque che la poesia sia studio de' poeti e giuochi de gli spettatori."

30 Ibidem, 17r: "Mi pare che voi abbiate descritte quelle che da alcuni son chiamate arti congetturali, qual è forse quella del capitano e del navigante."

31 Ibidem, 17v: "Ma di questi effetti né a voi pare che se ne possa rendere alcuna ragione, né io so chi n'abbia fatta osservazione alcuna; ma l'osservazioni si fanno più tosto de' tempi dell'invitare e dell'accettar l'invito, e di quel che soglia avenire ad un ch'inviti, o pur dell'animo e della risoluzione de gli avversari con la quale si muovono a fuggire o a far difesa; delle maniere de' giuochi, altre più ardite, altre più caute, altre più scarse, altre più liberali, e di quel che con ciascuna d'esse si faccia più facilmente o più difficilmente; misura oltre di ciò il giuocatore il suo resto e quel de gli avversari; tien memoria delle carte che ha scartate e di quelle che sono nel mazzo, e dall'une e dall'altre argomenta quel che gli avversari possono aver nelle mani; e da' sembianti e dal volto eziandio, ne' quali il timore e la speranza e la cupidità e l'allegrezza difficilmente posson ricorprirsi; e da queste osservazioni tutte farà quella che da voi arte de' giuocatori è stata detta."

Caravaggio's *The Cardsharps* pushes the viewer into a realm of deception and probability, transforming him or her into yet another player at the gaming table. All of the excitement bound up with a semi-artistic entertainment such as the card game resonates in the painting's compositional structure. By imitating what is already an imitation, the fictional contest of two adversaries, the picture in turn becomes a playing field: a new genre of fiction in which the determinacy of the *istoria*—its rules and conventions based on unshakeable facts and tenets, along with its claim for unrestricted legibility—yields to indeterminacy and duplicity. Conceived of as an open play, Caravaggio's comedic narrative brings the beholder through suspense to an intermediary state of involvement, one in which pleasure relies on expectancy and participation, and not on the possession of knowledge and certainty, a play whose outcome is perhaps predictable, yet far from assured. As Tasso demonstrates, players and spectators alike take pleasure in playing or watching a game:

> Even if the operation and imitation [of a contest] usually bring pleasure, the uncertainty of victory and the emotions felt on account of this uncertainty most greatly entertain not only the players, but also the viewers who tend to watch the game with a certain partiality.[32]

It is understandable that an essential shift in the history of pictorial narrative should have first occurred in a minor genre such as comedy. However, with his early paintings Caravaggio discovers and applies a paramount principle of narrative, regardless of its literary or visual manifestations: behind a told or represented story, there is a flux of energy, an appetite for unveiling, understanding and knowledge, and a flow of expectations that is in and of itself matter for inventiveness. This stream of narration, though it tends to an outcome feverishly awaited by readers or viewers, is independent from the plot's specificity, and as such can be channeled, manipulated, and occasionally frozen in order to multiply its effect. By choosing situations of low narratives that appeal to the beholder's emotions, but not to his memory, that is, narratives with unknown ends, and therefore radically different from the canonical subjects of the *istoria* whose contents were solidly engraved in the minds of the elite, Caravaggio focuses more on the narrative momentum than on the story itself, straddling its energy in a slow (the first version of *The Fortune Teller*) or fast (*The Cardsharps*) tempo. More specifically, *The Cardsharps* in this regard might well be Caravaggio's manifesto of a novel narrative thematically and analogically construed as a game of deception, that is, a machine for illusionary, conceptual, and interpretive misdirection, or in other words, a prelude to his poetics of dislocation, a play of mirrors in which beholders lose their cultural and social coordinates under the spell of an amusement-piece. Caravaggio would soon confront the challenges of the *istoria*, and especially tackle the delicate question of introducing indeterminacy and suspense into stories whose outcomes were instead firmly ensconced in his beholders' minds. Also at stake would be the idea of novelty and the urge to reform painting. The case of the *Conversion of Mary Magdalene* is thus of paramount importance in this connection. As I shall explain, Caravaggio endeavors there to recreate the dislocating effects of his early paintings, but in a religious subject. Despite the intensity of his efforts, he does not succeed entirely in

---

32 Ibidem, 11r: "Ma come ch'io non neghi che l'operazione e l'imitazione soglia apportare diletto, l'incertitudine nondimeno della vittoria e gli affetti ch'in questa incertitudine si sentono, non solo a' giuocatori, ma a' riguardanti ancora che con alcuna animosità di parte sogliono i giuochi rimirare, è di grandissimo trattenimento." See in this regard Castelvetro, 1: 39: "Ora il predetto soggetto [a miracle or prodigy] ci diletta per la sua novità miracolosa e non usitata, sì come ci dilettano non pure tutte le cose miracolose, ma le prosopopee ancora, senza che non ci porge poco piacere l'esser noi tenuti sospesi prima che veggiamo il fine dove si dee riuscire, il quale è d'insegnarci buoni costumi o d'indurci a fare o a fuggire alcuna cosa."

disjoining the narrative from the narration, or the canonical story from its actual enactment. Yet the essence of new meaning, the invention of a new poetics, and the possibility of dislodging a social and cultural order also lie in the gap between narration and narrative. For the time being, Caravaggio contents himself with unpacking painting's outcasts and sidestepping the margins of traditional genre distinctions, as if for fun.

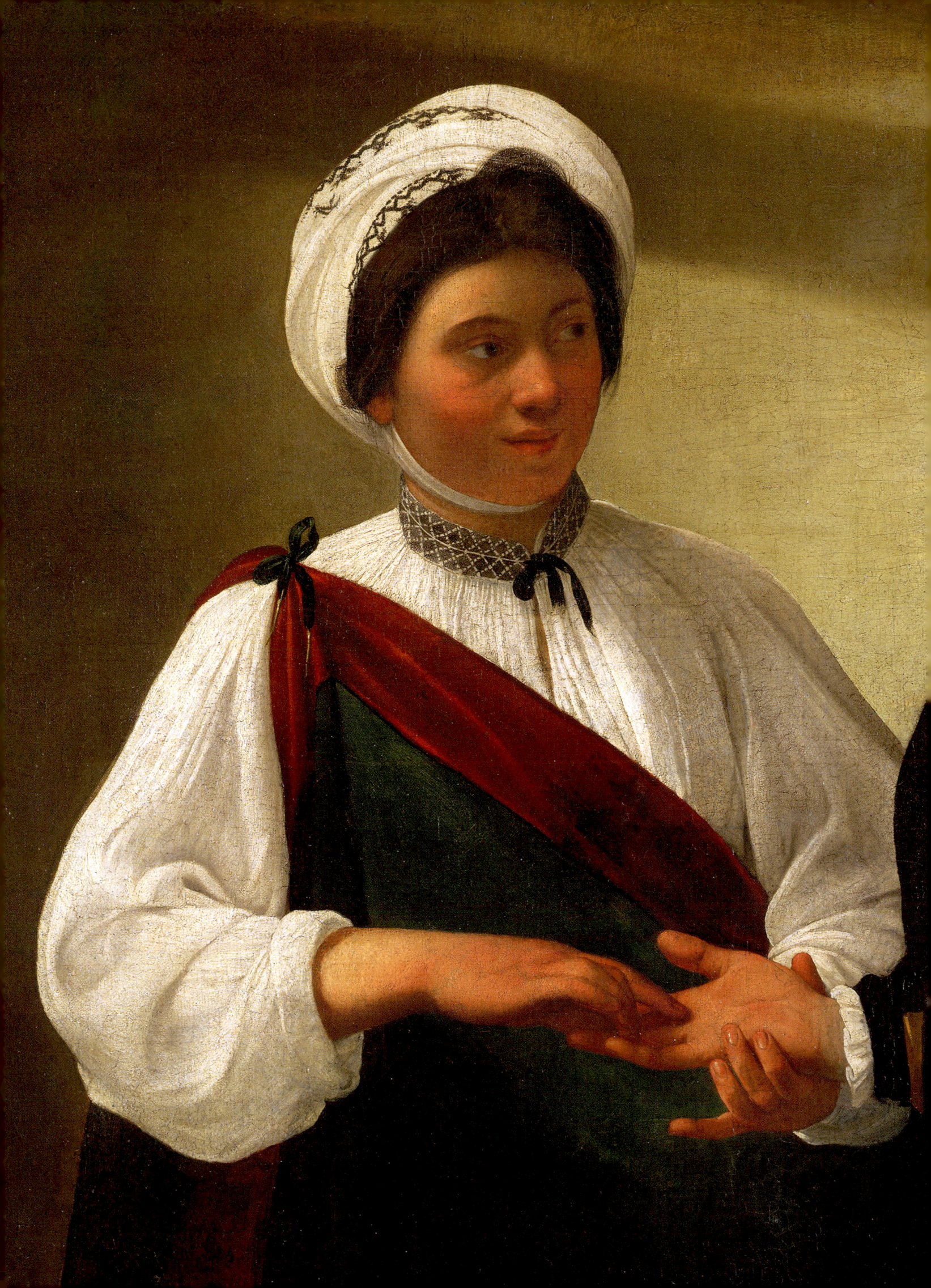

CHAPTER 4

Money and Seduction: Narrative Patterns in Caravaggio's Two Versions of *The Fortune Teller*

A Comic Scene?

Shortly after he is first recorded in Rome, in 1594,[1] Caravaggio painted the first version of *The Fortune Teller* (Pinacoteca Capitolina, Rome; Fig. 46).[2] Although it is impossible to ascertain its date, stylistic evidence indicates that it is one of Caravaggio's earliest extant pictures. A few years later, probably in 1596-1597, Caravaggio painted a second *Fortune Teller* (Louvre, Paris; Fig. 47).[3]

1   For these questions, see more recently Berra 2005, 245-58.

2   The painting belonged first to Cardinal Francesco Maria Del Monte, then to Cardinal Emanuele Pio. Cardinal Del Monte most probably bought it to accompany Caravaggio's *The Cardsharps* (now in Fort Worth, Kimbell Art Museum), which he commissioned at an indeterminate date, maybe around 1595-1596. It is also possible that Cardinal Del Monte commissioned *The Cardsharps*, after buying *The Fortune Teller*, as a pendant. See Mancini, 1:224; and Baglione, 136 ["Effigiò una Zingara, che dava la ventura ad un giovane con bel colorito"]. For the painting see Friedlaender 1969, 153 ["It is not necessarily an original, whereas the Louvre painting undoubtedly is. The features of the faces are blurred and the figures lack the square-shouldered firmness of the Louvre painting. In older literature it is always considered a free copy, often attributed to Saraceni"]; Frommel 1971, 16-8; Cuzin 1977, 10-1 [probably not an original]; Cinotti 1983, 519-21, no. 58; Hibbard 1983, 276-7 [as a copy of a lost original]; Christiansen 1985, 215-20 [catalogue entry by Mina Gregori]; Tittoni Monti 1989; Calvesi 1990, 228-30; Bologna 1992, 303-4; Bersani and Dutoit 1998, 16-8 [mostly erotic]; Puglisi 1998, 75; Guarino 1999; Longhi 1999-2000, 1:204 [1952]; Langdon 2001, 45; Marini 2005, 403-4, no. 19 ["percepibile substrato evangelico-morale"]; Schütze 2009, 249, no. 9. For a technical report of the painting, see Gregori 1991, 91-5. As already noted by Röttgen 1974, 125, the head of the Madonna underneath Caravaggio's *Fortune Teller* seems to be related to *The Crowning of the Virgin* by the Cavaliere d'Arpino for the Chiesa Nuova (Rome, Glorieri Chapel), commissioned in 1593, but finished in 1615. A preparatory drawing by the Cavaliere for the Virgin, dated to 1594-1596 by Röttgen 2002, 406-7, no. 165, now in a private collection, seems to be very close to the Virgin represented on the canvas of *The Fortune Teller*. The same applies to another Virgin by the Cavaliere d'Arpino, represented with the Child and Saint Jerome, and executed around 1594 according to Röttgen (Ibidem, 285, no. 54-54a). For Caravaggio's work in the Cavalier d'Arpino's workshop, see Van Mander, 3:191; Mancini, 1:224; Baglione, 136; and Bellori, 213. For the Cavalier d'Arpino's collection of paintings, which included works by Caravaggio, see Hermann Fiore 2000.

3   The painting belonged to Alessandro Vittrice, and later to Camillo Doria Pamphilj, who in 1665 sent it to France as a gift

for Louis XIV. As it was damaged in transit, it was restored in France. It was then enlarged at the top, and the feather in the hat almost entirely repainted. See Mancini, 1:109, 140, 224; Scannelli, 1:199; Chantelou, 207, 212 [Bernini, who saw the *Fortune Teller* upon its arrival in Paris, considered it "un pauvre tableau, sans esprit ni invention"]; Bellori, 202-3. For interpretations, see Francastel 1938, 51-2; Friedlaender 1969, 81-3, 152-3 [idyllic-erotic more than comic]; Salerno 1966, 109-10 [moralizing]; Frommel 1971, 16-8, 25; Wind B. 1974, 31-2 [Relying on a sixteenth-century engraving that represents a scene from a comedy, which he apparently misunderstands, Wind concludes: "Caravaggio could have been familiar with this vignette in a theatrical as well as a visual context. Caravaggio, whose companions were "herzhafter gesellen' (Sandrart, *Teutsche Academie*), was surely acquainted with the stock characters and actions depicted on the contemporary stage. In any event, the *Fortune Teller*, like a comedy, can be considered a witty statement on human failing." In my opinion, the French engraving considered by Wind as a possible point of departure for Caravaggio's painting, bears no more than a vague similarity to the *Fortune Teller*. It should be noted that the subject of the engraving is a comic swindle perpetrated by the three characters present in the composition, to the detriment of a fourth, absent but mentioned in the inscription below the engraving.]; Cuzin 1977, esp. 34 ["Sens moralisant ou sous-entendu évangélique? Les deux interprétations se complètent et s'enrichissent. La richesse d'interprétation du chef-d'œuvre résiste au décortiquage érudit; il assume toutes les interprétations, voulues et non par le peintre, saisies ou non par ses contemporains: seule compte la force novatrice de l'image. Mais il faut bien lire ici, au-delà de l'éclat des accoutrements et du chatoiement des couleurs, malgré les visages poupins et souriants (le seul sourire échangé de tout l'œuvre…) une pessimiste leçon de défiance: refus du jeune peintre des promesses d'avenir, et quelque vénéneuse amertume"]; Moir 1982, 68; Cinotti 1983, 484-7, no. 42; Hibbard 1983, 23-9 [idyllic-erotic]; Calvesi 1990, 228-30 ["Va ricordato che l'esemplare capitolino della *Buona Ventura* era stato eseguito per il cardinal Del Monte e che questi in una lettera del 2 settembre 1596 (…) citava a Federico Borromeo un'assonante massima di sant'Agostino: 'et si ricordi ch'io le dissi, e 'Mundus, Caro, Demonia movent nobis proelia diversa.' La vanità, la carne, il demonio. È ben probabile che il Caravaggio, per suggerimento del Del Monte, abbia tradotto

135

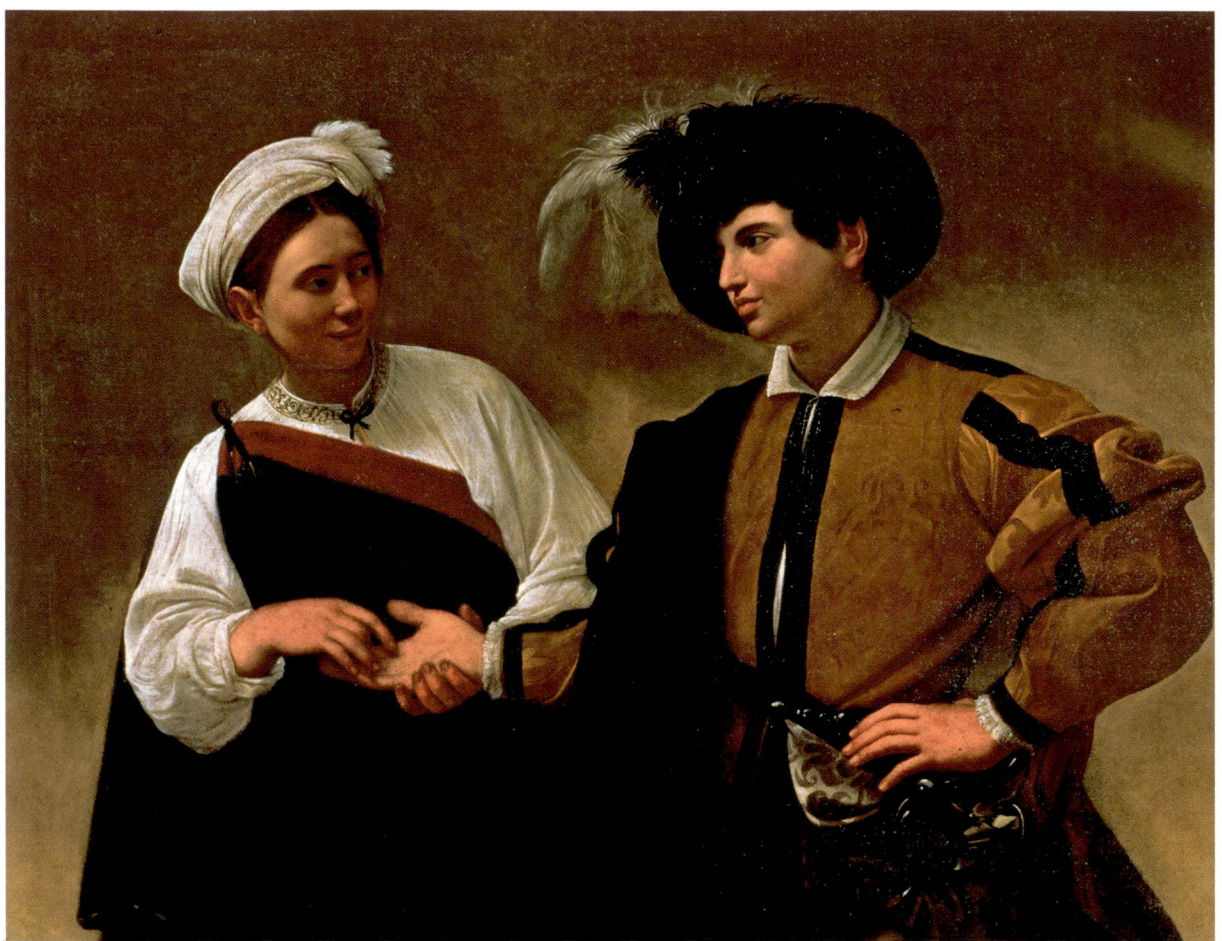

Fig. 46
Michelangelo Merisi da Caravaggio, *The Fortune Teller*, Pinacoteca Capitolina, Rome, oil on canvas, 115 x 150 cm.

Almost identical in composition, this version nevertheless differs from the Rome picture in several details, which I will discuss below.[4]

In his 1617-1621 *Considerazioni sulla pittura*, Giulio Mancini transliterates the narrative situation implied in Caravaggio's second *Fortune Teller*:

> The gypsy displays her craftiness through her feigned smile while removing the ring of the young man, and he [reveals] his simplicity and sensual attraction to the beauty of the gypsy, who tells his fortune and steals his ring.[5]

gradevolmente in allegoria l'insidiosa triade agostiniana. La zingara, imagine del demonio astuto e ladro e della seduzione della carne (mentre sfila l'anello accarezza infatti con un dito il Monte di Venere della mano protesa nella versione del Louvre); la vanità del giovane azzimato e compiaciuto con la grande piuma sul cappello (elemento di moda, ma simbolo di *vanitas)*"]; Gilbert 1995, 203 [idyllic-erotic]; Hirdt 1998; Puglisi 1998, 75-9 [moralizing]; Longhi 1999-2000, 1:6 [1943]; 171, 204 [1952]; Moffitt 2002; Moffitt 2004, 41-62; Marini 2005, 408-11, no. 22 ["forte monito morale"]; Loire 2006, 64-70; Olson 2006; Schütze 2009, 251-2, no. 13; Ebert Schifferer 2009, 73-8 [parallel reading of the two versions].

4 For the evolution of this iconographic subject in the painting of Caravaggio's followers, see more recently Feigenbaum 1997; and Hartje 2004, 185-210.

5 Mancini 1:109: "E di questa schuola [of Caravaggio] non credo forsi che se sia visto cosa con più gratia et affetto che quella zingara che dà la buona ventura a quel giovenetto, mano del Caravaggio, che possiede il signor Alessandro Vittrici, gentilhuomo qui di Roma, che, ancorché sia per questa strada, nondimeno la zingaretta mostra la sua furbaria con un riso finto nel levar l'anello al giovenotto, et questo la sua semplicità et affetto di libidine verso la vaghezza della zingaretta che le dà la ventura et le leva l'anello."

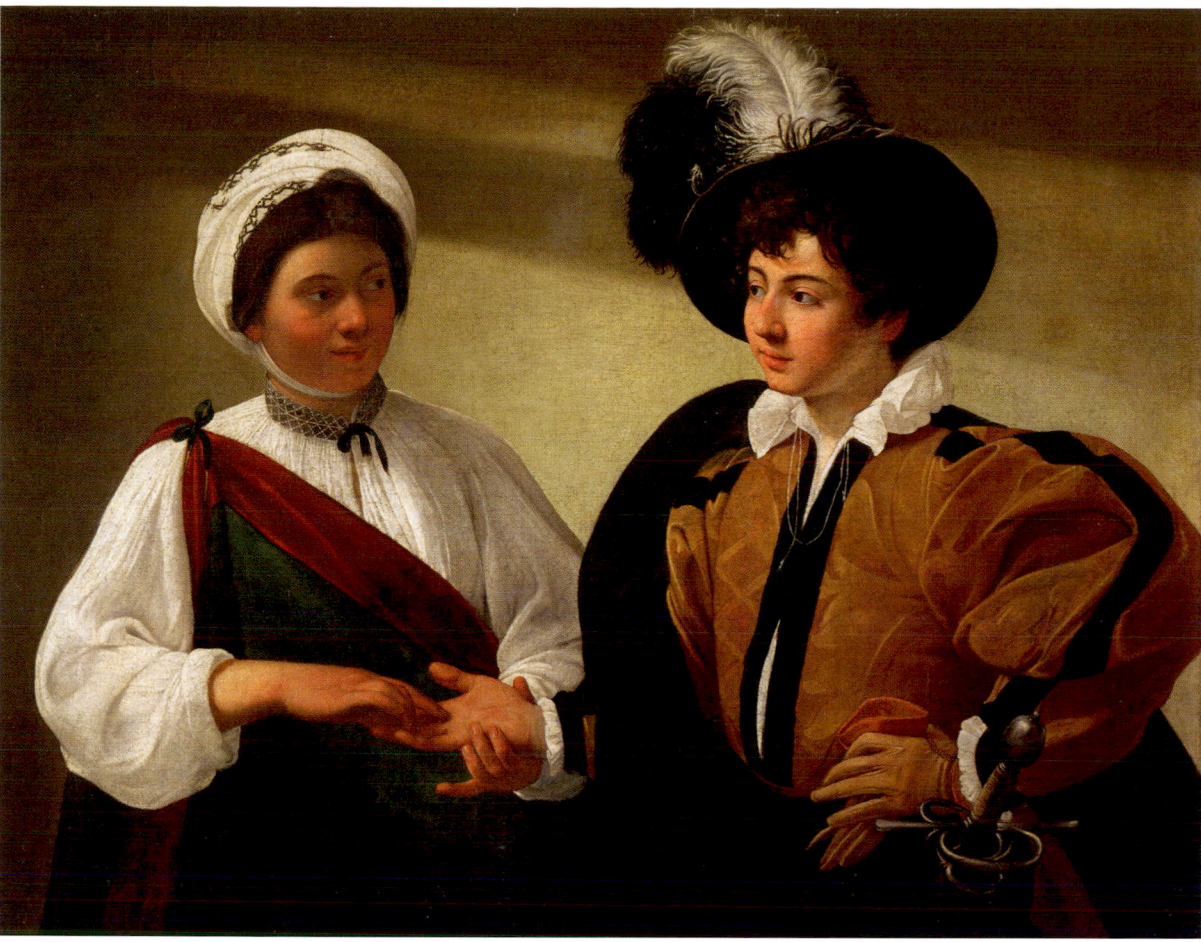

Fig. 47
Michelangelo Merisi da Caravaggio, *The Fortune Teller*, Musée du Louvre, Paris, oil on canvas, 99 x 131 cm.

By defining the woman as treacherous and seductive, and the youth as naïve and lustful, Mancini implicitly bestows a specific category upon the painting: its subject matter undoubtedly qualifies as comic. This implication must have been self-evident to a contemporary reader, since traditionally gypsies[6] and dandies belonged to the iconographic register of comedy. By no means could this trickery scene have been viewed as a heroic action, a subject suitable for an *istoria*. In Mancini's description, the painting thus yields to univocal interpretation. As a visual joke, the outcome was moreover highly predictable: to the young man's dismay, the gypsy will eventually escape with her bounty, the precious ring. Aided by lasciviousness, cleverness will overcome innocence.

Yet, despite its comic connotation, *The Fortune Teller* casts its undeniable spell on Mancini. As he admits, he had never seen a painting by Caravaggio or his followers endowed with more "grace and expression." Oddly enough, these terms likewise apply to the works of the Carracci, whom Mancini a few lines further would proceed to favor over Caravaggio as his more illustrious competitors. According to Mancini, their art demonstrated how to portray a figure with "grace and expression of affects" by composing pictorial narratives appropriately.[7] By extolling *The Fortune*

6   As Langdon 2001, 52, notes, the gypsy was an emblem of comedy in Ripa's *Iconologia*.

7   Mancini, 1:109: "Questa [the school of the Carracci] ha per proprio l'intelligenza dell'arte con gratia et espression

d'affetto, proprietà e composition d'historia, havendo congionto insieme la maniera di Raffaello con quella di Lombardia, perché vede il naturale, lo possiede, ne piglia il buono, lascia il cattivo, lo migliora, e con lume naturale gli dà il colore e l'ombra con le movenze e gratie".

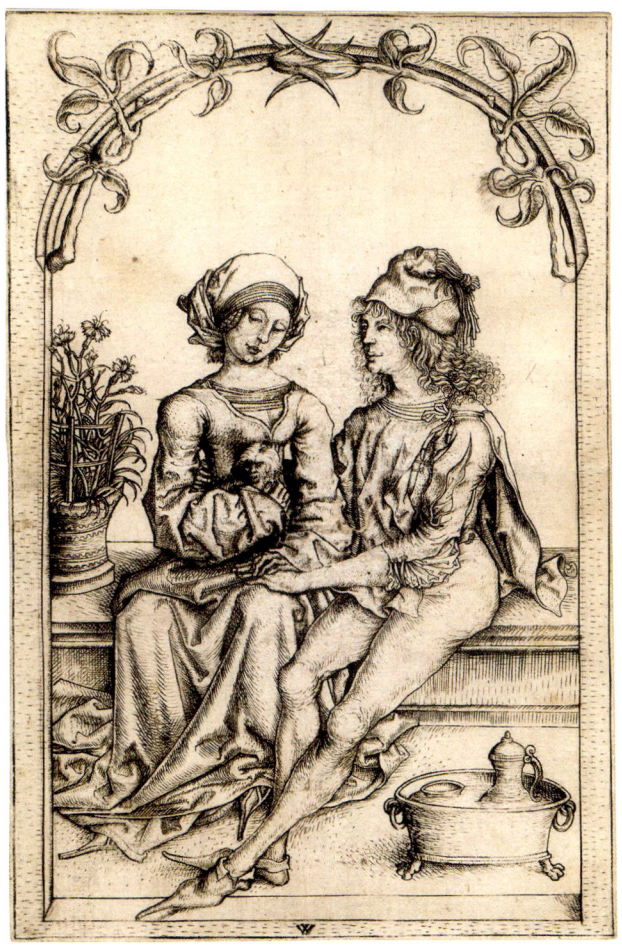

Fig. 48
Wenzel von Olmutz after the Master of the Housebook, *The Lovers*, engraving, 16.8 x 10.8 cm.

Teller, Mancini therefore suggests, indirectly at least, that Caravaggio had treated an intrinsically comic scene with the earnestness and congruity requested of an *istoria*. It would be unreasonable to extrapolate much more from Mancini's statement. Nonetheless, it is hard to conceive how so simple a plot might unveil Caravaggio's deepest ingenuity as a virtual *istoria* painter. Why should it be so difficult to depict the craftiness of a gypsy and the carefree sensuality of a youth, especially when compared to the full spectrum of noble features evoked by the Carracci in representing gods, saints, and heroes? Perhaps this question is not justified, since Mancini did not specifically betray any concern in this regard. Furthermore, these observations can be easily dismissed as speculative, if one concurs with Giovan Pietro Bellori's reductive interpretation of *The Fortune Teller*.

In his 1672 *Vite*, after illustrating Caravaggio's adherence to Giorgione's colorist methods, Bellori comments on the painter's contempt for antiquity as a source and measure of artistic perfection:

> Not heeding at all the most perfect ancient marbles and Raphael's celebrated pictures, but on the contrary disdaining them, he turned to nature as the exclusive object of his brush; accordingly, once he had been shown the most acclaimed sculptures by Phidias and Glycon as opportune for him to study, he replied by simply stretching out his arm toward a crowd of people, claiming that Nature had sufficiently provided him with masters. And to underscore the assertion, he hailed a gypsy who happened to be passing in the street, and he took her home and depicted her telling fortunes, as the women of that Egyptian race tend to do; and he also represented a young man, who rests his gloved hand on his sword and offers the other, bare, to the girl, who holds and observes it.

"In these two half-length figures," asserts Bellori, "Michele translated the truth so purely that he successfully proved his proposition."[8] Far from commending Caravaggio's pictorial purity and mimetic accuracy, Bellori subsequently disparages his art by equating it with the trivialities of Eupompos, the Greek painter who relied solely on nature in executing his pictures.[9]

---

8 Bellori, 214-5: "Datosi perciò egli a colorire secondo il proprio genio, non riguardando punto, anzi spregiando gli eccellentissimi marmi de gli antichi e le pitture tanto celebri di Raffaelle, si propose la sola natura per oggetto del suo pennello. Laonde, essendogli mostrate le statue più famose di Fidia e di Glicone, accioché vi accommodasse lo studio, non diede altra risposta se non che distese la mano verso una moltitudine di uomini, accennando che la natura l'aveva a sufficienza proveduto di maestri. E per dare autorità alle sue parole, chiamò una zingana che passava a caso per istrada, e condottala all'albergo la ritrasse in atto di predire l'avventure, come sogliono queste donne di razza egiziana: fecevi un giovine, il quale posa la mano col guanto su la spada

e porge l'altra scoperta a costei, che la tiene e la riguarda; ed in queste due mezze figure tradusse Michele sì puramente il vero che venne a confermare i suoi detti. Quasi un simil fatto si legge di Eupompo antico pittore, se bene ora non è tempo di considerare insino a quanto sia lodevole tale insegnamento."

9 See Pliny the Elder, *Natural History*, XXXIV, 61-2: "Lysippum Sicyonium Duris negat ullius fuisse discipulum, sed primo aerarium fabrum audendi rationem cepisse pictoris Eupompi responso. Eum enim interrogatum, quem sequeretur antecedentium, dixisse monstrata hominum multitudine, naturam ipsam imitandam esse, non artificem." In Bellori's account, Caravaggio thus repeated the reply Eupompos gave to

Truth be told, Bellori condemns Caravaggio's *Fortune Teller* more severely than it may at first glance appear by altogether disregarding its narrative content. In fact, he no longer expounds it as a scene of treachery, with its refined interplay of seduction, naïveté, and roguishness, but views it as reenacting a purely mechanical action: the fortune-telling ordinarily practiced by gypsies in Rome. His aesthetic prejudices furthermore led Bellori to misinterpret the picture: in fact, in neither version of *The Fortune Teller* does the gypsy read or behold the dandy's hand, as he wrongly assumes. Her gaze is always—though differently—locked on her incautious partner's eyes. Also, Bellori does not notice the gypsy's ability to flip the ring off the youth's hand. By overlooking these details, Bellori thus deprives the episode of pertinence and depth, thereby ignoring the possibility for it to develop into a narrative: in effect, instead of representing any action whatsoever, whether comic or otherwise, it simply "photographs" a situation without significant climax or denouement, hence wholly unsuitable for representation. Were it not for the human presence, Bellori would downgrade Caravaggio's painting to the rank of a still life. To be sure, the tactile and chromatic effects displayed in the *Fortune Teller* did seduce Bellori. In his condemnation, there is certainly more than a grain of admiration. Yet, by reducing its trivial subject to the equivalent of our photographic shot, or, in accordance with the early modern terminology, a picture of two "heads," Bellori brushes aside any temptation to read the composition as a narrative. Without this element, Caravaggio's *Fortune Teller* only preserved the shallow appeal of a wondrous painted surface. Like Giorgione and Titian, Caravaggio excelled in imitating the blood-tinged whiteness of flesh, the softness of its texture.[10]

Long before Bellori came to write on *The Fortune Teller*, around 1603, the poet Gaspare Murtola had praised Caravaggio's capacity to render flesh and life in quite different terms. In a madrigal devoted to the gypsy in the painting, Murtola claimed:

> I do not know who is the better magician,
> The woman you depict,
> Or you who paint her.
> Through her sweet charms,
> She is longing to dispossess us
> Of our heart and blood.
> You make her, who seems depicted,
> Look alive,
> You make others believe
> That she breathes and lives.[11]

Lysippus of Sicyon: "he pointed to a crowd of people and said that it was Nature herself, not an artist, whom one ought to imitate." It is important to note that in his so-called *Trattato della pittura*, Agucchi, 155, does not assimilate Caravaggio to the ancient painters specialized in depicting the worst: "Considerando Aristotile che necessariamente si dovevano dalla poesia imitare persone di qualità o migliori di quelle del suo tempo, o peggiori, o simiglianti, lo provò con l'esempio della pittura, perché Polignoto imitò i migliori, Pausone i peggiori e Dionisio i simiglianti. (...) Plinio racconta che Pireico conseguì somma gloria nell'imitare cose basse, come delle botteghe de' barbieri e de' calzolai e degli asinelli e delle robbe da mangiare e simili. (...) Quintiliano afferma che Demetrio, benché fosse scultore, andò tanto dietro alla simiglianza che alla bellezza non ebbe riguardo. Ma a' nostri tempi Rafaelle e la scuola romana di quel secolo (...) hanno sopra gli altri imitati i migliori, ed il Bassano è stato un Pireico nel rassomigliare i peggiori, ed una gran parte de' moderni ha raffigurato gli eguali, e fra questi il Caravaggio, eccellentissimo nel colorire, si dee comparare a Demetrio perché ha lasciato indietro l'Idea della bellezza, disposto di seguire del tutto la similitudine."

10   Bellori, 215: "E perché egli aspirava all'unica lode del colore, siché paresse vera l'incarnazione, la pelle e 'l sangue e la superficie naturale, a questo solo volgeva intento l'occhio e l'industria, lasciando da parte gli altri pensieri dell'arte" ["since he uniquely aimed at the praise for his colors, making the flesh, the skin, the blood and the natural surfaces appear true, he practiced his eye and put all his energies exclusively in that, leaving aside all the other principles of art"]. In this passage, Bellori echoes Vasari's definition of Giorgione's painting: "Diedegli [to Giorgione] la natura tanto benigno spirito, che egli nel colorito a olio et a fresco fece alcune vivezze et altre cose morbide et unite e sfumate talmente negli scuri ch'e' fu cagione che molti di quegli che erano allora eccellenti confessasino lui esser nato per metter lo spirito ne le figure e per contraffar la freschezza de la carne viva più che nessuno che dipignesse, non solo in Venezia, ma per tutto" (Vasari, 4: 42-3).

11   Murtola, Madrigal 472: "*Per una cingara del medesimo* [Caravaggio] Non so qual sia più maga/ O la donna, che fingi,/O tu che la dipingi./ Di rapir quella è vaga/ Coi dolci incanti suoi/ Il core e 'l sangue a noi./ Tu dipinta che appare/ Fa' che viva si veda./ Fai che viva e spirante altri la creda."

In accordance with the conventions of lyric poetry from Petrarch onward, a dialectic antithesis between concepts underpins Murtola's poem. At its core lies the assumption that the painter and his creation, the graceful gypsy, share an identical power, for both exert their witchcraft on the viewer, ineluctably the victim of their twofold sorcery. Surpassing Pygmalion, Caravaggio succeeds in infusing life and breath into the gypsy. Unlike Caravaggio, the girl, once alive, drains away life and breath from the beholder, who in turn, enticed into the painter's illusion, becomes devoid of flesh and blood almost like a painted figure. The conceptual tension between life and death, the animated and the inactive, the real and the illusionary stresses the lyrical—or erotic—passion that the fictive woman, a visual equivalent to Petrarch's Laura, and her creator, through his vivid creation, stir in the poet's heart. Of course, Murtola above all aimed to exalt Caravaggio's mimetic skills and outstanding expressivity. Consequently, his fondness for the gypsy is to be deemed in the main a rhetorical device of eulogy. Nonetheless, it is noteworthy that Murtola concentrates on the lyrical component of *The Fortune Teller*, interpreting it exclusively as a scene of seduction. After all, the inert beholder who cannot resist the glamor of the gypsy is indirectly identified with the youth in the canvas: a fictitious figure, without flesh and blood, at the mercy of the beautiful sorceress. This does not mean that Murtola was unaware of the treachery staged in Caravaggio's painting. In his poem, he alludes to it with the ambivalent verb *"rapire"* (here translated as "dispossess"), which signifies that simultaneously the viewer is fatally "rapt" with desire and "robbed" of his life. In Murtola's madrigal, the gypsy thus take away not the youth's ring but, more powerfully, the viewer's breath. Despite this subtle allusion to the swindle perpetrated by the "magician" in the painting, the poet deliberately neglects the role of comedy in *The Fortune Teller*. More remarkably, the fundamentally low-genre figure of the gypsy is transformed into a paradigm of lyrical beauty.[12]

Taken together, Murtola's encomiastic poem, Bellori's critical anecdote, and Mancini's concise description barely result in a completely trustworthy or thorough appraisal of *The Fortune Teller*. For this reason, these invaluable testimonies do not actually dovetail with each other in offering a definitive key to establishing the genre of Caravaggio's composition. The question remains: is this a comic or a lyrical episode? And if a mixture of both, which dominates, love or cunning, seduction or mischief? Otherwise, was Caravaggio, as Bellori insinuates, trying out a new genre, a "mechanical" one, regardless of conventions about comedy and lyric, inspired as he was by his obsessive fascination for surfaces and deceptive reality? To complicate the question, the inscription accompanying an early anonymous engraving of a *Fortune Teller* considered as inspired by Caravaggio's prototype seems to furnish a perceptibly different interpretation of the subject. As it reads *"Fur, demon, mundus"* ("The Theft, the Demon, and the World"), it explicitly admonishes the viewer against the dangers embodied by the seductive gypsy.[13] Hence Caravaggio's painting, as argued by some scholars, may be considered a moral allegory, supplying edification by setting up an exemplary case of treachery.

In analyzing Caravaggio's two versions of *The Fortune Teller*, most scholars have similarly pointed out either their humorous character, sometimes considered as relying on the theatrical tradition of the *commedia dell'arte*,[14] or their allegorical meaning, which has even been related—loosely, in my

---

12 For the lyrical connotation of the female figure in the pictorial tradition previous to Caravaggio, see Cropper 1976; Cropper 1986; and Cropper 1995, 178-83. For the lyrical connotation of male figures, see more recently Fend and Koos 2004; and Campbell 2005. The metamorphosis of the crafty gypsy into a Petrarchan beautiful creature is completely fulfilled by the poet Giovan Battista Marino. Hirdt 1998, 97-105, justly defines Marino's transposition of Caravaggio's *Fortune Teller* into his *Adone* as a "kaschierte Raub," a hidden theft; I will return to this point in the next chapter. For the

concept of literal and pictorial theft, see Cropper 2005, 129-58. For the relation between Caravaggio and Marino, see Cropper 1991.

13 For this anonymous print, dedicated to the Cavalier d'Arpino, see Salerno et al. 1966, 116-7.

14 Cuzin 1977, 22 mentions a painting by an anonymous French master now at the Ringling Art Museum (Sarasota), a *Scene of the Commedia dell'Arte*, wherein the Italian mask Pantaloon is fleeced by two gypsies. From this painting, it

opinion—to the iconography of the prodigal son.[15] Refuting Bellori's anecdote about the gypsy and the fortuitous genesis of the picture, some scholars, such as Rudolf Wittkower and, to a certain point, Walter Friedlaender, have celebrated the absolute novelty of the composition, analogous to a modern tableau vivant, hence similar to a "romantic narrative,"[16] or transposing the spirit of Cervantes' novels, perhaps the *Gitanilla*, into pictorial representation.[17] In these cases, Caravaggio's *Fortune Teller* is viewed as almost independent of iconographic conventions. To my knowledge, nowhere in the critical studies on Caravaggio have its ambivalent complexity and problematic pictorial genre been addressed. Furthermore, its lyrical components have predominantly been interpreted as subordinate to the treacherous plot, and never recognized as an alternative—both antithetical and concomitant—visual theme in the reading of the picture. My intention is to verify that the lyrical and the comedic strongly interfere in the pictorial structures of the two *Fortune Tellers*—if not to the same extent—and to prove that innovation in these compositions resides most specifically in the inherent ambivalence of their subject and narrative. Above all, I would like to demonstrate that Caravaggio, in innovating, is constantly acting within the boundaries of traditional iconographic codes. Strangely, scholars have often restricted their research to the iconography of the gypsy;[18] in light of the scarcity of pertinent parallels, they have come to the conclusion that somehow Caravaggio constructed a figurative theme destined for great success, which is only partly true. In *The Fortune Teller*, to be sure, the gypsy effectively makes her debut as an alluring, crafty actress. Yet, as I shall prove, other pictorial counterparts had already played

has been partially inferred that Caravaggio's *Fortune Teller* was an evocation of a theatrical scene. As recognized by Cuzin himself, the painting seems to postdate Caravaggio's *Fortune Teller*, and it was most probably executed at the beginning of the seventeenth century. Thus it is likely that Caravaggio's painting inspired the Sarasota picture. As for the sixteenth-century theatrical tradition of the *Zingaresca*, with its comic sketches centered on the figure of the gypsy, its relationship to Caravaggio's *Fortune Teller* is loose [the examples adducted by Hirdt 1988, 93-6, are not especially compelling, although he affirms that "Der Maler holt sich nicht eine zufällig die Straße überquerende Zigeunerin ins Atelier, er inspiriert sich vielmehr an der artifiziellen Welt des Theaters. Der Künstler setzt dramatische Kunst ins Werk, die ihrerzeits ein ebenso traditionsreiches wie problematisches Element des italienischen und europäischen Alltagslebens reflektiert"; see also in this regard Hartje 2004, 196-8]. Mina Gregori in Christiansen 1985, 215: "They [*The Fortune Teller* and *The Cardsharps*] belong, rather, to a tradition of theater-related genre painting, the intellectual basis of which was the Aristotelian comparison of the various arts as revived by Cinquecento theorists. The mental process by which an artist approached reality through the conventions of the theater may strike us today as both complex and artificial, but it was inevitable in Caravaggio's day. In any case, it should be mentioned that the artist probably deliberately exploited an ambiguity that his contemporaries would easily have recognized, for the characters he portrayed–even in their fictional, theatrical roles–were also parts of everyday life in the streets. Caravaggio's interest in the *commedia dell'arte* probably also stems from his familiarity with the places that the actors frequented and his sympathy–even in matters of dress–with the life that they led. A number of elements in *The Fortune Teller* and *The Cardsharps* relate directly to the *commedia dell'arte*, especially the theme of deception, which had been a *topos* in the theater since antiquity." Puglisi 1998, 78: "The staged look of both works [*The Fortune Teller* and *The Cardsharps*] reflects Caravaggio's recourse to contemporary theatre and the stock characters and situations of the *commedia dell'arte*, in addition to northern pictorial and literary sources." For the thetrical in Caravaggio, see also Danesi Squarzina 2000.

15 Puglisi 1998, 78: "In each picture [*The Fortune Teller* and *The Cardsharps*] Caravaggio explored the theme of a well-off young man being duped. Given the unregenerate pursuits of such feckless youths, the moral is unmistakable, and the gambling in *The Cardsharps*, like the gypsy's seductiveness, brings to mind the excesses of the Prodigal Son in the biblical parable. The image of fleeting youth also echoes here in the disillusionment that awaits the pair of inexperienced adolescents. Caravaggio shied away from blatant moralizing, however."

16 Wittkower 1973, 23: "It must be said that neither Caravaggio's *Cardsharps* nor his *Fortune Teller* reflect fresh observations of popular contemporary life. Suck slick and overdressed people were not to be found walking about; and the spaceless settings convey a feeling of the *tableau vivant* rather than of 'snapshots' of actual life. One looks at these pictures as one reads a romantic narrative the special attraction of which consists in its air of unreality."

17 Friedlaender 1969, 84: "The mood of the scenes represented by Caravaggio, wherein the elegant and frail youth is cheated by professional cardsharps or by a sweet young gypsy, has likewise a literary parallel: in the *Novelas Ejemplares* of Cervantes we find similarly insignificant events in the lives of adventurous young cavaliers, who have run away from home and made friends with gypsies, treated in this same gentle and romantic manner, smilingly and ironically. In this sense Caravaggio's *Fortune Teller* and the *Cardsharps* are 'novelistic.' They are not literal 'imitations of nature' but are scenes which he might have visualized in his imagination, after reading a story."

18 The most exhaustive study on the iconography of the gypsy in connection with Caravaggio's *Fortune Teller* remains Cuzin 1977, 16-24; Hibbard 1983, 26, mentions Boccaccino's *Gypsy Girl* at the Uffizi as an example of a positive portrayal of a gypsy. See also Langdon 2001, 51-63; and Moffitt 2002. For a study on the gypsy in the sixteenth-century northern tradition, see more recently Morrall 2002.

her role before. More precisely, two interrelated iconographic traditions prelude Caravaggio's composition: the *Lovers* and the *Ill-Matched Pairs*.[19]

Before introducing some examples of these iconographies, one point must be especially elucidated if only to avoid further confusion. The different representations of *Lovers* and *Ill-Matched Pairs* I am about to examine cannot be evaluated as direct sources for Caravaggio. What I mean is that Caravaggio did not have in mind any of these compositions in particular while imagining his *Fortune Teller*. Rhetorically speaking, these visual references do not attain the standard of citations. Put otherwise, Caravaggio did not intend to imitate—in the rhetorical sense of the term—or compete with a noble or classical prototype. By taking up schemes, attitudes or expressions specific to the iconography of the *Lovers* and the *Ill-Matched Pairs*, he instead uses, develops, and sometimes manipulates signs and codes of the pictorial tradition, which accomplish lexical and syntactical functions when properly applied by painters and correctly deciphered by viewers. These visual conventions are likely to be universally understood on account of their diffusion in the cultural imagery of Caravaggio's audience. Some of these motifs and gestures are not limited to a single iconographic tradition: if isolated, they become multivalent; but they take on a well-defined signification when activated by definite contexts, wherein they channel segmented messages transferable into narrative contents by beholders. As condensed fragments of an action, these schemes can ultimately be remolded and occasionally transformed into renewed sequences of narration by painters. Caravaggio thus modulates gestures, expressions, and postures in a subtle manner in order to bring out the delicate ambivalence of his narrative invention, suspended between love and money, seduction and trickery.

Equal and Unequal Lovers

It can be taken as a fact that Caravaggio was familiar with the iconographic tradition of the *Lovers* and the *Ill-Matched Pairs*, more typically northern, namely Flemish and German, but pervasively spread throughout southern Europe through engravings. It is perhaps no coincidence that among the artists who popularized this early modern iconography is Israel van Meckenem. According to Giovan Paolo Lomazzo, whose *Trattato della pittura* was published in Milan in 1584, the very year Caravaggio entered the Milanese studio of Simone Peterzano as an apprentice, numerous were the artists who "tainted by that curse which contaminates and annihilates the forces of the spirit," resorted to the "engraved papers recently invented in Germany by master Israel van Meckenem and in Italy by Andrea Mantegna,"[20] with the intention of copying them in order to fill out the

---

19 For these interrelated iconographical traditions, see Wescher 1938; Ringbom 1966; Hinz B. 1974; Olds et al. 1976; Stewart 1979; Moxey 1985a; and Schuttwolf 1998.

20 Lomazzo, 2:416: "Questa composizione nella idea chiunque averà famigliare, sappia certo che non sarà nel numero de gl'imprudenti che vogliono fare, o, come si dice, dar moto alle forme imaginate d'altri; le quali s'ancora da loro fossero imaginate, ma non composte, nell'idea, tuttavia malamente potrebbero esprimere, sì come ammorbati da quella maledizione che confonde e leva le forze allo spirito; io dico di quella gran quantità d'invenzioni, disegnate sopra le carte poste in stampa, ritrovate modernamente in Germania da Israel Metro et in Italia da Andrea Mantegna; le quali sono propriamente una confusione de gl'animi nostri, i quali senza dubio, se fossero privi di questi esempli, più sottilmente investigarebbero e, non risparmiando fatiche, produrrebbero da sé sempre alcuna bella invenzione secondo la natura e

genio loro." As will become evident by the end of this book, the influence of early Netherlandish and German prints upon Caravaggio is extensive. I will return to and expand upon this topic in Chapter 10. For Italian collections of prints, see the essential essays by Bury 1985; and Bury 2003. For the importance of early Renaissance prints in Italy, see Borea 1990; Borea 1992; and Borea 1993. More recently, McDonald 2004 (and to a certain extent, McDonald 2006) has demonstrated the overwhelming presence of early Netherlandish prints in the Sevillan collection of Ferdinand Columbus, a collection that an early seventeenth-century painter like Velázquez must have known and consulted. Unfortunately, it is impossible to establish to what extent the collection of prints gathered by Cardinal Francesco Maria del Monte, one of Caravaggio's most influential patrons, contained early Netherlandish and German works (see in this regard Waźbiński 1994, 2:629-32). It is well known that the Italian poet Giambattista Marino, a friend of Caravaggio, possessed an exhaustive collection of

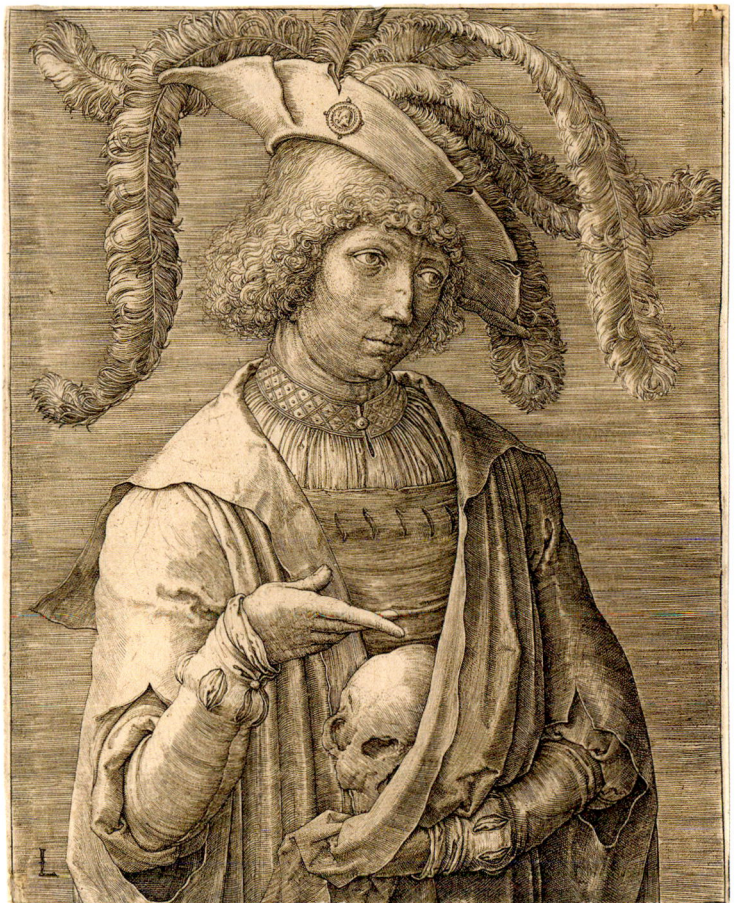

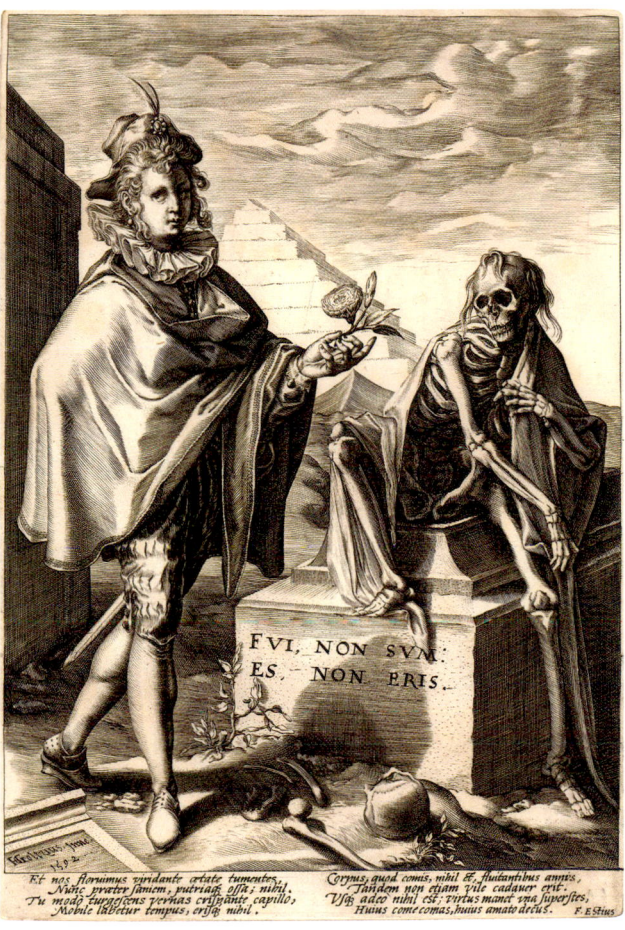

Fig. 49
Lucas van Leyden, *Young Man with a Skull*, engraving, 18.4 x 14.5 cm.

Fig. 50
Jan Saenredam after Hendrick Goltzius, *Allegory of Vanity*,
engraving, 22.9 x 17.3 cm.

blanks of their barren imagination. Lomazzo's testimony is extremely useful, since it confirms that painters in Milan at Caravaggio's time avidly sought early Netherlandish and German engravings, regarding them as valid examples of composition. To return to *The Fortune Teller*, it is important to analyze an engraving by Wenzel von Olmutz after the Housebook Master,[21] a composition also copied and popularized by Israel van Meckenem,[22] in which a couple of lovers is represented sitting on a sort of bench, caught up in a moment of graceful, yet lascivious affection.[23] If one focuses on the upper tier of the engraving, it is easier to distinguish a compositional scheme similar to that exploited in the two versions of *The Fortune Teller*: the woman's bust, almost parallel to the pictorial surface, though imperceptibly rotated toward the youth as if against her will, intersects with her partner's torso, which is three-quarter oriented, in order to evoke the preamble of a sensual contact. To signal the intensity of the young man's enthrallment in the view of his beloved, Olmutz represents his face in profile, showing but a small portion of his second foreshortened eye. Caravaggio in the Rome *Fortune Teller* almost exactly follows this pictorial device, through which

prints by Albrecht Dürer, Lucas van Leyden, and Heinrich Aldegrever, while at the same time collecting Renaissance Italian engravings, such as those of Marcantonio Raimondi and Giulio Bonasone. It is highly probable that, among the works by printers from "beyond the Alps" [Oltramontani], there were also prints by many other early Netherlandish and German printers. See Marino d, 227, a letter dated to 1619; and 330, a letter dated to *c*.1622-1623.

21   See Koreny 1986, 1:190, no. 493.

22   See Hutchison 1972, 63-4, no. 75; Kok 1985, 173-5, no. 75; Schuttwolf 1998, 25, no. 5.

23   For the Housebook Master, see Hutchison 1972; and Hess D. 1994.

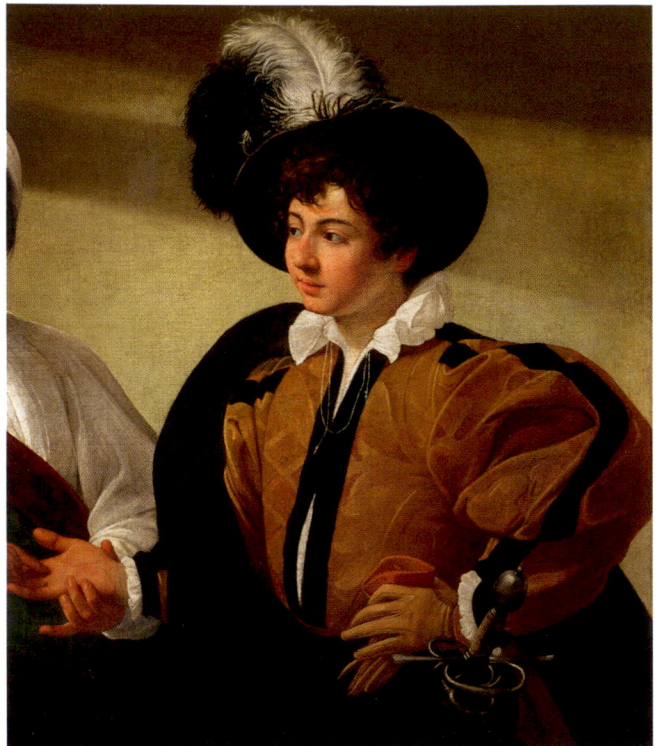

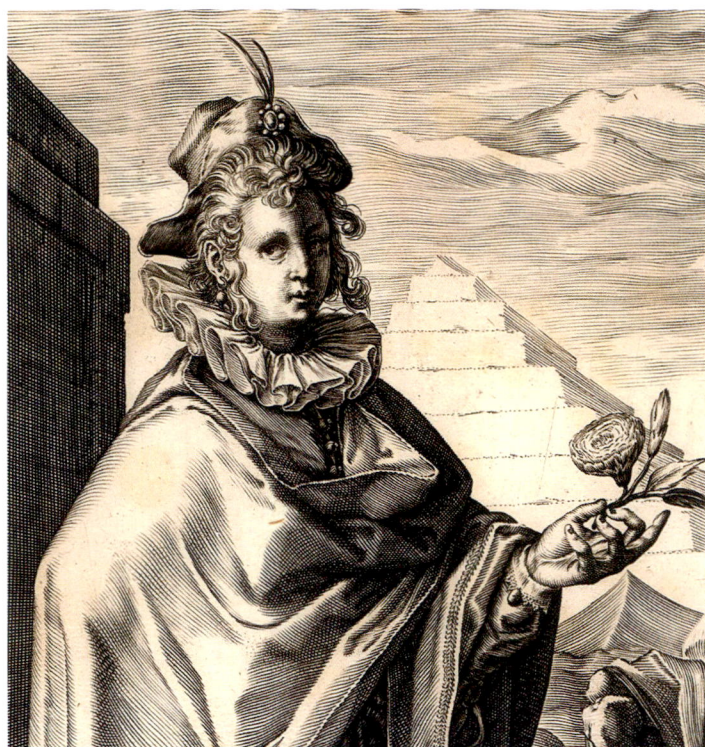

Fig. 51
Michelangelo Merisi da Caravaggio, *The Fortune Teller*, Musée du
Louvre, Paris, oil on canvas, 99 x 131 cm., detail.

Fig. 52
Jan Saenredam after Hendrick Goltzius, *Allegory of Vanity*, engraving,
22.9 x 17.3 cm., detail.

the intensity of lyrical passion is visually amplified, all the more so in that the youth, but also his
partner, seems to ignore the beholder's presence. Through the orientation of the lady's head artists
also nuance the narrative meaning of the episode. In Olmutz's print, the position of the woman's
face, tilted toward the youth, gives away her simultaneous attraction and hesitancy. In contrast, her
averted eyes disclose her demureness and determination to remain chaste. The visual dichotomy
between the nearly frontal position of her torso and the oblique movement of her head, intensified
by the adornment of an engirdling turban and swirling braids, is meant to underline her dilemma:
to succumb to, or to resist passion. The attitude of her arms and hands express the extent of her
quandary: with one hand, she accepts the youth's daring touch, while with the other she protects
her lapdog as if defending herself. Also, the printer gave visual relevance to the lovers' entangled
hands. Besides conventional attributes related to the lyrical subject, such as the vase of carnations
standing on the balcony, other fashion accessories help to connote the scene as partially allegorical.
The fanciness of the youth, who wears a doublet attached over the shoulder by laces, as well as
slashed sleeves revealing a puffy shirt beneath, and who exhibits a *Schnürlin*, a ring holding the
tassel on the top of his hat, unequivocally symbolizes vanity.

Despite the changes of fashion, the pompous accoutrement of young male figures over time
continued to be associated with vanity. For instance, in a 1519 engraving by Lucas van Leyden,[24]
an *Allegory of Vanity* (Fig. 49), the elegant youth, who holds a skull tucked under his mantle, is
characterized as a patent *memento mori*. More interesting, his curly hair is this time covered with a
large-brimmed hat from which several long feathers cascade. In a 1592 engraving by Jan Saenredam
after Hendrick Goltzius, another *Allegory of Youth* (Fig. 50),[25] vanity is again conjured up by a

24 See Kok et al. 1996, no. 174; Jacobowitz and Stepanek
1983, 197, no. 73.

25 The print bears the following hexameters at the bottom by
F. Estius: "Et nos floruimus viridante aetate tumentes/ Nunc

sumptuously clad youth. Apart from having his hat decorated with a gem and feathers, the young man in Goltzius' allegory wears a large fancy collar and slashed pantaloons. At the same time, he folds his right arm under his mantle, and his proud stride is punctuated by the presence of a sword. The gesture of the folded arm, the sword, the collar and the feathered hat are likewise characteristic of Caravaggio's dandy, especially the one depicted in the Paris *Fortune Teller* (Figs. 51, 52). Obviously, his fancy outfit does not designate him as an actor of the *commedia dell'arte*, as some scholars have claimed, but rather signals the swagger of youth.[26] In this sense, the figure of the dandy qualifies as comic as restrictively opposed to heroic. In addition, he incarnates the lightheartedness and proclivity to passion of youth. With the same implications, the figure of the young man appears in the tradition of the *Lovers* and the *Ill-Matched Pairs*.

In a *c.*1498 engraving by Albrecht Dürer,[27] *The Promenade* (Fig. 53), a young couple pauses momentarily, while at a distance Death, carrying an hourglass atop its skull and hiding behind a tree, spies on the partners' intimate encounter. Reversing the attitudes of the *Lovers* in the Housebook Master's original print, Dürer represents the youth's face and torso almost frontally, though slightly askew in order to intersect with the lady's bust. In contrast to the Housebook Master's scheme, Dürer does not show the woman's foreshortened second eye, but only her profile, for reasons clearly depending on the context; she seems to follow the young man's beckoning gesture,

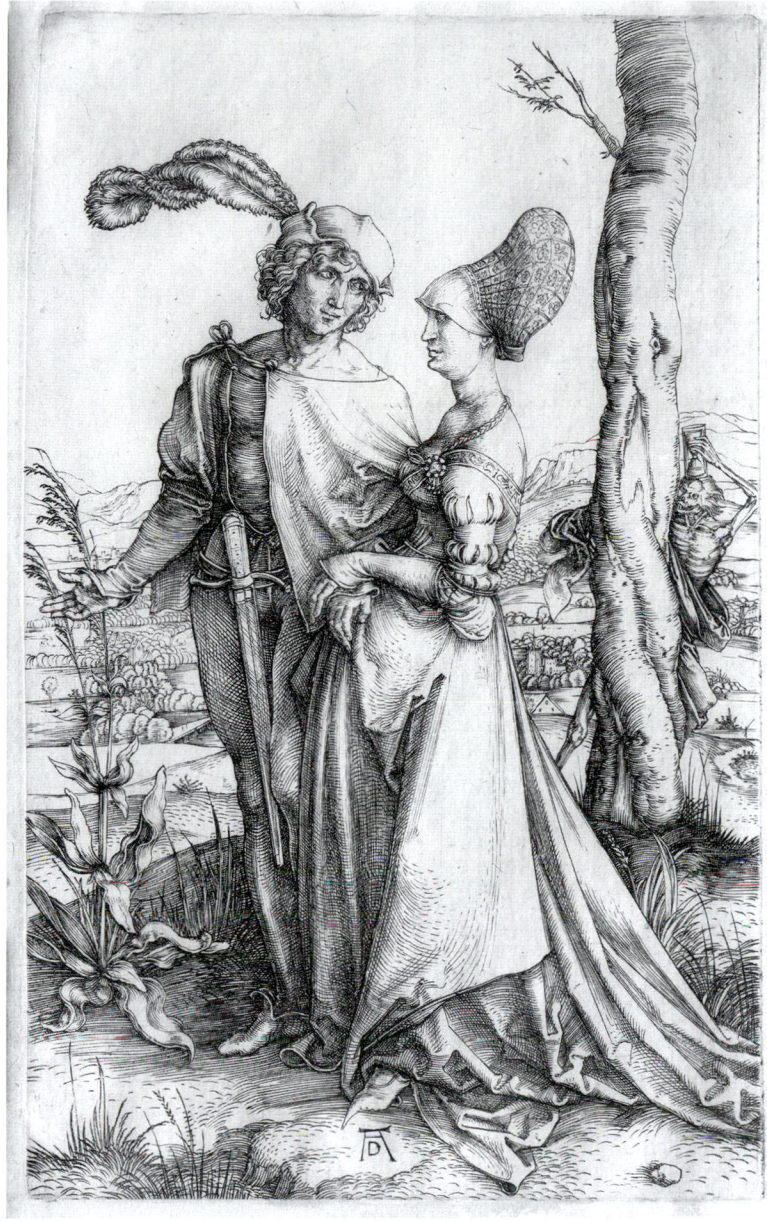

Fig. 53
Albrecht Dürer, *The Promenade*, engraving, 19.5 x 12.3 cm.

which oddly resembles the one performed by Caravaggio's dandy in the Rome *Fortune Teller* in offering his hand to the gypsy. Like the Housebook Master, Dürer aligns the couple's hands along a horizontal line, thereby underscoring essential nuances of the amorous episode: the restraint of the woman, who protects her womb by elegantly crossing her hands, and the undaunted allure-

---

praeter saniem, putriaque ossa nihil,/ Tu modo turgescens vernas crispante capillo,/ Mobile labetur tempus, erisque nihil./ Corpus, quod comis, nihil et, flu[c]tantibus annis/ Tandem non etiam vile cadaver erit./ Usque adeo nihil est; virtus mane tuna superstes,/ Huius come comas, huius amato decus." See Keyes 1980, 84, no. 111; and Strauss 1980, no. 123 (258).

26 Cuzin 1977, 13: "la position 'cavalière' (celle, ou peu s'en faut, de l'escrimeur), avec la main appuyée sur la hanche

ou sur l'épée, le bras plié et l'épaule en avant qui permet de developer le 'morceau de peinture' de la manche, est presque un poncif du portrait de jeune seigneur en Italie au XVIᵉ siècle"; Puglisi 1998, 75: "His lace collar and cuffs, plumed hat and sword with gloves stuffed in the hilt characterize him [the youth] as a *bravo*, or mercenary soldier."

27 See Schoch et al. 2001, 1:68-70, no. 19. For a subtle interpretation of this composition, see Meadow 1992.

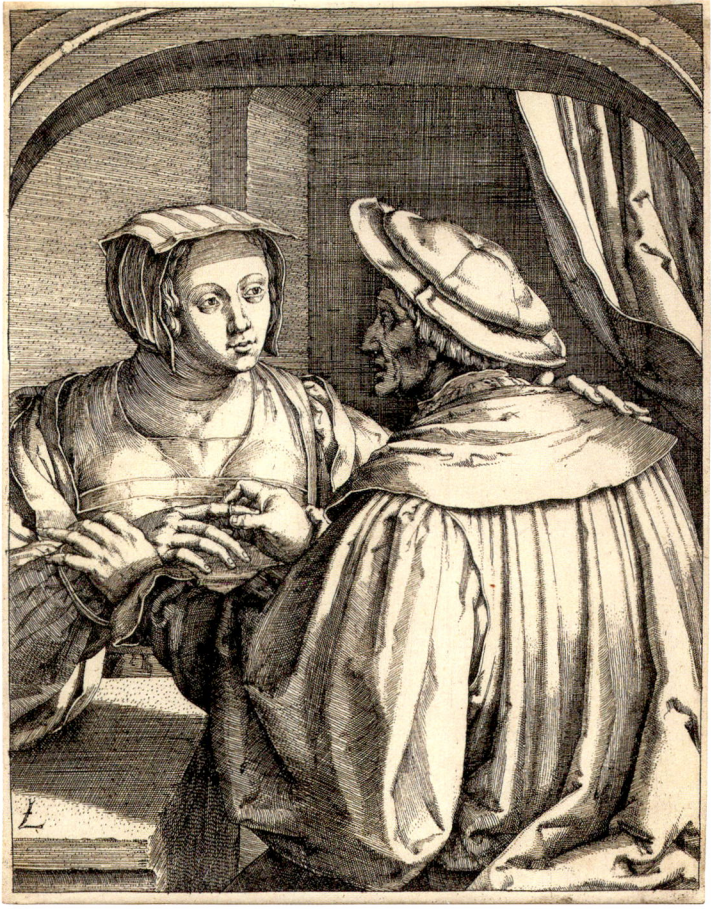

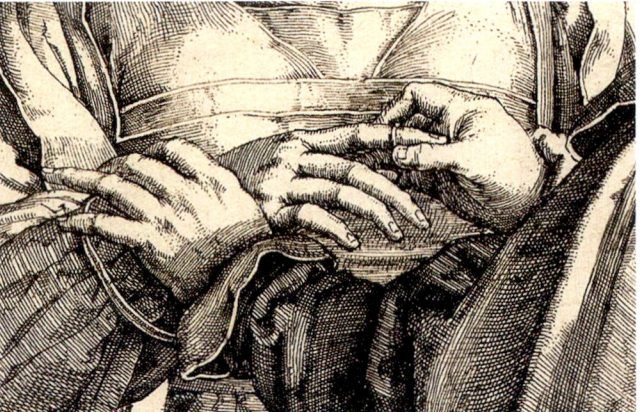

Fig. 55
Simon Frisius (attributed to) after Lucas van Leyden, *The Betrothal*, etching, 16.7 x 13 cm., detail.

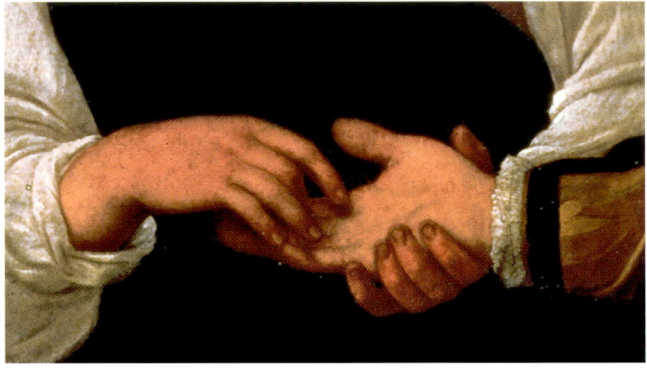

Fig. 54
Simon Frisius (attributed to) after Lucas van Leyden, *The Betrothal*, etching, 16.7 x 13 cm.

Fig. 56
Michelangelo Merisi da Caravaggio, *The Fortune Teller*, Pinacoteca Capitolina, Rome, oil on canvas, 115 x 150 cm., detail.

ment of the youth. In spite of some minor divergences, Dürer's engraving takes up and elaborates upon the same visual scheme used by the Housebook Master. In the evolution of this iconographic tradition, it is important to observe to what degree identical or similar attitudes can convey different, gender-based meanings: the oblique position of the damsel's face that, in the Housebook Master's engraving, originally uttered both demureness and enticement, when switched to a male figure marks intrepidity and intense desire. Of course, to vary the Housebook Master's original scheme, Dürer had to modify the quality of the lover's gaze, which is steadily fixed upon, instead of swerving off, the partner's eyes.

The iconography of the *Unequal Lovers* resorts to the same basic pattern as the *Lovers*. Before addressing this topic, an etching after Lucas van Leyden, *The Betrothal* (Fig. 54),[28] must be carefully analyzed, since it is probably related to Caravaggio's *Fortune Teller*. Even if the affective connotation of the scene is particularly akin to the cases hitherto taken into account—a couple fixedly exchanging a gaze in an amorous context—a different compositional pattern is used to underline visually the woman's expression to the detriment of the man's role in the scene. In a certain sense, Lucas rotates the point of view traditionally followed by artists, in an attempt to anchor the beholder's sight closer to the prenuptial ceremony. If one now focuses on the interplay of hands involved in the

28   See Kok et al. 1996, no. 11 (after Lucas van Leyden). For Lucas van Leyden's painting, now at the Musée des Beaux-Arts in Strasburg, see Parshall 1974, 113; Vos 1978, 97-114; and Smith 1992, 176-9. For an interpretation of the print, see Silver 1998.

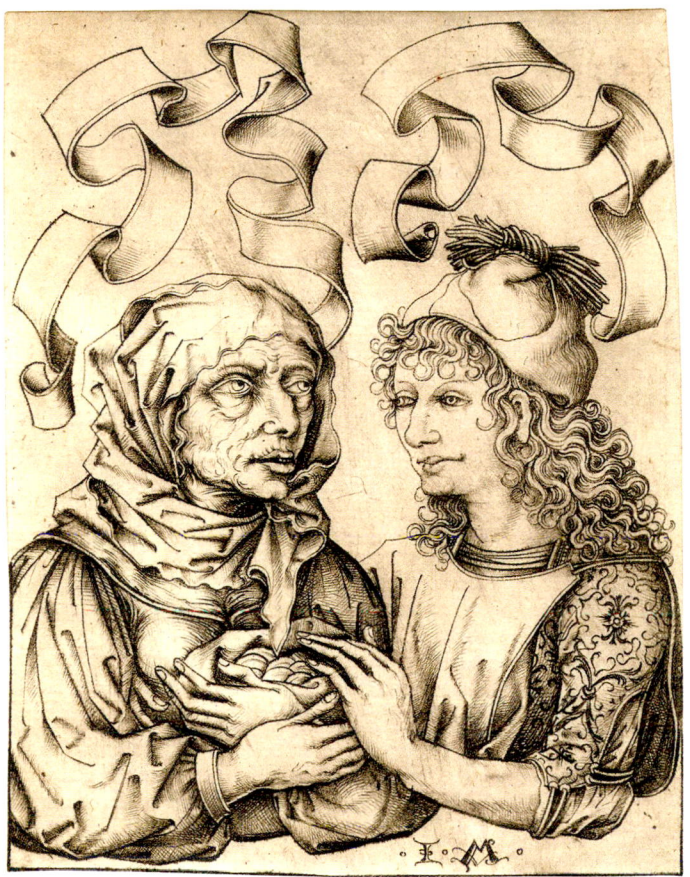

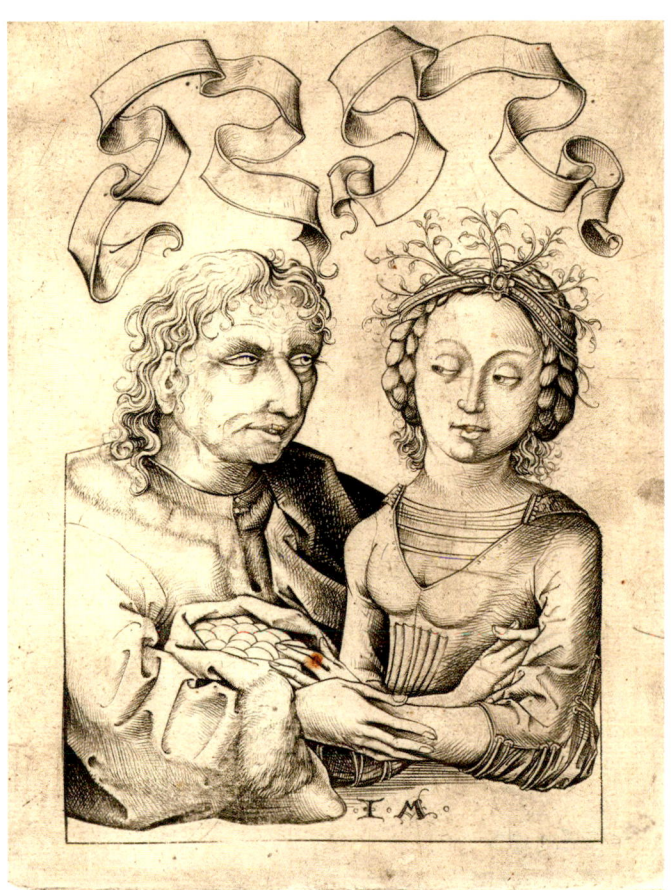

Fig. 57
Israel van Meckenem, *Old Woman and Young Man*, engraving,
14.6 x 11.4 cm.

Fig. 58
Israel van Meckenem, *Old Man and Young Woman*, engraving,
14.5 x 11.2 cm.

episode—respectively grasping the partner's wrist, accepting and placing the ring—one can easily recognize that Caravaggio employed an analogous scheme, but reversed, in the two versions of the *Fortune Teller*, more clearly in the Rome picture (Figs. 55, 56). The similarity of these postures, despite their inversion, is so striking that one is entitled to believe that Caravaggio actually wanted to quote Lucas, supplying a brilliant parody of his *Betrothal*. From this point of view, Caravaggio's swindle in the *Fortune Teller* might be interpreted as an anti-betrothal, therefore a comic visual antithesis of a lyrical commitment, whereby the man loses, rather than gives, the ring, and the woman fraudulently takes possession of the love token.

Before Caravaggio, Renaissance artists had already treated the theme of seductive deception that is equally integral to *The Fortune Teller*. In *The Young Man and the Old Woman* after the Housebook Master (Fig. 57), Israel van Meckenem[29] takes up the figure of the youth in the *Lovers*, turning him into a handsome swindler, charming a rich hag through his feigned adoring gaze, while his hand aims at his partner's purse. More relevantly, the Housebook Master uses a close-up framing, accommodating a parapet on the foreground, and imagining a neutral, close backdrop, which is almost the same structural device used by Caravaggio in his two versions of *The Fortune Teller*. In comparison to the iconographical tradition of the *Lovers*, some gestures of the far-fetched couple in the Housebook Master's engraving are appropriately inverted, or subverted, in order

29   For the print, see Kok 1985, 150-1, no. 56; and Schuttwolf
1998, 31-2, no. 9. See also Koreny 1986, 1:188-9, no. 488.

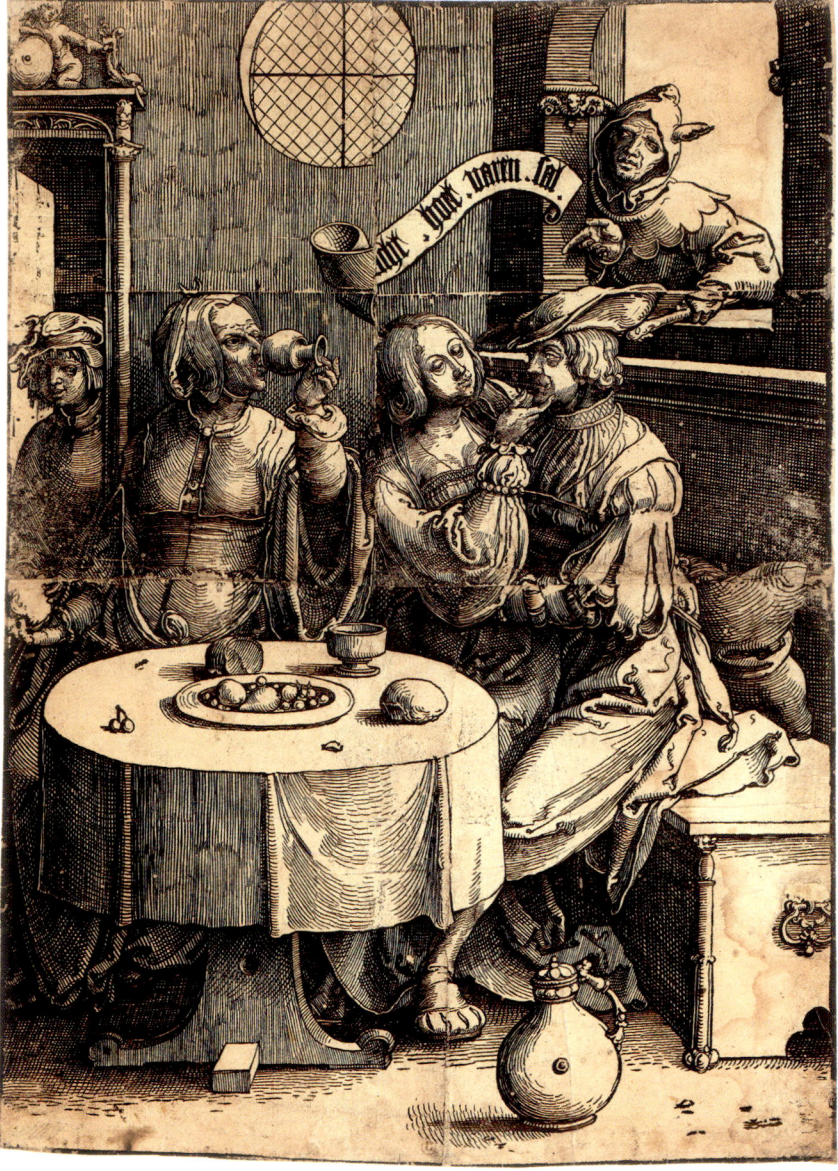

Fig. 59
Lucas van Leyden, *Tavern Scene* or *The Prodigal Son*, woodcut, 67 x 48.5 cm.

to suit the comedic mode. For instance, the crossed hands of the old woman—still, though vainly, protective of her belongings—seemingly parodies the gesture of protection performed by the woman of *The Lovers*. Similarly, in *The Old Man and the Young Woman* after the Housebook Master (Fig. 58),[30] Israel van Meckenem, by tilting the lady's face, and by making her express both revulsion at her partner's ugliness and attraction to his wealth, burlesques the pattern of demureness as evoked by the woman's bent head in the *Lovers*. One other element in the print rewards attention. The expressive gaze of the woman, furtively straying to her old partner, obviously differs from that of the gypsies in Caravaggio's two versions of *The Fortune Teller*, since the Housebook Master and the other artists who follow his example depict the woman's eyes as half concealed by heavy eyelids, this way insinuating her mischievous and sneaky intentions. On the contrary, in the Rome picture, although the gypsy's torso, clearly unbalanced, may reflect detachment from, rather than disgust toward the youth, the function of the gaze is undeniably more indefinite. The "magician's" doe-like charming eyes are overtly fixed on her partner's and they obey—and do not contrast with—the movement of her face. I shall return to this point later on.

Over time, artists multiplied the narrative intrigues involved in the swindles perpetrated on rich lovers, by adding complementary actors. Lucas van Leyden's *Tavern Scene* or *The Prodigal Son* (Fig. 59), a woodcut executed *c*.1517, is a good example of this iconographic diversification.[31] In this case, a beautiful harlot, sitting at the same table as a drinking procuress, enchants her partner, a sumptuously appareled man, through her enticing gaze and insistent caress, as she ferrets in his pouch. Here again Lucas resorts to the example of the Housebook Master's *Lovers*, representing the man in the same attitude as the lad in his predecessor's engraving, equally posing his face in profile, the second eye skillfully foreshortened. Furthermore, Lucas inverts the orientation of the chaste lady's face as reproduced in the *Lovers*: the chin pointed toward the man's lips translates the

30   For the first print, see Hutchison 1972, 53, no. 56; and Schuttwolf 1998, 31-2, no. 10. For the second print, see Koreny 1986, 1:188-9, no. 489. For the Housebook Master's original, see Hutchison 1972, 52-3, no. 55; Kok 1985, 150-1, no. 55.

31   See Parshall 1974, 123-4; Jacobowitz and Stepanek 1983, 195-6, no. 72; and Kok et al. 1996, no. 193.

slyness of the prostitute, unceasingly tempting and alluring; her gaze, roofed under heavy eyelids, betrays her dishonest goals. To unveil the allegorical meaning of the scene, Lucas represents a fool beyond a window, to the right, his finger directed toward the couple, while an inscription nearby admonishes: "(w)acht hoet varen sal" ["watch how it will turn out"].

In a woodcut by Urs Graf,[32] The Venal Lovers (Fig. 60), the traditional plot of the Ill-Matched Pair is developed into a paradigmatic sequel of swindles. In the center of the composition, a seductive damsel, wedged between two men, takes the money out of her older partner's purse to hand it over to her young beloved. Here, the woman's torso, almost frontal, is imperceptibly turned to the old man, as though accepting his lascivious touch purposely, whereas her tilted head and downcast gaze unmask her fatal, yet idyllic, attraction to the youth. Thus she is represented both as the perpetrator and the victim of the trickery. In Graf's woodcut, it must be also noted how easily the meaning of a traditional iconographic scheme can be inflected through slight variations: the canonical posture of the youth, whose face, bending inward, would

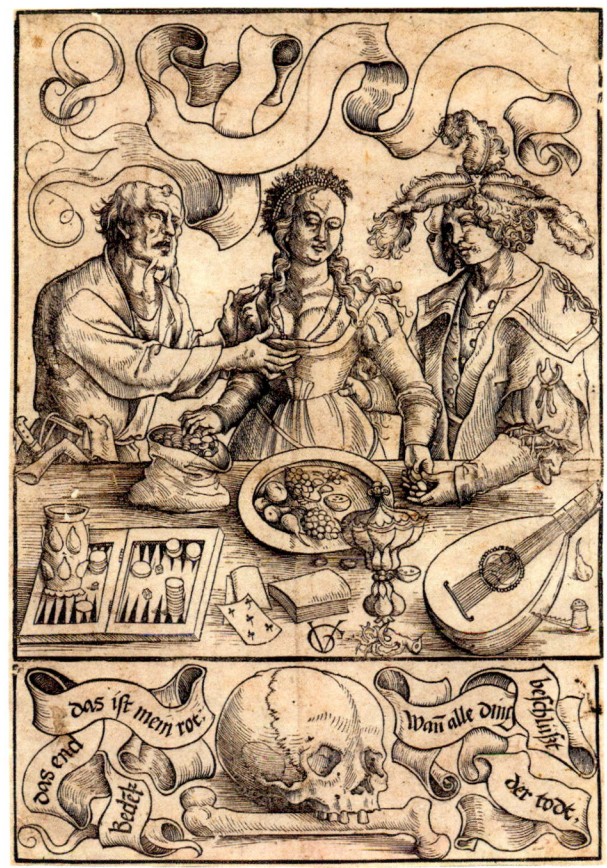

Fig. 60
Urs Graf, *Young Woman with an Old Man and a Youth*, engraving, 32.5 x 22.7 cm.

traditionally express the man's amorous engrossment in the beloved's sight, is to be decoded, in this particular context, as a faked, treacherous behavior, since the engraver shows the youth's hand promptly welcoming the woman's bounty. It should be once again remarked that the posture of the dandy's head perfectly matches the boy's in Caravaggio's first version of *The Fortune Teller*, almost to the smallest detail: the feather on the top of the hat, arching forward, that accompanies the movement of the face (Figs. 61, 62). Of course, in contrast to Caravaggio's picture, Graf's woodcut is clearly conceived as an allegory: the display of objects perceived as conducive to libido and deception—fruit, wine, games, cards, and a lute—laid out on the table in front of the venal lovers, are significantly juxtaposed with the skull in the lower register, surrounded by a scroll bearing an inscription: "bedenk das end das ist mein rot, wann alle ding beschlüßt der todt" ("here is my advice: mind the end, when Death dissolves everything").

After this survey of the visual patterns that underlie and latently operate in Caravaggio's two versions of the *Fortune Teller*, it is time for both pictures to undergo closer analysis. As Walter Friedlaender justly pointed out, Caravaggio was not the first painter to develop a subject of swindle and seduction. The *Ill-Matched Pair* by Quentin Massys (National Gallery of Art, Washington DC;

32   See Rowlands 1977, 52.

33   Friedlaender 1969, 82: "The artistic public of Rome toward the end of the sixteenth century had not yet become accustomed to the half-figure composition with secular subject matter, and was therefore attracted by its novelty. However, it was by no means an invention of the young Caravaggio. Almost from the

beginning of the century Flemish painters had used the limited frame of the half-figure painting to display as closely and shockingly as possible the facial expressions and significant gestures of their low-class figure types, mostly two or three figures of money changers, drunkards, lecherous old men and whores. The young Caravaggio had certainly seen half-figure compositions similar to the *Ill-Assorted Lovers* by Quentin

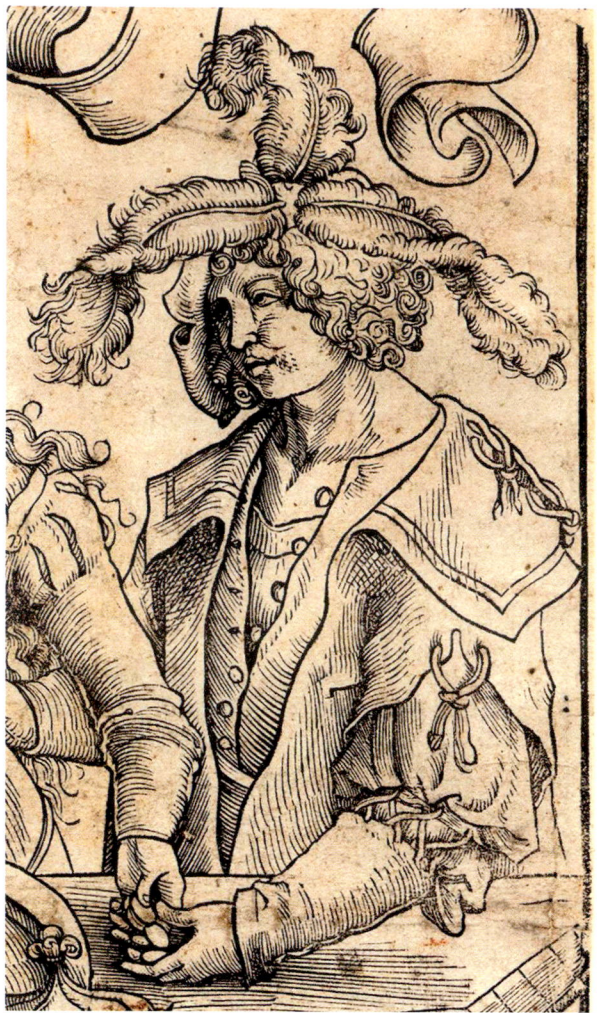

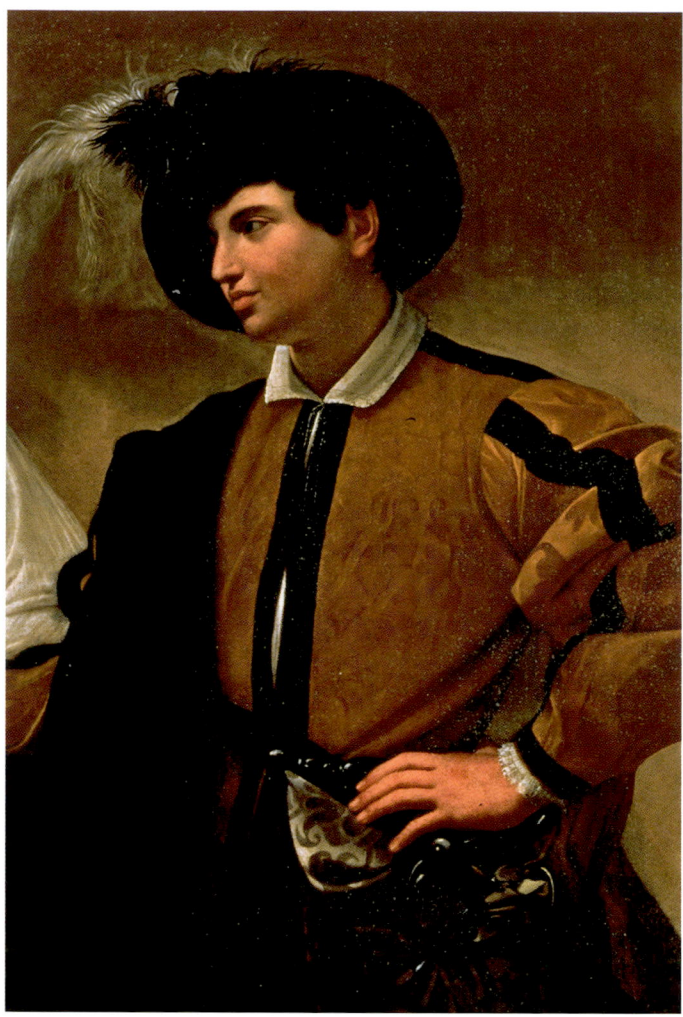

Fig. 61
Urs Graf, *Young Woman with an Old Man and a Youth*,
engraving, 32.5 x 22.7 cm., detail.

Fig. 62
Michelangelo Merisi da Caravaggio, *The Fortune Teller*,
Pinacoteca Capitolina, Rome, oil on canvas, 115 x 150 cm.,
detail.

Fig. 63), which Friedlaender mentions among the sources for *The Fortune Teller*, proves the point.[33]
Larry Silver has demonstrated that the Washington *Ill-Matched Pair* derives from Lucas van Leyden's
Tavern Scene.[34] Even if Caravaggio knew painted copies or versions of the same theme developed by
Massys, or, for that matter, by other northern painters, it should nevertheless be remarked that *The
Fortune Teller*, in its two variants, achieves a completely different effect. Caravaggio undoubtedly
dilutes the comic charge intrinsic to the subject. In this regard, for instance, one should consider
the narrower close-up chosen by Massys in his *Ill-Matched Pair*. It clearly functions as a magnifying
glass bringing out the damsel and the old man's almost caricatured faces, as well as the lacework
of arms and hands constituting the lower border of the composition. The assistance of a fool, to
the left, thirstily grabbing the pouch stolen from the man, explicitly stresses the comic character of
the episode. In other words, the hilarious feature of Massys' painting radically pervades the inner

Massys, and Jan van Hemessen's *Loose Company* during his
youth in Lombardy, or in central Italian collections; he may
actually have seen the *Money Changer and His Wife* by Marinus
van Roymerswaele in Florence. However, Caravaggio in his
Cardsharps and *Fortune Teller*, shows not the slightest didactic
or moralizing tendency; nothing of the satirical and defiant

mood of the northern artists can be found in these works. They
are tempered by his Italianism, not only in style, but also in a
certain humanism."

34   Silver 1974. See also Silver 1984, 143-6; 223-4, no. 35.

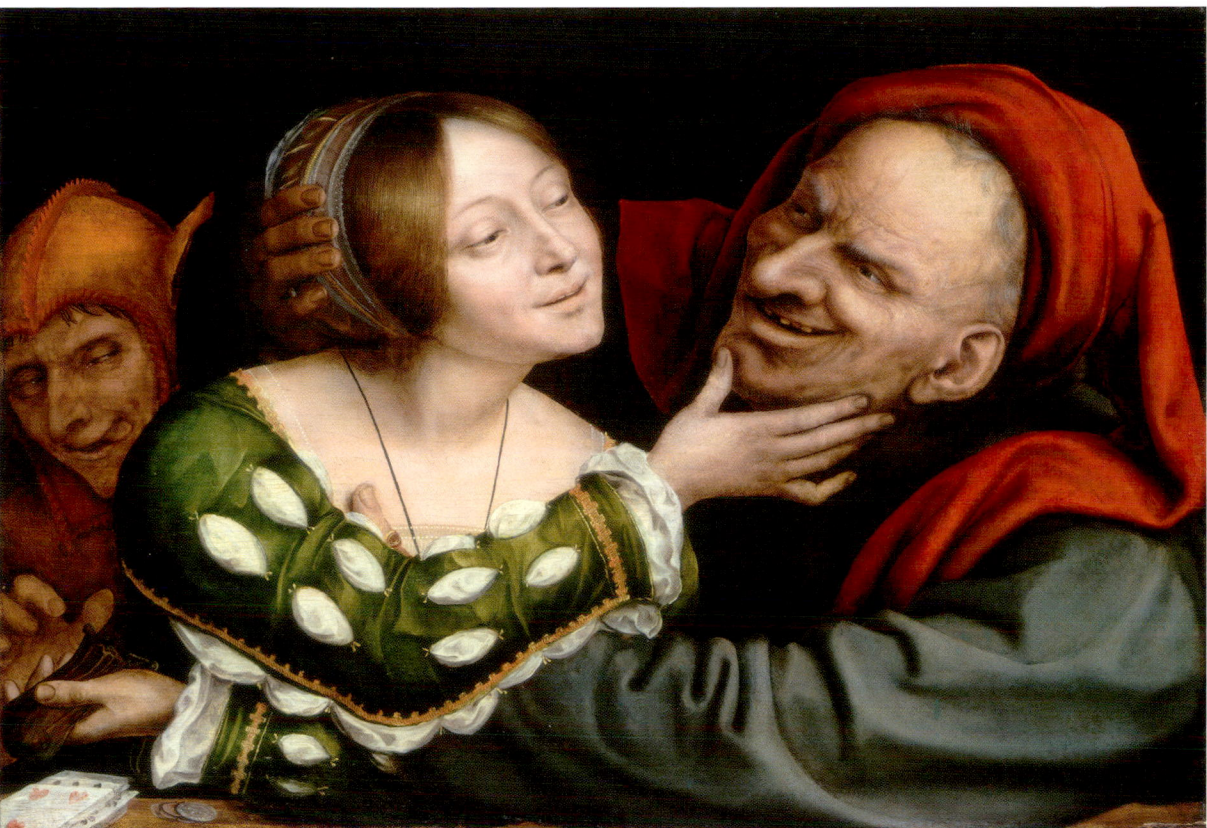

Fig. 63
Quentin Massys, *Ill-Matched Lovers*, National Gallery of Art, Washington DC, oil on panel, 43.2 x 63 cm.

structure of the composition, so much so that spontaneously, at the very first glance, beholders are driven both to understand the comic plot and to smile or laugh at the visual gag. Occasionally, they are also invited to meditate on the foolishness of human nature.

Caravaggio, however, masks the comic implications of the scene, by dissimulating or concealing those visual puns and devices specific to comedy. For instance, one element that explicitly characterizes the trickery unfolding in *The Fortune Teller* is money, more specifically the ring. Although it was once visible in both versions of the composition, it is indisputable that the ring never had the same visual prominence as the coins or pouches of money unfailingly deployed in the iconography of the *Ill-Matched Pair*. In connection with this, it should be recalled—if only partially to justify Bellori's misreading of Caravaggio's picture—that the act of removing the ring is so unclear, and its visual impact so tempered, that beholders may overlook it and be tempted to read the episode without recourse to it. Caravaggio, especially in the Paris *Fortune Teller*, misleads viewers by design—or tricks them into distraction, as his gypsy is supposed to do—by embedding the ring in the shade of the palm, so that viewers tend to misinterpret the very act of stealing, focusing instead on the erotic contact between the gypsy's finger and the boy's hand. In the Paris *Fortune Teller*, Caravaggio even covers the crime scene—the young man's palm—fractionally, by means of an upraised finger. Furthermore, the sinuous eurythmy of waving hands and curving fingers playing out the climactic momentum of the swindle belongs instead, more congruently, to the more delicate of idyll.

Another indispensable component of a visual comedy is patently absent in *The Fortune Teller*: the representation of the ugly partner, whether a man or a woman. Indeed, one of the reasons why Caravaggio's scene of treachery preserves its ambivalence resides in the physical equality of its two

151

actors. Bearing in mind the system of pictorial conventions previously analyzed, it is now more practicable to elucidate the scope of the iconographic elaboration developed by Caravaggio, if with differences, in the two *Fortune Tellers*.

Despite the paratactic disposition of the two figures in the Rome picture, roughly juxtaposed, Caravaggio deftly visualizes their divergences in expression and attitude. The youth, bending his head inward, transfixed in the contemplation of his sorceress, penetrates the space, inviting the viewer to follow the direction of his amorous gaze. By circumscribing his quasi-profile with the circular, ample brim of his dark hat, the painter attains an important result: beholders instinctively linger on the boy's face, thereby descrying the young man's physical and mental absorption in his passion. Much more complex is the gypsy's attitude. In the iconographic tradition of the *Ill-Matched Pair*, the contorted disposition of the woman's head and torso reveals the duality of her sentiments: love for money and disdain for her improvident partner. Therefore, the woman's torso in most cases is turned toward the man imperceptibly but unequivocally, whereas her head tilts away. Otherwise, if artists intend to highlight the woman's bawdiness, the female figure concomitantly directs her head and torso toward her victim, overwhelming him with her gaze and physicality. In the Rome *Fortune Teller*, the gypsy's posture does not correspond to these examples. Instead of seducing the youth by closing in, she eschews any bodily contact with him except through the hands. More importantly, her torso seems to pull back, as though she were ready to flee, should her partner sense her roguish intentions. On the contrary, her face, not simply her gaze, is riveted onto the youth's face, as though she were hypnotizing him with her beautiful eyes, stalking him attentively. Yet nothing in her physiognomy betrays her craftiness: neither her delicately rounded chin—used as a sign of treachery by the Housebook Master, who depicts it as asymmetrical with regard to the mouth—nor even her eyes—perfectly visible, unencumbered by heavy eyelids. In numerous examples, as already noted, this is an essential clue to uncovering the woman's mischief. When deciphered in light of iconographic tradition, the gypsy's posture accomplishes its comic function successfully only if the beholder realizes her robbery, and makes out her attempt to remove the boy's ring. Only in this case does her attitude transliterate her feline ability to enchant and chase the young man in her quest for gold. On the contrary, if the detail of the gliding ring happens to be overlooked—an effect that the painter himself seems to have sought—then the narrative takes another turn: a lyrical one. As already pointed out, the gypsy's intense gaze, even her nascent smile, which intrigued Mancini, could translate the affects of amorous attraction specific to the iconography of the *Lovers*, as elicited by Dürer's smiling male figure in *The Promenade*. If observed from this prospect, the attitude of the woman's torso might paradoxically indicate something else: a sudden, surprised restraint. Put otherwise, what is particularly disruptive in the Rome *Fortune Teller* is not the openness of its narrative plot—in the pre-existing iconography, narration is to a certain degree open, too[35]— but the impression it arouses in the viewer. The more one examines the composition, the more obscure the interpretation of its basic meaning and the identification of its subject becomes.

Somehow, Wittkower's definition of Caravaggio's composition as unreal has its own congruity. By dissimulating and concealing iconographic epithets, by modulating expression and attitude until the extremes of ambivalence and abstraction, Caravaggio not only blends different genres, lyrical and comic, in an inextricable manner, but he also compromises the subject itself, its fundamental coherence: the fortune-telling, as well as the theft of the ring, turn into an iconographic pre-text, a visual container whereby two actors interrelate in ways partially inaccessible to beholders. Whatever efforts viewers make in order to fit the image into the categories by which they are accustomed to decoding the comic or the lyrical, they end up fatally thwarted in coming to a

---

35 See, for example, Meadow 1992.

conclusive reading. In spite of its realism, or naturalism, Caravaggio's *Fortune Teller* exceeds the viewer's expectations; its pictorial indeterminacy engenders a gap between the image and the beholder's sense of comedy or lyric. In this interstice lies the essence of Caravaggio's "unreality." Of course, when referring to the spectator's comic and lyrical sense, I allude to the network of pictorial signs and conventions that constitute the perceptive and intellectual norms upon which an audience processes, acknowledges, and evaluates an image. In other words: the beholders' imaginative habits. As such, they are culturally and socially diversified. In the particular case of *The Fortune Teller*, the nature of its subject, whether lyrical or comedic, contributes to the viewers' bewilderment. In fact, compared to an *istoria*, in which the heroic, religious, allegorical dimension is instinctively perceived as remote and possibly beyond the limits of experience, a comic or lyrical subject features an abusing proximity, an illusionary immediacy that blurs the boundaries between subjective and objective, natural vision and fiction. By declaring that he contented himself with reproducing a gypsy directly in the canvas, Caravaggio intended to make the public believe that he wanted to abolish the fiction-factor of images themselves, as if pictures could really mirror actuality.[36] From this premise, it is easy to conceive the beholders' puzzlement when, looking at what appeared to be a fictive segment of actuality, they found themselves grappling with ambivalent signs and codes. To put it briefly, fictiveness peers back through the simple mirror the picture is supposed to be.

The complexity of Caravaggio's invention emerges in a more troubling way in the Paris *Fortune Teller*, in which pictorial description nonetheless plays a more fundamental role. Caravaggio reproduces vividly the slightest details of the couple's apparel: the hilt of the sword juts out from the foreground by reflecting the light that in turn orbits on its metal coils; the white rhomboidal patterns embroidered on the gypsy's black collar elegantly frame her décolleté; a filament of flashing pigment forms the shape of the lace on the youth's orange, dark-lined doublet.[37] Notwithstanding these visual and tactile effects of reality, Caravaggio enhances the ambivalence he had already introduced in his first *Fortune Teller*. I have already remarked that the act of stealing the ring is less conspicuous in the Paris version.[38] In addition, the artist insistently draws the viewer's attention to the axis linking the two actors' gazes, by casting the diagonal shadow of a window frame onto the wall serving as a backdrop. Therefore the gaze spontaneously follows the indication of this slanting, luminous vector of attention, dwelling on the couple's deep eye contact. As a consequence, the visual relevance of the gypsy's sleight of hand decreases, without entirely losing its importance. More astonishingly, Caravaggio reinforces the couple's spatial interrelation, by disposing their figures in almost perfect symmetry,[39] their faces tilting in reflection of each other, the gypsy's

---

36 Longhi 1999-2000, 1:166-7, particularly insists on the metaphor of the mirror and its importance for Caravaggio's painting. From this, Longhi comes to the following conclusion: "Che altro potesse conseguire a questa risoluzione di procedere per specchiatura diretta della realtà, non è troppo difficile intendere. Ne conseguiva la tabula rasa del costume pittorico del tempo che, preparandosi gli argomenti in carta e matita per via di erudizione storica e di astrazione stilizzante, aveva elaborato una complessa classificazione del rappresentabile, dove, per meglio servire alla società di allora, non poteva che preferirsi l'aspetto della classe dominante. Ma il Caravaggio pensa invece alla vita commune, ai sentimenti semplici, all'aspetto feriale delle cose che valgono, nello specchio, come gli uomini." My conclusions differ dramatically from this interpretation.

37 Hibbard 1983, 28: "We see Caravaggio's meticulously detailed attention to strings, bows, eyelashes, cast shadows, and other details, including a particularly intricate sword hilt of the kind that he himself carried and that often reappears."

38 Gilbert 1995, 203: "At the center of the painting, the specific detail of action is the seizure by the girl of the boy's wrist – much as in the 'guiding gesture' for an illiterate writer earlier discussed. With her forefinger, she then palpates the sensitive middle of his palm, the fortune-telling gesture. It is that sensuous touch of the flesh that got him started in responding to her. This is the gypsy girl whom Caravaggio asked to come into his house so he could paint her, according to Bellori. Even in the unlikely case that no erotic undertone was involved, this story and the cardinal's memories of the Artemisias of his youth suggest a bond of similar attitudes in artist and patron toward the image."

39 Cuzin 1977, 14: "Il [the painting] s'organise presque symétriquement par rapport à un axe central, les deux visages tournés du meme angle, les deux bras plies se répondant.".

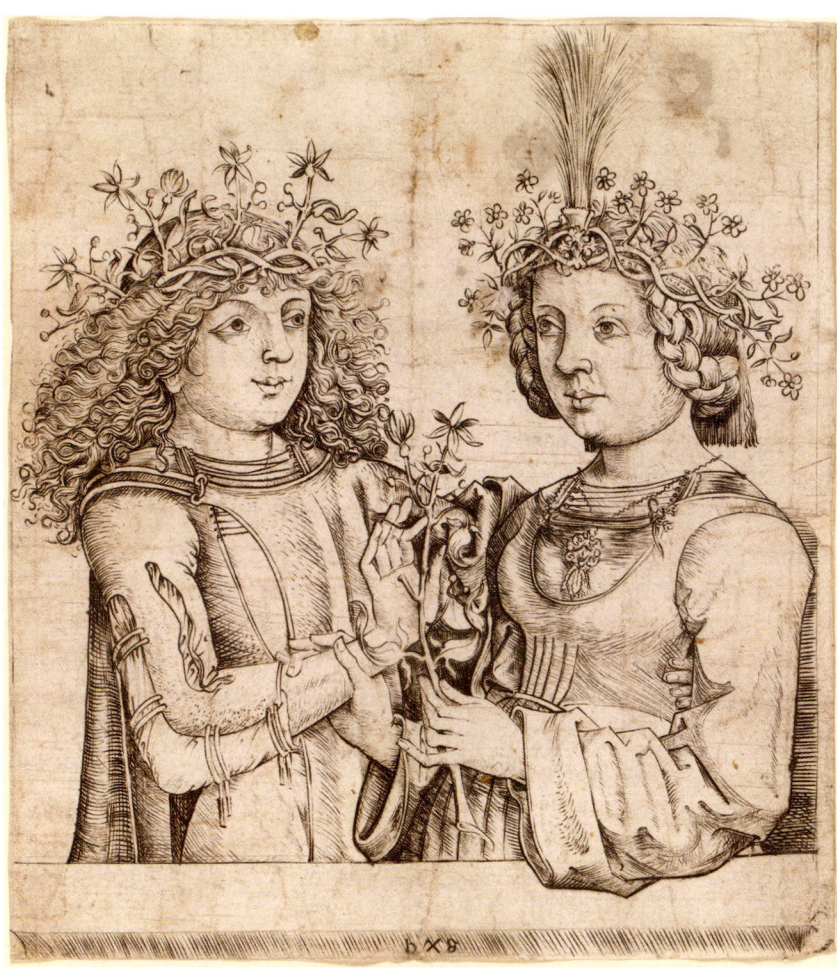

Fig. 64
Master b x g, *The Lovers*, engraving, 15.5 x 13.7 cm.

trapezoidal bust and the boy's elliptical torso suavely crisscrossing. Moreover, the artist suggests a kind of visual chiasmus[40] between the woman's face, plunged in a warm shade, but brought forth by the whiteness of her turban, and the young man's head, strongly spotlit, though circumscribed by the dark halo of the hat. Their symmetrical disposition reintroduces and underlines the lyrical mode specific to the *Lovers*, thereby signaling the equality of both the gypsy and the youth: visually, they are no longer an ill-matched couple. Caravaggio even resorts to the basic pattern from which the iconography of the *Lovers* sprang, as shown by a print by the Master b x g, generally considered a copy after a lost composition by the Housebook Master (Fig. 64).[41] There, the boy and the maid appear half-length, behind a parapet, their faces oriented three-quarter, their torsos almost frontally disposed, looking at each other's eyes with rapture. By reinstating the archaism of this pristine lyrical scheme in the second *Fortune Teller*, Caravaggio clearly underscores the artifice of his composition. At least unconsciously he could not ignore the

fact that this iconographic scheme was at variance with the comic action—the trickery—he was to develop, for two reasons. First and foremost, the quasi-immobility of both the gypsy and the youth somehow contradicts the very logic of a pictorial narrative, whether it be the telling of the fortune or the theft of a ring. Secondly, it stresses the lyrical theme in a comic context without suppressing comedy entirely. It would be inappropriate to define this combination and interference of pictorial codes as an iconographic clash, since Caravaggio's conflation of iconographies works out smoothly and imperceptibly. By intensifying the lyrical character of the image, and by strongly inhibiting its narrative charge, so much as almost to erase action altogether, Caravaggio thus betrays the fictiveness of his picture: the geometrical purity of these two bodies symmetrically aligned in the pictorial field makes them appear as if posing for the equivalent of the photographer's lens— the painter's inventive eye—in the analog of a snapshot framing—the margins of the canvas—as playing out both love and deception, attraction and youthful naïveté. On account of the different modes Caravaggio ingeniously blends together, the gaze his actors interchange remains suspended

40   Ibidem: "Mais le parti des valeurs est inverse: à gauche, sur un fond sombre, une silhouette blanche, un visage et des découpes sombres: cheveux, noeuds de rubans, triangle de la couverture; à droite une découpe sombre sur le fond blanc, un visage clair et des découpes blanches: collerette, échancrure du pourpoint, manchettes. L'effet est frappant au niveau des visages: demi-cercle blanc du turban découpé sur le fond

sombre, ovale sombre du visage; demi-cercle noir du chapeau, ovale clair du visage, fond blanc. D'où l'effet saisissant d'une image en négatif perçue dans un miroir."

41   According to Hutchison 1972, 77, no. 108, this print might be a copy after a lost work by the Housebook Master.

between absorption and artifice. However one interprets these absorptive looks—whether of lustful attraction or treacherous hypnosis—the fictiveness of the representation concomitantly taints their visual pertinence as signs of a narrative action and seduces the viewer into reading the scene as pure performance, a mere "reproduction" of two by-passers pretending to enact a "representation." In other words, the comedic plot is constantly reduced to the status of a two-bust portrait, while the latter lends itself to being read as a comedic or lyrical scene of a special kind: the spontaneous interaction of two sitters immortalized by the painter's brush. When describing *The Fortune Teller* as a tableau vivant, Wittkower pinpointed the quintessential feature of the Paris painting. Constructing it as a staged fiction, Caravaggio nonetheless lures beholders into a final illusion. In defiance of the roles they perform while posing for the painter, the youth and the gypsy suddenly seem to act out a quite different script, as though, when rehearsing their characters, they were caught by an unexpected affection that freezes their attitudes and deepens their gazes. From this point of view, Caravaggio's second *Fortune Teller* proves particularly to be a fiction-within-the-fiction device, a multi-layered visual mechanism whereby beholders alternatively question the visual congruity and the fictiveness of the image in a winding, marvelous short-circuit of multivalent pictorial ciphers.

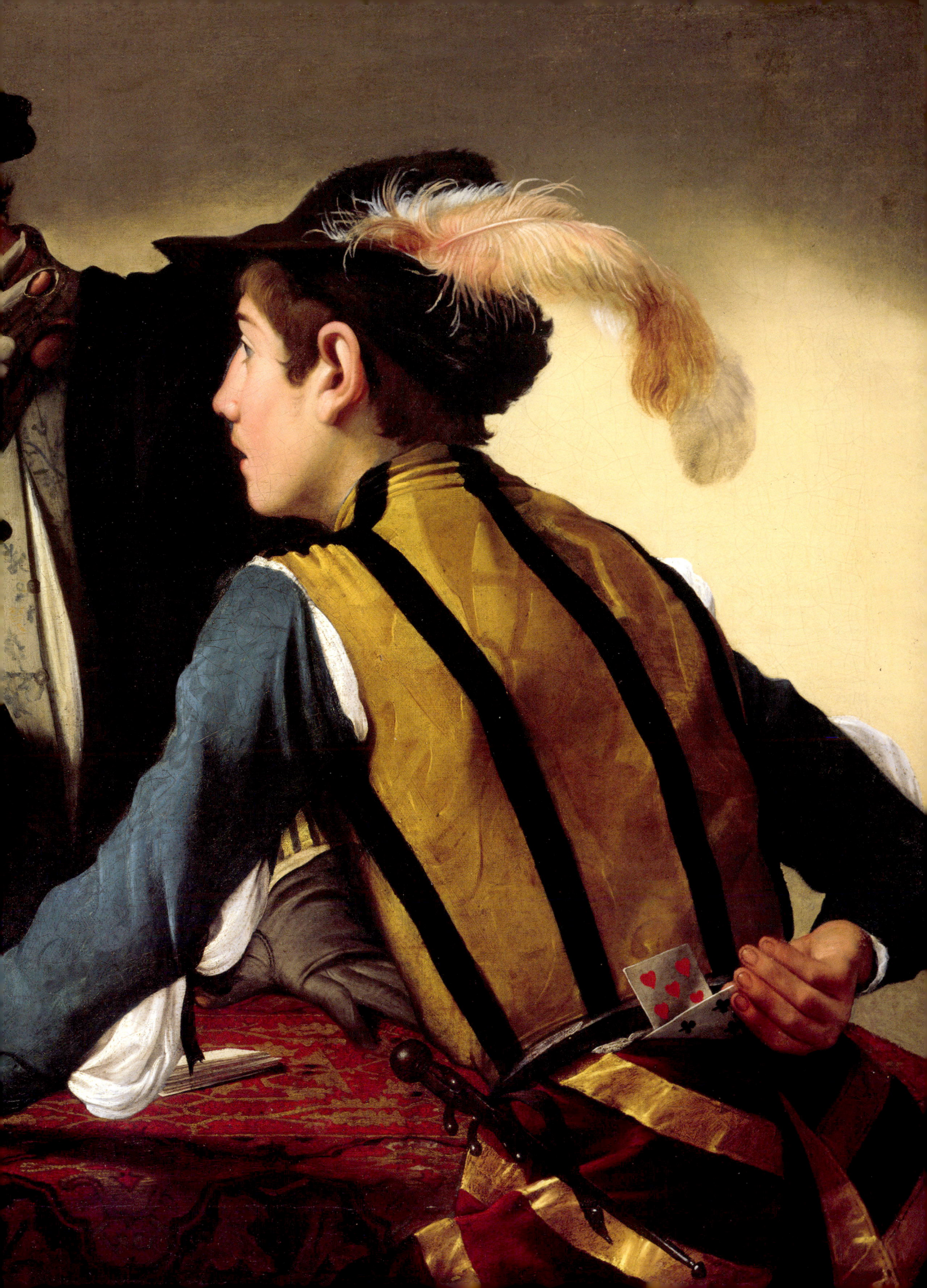

CHAPTER 5

Behind the Comical Trick: Caravaggio's *The Cardsharps* and Giovan Battista Marino's "Gioco di Primera"[*]

A Complex Text – Image Relation

The Italian poet Giambattista Marino was known to be extremely fond of works of art. He collected numerous pictures and drawings, executed by the most renowned artists of his time.[1] He also knew Caravaggio, whom he probably met in Rome in 1600. In his 1619 *Galeria*, Marino praised two paintings by Caravaggio, the *Medusa* (now Galleria degli Uffizi, Florence), and his own *Portrait*, now lost.[2] In accordance with the tradition of poetic eulogy, Marino did not describe these compositions, but rather used them as a pretext to celebrate respectively Ferdinand I de' Medici (for whom the *Medusa* was destined) and Caravaggio himself, capable of cloning and animating the poet's effigy. In both cases, the relation between text and image is rather loose, and Marino did not develop Caravaggio's pictorial subjects into a poetic or narrative situation. The same seemingly does not apply to a sonnet from Marino's *Amore*, the "Gioco di primera."

In her 1991 article on "Marino's Poetry and Caravaggio," Elizabeth Cropper singles out this poem, suggesting that it "may have been inspired" by Caravaggio's *The Cardsharps* (Fig. 65).[3] Although Cropper's suggestion is extremely compelling, it is problematic at first glance to acknowledge the presence, let alone specify the nature, of this inspiration. Indeed, Caravaggio's picture and Marino's sonnet do not deal with exactly the same topic. To be sure, since the poem's theme is practically unprecedented in the lyrical tradition,[4] it can be assumed that Marino reshaped the subject of *The Cardsharps* through subtle rhetorical variations. Marino's composition is given here in Cropper's translation (with a few variations):

> With twenty and twenty pictured cards
> (The weapons of Idleness) the sun of my thoughts
> Was training with three other warriors
> On a domestic battlefield at games of Mars.
> Proud champions of Fortune, they collect them up,
> They deal them out shuffled and scattered,
> And with moves now feigned, now true,

---

[*] This chapter is an expanded, revised version of my 2008 essay in the *Memoirs of the American Academy in Rome* (Pericolo 2008).

[1] See Fulco 1979; Fumaroli 1988; Guardiani 1988; Fagiolo Dell'Arco 1996; Fulco 2001; Pericolo 2001b; Stoichita 2004.

[2] Marini 2005, 453-4, no. 44, wrongly identifies this picture with a portrait in a private collection (London).

[3] Cropper 1991, 198-9.

[4] Alessandro Martini (Marino b, 94, no. 34) was the first to signal the "anomaly" of Marino's sonnet in the light of tradition and postulate that the poem was inspired by Caravaggio's *The Cardsharps*.

Now they divert feints, now with art they parry blows.
When turning his pious look toward me
(And Love gave him the cards with his own hand)
My beautiful idol picked up four of them,
There he was with the diamond, and with the club
The spade, the heart not yet there; but I gave him
The heart to make complete his victory.[5]

In the sonnet, the three interconnected themes of love, gaming, and war fuse together. The poet depicts four young men playing *primera*, a popular game of cards in the Renaissance and in the seventeenth century. The author, or his poetic "I," observes the match with loving care: he is the fifth actor on stage and, as will soon be clear, he is about to turn into a cheat. As his beloved happens to have a hand of three different suits (diamonds, clubs, spades),[6] the poet, who was spying on his cards, slips him the heart that would achieve his score. In *primera*, a hand of four suits constitutes one of the highest combinations. Since the youth through his "pious look" cajoles the poet into cheating, and apparently ends up accepting the false card, the poet actively takes part in the playful swindle. Moreover, the heart at the end of the poem is both an actual card and a metaphor for the poet's heart. Hence, the lyrical and the treacherous are so inextricably bound up with each other that it is not hard to predict that the youth will both triumph over the poet's heart and win the match, ensuring himself a complete victory in the kindred fields of love and gaming.

As for *The Cardsharps*, the only seventeenth-century source to describe the picture, originally executed for Cardinal Francesco Maria Del Monte around 1596, is Giovan Pietro Bellori in his 1672 *Vite*. Bellori praises the painting in which "three half-figures of men playing cards are arrayed." In it, Caravaggio depicted

> a naïve youth holding the cards with both hands, his face well portrayed from life, clad in dark clothes, and opposite him in profile a young swindler, turning toward him, leaning with one hand on the gaming table, while with the other he extracts a

---

5 Marino b, 94, no. 34: "Con venti e venti effigiate carte/ (armi dell'Ozio) il sol de' miei pensieri/ Esercitando gìa fra tre guerrieri/ In domestico agon scherzi di Marte./ L'accogliean, le spendean confuse e sparte/ Fatti di cieca dea campioni alteri,/ E con assalti or simulati or veri,/ Or schernian l'arte, or si schermian con l'arte./ Quando ver me volgendo il guardo pio/ (e gliene dié di propria mano Amore)/ Quattro ne prese il bell'idolo mio./ V'era col quadro e con la picca il fiore,/ Il cor non v'era già; ma gli died'io/ (per farlo apien vittorioso) il core." I deemed it opportune to modify Cropper's translation of v. 8 ("or schernian l'arte, or si schermian con l'arte"). "Now they mock art, now with art they fence with one another" is of course an excellent translation, but I wanted to stress the military aspects of Marino's metaphors. "Schermire" in fact means: "parare i colpi dell'avversario, fare sì che non giungano a segno, deviarli, arrestarli" (Battaglia 1961-2002, 17: 962, 3rd column, s.v. schermire). In Italian, it has the same root as "scherma" ("fencing"). In this regard, it is interesting to consult one of the definitions of this sport: "La scherma, la quale è arte di ben maneggiar l'armi, ha per fine principale la salvezza della nostra persona; e consiste in due parti, l'una è nella difesa nostra, l'altra nell'offesa del nimico" (Ibidem, 2nd column, s.v. "scherma"). Thus, "scherma", fencing, is ordinarily considered the art of handling weapons skillfully, in defense or attack. When Marino says: "schernian l'arte" ("mock the art"), he in my opinion means: "avoid the art of the adversary, their blows". As a matter of fact "schernire" also

means "avoid a blow" ("schivare un colpo, un'aggressione; stornare un pericolo, una minaccia" *Ibidem*, 969, 3rd column, s.v. "schernire"). I have translated "cieca dea" ("blind Goddess") as "Fortune," in order to make clearer the meaning of the metaphor.

6 Cropper 1991, 199, rightly remarks: "Marino's trick plays upon the fit between the numbers four and three—the numbers of the players (three plus the *sol*, or the one and only of his thoughts) and of cards (the three suits to which the heart must be added — and the quatrains and tercets of the poem." In his *Capitolo*, Berni insists on the symbolic importance of the number four in "primera." First of all, the winning combinations are always made of four cards (Berni, 220). The highest combination in "primera" consists also in four sevens of different suits (84 points). Whoever gets this kind of combination is practically master of the game (Ibidem, 220). In another passage, Berni ironically declares that playing "primera" requires the practice of the three theological virtues, and that the game itself involves the four humors (Ibidem, 242). It is noteworthy that in Caravaggio's picture and in Marino's poem the emphasis on the number three (the accomplice's signal; the beloved's current hand) seems to charge the composition with suspense, the viewer or reader expecting the combination of four cards to reveal the plot's outcome. On the rules of "primera," see Girolamo Cardano's *De Ludo Aleae Liber* (in Cardano, 1:269). See also Ore 1953, esp. 212-4.

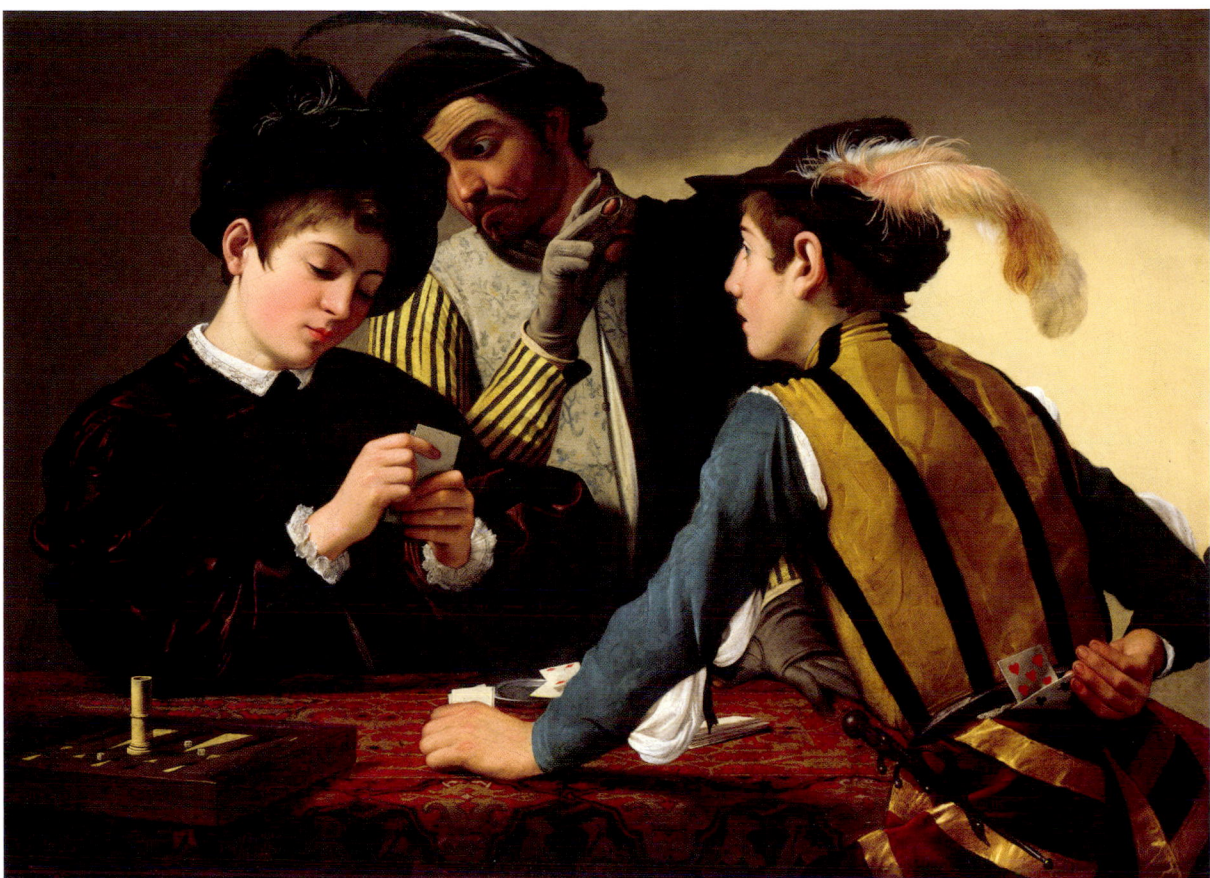

Fig. 65
Michelangelo Merisi da Caravaggio, *The Cardsharps*, Kimbell Museum of Art, Fort Worth, oil on canvas, 91.5 x 128.2 cm.

false card from his belt; near the boy, a third figure peeps at the marks on the cards, revealing their score to his mate by lifting three fingers; his companion, while leaning on the table, exposes his shoulder to the light along with his yellow doublet striped with black bands, whose imitation and coloring are anything but untruthful.[7]

A comparison of *The Cardsharps* with the "Gioco di primera" yields a few analogies and several apparent discrepancies. According to Cropper, Marino borrowed only Caravaggio's subject of a game swindle, thus encasing the trick at the core of *The Cardsharps* within a lyrical and erotic container. If one accepts this exegesis, one must wonder not only what pushed Marino to appropriate Caravaggio's idea for his own purposes, expanding the original script into a lyrical and (homo-) erotic poem, but also, more importantly, how to define this unwonted kind of poetic elaboration on a pictorial theme. In this regard, one single term comes to mind: literary theft.

7   Bellori, 216: "...ed un altro [quadro] degno dell'istessa lode nelle camere del cardinale Antonio Barberini, disposto in tre mezze figure ad un giuoco di carte. Finsevi un giovinetto semplice con le carte in mano, ed è una testa ben ritratta dal vivo in abito oscuro, e di rincontro a lui si volge in profilo un giovine fraudolente, appoggiato con una mano sulla tavola del giuoco, e con l'altra dietro si cava una carta falsa dalla cinta, mentre il terzo vicino al giovinetto guarda li punti delle carte, e con tre dita della mano li palesa al compagno, il quale nel piegarsi su 'l tavolino espone la spalla al lume in giubbone giallo listato di fasce nere, né finto è il colore nell'imitazione."

See also Scannelli, 199 ("Et appresso l'Eminentissimo Antonio Barberini si vede un quadro di meze figure al naturale, che dimostrano giocare mirabilmente alle carte, invenzione molto al di lui genio confacevole, e per conseguenza in tal particolare di rara bellezza"). As is well known, Caravaggio's *The Cardsharps*, after staying for several centuries in Rome, disappeared at the end of the nineteenth century; it was recovered in 1988. For the picture, see Friedlaender 1969, 81-4, 153-4, no. 9; Frommel 1971, 15-6, 24-5; Wind B. 1974, 32-4; Cinotti 1983, 554-6, no. 70; Mahon and Christiansen 1988; Wind B. 1989; Calvesi 1990, 229-30; Cropper 1991, 198-9;

This is not the place for a study of the rhetorical meaning and literary implications of seventeenth-century poetic borrowing. As he himself lucidly exposed, Marino made an art of literary robbery, and Cropper has pointed out the extent of his "stealing" in her *Domenichino Affair*.[8]

Another of Marino's raids into Caravaggio's inventions has passed almost unnoticed.[9] In Canto 15 of his 1623 *Adone*, Marino technically stole the subject of Caravaggio's *Fortune Teller* (Fig. 47), transliterating it into an episode of erotic chiromancy in which Venus, dressed as a gypsy and unrecognizable to her lover, the young hunter Adonis, foretells the future to him:

> …The youth, anxious to hear more
> [About his future], offers her his white hand.
> With a tremulous sigh, she holds it
> And, as she touches it, she senses an intense bliss,
> And feels the acute arrow that pierces her heart
> Quivering at once amidst her breast.
> The youth, his brows strained, his lips parted
> Fixes upon her his eyes, [already] directed to hers.[10]

It is relatively easy to imagine Venus as the gypsy and Adonis as the youth in Caravaggio's *Fortune Teller*. Like Adonis, the young man offers "his white hand" to the woman, by staring intently at her, "his brows strained, his lips parted." Like Venus, the gypsy holds the youth's hand, while locking her gaze on his. In a certain sense, Marino stealthily inserted an *ekphrasis* of Caravaggio's painting in the narrative action of his *Adone*. Furthermore, he unfroze the pictorial episode by providing it with a sequel and an epilogue; after the act of chiromancy, Venus abandons her disguise, losing her Egyptian tan and doffing her exotic headgear. She finally yields to love.

Although Marino dissimulated his theft, Caravaggio's imprint is still recognizable in this passage. Text and image thus mirror each other, or at least this can be our preliminary impression. Truth be told, the poet did not content himself with "transcribing" the picture's subject faithfully and transferring it directly into narration. By reversing the roles of Caravaggio's figures, Marino created a quite different situation. In fact, Venus—unlike the gypsy—falls for the youth, whereas Adonis, in contrast, is not charmed by the woman, but enthralled by her predictions. Moreover, Marino eliminates the swindle theme specific to the painting—the gypsy steals the youth's ring while telling his fortune—or, more appropriately, the only trick he alludes to is the one played by Venus on her lover, deceiving him with regard to her real identity. I chart in table 1 the similarities and differences between the picture and the sonnet.

Bologna 1992, 303-4; Gregori 1991, 96-109, no. 2; Puglisi 1998, 78-9; Longhi 1999-2000, 1:171, 178 [1952]; Langdon 2001, 46, no. 11; Bottacin 2002, 74-5; Moffitt 2002, 134-6; Moffitt 2004, 41-62; Marini 2005, 401-3, no. 18; Olson 2006; Schütze 2009, 248-9, no. 8; Ebert-Schifferer 2009, 78-81. Unlike the authors published in Benati and Paolucci 2008, I do not consider an ancient copy of Caravaggio's *The Cardsharps*, now in Denis Mahon's collection, to be a replica of the Fort Worth picture. Most of the interpretations of *The Cardsharps* insist on the moralizing message the painting is supposed to convey, a warning against the hazards of gaming. I recognize that ordinarily, in the seventeenth century, this kind of representation was given an "allegorical" content, as confirmed by many inscriptions on prints of gaming scenes. Yet I also believe that this allegorizing "patina" served as a pretext to justify the representation of what were considered low-genre scenes.

8   See Cropper 2005, 129-55.

9   Hirdt 1998, 97-105, is the only critic to remark on this poetic theft. He defines Marino's transposition of Caravaggio's *Fortune Teller* into his *Adone* as a "kaschierte Raub," a hidden theft.

10   Marino a, XV, 46: "A questo dir la bianca mano stende/ Vago d'udir più oltre il giovanetto./ Con un sospir tremante ella la prende/ E prende, nel toccarla, alto diletto./ E quel pungente stral che 'l cor l'offende/ Sente scotersi intanto in mezzo al petto./ L'altro con ciglia tese e labra aperte/ Gli occhi da lei pendenti a lei converte."

Roles	In Caravaggio's painting	In Marino's poem

The fortune teller	Loves secretly	Tries to seduce

but

	Looks at	Looks at
	Tries to deceive	Deceives through disguise
	Tells the fortune	Tells the fortune

The youth	Engrossed by the gypsy's beauty	Not engrossed by the gypsy's beauty

but

	Looks at	Looks at
	Curious (also) about his future	Curious (only) about his future
	Deceived	Deceived by the disguise
	Innocent	Innocent

From the scheme in table 1, it is obvious that the poetic theft, even when perpetrated at the expense of a picture rather than a poem, presupposes a transformation of its bounty. Therefore Marino's poetry not only attempts to conceal Caravaggio's borrowing by using it furtively, but also cashes in on its narrative charge by bending it into new action. At the same time, Marino may also seek to unveil his theft so the reader can detect it and appreciate its variations.

Although it is predictable that Marino, too, if he came to transpose the subject of the *Cardsharps* into a poem, would modify it through inversions and variants, it is doubtful whether he would challenge the prototype beyond recognition. Put otherwise, are the erotic and martial components of the "Gioco di primera" that, along with the swindle theme, underlie Marino's sonnet a pure caprice on the poet's part? And if so, do they lack any intertextuality? Should that be the case, it is difficult to understand to what end Marino would have pulled off a poetic theft with such vague scope and effect. Indeed, if the only common denominator between the picture and the poem were the card treachery, it would remain so obscure as to mar the text's allusive interplay with the image. Yet, another avenue could be considered. It is possible that a martial and erotic subtext operates concomitantly in Caravaggio's *The Cardsharps*, which enabled Marino to compose so sophisticated an elaboration of the painting.

Patterns of Assault

Like both versions of the *Fortune Teller*, executed around 1594-1597, the near-contemporary *Cardsharps* apparently belongs to the pictorial genre of comedy. There is no doubt, reading Bellori's description of the picture, that its subject is preeminently comic: a cheat scene whose climax Caravaggio admirably evokes. In an innovative way, Caravaggio sets up a dynamic narrative action, strongly articulated through the visual opposition between two geometrical schemes: the triangle determined by the cheater's arms, bracketing his shoulder, which culminates in the pointed silhouette of his plumed hat, and the trapezoid delineated by the boy's torso, timidly recoiling as

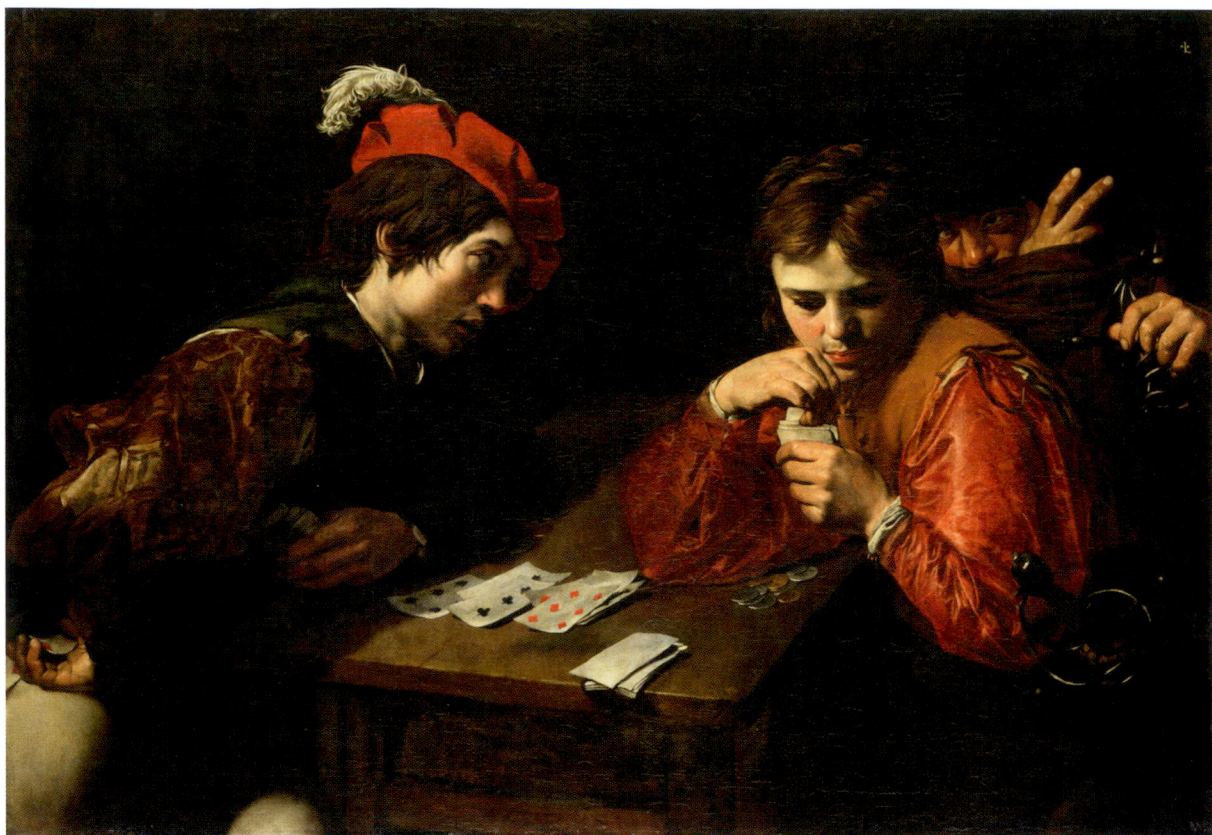

Fig. 66
Valentin de Boulogne, *The Cardsharps*, Gemäldegalerie Alte Meister, Dresden, oil on canvas, 94.5 x 137 cm.

if dodging his opponent's assault. Ingeniously, Caravaggio also tilted the youth's head rightward, in the direction of his adversary, thereby counteracting the oblique thrust of the swindler's rising figure. By the same token, he enhanced the dramatic tension between the players, whose respective calm and vehemence strongly contrast with one another, channeling the viewer's attention into a continuous short-circuited loop—the action winding and rewinding relentlessly, the eyes shuttling from one actor to the other. In a certain sense, the fast-paced unfolding of the scene is spatially dilated through the insertion, between the boy and the cheater, of a sloping table, which both deepens the pictorial space—despite its shallowness—and draws the beholder's attention from left to right (and vice versa), and from foreground to background (and conversely). In contrast, the presence of a third figure wedged between the two players contracts the timing of the action, compelling the beholder to focus on the climactic momentum of the swindle. To anchor the gaze at the center of the action, Caravaggio disposes the diagonals of the cheater's leaning arm and his mate's upraised forearm and hand as rhyming axes wittily linked together by the borders of a partially unbuttoned doublet. The patch of protruding shirt on the accomplice's chest and belly is a note of masterly lighting that serves as a breach between the youth and the swindler, and intensifies their mutual opposition.

By concealing a portion of the second cheater's grimacing face under the dark silhouette of the youth's velvet hat, Caravaggio intended to suggest a certain arbitrariness of the vision, as if the comic gag were by chance disclosed in the viewer's presence: a casual "snapshot" of an event inadvertently caught by the eye. Only after getting acquainted with the composition does the beholder become aware of all the geometrical harmonies that underpin its structure, from the principal ones—upon which I have already remarked—down to the smallest ones: for instance, the triangular shape of the gloved hand resting on the table and elegantly inscribed into the triangle outlined by the cheater's outstretched arm and the left contour of his shoulder, a marvelous *tour de force* that might otherwise go unnoticed.

The action conjured up by Caravaggio seems to function with clockwork precision. As usual in a comic scene, the denouement appears to be inevitable: cards will be exchanged and naïveté overcome by roguishness. However, a single detail does not perfectly square with the mechanism of the trickery: the swindler's parted lips, playing out puzzlement or—more surprisingly—admiration.[11] As will be demonstrated soon, Caravaggio inherited this attitude from the iconography on which he drew for his invention. At any rate, it is evident that the plot represented in the Kimbell picture is not as transparent as it may appear at first glance. In his *c.*1615-1617 *The Cardsharps* now in the Gemäldegalerie, Dresden (Fig. 66),[12]

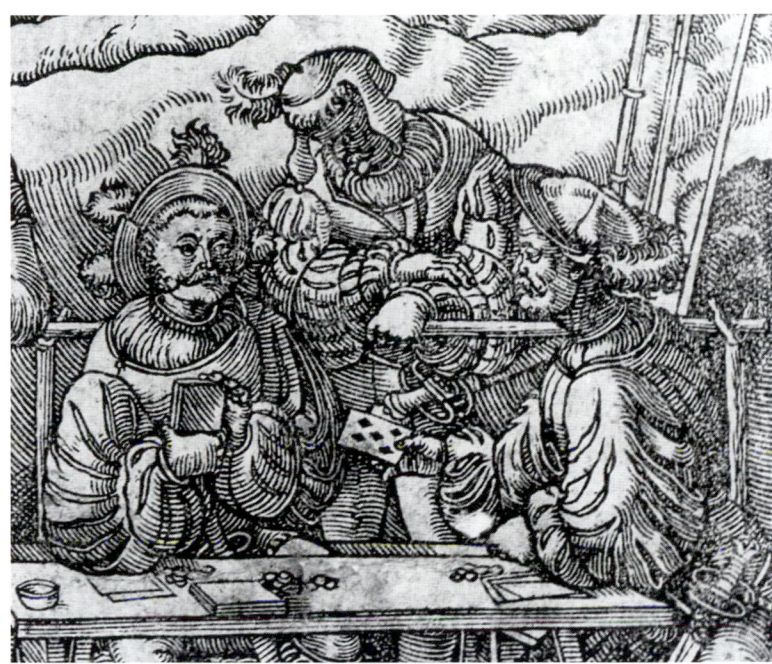

Fig. 67
Anton Woensam of Worms, *Two Soldiers Playing Cards*, engraving, 12.4 x 8.5 cm., detail.

Valentin de Boulogne attempted to eliminate all the ambiguities present in Caravaggio's prototype by suggesting a crystal-clear unfolding of the swindle episode. By varying the orientation of the gaming table, which now recedes askew toward the picture's background, and by showing one of its ends in the foreground, Valentin manages unambiguously to reveal the attitude and expression of the cheater: sitting on the left, he takes advantage of his adversary's absorption in the cards to catch the cue of his accomplice, who figures on the right, the lower part of his face masked by the border of his mantle: seizing his sword-hilt with his left hand, this third actor squints and crosses his eyes to indicate discreetly the victim's card score by lifting two fingers of his right hand. Accordingly, his companion extracts from his belt the card with which he will defeat his naïve adversary. Although the effect is caused by a perspective trick, the viewer has the impression that the youth rests his head on his bent hand, echoing the canonical pose of Melancholy: in reality, he is cautiously shifting his cards while pondering his score. Evidently Valentin visualized the swindle depicted in the Kimbell picture from another angle in order to clarify its plot and ensure that it would be read unequivocally as a pictorial comedy.

The general layout of Caravaggio's *The Cardsharps* seems to rely on an early sixteenth-century engraving by Anton Woensam of Worms, *Two Soldiers Playing Cards* (Fig. 67).[13] If one zooms in on the print's central episode, the many affinities between Woensam's and Caravaggio's compositions immediately become clear. In the engraving, a bearded landsknecht sits behind a table strewn with money and cards; almost motionless, his cards tightly held in his hands, he stares at his adversary's

---

11 Caravaggio also employs the *profil perdu* as a technical device to imply the figure's nascent bafflement at an unexpected situation. In the *Calling of Saint Matthew*, the young man seen from the back, whose affinity with the swindler in *The Cardsharps* must be noted, evinces his curious perplexity at Christ and Peter's sudden bursting onto the stage, or at least at Matthew's reaction to this irruption. Similarly, in the

London *Supper at Emmaus*, the apostle in the foreground, whose expression is half-hidden, and who occupies a position analogous to *The Cardsharps'* cheater, clearly shows his astonishment at recognizing Jesus' true identity.

12 See Mojana 1989, 56, no. 3.

13 For the print, see Strauss 1981, 206, no. 10 (491).

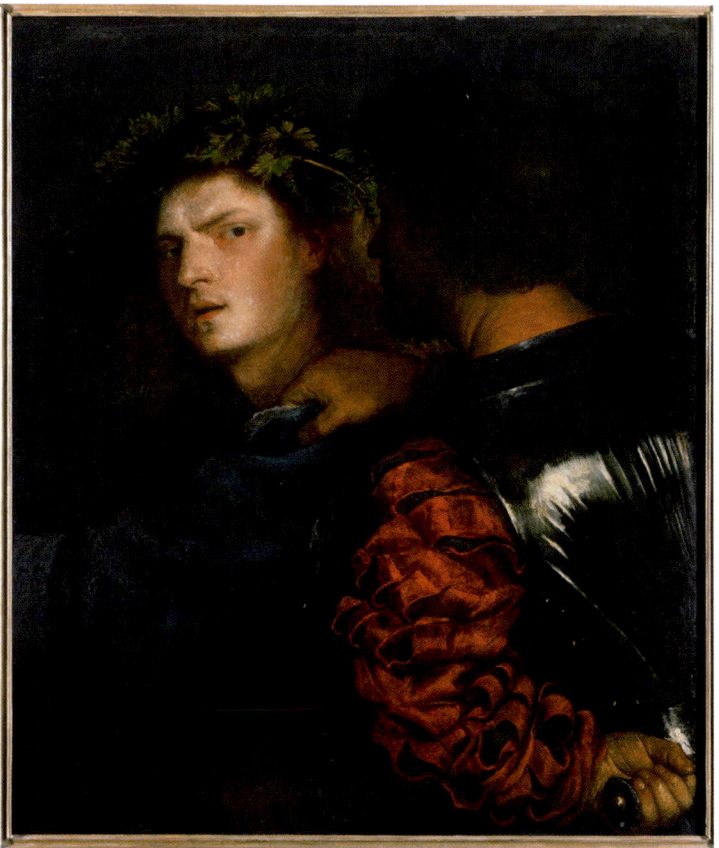

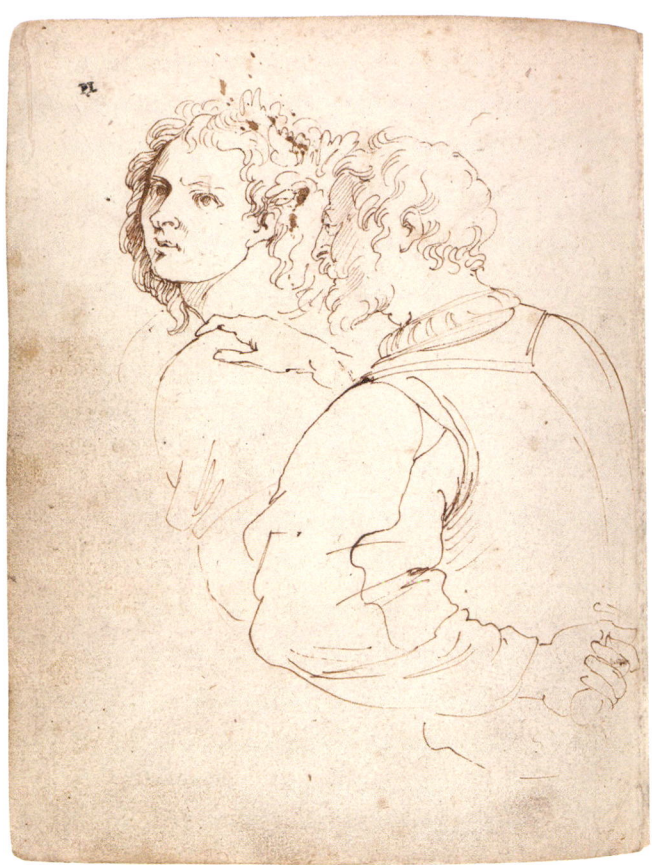

Fig. 68
Titian (Tiziano Vecelli), *The Bravo*, Kunsthistorisches Museum, Vienna, oil on canvas, 75 x 67 cm.

Fig. 69
Anton Van Dyck after Giorgione (or Titian), *The Bravo*, British Museum, London, pen and brown ink, 20 x 15.8 cm.

face as if gauging the man's intention in discarding a five of diamonds. His head in profile, the rival, a bearded soldier with almost identical features, appears to rise imperceptibly, his left arm bent over the table, his right arm stretched forward in presenting the card. A third landsknecht stands between the two men, his face, cast in shadow, leaning down as though reflecting on the imminent move of the soldier at his right. If, for the sake of experiment, the standing soldier is shifted downward and to the left so that his contours become partially overlapped by those of the player to his right, the figural configuration is very close to that used by Caravaggio in his *The Cardsharps*, the third actor in the print corresponding to the grimacing thug in the painting. Woensam's artistry in evoking the tense concentration specific to his duo of gamblers is prodigious. Besides the intensity of their exchanged gazes, each figure reacts to the other with calculated immediacy, the parted lips of both soldiers seemingly voicing the terms of their ongoing confrontation. Despite the similarities between the engraving and the picture, it is obvious that Caravaggio to a remarkable extent complexified and blurred the dynamics of the narrative scene depicted by Woensam. Not only does the Kimbell picture describe a swindle; the two main figures implicated in *The Cardsharps'* comedic action also behave as if independently from one another: as if the stake of the gaming were described from the inside, through the players' elusive inwardness more than through their external interaction. The dramatic leap between the tenor of the print and the painting becomes obvious if one considers Caravaggio's resorting to the examples of Giorgione and the early Titian in *The Cardsharps*.

In describing the Kimbell picture, Bellori noted: "these are the first traits of Michele's [Caravaggio's] brush in Giorgione's pure manner (in quella schietta maniera di Giorgione) with

164

attenuated shadows."[14] It has never been acknowledged that the figure of the young cheater in *The Cardsharps* stems from a prototype present in two pictures painted by the young Titian but attributed to Giorgione in the late Renaissance and beyond: an *Assault Scene* (usually identified with *The Bravo*, now in the Kunsthistorisches Museum, Vienna) and one of the frescoes for the Fondaco dei Tedeschi (known as *Judith*, now in the Ca' d'Oro).

There is wide agreement that the *Bravo* (Fig. 68)[15] corresponds to a picture described by Carlo Ridolfi in his 1648 *Meraviglie dell'Arte* as an original by Giorgione. In his text, Ridolfi declares:

> Also in Venice, there was [a painting of] two half-figures, the one featured Caelius Plotius assaulted by Claudius, who grabs him by the collar of the jacket, as he holds a dagger to his side; fear surfaces in the youth's face as mischief does in his assailant's, who ended up slain by Plotius, whose determination was praised by the Emperor Caius, the victim's uncle.[16]

Despite his muddled account, Ridolfi likely alludes to an episode related in Plutarch's *Life of Caius Marius* (14.3-5): Lusius' tentative attack on Trebonius, a soldier under his command, with whom he was infatuated.[17] Yet it is debatable whether Titian intended to represent a homoerotic aggression in the *Bravo*. During his sojourn in Venice in 1622-1623, Anthony Van Dyck copied a composition similar to Titian's *Bravo*, now at the British Museum, London (Fig. 69). This assault scene might be regarded as a variant of Titian's, and probably reflects a lost picture by Giorgione.[18]

14   Bellori, 216: "Sono questi li primi tratti del pennello di Michele in quella schietta maniera di Giorgione, con oscuri temperati." For Caravaggio and Giorgione in seventeenth-century sources, I look forward to the publication of Salvatore Settis, *Giorgione and Caravaggio: Art and Revolution*, Mellon Lectures, Center for Advanced Study in the Visual Arts, National Gallery of Art, Washington DC, 20 May - 17 June 2001.

15   Wethey 1969-1975, 3:130-1, no. 3.

16   Ridolfi, 1:101: "Si videro ancora in Vinetia due mezze figure, l'una rappresentava Celio Plotio assalito da Claudio, che lo afferrava pel collare del giubbone, tenendo l'altra mano al fianco sopra il pugnale; e nel volto di quel giovinetto appariva il timore e l'impietà nell'assalitore, che finalmente rimase da Plotio ucciso, la cui generosa ressoluzione fu commendata da Caio Imperatore, zio del morto Claudio."

17   Mistakenly, Ridolfi signals as the textual source for the painting a passage in Valerius Maximus' *Memorable Doings and Sayings* (VI. 8, 5), in which the author relates the exemplary case of C. Plotius Plancus, persecuted at the behest of the Roman Triumvirs, whose lair was heroically kept unknown by his slaves at the risk of their own lives. To prevent his servants from being further tortured, Plotius turned himself in to his persecutors. Apart from the presence of a personage named Plotius, Valerius Maximus' anecdote and Ridolfi's description of Giorgione's (or Titian's) painting have nothing in common. To explain these incongruities, Wind E. 1969, 7-11, suggested that Ridolfi alluded to an episode related by Plutarch—and not Valerius Maximus—in his *Life of Caius Marius* (XIV, 3-5). According to Plutarch, Lusius 'imperator,' Caius Marius' nephew, who had a weakness for young men, was infatuated with Trebonius, a soldier serving under his command. In spite of his many attempts, Lusius had never managed to seduce Trebonius, before he planned to lure the youth into his tent under a false pretext. When Caius to his despair tried to assault Trebonius, who had obeyed his order to show up at his tent, the latter drew his sword and slew his assailant. Plutarch also narrates how Caius Marius, although he was the victim's

uncle, not only admired Trebonius' exploit, but ordered that a crown be brought and given to him, in order to reward his courage. As E. Wind already pointed out, it is difficult to understand what misled Ridolfi in citing Valerius Maximus in place of Plutarch: most likely, he was fooled by the fact that Plotius, like Lusius, had been betrayed by his homosexuality: it was because of his "luxurious way of living and odor of perfume" that Plotius' persecutors could uncover his lair and capture his slaves. Ferino-Pagden 1990, 178-180, no. 13, rejects Wind's interpretation of the painting, suggesting that the Vienna *Bravo* rather represents *Pentheus Aggressing Bacchus*.

18   It is doubtful that Ridolfi in his *Meraviglie dell'arte* describes Titian's painting now in Vienna. In fact, he characterizes the young man's expression as fear, not courage or derision. Similarly Boschini, 56, in praising the same painting—which he equally considers an original by Giorgione—insists on the fright the assailed youth expresses: "Così quello Celio muove a compassion. /Se ghe vede la fazza tuta smorta,/ Da mezzo vivo, senza sangue adosso./ Quanto el sia natural dirlo non posso:/ Par che la Morte ghe bata a la porta (Likewise Caelius arises compassion./ His face appears entirely lifeless,/ He is half-alive, devoid of blood./ I cannot say how naturally he is painted./He looks like Death warmed over [literally: it seems that Death is knocking on his door]." More intriguingly, Boschini declares that the picture was not to be seen in Venice any more, for it belonged then to Archduke William Leopold of Habsburg, Regent of the Low Countries, whose works of art decorated his palace in Brussels. Since the *Bravo* certainly comes from the Archduke's collection, and since Boschini does not seem to describe the painting then in Brussels, it is necessary to explain the discrepancy between the author's testimony and Titian's composition. Boschini furnishes us a key to disentangling this question. After recalling that Giorgione's (or Titian's) picture had left Venice by the time he was writing, Boschini pointed out that a copy of it executed by Padovanino was still on view at the Grimani Palace. He himself had seen it six or seven years before (Ibidem, 56-57: "Dove de grazia adesso è sto tesoro [the *Bravo*]?/ No l'è più in sta città. Ché chi ebe inzegno/ El portè via, lassando

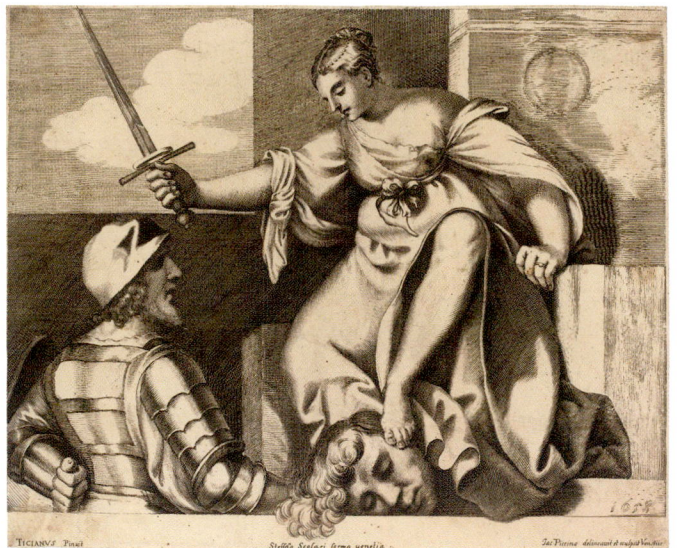

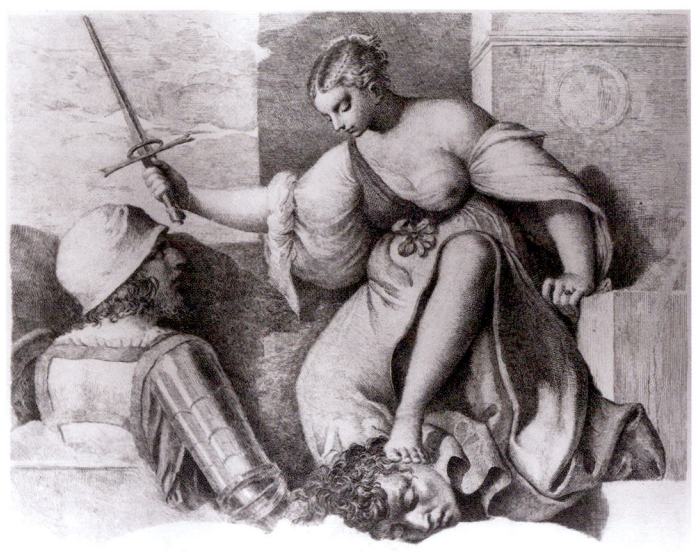

Fig. 70
Giacomo Piccini after Titian (Tiziano Vecellio), *Allegory of Venice-Justice*, 30 x 36 cm.

Fig. 71
Anton Maria Zanetti after Titian (Tiziano Vecellio), *Allegory of Venice-Justice*, 23.9 x 28.6 cm.

I believe that Caravaggio saw a version of the *Bravo* identical with or comparable to that reproduced by Van Dyck, and that it inspired him in his invention. Indeed, Caravaggio borrowed the figure of Giorgione's (or Titian's) assailant, reversing the attitude of his left arm, the one bent and disposed below the shoulder. By using and adjusting a Giorgionesque scheme of aggression,[19] Caravaggio evolved a pictorial microstructure, one that embodies a narrative content, which thereby encompasses a well-defined range of genre-oriented resonances. If Giorgione's (or Titian's) *Bravo* is regarded as an abridged *istoria*—as Ridolfi patently did—it is evident that, by taking up the posture of his forebears' assailant, Caravaggio used a high-genre figurative pattern, which at first seems at odds with the comic subject of his *Cardsharps*. In a sense, by endowing the cheater's figure with the grandiloquent promptitude of an assaulting soldier, Caravaggio inflects his visual trickery with rhetorical, quasi-heroic nuances: the swindle is in some measure displayed with the emphasis of a martial feat. If I insist on the plurality of registers to which the pose of the assailing cheater pertains, it is not only to stress Caravaggio's ability to merge and manipulate genres and pictorial conventions, but above all to unveil the scope of his blending procedures; surreptitiously or unconsciously, the beholder is beguiled into reading the episode as an *istoria*, not simply as a visual joke. In other words, extracting the false card from the waistband and carrying the dagger behind the back in attempting aggression and betrayal are visually equated. The very fact that the cheater is represented with his back to the viewer, allowing him or her to witness the mischievous exchange of cards, amplifies and almost exaggerates the climactic importance of the treachery.

un grosso pegno/ In cambio soo, che fu un profluvio d'oro./ Vero è ben che a San Boldo in Ca' Grimani/ Ghe xe una copia del gran Varotari [Padovanino]/ Ghe anche ela val montagne de danari;/ La vista che 'l puol esser sie o set'ani)." It is thus possible that Boschini's description concerns the copy, not the original now in Vienna, then in Brussels, which had left Italy by the late 1630s at least; even Ridolfi referred to it as not being present in Venice any more. It is also likely that the copy alluded to by Boschini was not perfectly identical with the *Bravo*, but resembled the composition in Van Dyck's London sketchbook, executed during his sojourn in Venice in 1622-1623, upon which I comment in the text. Ridolfi and Boschini's description coincides almost to the letter with the composition reproduced by Van Dyck: not only does the youth appear

startled and troubled, but his assailant's facial expression—defined as mischievous or daunting by these authors—is also visible. For Van Dyck's sketchbook, see Adriani 1940, 57, no. 65v. For other derivations from Giorgione (or Titian's) prototype, see the Doria-Pamphilj *Warrior Attacking a Youth* by Pietro Della Vecchia (Aikema 1990, 148, no. 202).

19 It has often been remarked that the figure with his back turned in the *Bravo* derives from a prototype by Giorgione, *The Man in Armor* (Vienna, Kunsthistorisches Museum). It is also interesting that some scholars have interpreted this painting as representing a homoerotic scene (see more recently Joannides 2001, 247-9). A much more pertinent reading of Giorgione's painting has been proposed by Brown 2008.

Besides Giorgione (or Titian's) *Assault Scene*, the representation of *Judith* (or more properly *Venice as Justice*), executed by the young Titian around 1510 on the southern façade of the Fondaco dei Tedeschi in Venice, inspired Caravaggio's *The Cardsharps*.[20] It is worth recalling that Titian's frescoes for the Fondaco were originally designed under Giorgione's supervision, and that the latter is the only painter to be explicitly mentioned as the author of the picture cycle in the documents (1505-1508) related to the decoration of the building. Even if Renaissance sources ordinarily recorded that Titian painted the frescoes on the southern façade, confusion sometimes arose about their authorship:[21] for instance, in the 1568 edition of his *Vite*, Giorgio Vasari erroneously assigned the *Judith* (or *Venice as Justice*) to Giorgione, describing the composition as somewhat exemplary of the artist's imagery. Unfortunately, Titian's fresco is ruined and barely visible. Nonetheless, an engraving and a colored etching, executed respectively by Giacomo Piccini (1658) and Antonio Maria Zanetti (1760), reproduce it reliably (Figs. 70, 71). Piccini's print is particularly interesting, because it still shows the back of the soldier standing at Judith's (or Venice's) feet, along with the motif of the concealed dagger. His attitude resembles that of Caravaggio's cheater; indeed, it is closer to it than the similar posture of the aggressor in Titian's *Bravo*, as evidenced by the detail of the parted lips and the triangular configuration of the bent arm, specific both to the Fondaco fresco and *The Cardsharps*.[22] In the so-called *Judith*, the soldier cautiously approaches a majestic female figure, sitting on an elevated pedestal, treading on a gigantic head, lifting a sword. The woman does not stare at the soldier, but at the trophy under her feet. For an unclear reason, the armored man seems to stop in front of her, his eyes riveted to her beautiful face, his lips parted in wonder or bewilderment. Like most of the frescoes by Giorgione and Titian for the Fondaco, the *Judith* (or *Venice as Justice*) is not easy to decipher. In this connection, it is useful to read Vasari's description and commentary on the fresco, despite its numerous inconsistencies:

> Above the main entrance to the Fondaco there is a sitting woman, who tramples on the head of a dead giant almost in the guise of a Judith, and who raises her face and a sword, as she speaks with a German at her feet; I could not understand what this figure stands for, unless Giorgione wanted it to be a personification of Germany.[23]

In Vasari's opinion, the meaning of the fresco was enigmatic, though apparently allegorical.[24] Most likely the woman in it was a personification not only of Judith, but also of Justice and Venice, as confirmed by the almost identical iconography of a female figure on one of the bronze pedestals that Alessandro Leopardi executed in 1505 to be placed before Saint Mark's in Venice (Fig. 72); they were originally meant to hold flagstaffs. According to Pietro Contarini (1541), Lombardi's goddess was to be identified with Astrea or Justice, but the context in which she appears, and the comparison with other representations of Venice from the late Middle Ages on, makes it unquestionable that she also personifies the city itself.[25] Therefore, in the Fondaco fresco, the woman served as

---

20 See Anderson 1997, 267-86; Joannides 2001, 51-71.

21 See Ridolfi, 1:155: "Ma più fiera è la figura di Giuditta, collocata sopra la porta dell'entrata, che posa il piè sinistro sul reciso capo d'Oloferne, con spada in mano vibrante tinta di sangue, ed a' piedi vi è un servo armato con berettone in capo, di gagliardo colorito; errando ancora in questo luogo Vasari, facendola di Giorgione."

22 The foreshortening of the hand which seizes the card from the waistband was modified by Caravaggio. In the X-ray photographs, it is still possible to discern the first draft, and to compare it to the soldier's hand holding the dagger in Titian's fresco: the similarities are interesting. See Mahon and Christiansen 1988, 26.

23 Vasari, 4:44-5: "V'è bene sopra la porta principale che riesce in Merzeria una femina a sedere, c'ha sotto una testa di gigante morta, quasi in forma d'una Iudditta, ch'alza la testa con la spada e parla con un todesco: né ho potuto interpretare per quel che se l'abbi fatta, se già non l'avesse voluta fare per una Germania."

24 Vasari's difficulty in interpreting the meaning of the Fondaco fresco reflects the elusiveness of subject matter characteristic of Venetian early sixteenth-century painting. For this topic, see Settis 1978.

25 See Wolters 1987, 228-38; Rosand 2001, 117-51, esp. 125-8; and Joannides 2001, 67-8.

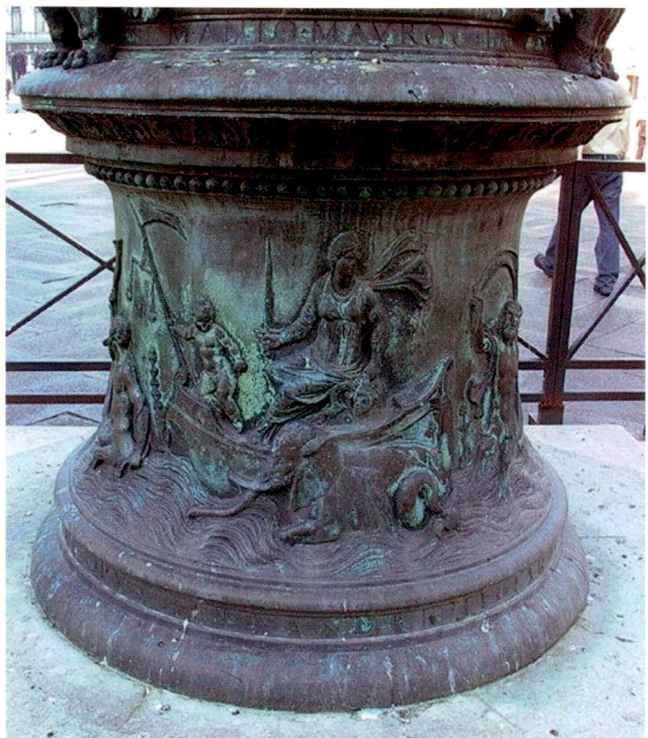

Fig. 72
Alessandro Leopardi (after Antonio Lombardo?), *Bronze Pedestal*,
Piazza San Marco, Venice, detail.

a visual admonition, warning the visitors of the risks of attacking the Venetian Republic. Whether a German or not, the soldier below Venice is consequently represented as menacingly closing in on her, hiding his dagger, but halting at her feet as he admires her courage and enticing beauty. As a matter of fact, Venice was often associated with, and likened to, the beautiful Venus, whose attributes she sometimes shares. If this reading is correct, the assault on Justice/Venice depicted above the main entrance to the Fondaco is obviously doomed to failure, so difficult it is to overcome the woman's virtuous beauty.

By representing the cheater in *The Cardsharps* from the back, concealing his false cards instead of the dagger— another dagger nonetheless keeps pointing toward the boy in the picture—with his face in profile while gazing at his rival, his lips parted in perplexity, Caravaggio thus consciously resorts to a figurative scheme of "thwarted assault" borrowed from Titian's fresco. It is important also to note that the boy in *The Cardsharps*, exactly like the female personification in the Fondaco, does not look at his aggressor, but casts his eyes downward, deeply immersed in his cards, with the same intensity with which Justice (or Venice) contemplates her trophy. The obvious question at this juncture is whether or not Caravaggio, by dint of this Giorgionesque (or Titianesque) pattern, intended to transpose the original narrative content of Titian's fresco into the swindle scene of *The Cardsharps*. Put otherwise, is it possible that, through the stunned figure of the cheater, Caravaggio also insinuated that the trickery is not necessarily bound to succeed? That, as the treacherous exchange of cards is about to be accomplished, the swindler could stop, and renounce his mischief? And if so, what would be the catalyst for such a dramatic reversal? In Titian's fresco, the soldier does not dare attack the woman, startled by her virtue and beauty. Could Caravaggio's cheater be sensitive to his adversary's contemplative grace?[26]

In this respect, it is no coincidence that, besides setting up a scene of amorous trickery, Marino resorted to a martial register in depicting his "gioco di primera." In the first and second quatrain of his sonnet, Marino transfigured the players into soldiers, the gaming table into the fields of Mars. On the table, the cards are arranged, shuffled, and scattered like swords before and during the battle; scores and bluffs, lunges and feints punctuate the matches; competitors thrust and parry like adversaries in fencing. If one postulates that Marino intended to elaborate on Caravaggio's *The Cardsharps*, one must admit that, intuitively at least, the poet discerned the martial component that the painter has ingeniously inserted into his swindle scene. From this premise, it is also possible to pry into Marino's procedure of robbery and elaboration. Instead of featuring three characters, he amplified the scene with five actors (4 + 1 rather than 2 + 1). At the beginning of the sonnet, the image of four players fighting against each other suggests the idea of a ludic battle. In comparison with Caravaggio, who practically narrates a duel, Marino's introduction of two additional warriors thus can be defined as rhetorical hyperbole.

26   A curiously similar example of an assault scene in which the aggressor seems to be struck with admiration at his victim's beauty in an ambivalent manner has been identified by Cole 2008 with regard to Giambologna's famous group of *The Rape of the Sabine Woman*.

The association of gaming and war was amply rooted in the literary tradition before Caravaggio and Marino. In his 1526 *Capitolo del gioco della primiera*, Francesco Berni affirmed that this game of cards is par excellence a game of twists [*travagliato*] "for the many varieties of chance [*fortuna*] and combinations that occur in it."[27] Even if chance plays an essential role in the game of *primera*, as Marino emphasizes when he characterizes its players as "proud champions of Fortune," it nonetheless requires recourse to strategy, a set of moves akin to those followed in fencing or fighting. In fact, in his *Capitolo*, Berni likens the game of *primera* to a battle,[28] but he also distinguishes his players from soldiers, because their tactics more closely resemble those of people who are trained in the more civilized art of fencing. In this context it is interesting to note Berni's comment on the expression "attack within shorter distance" (*venir a mezza spada*) used by players:

> A beautiful metaphor inspired by a fencing match or by the fight of two people who randomly assault one another with swords; in effect, whereas fighters ordinarily take their time by attacking and protecting themselves, proceeding step by step, and they even tend in the beginning to elude the blows rather than to hit [the adversary], people who do not care for their lives and play out of despair, thrust themselves into the fight incautiously and artlessly, coming within shorter distance ["a mezza spada"]; in other words, instead of keeping themselves out of range so that it is hardly possible even for an advanced lunge to reach its target, they come closer, getting straight to the point.[29]

If the affinities between playing cards, fencing, and combat were familiar to Renaissance literature, so too were the similarities between players and lovers. For instance, in a sarcastic passage of the *Capitolo*, Berni seems pleased to stress that almighty Gaming beats omnipotent Love:

> Nature found no greater or stronger bond between human beings than Love. (…) I saw with my own eyes the strongest [affection] ever between two lovers, one that nothing (or hardly anything) would break, and yet they had a wretched whim to play a game, one that is far from being worth a comparison with *primera*, and they ended up not only arguing vehemently, but fencing with each other, and the wretched whim that had driven them to fall in love transformed them into foes, and this solely for the pleasure of winning.[30]

In his "Gioco di primera," Marino unequivocally referred to this traditional opposition between love and gaming. But is this lyrical component also present in Caravaggio's *The Cardsharps*?

---

27 Berni, 220: "ella ["primera"] si dirà travagliata, per le molte varietà che in essa sono e della maniera e della fortuna sua."

28 Ibidem, 247: "E attaccata la battaglia, e' si rinforzano le poste, secondo che le carte vanno dando o togliendo speranza alle parti."

29 Ibidem, 250-1: "*E non venir al primo a mezza spada.* Bellissima translazione tolta o dalli giocatori di scrima o pur da due che a caso venghino alle mani con le spade: ché, ove si suole a poco a poco andare offendendo e difendendo, anzi più presto difendendo che altrimenti, chi ha poco cara la vita sua e gioca del disperato, bestialmente si mette innanzi senza riguardo alcuno e viene a mezza spada; cioè, dove ordinariamente si sta tanto lontano che a pena si può toccarsi con le punte, si viene a mezza spada, cioè alle strette, come si dice vulgarmente ; e vuol tuttavia intendere della bestialità della bassetta, de' tre dadi e delli altri simili, che alla prima voglion vedere quel che n'ha ad essere: argumento veramente manifestissimo di mera

avarizia e taccagneria." For the relationship between gaming and assault, see also Cardano, 1:268: "Commune habent cum aleis, ut quod desideratur, dolo occupetur, estque hoc genus doli exosum et gladio solet vendicari."

30 Berni, 243: "È ben grosso colui che crede, in qualunque diserto, furfantesco e vituperoso gioco, per desiderio di vincere aversi rispetto ad amici, a parenti, a fratelli, a madre o padre, a se stesso, per modo di dire che non si volesse vincer loro la vita e l'anima, se fusse possibile. Non ha trovato la natura maggior congiunzione fra li uomini né più potente che quella dello amore; venga Platone, venga Marco Tullio, venghino quanti filosofi fûr mai: quella che per nessuno accidente, o per rarissimi almeno, par che si possa separare; tuttavia i' ho visto due innamorati ben da maledetto senno giocare insieme, et a gioco che non saria degno di scalzare la primiera, non solo essersi crucciati ma venuti crudelmente alle mani; e sì come da maledetto senno prima erono innamorati, così poi da maledetto senno esser diventati inimici, non per altro che per desiderio di vincere."

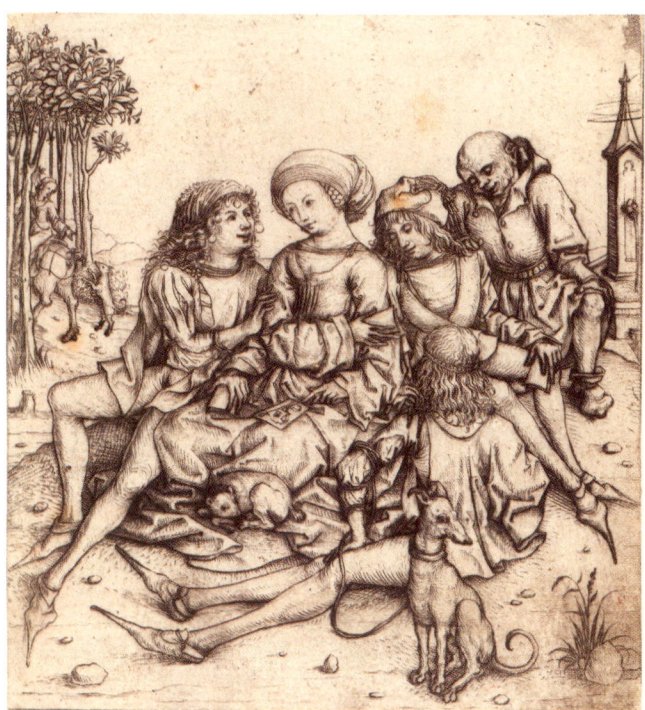

Fig. 73
The Housebook Master, *The Card Players*, engraving, 13.2 x 12 cm.

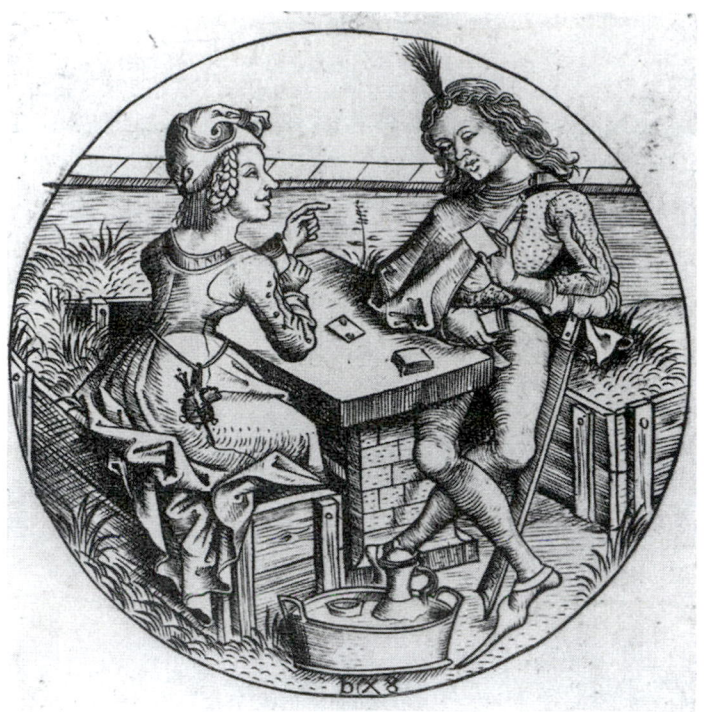

Fig. 74
Master b x g, *The Card Players*, engraving, 8.9 cm. (diameter).

The Lyrical Subtext

The visual arts provide several examples of players turning into lovers and conversely.[31] In a *c.*1485 print by the Housebook Master, *The Card Players*, three youths sit around a young lady, a victorious ace of acorns lying on her lap (Fig. 73).[32] To the left, a young man gazes at her, while putting the hand holding the cards over her thigh; to the right, another youth carefully considers her score. In the center, the lady seems to lead the courtly ceremonial of love, exchanging a gaze with one of his competitors, while showing another her cards. The fountain in the background marks the place as a garden of love. The jester designates the folly of erotic passion. In another print by the Master b x g, the *Two Card Players* (Fig. 74),[33] the diagonal surface of a gaming table separates the lovers; the woman urges her partner to play his trick, perhaps confident in her own victory; the young man studies his card meticulously, like the boy in *The Cardsharps*. Instead of uniting the pair, the game of cards divides them momentarily. This print is interesting because it, too, alludes to the theme of the war between the sexes. In his *Card Players* (Fig. 75),[34] Israel van Meckenem also represents two lovers opposing each other in a match. On the left, a smiling girl points to her winning card. On the right, a troubled youth utters his surprise by raising one hand, signaling his defeat. The visual theme of love and gaming expands well beyond Caravaggio's lifetime. In an emblem from Johan de Brune's 1624 *Emblemata of zinne-werck*, a beautiful lady and an elegant man play cards on the opposite sides of a table, on which lie a burning candle and a glass (Fig. 76). To the right, the man is about to discard a card, his gaze suggesting that he is sunk in thought. To the left, the

31 See Moxey 1980.

32 Hutchison 1972, 61-2, no. 73; Kok 1985, 170, no. 73; Koreny 1986, 230-2, no. 174. See also Koreny 1974, 230-2, no. 174.

33 According to Hutchison 1972, 76, no. 102, this print is a copy after a lost work by the Housebook Master. See also Kok 1985, 199, no. 99.

34 Hutchison and Koreny 1981, 240, no. 114 (302).

170

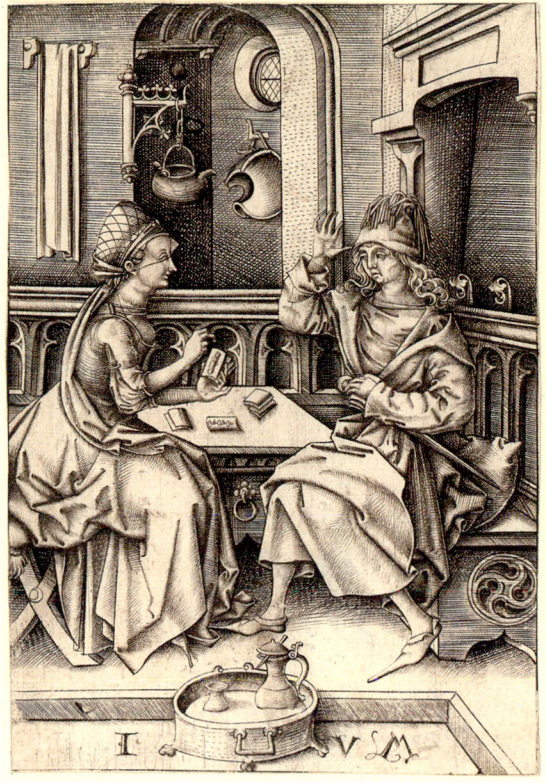

Fig. 75
Israel van Meckenem, *The Card Players*, engraving,
15.9 x 10.9 cm.

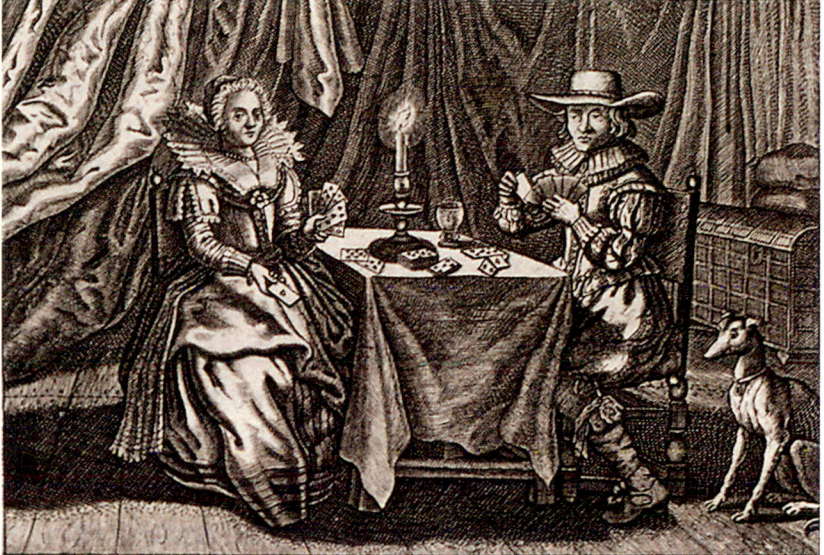

Fig. 76
The Card Players, reproduced from Johan de Brune's 1624 *Emblemata of zinne-werck*.

woman proudly and confidently shows an ace of hearts to the viewer in sign of anticipated victory. There is no doubt that the ace of hearts hints at the man's lyrical defeat by the woman, an amorous allusion that the burning candle—sometimes symbolizing passion's ardor[35]—may also convey. If one concedes that Caravaggio expanded this iconographic tradition into a swindle scene, it must be postulated that he replaced the conventional pair of a man and a woman playing cards with a couple of opposed boys. This kind of gender inversion is frequently practiced by Caravaggio: if in his two versions of *The Lute Player* (Metropolitan Museum, New York and The Hermitage, Saint Petersburg), an androgynous young man replaces the woman playing music of the iconographic tradition, his *Boy Carrying a Basket of Fruit* (Galleria Borghese, Rome) might well be a substitute for the gorgeous courtesans bearing flowers and fruits in Venetian Renaissance painting.[36] Yet the Kimbell painting, though it does not confirm or refute the possibility of such a gender inversion, seems particularly opaque in this regard, as though it were deliberately designed to discourage the viewer's certainty in either sense.

This opaqueness or potential ambivalence also applies to the figure of the young boy contemplating his cards. His attitude engenders disruptions of pictorial mode. Although his expression is analogous to that of Titian's Venice/Justice, it obviously does not derive from the same

---

35   For this motif as used by Nicolas Poussin in his *Triumph of a Poet* at the Corsini Gallery, Rome, see Pericolo 2003 and Pericolo 2005.

36   The androgynous character of Caravaggio's early models, their evident sensuality, and Caravaggio's possible homosexuality have been the subject of debate and innumerable essays. For Caravaggio's homosexuality, see Posner 1971b; and Gilbert 1995, 191-237. It is perhaps socially and culturally relevant that the most convinced supporters of Caravaggio's "heterosexuality" are Italian scholars. More recently, for instance, Berra 2007, has insisted on the exclusively allegorical significance of Caravaggio's *Boy Carrying a Basket of Fruit*. For Caravaggio's inversions of iconographical roles, see more recently Von Rosen 2009, 27-38.

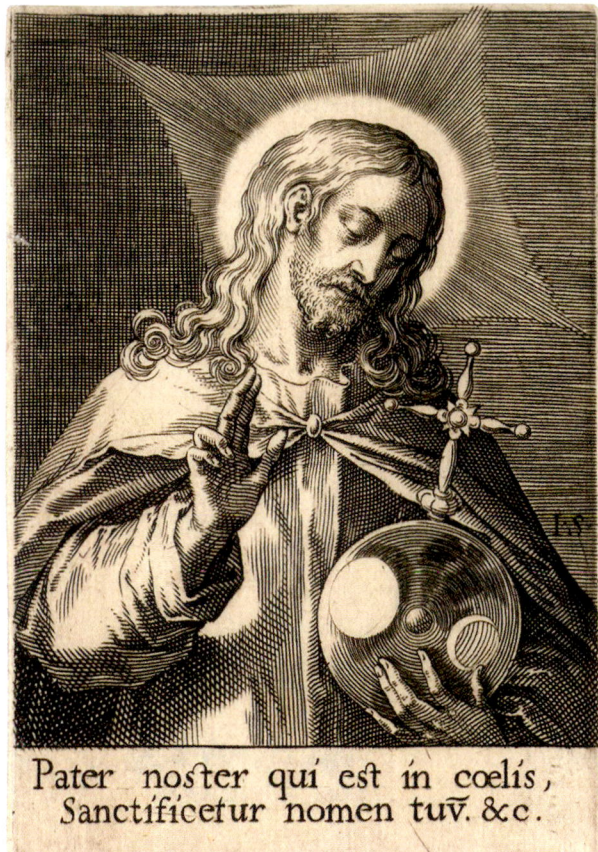

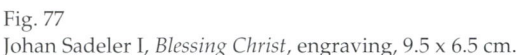

Fig. 77
Johan Sadeler I, *Blessing Christ*, engraving, 9.5 x 6.5 cm.

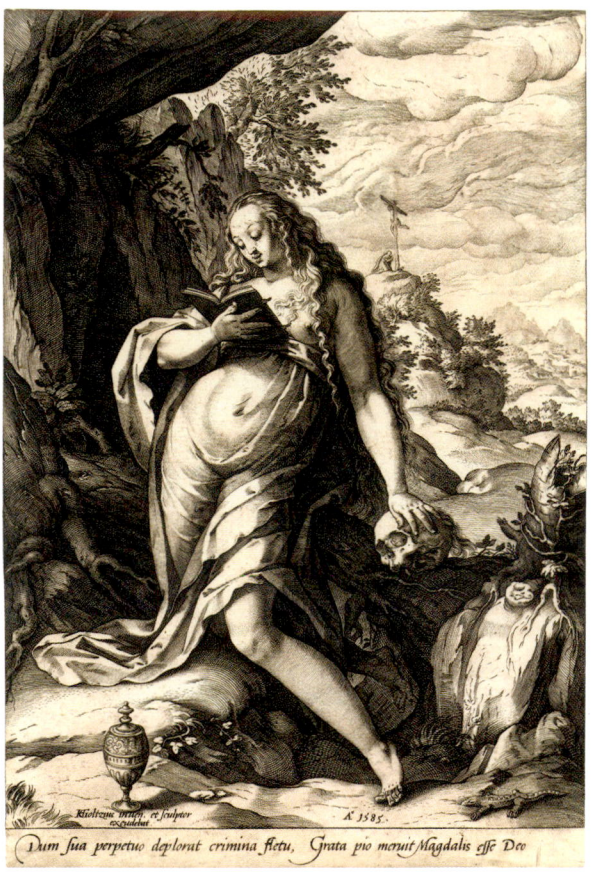

Fig. 78
Hendrick Goltzius, The *Magdalene in the Desert*,
engraving, 29 x 19.7 cm.

iconography. The pose of this figure can be found hundreds of times over in Renaissance art. In most cases the representation of a figure bending his or her head toward the torso at exactly the same, or a very similar, angle, whether it be oriented right- or leftward, his or her eyes turned downward and avoiding the beholder's gaze, qualifies as highly contemplative, and for this reason it specifically suits religious compositions. A few examples will elucidate the point. In a 1595 engraving by Johan Sadeler I that reproduces a *Blessing Christ* (Fig. 77),[37] the tilt of Jesus' face is precisely the same as that of Caravaggio's boy, down to the detail of the bare ear edged with a lock of hair. Of course, Sadeler's print cannot be regarded as a source for Caravaggio, and similarities exclusively concern their belonging to a common iconographic matrix. Another case in point is an engraving by Hendrick Goltzius, executed in 1585, which depicts a *Repentant Magdalene* (Fig. 78).[38] If reversed, the saint's down-turned face mirrors that of Caravaggio's youth in *The Cardsharps*. More interestingly, the torsion of the bust, and the attitude of the arm holding the Bible equally recall Caravaggio's figure: instead of the scripture, the youth holds his cards, and is as engrossed by them as the Magdalene is by her sacred book. Finally, a print by Israel van Meckenem,[39] representing Saint Lawrence immersed in the reading of the sacred text, provides a surprising comparison (Fig. 79). Not only does his head tilt at almost the same angle as that of the youth, but the regular contours of his shoulders, especially the right one, also match those of the boy. More intriguingly, the saint's bent left arm causes the folds of his dalmatic to revolve around his elbow, perhaps furnishing Caravaggio with the idea of

37   De Hoop Scheffer 1980, 137, no. 317, states that Raphael Sadeler collaborated with Johan on this series. See also De Ramaix 2001, 79, no. 278.

38   Strauss 1980, 1:58, no. 58 (26); 2:63-4.

39   Koreny 1986, 145, no. 368.

the swirling sleeve encircling the boy's foreshortened forearm. Moreover, the attitude of Lawrence's right hand, holding the palm of martyrdom, is identical to the boy's: the stretched finger serves this time to support the cards. Finally, the black velvet hat, akin to a turban, that girdles the youth's head visually echoes Lawrence's wide halo.

In the case of Caravaggio's *The Cardsharps*, this iconographic, high-genre attitude does not fit in with the comic plot of the swindle scene. Of course, one could object that the misplacement of a noble pictorial formula within a comic scene accentuates its hilarity: the more religious the youth absorbed in the vision of the cards appears, the wittier the cheat seems. However, the beholders' perception of the figure is certainly conditioned by its iconographic pedigree. This is why this contemplative pattern latently ennobles the representation of the youth. Also, since all the figures in the painting are turned toward the boy, beholders tend to focus on his face and expression; his seriousness and application are the visual pole of the action, especially in contrast to the fool's grimace nearby. At the same time, it is evident that, considering the subject, the youth's earnestness in contemplating his cards somehow exceeds the mechanism of the visual plot. This means that beholders may smile at his innocence, but are surely also struck by his contemplative absorption. Like Titian's figure of Venice/Justice, Caravaggio's youth arouses a sort of aesthetic admiration, determined by the alluring compound of his ephebic, lyrical beauty and his expressive profundity. Yet, is it possible that the cheater stares at the boy impressed by his lyrical contemplative grace, and not only in an attempt to check up on him before accomplishing his trick? Marino most probably interpreted it in this way, which clarifies the sense of his poetic theft and elaboration on Caravaggio's *Cardsharps*.

For Marino's artistic *paragone* to succeed, the various elements involved in the painting and the poem must be linked to one another in an interplay of conceptual similarities and oppositions. If Marino found the subject of *The Cardsharps* suitable for remodeling and reshaping, it was because, to his eyes, the picture also betokened a lyrical scenario. Marino then proceeded to switch Caravaggio's dramatic roles in the picture, as illustrated in table 2. Before looking at it, it must be recalled that the identification of the naïve youth and the cheater in the picture respectively with the beloved and the (potential) lover, albeit hypothetical, is required by the very mechanism of Marino's *paragone*.

Roles	In Caravaggio's painting	In Marino's poem

Cheater – (potential) lover	Inside the game	Outside the game
	Looks at	Is looked at
	Seems to cast aside the heart card	Picks up the heart card
	Seems to prepare the beloved's defeat	Contributes to the beloved's victory
	Opposes	Helps as an accomplice

(Potential) beloved	Inside the game	Inside the game
	Possesses a hand of three suits or a combination of three cards suitable for a winning score[40]	Possesses a hand of three suits

but

	Is looked at	Looks at
	Unaware of his beauty	(Likely) aware of his beauty
	Geared to defeat	Poised for success
	Innocent	(Likely) a cheater

40 This second reading is much less plausible, but it must be formulated, since there is no way to establish what game is taking place in *The Cardsharps*. First of all, it is not possible to distinguish how many cards are given each player: perhaps

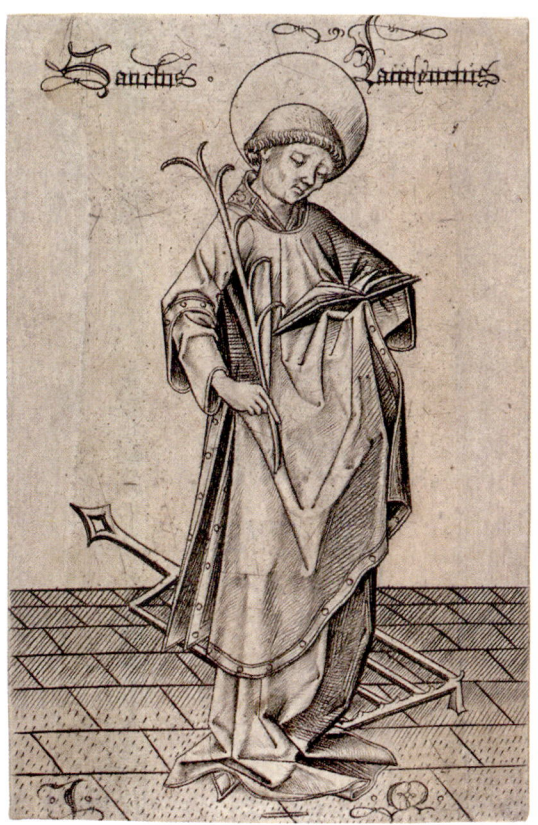

Fig. 79
Israel van Meckenem, *Saint Lawrence*, engraving,
12.3 x 7 cm.

Essentially, Marino brought to the fore the underlying lyrical component he had sensed, rightly or wrongly, in *The Cardsharps*. He thus expurgated from Caravaggio's subject its more comic, even slapstick, elements, such as the grimacing accomplice who in the poem disappears as an actor, but whose role is passed to the lover figure, magically able in the end to peep at his beloved's cards.[41] Although Marino tends to make explicit what might be implicitly hinted at by Caravaggio, the beloved's sexual identity is nonetheless carefully blurred in the poem, and Marino makes the reader infer it by deduction; because the beloved is playing with three male competitors, he is most likely himself a young man. It is worth signaling the diverse strategies followed by Marino, and possibly Caravaggio, in concealing the homoerotic implications of their compositions. Whereas Marino blurs the beloved's features to the point that his face as a metaphorical sun blinds the reader by fading into indistinctiveness, Caravaggio visually asserts the lover's sexual identity, obscuring instead the significance of his attitude. Marino especially revels in retouching Caravaggio's image, visualizing the invisible, pandering to the reader's imagination. The most telling example of this process is the theme of the beloved's gaze: whereas in *The Cardsharps* the beautiful youth deprives the beholder of his "pious look," in the "Gioco di primera" Marino unexpectedly reveals it to the reader, and the entire outcome of the sonnet depends on it: the lover's determination to cheat, the beloved's victory in gaming and love.

Yet, even though the gaze is literally and poetically unveiled, it never has the same graphic evidence as in a picture. In this mirroring relationship between the image—Caravaggio's painting—and the word—Marino's sonnet—the poem certainly improves on the image, but in doing so it betrays the very limits of its evocative powers. In fact, to be wholly understandable, to fulfill its mission, the poem has to refer back to the image, its innate complement. Marino knew that the more his verses hinted at the painting from which they originated, the more effective they proved.

By elaborating on Caravaggio's subject, Marino likewise supplied *The Cardsharps* with an epilogue. To clarify this statement, it is necessary to consider the painting again in an attempt to read

four (like in the "primera"). On the other hand, "primera" was a gambling game: it is possible to discern the equivalent of a "pool" or a "pot," on which lie the cards previously dealt out, but no coins are visible in it (though incidentally, in most cases there was no pot or pool on the gaming table, as the players put their bids directly in front of them). Also, it must be recalled that, on account of its wide diffusion, "primera" has numberless varieties. A last observation: "primera" is often played by at least four players, but some sources state that two people were sufficient. Unfortunately, early modern sources do not specify how kibitzers communicated with their accomplices. Cardano, 1:268-9 describes how cards could be marked in order to be recognized by cheaters, but he only mentions other techniques involved in the swindles without further explanation. See Ore 1953, 210-1.

41 I deliberately restricted my analysis of the grimacing figure to a few observations, although Caravaggio's "accomplice" rewards closer scrutiny. First of all, it is clear to me that Caravaggio, as he would do later in his *Incredulity of Saint Thomas*, here plays one of his visual tricks by inducing

the viewer to believe that the "accomplice's" gaze is locked upon the boy's cards, which is technically impossible. Indeed, in order to spy on the youth's score while orienting his eyes in the direction indicated by the painting, this figure should be standing beside, and not behind, the boy. One could justify this incoherence by assuming that the grimacing figure is a self-portrait of Caravaggio disguised as a cheater. In this case, the "displaced" gaze would suggest that the master, in representing himself, was working with two mirrors, one in front of him—to reproduce his torso—and the other at his left side, resting or leaning on a surface situated at the level of his torso—which would have helped him reproduce his grimacing face and bulging eye. In my opinion, the affinities between the features of the "accomplice" and those of Caravaggio's self-portrait in *The Martyrdom of Saint Matthew* are far from negligible and deserve serious consideration. If my intuition is correct, one could understand even better why Marino in his poem transposed himself into the figure of the cheater: Caravaggio had already preceded him in impersonating this character.

it through Marino's lens. The dark-clad youth "piously"—what adverb could be more pertinent?—assesses his score, perhaps a hand of three (indeterminate) suits as marked by the accomplice's uplifted fingers. Opposite him the swindler, cued by his companion, shifts from his waistband the false card that would determine his victory.[42] He jerks up, ready to deliver the fatal blow, but then instantly halts, looking bewilderedly at his opponent's contemplative face. It is noteworthy that Caravaggio froze the action at the point when the trick is not entirely accomplished, leaving the beholder to imagine the denouement. The visual prominence of the two cards tucked into the belt, clubs and hearts[43]—war or love?—presents the cheater's act as a sort of Herculean crossroads: what will prevail, love or play, seduction or betrayal? Marino must have decoded the episode as a dilemma. He chose to untangle it, by transforming the lover into a conniving cheater who, by picking out hearts instead of clubs, surrenders to the boy's "pious" beauty.

Despite its inherent, unsolved ambivalence, the originality of *The Cardsharps* paradoxically lies in its apparently unhermetic character. At first glance, the picture does not seem to call out for interpretation. Its unusual mixture of modes (serious, comic, martial) immediately ensnares viewers in the unfolding mechanism of the action, which they experience as a simple trick. Only the cheater's bewilderment may ultimately clue in the alert beholder to a subjacent action creeping beneath the pictorial text, lurking in wait for decoding. Like Titian's *Justice as Venice*, *The Cardsharps* "suspends" a scene of aggression, dilating it into reflective, unpredictable momentum. However, the Fondaco fresco, cryptic as it was to Vasari's eyes, was undoubtedly accessible to a wider Venetian audience, its weird combination of Eros and assault notwithstanding. Instead, *The Cardsharps* spoke to an elite of initiated viewers eager to read between the lines, savor its conceits, and occasionally, like Marino, develop them into keen variations. Viewed through the eyes of Marino, Caravaggio's painting leads into the playful dimension of Love and Fortune: like the startled swindler, the beholder may face the crucial moment in which the fate of the match intersects the quandaries of love, when betrayal and allegiance arise as alternatives. If, as Cropper rightly put it, Caravaggio, like Marino, "reveals to the spectator everything that is supposed to be concealed if the trick is to turn," it is likewise true that glancing at the trick does not offer the watchful beholder the certainty of an outcome. Instead, his or her mind may resonate with dilemmas: will the trick turn? Is the episode outrageously comic or lyrically dramatic? Whatever the answer may be—if indeed there is one—it is clear that Caravaggio somehow reduced the question to a visual conundrum by underlining the artifice of the composition.[44] In fact, it has already been remarked that the same model posed for both the boy and the cheater[45]; lover and beloved, on a certain level, are identical, conventional roles of poetry and painting, masks of a conceptual riddle. The fictional nature of this confrontation between lovers and players could not fail to amuse Marino, whose poetry thrived on the lyrical "conceits" of love, play, and war.

---

42 It is not clear how to interpret the accomplice's signal in Caravaggio's painting. If it refers to a secret code, I was not able to trace it in Renaissance treatises, but future scholarship might find new sources for this detail. On the other hand, the signal "three" could allude to the presence of three cards of different suits, or three cards of the same suit scoring high and suitable for "primera" or "flusso."

43 It is noteworthy that the choice concerns a seven of hearts (21 points in "primera," i.e. the highest score for a single card)

or six of clubs (18 points, the second highest score). Therefore, these particular cards can contribute to raising the score, if opportunely exchanged. Wind B. 1989 gives a different interpretation of the cards, which I do not find convincing: neither does Cropper 1991, 210-1, note 38.

44 Cropper 1991, 199, observes something similar in Marino's sonnet: "Marino's virtuoso poem exploits the power of lyric poetic, his medium, by calling attention to its artifice."

45 See for instance the observations of Hockney 2006, 226.

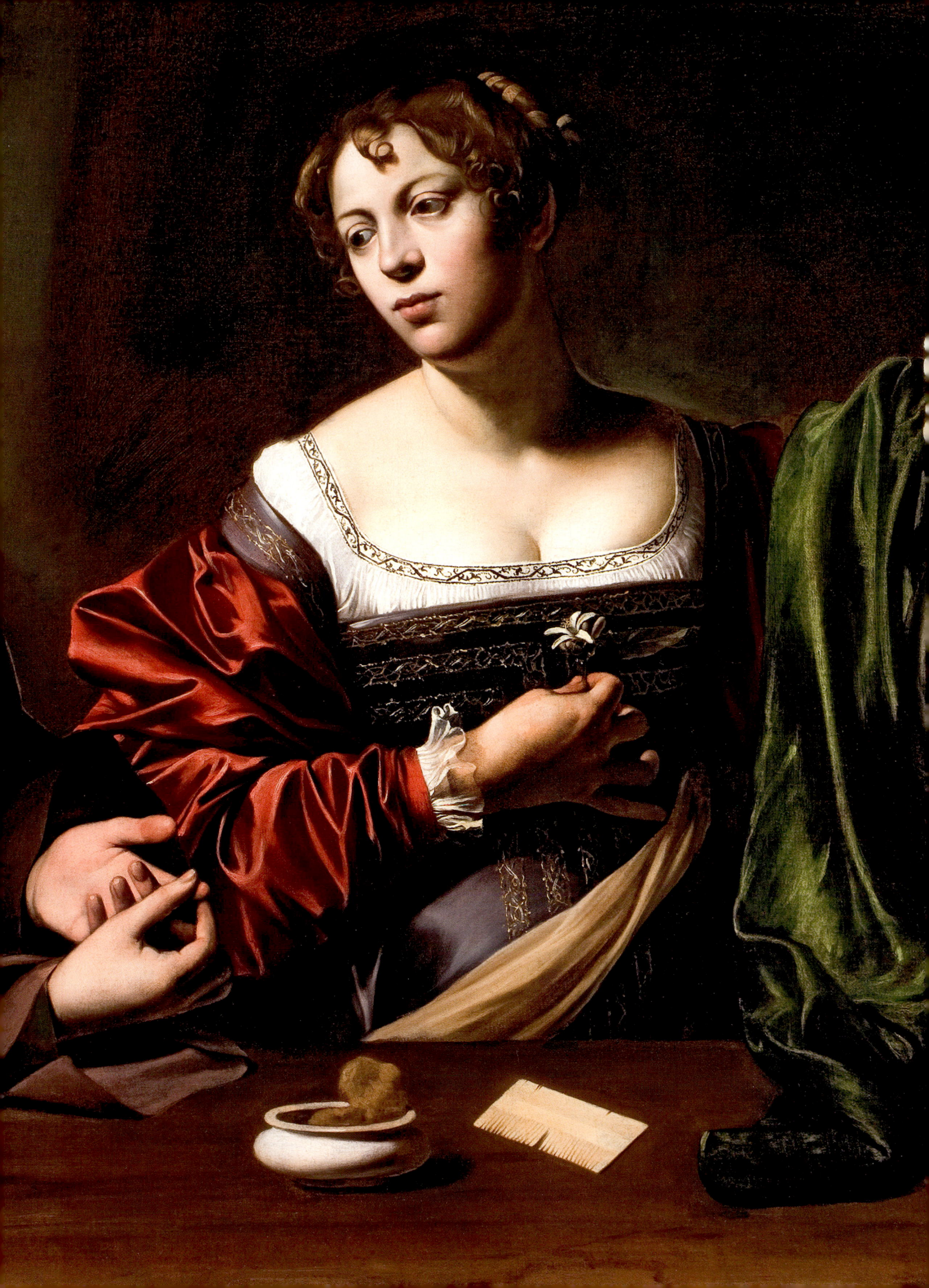

CHAPTER 6

Love in the Mirror: A Comparative Reading of Titian's *Woman at Her Toilet* and Caravaggio's *Conversion of Mary Magdalene**

"Veggendo in voi finir vostro desio"

Perhaps because it is so self-evident, the main source for Caravaggio's *Conversion of Mary Magdalene* (Detroit, Institute of Arts; Fig. 80),[1] Titian's *Woman at Her Toilet* (Paris, Louvre; Fig. 81) has not been discussed in detail. In his groundbreaking essay of 1943 on Caravaggio, Roberto Longhi had already signaled the connection, albeit vaguely. He remarked obliquely on "the sparkling vitality, akin to Courbet's," of the way Caravaggio interpreted the subject: "a brutalization of the ancient theme of vanity that Titian and Palma Vecchio had filtered through the serenity of their *Existenzmalerei* [everyday painting]."[2] Among the pictures by Titian that Longhi had in mind must have been *Woman at Her Toilet*, since it was then considered a *Vanity* on the basis of the two mirrors in which the lady admires her multiple charms. In 1974, Frederick Cummings, following in Longhi's footsteps, once again stressed the analogies between the Detroit picture and "Venetian paintings like those by Titian or Palma Vecchio."[3] He dwelt briefly on *Woman at Her Toilet*, commenting on the motif of the looking glass and its moral and philosophical implications.[4] In his opinion, the mirrors in Caravaggio's picture symbolize both the Magdalene's prudence and her self-love on the eve of her repentance.[5] It is noteworthy, however, that neither Longhi nor

---

* This chapter has already been published as an essay in *Villa I Tatti Studies*: Pericolo 2009b.

1 The Detroit *Conversion of Mary Magdalene* was considered a copy until 1971, when it was sold at Christie's (London). After cleaning (1973-1974), it became clear that it was an original, and ever since scholars have acknowledged its authenticity. See Cummings 1974; Salerno 1974; Greaves and Johnson 1974; Spezzaferro 1974; Hibbard 1983, 61-2 ["perhaps the Detroit picture was begun by Caravaggio but only blocked out at the right and then partially finished by another hand."]; Cinotti 1983, 424-7, no. 10; Christiansen 1985, 250-5, no. 73 [catalogue entry by Mina Gregori]; Calvesi 1990, 208-10 [focuses on the motifs of the orange blossom (mystic marriage with Christ) and mirror ("anima pura o contemplativa, amor di Dio, scienza come dono di Dio")]; Gregori 1991, 174-87, no. 7; Langdon 1998, 122-3; Puglisi 1998, 134-5; Longhi 1999-2000, 1: 7 [1943, as a copy]; Kroschewski 2002, 104-5; Marini 2005, 419-21, no. 28; Macioce 2007, 81-3; Ebert-Schifferer 2009, 105-6; Schütze 2009, 255-6, no. 20; Von Rosen 2009, 141-5.

2 Longhi 1999-2000, 1:7: "E resta pur sempre leggibilissima la vitalità scoppiettante, quasi courbettiana, dell'interpretazione: un brutalizzare l'antico soggetto della 'Vanitas' che Tiziano e il Palma avevano colato nella placidità della loro *Existenzmalerei*."

3 Cummings 1974, 572. Both Longhi and Cummings mention Palma Vecchio among Caravaggio's sources. Although deeply influenced by Titian, Palma does not seem to have treated the subject of the woman with the mirror. The only painting close to Titian's *Woman at Her Toilet*, *Portrait of a Young Woman* (present whereabouts unknown), depicts a lady holding the locks of her hair detachedly. See Rylands 1992, 221, no. 78.

4 Cummings 1974, 576. For the theme of the mirror in the visual arts, see Hartlaub 1951. For the topos of the mirror in French Renaissance literature, see Eymard 1975. For the conceptual relationship between the portrait and the mirror in Renaissance Venetian art, see Cranston 2000, 127-67.

5 Cummings 1974, 577: "According to this tradition, the mirror assumes an important dual role in defining the nature of the active and contemplative Christian lives, focusing both on vanity and the insight or *sapientia* which comes from deep reflection. The introduction by Caravaggio of the mirror into a painting about the Magdalen represents a new invention in the visual arts and was done expressly to connect the ancient literary tradition of the mirror with the prudence of the Magdalen as exemplar of the contemplative life. The mirror, as we have seen, refers to concept of sight, insight, wisdom and truth which are all central to the idea of the contemplative life that is an underlying level of meaning of this painting."

◀ Plate VIII: Michelangelo Merisi da Caravaggio, *Conversion of Mary Magdalene*, Detroit Institute of Arts, Detroit, oil on canvas, 97.7 x 132.7 cm., detail.

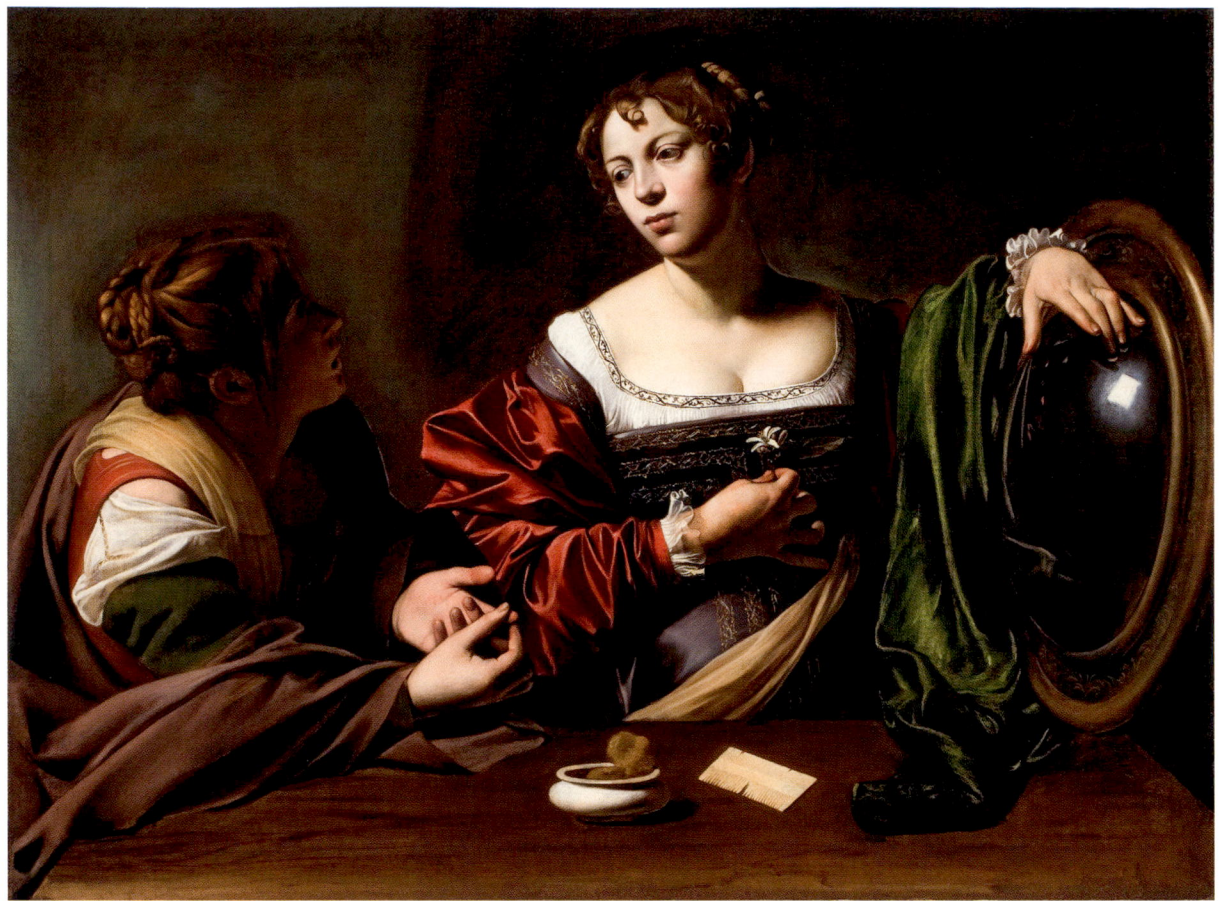

Fig. 80
Michelangelo Merisi da Caravaggio, *Conversion of Mary Magdalene*, Detroit Institute of Arts, Detroit, oil on canvas, 97.7 x 132.7 cm.

Cummings regard *Woman at Her Toilet* as a true source for Caravaggio's painting. For them, Titian's influence on Caravaggio is not so direct as to be construed as imitation, a concept essential to artistic practice during the Renaissance and beyond. *Woman at Her Toilet* is viewed rather as a repertoire of iconographic motifs that found their way into Caravaggio's *Conversion* almost incidentally. I contend instead that Titian's composition ignited Caravaggio's invention, and thereby played a paramount role in the painter's creative process.

Art historical disregard for this crucial and specific prototype does not spring from myopia: it depends rather on methodological prejudice. In a sense, unearthing a visual source often constitutes one step in, and not the grounds for, the evaluation of works of art. The search for iconography is meant to prove stylistic links, reconstruct the artists' imagery, and decode allegorical thoughts. Quoting or expanding on figures borrowed from other artists is thus normally perceived as resulting in self-referential winks destined for sophisticated beholders: by these means painters and sculptors show off the scope of their artistic knowledge and their ability to surpass even their most excellent predecessors. The discussion of elaboration as an early modern artistic practice barely seems to reach beyond the surface of self-referentiality, whereas one could describe it as "innervating" the deepest structures of creation itself: it sets off invention by mediating between memory and vision, tradition and originality. In fact, elaboration corresponds to a synaptic process of inventing and defining images.

In this chapter, I shall argue that Titian's *Woman at Her Toilet* supplied Caravaggio not only with figural patterns, but also with visual conceits. By elaborating upon Titian's image, Caravaggio discarded and reshaped the inner configuration of his predecessor's painted "sonnet"—a term to which I shall return—transfiguring it into a piece of religious art. Through elaboration, Caravaggio dissolved Titian's lyrical concision and ironic virtuosity into both allusive symbolism and narrative evasiveness. To demonstrate this, I will not only address the formal affinities between Titian's figure of a lady and Caravaggio's Magdalene, but also elucidate the complexity of *Woman at Her Toilet*, which—in my opinion—has been either misinterpreted or insufficiently probed. Without an accurate interpretation of this picture, any reading of Caravaggio's *Conversion* would be inconclusive.

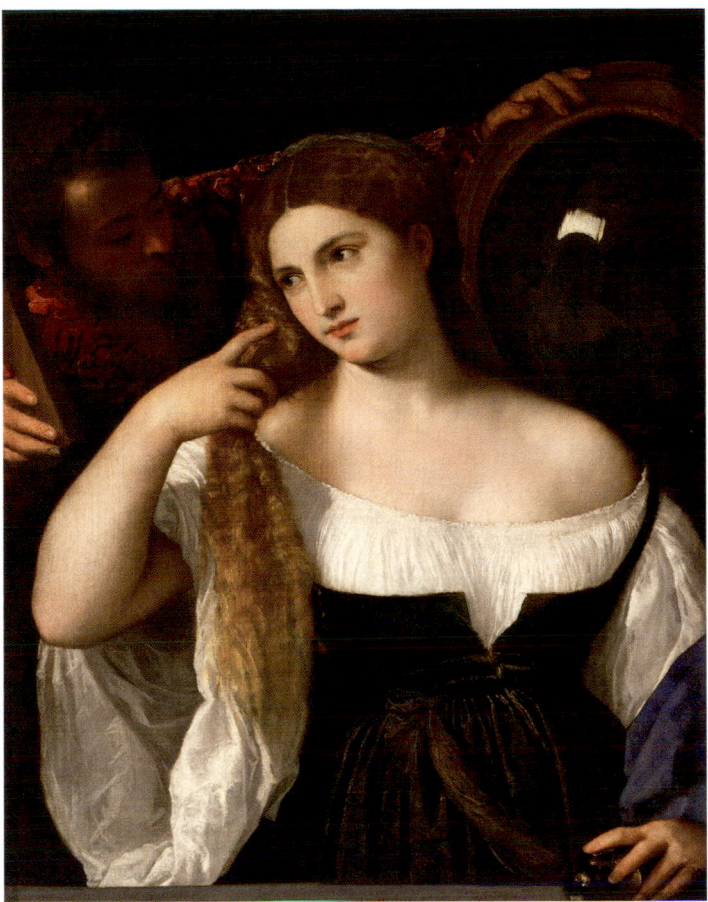

Fig. 81
Titian (Tiziano Vecelli), *Woman at Her Toilet*, Musée du Louvre, Paris, oil on panel, 93 x 76 cm.

Even at first glance, it is easy to discern how the silhouettes that circumscribe the face and upper bust of Titian's woman and Caravaggio's Magdalene match each other: an almost identical outline stretches from one shoulder to another, encompassing through its sinuosity a well-rounded, massive neck and a

voluptuous face. Bathed in warm sunshine, the women's heads tilt downward almost in absorption, the former's eyes riveted onto the effigy in the mirror, the latter's apparently fixed upon her interlocutor. Although he adjusted the posture of the woman's torso to the new context, Caravaggio faithfully took up Titian's stereography of her waist: a section of a cone tapering toward the bodice. Yet, he imagined a yellow scarf scrolling leftward across the Magdalene's lap to counteract the motif of the dark green ribbon that rolls down rightward over the skirt of Titian's woman. Caravaggio also modified Titian's *contrapposto* of the woman's arms, one lifted, the other lowered, inverting their relative posture, although he preserved the serpentine scheme they form together in unfolding around the bust. Some carefully thought-out details betray the extent of Caravaggio's elaboration: the Magdalene's right hand, holding the orange blossom, compares with the woman's, but its fingers, instead of clustering around the flower, fan out gracefully over the breast like uncurling petals. However, the Magdalene's little finger, completely unfurled, accomplishes a function analogous to that of the woman's forefinger in Titian's picture: the former is oriented to the mirror, the latter to the face. All this may not be merely fortuitous. Structurally, Caravaggio further compensated for the imbalance that resulted from his transformation of Titian's prototype: the Magdalene's upraised arm, deprived of the countervailing adornment of a whirling sleeve, leans on the mirror; a green drapery encircles it by drooping in a profusion of folds. Evidently, the ellipse of the mirror represented askew echoes and replaces the elliptical swirl of the woman's billowing sleeve in Titian's picture. As for lighting, the almost antinaturalistic effect of plunging Martha's profile into a brownish shade in opposition to the Magdalene's spotlit face and breast parallels Titian's idea of contrasting the man's shadowed figure

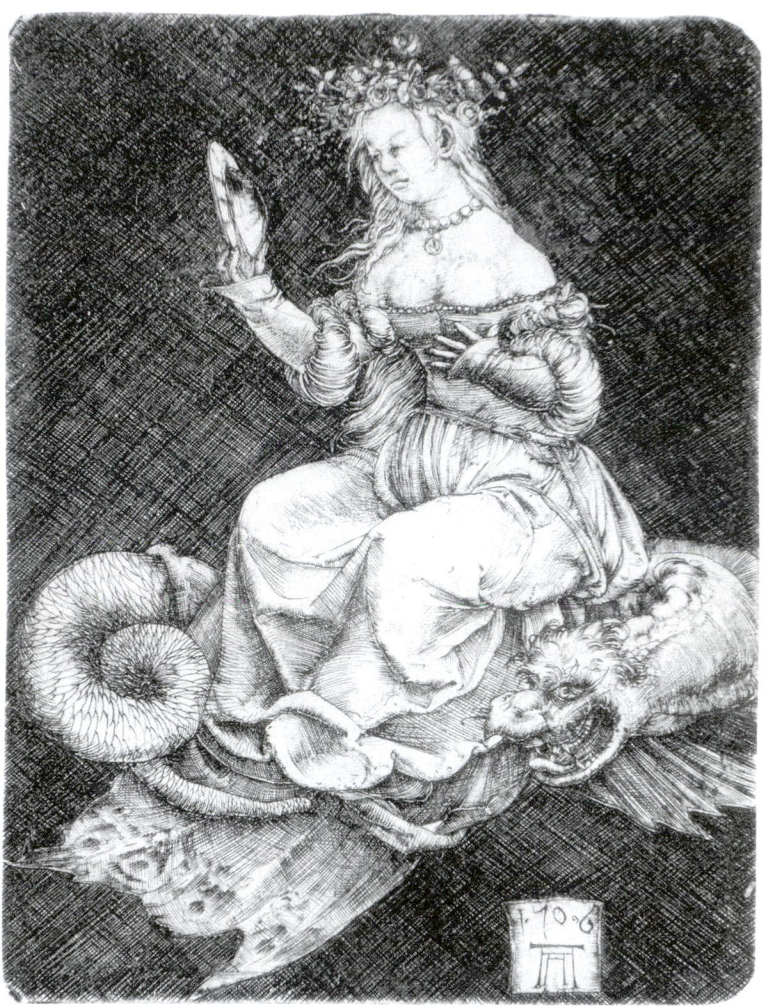

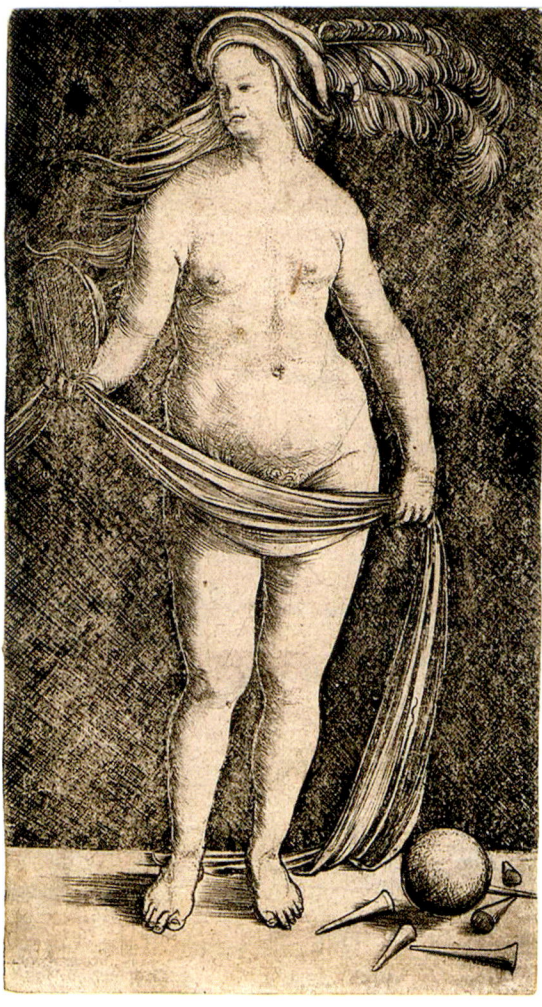

Fig. 82
Albrecht Altdorfer, *Allegory of Vanity*, engraving, 9.9 x 7.6 cm.

Fig. 83
Erhard Altdorfer, *Allegory of Vanity*, engraving, 8.8 x 5 cm.

with the woman's eburnean radiance. In sum, Caravaggio's elaboration operates on manifold levels such that one cannot deny his particular interest in Titian's *Woman at Her Toilet*.

By elaborating upon Titian's prototype, Caravaggio intended both to compete with his predecessor and to underscore the analogies between their respective figures: obviously, he also deemed the subject of *Woman at Her Toilet* iconographically contiguous, or even related, to the theme of Mary's conversion. The figure of the Magdalene therefore carries embedded in itself the diverse meanings of Titian's lady as a comparative substratum and interwoven subtext. But what did Caravaggio actually see in Titian's painting?

For many years, Erwin Panofsky's interpretation of *Woman at Her Toilet* prevailed: "the man is steeped in so deep a shadow (…) that, in spite of his presence, the woman seems to be alone with her thoughts; and the direction of these thoughts is revealed by the apparently unmotivated sadness of her glance." From this detail Panofsky inferred that "what we have before us is beauty looking at herself in a mirror and suddenly seeing there transience and death." To justify his laconic reading of the composition, he observed that the mirror, as a "standard attribute not only of Prudence and Truth but also of Vanity, came to be associated with death."[6] Panofsky's interpretation depends on two factors, the multiple and sometimes contradictory meanings of the looking glass, and the woman's expression, which he strangely characterized as "sadness." On preliminary analysis,

6   Panofsky 1969, 92-4.

Titian's lady seems absorbed rather than melancholic; she has already braided half of her honey-blond hair—seen in the convex mirror behind— and she prepares to arrange the rest of her tresses by perfuming them with ointment. If ambiguity is involved in her attitude, one can perceive it in the way she stares at the mirror: it is difficult to say whether she concentrates on her hair, verifying as if mechanically that she dresses it correctly, or contemplates herself, enraptured by her own image. Both interpretations, in my opinion, are legitimate. In any event, Titian does not seem to suggest the lady's sadness, much less her sudden meditation on transience and death.[7]

In this regard, it is helpful to compare Titian's picture (executed *c*.1515) with previous or contemporary allegories in which vanity and beauty are explicitly reproved.[8] In a 1506 engraving by Albrecht Altdorfer (Fig. 82), a woman sitting on a dragon with peacock-like wings looks fixedly at her face reflected in a convex mirror.[9] Her head, exuberantly crowned with germander, and her neck, adorned with a rich necklace, designate her as an allegory of Vanity, although some scholars outline her similarity with personifications of Prudence. Her downturned lips perhaps manifest self-disgust, but they may also refer to her moral wickedness. In an engraving of *c*.1506 by Erhard Altdorfer, a naked woman contemplates her face in a convex mirror (Fig. 83).[10] Her large-brimmed hat and luxurious feathers indicate her folly and lasciviousness. Once again, it is difficult to establish if her down-drawn lips evince bitterness or meanness. Erhard's print is also interesting for its analogies with Titian's painting. In spite of numerous discrepancies in the proportion of the bodies, the attitude of the face bent leftward, the motif of the swaying hair, the contours of the receding shoulder, not to mention the outline of the right upper torso and hip, are characteristics of both Erhard Altdorfer and Titian's figures of women at the mirror. Later, in a drawing of 1515 by Hans Baldung Grien, a standing nude woman, clasped by Death, combs her loose hair with her fingers while looking in the mirror.[11] Even though the rotting figure lurking behind her closes in menacingly, she expresses no jot of sorrow or regret: narcissistically, she is engrossed in her image as she is engaged in her toilet. In a 1530 woodcut by Hans Brosamer, *Allegory of Luxury and Foolishness*, a naked prostitute wearing an enormous feathered hat gazes at her face in the mirror (Fig. 84).[12] At her feet, a fool evokes the madness of vanity. Interestingly, Brosamer uses gestures and attributes similar to those employed by Titian, even though he inflects them quite differently. In his print, indeed, viewers can not only make out the effigy in the mirror—a grim double of the woman's face perhaps expressing self-disdain—but they are also able to read the composition as an allegory: the fool, the strange hat with its redundant feathers, and the overflowing curly hair clearly qualify as allegorical attributes.

All these prints unequivocally summon up vanity, by condemning it, even if allegory equally serves as a pretext to exalt the sensuality of the female body. Such a reading does not apply to Titian's picture, although he was certainly acquainted with the theme of vanity as developed in the early Renaissance tradition. In fact, if he did not accentuate the topic of death and decay graphically, this is simply because he did not intend to transform his picture into an allegory. For this reason, nothing

7   A different view is given by Titian's *Allegory of Vanity* at the Kunsthistorisches Museum, Vienna, in which a woman shows a mirror to the beholder. For the painting and its various repaintings, see Verheyen 1966.

8   I did not add to the list of representations of Vanity given later in the text a very important precedent to Titian's *Woman at Her Toilet*: Jacopo de' Barbari's *Naked Woman with a Mirror*. The subject of this woodcut, dated to c. 1504, is still the object of debate. For some scholars, the woman depicted in the print is an allegory of Vanity; for others, a personification of Prudence; and for others, a representation of Venus. See Ferrari 2006, 136-7, no. 22.

9   See Winzinger 1963, 89, no. 99; Mielke 1988, 30, no. 4; Hartlaub 1951, 167-8, identifies with germander the flowers with which the female figure is wreathed. He relates the figure to Dürer's *Melencholia I*, and considers it an *Allegory of Prudence*. For Dürer's personification, see Panofsky 1955, 157-71, esp. 163; Klibanski et al. 1964, esp. 325.

10   See Winzinger 1963, 126, no. 241; and Mielke 1988, 278, no. 178.

11   See Bernhard 1978, 177. For the place of the female nude in Baldung Grien's work, see Talbot 1981; Brinkmann 2007.

12   Hollstein 1957, 251, no. 442; and Koch 1980, 63, no. 1 (298) [as Jacob Bink].

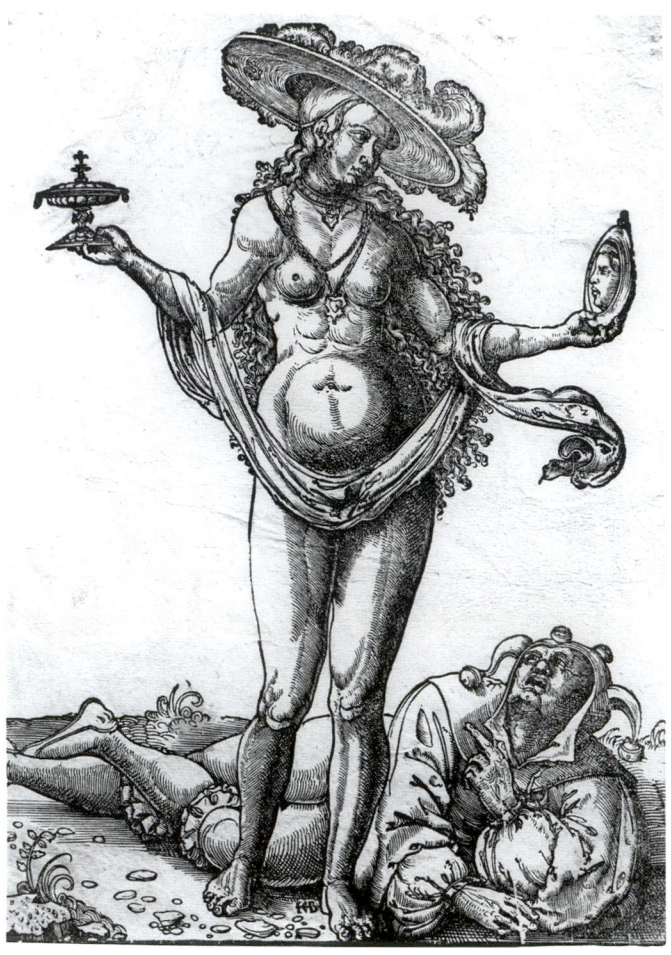

Fig. 84
Hans Brosamer, *The Prostitute and the Fool*, woodcut, 27.5 x 20 cm.

in the composition expresses disapproval of vanity or foreshadows the woman's impending decline.[13]

In 1983, Elise Goodman dismissed Panofsky's allegorical interpretation of *Woman at Her Toilet*, claiming with reason that the painting was indebted rather to the poetic theme of the mirror as inaugurated by Petrarch in his *Canzoniere*. In her opinion, figures and objects in Titian's painting transliterate conventional roles and functions specific to lyric poetry: the lady corresponds to the beloved, the man to the lover and suitor. Through the mirror, the woman's beauty is praised and the man's admiring jealousy[14] revealed.[15] This seems in general correct, and Goodman's contribution offers the ultimate key to unlocking Titian's imagery as embodied in *Woman at Her Toilet*.[16] However, it does not explain the picture's subtleties. Titian's composition does not simply incorporate lyrical topics; it presents itself as a pictorial "sonnet," the analog of an original amorous poem expanding on, and in competition with, lyrical material. In fact, *Woman at Her Toilet* also entails an artistic *paragone*: it opposes painting to poetry, the painter's illusionism to the poet's evocative skills.[17] The picture also responds to a commonplace widely diffused in lyrical poems, that neither words nor images can portray the woman's appearance, although poets are more likely to accomplish so bold an endeavor. Titian's painting instead underlines the painter's supremacy, his ability to visualize ineffable female beauty. By examining

13   In lyric poetry, the mirror can also convey the idea of transience and death. See Tebaldeo, II-1, 13, 141-2: "Non seranno i capei sempre d'or fino,/ Non seran sempre perle i bianchi denti,/ Non sempre aran splendor gli occhi toi ardenti,/ Né sempre rose il bel volto divino,/ Belleza è come i fior' che nel matino/ Son freschi e vaghi e poi la sera spenti,/ Né noi se renovian come i serpenti,/ Che nati son sotto miglior destino./ Deh, muta hormai questi costumi altieri,/ ché i giorni corron più che cervi e pardi,/ E stolta sei, se sempre durar speri./ Manca ogni cosa, e se nel specchio guardi,/ Vedrai che non sei quella che fusti heri:/ Però provedi a non pentirte tardi." The same topic appears in a sonnet by Pietro Bembo: "O superba e crudele, o di bellezza/ E d'ogni don del ciel ricca e possente,/ Quando le chiome d'or caro e lucente/ Saranno argento, che si copre e sprezza,/ E de la fronte, a darmi pene avezza,/ L'avorio crespo e le faville spente,/ E del sol de' begli occhi vago ardente/ Scemato in voi l'onor e la dolcezza,/ E ne lo specchio mirerete un'altra,/ Direte sospirando: eh lassa, quale/ Oggi meco penser? Perché l'adorna/ Mia giovenezza ancor non l'ebbe tale?/ A questa mente o 'l sen fresco non torna?/ Or non son bella, alora non fui scaltra." (Bembo, LXXXVII, 579). See also Dall'Aquila b, 202-4.

14   The theme of the man's jealousy is uncommon. See Dall'Aquila b, 204-5.

15   Goodman 1983a, 432-7.

16   Thoughtful and sensitive as it is, the interpretation of

Woman at Her Toilet proposed by Goffen 1997, 66-72, addresses the painting from a completely different prospective: that of gender studies. Cranston 2000, 156-63, also offers an interesting interpretation of Titian's painting and its relation to Petrarch's sonnet. For the evolution of this iconographical theme in Venetian painting, see Santore 1997. For a recent stylistic discussion of Titian's picture, see Joannides 2001, 258-60. For a critical discussion of the painting, see Laclotte 1993, 360-2, no. 48. For the motif of the woman with the mirror in Titian's painting, see Schäpers 1997, 111-34. For the representation of women in the lyrical tradition and its relationship to painting, see Cropper 1976; Cropper 1986; Pozzi 1993, 145-71; Shearman 1992, 108-48; and more recently Bolzoni 2008.

17   Besides the examples given later in the text, see Correggio, 51, 132: " Se a gli omin mostri qual tu fusti viva,/ Morti lor como te, nulla vedranno;/ Ma le parti invisibil tue staranno/ Puoi che dil secul questa età sia priva./ Laudo il pictor, ma più laudo un che scriva/ Quello a' futuri che i presenti scianno,/ Origin, stato, e che al triseptimo anno/ Morte spense ogni ben che in te fioriva./ Ma como excede tua forma il pennello,/ Ex">cederan le tue virtù la penna,/ E resterà imperfetto e questo e quello"; 108, 160-1: "Perché a le membra legiadrette e isnelle,/ Che 'l pictor con bella arte agli occhi adduce,/ Quest'alma non poss'io, che mi conduce,/ Dare, e fargli vestir carne, ossa e pelle?/ Io gli ho spirato già mille sospiri/ Per dargli vita: Amor, scio che tu 'l sciai,/ Che causi al cor gl'insoliti martiri./ Pigmalëon fu ben felice assai,/ Ma ne l'immagin sua (lei non si adiri)/ Simil bellezze non gli viddi mai"; 286, 249-

the poetic tradition from Petrarch onward, it will become evident how deftly Titian fashions poetic conventions into unwonted pictorial concepts.

In interpreting *Woman at Her Toilet*, Goodman postulates that a sonnet by Petrarch, "Il mio adversario" ("My adversary"), was Titian's principal source of inspiration:

> My adversary, in which you customarily see
> Your eyes, honor of Love and Heaven,
> Charms you with beauties that are not its own:
> Sweet and joyful beyond human comparison.
> At its instigation, my lady, you did
> Expel me out of my pleasant dwelling:
> Grievous exile! Although I do not deserve
> To live where you reside only by yourself.
> Yet, if I were attached there by firm nails,
> A mirror should not make you pleasing to yourself,
> Cruel and proud to my detriment.
> To be sure, if you remember Narcissus,
> His destiny and yours have the same end,
> Though the grass is not worthy of such a flower.[18]

The paradox that underlies Petrarch's poem becomes clear if one recalls the conception of love typical of Italian late medieval lyric poetry: the beloved's image lingers in the lover's eyes and heart constantly, without ever abandoning them.[19] By falling in love with her own effigy, the woman metaphorically banishes the man from her thoughts, replacing his effigy with hers. Even if the poet—or the lover—blames the mirror for effacing him from the woman's mind, his actual adversary is the woman herself who, entangled in her contemplation, is haunted by the vision of her own beauty. Thus she is compared to Narcissus, the handsome boy who fell in love with himself by looking at his image in the water. Like him, the beautiful lady might consume herself in self-indulgence and perish. Hence the poet admonishes her about the risks of vanity by alluding to Narcissus' fate: he was turned into a flower after drowning.[20] Maliciously, Petrarch implies that

50: "Non sia più chi sculpisca, pinga o scriva/ Umane forme né divine ancora;/ Copri pur, Fidia, Apollo e Apelle, Flora,/ Ché moderna opra oggi de fama i priva./ Questa è una donna sculpta in pietra viva/ Che natural vigor mostra di fuora/ Tal che Cipro ancor Venere adora,/ Dirà questa più bella e men lasciva./ Par ch'ella guardi, e pur tien gli occhi bassi;/ Par che si mova e pur tien fermo il pede,/ Par che respiri e odorata aura passi,/ Ma vano è tutto quel che in lei si vede,/ Che è pietra viva e fa de omini sassi,/ Né in pietra credo io mai trovar mercede." See also Tebaldeo, II-1, 199, 331; 224, 356.

18   Petrarca, 45, 237: "Il mio adversario in cui veder solete/ Gli occhi vostri ch'Amore e 'l ciel honora,/ Colle non sue bellezze v'innamora/ Più che 'n guisa mortal soavi et liete./ Per consiglio di lui, donna, m'avete/ Scacciato del mio dolce albergo fora;/ misero exilio, avegna ch'io non fôra/ D'abitar degno ove voi sola siete./ Ma s'io v'era con saldi chiodi fisso,/ Non devea specchio farvi per mio danno,/ A voi stessa piacendo, aspra e superba./ Certo, se vi rimembra di Narcisso,/ Questo et quel corso ad un termino vanno,/ Benché di sì bel fior sia indegna l'erba." See also commentary, Ibidem, 237-9.

19   This conception still operates in Renaissance poetry. See for instance Tebaldeo, II-1, 199, 331: "Credea me amassi, hor col timor combatto,/ Ché se ver fusse Amor pictor perfetto,/

T'aría l'effigie mia formata in petto,/ Né cercaresti aver altro ritratto."

20   The comparison between the woman and Narcissus is common in Renaissance poetry, and is usually related to the theme of the mirror. See Correggio, 81, 147: " Se con gli occhi costei penetra i cori/ Di porfidi, de diaspri e di diamanti,/ Como lì stai, tu o fragil vetro, inanti/ Che non ti spezzi, o il tuo lustro non mori?/ Quanto più natural li mostri fuori/ La sua bellezza e angelici sembianti,/ Tanto più, o specchio, a li infelici amanti/ La insuperbissi e a lor cresci dolori./ Deh, dimmi, o Ecco, tu, chi amò Narcisso/ E che vendicò in lui quel chiaro fonte/ E qual sua parte ebbe il suo cor avolto./ Cusì possa in te ancor star sempre fisso,/ Specchio infernal, quel suo superbo fronte,/ Puoi che l'empia a te solo ha il pensier vòlto"; Tebaldeo, II-1, 36, 165: "A che presti, superba, a un vetro fede?/ Se ben comprender vòi la tua belleza,/ Spècchiate in me, ché tanta è sua grandeza/ Quanto è l'incendio mio, che ogni altro excede;/ Non altrimenti in me quella si vede/ Che in un arbor del vento la forteza,/ Quando con furia a terra il piega e speza,/ Rompendol sin dove ha più fermo il piede./ L'effecto è da veder, non la figura:/ In questo è sua excellenza e, a dire il vero,/ Quel tuo specchiar non è cosa secura;/ Né a te verrà come a Narciso altiero/ Lui è un bel fior, tu serai pietra dura,/ Avendo di Medusa il guardo fiero." On the Medusa motif in Renaissance painting, see Shearman 1992, 48-50.

183

death cuts down even the prettiest flowers; like those less attractive, they, too, will lie extinguished on the humble grass.

Petrarch highlights the beloved's cruelty and narcissism in another sonnet centered on the mirror, "L'oro e le perle" ["Gold and pearls"]: after imputing his torments to the woman's imperishable beauty, the poet once again criticizes the mirror as the principal cause of her indifference. By contemplating her image relentlessly, the cruel lady wears out all the mirrors around her; even Love, the almighty god, cannot divert her attention from them, and renounces pleading the lover's case before the self-absorbed woman:

> Those [the mirrors] made my Lord [Love] mute.
> As he was intervening on my behalf, he fell silent
> Seeing that your desire ends in yourself
> ["Veggendo in voi finir vostro desio"].[21]

Titian's picture epitomizes the woman's narcissism as evoked in Petrarch's sonnets: not only does the lady seem to indulge in self-love by staring at the looking glass, but she also stands detachedly at the intersection of two crossed gazes—the suitor's and the beholder's—and between two mirrors. Moreover, through the convex looking glass and its evocative reflection, her figure is projected beyond the pictorial surface onto the viewer's space: she dwells outside the canvas even as she reigns within it. The picture becomes her metaphorical residence, a fictive spatial structure that ensconces her in its center, while visually eclipsing the suitor—a point to which I will return—and casting out the beholder: the mirror indeed does not acknowledge anybody else's presence in the room. It solely reflects the lady and, farther away, the detail of a silhouetted window.

To be sure, Titian was not the first to use the mirror as a device to show diverse facets of the female body at the same time. In his c.1450 *De viris illustribus*, Bartolomeo Fazio described a lost picture by Jan van Eyck in the collection of Cardinal Ottaviano Della Carda, in which several women emerged from the bath. Although "the more intimate parts of the body" were "veiled in fine linen," van Eyck managed to expose the naked shoulder and back of one of his bathers through a mirror in the painting.[22] Another picture probably by van Eyck, now lost, represents a similar subject. (At least one extant copy and a painting by Willem van Haecht reproduce it).[23] In it, a young woman exhibits her naked body frontally to the beholder, covering her loins with a towel; a servant assists her during the toilet. A convex mirror, affixed to a window at the left, partially reveals the lady's back. Even if Titian knew van Eyck's compositions—which is conceivable—he obviously turned his examples into a new pictorial formula. By focusing upon the half-length female figure, he adopted the point of view of the lyrical tradition in a mimetic manner. His close-up indeed imitates, or mimics, the poet's obsessive gaze, totally and uniquely transfixed upon his mistress' careless beauty. In a sense, Titian's picture is more about lyrical obsession than eroticism. The suitor's gaze to the left and the hypnotic sight of the mirror to the right form a pair of blind eyes in front of the viewer, re-echoing the woman's ubiquitous beauty symmetrically, though differently. In fact,

21   Petrarca, 46, 240: "L'oro et le perle e i fior' vermigli e i bianchi,/ Che 'l verno devria far languidi et secchi,/ Son per me acerbi et velenosi stecchi,/ Ch'io provo per lo petto e per li fianchi./ Però i dì miei fien lagrimosi et manchi,/ Ché gran duol rade volte aven ch'invecchi:/ Ma più ne colpo i micidiali specchi,/ Che 'n vagheggiar voi stessa avete stanchi./ Questi poser silentio al signor mio,/ Che per me vi pregava, ond'ei si tacque,/ Veggendo in voi finir vostro desio;/ Questi fuor fabbricati sopra l'acque/ D'abisso, et tinti ne l'eterno oblio,/ Onde 'l principio de mia morte nacque." See also commentary, Ibidem, 240-2.

22   See Baxandall 1964, 103: "Sunt item picturae eius nobiles apud Octavianum Cardam, virum illustrem; eximia forma feminae e balneo exeuntes, occultiores corporis partes tenui linteo velatae notabili rubore, e qui[bu]s unius os tantummodo pectusque demonstrans, posteriores corporis partes per speculum pictum lateri oppositum ita expressit ut et terga quemadmodum pectus videas."

23   See Seidel 1993, 206-18. For the importance of Jan van Eyck's lost picture to the Venetian tradition (especially to Giovanni Bellini's *Allegory of Prudence* and *Woman at Her Toilet*), see Schäpers 1997, 82.

the lady fills the pictorial field completely with her person or through the attention given her intentionally by the suitor and unwittingly by the mirror.

In transposing a lyrical topic into an image, Titian nonetheless offers his own version of the woman's narcissism. Her figure awakens wonder rather than resentment. As Titian imagines the lady undergoing the process of the toilet—the bodice is not yet laced, her breast is loosely enfolded by the chemise, parts of her tresses are still unfinished—uncertainty arises about the meaning of her action. Is she seduced by her image or fixated on her hair? Even the index finger that points to her face, as if signaling self-love, may well be a routine gesture. In other words, despite its lyrical connotations, the image preserves its exquisite, almost casual everyday character. Titian both observes

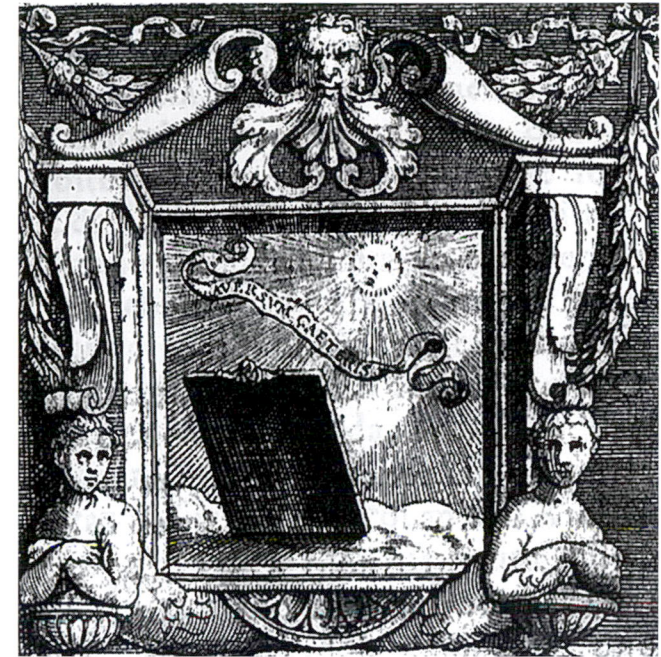

Fig. 85

Aversum Caeteris, reproduced from Camillo Camilli, *Imprese illustri*, 1586.

the woman with loving care and describes her toilet accurately. His passionate detachment recalls Ludovico Ariosto's evocation of his woman's tresses:

> The noble styles and the sweet modes
> That Greek and Latin poets taught
> Will not suffice for half, much less for all
> The praise of her golden, curling locks.
> Just beholding how bright and how even
> And long her rich golden threads are
> Could be the matter of endless poetry.[24]

Through smooth and lustruous brushstrokes, Titian recreates and celebrates the cascade of the lady's locks, a pure spectacle of Venetian blondness. Even the suitor seems as enthralled by the woman's hair as he is by her face. Yet his contemplation does not imply the torments conventionally associated with the beloved's indifference: the woman's hair is visualized as a simple object of desire. By holding her locks as if she were about to wring them out, Titian's lady transfigures momentarily into a local Venus Anadyomene, the goddess of Love whom Greek sculptors used to represent stepping out of the water after bathing. The allusion to this ancient figurative formula is

24 Ariosto, X, 134: "Com'esser può che dignamente io lodi/ Vostre bellezze angeliche e divine,/ Se mi par ch'a dir sol del biondo crine/ Volga la lingua inettamente e snodi?/ Quelli alti stili e quelli dolci modi/ Non basterian, che già greche e latine/ Scole insegnaro, a dire il mezzo e il fine/ D'ogni lor loda alli aurei crespi nodi,/ E 'l mirar quanto sian lucide e quanto/ Lunghe ed ugual le ricche fila d'oro/ Materia potrian dar d'eterno canto./ Deh! Morso avess'io, come Ascreo, l'alloro!/ Di queste, se non d'altro, direi tanto,/ Che morrei cigno, ove tacendo io moro." For the cruel implications of the contemplation of women's hair, see Tebaldeo, I, 106, 236; "O chiome parte de la treza d'oro/ De che fe' Amor il laccio ove fui còlto/ Qual simplice augelletto, e dal qual sciolto/ Non spero esser mai più se pria non moro,/ Io vi baso, io vi stringo, io v'amo e adoro;/ Perché adombrasti già quel sacro volto/ Che a quanti in terra sono il pregio ha tolto,/ Né lascia senza invidia il divin choro?/ A vui dirò gli affanni e i pensier' mei,/ Poi che longe è madonna e parlar seco/ Mi nega aspra fortuna e gli empii dei./ Lasso, guarda se Amor mi fa ben ceco!/ Quando cercar di sciogliermi io dovrei,/ La rete porto e le catene meco."

certainly the way by which Titian sought to extoll the woman's hair in "the noble styles and sweet modes" of classical art and poetry.[25]

The lover's absorption in the woman's beauty is frequently assimilated to the reflection of a mirror. Visually, Titian endorses the validity of this lyrical topos by depicting a second looking glass held by the suitor in front of the woman. Titian does not show what the mirror actually reflects; because of its position, it loses its individuality and becomes an opaque surface onto which the viewer projects the woman's envisioned profile. It can be assumed that, in this guise, the looking glass impersonates the lover's blind devotion to the lady. In his 1586 *Imprese illustri*, Camillo Camilli illustrates an emblem of a looking glass that may corroborate this assumption (Fig. 85):

> In this figure we see a mirror whose glass is directed to the sun, so that everyone who looks at it can only behold the part of it covered with ebony, or another similar material, and therefore cannot enjoy the brightness and splendor of the glass. Its significance is easy to interpret, since there is a symbolic parallel between the lover and the mirror on one hand, and the woman and the sun on the other. In fact, just as the glass receives the image of that which presents itself to it, so to does the lover adjust himself and his manners to the beloved woman's, seeking to resemble her as much as he can. The mirror, even the purest, does not shine in the darkness of the night, but only when the sun and the daylight hit it. Similarly the lover, though naturally most jovial, lives a dark and gloomy life, unless his beloved favors him with a glance.

Camilli sums up the meaning of the image: "its author intended to signal his fidelity in loving, as if to assure his woman by dint of this motto, *Aversum Caeteris* [with its back turned to others], that all his thoughts were fixed upon her entirely, and that nobody else shared his love."[26] Of course, Camilli's late testimony is not entirely conclusive in connection with *Woman at Her Toilet*. Yet it confirms that, a few decades after Titian's death, the motif of the mirror without a reflection, seen from behind or laterally, was interpreted as a symbol of the lover's staunch commitment to his mistress. Camilli also furnishes a valuable key to reading Titian's picture by suggesting that the comparison between the woman and the sun is a frequent literary and figurative topos. Does this similitude likewise operate in the painting? To answer this, it is necessary to explore two interconnected topics: the effects of the beloved's gaze on the lover and the paradoxes of the woman's poetic and visual representation.

As in front of a mirror, the lover metaphorically or physically loses his identity in front of the beloved woman.[27] In a sonnet of his *Rime* (1498), Antonio Tebaldeo transforms the lover into a metaphysical mirror of the devastating effects of the woman's gaze:

---

25 See Schäpers 1997, 13-43.

26 Camilli, 1:127-8: "e vedendosi in questa impresa uno specchio rivolto col vetro al sole di maniera che tutti gli altri, i quali lo mirano, veggono solamente quella parte ch'è coperta dall'ebeno o da altra materia tale, e per conseguenza non possono godere la chiarezza et lo splendor del vetro, è facil cosa interpretarla in questo significato, tanto più concorrendo qualche simboleità fra l'amante e lo specchio non meno che tra 'l sole e la donna che s'ama. Conciosia cosa che lo specchio riceve l'imagine della cosa che se gli presenta, e l'amante conforma se stesso et i costumi suoi alla cosa amata, cercando di divenire il più che gli sia possibile simile a lei. Lo specchio, benché purissimo, non risplende nelle tenebre della notte, ma solo quando è percosso dalla luce del giorno e del sole. Et così l'amante, benché di sua natura allegrissimo, se non riceve il favor della vista della cosa amata, mena vita tenebrosa et oscura. (...) sarebbe da dire che l'auttor suo avesse voluto mostrare in tal modo la fede sua in amando, quasi per accertar la sua donna col motto AVERSUM CAETERIS che i suoi pensieri fossero tutti rivolti a lei, e che nessun'altra avesse parte nell'amor suo."

27 A borderline case of the metaphorical absorption of the lover in the woman's figure is represented by Dall'Aquila a, XLVII, 86; to make the poet's portrait faithfully, the painter (Pinturicchio) is asked to represent the beloved woman first. Her portrait is the poet's real painter: "Se l'opra tua di me non ha già molto/ Non da te, Bernardin, vien da colei/ Che l'imagine mia porta con lei,/ L'aspetto mio non è donde m'hai tolto./ Son tutto un longo tempo in essa accolto;/ Onde per far del viso i membri mei,/ Prima te converria retrar costei/ E poi robbarmi intorno al suo bel volto." However, to depict the woman's face without going blind, Pinturicchio has to

Why do you trust a glass, proud woman?
If you want to know how beautiful you are,
Use me as a mirror: the greatness of your beauty
Is only reflected by my incomparable fire.[28]

In another sonnet, Tebaldeo more compellingly turns the beholder—the sculptor charged with carving Isabella d'Este's bust—into a mirror. He ends up turned to stone, and his identity is entirely absorbed by the woman:

Be careful, if you expose yourself to her face,
Cast your eyes down and do not mirror yourself
In it, lest from a sculptor you become a stone.[29]

The verb *specchiare* in this case takes on a specific meaning. In Tebaldeo's opinion, the woman's image forces its way through the eyes down to the heart and deep inside the soul, invading the lover's mind and senses radically: his identity consequently merges with hers as a mirror is filled by the beloved's image. As a result, Tebaldeo doubts the sculptor's capability to portray the woman without being "absorbed" by her image. Niccolò da Correggio, a near-contemporary poet of Tebaldeo, is much more explicit in this regard. In a famous sonnet, he challenges Leonardo to portray the effigy of an unidentified lady:

If Zeuxis, Lysippus, Polyclitus or Apelles
Were to draw the portrait of this woman,
By observing her every single feature
And the grace blended in all of them,
He would lose his sight along with his art,
As if staring at the sun or counting the stars,
Since Nature does not enable eyes
To discern the things in which she excels.
Hence, Leonardo, if you want to live up
To your name, and always be in-Vinci-ble,
Cover her face, and start painting her hair.
Otherwise, if you see all her beauties at once,
You, not she, will be the portrait.
For mortals cannot fix their eyes on her.[30]

---

represent her asleep: "Ma come la torrai che tu non ardi/ Al far degli occhi, e lei quelli volgendo/ Che tutti i sguardi soi son foco e dardi?/ Solo una via per tuo scampo comprendo:/ Pinger serrati i perigliosi sguardi,/ Ritrare il resto, e dir ch'era dormendo."

28 Tebaldeo, II-1, 36, 165: "A che presti, superba, a un vetro fede?/ Se ben comprender vòi la tua belleza,/ Spècchiate in me, ché tanta è sua grandeza/ Quanto è l'incendio mio, che ogni altro excede."

29 Ibidem, 251, 383: "Ma guarda, se al suo viso te apresenti,/ De chinar gli occhi e non specchiarte in ello,/ Ché pietra de sculptor tu non diventi."

30 Correggio, 189, 201: "Zeusi, Lisippo, Percotile o Apelle/ Che avuto avesse a ritrar questa in carte,/ Dovendo in lei mirar ciascuna parte/ E la grazia che è puoi mixta con quelle,/ Como a guardar el sole o contar stelle/ La vista in lui seria mancata e l'arte,/ Perché natura a l'occhio non comparte/ Potenzie in quel che essa natura excelle,/ Cusì, LEONARDO mio, se il tuo cognome/ Vòi conseguir, che ogni altro VINCI e excedi,/ Coprili il viso e incomincia a le chiome,/ Perché se a un tratto sue bellezze vedi,/ Tu el ritratto serai, non lei, ché some/ D'occhio mortal non son, vo' che mi credi." Correggio's poem was inspired by Petrarca, 77, 402: " Per mirar Policleto a prova fiso/ Con gli altri ch'ebber fama di quell'arte/ Mill'anni, non vedrian la minor parte/ De la beltà che m'ave il cor conquiso./ Ma certo il mio Simon fu in paradiso/ Onde questa gentil donna si parte:/ Ivi la vide, et la ritrasse in carte/ Per far fede qua giù del suo bel viso./ L'opra fu ben di quelle che nel cielo/ Si ponno immaginar, non qui tra noi,/ Ove le membra fanno all'alma velo./ Cortesia fe'; né la potea far poi/ Che fu disceso a provar caldo e gielo,/ Et del mortal sentiron gli occhi suoi." Unlike Leonardo, Simone

I would like to underline two points in this sonnet. Firstly, the poet warns the painter against the risk of becoming the equivalent of a mirror, should he gaze directly at the woman's face. Lest he become her portrait, Leonardo has to depict every detail of the lady's face separately. Only on this condition can he achieve his task. By reconstructing her effigy progressively, the painter recomposes her image as in a mirror: the drawing, or picture, mirrors and synthesizes the woman's aspect in a way that is tolerable to human eyes. Secondly, if the painter looks at the woman in her entirety, he is doomed to blindness: her beauty is as dazzling as the sunlight itself.[31] Accordingly, since the portrait makes the woman's face visible, it metaphorically succeeds in picturing the sunshine too. Tebaldeo approaches this question in different terms:

> Who is such a bold and foolish painter
> That tried to portray your figure on paper?
> Even Zeuxis and Apelles, who mastered
> Painting, and overcame all other artists,
> Would not be able to imitate and draw
> The smallest part of your gorgeous face.
> Nature herself, albeit most powerful,
> Would hesitate to make you anew.
> It is useless to put painters to the test:
> You are the sun, do not make yourself a star.
> Your figure does not have its honor in a drawing.
> If my heart, which alone knows how to depict
> Your beauty, could by chance show it outside,
> Everybody would exclaim: "that is she"![32]

Unlike Niccolò, who trusts Leonardo and his ability to depict, if analytically, the woman's face, Tebaldeo asserts that only the poet-lover can represent the beloved's figure truthfully. In addition, he claims that even the best portrait ever depicted could only represent the lady as a glimmering star, whereas she is a shining sun. In *Woman at Her Toilet*, Titian in a sense inverts Tebaldeo's statement: by capturing the sunlight through the window in the convex mirror, he reduces its reflection to a star in comparison with the radiance of the woman. Moreover, he sustains the superiority of painting, by contrasting the image itself to the mirror. Whereas the looking glass, disposed frontally as a picture-within-the-picture, exclusively reflects a warped segment of the woman's figure, the painting—like a full-scale mirror—renders the lady's beauty in its everlasting

Martini—called in to draw the portrait of Petrarch's beloved, Laura—succeeded in representing her, but only because he went to Paradise, and observed the eternal idea of the celestial woman. See also for a commentary Ibidem, 402-5, as well as the sonnet 79, 406-8.

31 For the theme of the sun-woman blinding the lover or the poet, see Dall'Aquila a, I, 39: "questo [the woman] è quel sol ch'ogn'altra vista abaglia,/ Che se 'l vedesse ognun come el vidi io/ Dirria ch'al mio nisiun stato se aguaglia"; XII, 50; CXII, C; Correggio, 292, 252-253; 304, 258-259; Tebaldeo, II-1, 87, 216: "Non già l'intenso ardor me increse e duole/ Che per mirarvi mi consuma drento,/ Ma duolme sol che star non posso intento/ Al vivo raggio che abagliar mi suole:/ Ché ognhor che quello a me mostrar si vole,/ Mi volgo altrove, e poi vòlto mi pento, / E diventar ocel serei contento,/ L'ocel che non offeso affronta il sole [the eagle]./ O possanza d'Amore invicta e stretta,/ Che a vedere ogni monstro staria forte,/ Né ardisco di guardare una angioletta!/ Maligno mio destin, maligna sorte,/ Che non sol darme morte se diletta,/ Ma de

privar d'ogni piacer mia morte!"; 179, 311: "Come posso aver facto del tuo volto/ Iudicio alcun, s'io non lo vidi mai?/ Ben vederlo più volte io me sforzai,/ Ma da quel mi fu sempre il veder tolto:/ Ché chiunque pò tenir l'occhio in te vòlto,/ Tenir lo pò ne gli apollinei rai"; 224, 356: "Scio che tutto infiammato alhor diresti:/ Io te scuso, Leon, se ardi per quella!/ Tolse il sculptor la minor parte de ella,/ Abagliato da gli occhi ardenti e honesti."

32 Tebaldeo, II-1, 91, 220: "Qual fu il pictor sì temerario e stolto/ Che ritrar volse la tua forma in carte?/ Ché Zeusi e Apel, che inteser sì ben l'arte/ E che hanno il pregio a tutti gli altri tolto,/ Imitar non saprian del tuo bel volto/ Col suo disegno pur la minor parte;/ Né se confidaria di novo farte/ Epsa Natura, benché possa molto./ Sì che non dar fatica a la pictura:/ Se sei un sol, non ti fare una stella,/ Non ha in carta il suo honor la tua figura./ Solo il cor mio scia farla come è bella,/ Che se di fuor potesse per ventura/ Mostrarla, odresti ognun gridar: Gli è quella!"

splendor.[33] Paradoxically, used as an ancillary device in evoking the back view of the female body, the looking glass adds to the painter's triumph: neither poet nor sculptor, for that matter, would be able to suggest diverse facets of the woman's figure in a single "shot." However, Titian's painting also dares depict the unconceivable: the sun itself, and not just a portion of it—the silhouette of the sunny window in the glass. That is, Titian opposes the lady's pictorial luminescence to the sun's subdued radiance. To understand the scope of this pictorial *paragone*, another poem by Tebaldeo may be helpful:

> Sun, what are you doing here still?
> The earth needs your light no longer.
> The day brings us a more beautiful sun.
> Turn your rays to other destinations.
> You will certainly not recover your rank
> As long as her light shines on the earth.
> I do not know why you are still coming back:
> It is better for you to hide, since if you
> Come down here just to be compared with her,
> You will be ashamed. Keep hiding, so that
> Nobody would be able to make a judgment.
> But I am afraid that, in love with her,
> Driven by passion, you come back to the earth:
> She has stolen your heart, as well as your office.[34]

In *Woman at Her Toilet*, Titian takes up Tebaldeo's comparison, by painting the lady and the sunlight side by side in the convex mirror. Ingeniously, he stages the defeat of the sun, literally overcome by the woman's silhouette that, superimposed, obscures its radiance. Furthermore, the lady illuminates the picture with the brilliance of her ivory-like flesh, the vibrancy of her flaming hair, the whiteness of her blouse. Compared to the miniaturized sun hovering nearby, her brightness proves absolutely victorious. The rays of her beauty eclipse even the suitor's presence: pictorially, he is a perfect foil for the woman's luminosity, a lyrical penumbra. The convex mirror provides the viewer with another insight into Titian's painted sonnet: turned toward the lady, the sun seems to aim at her in vain, since she casts her eyes toward the looking glass, while delicately holding the locks of her hair.[35] Like Tebaldeo, Titian ironically leads beholders to believe that the beautiful lady "has stolen [the] heart, as well as [the] office" of the sun. Yet the image also

33 For the conception of the portrait as a mirror in Renaissance art, see Cranston 2000, 127-50.

34 Tebaldeo, II-1, 73, 202: "Che vieni a far più qui, sole? Non sciai/ Che non bisogna al mondo più tua luce?/ Un più bel sole il giorno a nui conduce,/ Converti pur ad altro questi rai;/ E non sperar quel grado aver più mai/ Insin che questo lume in terra luce./ Non scio che causa a ritornar te induce,/ Ma il stare occulto è per te meglio assai,/ Ché venendo qua giuso al parangone/ N'arai vergogna; onde, se stai celato,/ Far non potran iudicio le persone./ Ma temo che de lui inamorato/ Descendi in terra, spinto da passione,/ E ch'el t'abia de officio e cor privato." See also Dall'Aquila a, LX, 98: "O ceco sol, che a noi remeni il giorno,/ A che pur vieni omai sì ben sicuro/ Che de qui non riporti altro che scorno?/ Che quando in ciel sei più fulgente e puro,/ Al paragon del suo bel viso adorno/ In mezzo al ciel te fa parere scuro."

35 In Renaissance lyric poetry, the poet sometimes pretends to be jealous of the sun. See Dall'Aquila a, CXII, 150: "El sol l'altrier m'assalse, e 'l fiero Amore/ Avanti alla mia dea tutti in un tratto,/ Tal ch'io mi persi e fui tutto disfatto,/ L'un dentro mi acceckò, l'altro di fuore./ L'un mi tolse la vista, l'altro il core/ Acciò restasse allor cieco et astratto,/ Ma a duo possenti dei non è degno atto/ A porre in terra un uom senza vigore./ El sol non volse che un bel sol vedesse,/ Ma volse amor fermasse una parola/ Acciò che 'l mio martir non li dicesse./ Ma ancor costei allor le forze invola,/ O divina beltà, or chi credesse/ Che 'l medesmo a lor dei facci lei sola"; Tebaldeo, II-1, 78, 207: "Io non te offesi mai, ma sempre in terra/ Adorato t'ho, Apol, come mio nume;/ Non scio per che cagion preso hai costume/ Di farme, come a un tuo nemico, guerra:/ Ché, quando gli occhi soi ver' me disserra/ Madonna, cerchi a me tòrre il suo lume,/ Né si sta chiuso tra le rive un fiume/ Come il tuo raggio fra nui dui si serra./ Tu sei pur sempre fastidioso e strano:/ Che ti facea già Marte e Vener bella,/ Che gli acusasti al fabro sciciliano?/ Che colpa han gli altri, s'el ti fo rubella/ Daphne? Ma contra me te adopri invano,/ Ché al lume del mio sol resti una stella." Tebaldeo, II-1, 301, 548, imagines that

entails an unexpected twist: without the sun streaming into the room, the woman's glowing beauty would fatally dim. The naturalism of the image both abets and belies the conventional language of lyric poetry: the lady's radiance relies on a misperception, and is enhanced by the close framing of the image. In other words, her brilliance is a function of the lover's obsessed sight. The multivalence of Titian's image resides in its ironic dissimulation; he assembles and condenses distinct components of the lyrical tradition in the form of an everyday toilet. By applying a contemplative point of view to a mechanical action, Titian both deploys and uncovers the conventionality of lyrical love.

Flames of Love in the Mirror

Elaboration entails displacement. In Caravaggio's *Conversion of Mary Magdalene*, figures and motifs grafted from Titian switch position and function. In shifting along the picture's surface in accordance with the painter's goals, they discharge, maintain or vary their initial meanings. As a general rule, Caravaggio tends to dissociate the woman from the mirror in two ways. First of all, instead of staring at a looking glass, the Magdalene's eyes focus on her sister's face. In a sense, Martha performs the task of the second looking glass, while simultaneously replacing Titian's suitor.[36] Second, the convex mirror no longer juxtaposes the woman and the sun. The Magdalene practically vanishes from the glass: all that survives of her reflected figure, besides the silhouette of her resting hand, are ripples of green drapery and shimmers of red satin. Sunshine rules supreme in the mirror without the Magdalene's rivalry. By arranging volumes in symmetry through lighting, Caravaggio brackets the figure of the Magdalene between her evanescent sister and the mirror's blind screen: a flash of light brightens these lateral masses, irradiating Martha's shoulder and hands, outlining a diamond of sunshine filtered through the window in the glass. On a narrower scale, Titian had imagined an analogous set-up.

All these pictorial shifts seem to be plainly justifiable: Caravaggio enlarges the perspective of *Woman at Her Toilet* to accommodate Martha's figure appropriately, remodeling Titian's amorous sonnet into a sacred narrative. Yet the transition from a lyrical to a religious mode does not explain the persistence of certain patterns: despite her role as a protagonist, Martha, like Titian's suitor, dwells in an inconsistent shade; the reflection of a sunlit window remains engraved within the convex mirror. To be sure, these details, and others, are reminiscences of Titian's prototype. However, they continue to convey meanings that, though specific to the new context, resonate with previous nuances.

Caravaggio's elaboration presupposes a deep comprehension of Titian's *Woman at Her Toilet*. The fact that the subject had become a worn-out topos in poetry and painting by his lifetime prepared Caravaggio to grasp its manifold subtlety.[37] The success of Titian's picture was remarkable. In

---

even the window is in love with the woman, who—like the sun—illuminates it during the night: "Ove è il bel sol che cum sua luce chiara/ Te facea giorno a meza nocte oscura,/ Nuda fenestra, che già tanto dura/ Me fusti a torto, e sì sdegnosa e avara?/ Hor prendi exempio, e da te stessa impara/ De esser discreta e d'aver più misura/ Ne la felicità, ché poco dura/ E alhor più fugge, quando è a noi più cara./ Tri cechi siamo: tu, fenestra, et io/ E Amor, da cui principio ebbe il mio male;/ Ma del vostro martir più forte è il mio,/ Ché tu sei vetro, e in te dolor non vale,/ Ché sei cosa insensata, e Amore è dio:/ A me dato è il sentire, e son mortale."

36   In a copy of *Woman at Her Toilet* now in Prague, considered by some scholars as an original by Titian, the suitor is replaced with another woman, a servant. On the table in the foreground, besides the flask, lies a comb, as in Caravaggio's *Conversion*. Most likely Caravaggio also knew this version of Titian's picture; he transformed the female servant into Martha. For the painting in Prague, see Joannides 2001, 258, 260.

37   Bargagli, 395, recognizes how widespread this topos was: "sicome costume antico e proprio de' veri innamorati, per le molte nobili e chiare qualità ch'essi ritrovano e pruovano verso di sé nell'amanze loro, similissime a quelle del celeste sole verso questo mondo e le parti sue, delle quali simiglianti virtù e proprietà si veggono ripieni tutti i volumi scritti de' poeti amanti e di coloro che di amore abbian trattato."

Torquato Tasso's 1591-1593 *Rime*, two sonnets are directly inspired by it. In both, the poet plays the role of the suitor. One of them reads:

> While holding in front of my sun
> A clear mirror, Love's select servant,
> My eyes happened to mirror a more
> Delightful and brighter object to me.
> In love with her beauty, she turned her eyes
> To her radiant face and lovely breast,
> Reveling in sharpening her sweet arrows,
> These fatal weapons of hers, destined for me.
> When she saw them lustrous and flaming,
> She launched more than one of her piercing
> Shafts from her serene brows to my heart;
> But I did not comprehend their threat.
> Yet, if my lady treats suitors this way,
> What wounds will she inflict on rebels?[38]

The many metaphors by which the woman and her gaze are defined all relate to a solar imagery: the lady is the sun; her face is radiant; her eyes shoot sharp rays at the lover's heart. Cultivated readers understood Tasso's metaphorical language because of its pervasiveness in late Renaissance culture.[39] A few years before Caravaggio painted the *Conversion of Mary Magdalene* (*c*.1598), Hendrick Goltzius vulgarized the subject of Titian's *Woman at Her Toilet* in a drawing of 1595-1596, now at the Boijmans-van Beuningen Museum, Rotterdam (Fig. 86), subsequently engraved by Jan Sanraedam. Towering in the foreground, the lady gives a sidelong glance to the mirror held by her lover who, in an attitude similar to Titian's suitor, but approaching her perilously, contemplates her face. His free hand lingers over her breast, longing for an intimate touch.[40] On account of her role, Goltzius' lady may well be perceived as the equivalent of Tasso's mistress, caught up by the draftsman shortly before diverting the amorous arrows of her eyes from the looking glass toward the lover or the beholder. As in Titian's painting, the mirror with its back turned echoes the lover's addiction to the woman. The popularity of this imagery extended beyond the kindred fields of poetry and painting. For instance, in his 1594 *Imprese*, Scipione Bargagli glossed upon an emblem in which a mirror reflects the face of the sun, explaining that it represented the lover's heart totally absorbed in the beloved's contemplation. Its motto accordingly reads: *Receptum Exhibet* ["it exhibits what it has received"] (Fig. 87).[41] All these testimonies are consistent with the lyrical message of Titian's

38   Tasso a, 1:95, XXX: "*Invitato da la sua donna a tenerle lo specchio, descrive quell'atto poeticamente.* A' servigi d'Amor ministro eletto/ Lucido specchio anzi 'l mio sol reggea,/ E specchio intanto a le mie luci io fea/ D'altro più chiaro e più gradito oggetto./ Ella al candido viso ed al bel petto/ Vaga di sua beltà gli occhi volgea/ E le dolci arme, onde di morte è rea,/ D'affinar contra me prendea diletto./ Poi come terse fiammeggiar le vide,/ Ver' me girolle e dal sereno ciglio/ Al cor volò più d'un pungente strale;/ Ma non previdi allor tanto periglio./ Or se Madonna a' suoi ministri è tale,/ Quai fian le piaghe onde i rubelli ancide?." Giovan Battista Marino develops this topic in a poem of his *Lira*: "A che pur donna il volto/ Ne lo specchio volgete,/ Se lo specchio del sol nel volto avete?/ Sia di noi, sia di voi solo il bel viso/ Lo specchio, e il Paradiso;/ C'ha in sé tal lume accolto,/ Che 'l vostro specchio ancor si specchia in esso,/ Et è lo specchio dello specchio stesso" (quoted in Mirollo 1963, 137).

39   On Tasso and painting, see Buzzoni 1985; Da Pozzo 1995; and Emiliani and Venturi 1997.

40   See Reznicek 1961, 306-7, no. 167. For Saenredam's print, see Strauss 1980, 411, no. 95 (249).

41   Bargagli, 394-5: "la prima impresa sarà d'uno specchio nel quale co' raggi suoi percotendo il sole vi disegna la forma del suo volto et esso, in segnale di ciò, rimanda indietro i medesimi raggi con voci scritte che di lui così parlano: EXCEPTUM [sic] EXHIBET. Il proposto dell'amico di Niccolò Gori scopritore di tali figure (…) mi persuado certo essere stato di voler per quelle manifestar la qualità dell'amor suo alla signora del suo cuore col figurarla per il suo sole in terra (…). Questo manifestamente ha preso di fare il Gori questa volta, dicendo d'aver segnata e ritratta la bella effigie di colei cui sola egli ama e pregia dentro il cuor suo, figurato per lo specchio da' raggi

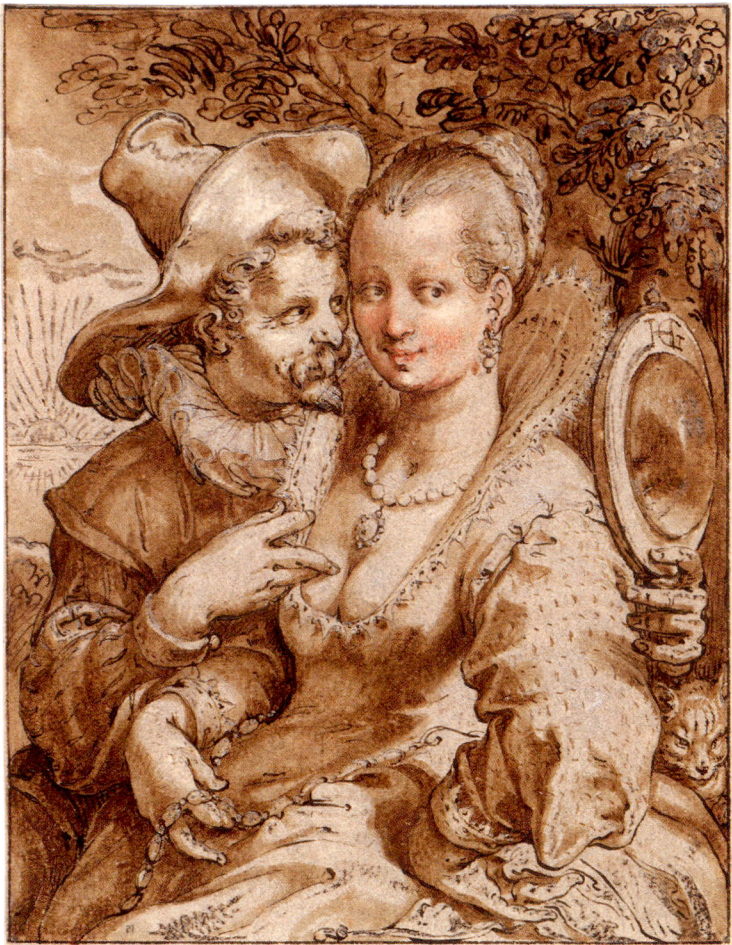

Fig. 86
Hendrick Goltzius, *Allegory of Sight*, Museum Boijmans-van Beuningen,
Rotterdam, pen, brown ink and wash with white heightening on pink paper,
16 x 12.4 cm.

painting. But do they also account for the presence of the sun in the mirror as depicted by Caravaggio?

Obviously, the lyrical comparison between the sun and the woman does not wholly apply to the *Conversion of Mary Magdalene*. By loosening the visual ties between the woman, the mirror, and the sun reflected in it, Caravaggio not only attenuates the theme of narcissism, but he in a sense also renounces the trope of likening the woman's beauty to the dazzling effects of the sunshine. In short, the sun no longer competes with the Magdalene; it is an entity of quite another league. However, the Magdalene's hands, both oriented to the diamond of light in the mirror, indicate that a relation still exists between the woman and the sun, one in which the latter almost certainly comes to symbolize God's merciful love.

In commenting on the emblem of the mirror turned to the sunshine, Camilli, after expounding its lyrical meaning—already quoted— proceeds to another explanation:

A figure composed of such noble things like the sun and the mirror, of which the former is the symbol of divinity itself, the latter of prudence, since both possess very profound and mysterious meanings in sacred literature, must hide a more secret and relevant significance; this figure was designed presumably to convey a concept not human, but spiritual and altogether divine. The mirror entirely turned toward the sun symbolizes a mind elevated and fixed upon the purest and brightest rays of eternal divinity. This is understandable, for the sun explicitly signifies God himself, who is named Sun of Justice, whereas the mirror represents a clear and shining mind, therefore particularly apt to grasp the influence of divine grace.

In this case, the motto, *Aversum Caeteris* [with its back turned to others], has to be interpreted differently:

solari percosso, et intendendo ciò dimostrare col ripiegamento di essi raggi vi si discuopre. Ché sicome quelli col loro vivo scintillare ivi dintorno fanno chiara mostra della solare imagine nello specchio impressa, così ancora tal nobile amante per le certe e chiare dimostrazioni amorose, che per lui ognora più belle si rendono e più onorevoli, intende che si debba conchiudere la verità da lui proposta del portare scolpita nel petto la sembianza delle amorose bellezze e dell'ardenti virtù e delle oneste grazie della sua amata donna."

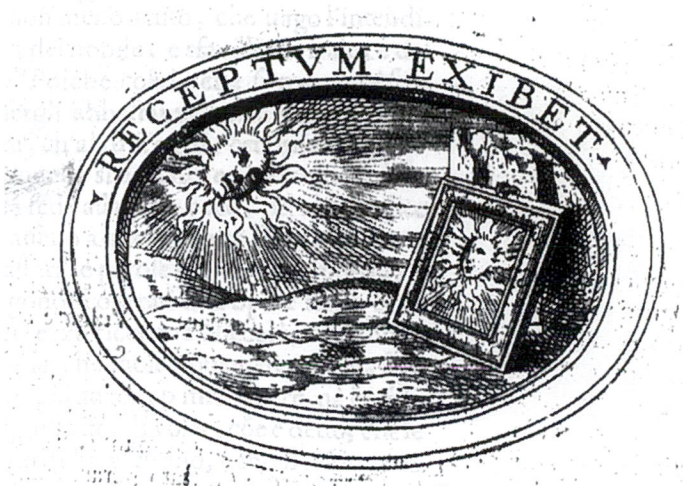 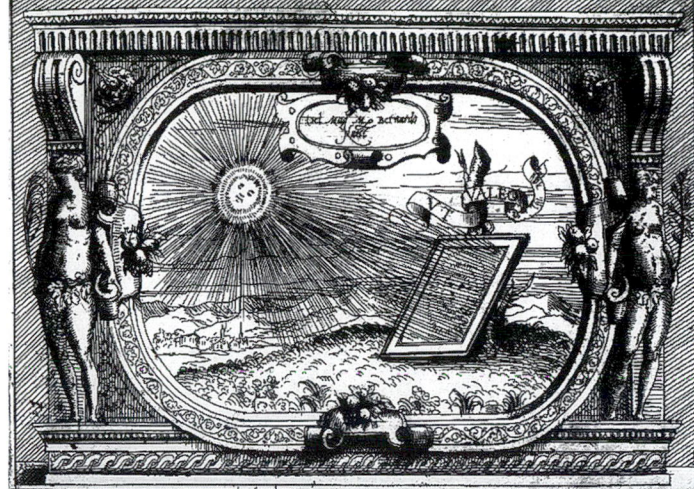

Fig. 87
Receptum Exhibet, reproduced from Scipione Bargagli, *Dell'imprese*, 1594.

Fig. 88
Ut Valeo, reproduced from Battista Pittoni, *Imprese*, 1562.

[A person] turning his own back away from the earthly things, and solely contemplating the lively rays of divinity, and by staring at them, receiving in his own soul the rays of divine grace, as the mirror turned to the sun receives the sunshine within itself.[42]

Camilli's exegesis is no exception. In his 1574 *Symbolicae Quaestiones*, Achille Bocchi had already compared divine love to the rays of the sun that, converging onto a concave mirror—the human soul—become the burning flame of grace and charity.[43] Bocchi's emblem in turn harks back to the lyrical tradition, according to which the woman/sun, whose eyes/rays collide with the man/mirror, engenders fervent passion in its target.[44] In his *Imprese*, Scipione Bargagli shows an emblem representing the sun, a concave mirror, and a flame originating from it. The image is accompanied by the motto *Unius Splendor Alteri Ardor*: "the one's brightness is the other's fire."[45]

In addition, the mirror stands for man's purified mind when imbued with divine virtues. In his 1562 *Imprese*, Battista Pittoni illustrates an emblem in which a mirror reflects the sun's effigy while leaning on a trunk around which curls an inscription: *Ut Valeo* ["As I am worthy"] (Fig. 88). Here is Pittoni's poetic interpretation:

42 Camilli, 128-9: "Ma io direi che un corpo d'impresa formato di due cose tanto nobili quanto sono il sole e lo specchio, che l'uno è il simbolo della stessa divinità e l'altro della prudenza, e d'ambidui de' quali si trovano per tutto il campo delle sacre lettere profondissimi e misteriosissimi significati, nascondesse in sé qualche senso più secreto e di maggiore importanza, e dovesse tenersi ch'ella fosse stata fatta per aver voluto spiegare qualche concetto non umano, ma tutto spirituale e divino. Et in tal proposito diremo che per lo specchio rivolto tutto al sole egli abbia voluto significare una mente elevata e fissa ne' purissimi e chiarissimi raggi dell'eterna divinità. Il che può quadrar benissimo, poiché nel sole viene espressamente significato Dio stesso, chiamandosi egli Sole di Giustizia; e nello specchio può esser significata una mente et una conscienza tutta chiara e risplendente, e però attissima a ricevere tutti gl'influssi della divina grazia, essendo la purità e la nettezza cose convenevolissime allo specchio. Così non averà egli voluto inferir altro con la figura e col motto se non d'aver voltato le spalle a tutte le cose del mondo e di mirar solamente ne' vivi raggi della divinità, in cui fissandosi voglia dire di ricevere dentro all'anima sua i raggi della divina grazia, come lo specchio rivolto al sole riceve in se stesso i raggi di lui."

43 Bocchi A., CXXVIII-CXXIX: "Mens pura quae Deum colit, amat, et statim divini amoris igne adurit caeteros ["A pure mind that honors and loves God, and all at once puts the flames of divine love in others"]. See Watson 1993, 77. See also Ruscelli, 1:125-8.

44 For the use of this metaphor in the seventeenth century, see Goodman 1983b.

45 Bargagli, 343: "Volendo l'amico nostro per ciò significare che la signora, per cui fu da lui tale impresa composta, tutta d'amore splendendo, ovvero che ricevendo ella ogni splendor di grazia, di leggiadria e di gloria da Amore, riscaldava et abbruciava gli altri di gentile amore."

As the sun wounds with its rays
A mirror of steel or of select crystal
Without damaging it anywhere,
Purifying and cleaning it instead,
So the man who mirrors himself in clear virtue
Wipes his stains out and emends his faults
Turning himself into a model
Through the light he derives from its rays.[46]

An analogous explanation of the same emblem is proposed by Vincenzo Ruscelli in his 1584 *Imprese illustri*. Moreover, Ruscelli remarks that "flat mirrors made of pure crystal not only reflect all the things that present themselves to them in a wondrous imitation of nature, but also render the very splendor of the sun, which [otherwise] would be incompatible with our eyes."[47]

By depicting the sun's reflection in the mirror, Caravaggio undoubtedly evoked both God's brightness as a source of love and grace and its irruption into the Magdalene's mind; as a mirror, albeit a convex one, the woman reflects the blinding brilliance of the divine sun. Through her own radiance, she somehow makes divinity compatible with human eyes. Oddly enough, the effects of God's supernatural intervention are not spelled out in the painting explicitly or systematically, unless one discerns them in the Magdalene's enlightened expression. According to Cummings, Caravaggio translated into visual imagery a then well-known account of Mary Magdalene's conversion, ascribed to an anonymous trecento writer. In it, the miracle unfolds during the preaching of Martha. While praising Christ's divine deeds, she looks at her sister, and remarks on an extraordinary change in her attitude: "and the gaiety which was usually on her face had vanished, and she was transformed, waiting to hear the words spoken by her sister." Apparently, she was entering "into the light of faith, whence she perceived in her heart that she was yielding love to the goodness she heard related to Him."[48] Cummings justly recalls a poem by Cardinal Roberto Bellarmino, composed about the same time as Caravaggio's *Conversion*, in which the prelate evokes the Magdalene's repentance through the similitude of the sun and God:

Father of the supreme light,
When you look at the Magdalene,
You generate flames of love,
Melting the ice within her heart.[49]

In light of these textual sources, which are essential to understanding the Detroit picture, Cummings argued that Caravaggio chose to depict the moment "when Mary is filled with light. In contrasting this special inner transformation with the figure of Martha," Caravaggio, according to Cummings, "created a psychological tension, which is the key to the extraordinary power of this painting." Cummings goes on, "the reflection of light in the mirror to which Mary points symbolizes divine truth and Mary's cognition of divine grace through love. It is light that comes

46 Pittoni, 40: "Perché ferisca co' suoi raggi il sole/ Specchio d'acciaio o di cristallo eletto,/ In parte alcuna danneggiar no 'l suole,/ Anzi quel n'è netto./ Tal, ch'in chiara virtù specchiar si suole,/ Purga ogni macchia e ogni suo difetto:/ E co' lumi che trae da' raggi suoi,/ Fa di se stesso paragone altrui."

47 Ruscelli, IV:19: "Gli specchi fatti di puro cristallo in forma piana ci raffigurano non solo tutte le cose che sono loro appresentate con emula e stupenda imitazione della Natura, ma ci rendono lo stesso splendore del sole incompatibile a gli occhi nostri."

48 Cummings 1974, 577.

49 Ibidem: "Pater superni luminis,/ Cum Magdalenam respicis,/ Flammas amoris excitas,/ Geluque solvis pectoris"

out of darkness and carries the message of I Corinthians: *We see now a dim reflection in a mirror, but then we shall see face to face.*"[50]

Cummings also remarks that the Detroit picture, albeit mostly inspired in his view by Bernardino Luini's various representations of *Martha and Mary Magdalene*, clearly differs from these previous compositions (Fig. 89). (A replica of Luini's painting, now in a private collection in Geneva, probably belonged to Cardinal Del Monte, the influential protector of the young artist).[51] Not only did Caravaggio modify the structure of Luini's paintings, in which the two saints, set side by side as joined icons, barely interact with each other, but he also decided "to portray a spiritual theme (…) within an everyday context" by introducing the mirror also as an allusion to a contemporary toilet.[52]

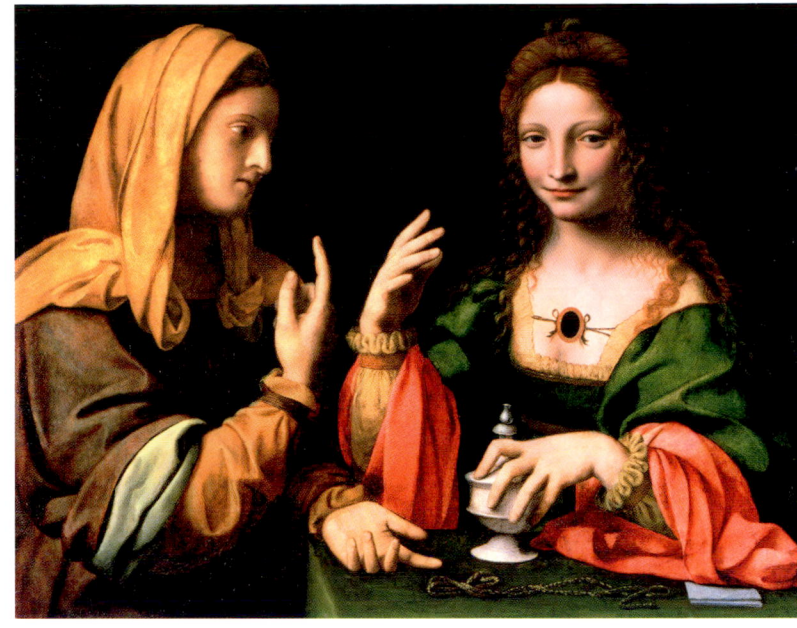

Fig. 89.
Bernardino Luini, *Martha and Mary Magdalene*, San Diego Museum of Art, San Diego, oil on panel, 63.7 x 82.5 cm.

The perfect coherence of the textual, visual, and symbolic structures of the painting as interpreted by Cummings is astonishing. He detects neither gaps nor contradictions between these three distinct hermeneutic levels. In his opinion, figures, objects, and narrative are felicitously combined to form a congruent theological message. Yet, despite Cummings' thoughtful reading of the picture, I still believe that the principal feature of the composition does not lie in its coherence, but in its intertextual discontinuities. As a matter of fact, the literary and the visual interfere with each other without fusing together, thereby disconnecting the narrative plot from its visual transposition. Moreover, the symbolic imagery does not convincingly heed the pictorial action. To grasp the extent of these disjunctions, it is necessary to analyze Caravaggio's painting both autonomously and through the lens of Titian's precedent.

From the outset, Caravaggio imagined the conversion scene as a metaphorical sequel to *Woman at Her Toilet*: like Titian's beautiful courtesan, Caravaggio's Magdalene is occupied with dressing, although she is almost finished. Her hair is combed and braided; her chemise, symbolically embroidered with vine and grapes, is properly tightened under the bodice, to which satin red sleeves have already been attached. As a final touch, she is about to adorn her breast with an orange blossom, and seems to be testing this detail at the mirror, when something seems to distract her attention. Suddenly, she turns to her sister, who exposes one by one, as if in a logical order, the reasons for conversion. Caravaggio represents Martha as the opposite of her self-loving sister. With her hands, she rehearses the canonical gesture of enumerating.[53] Martha thus incarnates here the ideal of active, somewhat rational spirituality as opposed to the future contemplative perfection of the Magdalene. Martha's parted lips may signal that, in amazement at her sister's expression, she

50   Ibidem, 577-8.

51   See Williamson 1907, 89-90 (with reproduction); Ottino della Chiesa 1956, no. 153. Waźbiński 1994, 2:613, notes that the Geneva painting does not match the dimensions given in Cardinal Del Monte's inventory. For the relevance of the iconography of Saint Martha and Magdalene in Luini's painting (especially in connection with the pictures he executed for the convent of Santa Marta), see Binaghi 1975, 64-9.

52   Cummings 1974, 575-7. According to Cummings, Luini's *Martha and Mary Magdalene* (now in the San Diego Museum of Fine Arts) is the painting that belonged to the Barberini collection, and probably to Cardinal del Monte.

53   Caravaggio represented the angel of his second *Saint Matthew* (Rome, San Luigi dei Francesi) in a similar attitude.

has paused, as Cummings pointed out, but also that she continues her argument.[54] However, no matter what her attitude stands for, Caravaggio visually suggests that Martha's role is secondary. Like the suitor in *Woman at Her Toilet*, her visual evanescence magnifies her partner's radiance, inciting beholders to focus on the Magdalene.

Yet, in Caravaggio's picture, the eclipse of Martha's figure is contradictory from a narrative and symbolic point of view. By making the Magdalene gaze at her sister's face with the same intensity as Titian's lady contemplates her own effigy in the mirror, Caravaggio insinuates the complementarity of the siblings: the one reflects the other in their twofold approach to God. If the Magdalene conceptually "mirrors" her sister to the point that, according to the textual tradition, she is "waiting to hear" her words at the very moment of her conversion, it is hard to understand why Caravaggio obscures Martha's presence, whereas he spotlights the gesture of her hands, which incidentally remain out of sight to her contemplative partner. On closer analysis, it is clear that, despite its many abrasions, the brightest zones of the picture gather around the axis formed by Mary Magdalene's head and Martha's hands, linked together by a rutilant satin sleeve. Observing the eerie, "crackly hardness" of its red folds, Longhi keenly noted that Caravaggio normally used "similar devices" to interrupt and abruptly rectify the uniformity of the pictorial surface in a view of intense illusionism and quasi-magical effects.[55] As a result, guided by the red slash of the sleeve, viewers tend to perceive Mary Magdalene's figure as segregated or independent from Martha's: as if, in the middle of her toilet, the Magdalene sank into a profound, solitary contemplation. Put otherwise, Mary Magdalene's "conversion"—and textual sources confirm that conversion it is—is initially perceived by viewers as unrelated to Martha's preaching. The chasm between text and vision, gestures and lighting, furtively and temporarily excludes the Magdalene from any narrative context. Her visual isolation, obtained with the same techniques of lighting used by Titian in evoking the sunlike brilliance of his lady, assumes here a miraculous nuance. It conveys a palpable notion of enlightenment. In *Woman at Her Toilet*, the lady's exceptional radiance read as lyrical. In Caravaggio's painting, Mary Magdalene's effulgence qualifies as religious, hence inducing viewers into a symbolic reading: her resplendence refers to the allegorical sun in the mirror.

Curiously, this symbolic level of interpretation, once hinted at, tends to fade away, and is even contradicted by the pictorial action. Were it not for the unintentional postures of her hands, discreetly indicating the light in the mirror, the Magdalene would be totally unconnected to the sun's presence. In Titian's painting, the lady's unawareness depends on her absorption or self-indulgence. Hers is also the victor's indifference; unknowingly, she is brighter than her bright rival and lover. Of course, these lyrical concepts have no direct equivalents in Caravaggio's conversion scene. In the Detroit picture, the relation between the Magdalene and the sun may be surmised, but is not demonstrable. Like Titian's lady, the Magdalene does not acknowledge the presence of the very sun that enlightens her: her eyes keep looking away from it. In her attitude, in the elegant way she poses next to the mirror, wielding the orange blossom with vanity, she still is the double of Titian's courtesan. Although the convex mirror—her metaphorical *alter ego*—may well symbolize her mind unpredictably visited by God's grace, it continues to be the quintessential instrument of narcissism as displayed in Titian's painting. In a certain sense, Mary Magdalene's conversion might equally be a misperception on the viewer's part. The sun's action operates in the painting completely on the surface. Like grace, of which it is a symbol, its effects are undetectable. By visualizing God's intervention as a reflection in the mirror, a secluded, anecdotal motif without

---

54 Cummings 1974, 577.

55 Longhi 1999-2000, 1:7: "Se a taluno la manica di seta dura e scricchiolante possa sembrare cosa quasi eteroclita, giovi rilevare che simili effetti d'interruzione e variazione improvvisa del tessuto pittorico a scopo intensamente illusionistico e ad effetto quasi magico, tornano persino in dipinti assai più tardi; per esempio in un particolare vistosissimo delle *Opere di Misericordia* di Napoli."

an apparent rationale in the narrative plot, Caravaggio paradoxically lessens its visual relevance, thereby inhibiting its allegorical value. In addition, he frustrates the expectations of the beholder, who, intrigued by the extraordinary brilliance of the Magdalene, is unable to unravel the faintest sign of a miracle, much less a conversion. The artist thus symbolizes, but does not represent, the divine. In fact, the allegorical disjoins from the gestural, gestures being the main means by which action and narrative clarify themselves. By uncoupling the *istoria* and the allegory, Caravaggio implicitly questions or make viewers question the efficacy of symbols, these conventional shortcuts of pictorial language, in conveying the impression of divine presence.

Moreover, in comparison with Titian's precedent, the figure of the Magdalene remains in pictorial suspension: she is neither a courtesan nor a saint. The religious content dislocates the lyrical matrix rooted within the figure without erasing it. The beautiful lady of Petrarch, as well as of Ariosto and Tasso, continues to hide behind the Magdalene, hindering her transformation into a religious character. As a result, the real subject of the painting is called into question. It is no coincidence that Caravaggio, unlike his predecessors and his own followers, played down the attributes of both Mary Magdalene and Martha. Cummings justified the absence of Mary Magdalene's epithetic jewels as a sign of ongoing repentance,[56] but he did not explain why Martha is deprived of the traditional nun-like veil that generally covers at least part of her head. I do not wish to imply that Caravaggio did not intend to represent Mary Magdalene and Martha. I merely point out that viewers, even those familiar with Christian iconography, might hesitate in front of Caravaggio's *Conversion* and misread it as a genre scene, the mysterious dialogue between two women in an early seventeenth-century interior.

In 1943, Roberto Longhi perceptively praised the novelty of the *Conversion of Mary Magdalene*. For him, the picture was a sort of manifesto, a clear polemical response to those "who blamed Caravaggio for not being able to represent action: that is, a moral or affective relationship."[57] The Detroit picture is assuredly one of the first attempts by Caravaggio to depict an *istoria*, that is, a religious or heroic action. It is noteworthy that, by bidding farewell to the swindlers, gypsies, and musicians who crowded his youthful canvases, he has recourse to the Venetian lyrical formulas and motifs specific to his earliest works. More intriguingly, in inaugurating a new phase in his career, Caravaggio introduces at the core of the noblest pictorial genre the unsettling principles of his poetics of dislocation. Instead of proving his ability to transpose a heroic action into a perfectly legible image, Caravaggio dismantles the coherence of the narrative by dislocating its visual referents and symbolic elements. Unlike Longhi, I believe that with the *Conversion of Mary Magdalene*, Caravaggio began not to grapple with the problem of heroic action, but to reassess the *istoria* by disarticulating its structural components in ways that were presaged by Titian, albeit in other pictorial genres.

56 Cummings 1974, 578: "Other details which might go unnoticed in another context underline the fact that the Magdalen has rejected the vanities of this world and has achieved a state of divine grace. Unlike traditional representations, she wears no earrings, necklace, nor jewels on her gown. Her only jewel is her tiny gold circlet on the finger of her left hand, linked closely with the ray of light, which may possibly suggest that she has become the bride of Christ. The orange blossom she holds stands for purity and would link well with the idea of a mystic marriage." Cummings' interpretation is particularly contradictory, in that he assumes that Mary has already converted before…the conversion itself. In fact, how can she be portrayed by Caravaggio at the moment of her enlightment, if she already renounced vanity and married Christ "mystically"?

57 Longhi 1999-2000, 1:7: "Palese insomma l'intento quasi polemico verso coloro che rimproveravano al Caravaggio di non poter rappresentare un'azione, un *rapporto* cioè morale ed affettivo." Immediately after this, Longhi states: "A questo fine, ecco che Marta spingendo le mani fuor della zona ombrosa, argomenta icasticamente, sulle dita, il pro e il contra di un'esperienza troppo mondana."

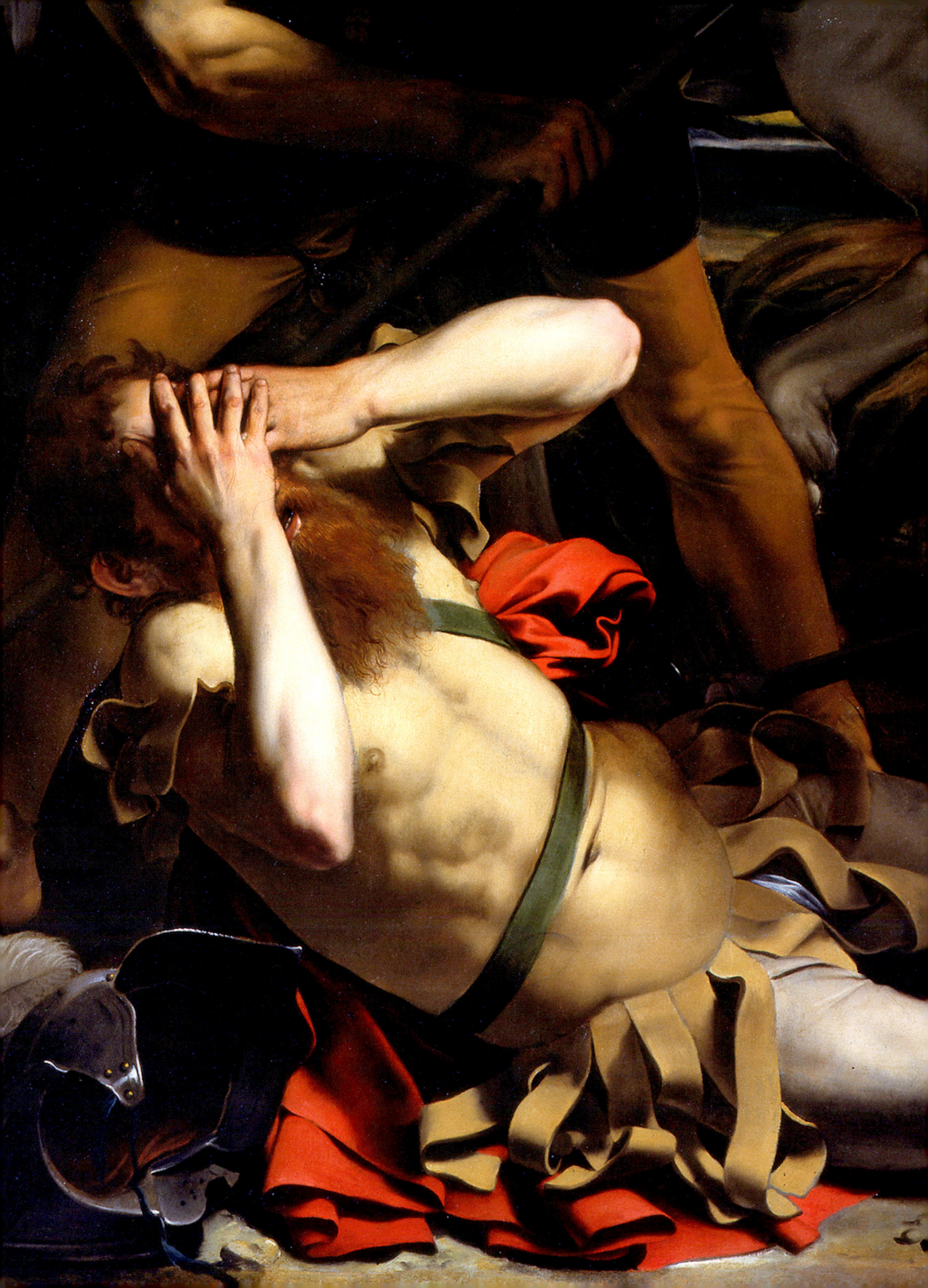

PART THREE

The Misplaced Hero: The Challenge of the *Istoria* in Caravaggio's Early Religious Narratives

Truth in Painting

> *"Back in those days I knew a painter in Rome whose mores were filthy, who always went around with clothes so worn out and dirty that it was a wonder, and who always hung out with the kitchen boys working for the Court's Signori. This painter never did anything good in his art but depicting innkeepers and gamblers, or gypsies reading hands, or else those porters and those despicable and miserable people sleeping in the piazze at night. And he was the most content man on earth when he represented an inn and those who eat and drink there. This was due to his mores, which resembled his paintings."[1]*

It is a truism to state that the Council of Trent's precepts in the matter of religious images exerted enormous pressure on the production of Catholic pictorial narratives at the end of the sixteenth century and throughout the seventeenth. Nor would one find an essay, article or book on Caravaggio in which the import of Counter-Reformation propaganda in his paintings would not stand as an assumption, be incidentally mentioned, or examined thoroughly. In several cases, scholars tend to describe Caravaggio as toeing the line of the most radical norms inspired by Counter-Reformation discourse on painting. Of course, according to this opinion, censorship intervenes—as it actually did—only when Caravaggio expresses radicalism at odds with the elitist views of the Church's hierarchy. I have already explained to some degree in Part One why I do not embrace this interpretation. At this point it should be clearly stated that Caravaggio's paintings do not by any means translate the most exacting instructions of Counter-Reformation art.[2] On the

---

1 This passage from Federico Borromeo's *De Delectu Ingeniorum*, a manuscript at the Biblioteca Ambrosiana, Milan, was first published by Marghetich 1988, 108: "Nei miei dì conobbi un dipintore in Roma, il quale era di sozzi costumi, et andava sempre co' panni stracciati e lordi a maraviglia, e si vivea del continuo fra i garzoni delle cucine dei signori di corte. Questo dipintore non fece mai altro che buono fosse nella sua arte salvo il rappresentare i tavernieri et i giocatori, overo le cingare che guardano la mano, overo i baronci et i fachini e gli sgratiati che si dormivano la notte per le piazze; et era il più contento huomo del mondo quando avea dipinto un'osteria, et colà entro chi mangiasse e bevesse. Questo procedeva dai suoi costumi, i quali erano simiglianti ai suoi lavori." There is no doubt that the painter evoked by Borromeo was Caravaggio, the only painter then in Rome who perfectly matches the cardinal's description. A similar passage, in Latin, is to be found in Borromeo's 1623 *De delectu ingegnorum*: Agosti 1997, 180, note 13. Borromeo, who owned Caravaggio's *Basket of Fruit* now at the Pinacoteca Ambrosiana, Milan, describes the painting in the most positive manner.

See Borromeo a, 192: "Michaelis Angeli Fiscella. Nec abest gloria proximae huic fiscellae ex qua flores micant. Fecit eam Michael Angelus Caravaggensis Romae nactus auctoritatem, volueramque ego fiscellam huic aliam habere similem, sed cum huius pulchritudinem incomparabilemque excellentiam assequeretur nemo, solitaria relicta est."

2 Some of the texts that I quote in this Introduction were also used by Bologna 1992, 10-137, although he comes to conclusions very different from mine. To prove this point, suffice it to quote some of Bologna's statements (77-8): "Anche senza bisogno d'impegnarsi in sottili disquisizioni teologiche, il primo punto chiaro è che il Caravaggio non può esser collocato al di fuori di una sostanziale adesione al cattolicesimo. E anzi, in quanto ogni parte della sua opera, come del resto tutta la critica—volente o nolente—ha sempre messo in risalto, rivela una profonda e non manierata religiosità, si tratta d'intendere che il rifiuto, o comunque il tipo di dissenso, che Caravaggio oppose al rigorismo di marca tridentina registrati nei testi autorizzati, nacque proprio dalla

---

◀ Plate IX: Michelangelo Merisi da Caravaggio, *The Conversion of Saint Paul*, Odescalchi Collection, Rome, oil on panel, 237 x 189 cm., detail.

contrary, the master purposefully flouts these prescriptions in ways that would doubtless qualify as sheer provocation were it not for his subtlety in doing so, and the seriousness with which he reinterprets the divine.

The paintings I will study in the following chapters elucidate the great extent to which Caravaggio reacts to Counter-Reformation aesthetic ideology:[3] the function of sacred images as vehicles of orthodoxy; the scope and interactions of the truth, the probable, and the verisimilar in religious narratives; and the role of the divine hero in the *istoria*. By inquiring into these interrelated questions, I am perfectly aware that, methodologically speaking, it is impossible to construe and evaluate Caravaggio's religious narratives without taking into account the insights of Counter-Reformation art theorists. By this I mean that, in a certain sense, Caravaggio's painting is the product of the most fertile reflections on images originating from the Council of Trent (1559-1563). In other words, Caravaggio's alertness and acuity in interpreting sacred history assuredly relies on the richness and complexity of this unprecedented and widely articulated meditation on art and images.

In Part One, I distinguished Leon Battista Alberti's model of the *istoria* from the near-contemporaneous Byzantine concept of painting. Not surprisingly—the vicissitudes of Calvinist iconoclasm certainly contributed to this phenomenon—art theorists of the Counter-Reformation harked back to Byzantine aesthetics, but without renouncing the Renaissance take on pictorial narratives. In his 1582 *Discorso intorno alle imagini sacre e profane*, Gabriele Paleotti[4] stresses:

> Turning now to the origin of images, I deem it appropriate to consider some aspects of their conformity to books, for we see that the sacred authors and the Gentiles, speaking about images, not only pair them often with books by assimilating one to the other, but the Greeks have also attributed the name of γραφεύς to the writer and painter alike, and the name γραφίς to writing and painting, and the term γραφή, or γράφειν, according to some, is attributed to both the pen or other tool with which one writes and the brush with which one paints.[5]

Heeding the theoretical positions of the patristic doctrine on images, Paleotti insists upon the importance of painting as an instrument for instructing the illiterate, teaching the dogmas and

non manierata profondità di quella 'religione,' e dalla volontà di contribuire autonomamente ad approfondirla ancora. (…) Solo con il prosieguo del tempo—dové convincersi ben presto il Caravaggio—la tradizione ha estrapolato, antologizzato e codificato gli eventi della storia sacra, per darne una versione strumentalmente apologetica ed esemplare. Nel momento in cui si produssero—e da parte di coloro che si trovarono ad assistere al loro prodursi—quegli avvenimenti non poterono invece non apparir—né essere percepiti—altro che come accadimenti comuni, con attori comuni. La loro sacralità, per conseguenza, nello stadio cruciale e storicamente originario della determinazione nel tempo, non poté manifestarsi altro che in termini di semplice umanità, e il loro grado di esemplarità coincidere con il grado di autenticità radicale con cui quell'umanità prese corpo, e con l'intensità con cui fu partecipata e sofferta. Il compito di un pittore che non voglia accontentarsi di conformità esteriori sarà perciò di liberare il tema agiografico sia dalle amplificazioni apologetiche e ripetitivamente rituali, sia dall'ostentazione pietisticamente devozionale, per restituirlo alla fragranza dell'accadimento: vale a dire (…) rendendo anche il sacro in termini di esperienza sensibile, e revocando tutto, sacro e profano, al grado zero della dimensione esistenziale." It is interesting that, on a certain level, Bologna's viewpoint, albeit simplified, continues to be adopted by scholars. See for instance Schütze 2009, 141:

"The aim of Caravaggio's interpretation of the *historia sacra* was to transport it into modern times and illuminate it from a human perspective, to provide a visual answer, as it were, to the question of what it could mean in concrete terms for his contemporaries and their religious convictions. (…) The religious history painting assumed the task of expounding the Scriptures and laying open their deeper significance in new ways through a visual exegesis."

3 For Counter-Reformation ideology in the matter of images in general, see Scavizzi 1992; and Hecht 1997.

4 For Paleotti, see Prodi 1967; Zacchi 1985; Salvarani 1994; Scorrano 2005; Caputo 2008; and Bianchi 2008.

5 Paleotti, 16: "Trattandosi ora della origine delle imagini, ci pare opportuno di considerare insieme alcune cose della conformità che tengono co' i libri, poi che veggiamo che gli autori sacri ed i gentili parlando delle imagini non solo l'accoppiano spesse volte co' i libri assomigliandoli insieme, ma ancora il nome dato da greci allo scrittore che è γραφεύς, l'hanno attribuito parimente al pittore, ed il nome γραφίς alla scrittura e alla pittura, e la voce γραφή overo γράφειν, secondo alcuni, così alla penna o altro istrumento con che si scrive come al pennello con che si dipinge."

mysteries of Christianity, and convincing the recalcitrant and the unbeliever. As they operate directly through the eyes, argues Paleotti, images are much more effective than words:

> Since our imaginative faculty is so capable of receiving [visual] impressions, there is undoubtedly no other instrument as strong and efficient to this end than images done from life, which almost inadvertently violate our senses.[6]

It cannot be emphasized enough that, because of their purity, Paleotti favors the senses over human intellect. In his view, senses are receptors that do not filter information; they are caught off guard by relentlessly ongoing images and incautiously let them in. Yet, in order to be trusted by the recipient, images must be graphically vivid; the divide between nature and artifact must wane, and even vanish, for the eyes to be wholly deceived. Only on this condition does the message reach its intended destination. Put otherwise, the efficacy of the religious image is proportionate to its naturalism. But naturalism is not a synonym of realism. By acknowledging the indispensable role of graphicness in painting, Paleotti restores and boosts the optical function of religious images as defined from Alberti onward, but reconsiders it in a more drastic manner. On this premise, pictorial narratives must indeed visualize scriptural texts with fidelity and transparently. I shall explain the intricate ramifications of this reasoning shortly, but for now I simply note a theoretical impasse determined by Paleotti's observation. Literary texts, including the Bible, are by definition rhetorical constructions: the raw material that they expose, that is, the account of the events to be represented visually, is already arranged in a fictitious and meaningful order. Does transliteration then equally imply the visual transposition of the rhetorical format inherent in the literary narrative? If so, does the painting's compositional layout replicate the textual one, or is it independent from it? And by assuming a rhetorical structure, does the image preserve the violent charge through which it aggresses the senses and convinces the viewer of its truth? Put otherwise, does painting's crude opticality diminish as a result of rhetoric's intervention? These questions are of utmost interest, and therefore should not be avoided. If, in accordance with the Byzantine model, painters are nothing but scribes encoding texts into images, there is almost no latitude for them to exercise invention. As a general rule, indeed, they are neither supposed nor requested to interpret sacred history. Essentially, they are translators, neither inventors nor exegetes of the Christian truth. Paleotti was absolutely cognizant of these theoretical conundrums. To resolve them, he differentiated between the truth and the verisimilar:

> As authors write, the truth is construed in diverse ways, but leaving aside its other definitions, I focus here on the truth in the sense that the sign matches the thing signified (*"prout est aequalitas signi ad rem significatam"*); I thus refer to paintings that accord entirely with what one aims to represent. Since every thing—whether natural, artificial, moral or of whatsoever sort—is arguably accomplished by a determinate person and occurs at a certain time and place, with a specific cause or mode, every narrative that intends to illustrate an action or any other fact that truly occurred will not omit any of these circumstances. Hence the painter, whose task it is to imitate the truth, will dwell particularly on the circumstances surrounding the truth's core, striving to understand clearly the whole span and order of the events, thereby forming his design in accordance. But because not all of the facts and sequences of things are known, for authors overlook an infinity of them, it is then necessary to resort to the verisimilar if one wants to depict what is not certain. Therefore, one will call verisimilar a narrative

---

6 Ibidem, 78: "Essendo dunque l'imaginativa nostra così atta a ricevere tali impressioni, non è dubbio non ci essere istrumento più forte o più efficace a ciò delle imagini fatte al vivo che quasi violentano i sensi incauti."

that similarly explains all the above-mentioned circumstances accompanying the truth. Since the verisimilar consists in reasonably representing those things that are unclear and uncertain with their own circumstances in such a way that they persuade people's common intellect by quieting it, it ensues that a painting is not verisimilar when it contradicts the truth—in this case, it would be false—or if it lacks some essential circumstances—it would be rather defective then—but only when it represents actions or things usually contrary to nature, common opinion, and the qualities and customs of man, animals, places, and other similar things.[7]

Before analyzing Paleotti's distinction of the true and the likely in painting—the false and the defective are summarily expounded in the previous quotation—it should be noted that, despite the author's explicit claims, truth in painting encompasses more than the relationship between the signifier and the signified. First of all, it is a metaphysical concept, circumscribing the innermost essence of the Supreme Being—the Christian God—as revealed to humankind. In and of itself, this truth is inaccessible to man's senses, and thus manifests itself through signs. In other words, text and image reflect, but do not equate with, the truth. Thus representing the truth necessarily draws on a mediated reality, replete with signs and therefore unsuited to be forthwith comprehensible: at best, it can be progressively deciphered. How painting as an optical, unfiltered, and uncomplicated device can represent truth is already a matter of paradox. Indeed, representing facts and events does not correspond to making their supernatural scope, significance, and finality understandable. As a corollary, painters must possess an almost prophetic insight in order to pierce the surface of facts and probe into the divine truth's eternal realm. Rather than simple translators, they should act as shamans of scripture and its true senses. I will return to this issue in the Introduction to Part Four. But even if it is painting's function solely to visualize the sacred text, the problem remains: scripture does not supply painters with enough data, and they are thus forced to interpolate. As Federico Borromeo puts it in his *Della pittura sacra*:[8]

> In order not to err, one must know that the Christian painter and sculptor may well amplify, ornate, and explicate sacred narratives, but it will always be illicit to oppose their truth and defy the best authors' opinions.[9]

Like Paleotti, but with broader insight, Borromeo concedes that painters need to submit the Christian truth to amplification and embellishment. As graphic as it might be, an image could never

7 Ibidem, 177-8: "Il vero si piglia in più modi come scrivono gli autori, ma noi lasciando l'altre parti pigliamo qui il vero 'prout est aequalitas signi ad rem significatam,' cioè quella pittura che si conforma intieramente con quello che si vuol rappresentare, e perché ogni cosa naturale o artificiale o morale o di qualunque altra sorte si presuppone fatta da certa persona ed accaduta in certo tempo, certo luogo, con certa causa e certo modo, però ogni narrazione che vorrà spiegare una azione o altra cosa vera e compita non doverà pretermettere alcuna di queste circostanze. Onde il pittore, cui ufficio è d'imitare il vero, doverà precipuamente avere l'occhio a queste circostanze con le quali sta accompagnato il corpo della verità, procurando di chiarirsi bene di tutto il contenuto ed ordine del fatto, e secondo quello formare il dissegno suo. Ma perché tutti i successi ed ordini delle cose non si sanno, ed infiniti sono tralasciati da gli autori, allora volendosi esprimere quelle cose che non sono certe, si viene al verisimile. Là onde narrazione verisimile si dirà quella la quale spiegherà medesimamente tutte le circostanze dette di sopra, le quali accompagnano

il vero. Dunque essendo il verisimile quello che le cose che non sono chiare e certe porge così ragionevolmente e con le sue circostanze che le rende persuasibili e quieta il commune intelletto delle persone, seguirà perciò che non verisimile sarà quella pittura la quale non contradirà già alla verità, perché quella saria falsa, né meno mancherà solo di alcune circostanze necessarie, perché questa saria più tosto imperfetta (...); ma solo rappresenterà azioni o cose contrarie ordinariamente alla natura, opinione, costumi e qualità de gli uomini, de gli animali, de' luoghi o di simile altra cosa."

8 For Federico Borromeo and his ideas on the subject of art, see Coppa 1970; Quint 1986; Marghetich 1988; Agosti 1992; Jones 1993; Agosti 1996; Bolzoni 2002; Mozzarelli 2004; Buzzi and Ferro 2005; Biscottini 2005; and Balestreri 2005.

9 Borromeo, 21: "E per non errare è da sapersi che al cristiano pittore e scultore sarà ben lecito amplificare e ornare e dichiarare le sacre istorie, ma non sarà giamai lecito opporsi alla verità di esse e contrastare col parere dei migliori scrittori."

simply translate a sacred text's visual core. The literary account, therefore, is to be conceived of as a bare subject ripe for elaboration. Artists re-invent the religious narrative through interpretation. It is their task not simply to reproduce sacred events, but also to recreate them in a pithily condensed form: one that incorporates—to paraphrase Paleotti—not only the circumstances absent in the literary text, but also the dogmas that it adumbrates. Once the principle of verisimilitude has been accepted, it remains to be understood which pictorial amplifications, adornments, and glosses are permitted, exacted or expected from a theological standpoint. Bearing Paleotti in mind, Borromeo enunciates a further distinction between the true, the likely, and the unlikely. Predictably, the truth is the domain of the past and the present—that is, of sacred history and its impending aftermath:

> As I have already said, art's proper objective revolves around things that have already been or still are; the more one distances oneself from this subject or goal, the more one strays from the art of representing.[10]

Furthermore, art on occasion censors the truth, at least every time that the truth should not be represented because it is religiously inconvenient:

> It will be the painter's task to represent faithfully what is or has been, but he will do so not indistinctively and carelessly, but with maturity of mind, since one cannot be allowed to say whatever things one might want to say, although they prove to be true.[11]

While unknowingly drifting from the optical model of painting as reformulated by Paleotti—being true is no longer a condition sufficient enough for representation—Borromeo instead resigns himself to the necessity of resorting to rhetoric in depicting the sacred. In his view, the category of the verisimilar might better suit the representation of an *istoria*:

> Reasoning eventually about things that are either probable or improbable, I say that it is permissible to avail oneself of probable things instead of true ones, and I would take this example: just as the orator loves the truth extremely, yet does not give up on or shun arguing through the probable, so too is the probable represented instead of the true, as it brings one pleasure, and as such is able to persuade one in an exquisite manner on account of its cherished novelty.[12]

Of course, Borromeo reiterates the idea that "composing a false book in painting is tantamount to writing a false story."[13] With slight regret, he even declares:

> On the other hand our faith is nonetheless so fond of the truth, and one must dodge the occasions that lay one bare to the blame and criticism of murmuring tongues with

10   Ibidem, 22: "Intorno poi alle cose che possono essere, parimente non si deono esprimere senza gran considerazione e riguardo, poiché, come abbiamo detto, il proprio oggetto dell'arte è intorno alle cose che sono già state over sono. E quanto maggiormente altri s'allontana da questo soggetto over scopo, tanto ancora si allontana dall'arte del rappresentare."

11   Ibidem, 21-2: "Intorno al primo capo, sarà officio del pittore di esprimere quello che è overo che è stato fedelmente, ma però non così indistintamente e senza riguardo questo far dee, ma con maturo senno agendo, sì come non sarebbe da approvarsi che si dicessero tutte quelle cose che dire si potrebbono, ancorché vere fossero."

12   Ibidem, 22: "Ragionando poi nell'ultimo luogo delle cose probabili overo improbabili, noi diciamo che è permesso il prevalersi delle cose probabili invece delle vere, e prendere potremo questo esempio, che sì come l'oratore ama sommamente le verità, ma non per questo rifiuta e ha a schiffo i probabili argomenti, così invece del vero rappresentasi ancora esso e dilettaci il probabile, e sì come tale ha forza di persuaderci con isquisita maniera sì come nuovo overo caro oggetto."

13   Ibidem: "E tanto è scrivere una falsa storia, quanto è formare un libro falso dipingendo."

such caution that I would rather prefer that one represents things as they occurred, transparently and without the supplement of new inventions.[14]

Yet, despite all his precautions, it is apparent to me that Borromeo is torn between two diverse paradigms of depicting the divine. Between the painter/translator and the painter/orator, his preference would doubtless go to the latter. More to the point, Borromeo's reflection betrays the intellectual pleasure he must certainly have experienced in detecting, interpreting, and savoring the painter's own interpretation of scripture—that is, his novelty. From this point of view, he imperceptibly but assuredly modifies Paleotti's conception of verisimilitude in painting: more than a logical inevitability due to scripture's brevity, the probable when opportunely buttressed by rhetoric might be a better instrument of imparting the truth. In any event, the aesthetic potential of verisimilitude intrigues and delights a refined and erudite intellect such as Borromeo's with undeniable intensity. Although Borromeo would not admit it, the model of rhetorical painting is more consonant with the expectations of an elite. When it comes to the populace—the mass of illiterate or poorly educated churchgoers—straightforwardness ought to prevail: neither novelties, nor intellectual intricacies should interfere with the reception of a sacred *istoria*. For this reason, it is completely understandable that Borromeo, in many instances in which a conflict arises between the truth of scripture and the verisimilar as crystallized in the iconographic tradition, feels compelled to endorse the latter to the detriment of the former:

> Some rightly state that [Jesus'] hands bore no wounds on the palms, but rather at the conjunction of the arm with the hand, for otherwise the Savior's most ponderous body could not hold up [on the cross]. However, it is always preferable to comply with the Holy Church's common usage. Nor should one want to introduce a new usage, the more so because scripture says: "He [Christ] showed them his hands and side" ("*ostendit eis manus et latus*").[15]

Similarly, Paleotti recommends that painters obey the common tradition of sacred images instituted during the Church's long and authoritative history, provided that the ordinary iconography does not prove false or defective on theological grounds:

> For instance, there is no Evangelist who says that, when our Lord was crucified, his genitalia were covered with a cloth or veil, and yet it is such a reasonable usage, and so often practiced by Christianity over the centuries, that it would be impious to question it. During the annunciation of the glorious Virgin, as the archangel Gabriel greets her, scripture does not tell us what she was doing, whether walking or sitting or sewing or working on something else, but painters have always agreed that she was kneeling, intent on praying, and this is how we must bring ourselves to believe it was. The Gospel does not recount how our infant Savior with his mother and Saint Joseph fled into Egypt, whether they walked or rode there. However, painters ordinarily depict the Madonna riding an ass with the Child in her arms, and it is reasonable it was as

14 Ibidem: "Ma tuttavia dall'altra parte è così amica la nostra fede del vero, e così saviamente fuggire si deono le occasioni che porgono materia di biasmare e di riprendere alle lingue mormoratrici, ch'io lodarei che schiettamente e senza alcuna mistura di nuove invenzioni si rappresentassero le cose come già furono."

15 Ibidem, 45: "Alcuni ancora hanno avuto ragione che le mani non fossero ferite nelle palme, ma sopra la [con]giuntura del braccio con la mano, affermando che in altro modo non si sarebbe potuto sostenere il corpo gravissimo del Salvatore. Ma tuttavia sarà sempre miglior cosa seguitare il commune consentimento all'usanza commune di Santa Chiesa, né volere in ciò introdurre nuove usanze e tanto maggiormente in quanto che la Scrittura dice: *ostendit eis manus et latus*."

such, for the Blessed Virgin was still vulnerable, and had to make a long trip, and it was customary for women to travel in that way.[16]

By defending verisimilitude in sacred images, both Paleotti and Borromeo justify and sanction the validity of Christian iconography: when reasonable, and sometimes even when inaccurate, the tradition of figurative formulas through which scripture had been visualized over the centuries must be preserved. Modifying the tradition would unsettle the viewer. In fact, Christian iconography had complemented and even replaced the authority of scripture: it had become a scriptural para-text. Yet, acknowledging the exceptional validity of visual habits in relation to sacred images led to theoretical inconsistency. First of all, if one adopts this principle, it follows that truth ceases to be the universal parameter of sacred representations. As I have shown, the true must surrender at times to tradition: that is, to the uncertainties of the verisimilar or the dictates of decorum. Secondly, in order to safeguard the image's orthodoxy, painters must work with figurative clichés and stereotypes. Once again, novelty is at risk, or at least at a farther remove. Needless to say, artists would find many ways to circumvent the threadbare fixity of Christian iconography, the more so because they were not facing a rigid system of norms, but guidelines that, if interpreted in their context, proved to be occasionally contradictory. As I have already said, Paleotti extols truth in painting while simultaneously championing its uncertain surrogate: verisimilitude. If Paleotti insists that images should act violently upon man's senses, especially sight, Borromeo instead likens pictures to orations, thereby describing them as rhetorical pieces: not devices reproducing the real or transliterating scripture faithfully, but fictions communicating the Christian truth's essence through adornments and magnifications. The fluctuations and occasional paralogisms characterizing Paleotti's or Borromeo's discussion of sacred images grant painters a certain latitude of options. At will, they can choose different models of representation, design strategies toward captivating specific audiences, and juggle with the theological truth and verisimilitude in order to achieve pictorial novelty. From this point of view, Caravaggio's rendition of sacred history does not differ from that of his contemporaries in Rome. All of them would exploit the chasm between the principles and the biases of the clergy with regard to religious images. The only pictorial criterion Paleotti, Borromeo or any other theorist of the Counter-Reformation would have never forgone is that of intelligibility. In explaining falseness in painting, Paleotti points out:

> Some tend to consider [falseness] a disproportion of many things together, when they are not assigned to their own place, as would be the case with a potter who, in making a vase, puts the bottom where the opening should be. It also applies to the painter who does not place the figures in accordance with their status and dignity, relegating to the margins what should figure at the center, and neglecting what is the *istoria*'s main goal by giving more relevance to what does not truly matter, which therefore stands out in greater view.[17]

16   Paleotti, 120-1: "Così possiamo dire delle pitture che, se bene non si troveranno tutte conformi alle parole sacre, non però si averanno a chiamare apocrife, purché siano conformi alla autorità de' santi padri ed uso universale della chiesa, ed in soma abbiano le condizioni che disse il Lirinense ricercasi alle cose ecclesiastiche, cioè *quod probatae fuerint semper unique et apud omnes*; sì come per essempio, non ci è Evangelista che dica che quando Nostro Signore fu crocefisso, gli fossero coperte le parti pudenda di alcun panno o velo, e nientedimeno è cosa tanto ragionevole e tanto frequentata già da tutti i secoli nella cristianità che il volere mettere in dubbio questo pareria quasi una impietà; nella nonziazione della gloriosa Vergine, quando l'arcangelo Gabriele la salutò, non dice la Scrittura quello che allora facesse la Madonna, se caminava o sedeva o cusciva o operava altro, nientedimeno tutti i pittori sempre hanno concordato che ella fosse genuflessa intenta all'orazione, e così ci abbiamo a persuadere che fosse; non dice lo Evangelio quando il Salvator nostro fanciullo con la madre e san Gioseffo fuggì in Egitto, se andassero a piedi o a cavallo o come, nientedimeno communemente dipingono i pittori la Madonna sopra l'asinello co 'l figliuolino in braccio, che è così ragionevole che fosse, essendo la Beata Vergine ancora tenera, e dovendo fare viaggio così longo, ed essendo usanza che le altre donne andassero in quel modo."

17   Ibidem, 187: "Si suol considerare da alcuni quella ancor

By the same token, Paleotti criticizes any element in the composition that would steer the viewer's attention away from the principal subject:

> Others pinpoint another type of disproportion relative to the whole composition when images, especially ones that are sacred or relating grave matters, combine with things that are beside the point and completely unrelated to the main action. These things the Greeks call accessories (πάρεργα), as would be the case if, in depicting our Lord at the column, one added to the side, albeit at a distance and in perspective, a child playing with a dog, or a battle of birds, or a peasant catching frogs, or whatever else painters might imagine without caring if this corresponds to the subject at hand.[18]

Paleotti's condemnation of misplacements and accessories in painting should be taken very seriously, since it betrays his profound concern with intelligibility, that is, with painting's anagogic and didactic function. Like authors and professors, painters must know how to elucidate "their concepts and subjects, however lofty or difficult" by making them "plain and intelligible to all" with an easy style of representation.[19] Here is what occurs when painters, on the contrary, disregard intelligibility:

> It happens every day that one sees in many places, and especially in churches, paintings so obscure and ambiguous that, instead of enlightening the intellect, arousing piety and moving the heart, they through their obscurity confuse the mind, distract it in infinite directions and keep it busy second-guessing what the figure might be, and this fosters a loss of devotion. As a result, even that bit of good intention with which one goes to church disappears, and often one takes one thing for another, to such a degree that, instead of being instructed, one remains confused or deceived.[20]

According to Paleotti, there are three substantial reasons for these "disorders" or anomalies in painting: painters' ill will, ignorance or incapability. It is particularly interesting to browse through Paleotti's arguments with regard to deliberate obscurity:

> As for the lack of will, it sounds strange that there might exist people who love obscurity and not being understood, and yet it is what happens. On account of his impenetrability, Heraklitos in antiquity was called the obscure (σκοτινός), and Quintilian reports that there was an orator who taught his disciples solely to obscure their speech, repeating:

---

per sproporziuone di più cose insieme, quando non sono distribuite a' suoi propri luoghi, non altrimente che faria un vasaio mettendo il fondo dove va la bocca del vaso. Così aviene quando il pittore non dà il luoco alle cose che figura, secondo la condizione e dignità loro, e mette da i lati quello che dovria esser posto in mezo: overo pretermettendo quello che è lo scopo principale dell'istoria, pone maggior diligenza in quello che non importa tanto, facendolo apparire più a gli occhi."

18 Ibidem, 187-8: "Un'altra sproporzione ancora rispetto al tutto pongono alcuni quando con le imagini massimamente sacre o di cose gravi s'aggiongono altre che sono fuori di quello soggetto, e che non hanno a fare punto con l'opera principale; le quali i greci chiamano πάρεργα, come seria dipingendosi il Signor Nostro quando alla colonna, l'aggiongervi da un lato, se bene con disegno di lontana prospettiva, un putto che scherza con un cane, o una battaglia d'ucelli, o un contadino che pesca ranocchi, o altre simil cose che s'imaginano i pittori, non avendo risguardo se ciò corrisponde a quello che hanno per le mani."

19 Ibidem, 209-10: "Una delle principali laudi che sogliono darsi ad uno autore o professore di qualche scienza è che egli sappia chiaramente esplicare i suoi concetti e le materie, se bene alte e difficili, renderle co 'l suo facil modo di parlare intelligibili a tutti e piane. Il medesimo possiamo affermare in universale del pittore, e tanto più quanto l'opere sue servono principalmente per libro de gl'idioti, alli quali bisogna sempre parlare aperto e chiaro."

20 Ibidem, 210: "A che non avertendosi da diversi, accade che ogni giorno si veggono in vari luoghi, e massimamente nelle chiese, pitture così oscure ed ambigue ch'ove doveriano, illuminando l'intelletto, eccitare insieme la divozione e pungere il cuore, elle con la loro oscurità confondono per modo la mente che la distraeno in mille parti e la tengono occupata in disputare tra se stessa quale sia quella figura, non senza perdita della divozione; onde ne fugge quel poco di buono pensiero che si era portato alla chiesa, e spesse volte si piglia una cosa per un'altra, talmente che in luogo di essere ammaestrato, si resta confuso o ingannato."

"σκότισον, σκότισον," which means: "blur it, blur it." In this respect, however, one must be aware that there are two types of intentional obscurities: the first is found to be used in ancient times by Hebrews, Egyptians, as well as by philosophers and others when they set out to speak about sacred matters, and this they called mysteries in the sense of "concealing" signified by the Greek word. In fact, they thought that God's great mystery should not be uncovered to the profane multitudes, but ought to be dealt with through enigmas and parables, of which our faith's holy Fathers approve in the major mysteries (…). But the theologian's reasons do not really apply to painters, who in religious matters represent but what our holy Fathers propose, which is consensually accepted by the Church. Therefore, painters should not add, diminish or alter anything that has been thus approved, neither in substance, nor in its modality or circumstances. I shall now pass on to the second type of intentional obscurity, which is criticized because at times it springs from one's hidden presumption or exhibited vanity of being held grand and marvelous: one thus treats or depicts not trifles, but sublime concepts as if derived from heaven. This obscurity is pure nonsense, not only because it is practiced for one's own sake and reputation, but also because it perverts the procedure of the science or art that one tackles.[21]

Without examining other factors of abstruseness[22]—for instance, painters tend to obscure their works through excessive concision—I will proceed immediately to Paleotti's antidote to these pictorial "disorders":

> Good painters must especially determine in their mind to benefit others and to do so in an appropriate manner, depicting those circumstances that are necessary and eschewing equivocations and other ambiguous figures as much as possible. (…) In order to resolve a question in any science, he who sorts out and analyzes its various points is more successful, and through his distinctions appeases altogether the intellect in suspension. Similarly, a painter who, in treating many sacred stories and mysteries, has the wise idea of ordering the subjects by separating them into various paintings or spaces—refraining as much as possible from piling up and squeezing together innumerable figures and actions, which confuses both the sight and the intellect— doubtless satisfies everyone and shows judgment and competence to a higher degree.[23]

21   Ibidem, 210-11: "Quanto al non volere, dovria parere strano che si trovino persone le quali amino l'essere oscure e di non essere intese, ed è pur così, onde anticamente fu nominato Eraclito σκοτινός dalla oscurità, e narra Quintiliano che fu già un retore, il quale non insegnava altro a' suoi discepoli ch'oscurare il parlare, dicendo 'σκότισον, σκότισον,' che vuol dire oscuralo, oscuralo. Ma in questo si ha da avertire che ci sono due sorti di questa oscurità che nasce da volontà, la prima si trova essere stata osservata sino da gli ebrei, da gli egizzi, da filosofi e da altri, quando volevano parlare delle cose sacre, che per ciò chiamarono misteri per il senso che ha la parola greca che è di occultare, giudicando essi che gli alti secreti di Dio non si avessero da scoprire alla profana moltitudine, ma più tosto con enigmi e sensi parabolici da trattarsi, il che da i santi dottori nostri è admesso ne i misteri maggiori della religione nostra (…). Ma questa ragione de' teologi non può avere molto luoco ne i pittori, i quali nelle cose sacre solamente rappresentano quello che si truova essere proposto da i santi dottori ed accettato dal commune consenso della chiesa, non aggiongendone né diminuendo né alterando punto quello che da essi è stato approvato, né quanto alla sostanza né quanto al modo o altre sue circonstanze. Però passeremo all'altra forma di oscurità procurata, la quale viene biasimata per che nasce alle volte da una occulta superbia ed afettata vanità di esser tenuto grande e meraviglioso, poi che non parla o non dipinge cose triviali, ma concetti sublimi e cavati come dal terzo cielo; la quale è una stolidità sciocchissima, non solo perché non ha per fine se non la propria e vana riputazione, ma ancor perché pervertisce il modo di quella scienza o arte che tratta."

22   Ibidem, 211: "Altre volte perché si vuol essere breve, e con poche parole o spazio abbracciare molto, onde ne segue quel detto volgare: *brevis esse laboro, obscurus fio.*"

23   Ibidem, 211-2: "Però per fuggire l'uno e l'altro, doverà il buon pittore avere proponimento nell'animo di volere giovare principalmente a gli altri, e tenere ancora modo a ciò fare conveniente, esprimendo le circostanze necessarie e fuggendo l'equivocazioni o altre figure ambigue più che si potrà. (…). E sì come a volere s[ci]ogliere bene una questione di alcuna scienza, chi va distinguendo e considerando vari capi riesce molto meglio e con quelle distinzioni quieta affatto l'intelletto

It is noteworthy that Paleotti assimilates paintings to theological arguments. Just as theology approaches and increasingly unveils the divine truth, proceeding through deductions or inductions articulated into syllogisms, so too should painting lead viewers to induce or deduce God's truth progressively, from one figure of the *istoria* to the next, in the clearest and most unequivocal manner. To be sure, Paleotti's position in this regard is utopian. Technically it is almost an insurmountable challenge to construct a picture as a visual syllogism. In his 1570 commentary to Aristotle's *Poetics*, Lodovico Castelvetro demonstrates that poetry is not suitable to carry out philosophy's tasks. Nor does it lend itself to perform as a philosophical discourse. The same could easily apply to painting and theology. Castelvetro notes that poetry is intrinsically the domain of verisimilitude; the truth it foreshadows is revealed only indirectly or allegorically.[24] As I have already emphasized, both Paleotti and Borromeo nonetheless recognize that painting cannot function without verisimilitude. Furthermore, images may require amplifications and adornments that exceed the nature of the theological discourse.

But even if painters cannot bend the picture to the principles of theology, it is still imperative that their narratives be perfectly legible and intelligible. From this prospect, the Counter-Reformation theorists go even farther than their Renaissance counterparts: clarity is no longer an aesthetic or rhetorical necessity; it is the *sine qua non* of art's pedagogy and morality. Regardless of the audience to which it is destined, whether the "happy few" of the clerical hierarchy or the larger mass of believers, the sacred image cannot afford obscurity, ambiguity, or contrived ingenuity. It is not the realm of conceptual wonder, but of devotional compunction and moral persuasion.

As I shall demonstrate, it is no coincidence that Caravaggio's *Calling of Saint Matthew* is instead devised as a narrative mechanism of latent obscurities: from the spatial layout to the chiaroscuro setting; from the cause-and-effect interrelations to the protagonists' ungraspable or eclipsed roles. Every element of the composition allows for second-guessing or, to paraphrase Paleotti, "keeps [the mind] busy" wondering who the main figure might be or what it might be doing. It would be excessive to assimilate Caravaggio to Quintilian's orator, who nagged his disciples to keep blurring their speech. But there is no doubt that, at the very moment that he confronts his first prestigious public commission, Caravaggio baffles his audience by offering a refined visualization of "equivocations" in such a simple form: to the left, a table of accountants and young men; to the right, the irruption of Christ and an apostle, the figures circumscribed by nothing but a rectangular box pierced through a window and lit by a powerful stream of oblique sunshine.

Neither is it a coincidence that in his *Conversion of Saint Paul* for the Cerasi Chapel—which Bellori would define as devoid of any action whatsoever —the viewer's gaze is filled with the impressive bulk of a steed, whereas the saint's supine body encroaches on the canvas' lower margin, as if exiting the scene. Perhaps Caravaggio does not behave here like the potter of Paleotti's metaphor, shaping the vase upside down, but he undoubtedly overturns the divine hero's centrality as requested of the *istoria* by substituting a horse for the saint—in lieu of the protagonist, a potential accessory (πάρεργον). As I will illustrate in Chapter 8, the Gospel does not mention the steed, whose insertion is defined by Paleotti as reasonable verisimilitude.

Finally, in his London *Supper at Emmaus*, Caravaggio does not disdain the figurative clichés that he inherited from the Venetian tradition in depicting the subject: Christ at the center, the two apostles almost symmetrically at either side, the innkeeper apparently peering as the Savior blesses the bread. But the master does so not to enforce clarity and foster legibility; here instead

---

ch'è sospeso, così sono molte istorie sacre e misteri i quali se il pittore averà questo giudicio di andarli compartendo con ordine e distinguerle in vari quadri o spazi, e si asterenà più che potrà di ammassare ed inculcare una moltitudine di figure e di azzioni, le quali confondono la vista e l'intelletto, senza dubbio più sodisfarà a tutti e darà maggiormente segno di giudicio e di perizia."

24 See for instance Castelvetro, 1: 45: "Quindi ancora si comprende che scienza o arte non può essere materia di poesia, né si possono con lode rinchiudere in poema, conciosia cosa che la scienza e l'arte, già considerate e comprese per ragioni necessarie e verisimili e per lunga esperienza da filosofi e da artisti, tengano il luogo d'istoria e di cose già avenute quanto è al poeta."

he stages a clash of iconographies that would dismantle the narrative and temporal structure of the sacred *istoria*. With its iconographic intermittences, its segmented temporality, and its unstable spatiality, the London picture is in a certain sense antipodal to the sacred image for which Paleotti or Borromeo might have wished.

In light of these observations, how is it still legitimate to consider Caravaggio a painter of the Catholic Counter-Reformation? I do not deny that the three paintings I will shortly explore to a certain extent constitute exceptional cases. To be sure, other works by Caravaggio may feel less rebellious or eccentric. But even so, how can modern scholars still claim that Caravaggio's painting is about inspiring devotion? The pictorial "anomalies" Caravaggio inserts into his sacred images do not merely qualify as instruments of wonder and captors of attention. As I have already pointed out in Part One, the master's use of graphic effects—his realism—does not definitely aim at enhancing the beholder's piety. It surely "violates" the spectator's senses, but not in the way Paleotti advocates. On the other hand, there is certainly a great deal of conceptualism in Caravaggio's works. Nevertheless, this conceptualism is not pursued for its own sake, for the pleasure of bewildering the viewer, but serves to reassess the divine, to investigate its *modus operandi*, and to put to the test the very foundation of the Counter-Reformation discourse on art: the didactic function of sacred images.

Through his pictures, Caravaggio exhibits the fracture between the Christian truth and its visual translation. His painting thrives along the lines of a discontinuity between dogma and fiction. When it comes to narrating, the divine and the human operate on two different levels. The painter can attempt, even pretend, to sew them together to make visual sense, but by doing so, he weakens and trivializes the import of the encounter between the two orders. For one thing, as Caravaggio demonstrates through his pictorial dislocations, the divine, along with its operational logic, challenges and clouds man's senses and intellect. In Caravaggio's painting, divinity repudiates clarity and acts obscurely: in its unfolding, it surpasses man's understanding. Looking at the divine through Caravaggio's lens implies renouncing art's pedagogic mission and doubting the visual heuristics that Counter-Reformation theorists construe as painting's innermost objective. Indeed, scripture's sense and meaning do not necessarily lie where the Church and iconographic tradition have lodged them. This discrepancy is the reason for the inherently desacralizing charge of Caravaggio's religious narratives, not because his paintings deny God's presence and intervention, but because they expose man's limits in sensing, recognizing, and interpreting divinity.

In this perspective, it will come as no surprise that the three pictures that form the object of the following analyses concern a critical seventeenth-century notion in the relationship between man and God: divine grace. Both *The Calling of Saint Matthew* and the *Conversion of Saint Paul* enact the traumatic encounter of Christ and an apostle. Both are paintings of enlightenment. Similarly, the London *Supper at Emmaus* pivots on man's blindness in identifying divinity. Christ's crucial epiphany through disappearance likewise ranks as an act of divine grace. It goes without saying that I am intimately persuaded of Caravaggio's religiousness. As I will show several times in the course of this book, many of his sacred narratives involve an extreme and quintessential interrogation about divinity, its manifestation, and the procedures through which painting represents it. Once again, I ought to distinguish between religiousness and devotion. Caravaggio's pictorial reassessment of the divine does not align with the practices of the devout painter as established by the Counter-Reformation Church. If Paleotti thought of sacred images as analogs of theological arguments, which traditionally relied on post-Aristotelian and Thomistic methods of reasoning, Caravaggio structured his religious narratives with a view to defying and inhibiting any pre-determined logic of arguing divinity through the figurative. Not only does the *istoria* as interpreted by Caravaggio disrupt the principles of Aristotelian mimesis, but Caravaggio's visual interpretation of the Catholic God also contradicts the neo-Aristotelian tenets on which the dogmas of the Counter-Reformation Church solidly rested during his lifetime.

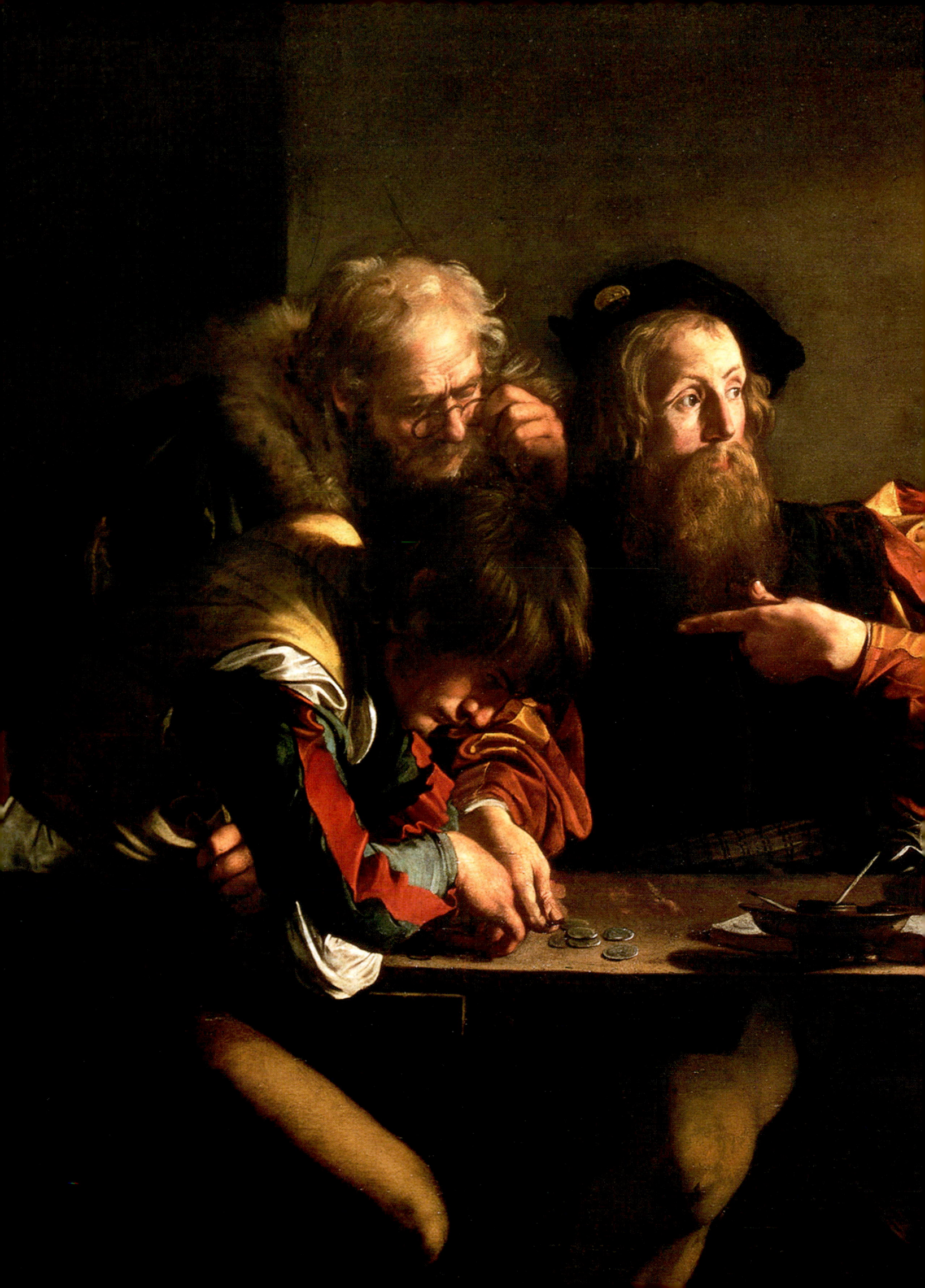

CHAPTER 7

The Calling of Saint Matthew in Retrospective: Experimenting with Narrative Disconnections

Fame and Controversy

Much has been said and written about the painting that established Caravaggio's name in early seventeenth-century Rome: *The Calling of Saint Matthew* (Fig. 90). Nor am I the first to argue that the picture is imbued with ambiguity on multiple levels. Where appropriate I shall acknowledge scholars' pertinent contributions to the understanding of *The Calling*, but I am convinced that much more still remains to be said about the painting. Indeed, a great deal of evidence waits to be culled, analyzed, and exploited. In this chapter, I intend to look at *The Calling of Saint Matthew* through the lens of early seventeenth-century first-rank painters, from Ludovico Carracci to Bartolomeo Manfredi, from Hendrick ter Brugghen to Matthias Stomer and Bernardo Strozzi.[1] In my opinion, the painting not only fascinated these artists, but also puzzled them to the point that, by elaborating upon Caravaggio's invention, they attempted either to interpret and clarify its multi-layered ambiguities, or expand upon and showcase them in full view. In other words, I firmly believe that the most efficient method to approach *The Calling* is a retrospective analysis of it. But first I need to reconstruct the picture's history and recapitulate scholars' most relevant interpretations in this regard.

No work by Caravaggio is better documented than the two companion pieces that he executed for the Contarelli Chapel in the French national church of Rome, San Luigi dei Francesi.[2] On 23 July 1599, the master received a down payment of 50 *scudi* for two large oil paintings, *The Calling of Saint Matthew* and *The Martyrdom of Saint Matthew*, destined for the chapel's lateral walls.[3] There is no doubt that he had already started working on this prestigious commission before this transaction. On 4 July 1600, Caravaggio obtained a final payment of 50 *scudi*: the outstanding remnant of the 400 *scudi* at which the paintings had been originally priced.[4] By the time the final receipt was issued,

---

1 To my knowledge, only two scholars have investigated the ways in which early seventeenth-century painters developed the iconographic formula inaugurated by Caravaggio in the Contarelli *Calling of Saint Matthew*: Burgard 1998 and Von Rosen 2009. I read Von Rosen's analysis after I had completed this chapter. Although Von Rosen examines some of the paintings on which I dwell here, her reading is rather broad and aims to establish which of the figures represents Matthew in Caravaggio's painting, a problem that is of lesser concern to me. In Von Rosen's view, the specificity of Caravaggio's *Calling of Saint Matthew* resides in its manipulation of the episode's temporality: instead of representing the climax of the depicted action, Caravaggio depicts the moment before the conversion. In this way, according to Von Rosen, Caravaggio enhances the perception of the Aristotelian "peripety." However pithy, Von Rosen's approach to the painting's narrative is in my view simplistic.

2 In addition to the sources I quote in this chapter, see also Mancini, 1:82, 124. For the painting, see Hess J. 1951;

Mahon 1953b; Bousquet 1953; Joffroy 1959, 300-18; Röttgen 1964 [reprinted and translated into Italian in Röttgen 1974, 11-44]; Röttgen 1965 [reprinted and translated into Italian in Röttgen 1974, 47-75]; Friedlaender 1969, 101-16; Röttgen 1969 [reprinted and translated into Italian in Röttgen 1974, 79-127]; Dell'Acqua and Cinotti 1971; Moir 1982, 92-4; De Marco 1982; Cinotti 1983, 525-33, no. 61; Hibbard 1983, 91-117; Prater 1985; Thomas T., 1985; Kretschmer 1988; Hass 1988; Treffers 1989; Calvesi 1990, 36-8, 280-2; Röttgen 1991; Lavin 1993; Prater 1995; Gilbert 1995, 159-89; Askew 1996, esp. 249-50; Pupillo 1996; Raabe 1996: 78-87; Burgard 1998; Puttfarken 1998; Puglisi 1998, 154-62; Longhi 1999-2000, 1: 147-50 [1951], 210-1 [1952], 258-63 [1968]; Schütze I. 2000; Marini 2005, 430-44, nos. 35-7, and 463-7, nos. 52-3; Varriano 2006, 111; Ebert-Schifferer 2009, 128-30; Schütze 2009, 97-110, 258-9, no. 24.I; and Von Rosen 2009, 241-68.

3 Macioce 2003, 77-9.

4 Ibidem, 86.

◄ Plate X: Michelangelo Merisi da Caravaggio, *The Calling of Saint Matthew*, Contarelli Chapel, San Luigi dei Francesi, Rome, oil on canvas, 322 x 340 cm., detail.

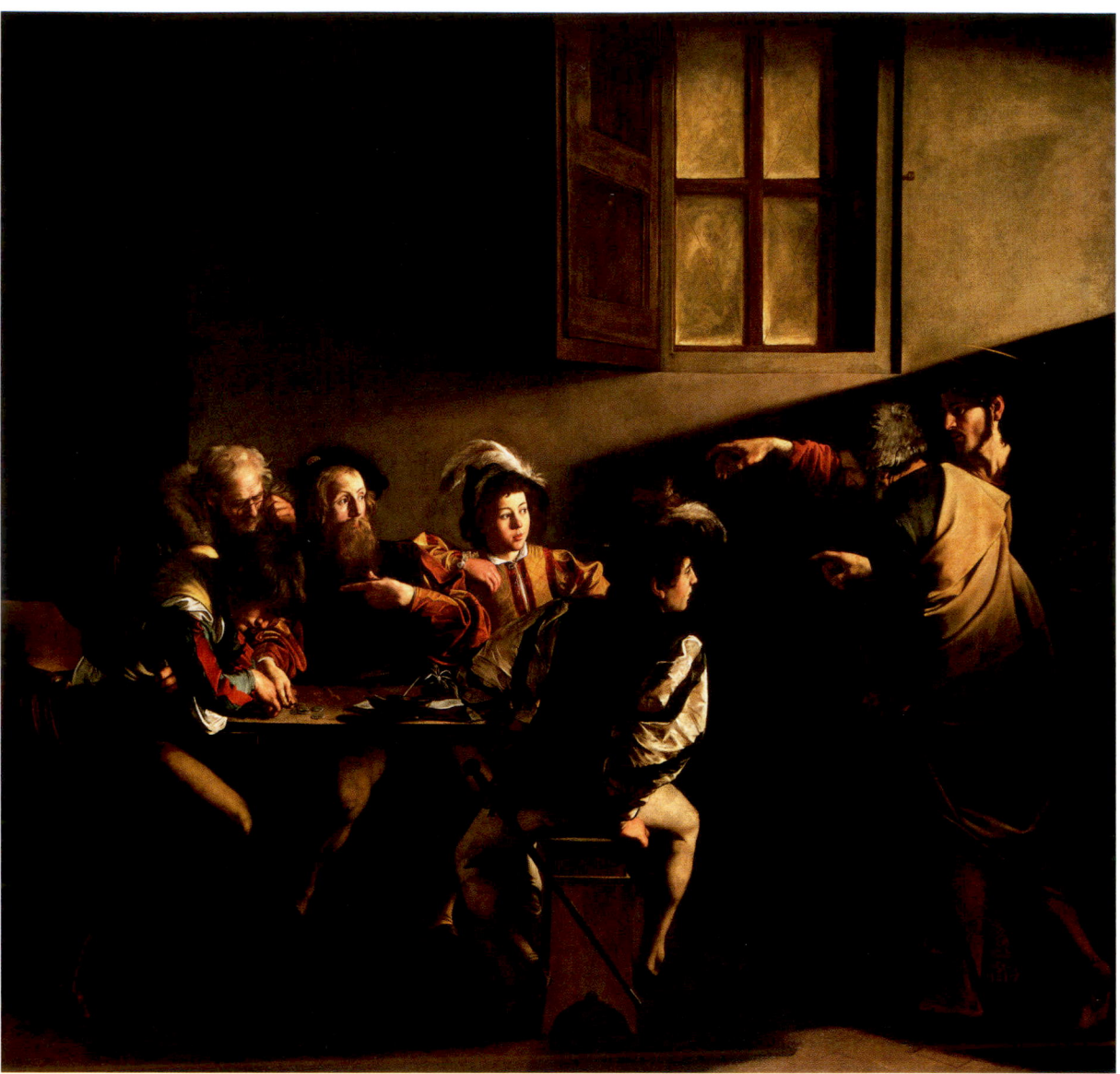

Fig. 90
Michelangelo Merisi da Caravaggio, *The Calling of Saint Matthew*, Contarelli Chapel, San Luigi dei Francesi, Rome, oil on canvas, 322 x 340 cm.

Caravaggio's pictures had already been installed in their frames in the Contarelli Chapel. According to Giovanni Baglione (1642), it was Cardinal Francesco Maria Del Monte, the owner of Caravaggio's Rome *Fortune Teller* and *The Cardsharps*, who recommended the young master for the job.[5] If one trusts Baglione's testimony, then one must deduce that Padre Berlingherio, the delegate of the *Fabbrica di San Pietro* in charge of the chapel's decoration, and Pietro Paolo Crescenzi, testamentary executor of Cardinal Matthieu Cointrel—the French prelate to whom the chapel had been assigned, and whose name had been Italianized as Contarelli—heeded Del Monte's suggestion. At any rate, they hired Caravaggio to replace the Cavalier d'Arpino who had been charged with the chapel's pictorial decoration on 27 May 1591, but had only completed the dome fresco—*Saint Matthew Resurrecting the Daughter of the Ethiopian King Egyppus*—and four *Prophets*, two on either side of the

5 Baglione, 136-7: "Per opera del suo cardinale ebbe in San Luigi de' Francesi la cappella de' Contarelli, ove sopra l'altare fece il San Matteo con un angelo; a man dritta, quando l'apostolo è chiamato dal Redentore, ed a man manca, quando su l'altare è ferito dal carnefice con altre figure."

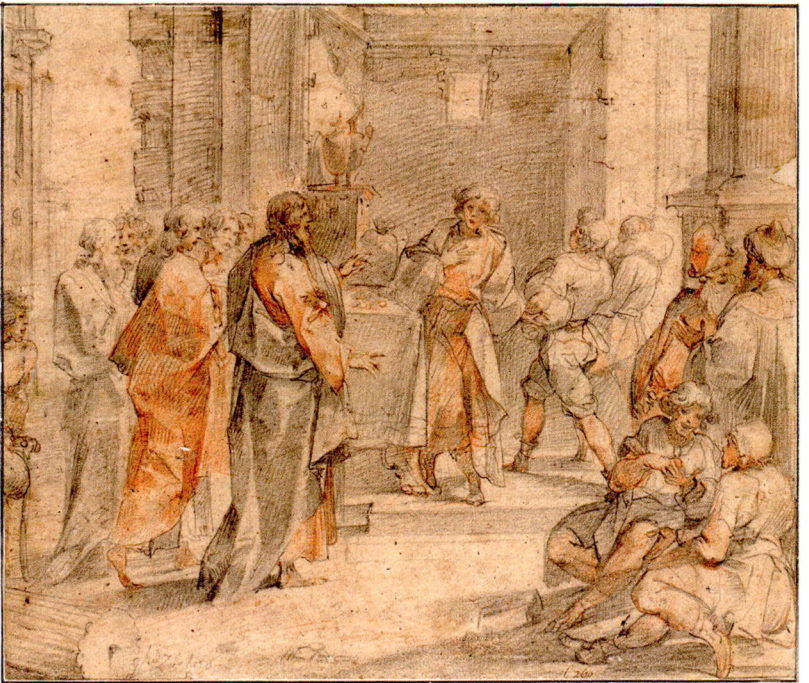

Fig. 91
Cavalier d'Arpino (Giuseppe Cesari), *The Calling of Saint Matthew*, Albertina, Vienna, black and red chalk, 22.3 x 26.4 cm.

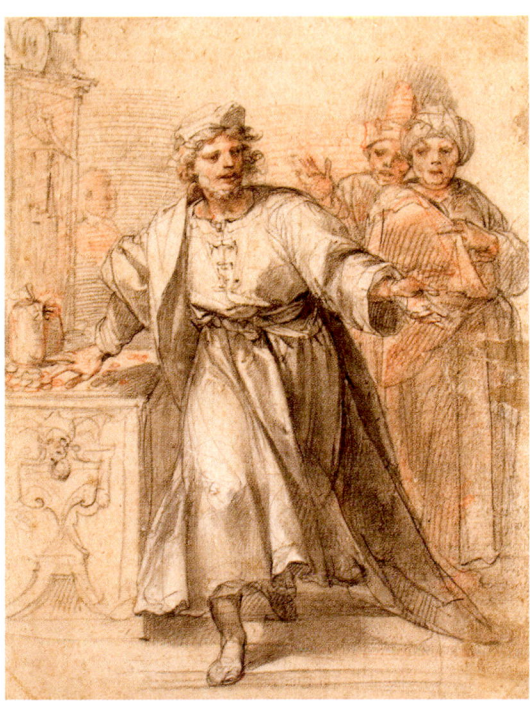

Fig. 92
Cavalier d'Arpino (Giuseppe Cesari), *Study for the Figure of Saint Matthew*, Holkham Hall, Lord Leicester's Collection, black and red chalk, 26.7 x 20.5 cm.

upper lateral walls.[6] Before his death in 1585, Cardinal Contarelli had determined and extensively described the subjects of the paintings that Caravaggio would depict nearly two decades later: to the right of the altar, Matthew's martyrdom, and to the left his vocation. In the latter painting, as Contarelli himself wrote in a note subsequently annexed to the Cavalier d'Arpino's 1591 contract, the saint was to figure "in a storehouse or hall where taxes are collected, with various props pertaining to this profession such as the counter used by tax-collectors, account books, and money, a certain sum of which he [will] appear to have just collected, or however it might seem better. Saint Matthew, dressed in a manner appropriate to his office, will rise from the counter eager to join Our Lord who, passing in the street with his disciples, calls him to the apostolate. And in Saint Matthew's act, as well as in the rest, the painter will show his artistry."[7]

It is often mentioned that the Cavalier d'Arpino, in whose workshop Caravaggio had begun his Roman career around 1595, had already made a few sketches in preparation for *The Calling*. In a sanguine and black chalk drawing now at the Albertina, Vienna, he staged a grandiose setting for the episode: a high-ceilinged hall supported by majestic columns, only partially visible, on pedestals, and a slightly elevated recess or alcove from which the soon-to-be apostle, relinquishing the table, heads toward Christ by pointing a finger to his chest (Fig. 91).[8] Escorted by his disciples, his face in profile, the Savior, on the left, singles out Matthew by raising his left hand toward him. To the right, two seated and two standing figures converse, oblivious to the miracle. Behind Matthew, two

6   For these works, see more recently Röttgen 2002, 249-53, nos. 29, 29.1, 29.2.

7   Röttgen 1964, 208: "Al lato destro dell'altare, cioè alla banda del Vangelio, si facci un quadro alto palmi dicesette et largo palmi quattordici di vano, nel quale sia medesimamente dipinto San Matteo dentro un magazeno, o ver salone ad uso di gabella, con diverse robbe che convengono a tal officio, con un banco come usano i gabellieri, con i libri et danari, in atto d'haver riscosso qualche somma o come meglio parerà, dal qual banco San Matteo, vestito secondo che parerà convenirsi a quell'arte, si levi con desiderio per venire a Nostro Signore che, passando lungo la strada con i suoi discepoli, lo chiama all'apostolato, et nell'atto di San Matteo si ha da dimostrare l'artificio del pittore, come anco nel resto." This passage is also transcribed extensively in Marini 2005, 432.

8   For the drawing, see Röttgen 2002, 250, no. 29g.

men exit the scene. This group of two figures might have inspired Caravaggio in his representation of two onlookers departing at the left of the *Martyrdom of Saint Matthew*: as is well known, one of them bears the master's likeness. In another drawing executed with the same technique (Holkham Hall, Lord Leicester's Collection; Fig. 92), the Cavalier d'Arpino isolated the figure of Matthew by rendering him as rushing suddenly toward the Lord, his robe swaying around his thighs and legs, his right hand open as if he had just dropped the coins that lie strewn over the counter while his head is directed toward the right off-scene.[9] Evidently d'Arpino planned to shift the figure of Christ rightward, as Caravaggio would do in his version of *The Calling*. At this point, I stress solely that in both cases d'Arpino followed Contarelli's instructions literally: the moment represented, the saint's gesture and expression, the crowd of apostles around Christ's figure, and the architectural setting correspond to the late cardinal's wishes. As d'Arpino's assistant, Caravaggio must have known these and other designs that the master might have prepared to illustrate the episode. As I shall demonstrate, he deliberately deviated from d'Arpino's formulaic decorum and narrative straightforwardness.

As soon as they were put on display, Caravaggio's two paintings stirred the awe and admiration of young painters. Baglione, who hated Caravaggio for personal reasons and disliked his pictures on account of what he considered to be their inherent vileness, maliciously attributed their success to the presence in the chapel of d'Arpino's dull frescoes, recording, as if to underscore the point, Federico Zuccari's veiled condemnation of *The Calling*. In front of the painting and in Baglione's presence, Zuccari allegedly exclaimed: "what is all this fuss about? I do not see here anything but Giorgione's idea."[10] I will return to this comment shortly. Despite Zuccari's affected indifference and Baglione's jealousy, *The Calling of Saint Matthew* was immediately submitted to closer scrutiny, re-elaborated several times over the following two decades, and most probably intensely discussed by numerous artists. In 1600 or 1601, the jurisconsult Marzio Milesi composed a few epigrams in honor of Caravaggio, the longest one devoted to the paintings in San Luigi dei Francesi. It is important to quote here the verses related to *The Calling*:

> Here is my beloved guide [my Muse] who supports my poem,
> Exhorting me to begin. I already see my Lord
> As he comes to convert publicans and sinners;
> Upon his first appearance he frees
> And enlightens Matthew's mind that,
> Greedy and blind, was constrained in the world
> By harsh chains. Jesus glows in such way
> That he pushes the viewers' eyes and minds to look
> At him again, and seems to make the mortals'
> Souls blissful. If he is like this on earth
> Through the artist's work and brush,
> How will he then appear in heaven![11]

9   For the drawing, see Ibidem, no. 29h.

10   Baglione, 137: "Quest'opera, per avere alcune pitture del naturale e per essere in compagnia d'altre fatte dal cavalier Gioseppe, che con la sua virtù si aveva presso i professori qualche invidia acquistata, fece gioco alla fama del Caravaggio, ed era da' maligni sommamente lodata. Pur venendovi a vederla Federico Zucchero mentre io era presente, disse: 'Che rumore è questo?' e guardando il tutto diligentemente soggiunse: 'Io non ci vedo altro che il pensiero di Giorgione nella tavola del santo quando Cristo il chiamò all'apostolato,' e soghignando e maravigliandosi di tanto rumore, voltò le spalle ed andossene con Dio."

11   These verses were first published by Fulco 1980, 88. See Macioce 2003, 101: "Ecco ch'a cominciare hormai m'invita,/ E che regge il mio dire amata scorta,/ E già veggio il mio Christo, ch'a chiamare/ E' publicani venne e peccatori,/ Come al primo apparir sgombra e rischiara/ La mente di Mattheo, ch'ingorda e cieca/ Si stava al mondo in duri lacci avvolta,/ E Giesù che risplende in guisa tale/ Ch'a rimirarlo attrahe gl'occhi e le menti/ De' risguardanti, e par beati renda/ De' mortali gli spirti. Et tal s'è in terra/ D'artefice per opra e di pennello,/ A rivederlo in cielo hor che fia, dunque?"

Needless to say, Milesi's poetic talent is scant, and his praise of Caravaggio's picture highly topical, to say the least. Yet, in my view, his verses are worth considering for they contain a tacit defense of *The Calling*.[12] By insisting on Christ's radiance, pivotal role, and charge of attraction in the painting, Milesi definitely exaggerates (if he does not quite lie about) the figure's centrality and clarity of expression. If one read his text without knowing the picture, one would never imagine that an unidentified apostle—commonly identified with Peter—to a remarkable extent occludes Christ's figure through the foil of his revolving body: a half-toned visual graft that interferes with, slows down, and in a sense impedes the beholder's ability to spot the Savior (Fig. 233).[13] Likewise, one would never realize that Jesus' glowing face is partly obscured through the cleavage of a shadow descending from his forehead to his chin, plunging his eye and mouth into a warm penumbra, while his hand lingers aloft in splendid isolation. In light of these facts, one must believe that Milesi either paid little attention to the painting or purposefully extolled Christ's brilliance in order to defend Caravaggio from an all too predictable objection with regard to the well established principle of intelligibility in the *istoria*: the evident opacity of the hero's figure, which in this case also happens to incarnate the very effigy of God. It would not be surprising that such criticism, among others, was directed at *The Calling* from the time that it was inaugurated and that it encountered both the approbation and censure of many painters.

At any rate, in his 1672 *Vite* Giovan Pietro Bellori surprisingly did not remark upon any defect in his laconic description of the painting:

> To the right of the altar, there is Christ calling Saint Matthew to the apostolate; he [Caravaggio] depicted some faces from life, among which that of the saint who, ceasing to count the money, turns to the Lord bringing his hand over his chest; nearby an elderly man rests his glasses on his nose, looking at a young man who, sitting at the edge of the table, shifts the coins toward himself.[14]

It is noteworthy that Bellori disregarded whole sections of the picture, including the pair of youths at the center of the composition, not to mention the figure of Peter to the right. If he disapproved of the visual form Caravaggio gave the biblical episode, he did not explicitly say as much. He merely criticized the companion piece, *The Martyrdom*, whose "composition and motions do not match the *istoria*," adding that—probably for the best—the gloomy chapel and Caravaggio's dark palette made it impossible to discern the paintings clearly.[15] However, Bellori's silence on the subject of some primordial aspects of *The Calling* should not be deemed fortuitous. The elusive phrasing of his description, and even more than this his fixation on what he undoubtedly regarded as anecdotal

---

12 Bologna 1992, 70, rightly stresses that Milesi's verses allude to "mistakes and neglects" present in Caravaggio's paintings for San Luigi dei Francesi. Bologna nevertheless believes that these allusions specifically concern the first version of Caravaggio's *Saint Matthew and the Angel*, once in Berlin, and destroyed at the end of the Second World War.

13 In this regard, see Hibbard 1983, 100: "The removal of Christ to a secondary plane, like the Michelangelesque quotation, were afterthoughts that make the picture more perverse, with the protagonist half-hidden at the far side of the canvas"; Puttfarken 1998, 169: "Christ's head and hand in the *Calling of Saint Matthew* are among Caravaggio's most impressive and dramatic inventions. Accompanied by the sharp shaft of light, they are the cause, the driving force of the whole narrative. And yet, in terms of pictorial composition and of the perspicuous display of meaning, they are curiously removed from the viewer's immediate attention by the

position of Christ (…) and by the addition of an apostle, who hides most of Christ's body and whose head separates his head from his hand." According to Puttfarken, the partial concealment of Christ's figure increases the impression of his divine "magnetism."

14 Bellori, 220: "Dal lato destro l'altare vi è Cristo che chiama san Matteo all'apostolato, ritrattevi alcune teste al naturale, tra le quali il santo, lasciando di contra le monete, con una mano al petto, si volge al Signore; ed appresso un vecchio si pone gli occhiali al naso, riguardando un giovine che tira a sé quelle monete assiso nell'angolo della tavola."

15 Ibidem 220-1: "Il componimento e li moti però non sono sufficienti all'istoria, ancorché egli la rifacesse due volte; e l'oscurità della cappella e del colore tolgono questi due quadri alla vista."

accessories—the old man putting on his glasses and the youth pulling the money toward himself—bespeak his reproach and dislike. In addition, by relating that Caravaggio used a portrait to represent the saint, Bellori hinted at the lack of ideality characteristic of the master's sacred figures.

Interestingly enough, some seventeenth-century critics celebrated *The Calling of Saint Matthew*, though on different grounds. In his 1657 *Microcosmo della pittura*, Francesco Scannelli defined the picture as "one of the most richly colored, rounded, and natural artworks that, through the imitation of the sheer truth, demonstrates painting's artifice."[16] The adjectives employed by Scannelli ("*pastoso*," "*rilevato*," and "*naturale*") tend to highlight Caravaggio's debt to the schools of Venice and Parma: his color techniques in reproducing nature—the optical paradigm to which I refer so many times in this book—resemble those of Titian and Correggio. Indirectly, though with a different theoretical resonance and in a positive manner, Scannelli embraced Zuccari's opinion about Giorgione's imprint on *The Calling*. In fact, Giorgione and Titian constitute a kind of conceptual dyad in the artistic taxonomy of seventeenth-century Italian painting. I will soon approach this issue in further detail.

Besides Scannelli, the German painter and art theorist Joachim von Sandrart also sang the praises of Caravaggio's picture. In his 1675 *Academie der Bau-, Bild- und Mahlerey Künste*, Sandrart misread the subjects of Caravaggio's two lateral paintings in the Contarelli Chapel, but his misconstructions reward serious reflection:

> He [Caravaggio] also painted two large canvases for San Luigi dei Francesi, opposite the palace of Prince Giustiniani. The first represents Christ, our Savior, chasing and driving the Jews, merchants, and tax collectors out of the temple with their booths and counters in disorder. But even more admirable is the second canvas, where he depicted Christ with two of his disciples entering a dark room as the publican Matthew sits, drinks, and plays cards and dice with a band of rogues. As if afraid, Matthew hides the cards in one hand, resting the other on his breast, his face expressing his fear and shame in considering that he is unworthy of being called to the apostolate by Christ. One of the men retrieves his money from the table by slipping it from one hand to the other, and is quite shameful of doing so. All of this is true to life and even to nature.[17]

In his life of Hans Holbein, Sandrart also mentioned Caravaggio's *Calling of Saint Matthew* with admiration. This passage equally deserves to be quoted in its entirety:

> Finally, in order to sum up his praises, [Holbein] during his lifetime was held in such high esteem that the most excellent of the Italians did not disdain to take up many of his ideas in their own works, as did Michelangelo Caravaggio in representing Matthew abandoning his office of tax collector upon Christ's call, especially in the figure of the player retrieving the money from the table, as well as in other things.[18]

16 Scannelli, 197-8: "E dello stesso Caravaggio (…) si vede nella chiesa di San Luigi della nazione francese l'ultima cappella nell'entrare a mano sinistra con la tavola che dimostra san Matteo con un angelo dalla parte di sopra, ed alla parete destra l'istoria pure del santo quando fu chiamato da Cristo all'apostolato, veramente una delle più pastose, rilevate e naturali operazioni che venga a dimostrare l'artificio della pittura per immitazione di mera verità, essendo in tal luogo quasi del tutto mancante il lume, in modo che opera tale per disgrazia de' virtuosi e dello stesso autore non si può vedere che imperfettamente."

17 Sandrart, 276: "Wiederum mahlte er zwey große Blätter zu San Luigi di Francesci, bey Prinz Justinians Palast über. Das erstte war, wie Christus, unser Seeligmacher, die Juden, Käuffer und Zöllner samt ihren Krämen und Kaufftischen

über Hauffen wirft und sie aus dem Tempel treibet; noch verwunderlicher aber ist das ander Blat, worinnen vorgestellt wie Christus in ein finster Zimmer mit zween der seinen eingetreten und den Zöllner Matthaeum bey einer Rott Spitzbuben mit Karten und Würflen spielend und trinkend sitzen findet. Matthaeus, als furchtsam, verbirgt die Karten in der einen Hand, die andre legt er auf seine Brust und gibt in seinem Angesicht den Schrecken und die Schamhaftigkeit zu erkennen, die er darüber gefast, daß er als unwürdig von Christo zum Apostelamt beruffen wird; einer streicht mit der einen Hand sein Geld vom Tisch in die andere und machet sich ganz schamhaft davon, welches alles dem Leben und der Natur selbst gleichet." For Sandrart's misconstructions, see also Simonato 2009, 229-30.

18 Ibidem, 102: "Schließlich sein Lob zusammen zu fassen,

Sandrart alludes here to Holbein's woodcut *Death and the Gambler* from the macabre series *Les images de la mort* (Lyons, 1547).[19] In the print, Death and the Devil fight over the soul of a gambler placed at the center of the composition behind a gaming table (Fig. 93). To the left, a player attempts in vain to stop the quarrel by thrusting his left arm toward the horned demon in an act of pleading. Unbothered by the surrounding hassle and unconcerned with his companion's fate, a third player bends over the table while retrieving his money. It is evident that Caravaggio borrowed this figure's attitude for the youngster at the left of *The Calling* (Figs. 94, 95). There, the young man sits on a chair with crisscrossed, ribbed legs forming a lancet arch akin to the support of Holbein's table. Bearing this in mind, it is now possible to explain Sandrart's "slip of the pen" in describing Caravaggio's painting. The German author somehow transferred the narrative situation enacted in Holbein's woodcut to the story of Matthew's conversion.[20] In his recollection, the open account book, inkwell, pen, and pouch lying on Caravaggio's table become cards. Christ

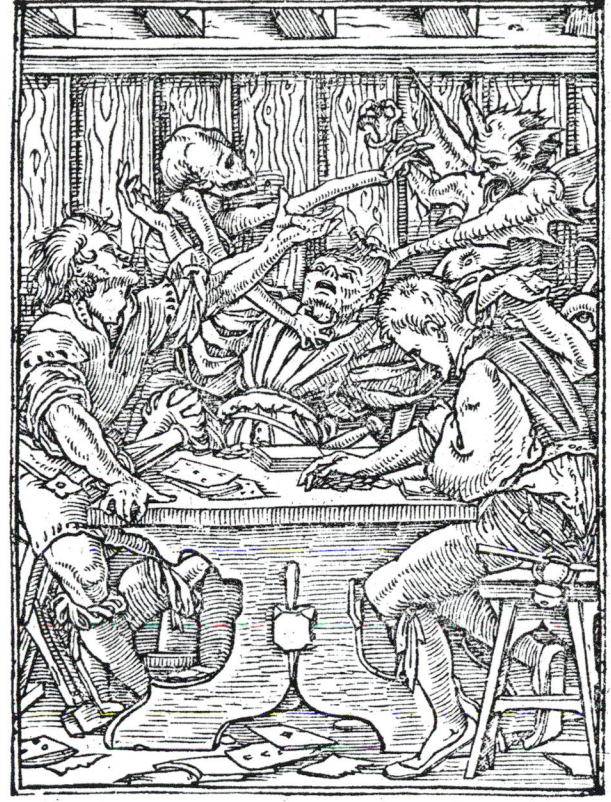

Fig. 93
Hans Holbein, *Death and the Gambler*, woodcut, 6.4 x 4.9 cm., reproduced from *Les Images de la mort*, Lyons, 1547.

and Peter's foray interrupts the imaginary game just as Death's and the Devil's quarrel catches the gamblers off-guard in Holbein's print. More importantly, Sandrart's imagination conflated the event depicted in Caravaggio's *The Cardsharps* with the epiphany scene of the Contarelli picture. As the swindler in the right foreground of the Kimbell picture conceals the fake cards tucked inside his belt, so too does Matthew hide his card upon Jesus' arrival. Needless to say, nothing like this seems to occur in *The Calling*. Nonetheless, Sandrart might have mistaken the youth's hand at the left—the one grabbing a pouch and ensconced under the red-stripped blue sleeve—for Matthew's hand. Most probably Sandrart imagined that this hand held a card instead of a pouch.

Be that as it may, one could easily justify Sandrart's confusion if one considers Caravaggio's sleight of hand in this portion of the picture. On a narrow table surface, the master imbricated Matthew's hand counting the money and the youth's hands, one shifting the coins, the other seizing the pouch. These three hands together with the figures' arms compose an uninterrupted chain of movement obviously conjuring the future saint's zeal in accumulating money. Moreover, through the imbrication of arms and hands, Caravaggio blurred the physical demarcation between Matthew and his young acolyte; although their gestures differ considerably, they end

so ist er [*sc.* Holbein] noch in seinen Lebzeiten in so hohem Wert gewesen, daß die fürnehmste Italiener keiner Scheu getragen, aus seinen Inventionen viel in ihre Werke zu bringen, sonderlich Michael Angelo Caravaggio, als da Matthaeus von dem Zoll durch Christum beruffen wird, auch den Spieler, der das Geld vom Tisch abstreicht und anders mehr."

19   For the woodcut, see Müller 1997, 284, no. 105. 43. On this series, see more recently Parshall 2001.

20   It is interesting that a scholar as experienced as Longhi, 1999-2000, 1:148-9, makes the same mistake as Sandrart a few centuries before: "Ma alle dogane, dove si cambia moneta, nulla di più facile che s'intavoli il gioco, e nulla perciò vieta che, per maggior maturalezza, il Cristo, entrando 'oggi' nella stanzaccia della dogana, venga a distogliere Matteo da una partita d'azzardo (…); sosta su Matteo mentre, raddoppiando con una mano la puntata, si addita con l'altra come dicesse: Vuol me? (…)."

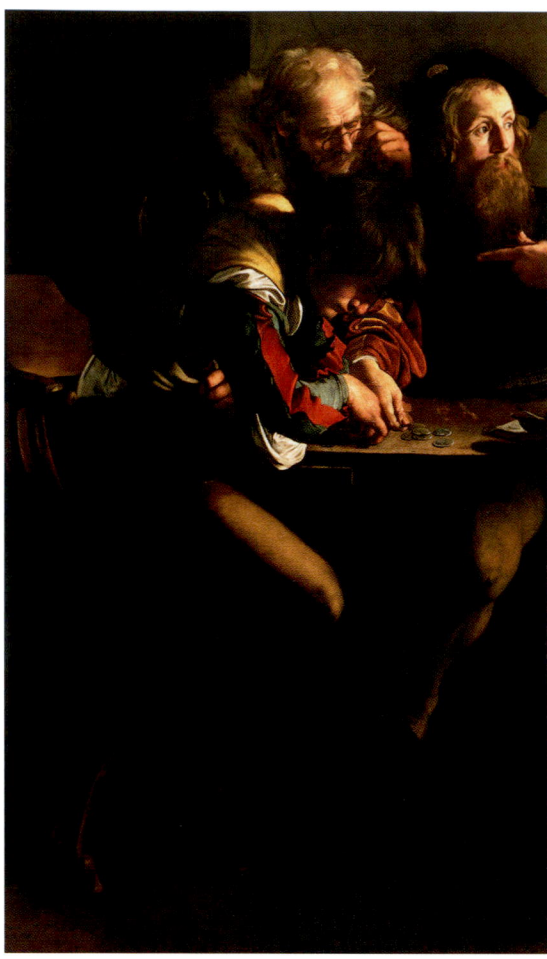

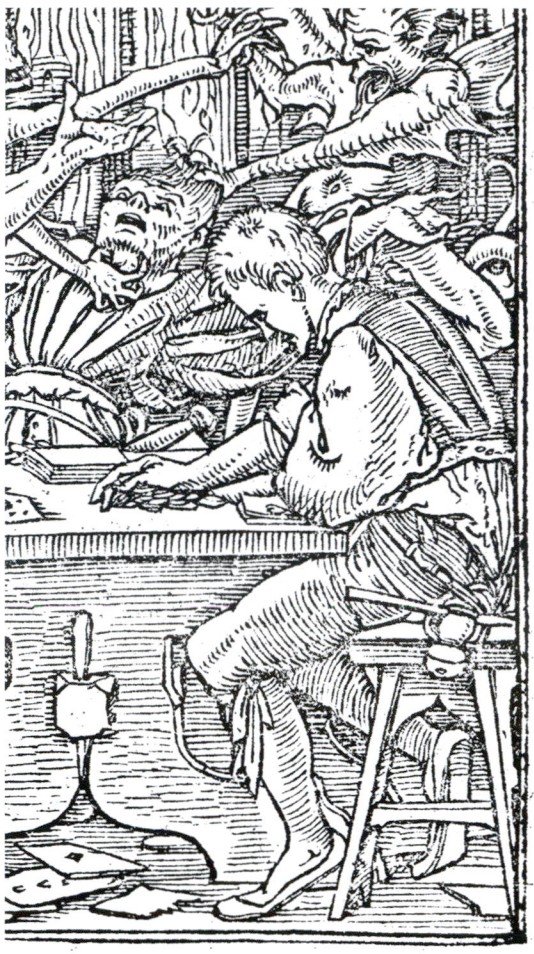

Fig. 94
Michelangelo Merisi da Caravaggio, *The Calling of Saint Matthew*, Contarelli Chapel, San Luigi dei Francesi, Rome, oil on canvas, 322 x 340 cm., detail.

Fig. 95
Hans Holbein, *Death and the Gambler*, woodcut, 6.4 x 4.9 cm., detail, reproduced from *Les Images de la mort*, Lyons, 1547.

up being visually amalgamated, as the beholder cannot comprehend one man's action without interpreting the other's. Put otherwise, the two figures are linked together in a relation that cannot be overlooked, especially because Caravaggio also bound them together through the ambivalent act of Matthew's pointing hand. I shall return to this detail shortly. By confusing a conversion scene with a game swindle, Sandrart in a sense stumbled into Caravaggio's pictorial trap. In recollecting the scene, the German author was indeed unable to tell apart a low-life episode from a religious image: gaming and sanctity fuse in his interpretation of the picture's subject. In other words, Sandrart was lured into perceiving an *istoria* as a genre scene, which in turn is dilated to the point of encompassing a sacred drama. Of course, this confusion is not coincidental. To be sure, Sandrart tends to be inaccurate in his descriptions. As I have already suggested, he read *The Martyrdom of Saint Matthew* as a scene of greedy tax collectors driven out of the temple; in his mind, the saint's torturer transforms into Christ and the martyr at his feet into a publican punished by the Savior's wrath. That said, it is imperative to highlight once again that Sandrart's misreading is not only the result of a fading memory and idiosyncrasy. While in Rome at the service of "Prince Giustiniani"—the Marchese Vincenzo—he must have gone numerous times across the street to see Caravaggio's paintings in San Luigi dei Francesi. His description betrays the curious intensity with which he sought to reconstruct their narratives after so many years, going so far as to remember the detail, unreal yet so significant, of the young man who is almost ashamed as he avidly pulls the money toward himself. In defense of Sandrart's inaccuracies, it must furthermore be said that Caravaggio himself from the outset made the "low-life" subtext of the tavern encounter operate within the conversion's religious text. It is above all this duality of genre that prompted Sandrart's equivocation. Latent in Caravaggio's table scene, there are indeed the tragic-burlesque situation of Holbein's woodcut and the mechanism of visual and conceptual deception first experimented with by Caravaggio in *The Cardsharps*.

In imagining Matthew's vocation as an inn scene unexpectedly disrupted by the divine epiphany, Caravaggio assuredly underlined the continuity between his youthful comedic scenes and his novel endeavor in the field of the *istoria*. Because he also detected the visual interrelation between the low and the high genres in Caravaggio's work, Zuccari dismissed *The Calling* as a product of the early Renaissance Venetian painting's influence upon the master. The allusion to "Giorgione's idea" thus marks Caravaggio's picture as an extemporaneous artwork done with an acute sense of color but without knowledge of drawing, reproducing figures from life without the filter of ideality, echoing the vagueness with which Giorgione and Titian failed or did not care to clarify their pictures' subjects. We have seen in Chapters 1 and 5 how this network of theoretical associations functioned at the beginning of the seventeenth century. I now return to the problem of narrative ambiguity in connection with *The Calling of Saint Matthew*.

Who and Where Is Matthew?

As a general rule, the most debated aspect of Caravaggio's painting in connection with ambiguity has almost exclusively revolved around an iconographic enigma: who and where is Matthew in the conversion scene? Is he the bearded man with the pointing hand, as Bellori first argued in his 1672 *Vite*? Or is it possible that any other figure at the table might be the soon-to-be apostle? Many scholars have already grappled with this complex question, and I list here the most salient or controversial arguments. In a 1985 article, Andreas Prater denied that the bearded man behind the table or counter—the one I have been considering thus far as the future apostle—is Matthew: "the bearded man's striking gesture of pointing does not necessarily mean that he identifies himself as the recipient [of Christ's calling]. In fact, if one wants to indicate oneself, one would hardly point his finger to some other person nearby."[21] In Prater's view, the bearded man's gesture might stand for "do you mean me or this man over here?" and hence Matthew could and must rather be the young man on the left,[22] whom Sandrart singled out in his description of the picture. In Prater's interpretation, the bearded man is most probably a merchant, escorted by two assistants (the youth next to him and the one with his back turned); he is counting the money destined to the young tax collector, alias Matthew. According to Prater, the compositional layout of the *istoria* corroborates his hypothesis, for the soon-to-be-enlightened young man appears at the opposite side of the incoming Christ; in his view, they constitute the dramatic poles of the narrative. More interestingly, by representing Matthew as still intent on counting the money, Caravaggio,

21 Prater 1985, 72: "Der auffallende Zeigegestus des Bärtigen signalisiert doch wohl daß er sich selbst nicht unbedingt als den Angesprochenen versteht. Denn wenn jemand auf sich selbst weisen will, dann wird er kaum mit seinem Zeigefinger auf einen anderen neben sich deuten." Of course, Prater's interpretation of the bearded figure's gesture has been submitted to much scrutiny (see esp. Schütze I. 2000), and the remainder of my text will confirm this point. To my knowledge, it has not been ascertained that the pointing gesture of the bearded figure appears as a gesture of self-designation in another iconographic tradition revolving around the theme of divine vocation: the Annunciation. In Duccio di Buoninsegna's

Annunciation for the Siena *Maestà* (National Gallery, London), the Virgin rehearses the gesture specific to Caravaggio's bearded figure as the angel approaches her. In other words, the Virgin reacts to the angel's greeting by replying: "Is it me you are addressing?" See Bellosi 1998, 266.

22 Prater 1985, 72: "Auch wenn man den fragenden Ausdruck und den Zeigegestus des Bärtigen etwa im Sinne einer Gegenfrage an Christus, 'meinst du mich oder diesen da?,' interpretieren wollte, bliebe doch der eindeutige Hinweis auf jenen am Kopfende des Tisches Sitzenden, der die Münzen anstarrt."

according to Prater, succeeded in inflecting the calling's canonical narration with original nuances: "Caravaggio shows the conversion, but Christ's call has not yet reached its addressee, or rather, [Matthew] has not yet become aware of it inside himself."[23] "The real revolution," argues Prater, "in Caravaggio's interpretation of the calling resides in the fact that he shows Christ's exhortation but not the publican's reaction to it, the call without its response: two elements that never split from one another in the iconographic tradition, but are always evoked simultaneously."[24] If I understand Prater correctly, Caravaggio introduced a rather bold anachronism in *The Calling*: by separating the cause from the effect—the call from the conversion—he left in suspension the episode's outcome; Matthew's enlightenment is displaced into the future. Prater's exegesis sparked a long and at times vehement controversy.

In 1991 Herwarth Röttgen vigorously (and sarcastically) refuted Prater's arguments on the subject of *The Calling*. Relying on Andrea De Jorio's 1832 *La mimica degli antichi*, Röttgen stated that the gesture of the bearded man's right hand, with the thumb and index rubbing against one another, does not designate counting, but rather requesting money. In other words, the figure at issue is not paying the tax, but exacting it from the young man hunched over the table. The latter, says Röttgen, "hides the money in the shade of his hand lest one see how much he owes and is still ready to pay. One can well imagine that he draws the money out from under his hand one coin at a time, unwillingly and reluctantly as his face suggests."[25] From this observation Röttgen came to the conclusion that Matthew must still be identified with the bearded man in Caravaggio's picture.

In 1998, Prater replied to Röttgen's objections. He proved that the gesture of the bearded man's right hand stands for counting, by reference to two paintings in which the same gesture appears: Maarten van Heemskerk's 1529 *Portrait of Pieter Bicker Gerritsz* (Rijksmuseum, Amsterdam),[26] and Orazio de Ferrari's *c.*1640 *The Almsgiving of Saint Charles Borromeo* (Private Collection, Lugano). Oddly enough, Prater did not mention that the gesture in question harks back to a sixteenth-century northern pictorial tradition, the representation of bankers, moneychangers, and tax collectors. As evidenced by Larry Silver and Keith Moxey in connection with paintings by Quentin Massys and Marinus van Reymerswaele, a hand literally clenched with the coin wedged between the bent index finger and protruding thumb commonly denoted avarice, and its depiction implied a strong criticism of this capital vice.[27] Once Prater ascertained what the gesture signifies, he strove to demonstrate—unconvincingly in my view—that despite his act of counting, the bearded man cannot be a tax collector, but is rather a merchant. The only evidence that Prater presented is extremely weak: since the figure's hat, adorned with a metallic pin or medal, was an anachronistic costume piece even in Caravaggio's time—which is unequivocally true—it could not suit a publican.[28] I shall not spend much time refuting Prater's assertion, which represents a secondary point in comparison with many other ambiguities in Caravaggio's picture. I simply note that in the sixteenth-century northern representations previously mentioned, bankers, moneychangers, and tax collectors sometimes don ridiculous, out-of-fashion, two-horned hats. This curious prop certainly betokened vanity and excessive wealth by burlesquing the painting's characters. Therefore, the fact that Caravaggio's bearded man also wears an obsolete hat might contradict, or even override, Prater's argument:

23   Ibidem, 73: "Caravaggio zeigt die Berufung, aber der Ruf Christi hat seinen Adressaten noch nicht erreicht oder besser, dieser hat ihn innerlich noch nicht wahrgenommen."

24   Ibidem: "Das wahrhaft Revolutionäre an Caravaggios Interpretation der Erzählung liegt darin, daß er die Aufforderung Christ ohne die Reaktion des Zöllners auf diese, die Berufung ohne die Bekehrung zeigt—zwei Inhalte, die in der Bildtradition nie voneinander getrennt, sondern stets simultan geschildert wurden."

25   Röttgen 1991, 98: "Und dieser verbirgt nun sein Geld im Schatten seiner Hand, damit niemand sähe, wieviel er hat und was er noch zu zahlen bereit wäre. Man kann sich gut denken, daß er widerwillig und verbockt wie sein Gesicht ein Stück nach dem anderen unter seiner Hand her durchschiebt."

26   See Grosshans 1980, 91, no. 3.

27   See Silver 1984, esp. 136-41, and Moxey 1985b. For a survey of this iconographical tradition, see Yamey 1989. See also Vlam 1977, for a survey of representations of *The Calling of Saint Matthew* in Flemish painting.

28   Prater 1995, 57.

in sum, on this basis, this figure might well be the publican Matthew.

Another point of critical dissension between Prater and Röttgen concerned *The Calling's* architectural setting. At the beginning, Prater maintained that, in spite of some inconsistencies, the dark site of the conversion represented an external location.[29] Predictably enough, Röttgen replied that Caravaggio instead depicted the interior of the hall where Matthew collected taxes, and this in accordance with Cardinal Contarelli's prescriptions. With reason, Röttgen pointed out that the yellow sheets of parchment or of oiled linen fabric displayed in the window were the equivalent of our blinds. These patches were pressed against the windowpanes and they were kept in place by wires, cords or strings. Notice that in Caravaggio's painting, a wire dangles loose over the window's upper left pane (Fig. 96). According to Röttgen, the wires were only visible from the inside, and consequently Caravaggio intended to depict a chamber's interior.[30] Unfortunately, it is not known whether these wires could also be used outside.[31] However, by focusing on this issue, one inevitably

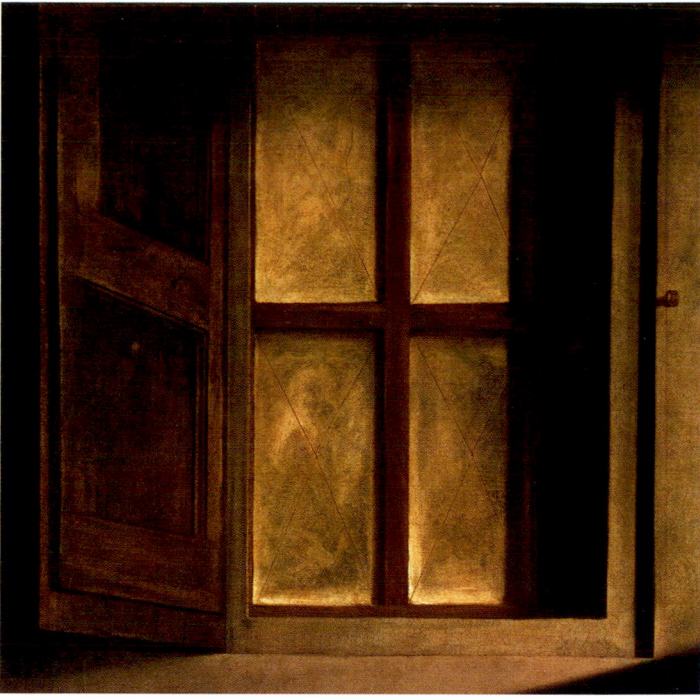

Fig. 96
Michelangelo Merisi da Caravaggio, *The Calling of Saint Matthew*, Contarelli Chapel, San Luigi dei Francesi, Rome, oil on canvas, 322 x 340 cm., detail.

misses a crucial point: the intrinsic indeterminacy of Caravaggio's architectural setting. Whether an interior or a passageway, the painting's dark space cannot be classified by any means as a tax collector's office. The presence of the publican's paraphernalia—account book, inkwell, and so forth—is deliberately generic and, as Sandrart's misconstruction has taught us, the scene's sparse furniture might as well be that of a humble inn or tavern. Similarly, there is no evidence that any of the figures at the table is represented in the act of paying taxes. As I will demonstrate later, it is quite possible that Caravaggio simply represented a group of accountants; any other attempt to sort out these figures' tasks would result unfailingly in over-interpretation.

In my opinion, both Prater and Röttgen, along with some other scholars involved in the debate, have erred in applying a traditionally iconographic method to the deciphering of *The Calling*. They have been more interested in establishing who is who in the picture than in exploring how the picture itself reads. Had they tried to analyze *The Calling's* narrative structure, they would certainly have concluded that the painting's obscurities are much more numerous and significant insofar as they concern the basic interconnections between the figures, the architectural setting, and the chiaroscuro layout—that is, between action, time, and space. To my knowledge, only Peter J. Burgard has realized that rhetorical amphibology—though not in the sense defined by Pomponio Gaurico[32]—is the painting's intrinsic characteristic. Visual indeterminacy indeed permeates all the elements at play within the composition.

29   Prater 1985, 72.

30   Röttgen 1991, 99.

31   A similar conclusion is reached by Burgard 1998, 99.

32   Von Rosen 2009, 252, refers to Gaurico's amphiboly with regard to *The Calling*, although she seems to misinterpret the specific meaning of this notion in Gaurico's treatise. Von Rosen, in fact, considers an amphiboly the representation of a moment "immediately before the reversal"—that is, immediately preceding the Aristotelian "catastrophe," and in this case, the saint's conversion—whereas Gaurico by amphiboly means the impossibility for a reader or viewer to establish whether the represented action refers to a moment before or still to come.

In his remarkable 1998 article on *The Calling of Saint Matthew*, Burgard described how Caravaggio's "art of dissimulation" is rooted everywhere in the composition:

> The painting is composed in such a way as to preclude final decisions in interpretation, even about such basic issues as the identity of Saint Matthew or the location of the scene. However, Caravaggio not only makes it impossible to decide who is who or what is where, he also prepares this final undecidability by articulating numerous other moments of ambiguity.[33]

To this end, according to Burgard, Caravaggio proceeded to a "de-centering" of the episode's protagonists: Christ is relegated to the right, half-hidden behind an apostle; Matthew, whether he is the bearded man or the young man bent over the table, appears on the left; whereas two walkons steal the center stage—one, his back turned, pivoting on a bench, the other resting his arm on the adjacent chair's back. As we have seen in the Introduction to Part Three, Counter-Reformation art theorists demand the hero's centrality in religious images. Yet I do not think that centrality must always be understood in spatial terms. The painter can move the main figures at will along the pictorial field as long as they remain immediately recognizable to the viewer. But even if one assumes that the bearded man is actually Matthew—which I personally believe for reasons I will explain later—then one also must admit that the picture's chiaroscuro fails to spotlight his persona with due intensity. In fact, the youth with the plumed hat at his side enjoys a greater concentration of lighting. At this point, it should be clear that neither the chiaroscuro nor the spatial layout brings to the fore the protagonists of *The Calling*.

As for expression, another substantial component of pictorial narrative, it is likewise apparent that the attitudes of Christ and the bearded man—let alone that of the youth hunched over the table—are far from being unproblematic. For this reason, I am convinced that Burgard interprets the bearded man's pointing gesture incorrectly:

> In the entire debate about the identity of Matthew that has arisen over the last decade or so, the one thing that has emerged that seems incontrovertible is this simplest of all observations: the fact that figure three [the bearded man] is not pointing at himself, but at someone to his right.[34]

As a scholar whose principal thesis relies on Caravaggio's art of dissimulation, Burgard strangely does not seem to consider that the pointing gesture is as ambivalent as other elements of the painting, although he admits in the end that the bearded man's gesture "sends the viewer off on the search for the true Matthew" by adding:

> For while those critics are right who insist that he is not pointing at himself, but off to his right, what none of them have realized is that this simple fact does not by any means prove that he cannot be Matthew. He could indeed be Matthew, but simply not yet realize that Christ is calling him. In the end, we cannot know who Matthew is.[35]

Burgard's last assertion seems to me compelling, and would be even more so had he recognized that the hand's orientation is in and of itself disorienting. With ingenuity, Caravaggio indeed arranged for the hand to linger in indeterminate suspension. As positioned, the hand gesture

33 Burgard 1998, 97.

34 Ibidem, 100.

35 Ibidem, 101.

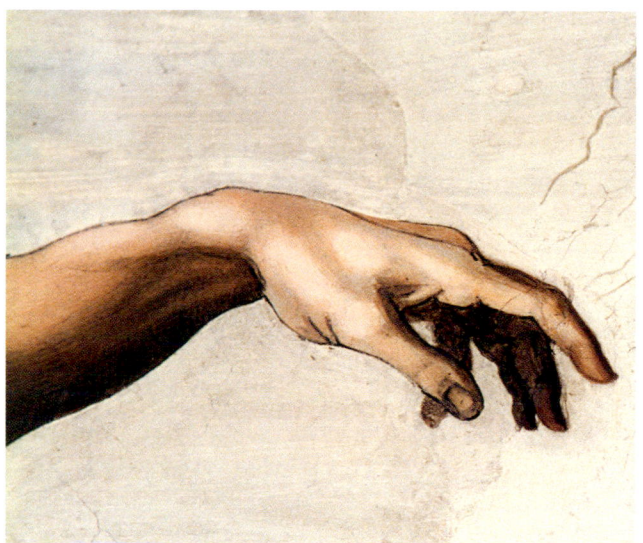

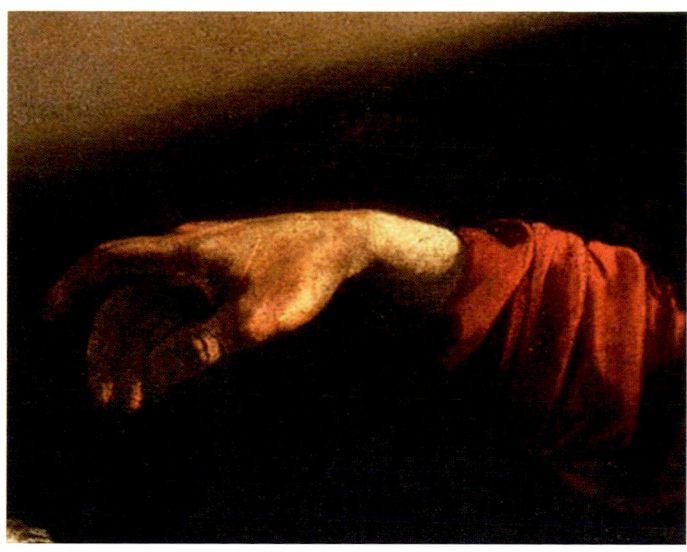

Fig. 97
Michelangelo Buonarroti, *The Creation of Adam*, Sistine Chapel, Vatican Palace, Rome, fresco, detail.

Fig. 98
Michelangelo Merisi da Caravaggio, *The Calling of Saint Matthew*, Contarelli Chapel, San Luigi dei Francesi, Rome, oil on canvas, 322 x 340 cm., detail.

definitely relates to both the bearded man and whatever figure might be to his right. I will come back to this observation shortly.

Similarly, if one now turns to Christ's calling hand, one will discover a few more inconsistencies. As has been frequently stressed, Jesus' hand patently mirrors Adam's in Michelangelo's *Creation of Man* in the Sistine Chapel (Figs. 97, 98). Burgard glosses the strangeness of this borrowing on a symbolic and narrative level:

> If we read the quotation correctly, then the very foundation of the image, its presentation of a scene in which Christ calls Matthew to the apostolate, is drawn into question, insofar as the hand tends to contravene Christ's identity as the agent of the act of calling and as the one who gives new life.[36]

In fact, in Michelangelo's fresco Adam's hand is essentially a passive receptor of outward energy: the vital input originating from God the Father transmitting the spark of life. By reversing Adam's hand literally and figuratively, and by severing it illusorily from Christ's body through the apostle's interposition, Caravaggio obscures the semantics of the calling gesture. By its integral passivity, Christ's hand performs almost in contradiction with Christ's willpower as evinced by his parted lips in proffering the calling's imperious elocution "Follow me." I will return to Jesus' hand and the charm that it exerted on the imagination of many painters in seventeenth-century Rome. For the time being, I want to underscore that the quotation of Adam's hand not only invites the viewer to compare Michelangelo's work with Caravaggio's, but also determines an effect of estrangement by depersonalizing the source of the miracle. This hand now acts as a transceiver of God's grace, and not as Christ's willful emitter.[37]

36 Ibidem, 97.

37 To my knowledge, the first to compare the gesture of Christ's pointing hand in the painting to Michelangelo's *Creation of Adam* is Friedlaender 1969, 108. In assessing Friedlaender's opinion, Hibbard 1983, 100, stressed that Christ's gesture in Caravaggio's picture resembles that of Adam, and not of God: an important detail, according to him, because in this way Caravaggio creates a parallel between Adam and Jesus, the new Adam. Puttfarken 1998, 169, dismisses this interpretation: "in choosing the passively receiving hand of Michelangelo's Adam rather than the precisely pointing one of the Father, Caravaggio has defined for us the nature of Christ's power: it is here not the life-giving force of the Creator, but the *magnetic* power of which Saint Jerome spoke." How a "passive" gesture could qualify as "magnetic" is difficult to understand.

Before going any further, I would like to declare that I agree with Burgard's conclusion as formulated in the following passage:

> Caravaggio's thematization of indecision should not surprise us once we have recognized the painting's manifold articulation of uncertainty. In its play with centers, its use of light and dark, its interpictorial allusions, its anachronism, its multi-directionality of figures and of light, and its dislocation of scene, which in turn sets the scene for the ultimate uncertainty, the undecidability of Matthew's identity, Caravaggio's *Calling of Saint Matthew* performatively enacts that indecision and forces the viewer to repeat the performance.[38]

From this felicitous sentence I want to extract a few key words that, in my view, are not satisfactorily examined in Burgard's essay: "play with centers," "anachronism," "multi-directionality of figures and of light," and "dislocation of scene."

For the sake of experimentation, let us rewind and relive the conversion episode as depicted by Caravaggio. To simplify our task temporarily, let us posit that the bearded man is Matthew. Thus, the publican is counting the money as he hears or sees someone or something calling him. Startled, he suspends the counting and responds to the call, doubting that he is the person addressed. Blind and deaf to the divine epiphany, the elderly man and the youth to Matthew's right continue their tasks with unflinching concentration. At the other end of the table, a young man who was apparently registering the amounts of money in the nearby ledger suddenly rotates over his bench. The suddenness of his movement expresses his bafflement at an unexpected fact or event. His face in profile is strongly lit, mysteriously in view of the fact that the apostle in front of him blocks the light streaming from the right. Not only does this young man ignore Christ's presence but, if one follows Caravaggio's cue, his eyes are transfixed on the apostle's pointing hand, a quasi-perfect double of Christ's. By the same token, the youth at Matthew's left has turned, almost distractedly, to see to whom or to what the tax collector is responding. More intriguingly, compared to Matthew's, his eyes do not necessarily aim at a figure or object close by. Rather, they seem to wander off in search of an objective. Hence, it is even doubtful that they are oriented toward Christ's calling hand or face. I shall return to this point later.

At first glance, this cursory, but fair description of Caravaggio's painting leaves us with many more questions than we could have predicted. The visual blanks of the narrative structure—its disjunctions, leaps, and inconsistencies—go well beyond the problem of Matthew's identity. Burgard's "multi-directionality of figures and of light" sounds like a euphemism compared to the drastic disconnections of the figures' movements, gestures and expressions from the already inconsistent chiaroscuro layout of the painting. Caravaggio's "play with centers" now also appears to be a timid definition: the picture's centers, in fact, carry within themselves the signs of, and urge for, de-centering: Christ's figure, visually dismembered, sinks into penumbra under the pressure of the sunshine's irresistible thrust directly above him; as for Matthew, the ambiguity of his gesture even deprives him of his own identity. The term "anachronism," interpreted by Burgard and others before him as the coexistence of contemporary and historical costumes in the painting, does not truly apply to *The Calling*. The window with its dangling wire and blinds, the table, chair, bench, account book, inkwell, and pen, were certainly everyday objects for beholders in Caravaggio's Rome. But what about Matthew's clothing? Did anybody at the time wear that kind of beret? Did tax collectors dress like that? And did accountants sport plumed hats and multi-colored striped sleeves like the young dandies—analogs of Caravaggio's gamblers—in the picture? In reality, these

---

38   Burgard 1998, 101.

costumes are incongruous and unsuitable for an accountants' scene.[39] Rather, they are Caravaggio's figments: signature pieces of his unprecedented inventiveness. Finally, Burgard's "dislocation of scene" refers solely to the ambiguity of the architectural space, one in which the interior and the exterior are merely indistinguishable. The point that I am making here is that the entire composition is innervated with dislocations: of lighting, temporality, narrative connectivity, and verisimilitude. In particular, the representation of the sacred event does not allow the beholder to make sense of the action's unfolding. More disturbing, Christ's and the apostle's figures might be invisible and inaudible to most of the actors in Caravaggio's *istoria*. At least, this is what other seventeenth-century painters inferred from *The Calling of Saint Matthew*.

The Painters' Viewpoints

In the summer of 1602, the Bolognese painter Ludovico Carracci visited Rome at the instigation of his cousin, Annibale. Unfortunately, no document or literary source reports which monuments and artworks Ludovico saw in the city. Nonetheless, it is conceivable that he was attracted by Rome's new artistic trends and, if so, he must have gone to San Luigi dei Francesi to observe Caravaggio's freshly inaugurated *Calling of Saint Matthew*. Not much is known about the Carracci's reaction to Caravaggio's paintings. Doubtless Annibale was well acquainted with the young master's early works in Roman churches, especially because the two of them, albeit independently, had been engaged in 1600 to decorate the Cerasi Chapel in Santa Maria del Popolo: Annibale executed the *Assumption of the Virgin* for the main altarpiece, and Caravaggio the two side paintings, *The Conversion of Saint Paul* and the *Crucifixion of Saint Peter*. In his 1678 *Felsina Pittrice*, Carlo Cesare Malvasia records Annibale's dry comment on Caravaggio's *Judith and Holofernes*: the painting was "too natural."[40] Malvasia's testimony seems reliable insofar as Annibale had then veered far away from the experimental naturalism of his early paintings and drawings. In 1602, Ludovico must have shared Annibale's opinion on Caravaggio, although *The Calling of Saint Matthew* apparently caught his attention. In 1939, Heinrich Bodmer first postulated that Ludovico's *c*.1607-1610 *The Calling of Saint Matthew* for the Chiesa de' Mendicanti in Bologna (now in the Pinacoteca Nazionale, Bologna) was indebted to Caravaggio's homonymous painting (Fig. 99).[41] Recently, scholars such as

39   Varriano 2006, 115-26, esp. 116-8, argues that the clothing of the figures in *The Calling* is perfectly contemporaneous, with the obvious exception of that of Christ and the apostle (a similar claim had also been made by Danesi Squarzina 2000, 93). In stating this, Varriano heavily relies on Pierce 1953, an essay that is both largely outdated and often inaccurate. Be that as it may, it is interesting to quote Pierce 1953, 151-2, in this regard: "The little boys in the *Vocation of Saint Matthew* are far more disturbing, but I believe that they have puzzled art historians unnecessarily. Their enigma lies not in the fact that their clothes are strange but in the fact that one cannot easily recognize the part these boys play in society. They are dressed in expensive damasks with fine tufts of plumes in their hats, yet they are certainly not young aristocrats; in the face of their confidence, their negligent ease, one cannot, on the other hand, regard them as guttersnipes. This familiarity, which alone should make untenable the theory that they have been specially dressed up, gives the clue to their identity: they are, like the little boys who appear in the paintings of Tintoretto, Aliense, Federico Zuccari, Santi di Tito and a score of other late sixteenth-century artists, the pages who were an indispensable part of the retinue of any man of substance." Apart from the fact that the clothes of the "little boys" in the paintings mentioned by Pierce do not truly compare with those of

Caravaggio's youths, and apart from the fact that Pierce in her essay several times remarks on essential incongruities in the ways Caravaggio supposedly reproduced the accoutrement of these lackeys, it must be said that the sumptuous dressing of the "pages" evoked by Pierce were specific to ceremonies and solemnities, and therefore unfit for an "everyday life" scene as Caravaggio's painting is held to be. Even more incongruous is Matthew's clothing, in particular the usage of the beret and of hose without apparent breeches. In Chapter 12, I deal with the outdated beret worn by the figure of Pilate. Albeit similar to berets from the mid-sixteenth century, Matthew's beret is difficult to define in terms of fashion. The usage of the pin, on the other hand, certainly harks back to the early sixteenth century, and is rather common in northern Europe, as evidenced by the one that adorns the hat of Emperor Maximilian I as represented in Albrecht Dürer's famous printed portrait.

40   Malvasia, 1:480-1: "Forzato pure a dire il suo parere sopra una Giuditte del Caravaggio, non so dir altro, rispose, se non ch'ella è troppo naturale."

41   Bodmer 1939, 66-7. For the painting, see Brogi 2001, 1:211-2, no. 97.

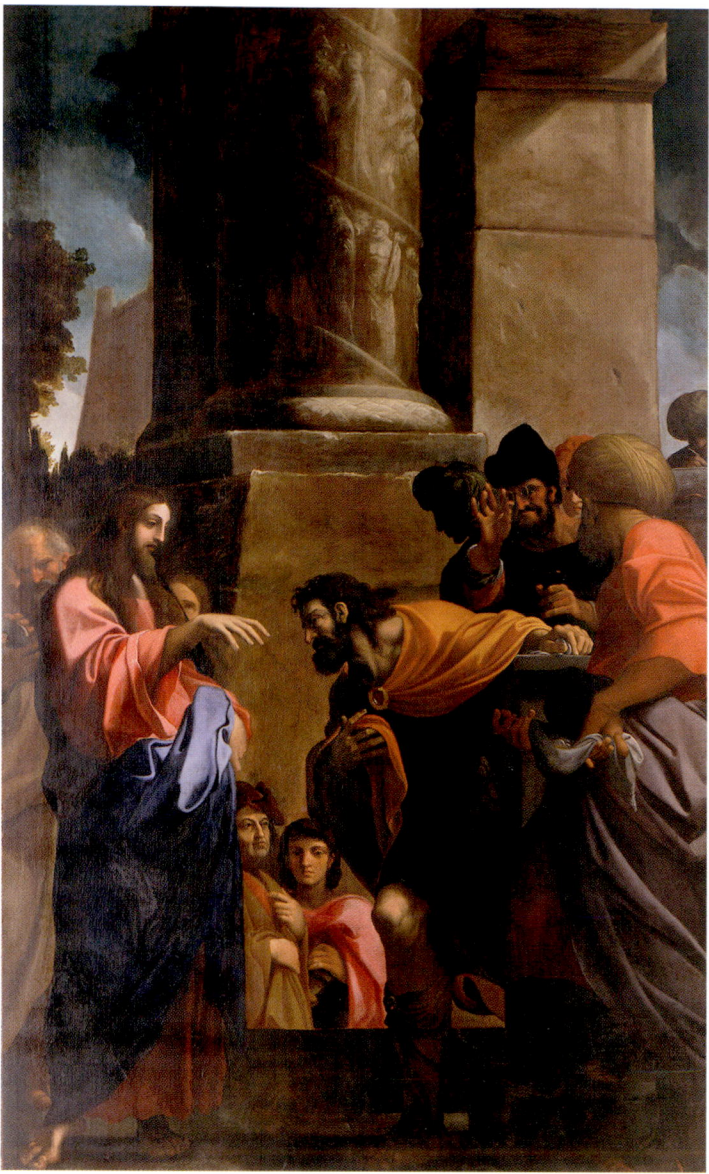

Fig. 99
Ludovico Carracci, *The Calling of Saint Matthew*, Pinacoteca Nazionale, Bologna, oil on canvas, 449 x 265 cm.

Gail Feigenbaum have attenuated the importance of this influence, enumerating the countless differences between the two paintings.[42] I am mostly inclined to agree with them, for it is evident that, on many counts, Ludovico strove to distance himself from Caravaggio. Yet, in declaring this, I implicitly admit that a tangible influence still exists, strong enough to be detectable in the Bologna picture.

Of course, Ludovico was called upon to paint a canvas whose gigantic format and vertical orientation demanded a treatment dramatically different from that of Caravaggio's *Calling*. To anchor Christ's and Matthew's titanic bulks to the painting's foreground, Ludovico planted high at the center of the composition a monumental pedestal and, atop it, a spiral column embellished with antique bas-reliefs, suggesting that the episode took place at the entrance of the holy city, Jerusalem. On the left, Christ soars in the foreground, his legs and thighs directed frontward, his torso solemnly swiveling toward Matthew as if he had halted in his tracks momentarily to accomplish the miracle. To the right, the publican kneels with deference in front of the Savior, one hand over his chest to voice his obedience, the other still grabbing a coin in a gesture that is exactly the same as that of Caravaggio's Matthew. It is important to dwell on this captivating detail: not only does it hint unequivocally at the Contarelli painting's precedent, but it also aims to improve upon Caravaggio's composition. Through his attitude, Ludovico's Matthew indeed conveys the impression of a longer span of temporality, inducing the viewer to imagine the tax collector quitting his office upon Christ's call and eagerly accepting the Savior's invitation.

In a certain sense, Ludovico could not have been more explicit in criticizing the temporal layout of *The Calling*—that is, Caravaggio's obscurity in evoking Matthew's response to Jesus. Immediately behind the publican, Ludovico represented a bearded man with a dark purple beret putting on his glasses and looking outward at the beholder. He holds a pouch of money and grimaces in a way that obviously bespeaks his comical function in the painting. In my opinion, Ludovico showed through this figure how Caravaggio should have treated the bespectacled elderly man at the left of *The Calling*. Like Bellori many decades later, Ludovico interpreted this feature as an "accessory" with great potential: an anecdotal insertion necessary to create variety in the *istoria*. For this reason, Ludovico made the figure's comicality transparent by endowing him with a burlesque attitude.

---

42   See Feigenbaum's catalogue entry in Emiliani 1993, 141-2, no. 65.

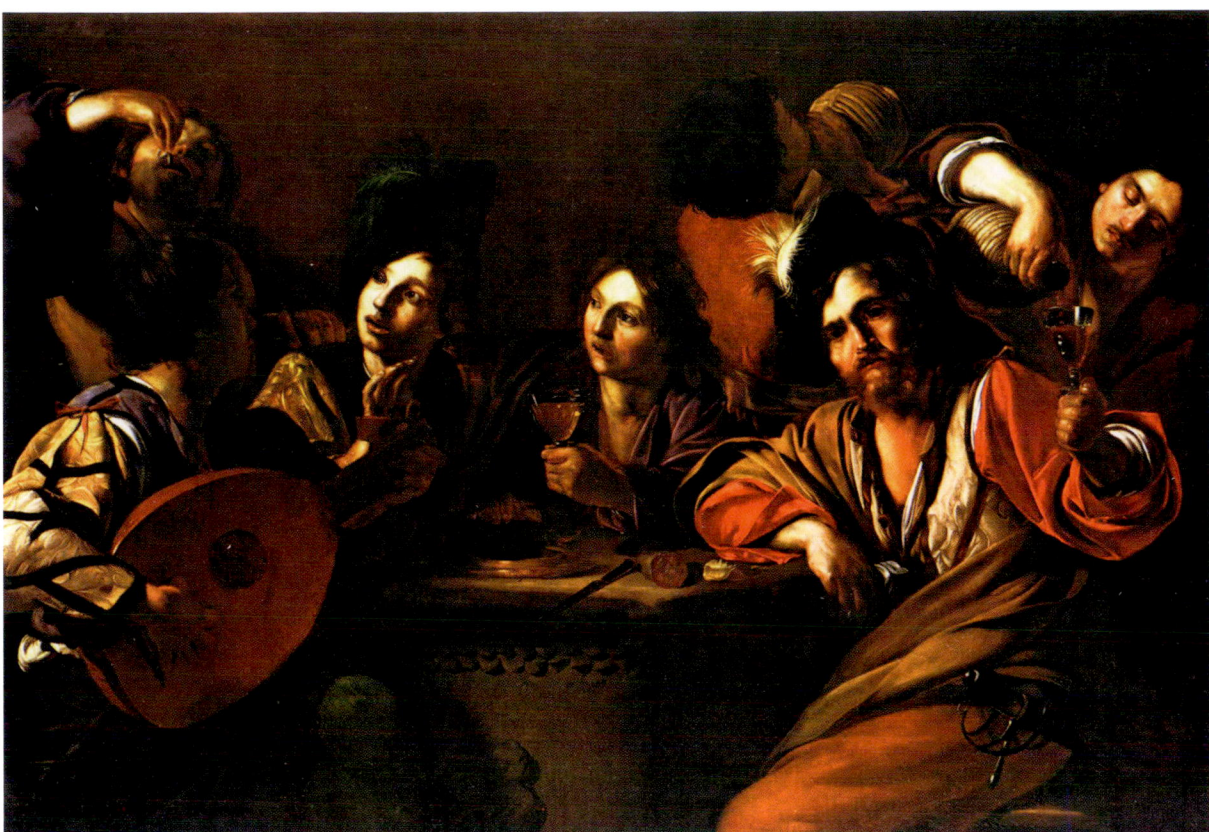

Fig. 100
Bartolomeo Manfredi, *Tavern Scene*, Trafalgar Galleries, London, oil on canvas, 120 x 190 cm.

Needless to say, scholars have strenuously focused on the hand gesture of Ludovico's Christ and on its connection with Caravaggio's *Calling of Saint Matthew*. It is a fact that Ludovico did not reproduce Caravaggio's quotation from Michelangelo. But is it legitimate to assume on this basis that Ludovico did not have Caravaggio's example in mind at all? Feigenbaum has pointed out that the hand gesture represented by Ludovico belonged to the traditional iconography of the conversion. I have been unable to trace it in the Renaissance tradition and it would seem to be a pithy and somewhat odd invention by Ludovico. In any event, thanks to its rhetorical relevance and narrative function, the hand gesture parallels that of Caravaggio's Christ. In fact, Ludovico purposefully isolated Jesus' disproportionate hand against the pedestal's brownish backdrop by spotlighting it powerfully, thereby making Matthew's sight converge toward, and close in upon, the gesture. Given the perspicuity of the new narrative context, the hand's excessive proximity to Matthew becomes emphatically redundant and the gesture itself proves to be unnecessarily affected. If Ludovico intended in this way to reassess and elucidate the cause-and-effect relationship between Christ's exhortation and Matthew's answer as staged in the Contarelli painting, he fulfilled his goal only in part, for the hand gesture in the Mendicanti picture loses the mysterious force of attraction that it originally possessed in *The Calling* as a result of Caravaggio's deliberate obscurities. Be that as it may, the hand gesture of Ludovico's Christ is yet another reaction to Caravaggio's work, a critical amendment to Caravaggio's indeterminacy in the *istoria*. However, other artists picked up on Caravaggio's novelty and elaborated upon it in ways opposite to Ludovico's.

At an unknown date, but probably at the beginning of the 1610s, the Italian follower of Caravaggio, Bartolomeo Manfredi, developed the situational theme at the core of *The Calling of Saint Matthew* in an astonishing *Tavern Scene with Musicians and Drinkers* (Trafalgar Galleries, London;

227

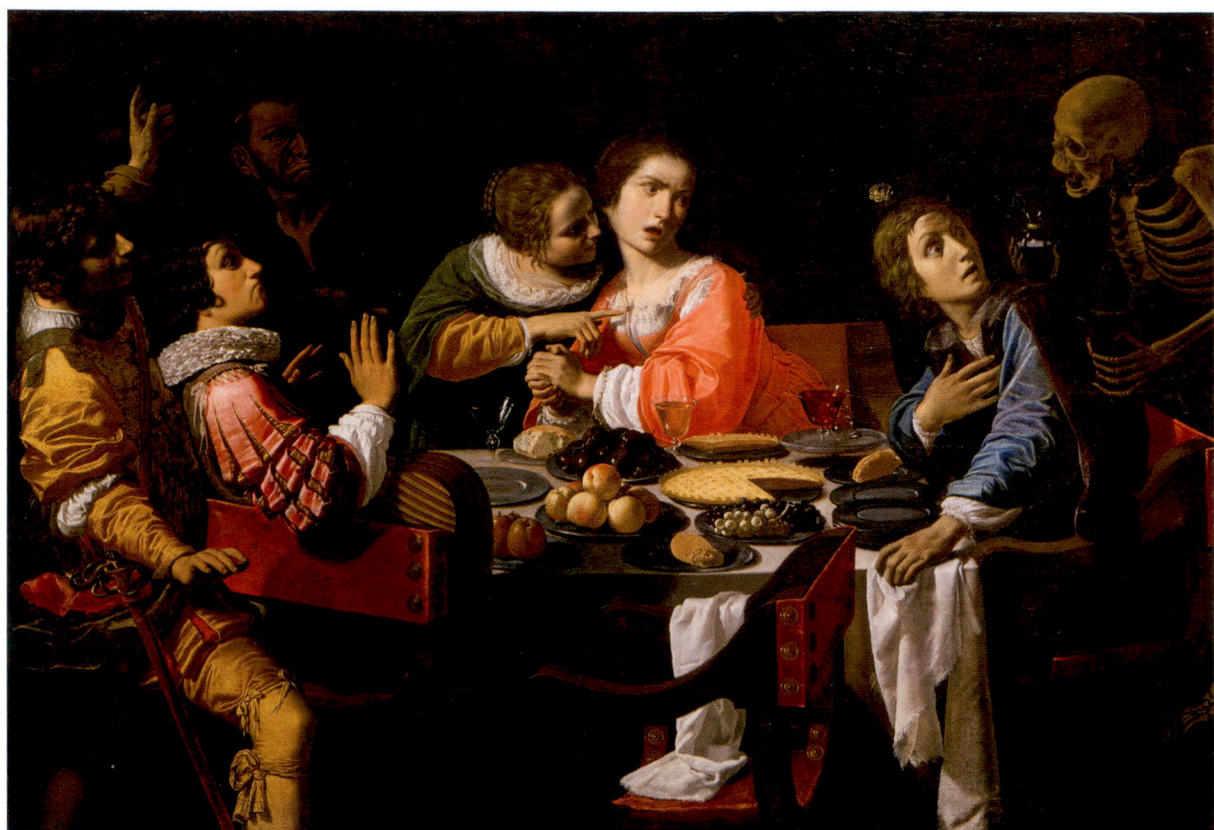

Fig. 101
Giovanni Martinelli, *Death Comes to the Banquet*, New Orleans Museum of Art, New Orleans, oil on canvas, 120.7 x 174 cm.

Fig. 100).[43] To a certain degree, Manfredi's composition is almost a cut-in of the table group in the Contarelli painting. Imagine a close-up view of Matthew and his acolytes with the noticeable omission of Christ and his companion to the right. Frame this visual sequence by leaving aside the window and the wall at the top, the figures being represented exclusively down to their thighs. And now invert the painting's orientation by letting the sunshine in from the left. By doing so, one will obtain the eerie effect of a tavern scene with an accountant's still life on the table, interrupted by an unspecified event that the viewer would intuitively associate with the in-pouring radiance of external lighting. If one now substitutes the table with the block of an ancient sarcophagus, the accountant's still life with a salami snack, and inserts into the scene a musician playing a lute as a soundtrack enjoyable to the figures but silent to us, one will come up with a script amazingly similar to that enacted in Manfredi's painting.

I shall now describe the action as depicted in the *Tavern Scene*. I shall not comment further on the three figures in the background: the man on the left bringing to his mouth something to eat; and, arranged in harmonious *contrapposto*, the two people carrying or drinking from a wine flask. On a narrative level and as anecdotal walk-ons, the figures serve overall to stress the continuity of the narrative flow: the action's uneventful backstage. In the right foreground, a bearded man with a plumed hat and a sword at his belt turns to the beholder as if in the act of toasting. Physically, the man is the analog of Caravaggio's Matthew, although his beret and sword recall the youth's in the foreground of *The Calling*. By drawing the viewer's attention, this prominent figure perversely makes the viewer overlook the very dramatic event unfolding in the painting, which undoubtedly

43   See Mina Gregori's catalogue entry in *Manfredi* 1987, 66, no. 5; and Hartje 2004, 312-5, no. A 11.

constitutes its main action: the unexplainable terror that overcomes the two boys behind the table. The boy on the left embraces his companion as if to protect him while shying away from a dreadful apparition: his open mouth, his wide-open eyes, and his lifted right hand convey sudden panic.[44] Warped through masterly foreshortening, the second boy's face expresses profound incredulity: the figure seems to have frozen out of fear, his glass of wine still suspended in mid-air. More difficult to understand is the lute player's attitude: either he pauses, alerted by the youths' dismay, or he keeps performing his music. In any case, by interposing himself between the visual field and the group of fearful boys, this figure, too, albeit with much less intensity, tends to distract the viewer's attention temporarily.

To my knowledge, only Nicole Hartje has truly questioned the meaning of the action narrated in Manfredi's *Tavern Scene*, although she has construed the youths' attitudes as a sign of melancholy, not of terror.[45] But if this is not melancholy—which it is certainly not—what then determines the boys' frightened reactions? And more to the point, what is the painting's subject? It is evident that this is not an ordinary "merry company," even if all the features of this iconographic theme reappear here. As a truncated elaboration on Caravaggio's *Calling*, one might be tempted to believe that the painting's off-scene element coincides with a divine epiphany. But why should God's manifestation frighten the two boys? Perhaps the only means of identifying the invisible actor or event is with the help of a picture attributed to Giovanni Martinelli, which presents close affinities to the painting of Manfredi and Cecco del Caravaggio: the c.1630 *Death Comes to the Banquet* (New Orleans Museum of Art, New Orleans).[46] There, a group of young men and women at a table become horrified at Death's abrupt irruption during a sumptuous meal (Fig 101). Predictably, Martinelli placed the lighting source at the opposite side of Death, implying that Death—a skeleton with a sandglass—comes from darkness. As Martinelli seems to have been familiar with the production of Caravaggio's followers, and more specifically with Manfredi's output, it is plausible that he completed and clarified what was unexpressed in this master's *Tavern Scene*: Death's unexpected presence. Of course, Martinelli might have interpreted the theme of Manfredi's painting incorrectly. Nonetheless, in one of Caravaggio's principal sources for the table group in *The Calling*, Holbein's *Death and the Gambler*, an analogous situation is evoked: Death and the Devil interrupting a tavern scene. Also, the posture and expression of Death's skull in Martinelli's picture mirror those of the Devil's head in Holbein's woodcut. This network of visual cross-references may be coincidental. But what if all these pictorial inter-textualities instead reflect a tenacious debate among Caravaggio's followers and even sympathizers concerning narrative ambiguities, the potential and limits of their developments, and the extent to which action should remain intelligible and legible in painting? Is it not true that, as Sandrart's misreading of the Contarelli pictures demonstrates, the tavern scene is a porous sub-genre, susceptible to hybridizations, and therefore open to multiple readings when adroitly manipulated?

To close the circle, it is important to mention Nicolas Tournier's c.1623 *Drinking Party with Lute Player* (Musée du Berry, Bourges).[47] In this painting, a figure's gaze directed off-scene once again

44 It is worth noting that Manfredi employed the same expression, though more accentuated, in a figure of his *Christ Driving the Merchants out of the Temple* (Musée des Beaux-Arts, Libourne): I refer to the young man with the plumed beret in flight from the Savior's outburst.

45 Hartje 2004, 226-30.

46 The painting, of which many versions and adaptations survive, has been attributed to numerous artists from the circle of Caravaggio's followers: Cecco del Caravaggio, the enigmatic Jean Ducamps, Domenico Carpinoni and, more recently, the Tuscan painter Giovanni Martinelli. See in this regard Spear 1971, 88-9, no. 24 [with extensive bibliography];

Chiara D'Afflitto in *Seicento Fiorentino* 1986, 3: 115-6; Papi 1997, 128-30; Papi 2001, 43. Ruggeri 1984, 242-3, no. 6, publishes two paintings from private collections in Bergamo and Milan, bearing the monogram "DC," and therefore executed by Domenico Carpinoni. As Ruggeri points out, the composition of these two pictures is almost identical to that of the New Orleans painting, which however seems to be a work by Martinelli, not Carpinoni. In the absence of better documentation, I content myself with noting this complicated issue, which nonetheless proves the wide diffusion of this composition. According to Ruggeri 1984, 215, Carpinoni's paintings date to the early 1620s.

47 See Hémery 2001, 88-9, no. 5.

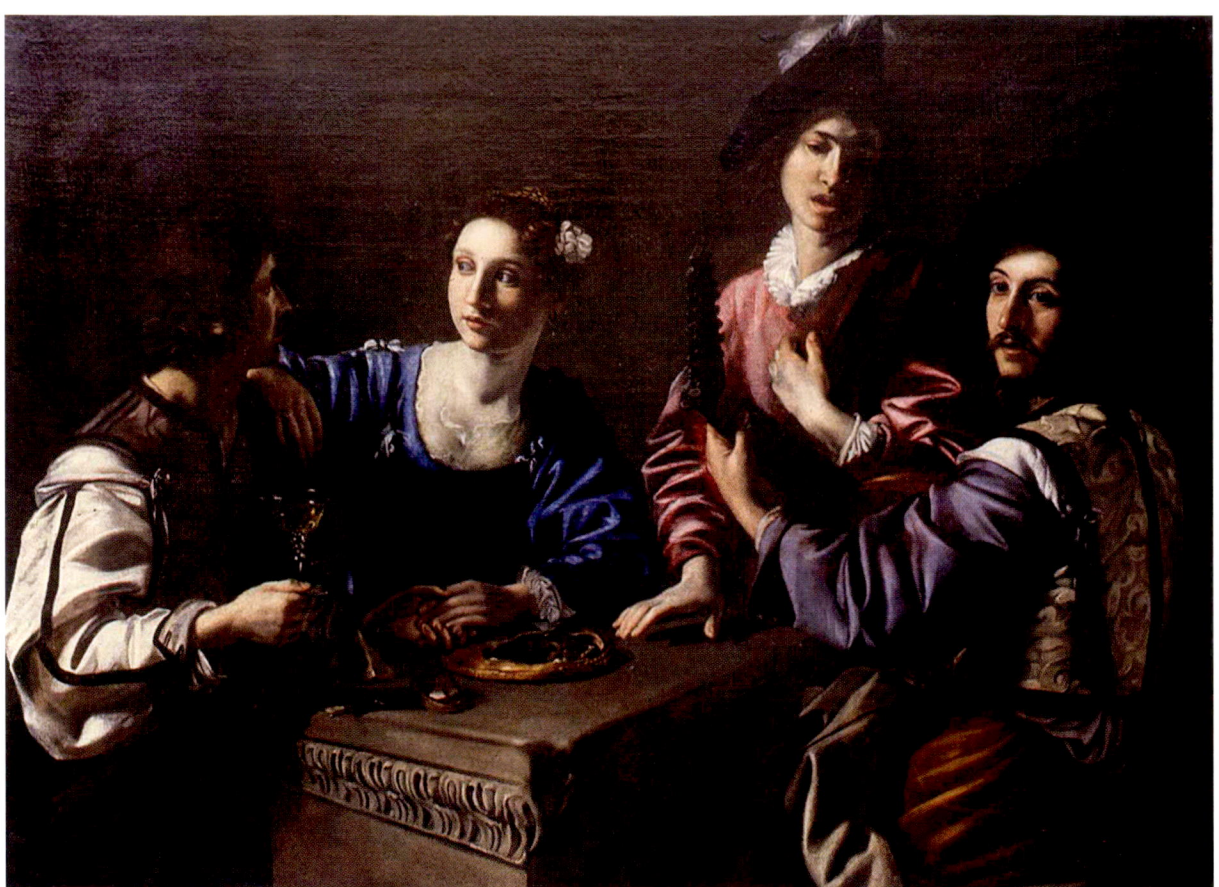

Fig. 102
Nicolas Tournier, *Drinking Party with Lute Player*, Musée du Berry, Bourges, oil on canvas, 120 x 60 cm.

introduces narrative indeterminacy (Fig. 102). A disciple of Manfredi, Tournier copied his master's works with a certain frequency, among them the London *Tavern Scene*.[48] In his Bourges painting, Tournier varied the narrative situation depicted in Manfredi's painting while preserving some of its key figures, a group of people at a table enjoying music's pleasure. To the right, a lute player with his back turned, his sight oriented forward, seemingly approaches the beholder. Next to him, a standing youth sings with enraptured concentration. To the left, another young man lifts a glass of wine, while tenderly holding his beloved's hand. He stares at the woman at his side almost transfixed, though her eyes veer toward the left off-scene, from where sunshine streams in. However, this time fear is not involved at all, so that the viewer is probably less curious about what truly distracts the woman's attention. More interesting, this female figure is taken directly from Caravaggio's *The Calling of Saint Matthew:* her attitude exactly mirrors that of the boy beside the bearded man. However one might interpret Manfredi's and Tournier's scenes, it is undeniable that both artists meditated on, and exploited, the narrative suspense of the Contarelli painting, the dramatically fraught interruption of a tavern episode with only one or two figures aware of the disruptive event—the catastrophe of Aristotle's *Poetics*—in the indifference of collateral actors.

What characterizes Manfredi's elaboration upon Caravaggio's suspense effect—Tournier simply follows in Manfredi's footsteps—is his concealment of the dramatic motive. In this manner, he plunges the viewer into narrative blindness; whatever frightens the London picture's boys is a matter of speculation that enormously amplifies, but never appeases, the beholder's curiosity.

48   The painting is now in the Musée de Tessé, Le Mans. See
Hémery 2001, 80-2, no. 1.

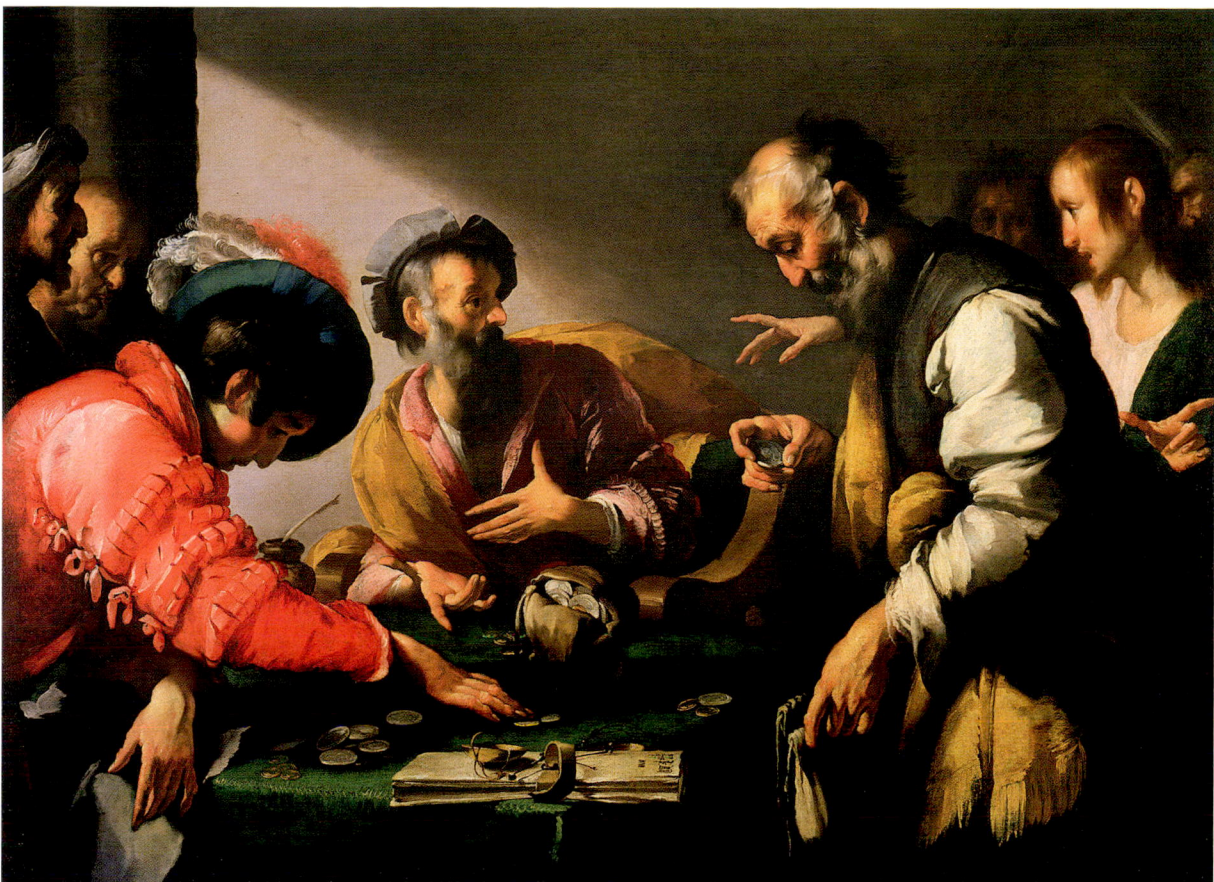

Fig. 103
Bernardo Strozzi, *The Calling of Saint Matthew*, Worcester Art Museum, Worcester, oil on canvas, 139 x 188.5 cm.

As a corollary, the unknown identity or scope of the off-scene actor or event makes it impossible to determine the painting's genre. Is this a tragedy? Death's precipitous irruption amidst youth's amusements? A kind of *Et in Arcadia Ego* with a tavern setting? Or is this a comedy? Is the thing or person causing the protagonists' disquiet merely insignificant and their reaction excessive? It is up to the viewer to complete the script suggested by the painting. In any case, the reason why I insist on Manfredi's manipulation of a suspense effect devised by Caravaggio is because I am convinced that the dramatic motive of the action unfolding in the Contarelli painting is, if not physically concealed, at least equally nebulous and indistinct. Put otherwise, Manfredi's suppression of the drama's efficient cause is a simple, albeit most audacious, radicalization of Caravaggio's narrative indeterminacy as orchestrated in *The Calling*. Indeed, the source for the viewer's blindness is already embedded in the Contarelli painting, but surprisingly enough, it lies undetected, that is, dissimulated by actors faking the congruousness of an *istoria*. In a certain sense, Manfredi accepted the possibility that Jesus and his disciple in *The Calling* might be invisible to most of the surrounding figures; he incorporated this invisibility into his London *Tavern Scene* through a strikingly innovative off-scene device. As I will show shortly, other painters went much farther than Manfredi in this regard.

Properly speaking, this is not yet the case with Bernardo Strozzi's *c.*1620 *The Calling of Saint Matthew*, now at the Worcester Art Museum, Worcester (Fig. 103).[49] Nevertheless, this painting calls for closer scrutiny owing to its many allusions to the Contarelli painting. There is no doubt that

49   See Mortari 1995, 344, no. 343.

Strozzi knew Caravaggio's works very well. His is a wonderfully executed copy of Caravaggio's *The Calling of Saints Peter and Andrew*, a painting probably lost.[50] Strozzi's copy now belongs to a private collection in Genoa. In the Worcester picture, the elongated perspective of a counter seen from its lateral end leads toward Matthew, his face in profile, one hand over his breast while the other points to the coins in front of him. He is obviously gazing at Christ who, just like his counterpart in the Contarelli painting, stretches his hand toward the tax collector in a gesture that clearly stems from Michelangelo's Adam via Caravaggio. This time, the Savior is cornered against the canvas' right margin, visually relegated off-center through the screen of an old man prominently standing in the foreground. More important, the figure of the elderly man separates Christ from the calling hand, a trick that Strozzi also borrowed from Caravaggio, although he increased its oddity by juxtaposing Jesus' gesture and the old man's face. Also in the foreground, a youth bends over the table, shifting some coins, his left hand wedged under his right elbow. Because of the youth's posture, his feathered hat, red jacket and sleeves adorned with slashed puffs—an even more archaic variant of Caravaggio's stripes—he is the peer of the youth on *The Calling*'s left. It is evident that Strozzi interpreted this figure as an accountant, and therefore made his activity less ambivalent. Since he fixedly inspects a coin that he holds in his right hand, Strozzi's old man also acts as a witty alias of Caravaggio's bespectacled elderly man; in a sense, this figure needs his counterpart's glasses to assess the coin's value. Incidentally, the wittiness of Caravaggio's old man was not lost on Strozzi, who reproduced him in a *Supper at Emmaus* now in a private collection.[51] There, Strozzi represented an apostle who dons his glasses as if to verify Christ's identity.

In some aspects, Strozzi's rendition of Matthew's conversion is more detailed than Caravaggio's. Not only are the figures' tasks neatly defined, but their attributes are also described with sharpness: for instance, the account book in the foreground with its buckle and the small balance with which tax collectors ordinarily weighed the money. Despite these clarifications, Strozzi also disorients the beholder by obscuring Christ's role, laying emphasis instead on the two foreground figures, which nevertheless are simple narrative accessories. At first glance, Strozzi's figure of the Savior is thus barely discernable: he is temporarily invisible, and his hand gesture, because of its isolation, becomes an enigmatic cipher. That is, until the viewer spots Jesus' presence in the background of the canvas' periphery and reconstructs Strozzi's tortuous narrative set-up. In his own way Strozzi, too, seems to have recognized the volatile status of Christ's presence in the Contarelli picture.

However, it must be said that only the Dutch followers of Caravaggio dared imply Christ's invisibility to Matthew's companions in their numerous adaptations of the Contarelli picture. First of all, consider Jan van Bijlert's 1625-1630 *Calling of Saint Matthew* (Museum Catharijneconvent, Utrecht).[52] Like Strozzi, Bijlert represented the already canonical figures of the young man with a plumed beret and the bespectacled old man in the foreground, situating Christ and Matthew in the second row at a considerable distance from one another (Fig. 104). Bijlert's young man is unmistakably related to Caravaggio's swindler in *The Cardsharps*: his turned back, his hand over the table, his face in profile and even the detail of the dagger tucked behind the belt confirm the kinship. Yet the posture of the leaning hand summons up that of *The Calling*'s young man who bends over the table. Next to him, a bald and bearded old man, equipped with glasses, weighs the coins on a balance as he tilts his head skyward. Both the young and the elderly men, comically

50 See Gavazza et al. 1995, 142, no. 23. Very recently, Caravaggio's original has been identified with a painting in the Queen's Gallery, Buckingham Palace, London. Although Rupert Featherstone's analysis of the X-ray photograph of this canvas tends to suggest that Caravaggio's is indeed the underpainting of the composition, the canvas as it is cannot by any means be assigned to the master. It is not unconceivable that Caravaggio left the painting unfinished and that an

artist in his circle finished it. I had the opportunity to assess Featherstone's ideas during a lecture he gave at the Getty Museum, Los Angeles, in 2008. To get a sense of his opinions, see Featherstone 2006.

51 See Gavazza et al. 1995, 148, no. 26.

52 See Huys Janssen 1998, 101-2, no. 20.

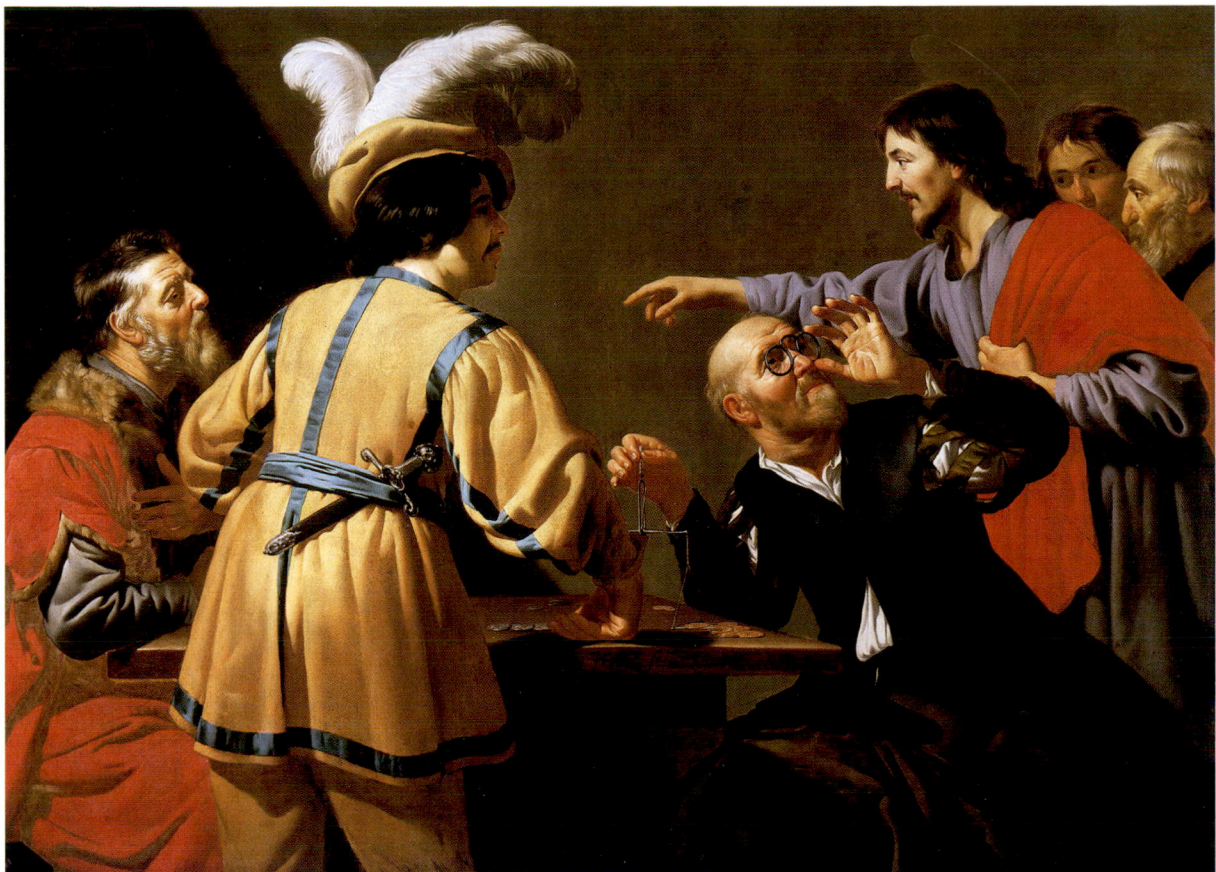

Fig. 104
Jan van Bijlert, *The Calling of Saint Matthew*, Museum Catharijneconvent, Utrecht, oil on canvas, 144 x 199.5 cm.

or tragically, depending on the viewpoint, are evidently at a loss to comprehend from where the call comes: the former looks directly to the right, and the latter adjusts his glasses in staring at the ceiling. It is even impossible to ascertain whether they react to a visual or an acoustic stimulus. Is it Christ's voice calling Matthew that alerts them? Or is it some unidentifiable visual sign? Or perhaps, something completely unrelated to the dramatic plot represented in the painting? Paradoxically, light enters the scene from the left, leaving the young man's face in the shade while illuminating his neck: hence it is not even divine sunlight that demands these figures' attention. In any event, they must be deaf and blind since they do not register the presence of the imposing Christ behind them, at the right, pointing to and unequivocally addressing Matthew, the elderly man who, sitting to the left, is dressed in a furred cloak, putting his hand over his chest while carefully listening to, and observing, the Savior.

One cannot dismiss Bijlert's multiple references to Caravaggio's painting, the most remarkable one being the very attitude of Christ with the typical hand gesture and face in profile. In my opinion, Bijlert's elaboration on Caravaggio's original idea becomes understandable only if one concedes that the unawareness of Bijlert's foreground figures echoes and develops that of Matthew's acolytes in *The Calling*. More specifically, by representing the empty gaze of the foreground youth, Bijlert not only recalls the young man pivoting on his bench in the Contarelli picture, but he also presupposes that Caravaggio's figure might be metaphorically blind to the divine epiphany nearby. In this context, note the ambiguous interplay of Christ's hand gesture and the youth's posture in Bijlert's painting. Inadvertently, the beholder might think that the Savior points to the young man, and not to Matthew. In sum, the spatial layout designed by Bijlert tricks the viewer into believing that

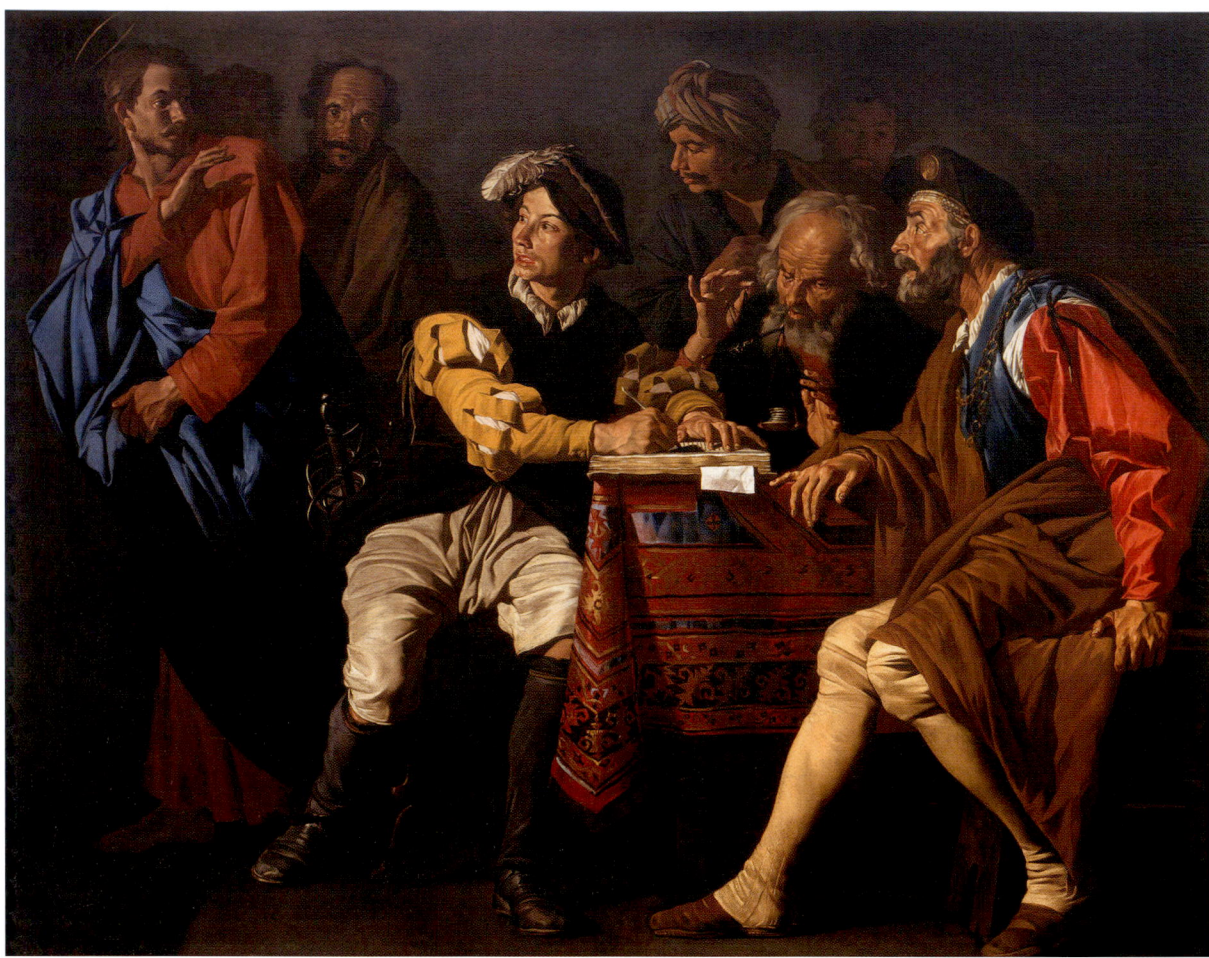

Fig. 105
Matthias Stomer, *The Calling of Saint Matthew*, Fine Arts Museum, San Francisco, oil on canvas, 174.9 x 224 cm.

these two figures respond to one another, though in fact no interaction is explicitly represented. Is it possible that the same applies to Caravaggio's picture? More to the point, is Caravaggio's young man with his back turned truly aware of the adjacent apostle's presence? What is certain is that in the Contarelli *Calling* Christ does not wave at the swiveling youth, although the hand gesture elegantly rhymes with the spanning feather of the young man's hat, another visual ruse subtly concocted by Caravaggio.

If one now rotates Caravaggio's figure of this young man so that he appears frontally, the result does not differ dramatically from the posture that Matthias Stomer imagined for the central actor of his *c.*1629 *Calling of Saint Matthew*, now in the Fine Arts Museum, San Francisco (Fig. 105).[53] Stomer's work is a complex masterpiece of misdirection. Probably because Stomer constructed the scene's spatial field with more clarity, distributing the figures as if on staggering friezes, the eeriness of the whole action transpires straightaway. At the right, a bearded man with a beret almost identical to his counterpart's in the Contarelli picture seems about to rise, his left fist clenched around the rim of the chair's seat. His open mouth betrays his surprise, as does his lifted eyebrow as he gazes at the Savior walking away at a distance across from him in the left background. Because of these two figures' relative positions, it might take some time for the viewer to realize their mutual relationship. At the same table, directly behind the bearded figure, an old man is wholly disconnected from the main event; he concentrates on the coins that he weighs with utmost delicacy. To his right, the young man that I have already mentioned appears dumbstruck: he must at once have quitted writing in the account book since the pen still presses against the open page, which his left hand keeps in place with diligence. It is obvious that an exceptional event or sound has interfered with his activity, forcing him to turn leftward. However, Stomer does not reveal what occupies the young man's attention. His face, though, is strongly spotlighted by an off-scene radiance that does not coincide with Christ's presence, but that on the contrary tends to eclipse the Savior's tan-hued figure. It goes without saying that this youth, too, like other analogous figures in the paintings of Strozzi and Bijlert that I have just investigated, is not only unable to see Christ, but his reaction is also directed to a target quite different from the narrative's sacred hero.

Even more curious, both the Savior's calling gesture and gaze ignore the bearded figure in the right foreground, the only one to be conspicuously aware of Jesus' presence, and are apparently oriented toward a turbaned man in the third row, completely extraneous to the ongoing miracle. To complicate the script, one of Christ's apostles glimpses at the young accountant with the plumed hat, the very same figure gazing at the left off-scene. If one examines with attention Stomer's painting, it becomes evident that no figure properly qualifies as Matthew. More than in the Contarelli painting, the beholder might hesitate over the future apostle's real identity. Of course, visual and narrative indeterminacy are not fortuitous features of Stomer's painting: the master intentionally shuffled all the elements of the composition in order to muddy the action's intelligibility. Shuffling seems the right term to define Stomer's operation; if one isolates the figures of the bearded man, the youth with the plumed beret and Christ, all aligned on a diagonal, one would immediately understand that they are deliberately misaligned—that is, misplaced on three distinct planes. For the narrative to function, one needs simply to shift Christ's figure to the foreground. Yet Stomer resorted to misalignment in view of obscuring the pictorial plot, and this to the point that even Jesus seems to have lost his Matthew. In this regard, it must be noted that in the Contarelli painting, Caravaggio had instead firmly incorporated alignment as a narrative device: Jesus and the bearded man, Peter and the youth with his back turned, appear on the same plane. Despite these convergences, Caravaggio's followers sensed that *The Calling*'s narrative connectivity presented its loose ends, and ingeniously tried to cash in on them.

In this respect, Hendrick ter Brugghen certainly distinguishes himself as one of the boldest and more perceptive interpreters of the Contarelli picture. At the center of his *c.*1618-19 *Calling of Saint Matthew* (Musée des Beaux-Arts André Malraux, Le Havre),[54] ter Brugghen positioned an unmistakable quotation of Caravaggio's painting: a youth with a hat and cascading feather swiveling on a stool and represented from behind (Fig. 106). In this manner, ter Brugghen deliberately activated a comparison with the Contarelli picture, thereby prompting the viewer to see one figure in light of the other. To the same end, he depicted to the right an old man hunched over the table, enthralled in the contemplation of a coin that he examines with the help of his glasses. This old man, too, is taken from Caravaggio's Contarelli painting, and replaces the young man to the left, although his physiognomy and attributes at the same time recall Caravaggio's bespectacled elderly man. Once one takes into account that ter Brugghen reversed the original orientation of the Contarelli *Calling*, it becomes easy to detect other affinities between the two paintings. First of all, a bearded man behind the table squeezes a coin between his index and thumb in a posture that is clearly indebted to his counterpart's in Caravaggio's picture. Similarly, he points a finger toward himself with hesitancy, so that the hand gesture, albeit in a different way, proves to be as ambiguous as that of Caravaggio's bearded man.

Surprisingly enough, ter Brugghen's Matthew seems not to look at Christ, but toward the left off-scene where two apostles, their backs turned, appear to exit. On an intermediary plane between the foreground youth and the bearded man, ter Brugghen placed Christ's figure, immersed in

---

53   On the painting, see Weller 1998, 193-4, no. 36.   54   See Slatkes and Franits 2007, 122-3, no. A 33.

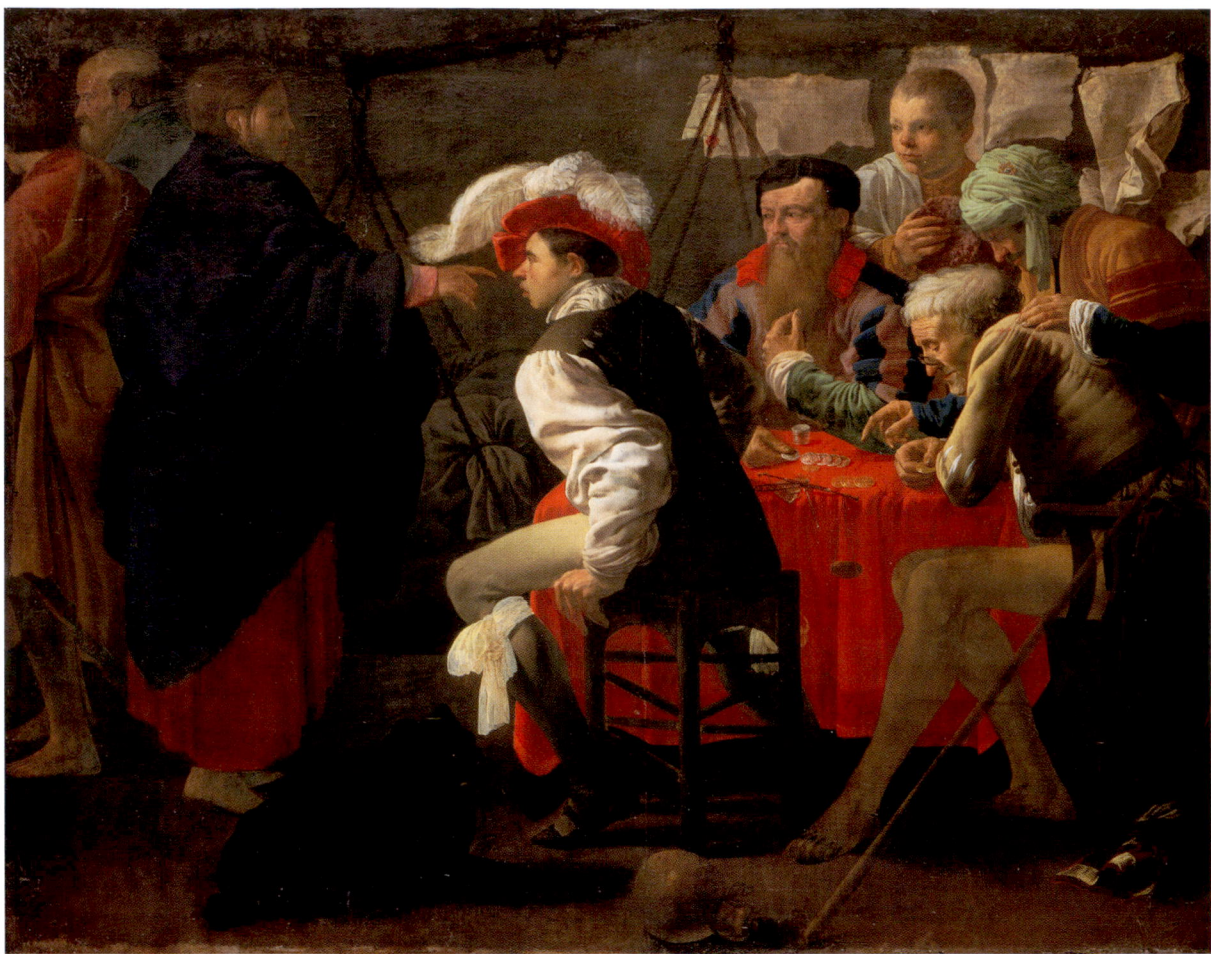

Fig. 106
Hendrick ter Brugghen, *The Calling of Saint Matthew*, Musée des Beaux-Arts, Le Havre, oil on canvas, 152 x 195 cm.

somber penumbra, inviting Matthew to the apostolate. Though invisible to the young man nearby, Jesus seems to point his finger toward the youth's profile, his body so dangerously close to the plumed hat of the latter that the feather illusorily grazes the Savior's hand and sleeve, which nonetheless would not be possible given the distance between the two figures. I do not need to prove again that, by using the foreground boy as a sort of smoke screen, ter Brugghen obscured the cause-and-effect relationship between Christ's calling hand and Matthew's response to it. More importantly, the master also suggested that, in spite of Jesus' presence, Matthew's answer might not be addressed to him. In other words, ter Brugghen explicitly implied the Savior's invisibility by disconnecting him from the composition's narrative causality and by immerging his figure into the haze of pictorial shade.

The visual link between the youth and Christ in ter Brugghen's painting conjures and elaborates upon the interrelation between the young man with his back turned and the apostle as evoked in the Contarelli *Calling*. But does this mean that Caravaggio also made Peter invisible to the youth nearby? It is noteworthy that Caravaggio added, or rather superimposed, the figure of Christ's disciple later, when the compositional layout of the painting had already been fixed. In the original version of the Contarelli *Calling* the young man, turned to the right, faced nothing but the void. From this point of view, one would be inclined to believe that Caravaggio inserted the apostle's figure as a narrative counterpoint to clarify the youth's attitude, were it not for the fact that, as I have already noted, through chiaroscuro Caravaggio irreparably blurred their interconnection: if the apostle truly remained in front of the young man, he should cast his shadow upon him, which is by

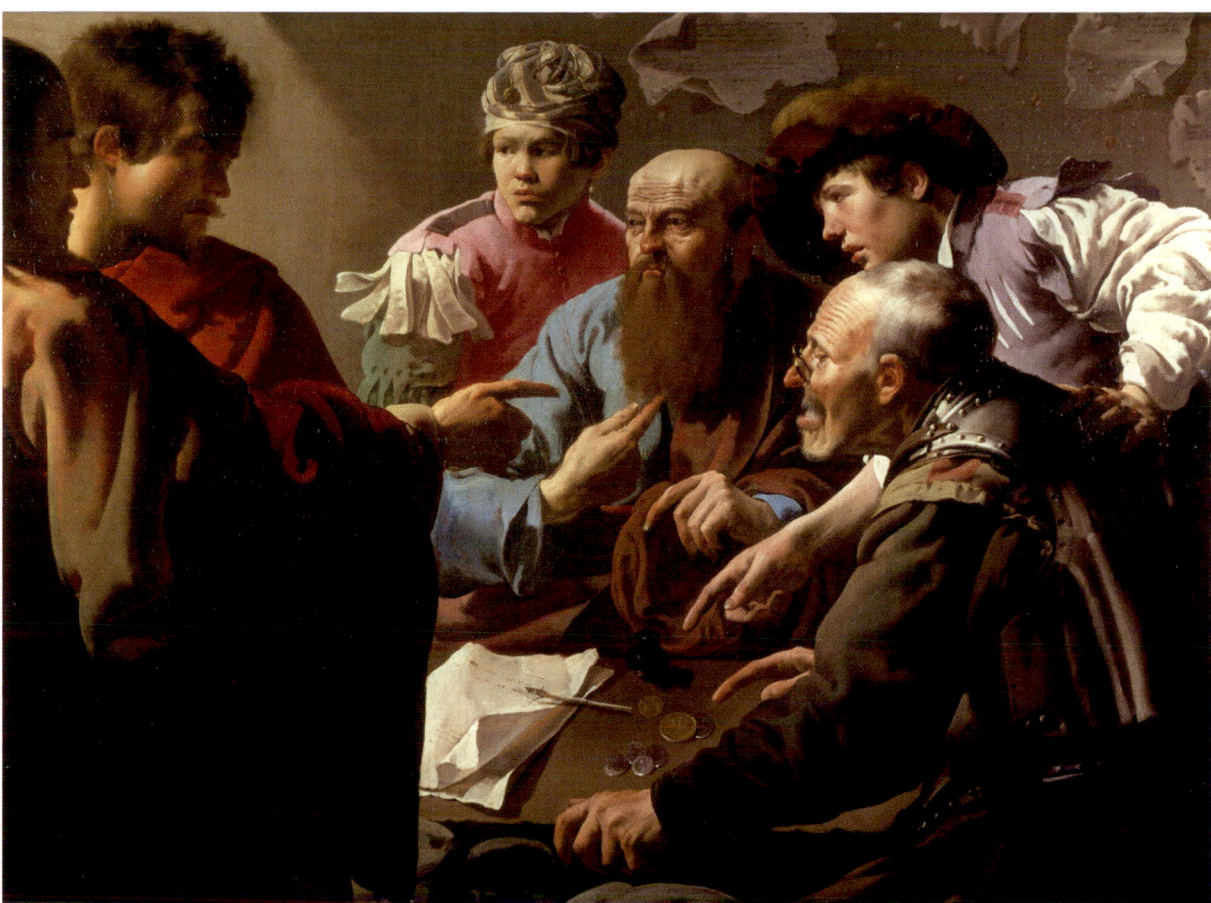

Fig. 107
Hendrick ter Brugghen, *The Calling of Saint Matthew*, Centraal Museum, Utrecht, oil on canvas, 102.3 x 136.9 cm.

no means the case. In a sense, through lighting Caravaggio insinuates either that the apostle lingers in an intermediary space between the two youths at the table's right end (although the painting's compressed and shallow depth seems to rule out this possibility) or that his presence is symbolic, not actual: that is, he is there for the viewer, but not for the young man's figure nearby. It is clear to me that ter Brugghen not only perceived the ambivalent status and function of Caravaggio's apostle, but he also enhanced this ambiguity in his rendition of the figure of Christ, an equivalent to Peter in *The Calling* owing to his proximity to the pivoting youth.

As if to emphasize the point, ter Brugghen reinforced the tricks of invisibility that he had inherited from Caravaggio when he dealt with the same iconographic subject a second time. I refer here to his 1621 *Calling of Saint Matthew*, now at the Centraal Museum, Utrecht (Fig. 107).[55] With intelligence and inventive audacity, ter Brugghen opted here for a diving view of the tax collector's table and the accountants, moving the spectator's viewpoint to a position right beside the cropped figures of Christ and a young apostle. The Savior is so close to the beholder that his mantle, wrapped around his lifted arm, heavily droops across the foreground. It cannot be highlighted enough how deftly ter Brugghen managed to create the impression of an orbiting sight. Intuitively, the beholder's eyes derail toward the adjoining group of Christ and the apostle, then proceed leftward as if to ascertain who or what catches the attention of the figures around the table. In this manner, ter Brugghen made it clear that the Savior's irruption into the scene does not

55 See Ibidem 123-6, no. A 34; and Silver 2000, for
Caravaggio's influence on ter Brugghen.

correlate with the accountants' reactions. Unequivocally, the divine and the human have parted ways in this painting.

The visual disassociation of Jesus and Matthew, two essential components of the calling narrative, here reaches its climax, for ter Brugghen pushes the viewer to doubt whether Matthew indeed responds to a divine invitation. As the tax collector—undoubtedly, the bearded man with an antique tunic—points to himself in the well-known gesture staged by Caravaggio in the Contarelli *Calling*, and the youth behind him fixedly gazes off scene, it is evident that the two other figures are exclusively concerned with money. The young man with the plumed hat, resting a hand on the shoulder of the bespectacled elder at his left, clearly indicates the sheet of paper on which Matthew was recording the revenues—the pen lies inert across the folio's puckered margins—even as his eyes dwell on the off-scene intruder or intruding event on the left. The old man with glasses, his torso sheltered with a metallic cuirass—a striking alter ego of the old peasant in Marinus van Reymerwaele's *The Lawyer's Office* at the Alte Pinakothek, Munich—intently considers the coins on the table, his right hand pointing toward the money, his jaw protruding as a sign of utter concentration. Judging from the figures' expressions and attitudes, it is clear that whoever or whatever addresses Matthew is perfectly visible or audible to all of the characters in the Utrecht picture, with the exception of the old man at the right. Paradoxically, the subject or cause of the calling cannot be Christ because, as I have already established, his profile and pointing finger are not directed toward Matthew and his acolytes. To complicate this comedy or drama of misdirection, ter Brugghen seems to have created a triple source of lighting: one investing the Savior from behind; another streaming from the left and vigorously illuminating the figures around the table; and a third coming from above and revealed by the oblique sign that it traces on the background wall.

Like Caravaggio before him, ter Brugghen disjoined the representation of divinity from light, engendering the impression—already familiar to us through Manfredi's example—that Matthew and his companions respond to the sunshine while distinctly overlooking Christ. But once again, had it not already been Caravaggio's idea to tamper with the scene's lighting by engendering effects that, though apparently all too natural, resist the logic of optics? Does one not see in the Contarelli painting a source of syncopated light bringing out the apostle's back, as well as Christ's neck, cheek, nose, and wrist? And despite these two bodies' interposition, is it not a fact that dense lighting continues to illuminate the figures around the table? And what about the light coming once again from the right, but slanting from above toward Matthew, revealing a lightless and blind window but avoiding Jesus' figure beneath? I will not discuss the inconsistency of the chiaroscuro system laid out by Caravaggio for his *Calling*: no one would deny the point. Instead, I will remark upon the fact that, as the various paintings previously examined have keenly demonstrated, viewers easily cope with a certain lack of optical and narrative verisimilitude when it comes to "reading" pictorial fictions. Without this premise, it would be inconceivable that artists like Caravaggio and his followers could in the first place have afforded dismantling narrative coherence in painting. Caravaggio's profound awareness of the pre-conceptions and simplifications to which pictorial narratives are submitted when first approached by beholders is exactly one of the facts that I seek to prove in this chapter. For this reason, I am moreover convinced that the master's celebrated realism is highly instrumental in camouflaging the numerous discordances of the sacred event that he represented in the Contarelli painting. I now return for the last time to *The Calling of Saint Matthew*.

Truth Is Not To Be Seen

Certainly more than its companion piece, *The Martyrdom of Saint Matthew*, *The Calling* constituted a telling manifesto of an entirely renovated art of painting. From Manfredi to Strozzi, from Stomer to ter Brugghen, many young masters from Italy and abroad scanned the painting, extracted from it a lexicon of postures and gestures destined to become canonical, and interpreted its syntax—the interrelation between figures and their interactions with space and chiaroscuro—as a portentous machine of dissimulation and dislocation. In some cases, these painters contributed to the durable celebrity of some of the master's formulas, for instance, the often elaborated-upon figure of the young man with his back turned. As I have demonstrated, most of these artists focused upon the potential invisibility of Christ and his disciple as implied in the Contarelli *Calling*. If anything, they tested Caravaggio's obscurities and pushed their implications to the extreme. Yet none of their paintings rivals Caravaggio's achievement. The reason is simple: by elucidating Caravaggio, they fatally compromised the effect of suspense and uncertainty that the master deeply enshrined within his work. Because every detail of the representation is apparently true to life, because the representation pretends to mirror reality, one abandons oneself to the gratifying impression that all makes sense in the Contarelli painting.

The optical enhancements and magnifications that Caravaggio activated with such unprecedented success in *The Calling* prevent the viewer from discovering that, in the matter of optics, and especially of lighting and spatiality, nature has been subverted and vision manipulated. Optics conceals fiction and permits pictorial appearance to form a blurring film between the beholder and the action enacted, that is, the painting's event. In contrast with Gabriele Paleotti's conviction about sight's effectiveness in channeling knowledge, Caravaggio here demonstrates that graphicness and meticulous rendition of optical effects might very well disobey the sacred episode's content and distort its message. More subtly, optics only conveys a surrogate truth, or a conventional representation of it. By lining up figures and facts in an apparently comprehensible order, and by assigning to light and space the task of jeopardizing and belying that same order, Caravaggio dramatically underlines how much vision is a matter of prejudice: seeing does not compare at all with knowledge, but only with pre-fabricated intuitions. Seeing is not observing, let alone understanding. Out of habit, their minds nurtured by a long iconographic tradition, viewers, if the painter knows how to handle them, jump to conclusions, anticipate the outcome, and simplify the action. Inconsistencies, when they are keenly dissimulated, and sometimes even when they are not, go unnoticed, and elude the eye that sees what it has been trained to see:[56] in the case of the Contarelli painting, a linear and univocal cause-and-effect relation between Christ's calling gesture and Matthew's response.

By now, it should be evident that Caravaggio, much more than his followers, relies on the viewer's expectations. More importantly, through the numerous and subtle breaches of verisimilitude and narrative connectivity that he inserted into *The Calling*, he denounced the process of trivialization induced by the conventions of iconography and its inappropriateness in transmitting the truth; visual habit weakens the act of processing and interpreting images, as it blinds beholders and hampers their aptitude to interrogate the artwork's true meaning. Is it possible to imagine a more compelling refusal of Counter-Reformation theorists' faith in the didactic value of sacred images? And can one conceive of a more efficient way to undermine what is probably the most radical tenet of Catholic iconography, that is, Christ's visibility? Even by the standards of Federico Borromeo,

---

56 The subtlety with which Caravaggio introduces and calibrates misperceptions in his paintings might reflect the interest with which artists in Milan at the end of the sixteenth century experimented with what DaCosta Kaufmann 2009, 10, 92-3, defines the "paradox of perception" in Arcimboldo's composite portraits.

the suggestion of Jesus' invisibility would certainly rank as an excessive manifestation of pictorial novelty, something to be remedied by resorting to the duller but more reassuring practice of traditional iconography.

Nonetheless, instead of representing Christ and Peter distinctly and as easily recognizable, Caravaggio invented what at first glance would qualify as an almost incomprehensible hieroglyph: the duplicitous fusion of two figures and bodies into a single entity, rehearsing the act of pointing and calling twice, their hands harmoniously configuring a flying buttress; in other words, the mysterious logogram of God's invitation to the apostolate.[57] To comprehend how illogical these two figures are on a narrative level, suffice it to consider the position of their feet, designing a pattern of misaligned and misdirected movements, as Burgard ingeniously put it.[58] In a sense, Christ and Peter come from, and go, nowhere: they literally materialize in front of the viewer. Of course, the potential invisibility of the divine figures suggested by Caravaggio in *The Calling* equally targets the relation between man's senses and intellect and God's acts as represented in painting. It is incontrovertible that by disjoining the source of light from the figure of Christ—pace Marzio Milesi and his claim to the contrary—Caravaggio disassociated the two signifiers through which divinity was, and still is, alluded to in religious images. Thus the question remains: where is God in *The Calling*? What really stimulates the diverse and irreconcilable reactions of Caravaggio's figures? How are we to explain the discrepancies of narrative tempos as elicited by the foreground young man's sudden swiveling and by the indolent, almost distracted staring of the youth near Matthew? And what about the other figures' indifference?

Evidently, it is divinity's epiphany that unsettles the episode's temporality to so great an extent. One can infer its destabilizing and prodigious presence from the action's reciprocal inconsistencies, but this fact does not solve the basic question of God's identity: what, who, and where is the divine in the painting? It is no exaggeration to state that, in concealing God's true presence, and in reducing Christ's figure to a pictorial sign, Caravaggio expressed the divine's transcendence and grace's mystery in a disturbing manner: by relativizing the conventions and symbols through which divinity had preserved its identity over the centuries in the sacred image. Compared to the controversial issue of Matthew's identity and location in the painting, the concealment of God's operations seems to me more salient and historically urgent. Yet, were I to enter the debate, I would incline to the view that, on account of his physiognomy and relevance in the composition, the bearded man at the center of the table is assuredly Matthew. None of the painters who developed Caravaggio's idea doubted this identification, whereas some of them certainly played with the invisibility of Christ and Peter in their many versions of *The Calling*.

In any event, I would argue that the most important aspect of this debate is not Matthew's identity in the painting, but the beholder's disorientation while processing Matthew's ambiguous act of indicating himself. Just as God's presence and act of calling are difficult to pinpoint and assess, so too does the recipient of his grace metaphorically vanish out of sight by losing his

---

57 Puttfarken 1998, 170, discerns a contrast of functions between the hand of Peter and that of Christ: "the disciple, arguing with a listener immediately in front of him, needs to direct his finger at him in order to stress a point. Christ's command, by contrast, does not allow for arguments; with his feet turned to leave, his hand exerts its irresistible magnetic power across most of the picture without having to point at its object." It is difficult to understand why, in the scene of Matthew's conversion, Peter should be arguing with a nearby listener. Furthermore, the apostle's gesture of the pointing hand is identical to Christ's, and therefore seems to reiterate the act of calling.

58 Burgard 1998, 98: "Within the image, there is a confusion of direction in the figures of Christ and Saint Peter. The latter stands not as if he has just turned around when walking by toward the right (...), but rather as if he had approached the group at the table from the right and foreground (...); the position of his right foot and leg indicates that he has either just stopped moving in this direction or that he is about to turn and walk away—yet another, if minor, undecidable point. Christ's foot indicates that he has come from *no* direction, for in this position, with his foot pointing straight out at the viewer, he has either just emerged from the wall, since the painting depicts no other egress whence he might have come, or he has simply been standing there."

traditional identity. In sum, Caravaggio's art of dissimulation not only stages the "undecidability" of God's calling, but also overthrows the principle of "dramatic irony" that granted the viewer the privilege of understanding the action's plot and the possibility of deducing its meaning. This time, Caravaggio's optical graphicness brings about the strangest of all the effects in the domain of fiction: the beholder's hermeneutical unsettlement.

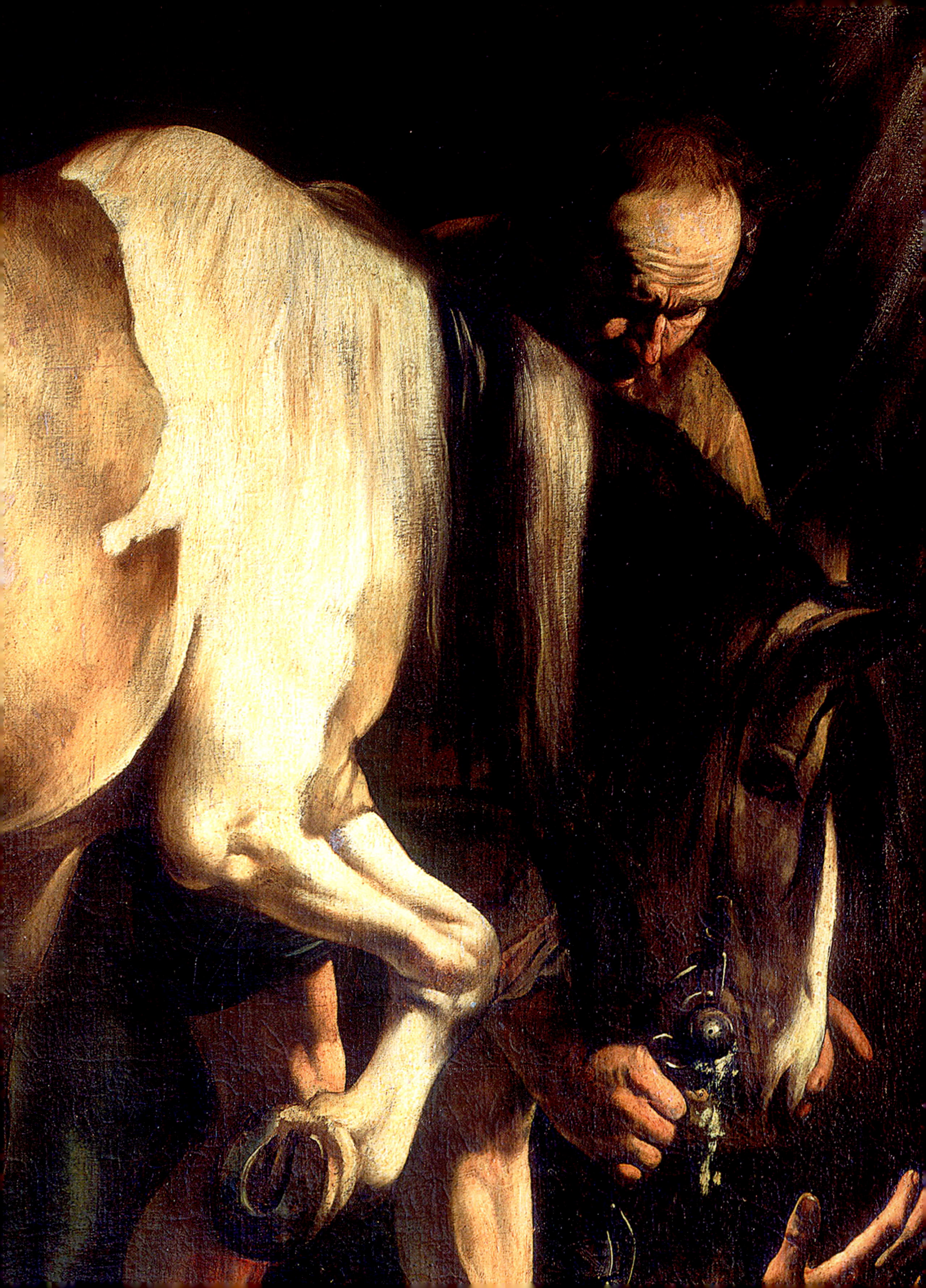

CHAPTER 8

"Completely Bereft of Action": Narrative Blindness and the Heroic Horse in the Cerasi *Conversion of Saint Paul*

A Tale of Blindness

In the previous chapter, I introduced a concept that will prove particularly useful in my analysis of Caravaggio's *Conversion of Saint Paul* in the Cerasi Chapel, Santa Maria del Popolo, Rome: narrative blindness. In interpreting *The Calling of Saint Matthew*, I have been using this concept in a twofold manner with regard to both the painter's strategies in obscuring the pictorial action and the beholder's uncertainties in reconstructing the *istoria* as represented by the master. On the one hand, it is the painting's structure—its overall composition—that is punctuated with subtle, almost imperceptible disconnections such as narrative short circuits, spatial inconsistencies, and incongruous chiaroscuro effects. Through these disjunctions, Caravaggio manages to disseminate blind spots throughout the pictorial field of the sacred representation, thereby sneaking discontinuities and fractures into the action's visual concatenation. On the other hand, it is the viewer who, on closer inspection of the painting, ends up frustrated in his or her efforts to reconstruct the pictorial narrative as a logically ordered sequence of figures playing, and events unfolding, in a condition of temporal, spatial, and optical verisimilitude. As a consequence, the inner sight—a metaphor designating the beholder's ability to visualize, and therefore piece together the *istoria*'s logic in retrospect—is clouded, for the viewer is unable to fill in the action's blanks. Needless to say, these two kinds of blindness interface with one another continuously insofar as the painter predetermines the beholder's perception of, and reaction to, the pictorial narrative. A third form of blindness, already alluded to in the Contarelli *Calling*, serves as the conceptual fulcrum and thematic substratum of the Cerasi *Conversion*: theological blindness. In order to explain this concept, I quote the passage from Acts (9, 3-10) in which Paul's conversion is narrated:

> On his journey, as he [Saul, alias Paul] was nearing Damascus, a light from the sky suddenly flashed around him. He fell to the ground and heard a voice saying to him, "Saul, Saul, why are you persecuting me?" He said, "Who are you, sir?" The reply came, "I am Jesus, whom you are persecuting. Now get up and go into the city and you will be told what you must do." The men who were traveling with him stood speechless, for they heard the voice but could see no one. Saul got up from the ground, but when he opened his eyes he could see nothing; so they led him by the hand and brought him to Damascus. For three days he was unable to see, and he neither ate nor drank.

In another passage from Acts (22, 6-11), Paul himself recounts his conversion on his way to Damascus, declaring—counter to what is said in the previous account—that his "companions saw

243

the light but did not hear the voice of the one who spoke to [him]." He also remembers that he "could see nothing because of the brightness of that light." Finally, in Acts 26, 12-19, Paul recalls Jesus' speech to him in detail:

> I have appeared to you for this purpose, to appoint you as servant and witness of what you have seen and what you will be shown. I shall deliver you from this people and from the Gentiles to whom I send you to open their eyes that they may turn from darkness to light and from the power of Satan to God, so that they may obtain forgiveness of sins and an inheritance among those who have been consecrated by faith in me.

By definition, the sequence of events that forces Paul to convert is a matter of paradox and an act of blindness. Indeed, the future saint's vision of God is recorded as purely acoustic—Jesus uncovers his own identity through his allocution to Paul—and results in Paul's temporary lack of sight as a consequence of his exposure to excessive brightness. Even as the apostle opens his eyes to the true faith, he loses his capability to see for a time. From this prospect, blindness is a spiritual state of mind, and hence can be construed in two different ways. It is either the condition of the unbeliever living in ignorance and disregard of God, or the ephemeral stigma of man's contact with divinity: a testimony of how God's transcendence exceeds human senses. It is this second definition of theological blindness that I deem of utmost importance with regard to the Cerasi *Conversion*.

It is important to note that sight is not the only sense affected by the overwhelming violence of God's manifestation. Just like Paul, his companions hear Christ's voice, yet remain speechless, for they are unable to see the Savior. Or, as the second version of the events records, they cannot hear Jesus' allocution but only see the supernatural light. Dramatically speaking, the tense silence of Paul's assistants amplifies the epiphany's direness—that is, Paul's desperate questioning and Christ's imperious speech: the vibrant and solitary dialogue between man and God. Of course, paintings lack sound and, on this account, one might be willing to believe that painters renounce suggesting acoustic effects. This is not entirely true, as I shall argue especially in Chapter 15. Surprisingly enough, however, Caravaggio strove to suppress any hint at, or impression of, sound in *The Conversion*, thereby conjuring muteness in addition to blindness, as can be seen by comparing the Cerasi picture with Caravaggio's first version of it, the utterly eccentric Odescalchi *Conversion of Saint Paul*. As I will demonstrate in the course of this chapter, these two paintings—the Odescalchi one to a lesser degree—stage, explore, and thematize the incommensurability of man's interaction with the divine; in other words, the inexorable blindness brought about by this crucial encounter and revelatory clash. To insinuate and demonstrate the extent of man's finitude in comprehending God, Caravaggio once again resorted to blinding viewers, thereby putting them in a situation whereby they are unable to see God's presence or intervention, let alone the cause of Paul's fall. In this manner, Caravaggio makes beholders experience, albeit on a narrative level, Paul's blindness. Although Caravaggio's attempt at obscuring action in order to engender the viewer's blindness is not unprecedented—remember the previous case of the Contarelli *Calling*—the visual strategies through which he fulfills this goal in the Cerasi *Conversion* prove to be radically novel and groundbreaking, to say the least.

Before proceeding further to analyze Caravaggio's two versions of *The Conversion of Saint Paul*, it is useful to examine the interest with which Counter-Reformation art theorists investigated the traditional iconography of this biblical episode. In the 1570 edition of his *De historia sacrarum imaginum et picturarum*, Johannes Molanus illustrated the various reasons why it was acceptable for painters to depict what is missing in scripture, as long as this is done appropriately. Among the examples that he took into consideration, one concerns the notorious horse frequently represented in Conversions of Saint Paul:

> Luke reports that Saul, still muttering threats [against the disciples of the Lord], fell to the ground as he was nearing Damascus. Painters add a horse to this episode. In fact, Saul was not likely to walk on his journey to Damascus after he had accepted from the high priests the mission to bring back into Jerusalem and put in chains any men or women of the Christian sect that he should find. What will we say about these cases and other similar ones? Would one say that the Church tolerates uncertain things in its paintings? No. Even if one concedes that it is not clear whether (…) Paul fell to the ground from a horse, it does not ensue that these images are uncertain.[1]

It is noteworthy that Cardinal Gabriele Paleotti, in his 1582 *Discorso intorno alle imagini sacre*, essentially transcribed Molanus' opinion to buttress the same arguments. In another passage that I have partially cited in the introduction to Part Three, Paleotti blames the artists who execute a sacred image by overturning the strict hierarchy and narrative relevance of the holy figures they represent. More to the point, Paleotti asserts that, in depicting Paul's conversion, "several painters apply all of their minds to representing a beautiful and vigorous horse, and consider this animal the main subject, and do not care about anything else."[2] Paleotti's criticism is completely understandable if one considers the visual and dramatic prominence of the rearing horse in Christian iconography as established over the centuries. Not that the figure of Paul was truly disregarded, but it is undeniable that the steed ordinarily competes with the apostle in capturing the viewer's attention. From a theoretical viewpoint, it was not an easy task to justify the horse's pictorial predominance; a technical accessory, however acceptable in light of verisimilitude, should not usurp the sacred hero's pride of place. Here is Cardinal Federico Borromeo's opinion on this very point (I quote it from his *Della pittura sacra*):

> Returning to discuss the pictorial field, one should strongly criticize those artists who in a painting turn the accessory into the principal, and the principal into an accessory. For instance, if they represent Saint John in the wilderness, they place his figure in a dark and dashed out spot, so that he is barely visible, and they fill the most majestic and noble parts of the pictorial field with animals, plants, rocks and perspectives. In this case, it would have been preferable to depict all these things in a landscape, as a distinct painting, and to carefully represent [the saint's] figure, entirely devout, in another canvas destined for the religious cult, so that it could be worshipped and revered.[3]

1 Molanus, 82-3: "Saulus adhuc spirans minarum cum appropinquaret Damasco cadit in terram, habet Lucas: pictores addunt ei aequum. Non enim verisimile est peditem fuisse Saulum, quando commissione accepta a principibus sacerdotum, in Damascum iter faciebat, ut si quos ibi inveniret Christianae viae viros ac mulieres, eos vinctos perduceret in Ierusalem. Quid igitur ad haec et similia multa dicemus? Quod Ecclesia multa habeat incerta in suis picturibus? Absit. Quantumvis enim admitteretur incertum esse (…) an e caballo in terram ceciderit Paulus, ex his tamen non consequeretur incertas esse superius indicatas picturas." For an almost identical argument, see Paleotti, 120-1.

2 Paleotti, 187: "Sì come nella conversione di san Paolo si vedono molti pittori consummare tutta la sua cura in figurare un cavallo bello e gagliardo, e questo hanno per principale, né del resto si curano più di tanto."

3 Borromeo, 30: "Ritornando poi a dire del campo, sono grandemente da biasmare quei pittori che in una tavola fanno ciò che è principale accessorio, e ciò che è accessorio principale. Se dipingeranno san Giovanni nel deserto, e' porranno l'istessa figura in una parte oscura e mal fatta che appena potrà vedersi, e poi riempiranno il campo nelle parti più signorili e nobili d'animali, di piante, di scogli e di prospettive. Meglio sarebbe stato in questo caso dipingere queste cose sì come rappresentanti alcun paese [in altra tavola, e poi in quella che si doveva destinare al culto divino] decentemente rappresentare l'immagine [tutta devota e fatta con gran studio] per adorarla e riverirla."

If, on the one hand, it was advisable, even mandatory, to depict the horse as an attribute in the representation of Paul's conversion not only because verisimilitude dictated the animal's presence, but especially in consideration of the viewer's visual habits, on the other hand it was essential to downplay the steed's role by representing it as clearly as subordinate to the figure of the saint. As Borromeo rightly suggested in connection with other iconographic accessories, the horse's predominance, on the practical level of the religious cult, would have been conducive to idolatry and blasphemy: churchgoers would have adored a "beautiful and vigorous" steed instead of the saint's prototypical likeness. I shall show that Caravaggio, on the contrary, upgraded the horse's role in the Cerasi *Conversion* by turning it into the painting's protagonist: a classic example of "the accessory" substituting for "the principal," to paraphrase Borromeo. How this obvious fault or, to be more in keeping with Caravaggio's intention, unequivocal transgression in matters of decorum and propriety might have borne on Giovan Pietro Bellori's lapidary and much glossed condemnation of the Cerasi *Conversion*—a painting, in his own words, lacking action altogether— is an essential issue I will deal with later while examining the composition closely.

Before scrutinizing the two versions of *The Conversion of Saint Paul*, I shall sum up the history and vicissitudes of the Cerasi commission. On 24 September 1600, some two months after Caravaggio had received the final payment for the two laterals in the Contarelli Chapel, Tiberio Cerasi, general treasurer to the Pope and the Apostolic Chamber, commissioned the master to execute two large paintings, both on cypress panels, representing *The Crucifixion of Saint Peter* and *The Conversion of Saint Paul*.[4] Their price was fixed at 400 *scudi*, and Cerasi destined them for the chapel he was having built in Santa Maria del Popolo after a design by Carlo Maderno. In the contract, it was stipulated that Caravaggio, prior to the paintings' execution, should provide Cerasi with "examples and drawings of the figures and any other thing with which the painter, out of his own invention and ingenuity, intended to embellish the [sacred] mystery and martyrdom."[5] Caravaggio then received a down payment of 50 *scudi*, and promised to deliver the paintings within eight months, that is, by 24 May 1601. As it turned out, Cerasi would never see Caravaggio's works finished, for he died on 3 May 1601. In his will, he urged his heirs and testamentary executors, the priests of the Ospedale della Consolazione, to put all their efforts toward completing the chapel's decoration with no further delays.[6] Caravaggio finished his two paintings quickly, a few months after Cerasi's death, but he was paid 300 *scudi* instead of the 400 agreed upon in the 1600 contract, as evidenced by the receipt for the last payment issued on 10 November 1601.[7] Moreover, instead of being on cypress panels, the two paintings installed in the Cerasi Chapel in May 1605—that is, four years after their completion—were on canvas. These two laterals are still in place, on either side of an altarpiece by Annibale Carracci, *The Assumption of the Virgin*. Malicious as ever, Giovanni Baglione records in his 1642 *Vite*: "Caravaggio first executed these paintings [in Santa Maria del Popolo] in another manner, but because the patron disliked them, they were purchased by Cardinal Sannesio, and Caravaggio himself made those now in view, which are painted in oil, because he never worked in any other manner."[8] In his 1617-1621 *Considerazioni della pittura*, Giulio Mancini corroborates Baglione's testimony as to the presence of two other paintings by Caravaggio in Cardinal Giacomo

---

4 First published by Mahon 1951a, 226-7. See Macioce 2003, 91.

5 Macioce 2003, 91: "Ipse pictor teneatur, prout promisit, ante dictarum picturarum confectionem exhibere specimina et designationes figurarum et aliorum quibus ipse pictor ex sui inventione et ingenio dicta misterium et martyrium decorare intendit."

6 For these documents, first published by Luigi Spezzaferro and Almamaria Mignosi Tantillo in Bernardini 2001, 108-17, see also Macioce 2003, 103.

7 For this document, first published by Mahon 1951a, 227, see Macioce 2003, 106.

8 Baglione, 137: "Questi quadri prima furono lavorati da lui in un'altra maniera, ma perché non piacquero al padrone, se li prese il cardinale Sannesio, e lo stesso Caravaggio vi fece questi che ora si vedono, a olio dipinti, poiché egli non operava in altra maniera."

Sannesio's collection, although Mancini relates that they were "copied and remade after those in Santa Maria del Popolo."[9]

Fortunately, one of these two pictures has survived, and is now in the Odescalchi Collection, Rome (Fig. 108).[10] The painting, a cypress panel, differs so conspicuously from the Cerasi version that one must conclude that Mancini was misinformed about its status as a simple copy. In any event, there is no doubt that Cardinal Sannesio owned the two paintings on panel that Caravaggio had originally executed for Cerasi, since both are mentioned in the 1644 inventory of Francesco Sannesio's possessions (Francesco was Giacomo's nephew and heir).[11] In 1646, Juan Alfonso Enríquez de Cabrera, Duke of Medina de Rioseco, bought Caravaggio's two paintings, which were shipped to Madrid immediately afterward. A year later, upon the Duke's death in 1647, the Genoese nobleman Agostino Ayrolo bought *The Conversion of Saint Paul*, which therefore returned to Italy, namely to Genoa.[12] For unknown reasons, The *Crucifixion of Saint Peter* remained in Madrid in the collection of the Medina de Rioseco family until the beginning of the eighteenth century.[13] The painting has been lost ever since. In all likelihood, Baglione's statement about Cerasi's dissatisfaction with Caravaggio's paintings is equally incorrect. In fact, Caravaggio would have never begun working on the two panels had Cerasi disapproved of his designs—as I have already pointed out, the 1600 contract specified that the master present the preparatory drawings to the patron prior to execution. On the other hand, Luigi Spezzaferro's suggestion that the priests of the Consolazione accepted Caravaggio's replacement of the two panels with two canvases in order to save money cannot be verified, and hence remains but an intriguing hypothesis.[14] At this point, it must be confessed that it is impossible to understand why Caravaggio brought to completion two different sets of paintings with the same subject. Whether this occurred at the behest of Cardinal Sannesio, who, taking advantage of Cerasi's death, decided to snatch the two panels for Santa Maria del Popolo and negotiated with the priests of the Consolazione to this end, is also a matter of speculation. In fact, it is even unknown when exactly Cardinal Sannesio purchased his two paintings, and it is possible that one of them stayed in Caravaggio's house for a while, since, as Maurizio Marini and Spezzaferro noted, the inventory of the master's possessions, drawn up on 26 August 1605, mentions "a large painting on panel,"[15] which might have been either the Odescalchi *Conversion* or the lost *Crucifixion*, owing to the rarity of wooden supports in Caravaggio's work. I emphasize this, because it cannot be ruled out that Caravaggio achieved the two Sannesio panels at a subsequent date. In other words, he might have begun them in 1600, put them aside in 1601 when he executed the two canvases for Santa Maria del Popolo as replacements, and then subsequently resumed working on the panels so that they could be delivered to Cardinal Sannesio. As Spezzaferro suggested, these factors might account for the stylistic oddities of the Odescalchi *Conversion*. Many scholars indeed have had trouble fixing its chronology, for some elements hark back to Caravaggio's early productions, and others, for instance the angel on the upper right corner, match or recall the master's techniques around 1602-1603.

9   This passage is a variant of Mancini's manuscript. See Mancini, 1:225, note 2: "…che sono copiati e ritoccati da quelli che sono nella Madonna del Popolo, nella cappella del Prato."

10   For this painting, see Mahon 1951a, 227, 234; Friedlaender 1969, 184-5; Röttgen 1974, 107-11; Cinotti 1983, 540-2, no. 63; Moir 1982, 104; Hibbard 1983, 123; Boccardo 1988, 100; Calvesi 1990, 95-9; Gregori 1991, 200-5, no. 9; Puglisi 1998, 165-6; Longhi 1999-2000, 58 [1943; as not by Caravaggio], 80-1, no. 13 [1951; as an original], 147, 255 [as unrelated to the Cerasi commission]; Spezzaferro 2001; Marini 2005, 447-9, no. 39; Vodret 2006; Merlini and Storti 2008; Schütze 2009, 261, no. 25.I.

11   This inventory was published by Luigi Spezzaferro and

Almamaria Mignosi Tantillo in Bernardini 2001, 117-24. See Ibidem, 118: "doi quadri grandi in tavola che rappresentano un San Pietro crocifisso e l'altro la Conversione di San Paolo corniciati e filettati d'oro."

12   See Boccardo 1988, 100; and Burke and Cherry 1997, 1:412, nos. 86-7.

13   See Burke and Cherry 1997, 1:957, no. 910; and Vannugli 1999.

14   See Spezzaferro 2001, esp. 22-3.

15   First published by Marini and Corradini 1993, 162; see Macioce 2003, 173: "Item, un quadro grande de legname."

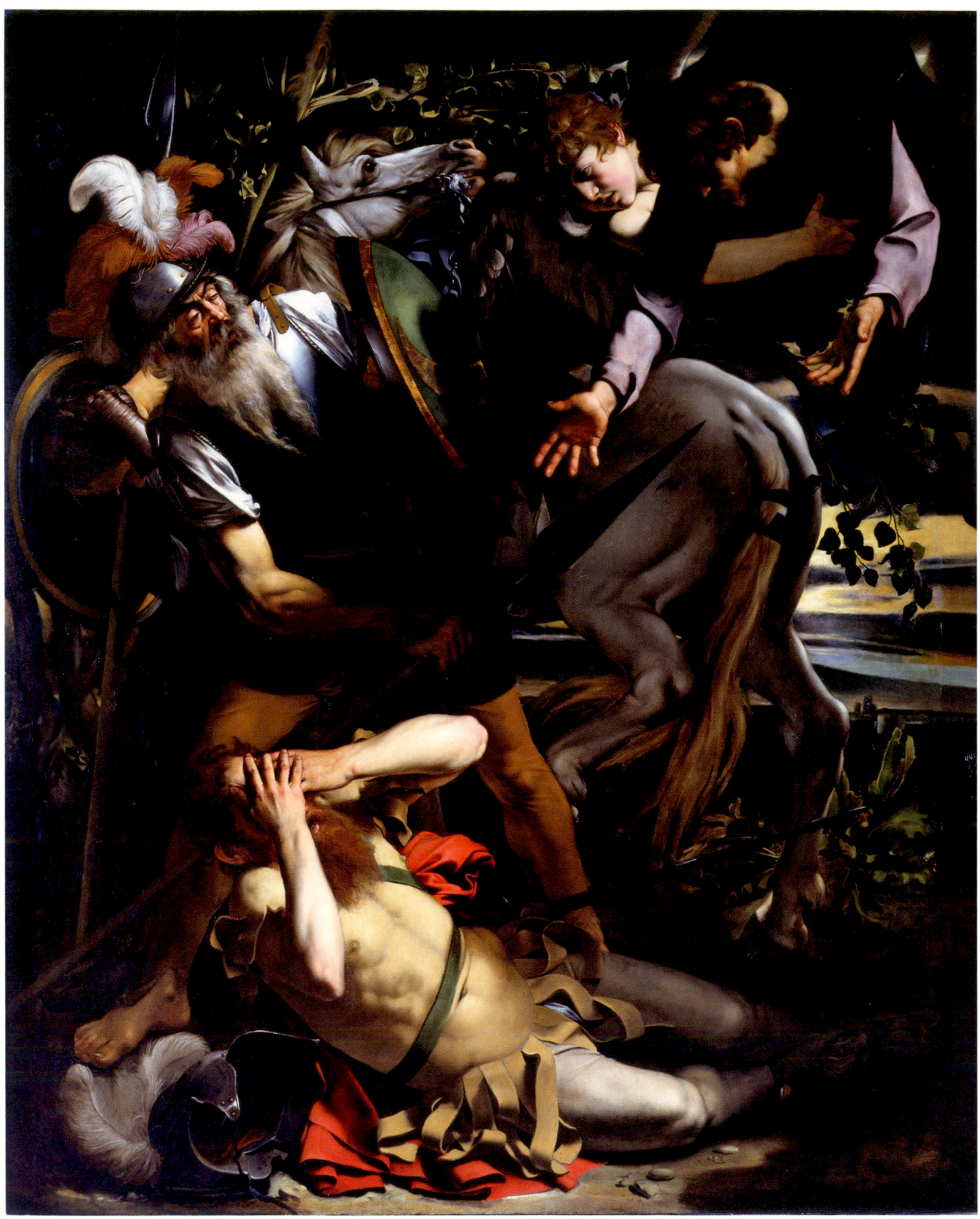

Fig. 108
Michelangelo Merisi da Caravaggio, *Conversion of Saint Paul*, Odescalchi Collection, Rome, oil on panel, 237 x 189 cm.

Be that as it may, it is beyond doubt that, compared to *The Martyrdom of Saint Matthew*, the Odescalchi *Conversion* marks a new experimental phase in the evolution of Caravaggio's painting. After the intense experience of the Contarelli laterals, Caravaggio once again focuses on the interplay of the image's surface and periphery, distributing all his figures along a virtual crescent in the foreground, framing them tightly by ensconcing them in proximity to the composition's margins. As a result, the pictorial drama is entirely articulated on a single plane at close range, unfolding as a chain of events from the upper right corner down to the left lower stage or vice versa, allowing a breach of crepuscular landscape to loom into view at the opposite side of Paul and his acolytes. There, at a distance, the towering profile of a town detaches itself from the sunset dusk, the sky exhibiting its alternating layers of dark clouds and bright clearings, as if a storm had just broken and suddenly calmed down. Above, in a flash, Christ stretches his arms toward Paul, while an angel, his torso bare, his wings deployed as if landing, circles the Savior's chest with his right arm. In one of his usual tricks, Caravaggio opposes the angel's radiance to the penumbra bathing Christ's face. In this manner, the two figures fuse together in a logogram, the angel's profile and Jesus' outflung arms combined in a unique action, a gesture of acceptance and exhortation rather than a reprimand against the former persecutor of Christians. Behind the angel's face, a branch of poplar bends down after having been split from the trunk by a thunderbolt: an eloquent yet minor detail evoking God's fulgurating omnipotence. The Savior's arms open directly upon, and are clearly oriented toward, the fallen Paul on the ground, the apostle's torso and covered face powerfully lit by a dense stream of sunshine, a substitute for and immanent variant of the Gospel's miraculous lightning.

In response to Jesus' speech—albeit difficult to see, the Savior's lips are evidently parted and his eyes turned downward—Paul raises his torso and asks who is addressing him. Around him, to the left, a plumed helmet shows its concavity to the viewer; to the right, pointing toward the distance, Paul's lance indicates that he has been recently unhorsed. Behind the apostle and the soldier protecting him, the rump, tail, and hind legs of a silvery steed can be seen, a chromatic counterpoint to the orange swaths of the sky at a distance. To find the horse's face, one must look at the panel's upper margin; there, in profile, the head appears as it tilts heavenward, the animal's eyes wide open, its mouth still foaming out of panic. Arcing forward, the steed's profile bridges the two soldiers' faces to the left and Christ's and the angel's faces to the right. The poplar's fractured bough and frail trunk, as they span over and crown the horse's head, amplify but also contain the figures' fanning out in the upper register, a visual connection from which Paul is excluded. Wedged between the divine apparition and Paul beneath, an old soldier with an iron helmet adorned with multicolored feathers and a metallic cuirass, puts up a fight with Christ and the angel by protecting himself with a round shield bearing a crescent on the outside; he points a sharp and menacing spear against the divinity in order to defend the apostle. Behind the old soldier, a figure shelters the back of his lowered head with his left hand's metallic glove, obviously retreating and overwhelmed by both the flash's radiance and the thunder's roar. Caravaggio's signature or trademark, a mullein,[16] grows at the horse's feet, its leaves delicately and accurately brought out by lighting.

At first glance, it is perhaps difficult to uncover the refinement of the Odescalchi *Conversion*'s references to early Renaissance canonical masters, especially Titian, Raphael, and Michelangelo. The horse's profile in the Odescalchi *Conversion*'s upper register recalls a detail from Titian's woodcut of *The Crossing of the Red Sea*, or more specifically a reduced version of it engraved in 1583 by Orazio Farinati after Paolo Farinati's design.[17] At the center of the print, one can easily

---

16 For the presence of the mullein in Caravaggio's painting, see Di Vito 2007.

17 For Farinati's print, see Zerner 1979, 269, no. 1(168). For Titian's original woodcut representing *The Submersion of Pharaoh's Army and the Red Sea*, see Rosand and Muraro 1976, 70-3, no. 4.

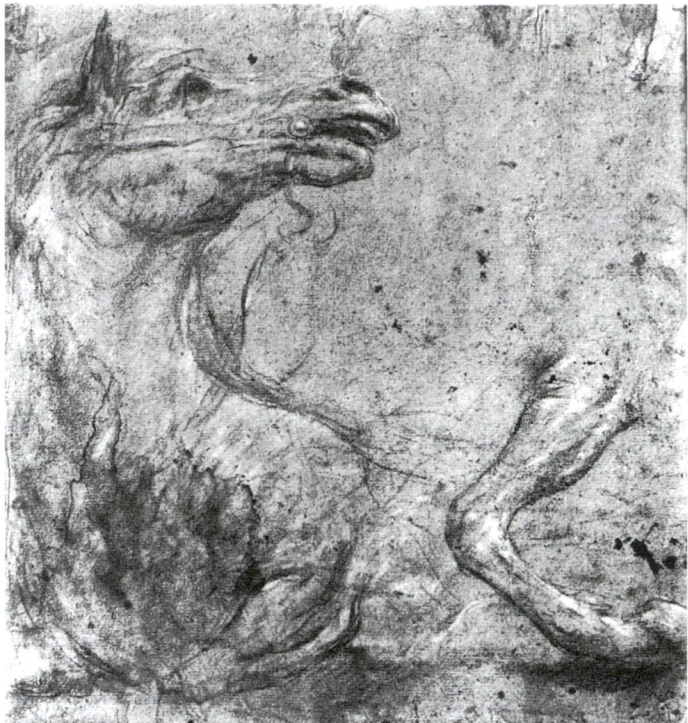

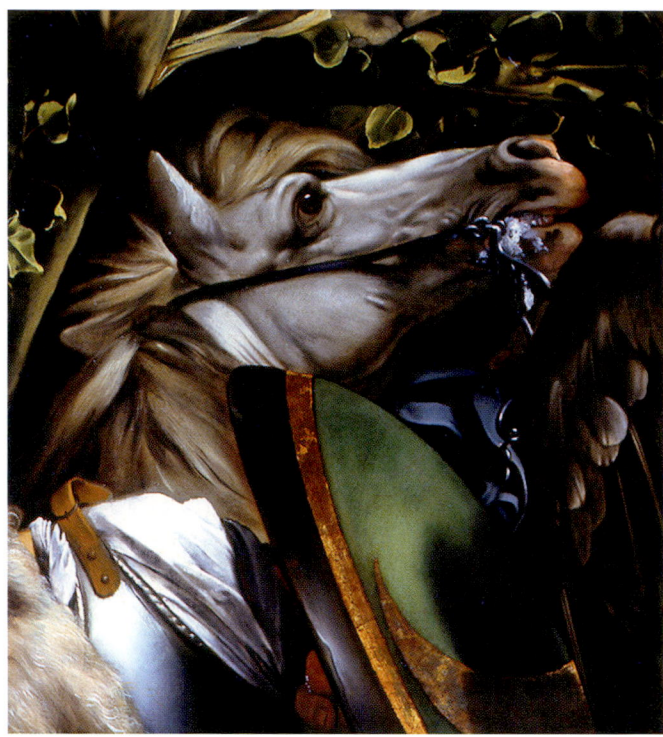

Fig. 109
Titian (Tiziano Vecelli), *Head of a Frightened Horse*, location unknown, black chalk on gray paper heightened with white, 20.9 x 20.7 cm, reproduced from Harold Wethey, *Titian and His Drawings*, 1987.

Fig. 110
Michelangelo Merisi da Caravaggio, *Conversion of Saint Paul*, Odescalchi Collection, Rome, oil on panel, 237 x 189 cm., detail.

discern a neighing steed sinking into the water, its face in profile and its eyes wide-open and empty. A drawing in black chalk with white heightening attributed to Titian, once in the Johann Török Collection and now lost,[18] represents the head of this frightened horse, and resembles the profile of Caravaggio's steed—observe its spindle-shaped, slender muzzle, as well as the way its mane unfurls around its pricked ear (Figs. 109, 110). Moreover, to celebrate his superiority over Titian's prototype, Caravaggio masterfully rendered the froth at the horse's mouth, a naturalistic touch in which only Apelles of antiquity had been successful, but only by chance. As recounted, though with some divergences, by Dio Chrysostom and Sextus Empiricus, the great Apelles depicted a horse returning from battle, "its neck arched up high, its ears perked, and its eyes glaring, like a horse returning from war, retaining the furor of the charge in its visage." Although Apelles had "succeeded in nearly every respect in the drawing and color," he was unable to represent "the frothy appearance of the foam from champing the bit, and the rush of the foam-flecked breath," which he had tried "again and again to paint, but without success, and each time had wiped it out until finally, in a rage, he threw his sponge, just as it was, full of pigments, at the canvas, and this, as it struck, transferred its contents in some amazing manner to the canvas, and effected the desired result."[19] It is noteworthy that Caravaggio's rendition of the steed's foam—a sign of technical virtuosity and, as such, a token of pictorial superiority over Apelles—is not the only allusion to the excellence of ancient artists in the Odescalchi *Conversion*, and assuredly adds to the many elaborations upon well-known models by Renaissance masters deployed in the painting.

Predictably, Paul's figure constitutes the most sophisticated case of emulation. It has been just-ly advanced that Caravaggio was inspired by two particular sources in representing the unhorsed saint: Michelangelo's figure of the apostle from the *c.*1542 *Conversion of Saint Paul* in the Pauline

18   See Wethey 1987, 134-5, no. 5 D.

19   Dio Chrysostom, 5:39. See also Sextus Empiricus, 19.

Chapel (Fig. 111); and Raphael's figure of Heliodorus in the 1511 *Expulsion of Heliodorus from the Temple* in the Vatican Palace (Fig. 112). There is no doubt that Raphael's prototype is closer to Caravaggio's Paul, not only in the identical, albeit reversed, position of the legs and hip, but more particularly the arched torso. In fact, from the viewpoint of anatomical verisimilitude, the inclination of the apostle's torso in the Odescalchi *Conversion* would make better sense if the figure leaned on his arm as does Raphael's Paul. On the other hand, it is equally undeniable that Caravaggio also had in mind Michelangelo's Paul: besides the similar posture of the saint's legs, the idea of evoking not only the apostle's blindness, but also his allocution, represents a common denominator between the two figures. Yet if the detail of the open mouth is basically the same, the way of conveying the impression of blindness is radically different: Michelangelo's closed eyes and Caravaggio's covered face embody a profound divergence in expressivity and significance. Before interpreting these factors, I would like to reflect on Caravaggio's beautiful invention of Paul's crossed hands concealing his face. This detail in my view confirms Raphael's influence. To the best of my knowledge, this gesture of the hands is indeed specific to Raphael's *Moses and the Burning Bush*, one of the frescoes decorating the ceiling of the Stanza d'Eliodoro.[20] It is perhaps no coincidence that this composition appears directly above *The Expulsion of Heliodorus From the Temple*. In the ceiling fresco, the biblical patriarch appears

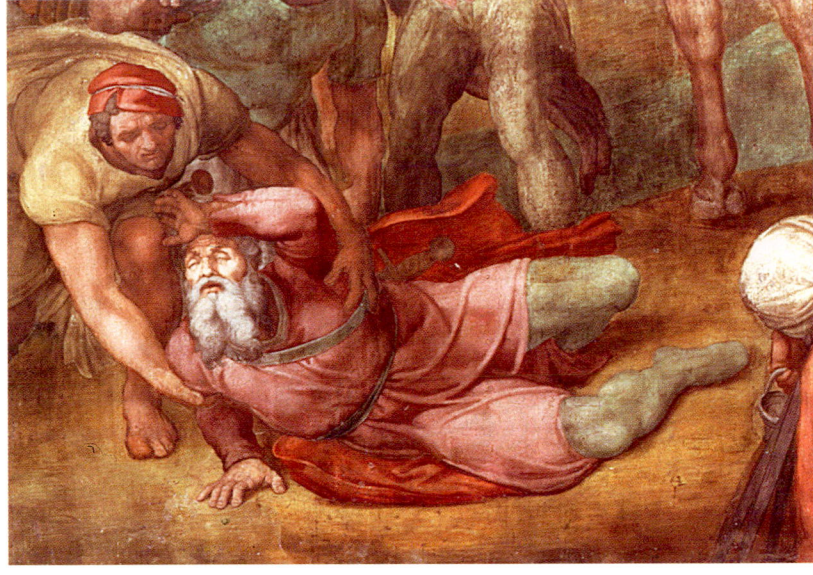

Fig. 111
Michelangelo Buonarroti, *Conversion of Saint Paul*, Pauline Chapel, Vatican Palace, Rome, fresco, 620 x 670 cm., detail.

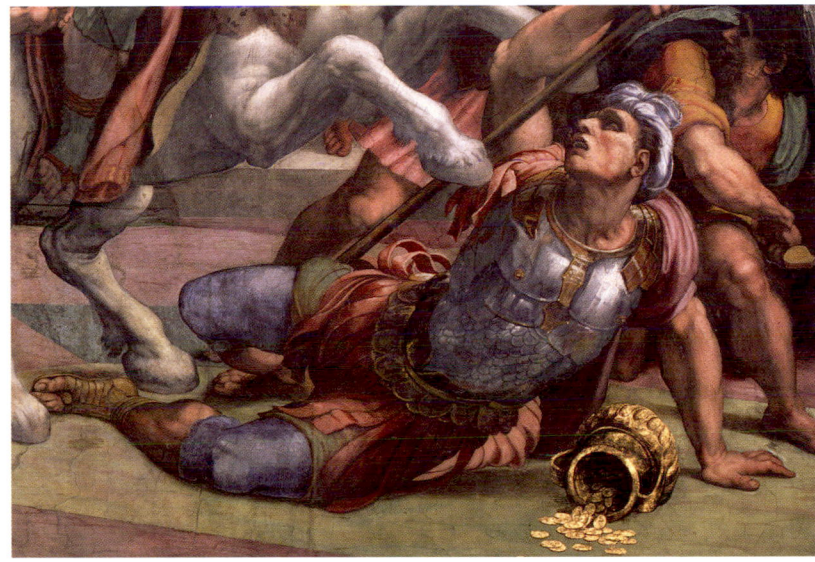

Fig. 112
Raphael (Raffaello Santi), *The Expulsion of Heliodorus from the Temple*, Stanza d'Eliodoro, Vatican Palace, Rome, fresco, 750 cm., detail.

partially kneeling, his right leg stretched forward, his torso and face in profile. One can better study this figure in Raphael's original cartoon at the Museo di Capodimonte, Naples (Fig. 113). Afraid of laying his eyes on the burning bush, God's miraculous surrogate, Moses diligently hides his face behind both hands, of which only one is visible, fingers displayed entirely in view. Most interesting, Raphael suggests that the patriarch's hands overlap one another, intersecting at the level of the wrists. Caravaggio's motif of the crossed hands seems to depend on Raphael's, although in the Odescalchi *Conversion* only the hands, and not the forearms, are superimposed.

I stress Caravaggio's reliance on Raphael since in my opinion it goes deeper than it may ap-

20   See Knab at al. 1983, 627, no. 488.

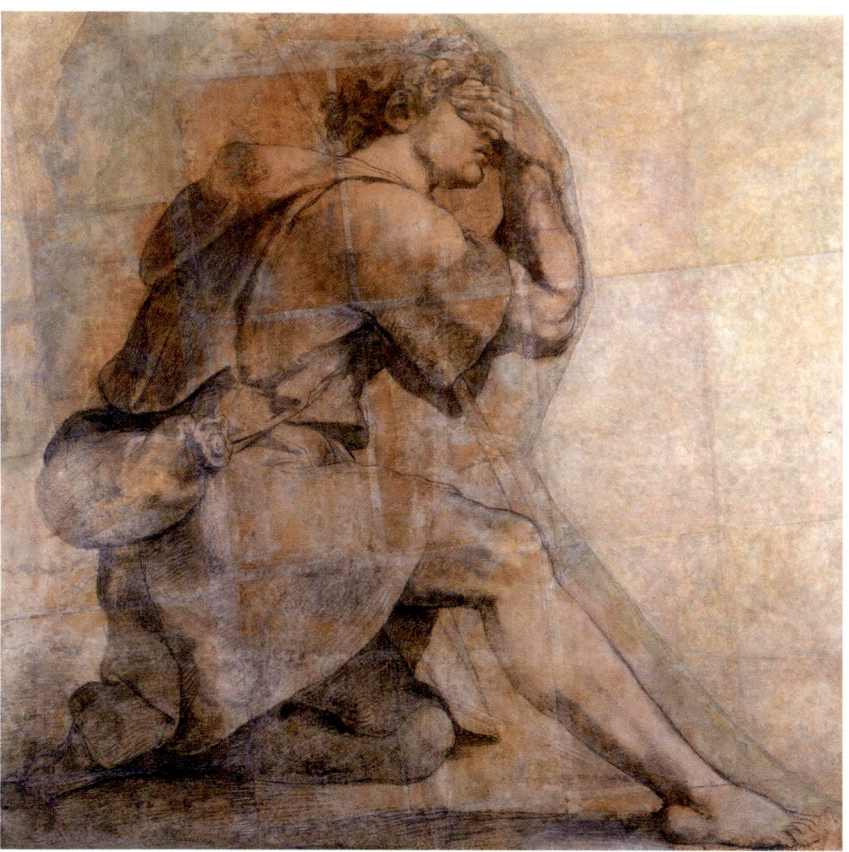

Fig. 113
Raphael (Raffaello Santi), *Cartoon for the Figure of Moses in The Burning Bush*, Museo di Capodimonte, Naples, black chalk with white highlights, 140 x 138 cm.

pear at first glance. To this end, I will produce here a *c.*1513 drawing by Raphael in black chalk (Devonshire Collection, Chatsworth) representing three fallen soldiers for a *Resurrection* that Raphael never executed (Fig. 114).[21] The sheet's main figure, a prostrate nude trying to screen himself from the lightning and thunder contemporaneous with, and consequent to, Jesus' resurrection, might well be a model for Caravaggio's Paul: the position of his legs, but especially the rendering of the lower abdomen, are a perfect match. More intriguingly, Raphael's soldier lowers his head while resting his left hand over his skull in an attitude that recalls that of Caravaggio's warrior at the extreme left of the Odescalchi *Conversion*. Unfortunately, we do not know where Raphael's drawing was kept at the beginning of the seventeenth century. However, it is well known that drawings like these were frequently copied and examined by artists at the time, and it would seem that Caravaggio was familiar with either the Chatsworth sheet or a copy after it.[22]

By recalling the extent of elaboration to which Caravaggio submitted Raphael's prototypes, I am not implying that the master, as it were, nipped and tucked diverse anatomical parts from a single figure in an ostentatious act of pictorial plastic surgery. What I am arguing is that Raphael's and Michelangelo's precedents stuck almost obsessively in Caravaggio's mind while he was depicting the Odescalchi *Conversion*, swarming and recombining relentlessly until the painter found the right configuration for his work. If Raphael's inventions inhered so tenaciously in Caravaggio's mind, this is not only because the master sought to compete with, and surpass, his predecessor's exploits, but especially, in my view, because Raphael's models resonated with conceptual implications and associations that, to diverse degrees, incorporated the theme of man's blindness so integral to Caravaggio's Odescalchi *Conversion*. Whether Moses' fear of God's vision or the soldier's prostration and disorientation at Christ's epiphany, both of these episodes visually and conceptually parallel Paul's enlightenment. More specifically, by masking the apostle's face through a shield of hands, Caravaggio activated a correspondence between Moses' deliberate action in front of God's burning bush and Paul's involuntary reaction to God's lightning. Like the soldiers around Christ's tomb during the Resurrection, Paul is the victim, not merely the interlocutor of the divine epiphany. In and of themselves, these cross-references between the Old and the New Testament, between Christ's saga and Paul's apostolate, deepen the visual impact of Caravaggio's figure.

21   See Ibidem, 626, no. 478, and for a technical analysis of the drawing: Ames Lewis 1986, 110.

22   A sixteenth-century engraving by the Monogrammist H.E., *The Effects of Wine,* is partially based upon Raphael's drawing. See Boorsch and Spike 1986, 302-3, no. 5 (464).

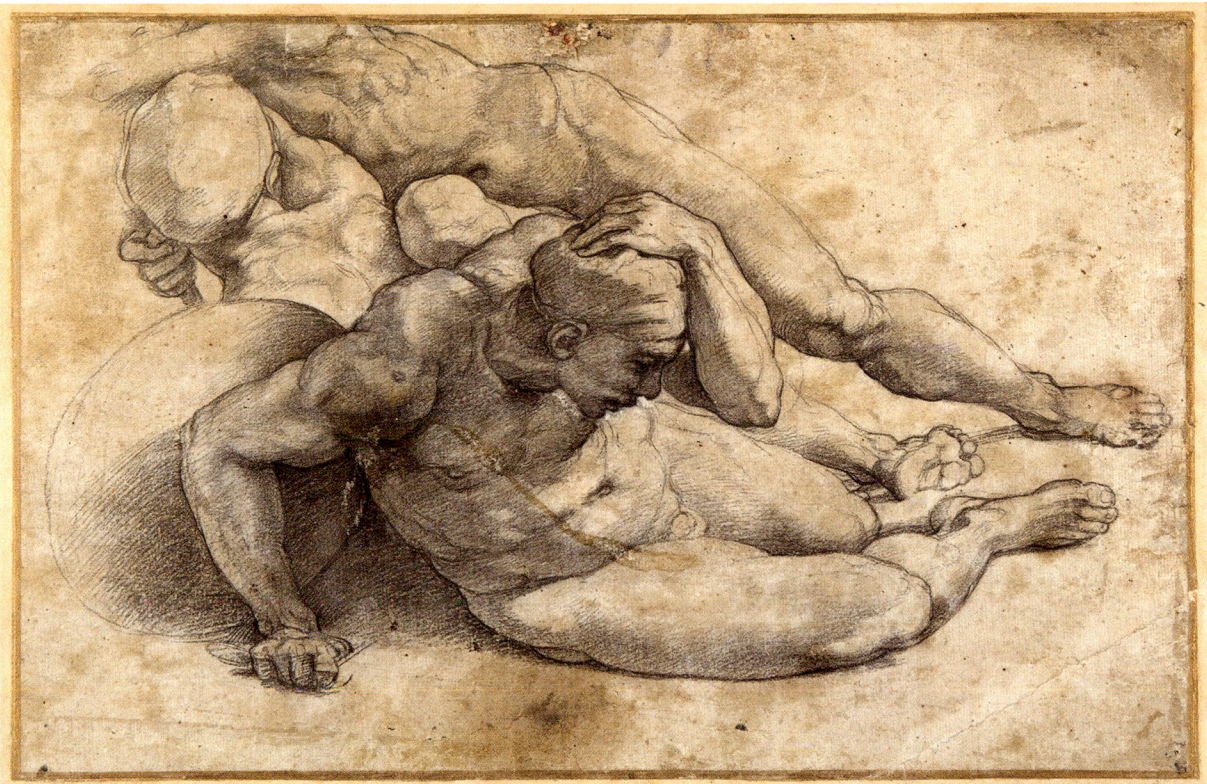

Fig. 114
Raphael (Raffaello Santi), *Study of Three Male Nudes*, Devonshire Collection, Chatsworth, black chalk, 23.4 x 36.5 cm.

In a sense, as Raphael had also done in *The Burning Bush*, Caravaggio eloquently described the encounter of man and God as an imbalanced exchange: of all the senses, only hearing, not seeing, is the designated channel of communication. Sight indeed is barred on two counts: Paul's vision of God culminates in sheer blindness, that is, the total concealment of the figure's eyes. Secondly, the beholder's experience of Paul's vision corresponds to a visual blackout, the viewer's eyes being unable to see the major effect of the apostle's enlightenment, namely his blindness. One would undervalue Caravaggio's unique rendition of Paul's blindness by judging it as a mere conceit. Just as the Greek painter Timanthes in his *Sacrifice of Iphigenia* veiled Agamemnon's face to suggest the father's ineffable pain, so too does Caravaggio cover Paul's face to indicate the apostle's overpowering blindness.[23] Like the horse's foaming mouth, the saint's crossed hands mark a challenge to past ideas of pictorial excellence. Yet Agamemnon's concealed pain does not equate with Paul's covered blindness. Blindness is not an emotion, nor does it result in expression. Hence, on the visual and narrative level of Paul's conversion, disguising the apostle's blindness entails the erasure of the action's principal event. In this manner, the effect of God's revelation to man is hinted at, but simultaneously vanishes out of sight. Put otherwise, if the concealment of Paul's blindness is a rhetorical figure, the visual equivalent of litotes, then it can be said that Caravaggio employs a blank to replace a blank, or rather to strengthen the notion of blankness. Litotes indeed requires that one negate in order to affirm, and pictorially that one cover in order to show; but in this case covering blindness to show blindness does not enhance the visualization of blindness. In his *Sacrifice of Iphigenia*, Timanthes had exhausted all the possibilities of rendering

23   On the topos of Timanthes' *Sacrifice of Iphigenia*, see more recently Moffitt 2005.

pain by extensively endowing his figures with as many attitudes of sorrow as possible before he resolved to veil Agamemnon's face, whose torment thus could be measured against the surrounding expressions. In the Odescalchi *Conversion*, nothing preludes Paul's blindness: the saint's hidden face is both the zero degree and the climax of the figurative formula through which blindness is rendered. On this account, the pictorial expression of blindness is reduced to an absolute lack of expression. This is why the visual litotes designed by Caravaggio backfires on the viewer who, instead of neatly visualizing Paul's state, ends up both perceiving blindness as unrepresentable and internalizing it as a primordial condition of the painting's experience. For this reason, I previously posited that Caravaggio's depiction of Paul's conversion generates narrative blindness: the beholder's visualization of the saint's blindness as pure pictorial blankness is in turn a situation of extreme blindness.

By making the effect of God's epiphany in Paul invisible, Caravaggio intended not only to convey the impression of the apostle's blindness, but also to test painting's ability to represent God's operation—I refer not to Christ's apparition, but to Paul's loss of sight. By doing so, he resorted to pictorial devices, such as the visual litotes that I have just illustrated, that allowed him to insinuate the notion of divine unrepresentability, but had detrimental consequences to the *istoria*'s normative principles as endorsed by his contemporaries. Paradoxically, as Caravaggio demonstrates in the Odescalchi *Conversion*, clarifying the cause-and-effect order of an action does not necessarily awaken, or even intensify, the beholder's empathy with the sacred image. On the contrary, if the painter's task is to coax viewers into sharing the sacred hero's inner emotions, as all the Counter-Reformation theorists claimed (albeit with diverging tones), then the warping of the visual action's coherence might prove to be a more efficient means to that end.

Nevertheless, in the Odescalchi *Conversion* Caravaggio inexplicably attenuates the innovative charge of this tacit statement. The elderly soldier's insertion between Paul and Jesus steers the beholder's attention away from the apostle, and therefore away from the compelling dialogue the master imagined in order to stage the incommensurability of man's and God's encounter. Unlike Paul, the old soldier in the Odescalchi *Conversion* is doubtless able to see Jesus, and fights him in a way that engenders a major comical digression in the scene. The eeriness of this figure has thus far gone unnoticed and rewards closer scrutiny. It would be no exaggeration to state that Caravaggio extracted this old warrior from northern Renaissance iconography. A single artwork will illustrate the point: Niklas Stoer's 1543 woodcut of *Eusterwon, King of the Germans*.[24] Stoer's xylograph depicts a frontal figure fully armored, sporting a metal cuirass and, more important, a helmet adorned with multicolored feathers cascading in various directions. King Eusterwon's physiognomy, as imagined by the printer, does not substantially differ from that of Caravaggio's old warrior (Figs. 115, 116). Note also both figures' long, two-pronged beard. Although the costume of Caravaggio's old man is simpler, or simplified, it is irrefutable that it relies on northern prototypes (even if it is unlikely that Caravaggio knew this book illustration, the helmet, armor, and facial features specific to Stoer's Eustorwon can be found in other German sixteenth-century prints, such as Heinrich Aldegrever's *Titus Manlius Torquatus Attending His Son's Decapitation*).[25] For this reason, not only does the figure's accoutrement constitute a blatant case of anachronism, which is extremely common in Caravaggio's painting, but it also contradicts the impression of actuality that Caravaggio so often endeavors to bring about in order to reinforce the reality effects of his paintings.

In light of these northern sources, it is evident that beholders in Caravaggio's time must have found the old soldier's figure a visual rarity, almost the analog of a circus attraction;[26] an amusement,

---

24   For the print, see Strauss 1984, 574-5, no. 009.

25   See Koch 1980, 178, no. 72 (388); Mielke et al. 1998, 83, no. 72.

26   In this regard, see the comment of Berenson 1953, 20-1, note 1: "And yet (...) there is no lack of incongruities: the groom who is dealing with the hysterical horse, instead of being young and alert, is a plumed and majestic patriarch."

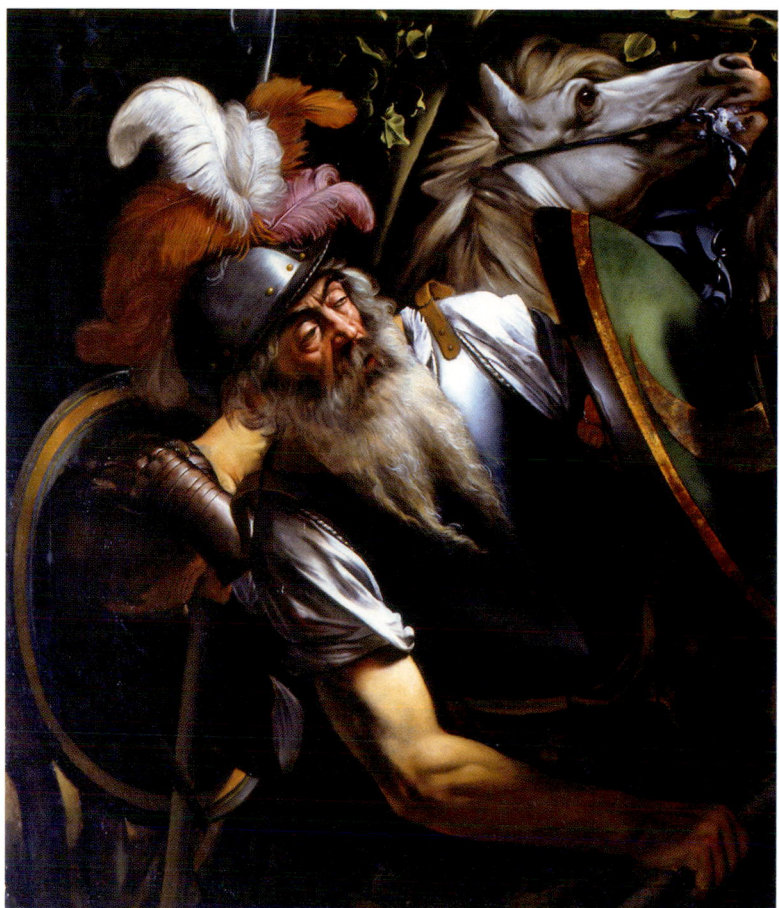

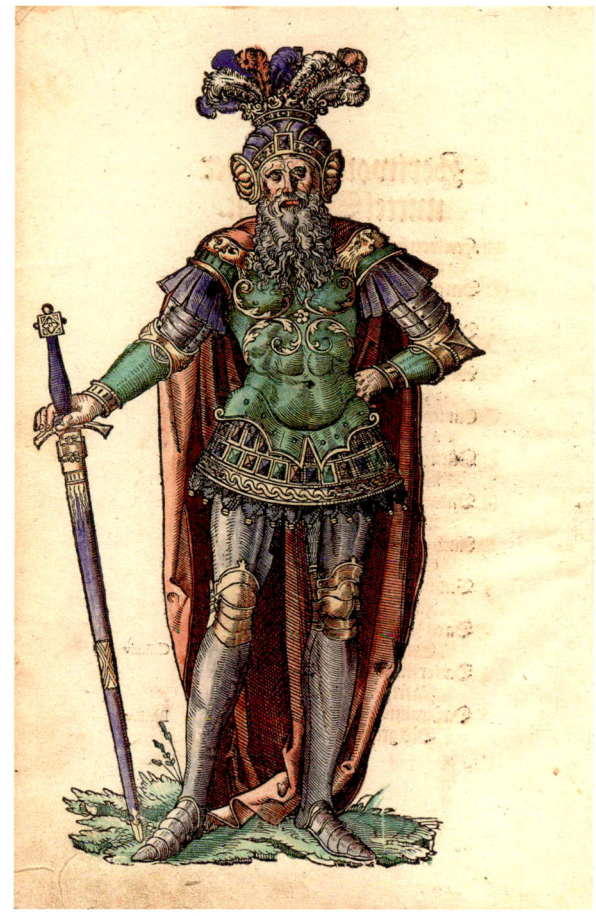

Fig. 115
Michelangelo Merisi da Caravaggio, *Conversion of Saint Paul*, Odescalchi Collection, Rome, oil on panel, 237 x 189 cm., detail.

Fig. 116
Niklas Stoer, *Eusterwon, King of the Upper Germans*, from Burchard Waldis, *Ursprung und Herkümen der zwoelff ersten alten Koenig und Fürstem Deutscher Nation…* (Nuremberg, 1543), woodcut, 27.7 x 15.3 cm.

indeed, on account of the warrior's out-of-fashion helmet, extravagant feathers and, last but not least, his dazed expression—he squints his eyes, attempting to focus on the target he is unable to discern with clarity since he is still stupefied as a result of the divine lightning. By his extravagance, the figure tends to usurp Paul's main role in the Odescalchi *Conversion*. This risk becomes even more manifest if one considers that, dramatically speaking, the old warrior is the exact counterpart of the apostle: one is able to see whereas the other cannot; one stands whereas the other lies; one is the passive prey of God's inner vision, whereas the other struggles with God's apparent image. In sum, the figures are not only associated with one another, but Paul's covered face intuitively serves as a foil to the old soldier's facial expression, so that through their assimilation Caravaggio creates two alternative foci of action. Why Caravaggio gave such relevance to the old warrior remains a mystery to me. It is a fact that this figure's role in the Odescalchi *Conversion* introduces an anecdotal, and comic interference, or disturbance, within the subject matter's main theme, thereby lessening the impact of narrative blindness that, as I have already explained, represents an unparalleled innovation on Caravaggio's part with regard to the traditional iconography of Paul's Conversion. In any event, Caravaggio developed the potentialities of narrative blindness in the Cerasi painting in a completely new manner; there is no doubt that the second *Conversion of Saint Paul* is one of the boldest and most radical pictorial statements of the master's entire output.

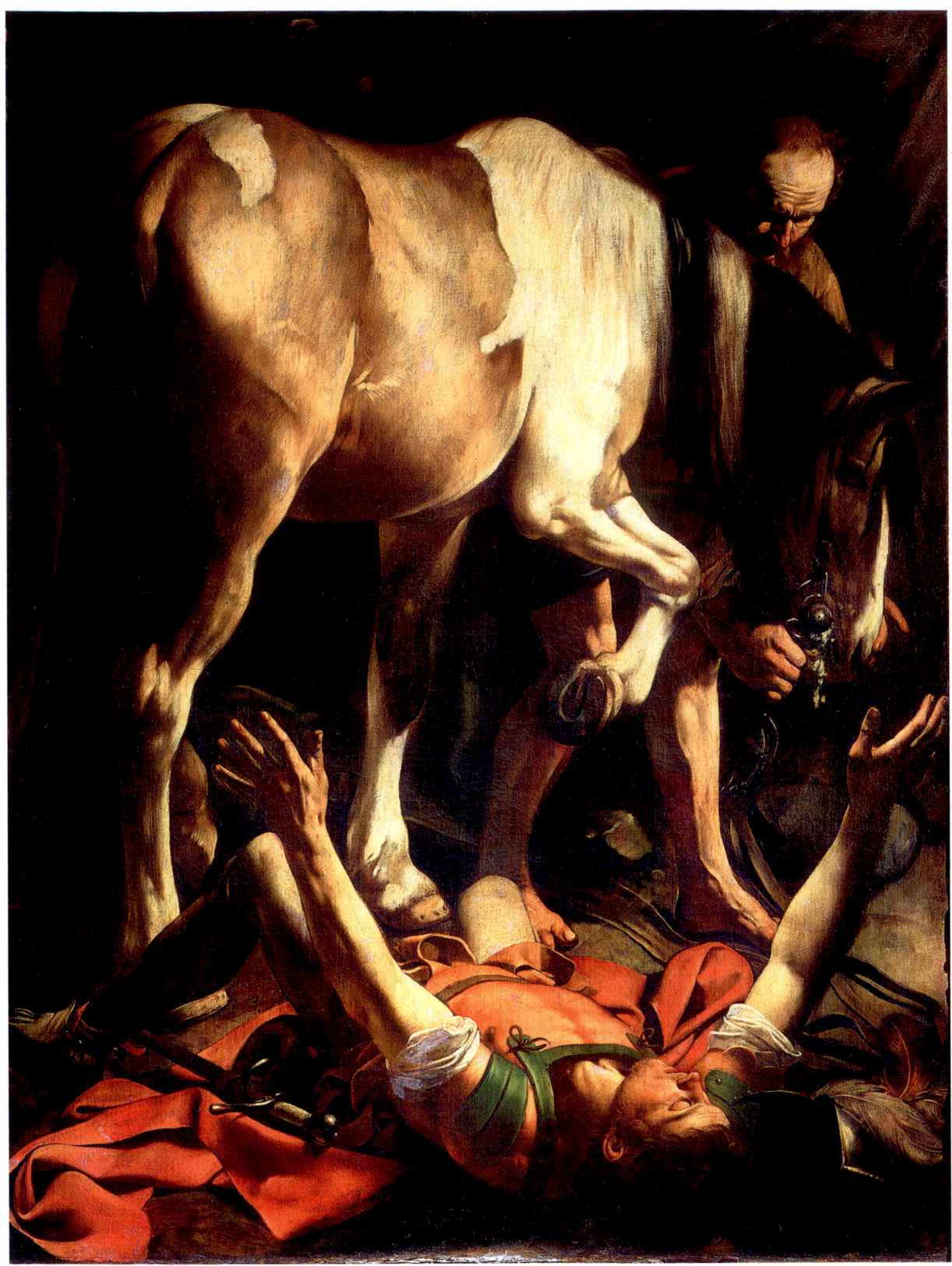

Fig. 117
Michelangelo Merisi da Caravaggio, *Conversion of Saint Paul*, Cerasi Chapel, Santa Maria del Popolo, Rome, oil on canvas, 230 x 175 cm.

Bellori's Censorship

In her seminal 1976 article "Describe or Narrate? A Problem in Realistic Representation," Svetlana Alpers claimed that, with Caravaggio, narrative painting underwent a drastic change that, doomed to failure in Italy, was fully accomplished in seventeenth-century Holland.[27] There, a newly sprung art of description unsettled and eclipsed the humanistic foundations of pictorial narration as established by Leon Battista Alberti in his 1435 *De Pictura*, and agreed upon consistently by artists throughout the Renaissance. Although Alpers argued her thesis with subtlety, she drew an almost insurmountable watershed between Italian and Dutch painting, one neatly bisected by Caravaggio's work. I do not intend here to challenge Alpers' influential theory on description and narrative, but rather to appraise the validity of its cornerstone, Caravaggio's alleged role in the genesis of a non-narrative painting. Relying on a passage from Bellori's *Vite* in which Caravaggio's Cerasi *Conversion of Saint Paul* (Fig. 117)[28] is fiercely blamed for its lack of action, Alpers came to the conclusion that Caravaggio's *istoria* did indeed favor description over narration. More importantly, narration is dismissed as secondary in Caravaggio's oeuvre. Bellori's sentence in this regard is direly laconic. After mentioning Annibale Carracci's *Assumption* on the altar of the Cerasi Chapel, he states: "Caravaggio executed the two lateral paintings, the Crucifixion of Saint Peter and the Conversion of Saint Paul; this *istoria* is completely bereft of action" ("*la quale istoria è affatto senza azzione*").[29]

There is no doubt that Bellori meant to denigrate Caravaggio's picture, and dismissed it by means of a conceptual oxymoron: because the *istoria* canonically represents action, *The Conversion of Saint Paul* is consequently "action without action." In other words, the painting is the opposite of what painting should be; it is a non-painting. Albeit somewhat sophistic, this conclusion logically translates the paradox of Bellori's scathing phrase. Yet on what basis can Caravaggio's painting be accused of lacking action? Guided by an old man, a horse acquiescently ambles beside and over Paul's body. In the foreground, the supine saint encroaches headfirst upon the canvas's lower margin. Eyes shut, he raises both arms heavenward; a red mantle serves as an improvised bed; on it, Paul's epithetical sword visually links the bent left leg to the head. Caravaggio ingeniously arranges the limbs of the prostrate body and the weapon as a set of diagonals fanning out across the painting's lowest register. At first glance, it is clear that a kind of action, if unconventional, is unfolding. Then, why did Bellori find the painting devoid of action altogether? Is it because action is so secondary here that, as Alpers suggested, viewers, overlooking the story, are cajoled into admiring its figures and objects, which light and shadow describe most minutely? Perhaps, but before tackling the issue of action in Caravaggio's Cerasi *Conversion*, it is necessary to point out the intrinsic canonicity of its sources.

It has been noted frequently that the figure of Paul results from a refined elaboration upon a model by Raphael via Taddeo Zuccari, brother of Federico, one of the most renowned painters in Caravaggio's Rome.[30] Around 1560, Taddeo painted an altarpiece for the Frangipani Chapel in San Marcello al Corso, Rome, a large *Conversion of Saint Paul* still in situ, and reproduced in a

---

27 See Alpers 1976, esp. 18-20.

28 For the painting's sources, besides Bellori quoted and commented upon here, see Mancini, 1:225; Baglione, 137; Scannelli, 197; Sandrart, 276; and Dezallier D'Argenville, 1: 262. See also Berenson 1953, 20; Steinberg 1959; Friedlaender 1969, 3-28; Moir 1982, 108; Hibbard 1983, 123-8; Cinotti 1983, 538-40, no. 62B; Bologna 1992, 47-51; Puglisi 1998, 166; Longhi 1999-2000, 152-3 [1951], 191-2 [1952], 274 [1968]; Bernardini 2001; Spezzaferro 2001; Marini 2005, 450-1, no. 42; Vodret 2006; Schütze 2009, 262, no. 25.III; Ebert-Schifferer 2009, 137-9.

29 Bellori, 221-2: "Nella chiesa della Madonna del Popolo, entro la cappella dell'Assunta dipinta da Annibale Carracci, sono di mano del Caravaggio li due quadri laterali, la Crocifissione di san Pietro e la Conversione di san Paolo, la quale istoria è affatto senza azzione."

30 See particularly Friedlaender 1969, 3-28. Interestingly, Pomarancio (Cristoforo Roncalli), picked up the motif of the falling Paul in his circa 1606 *Death of Sapphira* for Santa Maria degli Angeli, Rome. For the painting, see Chiappini di Sorio 1975, 117-8, no. 45. Also, Röttgen 1974, 122, note 92, noted

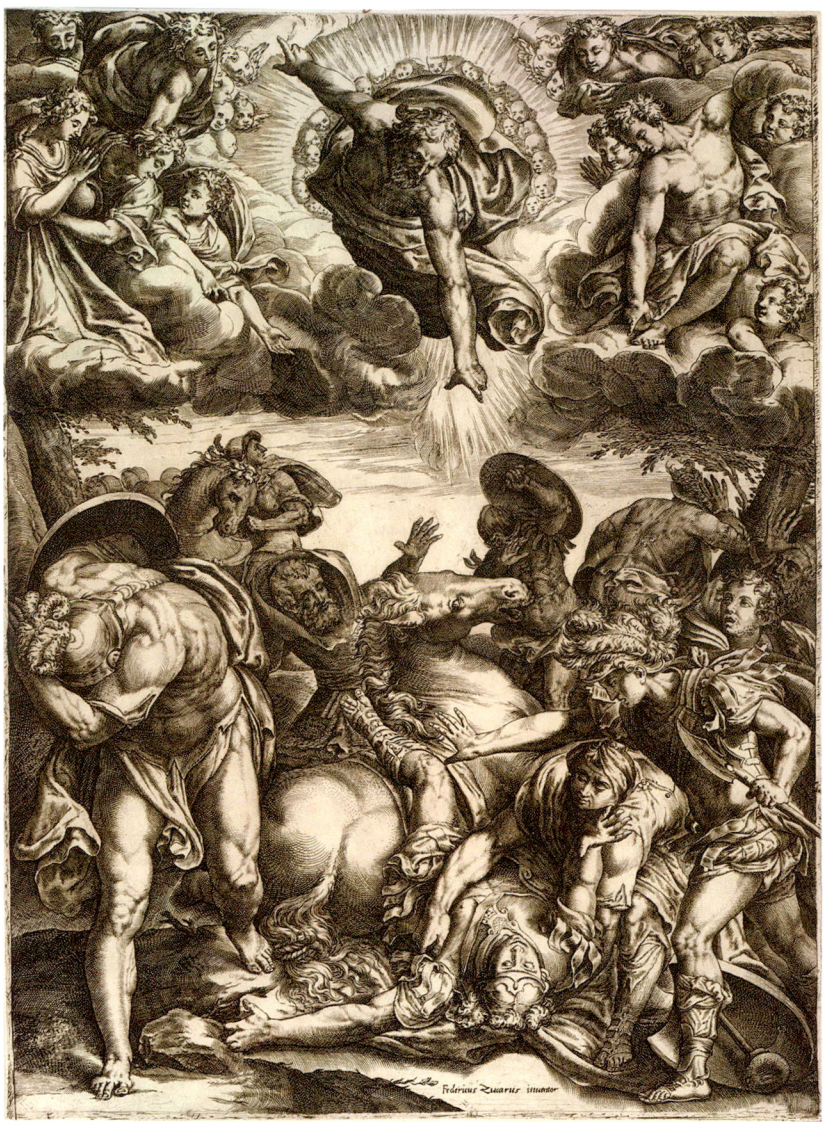

Fig. 118
Cherubino Alberti after Taddeo Zuccari, *Conversion of Saint Paul*, engraving, 46.5 x 34 cm.

1575 engraving by Cherubino Alberti (Fig. 118).[31] In accordance with the iconographic tradition, Taddeo represented a rearing and panicked horse at the center of the painting, aligned with the figure of Jesus above, and with the body of the unhorsed saint below. Saul falls headfirst toward the foreground, his torso nestled within a red mantle, one arm lifted as if in wonder, or perhaps as a counterpoint to Jesus' accusing hand. More interestingly, his eyes remain sealed to mark the saint's temporary blindness and enraptured contemplation. In representing the apostle's conversion, Taddeo sought to improve upon the works of Raphael and Michelangelo. Observe, for instance, the young man who tries to lift Paul in Taddeo's painting; he is almost a copy of the analogous figure in Michelangelo's *Conversion of Saint Paul*. Similarly, Taddeo's Christ, his arms splayed as if mimicking the trajectory of a thunderbolt, constitutes a variant of Michelangelo's Savior.

In imagining the stumbling saint, Taddeo also had in mind Raphael's design for the *Conversion of Saul*, one of the tapestries for the Sistine Chapel commissioned by Pope Leo X around 1515 (Fig. 119).[32] There, Raphael imagined Saul lying to the left, his horse dashing away at a distance while a squad of disconcerted soldiers and knights rush toward him. Saul's arms, almost symmetrically raised, voice his bafflement as he, alone among his companions, rivets his gaze onto the wrathful Jesus above him. It is evident that Caravaggio took up the attitude of Raphael's Saul by turning it nearly upside down, and by inverting the posture of his legs: the right stretched, the left bent, with which a fallen sword also happens to rhyme in the tapestry. With pertinence, Caravaggio directed Paul's arms upward, and outstretched them with the purpose of anchoring the torso to the ground. As a result, the contours of the shoulders and arms take on the form of an open trapeze. Moreover, like Taddeo Zuccari, Caravaggio closed Paul's eyes. In this way, he created a chronological sequel to Raphael's story. If there the apostle has been recently unhorsed, in Caravaggio's painting he by contrast is already transfigured in sightless bliss.

another similarity between Caravaggio's falling Paul and a figure in a painting by Roncalli, a falling soldier represented in the *Resurrection of Christ* for San Giacomo degl'Incurabili, Rome. Röttgen equally reproduces the preparatory drawing (Cologne, Wallraf-Richartz-Museum) for Roncalli's falling figure. For Roncalli's *Resurrection of Christ*, see Chiappini di Sorio 1975, 114-5, no. 41.

31   For Taddeo Zuccari's painting and his works at the Frangipani Chapel, see Acidini Luchinat 1998, 1:62-75. For the print, see Buffa 1982, no. 57-II (70).

32   For this tapestry and the set of cartoons related to Leo X's commission, see Shearman 1972.

Acquainted with Raphael's work, Bellori would surely have guessed that his tapestry was among Caravaggio's sources of inspiration. But he did not, or did not care to, since something in the painting bothered him to the point of repulsion. It cannot be that Bellori disliked Caravaggio's skills of description, as he himself praised them as the painter's unique talent. So what ultimately was so wrong with the *Conversion*? The answer may be found in Bellori's own text.[33] Two or three passages will elucidate the concept of action to which Bellori was wholly devoted. Quoting Nicolas Poussin,[34] Bellori offers a crystal-clear definition of what painting, in his opinion, should be:

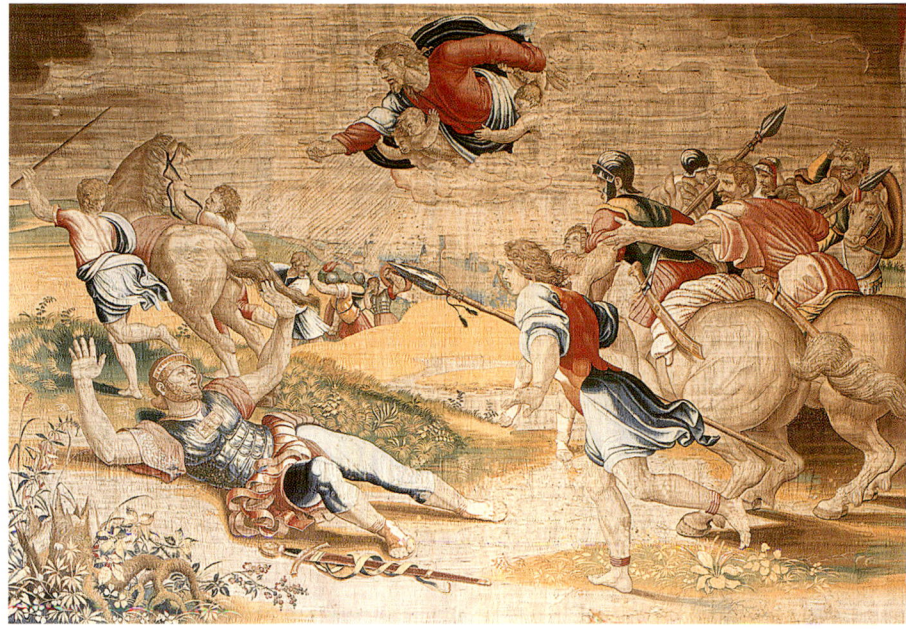

Fig. 119
Workshop of Pieter van Aelst after Raphael (Raffaello Santi), *Conversion of Saint Paul*, Musei Vaticani, Rome, wool, silk and gilt-metal-wrapped thread, 484 x 540 cm.

> Painting is nothing but the imitation of human actions, which properly are the only actions to be imitated; others are not imitable in and of themselves, but only contingently, and not as primary parts, but as accessories; in this sense, it is possible to imitate not only the actions of animals, but furthermore those of all natural things.[35]

The visual relevance of the human figure, the *istoria*'s hero or heroine, was so integral to the achievement of a painting that Bellori insistently underscores its importance whenever the occasion manifests itself. In commending Domenichino's 1614 *Communion of Saint Jerome* (Pinacoteca Nazionale, Bologna),[36] he declares: "[Jerome's] figure is the principal subject over which the gaze first lingers, and therefore is entirely exposed to the light that flows onto his face; the other [figures] around him function as a backdrop darkened by the priest's shadow."[37] In Bellori's eyes, Domenichino embodied the idea of excellence in his rendition of action:[38]

> His genius inclined him to [care] for action in the story; he dressed it, if it proved to be bare; in his quest for propriety, he sought the most arduous expressions, and went as far as to express soul and mind.

33 For Bellori, see Pallucchini 1971; Borea 1992; Sparti 2002; Perini 2002b; Davis M. 2007; and the numerous essays published in Borea and Gasparri 2000. On Bellori's biography of Caravaggio, see also Borea 2000.

34 For Poussin's concept of "novelty," for which there is a vast bibliography, see most recently Unglaub 2006, 38-70.

35 Bellori, 478: "La pittura altro non è che l'imitazione dell'azzioni umane, le quali propriamente sono azzioni imitabili; l'altre non sono imitabili per sé ma per accidente, e non come parti principali ma come accessorie, ed in questa guisa si possono ancora imitare non solo l'azzioni delle bestie, ma tutte le cose naturali."

36 For the painting, see Spear 1982, 1:175-78, no. 41; and Cropper 2005, 67-97.

37 Bellori, 322: "Questa figura è il soggetto principale, dove prima l'occhio si ferma e resta però tutta esposta al lume che le viene in faccia; l'altre che la circondano servono di fondo oscurato dall'ombra del sacerdote."

38 For Domenichino and the *istoria*, see more recently Popp 2007.

With admiration, Bellori concludes: "and this is the utmost difficulty in painting, which without the movements of the soul is nothing but dead imitation."[39]

At this point, it is worthwhile to approach the Cerasi *Conversion of Saint Paul* through Bellori's academic lens. It is undeniable that the story's main subject, that is, the one that first strikes the eye, is not Saul, but the horse passing over him.[40] With intensity, the light brings out its mottled brown and cream markings, so that viewers feel its downy coat and its soft mane, while sensing the stasis or vibrancy of its muscles and tendons. Like Walter Friedländer, I am convinced that Caravaggio imitated Albrecht Dürer's most famous print, *The Large Horse* (Fig. 120).[41] And indeed, it is no coincidence that both Dürer's and Caravaggio's steeds exhibit their bulky, powerful hindquarters, whereas the rest of the body imperceptibly recedes rightward askew. From this prospect, it must be inferred that the hero, or protagonist, of Caravaggio's picture is not Paul, but his horse. Put bluntly, the saint here risks being downgraded to a visual accessory. According to Poussin and Bellori, however, beasts cannot provide matter for imitation, unless they perform a secondary role: a starring horse's action is no action. Caravaggio's painting thus is no painting: it is nothing but "dead imitation."

As usual, however, Caravaggio pushed transgression much farther. In many passages, Bellori remarks upon the finality of pictorial narration; the visual configuration of an *istoria* remains strictly subordinate to a superior, moral message—its goal consists in constituting a paradigm of transcendental truth. To this end, artists are entitled to disrespect the textual plot by manipulating visual action even to the detriment of history. This practice is what Bellori names anachronism: a technical device through which painters "reduce to a single action and time [an event] that poets relate at leisure in many actions and times."[42] It comes as no surprise that Bellori permits this kind of poetic license. However, its use is legitimate only on one condition: anachronism must enhance the legibility and intelligibility of narrative. In the *Conversion of Saint Paul*, Caravaggio instead commits an unforgivable infraction: his *istoria* qualifies as a case of inconsequential anachronism.[43]

To justify my assumption, let us return to Raphael's and Taddeo Zuccari's versions of Paul's conversion. In Taddeo's picture, the most orthodox with respect to Renaissance iconography, verisimilitude in the depiction of time is obviously heeded: Christ's divine intervention is visually related to Paul's collapse and to the horse's rearing. More boldly, Raphael rids the scene of the

39   Ibidem, 360: "Dal suo genio era egli tirato all'azione dell'istoria, ritrovandola nuda la vestiva, e nella proprietà cercava il più difficile dell'espressione, ed esprimeva sino all'anima ed alla mente (…). E questa è la maggior difficoltà della pittura, la quale senza li movimenti dello spirito non è altro che una morta imitazione."

40   Among others, see Longhi 1999-2000, 1:274: "Non fosse che qui si tratta di un dipinto 'laterale,' potrebbe anzi sorprendere che il Caravaggio riuscisse a 'pubblicarlo' senza incorrere in un rifiuto o almeno in serie censure. E quasi si amerebbe sapere se, nel ceto dei dilettanti, mancò chi, usando il titolo nel senso cinetico, galileiano, chiamasse il quadro la 'conversione di un cavallo'; resta però lo stupore del biografo più famoso nel rilevare che 'la storia è affatto senza azzione.' Lo stupore verrà corretto più tardi dall'elogio per 'il cavallo pomellato che è simile al vero' o, addirittura, 'mirabile.' Ma queste son già frasi di amatori." Berenson 1953, 20: "We are to interpret this charade as the conversion of Saint Paul. Nothing more incongruous than the importance given to horse over rider, to dumb beast over saint. No trace of a miraculous occurrence of supreme import." Hibbard 1983, 126, comments: "Nevertheless Caravaggio retained what he wanted from tradition, most obviously the horse. Although Acts does not mention a horse, it had become iconographically indispensable in the Renaissance, and Caravaggio, among other things, needed it to fill up the picture."

41   Friedlaender 1969, 7-8. For the print, see Schoch et al. 2001, 1:120-1, no. 43.

42   Bellori, 55: "Però li pittori sono necessitati servirsi spesso dell'anacronismo, o riduzioni d'azioni e di tempi vari in un punto ed in una occhiata dell'istoria o della favola, per far intendere col muto colore in uno istante quello che è facile al poeta con la narrazione, ed in tal modo certamente l'artefice diviene inventore e si fa proprie l'invenzioni altrui, accrescendo e diminuendo, con lode grandissima." For anachronism in Bellori, see above all Tomasi Velli 2007, 143-203.

43   In a four-block woodcut of the *Conversion of Saint Paul* dating to 1515-1520 and formerly ascribed to Titian, Saint Paul appears lying on the ground in the center of the print, while, to his right, a groom tries to calm his horse by leading it away from the saint. The horse appears to amble. To my knowledge, this is the only example of a Conversion of Saint Paul in which the moment represented corresponds almost exactly to the one evoked by Caravaggio in his painting. For this reason, this print may be considered a remarkable source for the Cerasi *Conversion*. For the woodcut, see Rosand and Muraro 1976, 111-2, no. 13.

encumbering, though highly theatrical, steed, by focusing on the recumbent Paul, whose body, shaped into a cross, seems both to react to the prodigy and to await divine inspiration. In Caravaggio's painting, by contrast, time seems to be eerily suspended. Evidently, an old groom, not the traditional soldier, has calmed the horse, and now prevents it from treading upon Paul. Both the old man and the steed pay no attention to the saint, abandoned on the ground, his eyes shut, while his arms grope inexplicably upward. Or rather, almost inexplicably, since Caravaggio did depict a few rays, streaming in above from the right, through which he perfunctorily evokes Jesus' epiphany. Nonetheless, the real source of lighting is practically invisible, although it spotlights the scene with vehemence, tearing darkness apart and asserting its presence. By concealing the cause of the action, and by steering the attention from the portent to its almost anecdotal outcome, Caravaggio contravened the principle of finality and intelligibility endorsed by Bellori.[44] Without these substantial components, there is no action worthy of the term. In this respect, *The Conversion of Saint Paul* once again embodies no action.

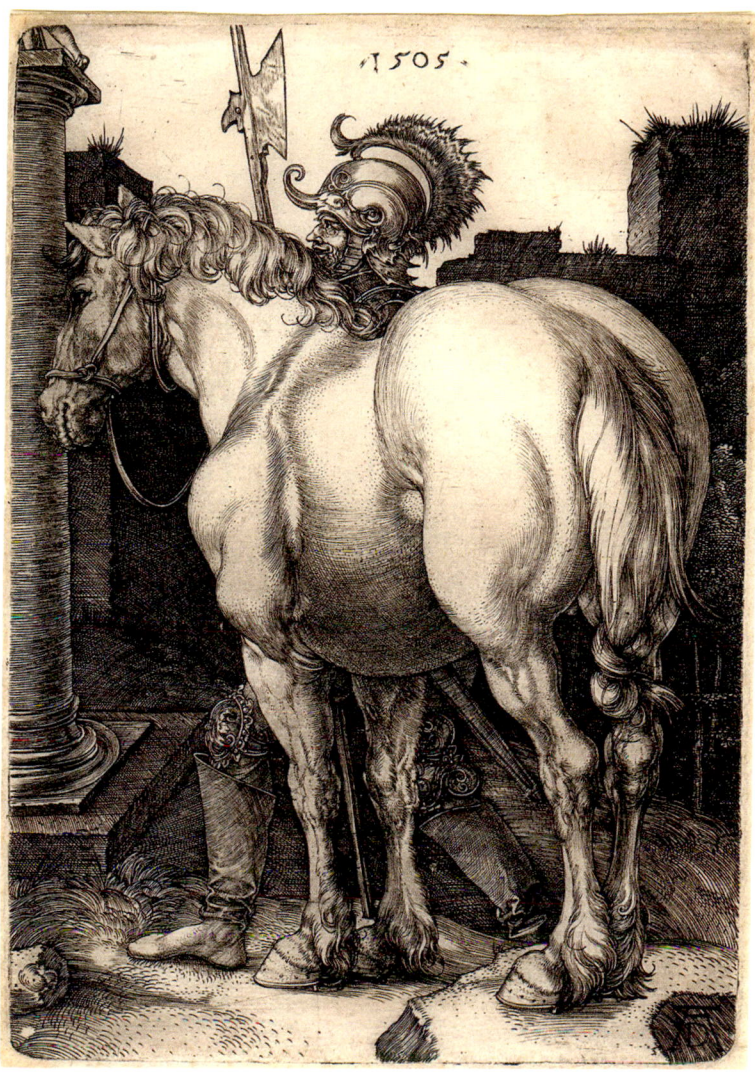

Fig. 120
Albrecht Dürer, *The Large Horse*, engraving, 16.7 x 11.9 cm.

By casting the horse rather than the biblical hero as the painting's protagonist, and by disrupting the narrative momentum, Caravaggio inflects the sacred episode with pithy implications. I will expand on this shortly. Regardless of this fact, it has become clear why Bellori viewed the Cerasi *Conversion of Saint Paul* as "bereft of action." He did not intend to say that the painting lacks action completely, but instead that its action does not pertain at all to the category of the *istoria*. From this point of view, Caravaggio's picture does indeed represent the opposite of the *istoria*. In this case, a dislocation of character—a horse as the main feature—and of momentum—a slumbering rather than a stumbling Paul—aroused Bellori's indignation. But the scope of Caravaggio's poetics of dislocation extends to many other aspects of pictorial narrative. By attacking the principles of art's loftiest institution, the *istoria*, Caravaggio nevertheless did not aim to stifle visual action. As I have already stated in Part One, the master instead tried to enlarge the *istoria*'s potentialities beyond its conventional confines. This disruptive endeavor does not entail

---

44 For Caravaggio's focus on the action's outcome, see Röttgen 1974, 109, who assigns a "psychological" function to it: "L'azione drammatica della prima versione è stata completamente trasformata in un linguaggio psicologico che prescinde dall'antefatto per esprimere un 'dopo' soltanto in quanto si manifesta nell'avvenimento e solo per mezzo di braccia tese."

the beginning of an art of description, as Alpers claimed, but prefigures the end of normative, neo-Aristotelian forms of narration.

Compared to the Odescalchi painting, the Cerasi *Conversion of Saint Paul* is a monument of pictorial concision. By shifting Paul's companion to the right background and illuminating part of his downcast face, right foot, and left leg, Caravaggio greatly downplayed this figure's relevance. In a certain sense, the groom appears as an appendage of the mottled steed, his foot and leg prolonging those of the animal, his face echoing the downward orientation of the horse's face as if both were intent on the same objective:[45] to avoid treading upon Paul's body by exiting the scene, as the old man's pointing finger indicates. In this manner, Caravaggio structured the composition as a bipolar field of interaction: one dominated by the fallen apostle below and the ambling horse above, the trapeze of the saint's shoulder and arms responding to the triangular outline of the steed's muzzle and bent neck on the one hand, and to the trapezoid of its right rear leg and angled foreleg on the other. Even though these two figures, the horse and the saint, fill and circumscribe the whole pictorial space, their opposition proves to be uneven: the apostle's flattened and foreshortened body delimits a void counterbalanced, or rather pressured, by the fullness of the steed's massive bulk. Through this pictorial device, Caravaggio managed to reduce Paul's figure to a colored silhouette relegated to the periphery of the beholder's visual field, thereby undermining and strongly diminishing his visual salience. In other words, the viewer cannot help but turn his or her eyes toward the horse's planar volume, a blind screen of cream and brown hair,[46] whereas the animal's face fades into apparent shadow under the camouflage of its black mane, its eye's indefinite darkness contributing even more to this effect. In my opinion, the dissimulation of the horse's face as opposed to the theatrical display of its body deprives the animal of its narrative role and transforms it into abstract surface: the point zero of pictorial action and an impenetrable, voluminous curtain to the beholder's eyes.

If one ponders the scope of the compositional layout devised by Caravaggio for the Cerasi *Conversion*, it will become clear that, visually speaking, the painting's main figure is not even the horse, but the physical barrier it opposes to the viewer's sight, blocking the pictorial depth, deviating the attention from Paul's figure toward the painting's mottled blankness. Caravaggio's steed is above all a figuration of narrative blindness. In the Cerasi *Conversion*, the master did not content himself with hiding the saint's loss of sight and by covering his face. The visual litotes that I have previously discussed at length with regard to the Odescalchi painting becomes useless here insofar as the whole action turns out to be an extensive narrative litotes. By slowing the action almost to stillness, by focusing furthermore upon the story's insignificant moment—the one that, as a corollary to Bellori's academic aesthetics, painters should carefully dodge because it makes it impossible for beholders to reconstruct the action's premise, outcome, and implications—Caravaggio eradicates the hero and his living attribute, the horse, from the iconographic tradition of Paul's conversion, their simple juxtaposition on the canvas sufficing to evoke the biblical episode.[47]

Yet the horse without its rearing, Paul without his collapsing, the old man without his astonishment and the sunshine without Christ, as allusive as they might be to the saint's conversion, do not add up to the Gospel action. The event, it must be avowed already, has been lost in the passage

---

45 See the way in which Longhi 1999-2000, 1:274, describes the figurative assemblage of the horse and the groom: "quell'intrigo indecifrabile, tra quadrupede e servente, di vene nodose e varicose."

46 The importance of the horse's coat in Caravaggio's painting is a sort of early topos. See Sandrart, 276: "Das Pferd ist ein Scheck und scheint lebendig zu seyn"; and Dezallier d'Argenville, 1:262: "son cheval gris pommelé est admirable."

47 See the interesting remark of Longhi 1999-2000, 1:274: "Con questo sottinteso discreto, che sta per sommessa ironia dell'erudizione corrente e che, eliminando fino all'osso la tradizione iconografica del tempo, non manca di fermare un punto nell'immenso percorso mentale del maestro, questi licenzia il dipinto forse più rivoluzionario in tutta la storia dell'arte sacra."

from one point to the next of the story's chronological sequence. Assembled together, the ecstatic Paul and the ambling horse give rise to a novel *istoria*, one in which nothing miraculous occurs; one deserted by the divine epiphany but still unfurling in time, as the horse continues to foam at the mouth, its hoof still hanging in mid air, while Paul keeps his arms stretched as if embracing his vision, although the commotion of God's flash and thunder have receded and vanished and silence is all that remains. In a sense, Bellori is right when he affirms that Caravaggio's painting is "completely bereft of action." To him, action is a culminant point in time, the climax of a story, and the Cerasi *Conversion* is rather a narrative anticlimax. None of these factors are fortuitous; the stroke of a sponge on a canvas cannot account for the pictorial blindness and muteness the master summoned so masterfully in this painting. Caravaggio indeed calculated every detail, as evidenced by X-rays of the painting. At the beginning, Paul appeared in the lower right foreground, his torso lifted, one hand open and rising to halt the divine radiance's onslaught coming from the left.[48] In this first version, the apostle still accomplishes his traditional function, and his relation to God's lightning is perfectly legible.

But Caravaggio changed his mind, deliberately, and never bothered to modify the picture's lighting, which still streams from the left and above, but now does so incoherently. As if to remedy this incongruousness, Caravaggio depicted a few sunrays to the right: a symbol of God's intervention devoid of narrative mission because visually unrelated to Paul's fallen body. In the end, God is nowhere to be seen in the Cerasi *Conversion*. Paul's blindness becomes the blindness of the viewer, whose sight remains fascinated and occluded by the horse's imposing mass. Tragically, nothing in the painting allows the beholder to feel or share Paul's bliss, certainly not the saint's sightless face, so impassible and inert. One can only perceive the apostle's impression of falling ever so calmly through the posture of his stretched arms. If there is bliss in this painting, it can only be imagined despite the painting's action and beyond its narrative blindness.

---

48 For the X-ray photographs, and a reconstruction and discussion of the first version of Paul's figure in the Cerasi painting, see Bernardini 2001, 126-33.

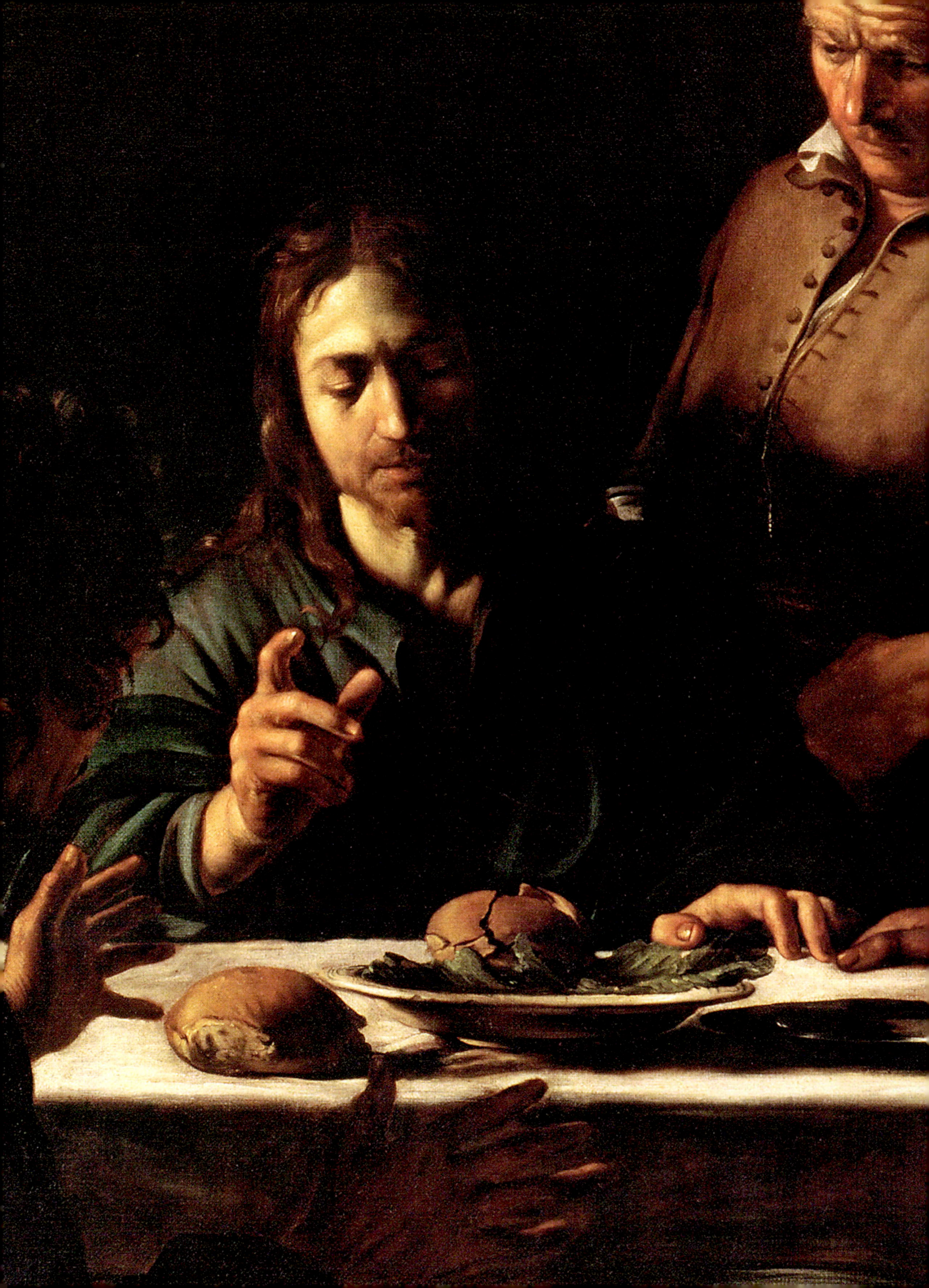

CHAPTER 9

Visualizing Appearance and Disappearance: Caravaggio's Two Versions of the *Supper at Emmaus*[*]

"No form can be found that might either convey divinity to mortal eyes or represent the image of God's Son in his being God (…). Whatever one reads as referred to God in the sacred texts is indeed formulated but in a metaphorical manner and quite inadequately."[1]

The Visibility of God

In his first *Supper at Emmaus*, painted for Cardinal Ciriaco Mattei in 1601-1602 and now in the National Gallery, London (Fig. 121),[2] Caravaggio once again manipulated the conventional techniques of Renaissance narration to incorporate ambivalence and subjectivity into the painting's action. To demonstrate this, it is appropriate to consider the London picture within the purview of the iconographic tradition. Although the Mattei *Supper at Emmaus*, as a figurative text, is interwoven with multiple references to a preexisting iconography, intrinsically informed by the reflection and inventiveness of Renaissance artists from Bellini to Titian, from Moretto da Brescia to Paolo Veronese, it nonetheless detaches itself from its antecedents in a disruptive manner. By inquiring into the theme of *The Supper at Emmaus* before Caravaggio, I intend to demonstrate how figures, expressions, and gestures were to translate facets and nuances of the subject in a pictorial structure that, unlike that of the London painting, can be most appropriately defined as a symbolic narrative. This definition notwithstanding, I shall not investigate here the symbolism or the allegorical significance of *The Supper at Emmaus*. Moreover, in interpreting Caravaggio's picture, I shall continue to prefer visual sources to literary ones. As a matter of fact, if there is no certainty that theological treatises might have inspired Caravaggio, who in his own time was not renowned for his erudition, it is undeniable that in depicting his *Supper at Emmaus*, he grappled with schemes, motifs, and accessories derived from other artists, which were stocked in his memory as raw material and organic matter for inspiration. If correctly identified and construed, these visual sources may help us grasp the specificity of Caravaggio as both an inventor of sacred images and an original interpreter of the visibility of Christ, a concept crucial to the evolution of Christian iconography that is inherently linked to the early modern representations of *The Supper at Emmaus*. The notions of Christ's visibility and invisibility in religious compositions thus merit an introduction.

[*] This chapter is an expanded, slightly modified version of my 2007 essay in the *Art Bulletin*: Pericolo 2007.

1 Gabriele Paleotti, fragment of Book 4 of his unfinished *De imaginibus sacris et profanis*, transcribed by Bianchi 2008, 229, note 61: "Imaginem Dei Filii representare pro ut Deus est, de quo modo diximus, nullam inveniri formam quae oculis mortalium divinitatem possit referre, cum quicquid in sacris literis Deo ascribendum quisquis legitur, id non nisi metaphorice et valde improprie sit positum."

2 For the London *Supper at Emmaus*, see Celio, 134; Baglione, 137; Manilli, 88; Scannelli, 198-9; Bellori, 174. For an interpretation of the painting, see Friedlaender 1969, 164-7, no. 18; Moir 1976, 87-8, no. 17; Scribner 1977; Moir 1982, 102; Cinotti 1983, 450-3, no. 25; Marini 1983, esp. 136-43; Hibbard 1983, 75-80; Christiansen 1985, 271-6, no. 78 [catalogue entry by Mina Gregori]; Varriano 1986, 218-24; Pfatteicher 1987; Calvesi 1990, esp. 10-1, 255; Warma 1990; Bologna 1992, 42-3; Cappelletti and Testa 1994, 104-6, no. 8; Gilbert 1995, 143-50; Strinati and Vodret 1995, 118, no. 1; Schröter 1995; Bell 1995; Puglisi 1998, 209-13; Longhi 1999-2000, 1: 174 [1952]; Lavin 2000, 30-3; Marini 2005, 456-8, no. 47; Schütze 2009, 263, no. 27; Ebert-Schifferer 2009, 141-6.

◄ Plate XII: Michelangelo Merisi da Caravaggio, *The Supper at Emmaus*, Pinacoteca di Brera, Milan, oil on canvas, 141 x 175 cm., detail.

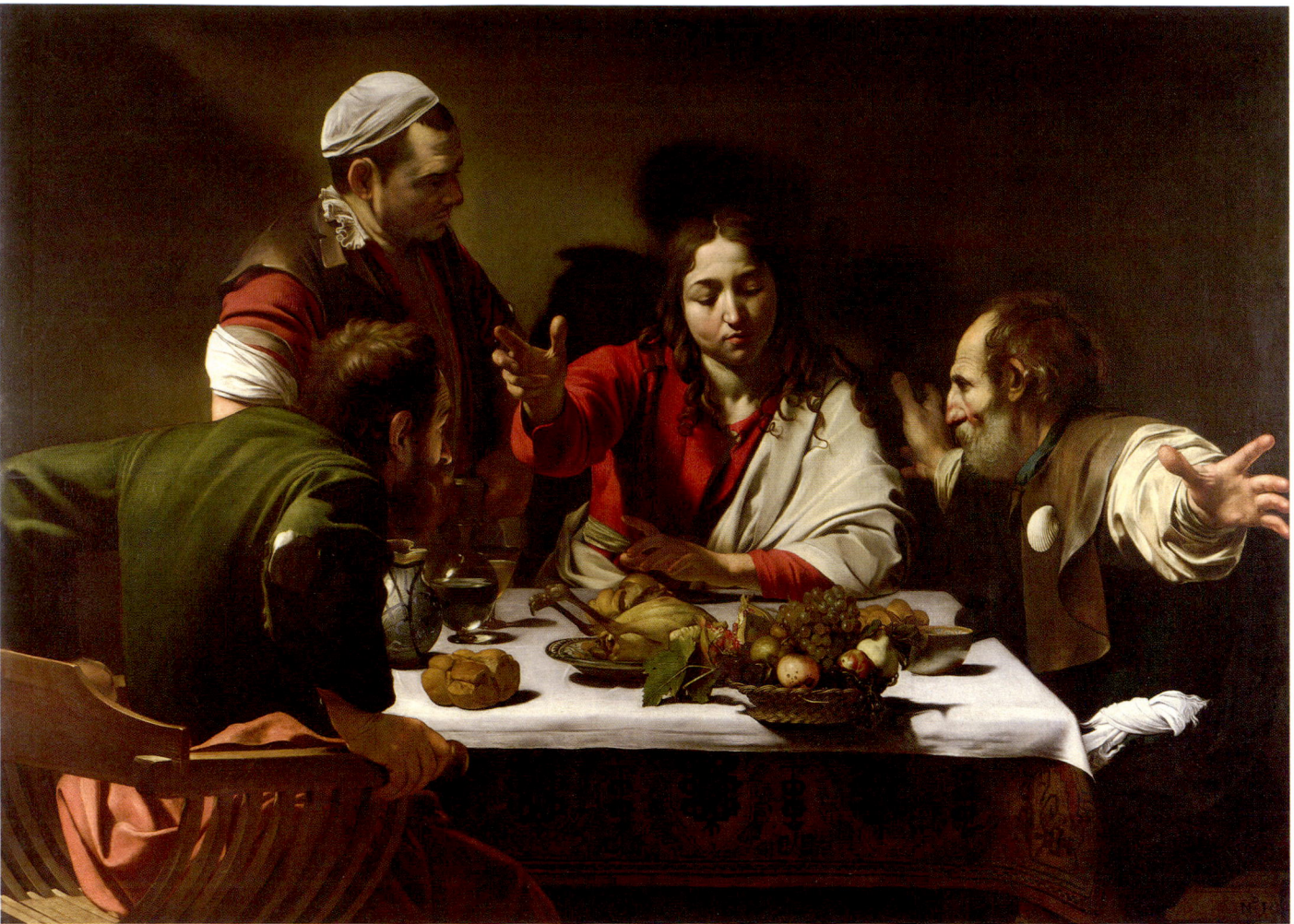

Fig. 121
Michelangelo Merisi da Caravaggio, *The Supper at Emmaus*, National Gallery, London, oil on canvas, 141 x 196.2 cm.

Even for such a convinced defender of sacred images as John of Damascus, visualizing God was undoubtedly a matter of the "utmost foolishness and impiety."[3] In his *Treatise on Divine Images*, composed shortly after 726, he concisely explained the point by means of a metaphysical argument: "one would certainly be wrong, if one tried to make the image of God, since it is impossible to represent what is devoid of body and invisible to human eyes, what cannot be circumscribed and is shapeless."[4] Relying specifically on John's authority, Cardinal Gabriele Paleotti underscored centuries later in his *Discorso intorno alle immagini sacre* (1582) that divinity in itself is not to be reproduced. Yet since the Bible metaphorically visualizes the divine, describing its presence and actions in perceptible figures, divinity "can and must be represented through likenesses proportionate to our senses, [especially] on account of their weakness, so that we ascend to the contemplation of the invisible by comprehending and imitating the visible that is known to us."[5] Thus, when it comes to representing divinity, the ecclesiastical tradition going back to John of

3   John of Damascus a, 4.17.

4   John of Damascus b, 730: "Erraremus profecto si vel Dei, qui cerni non potest, imaginem faceremus, cum id, quod est corporis expers, quodque nec oculis videtur, nec circumscribitur, nec figuram habeat, effingi nequeat." See also Paleotti, 89. For the debates about the invisibility of God and the use of images in early Christianity, see Finney 1997.

5   Paleotti, 89-90: "E di questa maniera è stato sempre dalla antichità giudicato che si possano e si debbano con tali somiglianze proporzionate a' sensi nostri, per la debolezza di quelli, rappresentare le cose celesti, accioché dalla significazione ed imitazione di queste cose visibili a noi note, ascendessimo alla meditazione delle invisibili." See John of Damascus b, 704.

Damascus and culminating in Paleotti's precepts on art makes it clear that the visible and the invisible, albeit strongly related, are unambiguously distinguished from each other.[6]

Sacred images, if appropriately constructed, incite beholders to transcend the limits of their senses so that they can perceive, imagine, or contemplate the divine that they can in no way see. However, there is an exception to this principle, a particular case in which visible and invisible might fuse together, in which divinity plainly unfolds, manifesting itself in a visible manner. Only in this case could reproducing and representing the divine be almost equated. This is the image of Christ, according to John of Damascus: "I dare make the image of the invisible God, not because he is invisible, but because he made himself visible for our sake, partaking of flesh and blood."[7] As stated by John in several passages of his text, Christ's historical figure embodies the essence of God himself: "the Son is the image alive, natural and perfectly similar of the invisible God; he carries in himself the Father, and is identical with him in everything, except for this single fact, that he derives from him as from his [primary] cause."[8]

Strangely enough, neither Paleotti nor any other art theorist of the Counter-Reformation seems to have adopted John's point of view. Without explicitly rebutting it, Paleotti placed the images of the Father, the Son, and the Holy Spirit in the same category, thereby implying that all these effigies, despite their highest nobility, refer to divinity in a symbolic, indirect way.[9] As the chapter in which Paleotti planned to deal with the figure of Christ was never completed, it would be rash to draw any unequivocal conclusion in this regard.[10] Maybe, to explain his reticence, it should just be assumed that the specificity of Christ's image, or his pictorial visibility, was taken for granted and too universally acknowledged to be theorized. By insisting on this point, Paleotti would have laid himself open to criticism, being suspected of giving grounds for a milder sort of idolatry. In any event, whether theoretically justified or barely alluded to, the particular status of Christ's image factually exerted a radical influence on the structure and iconography of sacred images. As the Son visually incarnates the invisibility of the Father, his pictorial representation was to be endowed with a supplementary charge of visibility. Rhetorically speaking, his was a prosopopoeial figure. To be entirely efficient, his image had to be forthwith identifiable and pictorially conspicuous.[11]

To this end, Western artists were often driven to reduce the range of expressions and attitudes used in representing Christ to a canonical repertoire. As a result, beholders could easily recognize his majesty and divinity, interpreting by force of habit the biblical episodes in which he was shown. This practice virtually led to two interconnected side effects in Christian iconography, which I would define as *inhibition* and *erosion*.[12] On the one hand, narrative pertinence in sacred images can be either inhibited or perturbed by an excessive or overly conventional visibility of Christ's figure

---

6   See also Molanus, 38; Borromeo, 37-8.

7   John of Damascus b, 701: "Itaque Dei invisibilis imaginem audio conficere, non quatenus invisibilis est, sed quatenus propter nos visibilis factus, carnis et sanguinis particeps."

8   Ibidem, 704: "Ac viva quidem, naturalis ac nulla re dissimilis imago Dei invisibilis est ipse filius, qui in se ipso patrem gerit, et in omnibus idem cum illo est, praeter unum id, quod ab eo, tamquam a causa est." See also ibidem, 730. For John of Damascus' conception of sacred images, see Freedberg D. 1989, 393 ff. For the concept of Christ's image as the *vera icon* and its importance in German Renaissance art, see Koerner 1993, 80-126.

9   See Paleotti, 90. Paleotti does not seem to acknowledge the specificity of Christ's image as a historical one, since he claims that any figure of Jesus is nothing but representation. Furthermore, Paleotti does not consider the common iconography of Christ's image as stemming from at least two prototypes, the Mandylion and especially the Veronica, which

were viewed as true portraits of Jesus and whose authenticity he himself deemed as proved (86-8). See also Molanus, 48-51; 381-4; Alberti R., 52-3; Comanini, 117, 125 ff.; Bocchi F., 78-9; Ghini, 45, 52; Borromeo, 41-3; and Baronio, 475. For the history of these prototypes, see Belting 1990, 208-24.

10   For this point, see Prodi 1967, 2:526-62; and more recently Bianchi 2008, 221-3.

11   When alluding to an easily identifiable type, I do not mean that images of Christ should be identical. Nevertheless, they must share a set of specific features, characterizing them as a distinctive type, an *eikonismos*, as Byzantine theologians used to refer to it. See Dagron 1991, esp. 25-30. See also Hinz P. 1973; Kessler and Wolf 1996; Finaldi 2000; McGregor and Langmuir 2000; Morello and Wolf 2000; Wolf et al. 2004.

12   To my knowledge, there is no study that deals with these specific notions. An interesting study of the figure of Christ in the early Renaissance is in Nagel and Wood 2010, 241-50.

and attitudes. On the other hand, the frequency and invariability of his prototypical representation inevitably erode and diminish its evocative power. In other terms, Christ's overexposed image might fail to hint at the invisible divinity to which it is symbiotically related.

To avoid both these risks without transgressing the codes of pictorial tradition, artists over time came up with a surprising array of visual solutions, some successful. Yet, as a general rule, the visibility of Christ is never doubted nor reassessed, even in those borderline cases in which, according to the Bible, Jesus himself revealed his supernatural, invisible divinity by disappearing or becoming transfigured.[13] It would be extremely interesting to zero in on those biblical representations of disappearance and transfiguration, for upon closer analysis of their structures we can positively understand to what extent the visibility of Christ stood out as an artistic axiom. More often than not, we shall see that it hindered pictorial narration from developing coherently, occasionally trivializing the miraculous character of theophany. Of course, it would take much more time to examine all the pictures, drawings, or engravings that, in the Western tradition, and especially in the early modern period, depict the sudden manifestation of Christ's divinity. For this reason, it is appropriate to concentrate on a single picture. Because of its complexity, Caravaggio's London *Supper at Emmaus* provides us with an example of all the technical and theoretical problems that a painter had to tackle when conjuring up the divine presence and miraculous disappearance of Christ.[14]

Before dwelling on the London painting, it is useful to underline some aspects of the biblical subject illustrated by Caravaggio. As Saint Luke narrates (24,13-35), immediately after the Passion and the Resurrection, Jesus addressed two apostles, Cleophas and another whose name is not given, on their way to Emmaus. As "their eyes were prevented from recognizing him," they did not know him. Unrecognized, Christ chastised his two disciples for their skepticism about his divine nature and miracles, reminding them that the prophets of scripture had forecast his actions. While approaching Emmaus, as the sun was about to set, the two apostles begged Christ not to depart but to abide with them, sharing their meal in a local inn. During the supper, Jesus "took bread, said the blessing, and broke it, and gave it to them." Only then could Cleophas and his companion identify him: then "their eyes were opened, and they recognized him; and he vanished from their sight." Later on, after recovering from their astonishment, the two told the other apostles about the miracle: "what had taken place on the way, and how [Jesus] was made known to them in the breaking of the bread." More concisely, Saint Mark's Gospel (16,12) reports that Christ appeared to his disciples after the Passion "in another form." As a theatrical and literary subject, the episode of the supper at Emmaus constitutes a classical scene of recognition, or *anagnorisis*.[15] As such, it should have offered artists an amazing opportunity to describe both the surprise of the apostles and the prodigious disappearance of Christ. But, unexpectedly, painters seldom, if ever, depict Jesus vanishing as his disciples lose their momentary blindness, gazing at him with incredulous understanding. On the contrary, in most versions of *The Supper at Emmaus* dating from the fifteenth through the seventeenth centuries, the visibility of Christ is preserved as a substantial component of the iconography.

Artists' reluctance to visualize a disappearing Christ cannot be dismissed as a lack of technical capability. In fact, painters practiced effects of fade-in and fade-out in various subjects, as, for example, in innumerable Annunciations. Even in the seventeenth century, a period in the history of

13 For the representation of a disappearing Christ in the Middle Ages, see Schapiro 1943, reprinted in Schapiro 1979, 267-87; and Deshman 1997.

14 For the iconographic tradition of the Supper at Emmaus, see Vloberg 1946, 1:125-33; Rudrauf 1955-1956; Stechow 1967; Corsato 1997; and Canova and Spiazzi 1997.

15 For the importance of the concept of *anagnorisis* in the theory of narrative as derived from Aristotle's *Poetics*, see Ricœur 1983, 86-92.

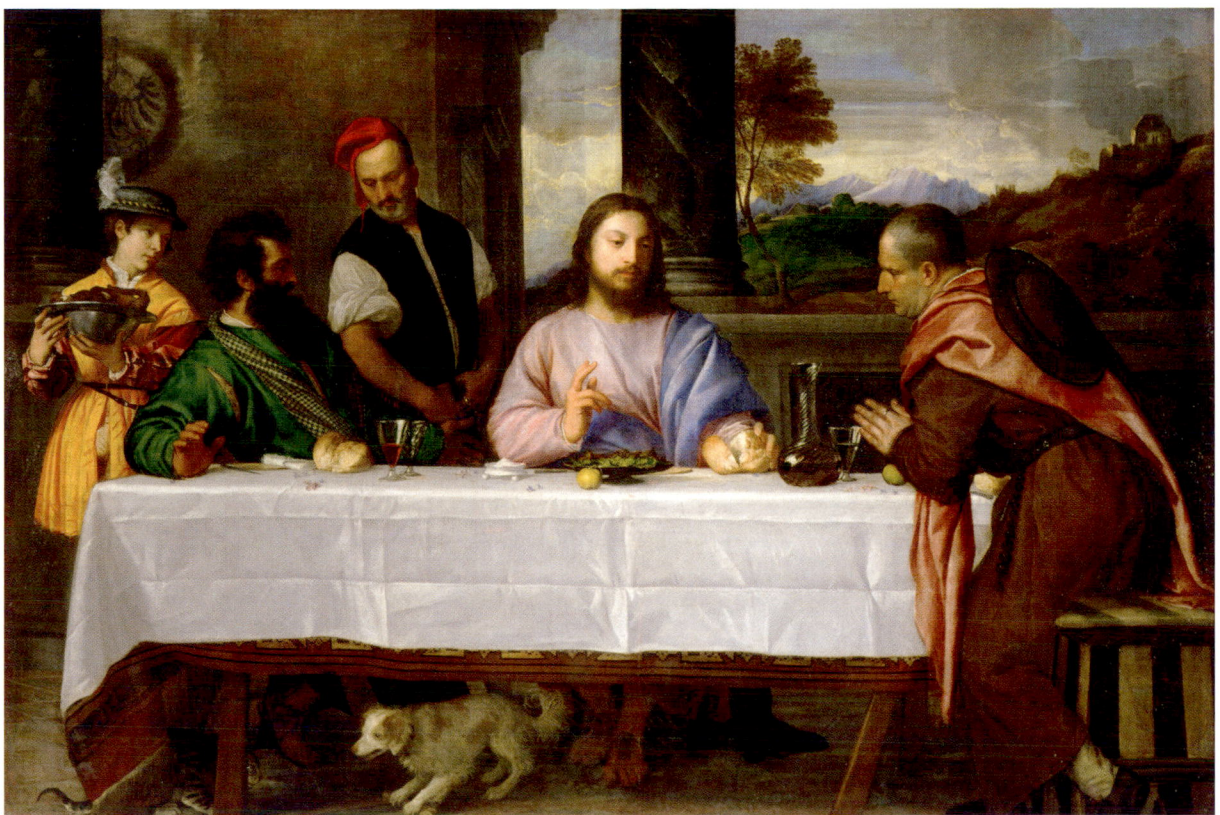

Fig. 122
Titian (Tiziano Vecelli), *The Supper at Emmaus*, Musée du Louvre, Paris, oil on canvas, 169 x 244 cm.

art notorious for its sensitivity to verisimilitude, a textually accurate reconstruction of this biblical episode seems not to have been required, as proved, for instance, by Jean-Baptiste de Champaigne's comment on Titian's *Supper at Emmaus* (Musée du Louvre, Paris), a famous picture then in the collections of Louis XIV (Fig. 122).[16] In a lecture given at the Académie Royale de Peinture et de Sculpture, in October 1676, Champaigne, an eager supporter of history painting and a severe critic of narrative inconsistencies, had nothing but praise for the way Titian had depicted the episode, especially the figure and attitude of Christ:

> [The figure] does not cease to be majestic, and succeeds very well in featuring the object to which the apostles' attention is turned, [acting out] the moment that would unclose their eyes and make them understand the maxims he had given them on their way [to Emmaus], since he had chosen this very instant to let them know the truth of his Resurrection through the consecration of the bread [he performed] while being present in his own body, as witnessed by the holy Fathers of the Church.[17]

16 See Laclotte 1993, 515-7, no. 161 [with extensive bibliography].

17 *Conférences*, 2:610: "Mais il faut convenir que le tout ensemble de l'intention de cette figure est à considérer pour la beauté du pinceau, et que l'on passe volontiers par-dessus toutes les réflexions qu'on pourrait faire, car elle ne laisse pas d'avoir de la majesté, et réussit très bien comme ayant voulu représenter l'objet de l'attention des disciples et le moment qui leur devait ouvrir les yeux et qui devait faire l'effet des instructions qu'il leur avait faites par le chemin, s'étant réservé cet instant pour leur faire connaître la vérité de sa Résurrection par la consécration du pain en la réalité de son corps, comme le témoignent les Pères de l'Église." Unfortunately, the letter written by Jean-Baptiste de Champaigne to the abbot of Saint-Cyran in 1674 (in which he criticized Titian's *Supper at Emmaus*, comparing it with another painting of the same subject painted by Philippe de Champaigne, which Jean-Baptiste completed after his uncle's death) has not been preserved. See the response to Jean-Baptiste de Champaigne by the abbot of Saint-Cyran in Gazier 1891, esp. 115. In his 1676 lecture at the Académie Royale, Jean-Baptiste noted some anachronisms in Titian's painting, exclusively in connection with clothing, but he justified them as imposed by the patron.

Obviously, the image of Christ is commended not on its narrative pertinence, but on its paradigmatic conspicuousness: as an "object," or icon, of the divine majesty, it appeals not only to the apostles, enthralled in its contemplation, but also to the viewer, equally absorbed in its glorious display. In addition, the painting fully represents a symbolic action, one that uncovers the mysteries of the Resurrection and the Eucharist.

Yet, in exalting Titian's painting, Jean-Baptiste de Champaigne ignores the incongruity of the attitude of Christ, who blesses the bread he has broken beforehand, thereby bypassing the steps of the ritual, while Cleophas is about to bend forward to honor him upon untimely recognition. This proleptic, short-circuited portrayal of Christ's theophany cannot be properly characterized as an *istoria* in the specific terms of the Counter-Reformation. As an abridged and condensed version of a biblical episode, the subject can thus be easily identified by beholders, although it is scarcely suitable to be read and reconstructed as a chronologically and logically coherent narration. In other words, this kind of figurative device is meant to instantaneously trigger the memory of the scriptural passage in the viewer's mind, topically recalling its theological significance, namely, the dogmas of the Resurrection and the Eucharist. Thus, by modeling his figure of Jesus on the traditional icon of the Blessing Christ—in *The Supper at Emmaus*, the Eucharistic bread is exhibited as a near equivalent to the crystal sphere usually associated with God's earthly and universal power—Titian above all intended to accentuate the visibility of the Son. If, as a consequence, the narrative pertinence of the episode was inhibited and disrespected (as in fact it is), this was, for the painter and for many other artists drawing on the same iconographic tradition, a secondary matter.

Caravaggio's first version of the *Supper at Emmaus* substantially appears to toe the line of the traditional iconography. Nowhere in the documentation related to it is a trace of any confusion to be found about its subject or any objection to the verisimilitude of the action it places on view. In a document dated 7 January 1602, Cardinal Ciriaco Mattei described the painting he had just purchased as "a representation of our Lord *in fractione panis*" [breaking the bread].[18] A few years later, the picture was offered, or sold, to Cardinal Scipione Borghese. In 1672, Giovan Pietro Bellori appraised Caravaggio's composition in his *Vite*, admiring its coloring, but reproving the painter's proclivity to vulgarity and incongrousness: "in the Supper at Emmaus, besides the rustic figures of the two apostles, and that of Christ represented as young and beardless, there is an innkeeper wearing a cap, and on the table sits a basket filled with grapes, figs, and pomegranates, out of season."[19]

Bellori's criticism pointed in the first place to Caravaggio's lack of pictorial decorum; in his opinion, the painter should have chosen other models for Christ and his disciples, models whose features and physical proportions would express the nobility of a sacred story. The unusual typology of a young and beardless Jesus is criticized less for its strangeness than for its triviality. In a sense, this detail does not seem to Bellori more bewildering than the basket of unseasonal fruits suspended on the edge of the table. In any case, he never questioned the way Caravaggio conceived the narrative structure of the scene, or the dynamics of its action; neither do modern scholars, for that matter, with very few exceptions.[20] Perhaps, the traditional—or apparently so—structure of

---

18   See Cappelletti and Testa 1994, 104-5.

19   Bellori, 231: "Nella Cena in Emaus, oltre le forme rustiche delli due apostoli, e del Signore figurato senza barba, vi assiste l'oste con la cuffia in capo, e nella mensa vi è un piatto d'uve, fichi, melagrane, fuori di stagione."

20   The weirdest and least understandable interpretation of the narrative involved in Caravaggio's *Supper at Emmaus* comes from Gilbert 1995, 147, who, relying on a personal interpretation of the iconographic tradition, claims that the gestures of surprise performed by the apostles do not involve the idea of recognition. Criticizing both Scribner 1977 and Hibbard 1983, he affirms: "Despite the insistence in it [the medieval *Glossa ordinaria*] that the disciples recognized Christ only 'in the breaking of the bread,' Scribner does not point out that Caravaggio shows unbroken bread, and so is able to read the disciples as recognizing Christ when he blesses. Like Hibbard, he treats the painting as both Eucharistic, which it is, and also a recognition scene, which it is not, these being incompatible moments." To my knowledge, the recognition, represented through the gestures of surprise and puzzlement, is an iconographical element integral to every Supper at Emmaus.

the painting, and its close relation to a well-established iconography beguile both beholders and scholars into a satisfying impression of recognition and understanding.

Once again, the visibility of Christ, brought out by means of a traditionally recognizable scheme, obtrudes into our reading of the subject and our comprehension of the whole composition as an articulated narrative. Of course, the way we usually react to Caravaggio's painting is anything but fortuitous. By exploiting a traditional formula, Caravaggio expected the beholder to identify the subject right away, passing over even the unprecedented disguise of Christ, which—as pointed out by Charles Scribner, Howard Hibbard, and especially by Irving Lavin[21]—might paradoxically add to his visibility and divine majesty as a visual reference to his transfigured nature after the Resurrection. We shall return to this detail later, but, on a preliminary assumption, it must be admitted that, if the only discrepancy between Caravaggio's painting and the compositional formula on which he relied is the disguised figure of Jesus, then his *Supper at Emmaus* is to be gauged simply as a renewed and relevant example of the visibility of Christ in Western painting.

Yet this judgment would be premature. We might be tempted to come to a different conclusion if we inquire carefully and deeply into the compositional structure of Caravaggio's painting. By the end of this inquiry, we will be likely to conclude that setting up disappearance is not the only available means for an artist to suggest the invisibility of Christ. Also, we will see that Caravaggio found a subtler way to blind viewers, misleading them about what they actually perceive as a plainly visible Christ. He managed to do so primarily, but not exclusively, by meticulously pondering the narrative set-up of his *Supper at Emmaus*.

Visualizing Appearance:
The Supper at Emmaus *and its Venetian Background*

To measure to what extent Caravaggio juggled with the conventions inherent in the iconographic tradition requires an overview of its most remarkable examples, all of them originating in Venetian Renaissance painting. I shall begin with a *Supper at Emmaus* by Giovanni Bellini, painted in 1494, destroyed in a fire in the second half of the eighteenth century, but reproduced in a print by Pietro Monaco dated to 1760 (Fig. 123).[22] In it, Bellini clearly reenacted the compositional scheme of the *Last Supper*, placing the figure of Christ exactly on the main longitudinal axis, behind a table that marks the horizontal, pivotal line around which the scene is structured. At the ends of the table, symmetrically disposed right and left and opposite each other, the two disciples sit motionless, expressing their nascent astonishment by petrified, almost unremarkable gestures: a hand upraised, a finger discreetly pointing upward. Next to the Savior, two other figures appear, one sitting— playing out stupefaction, absorption or incredulity—the other standing, staring forward at the viewer. In every respect, Bellini's picture is an almost archetypical example of what I have already defined as a symbolic narrative. Enthroned as a sublimely majestic Pantocrator at the center of the composition, exposing to view the broken Eucharistic bread as a divine insignia, his Christ detaches himself from any narrative contingency. At the ends of the table, the two apostles do not even seem to remark his permanent presence, as though he were already out of sight.

The distinctive feature of Bellini's representation consists in its relative independence from the

21   Scribner 1977, 379-82; Hibbard 1983, 76-7; Lavin 2000, 30-2.

22   For the painting, see Vasari, 3:434-5; Ridolfi, 72. The painting was taken to Vienna, and it was destroyed in the fire at the Razumowski Palace. For the many copies after Bellini's original, see Berenson 1916, 119-23. See also Gronau 1930, 217; and Goffen 1989, 277-80. A *Supper at Emmaus* in San Salvador, Venice, was also celebrated as an original by Bellini. The painting is now considered a work by his studio. See Sansovino, 47; and Ridolfi, 71.

271

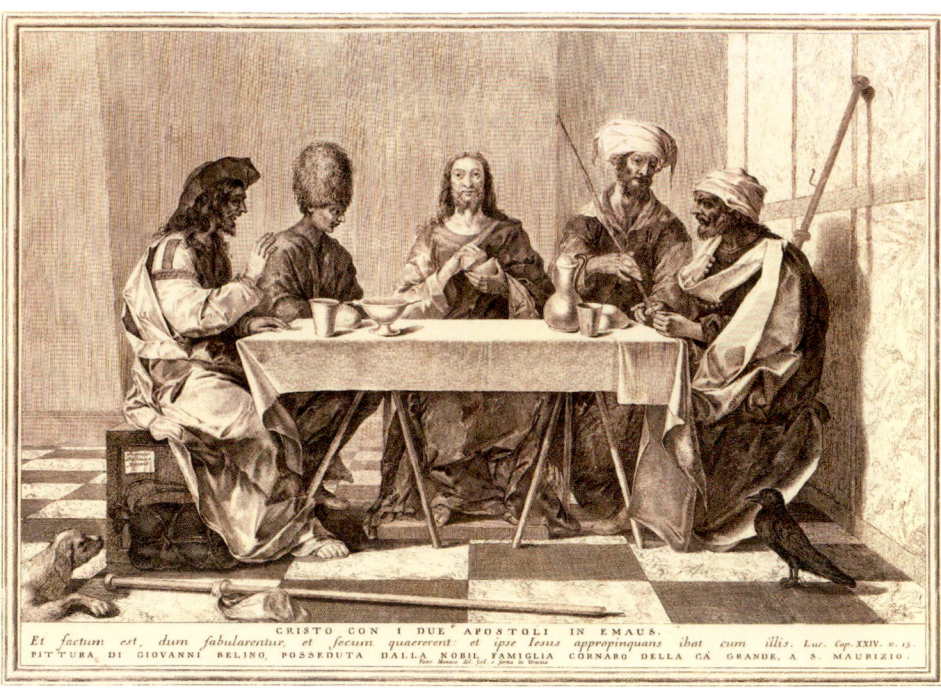

Fig. 123
Pietro Monaco after Giovanni Bellini, *The Supper at Emmaus*, etching and engraving, 36.3 x 50.5 cm.

literary source it refers to. Actually, in all the paintings inspired by Bellini's iconographic formula, we can observe a persisting hiatus between the scriptural text and its pictorial translation. As I have already shown in the introduction to Part Three, pictures held the same authority as the literary episode they represented, serving as vulgate versions of the biblical event itself. A remark by Cardinal Federico Borromeo about the iconography of the Supper at Emmaus demonstrates to what extent believers relied on images in recollecting scripture. I quote from Borromeo's *Della pittura sacra*:

As I have seen in some pictures, painters may depict our Lord at the table with his disciples, after he was resurrected and appeared to them on their way to Emmaus. The Savior must hold a loaf of bread in his hand, being about to break or split it in two parts, but not as evenly as if he were to cut it with a knife or razor, lest this confirm a foolish opinion of some people who believe that our Lord was recognized as the bread split miraculously, with no knife.[23]

This ridiculous and "foolish opinion" could solely spring from the believer's habit of reconstructing biblical narratives with the support of images. Be that as it may, in all of these symbolic representations of the supper at Emmaus, there is no cause-and-effect connection between the attitude of Christ and those of his apostles. In other terms, the acts of these actors are not necessarily interconnected in a logically synchronized development. As artists' primary purpose is visually to underscore Christ's divinity, the apostles' reaction often achieves a purely epithetic function; their gestures are meant to signal the prodigy of Christ's theophany in the specific context of a supper at Emmaus. Strictly speaking, it would be inappropriate to define as epiphany a scene in which divinity is not visualized as appearing or disappearing, but is experienced by beholders as an axiomatic presence. In fact, the viewers' position in regard to the scene is preeminently one of dramatic irony: unlike the apostles, the audience is totally acquainted with the outcome and implications of the pictorial event. The traditional iconography of *The Supper at Emmaus* therefore poses a neat disjunction between the surprise of the apostles and the detachment of the beholder, who usually is not involved in the unveiling of the hidden divinity on an emotional level.

The polarity between awareness and surprise embedded in the iconography of *The Supper at*

23 Borromeo, 80: "E resuscitato che fu il Salvatore e che apparve ai discepoli che andavano in Emaus, si può dipingere a tavola con esso loro, sì come ho pure veduto che alcuni pittori hanno fatto, e che il Salvatore abbia un pane fra le mani, e che lo spezzi e lo divida, ma non così egualmente in due parti come se alcun coltello o rasoio l'avesse diviso, imperocché ciò confirmarebbe una stolta opinione che hanno alcuni che il Salvatore fosse conosciuto dai discepoli allora, perché il pane si divise senza coltello per via di miracolo."

Emmaus is frequently enriched and emphasized by a figure playing a transitional part in the composition: the clueless spectator. Often, but not systematically, identical with the innkeeper (or cook), this actor functions as a witness to the epiphany, although his attitude indicates that he fails to perceive or understand the miracle unfolding right in front of him. In Bellini's destroyed *Supper at Emmaus*, this role might be given to the figure to the left of Christ, paralyzed in his effort to process the theophany.

In Titian's painting, it is certainly performed by the innkeeper who stands close to Jesus and, according

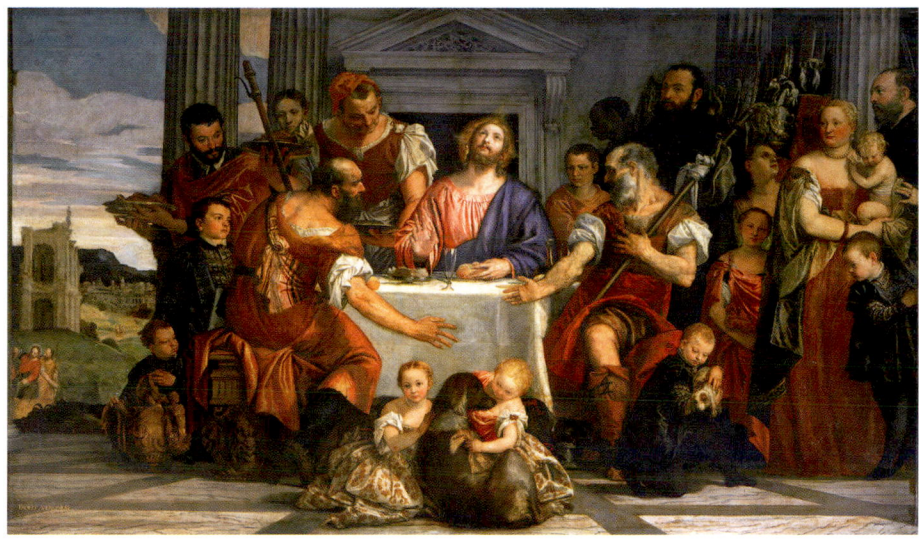

Fig. 124
Veronese (Paolo Caliari), *The Supper at Emmaus*, Musée du Louvre, Paris, oil on canvas, 242 x 416 cm.

to Jean-Baptiste de Champaigne, "intently looks at the action, [considering] it as an extraordinary mystery he is completely at a loss to understand." Turning his eyes away from Christ, he scans a second loaf of bread on the table as though wondering what sort of prodigy it might contain. As a low-genre actor, the clueless spectator may connote a potentially comic role. Affected by a sort of intellectual blindness, he is almost the only figure to suggest the invisibility of Christ, for riveted as he is on the epiphany, his eyes seem to pass through it.

A good example of this latter case is provided by Veronese's *Supper at Emmaus* at the Louvre, in which the cook to the left of Christ apparently fixes his gaze on the blessing hand, without recognizing or questioning the sacred gesture (Fig. 124).[24] As pointed out by the French painter Jean Nocret in a lecture on Veronese's picture delivered to the Académie Royale in 1667, "he is bringing a dish, and looking for a spot on the table to put it down. His posture and sight evoke quite well his concentration on the task."[25] Nocret obviously overlooks the ambiguity of the cook's attitude; besides waiting on guests, he might have stopped to consider Jesus' blessing of the bread, which he possibly perceives just as an incidental movement preventing him from setting down the dish. If so, he fills the role of not only the clueless spectator, but also the indifferent walk-on part. Unaware of the miracle that takes place around them, these actors are shown as immersed in a mechanical action or peering hypnotically forward in the direction of the viewer. The standing figure in Bellini's destroyed *Supper at Emmaus* belongs to the latter category. Through his unawareness, the indifferent walk-on part might surreptitiously convey the impression of a partially invisible epiphany: in other words, he does anything but behold a theophany to which only the viewers and their fictitious counterparts, the devout figures occasionally present in the painting, have full access.

The pious onlookers depicted in various versions of *The Supper at Emmaus* are evidently to be identified as the patrons who commissioned the pictures, their features and clothes meticulously portrayed.[26] In Titian's *Supper at Emmaus*, the patron is, exceptionally, disguised as the apostle

24   See Pignatti and Pedrocco 1995, 1:135, no. 100. For other paintings by Veronese representing the same subject, see Ibidem, 295, no. 200; and much earlier Fiocco 1928, 197, no. 233.

25   *Conférences*, 1:152: "Auprès de ce cuisinier, l'on en voit un autre qui porte un plat et qui regarde en quel endroit de la

table il le posera. Sa posture et ses regards montrent assez bien qu'il est appliqué à ce qu'il fait."

26   According to Vasari, 5:319-22, Jacopo da Pontormo represented some lay brothers from the Certosa at Galluzzo in his 1525 *The Supper at Emmaus*. See more recently Cropper 2004, 11-4.

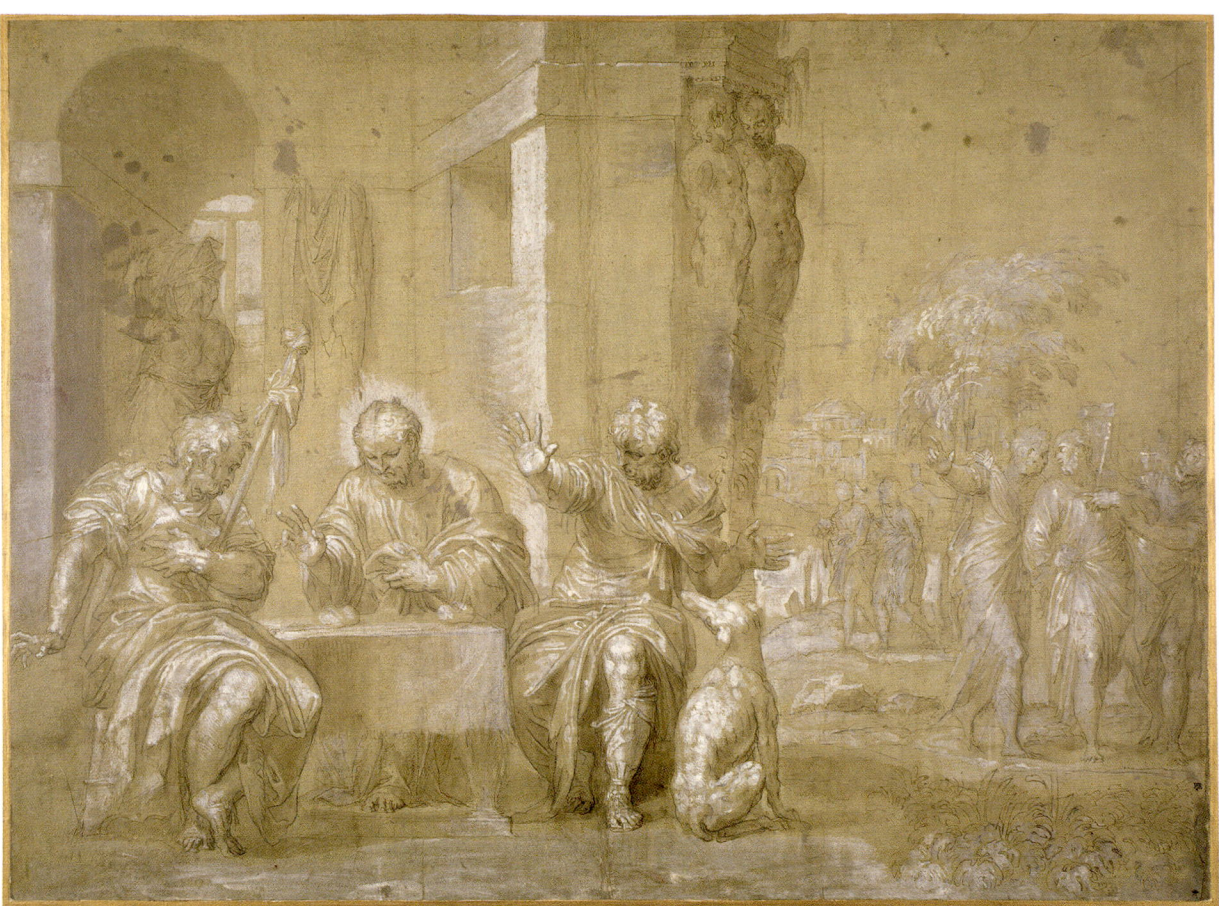

Fig. 125
Veronese (Paolo Caliari), *The Supper at Emmaus*, Devonshire Collection, Chatsworth, pen, ink, and wash on green prepared paper heightened with white, 42.1 x 57.5 cm.

Cleophas. But Veronese, for example, in his Louvre version of the subject, introduced all the members of his patrons' families into the composition as either absorbed or distracted witnesses, their attitudes mostly dependent upon their ages. In all these cases, however, the devout figures prove to be a projection, whether real or symbolic, of the beholder. As such, they are intended to contemplate the epiphany as an everlasting revelation of Christ's divinity.

A final observation must be made before examining Caravaggio's *Supper at Emmaus* in light of the iconographic elements hitherto taken into account. Since Bellini's first attempt at the subject, the traditional figures of the apostles, in spite of their epithetic function, have been increasingly provided with dramatic and fidgeting postures, which more or less appropriately translate their astonishment in recognizing Christ. As a general rule, though, only their arms and legs are meant to express the climactic degree of their surprise. In contrast, painters very often portrayed their faces in immobile profiles, symmetrically opposing each other, in order to frame and bring forward the figure of Jesus. To preserve these traditional profiles and to enhance their visual opposition, artists also tended to rotate the apostles' torsos and arms in opposite directions. In Veronese's Louvre *Supper at Emmaus*, the two disciples' outstretched arms, the one thrust inward, the other jutted outward beyond its anatomical flexibility, seem to project ideally toward each other, forming an elliptical chain that serves to frame the central epiphany. There is no doubt that Veronese managed to make the concomitant rotation of his apostles' bodies interact with the surrounding space by seating these figures on two differing grounds, one at the bottom of the table, the other in front of it. In another *Supper at Emmaus* (Fig. 125), now at Chatsworth, drawn in pen, ink and wash on green prepared paper and heightened with white, Veronese[27] carries this spinning tension of diverging movements to its extremes by projecting it into the foreground; the apostle at the right stretches one arm toward the viewer, almost piercing the pictorial surface with his open palm. His protruding gesture is pointed out by the intrigued muzzle of a dog crouching nearby, which Veronese shows from behind. The illusory device set up by Veronese explicitly aims to capture the viewers' attention, somehow involving them in the pictorial fiction and, more precisely, in the mechanics of the recognition plot.

At the same time, by framing the scene from a distance, and by evoking accessory details, not least the landscape to the right and the ruins of an improvised inn to the left, Veronese dilutes the charge of illusion intrinsic to his composition. As a result, the beholder is invited to experience the epiphany through the lens of a theatrical display. This especially applies to Titian's and Veronese's painted versions of *The Supper at Emmaus*, in which the hieratic figure of Christ, pictured in a meditative and symbolic act of blessing, is essentially inset into a theater-like stage, between his two disciples, among clueless or indifferent spectators and contemporary onlookers. This theatrical set, so typical of Venetian narrative painting from Carpaccio onward,[28] inevitably works as a filter in the beholder's emotional involvement. Such a scene is perceived as a meta-theatrical performance, and not as an illustration, of the biblical episode. Of course, the transposition of *The Supper at Emmaus* into a theatrical set does not compromise the religious significance of the subject: it transfers it into a magnifying dimension in which the seriousness of the theophany and its mysteries can blend with the conviviality of a country inn supper or the formality of a banquet.

Caravaggio's London Supper at Emmaus: Closeness and Immediacy versus Distance and Duration

Caravaggio must have known all the Venetian compositions I briefly commented on either as originals or in copies. From the outset, he decided to condense the episode visually and dramatically by sifting out any complementary figure, except for that of the clueless spectator, performed once again by the innkeeper, and by eliminating any trace of an ambient setting, architecture as well as landscape. In framing the scene, as in previous paintings, he revitalized a then-obsolete compositional scheme, the dramatic close-up, as defined by Sixten Ringbom in his memorable book, *Icon to Narrative*.[29] Already used by Andrea Mantegna in the middle of the fifteenth century, this pictorial formula had thrived particularly in Venice, attaining its full accomplishment in the work of Giovanni Bellini and prolonging its influence well into the sixteenth century, not only in the Veneto but also in Lombardy. Oddly enough Bellini, whom I have recognized as the inventor of the early modern iconography most frequently used for *The Supper at Emmaus*, never employed the dramatic close-up in conjuring up this biblical subject. Neither did Titian. Whether consciously or not, Caravaggio thus imagined a sort of revivalist close-up version of *The Supper at Emmaus* in the manner of Bellini's *Circumcision* in Venice (Pinacoteca Querini Stampalia),[30] his *Deposition* in Florence (Galleria degli Uffizi),[31] or in the spirit of Giorgione's—or Titian's—*Christ Carrying the Cross* (San Rocco, Venice).[32] This perfectly corresponds to the controversial statement made

---

27   See Cocke 1984, 104, no. 35, and also 336, no. 160. For an early copy of this drawing, see Coutts 1987.

28   See Zorzi 1988; Fortini Brown 1988; and Rosand 1997.

29   Ringbom 1965.

30   Some have considered *The Circumcision* to be executed by a painter from Bellini's studio. See Goffen 1989, 281 ff.

31   Ibidem, 178-81.

32   See Anderson 1997, 303.

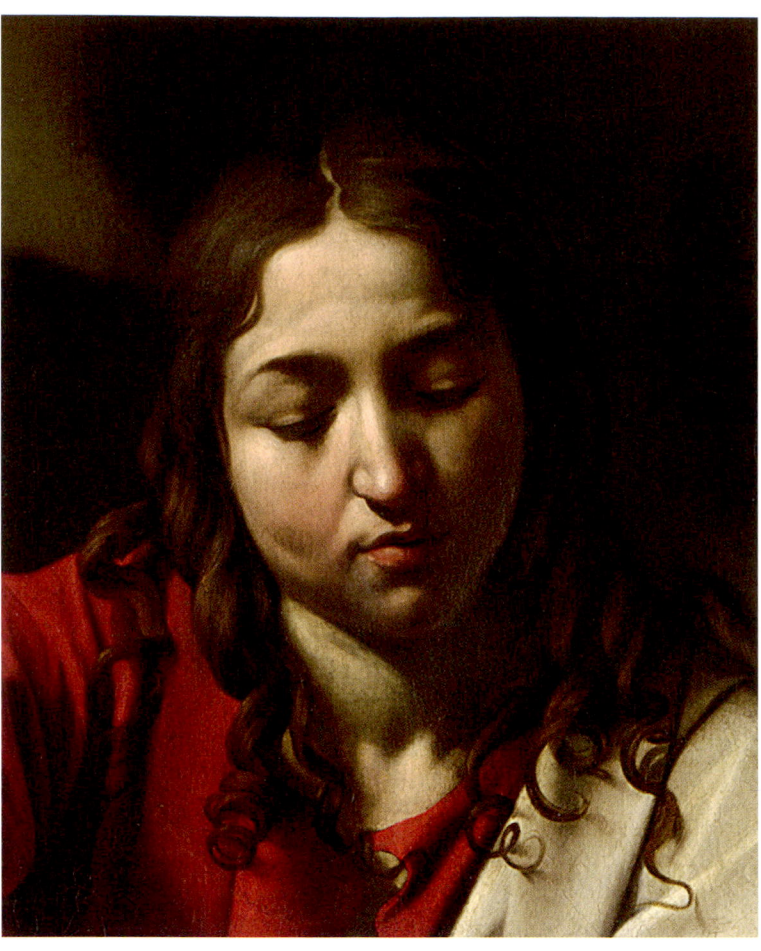

Fig. 126
Michelangelo Merisi da Caravaggio, *The Supper at Emmaus*, National Gallery, London, oil on canvas, 141 x 196.2 cm., detail.

by Caravaggio's biographers on his belonging as a painter to the early Renaissance Venetian tradition.[33]

Nevertheless—and there is no contradiction in this—the reference point for Caravaggio's painting was undoubtedly Leonardo's *Last Supper* in Milan, which he constantly tried to evoke in his *Supper at Emmaus* in different, subtle ways.[34] Roberto Longhi already claimed that Caravaggio's beardless Christ appears to be a "nearly ironic reminiscence" of Leonardo's.[35] Although the definition is not entirely correct—Caravaggio was far from arousing any sort of irony by alluding to Leonardo—it is unquestionable that Caravaggio's figure of Christ, through his expression, stunningly parallels Leonardo's: both seem deeply engrossed in the intense and highly contemplative act of blessing and consecrating the bread,[36] as indicated by their half-closed, downcast eyes, and their parted, whispering lips (Figs. 126, 127).[37] In Caravaggio's case, the asymmetric posture of the mouth may also take on a nuance of indeterminate bitterness that to my knowledge has never been accounted for. If one interprets Caravaggio's image of Christ as an allusive and disguised double of Leonardo's, his expression could then reflect the awareness of the Passion *a posteriori*, and not *a priori*, as in the *Last Supper*.

Also the face of Christ in Caravaggio's *Supper at Emmaus* derives from Leonardo, though indirectly. Typologically, it presents the same features and proportions of a pictorial prototype largely used by Leonardo's followers in Lombardy.[38] A drawing in London (British Museum), executed in metalpoint heightened with white, formerly ascribed to Giovanni Antonio Boltraffio and recently attributed to the Master of the Pala Sforza, corroborates the point (Fig. 128).[39] It shows a female head bending to the left, faintly smiling while gazing downward. The broad structure of her face, characterized by a large and triangular forehead, wide-set eyes, flat nose, bulgy cheeks, and pointed chin, unequivocally recalls the physiognomy of Caravaggio's Christ. Likewise, the

33 For this issue, and the possibility that Caravaggio sojourned in Venice as reported by Bellori, see Berra 2005, 246-8, with extensive bibliography.

34 See Spear 1987, reprinted in Spear 2002, 129-68, esp. 136; and Brown 2001.

35 Longhi 1999-2000, 1:174: "Un Cristo sbarbato, quasi ironico ricordo della 'Cena lionardesca' vista negli anni di Milano."

36 I agree with Steinberg 2001, 35, when he claims that Leonardo's Christ is represented as both having just said, "one of you shall betray me" and as consecrating the bread in a silent prayer. According to Steinberg, "again and again the narrative and the sacramental are syntactically intertwined." To prove his interpretation, Steinberg appropriately recalls

Federico Borromeo's description of Leonardo's *Last Supper*. See Borromeo, 79: "Intorno all'istituzione del santissimo sacramento, si può rappresentare il pane e il vino posto dinanzi [al Salvatore e sopra] alla tavola dove esso mangiò coi suoi discepoli, ma non conviene porre atto che dimostri ch'esso Salvatore facesse sopra il pane e il vino una croce con la mano, poiché innanzi alla Passione (e così nell'antica legge come nella nuova) in fino a tanto che il Salvatore non fu morto in croce, le benedizioni non si facevano formando il segno della croce [sì come sanno i periti delle sacre lettere] e perciò Leonardo in quel suo Cenacolo tanto memorabile, il quale era già uno degl'ornamenti della nostra città (…) Leonardo, dico, in questa memorabile opera è degno ancora di laude, poiché pingendo il Salvatore, lo pinse in atto come se egli parlasse, overo avesse poco inanzi parlato, e facesse orazione."

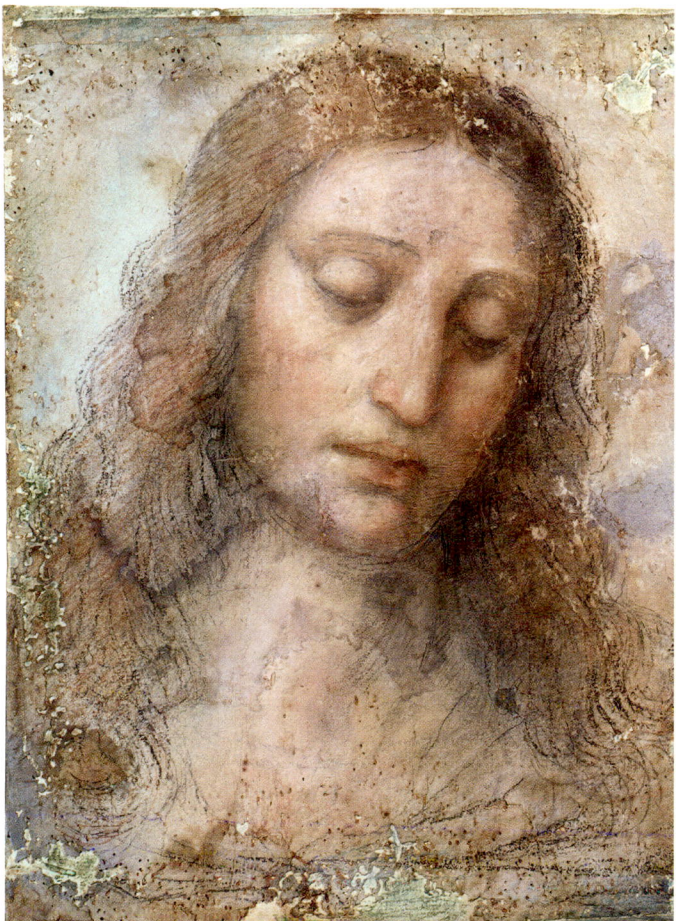

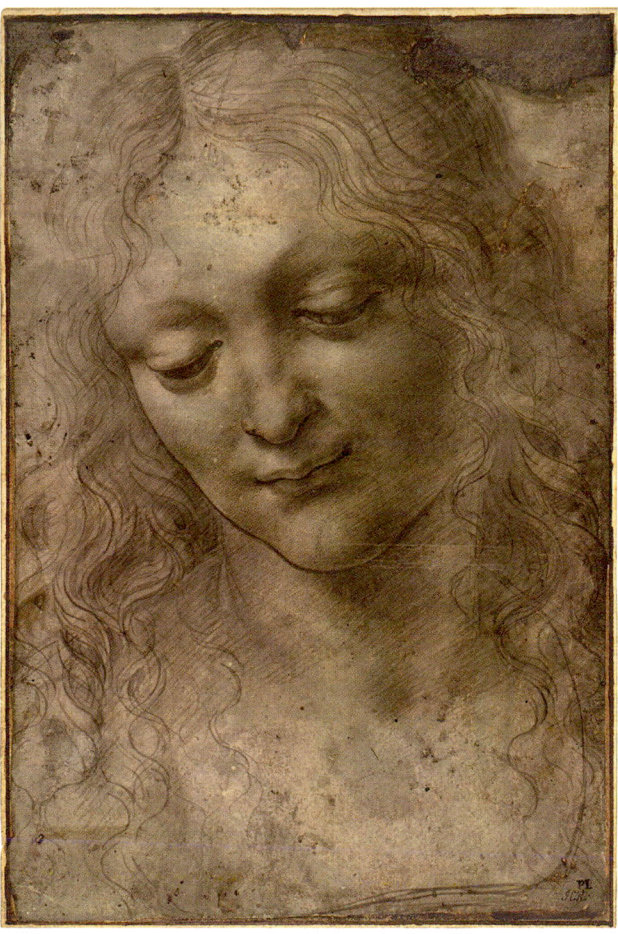

Fig. 127
Leonardo da Vinci (attributed to), *Head of Christ*, Pinacoteca di
Brera, Milan, black and red chalk, tempera on light green paper,
40 x 32 cm.

Fig. 128
Master of the Pala Sforza (attributed to), *Head of a Female Figure*,
British Museum, London, metal point on green-brown prepared
paper heightened with white, 24 x 15.8 cm.

iconographic type of the young blessing *Redemptor*, common in Venice and especially in Lombardy
at the beginning of the sixteenth century, has its roots in Leonardo's oeuvre:[40] a *Salvator Mundi*
(Galleria Borghese, Rome) by Marco D'Oggiono,[41] a follower of Leonardo, has already been linked to
Caravaggio's representation of a youthful Christ, but there are many more examples of this specific
iconography. Finally, the sharp-cut profile of Caravaggio's apostle who, in *The Supper at Emmaus*,
extends his arms in an astounded reaction seems a shrewd variation on a Leonardesque theme,[42]
as exemplified by a study in sanguine (Royal Library, Windsor Castle) for the figure of Simon in
The Last Supper, which most scholars consider an early copy after a lost original by Leonardo (Fig.
129).[43] By enhancing the definition of the contour and bringing out the profile, Leonardo intended
to stress the discontinuities of the otherwise regular structure of the head, whose silhouette can

37 Despite its poor state of conservation, the *Study for
the Head of Christ*, maybe by Leonardo himself and heavily
retouched by a follower, is well suited for comparison with
Caravaggio's Christ. For this drawing, see Marani 2001, 150,
no. 40 [with extensive bibliography].

38 For Leonardo and his followers in Lombardy, see Bora et
al. 1988.

39 See Fiorio 2000, 199, no. D38. See also Bora 1987, 162.

40 See Snow-Smith 1978; Brown 1981; and Snow-Smith 1982.

41 See Della Pergola 1955, 1:82, no. 146.

42 See Hibbard 1983, 77. The outspread arms of the disciple
seem also to be an elaboration on a similar gesture performed
by James the Less in Leonardo's *Last Supper*. As Spear 2002,
136, has correctly pointed out: "James the Less in the Last
Supper I believe inspired Caravaggio's apostle at the right of
the *Supper at Emmaus* in London, not only in formal ways, but
because the Eucharistic meanings of the two images are so
closely linked."

43 See Marani 2001, 144, no. 37.

be substantially inscribed into a rectangle. In contrast to Leonardo, but in his footsteps, Caravaggio lines up the salient parts of his apostle's profile, turning its convex outline into a strained bow, wittily evocative of the scallop shell attached to the jacket (Fig. 130).

The numerous references to Leonardo's art, along with the reenactment of an iconographic formula borrowed from the Venetian pictorial tradition, concomitantly designate Caravaggio's *Supper at Emmaus* as an oddly "primitive" composition. Visually and structurally, indeed, it recalls a phase in the Italian artistic evolution that precedes the foremost achievements of the mature Renaissance. It is difficult for us to imagine how provocative the painting might have appeared at the time; without doubt, its vanguard elaboration of early Renaissance naturalistic styles and schemes reified the most radical aspect of the pictorial reform then in vogue.[44] Its pre-classical radicalism must have startled contemporary viewers, all the more so in that it was accompanied by two major technical innovations, a

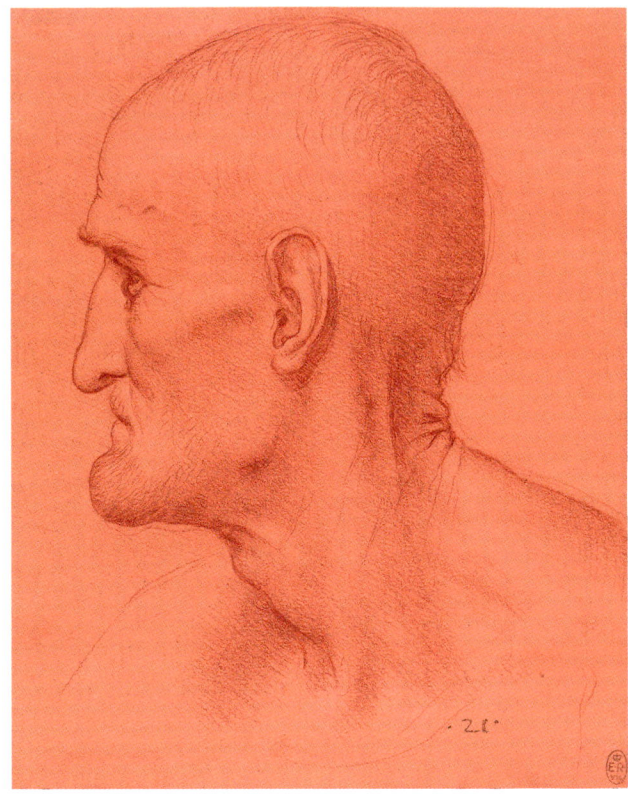

Fig. 129
Leonardo da Vinci (after), *Head of an Old Man in Profile (Study for Saint Simon in the Last Supper)*, Royal Library, Windsor Castle, red chalk on red prepared paper, 19 x 15.2 cm.

spectacular enhancement of optical and tactile effects and an unprecedented narrative structure. The combination of both these devices obviously modified the way the beholder was driven to perceive the biblical subject. In one sense, these were the means by which Caravaggio could push back the boundaries of the traditional devices he intended to use, disclosing the unsuspected potentials not solely of the dramatic close-up and the compositional formula inherited by the Venetian masters, but also of the rhetoric of physiological expression specific to Leonardo and his disciples.[45]

In adopting, combining, and adjusting these pictorial conventions, Caravaggio above all planned to steer the beholder's attention toward a three-pronged, virtually contradictory approach to the picture. More concretely, the viewer, who is spontaneously induced to experience the scene in its closeness, immediacy, and intelligibility, is consequently enticed into a process of comprehension that instead triggers distance, duration, and ambivalence. By manipulating the perception of space and time as interplaying factors in the reading of a pictorial narrative, Caravaggio succeeded in involving the beholder in the mechanism of recognition, or *anagnorisis*, potentially inherent in *The Supper at Emmaus*: like the apostles, though on a different level, viewers may hesitate to recognize or decipher the acting figure of Jesus. Hence, the visibility of Christ itself turns out to be both reassessed and invigorated.

The dramatic close-up framing is traditionally used by early modern painters to contract and condense the beholder's field of vision. By aligning the main characters of the sacred story in the foreground, usually but not exclusively behind a parapet, and by depicting a neutral, dim backdrop, painters project the action onto the pictorial surface, which practically serves as a screen,

44 For the eclectic preference for the models of the High Renaissance in Caravaggio's time, see Dempsey 2000. For the reception of the Italian "primitives," see Previtali 1989.

45 For Leonardo's influence on Venetian painters during the Renaissance, see Brown 1992; Humfrey 1992; and Marani 1992.

thus making the viewer perceive the scene as contiguous and close at hand. As a consequence, the fictitious space of the composition is compressed into shallowness. In his *Supper at Emmaus*, Caravaggio employed the slope of the table as a visual equivalent to a parapet. Its foreshortened brightened surface and, especially, its visible retreating border direct the view toward the main figure of Christ, who seems to lean over the table, thrusting his right arm toward the viewer. Technically speaking, this compositional setting creates an almost picture-within-the-picture effect, bringing to the fore the image of the blessing Jesus while paradoxically relegating him to the background. However, the mighty diagonal traced by the outflung arms of the apostle on the right similarly helps shorten the distance between the foreground and the figure of Christ.

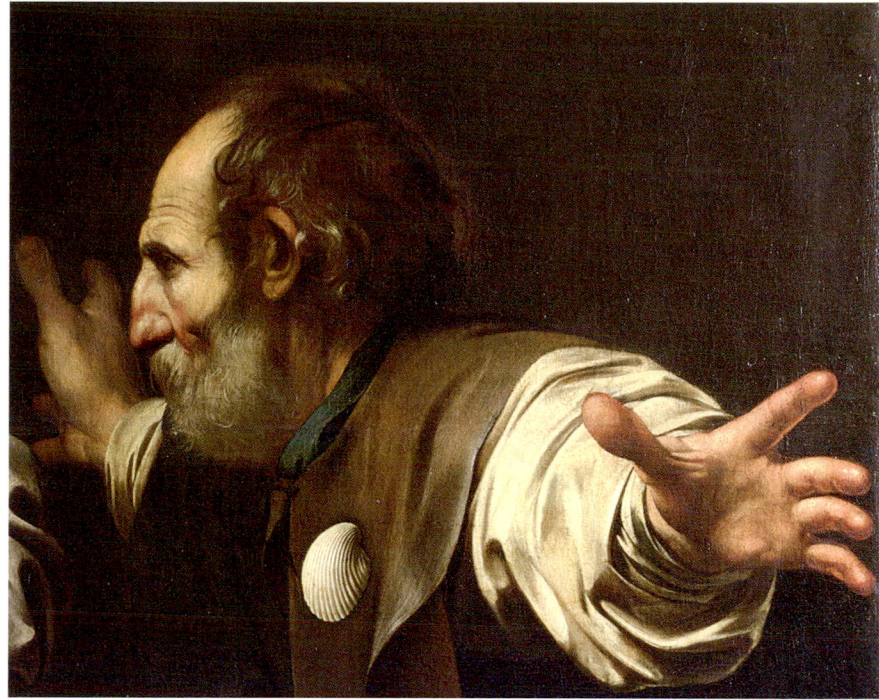

Fig. 130
Michelangelo Merisi da Caravaggio, *The Supper at Emmaus*, National Gallery, London, oil on canvas, 141 x 196.2 cm., detail.

Like Veronese in his Chatsworth *Supper at Emmaus*, Caravaggio imagined an open palm piercing the pictorial surface in order to lure the viewer into the picture.[46] In contrast to Veronese, however, Caravaggio suppresses the wheeling movement of the astonished apostle, expanding the gesture of the protruding arm into an oblique axis that operates both as a vector of attention and as a scale to probe and intrude into the fictive space.[47] Prodigiously, the swirl of the white sleeve around the closer arm, causing the light to roll and spiral down toward the background, also makes the viewer's eye rush in the direction of the blessing divinity. Jesus' extended arm is apparently given a similar function. Along with the diagonal of the apostle's outstretched arms, this second axis once again helps propel the viewer's attention in the direction of Christ. At the same time, this circuit of propulsive visual vectors may accomplish an opposite task, directing the sight back to the outside.

In any event, the geometrical clarity of this centripetal and partially centrifugal structure forces beholders to concentrate intuitively on their relationship to the blessing Jesus, momentarily forgetting about and stepping over the interposed table, as well as the figure of the second apostle, who nevertheless occupies an intermediate position nearer theirs.[48] As already remarked, the iconographic tradition permitted painters to shift one of the apostles to the foreground, straight in front of the table. Cut off by and wedged into the left lower corner of Caravaggio's *Supper at Emmaus*, the figure of the apostle with his back turned should have been able to intercept the viewer's eyes,

---

46 Hibbard 1983, 77-8: "The left arm of the gesticulating disciple unites the painted actors with us, the living viewers, in a manner that signals a new age of participatory art; the spectator is almost forced to take part in the painted religious drama. Mannerist artists had long been toying with the illusion of continuity between spectator and painted scene, but in general these were *tours de force* that called attention to themselves as illusions, rather than to the subjects and their meaning. (…) Caravaggio adapts Mannerist tradition only to the extent that he again seems to penetrate the picture plane, not as an exhibitionist but as a dramatist who seizes our attention in order to illuminate the meaning of the story within the frame."

47 Puglisi 1998, 212: "The tightly grouped protagonists are closely framed in a shallow space measured in depth by the extended arms of the apostle on the right."

48 Hibbard 1983, 77: "We see this disciple only from the side and back, in the darkness; the focus of our attention is on the illuminated Christ."

279

but the painter greatly weakened his visual impact by plunging him in a local secondary light and depicting his face as three-quarter hidden. In this way, the artist breached another tacit rule of the iconographic tradition that required the opposition of the apostles' facing profiles as an echoing device meant to utter the surprise of the theophany. On the whole, Caravaggio thus aimed at arousing an impression of closeness to the figure of Christ. This effect of proximity is deliberately engendered by the close-up framing and the mostly centripetal structure of the picture, but is factually and systematically contradicted by the presence of two interposed grounds: a transitional foreground space, which beholders are led to share with one of the apostles, and a dilated area traditionally intended to accommodate a parapet and here morphed into a table strewn with a frugal spread of meals. To punctuate these intermediate grounds and their virtual intersections, Caravaggio disposed a set of protruding elements: a blank hole analogous to an elbow patch on a worn-out jacket,[49] an emerging open palm, a poised-for-blessing hand, and last but not least, an overloaded basket of fruit, casting its shadow onto the tablecloth, and teetering perilously on the brink of the table.

Logically, the calculated disposition of the figures and objects interacting in the picture, and projected onto the surface by the close backdrop, should provide viewers with a crystal-clear perception of space and distance; one should even be able to measure the depth of the scene, using the compasses of the apostle's outstretched arms as a geometrical scale. However, any attempt to do so makes one realize how remote and inaccessible the figure of Christ and, generally, his divinity appears. In fact, the closer one tries to get to Christ, the farther his image, both as an optical and tactile representation, moves away. As for its tactility, it has never been clearly stated that, in spite of its considerable elongation,[50] the extended right arm of the bald apostle inexplicably fails to reach out to Christ. Consequently, any effort on the beholder's part to verify Jesus' exact location in the fictive space falls short. It is barely possible, indeed, to quantify the distance between Christ and the silhouette of the apostle's farther hand—an out-of-scale "stump"[51] suspended between light and dark, pointing to the shadow apparently cast by Jesus' head and torso—that blindly gropes for a contact never to be achieved. Of course, there is a sort of witticism in the attitude of the apostle, whose hand is oriented to what viewers regard as the true epiphany of Christ, whereas his eyes swerve off from it toward the upraised arm of the resurrected God. Caravaggio must have intentionally depicted the apostle's right hand as a visual parody, almost a caricature, of Christ's blessing hand, as confirmed by the identical posture of their thumbs and forefingers. This parallelism notwithstanding, the functions of these hands are symmetrically opposed: the gesture of Christ's hand is fraught with a conscious and divine intensity, whereas the apostle's hand unconsciously reveals the extent of a human conditioned reaction. The diverging directions of the apostle's hand and sight also accentuate the impression of remoteness felt by viewers while focusing on Jesus' figure and action. As a matter of fact, besides being unable to touch the divinity through the apostle's hand, beholders, after dwelling on the main figure of Christ, are compelled to divert their attention to an unexpected target, the blessing hand.

Caravaggio also puts in jeopardy the optical consistency of Jesus' image. At first glance, it looks

---

49 Bell 1995, 151: "Caravaggio took advantage of these effects, placing an area of white wherever he wanted to indicate the full intensity of light. For example, in the dark green jacket of the apostle on the left, a small patch of the white shirt is revealed by a hole in the elbow. Because the value of the dark green is significantly lower than the other illuminated areas, the white patch is necessary to bring the elbow forward."

50 Hibbard 1983: "There are 'errors' in the *Supper at Emmaus* that might place it earlier rather than later: the extended hands of the disciple at the right are of about the same size, even though one is thrust toward us and the other, if anything the largest of the two, is as far from us as possible."

51 In this regard, see Moir 1987, 139: "Se si guarda *La cena in Emmaus* di Caravaggio alla Galleria Nazionale di Londra, non si può fare a meno di notare la mano destra del discepolo che si trova a destra: questa mano è troppo grande. La proporzione è sbagliata, e questo non è l'unico errore del dipinto." According to Moir, the out-of-proportion hand, along with many other anatomical "mistakes" in Caravaggio's painting, depends on the painter's procedure of montage. On this detail, see also the fanciful remarks of Hockney 2006, 120.

perfectly secure, particularly given the way Caravaggio literally spotlighted Christ's face and torso, once again pushing his image toward the foreground. Yet, by placing the half-lit figure of the innkeeper nearby and directing his massive shadow askew onto the backdrop behind Jesus himself, the painter optically engendered an effect of transparency; temporarily, as long as the body of Christ shows no sign of intersecting with the innkeeper's shadow, the viewer may question the very presence of the Savior in the pictorial space. This lurking and troubling illusion is all the more unavoidable in that Caravaggio himself encouraged it through the innkeeper's clueless expression. As a patent quotation from Titian's Louvre *Supper at Emmaus*, this actor, who clutches his belt exactly as does his prototype, and who "intently looks at the action, [considering] it as a mystery he is completely at a loss to understand," has also the ambiguous gaze of someone who simply stares into space.[52] By inserting Titian's clueless innkeeper into the scene, by rotating him in order to adapt him to a different context—in the London painting, he does not look at a second loaf of bread on the table—Caravaggio turned a comic and anecdotal note into a primary and highly dramatic one; somehow, the innkeeper's attitude defies viewers to acknowledge and recognize Christ's divine icon. In effect, his simultaneously intrigued and blank gaze is locked not on a secondary aspect of the theophany—the second loaf—but on the figure of Christ himself, who, though expanded by the special lighting and imperceptibly out of proportion—and perhaps because of his hypervisibility—appears to exceed the onlooker's visual field.

The process of bewilderment that Caravaggio forces beholders to go through by altering the perception of distance does not exclusively concern Jesus' image; it also applies to the still life displayed on the table. The suspended basket of fruit attracts the viewers' attention, inviting them to approach the dishes set up on the table for the supper. Their extraordinary optical and tactile evocation, a quality that painters had neglected for decades, provides the viewer once again with an impression of proximity and accessibility, as though every single constituent of the still life were to be visually singled out and possibly enumerated. And this is indeed the case, except for the Eucharistic bread that, partially concealed behind a roast fowl, practically merges with it and momentarily disappears at first glance.[53] To spot it, the viewer's gaze must veer and wind amidst the dishes laid out on the table. In addition, Caravaggio deliberately misleads the viewer as to its location, since Christ's upraised arm waves in the direction of an alternative loaf situated by the edge of the table, whereas the hand that supposedly is about to "take" or "break" the bread hovers over an indefinite space, somewhere between the Eucharistic bread and the roast fowl.

It can hardly be a coincidence that the Eucharistic bread, the only sacred attribute that qualifies as a symbolic alias of Christ's body, seems to vanish out of sight, allusively roofed by a hand that, in turn, lingers aloft in the shade of the blessing arm. This bold chiaroscuro arrangement undeniably refers to the mystery of Eucharist, whose symbolic and theological implications deserve much more development than I can afford here, beyond pointing out that even the ambivalent gesture of the hand, performing not only the mechanical act of seizing the bread but also the ritual one of consecrating it,[54] allows for an allegorical reading. That said, what really matters for us is the way Caravaggio draws attention to the figure of Christ—or hints at its equivalent, the Eucharistic bread—by constantly misguiding the beholder. Most important, this discontinuous approach to divinity, a sort of back-and-forth circuit, is processed and legitimized within the boundaries of the iconographic tradition. Even the idea of duplicating the bread, which is meant to play a trick on the

52 Hibbard 1983, 80: "The innkeeper, who sees and understands nothing, represents the world of pagans who do not recognize Christ and his Church." I am not convinced that the innkeeper has such an allegorical connotation. See also Puglisi 1998, 213: "The innkeeper's puzzled expression, as he witnesses the scene at first hand but fails to grasp its meaning, provides a foil to the disciples' agitation."

53 See Hinks 1953, 58: "But in fact the bread is almost hidden behind an irrelevant roast chicken on a majolica dish, which is again partly concealed behind an elaborate basket of rare hot-house fruits."

54 For the imposition of the hands and its significance as a gesture of consecration, see Barash 1987, 117 ff.

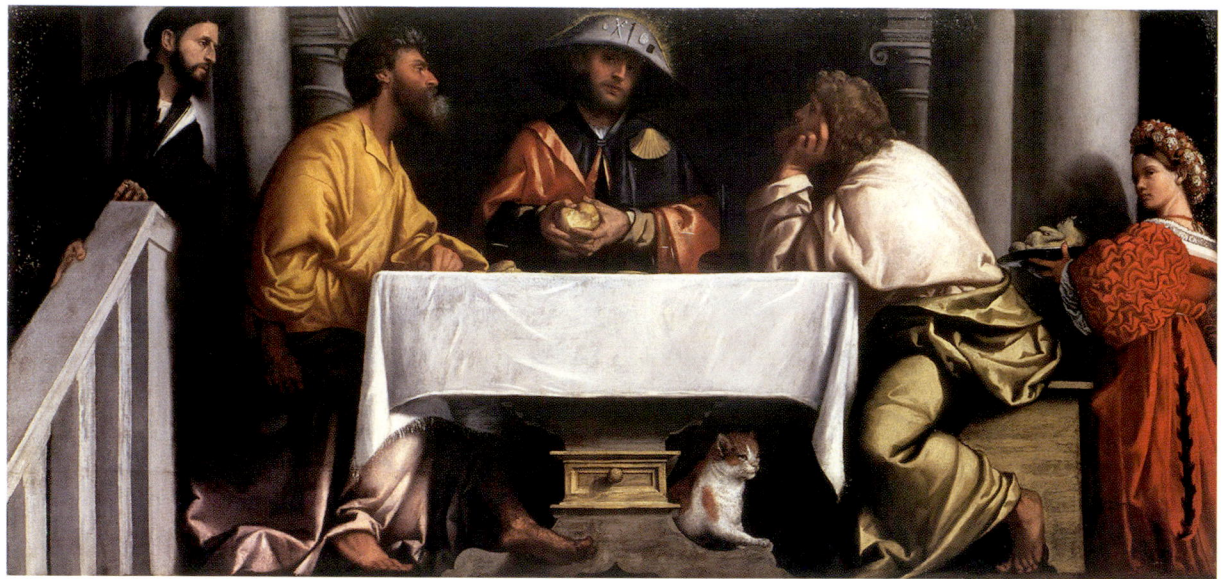

Fig. 131
Moretto da Brescia (Alessandro Bonvicino), *The Last Supper*, Pinacoteca Tosio e Martinengo, Brescia, oil on canvas, 147 x 305 cm.

viewer's attention, goes back to Titian's *Supper at Emmaus*.

If the perception of proximity and distance plays a capital role in my reading of Caravaggio's painting, the interconnected effects of immediacy and duration are no less important. By choosing a close-up framing for his *Supper at Emmaus*, Caravaggio did not necessarily intend to underscore either the synchronous or the diachronic development of his sacred story. Traditionally, the close-up framing does not increase the dramatic potential of the pictorial subject, especially if by drama one means the graphic translation of a multifaceted, highly expressive action. Rather, this compositional formula "freezes" the narration in an exemplary, climactic, almost timeless shot, in which the main characters' expressions, brought out by their closeness to the foreground, capture the beholder by inducing a state of contemplation. Nonetheless, in his *Supper at Emmaus*, Caravaggio conspicuously attempted to suggest a "chronology." In a sense, he devised a clockwork narrative, whose wheels and springs, however, seem not to be perfectly synchronized.

This temporal disjunction appears to be common in the iconographic tradition; before Caravaggio, Bellini, Titian, and Veronese had also overlooked verisimilitude. But the extent to which Caravaggio visually developed the gestures of his figures through a pervasive network of propulsive diagonals and orthogonal axes obliges the viewer to perceive the scene as an action in progress, not as a symbolic narrative. Time and duration matter. What specifically characterizes the chronological set-up of the composition is its contradictory mixture of contemplative expressions and dramatic gestures. It is difficult, for one thing, to reconcile the persistently enthralled gaze of the apostle on the right, which recalls the timeless version of Bellini's destroyed *Supper at Emmaus*, with the instantaneous reaction of his outflung arms: contemplation and marvel happen to be perceptibly at odds with each other here. More difficult to explain is that the act of Christ's blessing hand, depicted as practically unfurling, strangely antecedes that of taking the bread. However one interprets these gestures, one cannot push aside an impression of disconnected actions, as though Caravaggio fast-forwarded the scene of the consecration enacted by Christ while freezing a partial shot of it: the act of the hand suspended over the bread with which the ritual would have begun. Moreover, the strangeness of Christ's attitude is somehow intensified by the grandiose thrust of the upraised arm, which drastically exceeds the dynamics of the pictorial event. Even if one does not take into account the grandiloquence of this gesture, it could be said in modern terminology that Caravaggio spliced together two different sequences of an episode to create what might be interpreted as the illusion of a diachronic development.

Yet this syncopal dilation of time, if real, is not to encompass a significant prolepsis, as in the versions of *The Supper at Emmaus* by Bellini, Titian or Veronese, insofar as the actions placed before us do not have a symbolic value: Jesus does not take the bread, he is going to; he does not bless it, he is about to. For a painting that reportedly represents "our Lord *in fractione panis*," Caravaggio's *Supper at Emmaus* goes visibly beyond the mark of its subject. At this point, it must be clear that its multiple incongruities cannot easily be disregarded. They are rooted in the compositional structure of the painting and are quite deliberate. One can overrule them as irrelevant, or try to explain their function. In the latter case, it is necessary to grapple with two interrelated questions: what specifically are viewers supposed to perceive in the figure and attitude of Christ? And how do they process and experience his action?

Overlapping Identities and Narrative Disjunction

In another *Supper at Emmaus* (Pinacoteca Tosio e Martinengo, Brescia) painted about 1526 by the Lombard Renaissance painter Moretto,[55] the Christ at the center of the scene, behind the table, appears incognito; a wide-brimmed pilgrim hat covers his head and overshadows his eyes, while a mantle embroidered with a scallop shell protects his shoulders (Fig. 131). His canonical bearded face, albeit partially hidden, nonetheless betrays his real identity, as does the radiant aureole spreading out from behind the top of his hat. He breaks the bread as his two disciples stare at him motionless, absorbed in peaceful contemplation. On the right, in an indifferent walk-on part, a sumptuously dressed servant distractedly shifts her eyes away from the prodigy, looking toward the viewer. An onlooker on the left intently and almost piously witnesses the theophany: he is surely the patron who paid for the composition. Every single element of the pictorial representation seems to derive from the iconographic tradition I have been examining above—everything but the simulated pilgrim. It is difficult to estimate the effect this iconographic camouflage exerted on viewers. It must have been remarkable in the beginning, as they first set eyes on the picture and encountered the disturbing image of a Christ wearing the traditional mask of his apostles, their pilgrim attire.[56] Then, after considering the context, beholders would certainly have recognized both Jesus and the Gospel episode, and perhaps appreciated the novelty introduced by Moretto in the depiction of Christ. In other terms, their bewilderment, like ours, in failing to identify the divine image was and is restricted to initial stupefaction.

Caravaggio's *Supper at Emmaus* does not call out for a similar reaction. Though disguised, his Christ keeps some of his recognizable features; his identity and the character of his gesture, on the contrary, become more and more questionable as the viewer delves into the composition. Caravaggio himself deliberately planned all of this. Although he must have known Moretto's *Supper at Emmaus*—the picture was on view from the sixteenth through the eighteenth century in San Luca, Brescia, not far from Caravaggio's family town—he decided to modify the identity of his Christ in a much more refined manner. As we have seen, Caravaggio drew on the iconographic tradition of the blessing *Salvator Mundi* in depicting Jesus as a young, beardless God. Also, the

55 See Begni Redona 1988, 192-5, no. 27; and Strinati and Vodret 2000, 207, no. 30 [catalogue entry by Francesco Rossi].

56 The figure of Christ in Romanino's *Supper at Emmaus* (Pinacoteca Tosio-Martinengo, Brescia) wears a similar outfit. Furthermore, he is represented as an old man with a long beard. At first glance, he thus qualifies as a representation of Jesus *in alia effigie*. Nevertheless, the same features appear in two other pictures related to the same cycle to which the *Supper at Emmaus* originally belonged: *Christ with the Samaritan Woman* and *Christ at the House of Simon the Pharisee*. Since the specificity of Christ's figure does not seem linked to the iconography of the *Supper at Emmaus*, I do not deal with this composition here. For Romanino's *Supper at Emmaus*, see Panazza 1965, 98-9; and Nova 1994, 268-9, no. 54.

colors of Christ's robe and mantle, purple and white, allude to the Passion and the Resurrection, which perfectly matches the symbolism of a *Supper at Emmaus*. The Jesus appearing in the painting has endured the Crucifixion and triumphed over death. In spite of their symbolic meanings, the unusual features of this transfigured Christ still trouble the viewer, since they persistently clash with a context in which another traditional iconography is involved and alluded to, that of the *Last Supper*. In the adolescent traits and yet grave expression of Caravaggio's Jesus thus collide the past, present, and future of the incarnate divinity.

On a subliminal level, the interplay and tension of various iconographic traditions must have been apprehended by beholders as a visual interference, therefore bringing about an effect of latent surprise; Bellori's scathing remarks about the lack of "decorum" of Caravaggio's beardless Christ somehow signals the marvel and discomfort experienced by a cultivated viewer in front of the figure. In addition, the illuminated face and torso of the blessing Savior emerging from the dense shadow thrown by the innkeeper engender a twofold eerie illusion; a sort of dark aureole, perceived as an unfitted, looming, and distorted silhouette of Christ himself, crowns his figure, projecting forward his glowing face.[57] As a result, Jesus' identity and majesty are subtly undermined, since beholders would anticipate seeing either his epithetic aureole or at least a less deceptive shadow. The opposition of light and darkness that underlies Christ's epiphany is likely to suggest the dialectical relation between visibility and invisibility inherent not only in the iconography of *The Supper at Emmaus*, but also in the notion itself of a visible, figurative God, as espoused, for instance, by John of Damascus. By linking together the brilliant image of Christ and the mysterious shadow behind him, Caravaggio both reasserts and reassesses the cultural and visual dialectic between visible and invisible, insinuating that both define divinity, though neither in an exclusive way. In Caravaggio's picture, however, Christ's identity remains constantly entangled in an unsolvable dialogue between opposing concepts and, as far as iconography is concerned, ambivalent features and attributes. If light is assimilated to sight and knowledge, darkness no longer connotes blindness and ignorance, insofar as it also encapsulates a relevant part of Jesus' divine identity, its potential invisibility.

This visual ambivalence pertains to the figure and attitude of Christ alike. In fact, beholders are systematically misled in their attempt to interpret his gesture correctly. As already observed, the centripetal structure of the painting invites viewers to focus on the figure of Christ, especially on his spotlit face. The axis of the bending head, marked by the bridge of the nose, seems to direct the beholders' eyes downward, where Jesus also appears to be gazing. Unexpectedly, in the prolongation of the axis, nothing seems worthy of consideration. Instead, the beholder's sight is rerouted toward two other focal points, the hovering hand and the upraised arm. As in a circuit, the figure of Christ thus channels and refracts the viewer's attention along at least three different axes. Consequently, Jesus' action seems to unfold with a certain vastness, virtually expanding its visual impact across the pictorial surface. Besides the large scale of the figure, the dislocation of its main axes in their connection to each other leads to a dispersal of the viewers' focus; as a consequence, viewers tend to discern the self-absorbed expression on Christ's face and the gestures of his two

---

57 Oddly enough, the detail of the "dark halo" behind Christ has aroused little curiosity. Longhi 1999-2000, 1:174, first dwelt on it: "The almost caricatural shadow that Caravaggio makes the figures of the innkeeper and Christ cast together onto the backdrop is a first element of dramatic inflection." Scribner 1977, 376, note 10, considering the shadow cast by the basket of fruit on the table, points out: "Even the shadow cast by the basket of fruit may have emblematic significance for, as Professor Walter Liedtke has called to my attention, it describes the partial outline of a fish, the early Christian symbol for Christ. The probability of a symbolic meaning here is strengthened by Liedtke's further observation that the innkeeper's shadow creates a naturalistic halo around Christ's head. This dark, 'negative' halo in a form of a foreshortened disc is effectively juxtaposed with Christ's fully illumined face—a clear indication of the metaphysical qualities of Caravaggio's chiaroscuro." See also Hibbard 1983, 80: "The innkeeper casts a shadow that seems to form a negative halo around the brilliant head of Christ, as if to indicate that we honor the Savior even while ignoring or denying him"; and Puglisi 1998, 213: "Rare in Italian painting and used sparingly by Caravaggio, the cast shadows serve here more than one purpose: to reaffirm the corporeality of forms, to project a halo shape on the wall above Christ's head, and to imply the transient nature of the moment represented, for immediately after the theophany, Christ disappeared."

hands separately. More precisely, the beholder's sight alternately shuttles between Jesus' head and his upraised arm, toward which the apostle's transfixed profile on the right is pointed. There is no doubt that Caravaggio consciously underscored the visual polarity of these focal points.

The act of blessing, with its powerful eloquence, has particularly intrigued scholars.[58] It is not difficult to understand why the gesture, as well as its structural and visual importance, has raised such curiosity. If one considers the picture as an equivalent to a literary text, it must be agreed that the act Christ performs by lifting his arm and uncurling his hand is both lexically and syntactically disproportionate. It is, furthermore, unparalleled in the iconographic tradition. Regarded in terms of verisimilitude, it is simply incongruous, since it does not seem directly related to the object—the Eucharistic bread—that would justify it. To explain what has been designated the *terribilità* of this gesture, that is, its capacity to induce dread, some scholars have compared it with the attitude of Michelangelo's wrathful Christ in the *Last Judgment*.[59] In fact, Jesus' hovering hand exactly mirrors the downturned hand of Michelangelo's Christ, even if, in a different context, Caravaggio's quotation apparently cannot convey the same narrative significance. Therefore, one cannot simply interpret the gesture of Caravaggio's Christ as one of judging and condemning, although by evoking Michelangelo's precedent, Caravaggio assuredly intended to imitate its dramatic intensity. Then, if the acts of the upraised arm and the blessing hand do not express the wrath and implacability of a judging Christ,[60] they may refer to the triumph and prodigy of a risen Savior. The iconographic tradition underpins this interpretation.

Among the canonical gestures attributed to Christ in the iconography of the *Resurrection*, one often finds the act of raising the right arm in a sign of victory associated with an unfurling hand poised for a blessing. An engraving by Marcantonio Raimondi after a drawing by Raphael epitomizes the main elements of this iconographic theme (Fig. 132).[61] Jesus stands in the foreground, framed by a mandorla, his head sparking rays like a glowing star; his left arm adheres to his torso and hip, as his hand holds the pole of the Christian banner. His right arm is lifted in a position similar to that of Caravaggio's Jesus. The same can be said of the blessing hand. More interesting, in Raimondi's engraving a source of light illuminates from above the upraised arm of the resurrected Christ, casting its shadow on the torso and leaving the palm of the blessing hand unlit. These similarities could be purely coincidental, and there is no evidence that Raimondi's engraving actually inspired Caravaggio. Yet a 1619-1620 *Resurrection* by Cecco del Caravaggio (Art Institute, Chicago),[62] which I will examine in Chapter 15, confirms without any doubt that the gesture of Caravaggio's Christ in *The Supper at Emmaus* might be perceived as perfectly suitable for a resurrected Jesus (Fig. 133).

One knee leaning on a cloud suspended above the sepulcher, the risen Christ turns his eyes down to the guardians frightened by the dreadful sound of the thunder that had preceded his Resurrection. He holds the pole of the banner in his left hand, while lifting his right arm in a sign of triumph. At the same time, he uncurls his hand in an act of blessing. Like Caravaggio, Cecco depicts his Christ as deeply immersed in contemplation, his head bent down, his eyes escaping any contact with the viewer. Like Caravaggio, Cecco also imagined strong lighting coming from above, hitting the raised arm and casting its heavy shadow across Jesus' torso. Incidentally, it must be observed that the posture of the arm and especially the gesture of the blessing hand in Cecco's *Resurrection* appear also to be literal quotations from Raimondi's *Blessing Christ*. In any event,

---

58   As evidenced by Kroschewki 2002, 127, the blessing hand is situated exactly on the golden section of the composition, which underscores its visual relevance.

59   A lot of ink has been spilled over the gesture of Michelangelo's judging Christ. Vasari's description of Michelangelo's figure is unfortunately too vague (Vasari, 6:71). More detailed is Ascanio Condivi's description of the gesture

(Condivi, 50). For interpretations of Michelangelo's judging Christ see Steinberg 1975; Hall 1976; Dixon 1983; Barnes 1998 [with extensive bibliography]; and Hall 2005.

60   For a different interpretation, see Lavin 2000, 32.

61   See Oberhuber 1978, 1:92, no. 64.

62   See Papi 2001, 132-5, no. 16.

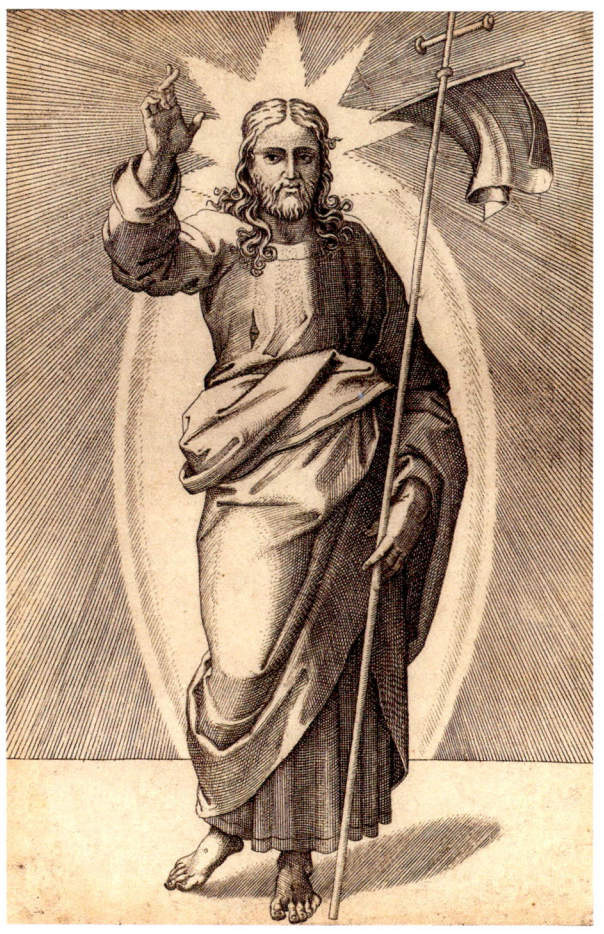

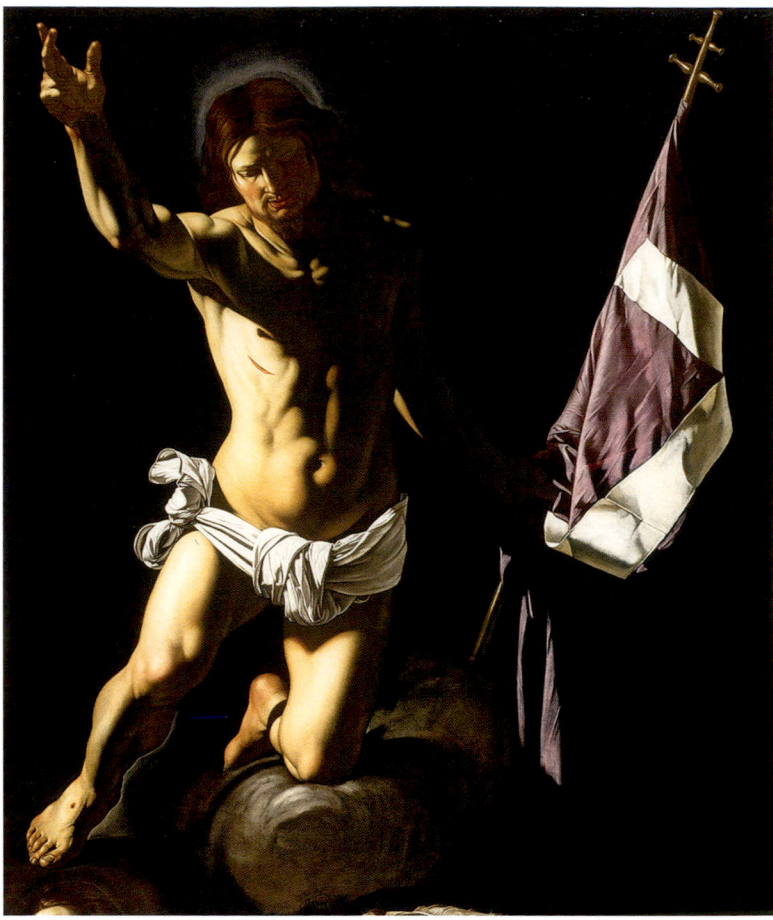

Fig. 132
Marcantonio Raimondi after Raphael (Raffaello Santi),
Resurrected Christ, engraving, 20.8 x 13.6 cm.

Fig. 133
Cecco del Caravaggio (Francesco Boneri), *The Resurrection*, Art Institute, Chicago,
oil on canvas, 339 x 199.5 cm., detail.

if Cecco, in depicting his triumphant Christ, elaborated on a visual formula excerpted from his master and mentor's *Supper at Emmaus*, it must be inferred that, intuitively at least, he was aware that Caravaggio's blessing figure of Jesus somehow belonged to the iconographic theme of the *Resurrection*.

Another *Supper at Emmaus* (J.P. Getty Museum, Los Angeles) by a follower of Caravaggio, Bartolomeo Cavarozzi, corroborates this interpretation (Fig. 134).[63] Cavarozzi depicted a beardless Christ swathed in the pure linen of his shroud, bare chested, uplifting his right arm in the typical gesture of the Resurrection or, for that matter, of the Incredulity of Saint Thomas, thus offering his torso to view. It is no coincidence that Christ's left arm, strangely also poised for blessing, points to the wound in his side, which opportunely remains invisible under the unfolding drapery of his mantle. The apostle at the right, leaping to his feet, contemplates Jesus' upraised arm and uncurling hand. His companion seems to gaze into space, thereby performing the role of the clueless spectator. There is no doubt that Cavarozzi, in representing Christ as he did, created a visual interference

63 As evidenced by Marini 1981a, esp. 127, the apostle stretching his arms out in the Getty *Supper at Emmaus* is almost identical with a figure at the left in the *Martyrdom of Saint Stephen* (Cathedral of Monterotondo) that a 1624 source assigned to Bartolomeo Cavarozzi. Equally, the apostle at the right in the Getty picture has the same features as the torturer at the center of the Monterotondo painting. Marini's attribution of both paintings to Giovan Battista Crescenzi is far-fetched. On Cavarozzi's *Martyrdom of Saint Stephen*, see Schleier 1969; Pagliara 1980; and Spezzaferro 1985, esp. 55. For Cavarozzi as the author of the Getty *Supper at Emmaus*, see Papi 1996, especially 91-2. According to Papi, the Getty *Supper at Emmaus* must have been executed before 1614-1615. See also Spear 1971, no. 25 (as Aniello Falcone); Causa 1972, 933, 975, no. 66 (as Alonso Rodríguez); and Nicolson 1979, 38 (as Caravaggesque Unknown-Neapolitan).

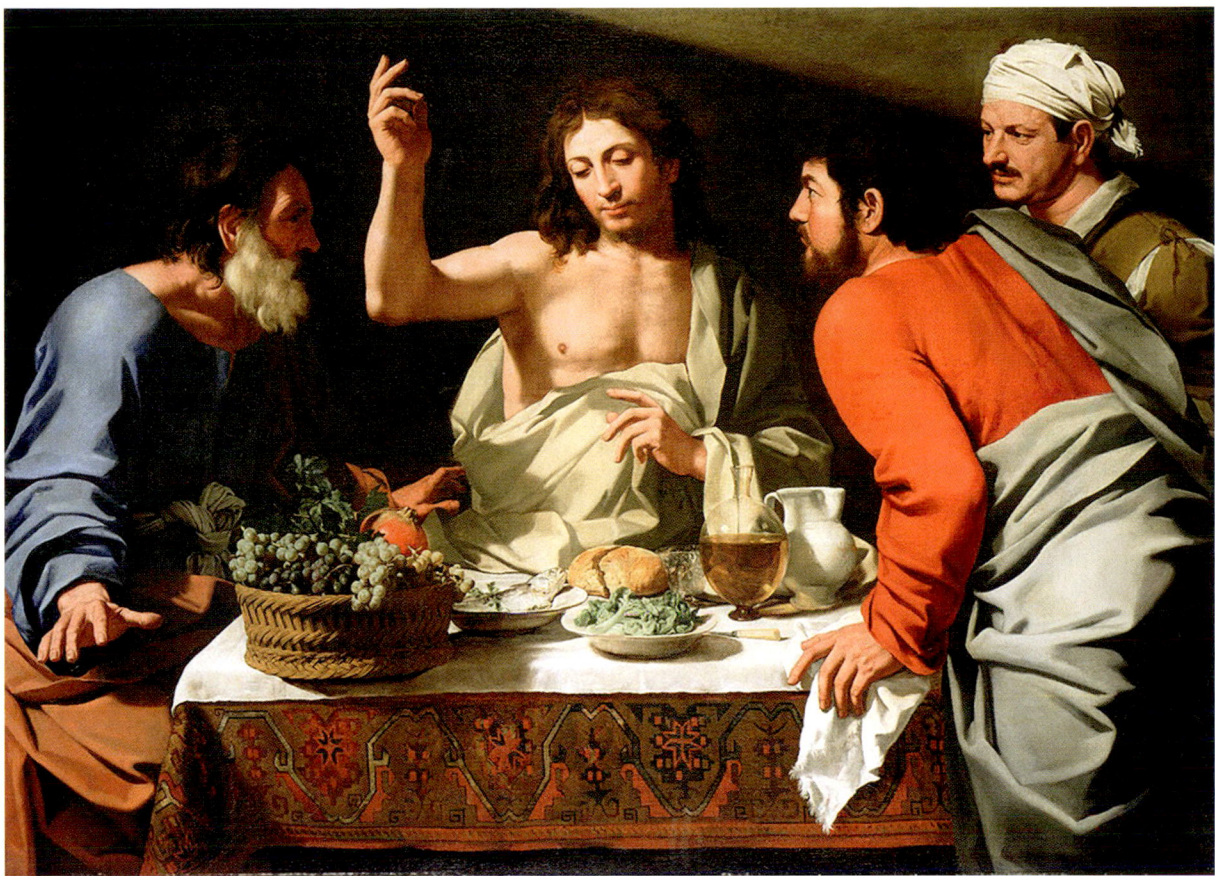

Fig. 134
Bartolomeo Cavarozzi, *The Supper at Emmaus*, The J. Paul Getty Museum, Los Angeles, oil on canvas, 139.7 x 194.3 cm.

between at least two different iconographies: the Supper at Emmaus and the Resurrection. Of course, his iconographic boldness relies on, and stems from, Caravaggio's precedent.

By raising his arm in a graphically overwhelming gesture, Caravaggio's Christ subliminally evokes the mystery of the Resurrection. In other words, Caravaggio, in setting up the composition, tried to adjust the figure of a glorious risen Christ to fit the context of *The Supper at Emmaus*. Therefore, he charged the gesture of raising the arm during the consecration of the Eucharistic bread with the exceptional strain of a silent triumph. The superimposition of two distinct iconographies that, inextricably interconnected, coalesce in the viewer's perception enhances the visual pertinence of the figure of Christ, that is, his visibility, but in a way that latently puzzles the viewer. As a matter of fact, the allusion to the iconography of the Resurrection is hard to detect, skillfully dissimulated as it is, though continuously challenging and prompting the beholder for recognition. Through its dissimulation, Caravaggio succeeded in stimulating the figurative memory of his contemporary beholders at its core, that unconscious portion of it operating underneath as a "white noise" of Christian imagery.

With his overlapping identities and ambivalent gestures, Caravaggio's figure of Christ unsettles the confident impression of recognition intrinsic to the pictorial tradition of *The Supper at Emmaus* from Bellini onward. As a consequence, viewers are denied that degree of dramatic irony that traditionally prevented them from sharing the apostles' surprise at the impending theophany. At the same time, they are also thwarted in their effort to comprehend fully the mechanism of the pictorial event. For this reason, they cannot partake in the emotion of any of the actors in the presence of Christ. Theirs, then, is not the apostles' surprise, nor even the innkeeper's clueless

287

incredulity. Indeed, even if all these actors seem to turn their attention to Christ, none of them appears to consider the same aspect of the theophany. The innkeeper apparently fixes his gaze on Jesus' face, whereas the disciple on the right intently contemplates the Savior's blessing hand.[64] As for the second apostle, it is impossible to understand what actually makes him jerk upward, as Caravaggio hid his eyes and therefore the specific object of his astonishment.[65] As a result, the viewer's sight revolves around the epiphany without being able to reconstruct it in its dramatic coherence. What is truly evident at least is that the visual catalyst for recognition cannot be the same for the aghast apostle on the right as for the beholder who, from his point of view, barely realizes what prodigy can possibly be revealed by the isolated gesture of both an upraised arm and a blessing hand. Ironically enough, if one concentrates on them as the apostle does, one is at a loss to identify the sign of divinity they reveal as a hieroglyph of Resurrection, especially if the detail of Christ's pierced, wounded palm, invisible to us, made itself visible to the baffled disciple.[66]

Whatever one's position toward Caravaggio's Christ might be, whether one takes the viewer's point of view or adopts the fictive angle of every single actor in the picture, his image and the meaning of his gesture end up eluding one. Paradoxically, his visibility skips away because of its visual many-sidedness. As a corollary, the action Christ performs loses its narrative congruity, shattering into a diversity of sequences and pandering to multiple points of view that eventually prove to be unfit to dovetail in an objective reconstruction of the pictorial event. The concept of objectivity is crucial here. As fiction, Caravaggio's *Supper at Emmaus* naturally lacks the objectiveness of historical fact. Yet there is a kind of pictorial objectivity that consists in allowing the viewer to read the scene as a coherent interrelation of actions and reactions with the highest degree of certainty. Therefore, a picture is objective when its reading does not afford any ambiguity or uncertainty. In any case, this is what Counter-Reformation art theorists such as Paleotti and Borromeo unequivocally asserted.

As a narrative structure, Caravaggio's *Supper at Emmaus* keeps beholders in twofold indeterminacy, both perceptive and intellectual. At every step, they believe they see, almost touch and understand the scene, whereas the unseen, the intangible, and the ambivalent are relentlessly conjured up or insinuated in a context where time (duration) and space (distance) constantly fluctuate. Caravaggio's pictorial narrative, as articulated in his first *Supper at Emmaus*, is thus characterized by its insistent addressing of the viewer's subjectivity, insofar as it arouses a sequence of open, sometimes contradictory, reactions to the picture's optical, tactile, and dramatic effects. This narrative machinery of underlying visual surprises, which deftly exploits opposing concepts and is destined to engender a state of subtle bewilderment, certainly preludes the "poetics of the marvelous" and the *concettismo* that would soon be in vogue in Italian literature at the beginning of the seventeenth century. However, the temporal leaps, narrative lacunae, and indeterminacies of the painting's visual plot do not find any contemporary literary parallel. Like the reader of James Joyce's *Ulysses*, it is the beholder of Caravaggio's *Supper at Emmaus* who, "almost abandoned by the work, [must] carry on his own shoulders the burden of [reconfiguring] the intrigue," even if—or perhaps the more so in that—he already knows its outcome.[67]

Whatever pictorial subtleties might be involved in Caravaggio's picture, one eventually has to acknowledge the profound seriousness with which he has questioned and strengthened the notion of visibility as traditionally conveyed by the image of Christ. Caravaggio's success in manipulating Jesus' canonical figure relies on his capacity to modify the sacred image from the inside, in its

---

64 See Gilbert 1995, 147: "Because he is at the side of the table, forward of Christ, his gaze must pass far in front of him, too. It thus focuses on Christ's blessing hand, the motif in some of the Venetian paintings."

65 Ibidem: "The face of the left disciple is hidden, so we are not to know what he sees."

66 The pierced palm can appear as an attribute of the Risen Christ, as evidenced by an engraving by Maarten van Heemskerk, *Christ as the Way, the Truth and the Life*, 1556. See Veldman and Luijten 1994, 44, no. 337.

67 Ricœur 1983, 1:145-6.

basic connections with the iconographic tradition. Without a doubt, this is what defines the essence of Caravaggio's rebellion and genius: his "inside job" in Christian iconography. Even if he does not actually vanish from sight, his Christ nonetheless loses his univocal appearance in a multiplicity of identities and gestures. By disappearing as a prototypical, immediately identifiable image, Caravaggio's Jesus transfigures into the unwonted icon of an eternally youthful divinity, consecrating the Eucharistic bread by casting the mysterious shadow of his resurrected body over it in a gesture of mute, hieroglyphic triumph and blessing.

The Presence of Darkness: On the Brera Supper at Emmaus

Caravaggio's second version of *The Supper at Emmaus*, now in the Pinacoteca di Brera, Milan (Fig. 135), is the work of a fugitive.[68] On 28 May 1606, the painter murdered Ranuccio Tomassoni. To avoid prison and the death penalty, Caravaggio fled Rome soon afterward, on 31 May; he was "badly wounded." He spent the entire summer in the properties of the Colonna family, in Zagarolo and in Paliano, not far from Rome, then moved to Naples at the beginning of the fall. From the extant documentation, it is evident that he was easily accessible while in exile. On 15 July 1606, Fabio Masetti, agent of Cesare d'Este, Duke of Modena, reports: "I let the painter [Caravaggio] know that if he sends me the finished painting by next week, I will take it; otherwise, it is useless for him to work on it any further, since we have been awaiting it for too long."[69] Masetti refers to a painting commissioned by the Duke a year earlier, in August 1605. Caravaggio had already received 32 *scudi* as a down payment for the job, and had even promised Masetti that the painting would be ready in November 1605. If Caravaggio ever began working on this picture—its subject matter is unknown, and scholars' attempts to identify it are inconclusive, if not wholly unsubstantiated— he eventually abandoned its completion. On 23 September 1606, Masetti indeed records that "Caravaggio sojourns in Paliano, with the intention of obtaining a speedy pardon; I'll try to get back the 32 *scudi* I gave him," which means that, despite his previous letter, Masetti had resigned himself to never obtaining the painting.[70] From other letters, it is also apparent that Caravaggio never replied to Masetti's requests. I stress this point since, according to Giulio Mancini, after the murder and flight from Rome, Caravaggio went to Zagarolo, "where he made a Magdalene and Christ on his way to Emmaus that was purchased by Costa in Rome." In a variant of this passage, Mancini instead declares that Caravaggio sent the Emmaus painting "to Rome for sale."[71] Although Mancini describes the picture at issue as "Christ on his way to Emmaus," a subject never mentioned by any other source or documentation pertaining to Caravaggio, he was most likely referring to a *Supper at Emmaus*.

This assumption is corroborated by Bellori's testimony. In his *Vite*, Bellori indeed mentions a "Christ in Emmaus between his two apostles" painted by Caravaggio "in Zagarolo."[72] If this is true,

68 For the painting, see Venturi 1912; Spezzaferro 1974, 118; Moir 1982, 132; Cinotti 1983, 462-3, no. 31; Hibbard 1983, 211-2; Christiansen 1985, 306-10, no. 87; Bologna 1992, 332; Puglisi 1998, 243; Longhi 1999-2000, 1:85 [1951]; Varriano 1999b, 192-203; Borea and Gasparri 2000, 2:280-1, no. 5; Pedrocchi 2000, 218; Cassani and Sapio 2005, 100-2, no. 2; Marini 2005, 504-6, no. 74; Varriano 2006, 124-5; Terzaghi 2007, 293-5; Ebert-Schifferer 2009, 200; Schütze 2009, 273-4, no. 46. Only when the book was in production did I find out that Kloek 2002 has already linked the Brera painting to the prints by the Sadeler after Candido.

69 First published by Venturi 1910, 282. See Macioce 2003, 202: "Al pittore ho fatto sapere se mi manderà il quadro finito per la prossima settimana ch'io lo pigliarò, altrimenti non occorre che più vi affatica perché pur troppo s'è aspettato."

70 First published by Dell'Acqua and Cinotti 1971, 110. See

Macioce 2003, 209: "Commesse il Caravaggio l'homicidio già scritto et si trattiene a Pagliano con dissegno di dover esser presto rimesso; procurerò da lui recuperar 32 scudi ch'io gli diedi come per sue ricevute ch'io mandai in mano del Milani che le mostrasse a Vostra Signoria Illustrissima."

71 Mancini, 1:225: "In ultimo, per alcuni eventi che corse pericolo di vita che, per salvarsi, aiutato da Onorio Longo, ammazzò l'inimico, fu necessitato fuggirsi di Roma, e di primo salto fu in Zagarolo, ivi trattenuto secretamente da quel Principe, dove fece una Madalena e Christo che va in Emaus che lo comprò in Roma il Costa [lo mandò a vendere a Roma]."

72 Bellori, 225: "Fuggitosene di Roma, senza denari e perseguitato, ricoverò in Zagarolo nella benevolenza del duca don Marzio Colonna, dove colorì il quadro di Cristo in Emaus fra li due apostoli ed un'altra mezza figura di Madalena."

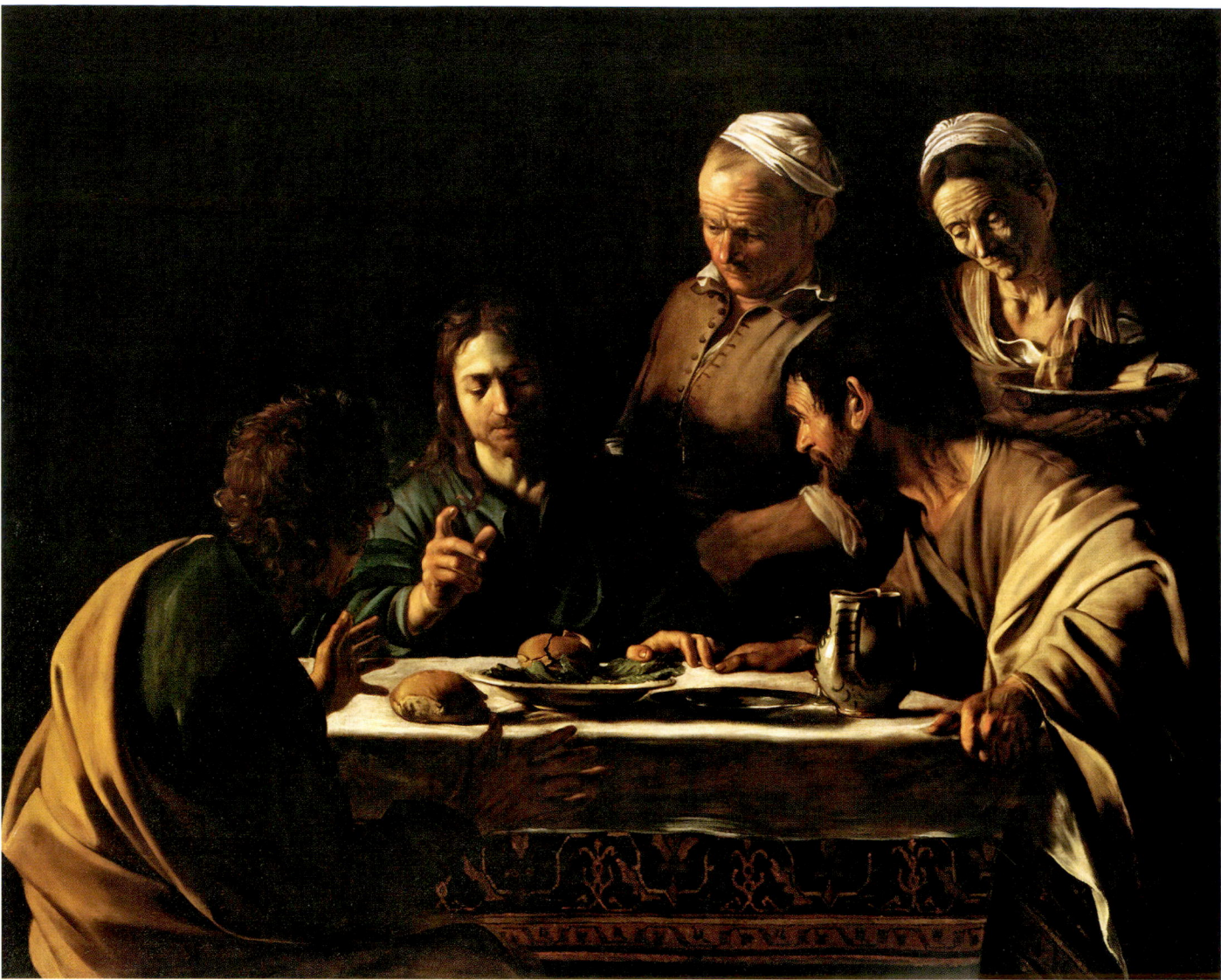

Fig. 135
Michelangelo Merisi da Caravaggio, *The Supper at Emmaus*, Pinacoteca di Brera, Milan, oil on canvas, 141 x 175 cm.

then there is no doubt that the work Caravaggio executed at the beginning of his exile was the Brera *Supper at Emmaus*, which on stylistic grounds is not only possible, but also extremely probable. In any event, whether shipped to Rome for sale, bought by the banker Ottavio Costa or even paid for by him at a client's behest or in view of speculation, circumstantial evidence suggests that the painting did not result from a commission. In other words, at the very moment Caravaggio required money to survive during the difficult times of his exile and was certainly requested to execute or finish other paintings—the d'Este commission confirms this fact—he might have preferred to give free rein to his inspiration, thereby returning to a subject he had already dealt with in better times, that is, the representation of the supper at Emmaus. It is important to underline this possibility, because this means that, in representing the biblical episode for the second time, Caravaggio approached it in a very personal manner: as a meditation on the divine and its epiphany to man's eyes.

Be that as it may, the Brera *Supper at Emmaus* is, in my opinion, among Caravaggio's most thrilling creations, a masterpiece whose eloquence does not solely unfurl through the traditional means of expression, attitudes, and composition—which nevertheless prove to be more conventional when compared to those deployed in the London version—but is rooted in, and magnified by, its facture.

More to the point, the crucial theme of divinity's appearance and disappearance, conceptually exemplified by the pictorial dialectics of light and dark, manifests itself in the Brera painting not so much on the level of the narrative, but above all on that of technique and chiaroscuro. Action and temporality are therefore set in motion by the work's spectacular opalescence, a phenomenon that, unfortunately, no reproduction, however good, can render appropriately. I shall examine the conceptual repercussions of this opalescence shortly. Even Caravaggio's most severe censor, Bellori, acknowledged the work's intriguing beauty. In his 1654 *Nota delli musei di Roma*, he singled out "the Supper of our Lord at Emmaus with his disciples, very beautiful"[73] in the Patrizi Collection, Rome; the first mention of the painting's ownership by this Roman family can be traced in a 1624 inventory of the artworks at the Patrizi Palace.[74] Even if he did not express any aesthetic appreciation of the picture in his subsequent *Vite*, Bellori honored Caravaggio's work with a short description, without criticizing it:

> There is Christ in the middle who blesses the bread, and one of the apostles, seated, opens his arm upon recognizing him, as the other rests his hands on the table, looking at him in wonder; behind, there is the innkeeper with a cap on his head, and an old woman bringing in the meal.[75]

As Bellori points out, this second version of *The Supper at Emmaus* is "somewhat different" from, and "darker" than, the first one. Notwithstanding Christ's quasi-centrality, the Brera painting is structurally based on asymmetry and a noticeable imbalance between its left and right sides. The apostles' position in the left foreground and to the right echoes that of their counterparts in the London picture. Nonetheless, by omitting the chair of the disciple with his back turned, Caravaggio mitigated the effect of pictorial depth specific to the Mattei *Supper at Emmaus*. Also, the London version's wide slope of the table with its luscious spread of victuals loses much of its relevance in the Brera picture, where it shrinks to a narrow, almost planar, surface. At its center, the table offers to view an empty dish—only a salad leaf inside it attests to the food's former presence. Nearby lies another dish, as well as two loaves of bread, the closer one framed by the apostle's open arms, the farther, already broken in two, lying next to Christ ready to be blessed. At the right of the table, a terracotta jug, cursorily but skillfully decorated with the rudimentary motifs of strias, commas, and spirals, stands between the second apostle's clenched hands. An Anatolian rug covers the table, its borders appearing below a light-colored tablecloth.

Scholars have rightly indicated that Caravaggio drew on his memory in depicting both the innkeeper (the posture of his arms bracketing his ponderous belly as his hands grasp his belt harks back to the Mattei painting) and the old servant (her face, tilted down- and rightward, and her craned and wrinkled neck are excerpted from the figure of the elderly Saint Anne in the 1606 *Palafrenieri Madonna*, now at the Galleria Borghese, Rome),[76] thereby inferring that the master, deprived of his studio, renounced working from live models altogether. In Part Five, I will tackle the complex question of Caravaggio's pictorial memory. But working from memory does not necessarily entail the absence of live models; in the Brera painting, for instance, the innkeeper has an all too specific physiognomy, which might derive from an actual portrayal. Moreover, the painting's alleged extemporaneousness should not discourage scholars from seeking visual sources for Caravaggio's invention.

73 Bellori a, 43-4: "La Cena del Signore in Emaus co' due discepoli di Michele da Caravaggio, bellissima."

74 For the Patrizi inventories, see Pedrocchi 2000.

75 Bellori, 223: "Alli signori Massimi colorì un Ecce Homo che fu portato in Ispagna, ed al marchese Patrizi la Cena in Emaus, nella quale vi è Cristo in mezzo che benedice il pane, ed uno de gli apostoli nel riconoscerlo apre le braccia, e l'altro ferma le mani su la mensa e lo riguarda con maraviglia; evvi dietro l'oste con la cuffia in capo ed una vecchia che porta le vivande."

76 The first to note this is Baroni 1947.

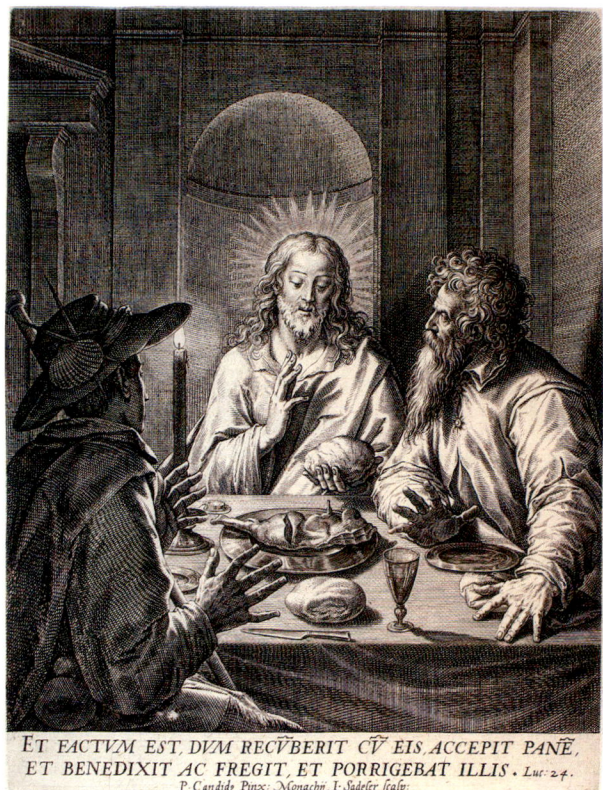

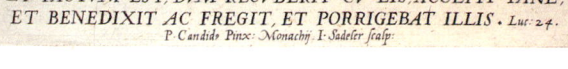

Fig. 136
Johan Sadeler I after Pietro Candido (Pieter de Witte), *The Supper at Emmaus*, engraving, 20 x 15.3 cm.

Fig. 137
Aegidius Sadeler II after Pietro Candido (Pieter de Witte), *The Supper at Emmaus*, engraving, 24 x 18 cm.

In this regard, it is noteworthy that a detail from a print by Johan Sadeler I after Pietro Candido (alias Pieter de Witte) supplied Caravaggio with a gripping idea for the Brera painting (Fig. 136).[77] In this engraving, also a *Supper at Emmaus*, a young apostle at the left wearing a pilgrim hat with a scallop shell (the attribute of Saint James), his face nearly entirely hidden, opens his arms in surprise as he recognizes Christ's identity. Candido's figure as represented by Sadeler is a wondrous example of back-lighting: not fortuitously, a tall candle soars at the left upon the table, illuminating Christ with vigor, making his blessing right hand cast a dense shadow across his chest. More important, the brim of the young apostle's hat interposes itself between the candle's circular glow and the foreground. As a consequence, the disciple's figure plunges into thick penumbra, his profile, right forearm and arm thinly silhouetted by the reverberation of light. It is not difficult to ascertain that Caravaggio's analogous figure to the left of the Brera painting recalls Candido's young apostle, whose two open hands counter the incoming light: two dark masses hovering mid-air, brought out exclusively through their luminous contours.

Without insisting on these analogies, I ought to signal another *Supper at Emmaus* engraved by Aegidius Sadeler II after Pietro Candido, very similar to the previous one, though with some salient divergences (Fig. 137).[78] In this second print, the young apostle at the left with his back turned reacts to Christ's theophany with greater awe, pushing his torso backward; his right hand, completely unfurled, detaches itself in half-tone against the dark background of the tablecloth's drooping

77 De Ramaix 1997, 105, no. 065. As Johan Sadeler I lived from 1589 to 1594 at the court of William V of Bavaria, in Munich, for whom Pietro Candido also worked, the print must date to those years. See also Volk-Knüttel 2010, 351, no. D13.

78 De Ramaix 1999, 276, no. 223. Pietro Candido's original drawing is now at the Art Institute, Chicago. This print was executed before 1597, when Aegidius Sadeler II, the nephew and apprentice of Johan Sadeler I in Munich, left for Prague. See previous note. See also Volk-Knüttel 2010, 211, no. Z14 and 351, no. D14.

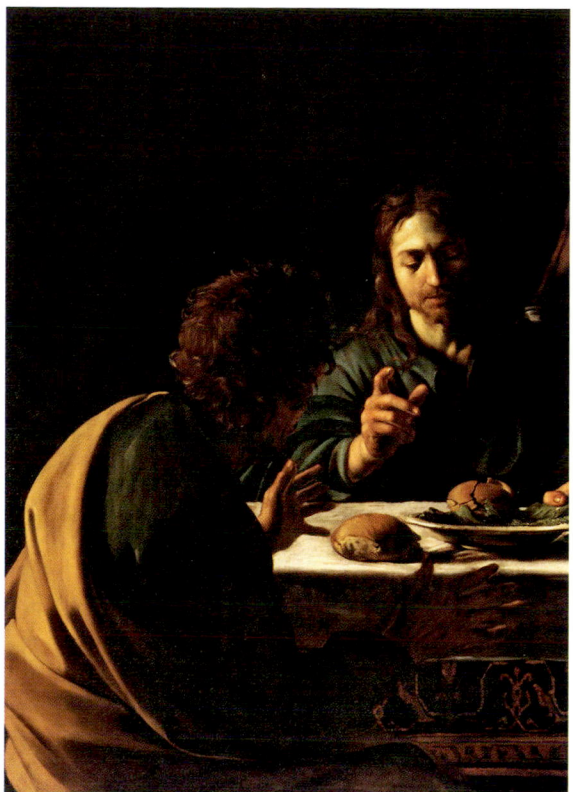

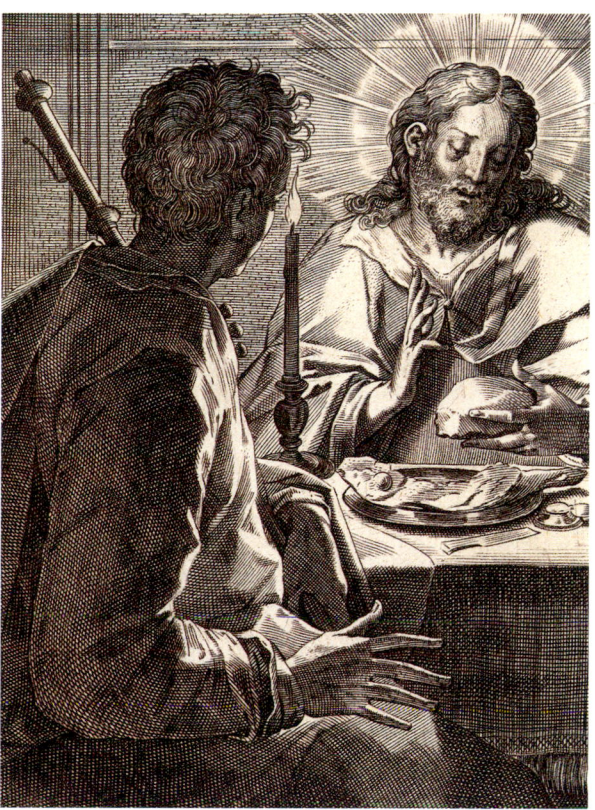

Fig. 138
Michelangelo Merisi da Caravaggio, *The Supper at Emmaus*, Pinacoteca di Brera, Milan, oil on canvas, 141 x 175 cm., detail.

Fig. 139
Aegidius Sadeler II after Pietro Candido (Pieter de Witte), *The Supper at Emmaus*, engraving, 24 x 18 cm., detail.

border. His bare head and concealed face generate an extraordinary chiaroscuro effect as his locks of hair vibrate in penumbra, some of them flaring against the refulgent candlelight: details not lost on Caravaggio, as can be proved by merely comparing the two figures of this apostle in the print and in the painting (Figs. 138, 139). Nor can it be a coincidence that Caravaggio adopted some of the chiaroscuro devices employed by Candido in representing the table with the remains of the supper, particularly the contrast between the table's bright surface and its shaded border in the foreground. By the same token, consider the older disciple to the right of Sadeler's engraving, his face in profile, his eyes fixed upon Christ's face, his uplifted and open right hand screening the Savior's radiance while casting an ominous shadow across his chest, as if an invisible hand was seizing him. To a certain degree, this figure's profile evokes his counterpart in the Brera painting, although Caravaggio lessened the physiognomic sharpness of Candido's old man by "rounding" his apostle's traits, as evidenced by the crescent-like protuberance of his ear. Of course, one could object that the bearded apostle in Caravaggio's painting is reminiscent of the disciple with his back turned in the left foreground of the London *Supper at Emmaus*, the profiles of these two figures bearing an undeniable resemblance. In the end, it must be said that the one assumption does not rule out the other's authenticity. Yet matching the postures of figures seems to me somewhat secondary in this case.

Rather than being interested in pictorial attitudes, I am profoundly intrigued by the complexity of the print's chiaroscuro and the influence it exerted on Caravaggio: both Candido with his design and Sadeler with his burin express light's motion and drama in their images of *The Supper at Emmaus* with artistry, that is, with groundbreaking results. Although one does not detect the same chiaroscuro arrangement in the Brera painting, it is evident that Candido's inventions sparked, if they did not ignite, Caravaggio's imagination. However, unlike Candido, Caravaggio in the Brera picture, while

293

not downplaying the contrast of light and shade, as a general rule attenuated the stereography of bodies and objects that intense chiaroscuro ordinarily spawns in painting. To be sure, the opposition of lit and shaded parts in the picture's figures begets an impression of three-dimensionality, yet the relief effect is mitigated by at least two concomitant factors: the scarcity of shadows—the only one cast by a figure is that of Christ upon the innkeeper's belly, which rather than projecting the Savior's face and torso forward serves to accentuate his physical separation from the adjacent figure—and the painting's spatial compression—the figures being clustered together within a narrow section of the pictorial field. I do not mean by this to characterize the Brera painting as merely flat, which is far from being true. Rather, I highlight the fact that, compared to the London *Supper at Emmaus*, in which the interplay of space and volume is pushed to extremes, the Patrizi picture does not aim at dilating spatiality by simultaneously obscuring the correlation between proximity and distance. In sum, there are no tricks and sleight of hand in the Brera *Supper at Emmaus*.

In this connection, consider the hands of Jesus and his two disciples around the table. Not only are they interrelated separately, figure by figure, at regular intervals, but their reciprocal position with regard to space also precludes ambiguity. This time, the older apostle's hand would truly manage to touch Christ's: a telling detail, expressive of a physical contiguity on the verge of dissolution. This observation helps me draw attention to the clarity of the narrative arrangement: whispering the ceremonial blessing, Christ is about to consecrate the bread as his apostles finally recognize his true identity; both utter their bafflement, one opening his arms, the other clutching his hands around the table's corners and leaning forward as if second-checking his fulgurating intuition. From the viewpoint of synchrony, not only is the scene structured coherently, but its tempo is also deliberately protracted. Here Caravaggio avoids angles as much as possible, the figures and objects' outlines being shaped into soft curves. We have seen in Chapter 3 how curvilinear patterns influence the action's pace and mode in accordance with Volpato's artistic theory. To Christ's right and behind him, the canonical figures of the clueless actor and the indifferent walk-on—the innkeeper and maidservant—witness the epiphany in deep silence. The old woman halts as she brings out a plate with the remains of some roast lamb, keeping it aloft just as Salome would hold the plate with Saint John the Baptist's head. Like Saint Anne in the *Palafrenieri Madonna*, she gazes downward, but whereas her counterpart's sight was directed to the snake upon which the infant Christ treads with his mother's assistance, in the Brera painting the maidservant's eyes have lost their target. As a result, the old woman, a true sibling to Giorgione's *La Vecchia* at the Venice Accademia, appears immersed in serious and bitter contemplation, her lips twisted and pursed, her chin moving almost imperceptibly. The quasi-immobility of the innkeeper and maidservant strengthens the impression of a slow-paced tempo coming progressively to a standstill. Were it not for the astonishment of the two apostles, it would be difficult to realize that a miracle is occurring.

But what kind of miracle? Is Caravaggio simply toeing the line of tradition and, like Giovanni Bellini before him, depicting Christ's imminent disappearance as divinity's unproblematic immanence? A viewer who has never seen the Brera painting would be prone to embrace this interpretation, although, when looking at the photographic reproduction, one would wonder why Caravaggio doubled the plot's secondary roles by pairing the innkeeper with a maidservant and placing both on the same side as if to counterbalance the painting's opposite void. The response to this crucial question is double-edged, so to speak. It makes sense that these two figures are not only visual counterweights to the opposite emptiness, but that they in the first place generate that void. Put otherwise, Caravaggio bundled together the innkeeper and the old woman because he meant to widen the void's scope and endow it with a pictorial role and physical relevance. But for what purpose? Herein lies the explanation to my previous insistence on seeing the Brera painting in person.

More than any other work by Caravaggio, the Patrizi *Supper at Emmaus* is a relentlessly shifting surface, what I have previously described as the painting's opalescence. In it, nothing is, feels or looks fixed. Technically speaking, Caravaggio discovered in this work how to unleash light into unabating motion. The tablecloth constitutes the best example of this refined technique: its bright field undulates over, and does not adhere to, the table's surface, while the dark shadows of the food and plates on it, similar to shallow puddles, fail to anchor the tablecloth's fluctuation to the fictive space. The tablecloth's shaded section furnishes further evidence of, and metaphorically epitomizes, the continuous undulation of forms across the pictorial field: Caravaggio here and there deftly heightens its extreme borders with broad yet parsimonious strokes of white pigment emerging into view like the surf of the waves. Even more prodigious, the younger apostle's right hand pulsates against the tablecloth's shade as if disengaging itself from their common half-tone, which almost, but not entirely, corresponds to the painting's priming. Many scholars have already remarked upon this shift in Caravaggio's color technique, commenting on the fewer pigments used by the artist—notice how the young apostle's orange mantle juts out against the painting's earthly hues—and have particularly underscored the new function of the priming from which figures and objects seem to extricate themselves with a *non-finito*, almost crude, effect.

However, the end result of this new technical procedure has not been sufficiently investigated with regard to the Brera painting. Here, the pictorial surface appears as a luminous projection of the dark background, as if forms surface from the pictorial blackness while still remaining tethered to it. Although I am unable to say to what extent this technique is an independent evolution, I suspect that Vasari's view of the *non-finito*, which I shall examine in Chapter 13, relates to Caravaggio's new model of painting. Not that the painted work would eventually appear half-way interrupted; what Caravaggio endeavors to convey through this technical development is the process through which figures and objects come to life in painting. Caravaggio's, however, is not an evocation of the artist's creative process, a kind of perennial commemoration of the artwork's genesis. Rather, the pulsing in and out, and back and forth, of the image is an endless re-enactment of the dialectics between light and dark by dint of which every painting achieves its final configuration. Metaphorically— and this principle may apply to all the paintings Caravaggio would subsequently execute with this technique—the visual instability of forms through the chiaroscuro layout points to the uncovering of the common source of pictorial invention: the nothingness and blankness from which, almost miraculously, the image springs forth.

In the Brera painting, the tension between light and dark, as well as the luminous oscillation of figures and objects against the background's pervasive blackness, assumes a different and more pertinent meaning. Here, structurally, the presence of darkness becomes an acting entity: a pictorial force that takes over, or even annexes, the painting's left side by irreparably unsettling the composition's balance and symmetry. Through this imbalance and blatant asymmetry, through the figures' and objects' implicitness in, and detachment from, the background, the pictorial field turns into a battlefield in which light and dark compete for hegemony. As a result, the painting's fluttering surface mimics the solemn and slow-paced systole and diastole of unfolding time: synchrony and diachroneity here are the matter of light's pulse. At the intersection of the painting's right and left zones, the figure of Christ represents both the suture and the breaking point of this pictorial contention: a provisory barycenter to the chiaroscuro's instability. Tilted leftward, the Savior's strongly lit face both resists and gravitates toward the surrounding darkness, emerging from and verging onto it unceasingly. From the prospect of optics and verisimilitude, the presence of darkness around Christ's bright image is in and of itself baffling; in the London *Supper at Emmaus*, the light streaming from the left, in fact, illuminates the wall directly behind Christ. In the Brera painting, though, light is inexplicably unable to tear apart the thick darkness lingering at the left, which the viewer hence tends to perceive as impenetrable as well as materially concrete. In his last *Supper at Emmaus*, Caravaggio therefore not only visualizes Christ's glowing epiphany, but also animates the vehicle of his divine disappearance: the pitch-black darkness that will soon engulf him.

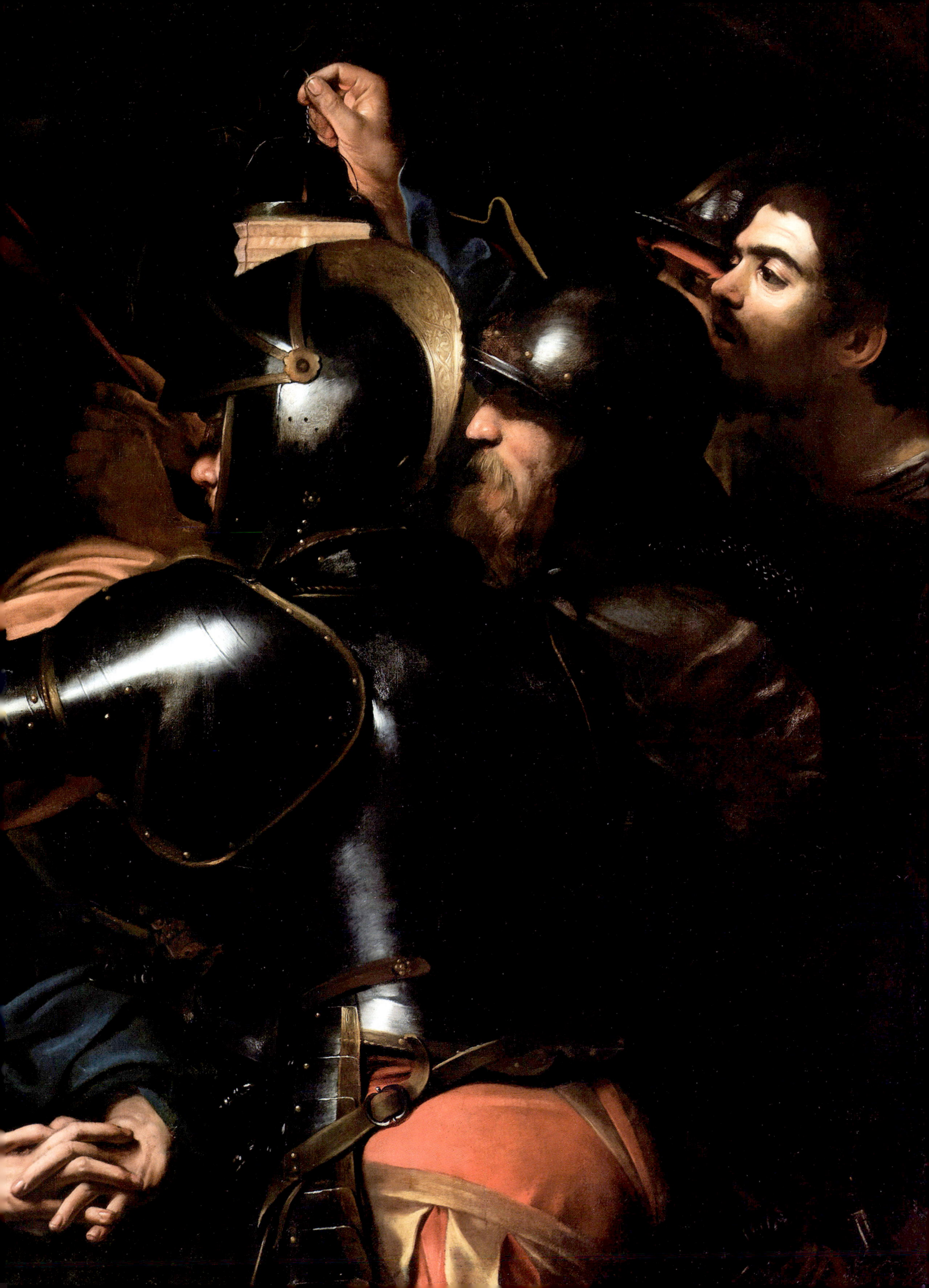

PART FOUR

"With the Mind's Eye": Self-Representation and Self-Referentiality in Caravaggio's Pictorial Narratives

The Shaman Painter or The Metaphysics of Pictorial Invention

In my opinion, it has not been stressed enough that even as the name of Caravaggio ascended to fame and glory in Rome at the beginning of the 1600s, the most current interpretation of artistic creation assimilated the painter's intellect to the light of divine generation, qualifying the artist's craftsmanship and work, especially in the domain of the *istoria* and religious art, as the empirical ability and final embodiment of a transcendental "power"—I use this term in its Aristotelian and Thomistic sense. Unanimously, late sixteenth- and early seventeenth-century artists designated this intellectual and spiritual power as *disegno*, that is, design. By translating *disegno* as design, I am of course oversimplifying; the Italian term also came to signify drawing, both the manual practice and the product thereof. However, in this introduction to Part Four I will grapple largely with *disegno* as design insofar as I am concerned with establishing the intrinsic quality, conceptual extension, finality, and meaning of the faculty through which painters visualize their nascent artworks. In my view, this aptitude constituted the cornerstone of artistic identity during Caravaggio's time. In other words, what distinguishes a painter, and for that matter an excellent one, from an artisan, is the power or principle of *disegno* inherent in his persona; *disegno* drives his mind to visualize concepts while prompting his hand to try out, reproduce, and hone the multiple, at times blurry offspring of these visualizations; it is only then that the artist can turn the flurry of these ideas into felicitously interlocked narratives.

As a general premise, I am interested in *disegno* only indirectly, insofar as this concept, and the idea of artistic identity with which it is inextricably bound up, will help to shed light on the role and significance of a portrait and two self-portraits present in three paintings by Caravaggio: *The Entombment*, *The Taking of Christ*, and the *Ecce Homo*. As I will show in the following chapters, the figure of Nicodemus in the first painting conjures up the effigy of Michelangelo—the celebrated painter, sculptor, and architect whose first name was the same as Caravaggio's—whereas that of Pilate in the third picture is a parodic disguise of Caravaggio himself, a caricatural self-portrait. As for *The Taking of Christ*, it is well known that the soldier carrying the lantern to the right bears Caravaggio's likeness. It goes without saying that the presence, evocation, and parody of the painter himself or his homonymous predecessor do not amount to authorial signatures or, in the case of Michelangelo, referential winks; the very fact that these portrayals participate in the pictorial action with well-defined, and mostly primary roles suggests, or even sparks the reasonable doubt, that they serve to stage, probe, and reassess the crucial relation of the artist to his artwork. These self-representations—in a sense, the evocation of Michelangelo may also belong to this category—redefine the function of the artist and put to the test his faculty of visualization and its efficiency in ways that dislodge, contemporary notions of invention and

297

◀ Plate XIII: Michelangelo Merisi da Caravaggio, *The Taking of Christ*, National Gallery of Ireland, Dublin, oil on canvas, 133.5 x 169.5 cm., detail.

artistic identity. For the sake of clarity I now need to introduce the complex ramifications of *disegno* as an aesthetic notion.

The idea that the artwork's genesis depends on a transcendental faculty had already gained momentum and authority in late sixteenth-century Rome, that is, at the time Caravaggio first arrived in the city. Although Michelangelo had already posited in many of his sonnets that the artist's creativity paralleled God's generative power, art theorists had not embraced the validity of this theory wholesale. Even Giorgio Vasari,[1] for whom Michelangelo embodied the very idea of perfection in art, felt compelled to dilute and remold the notion of *disegno* as construed by the great master, as can be seen from the following passage from Vasari's 1568 *Vite*:

> Because design, which is the father of our three arts—architecture, sculpture and painting—proceeds from the intellect and extracts from many things a universal judgment similar to a form or an idea of all the things of Nature, which is very particular in its measures, the intellect therefore knows the proportion that the whole has with the parts, and the parts have with one another and with the whole, [and this] not only in the bodies of men and animals, but also in those of plants and in buildings, sculptures, and paintings. And because a certain concept or judgment springs from this knowledge, as the mind forms that which is called design once it has been rendered through [man's] hands, it can be concluded that design is nothing but the outward rendition and clarification of the concept in our mind or of what others have figured in their minds and conceived as an idea. The Greek adage "knowing a lion from its claw" has its origin herein, since from the dimension and form of a lion's claw that was sculpted in stone, a good artist with the help of his intellect surmised [the dimension and form of] the animal's parts and its entire body, as if it had been before his eyes.[2]

What does Vasari mean by declaring that design is a "universal judgment," a "form" or "idea" of all the things engendered by Nature? If I understand this passage correctly—its meaning is not completely clear—then design is not a power or aptitude, but a principle or canon of proportions in light of which artists sift out whatever turns out to be aberrant as Nature's defect by decoding natural things and rendering them as ideal prototypes. In other words, design is an internal, habit-based, and hence intuition-driven, compass that enables artists to see natural things not as they are, but as they should be, in accordance with symmetry and proportion. To be sure, the notion of design in Vasari's terminology partakes of aesthetics: it is a parameter of beauty. However, inasmuch as proportion is an intrinsic quality of Nature's prototypes—that is, the eternal matrices through which transcendental ideas impregnate and configure the matter of all existing things—it also encompasses a metaphysical value. Although Vasari does not seem to draw the consequences of his assumptions, the artist's intellect is able not only to visualize Nature in its pristine, conceptual form, but also to materialize perennial canons of proportionality through lines and contours. From this point of view, design is not an epistemological tool—the knowledge to which Vasari refers is

1 For *disegno* and Vasari's interpretation of the concept, see Kemp 1974; Barzman 1991; Roggenkamp 1996; Pozzi and Mattioda 2006; and Dempsey 2009.

2 Vasari, 1:111: "Perché il disegno, padre delle tre arti nostre architettura, scultura e pittura, procedendo dall'intelletto cava di molte cose un giudizio universale simile a una forma overo idea di tutte le cose della natura, la quale è singolarissima nelle sue misure, di qui è che non solo nei corpi umani e degl'animali, ma nelle piante ancora e nelle fabriche e sculture e pitture, cognosce la proporzione che ha il tutto con le parti e che hanno le parti fra loro e col tutto insieme; e perché da questa cognizione nasce un certo concetto e giudizio, che si forma nella mente quella tal cosa che poi espressa con le mani si chiama disegno, si può conchiudere che esso disegno altro non sia che una apparente espressione e dichiarazione del concetto che si ha nell'animo, e di quello che altri si è nella mente imaginato e fabricato nell'idea. E da questo per avventura nacque il proverbio de' greci *Dell'ugna un leone*, quando quel valente uomo, vedendo sculpita in un masso l'ugna sola d'un leone, comprese con l'intelletto da quella misura e forma le parti di tutto l'animale e dopo il tutto insieme, come se l'avesse avuto presente e dinanzi agl'occhi."

by no means an explanation of Nature and her foundations—but the revelatory comprehension of Nature's metaphysical structure as reflected in the practice of drawing. To develop Vasari's simile of the lion's claw, I would infer that the Greek artist he mentions could reconstruct the sculpted animal's forms and dimensions exactly, but on one condition: if they truly accorded with an artistic and metaphysical canon. More important, design allows artists to teleport into the realm of proportion: their seeing is a first-hand witness of Nature's occult principles.

At this point, I ought to make a distinction between Vasari's and Michelangelo's interpretation of design. In Michelangelo's view, the concept that manifests itself through *disegno* is the artwork's visualization as it looms in the artist's mind; to a certain extent, it includes the work's subject matter in its broader sense. Compared to Michelangelo's, Vasari's design limits itself to operating as a principle of proportion, although the ambiguous tenor of Vasari's definition, especially at the end, seems to imply that design also incorporates the visualization of the artwork to come. I would interpret Vasari's haziness in this regard as a sign of his hesitancy in accepting Michelangelo's wider-ranging interpretation of concept and design. On the other hand, it is apparent to me that Vasari's main goal in the previous passage is rather that of ennobling the practice of drawing by describing it as the technical transcoding of Nature's metaphysical order. In any case, Vasari's interpretation of design, thoughtfully revised and considerably extended, would prevail in Caravaggio's time. This point is of paramount importance; as is well known, design is the mainspring of an artistic paradigm characteristic of Florence's pictorial tradition.

Turning to Venice, and more specifically to Paolo Pino's 1548 *Dialogo di pittura*, it becomes clear that design does not at all signify what Vasari would like it to signify. According to Pino's fuzzy and overstretched definition, design is an aptitude of sorts: it is innate, yet subject to improvement; it instructs artists how to circumscribe, illuminate, and shade figures and objects, and thus results in sketches preliminary to the final work; it is the customary practice of configuring the image and its components appropriately, and indicates furthermore how to adapt the form to the content with pertinence and judgment.[3] I do not need to emphasize the fact that, whatever design means to Pino, it is certainly not an intellectual act and procedure of transfiguring natural forms according to transcendental patterns of proportionality. Should I select an equivalent of Vasari's *disegno* in Pino's treatise, I would opt for invention in default of a better solution. Pino elucidates this term in a twofold sense: it is either the ability to invent the subject of a poem—in this case, an allegoric or mythological plot—or an *istoria*, or the capacity to comprehend, arrange, and articulate "things said by others, by adjusting the figures' attitudes to the subject appropriately, so that all of them [the figures] serve to expose the [painting's] finality."[4]

Arguably, invention involves the intellect's aptitude to visualize pictorial concepts, but, as

3 Pino, 107-8: "Quanto alla prima parte detta disegno, io voglio anco dividerla in quattro parti: la prima diremo giudicio, la seconda circunscrizzione, la terza pratica, l'ultima retta composizione. Circa alla prima detta da me giudicio, in questa parte ci conviene aver la natura e i fatti propizi, e nascere con tal disposizione come i poeti; altro non conosco come tal giudicio si possa imparare; è ben vero ch'isercitandolo nell'arte egli diviene più perfetto, ma avendo il giudicio voi imparerete la circonscrizzione, il ch'intendo sia il profilare, contornare le figure e darle chiari e scuri a tutte le cose, il qual modo voi l'addimandate schizzo. La terzia è la pratica del saper accomodar il vivo e buon lume; conoscere il bello, perché molte cose propie sono belle in sé che fatte in pittura paiono isgraziate e goffe; aver buona maniera nel disegnare; saper l'invenzioni, come in carte tinte, con lapis nero e biaca, toccar d'acquaticie, trattegiar di penna; ma lo chiaro e scuro è il più presto e più util modo, e il migliore perché si può ben unire il tutto e dar più mezze tinte e più chiare. L'ultima poi è detta composizione: in questa s'include tutte l'altre,

cioè il giudicio, la circonscrizzione e la pratica. Imperò che questa retta composizione consiste nel formar integramente le superficie, le quali sono parte de' membri come parte del corpo, il corpo poi come integrità dell'opera; questa dà la giusta porzione al tutto; imita ben il proprio, come un vecchio, un giovene, un fanciullo, una femina, un cavallo e l'altre diverse cose sì ch'uno non assomiglia all'altro; contrafà ben gli scurci, parte più nobile nell'arte nostra; figne ben li drappi senza confusione di pieghe, sempre accenando il nudo sotto; dà gran rilievo al tutto, e quest'è lo spirto della pittura."

4 Ibidem, 108: "Or alla seconda parte, già detta invenzione, questa s'istende nel trovar poesie e istorie da sé, virtù usata da pochi delli moderni, ed è cosa appresso di me molto ingegnosa e lodabile. (…) È anco invenzione il ben distinguere, ordinare e compartire le cose dette dagli altri, accommodando bene li soggetti agli atti delle figure, e che tutte attendano alla dechiarazione del fine (…)."

defined by Pino, this visualization does not seem to rely on an interior experience ushering in the realm of ideas. One might object that, culturally speaking, the transcendental character of invention was so solidly engrained in Renaissance art theory, especially in the light of its neo-platonic foundations, that Pino ought not to highlight these implications. And indeed, in another passage of his treatise Pino clearly outlines the function of man's intellect in the artwork's genesis.[5]

Nonetheless, what particularly matters here is that in defining invention and design, Pino did not care to bring up the metaphysical source of the former, and even less of the latter. Albeit mind- or intellect-rooted, invention and design are above all articulations of an artistic practice: a high-standard and "liberal" craftsmanship. Following in Vasari's footsteps, though in clearer and more distinct terms, Giovan Paolo Lomazzo places design at the core of any artistic production. In his 1590 *Idea del tempio della pittura*, Lomazzo explains:

> But first we need to know that the foundation of everything—that is, of [art's] principal parts and its genres—upon which everything rests as if upon the firmest basis, and from which all beauty derives, is what [ancient] Greeks call eurythmy, and we call design.[6]

Lomazzo, unlike Vasari, specifies the aesthetic nature of design: it is a principle of beauty and proportion, though it does not give rise to a single canon, but to a plurality of aesthetic models in conformity with what Lomazzo classifies as pictorial "genres" or "manners." This is not the place to elucidate these aspects of Lomazzo's thought, beyond saying that he singles out several canonical styles originating in the work of Italian Renaissance masters, among them Michelangelo, Raphael, and Titian, but also Gaudenzio Ferrari. A few years before publishing his *Idea*, Lomazzo was even more specific in defining the essence and function of *disegno*. I quote here some of the passages he devoted to this notion in his 1584 *Trattato della pittura*:

> [The most famous and celebrated masters of this art] first and foremost mentally conceived the form of whatever thing they set about to make and, before they resolved to start drawing, visualized everything most distinctly in their imagination. Thus, by imitating these masters, after reading and pondering the *istoria* or the *capriccio*, one must fix it in one's mind as clearly and distinctly as if one truly saw it with one's own eyes; then, one will continue to consider in one's intellect the place where one wants to represent the read or imagined event, which by any means will not unsettle viewers. I have to point out that the work's primary perfection rests herein, because a perfect principle cannot subsist without the knowledge of its means and goal. He who is acquainted with [the procedure of] mentally composing must avoid being among the foolish who set out to copy or, as is commonly said, animate the forms imagined by someone else. However, even if they [the foolish painters] imagine these forms, since they do not compose them mentally, they will express them badly, as if they were afflicted by a curse that confounds, and drains the vigor from, their minds.[7]

---

5 Ibidem, 99: "Furono alcune più nobil arti chiamate dagli antichi liberali, come propie dell'intelletto e agli uomini liberi, e fu la pittura tra quelle celebrata e approbata da tutti e filosofi, come referisce Laerzio, Diogene e Demetrio, e che cusì sia la ragione è ch'uno pittore non può nell'arte nostra produrre effetto alcuno della sua imaginativa, se prima quella così imaginata non vien da gli altri sensi intrinseci ridotta al cospetto dell'idea con quella integrità ch'ella s'ha da produrre, tal che l'intelletto l'intende perfettamente in se stesso, senza mecare fuori del suo proprio ch'è l'intendere, similmente come intese l'altre arti liberali come dialettica, grammatica,

retorica e l'altre, onde noi pittori siamo intelligenti nell'arte nostra teoricamente senza l'operare."

6 Lomazzo, 1:281: "Ma prima abbiamo da sapere che il fondamento di tutto, cioè delle parti principali e de i suoi generi, sopra il quale ogni cosa come sopra saldissima base si riposa ed onde deriva tutta la bellezza, è quello che i greci chiamano euritmia, e noi nominiamo disegno."

7 Ibidem, 2:415-6: "[I più famosi e celebrati in quest'arte] innanzi a tutte le cose solevano concipere nella sua idea la forma di qualunque cosa si proponevano di fare e, prima

300

I will comment on Lomazzo's interpretation of originality and imitation in the introduction to Part Five. For now, I shall demonstrate that Lomazzo's take on artistic creation as a process of mental composing requires that painters cut themselves off from the external world entirely, by seeing only through their inner eyes:

> I shall always commend him who, before he sets out to work, endeavors to see in his mind everything that he wants to make. In fact, judgment is less affected by the mental composition, which is not to be seen, than by the practical composition, which is to be seen, and which interrupts the comprehension due to the eyes through which one sees. It is certain that those who imagine subtle things tend to believe that not seeing or hearing is greatly helpful, for they are not disturbed by the nuisance that seeing objects and hearing sounds engender. For this reason, as I have said from the outset, all the talented painters have seen to it that they first form in their minds all the things they mean to represent. To make this task easier, it is necessary to avoid noise, and especially any occasion for seeing, because nothing more than objects distracts men and precludes one from staying focused. We thus see that those whose pen and stylus storm over the paper amidst [men's] noises and hubbub are eventually unable to pin down the invention of whatever they intend to represent. Nor can they set into motion, as is ordinarily said, the figures they imagine. In this regard, one reads that Homer, Democritus, and Plato deliberately deprived themselves of their sight in order to better and more subtly investigate the nature of what they had conceived and imagined in their minds.[8]

I quote this passage in its entirety despite its occasional vagueness, because it expounds the dialectics between inward and outward seeing in the most complex manner. First of all, Lomazzo distinguishes between a mental and a practical procedure of composing. As for the former, its function and meaning are crystal clear. But how is one to construe the notion of practical composition? There is no obvious explanation of this procedure in the passage. Neither does Lomazzo offer any valuable insight in this respect elsewhere. In which ways can "seeing objects" disrupt the faculty of composing pictorially? And what kinds of objects does he bear in mind? Any object, or only those related to the ongoing composition? Probably both. Nonetheless, my hunch is that Lomazzo alludes to the Venetian method of composing, that is, working directly on the canvas without preliminary drawings with the assistance—at least, occasionally—of

che si ponessero a voler disegnare, tutta benissimo vederla con l'imaginazione. Però ad imitazion di questi, letto prima o pensato che si ha l'istoria o capriccio di quello che si vuol dipingere, conviene averla nella mente così formata e distinta come s'ella si vedesse in fatto con gl'occhi; e poi con l'ingegno andar considerando lo spazio dove la cosa letta, overo imaginata, si vuol rappresentare, e riuscirà in atto senza offensione alcuna de i riguardanti. E si ha da avvertire che quivi consiste la principal perfezion dell'opera. Però che 'l perfetto principio non può stare senza la cognizione del suo mezzo e fine. Questa composizione nell'idea chiunque averà famigliare, sappia certo che non sarà nel numero de gl'imprudenti che vogliono fare o, come si dice, dar moto alle forme imaginate d'altri; le quali s'ancora da loro fossero imaginate, ma non composte, nell'idea, tuttavia malamente potrebbero esprimere, sì come ammorbati da quella maledizione che confonde e leva le forze allo spirito."

8   Ibidem, 2:416-7: "Però loderò sempre colui il quale, prima che si accinga all'opera, cerca prima di veder nell'idea tutto quello che vuol fare. Imperò che manco offende il giudizio la composizione della mente che non si vede di quello che fa la composizione della pratica che si vede, la quale interrompe la cognizione per gl'occhi onde si vede. Ed è certo che a coloro che sottili cose imaginano, pare che 'l non vedere e sentire gl'apporti aiuto, non sentendosi offendere da gl'incommodi che gl'occhi per gl'oggetti e l'orecchie per li suoni apportano. Quindi tutti i valenti pittori, come dissi da principio, hanno avuto questo, di formar prima tutte le cose che volevano fare nella loro idea; per cui più facilmente fare è necessario ad ogni modo fuggir gli strepiti, e massime l'occasioni di vedere; perché non vi è cosa che più tragga l'uomo fuor di proposito e non lo lasci stare in sé raccolto de gl'oggetti. Onde vediamo che quelli che tra romori e strepiti stanno con lo stile e con la pena tempestando sopra le carte, all'ultimo non possono trovare invenzione d'alcuna cosa che vogliono fare, né manco dar moto, come si dice, alle figure imaginate. Leggesi a questo proposito che Omero, Democrito e Platone da se stessi si privarono della luce de gl'occhi per meglio e più sottilmente investigare la natura di quello che nella sua mente concetto ed imaginato s'avevano."

live models.[9] Of course, Lomazzo's criticism of painters who work in the chaos of a studio, a house, a tavern, or even a street, extends well beyond the Venetian "path of composing," and undoubtedly aims to endorse the myth and ideology of the painter-poet, the painter-orator, and the painter-philosopher (the allusions to Homer, Democritus, and Plato confirm this assumption). Yet Lomazzo's statement that objects surrounding artists impede the comprehension of the mind's pictorial visions and stifle inspiration, makes sense within the context of a straightforward practice of composing as that generally associated with Venetian masters. Another passage, though somewhat confused, points in this direction:

> And finally I conclude, heeding natural judgment, that any person, however a great and diligent colorist he might be, if bereft of invention or lifting figures whole from someone else's papers or works, must not be called a painter, but an imitator, or even a destructor of art, for in his productions he satisfies himself with somebody else's inventions, abhorring the painful study that whoever aspires to a certain degree of excellence must apply to this art.[10]

In reading this passage, I have always been, and am still, struck by a few inconsistencies. First of all, it is a partial mystery to me why Lomazzo in the first place mentions the virtuosity of colorists in connection with painters whom one might connote as plagiarists of ideas or mediocre designers in today's terminology. To be sure, because invention is strictly correlated with design and drawing, the notion of color might bubble to the surface unexpectedly—as indeed it does here—in opposition to *disegno*. That said, the censure of great colorists as opposed to original inventors remains, if not gratuitous, at least impertinent. Secondly, what exactly does Lomazzo mean by "painful study"? It would seem obvious that he refers to the practice and training of composing well, which in Lomazzo's view incorporates the mastering of many tedious techniques, such as perspective, foreshortening, arithmetic, and so forth. But how does this course of studies pertain specifically to mental composing? To put it in a different way, what is Lomazzo omitting or dissimulating in this passage? Underneath Lomazzo's indeterminateness, one may detect the terms of Vasari's polemic against Venetian painters. In his *Vite*, Vasari unequivocally criticizes the practice of painting set up by Giorgione and elaborated upon by Titian. Although Giorgione's work, argues Vasari, is endowed with softness and relief, in a "*bella maniera*" [beautiful style], it imitates life and Nature to the extreme without relying on invention and design:

> He [Giorgione] did not realize that he who wants to set up his compositions and adjust his inventions effectively must first put them down on paper in diverse ways to

---

9   In the so-called Düsseldorf notebook, Pietro Testa asserts that it is not enough for the artist to paint from nature by "having the objects" in front of himself in order to achieve perfection. On the contrary, this form of rudimentary imitation, though necessary in the beginning, is condemned and ridiculed. According to Testa, painting is essentially a work of the intellect, and his point of view undoubtedly corresponds to that of Lomazzo. See Testa, 209: "Io dico che chi sa, cioè chi à le prime notitie, hopera sensa oggetti e tutto nel suo genere farà ottimamente. (…) E chi non ha queste ragioni, dico non poter hoperar bene né meno col' aver l'ogetti avanti li ochi." The "folly" of working with "the eyes" rather than with "the mind" is expressed by Testa in an amusing anecdote: "E io ho visto con risso e compassione che a un dio Padre farli il g[i]ubbone allac[i]ato con stringa, messo per via di puntelli a giacere e dal patimento tremare con rui[na] della macchina del vecchio e della povera dipintura." By evoking the collapse of the old man representing God the Father with his vest strung up so as to remain suspended and enable the painter

to copy him on the canvas, Testa allows us to glimpse an artistic practice for which there is only scarce evidence. That this practice was more widely diffused than we can imagine is confirmed by Testa, 227: "Per fare uno che corra, l'apuntellano in aria una gamba, se uno che grida l'aprono con li stecchi la boccha e simile." Of course, this last passage also involves a great deal of parody.

10   Ibidem, 2:418: "E finalmente io concludo, seguendo il giudicio naturale, che niun, per gran coloritor che sia e diligente, ma senza invenzione e che levi di peso le figure dalle carte ed opre altrui, non si deve chiamar pittore, ma imitator, anci distruttor dell'arte, per appagarsi solamente nelle fatiche sue delle invenzioni de gl'altri ed aborrire il faticoso studio che necessariamente convien porre in quest'arte a chiunque aspira a qualche grado d'eccellenza, come ho inculcato più e più volte in molti luoghi di questi libri per esser cosa importantissima."

see how the whole thing comes along. In fact, an idea cannot perfectly visualize and imagine its own inventions unless it opens and shows the concept to the corporal eyes so that they can assist the idea in making the right judgment. Without this [procedure], one must toil away to understand the nude well, which is not, and cannot be, done without having recourse to paper, and it is a great inconvenience [for a painter] to keep people, whether naked or dressed, in front of him while applying the colors.[11]

Through the practice of drawing, artists instead

fill their minds with beautiful concepts and learn how to represent from memory all the things of Nature without keeping them always in front of their eyes, or being forced to conceal the trouble of not mastering drawing under the beauty of colors, as many Venetian painters had done for many years, such as Giorgione, Palma, Pordenone, and others who did not see Rome or any other work of utter perfection.[12]

Bearing in mind Vasari's criticism of Venetian painting, and Lomazzo's description of practical composition and its effects on artists, it will become evident that the objects that hamper the process of mental visualization by interfering with the corporal eyes might well be those figures and things that artists must keep "before their eyes" while painting, unless they are able to summon up by heart a repertory of forms previously gleaned through the practice of drawing. Lomazzo's unwillingness or reluctance to unveil his thought plainly, as if afraid of laying himself bare to criticism, is noteworthy. There is no doubt in my mind that the indeterminacy of Lomazzo's passage betrays a kind of self-repression or self-censure. The only reason I can envision for this is Lomazzo's diplomacy and attention to the sensitivity of his colleagues, those painters in Milan to whom his treatise was originally addressed in 1584. An excessively harsh condemnation of the Venetian practical composition might have touched a raw nerve in artists who, although they shared Lomazzo's convictions, were indebted to the tradition of painting in Venice, such as, for instance, Simone Peterzano, a disciple of Titian and himself the master of Caravaggio. This is one of the main points toward which I have been headed from the beginning.

Even if not much is known of Peterzano's work,[13] and nothing has emerged about his theoretical biases in the matter of art, it can be fairly assumed that he recognized the importance of drawing and assiduously strove to demonstrate that he was steeped in its knowledge. His numerous designs certainly corroborate the point. In his paintings, beside the unmistakable imprint of the Venetian tradition—not only through Titian, but also Veronese and Tintoretto—one can easily discern the efforts he made to show off the correctness of his lines and contours: indisputable evidence that Peterzano, along with many other painters of his generation, was inching his way toward a reformed art by resorting to an eclectic model of painting—one in which Florence and Venice interact with, and blend into, one another. As an apprentice of Peterzano in Milan since 1584, the same year in which Lomazzo's treatise was published, the young Caravaggio could not have ignored how

11   Vasari, 6:155: "Ma non s'accorgeva ch'egli è necessario a chi vuol bene disporre i componimenti ed accommodare l'invenzioni ch'e' fa bisogno prima in più modi diferenti porle in carta, per vedere come il tutto torna insieme. Con ciò sia che l'idea non può vedere né imaginare perfettamente in se stessa l'invenzioni, se non apre e non mostra il suo concetto agl'occhi corporali che l'aiutino a farne buon giudizio; senzaché pur bisogna fare grande studio sopra gl'ignudi a volergli intendere bene: il che non vien fatto, né si può, senza mettere in carta; ed il tenere, sempre che altri colorisce, persone ignude innanzi overo vestite, è non piccola servitù."

12   Ibidem, 6:155-156: "per non dir nulla che, disegnando in carta, si viene a empiere la mente di bei concetti e s'impara a fare a mente tutte le cose della natura, senza avere a tenerle sempre innanzi, o ad avere a nascondere sotto la vaghezza de' colori lo stento del non sapere disegnare, nella maniera che fecero molti anni i pittori viniziani, Giorgione, il Palma, il Pordenone ed altri che non videro Roma né altre opere di tutta perfezione."

13   I give extensive bibliography on Peterzano in Chapter 1.

much invention and design both practically and theoretically buttressed the ideal of a renewed and perfected painting. He certainly knew, because he heard their opinions and learned their methods, that for painters in Milan pictorial composition consisted of a mental and abstract process through which the image came out purified, as it were. In sum, Caravaggio must have been taught that, to become an accomplished painter, he needed to see with his mind's eye, thereby distrusting whatever allure the living image might have exerted upon him. Needless to say, years later, when in Rome, he would forge his own trademark around the very practice that Lomazzo, if he did not despise, assuredly disqualified: the practice of seeing with his own, corporal eyes, directly in front of him, what he planned to depict. I have already claimed that Federico Zuccari and Giovan Pietro Bellori's interpretation of Caravaggio's early paintings as the product of Giorgione's ascendancy most likely hark back to Caravaggio himself. Even if this assumption were not true, it is a fact that Caravaggio, through his own practice of painting, favored practical composing over mental. Or at least, he pretended to do so. As a corollary, it can be assumed that Caravaggio also disapproved of the entire transcendental apparatus that Michelangelo and Lomazzo—but also Zuccari, as I shall explain shortly—built around the concept of invention and artistic creation. Or perhaps, he turned it to his own advantage. As usual, Caravaggio has a knack for making complex even the simplest issues in the simplest way.

Before I proceed further, it is important to underscore that the refusal or parody of a metaphysical paradigm of artistic creation resonated with even more tremendous implications in Caravaggio's Rome than it did in Milan. The divine origin of *disegno* had in the meantime metamorphosed into a touchstone of Catholic orthodoxy; design was the privilege and token of the Christian painter. Pivotal in this connection was Federico Zuccari and the artistic ideology that he sought to impress upon the newly founded Accademia di San Luca in Rome. On 17 January 1594, Zuccari as the *"principe"* or chief of the Academy entertained its members, mostly artists, with a lofty discourse on *disegno*. To expound the importance of this artistic concept, Zuccari did not balk at resorting to theology:

> We know that God is not only the first cause of all the things in this world, for he created them all from nothing and through his simple willpower, but he is also the prime mover through which they operate; in particular, as the supreme good, wisdom, and power, he is the prime mover of man's understanding and operations. However, we have to be acutely aware that, because he operates in all created things through secondary causes in view of marshaling and ruling them all more smoothly, it is necessary that all these things owe their exclusive and interior principles of motion— that is, the proximate causes of their operations—such as the [angelic] motors in heaven, the qualities in the elements, the souls in living creatures, and so on. Here is a clearer example: just as the sun, which is the prime star and vice-regent of the first cause, in the elementary world enlightens, moves, and enlivens the generable and corruptible things of Nature—otherwise they would be unable to create and produce stones, plants, flowers, animals, and so on, without the sun's assistance and virtue—so must we infer that design in ourselves is the prime and proximate internal principle and formal mover of our understandings and operations. Design indeed first moves our intellect, and after the intellect, our will, which in turn [prompts] our practical faculties so that we can operate outside. Thus, [internal] design is another sun in man's soul and intellect, thereby moving, enlivening, and enlightening all our operations, and it is as indispensable to us as the sun is to the world.[14]

14 Alberti and Zuccari, 17-8: "Sappiamo che Iddio non solo è la prima causa di tutte le cose di questo mondo, avendole tutte di niente e con il semplice suo volere create, ma anco che è primo motore di quelle accioché oprino, ed in particolare motore delle nostre umane cognizioni ed operazioni, come sommo bene, somma sapienza e somma potenza; tuttavia

As he rushes to boast immediately afterward, Zuccari's definition of design is indeed unprecedented. Never before has an art theorist or an artist, not even Michelangelo, dreamed of transforming *disegno* into a human hypostasis of God's intellect and essence. There is no ambiguity in Zuccari's statement. On the contrary, his terse and lapidary prose makes plain the new nature and function bestowed upon design:

> As for its main meaning, we will say that design is essentially the object and purview of our intelligence; in design, as if in the most lucid mirror, the intellect clearly and neatly sees the things represented in itself under the intelligible forms with which it is equipped. Or, reasoning through metaphor and similitude, we will define design as the intellect's general light, the nurture and life of our operations. (…) However, one must know that design is not of one, but two kinds: intellective and practical. Just as there are two intellects in us, of which the one called speculative properly and solely serves to comprehend the universals, and the other, named practical, ultimately and specifically aims at operating, being—so to speak—the principle of our operations, so too is it necessary that two kinds of design enlighten our intellects: namely, the one that constitutes the object and purview of our cognitive intellect, which represents the things under the form of universals to the intellect; and the other that is the object and purview of the practical intellect, which represents the things in particular and in their singularity to the intellect. In this discourse, I use the term of intellective and practical design, and not that of concept, like the metaphysicians, or of Verb, like the theologians, because I reason as a painter and for the sake of painters, sculptors, and architects, who must work with the intellective and practical design by which the intellect is regulated.[15]

In Chapter 10 I shall examine Zuccari's metaphysics of artistic creation in detail. For the time being, I merely point out that despite Zuccari's intricate casuistry of the ways in which it acts, design is evidently the faculty through which painters, in visualizing scripture, manage to represent the sacred as if they could see it before their eyes. As Giovan Battista Armenini put it in his 1586 *De' veri precetti della pittura*:

abbiamo molto bene ad avertire ch'oprando lui in tutte le cose create con li mezi delle seconde cause acciochè con maggior suavità disponga e governi il tutto, è necessario ch'in queste cose tutte siano i propri ed interni principi moventi, cause prossime delle loro operazioni, come i motori ne i cieli, le qualità ne gl'elementi, l'anime ne i viventi, e cose simili. O con più chiaro essempio, come il sole in questo mondo, poiché essendo egli il primo pianeta e viceregente della prima causa, qua giù nelle cose elementari è quello ch'alluma, move e vivifica tutte le cose generabili e corruttibili della natura prodotte, ove ch'elle sarebbero impotenti a produrre e generare pietre, piante, fiori ed animali, e cose simili, senza l'aiuto e virtù del sole; così vogliamo noi inferire ch'il disegno entro di noi è il primo e prossimo interno principio, formale motore delle nostre istesse cognizioni ed operazioni, conciosia che movendo questo prima l'intelletto nostro, e dopo l'intelletto la volontà, ed in oltre questa le virtù nostre essecutive, noi operiamo al di fuori. Sì che questo disegno è quasi un altro sole nell'anima e nell'intelletto umano che move, vivifica ed alluma tutte le nostre operazioni, e necessario in noi come il sole nel mondo."

15 Ibidem, 18-9: "Diciamo che il disegno quanto al suo principale significato altro non è in sostanza che un oggetto ed insieme un termine della nostra intelligenza, in cui come in lucidissimo specchio l'intelletto chiaramente ed espressamente vede le cose rapresentate in lui per le forme intelligibili ornanti l'istesso intelletto, o ragionando in metafora e similitudine, lo difiniremo luce generale dell'intelletto ed alimento e vita dell'operazioni nostre, e questo per diffinirlo più chiaramente e più sensibilmente ancora, acciochè possa essere da tutti voi signori inteso. Si deve però sapere che non d'una, ma di due sorti è il disegno, cioè intellettivo e prattico, perché sì come sono duoi intelletti in noi, uno chiamato speculativo, il cui fine proprio è l'intendere solamente in universale, e l'altro adimandato intelletto pratico, il cui termine proprio ed ultimo è l'operare, o per dir meglio esser principio dell'operazioni nostre, è necessario che anco siano due i disegni alluminanti gl'intelletti nostri, cioè uno ch'è oggetto e termine dell'intelletto cognoscitivo, e questo rappresenta all'intelletto le cose universalmente intese, e l'altro che è oggetto e termine dell'intelletto pratico, e questo rappresenta all'intelletto le cose in particolare ed in singolare. E di qui nasce ch'io usi in questo discorso questa voce di disegno intellettivo e pratico, e non di concetto, come i metafisici, o di Verbo, come i teologi, perché ragiono come pittore, ed a' pittori, scultori ed architettori a' quali conviene operare con questo disegno intellettivo e pratico."

> A painter is whoever, thanks to a certain and marvelous judgment and artistry, is able to accomplish the things he has previously conceived in his mind and intellect, thereby representing them (…) through lines and color so true to life [*così al vivo*] that sight remains deceived.[16]

In the case of a religious picture, a fundamental quality adheres to the mental image of divinity as visualized by artists: as design bursts into view and pans out according to the standard procedure espoused by Counter-Reformation art theorists, it necessarily reveals the truth of the *istoria* to be represented: in the end, the painting becomes also true to its subject. In my view, Zuccari's main goal in upgrading design as the analog of the theological Verb or the metaphysical concept is, among others, to validate and sacralize the *istoria*. What the painter sees in his mind and filters through the laborious practice of drawing turns out to be the visual manifestation of a religious truth. I have tackled the question of pictorial truth at length in the introduction to Part Three, but I will add a few observations with regard to the metaphysics of the sacred *istoria* as interpreted by Zuccari.

Because design is the noble surrogate of God's creative and speculative faculty, the act of visualizing the divine and its deeds, albeit compromised by man's finitude, logically unfolds as a process of anamnesis or metaphysical reminiscence. As if "in the most lucid mirror," artists can contemplate, divinely enlightened in the intellect, the indistinct forms of Christian truth. Step by step, drawing after drawing, in accordance with Zuccari's theory, the vision as first sketched out by the intellective design eventually acquires the neatness of a mirror-like image, or should, if the artist follows the protocols necessary to guarantee the excellence of his *istoria*. As Armenini points out, even the most finely wrought artwork will be doomed to censure if its author does not mull over the subject of the sacred episode with due profundity:

> It is appropriate that I unveil some defects that are to be seen in many [painters], which must be greatly avoided as they stray far from the true principles of good composing. Indeed, whether they do not know the [right] way or do not mind to adequately take in and comprehend the subject matter, they compose their narratives very differently from the truth of good scripture, and therefore knowledgeable people blame them with great reason. [17]

Of course, the contrary is equally true; when the religious subject matter is well absorbed and comprehended, the image mirrors "the truth of good scripture." As described by Armenini and especially Zuccari, the cosmogony of artistic creation, that is, the quasi-miraculous process through which the divine light dissipates the darkness of the painter's intellect and uncovers the purest vision of the divine truth to the painter's eyes, seems to have fascinated and stimulated Caravaggio's imagination. As we have seen in Part Three, the twists, misreadings, and tensions of seeing the divine, including man's real or metaphorical blindness as revealed in the artist's attempt to represent God, had constantly been at the heart of Caravaggio's early sacred narratives.

Yet, in the three paintings that I am about to analyze, Caravaggio raises yet another pictorial bar;

---

16   Armenini, 38: "Conoscasi dunque, dalle cose sudette, che il pittore sarà colui il quale, per un suo certo e maraviglioso giudicio ed arte, saprà condurre a fine le cose ch'egli prima avrà concetto nell'animo e nella mente, e con maniera antica e col mezzo delle linee e colori rappresentarle così al vivo che il senso dell'occhio ne rimanga ingannato."

17   Ibidem, 87: "Ma è bene ch'io prima vi discuopra alcuni diffetti che si veggono essere in molti, i quali sono da essere fuggiti assai come troppo lontani da' veri termini del buon comporre; imperò che, o che questi non sanno il modo o pur che non fanno caso d'intendere né di sapere il soggetto delle materie bene, e' compongono l'istorie loro molto diverse dalla verità delle buone scritture, ond'essi poi vengono biasimati, e con gran ragione, da gli uomini intendenti."

one way or another, he inserts the seer inside the vision, the author inside the work, and the artisan inside the manufacture. Caravaggio thus enters his own fictions either playing himself, disguised, or as an avatar: not an alter ego, but a counter-ego, of himself—the allusion is to Michelangelo. If Caravaggio trespasses the fictive boundaries of his own visions by transposing himself into his narratives as a performing figure, this pictorial challenge was conceivable because, theoretically, the painter was required not only to "eyewitness" his *istoria* in order to reproduce it with authenticity, but also to feel it while visualizing it, as if the events to be represented were tapping onto, or rubbing against, his skin. This should not be interpreted as a mere metaphor. Counter-Reformation art theorists, for instance, insisted on the fact that painters could not "touch" the heart of the devout if they had not been originally touched by the subject they set out to treat. This is Cardinal Federico Borromeo's opinion as reported in his *Della pittura sacra*:

> We can say that, just as the orator attempts in vain to move others if he himself is not moved, so—I believe—does this apply to the painter: if he does not try to move himself through devout thoughts, he will not be able to convey in his figures what they lack: that is, devotion and commendable affects.[18]

In his 1582 *Discorso delle imagini sacre*, Cardinal Gabriele Paleotti goes so far as to inscribe this sort of religious empathy into the very definition of the Christian painter:

> As for the artificer, who is called [painting's] efficient cause, numerous are the features required for his persona to fit in within his mission (…). Let us recall just two of [these features]: first, the artificer must be an expert in what he does (…); secondly, it is not enough for him who is by name and profession a Christian to be a good artificer; the images he makes likewise require a Christian mind and affection; this is an inseparable quality of his persona, and therefore he is compelled to show it whenever it is necessary.[19]

Truth be told, far from being an exclusive requirement for a Christian painter, the ability to move the beholder's heart and mind through the figures' "movements" concerns the whole art of painting: it was an indisputable sign of artistic excellence. Lomazzo explains why this aptitude is so crucial:

> But men are moved much more through seeing than hearing (…). In fact, each of us, seeing someone die, or suffer, experiences [the same] in himself, and is deeply moved, becoming sad for the dead, and feeling pain for him who is suffering; if one sees that a leg, or arm, is severed from someone's body, one twists one's hip and experiences the pain in that part [of the body] in which the other has been affected, as if one could feel a hint of that suffering. In this way, if we want to browse through the other effects to which the human body can be submitted, we will constantly come across a certain power or hidden force that, by dint of similitude, induces men to partake of it and react accordingly. For this reason, in conformity with philosophers, it comes as no surprise

---

18 Borromeo, 34: "[E procedendo ancora più avanti] dir possiamo che, sì come l'oratore invano s'affatica di muovere gl'altri s'egli stesso non muove, così io credo che avvenga generalmente dei pittori, che essi in prima se stessi non cercano di muovere con alcuni divoti pensieri, non potranno nelle loro figure imprimere ciò che non hanno, cioè la divozione e i lodevoli affetti."

19 Paleotti, 11-2: "Quanto all'artefice, che si chiama causa efficiente, molte sono le parti che si ricercano nella persona sua per corrispondere a questo ufficio (…). Ora ricordiamo sol due cose: l'una, che deve essere perito l'artefice di quello che vuol fare (…); l'altra, che non basta solo esser buono artefice, ma oltre l'eccellenza dell'arte, essendo egli di nome e di professione cristiano, ricercano da lui l'imagini ch'egli farà un animo ed affetto cristiano, essendo questa qualità inseparabile dalla persona sua, e tale ch'egli è ubligato di mostrarla ovunque sia bisogno."

that a man's body and soul are equally able to affect the soul of another (…). This is why it is said that a man only through his affect and custom acts upon another man.[20]

In Lomazzo's opinion, mimesis, that is, the representation of a human action, not only stirs up empathy in the audience, but also contaminates, as it were, the performer's body and soul:

> We see that a man who recounts a prodigious event to another acts relatively in accordance with what he says, and the audience, moved with him by the same emotions, to various degrees enact similar movements with their bodies. And this occurs all the time, because we see the public react diversely: fiercely to the evocation of war, sadly to that of pain, with compassion to that of misery, laughing to that of fancy, or carelessly and merrily to that of joy. In the same manner, a man who, laughing, narrates some risible event, induces the others to laugh along with him.[21]

At the intersection of the raw material to be narrated or depicted with the audience, the artist like a shaman relives the action and funnels its emotional content through his tale or *istoria*; his psychagogic power—a by-product of his *disegno*—if appropriately conveyed, moves the spectator or beholder through empathic symbiosis. One sees, feels, and experiences exactly what the artist has first seen, felt, and experienced. This shamanic conception of mimesis pertains not only to the domain of alchemy and physiology, from which Lomazzo adopted it, but also to that of rhetoric, poetry, and even theology. What else are the "spiritual exercises" of Ignacio de Loyola and the Jesuits but a procedure through which the believer, by him- or herself and without the intervention of an artist, internalizes the emotions of sacred scripture by experiencing them? And what else is the goal of this practice than recovering the truth of divinity?

It would be perhaps superfluous to remember that this psychagogy of the image must have permeated Caravaggio's culture. As the painting's author, Caravaggio must have known that he was deemed the seer of a transcendental truth, but he did not seem to accept this role flatly. Rather, he displays the limits of metaphysical authorship by staging a real clash of artistic spheres: by materializing the authorial voice—more to the point, the painting's narrator—as an acting figure. In the Dublin *Taking of Christ*, Caravaggio seeks to no avail to illuminate the figure of the Savior who is at the center of his own vision. Unable to see his *istoria*'s hero, he represents himself in a state of blindness: a visual paradox, because he appears temporarily blind in the vision he has created. Like Homer, Plato or Democritus, he also happens to be deprived of his sight for the sake of, or as a consequence of, his vision, yet, unlike his Greek predecessors, he is unable, once in the painting, to "better and more subtly investigate the nature of what [he has] conceived in his mind." Even worse, he is literally incapacitated and unable to gaze at the hero of his own vision.

In the Genoa *Ecce Homo*, Caravaggio transfigures his persona into a comedic mask—the Italian sanctimonious *dottore*—offering to view the artistic product of his own visualization: a miserable

---

20 Lomazzo, 2:106-7: "Ma di gran lunga più che per l'udire si muove l'uomo per vedere (…). Imperò che non è di noi che in se stesso non pruovi che, vedendo un altro morire, o stentare, tutto si commuove e s'attrista per il morto, e pare che patisca per colui che stenta; vedendo ad alcuno tagliare gamba, o braccio, si risente e si torce con la vita, anch'egli, in quella parte dove quello è offeso, come che senta un certo che di quella pena. E così se vogliamo discorrere per tutti gl'altri effetti che un corpo umano può fare, troveremo sempre in loro un certo che di potere e quasi occulta forza che per via di similitudine induce gl'altri a contrarre di quello, e secondo esso muoversi. Di qui vogliono i filosofi che non si maravigli alcuno se il corpo e l'animo di uno non possa similmente dell'animo d'un

altro essere affetto (…). Perciò si dice che l'uomo solamente con l'affetto ed abito opera nell'altro uomo."

21 Ibidem, 2:106: "E però vediamo che uno che racconti un qualche caso maraviglioso ad altri, egli principalmente si muove secondo la natura di quello che racconta, e gli ascoltanti chi più e chi meno, mossi con lui da quei medesimi moti, fanno col corpo simiglianti effetti; così avviene in tutti i casi, perché si veggono diversamente ne i bellicosi motti fieri, ne i dolenti mesti, ne' pietosi compassionevoli, ne' capricciosi ridicoli e ne gl'allegri spensierati e contenti: sì come vedesi, per essempio, in uno che, ridendo, narri qualche facezia, incita gl'altri a ridere."

Christ despised by a brutal torturer. "Behold the man": the painter beckons the viewer to see his own vision, his fictive truth; but by putting himself—his comedic alter ego—in the shoes of Pilate, or in the clothes of an obsolete Baccio Bandinelli (see Chapter 12), he drags the figure of the author into a cruel parody of authorship. As is always the case with the *dottore*, the Latin of Caravaggio's *istoria*, the nobly crafted language through which the painter is supposed to narrate the sacred event, likewise betrays its inappropriateness in conjuring up the Passion's true vision—or so it pretends. As a result, the author ridicules his own pretense of making the beholder relive the *istoria*, that is, his pretense of making the beholder truly "behold the man."

In the Vatican *Entombment*, Caravaggio challenges Michelangelo in a staged *paragone* of painting and sculpture. As in his famous Florence *Pietà*, Michelangelo reappears in the guise of Nicodemus holding Christ's dead body, an author lifted wholesale from his own vision and put to use in another author's work. In a certain sense, Caravaggio's *Entombment* proves to be a sculpture-within-a-painting, a *mise en abîme* of authorship, its functions and, once again, its limitations: a hall of mirrors where one author reflects himself through another. Tragically or comically enough, Caravaggio's Michelangelo/Nicodemus cannot by himself support either Christ or the machine of the whole composition orbiting around Christ. Michelangelo, the very endorser of *disegno* as a metaphysical aptitude inherent in art's practice, is here entrapped in a compositional mechanism that literally weighs too much to be carried with his bare hands: an ironic but at the same time poignant spectacle of the author's physical and intellectual implicitness within his own artwork. In these three cases Caravaggio shows the disenchantment of transcendental authorship; pace Lomazzo, Armenini, Zuccari, and Paleotti, fiction, albeit a vision, is no substitute for the truth.

With unmatched ingenuity and irony, Caravaggio demonstrates the fictiveness of the *istoria* by representing its prime mover—its author—as both a fictive figure and a figure of fiction. The painter within the painting ceases to be an artistic signature, as in the Renaissance tradition; he is no longer the detached if proud visitor in his own vision. By interacting with the *istoria*, the author's omnipresence in his creation is theatrically questioned. The seer-painter, in fact, only happens to cover a unique visual angle of his representation; by being in two places simultaneously—in front of, and inside, the painting—the master's authoritative sight doubles into two alternative perspectives on the represented action. Far from embodying the truth, the *istoria* is essentially a "point of view," and the painter's eye—the one through which the beholder observes the scene—proves to be a conventional figment, nothing but an authorial lens into the fictitious realm of painting. It is probably disconcerting that Caravaggio's originality—what Lomazzo would have considered the uniqueness of his invention—ends up asserting itself in the *istoria* through the insertion of the author as a performing figure, that is, through the very device meant to uncover the author's inadequacy and relativity in relaying the transcendence of vision. It is certainly less disconcerting that the unveiling of the author as a figure of fiction—what I will call the discovery of the meta-author—comes to fruition through the work of a painter who has renounced the practice and theoretical implications of *disegno* from the beginning. Perhaps because the practical method of composing demands that the image remain directly in front of the painter's eyes, thereby allowing for multiple points of view as the painter moves before his models, the relativity of authorship must have dawned as a fact on Caravaggio's mind.

I have employed the term "disenchantment" to describe Caravaggio's take on transcendental invention, and it is indeed disenchantment which is foreshadowed by the tragicomic roles of the author's doubles in the three pictures that I am about to discuss. Yet, for all his disenchantment, Caravaggio always manages to exalt the sheer enchantment of artistic creation through the religious seriousness with which he evokes the sacred *istoria*: what other painter could have depicted the Savior's revulsion at Judas in a more lifelike manner than Caravaggio in his *Taking of Christ*?

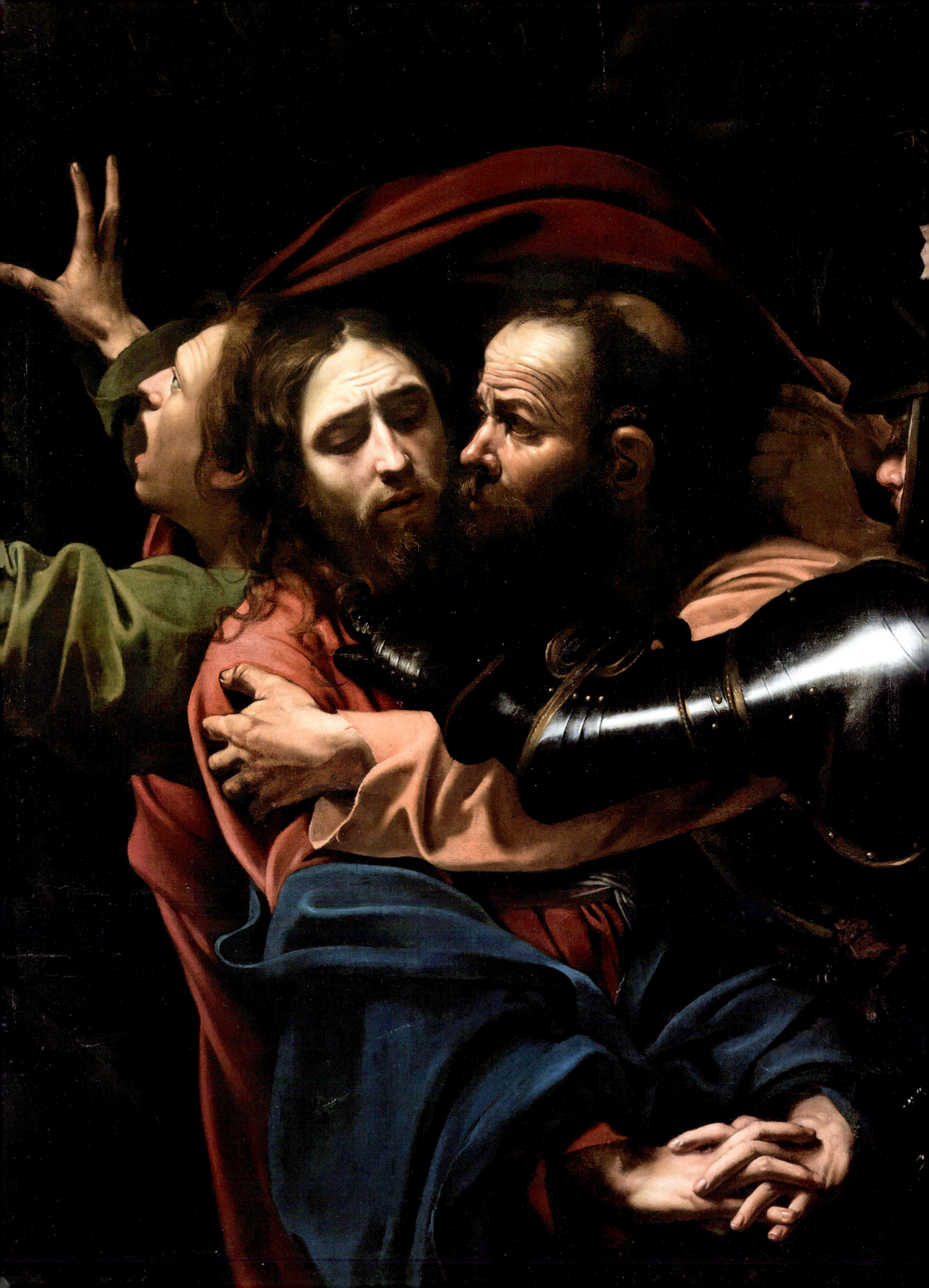

CHAPTER 10

Zuccari's Lantern:
The Blind Spot of Painting in
Caravaggio's *The Taking of Christ*

The Novelty of the Subject

Some time around 1604-1605, Caravaggio reportedly confronted his fellow painter Guido Reni, accused him of plagiarism, and threatened to beat him to death. This well-known episode, related by Carlo Cesare Malvasia in his 1678 *Felsina Pittrice*, is worth reading carefully. Upon his arrival in Rome, the Bolognese Guido became a sort of strategic weapon in the war between Caravaggio and the Cavalier d'Arpino. According to Malvasia, Guido was then "well served and assisted" by the Cavaliere who, "in order to counter Caravaggio, his declared enemy, set out to support him by procuring for Guido even those works he knew destined for Caravaggio, as was indeed the case of the Crucifixion of Saint Peter at the Tre Fontane outside Rome." To persuade Cardinal Scipione Borghese, the commissioner of the picture, to favor Guido over Caravaggio, the Cavaliere promised that the former "would metamorphose" into the latter, "and paint [the Crucifixion of Saint Peter] in that dark and contrasted manner, as he in fact did skillfully."[1] In partial contradiction to his previous statement, Malvasia further reports that Caravaggio, "quite afraid of a new manner completely opposed to, and as well-appraised as, his," used to slander his competitor "too overtly," defining Guido's style as "affected and altogether fanciful."

Apparently Caravaggio's grudge grew stronger as another prestigious commission, the decoration of the Sala del Tesoro in the Loreto Basilica, likewise pitted him against Guido.[2] This

---

1 Malvasia, 2:14-5: "Gionto colà assieme col sudetto Albani, vi fu ben veduto e servito, massime dal detto Arpini che, per far anche contraposto al Caravaggio suo dichiarato nemico, si era posto a portarlo, procacciandogli anco que' lavori stessi che al Caravaggio intendeva esser destinati, come poi avvenne del San Pietro crocefisso alle Tre Fontane fuor di Roma, promettendo egli al cardinal Borghese che sarebbesi Guido trasformato nel Caravaggio, e l'avrebbe fatto di quella maniera cacciata e scura, come bravamente eseguito si vede".

2 As is well known, Pomarancio was to carry out this pictorial cycle. See Chiappini di Sorio 1975, esp. 9-13, 95-98, no. 9, and more recently Polichetti 2001. For other early testimonies of the Loreto commission, see Baglione, 291: "ma perché tra gli altri che a quest'opera concorsono v'era Michel Agnolo da Caravaggio in paragone del Roncalli, essendone quegli stato escluso, sì fattamente sdegnossene che per via d'un traditore siciliano il fece ferire, se bene con taglio leggero, là dove il contrario ad esso Michelagnolo occorse in Napoli, ov'egli restò sì fortemente segnato che più non si riconosceva"; and Passeri, 373-4, who does not mention Guido, but Guercino, as Caravaggio's victim: "nel quale tempo [under Paul V] si negoziava l'opera della cupola della chiesa nella quale è la Santa Casa di Loreto, e doppo varietà di pareri nel darla ad un pittore di qualche fama, per essere quella opera di considerazione, si conclude dai deputati nella

persona di Michel Angelo per esser egli di stima universale in una nuova maniera. Ma perché il concetto della sua persona, quanto al costume, era sinistro per la sua bestialità, stavano alcuni altri perplessi. Pensando di dargli un compagno moderato o ben composto come per freno delle sue furie, elessero Giovan Francesco, il quale era uomo quieto, pacifico e timorato di Dio, tanto più che pareva a quei signori che in loro fosse gran somiglianza nel modo di dipingere. Andarono a trovare il Barbieri e gli conferirono questo loro stabilimento, imponendogli che andasse a comunicarlo da parte loro col Caravaggio. Andatosene il Barbieri allegramente a trovarlo a casa perché passava tra di loro buona amicizia, lo accolse il Caravaggio amorevolmente non sapendo quello che voleva trattare con esso lui. (…) Dopo averlo riverito, ed essendosi anch'egli assiso accanto al bragiere, così si introdusse a favellare. 'Suppongo, signor Michel Angelo, che a un d'appresso v'immaginiate la ragione della mia venuta; ma quando questo non sia, mi dichiaro che sono per parlarvi con ogni apertura e sincerità. Questi signori deputati della Santa Casa, come già ben sapete, hanno eletto voi per l'opera della cupola, ma non so da qual genio mossi, hanno destinato me per vostro compagno in questo lavoro. Sono venuto dunque non solo per darvene parte, ma per esibirmi in questo particolare non per compagno, ma per discepolo, per suddito ed anco per vostro servitore, rimettendovi del tutto al vostro arbitrio ed alla vostra disposizione senza replica né doglianza alcuna.'

311

◄ Plate XIV: Michelangelo Merisi da Caravaggio, *The Taking of Christ*, National Gallery of Ireland, Dublin, oil on canvas, 133.5 x 169.5 cm., detail.

episode sparked the famous argument between the two painters that I have just described. Stumbling into his competitor, Caravaggio discouraged Guido from challenging him, adding menacingly that he was eager to "blow these airs out of his head." As on other occasions, Guido feigned humility, claiming that, on Caravaggio's demand, he would withdraw from the competition. Instead of calming him down, Guido's words infuriated Caravaggio, who—with reason—doubted his sincerity. "If he truly considered himself such a gentleman," argued Caravaggio, "why was he constantly seeking my works, purchasing any picture [of mine] he could find? What mystery lay behind it all, and to what end was he doing such things? Why did he steal my manner and color technique in the Crucifixion of Saint Peter at the Tre Fontane?" Eventually, Caravaggio reminded Guido that, even if he obtained the commission, he could not rob him of his celebrity as well. More importantly, he made it clear that "he was capable of taking out the Cavalier d'Arpino, the rogue who hatched the plot, and coaxed from Cardinal Borghese a painting that was meant for him."[3]

Some scholars have questioned the authenticity of this anecdote. I believe that Malvasia's testimony is credible, if not entirely reliable, despite some obvious inaccuracies. There are a number of reasons to trust this source, but I think that Guido's *Crucifixion of Saint Peter* (now at the Pinacoteca Vaticana) proves to be irrefutable evidence (Fig. 140).[4] Not only did Guido patently try to appropriate and improve upon Caravaggio's pictorial language in this ambitious picture, but his antagonist's style also seduced him so deeply that it affected his production for years. On the other hand, Caravaggio's aggression is not at all unexpected; his vehement temper is sufficiently documented, and his claim to artistic supremacy all too comprehensible.[5] To paraphrase Malvasia, I would say that "the dark and contrasted manner" of the *Crucifixion of Saint Peter* is an obvious

Quando il Barbieri esponeva questo suo sentimento, teneva Michel Angelo in mano quel ferro col quale si va attizzando il fuoco, e mentre quegli si affaticava all'esplicazione del suo desiderio, percuoteva il Caravaggio la terra senza intermissione. Avendo Giovan Francesco terminato il suo dire, si rivoltò a lui quella fiera indomita con ira grandissima, e tutto rabbia così gli rispose: 'Ché siete venuto, per burlarmi? Che mezzaria è questa? Quanto alla cupola, o sarà tutta vostra o tutta mia, ed andate a fare i fatti vostri, ché io non vi voglio più sentire' e, levatosi in piedi, voltandogli le spalle, si partì da quella stanza lasciandolo tutto confuso ed intimorito, dubitando di qualche bestiale risoluzione, com'era solito." Of course, Passeri's anecdote is mostly fabricated, but it in part matches Malvasia's if one replaces Guercino's name with Guido's. As I demonstrate in the Introduction to Part Six, it is possible that the source of this episode as related by Malvasia and Passeri was Guercino, which may explain Passeri's confusion between Guido and Guercino.

3   Malvasia, 2:15-6: "Ma se non piacque ad Annibale, tanto più spiacque al Caravaggio che temette assai di una nuova maniera totalmente alla sua opposta, ed altrettanto quanto la sua gradita. Ne sparlava però egli con troppa libertà, chiamandola leccata e tutta fantastica; cercava, come uomo brigoso ch'egli era, occasione di romperla, minacciando di voler menar le mani un giorno con altro che col pennello, e l'avrebbe fatto al certo, se Guido con gran destrezza non avesse scansato ogn'incontro, né si fosse coperto con la protezione de' grandi che lo favorivano. Incontratolo un giorno gli disse ch'ei non lo stimava punto, e che se fosse venuto a Roma con pensiero di competere seco, egli era pronto a dargli ogni soddisfazione in qual si fosse modo, e gli avrebbe levato l'albagia di capo ed insegnato di starsene a casa sua, e non andare nell'altrui a fare da bell'umore e cattar risse. Al che rispose Guido che gli era servitore; esser venuto alla corte per dipingere, non per duellare, né per sua elezione, ma per servire a' padroni che ve l'avean chiamato; stimare il suo valore al pari d'ogn'altro, né competere con alcuno, conoscendosi a tutti inferiore. Usò

anche questa finezza che, concorrendo dopoi il Caravaggio anch'egli co' gli altri al lavoro della cupola della Santa Casa di Loreto, ed essendo a quello efficacemente portato Guido dalli cardinali Sfondrato, Sanesio, Santi Quattro ed altri, fece significargli per Giovan Battista Croce che, avendo inteso ch'anch'egli addimandava quell'opra, se comandava si ritirasse egli dal procurarla, volentieri l'avrebbe fatto; anzi che a lui tocca, saria stato a fargli compagnia od a servirlo nel modo che a lui fosse piacciuto di trattarlo, ma o che dubitasse di non esser in tal guisa burlato da Guido, del quale pubblicamente diceasi dover esser indubitatamente quel lavoro (ed accadeva certo, se maliziosamente non ne venisse escluso da quel prelato governatore) o che questo atto umile troppo dasse maggior franchigia a quell'altiero, diede nelle scandescenze. Rispose che badasse a' fatti suoi, né gli stasse a scocchiar il capo; ch'egli gli avrebbe rotto le corna da dovero, e gli avrebbe insegnato il vero modo di burlare il prossimo; che il lavoro o non lo voleva, o voleva farlo solo, né per mezzo suo o col suo aiuto, dandogli ben l'animo d'uscirne in bene, senza tanti protomastri sopra; che s'egli professava d'esser sì grand'uomo, perché dunque tutto il giorno cercare quadri di sua mano, e comprare quanti gli ne dassero nelle mani? Che mistero era questo ed a che fine ciò facesse? Perché nel quadro del San Pietro crocefisso alle Tre Fontane rubargli la maniera e 'l colorito? Che se gli avea tolto quell'opra, non gli avea però tolto per anche la fama; ch'era egli ben uomo da tor la vita e quel maluomo dell'Arpino, che ben sapea aver ordito questa trama e procuratagli questa tavola dal cardinal Borghese, che doveva esser la sua."

4   For the painting, see Pepper 1988, 220-1, no. 17. For the relation between Caravaggio's painting in the Cerasi Chapel and Reni's *Crucifixion of Saint Peter* at the Tre Fontane, see Friedlaender 1945; Pepper 1971; and Spear 1997, 82-8. For Caravaggio's influence on Guido Reni, see Landrus 1998; Cosmo 1999; and Benati 2005.

5   For an overview of Caravaggio's propensity for violence, see Varriano 1999a; and Varriano 2006, 73-86.

attempt on Guido's part to turn himself into an "emended" Caravaggio. The results of this metamorphosis, as Caravaggio himself maliciously predicted, are perhaps not "affected and fanciful," but certainly polished and tendentiously ornamental.

Be that as it may, Malvasia's story, though trustworthy, raises a series of crucial and hitherto unformulated questions. If Caravaggio's concern with originality is certain, the way in which the painter himself interpreted his pictorial novelty is far from being self-evident. For instance, when blaming Guido for "stealing his manner and color technique," was he alluding exclusively to the specific practice of chiaroscuro that still remains for us, centuries later, the hallmark of his creativity? Truth be told, even Caravaggio's expression as quoted by Malvasia lacks definition. Do "manner" (*maniera*) and "color technique" (*colorito*) form a type of hendyadis, as if to say: "a manner of coloring?" Or does "manner" differ conceptually from "color technique," as if to stress the fact that Guido imitated both Caravaggio's chiaroscuro and compositional principles? If so, does "manner" equally include invention, and therefore the way in which the subject matter is conceived and visualized? All of the above interpretations are virtually correct. I wish only to point out that Guido did not confine himself to emulating Caravaggio's chiaroscuro. The posture of Saint Peter in his *Crucifixion* derives from that of Caravaggio's Saint Paul in the *Conversion* for the Cerasi Chapel: both figures, supine and head-down, offer themselves to view in bold foreshortening, stretching their outflung arms upward. Subtly, Guido developed his competitor's idea into a distinct action, thereby correcting Caravaggio's own version of the *Crucifixion of Saint Peter*, hanging opposite the *Conversion of Saint Paul* as its pendant in the Cerasi Chapel. There would be much to remark upon in Guido's visual reaction to his rival's pictures, but these comments would not explain what exactly Caravaggio intended by originality, less so whether it also applied to invention and, in general, to the treatment of the subject.[6]

Nowhere in the literary sources is Caravaggio recorded to declare explicitly on what premises he deemed his creations to be original. However, in two of his pictures, the *Ecce Homo* in Genoa

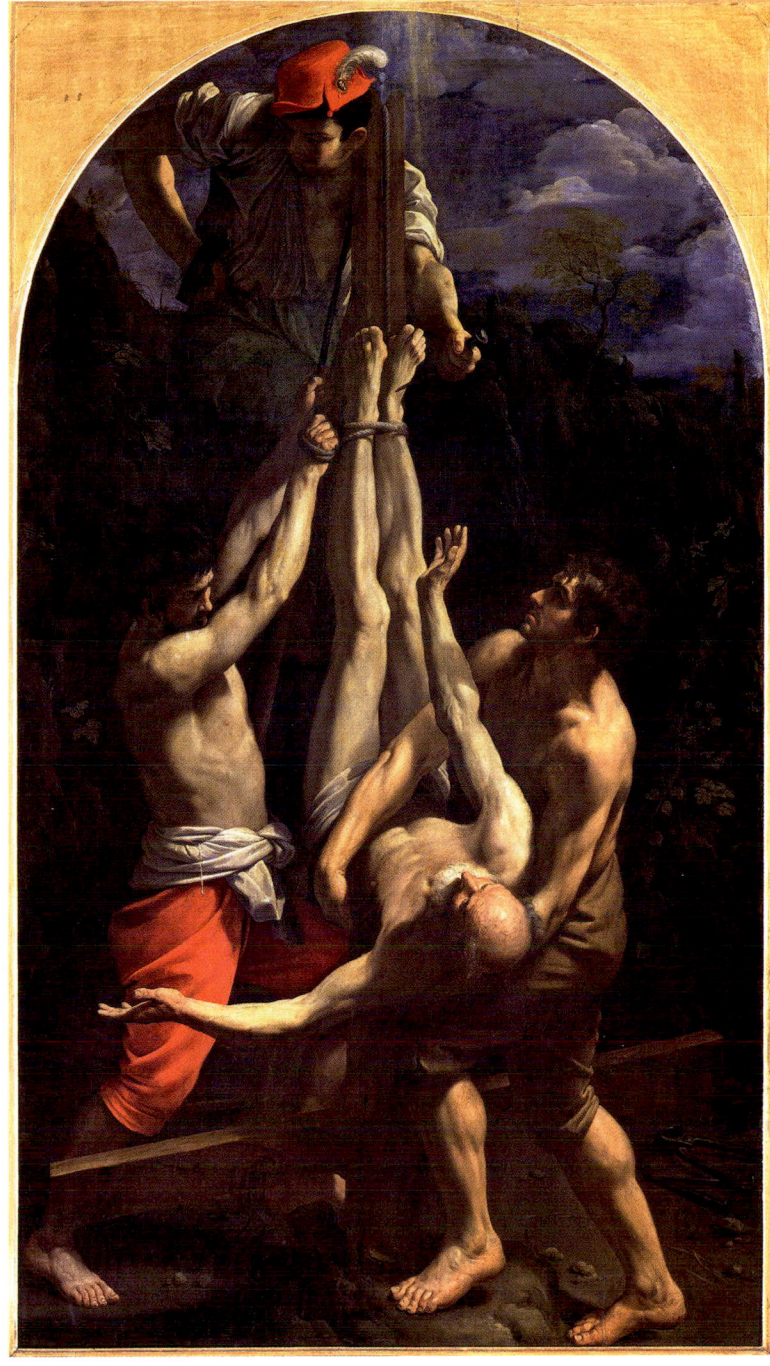

Fig. 140
Guido Reni, *The Crucifixion of Saint Peter*, Pinacoteca Vaticana, Rome, oil on canvas, 305 x 175 cm.

6   For a discussion of the concept of novelty and originality in the seventeenth century, see Cropper 2005.

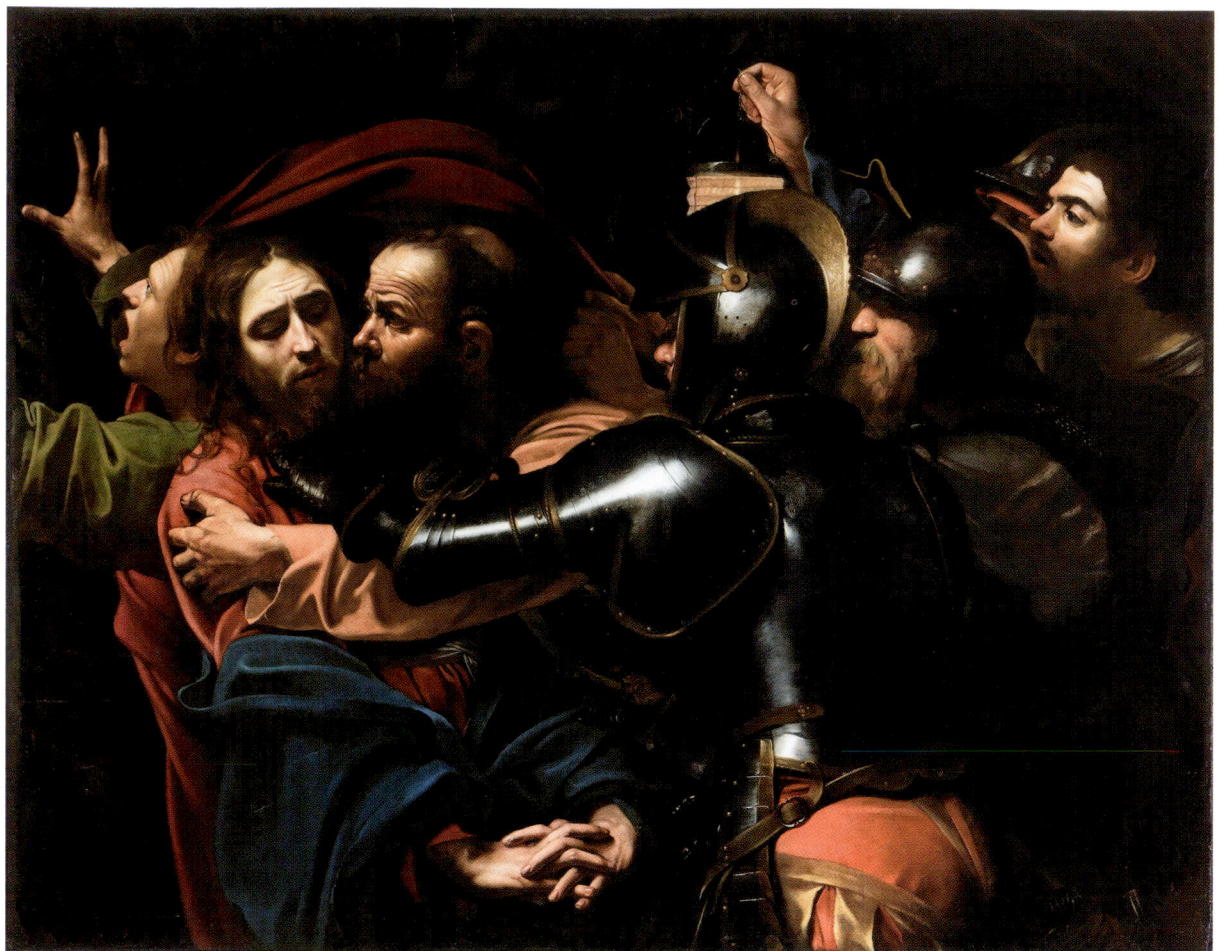

Fig. 141
Michelangelo Merisi da Caravaggio, *The Taking of Christ*, National Gallery of Ireland, Dublin, oil on canvas, 133.5 x 169.5 cm.

and *The Taking of Christ* in Dublin (Fig. 141), the painter undertook an audacious reflection on his role as an inventor. In both compositions, he represented himself as a participant, thus introducing almost unprecedented elements of self-referentiality into his narratives.[7] Of course, artists had been depicting their own effigies in religious works for centuries before Caravaggio. Yet, in the Western tradition, they appear mostly as walk-on parts celebrating their achievements by proxy through their doubles in the composition, or manifesting their devotion in front of sacred figures. In the *Ecce Homo*, on the contrary, Caravaggio usurps Pilate's role by delivering the tortured Jesus to the beholder. In *The Taking of Christ*, he belongs to the group of Roman soldiers arresting the Savior, attempting to glimpse the sacred figure by dint of a lantern that he holds aloft over the scene. By these means, Caravaggio either ceases to witness the event as an outsider, or extends his task of witnessing to a vain quest for the pictorial hero: in the Dublin picture, notwithstanding his efforts, the painter's *alter ego* is hindered from approaching the central episode and observing the nefarious kiss. Furthermore, his lantern does not reach the group of Judas and Christ: oddly enough, its light seemingly irradiates only the right portion of the picture, reflecting back onto Caravaggio's face.

7   To my knowledge, the first to identify the lantern-bearer as a self-portrayal of Caravaggio was Roberto Longhi in 1960, after examining an ancient copy of *The Taking of Christ* in Odessa (the original painting was not discovered until after Longhi's death, in 1993). See Longhi 1999-2000, 2:248: "A chi conosca infatti la somatica del Caravaggio come persona fisica (…), non può sorger dubbio che anche in questo giovinetto pallido e scavato, dalla chioma a ricci compressi e che si sforza di metter su per la prima volta una lanugine di barba e baffetti, si abbia, in ordine di serie, il terzo autoritratto del Caravaggio, qualche anno innanzi a quello già citato del *Martirio*." Of course, Longhi's assumption that the *Taking of Christ* preceded *The Martyrdom of Saint Matthew* is false.

Because of their specificity, one cannot dismiss these self-representations as simple signatures. Unlike *The Martyrdom of Saint Matthew*, in which Caravaggio depicted himself stepping out of the scene in the left background while peeping back to the ongoing murder as if in contempt, the *Ecce Homo* and *The Taking of Christ* stage and presuppose the painter's involvement as an integral part of the composition. Different again is the case of the Borghese *David*, where Caravaggio lent his features to the beheaded Goliath: structurally, the picture partakes rather of allegory than narrative.[8] Although the artist's presence assumes a self-referential meaning, this visual meditation concerns less the act of painting than the artist's identity in its broader sense. I thus contend that, by representing himself in both the Genoa and the Dublin pictures, Caravaggio intended to illustrate the puzzling relation between the artist and his own invention, as well as his role as a creator of religious images. Evidently, the *Ecce Homo* and *The Taking of Christ* tackle this issue from diverging standpoints. For this reason, I will focus first on the Dublin painting, and try in this chapter to penetrate its multi-layered structure. Even if I cannot prove it irrefutably, I assume that, in *The Taking of Christ*, Caravaggio also aimed to signal the newness of his invention; by imagining himself as unsuccessfully shedding light onto, and witnessing, the betrayal, he intentionally turns the viewer's attention toward the kiss scene in an invitation to closer reading.[9]

Lost for decades and felicitously rediscovered in 1993 in Dublin, *The Taking of Christ* was executed in 1602, and delivered on 2 January 1603 to Cardinal Ciriaco Mattei,[10] who had formerly commissioned from Caravaggio another painting, *The Supper at Emmaus* now in the National Gallery, London. In his 1672 *Vite*, Giovan Pietro Bellori described the picture as follows:

> After the kiss, Judas keeps his hand on the Lord's shoulder; in the meantime a soldier, in full armor, stretches his arm and hand clad in iron onto the chest of Christ, who halts patiently and humbly, interlocking his hands, while Saint John, behind him, escapes by thrusting his arms ahead. [Caravaggio] imitated the rust on the armor of this soldier, whose head and face are covered with a helmet, his profile jutting out slightly; and behind, a lantern rises, followed by two other heads of armored [soldiers].[11]

8 For a thoughtful reading of this picture, see Stone 2002 and esp. Stone 2006. For an interpretation of Caravaggio's self-portraits in terms of Counter-Reformation religiosity, see Rossi S. 1996.

9 Although it has been unanimously acknowledged that Caravaggio represented himself as the lantern-bearer in the Dublin painting, scholars have rarely sought to interpret the function and meaning of this self-portrayal. Here are a few relevant examples of how Caravaggio's presence in the painting has been interpreted: Herrmann Fiore 1995, 25: "It is Caravaggio, the artist, who looks up and raises a lantern which occupies the most prominent position of the composition, so as to bring light to the night scene and, with his upraised hand, reveal the true story"; Puglisi 1998, 221: "The thirty-one-year old painter strives to illuminate the scene although his lantern barely penetrates the darkness; thus, Caravaggio implies, the artist tries, however vainly, to enlighten the world"; Ebert-Schifferer 2009, 148: "Die spirituelle Zeugenschaft, die Caravaggio dem Maler bereits im *Martyrium des hl. Matthäus* zugesprochen hatte, wird hier als selbstbewußtes Manifest im Rahmen einer zeitgenössischen Diskussion über das Künstlertum wiederholt. Malerei, so eine der jahrhundertelang diskutierten Thesen, kann Betrug sein; sie kann aber auch, beispielsweise im Dienste des Glaubens, Unvorstellbares sichtbar, erlebbar machen. Das glaubte noch Paul Klee: 'Kunst gibt nicht das Sichtbare wieder, sondern macht sichtbar'." A broader discussion of Caravaggio's self-portrayal in the Dublin picture is in Corrain 2002, 224-9. I will quote some of Corrain's observations in the notes when the opportunity arises.

10 Apart from Bellori, quoted in the text, Celio, 134, mentions Caravaggio's painting at the Mattei Palace: "quella pittura della Presa di Cristo mezze figure." The Dublin picture is also recorded in Bellori a, 43. Cappelletti and Testa 1990b, 237-38 (and again 1994, 101-4, no. 7) first published the receipt delivered by Ciriaco Mattei to Caravaggio (January 2, 1603). See also Macioce 2003, 116. For the painting, see Friedlaender 1969, 172-5; Cinotti 1983, 479-81, no. 39; Bologna 1992, 322-3; Benedetti 1993a; Benedetti 1993b; Cappelletti 1993; Benedetti 1995; Strinati and Vodret 1995, 124-5, no. 3; Hermann Fiore 1995; Schröter 1995; Treffers 1996, 277-81; Bersani and Dutoit 1998, 54-9, 65-73; Puglisi 1998, 220-1; Longhi 1999-2000, 1:9 [1943], 2:247-8 [1960], 265 [1968]; Lavin 2001, 632-7; Corrain 2002; Biscottini 2004; Curzietti 2004; Marini 2005, 478-80, no. 59; Preimesberger 2007; Koos 2007, 77-9; Schütze 2009, 265-6, no. 31; and Ebert-Schifferer 2009, 146-8.

11 Bellori, 222-3: "Concorsero al diletto del suo pennello altri signori romani, e tra questi il marchese Asdrubale Mattei gli fece dipingere la Presa di Cristo all'orto, parimente in mezze figure. Tiene Giuda la mano alla spalla del Maestro, dopo il bacio; intanto un soldato tutto armato stende il braccio e la mano di ferro al petto del Signore, il quale si arresta paziente ed umile con le mani incrocicchiate avanti, fuggendo dietro san Giovanni con le braccia aperte. Imitò l'armatura rugginosa di quel soldato, coperto il capo e 'l volto dall'elmo, uscendo alquanto fuori il profilo; e dietro s'inalza una lanterna, seguitando due altre teste d'armati."

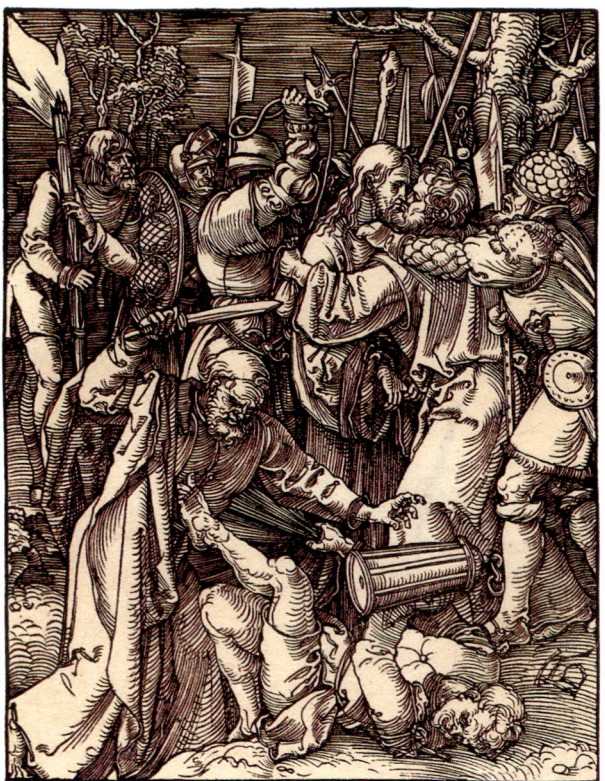

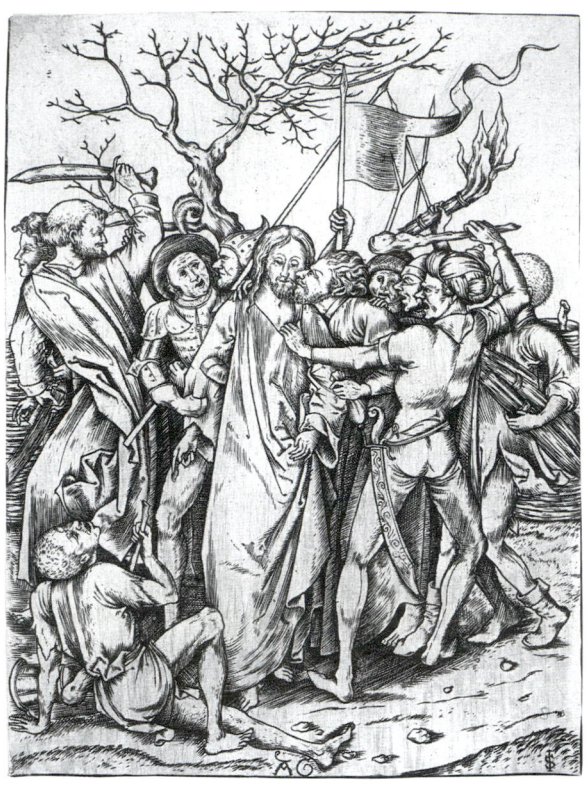

Fig. 142
Albrecht Dürer, *The Taking of Christ*, woodcut, 12.7 x 9.7 cm.

Fig. 143
Master AG (Anton Gerbel of Pforzheim?), *The Taking of Christ*, engraving, 14.5 x 10.8 cm.

Not surprisingly, Bellori fails to recognize Caravaggio's likeness in the figure holding the lantern; nor does he mention in his *Vite* that *The Martyrdom of Saint Matthew* contains another self-portrait of the painter. Although properly speaking he does not judge the picture, his description, precise in some respects, betokens a certain admiration, especially in connection with Caravaggio's naturalistic rendering of the soldier's armor, down to the detail of the rust. It is interesting that Bellori, along with most modern scholars, read Christ's gesture as expressing resignation and patience, whereas in my view it suggests despair and repugnance. Also important is Bellori's identification of the fleeing figure with Saint John, an iconographic rarity that to a certain extent also constitutes a relevant novelty. Even if Bellori points out that Caravaggio chose the moment immediately subsequent to Judas' kiss, the image is definitely ambiguous in this regard: a classical example of Gaurico's amphiboly. Yet this ambiguity is inherent to the iconographical tradition, and as such does not represent a distinct hallmark of Caravaggio's originality. Yet, unlike Bellori, an early modern viewer would probably perceive the episode represented in the Dublin picture as preliminary to the fatal kiss.

In her remarkable 1995 article on *The Taking of Christ*, Kristina Hermann Fiore states that a woodcut by Albrecht Dürer from the 1509 *Small Passion* inspired Caravaggio for his Dublin painting (Fig. 142).[12] In Dürer's *The Taking of Christ*, the Savior, Judas, and the adjacent soldier cluster together in an indissoluble block:[13] the knot-work of intercrossed arms piling up over Christ's figure acts like a single, implacable machine to fulfill the arrest (Figs. 146, 147). By framing into a close-up frieze this chain of three actors, Caravaggio visually accentuated the silent violence and ineluctability of the episode. In fact, the armored soldier, cut off just below the waist, his face practically hidden under his helmet, both creates a foil for the group of Christ and Judas, and transfigures into a

12 Hermann Fiore 1995, 24-5. For Caravaggio and Dürer, see also Heimbürger 1998.

13 See Hütt 1980, 2:1603; and Schoch et al. 2001, 2:304-5, no. 197.

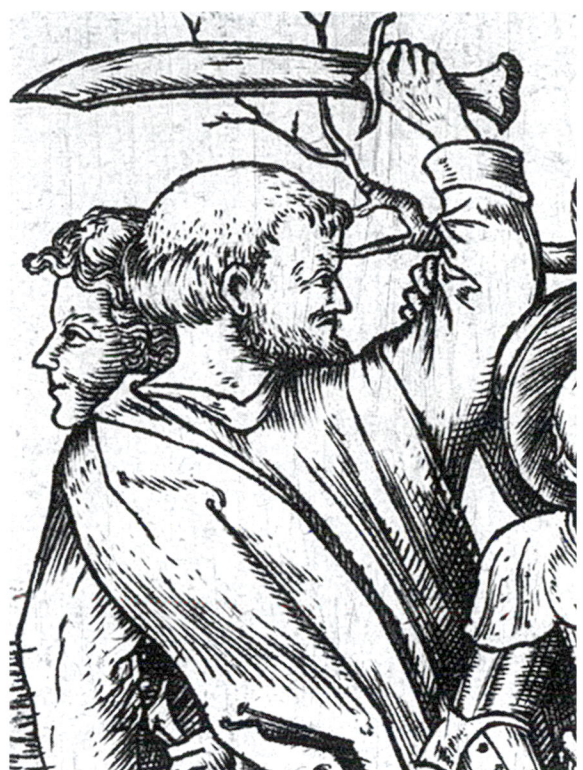

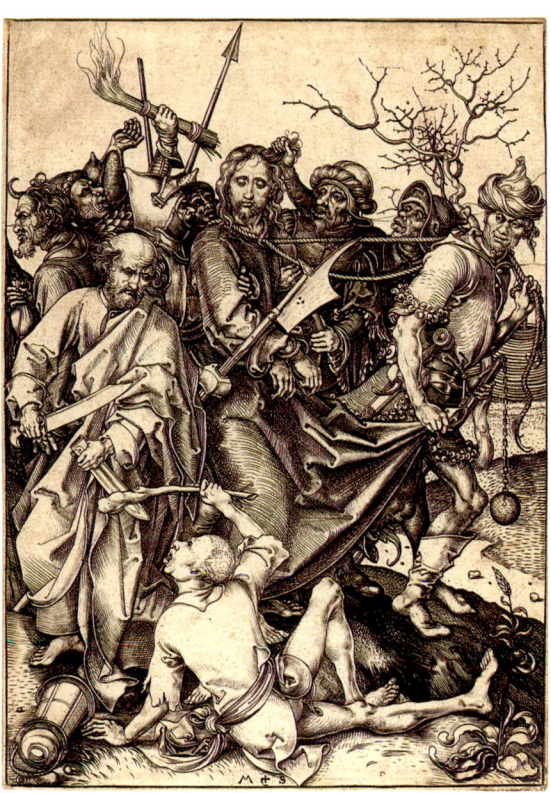

Fig. 144
Master AG (Anton Gerbel of Pforzheim?), *The Taking of Christ*, engraving, 14.5 x 10.8 cm., detail.

Fig. 145
Martin Schongauer, *The Taking of Christ*, engraving, 16.4 x 11.6 cm.

dark, reflecting screen, thereby distancing the viewer from the scene and conjuring up the blind impersonality of the Roman soldiers. In concealing most of this soldier's face, Caravaggio perhaps had in mind the assaulting figure in Titian's *Bravo*. Like Dürer and Titian, Caravaggio underscores the detail of the hand seizing the victim by the collar, but he amplifies its effects through the contrast between the glimmering black metal of the iron glove and the shade surrounding Christ's face.

Although Dürer's woodcut provided Caravaggio with an ingenious invention, one particularly suitable for revision and refinement, it can be proved that *The Taking of Christ* is indebted to other sources, some of them atypical, some canonical but astounding. In composing the Dublin picture, Caravaggio thus sifted through patterns and schemes stemming from the iconographical tradition, blending them in a unique pictorial synthesis. A late fifteenth-century print of *The Taking of Christ*, by the Master AG, tentatively identified as Anton Gerbel of Pforzheim, exerted a certain influence on Caravaggio (Fig. 143).[14] If isolated in a frieze-like image, the cohort of mercenaries to the right rushing at Christ on Judas' infamous cue recalls Caravaggio's composition. The painter in a sense inverted the order of these soldiers, shifting them outward to the right margin, staggering their heads in a wavy curve (Figs. 146, 148). In the center of the print, the group of Jesus, seen frontally, and Judas in profile, barred by the stretched arm of a snarling soldier with his back turned, also resembles that in Caravaggio's picture. More important, Caravaggio borrowed the detail of the face detaching itself from behind Christ's head as depicted in the engraving. Taken together, the trio of aligned heads at Judas's right, as well as the outcrop of the soldier's profile behind Jesus, so characteristic of the Master AG's invention, must be regarded as unequivocal sources for Caravaggio. There is no doubt that these rhythmical alignments and binomial junctions of figures subtly intrigued the painter,

14   See Koreny and Hutchison 1981, 320, no. 5-1 (346); and Hutchison 1991, 205, no. 009.

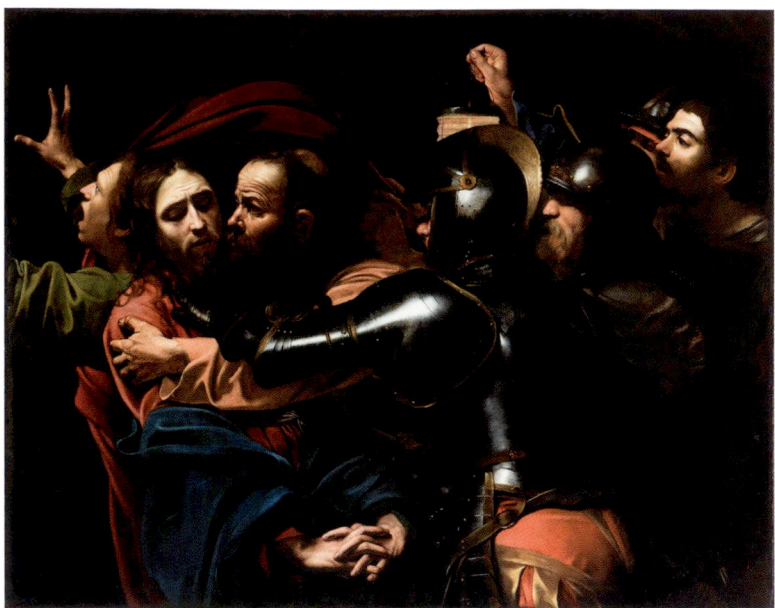

Fig. 146
Michelangelo Merisi da Caravaggio, *The Taking of Christ*, National Gallery of Ireland, Dublin, oil on canvas, 133.5 x 169.5 cm.

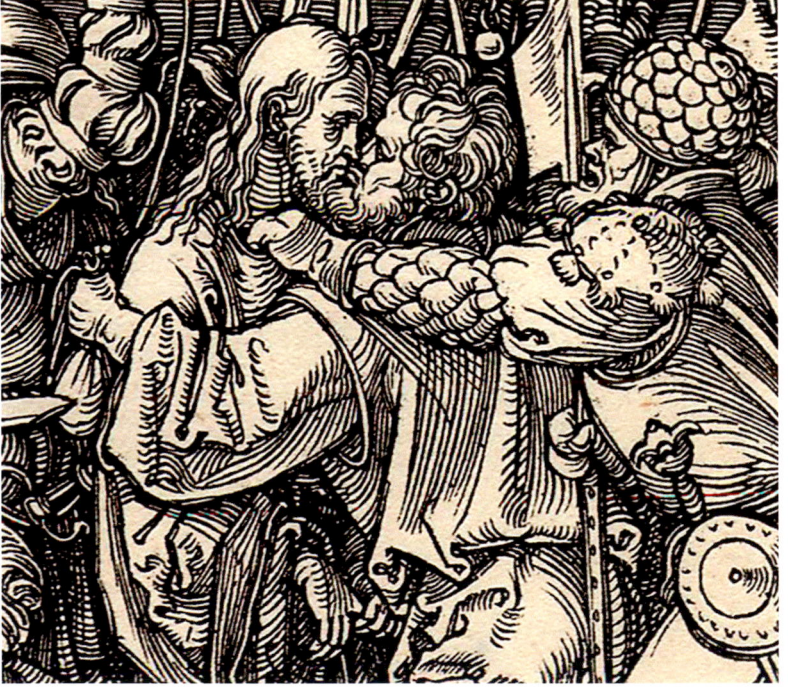

Fig. 147
Albrecht Dürer, *The Taking of Christ*, woodcut, 12.7 x 9.7 cm., detail.

who used them upon elaboration, and extracted from them unexpected implications. Aside from transforming the soldier's face behind Jesus into Saint John's, thereby inflecting the narration with thoughtful nuances, Caravaggio developed other structural singularities of the Master AG's composition, to wit, certain visual syncopes through which relevant segments of the ongoing action are concealed. The more eloquent example of this narrative device takes place on the far left of the print. A hand, mysteriously reemerging from behind a hat and belonging to the figure near Christ, holds back Saint Peter, his arm heroically soaring as he wields his sword, while the face of the bolting Saint John protrudes from behind Peter's head (Fig. 144). By the juxtaposition of the two apostles' profiles, the Master AG duplicates the effect of the junction between Jesus' head and the soldier's at the center of the print. Similarly, in Caravaggio's *The Taking of Christ*, a pair of powerful hands ambiguously abutting the foreground soldier's profile grasps the mantle of the escaping Saint John; they assuredly belong to the bearded figure contiguous to Caravaggio's double.

One can discern analogous cases of narrative fragmentation and figurative coagulation in Martin Schongauer's *The Taking of Christ* (Fig. 145).[15] In this print, the insertion of interposed figures partially blocks out the actions of two ugly soldiers, almost symmetrically situated on each side of the Savior, but not contiguous to him. The soldier at the right raises his head as he tugs at a lock of Christ's hair. The one at the left lifts his arm while holding a torch in a thwarted attempt to look more closely at Jesus' capture: like in Caravaggio's picture, a helmeted soldier prevents him from witnessing the scene by inserting himself in between the two (Fig. 146, 149). It cannot be coincidental that this torchbearer's attitude echoes that of Caravaggio's self-portrait in *The Taking of Christ*, and that his upraised arm holding the light appears temporarily mutilated through the helmet's interposition exactly as in the Dublin painting. Also remarkable is the fact that, in Schongauer's composition, Judas' fleeing profile merges with the torch-bearing soldier's: the traitor clutches the money pouch while stepping out of the scene.

15   See Bernhard 1980, 59; and Béguerie 1991, 372, no. G 85.

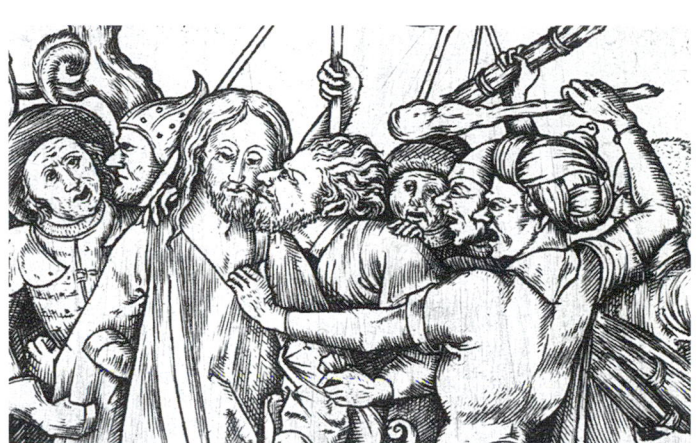

Fig. 148
Master AG (Anton Gerbel of Pforzheim?), *The Taking of Christ*, engraving, 14.5 x 10.8 cm., detail.

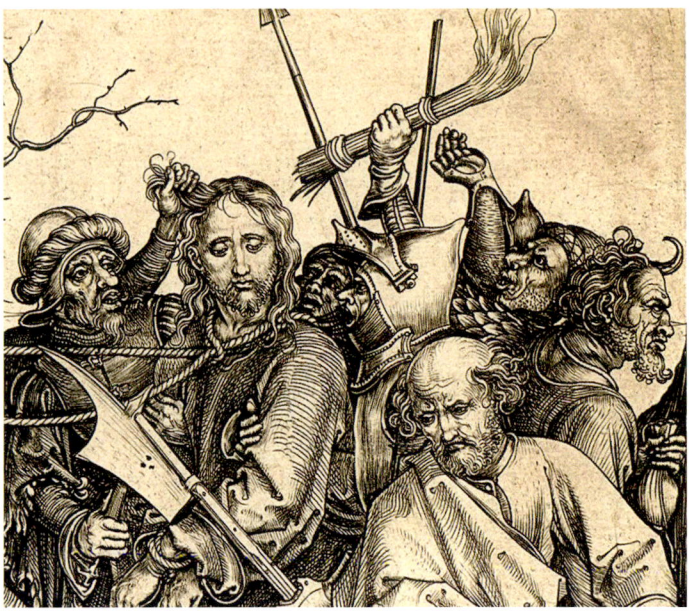

Fig. 149
Martin Schongauer, *The Taking of Christ*, engraving, 16.4 x 11.6 cm., detail reversed.

Of course, the similarities between Dürer's, the Master AG's, and Schongauer's prints depend on their common cultural matrix. By contrast, Caravaggio's systematic raids on the German primitive tradition, mustering whatever microscopic detail he found useful to renew the iconographic theme of *The Taking of Christ*, reward consideration. Before dwelling on this issue, it will be appropriate to uncover another strange precedent to the Dublin picture: Lucas van Leyden's *Embrace* or *The Fool and the Servant* (Fig. 150).[16] In this 1520 print, a hideous old man, dressed as a fool, his belt loaded with a huge pouch, seeks to embrace a young lady who, disgusted, strives vainly to sneak out of his grip. When inverted, the profile of the foolish lover, the position of his arm over the woman's breast, and the motif of his rapacious clutch at her shoulder, evoke Caravaggio's kissing scene. More relevant, the tilt of the lady's head in rebuking the old man, her averted eyes covered by heavy eyelids, and the sigh escaping from her parted lips undoubtedly compare with Christ's expression in the Dublin painting. In Chapter 4, I noted the influence of northern primitive prints on Caravaggio's two versions of the *Fortune Teller*: the artist was assuredly well acquainted with the iconographical tradition of the *Ill-Matched Pairs* as exemplified by Lucas' *Embrace*. Thus, it is no surprise that, in imagining Judas' kiss in *The Tak-*

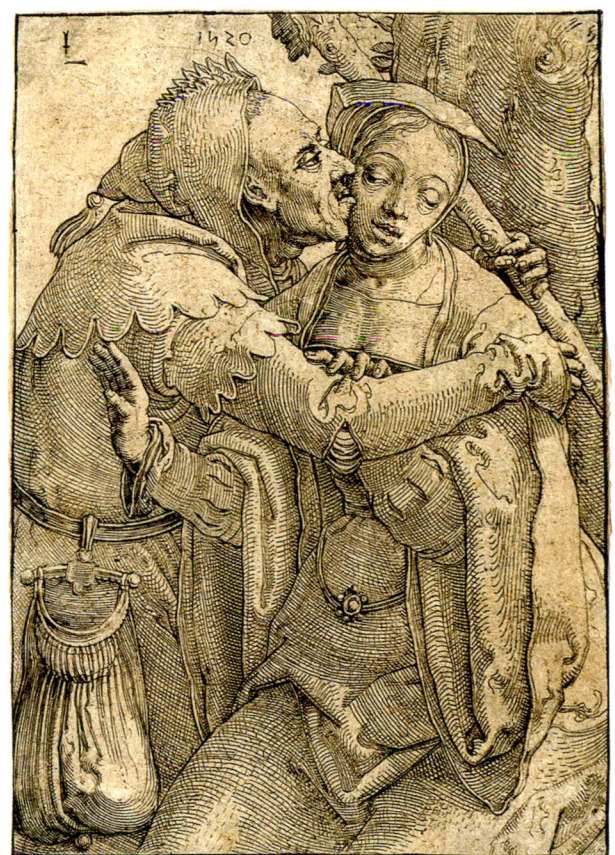

Fig. 150
Lucas van Leyden, *The Embrace*, etching and engraving, 10.5 x 7.4 cm.

16   See Kok et al. 1996, 140, no. 150.

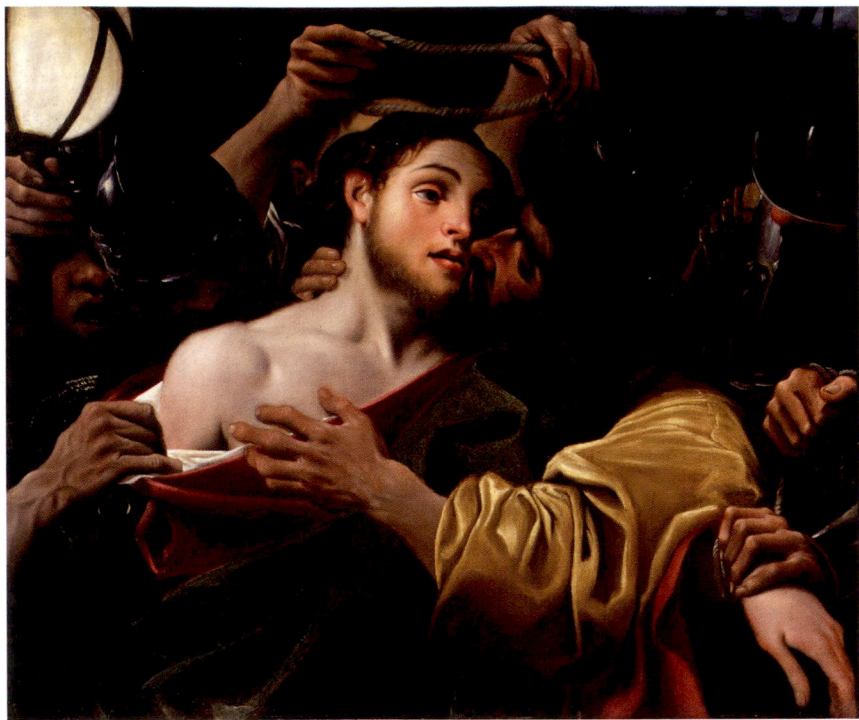

Fig. 151
Ludovico Carracci (after), *The Taking of Christ*, Princeton University Art Museum, Princeton, oil on canvas, 80 x 97 cm.

ing of Christ, Caravaggio also relied on this imagery. I will explain later to what end the artist drew on this unusual repertoire of images, but first I shall explain why the recourse to these rare sources falls within the purview of a widerspread debate on originality among artists in Rome and beyond.

In interpreting the Dublin painting, Hermann Fiore remarked that Caravaggio's elaboration of Dürer's ideas was by no means an anomalous case at the time; in an anonymous copy after Ludovico Carracci's *The Taking of Christ*, now in the Princeton Art Museum (Fig. 151),[17] the motif of the noose hovering over Christ's head as an "ironic halo" likewise harks back to a 1508 print by Dürer from the *Engraved Passion* representing the betrayal episode.[18] In the main, I agree with this observation, but I wish to pick upon Hermann Fiore's consideration in order to enlarge its scope. Painted *c*.1590, Ludovico's *The Taking of Christ* owes a great deal to northern early Renaissance prints, whose patterns and motifs it combines in a groundbreaking manner. A 1514 woodcut by Jacob Cornelisz van Oostsanen, *The Taking of Christ*,[19] probably figures among Ludovico's sources (Fig. 152). In it, Jesus, by bending his head and torso rightward, his face oriented in three-quarter view, gazes intently at Judas who, in profile, rests his right hand over the Savior's shoulder as he kisses him. Behind Christ, a landsknecht, both his arms lifted, is about to encircle his neck with a noose that, before landing on its target, perilously hangs over him. Oostsanen's composition is closer to Ludovico's than Dürer's, although it does not present the detail of Judas's left hand suspended over Christ's chest, so crucial to the Princeton picture (Figs. 154, 155). However, this motif is not uncommon in other northern prints. In an extremely rare woodcut ascribed to the Master of the Berlin Passion,[20] Judas clings on to Christ's torso in an attitude similar to his counterpart's in Ludovico's painting: his open left hand, after sweeping over the Savior's chest, aims at his shoulder. In a woodcut by Urs Graf, illustrating both *The Agony in the Garden* and *The Taking of Christ* (Fig. 153),[21] Judas' hand lingers exactly in the center of Jesus' torso, in a posture noticeably identical to his counterpart's in Ludovico's picture (Figs. 154, 156).

It is difficult to acknowledge the importance of such peripheral and unwonted sources for Ludovico, whom one would expect to be more sensitive to other sorts of models. But the evidence indicates otherwise: even the sensual and perverted character of Judas' kiss in the Princeton picture, as Gail Feigenbaum characterized it, seems related to northern patterns.[22] For instance, in Ludwig

17 See Feigenbaum 1989; Emiliani 1993, 52-4, no. 24 [as an original; catalogue entry by Feigenbaum]; and Brogi 2001, 1:243-5, no. A3 [as doubtful].

18 Herrmann Fiore 1995, 26. For the print, see Hütt 1980, 2:1851.

19 For the print, see Strauss 1981, 11, no. 3 (445).

20 See Hollstein 1955, 86, no. 9-I.

21 For the print, see Ibidem, 57, no. 2j (459).

22 See Feigenbaum's catalogue entry in Emiliani 1993, 52: "a occhi chiusi, sporge la bocca per deporre un bacio sulle labbra socchiuse di Cristo. È l'abbraccio tenero e appassionato di un amante, un gesto che porta con sé una carica erotica concepita per turbare lo spettatore."

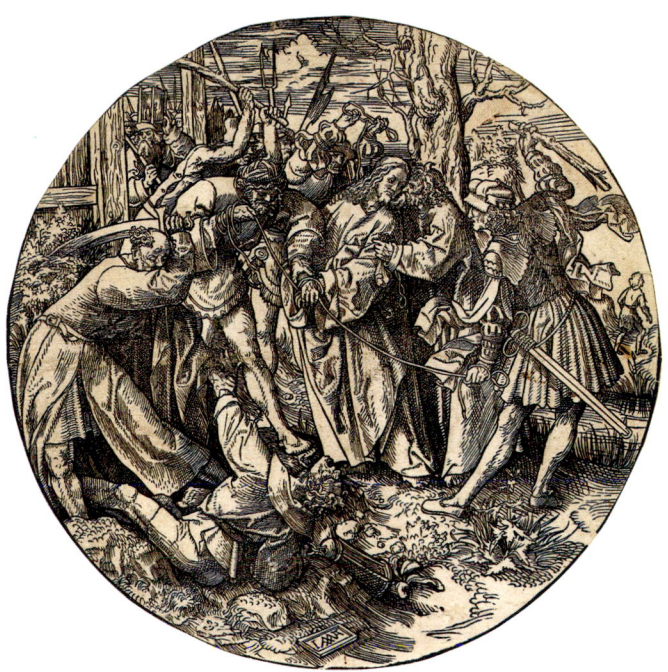

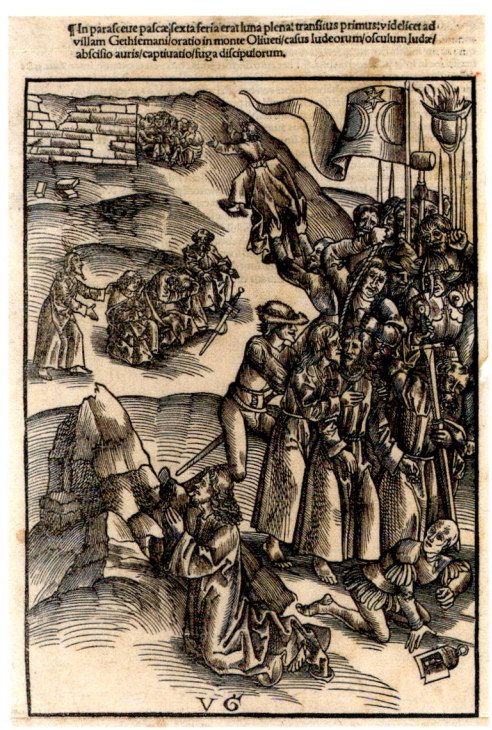

Fig. 152
Jacob Cornelisz van Oostsanen, *The Taking of Christ*, engraving,
23.2 cm. (diameter).

Fig. 153
Urs Graf, *The Agony in the Garden and The Taking of
Christ*, engraving, 21.6 x 15.7 cm.

Krug's *The Embrace* (Fig. 157),[23] a young fool snatches a lascivious kiss from a female peasant. Not only is the man's face represented in profile, his lips sticking out toward the woman's cheek, but he also seizes his partner's head in a powerful hold. Albeit not identically, Ludovico's Judas takes possession of Jesus' torso in an analogous way. Krug's print belongs to the same tradition as Lucas van Leyden's *The Embrace*. Like Caravaggio a decade later, Ludovico fashions comedic and serious formulae into religious tragedy.

Caravaggio's inventive process in imagining The *Taking of Christ* parallels Ludovico's: both artists browse through selected northern compositions searching for rare details that would enliven their interpretation of the subject. Both dissimulate their thefts by magnifying apocryphal, even minuscule, iconographic motifs: indeed, unless through zooming in, these details become paradoxically undetectable. In the Princeton picture, Ludovico unabashedly exhibits to view the ill-matched kiss between Judas and Christ, transforming the betrayal gesture into a rebutting embrace. By omitting the face of the soldier behind Christ, he changes an instrument of torture, the noose, into a sign of holiness and salvation. Moreover, by limiting the pictorial field to the central group of Judas and Christ, blurring the soldiers' faces through daunting foreshortening, Ludovico enhances the imaginative impact of the episode: the stumps of grasping hands swarming around Christ's radiant figure function as a visual synecdoche, increasing the impression of violence in the viewer's imagination. If Ludovico did not invent all the motifs that individually characterize his picture, by assembling them together he created an effect of astounding novelty. In other words, Ludovico's incursion into early Renaissance prints is the prerequisite for his originality. Through these exceptional sources, the déjà-vu rooted in the traditional subject explodes into a brand new vision.

23   See Strauss 1981, 308, no. 10 (540).

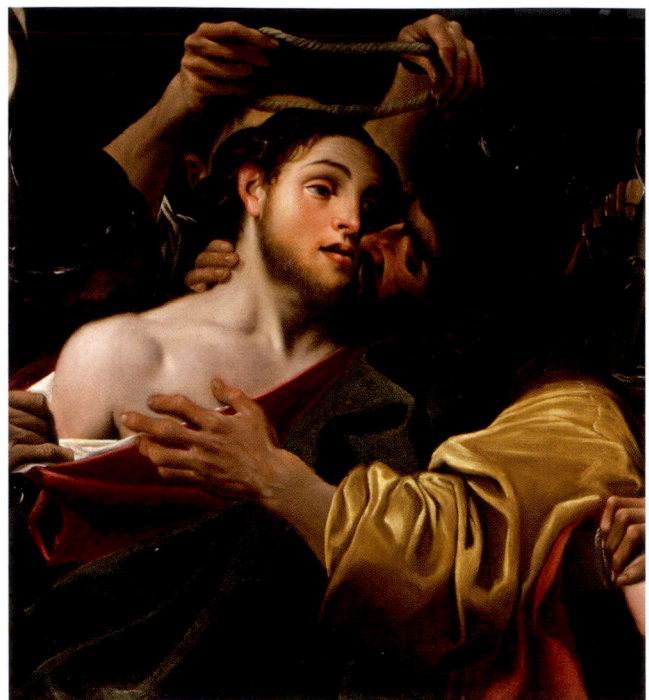

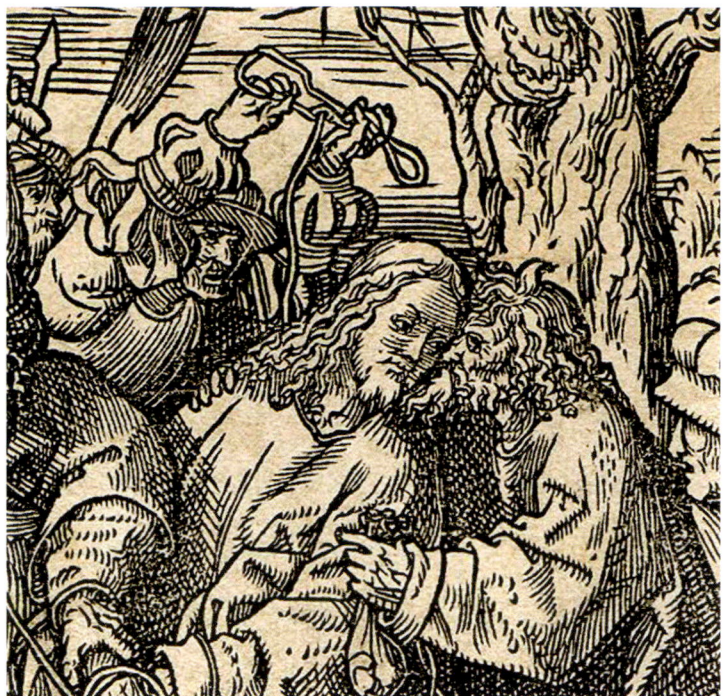

Fig. 154
Ludovico Carracci (after), *The Taking of Christ*, Princeton University
Art Museum, Princeton, oil on canvas, 80 x 97 cm., detail.

Fig. 155
Jacob Cornelisz van Oostsanen, *The Taking of Christ*, engraving, 23.2 cm.
(diameter), detail.

The analogies that I have unraveled between Ludovico's and Caravaggio's working methods
in depicting their versions of *The Taking of Christ* are not fortuitous. Caravaggio might have visited
Bologna if, as Bellori declares in his *Vite*, he spent time in Venice before heading to Rome. Also, he
must have been intrigued by a close-up, half-figure composition like Ludovico's that is frequently
viewed by scholars as an anticipation of his own mature style. In this connection, the Dublin
picture looks like an untimely—or maybe too timely—response to Ludovico's painting of the
1590s. Compared to the pictures that Ludovico's cousin and former associate, Annibale Carracci,
was executing in Rome around 1602-1603, Caravaggio's *The Taking of Christ* constitutes what could
have been one of the most sophisticated products of the Bolognese reform, had the Carracci not
strayed from their pristine naturalism and experimental syncretism.

But Caravaggio is not one of the Carracci. Even if his *The Taking of Christ* structurally lends itself
to a comparison with Ludovico's, it also differs from the Princeton picture in many respects. It is
not simply that Caravaggio widens the pictorial field to accommodate more figures, visualizing
an articulate action where Ludovico's painting is substantially a contemplative image: a near
equivalent of a Man of Sorrows. Were it not for the fuss of truncated anatomies and swirling
movements around Jesus' figure, Ludovico's painting would easily compete with Mantegna's
close-up narratives.

The real originality of Caravaggio's *The Taking of Christ* lies in two specific points: its interpretation
of Christ's reaction to Judas' kiss, and the insertion of John's figure disengaging himself from the
Savior's body. Along with the innovative presence of the painter cast as a lantern-bearer, these
two elements deserve further analysis. I have already remarked that Christ's expression seems to
convey revulsion rather than acceptance, as suggested by the parallel of Lucas' *Embrace*. The gesture
of the interlocking hands confirms this interpretation, for it traditionally expresses desperation
before an irreparable event. A few examples will corroborate the point. In a print attributed to the
Master ES, a *Crucifixion*, the Virgin rehearses this posture while sunk in mourning at the foot of the

322

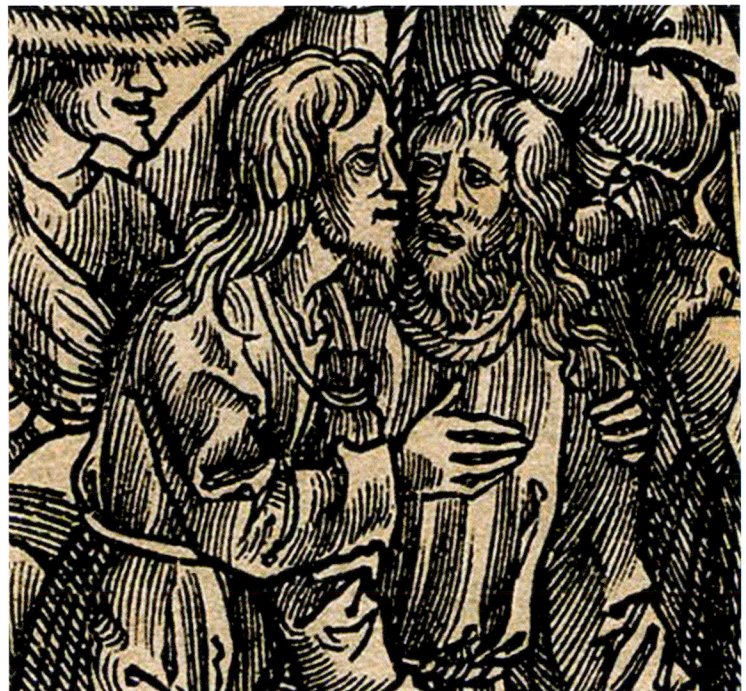

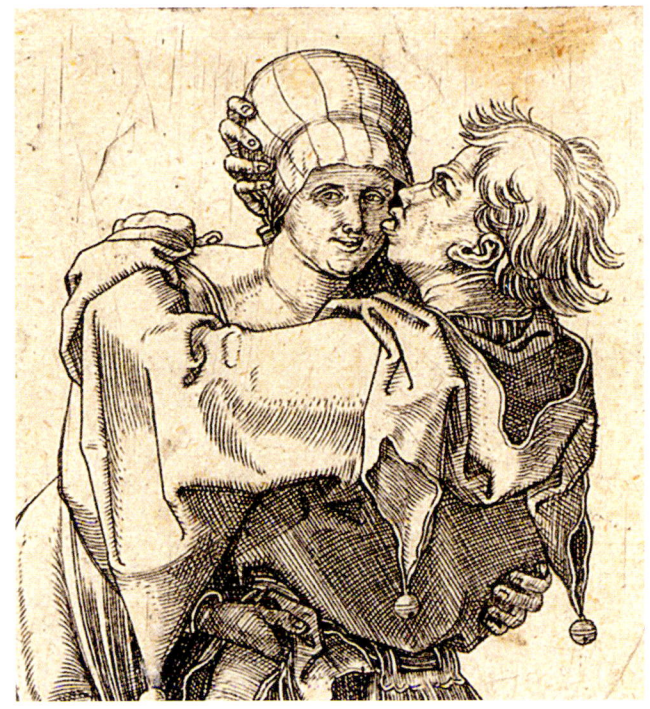

Fig. 156
Urs Graf, *The Agony in the Garden and The Taking of Christ*, engraving,
21.6 x 15.7 cm., detail.

Fig. 157
Ludwig Krug, *The Embrace*, engraving, 11 x 7.8 cm., detail.

cross.[24] Similarly, Saint John performs the same attitude in a woodcut by Hans Schäufelein, another *Crucifixion*.[25] As another woodcut by Schäufelein demonstrates, the gesture was not limited to religious subjects: in his *Pyramus and Thisbe*,[26] the heroine poses in an attitude almost identical with Caravaggio's Christ. By entangling her hands, Thisbe communicates her despair before Pyramus' dead body (Fig. 158). Nor does this gesture apply exclusively to the northern tradition, as is shown by the case of Guido Reni's famous *Crucifixion* for the Capuchins (Bologna, Pinacoteca Nazionale), painted in 1617-1618.[27] The painting shows Saint John contemplating the crucified Christ as he entwines his hands in desperation.[28] Though similar to a praying gesture, this posture translates something both related and different: grief and hopelessness. As such, it is fitting to use it to refer to Christ's momentary despair before his arrest and Passion. In Guido Reni's *The Agony in the Garden* (Louvre, Paris), painted in 1607 (a few years after the artist's alleged confrontation with Caravaggio), Jesus kneels in the foreground, his arms stretched obliquely alongside his torso, his hands interlocked as his face turns heavenward (Fig. 159).[29] To my knowledge, only Hans Sebald Beham uses this gesture in relation with Jesus' capture. In his 1535 woodcut of *The Taking of Christ*,[30] the Savior clenches his hands even as Judas, surrounding him with one arm, is about to give him the fatal kiss (Fig. 160).

By representing Christ leaning away from Judas' kiss and the soldier's grip, and by making him perform the gesture of helpless despair, Caravaggio introduces an element of great novelty in the iconographical tradition. As a prolepsis, the interlocked hands prefigure the Virgin's and

24 For this *Crucifixion*, see Geisberg 1924, 28, no. L. 32.

25 See Falk 1980, 206, no. 31 (252).

26 See Ibidem, 275, no. 95 (265).

27 See Pepper 1988, 240-1, no. 55.

28 Treffers 1996, 278, had already noted this iconographical detail.

29 For the painting, see Pepper 1988, 226-7, no. 27.

30 For the print, see Koch 1978, 86.

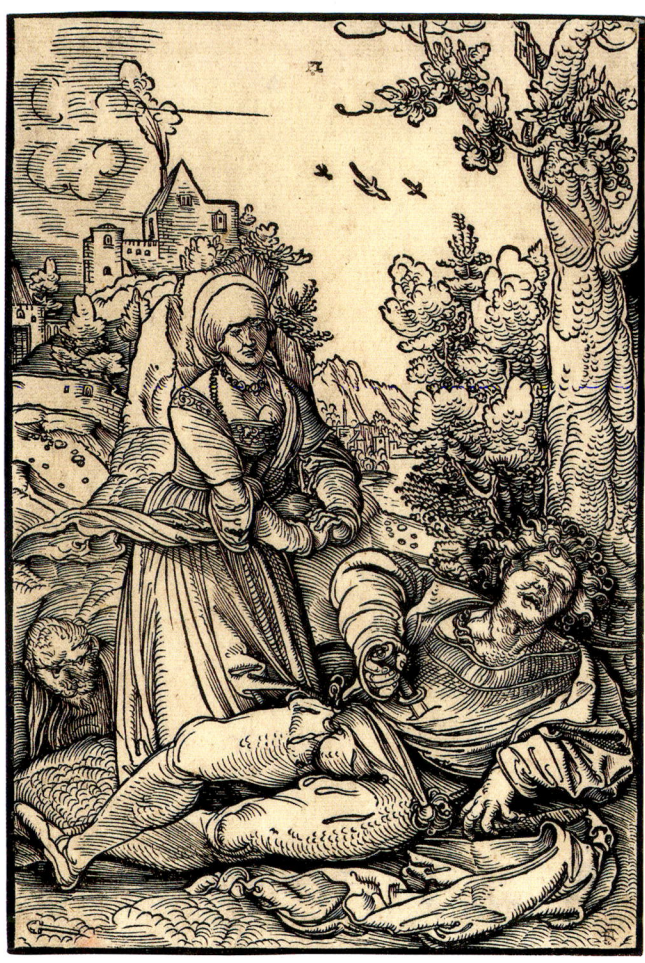

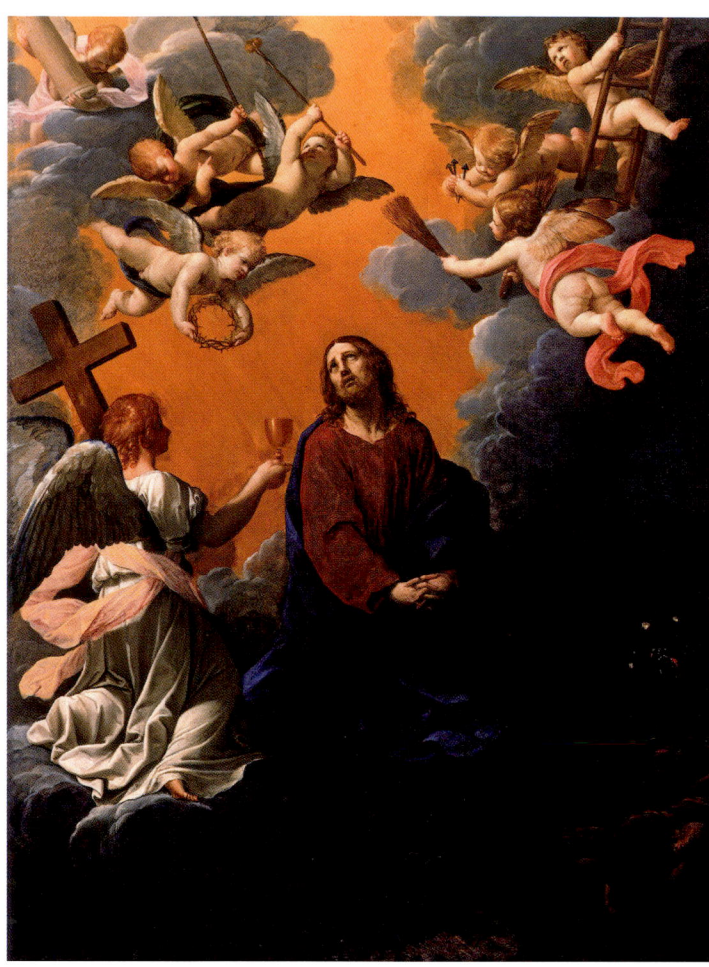

Fig. 158
Hans Schäufelein, *Pyramus and Thisbe*, woodcut, 22.9 x 15.5 cm.

Fig. 159
Guido Reni, *The Agony in the Garden*, Musée du Louvre, Paris, oil on copper, 67 x 43 cm.

Saint John's desolation once the Passion is accomplished. Foreseeing his martyrdom, whose accomplishment is officially triggered by Judas' kiss, the figure of Christ in the Dublin picture enacts the desperation of his crucifixion and death.[31] In retrospect, the gesture evokes Christ's abhorrence of his sacrifice during his prayer in the garden.[32] In a sense, Judas in this context incarnates the bitter chalice that the Savior wished, however temporarily, to be taken away by his Father, as well as the horror of his imminent crucifixion. Instead of endowing him with a conventional heroism, Caravaggio gives Christ the terrible awareness of his Passion: he accepts, or is going to accept, the sacrifice, but at what price! Caravaggio's use of a dislocated gesture—that is, a gesture that pertains to other iconographies—in so appropriate a manner, through collapsing time and condensing past, present, and future in a single shot, qualifies as pure originality. In this manner, the subject matter undergoes a meaningful and unusual elaboration.

31 With regard to the visual prolepsis employed here by Caravaggio, see also Corrain 2002, 228: "il Maestro con le braccia rivolte verso il basso, con le mani incrociate, sembra, invece, assumere la postura tipica di Giovanni ai piedi della croce (…). Uno scambio che non si circoscrive alla gestualità, ma sembra toccare anche la resa dei volti. La testa leggermente piegata, gli occhi ribassati del protagonista principale potrebbero, infatti, essere quelli di Giovanni nell'iconografia della crocefissione e i segni di contrazione e di paura del viso di Giovanni potrebbero essere assimilabili, o meglio far tornare alla mente quelli di Gesù sulla croce, nel momento antecedente la morte. (…) È una narrazione che, attraverso la rappresentazione dell'inizio, della fase incoativa, 'include' la fase terminativa."

32 Some scholars view Christ's gesture and attitude in the Dublin painting in heroic terms. Among others, see Puglisi 1998, 221, who speaks of "stoical resignation."

The conjunction of the heads of Jesus and Saint John in an awkward evocation of an ancient *Janus Bifrons* may also rank among the most outstanding originalities of Caravaggio's *The Taking of Christ*. Saint Mark (14, 50-52) is the only one to mention this secondary episode of Jesus' capture:

> Then [after the kiss] all his disciples left him and fled. And a certain young man was following him, having a linen cloth wrapped about his naked body, and they seized him. But leaving the linen cloth behind, he fled away from them naked.

Mark does not explicitly say that the young man who lost his dress was John, although he reports that all three apostles accompanying Jesus escaped arrest. But nor does he relate that the "bystander" who cut Malchus' ear during the capture of Christ was Saint Peter, as specified solely by Saint John's Gospel. Therefore, it comes as little surprise that "the young man" of Mark's account was identified in Caravaggio's time with the youngest of the apostles, Saint John, and this is certainly the reason why Bellori did not hesitate to recognize the fugitive in *The Taking of Christ* as John. This identification, incidentally, must have been very common. For example, in the 1569 inventory of Gerolamo Garimberto's collection, a painting after Correggio is quoted: "a little canvas with Saint John escaping when Christ is captured in the garden."[33] Caravaggio's idea of fusing John's head with Jesus' is thus a stroke of genius.

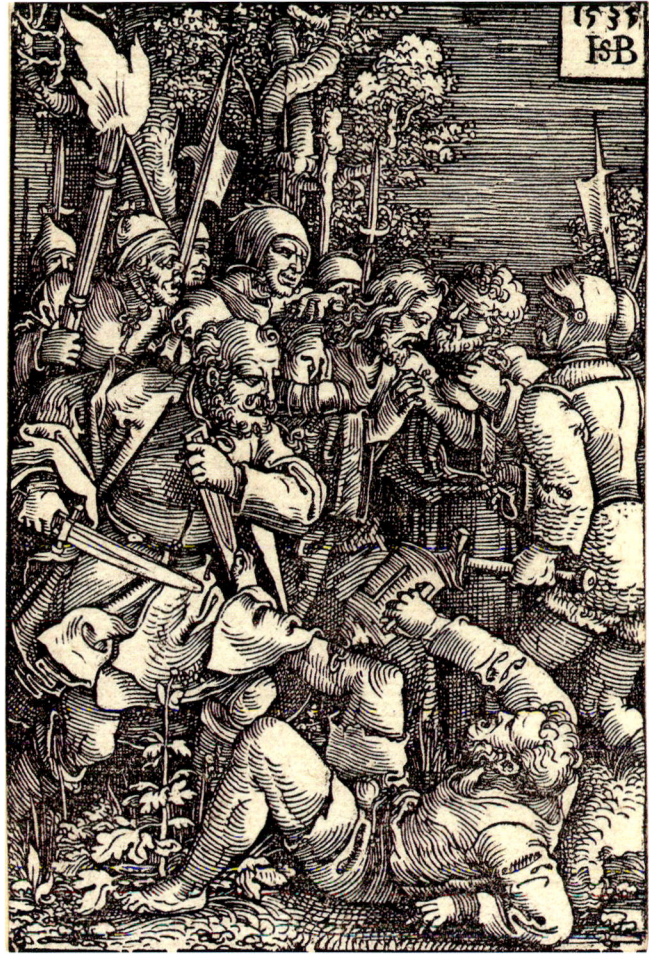

Fig. 160
Hans Sebald Beham, *The Taking of Christ*, woodcut, 12.5 x 8.5 cm.

According to the textual sources and Christian authorities, John was Christ's favorite. His presence at the foot of the cross, near the Virgin, bears witness to his privileged status. In the iconography of the *Last Supper*, artists used to highlight his closeness to the Savior by ensconcing his face and torso within Jesus' chest, as in a woodcut by Dürer from the 1509-1511 *Small Passion* (Fig. 161).[34] Valentin de Boulogne's *Last Supper* (now in Rome, Galleria Nazionale di Palazzo Barberini),[35] originally destined for Cardinal Ciriaco Mattei as a sequel to Caravaggio's *Supper at Emmaus* and *The Taking of Christ*, represents Jesus and Saint John equally united in a triangular scheme (Fig. 162). There, the Savior's arms and shoulder encompass the figure of the sleeping young apostle. This iconographic formula implies that, on an affective level, John and Jesus are but one person, the former being almost the double of the latter.

It is evident that Caravaggio somehow overturns the conventional scheme linking the figure of Christ to the young apostle: instead of standing by the Savior, John runs away in panic. As Sergio Benedetti pointed out, the apostle's attitude mirrors that of a furious Maenad in an antique

---

33   Brown C. 1990, 203. An early copy (or uncertain original) of this painting has been published in Fornari Schianchi 2008, 322-3, no. III.36 [catalogue entry by Angelo Loda]. Correggio's picture certainly sheds light on the Cavalier d'Arpino's strange invention of a fleeing nude in his own version of *The Taking of Christ*.

34   See Hütt 1980, 2:1600; Schoch at al. 2001, 2: 184-5, no. 155.

35   See Mojana 1989, 140, no. 44.

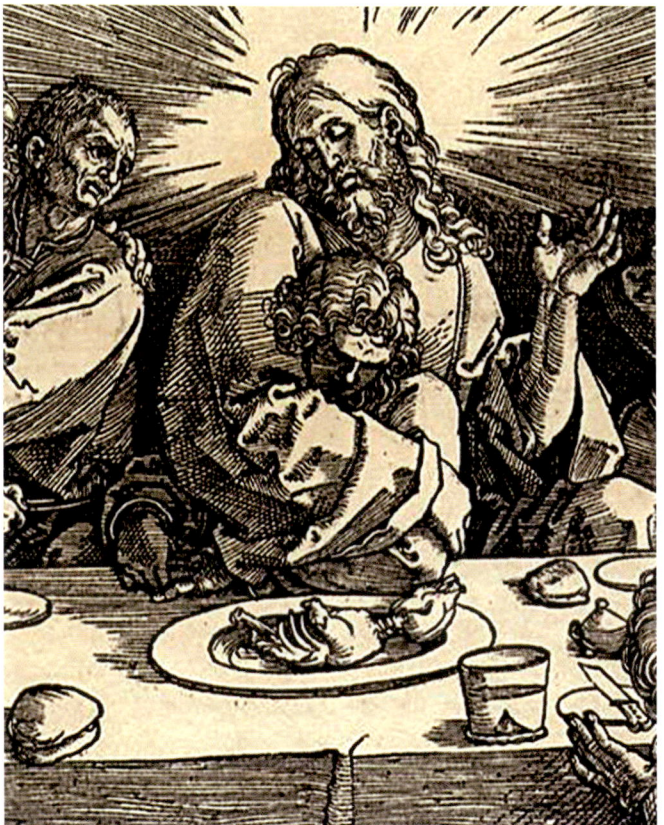

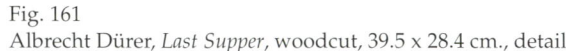

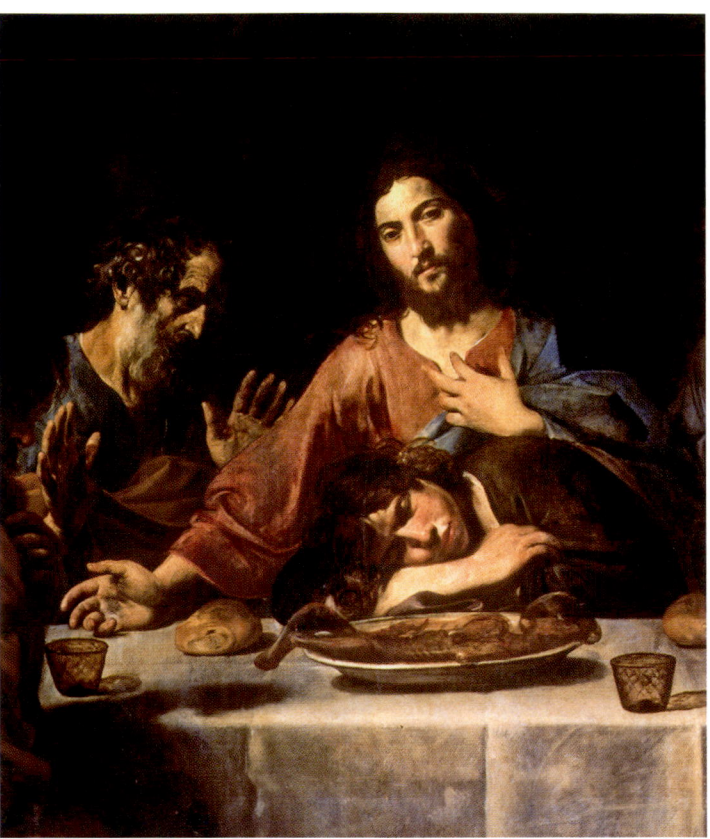

Fig. 161
Albrecht Dürer, *Last Supper*, woodcut, 39.5 x 28.4 cm., detail.

Fig. 162
Valentin de Boulogne, *Last Supper*, Galleria Nazionale d'Arte Antica, Palazzo Barberini, Rome, oil on canvas, 139 x 230 cm., detail.

bas-relief or vase, head tilted backward, drapery swelling and waving behind due to the hectic motion.[36] However, I believe that Caravaggio intended something else by dislodging John's profile from behind Jesus' head. Linked together by a diagonal axis, the two figures coalesce into a single contradictory action, Christ's arms and entangled hands acting as powerful brakes to counteract John's escape. As an *alter ego* of the Savior, John visually suggests that a part of Christ would long to bolt and escape the loathsome embrace of Death, whereas another part of him thinks better of it, surrendering to Judas' kiss and God's will.[37] From this point of view, Caravaggio's attempt at originality reaches its climax. His representation of a torn Jesus, heroically resisting the idea of fleeing, inwardly conscious of the Passion's torments, is a *hapax legomenon*, an unmatched, unrivaled version of *The Taking of Christ*. This reassessment of Jesus' behavior during his betrayal and capture might have had devastating implications for a contemporary beholder. Accordingly, Bellori's misreading of Christ's attitude as expressing humility and resignation may depend on a religious and cultural taboo. In a civilization exalting the heroism of unflinching saints and martyrs, the evocation of Christ's wavering from death, however ephemeral and spontaneous, would barely be tolerable.

36   See Benedetti 1993b, 30-1.

37   A similar observation is made by Bersani and Dutoit 1998, 56: "The figure himself [the authors do not recognize him as John] is, in some ways, a double of Christ. He seems to be a growth on Christ's body. They have identical hair, and they seem to be attached like Siamese twins. (…). It is as if the nonresistant Christ were also running away, rushing out from his own head to escape his imminent death only, perhaps, to meet that predestined, inescapable fate also rushing toward him from the opposite direction." To understand the final sentence, one must take into account that the authors postulate that the running John might also be preventing the arrival of other soldiers coming from the left, and therefore from off-stage, which is false.

326

The Cavalier d'Arpino's 1596-1597 *The Taking of Christ* (Rome, Galleria Borghese), of which a workshop copy from *c*.1610 is now at the Accademia di San Luca, Rome (Fig. 163), allows us to measure the extent of Caravaggio's originality.[38] In it, the Cavaliere placed the naked figure of an escaping apostle at the left: a soldier behind seizes his "linen cloth" vainly. When compared to Caravaggio's invention, this nude looks bland and anecdotal, although in a sense it was also original, and truer to the letter of the Gospels. Interestingly enough, Bellori praises the Cavaliere's *The Taking of Christ* for being "the most beautiful picture he ever painted."[39]

Considered together, Ludovico's, the Cavalier d'Arpino's, and Caravaggio's paintings attest to a discourse on originality practically undocumented in contemporary sources. Although style is an essential part of newness, it is undeniable that the treatment of the subject ranks as a basic component in the definition of artistic originality. It is no coincidence that Ludovico and Caravaggio strewed their inventions with unanticipated twists and insights derived from an iconographic tradition perceived as generally out-of-date and non-canonical. From this point of view too, the insertion of a naked figure in the Cavaliere's *The Taking of Christ* responds not only to a demand for textual trustworthiness, but also provides beholders with an unpredicted visual invention: one able to invigorate a worn-out tradition, even in a shocking way.

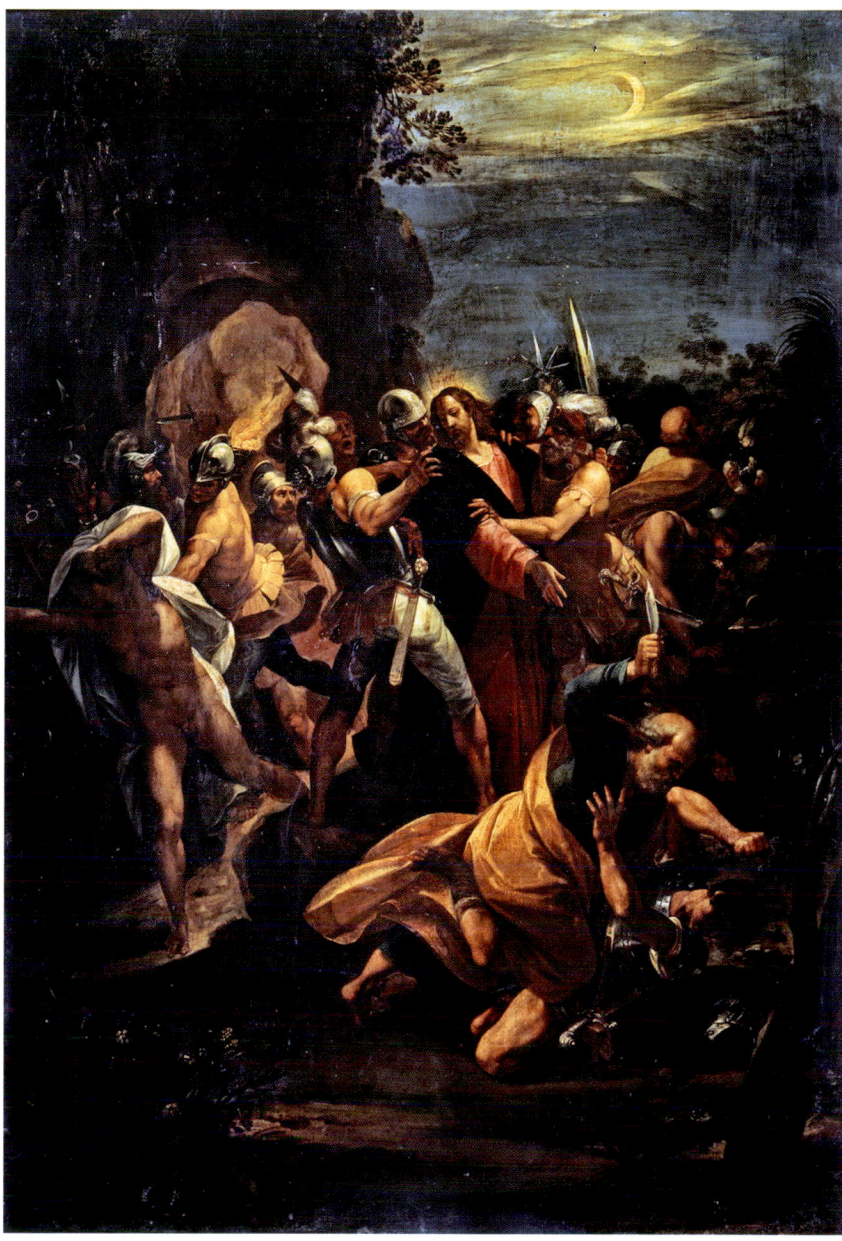

Fig. 163
Cavalier d'Arpino (Giuseppe Cesari) and workshop, *The Taking of Christ*, Accademia di San Luca, Rome, oil on canvas, 100 x 70 cm.

In this regard, the elements of novelty displayed by Caravaggio's interpretation of *The Taking of Christ* are less immediate; unlike the Cavalier d'Arpino, Caravaggio does not show off at first the many originalities of his painting. In this regard, it is understandable that the artist was proud of his creation, so much so as to replicate his effigy in the painting, directing the viewer's attention toward his new vision of the kiss scene. This is why he ingeniously sheltered the group of Christ, Judas, and John under the artificial niche of a flying mantle.[40] However, by envisioning himself as

38 See Röttgen 2002, 308-9, no. 68; 398, no. 156.

39 According to Röttgen 2002, 308, this remark ("la più bell'opera che facesse il Cavaliere") is to be found in a manuscript note by Bellori to Baglione's 1649 *Vite*.

40 See Longhi 1999-2000, 1:265: "Contro la citazione antica del manto che avvolge quasi in un dittico la testa di Cristo e di Giuda, il gruppo, schiarato dal lampione oscillante, sembra incrinarsi come un calice di vetro entro l'orrore notturno."

a lantern-bearer making ineffectual efforts to watch the betrayal, Caravaggio did not intend merely to celebrate his artistic achievement. To corroborate this assumption, I shall elucidate the situation of self-ironic frustration in which the master put himself in the picture, and the function of the lantern that he holds aloft ineffectually.

Igniting Invention

It was Maurizio Marini who first suggested that Caravaggio's self-representation as an escort of the Roman cohort holding a lantern in the Dublin picture may allude to Diogenes' famous "quest for the man."[41] According to Diogenes Laërtius, the Greek cynic philosopher Diogenes once lit up a lantern in plain daylight, declaring: "I seek the man." An engraving in Jan Moerman's 1608 *De Cleyn Werelt* shows Diogenes as a pilgrim, erring among people, looking for the man—that is, the honest man—with his lantern.[42] Unfortunately, Diogenes' search only thrived as a figurative subject after Caravaggio's lifetime, and above all in northern Europe.[43] Even if representations of this theme existed before, they are so scarce that it is impossible to establish Caravaggio's acquaintance with them. However, I would be inclined to agree with Marini's hypothesis, since the allusion to Diogenes in The *Taking of Christ* matches Caravaggio's both playful and thoughtful interpretation of Pilate's well-known dictum, "Ecce Homo," in the Genoa depiction of this subject, as I will explain in Chapter 12. In fact, Diogenes' statement in connection with the lantern was usually known as a Latin aphorism: "Quaero hominem" ["I seek the man"]. On the other hand, the iconographic subject of the Genoa picture, "Ecce Homo," refers to the sentence pronounced by Pilate when presenting Christ to the crowd of Jews: "behold the man." It is difficult to disregard the subtle connection between the two paintings: in *The Taking of Christ*, Caravaggio holds a lantern as he "seeks the man"; in the *Ecce Homo*, the painter, in the guise of a caricatural Pilate, offers "the man" for the crowd to behold. In other words, the two pictures thematically dovetail with each other, configuring a sort of artistic parabola or itinerary in Caravaggio's reflection on the divine, from the quest to the discovery of "the man" by definition: that is, Christ. Therefore, the role of the painter changes from one painting to the other: he is first an accomplice in Christ's betrayal and capture, and then the involuntary cause for Jesus' condemnation and murder. I stress this evolution in Caravaggio's self-representations all the more so in that it culminates in the Borghese *David*. There, the painter symbolically decapitates himself in a kind of self-punishment, by giving his own likeness to Goliath. I personally believe that this pathological tendency to self-degradation and self-destruction was deeply rooted in Caravaggio's personality, but as I have neither the competence nor the evidence to examine the artist's psyche, I willingly leave this topic to more expert scholars. Nevertheless, I am convinced that the artist's self-portrayal in both *The Taking of Christ* and the *Ecce Homo* takes on a very specific self-referential value.

Once again, Hermann Fiore furnishes us with an ingenious clue as to the meaning of the lantern in Roman artistic milieus in Caravaggio's time.[44] As she rightly noted, Federico Zuccari, one of

---

41 Marini 1981b, 368, note 17: "l'immagine allude verosimilmente a un'allegoria di Diogene, che cerca l'uomo con una lanterna, da cui Caravaggio-Diogene cerca Cristo, l'uomo per eccellenza, tra le tenebre e le forze del male. Quindi un emblema stoico di fede e redenzione." See also Treffers 1996, 281.

42 See Moerman, s.p. The print is illustrated by these verses: "Diogenes leert met een vreemt bediet,/ Wie menschen gheheeten moghen syn oft niet," and accompanied by Psalm 39: "Och hoe gants ydel is alle mensche/ Die hier is levende near synen wensche."

43 See Schmitt 1993.

44 Hermann Fiore 1995, 25-6: "The idea that the artist's task is that of enlightenment is one that is articulated in the writings of Dürer, Benvenuto Cellini, Lomazzo and others, and was of particular relevance in the discussion of the Accademia di San Luca during Caravaggio's Roman years. Federico Zuccaro, Prince of the Accademia, proposed a lantern as the academy's emblem, and used the term lanternini to refer to its members. Caravaggio, who was clearly opposed to the spirit of the Accademici del Disegno, presented his new style of painting in a very different, but related, light." The assimilation of the lantern or lamp with *disegno* is indeed to be found in Cellini's statement of the seal he proposed as the emblem of the

the most renowned painters then in Rome, urged the Roman Accademia di San Luca to adopt the lantern as its own emblem. Romano Alberti, in his 1604 *Origine e progresso dell'Accademia del disegno*, relates the circumstances under which the academicians discussed the image of the lantern. On 26 January 1594, Zuccari proposed that the Academy choose its emblem. As if by accident—though everything had been set up previously—a boy interrupted the assembly, carrying a sheet with a proposal by an anonymous member, who we now know was Zuccari himself. Enclosed therein was an emblem with a cube and an oil lamp. Shortly afterward, a second letter arrived, endorsing another design composed of three branches of an olive tree with a mirror. A discussion ensued; other emblems were brought forth, but none was unanimously approved, so that Zuccari was compelled to adjourn the assembly. On 3 February 1594, the academicians were presented with another anonymous proposal (again by Zuccari). In this proposal, a lantern was drawn,

> having three main shutters to let the main light out; above, below, and around, very tiny holes pierced it like a sieve, so that the light burning in the lantern in one way or another streamed outside from everywhere, but particularly from those three shutters. Around it was a motto that read SIC OPERATUR [it operates in this way].[45]

After an animated debate, the academicians voted and opted for this emblem as their own. It is important to explain the emblem's symbolism. Usually associated with assiduous labor, the lantern, curiously enough, was an uncommon motif in Renaissance treatises on emblems. In Mathias Holtzwart's 1571 *Emblematum Tyrocinia*, a woodcut by Tobias Stimmer represents Intellect, his head flaming with sunrays, holding a lantern; behind him, an old man avidly reads a book.[46] The motto "Quae doctum efficiant" ["things that make an accomplished savant"] suggests that culture and science climax when underpinned by assiduity and vigilance. Zuccari's symbolism of the lantern also relates to the notion of an alert intellect, though in a more radical way.

"By illuminating and defeating the darkness," Zuccari stated in the February 1594 session of the Roman Academy, "the lantern obviously signifies the effects and operations enacted by intellective and practical *disegno* in human intelligence and practice." The metal armature of the lantern "means that every faculty of the intellect is dark until the pristine divine spark of light illuminates it." For this reason, "just as this resplendent and bright lantern lightens and casts away darkness, unveiling every hidden appearance to human eyes, so too is such a luminous lantern an appropriate symbol, as well as a decent and adequate emblem of drawing and of this most noble Academy."[47]

As for the motto, SIC OPERATUR, Zuccari noted: "drawing operates like the lantern, since the essential operation of lighting consists in illuminating darkness, and revealing every thing concealed or veiled by darkness." To expound his motto, Zuccari relied, if partially, on Plato's theory of anamnesis, or reminiscence:

Florentine Accademia del Disegno. See Cellini, 145, a passage that resonates with ideas further to be developed by Zuccari: "Sì come questo [*disegno*] è la vera lucerna di tutte le azzioni che fanno gli huomini in ogni professione, perché il disegno è di due sorte, il primo è quello che si fa nell'immaginativa, e il secondo tratto da quello si dimostra con linee (…)." On this concept, see Winner 1968; Kemp 1974; and more extensively with regard to Cellini, Cole 2002, 94, and esp. 121 ff.

45   Alberti and Zuccari, 31: "E questa fu una lanterna la quale aveva tre sportelle principali di dove usciva il maggior lume, al intorno poi minutissimi spiragli sotto e sopra, essendo per tutto forata come crivello, di maniera che il lume acceso dentro a detta lanterna da tutte le parti in qualche maniera spirava la sua luce, ma principalmente dalli tre sportelli, con un motto attorno che diceva: SIC OPERATUR."

46   Holtzwart, 30-1, 171-2.

47   Alberti and Zuccari, 32: "La lanterna risplendente che d'ogn'intorno spande ' raggi della sua luce, sì per li minuti [spiragli] d'ogn'intorno come per li tre sportelli principali che alluma e vince ogni tenebra, denota assai chiaramente gl'effetti e l'operazione che fa il disegno intellettivo e prattico nell'intelletto umano e nell'umane intelligenzie e prattiche; il corpo della lanterna oscuro dinota come ogni virtù dell'intelletto è oscura prima che sia da quella scintilla divina allumata, e sì come questa lanterna risplendente e chiara viene ad allumare e scacciare ogni tenebra e discoprire all'occhio umano ogni nascosta ed apparente cosa, così il disegno viene ad allumare l'intelletto in ogni sua intelligenza, e così in tal maniera pare che questa lanterna così luminosa possa essere e sia proprio simbolo ed impresa dignissima e particolare del disegno e di questa nobilissima Academia."

Plato used to say that our soul, being divine, is endowed with every kind of knowledge before it lands in the mortal body. Once covered with flesh, it loses, but does not forget, its knowledge and learning. Only practice and study make the soul remember that knowledge.

Therefore, he concluded: "the intellective *disegno* acts in our soul like light, inducing us to recover or recollect every science and knowledge."[48]

Exposing Zuccari's theory on *disegno* in all its tenets and logical deductions is beyond the scope of this chapter.[49] However, a few words on Zuccari's hermeneutics may be helpful in decoding the meaning of the lantern in Caravaggio's picture. In a lecture given at the Roman Academy on 17 January 1594, Zuccari reconstructed the mechanism of knowing and creating in a manner that is clearly related to the topic of divine and intellective light:

First of all, our external senses, like tools or ministers, apprehend and come to know all things sensitive. By depositing and stocking their forms in our deepest and most secret senses, our intellect, acting through its own spiritual light, illuminates them in the same way as the sun enlightens colors. Hence, it extracts and creates diverse, more spiritual forms, and marvelously depicts them in our intellect. Indeed, the human intellect is unable to either understand or operate without these forms.

Following in Aristotle's footsteps, Zuccari asserts that there is nothing in the intellect that has not previously been in the senses, and that our intellect is a "*tabula rasa*, albeit able and ready to receive in itself every image and figure of science and practice."[50]

Unfortunately, Zuccari did not explain in his Academic discourse of January 1594 how internal light, or intellective *disegno*, bears on the process of inventing and conceiving an image from the stock of diverse imaginative forms that the soul unceasingly accumulates, and how the intellect transmutes these figurative patterns into the actual artwork. However, Zuccari returned to these crucial topics in his 1607 *Idea de' pittori, scultori et architetti*, in which he elucidates the mechanisms of art-making by integrating them in a broader philosophical discourse: one in which he brilliantly proves that painting, sculpture, and architecture count among the most sophisticated "sciences" insofar as they are regulated by both intellect and knowledgeable practice. To begin with, Zuccari defines the internal *disegno* by specifically resorting to the example of the painter's practice:

By internal design I mean the concept formed in our mind in order to know everything and operate outside in conformity with this knowledge. In the same manner, we

---

48 Ibidem: "Poiché l'istesso disegno fa l'istessa operazione che fa l'istessa lanterna, essendo che l'operazione sustanziale della luce è d'allumare ogni tenebra e di scoprire ogni nascosta e velata cosa da esse tenebre celata, tal dunque fa l'istesso disegno a guisa di luce (…). Platone soleva dire che l'anima nostra come cosa divina sia d'ogni scienza ornata prima che discenda in questo corpo mortale e, vestita di questa spoglia, abbia non perduto, ma sdimenticato le sue scienze e intelligenze, e che li essercizi e gli studi fanno ritornare alla mente l'istesse scienze a chi piacesse con Platone aver tal opinione, la quale però io non tengo, non sarà anche indecenza dire che il disegno intellettivo sia a guisa di lume nell'anima nostra, che ne fa credere di nuovo e ricordare ogni scienza ed ogni intelligenza."

49 For Zuccari as theorist, and his interpretation of *disegno*, see Hermann Fiore 1982; some of the essays published in Cleri 1997; Moralejo Ortega 2001; Pierguidi 2006; Gareffi 2009; Capretti 2009.

50 Alberti and Zuccari, 21: "Prima i sensi nostri esterni, come stromenti o ministri, aprendono e conoscono tutte le cose sensibili, le cui forme poi riponendo e conservando ne i più interni e secreti sensi, l'intelletto nostro, agente col lume suo spirituale, quelle illumina nel modo che il sole illumina i colori, e così ne trae diverse forme più spirituali, e quelle con modo maraviglioso dipinge nel nostro intelletto, poiché questo umano intelletto, sì come è noto, non può senza queste forme ed instrumenti né intendere né operare, essendo vero, come è verissimo, e volgarmente noto quello che Aristotele e tutta la scola de' filosofi vogliono, che non sia cosa nell'intelletto che prima non sia stata ne i sensi, essendo egli qual tavola rasa, se bene però atta e disposta a ricevere in sé ogni imagine e figura di scienza e prattica con i sudetti mezi, ché di altra maniera non sarebbe qual tavola rasa."

painters, willing to draw or paint a proper *istoria* (for instance the Annunciation to the Virgin, when the celestial messenger announced that she would become the mother of God), we preliminarily form in our minds a concept of what we think might have occurred on earth and in heaven (from the point of view of the committed angel, the Annunciate, and God who sent the message). Afterward, in accordance with this internal concept, we set about sketching and drawing [it] with a pen on paper, and then with brushes and colors on a canvas or a wall. [51]

Of course, this internal design—a concept which will require further consideration—is technically insufficient to implement the entire production of the artwork. In Zuccari's terminology, this kind of *disegno* is indeed merely speculative and therefore lacking its operative counterpart, practical drawing:

> There are two intellects in us that, albeit distinct in name, are essentially the same: the one is defined by philosophers as the speculative intellect, whose main and principal goal it is exclusively to comprehend; the other is called practical, whose main goal it is to operate or, more appropriately, to be the principle of our operations.[52]

According to Zuccari's hermeneutics, the practical intellect also possesses a twofold nature, ethical and artistic:

> Thus, man's practical intellect (…) not only knows, but is also the principal cause that predisposes and regulates two kinds of operation: those defined by philosophers as virtuous, whether internal or external, like virtuous thoughts, words, and deeds; and those called artificial, both internal and external, such as comprehending the reason for painting, sculpting, and building, as well as the external acts of painting with a brush, sculpting with a scalpel, and building with other tools.[53]

Not only does Zuccari associate the moral and the technical spheres of virtue and artistic excellence, but he deems theory unable to ensure on its own—without the assistance of practice—the perfection of both man's behavior and the artist's work:

> In truth, if one wishes to become virtuous, for instance demure and chaste, it would be of little or no utility—or if so, only by accident—to be a metaphysician, a mathematician, a physicist or an expert in logic; in the same way, it would be of little utility to know in general what virtue is and what a virtuous action or demureness and chastity are. Only

51 Zuccari, 1:4: "Dirò che per dissegno interno intendo il concetto formato nella mente nostra per potere conoscer qual si voglia cosa ed operare di fuori conforme alla cosa intesa, in quella maniera che noi altri pittori volendo dissegnare o dipingere qualche degna istoria, come per essempio quella della Salutazione angelica fatta a Maria Vergine, quando il messagger celeste gli annunciò che sarebbe diventata madre di Dio, formiamo prima nella mente nostra un concetto di quanto allora potiamo pensare ch'occorresse così in cielo come in terra, sì dal canto dell'angelo legato come da quello di Maria Vergine, a cui si faceva la legazione, e da quello di Dio che fu il legante. Poi conforme a questo concetto interno andiamo con lo stile formando e dissegnando in carta, e poi co' pennelli e colori in tela o in muro colorando."

52 Ibidem, 1:15: "Perché in noi sono due intelletti, se bene

però distinti solamente di nome, ché nel resto sono l'istesso. Uno chiamato da i filosofi intelletto speculativo, il cui fine proprio e principale è l'intendere solamente. L'altro chiamato prattico, il cui fine principale è l'operare o, per dir meglio, esser principio delle nostre operazioni."

53 Ibidem, 1:18: "L'intelletto dunque umano prattico, del quale abbiamo ragionato di sopra, non solo conosce, ma è causa principale dispositiva ed ordinativa di due sorti di operazioni: di quelle che sono da' filosofi chiamate virtuose, siano mo' interne od esterne, come de i pensieri, delle parole e de i fatti virtuosi; e di quelle che sono chiamate opere artificiali, sì interne come esterne, come l'intendere la ragione del dipingere, dello scolpire e dell'edificare; e poi al di fuori col pennello pingere, e con lo scarpello scolpire e con altri istromenti edificare."

by forming a concept in particular about these things, and by behaving in conformity with the concept preliminarily formed, will one become virtuous, acquiring a virtuous habit and acting accordingly.[54]

Zuccari's eagerness in carefully distinguishing theory and practice in the field of ethics by describing the latter as subordinate to, as well as indispensable for, the former, rewards reflection even from the standpoint of the early modern discourse on art. Although he does not suggest here that artists should be virtuous, he assimilates the artists' manual practice, their craftsmanship, to the exercise of virtue. In a sense, by forming a specific ideal of artistic perfection and by making it an innate habit, artists show an aptitude and behavior as rigorous as those of virtuous men. Drawing, carving, coloring, and building in their turn should be equated with ethical practices and, as such, they display moral virtue. For Zuccari, the righteousness of practicing art relies entirely on *disegno*:

> The necessity for art to be effective is evident, since art guides the practical intellect in its operations so that it may achieve its prefixed goal without errors, as we see is the case for all the arts. This is why Aristotle defines art as an effective habit that dominates and orders those things which are feasible. Moreover, the necessity of the internal drawing in all these operations can be inferred from this fact: since art is a principle, though common and general, to be effective outside, if it were deprived of *disegno*—which determines in particular what can be achieved as well as how to achieve it—art would be unable to produce any effect. For this reason, although we painters have mastered the art of painting with great hardship and practice, if we need to paint something specific, we need to form the design of that thing in our minds, as all the arts that operate outside do, and some call these designs new inventions. Just as the internal design thus conceived by deft artificers helps art, not as its instrument or internal cause, but as its objective and as the formal cause prompting the practical intellect to operate, so too is it necessary, before acquiring our art, that one acquire *disegno*, for it is the cause and source of all the arts. Indeed, art, however easy, can only be rooted in us through much practice, as Aristotle says, and we experience this every day, as an apprentice will consume thousands of sheets and models before he is able to form a figure.[55]

Disegno therefore not only guarantees the excellent quality of an artwork's invention, but also the excellence of its making and completion. I emphasize Zuccari's interest in connecting theory and

54   Ibidem, 1:19: "Ché, a dirne il vero, s'uno vorrà diventar virtuoso, come per esempio pudico e casto, nulla o poco gli gioverà l'essere metafisico, o matematico, o fisico, o logico, se non per accidente; così poco gli gioverà il sapere in commune che cosa sia virtù, che cosa operazione virtuosa, che cosa pudicizia e castità. Ma quando intorno a queste andarà in particolare formando un concetto, e poi conforme al concetto formato in se stesso praticando, allora diverrà virtuoso, acquisterà l'abito virtuoso e secondo questo operarà."

55   Ibidem, 1:20: "La necessità dell'arte all'operare è manifesta, perché lei è quella che guida l'intelletto prattico nelle sue operazioni acciò senza errori possa pervenire al fine intento, come vediamo che fanno tutte le arti, onde Aristotele difinisce l'arte in questo modo: l'arte è un abito operativo il quale ha retta ragione ed ordine delle cose fattibili. La necessità poi del disegno interno in tutte queste operazioni si conosce di qui, ch'essendo l'arte un principio, ma commune e generale ad operare al di fuori, se non avesse il disegno, che determina in particolare e quello che si deve operare e come si deve operare, l'arte non potrebbe produrre più questo che quell'altro effetto. Onde esperimentiamo noi altri pittori che, se bene abbiamo acquistato con molta fatica e molta isperienza l'arte del dipingere, nondimeno, se vogliamo pingere qualche cosa in particolare, è necessario formare nell'intelletto nostro qualche disegno di quella cosa, e così fanno tutte l'arti che operano al di fuori, e questi disegni alcuni li chiamano nuove invenzioni. Et sì come questo disegno interno così formato da gl'artefici provetti aiuta l'arte, non come istromento o causa interiore di lei, ma come oggetto e causa formale movente l'intelletto prattico all'operare, così, prima che alcuno acquisti questa nostra arte, fa bisogno che acquisti il disegno, come causa e genitore dell'arti, perché l'arte non si può generare in noi, e sia qual si voglia, benché facile, se non per molti atti, come dice Aristotele, e l'esperimentiamo ogni giorno, ché prima che un discepolo sappia formare una figura, consumerà mille fogli e mille esempi."

practice into an inextricable compound. Based on drawing, the training of the painter makes him capable of "effecting," not merely of "ideating." Although "new inventions" originate in the artist's mind as visual concepts, or designs without paper, only the painter who masters the technique of drawing will be successful. Zuccari's transcendental idea of *disegno* has a perversely concrete application: it encompasses practice and craftsmanship, so that no excellent painter can exist without mastering drawing. As a general rule, the hand that paints is the hand that accomplishes the prime finality of *disegno*. *Disegno* intervenes in the shading and coloring of the artwork's intellective visualization; it is the cause of the image's optical unveiling in the painter's mind. Here is how Zuccari describes the divine fire of artistic invention, or the process through which a painter's mind becomes enlightened:

> Just as, in order to light a fire, the steel strikes the flint, and from the flint spring sparks, and sparks ignite the tinder, and then, by nearing the sulfur wicks to the tinder, one lights the lamp, so too does the intellective faculty strike the flint of concepts in man's mind, and the first concept that sparks from it ignites the tinder of imagination and stirs phantasms and imaginative ideas. The first concept is indeterminate and very confused, and thereby cannot be comprehended by the soul's faculty or by the actual and potential intellect. However, this spark little by little turns into form, idea, and real phantasm: a spirit formed by the speculative and formative soul. Thereupon, the senses, similar to sulfur wicks, take fire and light the lamp of the actual and potential intellect; once lit, the lamp spread its light by pondering and analyzing all things. In this manner, there spring clearer ideas and more certain judgments through which the intellective faculty waxes into comprehending and forming things. From the forms spring order and rule, and from order and rule, experience and practice. In this manner, the lamp of the intellect becomes bright and luminous.[56]

The lamp metaphor developed by Zuccari in this passage is the perfect equivalent of the lantern metaphor, the only difference between the two being that the former provides Zuccari with a more complex procedure of activation, one that most graphically conjures up the machinery of artistic invention in the reader's mind. Regardless of Zuccari's indulgence in an over-analytical description of the artist's creative process, the physiological mechanism through which the intellective mind stimulates the internal senses toward defining and perfecting a visual concept is far from being incoherent, and I do not doubt that Zuccari meditated carefully on this issue. Artistic creation operates as visual hermeneutics: indeed, it can be construed as the self-triggered method through which the intellect produces a vision that is not only crystalline, but also perfectly self-explanatory. In other words, the pristine concept spawn by the artist's mind, however valuable it might be, partakes of chaos and blurriness, and only through self-reflection—Zuccari uses the metaphor of the mirror reflecting the inventor's ideas (that is, by wholly manifesting and apprehending itself as a visual discourse)—does it break free, configured as a working template, and hence analogous to a moral or a philosophical proposition. At the end of this process, vision is intrinsically imbued

---

56   Ibidem, 1:25: "Però dico che, sì come per formare il fuoco il focile batte la pietra, dalla pietra n'escon faville, le faville accendon l'esca, poi appressandosi all'esca i solfarelli s'accende la lucerna; così la virtù intellettiva batte la pietra de i concetti nella mente umana, ed il primo concetto che sfavilla accende l'esca dell'imaginazione, move i fantasmi ed imaginazioni ideali; il qual primo concetto è indeterminato e confuso, né dalla facoltà dell'anima o intelletto agente possibile è inteso. Ma questa favilla diviene a poco a poco forma, idea e fantasma reale, e spirito formato di quell'anima speculativa e formativa; poi s'accendono i sensi a guisa di solfanelli, ed accendono la lucerna dell'intelletto agente e possibile, la quale diffonde il suo lume in ispeculazione e divisione di tutte le cose. Onde ne nascono poi idee più chiare e giudizi più certi, presso de' quali cresce l'intelligenza intellettiva nell'intelletto alla cognizione e formazione delle cose, e dalle forme nasce l'ordine e la regola, e dall'ordine e regola l'esperienza e la prattica; e così vien fatta luminosa e chiara questa lucerna dell'intelletto."

with "order and rule," which means, among other things, that the image's components have been filtered and purified into ideal forms or encoding:

> It [the cognitive intellect] at once forms a concept of the thing that it aims to understand, or of which it keeps the form stored, and thus it sees in [this concept] clearly and distinctly what it contains, and so it comprehends, and discourses, and judges, and becomes learned, knowledgeable, and accomplished. If it at the outset is called potential intellect, for it might or might not be in a state of comprehending, it is then called actual and knowledgeable ["*scienziato*"] intellect. This is the truly marvelous way in which the intellective *disegno* surges in us, the reason of all of our knowledge, of all the sciences and practical operations.[57]

Surprisingly enough, and not without a few contradictions, Zuccari in another passage of his 1607 treatise regards the intellective *disegno* as imperfect until painting succeeds in achieving it concretely:

> I shall also say something worth knowing about painting's greatness and excellence: from being in a sense the daughter of *disegno*, she becomes its mother by nourishing and nursing it. (…) The perceptible internal *disegno* conceived in the imagination is not to be seen, although it is known through the internal sense. When it is materialized externally through simple outline, it is rather shapeless like the she-bear's offspring, so that it cannot provide the senses, not to mention the intellect, with an accomplished knowledge of itself. Therefore, for it to emerge before our eyes in its perfection, it must be assisted and smoothed by its mother, just as the she-bear does with her cub. And just as the sun extracts itself from the clouds that cover and hide him, it is necessary that this *disegno* show itself accomplished, and as the clouds disperse, it appears terse and luminous. In this way *disegno*, reshaped by painting—its daughter, mother, and nurse—is fashioned into three states, that is, into visible form, impalpable body, and adorned accessory: only then is it perfectly achieved. And this happens when painting embellishes, complements, and achieves it with its light and dark shades.[58]

This is not the place to comment in detail on Zuccari's use of figurative emblems as metaphors of artistic creation—the image of the sun triumphing over the clouds and of the she-bear licking and smoothing her shapeless offspring into a cub. Nevertheless, I ought to remark upon the paradoxical understatement that buttresses Zuccari's celebration of painting. If I understand correctly, *disegno* is unable to subsist without painting's intervention, yet what painting specifically brings to *disegno* is a refined form of materiality or corporality that Zuccari reduces to mere adornment. Painting in

---

57 Ibidem, 1:28: "Il quale forma subito un concetto della cosa che vuole intendere o della quale ha appresso di sé la forma, e così in quello vede chiaramente e distintamente quanto si contiene, ed intende e discorre e giudica e si fa scienziato, dotto e compito, e come prima si chiamava intelletto possibile, perché poteva intendere e non intendere, si chiama poi intelletto in atto scienziato. Ecco il modo veramente meraviglioso come in noi si formi il disegno intellettivo, cagione di ogni nostro intendere, delle scienze e dell'operazioni prattiche."

58 Ibidem, 2:22-3: "Dirò di più cosa degna da sapersi intorno alla grandezza ed eccellenza della pittura, cioè ch'ella di figlia diviene in un certo modo nodrice, balia e madre del disegno. (…) Il disegno parimente interno sensibile formato

nella fantasia non si può vedere, se bene si conosce col senso interno, e quando è formato esteriormente in semplice linea, è assai confuso a guisa del parto dell'orsa, né può dare al senso, non che all'intelletto, compita cognizione di se stesso, onde, acciocché appaia a gli occhi nostri e comparisca perfetto, conviene sia lisciato e levato dalla madre come il parto dell'orsa. Così questo disegno a guisa del sole che esce fuora delle nuvole che l'occupano e nascondono, è necessario a far di sé compita mostra, e dileguandosi le nuvole, si dimostra chiaro e lucido. Così il disegno riformato da questa sua figlia, nodrice e madre, la pittura, vien posto in questi tre stati di forma visibile, di corpo impalpabile e d'accidente vestito, allora è compitamente perfetto, e questo avviene quando la pittura con ' suoi chiari e scuri l'abbellisce, l'orna e perfezziona."

fact gives color (visible form) and relief (impalpable body) to the artist's spiritual design: features that connote as simple "accidents" (accessory or "*accidente*" in Italian) of the *disegno*-substance. More interesting, although Zuccari explicitly singles out the chiaroscuro technique, he astutely omits the key term that epitomizes painting's specificity: color. It is a fact that Zuccari was strongly attuned to color's essential role in painting despite his Florentine training.[59] Yet theoretically speaking he is unable to pronounce the word "color" without compromising the loftiness of his discourse on painting: on a philosophical, and on a more strictly Aristotelian level, color is but an accident adhering to substances.[60] I stress Zuccari's hesitations and contradictions in this regard because they betray an interpretation of painting and artistic creation that Caravaggio opposed and publicly repudiated by endorsing an anti-*disegno* position.

Even if Zuccari's *Idea* was published after Caravaggio had fled Rome in 1606, its contents—essentially, the treatise was a further elaboration on Zuccari's 1594 lecture on drawing—were assuredly familiar to the painter. As an assistant to the Cavalier d'Arpino around 1595, he must have been acquainted with Zuccari's precepts and doctrine. In February 1594, the Cavalier d'Arpino, already a respectable academician, was invited to the Accademia to discourse on the definition of "figure" as a sequel to Zuccari's lectures.[61] Zuccari's enthusiasm notwithstanding, the Academy as an institution failed to attract the interest and involvement of all the artists working in Rome. For decades, it survived almost as an empty container. However, there is no reason to assume that the Academy's failures affected Zuccari's popularity, or eclipsed the importance and ascendancy of his theories on art. On the contrary, the publication in 1607 of Zuccari's *Idea* confirms, if confirmation were needed, the actuality and validity of his ideas.

Caravaggio's artistic practice did not conform to Zuccari's precepts. Provocatively, the painter refused to sketch and test his compositions on paper, working instead directly on canvas. Yet Zuccari's metaphor of the lantern would surely have appealed to Caravaggio. The assumption that the artist's mind, through invention, separates darkness from light in the picture, untangling figures, objects, and actions by means of a sensitively induced naturalism, as if in a mirror, likewise accords with Caravaggio's method of painting. "With light and dark shades," Caravaggio gave his pictures "visible form, impalpable body, and adorned accessories." Although the lantern held by Caravaggio's *alter ego* in *The Taking of Christ* is devoid of shutters—Zuccari thought of them as allusions to the three arts of painting, sculpture, and architecture—it seems to be credited with an analogous function: illuminating the darkness while unveiling the composition.

By stepping into the pictorial action with a lantern, Caravaggio reenacts the process of artistic creation: he is about to shed light upon the *istoria*—the arrest of the Savior—as he endeavors to witness it with his own eyes. Accordingly, he raises his head, his open mouth mimicking the intensity of his expectation, but to no avail, since the more he approaches the main scene in order to see it "clearly and distinctly," the more the cluster of figures around Judas and Christ block his vision; despite the short distance that separates him from the betrayal scene, and the effort with which he lifts his lantern, he is doomed to remain blind to his own *istoria*.[62]

---

59   For Federico Zuccari and Venice, see more recently Acidini Luchinat 2001.

60   For the complex and contradictory definitions of color in seventeenth-century art theory, see Lichtenstein 1993.

61   D'Arpino is mentioned in a document of the Accademia di San Luca as early as 31 October 1593. For this and other documents relating to the Accademia, consult CASVA's excellent website: www.nga.gov/casva/accademia. For a history of the Accademia, see Missirini 1823; and more recently Cohen E. 2009.

62   See the interesting remarks by Sapir 2005-2006, 70:

"Caravaggio has deprived the scene of its context, and created instead an episode floating in an undefined space. The cold shoulder this turns to the knowledge-avid spectator is further enhanced by the impenetrable shield, another obstacle for our direct, immediate comprehension of 'what is going on,' and by the curious-but-eventually-frustrated attitude of the figures themselves, especially of Caravaggio's doppelganger trying to spread some light around, striving to see the crucial moment of Judas' kiss—and apparently arriving just too late and standing just too far to see anything. We are compelled, in a way, not only to 'identify' with him, but also to re-enact his thwarted act of seeing. If the painting was intended simply to 'tell a story,' then it seems to have failed miserably."

One can construe Caravaggio's attitude in the painting in a twofold way. His approaching the event and enlightening it with a lantern may demonstrate the immediacy and directness of his creative process;[63] sidestepping the Florentine practice of preparatory drawings, he enters the subject straightaway and attempts to visualize it even as the sacred action unfolds: here and now, before his own eyes. By the same token, his firsthand vision of the religious drama becomes his personal signature; his presence in the painting therefore serves not only as a device of self-celebration, but also as evidence of his novel method of artistic invention. From this prospect, Caravaggio's usurpation and ironic misuse of the Roman Academy's lantern reveals a conception of painting profoundly at odds with Zuccari's. It is no coincidence that the somewhat elevated position of his changeling's lantern with regard to the picture's figures, as well as the author's eyewitness of the biblical event, bring to mind Caravaggio's workshop practice: the pose of live models in front of the painter illuminated by light coming usually from above. Wittily, Caravaggio burlesques Zuccari's metaphysics of the pictorial vision by teleporting physically, not only spiritually, into the main scene, and by experiencing it as if in the flesh. Nonetheless, one cannot overlook Caravaggio's *alter ego*'s blatant shortcoming in glancing at Christ's capture in the Dublin picture. Through the stifled act of this figure, Caravaggio may instead indicate the inescapable variability of the artist's point of view while working directly on the canvas, as his models vary postures and expressions, so that the vision of the action to be represented might, however momentarily, grow blurry and even black out. In fact, creating for Caravaggio must have occurred amidst a fluctuant tide of diverse views, and the outcome—the final "shot"—was to a certain degree destined to remain unpredictable until the very end.

In my view, the inability of Caravaggio's *alter ego* to catch a significant glimpse of Christ's betrayal voices a more radical opinion on the master's part: the conviction that, in the end, the *istoria* as the true representation of an event is logically and pictorially inaccessible. I am not here using the concept of "truth" in metaphysical terms, but in artistic ones: artistic truth involves the possibility, and necessity, for an artist to represent an event in its completeness, true to the letter of the account though adorned by the legitimate cosmetics of verisimilitude. To put it more bluntly, in the Dublin picture Caravaggio refutes both the principle of the univocal point of view—that is, the pretense that the author, by selecting the culminant point of an action, might be able to offer a global vision, or otherwise an intellectually satisfying "discourse," on a sacred event, including its theological implications, teleology, and aftermath—and the Aristotelian criterion of the action's unity.

Screened by the mantle of the fleeing apostle, Judas' betrayal becomes invisible to Caravaggio's *alter ego*, and hermetically inaccessible to his lantern. A dense light, slanting from the left above, powerfully illuminates Christ's disgust and Judas' kiss, John's dreadful escape and the armored soldiers' brutality as they grip the Savior's unprotected body. The effect of this primary source of light is purposefully enhanced by the reflections it casts upon the warriors' armors: razor-cold shimmers upon black metallic opacity. The primary light's silvery reverberation upon the two foreground soldiers' helmets competes and contrasts with the warm light of the much-concealed lantern. As is evident in the visual representation of Christ's capture in the Dublin picture, the

---

63   In this regard, see Longhi 1999-2000, 2:248: "Il Caravaggio non era certamente un pittore simbolista, ma non disdegnò talora, e quasi sempre a sfondo polemico, di esprimere, nei suoi dipinti, un senso 'riposto.' E qui il senso sarebbe che è proprio soltanto del pittore 'dar lume' all'opera: sia il 'lume naturale' che è quello della luna che inonda da sinistra la scena; sia quello 'artificiale' che sopraggiunge da destra con la lanterna e che dà l'abbrivo agli sviluppi fin troppo 'artificiosi' dei caravaggeschi nordici da Gherardo in poi." A consideration analogous to mine is formulated by Corrain 2002, 225: "La lanterna si comporta in modo analogo all'operare pittorico dello stesso Caravaggio che, come scrivono i biografi a lui contemporanei, consiste sì nell'impiegare la luce naturale, ma manipolandola in maniera da creare una spazialità attraverso un singolare rapporto di luce e ombra. (...) Caravaggio, allora, si è effigiato nell'atto di compiere l'azione che costituisce la caratteristica saliente del suo modo di dipingere. (...) È Caravaggio che si mostra mentre mostra come lui lavora con la luce."

lantern carried by Caravaggio's counterpart sheds a restricted light. In other words, the divine light handed down to painters as their appropriate privilege to rescue the intellectual image from the inchoate darkness of inert creation does not succeed in enlightening the vision. A more powerful lamp, indeed, seems to have already illuminated the scene, so that this humble lantern is barely able to edge its way through the already performed *istoria*. Paradoxically, the lamp and the lantern belong to the same persona, Caravaggio, but their role noticeably changes; the former pertains to the author—the inaudible narrative voice, or the invisible eyes through whose exclusive viewpoint beholders access the painting—the latter to a figure of authorship—the embodiment of the author's metaphoric path toward creation.

As a metaphor of the painter's creative process in visualizing the *istoria*, Caravaggio's self-representation as a lantern-bearer thus seems to formulate the subject matter's inaccessibility to the artist's investigative eyes. Yet this assumption does not seem to make much sense. By finishing his picture, Caravaggio undoubtedly shows otherwise, for the subject matter, plainly accessible through the work's completion, is eventually exposed to view. But what if Caravaggio does not allude here to the subject matter as the pictorial transposition of an account, but rather to the event that the subject matter translates into image? Is Caravaggio pointing here to the inaccessibility of pictorial truth? As I have stressed in the Introduction to Part Four, the artwork's genesis—especially that of the *istoria*—entails not only the artist's intellectual involvement, but also his quasi-physical participation in the episode that he sets out to depict. Lomazzo even theorizes that what he considers the universal phenomenon of artistic empathy is the foundation of, and a prerequisite to, the successful rendering of pictorial motion and figural emotion in the *istoria*. In this connection, we should remember that feeling and experiencing the figures' affects allow the painter to attain the truth of his work—a fictional truth, of course, but material in its effects because it is redirected to arousing real responses on the beholders' part: their involvement in the painting as if the action depicted was indeed perceived as reality. Hence, empathy is conceived of by Lomazzo and by other Counter-Reformation art theorists as the specific means by which the viewer is lured into the classical "suspension of disbelief," when the fiction is perceived as an ongoing "event."

By appearing in his painting as an acting figure, and not as a real witness, Caravaggio, like the beholder, relives the representation—that is, Christ's betrayal—as if it were occurring directly in his presence. However, unlike the viewer, the viewpoint from which he enters and experiences the episode turns out to be a blind spot.[64] Both his effort to illuminate and participate in the *istoria* therefore prove to be drastically and irreparably thwarted. In other words, Caravaggio's *alter ego* in the Dublin painting is a living emblem of the author's and the spectator's incapability of visualizing and reliving the truth of the *istoria*; as a representation, and hence a product of fiction, the religious painting necessarily presupposes a point of view—an angle of approach—and for this reason it is nothing but artistic interpretation: it unequivocally does not qualify as divine revelation. Truth indeed requires an identity of views, whereas the figure of Caravaggio sneaking into his artwork holding a lantern obviously establishes the opposite fact. If viewed from another angle, the representation of Christ's capture might depict sheer blindness—namely, darkness in spite of the lantern. Once again, Caravaggio's painting pivots around the complex concept of truth and its manifold meanings and applications in the matter of art.

To comprehend fully how essential the adoption of an authorial viewpoint was in Caravaggio's time, I shall consider briefly a *c*.1603 drawing in pen by Annibale Carracci (The Royal Library,

---

64 A viewpoint completely opposed to mine, and which I find utterly absurd, is expressed by Corrain 2002, 227: "lo spettatore, infatti, da quella posizione [in front of the painting] ha una visione non nitida, una visione intaccata dalla troppa luce, qualcosa di percettivamente analogo a un abbagliamento (…). Se dalla posizione centrale la visione non è nitida (…) l'osservatore potrà assumere un punto di vista da cui vedere meglio: quello dell'uomo con la lanterna, quello che gli permetterà di non subire l'effetto di abbagliamento."

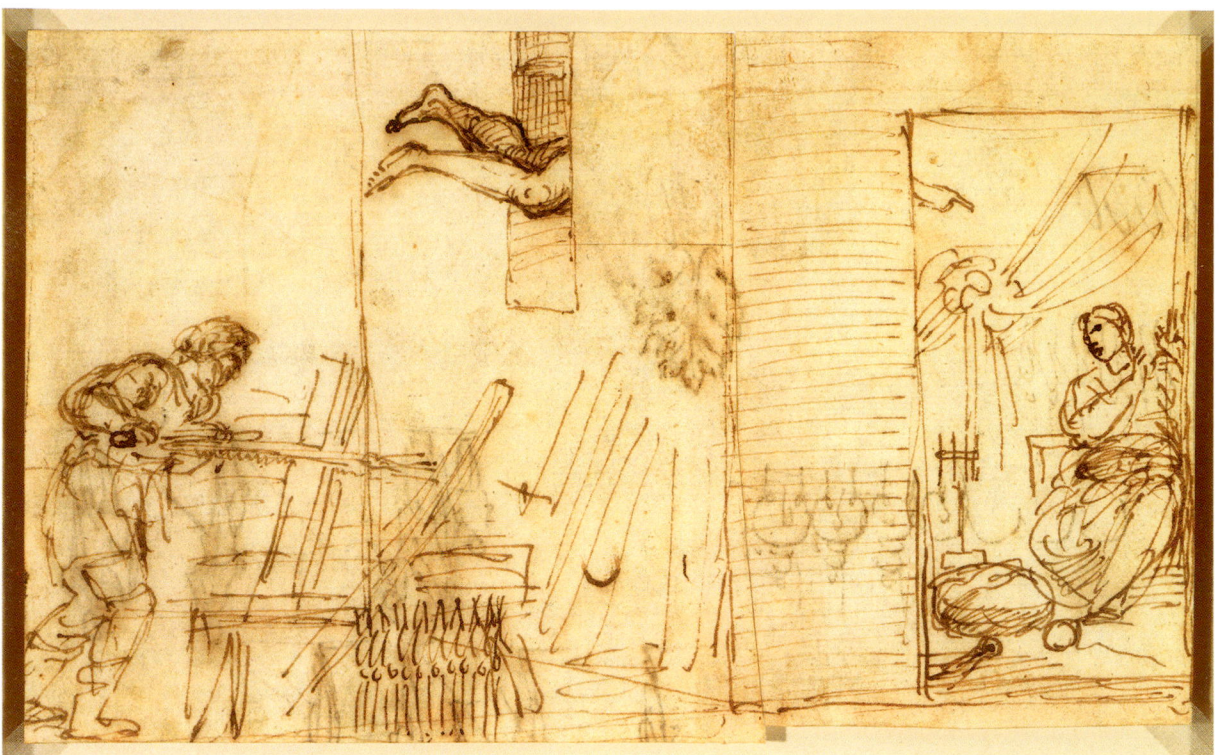

Fig. 164
Annibale Carracci, *The Annunciation*, Royal Library, Windsor Castle, brown ink on paper, 11.5 x 18.8 cm.

Windsor Castle) representing *The Annunciation* (Fig. 164).[65] In this drawing, as many scholars have already noted, Annibale parodied a famous composition by Tintoretto, an *Annunciation* executed around 1583-1587 for the Scuola Grande di San Rocco, Venice (Fig. 165).[66] Since Annibale's sojourn in Venice took place in the 1580s, the drawing results from a fairly trustworthy, but not entirely accurate, reminiscence of Tintoretto's picture, which Annibale pretends to observe from a different angle by a mere shift of the composition's main architecture. At the center of the sheet, Annibale lodged the outside edge and lateral wall of a house, receding askew toward the left, and summoning the ruined partition through which Tintoretto's Gabriel bursts into the Virgin's bedchamber. However, if in Tintoretto's *Annunciation* the wall, receding rightward, invites the viewer into the scene by framing the figures of the Virgin and the angel with emphasis, in Annibale's drawing the house's exterior blocks out the viewer's gaze, so that only the pedaling legs of a flying figure animate the center of the composition. More interesting, Annibale moved Tintoretto's sawing Saint Joseph to the left foreground, making the planks of the already sawn wood lean against the house's

65   See Posner 1971a, 84: "Annibale's study of Roman design was naturally accompanied by critical reflections on his earlier work and on North Italian pictorial modes in general. An amusing example of his 'art criticism' at this time is a drawing at Windsor Castle, a parody—one might say a caricature—of Tintoretto's *Annunciation* in the Scuola di San Rocco, Venice. By a witty, relatively small, and not so illogical change in the image, the marvelously expressive spatial configuration in Tintoretto's painting is transformed into an architectural and presentational absurdity. The drawing thus unmasks what Annibale considered the underlying indecorousness, that is, the visual and contentual inappropriateness, of the painting"; Benati and Riccomini 2006, 390, no. VIII.12: "l'attenzione di Annibale si appunta piuttosto sugli strumenti della visione pittorica e sembra riflettere sull'importanza della prospettiva che, con la scelta di un punto di vista piuttosto che di un altro, può cambiare il senso di una raffigurazione"; and Robertson 2008 (taking up ideas published in 1996 and 1997), 62: "He [Annibale] was also able to parody his [Tintoretto's] bombast, as in a hilarious parody of the *Annunciation* in the Scuola di San Rocco. Merely by shifting the angle from which the composition is seen, he gives the impression that the unfortunate angel has become wedged in the window opening."

66   For the painting, see Pallucchini and Rossi 1982, 1:225, no. 435.

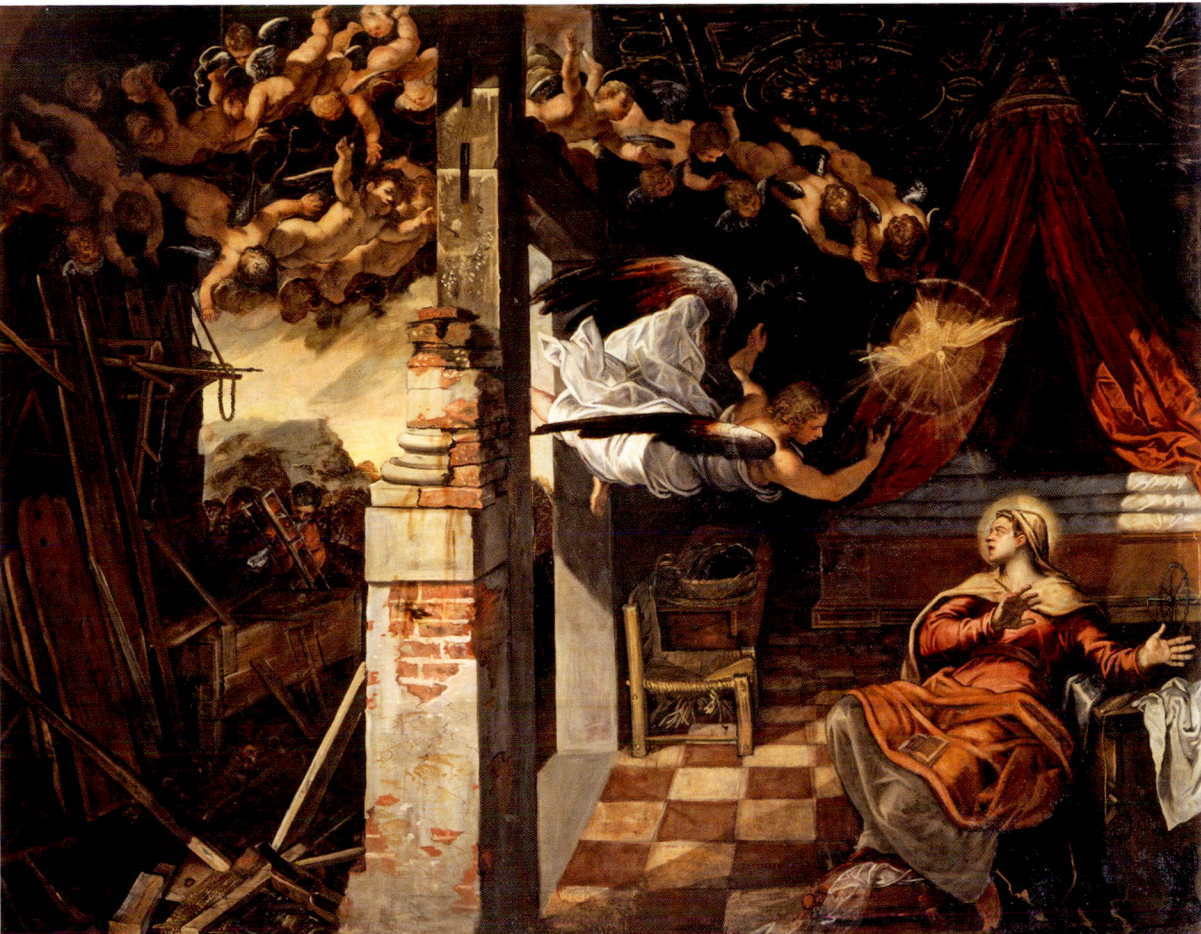

Fig. 165
Tintoretto (Jacopo Robusti), *The Annunciation*, Scuola Grande di San Rocco, Venice, oil on canvas, 422 x 545 cm.

outside wall, and thereby expanding on what Tintoretto had conceived as an anecdotal secondary scene. Through the divergent orientation of Annibale's partition, beholders now focus on the left portion of the sketched *istoria*; as a consequence, they tend to notice the Annunciate at the extreme right only subsequently, intrigued as they are at first by the hovering legs figuring at the center of the drawing, and then by Joseph's activity.

As Daniele Benati has pointed out, in his Windsor drawing Annibale "seems to reflect upon the importance of perspective that, through the choice of a viewpoint rather than another, can change the meaning of a representation." To be more precise, I would say that Annibale is particularly interested in the pictorial viewpoint as a means toward, or an inhibitor of, narrative meaning. In other words, although Annibale's drawing must be understood as a parody, I believe that Tintoretto was not its immediate target, but that it rather aimed at mockingly reassessing the complex issue of the authorial viewpoint. By laying emphasis upon the angel's feet, Annibale not only transforms a religious mystery into an odd comedy—in this prospect, even the Virgin's gesture of surprise and disquiet at Gabriel's acrobatics loses its miraculous undertones and calls for a disenchanted smile— but overall tarnishes the coherence of the Annunciation episode; through the mutilated messenger, Annibale also mutilates the message's function in the scene. Of course, Annibale's visualization of the Annunciation does not contradict the truth, properly speaking. Nonetheless, from a theological perspective, the decentering of the *istoria*'s heroine and the concealment of her sidekick by a blind wall irreparably compromise the intelligibility of the episode and the effectiveness of its pedagogy;

therefore its truth—the systematic unveiling of its religious significance—is equally inaccessible as partially hinted at. If in the Windsor drawing, Annibale's mockery is channeled through the parody of a Tintoretto painting, in the case of the Dublin picture, the main target of Caravaggio's visual discourse on pictorial truth is, as has become clear already, Zuccari's metaphysics of artistic invention.

Since the intellective *disegno* is God's emanation, one must deduce in accordance with Zuccari that the act of painting, grounded on anamnesis, results in "true" revelations. Yet Zuccari never comes to this conclusion. Instead he busies himself with the painter's status and high-standard knowledge and practice: his theory on *disegno* tends to evince the nobility of sculpture, architecture, and especially painting. Truth in religious images, nevertheless, is an issue with which most theorists of the Counter-Reformation deal in their treatises, as I have explained in the introduction to Part Four. Johannes Molanus, Gabriele Paleotti, and Federico Borromeo among others, because they intended to preserve the truth or dogmatic content of religious images, more often than not judged pictorial originality with suspicion. However, if innovation must undergo serious evaluation and severe censure, this does not imply at all that artists should renounce novelty altogether. On the contrary, as members of a cultivated elite, prelates like Paleotti or Borromeo are not insensitive to novel ways of representing the divine, as long as they heed orthodoxy. A brief note by Cardinal Borromeo can help clarify this point. In his treatise *Della pittura sacra*, he declares:

> Raphael deserves great praise, since he, in representing Jacob's ladder ascending to heaven, did not depict a ladder—as many other painters did—akin to that used by peasants to climb onto their hay-lofts and dovecotes. Instead, he painted heavenly clouds forming steps similar to those through which one goes up to a throne or altar. Through these, he made the angels move up and down.[67]

Borromeo's testimony is crucial to comprehending how a cultured prelate would have responded to originality in sacred images. The iconography of Jacob's ladder relied on a long, well-accepted tradition, of which the Church would by no means have disapproved. By transforming the ladder into a celestial staircase, Raphael modified an iconographic convention in such a way that his invention both stirs up curiosity and, upon reflection, meets the criteria of truth and verisimilitude. In fact, Raphael dissolves the metaphor intrinsic to the image of the ladder, rendering its referent more congruous on a visual level: the gradual ascension to heaven becomes an imaginative trekking across clouds. It is impossible to establish Paleotti's or Borromeo's response to Caravaggio's *The Taking of Christ*. One may suppose that, being sensitive to iconographic discrepancies, they would have noted Christ's interlocked hands and the escaping figure of John, thereby remarking upon the anti-heroic connotations of the picture. Neither of them would have censured Caravaggio's painting as untrue or unlikely. Only the contemporary armor of the soldiers might have qualified as anachronistic, but these kinds of anachronisms were so diffused at the time as to go often unnoticed. On the other hand, they might have been disconcerted by the message that the insertion of the author as a powerless lantern-bearer conveyed, had they known that the figure indeed portrayed the painter. I do not refer uniquely to Caravaggio's subtle refutation of the pictorial truth and of Aristotle's unity of action, but also to his denunciation of authorial fallacy.

It would be no exaggeration to say that the whole building of artistic theory and practice rested upon an ideal of perfection, and therefore the infallibility, of the creator's authority. Conceptualizing,

---

67 Borromeo, 121: "Per questo è degno di somma laude Raffaele, il quale dovendo [dipingere] quella scala di Iacob che ascendeva al cielo, non dipinse una scala quale hanno dipinto altri pittori, simile a quella che adoprano i contadini per salire sopra il loro fenile o sopra la colombaia, ma effiggiò le nuvole in cielo, che formassero certi gradi simili a quelli per i quali si sale ad alcun trono o altare, e per questi fece ascendere gl'angeli e discendere."

visualizing, and crafting the *istoria* is ideally construed as an artistic epiphany whereby the artist's seeing is invested with an authorial validity: the author's paradigmatic take on the subject matter turns into a normative viewpoint. This is one of the reasons why Borromeo, seduced by Raphael's newness, presented the artist's interpretation of *Jacob's Dream* as exemplary to other painters. It might seem strange that Caravaggio in his Dublin picture, after such strenuous elaboration and improvement upon the iconographic tradition of Christ's betrayal in view of impactful originality, also staged the painter's limits, his own limits, as an author and a principle of narrative authority. With *The Taking of Christ*, Caravaggio indeed asserts the relativity of the authorial viewpoint, by the same token denouncing the relativity of the pictorial truth in the *istoria*. Moreover, his self-portrayal as an ineffectual lantern-bearer, groping for a close-up vision and reduced to missing the key episode of the kiss, constitutes the most eloquent debunking of Zuccari's artistic omniscience and polymathy.

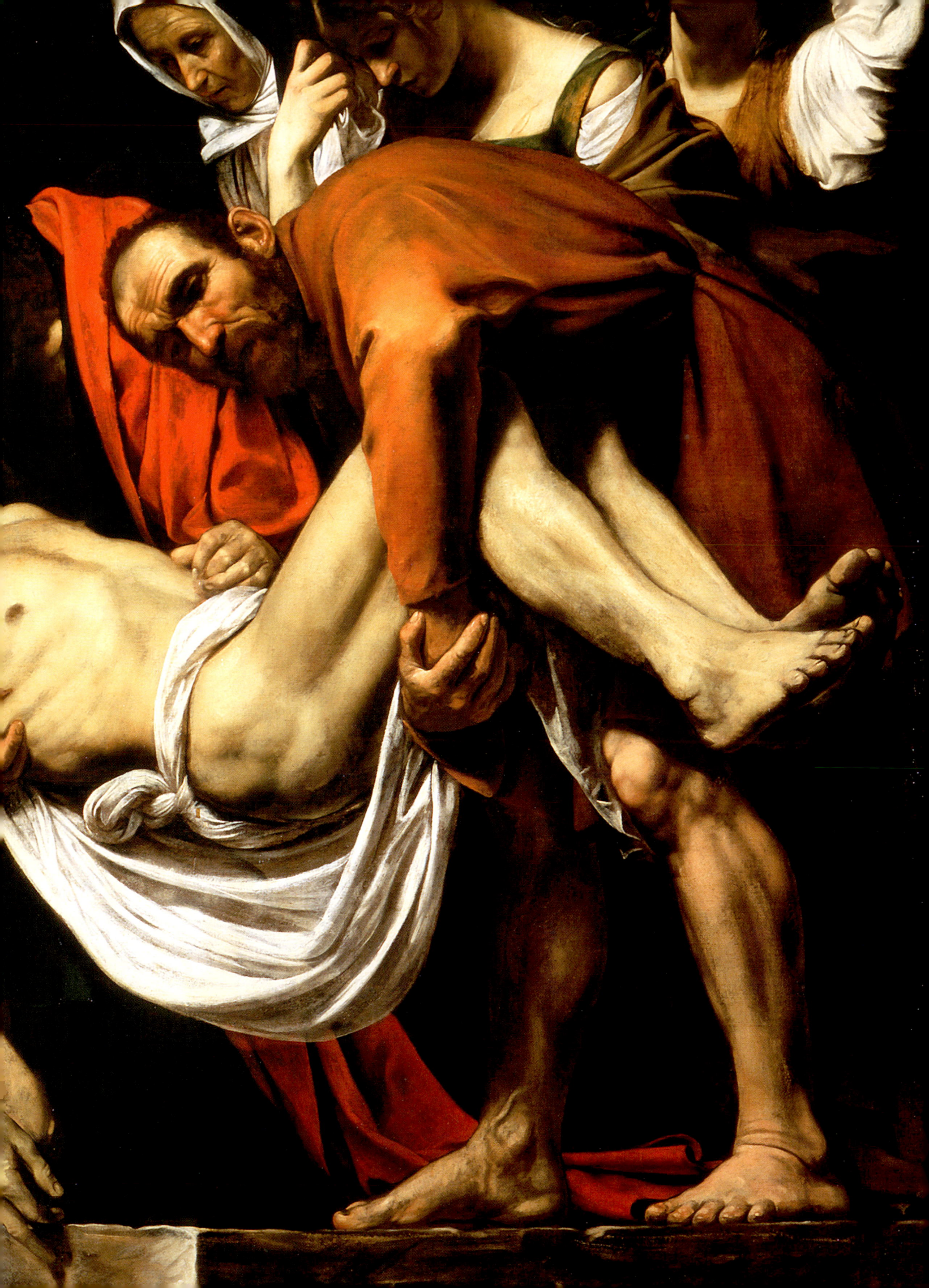

CHAPTER 11

The Other Michelangelo: The Weight of Composition and Artistic *Paragone* in Caravaggio's *Entombment*

A Flawless Masterpiece

"And this—they say—is his best work."[1] Giovanni Baglione, the source of this backhanded compliment, loathed Caravaggio on several counts, both personal and artistic. As a general rule, though, Baglione feigned a certain fairness and equanimity while judging his enemy's works. Systematically, he sought subtle ways to denigrate Caravaggio and belittle his paintings, whether with a single adjective or a succinct, snide sentence, all done as though inadvertently or unwillingly. In the case of the work he defines as Caravaggio's best, Baglione could not find a pretext to vilify the painting; he simply drops it in the hope that the reader will not give much thought to the work. However, it was difficult even for the most obdurate detractors of Caravaggio not to acknowledge the exceptional quality—in the seventeenth century, it would have been called excellence—of his *Entombment*, executed around 1603-1604 for the Vittrice Chapel in the Chiesa Nuova, Rome, and now in the Pinacoteca Vaticana (Fig. 166).[2] Both on a formal and a narrative level, the painting seemed to be beyond criticism:

> Among the most outstanding works produced by Michele's [Caravaggio's] brush, the Entombment of Christ in the Chiesa Nuova of the Oratory's fathers is deservedly held in esteem; the figures are located upon a stone at the brink of the sepulcher. One sees the sacred body at the center, supported by Nicodemus who is standing and grabs it under the knees, and as Christ's thighs move down, his legs jut outward. On the other side, Saint John puts his arm under the shoulders of the Redeemer, whose face and deathly-pale chest remain supine while his arm dangles along with the shroud, and the entire nude is portrayed with the vigor of the most accurate imitation. Behind Nicodemus, the three mournful Marys are to be seen only partially; one lifts up her arms, the other holds her veil to her eyes, and the third gazes at the Lord.[3]

1 Baglione, 137: "Nella Chiesa Nuova alla man diritta v'è del suo nella seconda cappella il Cristo morto che lo vogliono sepellire con alcune figure, a olio lavorato; e questa dicono che sia la migliore opera di lui."

2 Besides Baglione and Bellori, the painting is mentioned in the seventeenth century by Mancini, 1:224; Celio, 51; Scannelli, 199; Silos, 32; and Sandrart, 276. For the painting, see Graeve 1958; Friedlaender 1969, 186-9; Moir 1982, 118; Cinotti 1983, 493-6, no. 46; Hibbard 1983, 312-4; Zuccari 1983; Grossman 1984; Calvesi 1990, 312-8; Bologna 1992, 108-11; Puglisi 1998, 173-6; Langdon 1998, 241-6; Longhi 1999-2000, 1:274-5 [1968]; Papa 2001; Sickel 2001; Kroschewski 2002, 118-21; Sickel

2003, 64-73; Marini 2005, 470-73, no. 55; Lechner 2006, 165-80; Varriano 2006, 45-6; Schütze 2009, 267, no. 34; and Ebert-Schifferer, 170-2.

3 Bellori, 221: "Ben tra le megliori opere che uscissero dal pennello di Michele si tiene meritamente in istima la Deposizione di Cristo nella Chiesa Nuova de' padri dell'Oratorio, situate le figure sopra una pietra nell'apertura del sepolcro. Vedesi in mezzo il sacro corpo, lo regge Nicodemo da' piedi, abbracciandolo sotto le ginocchia, e nell'abbassarsi le cosce, escono in fuori le gambe. Di là san Giovanni sottopone un braccio alla spalla del Redentore, e resta supina la faccia e 'l petto pallido a morte, pendendo il braccio col lenzuolo; e

◄ Plate XV: Michelangelo Merisi da Caravaggio, *The Entombment*, Pinacoteca Vaticana, Rome, oil on canvas, 300 x 203 cm., detail.

"Deservedly held in esteem" says Bellori of Caravaggio's *Entombment*, before describing it in terms that unequivocally betoken the painting's conformity with his own aesthetic tenets. As far as I know, it has not yet been pointed out that Bellori's description echoes the passage from Leon Battista Alberti's 1435 *De Pictura* (quoted in Chapter 1), in which the author praises the figures' pertinence of expression and attitude in the *istoria*:

> In Rome, people commend a story in which the dead Meleager is carried, and those who support his weight seem to suffer and endure pain with all their limbs. Yet in the figure of the dead, there is no limb that does not appear lifeless: everything dangles; hands, fingers, head, all droop inertly, and accordingly all the limbs converge toward expressing the lifelessness of the body.[4]

Although in Caravaggio's painting the only dangling limb is Christ's right arm, Bellori's description obviously aims to extol the nude of the Vatican *Entombment* as a model of pictorial deadness alternative to, or in competition with, the figure of Meleager from the ancient sarcophagus.[5] In fact, Bellori carefully justifies the supine orientation of Christ's face and chest, as well as the zigzagging disposition of his thighs and legs, as the mechanical results of two concomitant pulls, those exerted by John and Nicodemus from beneath Jesus' upper torso and bundled knees. In Bellori's view, the coherent correspondence of the figures' movements—the fact that "all the limbs converge toward expressing the lifelessness of the body"—apparently succeeds in scaffolding the structural verisimilitude of the *istoria*, the cause-and-effect interconnectedness of the visual plot. No one would contest the opinion that this interpretation is extremely rare in the scope of Bellori's assessments of Caravaggio's painting; throughout his biography, the cases in which Bellori at best tempers his disapproval of Caravaggio's art predominate. But not in this specific instance: not only has narrative congruousness been respected in the Vatican *Entombment*, but also—perhaps uniquely—Caravaggio's mimesis—his "accurate imitation" of Christ's dead body—has been put to good service. In other words, Caravaggio's "true-to-lifeness" finally obeys the principles of the *istoria* (I would not go as far as to say that it incarnates the "ideal nature" of which Bellori was so fond, although it certainly tends toward it) and does not deviate in its usual quest for low-life and crude naturalness.

In this regard, it is noteworthy that Bellori does not criticize the proportions of Christ's body—for one thing, the Savior is no longer a "beardless plebeian" as in the London *Supper at Emmaus*—so that it is fair to infer that, in the Vatican *Entombment*, mimesis is practiced within the purview of decorum, a winning combination for Bellori. Predictably, Bellori also signals—or rather hints at—Christ's lividness, a remark that incidentally indicates that the temporality of the sacred episode represented has also been taken into account so that the paleness of the Savior's chest appropriately expresses how long and how truly he has been dead. In sum, no anachronism undermines the *istoria*'s excellence. Oddly enough, Bellori does not comment on Nicodemus' blatant effort in supporting Christ's body, or on what seems to be John's absorbed consideration of the Savior's side wound, upon which the apostle's right hand has happened in his attempt to lower Christ's cadaver delicately into the sepulcher. Observing these elements would have stressed even more greatly the idea of "factual consistency" in the depiction of a dead body: "and those who support the

---

tutto l'ignudo è ritratto con forza della più esatta imitazione. Dietro Nicodemo si vedono alquanto le Marie dolenti, l'una con le braccia sollevate, l'altra col velo a gli occhi, e la terza riguarda il Signore."

4 Alberti, 65: "Laudatur in Roma historia in qua Meleager defunctus asportatur, quod qui oneri subsunt angi et omnibus membris laborare videantur; in eo vero qui mortuus sit,

nullum adsit membrum quod non demortuum appareat, omnia pendent, manus, digiti, cervix, omnia languida decidunt, denique omnia ad exprimendam corporis mortem congruunt."

5 The relationship between Caravaggio's figure of Christ and the iconographical tradition of the *Death of Meleager* is evoked by Ebert-Schifferer 2009, 170-1.

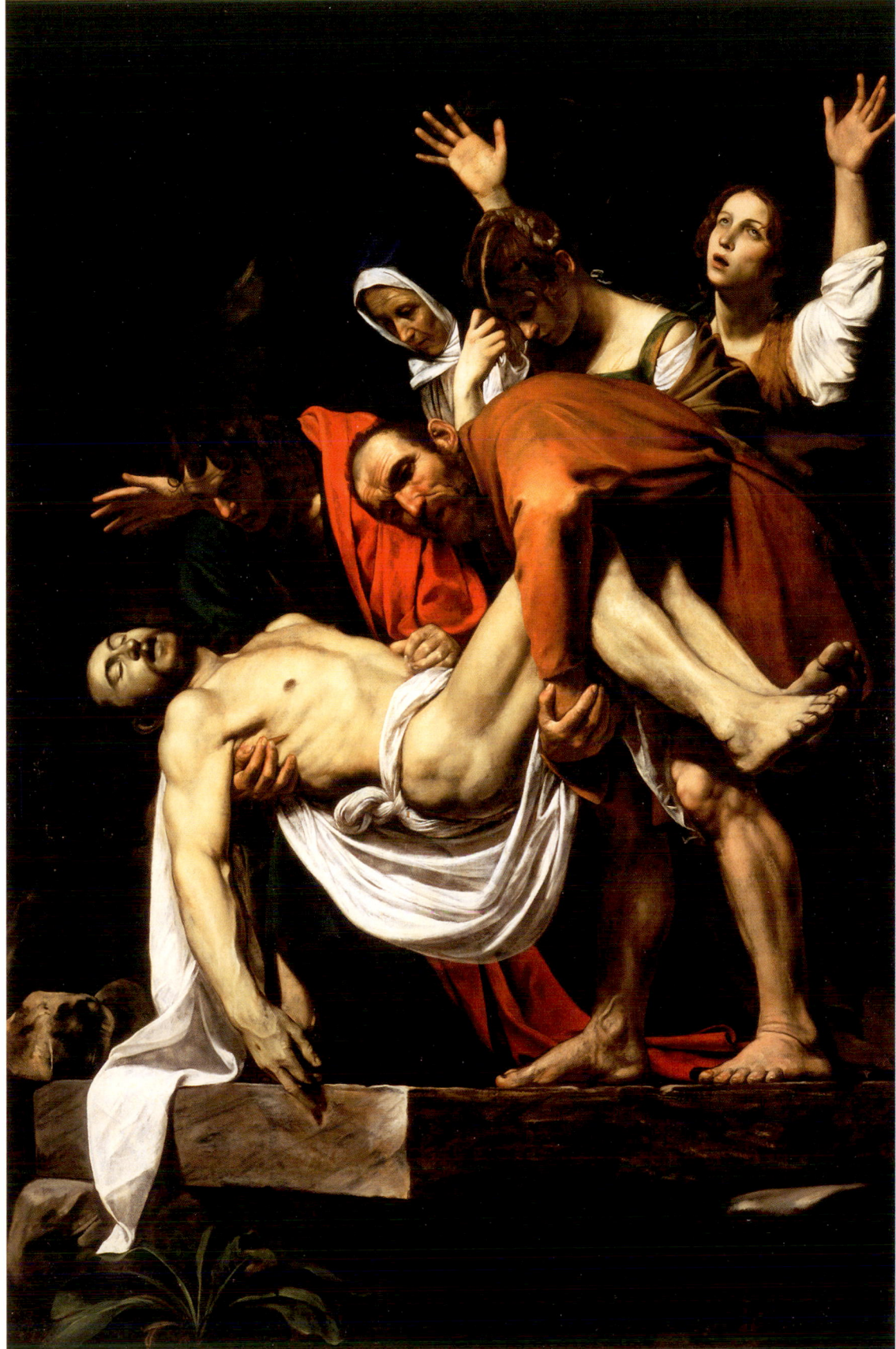

Fig. 166
Michelangelo Merisi da Caravaggio, *The Entombment*, Pinacoteca Vaticana, Rome, oil on canvas, 300 x 203 cm.

weight seem to suffer and endure pain with all their limbs," as Alberti says of the figures carrying Meleager in the ancient sarcophagus. Nor does Bellori realize that the veiled old woman directly behind John is the Virgin, and not one of the Marys, an identification that would most probably have upset Bellori given the minor relevance assigned by Caravaggio to the Mother of God in the painting. I shall return to these details in the following pages. For the time being, I intend to use Bellori's acknowledgment of the Vatican *Entombment*'s canonicity—its exemplary respect for the *istoria*'s canonical principles—as a linchpin of a deeper reflection on the picture.

For the first time in this book, I agree entirely with Bellori's opinion. I believe that with the *Entombment* Caravaggio intended to produce an impeccable artwork, his own version of an excellent *istoria*. For this reason, it comes as no surprise that Bellori perceived the painting as embodying the principles of Alberti's mimesis. However, I do not think that Bellori imagined the extent to which Caravaggio used the *Entombment* in order to show off the newness of his painting: to the point that he staged in his *istoria* an artistic *paragone* of which the main referent, and in a sense the target, is none but the other Michelangelo—Buonarroti, the author of the Vatican *Pietà*.[6]

Scholars have repeated endlessly (sometimes opportunely, sometimes mechanically) how much Caravaggio's Christ depends on Michelangelo's prototype in Saint Peter's. Maurizio Marini, although he recanted immediately afterward, even formulated the hypothesis—which I shall defend and substantiate—that the figure of Nicodemus in the Vatican *Entombment* personifies Michelangelo.[7] However, it has never been recognized that, more than with the Vatican *Pietà*, Caravaggio's *Entombment* engages in unflinching competition with Michelangelo's Florence *Pietà*, the one the old master so feverishly worked upon, toiled away at, and allegedly hammered into pieces out of desperation: the one in which he represented himself as a hooded Nicodemus supporting Christ's dead body. Perhaps because Michelangelo's sculptural group is now in Florence, scholars have not considered that it might have exerted a real influence on Caravaggio; but the Florence *Pietà* was still in Rome at the beginning of the seventeenth century, ready to be studied and mulled over by artists who most likely knew about its containment of Michelangelo's self-portrait. By highlighting on a preliminary basis the importance of the Florence *Pietà* for the Vatican *Entombment*, I do not wish to give the impression that Michelangelo's imprint is exclusively a matter of quotation.

In truth, Caravaggio's painting does not indulge in mere quotation of any prototype ideated by Michelangelo, but rather elaborates radically and profoundly upon theoretical problems that all hark back to Michelangelo: the artist's role in the artwork's conception and execution, the relation between painting and sculpture, the function of the figure in the machinery of the composition, and the challenge constituted by the harmonious and successful imbrication of multiple actors in a coordinated action. A full-range *paragone* is, I contend, what the Vatican *Entombment* represented for Caravaggio. In the background of this confrontation with the titanic persona of Michelangelo a greater ambition is at stake: the possibility for painting to recover from what might be called the "Mannerist decline," and renew itself in a modern configuration that would be entirely Caravaggio's hallmark. In my opinion, the Vatican painting represents a telling manifesto of Caravaggio's avant-garde. Before embarking upon an analysis of the picture, it will be helpful to know more about Caravaggio's feelings toward his great predecessor. Of course, the homonymy between the two Michelangelos was not lost on Caravaggio's critics; it became a witty pun, and yet another way to put down the detested Lombard master. Francesco Albani, as I have already pointed out in the introduction to Part One, played with this homonymy, as did Vicencio Carducho—as I will explain

6 The bibliography on the concept of the *paragone* is vast. A few of the most relevant essays in this regard are: White 1967; Collareta 1988; Winner 1989; Preimesberger 2001; Thomas B. 2001; Nova 2003; Collareta 2007; Ostrow 2007; Payne 2007; Dempsey 2009.

7 See Marini 1974, 70, note 249: "Si potrebbero riconoscere (del tutto ipoteticamente) i tratti somatici di Michelangelo Buonarroti: un omaggio al creatore del prototipo della Pietà?"

in Chapter 16—who referred with contempt to Caravaggio as the anti-Michelangelo: the Antichrist of art. Less well known is Carlo Cesare Malvasia's parallel between Michelangelo and Caravaggio, which he introduced in his 1678 biography of the Bolognese painter Giacomo Cavedone as a demonstration of how artists with superficial talents manage to meet with success:

> It is not because Caravaggio was so far removed from the knowledge of Buonarroti— whose name, Michelangelo, was instead so close to his own—that Caravaggio's shallow and facile manner—because it was well accomplished in its own way—did not encounter universal consensus. Caravaggio indeed deserved compliments as much— if I dare say—as that great master of all [Michelangelo] merited the praises due to him.[8]

Lest Malvasia's diplomatic phrasing at the end of the passage deceive anyone, the assimilation of Caravaggio with Cavedone was not supposed to be flattering for either of the artists. In any event, from these few, but valuable, testimonies, it is evident that Caravaggio was constantly characterized as the bad Michelangelo, the one who corrupted, and even destroyed, painting instead of raising it to its perfection as his forebear had done. But what about Caravaggio himself? Besides the fact that his paintings allude very often to Michelangelo's antecedents in view of emulation, there is unfortunately not the slightest trace as to whether he admired or looked down upon his predecessor. Although Caravaggio's enemies all too naturally tended to abound in slander, there must have been a grain of truth in the reports of Caravaggio's arrogance and self-confidence. According to Baglione:

> Michelangelo Amerigi [Merisi] was a mocker and a haughty man; sometimes, he came to speak ill of all the painters, past and present, however illustrious they might have been, for he believed that he alone had surpassed all the men of his profession with his works.[9]

On the other hand, while it is clear that Caravaggio held his art and persona in high esteem, there is also evidence that he was able to recognize other painters' talents. In an oral deposition he made in the so-called Baglione trial[10]—Baglione had accused Caravaggio and others of having composed satirical poems about him—on 13 September 1603, around the time he executed the Vatican *Entombment*, Caravaggio, when asked to define what he meant by "*valentuomo*" (literally, a gentleman, but in the terminology of art, an accomplished artist), declared:

8 Malvasia, 2:215: "Perché tanto fosse lontano al sapere del Buonaroti, quanto vi si approssimò col nome anch'egli di Michelangelo il Caravaggio, non è che quel suo modo compendioso e superficiale (perché in suo essere ben fatto) non incontrasse nel genio universale e non abbia anch'egli i suoi encomi, sto per dire, uguali alle lodi tanto dovute a quel gran maestro di tutti".

9 Baglione, 138: "Michelagnolo Amerigi fu uomo satirico ed altiero, ed usciva talora a dir male di tutti li pittori passati e presenti per insigni che si fussero, poiché a lui parea d'aver solo con le sue opere avanzati tutti gli altri della sua professione." A similar observation was already made in 1604 by Van Mander, 3:191: "Hy heft ghedaen een Historie tot S. Laurens in Damas, neffens die van Iosepino (...). Hier in heft hy gemaect een Naenken oft Reusken dat nae Iosephs Historie toe siende de tongh uyt steeckt schjinende of hy aldus Iosephs wreck wilde bespotten: want hy is een die van geen Meesters dinghen veel houdt: doch sy selven niet openlikj prijsende. Dan zijn segghen is dat alle dinghen niet den *Bagatelli*, kinderwerck oft

bueselinghen zijn, t'zy wat oft van wien geschildert, soo sy niet nae t' leven ghedaen en gheschildert en zijn, en datter niet goet oft beter en can wesen dan de Natuere te volghen [He did a story at San Lorenzo in Damaso, next to that of the Cavalier d'Arpino [Giuseppino] (...). In it he has painted a dwarf or little fellow who, looking at the Cavalier's picture, sticks out his tongue, as if he wished to ridicule the Cavaliere's work. For he is one who cares little for the work of other masters, yet will not praise his own openly. He holds that all works are nothing but bagatelles, child's work, or trifles, whatever their subject and by whomever painted, unless they be done and painted after life and that nothing could be good and nothing better than to follow Nature." Nevertheless, in an appendix attached to his *Schilder-boek*, Van Mander stated that he had been ill-informed about the figure of the dwarf mocking the Cavalier d'Arpino's work.

10 For a general survey of the trial, see Smith 'O Neil 2002, 7-39.

> *Valentuomini* are people who are knowledgeable about painting, and they will consider good [or bad] painters those whom I have called good or bad; but those who are ignorant and bad painters will consider ignorant painters just like themselves to be good.[11]

Among the painters he deemed to be *valentuomini*, Caravaggio mentioned the Cavalier d'Arpino, Federico Zuccari, Pomarancio, and Annibale Carracci, although he had stated earlier that the Cavalier d'Arpino was not a friend of his. The fact that he made a distinction between friendship and artistic quality seems to me the sign of a certain levelheadedness. I do not doubt that Caravaggio sincerely admired Michelangelo's art at least for one reason: he chose Michelangelo, rather than Raphael or Titian, as his partner in the fictive duel for artistic preeminence that he set up in the Vatican *Entombment*. If, as I shall demonstrate, Caravaggio evoked the figure of Michelangelo in a state of artistic frustration, such evocation does not entail any attempt at diminishing his adversary's genius: as I have already pointed out in the previous chapter, Caravaggio also put himself in a frustrating situation in *The Taking of Christ*, so that, by pairing himself with Michelangelo in the hopeless task of either illuminating or supporting the whole *istoria*, he rather intended to convey his own outlook on artistic invention. Needless to say—and Baglione's opinion was right on the mark in this respect—Caravaggio was an inveterate mocker; however, his taste for mocking overall extends to his own persona and is never free of tragic facets. I will deal extensively with Caravaggio's self-mockery in the next chapter.

Before elucidating the complex relationship between Michelangelo and Caravaggio, it is essential to ascertain the originality of the Vatican painting; nothing in the Renaissance tradition truly compares with *The Entombment*'s sophisticated visual configuration. In its composition, the Vatican picture conjures up and brings to a synthesis a three-pronged iconographic tradition: that of the Deposition, the Lamentation, and the Entombment. Over the previous two centuries or so, artists had sought in many ways to resolve the technical problems that multi-figured actions like these, which almost by definition should move along by themselves like well-oiled machines, had come to incorporate. In some cases, the artists' ingenuity had reached an extraordinary climax. Since Caravaggio takes up or elaborates upon various formulas from his predecessors, the scope of his achievement will emerge more clearly by means of a comparison with some of their works.

To begin with, I shall briefly consider Hans Baldung Grien's 1515-1517 woodcut representing the *Lamentation* (Fig. 167).[12] Most interesting and extraordinary is the three-tiered structure within which Grien succeeded in clamping together the wing-nut of the Magdalene's torso and outstretched arms, the trapezoidal rivet of the Virgin bowing her head and clasping her hands, and the boldly foreshortened tripod of Christ's prostrate dead body, anchored to, and pressed against, the ground through his folded right arm, his supine torso, and bent legs. Masterfully, Grien flung the Savior's left arm upward so that the Lamentation group is equally fastened to the figure of the mourning John to the right, his hand at his eye to dab a tear, his lips parted in a sigh. The lexicon of gestures and attitudes—outstretched and skyward-tilted arms, downward-tipped, three-quarter heads, and clenched fists concealing portions of faces, among others—is particularly adaptable to diverse settings and aspects of a burial ceremony.

Grien's wondrous clockwork of mourners responded to Albrecht Dürer's *tour de force* in his 1507 *Lamentation* from the *Engraved Passion* (Fig. 168).[13] Akin to a descending wave, a parabolic

---

11   This document was first published by Bertolotti 1881, 2:58-69. See Macioce 2003, 128: "Li valent'huomini sono quelli che si intendono della pittura et giudicaranno buoni pittori quelli che ho giudicato io buoni et cattivi; ma quelli che sono cattivi pittori et ignoranti giudicaranno per buoni pittori gl'ignoranti come sono loro."

12   See Marrow and Shestack 1981, 201-2, no. 49.

13   See Hütt 1980, 2:1860; Schoch et al. 2001, 1:145-6, no. 56.

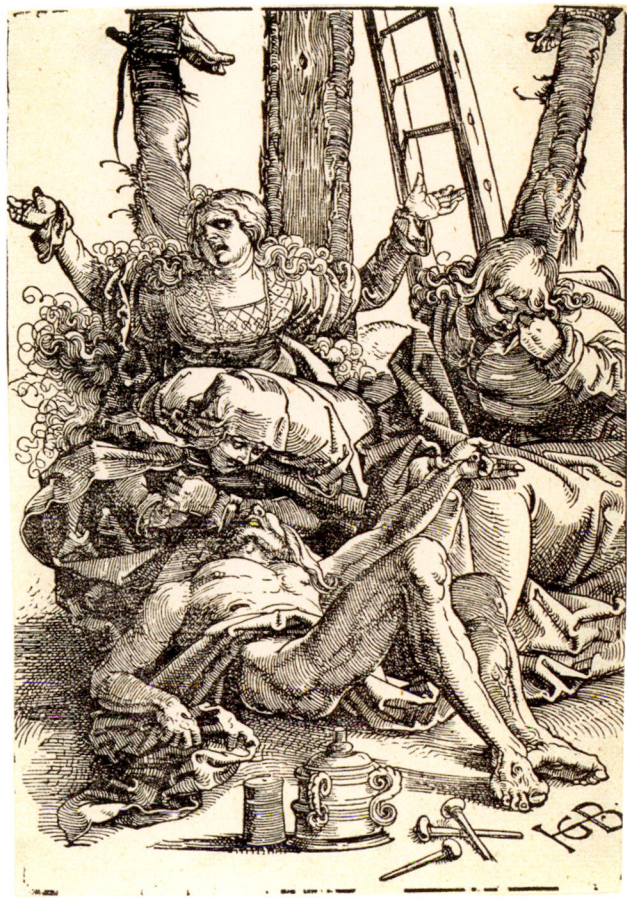

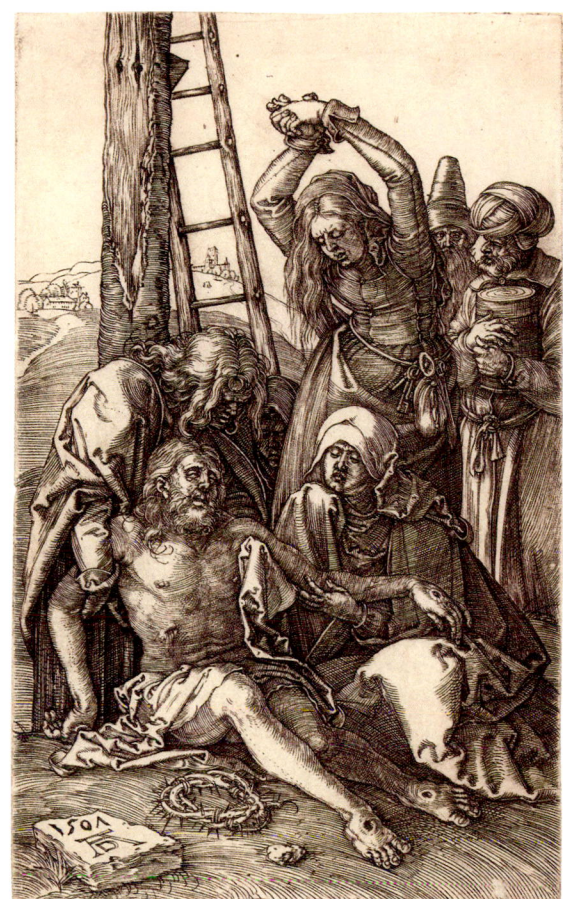

Fig. 167
Hans Baldung Grien, *Lamentation*, woodcut, 22.5 x 15.2 cm.

Fig. 168
Albrecht Dürer, *Lamentation*, engraving, 11.5 x 7.1 cm.

curve circumscribes the figures of John, standing on a farther, lower level as he pulls up Christ's torso, and the Virgin, kneeling beside her Son and supporting his left arm. The overhanging Magdalene constitutes the crest of this metaphoric wave and the apex of the episode's pathos; like a New Testament maenad, her hair disheveled, she raises both her arms while her hands, tightly interlocked, form the top of a living canopy covering the *Pietà* at her feet. To say that Dürer's composition—the elegantly overlapping parabolas of his figures—constituted an immense challenge of originality for artists who wished to depict the same theme, is an understatement. By placing atop the reeling machine of his mourners the outflung arms of one of the Marys, Caravaggio in my opinion bore in mind Dürer's example. Although there is no neat quotation from the German master in *The Entombment*, I think that Caravaggio's gripping idea of shading John's bent face by very slightly lightening the ridge of his eyebrows, his nose and the salience of his lips owes a great deal to Dürer's *Lamentation*. By the same token, I suspect that Dürer's 1512 *Deposition*,[14] also from the *Engraved Passion*, might to some degree have been in Caravaggio's mind when he painted the Vatican *Entombment*. Although not uncommon, the detail of the veiled Virgin's downcast, three-quarter face as evoked in Dürer's engraving reappears in Caravaggio's mourning Madonna. Nonetheless, some motifs present in the Vatican picture are not inspired by specific prototypes, but may well be merely formulaic. For instance, Caravaggio's young Mary with braided hair and bringing a handkerchief to her face recalls the figure of the Virgin in Hans Schäufelein's *Lamentation*, a woodcut from the Nuremberg 1507 *Speculum Passionis*.[15] In the print

14   See Schoch et al. 2001, 1:146-7, no. 57.

15   See Falk 1980, 229, no. 34-21 (253).

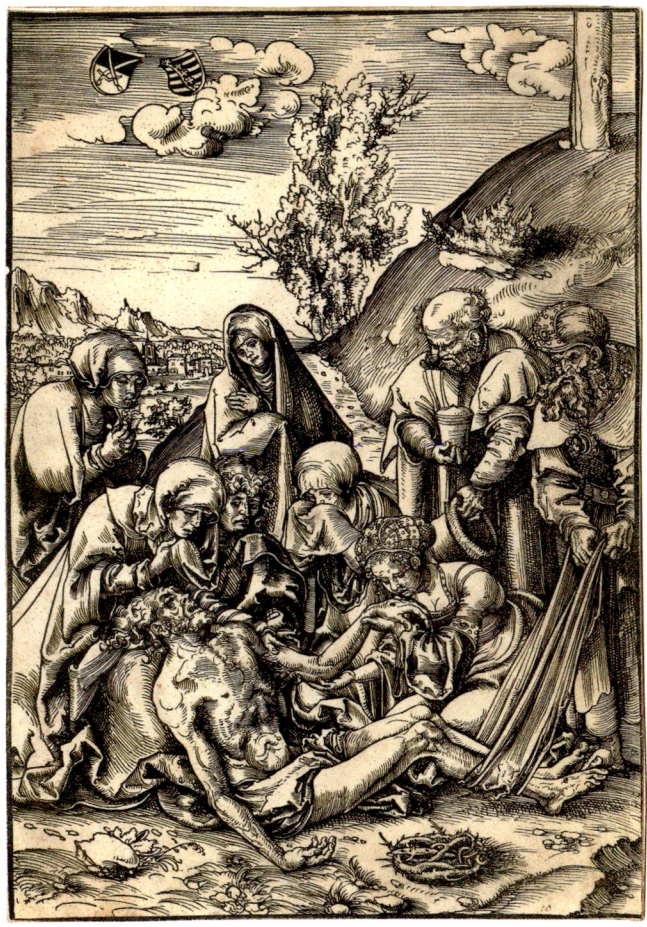

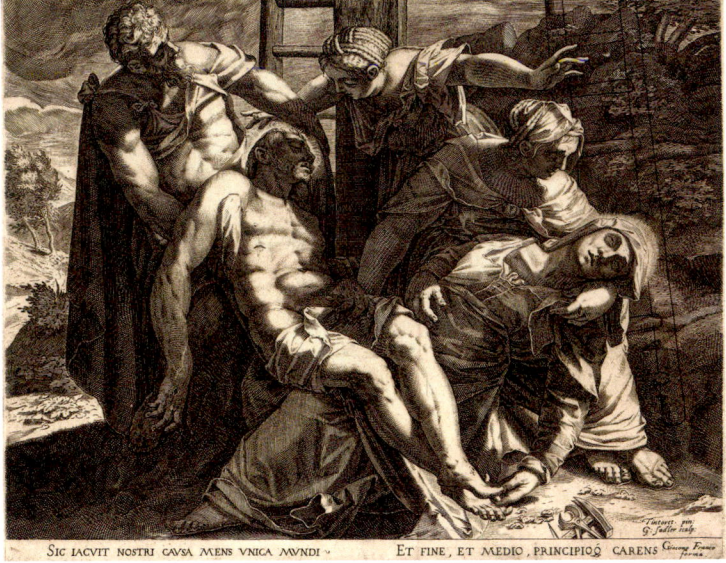

Fig. 169
Lucas Cranach the Elder, *Lamentation*, woodcut, 24.5 x 17.1 cm.

Fig. 170
Aegidius Sadeler II after Tintoretto (Jacopo Robusti), *The Deposition*, engraving, 31.7 x 39 cm.

the elderly Madonna is veiled and dabs her tears with the veil wrapped around her hand. The affinity, in any case, may be fortuitous, as the gesture is widely diffused in the iconography of the Lamentation.

On the other hand, I would not rule out the possibility that Caravaggio studied Lucas Cranach's *Lamentation* from his 1509 *Passion*, a series of fourteen xylographs (Fig. 169).[16] In this work, Cranach disposed the mourners into two concentric semi-circles around Christ's dead body, which lies almost parallel to the print's surface in the foreground. If one mentally isolates the group of the Virgin, Saint John, one of the Marys, and the Magdalene, one will notice that, albeit perceived as leaning in a single row, their faces are coupled in a twofold sequence: to the left, those of the Virgin and John are aligned with one another, the undulating motion of her veil and his mantle beneath serving as a common base to their shoulders; to the right, the heads of one of the Marys and the Magdalene, on two different planes, relate to each other along an oblique line. Even though nothing in Caravaggio's painting literally mirrors Cranach's composition, Caravaggio's idea of both superposing two friezes of aligned and paired faces and linking the lower ones to the higher ones diagonally might be interpreted as a clever variation on Cranach's *Lamentation*.

With respect to the iconographic tradition, these analogies are startling and anything but hackneyed. On the contrary, great artists tended to indulge their whims, as it were, in imbricating the mourners' figures together in the most varied schemes. Tintoretto is a case in point: in his mid

16   See Jahn 1975, 216-7, 240.

1550s *Deposition of Christ* now at the Gallerie dell'Accademia, Venice,[17] and reproduced by Aegidius Sadeler II in an engraving (Fig. 170),[18] Tintoretto bound the figures together in what at first glance appears to be a monumental X. Furthermore, the group of the Virgin to the right and the figure of Christ with his dangling arm to the left delineate two intersecting triangles crowned by the open and closed curves of the Magdalene's and Nicodemus' (or Joseph of Arimathea's) arms respectively. The compound of straight lines and ellipses specific to Tintoretto's group, extremely refined as it is, does not bear any resemblance to Caravaggio's millwheel—I will expand on this metaphor later—beyond the fact that both compositions are artistic feats in their own right. Nor would one find any similarity between Caravaggio's fanning layout of actors and, say, Battista Franco's rather canonical frieze-like disposition of the mourners as depicted in an engraved *Deposition* difficult to date, but most probably from the 1540s or 1550s (Fig. 171).[19] I would draw attention to the figure of the Virgin at the left of this print, riveting her gaze on her Son's dead body while opening her hands in awe and sorrow; the hovering silhouette of her right hand with its shaded palm reminds one of the analogous

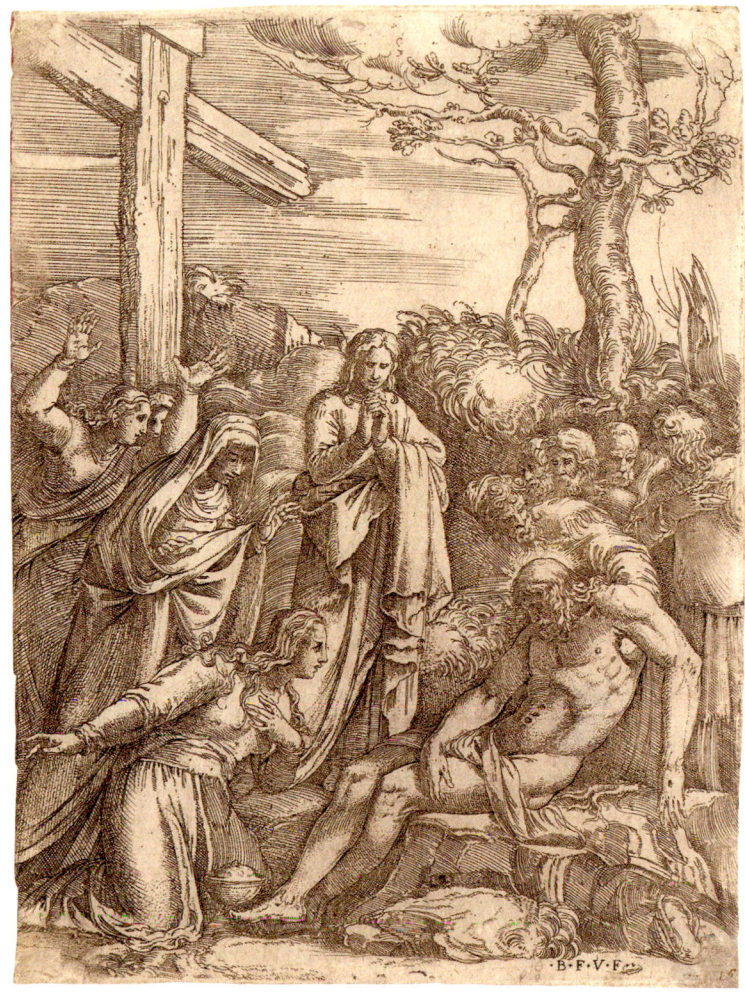

Fig. 171
Battista Franco, *The Deposition*, engraving, 22.3 x 15.8 cm.

motif of the Virgin's suspended hand in the Vatican *Entombment*. Of course, I am not implying by this that Franco's *Deposition* should qualify as a source for Caravaggio's painting.

Rather, what interests me is to underscore two facts: first, the figures' disposition in the Vatican picture assuredly ranks as a *hapax legomenon*, a unique instance of visual rhetoric; secondly, the painting's uniqueness nonetheless relies on an amazing knowledge of the iconographic vocabulary, that is, of the figurative patterns embedded in, and swept along by, the traditional iconography. The fact that only bits and pieces of this lexicon can be traced back in *The Entombment* shows how far Caravaggio pushed the process of elaboration upon canonical formulas: he distilled his prototypes not only to conceal any trace of influence—with the exception of Michelangelo, as I will determine shortly—but especially to endow the uniqueness of his invention with an indeterminate aura of canonicity.

When examined in the context of seventeenth-century aesthetics, the procedure by which Caravaggio ensured his work's originality naturally required the evocation of an artistic touchstone: the more ambitious the enterprise, the greater the master to be challenged. In other words, to be wholly effective, the discourse on novelty that Caravaggio deployed in the Vatican

---

17   See Pallucchini and Rossi 1982, 180, no. 227. The painting has been recently cleaned and exhibited in Boston. See Ilchman 2009, 140-2.

18   De Ramaix 1997, 87, no. 056.

19   For the print, see Zerner 1979, 173, no. 17 (125).

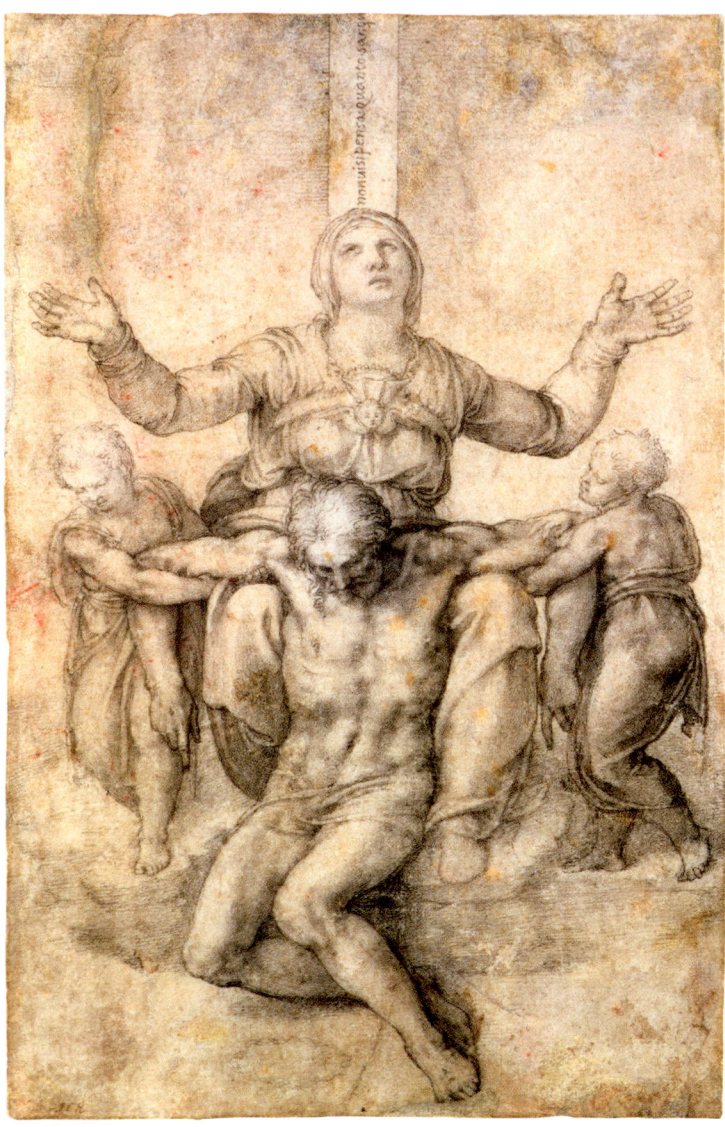

Fig. 172
Michelangelo Buonarroti, *Lamentation (Pietà for Vittoria Colonna)*, Isabella Stewart Gardner Museum, Boston, black chalk, 29.4 x 18.1 cm.

picture demanded that Michelangelo's paradigm of perfection should be put to the test, constantly alluded to, and eventually transcended. As a corollary, Michelangelo's art ought to be evoked, but never copied to the letter; to put it more strongly, the use of Michelangelesque patterns ought to be less in the nature of scavenging and more of reinterpretation. I illustrate this point by an example that will also serve as an introduction to the diverse ways in which Caravaggio adjusted and improved upon Michelangelo's art.

As we have seen, the gesture of the young Mary at the top of *The Entombment*, lifting her arms in desolation, relates to the iconography of the Lamentation and Deposition. Thus it should be viewed as a topical gesture and should not be expected to hint at any specific prototype. Nonetheless, I am convinced that, in depicting the figure of this Mary, Caravaggio had in mind the drawing of the *Pietà* that Michelangelo had donated to Vittoria Colonna around 1546.[20] This drawing in black chalk now belongs to the Isabella Stewart Gardner Museum, Boston (Fig. 172), and although its whereabouts at Caravaggio's time is unknown, the composition was available not only through copies, but especially through three engraved reproductions:[21] one by Giulio Bonasone dated 1546 (Fig. 173),[22] one by Nicolas Béatrizet,[23] and another by Agostino Carracci from 1579 (Fig. 174).[24] I shall look at both the first and the last of these works, because Agostino's print bears a detail absent in Michelangelo's drawing and Bonasone's engraving: the Virgin's mouth is open in a fierce shriek. In his 1553 *Vita di Michelagnolo Buonarroti*, Ascanio Condivi describes the drawing as follows:

A naked Christ being laid down from the cross, whose inert body would collapse to the feet of his most holy Mother if two little angels did not support his arms. She [the Virgin] sitting under the cross, her face tearful and sorrowful, flings both arms out raising them heavenward; a sentence on the cross's surface reads: "none considers how much blood it costs."[25]

20 Calvesi 1990, 313-4, points out that the female figure with the outflung arms in Caravaggio's picture stems from an analogous figure in Pomarancio's *Deposition* in Santa Maria in Aracoeli, Rome, although, he argues, both artists relied on Michelangelo's figure of the mourning Virgin in the *Pietà* for Vittoria Colonna. On this drawing and its meaning, see De Tolnay 1953; Nagel 1996, 554-63; Nagel 1997; Campi 1997; Nagel 2000, 167-8; Gabrielli 2009.

21 On sixteenth-century printed reproductions after Michelangelo's Colonna *Pietà*, see Barnes 2010, 78-80.

22 See Massari 1983, 70-1, no. 77.

23 See Boorsch 1982, 268, no. 25 (251).

24 See DeGrazia 1979, 84-5, no. 10.

25 Condivi, 61: "Fece a requisizione di questa signora un Cristo ignudo quando è tolto di croce, il quale come corpo

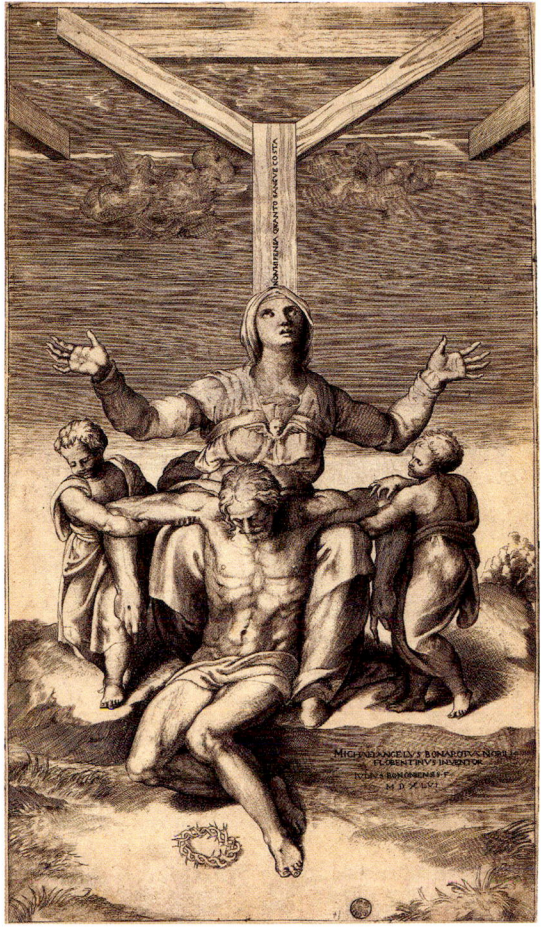

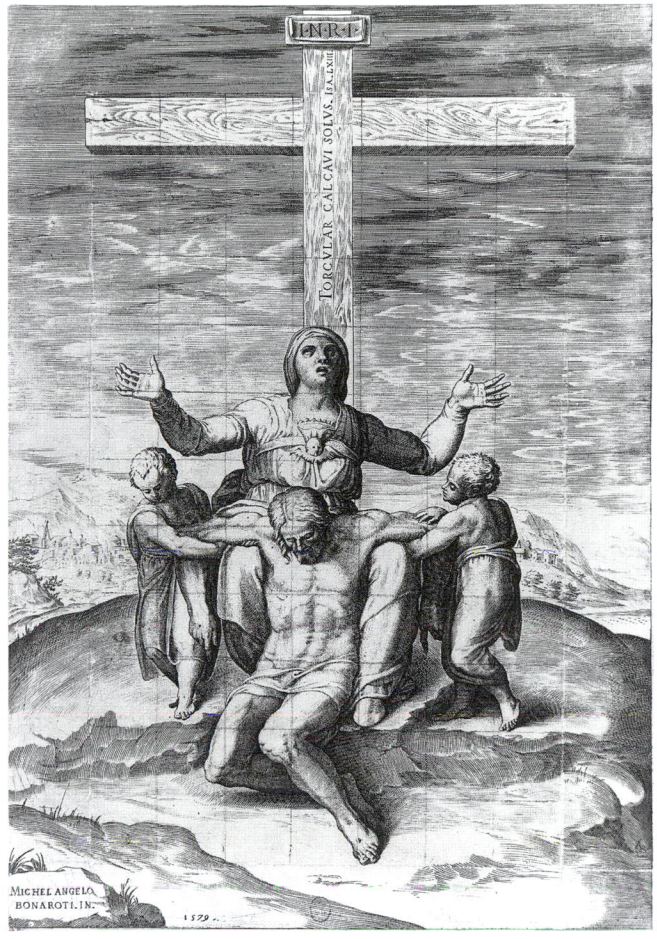

Fig. 173
Giulio Bonasone after Michelangelo Buonarroti,
Lamentation, engraving, 36 x 20.6 cm.

Fig. 174
Agostino Carracci after Michelangelo Buonarroti, *Lamentation*,
engraving, 41.1 x 28.7 cm.

Although Michelangelo's drawing was cropped at the top at an indeterminate date so that only the cross's trunk is now visible, it is still possible to reconstruct the impact of what Alexander Nagel has defined as the "yoke-like" disposition of Christ's arms[26] and its reiteration through inversion in the Virgin's outstretched arms and in the diagonal arms of the cross; these are to be seen in Bonasone's engraving, but were nonetheless "regularized" by Agostino Carracci into a long horizontal. It is evident, in any case, that Michelangelo conceived of the Virgin–Christ dyad as a single, sculptural block, almost able to stand in symmetric balance on its own were it not for the dead body's natural tendency to slide downward, a gravitational pull against which the Virgin's outcropping knees cannot offer adequate resistance. In Condivi's description, emphasis is also laid on the body's lifelessness, and hence on the necessity of its drooping, dangling or collapsing.

Returning to the Vatican *Entombment*, I would argue that its shrieking Mary is intended to evoke Michelangelo's Virgin in the Colonna drawing; if Caravaggio's figure does not angle her outflung arms into brackets, this deviation from the prototype can be easily accounted for through the painting's specificity—the gesture, here, serves as the culminating pediment, a kind of acroterion, to a six-figure action, and therefore is supplied with greater relevance. Moreover, Caravaggio

morto cascherebbe a' piedi della sua santissima madre se da due agnioletti non fusse sostenuto a braccia. Ma ella, sotto la croce stando a sedere con volto lacrimoso e dolente, alza al cielo ambe le mani a braccia aperte, con un cotal detto che nel

troncon della croce scritto si legge: 'Non vi si pensa quanto sangue costa'."

26   Nagel 2000, 168.

353

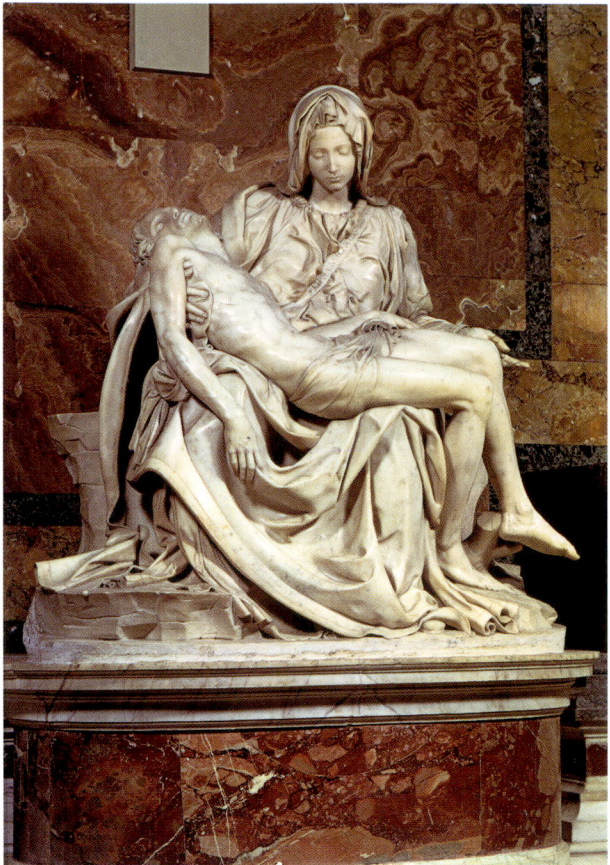

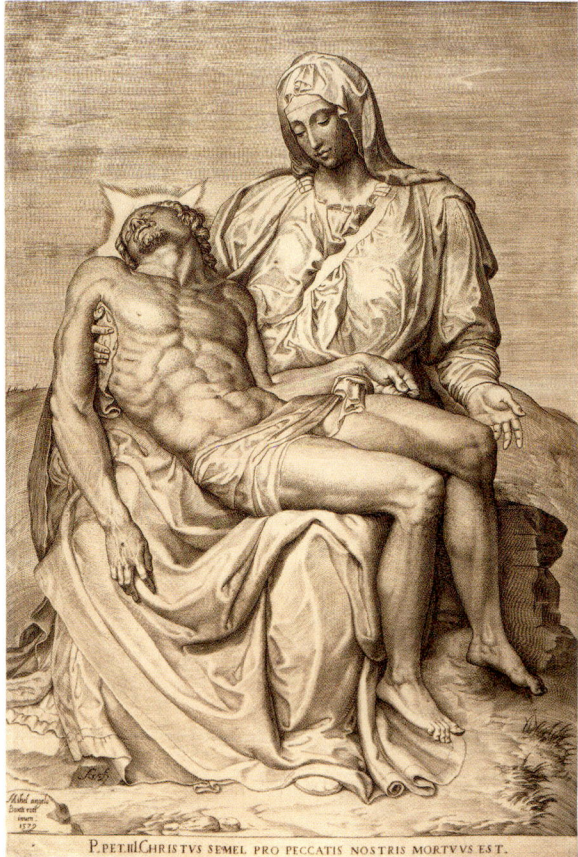

Fig. 175
Michelangelo Buonarroti, *Pietà*, Saint Peter's, Rome, marble,
175 cm.

Fig. 176
Agostino Carracci after Michelangelo Buonarroti, *Pietà*,
engraving, 44.9 x 30.4 cm.

designed the two uplifted arms to operate as a mechanical counterweight to the lowering machine
consisting of the lamenters. This main divergence notwithstanding, Mary's cocked face, upturned
eyes and craned, cylindrical neck in Caravaggio's picture echo those of Michelangelo's Virgin.
In addition, the lively graphicness of Mary's exposed palms—Caravaggio singled out the back
of every finger at the risk of unnatural elongation and did not hesitate here and there to bend
subtly an index or a little finger, thereby engendering a discreet ornamental effect—corresponds to
Michelangelo's drawing as rendered by Bonasone's burin. Even the act of the open, screaming mouth
in Caravaggio's Mary might derive from the Colonna *Pietà* via Agostino Carracci's interpretation
of it. It is thus clear that, in one way or another, Caravaggio's *Entombment* systematically points
toward Michelangelo.

Sculpture in Painting

Doubtless Caravaggio himself planned to trigger instantaneously in the beholder's mind the
reminiscence of Michelangelo's Savior from the Saint Peter's *Pietà* with the view of Christ's dead
body in his Vatican *Entombment*. Despite its execution toward the end of the quattrocento—more
precisely, in 1498-1499—Michelangelo's sculpture continued to be celebrated and popular in
Caravaggio's time (Fig. 175).[27] The temptation for artists to compete with the paradigm of excellence

27 For Michelangelo's Roman *Pietà*, see De Tolnay 1969,   Niebaum 2007.
1:145-50, no. V; Wallace 1992; Schwedes 2000. Pestilli 2000;

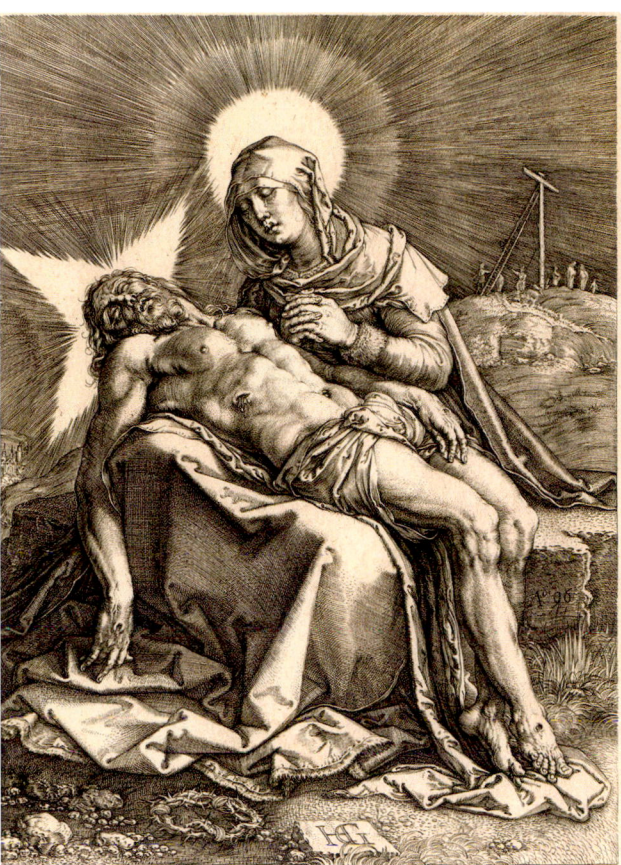

Fig. 177
Hendrick Goltzius, *Pietà*, engraving, 17.5 x 12.6 cm.

it embodied was therefore strong, and re-elaboration was not at all uncommon.

In 1579, the same year that he reproduced and published Michelangelo's drawing for Vittoria Colonna, Agostino Carracci engraved a large sheet representing the Vatican *Pietà* (Fig. 176).[28] It has been argued that Agostino was not able to study the sculpture first-hand—he had not yet traveled to Rome at the time—and most probably worked after a (now lost) design by another artist. Even though Agostino's print limits itself to rendering faithfully the overall configuration of Michelangelo's sculpture, the viewpoint opted for to envision the work in its integrity—or as much as could be seen from a single angle—generates an effect of subtle estrangement. Michelangelo indeed carved the marble block in order to emphasize the frontal view, whereas in Agostino's engraving one gazes at the Virgin and Christ from above and from the right, so that the detailed anatomy of Christ's body is fully disclosed to the viewer. Agostino also enhanced a detail that might go unnoticed at first glance in the Vatican *Pietà*: the audacious foreshortening of Christ's drooping head. In a certain sense, Agostino's print recreates Michelangelo's sculpture by shedding an unusual light upon it, and by inserting the work into a pictorial setting; the Virgin and Christ now loom large, even monumentally, against the backdrop of a makeshift sky, delicate parallel strias mimicking the diverse density of the air by their varying thickness.

More important for our purpose is Hendrick Goltzius' engraved *Pietà* from 1596 (Fig. 177).[29] In my opinion, the oblique point of view adopted here is indebted to Agostino's precedent, so that through his ingenious elaboration of the Vatican *Pietà* Goltzius sought to rival not only Michelangelo's feat, but also the model of outstanding craftsmanship in the domain of printing that Agostino had come to represent later in his lifetime. By depicting the group of the Virgin and Christ from a lateral standpoint, Goltzius also tried to capture a comprehensive glimpse of Christ's anatomy—like Michelangelo, he staggered the Virgin's thighs on two different levels in order to form a gentle slope upon which to lay and exhibit Jesus' body. Yet Goltzius could not help but improve upon Michelangelo's invention; for one thing, the Virgin's raised knee operates as a watershed between Christ's torso and his dangling arm, which as a consequence lends itself to exclusive contemplation on the viewer's part. In this manner, the rather large crater of Jesus' hand wound emerges strongly into view; incidentally, the same applies to the side wound, from which drops of blood are seeping. Secondly, Goltzius managed fully to uncover the Savior's collapsing face, whereas Michelangelo's group causes the viewer's attention to veer toward the

28 See DeGrazia 1979, 82, no. 9. For the numerous reproductions of Michelangelo's Roman *Pietà* printed in the sixteenth century, see Barnes 2010, 149-53.

29 See Strauss 1977, 608, no. 331.

majestically contemplative face of the Virgin. Thirdly, Goltzius animated Michelangelo's invention by incorporating its two figures into a narrative framework—the Virgin's interlocked hands and falling tears attest that the lamentation is unfolding, while Michelangelo magnifies the group's stillness and muteness to the point that the sculpture's only acting gesture—the Madonna's stretched left hand uttering resignation and distress—vanishes out of sight behind Christ's thighs.

Michelangelo's mastery of drapery and its folds represented a point of unsurpassed excellence for late sixteenth- and early seventeenth-century artists. Interestingly enough, Goltzius renounced the elliptical interplay of wide folds that punctuate the landing of the Virgin's mantle upon the sculpture's base. In the engraving, Goltzius reshaped this part of the drapery into a solid cube, whose perimeter is occasionally interrupted by two major, angular breakings of the folds. The treatment of this section of the Virgin's mantle clearly contrasts that of Christ's underlying shroud, bristling with small crevasses and tubular ridges, and hence vividly illuminated. These details are of primary importance: rather than decorative, the system of folds in Goltzius's print is in fact performative. In other words, Goltzius replaced Michelangelo's reiterated "motifs of cascading folds" with an antique-style pedestal of drapery, while simultaneously, in Christ's shroud, recalling the minute and calligraphic handling of northern Renaissance print-making, particularly Dürer's artistry.[30] What I have just highlighted to a certain degree epitomizes Goltzius' "path to newness," the search for an originality that does not deny, but relies upon, previous patterns of artistic excellence. In the case of Goltzius, the new art condenses the features of various traditions—antiquity, the Italian and northern Renaissances, and so forth—and thus connotes a reformed eclecticism.

Caravaggio's intention does not radically differ from Goltzius'; for the Italian master, art's new language also proceeds from a synthesis, or condensation, of diverse canonic artistic idioms. But of course, Caravaggio's response to this supreme form of eclecticism is unique on several counts. Before comparing the figure of Christ in Caravaggio's *Entombment* with its prototype in the Vatican *Pietà*, it is appropriate to assess what exactly the representation of Michelangelo's dead body of Christ implied during Caravaggio's time.[31] This is Giovan Paolo Lomazzo's reading of this figure in his 1584 *Idea della pittura*:

> One can see death's true motion [in Michelangelo's Christ], as one discerns all the limbs dangling, bereft of any vigor that might allow them to support themselves. One must follow this [example] with utmost diligence so as not to incur the errors of those who furnish the limbs of the dead with vigorous motion and, in a sense, make [their bodies] support themselves on their own.[32]

Caravaggio's rendering of Christ's dead body not only responds to Alberti's principles of mimesis in the *istoria*, but also to the difficult challenge that Michelangelo's prototype presented to artists in matters of narrative pertinence and naturalism. What characterizes Michelangelo's configuration of the dead body is its quasi-circular profile when looked at frontally: an uninterrupted curve that spans from the point in which the Virgin's right hand holds her Son's torso down to Christ's right knee. However, nothing like this is to be found in Caravaggio's picture (Figs. 178, 179). There, on the contrary, Christ's torso and buttock are stretched almost along a straight line, so that his chest seems to tilt forward toward the beholder's visual field. As a consequence, the right arm disengages

---

30 For this point, see Melion 1991, esp. 143-72.

31 For Lomazzo's interpretation of Michelangelo and his art, see more recently Squizzato 2004.

32 Lomazzo, 2:147: "...sì come giudiciosamente osservò (…) Michel Angelo nel Cristo morto di marmo in grembo alla

Madre che è in San Pietro in Vaticano, ne i quali si veggono i veri moti che fa la morte, vedendosi tutti gli membri cadenti e senza alcun vigore da potersi più in sé sostenere. Il che ha da essere diligentissimamente avertito per non incorrere ne gli errori di quelli che danno alle membra de i morti moti di gagliardia et in certo modo gli fanno da loro medesimi far atto di sostegno."

itself from the torso and spins out toward the tomb's slab in a manner not dissimilar from what Goltzius ideated in his 1596 *Pietà*. Again, as in Goltzius' print, the Savior's face in Caravaggio's *Entombment* is free to fall sideways and downward, making itself more visible to the viewer. As I have already stated, none of this necessarily points to Michelangelo's example.

Yet it is undeniable that the zigzag designed by the ascending thighs and collapsing legs of Caravaggio's dead body recalls that of Michelangelo's prototype, although this motif is obtained through opposite dynamics. In the sculpture, Christ's thighs and legs form an approximate 90 degree angle by naturally dangling alongside the Virgin's left leg, whereas in Caravaggio's painting the similar disposition of Christ's lower body results from an exterior thrust, an element that engenders an indissoluble bond between the Savior's body and Nicodemus. By this, I mean to stress a crucial fact: as a general rule, the configuration of Christ's dead body in Caravaggio's painting enhances the interdependence between the suspended figure of the Savior and his carriers. How indeed is one to separate the telling motif of Christ's hovering legs from the tight grasp of Nicodemus' arms around them? How is one to neglect the strong buckle constituted by Nicodemus' massive clasped hands under Christ's knees? And how is one to forget that, despite their fiery hold, these hands and arms would necessarily destabilize the position of Christ's body to the point of making it collapse were it not for John's concomitant support? It might seem a paradox that, even as he increases the effect of the body's deadness by visually strengthening the magnitude of Nicodemus' pull, Caravaggio indicates the partial ineffectiveness of the effort; unlike the seated Virgin of Michelangelo's *Pietà*, Nicodemus is here unable to carry the weight of Christ's corpse by himself. One figure is not enough to keep Michelangelo's Christ aloft.

There are at least two reasons for such an elaboration upon Michelangelo's prototype. On the one hand, Caravaggio evidently intended to give visual relevance to Nicodemus by underscoring both his absorbing endeavor and its inadequateness. On the other hand, the artistic competition with which Caravaggio had engaged entailed that Michelangelo's prototype should be "set in motion"—to paraphrase Lomazzo—that is, varied in such a way that it could adapt to the new narrative context. From this prospect, Nicodemus's incapacity to support Christ on his own is the *sine qua*

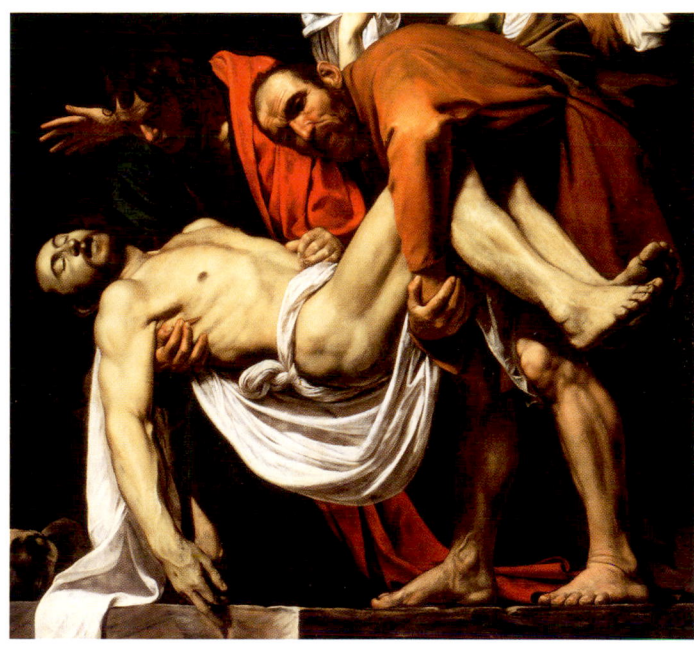

Fig. 178
Michelangelo Merisi da Caravaggio, *The Entombment*, Pinacoteca Vaticana, Rome, oil on canvas, 300 x 203 cm., detail.

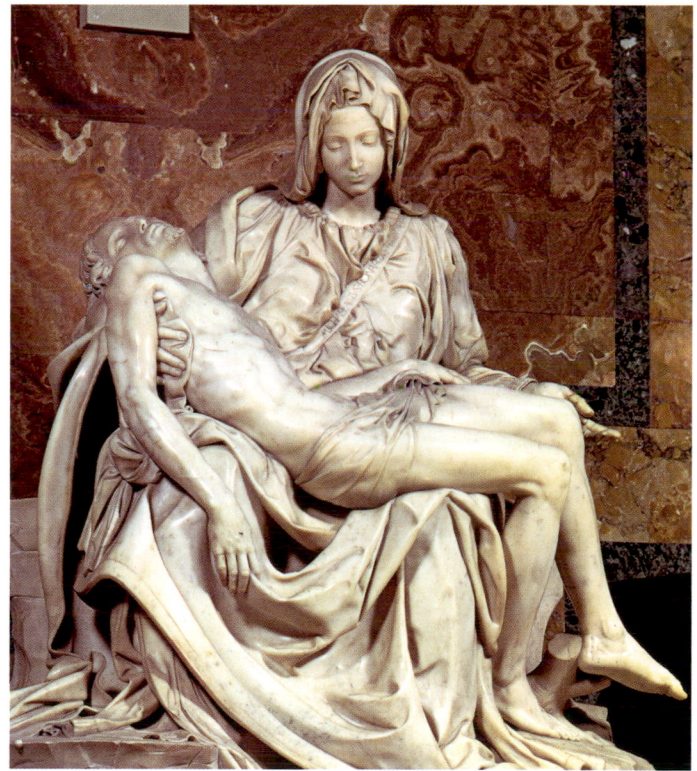

Fig. 179
Michelangelo Buonarroti, *Pietà*, Saint Peter's, Rome, marble, 175 cm., detail.

non of Caravaggio's enterprise in the Vatican *Entombment*, the means by which he could scale up Michelangelo's *Pietà* into a wider-ranging Deposition.

Of course, by adapting Michelangelo's Christ to a different script, the visual affinity between the prototype and its elaboration might considerably wane, becoming nothing but a wink. Yet, lest the tether between his and Michelangelo's figures of Christ disappear altogether, Caravaggio insisted on multiplying the traces of his artistic elaboration. For instance, John's right hand under Christ's armpit, or around his upper ribs, in the Vatican *Entombment*, evidently mirrors the Virgin's right hand at almost the same level in Michelangelo's *Pietà*. But there are some crucial variations: instead of resting on the mantle's border so as not to touch the Savior's body, John's hand presses directly against Christ's skin, opening his side wound and poking it inadvertently as if rehearsing or prefiguring Thomas' incredulity. John's ineffable expression is also worthy of note: the surprise at his involuntary gesture; the profundity of his contemplation in staring at the wound; and his whispering lips, either uttering marvel at, and regret for, the incident, or murmuring his sorrow.

Moreover, if Caravaggio's Christ lacks the footing of drapery that Michelangelo had accommodated under his counterpart's body, a parachute of billowing shroud substitutes for it, configuring a rippling pattern of ellipses echoing the reiterated, yet heavy waves of the Virgin's lower mantle in Michelangelo's Vatican *Pietà*. Last but not least, the stretch of shroud cascading alongside Christ's dangling arm in Caravaggio's *Entombment* represents, in my opinion, an ingenious elaboration upon the sweep of drapery gushing down from the Virgin's right hand in Michelangelo's sculpture. The subtlety of these allusions proves the degree of refinement that the reshaping of canonical formulas into original solutions could, and was supposed to, reach in Caravaggio's time. Yet I do not think that Caravaggio's revision and revival of Michelangelo can be comprehended satisfactorily without investigating the theoretical repercussions of his elaboration upon the Vatican *Pietà*. This is the passage in Giorgio Vasari's 1568 *Vite* in which Michelangelo's famous sculpture is introduced, glossed upon, and exalted as an unrivaled masterpiece:[33]

> His [Michelangelo's] sojourn in Rome made him advance so much in the study of art that one would not have believed one's own eyes in seeing the loftiness of his inventions and the simplest ease with which he practiced his difficult style, so that this intimidated both those who were not used to seeing such things and those who were familiar with good things, for the works that were [then] done seemed to be nothing compared to his. Seeing these things, the Cardinal of San Dionigi, a Frenchman called Cardinal Rovano [Rouen], conceived the wish to leave some worthy memorial of his persona in such a famous city [Rome] by dint of so rare an artificer, and engaged him to carve a marble Pietà in full relief. When it was finished, it was installed in Saint Peter's in the Chapel of Santa Maria della Febbre, in the [ancient] temple of Mars. Do not ever think, sculptor or rare artificer, that you will be capable of adding more design or grace, or that you could strive to pierce the marble with more minuteness, polish, and subtlety than Michelangelo did here, since one can see all the virtue and power of art in this sculpture. Among its beautiful things there is, besides the divine draperies, the dead Christ; regarding the beauty of his limbs and the artistry of his body, no one would ever hope to see a nude so well depicted with his muscles, veins, nerves [as those] covering the bones of this body. Nor would one come across a dead figure more similar to a dead man than this one. His face is of the most suave form and expression, and the conformity in the articulations and junctions of his arms, body, and legs, as well as the facture of his arteries and veins, are such that Marvel itself remains

---

33   For Vasari's interpretation of Michelangelo's Roman *Pietà*, the importance of the topos of living stone, and its reception   in the sixteenth and seventeenth centuries, see Smick-McIntire 1996a and Smick-McIntire 1996b.

marveled at the fact that an artificer's hand might have been able to execute something so admirable, and so divinely and appropriately, within such a short delay. And indeed it is a miracle that a stone, initially completely shapeless, might have been reduced to a perfection that Nature tends hardly to attain in forming the flesh. The fondness of his own work and endeavor pushed [Michelangelo]—something he would never do again in any other work—to leave his name written on the belt crossing and girdling the breast of our Lady. One day, in fact, as he entered [the chapel] where the sculpture was placed, he found a great number of foreigners from Lombardy who praised it fiercely, and as one of them asked another who had done it, the answer was: "our Gobbo [hunchback] from Milan." Michelangelo remained silent and thought it was somewhat strange that his works might be attributed to someone else. Thus, one night, he closed himself inside [the chapel] with a lamp and, as he had brought his tools, he engraved his own name. And the sculpture, a true and living figure, is such that a most brilliant mind said:

> Oh beauty and honesty,
> Oh pain and misery, lifeless in a lively marble,
> How is it that you
> Do not cry so intensely
> As to awaken from death and before time,
> Against his will,
> Our Lord and your
> Groom, Son, and Father,
> Oh you, his only bride, daughter, and mother?[34]

Vasari's description of Michelangelo's *Pietà* easily qualifies as a set piece of laudatory rhetoric, and was certainly intended from the outset as such. At times, the eulogy of the author's unmatched craftsmanship takes the turn of a ritualistic, alliterating mantra ("difficile con facilissima facilità"; "un morto più simile a un morto"; "appiccature e congiunture"), while the prosopopeia—in this case, the personification of Marvel—aims not only to celebrate the artwork's perfection, but also to describe it as a miracle by playing with the Latin and Italian root: *mira-* ("si *mara*viglia lo stupore... cosa sì *mira*bile, ché certo è un *mira*colo"), indicating both the intensity of man's gaze ("*mirare*,"

---

34   Vasari, 6:15-18: "Per il che nel suo stare a Roma acquistò tanto nello studio dell'arte ch'era cosa incredibile vedere i pensieri alti e la maniera difficile con facilissima facilità da lui esercitata, tanto con ispavento di quegli che non erano usi a vedere cose tali, quanto degli usi alle buone, perché le cose che si vedevano fatte parevano nulla al paragone delle sue. Le quali cose destarono al cardinale di San Dionigi, chiamato il cardinale Rovano franzese, disiderio di lasciar per mezzo di sì raro artefice qualche degna memoria di sé in così famosa città; e gli fe' fare una Pietà di marmo, tutta tonda, la quale finita fu messa in San Pietro nella cappella della Vergine Maria della Febbre nel tempio di Marte. Alla quale opera non pensi mai scultore né artefice raro potere aggiugnere di disegno né di grazia, né con fatica poter mai di finitezza, pulitezza e di straforare il marmo tanto con arte quanto Michelagnolo vi fece, perché si scorge in quella tutto il valore et il potere dell'arte. Fra le cose belle che vi sono, oltra i panni divini suoi, si scorge il morto Cristo: e non si pensi alcuno di bellezza di membra e d'artificio di corpo vedere uno ignudo tanto ben ricerco di muscoli, vene, nerbi sopra l'ossatura di quel corpo, né ancora un morto più simile al morto di quello. Quivi è dolcissima aria di testa et una concordanza nelle appiccature e congiunture delle braccia e in quelle del corpo e delle gambe, i polsi e le vene lavorate, che in vero si maraviglia lo stupore che mano d'artefice abbia potuto sì divinamente e propriamente fare in pochissimo tempo cosa sì mirabile: ché certo è un miracolo che un sasso, da principio senza forma nessuna, si sia mai ridotto a quella perfezzione che la natura affatica suol formar nella carne. Poté l'amor di Michelagnolo e la fatica insieme in questa opera tanto che quivi (quello che in altra opera più non fece) lasciò il suo nome scritto attraverso in una cintola che il petto della Nostra Donna soccigne: nascendo che un giorno Michelagnolo, entrando drento dove l'è posta, vi trovò gran numero di forestieri lombardi che la lodavano molto, un de' quali domandò a un di quegli chi l'aveva fatta; rispose: 'il Gobbo nostro da Milano.' Michelagnolo stette cheto e quasi gli parve strano che le sue fatiche fussino attribuite a un altro; una notte vi si serrò drento e con un lumicino, avendo portato gli scarpegli, vi intagliò il suo nome; et è veramente tale che, come a vera figura e viva, disse un bellissimo spirito: 'Bellezza et onestate,/ E doglia e pieta in vivo marmo morte,/ Deh, come voi pur fate,/ Non piangete sì forte/ Che anzi tempo risveglisi da morte,/ E pur, malgrado suo,/ Nostro Signore e tuo,/ Sposo, figliuolo e padre,/ Unica sposa sua, figliuola e madre'." An excellent commentary on Vasari's passage is to be found in Barocchi 1962, 2:174-88.

"ammirare") and the supernatural character of the artwork ("miracolo"). More important, Vasari resorts here to Michelangelo's metaphysical conception of artistic invention. In fact, the sculptor extracts from the shapeless, inert, and dead matter a reanimated figure, the compound of a living mother mourning to death and her dead son animated through the rendering of his lively flesh. The conceited oxymoron underlying Vasari's appreciation of Michelangelo's sculpture rewards further examination.

As raw material, the block of stone that the sculptural group sloughs off through artistic invention is perceived as latently dead; Michelangelo's chisel therefore accomplishes the double somersault of enlivening the dead matter by bringing to artistic life a dead body: a dumb-founding miracle indeed. Michelangelo's miracle likewise occurs to the detriment of painting, whose paramount task it is to duplicate man's flesh like second nature, a task that sculpture has usurped in the Vatican *Pietà*. Vasari's insistence on Christ's "muscles, veins, [and] nerves covering the bones," and on his "arteries and veins" underscores this usurpation: the process of self-duplicating flesh through which painters, especially from Venice, recreate life, must yield to Michelangelo's mastery of sculpture. Michelangelo's challenge to the brush is a not infrequent theme in Vasari's *Vite*. This is the beginning of Vasari's comments on Michelangelo's *Moses* in San Pietro in Montorio, Rome:

> [Then] he finished the Moses, ten feet tall, whose beauty will never be equaled by any modern work, and the same even applies to ancient sculpture. In fact, sitting in the most earnest attitude, Moses rests his arm upon the tablets [of the Law] that he holds in one hand, and with the other hand he grabs his beard, which, long and parted in locks, is rendered in the marble in such a manner that the strands of hair—which sculpture finds so difficult to make—are executed one by one, downy and soft in the extreme, so much so that it seems impossible that the chisel might have morphed into the brush.[35]

It is understandable that Vasari, as the occasion arises, exhumes the terms of the artistic *paragone* or contest that opposed painters to sculptors in mid sixteenth-century Florence. Needless to say, in Vasari's view Michelangelo both wins and resolves the *paragone* inasmuch as the then old artist, by mastering the art of drawing, excelled equally in painting and sculpture—to say nothing of architecture—so that the chisel and the brush become perfect analogs through his art. I am not concerned here with the Florentine debate on the preeminence of painting or sculpture, but rather with its aftermath as reflected and developed in Caravaggio's *Entombment*. I have already established that Caravaggio intentionally alludes to the dead Christ in Michelangelo's Vatican *Pietà* in order to proclaim his own artistry, originality, and excellence. In the most natural way, the process of emulation operating in the Vatican picture entails a visual *paragone* between painting—the medium in which Caravaggio worked—and sculpture—the medium in which Michelangelo's *Pietà* was made.

Caravaggio thus explicitly reminds the viewer of this *paragone* by means of a detail that has been partially overlooked in previous scholarship: Christ's dangling arm pointing to the stone slab on which the episode takes place. It has rightly been said that, in depicting the angular corner of the sepulchral marble, Caravaggio referred to the biblical metaphor of Christ as the Church's cornerstone.[36] Scholars have also highlighted the mighty illusionism of the sepulcher's depiction,

---

35 Vasari, 6:28: "Finì il Moisé di 5 braccia, di marmo: alla quale statua non sarà mai cosa moderna alcuna che possa arrivare di bellezza, e delle antiche ancora si può dire il medesimo; avvengaché egli, con gravissima attitudine sedendo, posa un braccio in sulle Tavole che egli tiene con una mano, e con l'altra si tiene la barba, la quale nel marmo svellata e lunga è condotta di sorte che i capegli, dove ha tanta difficultà la scultura, son condotti sottilissimamente, piumosi,

morbidi e sfilati, d'una maniera che pare impossibile che il ferro sia diventato pennello." An excellent commentary on the *paragone* between the brush and the chisel as developed by Vasari in this passage is in Barocchi 1962, 2:350 ff.

36 Many scholars have insisted on the symbolism of the marble slab in Caravaggio's picture, first of all Graeve 1958.

which invited the viewer, when the painting still hung over the altar, to imagine Christ's body lowered upon the Eucharistic tabernacle, in order to accentuate the divine presence of Christ's body in the Host. All of this makes sense and was certainly in Caravaggio's mind. But apart from these liturgical reasons, Christ's dangling arm in the *Entombment* also suggests a visual parallel between the flesh and the marble, that is, between the enlivened rendition of Christ's dead body and the lifeless surface of the streaked marble serving as the opening of his sepulcher. It is no coincidence that nowhere more than in the dangling arm did Caravaggio strive to animate "the arteries and veins," the implausible pulse, of Christ's dead body. Nor is it fortuitous that the point of maximal lividness in the Savior's corpse concentrates in the very hand that grazes the sepulchral marble through the extension of a dangling finger; on a chromatic level, the sand-hued pigments of the hand and the marble prove to be remarkably similar.

I emphasize the extraordinary color technique deployed by Caravaggio in Christ's dead body because it is extremely pertinent to the *paragone* that the master formulates in his Vatican *Entombment*. By juxtaposing the bright whiteness of Christ's loincloth and shroud to the dim paleness of his body, Caravaggio throws down the gauntlet at Venetian chromaticism—compare Titian's *Deposition* now in the Louvre—as a provocative response to Michelangelo's design-grounded mimesis.[37] In other words, flesh is not only the product of skillful drawing and anatomic knowledge, but reaches its perfection through color, that is, through the brush's work. If, according to Vasari, Michelangelo transformed the chisel into the brush, Caravaggio in the *Entombment* turns his brush into a chisel by squaring a block of marble into a tomb slab by dint of painting. If, in Vasari's opinion, the way Michelangelo had transfigured a shapeless stone into the living flesh of a dead body was a portent, Caravaggio demonstrates that, compared to the marble it refers to, the body of Christ in his Vatican picture takes on a truly human form and transcends its sculptural prototype. If, according to Vasari, Michelangelo animated "the veins and arteries" of his Savior, Caravaggio exhibits the superiority of his own "veins and arteries" in Christ's figure with respect to the marble's streaks, their equivalents in stone.

It goes without saying that Caravaggio might not have read Vasari's description of Michelangelo's *Pietà*, and therefore was simply reacting to the paradigm of perfection that the Vatican sculpture incarnated in his eyes. But I am convinced that Vasari's text is among the main referents of Caravaggio's *Entombment*. As evidenced by Annibale Carracci's demeaning gloss on the famous—or infamous—*Vite*, artists avidly read, and vehemently disapproved of, Vasari's work.[38]

Let us return to the painting: although they share a roughly common space, John and Nicodemus stand out before the viewer in very different ways. John's face plunges into penumbra, sinking into the abyss of his dark green tunic. The red mantle flung above his shoulder ought to remedy his minor visual relevance, but instead it acts as a powerful foil to Nicodemus' bent face. Beholders at first glance notice only two figures: Christ's pale corpse and Nicodemus' hunched body. Wittily enough, Caravaggio also represents Nicodemus' bare feet and leg as if they alone were supporting the entire group of mourners. Furthermore, although one is alive and the other dead, Christ's and Nicodemus' faces strongly interrelate with one another through the common detail of the open mouth: that of Jesus gasping in deadly slumber, and that of Nicodemus panting as a result of his extreme effort in carrying the corpse. Yet to my knowledge, the unusual importance of Nicodemus' figure has not hitherto aroused the slightest curiosity on the part of scholars.

---

37   For the painting, see Wethey 1969-1975, 1:89-90, no. 36. One can find a very detailed bibliography on Titian's picture in Laclotte 1993, 565-6, no. 159.

38   On Annibale's comments on Vasari, see above all Dempsey 1986. Besides Annibale Carracci, on whose reaction to Vasari's *Lives* I have already touched in Chapter 1, Federico Zuccari is also known to have commented on Vasari with severity. See Hochmann 1988; and Pierguidi 2006.

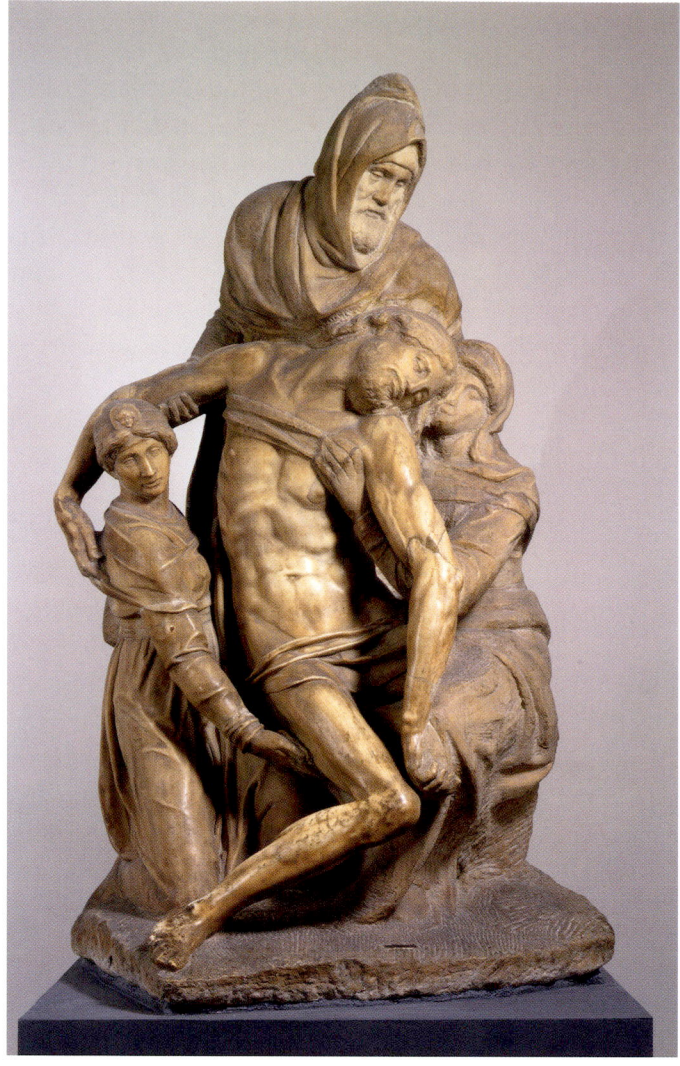

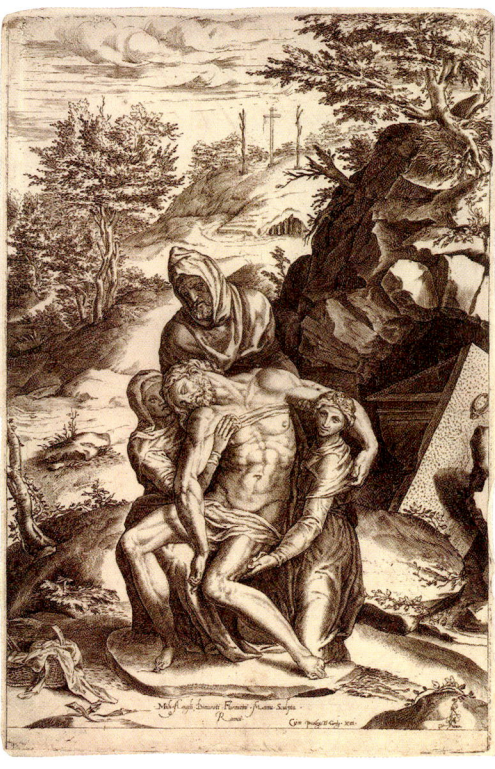

Fig. 180
Michelangelo Buonarroti, *Pietà*, Museo dell'Opera del Duomo, Florence, marble, 226 cm.

Fig. 181
Cherubino Alberti after Michelangelo Buonarroti, *Pietà*, engraving, 44.5 x 30.1 cm.

Nicodemus as Michelangelo

The Vatican *Pietà* is not the only sculpture in which Michelangelo treated the theme of the Deposition in its broader sense. Sometime around 1547, Michelangelo began working on a grand sculptural group that turned out to be a technical and theoretical challenge to the old master.[39] This is how Vasari describes the sculpture now known as the Florence *Pietà* (Fig. 180):

> Michelangelo's spirit and virtue could not idle. As he was unable to paint, he set out
> to work on a piece of marble by carving four figures in full relief larger than nature,
> sculpting a dead Christ in it for his own pleasure, to kill time and, as he used to say,
> because the practice of the chisel kept his body healthy. This [sculpture] represented
> Christ as he was laid down from the cross, supported by our Lady while Nicodemus,
> standing and sneaking in, powerfully helps to support them; one of the Marys helps

39 For the Florence *Pietà*, Michelangelo's self-portrait as Nicodemus, and the reasons for the attempted destruction of the sculptural group by Michelangelo himself, see Von Einem 1940; Von Einem 1956; De Tolnay 1969, 5:86-8, 149-52; Liebert 1977; Steinberg 1988; Kristof 1989; Shrimplin Evangelidis 1989; Nagel 1996, 563-7; Arkin 1997; Nagel 2000, 202-12; Wallace 2000; Wasserman 2001; Fehl 2002; Forcellino 2002, 182-201; Steinberg 2006; and esp. Wasserman 2003.

him, as she sees that the Mother, overwhelmed with sorrow, loses her grip and cannot maintain a hold. Nor can one see a dead body similar to that of [this] Christ, which, all his limbs collapsing inertly, appears in postures wholly different not only from those of Michelangelo's other [Saviors], but from those of any Christ ever executed. A laborious work, outstanding if one considers it is in stone, and truly divine. As I will say farther, this work remained unfinished, and went through many misadventures, although Michelangelo wanted it to be destined for his tomb, [which would have been] at the feet of the altar upon which he planned to place it [the sculpture]. [40]

In another passage, Vasari recounts the misfortunes that befell Michelangelo's sculpture after many years of being chipped away at by the master:

> As a hobby, Michelangelo worked almost every day on the Pietà with four figures that I have already mentioned, and then he broke it for these reasons: either because the stone had several dark spots, was hard, and caused the chisel to spark, or because this man's judgment was so great that it was never satisfied with what he did; that this is the truth [is proved by the fact that] only few of his sculptures were finished during his maturity.[41]

As Vasari elucidates in the first passage, the main difficulty for Michelangelo in sculpting the Florence *Pietà* consisted in lodging four interacting figures in a single block of marble, making their bodies interface with one another, and their attitudes dovetail into coherent action. This is not the place to add to the debate on why Michelangelo tried to smash his work, but it is necessary to consider to what extent the old master succeeded in this arduous enterprise. Here is Condivi's description of the Florence *Pietà*, and in particular, the passage in which the author describes the coordination of the group's figures:

> He [Michelangelo] has now set his hand to a work in marble, which he makes for his own delectation, because, rich as he is in inventions, he cannot help but produce a few every day. This is a group of four figures larger than nature: that is, a Christ that is laid down from the cross, whom the Mother, as he is dead, supports by gathering his body from below with her breast, arms, and knee in a wondrous attitude; from above, Nicodemus nevertheless assists her; he stands firmly on his feet, holding Christ under his arms with extreme vigor; at the left, one of the Marys also helps the Virgin; although she appears to be in much pain, this Mary does not fail to accomplish the task that the Mother, overwhelmed with sorrow, cannot carry on.[42]

40 Vasari, 6:77: "Non poteva lo spirito e la virtù di Michelagnolo restare senza far qualcosa; e poi che non poteva dipignere, si messe attorno a un pezzo di marmo per cavarvi drento quattro figure tonde maggiori che 'l vivo, facendo in quello Cristo morto per dilettazione e passar tempo e, come egli diceva, perché l'esercitarsi col mazzuolo lo teneva sano del corpo. Era questo Cristo, come deposto di croce, sostenuto dalla Nostra Donna—entrandoli sotto et aiutando con atto di forza Niccodemo fermato in piede—e da una delle Marie che lo aiuta, vedendo mancato la forza nella Madre, che vinta dal dolore non può reggere; né si può vedere corpo morto simile a quel di Cristo che, cascando con le membra abbandonate, fa attiture tutte diferenti non solo degli altri suoi, ma di quanti se ne fecion mai. Opera faticosa, rara in un sasso e veramente divina; e questa, come si dirà di sotto, restò imperfetta et ebbe molte disgrazie, ancora che gli avessi avuto animo che la dovessi servire per la sepoltura di lui, a pié di quello altare dove e' pensava di porla." An excellent commentary on Vasari's passage is to be found in Barocchi 1962, 3:1437 ff.

41 Vasari, 6:92: "Lavorava Michelagnolo quasi ogni giorno per suo passatempo intorno a quella Pietà che s'è già ragionato, con le quattro figure, la quale egli spezzò in questo tempo per queste cagioni: perché quel sasso aveva molti smerigli et era duro e faceva spesso fuoco nello scarpello; o fusse pure che il giudizio di quello uomo fussi tanto grande che non si contentava mai di cosa che e' facessi: e che e' sia il vero, delle sue statue se ne vede poche finite nella sua virilità." For this passage, see the comment of Barocchi 1962, 4:1645 ff.

42 Condivi, 51: "Ora ha per le mani un'opera di marmo, qual egli fa a suo diletto, come quello che, pieno di concetti, è forza che ogni giorno ne partorisca qualcuno. Quest'è un

At the time Condivi wrote this passage, Michelangelo had not yet attempted to destroy the sculpture, which was in progress and far from being completed. In light of these events, it is clear that Condivi, at Michelangelo's suggestion, described the action represented in the Florence *Pietà* as the author meant it to be. Since the sculpture now lacks an important component—Christ's bent left leg astride the Virgin's left thigh—it is perhaps difficult to construe the intricate dynamic of motions in which the figures are wholly involved inside the marble block. However, one can use Cherubino Alberti's *c.*1580 engraving representing Michelangelo's sculptural group[43]—which the engraver reconstructed in its entirety, though it appears reversed—in order to envisage better the *Pietà*'s global effect (Fig. 181). As Vasari and Condivi implied, Nicodemus indeed lowers Christ's body upon the Virgin's lap, but he only supports Christ's right arm: his left hand, invisible to the viewer in front of the sculpture, is pressed against the Virgin's back. One must infer that most of the dead body's weight is therefore already secured and stabilized upon a double basis—the sculptural ground and the Madonna's thigh—otherwise Christ's figure could not stay in place as it is. In other words, Nicodemus and one of the Marys are trying to lay Christ's body across the Virgin's thighs, that is, to put the Savior in the position he occupies in the Vatican *Pietà*. For this reason, the Mary on the left seems to support and lift Christ's right leg as if to shift it upon the Virgin's thigh.

If then the action imagined by Michelangelo for his monumental group unfolds with coherence, it is also true that, once looked at frontally and upon an altar, which was their intended emplacement, the figures' attitudes and motions become convoluted, if they do not seem to be incoherent altogether. For one thing, the Virgin almost disappears behind Christ's out-of-proportion and cumbersome body, and this is especially evident if one mentally adds Christ's missing leg to the sculpture. Moreover, the cause-and-effect dynamic of the represented action cannot be discerned fully unless viewed from behind the sculpture, which would be impossible for a funeral monument intended most probably to be placed against a wall and above an altar.[44] More importantly, despite the presence of four figures, the group essentially relies on the interconnection between Nicodemus and Christ alongside a vertical axis; in sum, it ends up being a two-figure artwork with the unhinged appendix of a lateral female figure, namely one of the Marys. This impression is intensified by the fact that Michelangelo left the Virgin mostly unfinished, so that, akin to a summarily chiseled block of stone, she barely surges into view. Thus, as it was progressing under Michelangelo's chisel, the Florence *Pietà* must have begun to constitute an insurmountable impasse to its author. To give the Virgin visual relevance, Michelangelo would have had to develop the sculpture's side view; but this, in turn, would have implied that the sculpture could no longer figure on an altar and above Michelangelo's tomb. In addition, it certainly was too late to correct the disproportions in scale between Jesus' body and the Virgin's figure.

Put otherwise, if one considers both Michelangelo's intention for, and ambition in executing, his late *Pietà*, it must be confessed that the endeavor was mostly unsuccessful. Perhaps Michelangelo's wrath and fury against his own artwork depends much more than has been thought on a technical flaw. In a certain sense, his assault on Christ's left leg and arms might be read as an ultimate desperate attempt to bring the Virgin's figure to the fore. At any rate, it is certainly understandable why the old master rid himself of the sculpture by offering it as a gift to his friend Francesco Bandini, who engaged Tiberio Calcagni, Michelangelo's disciple, to complete the master's unfinished work. Fortunately, Calcagni did not go beyond the figure of the Mary at the left. The somewhat

groppo di quattro figure più che al naturale, cioè un Cristo deposto di croce, sostenuto, così morto, dalla sua Madre, la quale si vede sottentrare a quel corpo col petto, colle braccia e col ginocchio in mirabil atto, ma però aiutata di sopra da Nicodemo che, ritto e fermo in sulle gambe, lo solleva sotto le braccia, mostrando forza gagliarda, e da una delle Marie della parte sinistra; la quale ancora che molto dolente si dimostri, nondimeno non manca di far quell'uffizio che la madre per lo estremo dolore prestar non può."

43   For the print, see Buffa 1982, 141, no. 23 (58).

44   For the sculptural group's original destination, see Wasserman 2003, 25-9.

unpredictable way in which the sculpture evolved as Michelangelo progressively carved it, with the preeminence of the vertical axis linking Nicodemus to the Savior's dead body at the expense of the Virgin's figure, is contingent upon Michelangelo's idea of portraying himself as Nicodemus; consciously or unwillingly, the master focused his attention on his devout *alter ego* gazing lovingly at the Savior's body while helping unite the Son and the Mother in an ultimate embrace.

It is noteworthy that Vasari, who knew that "the old man" in the Florence *Pietà* was a self-portrait, as he declares in a letter of 18 March 1563 to Lionardo Buonarroti, did not mention this detail in his 1568 *Vite*.[45] Nonetheless, he reports in Baccio Bandinelli's biography that this sculptor, a longtime rival of Michelangelo, as soon as he learned about the old master's intention of sculpting a *Pietà* for his own tomb, started working on a similar project with the assistance of his son, Clemente.[46] In this sculptural group, as Vasari confirms, Baccio portrayed himself in the figure of Nicodemus supporting Christ's dead body (Bandinelli's *Pietà* remains *in situ*, in the church of Santissima Annunziata, Florence).[47] If the analogy between Michelangelo's and Baccio's designs for a funerary *Pietà* did not make it clear to Vasari's readers that Michelangelo, too, had represented himself as Nicodemus in his own sculpture, it is fair to assume that Francesco Bandini's heirs—who exhibited Michelangelo's work in the garden of their Roman palace until 1674, when it was sold and transported to Florence—must have known and boasted about the presence of the master's self-portrait in their *Pietà*.[48]

Be that as it may, it is inconceivable that Caravaggio, like many other artists of his time, was not acquainted with both Michelangelo's Bandini *Pietà* and the old master's self-portrait as Nicodemus in the sculpture. That said, at first glance there is no compelling visual connection between Michelangelo's late work and Caravaggio's *Entombment*. Yet I contend that the paramount role played out by Nicodemus's figure in the Vatican picture must be regarded as an allusion and a response to the technical and symbolic problems put forth by the Florence *Pietà*. First of all, Nicodemus's figure as represented by Caravaggio must be interpreted as an evocation of Michelangelo's persona. Do I mean by this that Caravaggio portrayed Michelangelo as Nicodemus? To answer this question, it is necessary to investigate whether there is any resemblance between the old master and Caravaggio's figure: not an easy task, since, despite the painting's overall fair state of preservation, Nicodemus's head presents several abrasions.

If one compares Nicodemus's face with the *c*.1545 unfinished *Portrait of Michelangelo* attributed to Jacopino del Conte (Metropolitan Museum, New York), the affinities are too tenuous to be conclusive.[49] Some details of Michelangelo's physiognomy as depicted in the Metropolitan panel lend themselves to comparison, particularly the frontal bone and the puckered protuberance that it forms atop the nose as a result of the furrowed eyebrows, as well as the grooves of arching wrinkles

45 See Frey 1923-1930, 2:59: "È venutomi considerazione che Michelagnolo, d'udita io e che lo sa anche Daniello e messer Tomao Cavalieri e molti altri suoi amici, che la Pietà delle cinque figure ch'egli rope, la faceva per la sepoltura sua; e vorei ritrovare, come suo erede, in che modo l'aveva il Bandino: perché, se la ricercherete per servirvene per detta sepoltura, oltre che ella è disegnata per lui, evvi un vechio che egli ritrasse sé; non essendo stata poi tolta da Tiberio, procurerei di averla e me ne vorrei servire per ciò."

46 For the Santissima Annunziata monument and its significance, see more recently Hegener 2008, 564-87. In this regard, I must also signal that Titian, most likely on the model of Michelangelo, represented himself as an old man at the feet of the Virgin and dead Christ in his 1576 *Pietà*, which remained unfinished and was completed by Palma Giovane. Similarly, Titian represented himself as Nicodemus laying Christ down into the sepulcher in his 1559 *Entombment* for Philip II of Habsburg, now in the Prado, Madrid. For Titian's *Entombment*,

see Wethey 1969-1975, 1:90-1, no. 37; and for the *Pietà* at the Gallerie dell'Accademia, Venice, Ibidem, 122-3, no. 86. One can find updated bibliography on the 1576 *Pietà* in Ferino-Pagden 2007, 308-11, no. 3.20 (catalogue entry by Giovanna Nepi Sciré).

47 Vasari, 5:270: "Lasciò ancora Clemente molto innanzi un Cristo morto che è retto da Niccodemo, il quale Niccodemo è Baccio ritratto di naturale; le quali statue, che sono assai buone, Baccio pose nella chiesa de' Servi, come al suo luogo diremo." See Ibidem, 5:272-3.

48 For the original collocation of Michelangelo's *Pietà* in the Bandini Palace, Rome, see the essay by Franca Trinchieri Camiz in Wasserman 2003, 99-108.

49 The painting is almost unanimously assigned to Jacopino del Conte. To my knowledge, the first to support an attribution to Daniele da Volterra is Weisz 1984, 69, 164 note 2.

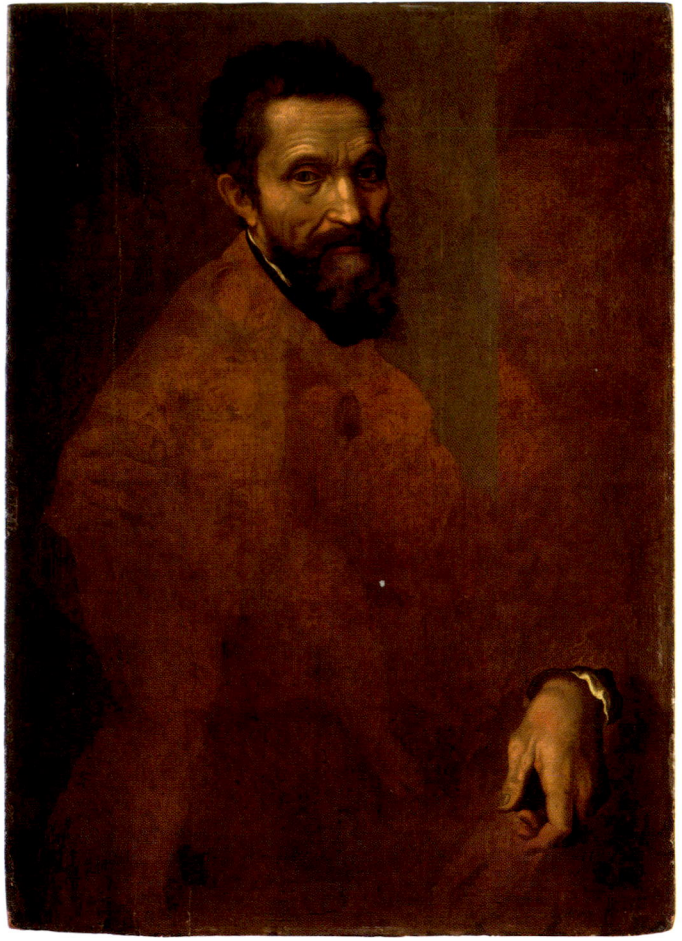

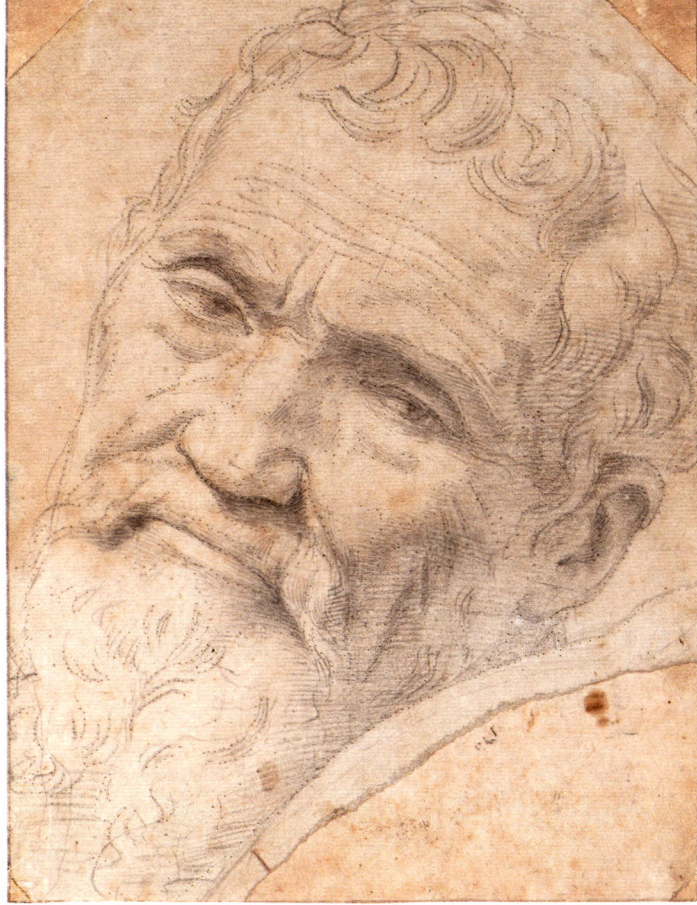

Fig. 182
Jacopino del Conte (attributed to), *Portrait of Michelangelo*,
Metropolitan Museum of Art, New York, oil on panel, 88.3 x 64.1 cm.

Fig. 183
Daniele da Volterra, *Head of an Apostle with the Likeness of Michelangelo*,
Teylers Museum, Haarlem, black chalk on lead point heightened with
white on paper, 29.5 x 21.8 cm.

above the eyebrows (Fig. 182). The deep crease departing from below the nostrils and plowing through the cheek is also characteristic of Michelangelo.[50] But Nicodemus's face in the *Entombment* is fuller and rounder; his nose does not seem broken and the uppermost part of his forehead appears to be lower and less square, although it is impossible to make out the configuration of this figure's hairline in the picture, so that this point must remain in doubt.

Caravaggio might also have been familiar with the portrait of Michelangelo that Daniele da Volterra had depicted in his 1550-1552 frescoed *Assumption* in the Della Rovere Chapel, Trinità dei Monti, Rome. There, the apostle to the right looking toward the viewer and pointing to the ascending Virgin bears the likeness of the then old sculptor. A beautiful drawing by Daniele at the Teylers Museum, Haarlem, executed mostly in black chalk (Fig. 183), has been identified as a vestige of the preparatory cartoon for Michelangelo's figure, and as such can be used for comparison.[51] Regardless of the differences in expression, which are justifiable on account of the diverse narrative contexts in which the figures appear, the modeling of the two faces—that of Nicodemus in Caravaggio's painting and that of the apostle-Michelangelo in Daniele's drawing—are unequivocally similar, especially with regard to the cheekbones and the forehead, but Daniele's Michelangelo has slightly

50 For Michelangelo's physiognomy and the innumerable portraits of the master done since the sixteenth century on, see more recently Ragionieri 2008.

51 For the drawing, see Romani 2004, 110-2, no. 27. It must be noted that Michelangelo's expression in Daniele's drawing corresponds to that of Caravaggio's self-portrait in the Contarelli *Martyrdom of Saint Matthew.*

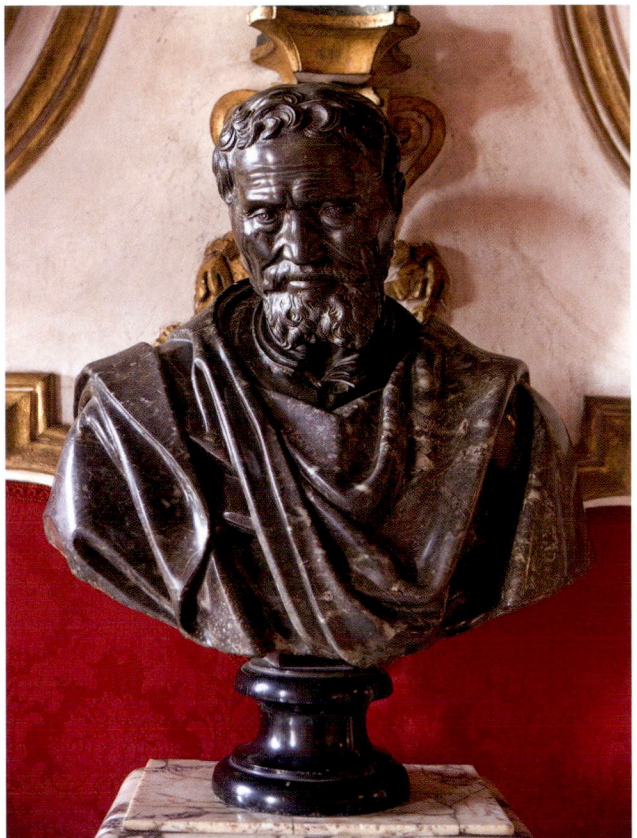

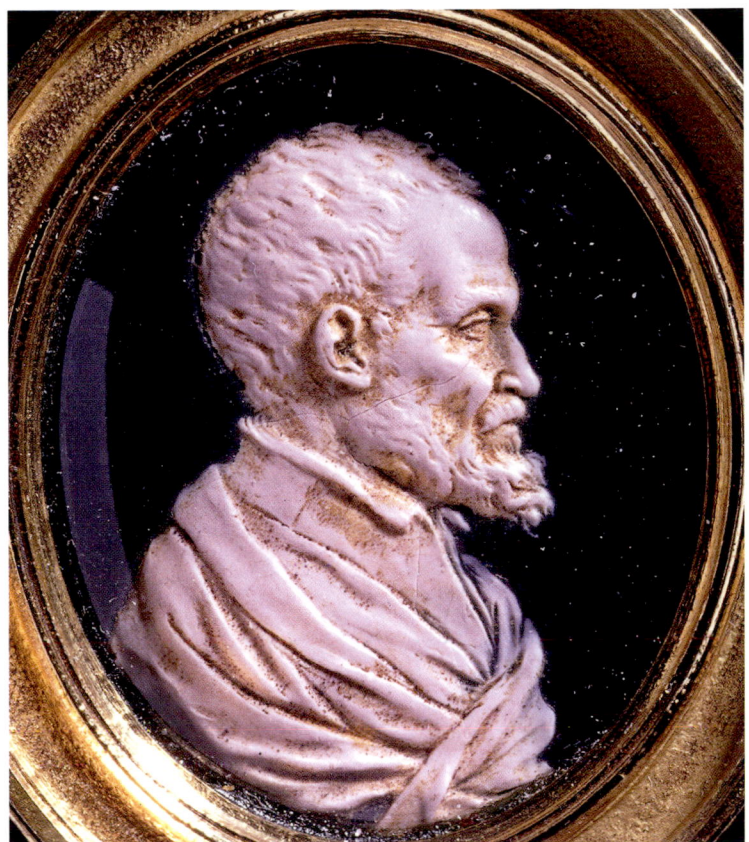

Fig. 184
Daniele da Volterra, *Portrait of Michelangelo*, Musei Capitolini, Rome, bronze, 30 cm. (head).

Fig. 185
Leone Leoni, *Portrait of Michelangelo*, British Museum, London, pink wax on black slate, 43 cm. (diameter).

finer features, so that his similarity with the figure of Nicodemus in the *Entombment* cannot be satisfactorily substantiated. Even a comparison with Daniele's many busts of the old master (Fig. 184),[52] or Michelangelo's profile reproduced in medals by Leone Leoni (Fig. 185),[53] or engraved by Enea Vico and others,[54] would not produce an irrefutable conclusion. To be sure, there is a certain resemblance, but this is not enough to corroborate such a consequential hypothesis.

In my view Caravaggio based the physiognomy of his Nicodemus on that of Michelangelo as represented in the Bandini *Pietà*; by putting side by side the sculpted and the painted Nicodemus, their common identity is uncovered (Figs. 186, 187, 188). Probably because Michelangelo left his portrait unfinished, or perhaps because he perceived his own physiognomy differently from the way in which Daniele did, one finds in his hooded Nicodemus the sharp, arched frontal bone, the narrow and tapering eyes, the dug-out puckers circumscribing the mouth, and even better, the strong, asymmetric nose bridge that also characterize Caravaggio's Nicodemus. The figure of Nicodemus in the Vatican *Entombment* is first and foremost a faithful evocation of Michelangelo's figure as summoned by the old master himself in the Nicodemus of his late *Pietà*. Therefore, through his figure of Nicodemus, Caravaggio intended to allude specifically to the Bandini sculpture. Not content with evoking Michelangelo/Nicodemus in the attitude of carrying Christ, whose body is depicted not in the vertical, but in the horizontal posture specific to the Roman *Pietà*, Caravaggio

52 For Daniele's busts, see Romani 2004, 170-2, nos. 54, 55; and Ragionieri 2008, 90, no. 38.

53 For the medal, see *Los Leoni* 1994, 190-1, no. 43; and Ragionieri 2008, 92-3, no. 39.

54 For Enea Vico's 1545 engraving, see Massari 1983, 74,

nos. 86, 87, who also catalogs Giulio Bonasone's prints after Vico's (see Ibidem, 73-4, no. 85). For Michelangelo's engraved portrait in Vasari's 1568 *Vite*, see Ragionieri 2008, 86, nos. 36, 37. For Giorgio Ghisi's engraved portrait of Michelangelo, see Boorsch et al. 1985, 139-41, no. 39; and Ragionieri 2008, 98, no. 44.

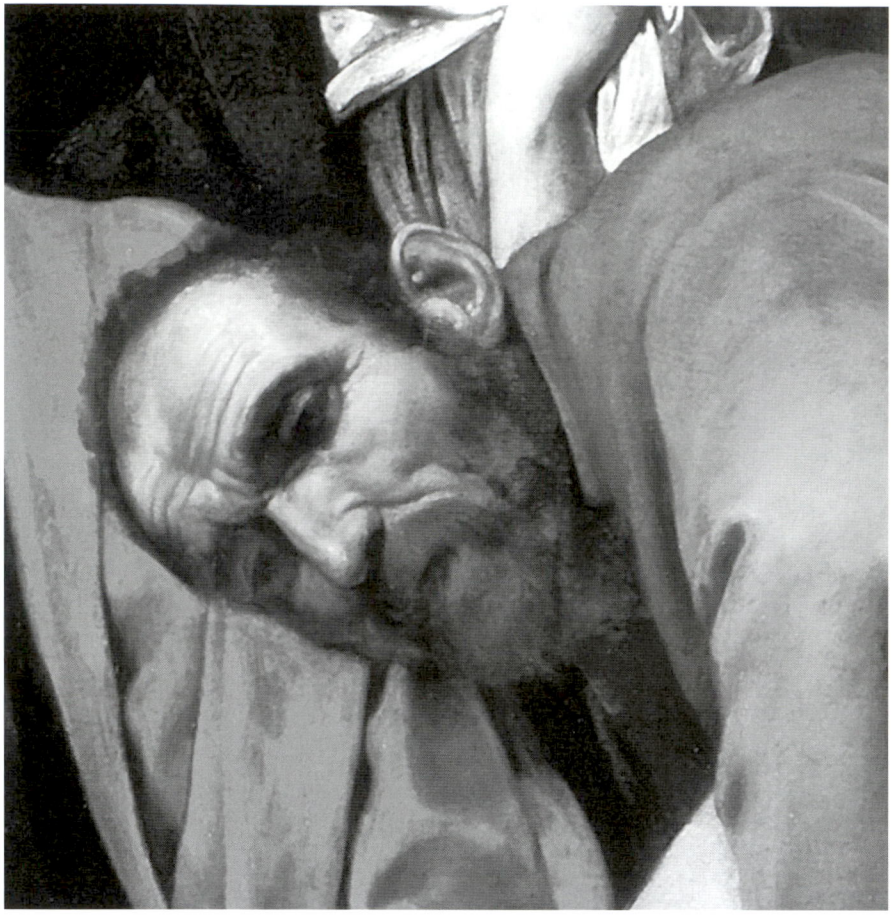

Fig. 186
Michelangelo Merisi da Caravaggio, *The Entombment*, Pinacoteca Vaticana, Rome, oil on canvas, 300 x 203 cm., detail.

added a comic twist to his evocation, a sort of witty signature. According to Vasari, Michelangelo felt compelled to carve his name upon the Madonna's belt because foreigners misattributed his Roman *Pietà* to Il Gobbo from Milan, the nickname of the Milanese sculptor Cristoforo Solari. In Italian, "gobbo" means "hunchback," so that Vasari's text is somewhat ambiguous: the Vatican *Pietà* might also be the work of the "Milanese hunchback."

I have always been amazed by the configuration of Nicodemus's shoulders and back in Caravaggio's *Entombment*. Owing to the considerable weight of the dead body, Nicodemus hunches forward so much in pulling Christ's legs up that he unequivocally appears to have a hunchback. To put it more bluntly, the effort of supporting Christ is so backbreaking that it temporarily transmutes Michelangelo/Nicodemus into a hunchback or "gobbo." Bearing in mind that Caravaggio was born in Milan, and that Michelangelo's emotive reaction to his work's misattribution in Vasari's text, among other things, relied on the Florentine artist's surprise at being mistaken for a Milanese—a classic example of Italian *campanilismo*—then the apparent hunchback of Nicodemus's figure turns out to be a visual pun.

In the Vatican *Entombment*, the usurpation of Michelangelo's identity, and accordingly the plunder of his inventions through elaboration, is due to a Milanese, and the hunchback is the trace of his misdeed. To reveal his artistic larceny, the Milanese Caravaggio thus morphs Michelangelo into the "hunchback from Florence." But the depiction of Michelangelo/Nicodemus's strenuous labor in helping John to lower Christ's dead body into the sepulcher is fraught with more serious and thoughtful implications than may at first appear. In fact, the figure not only reminds us of the similar situation of carrying Christ's body in which Nicodemus finds himself in the Florence *Pietà*, but it also invites the viewer to compare the painting and the sculpture more largely—that is, to judge who—Michelangelo or Caravaggio—has succeeded better in coordinating Nicodemus's figure to the mechanism of the whole composition. To paraphrase Condivi, the comparison simply boils down to ascertaining who has crafted the more harmonious and coherent "group of figures" interconnected in action. It can be assumed that, during Caravaggio's apprenticeship in Milan, Michelangelo was viewed as the unattainable master of composition. Lomazzo unequivocally endorsed this view both in his 1584 treatise on painting, and his 1590 *Idea del tempio della pittura*:

> Although, in this no less difficult than important part of painting [the representation of motion], all these great masters have also differed from one another, they have generally

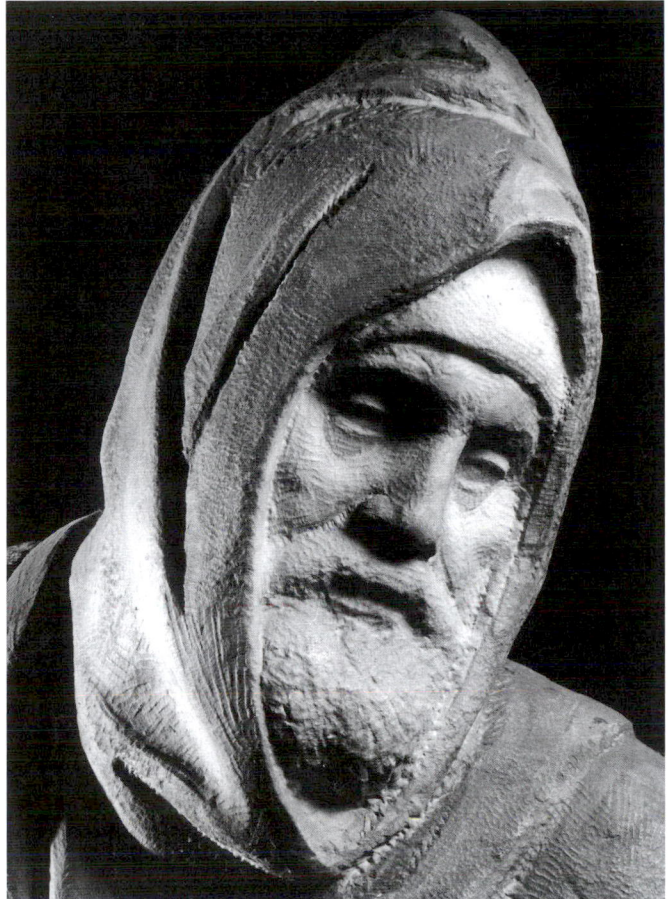

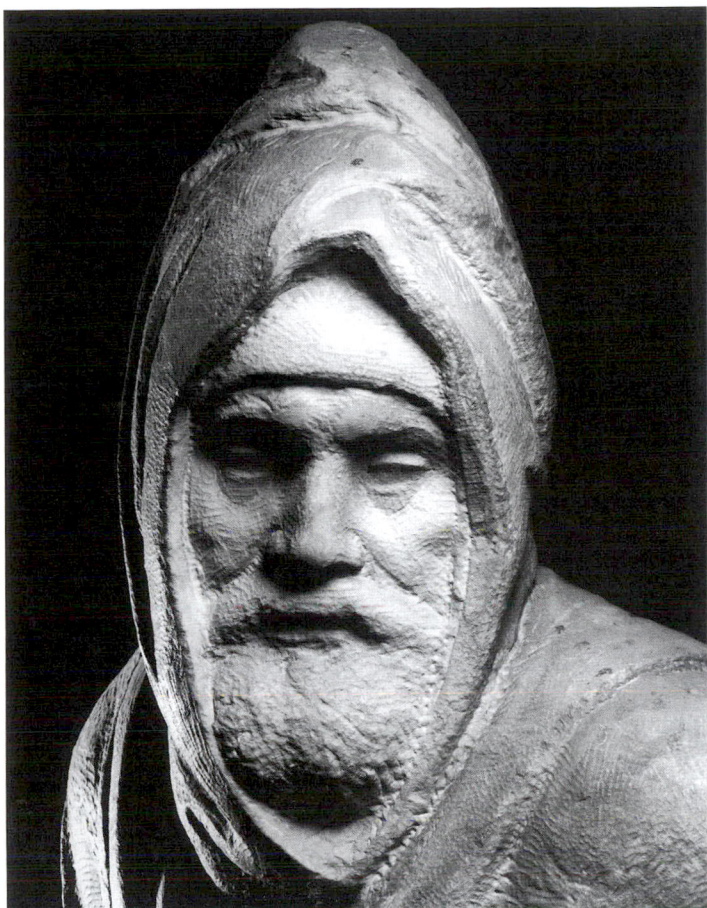

Fig. 187
Michelangelo Buonarroti, *Pietà*, reproduced from Jack Wasserman, *Caravaggio's Florence* Pietà, 2003.

Fig. 188
Michelangelo Buonarroti, *Pietà*, reproduced from Jack Wasserman, *Caravaggio's Florence* Pietà, 2003.

agreed in similarly representing motion in the pyramidal form of fire, avoiding acute angles and straight lines, as can be particularly observed in the practice of the master of all, Michelangelo, who has never used them. From here springs the grace of their figures, which pleases the eyes so greatly.[55]

In the following passage from his *Trattato della pittura*, Lomazzo explains what exactly the "pyramidal form of fire" is meant to be:[56]

Since [reporting] a precept of Michelangelo comes so appropriately here, I will relate it as it is, leaving the keen reader to interpret and elucidate it. It is then said that Michelangelo once advised the painter Marco from Siena, his disciple, that he should always make the figure pyramidal, serpentine, and susceptible to being modulated in accordance with a one-to-two-to-three [scale of] proportions. Herein lies, I believe, the entire secret of painting, because the greatest grace and beauty is for a figure to appear

55 Lomazzo, 1:283: "In questa parte non men difficile che importante nel pittore, se ben diversi parimenti sono stati fra sé questi grandi, tuttavia in generale sono stati simili e concordi tutti in esprimere il moto in forma piramidale di foco, e fuggire gli angoli acuti e le linee rette, come principalmente si vede che ha osservato sempre il primo di tutti Michel Angelo,

che già mai non li ha usati. E da qui nasce tutta la grazia che si vede con tanto diletto dell'occhio nelle figure loro."

56 For Michelangelo's "figura serpentinata" see Summers 1972; Summers 1981, 80-3; Maurer 1995; Maurer 2001; Davis C. 2009.

to be in motion [by itself], which painters define as the figure's fury. To represent this motion there is no better form than that of the fire's flame; according to Aristotle and all the philosophers, fire is indeed the most active element and the form of its flame is the most suited to motion, its cone and acute tip seemingly piercing the air in order to ascend to [fire's] own sphere. Therefore, when the figure presents this form, it will be most beautiful. And this can be obtained in a twofold manner, by setting the cone of the pyramid—which corresponds to the tip—at the top—and its base—which is the widest part of the pyramid—below, as is the case of fire (and then, the figure will display amplitude and largeness, for instance, in the legs and lower drapery, while its upper part will taper like a pyramid, showing but one shoulder, the other receding through foreshortening, so that the body twists as one shoulder hides and the other is brought out into view). By the same token, the figure that one depicts can be configured like a pyramid having its base and broader part turned upward, while the cone is directed downward (thus, the figure will display largeness in its upper part, by either showing both shoulders, or stretching its arms, or by showing but one leg while the other remains concealed, or in a similar way, as the wise painter considers it to be better). However, because there are two kinds of pyramids, one linear—like that near Saint Peter's, called the pyramid [obelisk] of Julius Caesar—and the other akin to the fire's flame—which Michelangelo defines as serpentine—the painter must accompany the pyramidal form with the serpentine form, representing the sinuousness of a living snake when it creeps, which is the characteristic form of an undulating flame. This means that the figure will configure itself as an S either straight or reversed—like this ς—and only so will it achieve beauty. And not only should the figure in its entirety conform to this configuration, but also all its parts should do so. Consequently, in a leg, when a muscle juts out in a part, in another part, responding and diametrically opposed to the former, it will subside and retract inward, as it naturally occurs in man's legs and feet.[57]

Although Lomazzo's description of the pyramidal and serpentine configuration has been frequently perused and related to Michelangelo's practice, it is worth examining briefly the Florence *Pietà* in light of these precepts, in order to determine in what sense the figures' disposition in Caravaggio's

57 Lomazzo, 2:29-30: "E perché in questo loco cade molto a proposito un precetto di Michel Angelo, non lascerò di riferirlo semplicemente lasciando poi l'interpretazione et intelligenza di esso al prudente lettore. Dicesi adunque che Michel Angelo diede una volta questo avvertimento a Marco da Siena, pittore suo discepolo, che dovesse sempre fare la figura piramidale, serpentinata e moltiplicata per uno, doi e tre. Et in questo precetto parmi che consista tutto il secreto della pittura, imperò che la maggior grazia e leggiadria che possa avere una figura è che mostri di moversi, il che chiamano i pittori furia de la figura. E per rappresentare questo moto non vi è forma più accommodata che quella de la fiamma del foco la quale, secondo che dicono Aristotele e tutti i filosofi, è elemento più attivo di tutti e la forma de la sua fiamma è più atta al moto di tutte, perché ha il cono e la punta acuta con la quale par che voglia romper l'aria et ascendere a la sua sfera, sì che quando la figura averà questa forma sarà bellissima. E questa anco si può servare in due maniere, una è che 'l cono de la piramide, che è la parte più acuta, si collochi di sopra, e la base, che è il più ampio de la piramide, si collochi ne la parte inferiore, come il foco; et allora s'ha da mostrare ne la figura ampiezza e larghezza, come ne le gambe o panni da basso, e di sopra si ha di assottigliare a guisa di piramide, mostrando l'una spalla e facendo che l'altra sfugga e scorzi, che 'l corpo si torca e l'una spalla s'asconda e si rilievi e scopra l'altra. Può ancora la figura che si dipinge stare a modo di piramide ch'abbia la base et il più ampio rivolto verso la parte di sopra, et il cono verso la parte da basso: e così mostrerà la figura larghezza ne la parte superiore, o dimostrando tutti doi gl'omeri, o stendendo le braccia, o mostrando una gamba et ascondendo l'altra, o d'altro simil modo, come il saggio pittore giudicherà che gli venga meglio. Ma perché sono due sorti di piramidi, l'una retta, come è quella che è appresso San Pietro in Roma, che si chiama la piramide di Giulio Cesare, e l'altra di figura di fiamma di foco, e questa chiama Michel Angelo serpentinata, ha il pittore d'accompagnare questa forma piramidale con la forma serpentinata che rappresenta la tortuosità d'una serpe viva quando camina, che è la propria forma de la fiamma del foco che ondeggia. Il che vuol dire che la figura ha da rappresentare la forma de la lettera S retta o la forma rovescia, che è questa ς, perché allora averà la sua bellezza. E non solamente nel tutto ha da servare questa forma, ma anco in ciascuna de le parti. Imperoché ne le gambe, quando l'un muscolo da una parte rilieva in fuori, da l'altra che gli risponde e gl'è opposta per linea diametrale ha d'essere nascosto e ritirato in dentro, come si vede nel piede e ne le gambe naturali."

Entombment constitutes provocative feedback with regard to Michelangelo's artistic paradigm. As Vasari and Condivi opportunely pointed out, Michelangelo's idea of sculpting four figures in a single block of marble represented a legendary exploit; even the Greek authors of the much celebrated *Laocoön*, with its three standing figures allegedly carved in a single piece of stone, had never attempted such bravado. The most complex part of Michelangelo's endeavor resided in the congruous and graceful imbrication of four serpentine figures into a pyramid, whose uppermost acute tip was to coincide with Nicodemus' hood.

It is evident that the Savior's dead body roughly accords with what Lomazzo defines as both a reversed pyramid and a serpentine figure collapsing into a ς-scheme. At first glance, Christ's dangling arms, by being mechanically stretched and by angling downward naturally, enhance the figure's amplitude and largeness in the body's upper part, whereas the isolated right leg, lifeless and powerless, constitutes the corpse's tapering final extension. This becomes particularly obvious if one looks at the sculpture from the left side. Furthermore, by spiraling down in mortal inertia, Christ's torso is submitted to two opposing movements, that of the outflung arms oriented leftward, and that of the falling right leg pushed up and rightward. As a result, Christ's left shoulder and head drop, while his right shoulder jerks upward, supported by Nicodemus's grip. Similarly, whereas Christ's lower right leg retracts backward, his thigh soars and is brought forward. One will easily verify a similar mechanism of rotation and chiasmus of the body's limbs in the figure of Nicodemus, especially as regards the balancing of his shoulders.

Of course, the Florence *Pietà* cannot be reduced to a sheer interplay of chiastic and oppositely swiveling limbs, but it is undeniable that through the intricacy of its compositional layout, Michelangelo conceived of this work as an ultimate disclaimer of his theoretical tenets about the serpentine and pyramidal figure. In other words, no other sculpture by Michelangelo embodied the principles of the flaming pyramid more intrinsically than the Florence *Pietà*. However, in the Vatican *Entombment*, Caravaggio carefully avoided conjuring up the last motif of a serpentine or a pyramidal motion in his painting. While deliberately facing the same problem developed in Michelangelo's Bandini *Pietà*—that is, how to connect Nicodemus's carrying figure with a cohort of interrelated actors—he disregarded Michelangelo's solutions wholesale, proposing instead a completely alternative paradigm of figural interweaving in the field of the sacred *istoria*.

For one thing, Caravaggio distributes his figures into superposed tiers or friezes, piecing them together into a unique moving compound: first the Savior, then John and Nicodemus, then the Virgin and one of the Marys, and eventually the screaming Mary. As a general rule, the figures remain confined within shallow depth—indeed, only Nicodemus with the ponderous outcropping of his left arm and shoulder and, in part, Christ's dangling arm, disrupt the low-reliefs formed by the painting's figures. More importantly, by staggering his actors on climbing and slightly receding planes, from the horizontal Christ up to the vertical shrieking Mary, Caravaggio encompasses the group of mourners within the arch of a circle, or more exactly within the left half of a semi-circle, engendering the impression of an ascending thrust proportionate to the lowering of Christ's body.[58] As I have already suggested, the radial disposition of Caravaggio's figures, fanning out across the painting's surface, mimics the motion of a millwheel, or more precisely any circular mechanism for hoisting and lowering weights, a synchronized machine of figure-leverages that are gradually craned into position as the dead freight proceeds to its landing. In a sense, Caravaggio's machinery recalls the extensive array of moving wheels designed by Leonardo for a variety of purposes, from cogs to hoists, from automated potter's wheels to hydraulic devices: from unwinding springs to clockworks, from rolling mills to giant crossbows. I am not implying that Caravaggio truly adapted the motion and disposition of his figures to any of Leonardo's engineering inventions, although he

---

58　See in this regard Kroschewski 2002, 118-21.

must have been well acquainted with the Florentine master's drawings and projects that abounded in his native Milan.[59] Rather, I argue that Caravaggio responded to Michelangelo's challenge of the pyramidal and serpentine composition, and generally, to the principle of coherent motion as requested of the sacred *istoria*, by literally assembling a mechanical device of weight-lowering: a wheel of figures whose metaphorical vanes protrude beyond the circle's perimeter in the form of the Mother's hovering hand above her Son's beloved head (a gesture of protection and blessing performed, among others, by Leonardo's Madonna in the *Virgin of the Rocks*, originally in Milan, but which here assumes the appearance of a distant caress)[60] and in the form of the two outstretched palms of the shrieking Mary at the top of the composition.

It is important to remember that Caravaggio's millwheel of mourners radiates from, and is set in motion through, a near-quotation of Michelangelo's Christ from the Roman *Pietà*. In competing with Michelangelo's model of artistic perfection, Caravaggio seems to distinguish between Michelangelo's late-quattrocento style and his mature, mid-cinquecento artistry, favoring the former over the latter, and bidding farewell to the "figure's fury," the neo-Mannerist speculations on the human body that Michelangelo's "*figura serpentinata*" had irreparably triggered. I take this as supplementary evidence of Caravaggio's self-awareness in matters of artistic reform and painting's renewal, so crucial, too, for many of his contemporaries. The historical perspective adopted by Caravaggio in coming to terms with, and improving upon, Michelangelo's excellence as extolled by Vasari and, in part, by Lomazzo, is dramatically epitomized by the figure of Nicodemus/Michelangelo in the Vatican *Entombment*; it is no coincidence that the old master's *alter ego* is unable to sustain by himself the Christ of his Roman *Pietà* despite his extreme vigor and strain. The precariousness of Nicodemus' support therefore betrays not the defeat, but the flinching relativity of the aesthetic canon incarnated by Michelangelo and, *a fortiori*, by any other master of the past. From this prospect, the Vatican *Entombment* stages the fallacy of Vasari's take on the historical evolution of arts in Italy from the Middle Ages up to the zenith of the Renaissance, that is, up to Michelangelo's art. On the other hand, the personification of Michelangelo as Nicodemus introduces another theme inherent in the concept of artistic invention as construed during the early modern period in Italy: the artist's role and involvement in his own work.

I will not discuss here why Michelangelo represented himself as Nicodemus in the Florence *Pietà* in the first place. It is doubtful that the old sculptor through his disguise wished to display his sympathy for the heretic movement of Nicodemism. More likely, Michelangelo could recognize himself in Nicodemus because, according to late medieval legends that the old master would undoubtedly have known, the Gospel's carrier of Christ carved out of cedar wood a crucifix whose face was fabricated by divine intervention.[61] Thus Nicodemus was the archetype of the Christian sculptor. Furthermore, the fictive act of carrying the Savior's dead body, of sensing its weight and lifelessness through the practice of sculpture, might well qualify as one of the many means by which Michelangelo could psychophysically endure the experience of Christ's Passion: a pious exercise of "*imitatio Christi*." By inserting the figure of Nicodemus-Michelangelo into his own *Entombment*, Caravaggio also theatricalizes the notion of creative empathy so specific to his own time, as I have already suggested in the introduction to Part Four. From this point of view, the figure of Nicodemus in the Vatican painting is not only an avatar of Michelangelo, but also a living representation—wittily mechanistic, yet concretely grueling—of the artist's self-implication in his own invention, a metaphor for the painter's reliving of the sacred *istoria* through his own vision.[62]

59   A complete catalog of Leonardo's drawings accompanied by excellent reproductions is to be found in Zöllner 2007, esp. 570 ff.

60   I illustrate the meaning of this gesture in Pericolo 2009a, in relation to Antonello da Messina's Palermo *Annunciate*.

61   For this specific point, see Stechow 1964.

62   A similar conclusion, with regard to Michelangelo's self-portrait in the Florence *Pietà,* is expressed by Nagel 2000, 208: "But Michelangelo was doing more than applying his features to a patron Saint. The very work that this figure is

In *The Entombment*, this vision connotes not only as a spiritual experience—attendance at the event represented—but overall as the physical participation in the pictorial machinery of composition.[63] By depicting the artist's inability to sustain his—or someone else's—machine by himself, with his bare hands, Caravaggio once again relativizes the omnipotence of the creative act as illustrated by his contemporaries, and especially by the neo-Platonic and neo-Aristotelian Federico Zuccari. Whatever his effort might be, the painter remains but a part of his work; he is less the shaman of God's history through divine revelation than the elaborator and developer of previous inventions—as Caravaggio was of Michelangelo's—as well as the heir and emulator of those skills by dint of which artists manually "carry" their compositions—an allusion to either Caravaggio's brush or Michelangelo's chisel. Viewed from this perspective, the Michelangelo/Nicodemus of the Vatican *Entombment* becomes an analog of Caravaggio himself, the "porter" of his views about invention. Having Michelangelo bear the weight of *The Entombment*'s composition must have been for Caravaggio the greatest honor he could have bestowed upon his own painting.

doing in the group symbolizes the labor of sculptor and embodies the material virtue of the stone. The mountainous figure of Nicodemus-Michelangelo physically holds the group together, epitomizing the efforts of the artist to craft and sustain a meaningful union among his figures (...). His work in the group, symbolizing his work on the group, is the expression of a piety that belongs specifically to the sculptor."

63 Throughout this chapter, I have deliberately used the term "machine" and its derivates to define the specificity of the composition delineated by Caravaggio in his *Entombment*.

In early modern Italian, "*macchina*" may refer to a building, a sculpture or a painting whose structure is perceived as elaborate, complex or monumental. See Battaglia 1961-2002, 9:359. Relying on Daniele Barbaro's 1556 commentary to Vitruvius' treatise on architecture, Pietro Testa in his so-called Düsseldorf sketchbook notes: "machine dette dal machinare cio[è] considerare, studiare con fini mattematic[i] di giri o circoli." The association of "machine" with circle and circular movement can already be found in Barbaro's treatise: "la forma et il principio delle machine è il moto circolare." See Testa, 195.

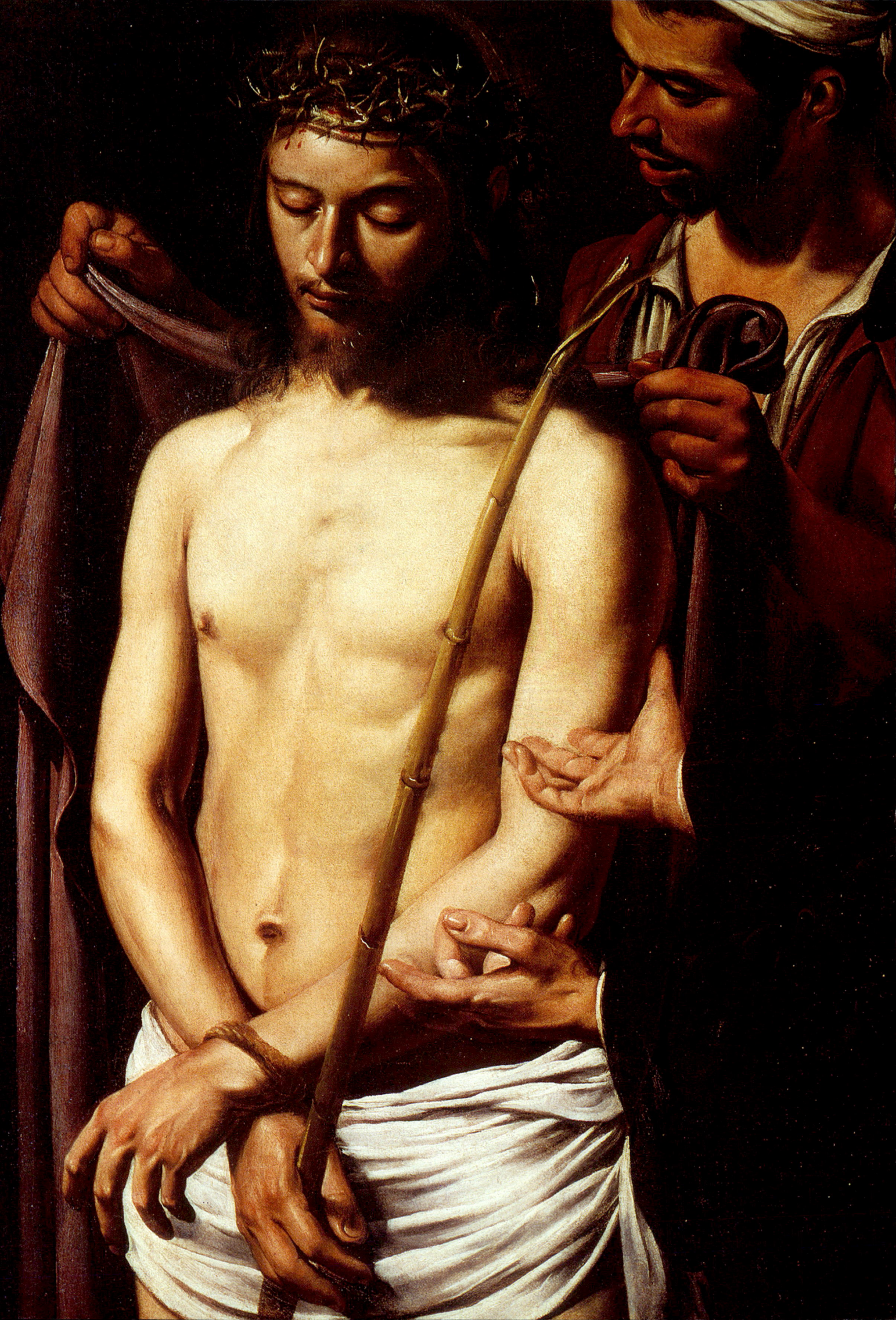

The Impossible Banality of Representing Christ: Self-Parody and Tragicomedy in Caravaggio's *Ecce Homo*

"Pilate-The-Realist-Painter"

It is perhaps the eerie and unsettling figure of a black-clad, black-bereted, swarthy Pilate with hirsute beard that has thus far discouraged scholars from approaching with sympathy and analyzing Caravaggio's *Ecce Homo* at the Galleria di Palazzo Bianco, Genoa (Fig. 189).[1] Or maybe it is the poor condition of the canvas. In some cases, I suspect scholars have doubted even the painting's attribution to Caravaggio, not because of its pictorial quality—which is outstanding, and worthy of inclusion among the master's most virtuoso works—but because of the composition's strangeness, an alienating effect that is difficult to chart. The fact is that, among Caravaggio's pictures, the Genoa *Ecce Homo* has often been overlooked by scholarship, whereas one would expect that at least the iconographic anomaly of the dark Pilate would have lured scholars into studying the painting with unwavering curiosity. In his often neglected but admirable 1954 essay, Roberto Longhi—who deservedly earned the title of Caravaggio's discoverer for having so felicitously pioneered the reconstruction of the painter's oeuvre after centuries of critical misfortunes—recounts the almost random recovery of the until-then lost *Ecce Homo*.

Probably because he saw the painting coming to new life under his eyes, Longhi's analysis of the Genoa picture must be counted among his sharpest, most thrilling readings of Caravaggio's works. I shall quote at length from Longhi's text in the following pages, since it is the best introduction to the *Ecce Homo* and the most stimulating counterpart to my analysis of the painting. At the same time, I shall present all the scant and uncertain documentation about the painting that has been mustered by scholars and interweave it into Longhi's reasoning when required. Although this shuttling back and forth between Longhi's text and documentary sources may entail some limited digressions, I am confident that in this way the painting's reading will be enriched.

Longhi's interest in the composition of the *Ecce Homo* is first documented in his 1943 *Ultimi studi sul Caravaggio*. In a list of works possibly derived from lost or destroyed paintings by Caravaggio, Longhi mentioned an *Ecce Homo* in the Museo di Messina, which he deemed a "coarse, but rather faithful copy" after a late picture by the Lombard master. "Surprisingly," he added, "the tradition according to which Caravaggio portrayed himself in the figure of Pilate is punctually corroborated by his unmistakable physiognomic traits, [which] bear such dire testimony to the physical and moral

---

1 For the painting, see Morassi 1947; Friedlaender 1969, 222-3; Cinotti 1983, 438-40, no. 18; Hibbard 1983, 337-8 [as uncertain]; Christiansen 1985, 303-6, no. 86 [catalogue entry by Mina Gregori]; Cinotti 1987; Calvesi 1990, 322-4; Bologna 1992, 325 [rather a copy]; Gregori 1991, 428-61, no. 13; Spike 2001, 158-61; Puglisi 1998, 229-31 [as uncertain]; Longhi 1999- 2000, 1:31 [1943], 91 [1951], 276 [1968]; 2: 121-30 [1954], 183-5 [1954]; Strinati and Vodret 2000, 212-3, no. 37 [catalogue entry by Clario Di Fabio]; Milicua and Cuyàs 2005, 64-7 [catalogue entry by Piero Boccardo and Clario Di Fabio]; Marini 2005, 496- 9, no. 70; Schütze 2009, 293-4, no. 80 [as uncertain]; Cappelletti 2009, 131 [as uncertain]; Vannugli 2009, 360-81.

◀ Plate XVI: Michelangelo Merisi da Caravaggio, *Ecce Homo*, Galleria di Palazzo Rosso, Genoa, oil on canvas, 128 x 103 cm., detail.

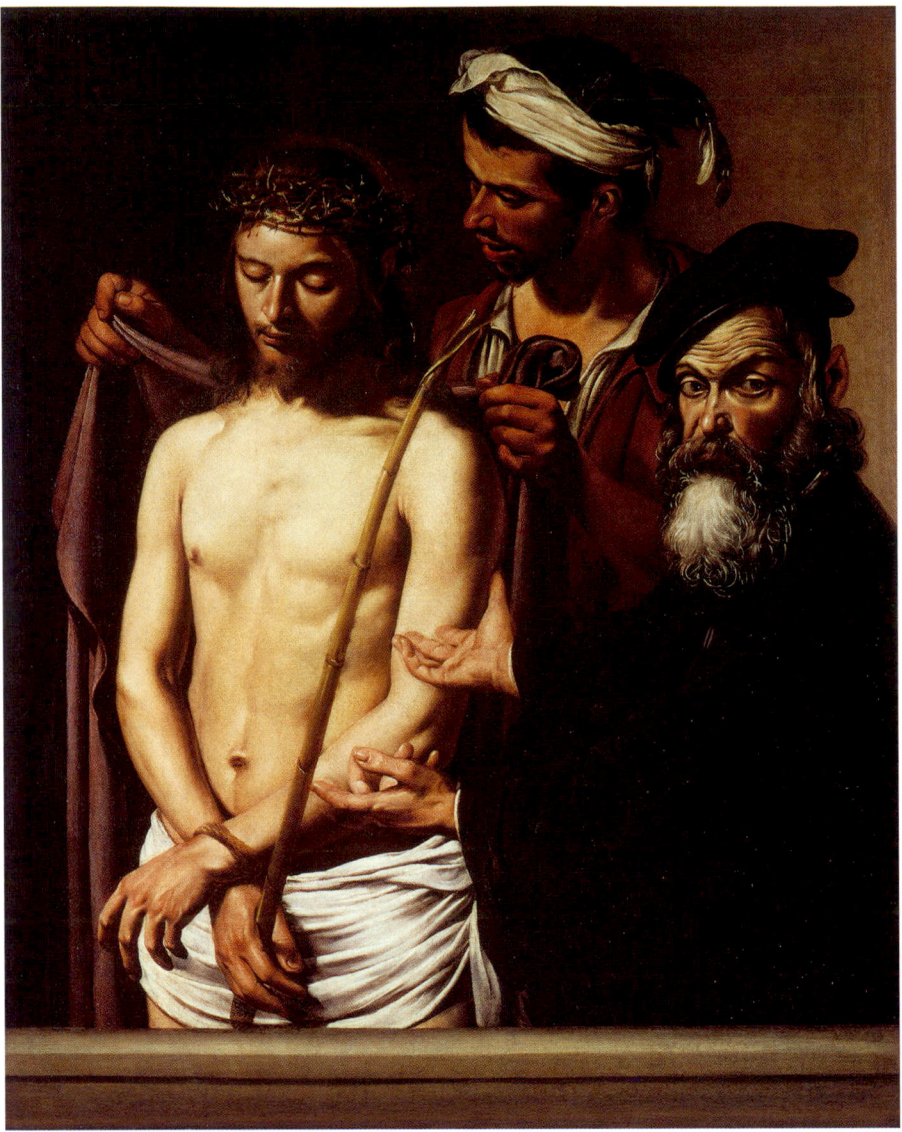

Fig. 189
Michelangelo Merisi da Caravaggio, *Ecce Homo*, Galleria di Palazzo Rosso, Genoa, oil on canvas, 128 x 103 cm.

ordeal of the painter's final year."[2] As it turned out, the Messina *Ecce Homo* was indeed an early copy after what would prove to be the Genoa original many years later. In any case, trusting his intuition, Longhi requested the Messina painting for the 1951 Milanese retrospective on Caravaggio, labeling the picture once again as a copy after a lost *Ecce Homo*.[3]

Given his intimate conviction about the existence of an unidentified prototype, it is comprehensible that, as soon as he was alerted in 1953 to the recovery of a plausible original in the deposits of the former Musei Comunali at Genoa, Longhi immediately offered his expertise, intuited the painting's superb quality, and had it restored and cleaned—the canvas, drastically resized, was at the time heavily overpainted and considerably damaged. Upon restoration, it became obvious to Longhi that he had finally come across Caravaggio's longed-for *Ecce Homo*, and he proudly presented his discovery in his 1954 essay. Besides extolling his connoisseur's hunch—with good reason—Longhi rectified some of the opinions he had expressed in 1943 on the basis of the Messina copy: first of all, his dating

of the original to Caravaggio's sojourn in Sicily around 1608-1609, which he now considered an "exaggeration." To justify his error, Longhi confessed that he had been misled "not only by the location of the copies"—other paintings derived from the *Ecce Homo* had been unearthed in the meantime, all in Sicily—"but also by the almost archaic simplicity of Christ's torso, consummate and austere like an Antonello [da Messina]: almost an ideal, on-site homage (…) attributed to the great Sicilian 'realist' of the quattrocento."[4] Wisely and rightly, Longhi renounced his former idea

2 Longhi 1999-2000, 1:31, note 25 [1943]: "L'Ecce Homo con Pilato e un manigoldo nel Museo di Messina: (…) a mio avviso, cruda copia, ma abbastanza fedele, da un'opera tarda del maestro. E, per quanto sorprendente, anche la tradizione che il Caravaggio abbia ritratto se stesso in figura di Pilato trova conferma precisa nei tratti somatici inconfondibili, e tremendamente significativi del travaglio fisico e morale dell'ultimo anno di vita del maestro. Commuove poi, quasi più che sorprenda, il rilevare come nel torso e nella testa del Cristo il pittore abbia insistentemente evocato in Messina, dal buio dei secoli, un modulo di Antonello, sì, di Antonello

da Messina." The "tradition" to which Longhi alludes in this passage was already evoked by Saccà 1906-1907. Longhi's identification of Caravaggio's self-portrait in the *Ecce Homo* has been contested in particular by Czobor 1955. Marini 2005, 499, believes that Caravaggio represented Galileo as Pilate in the Genoa *Ecce Homo*.

3 Ibidem, 1:91, no. 61.

4 Longhi 1999-2000, 2:123-4: "Il recuperato originale, uno dei più commoventi, ripeto, che ci siano pervenuti del maestro

of a Sicilian influence on, and origin of, the Genoa picture, which he then placed at the end of Caravaggio's Roman period, and associated it with an *Ecce Homo* that the master had executed for the Massimi family as reported by Giovan Pietro Bellori in his 1672 *Vite*: "for the Signori Massimi he painted an Ecce Homo that was sent to Spain."[5] By the same token, Longhi mentioned the important testimony of Giovan Battista Cardi, who in his *c.*1628 biography of his uncle, the Florentine painter Ludovico Cigoli, supplies further information about Caravaggio's *Ecce Homo*:

> As Monsignor Massimi desired [to possess] an Ecce Homo to his taste, he commissioned one from Passignano, one from Caravaggio, and one from Cigoli, each one unbeknownst to the others. As the [paintings] were finished and compared with one another, [Massimi] liked Cigoli's better, and hence the monsignore kept it at his house as long as he stayed in Rome, and it was then transported to Florence…[6]

Domenico Passignano's *Ecce Homo* is lost, but Cigoli's painting has survived and is now on view at Palazzo Pitti, Florence (Fig. 190).[7] The discovery in 1987 of two autograph notes, one by Caravaggio and the other by Cigoli, in relation to two unspecified paintings for Massimo Massimi (he was no Monsignore), came to buttress Cardi's testimony only partially. The first document reads:

> I, Michelangelo Merisi from Caravaggio, bind myself to paint for the most illustrious Signor Massimo Massimi, who has already paid, a painting of the same value and size as the one of Christ's Crowning that I did for him, [and to deliver it] by August 1st, 1605. In witness whereof, I myself have written this [note] and signed, today, June 25, 1605.[8]

The second is as follows:

> March 1607, I Lodovico, son of Giambattista Civoli, have received from noble Signor Massimo Massimi twenty five *scudi* for a large painting companion to another by Signor Michelangelo Caravaggio (…). In witness whereof, I myself have written [this note], in Rome, the aforementioned day, I, Lodovico Civoli.[9]

(…) viene anche a rettificare lievemente l'immagine che, in un primo tempo, avevo cercato di presumerne, in accordo con le opere estreme del tempo siciliano; un eccesso cui ero stato spinto non soltanto dalla ubicazione delle copie, ma dalla semplicità quasi arcaica del torso del Cristo, polito e mesto come in un Antonello: quasi un omaggio ideale, ero scivolato a credere, reso sul luogo al grande 'realista' isolano del Quattrocento."

5   Bellori, 223: "Alli signori Massimi colorì un Ecce Homo che fu portato in Ispagna."

6   Cardi, 37-8: "Volendo Monsignor Massimi un Ecce Homo che gli soddisfacesse, ne commesse uno al Passignano, uno al Caravaggio ed uno al Cigoli senza che l'uno sapesse dell'altro; i quali tutti tirati al fine e messi al paragone, il suo piacque più degli altri, e perciò tenutolo appresso di sé Monsignore mentre stette a Roma fu di poi portato a Firenze e venduto al Severi." See also Baldinucci, 3:266-7: "Lo stupendo quadro dell'Ecce Homo, che è quello stesso che oggi ha luogo in propria camera del serenissimo granduca. Aveva il Cigoli fatta quest'opera per monsignore de' Massimi, il quale desiderando di avere una sacra istoria di mano di uno de' maggiori uomini del suo tempo, diedene la commissione a tre pittori, senza che l'uno nulla sapesse dell'altro, e tali furono il Passignano, il Cigoli e 'l Caravaggio; ma essendo tutti i lor quadri rimasi finiti, riuscì di sì eminente perfezione quel del Cigoli che quel prelato

diede via i due, e questo solo a sua devozione si riservò"; and Ibidem, 3:685: "[Caravaggio] dipinse per i Massimi un Ecce Homo, che poi fu portato in Ispagna, ove pure furon mandate altre sue opere, e per altri, molti quadri ebbe a fare, a cagione dell'essersi ormai tutta Roma impegnata nel gusto di sua maniera."

7   See Contini 1991, 82, no. 22.

8   For this document and the following one, discovered by Rosanna Barbiellini Amidei and first published by Maurizio Marini in 1987 (see Barbiellini Amidei 1989 and Marini 2005, 496), see Macioce 2003, 165: "Io Michel Angelo Merisi da Caravaggio mi obligo di pingere al Illustrissimo Signor Massimo Massimi per esserne statto pagato un quadro di valore e grandezza come quello ch'io gli feci già della Incoronatione di Cristo per il primo di Agosto 1605. Di fede ò scritto e sottoscritto di mia mano questa. Questo dì 5 Giunio 1605. Io Michel Angelo Merisi."

9   See Macioce 2003, 221: "A dì marzo 1607. Io Lodovico di Giambattista Civoli ò ricevuto da nobil Signor Massimo Massimi scudi venticinque a buon conto di un quadro grande compagno d'un altro di mano de Signor Michelangiolo Caravaggio; resto contanti scudi sopradetto Giovanni Masserelli suo somministratore et in fede di mia mano ò scritto questo dì sudetto in Roma. Io Lodovico Civoli."

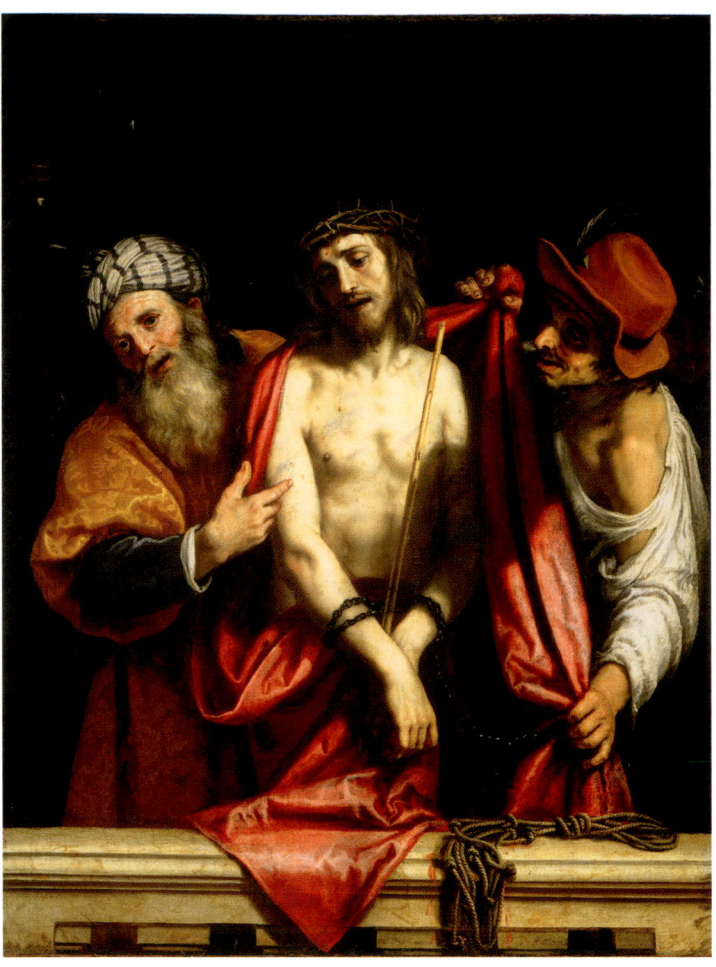

Fig. 190
Cigoli (Ludovico Cardi), *Ecce Homo*, Palazzo Pitti, Florence, oil on panel, 175 x 135.5 cm.

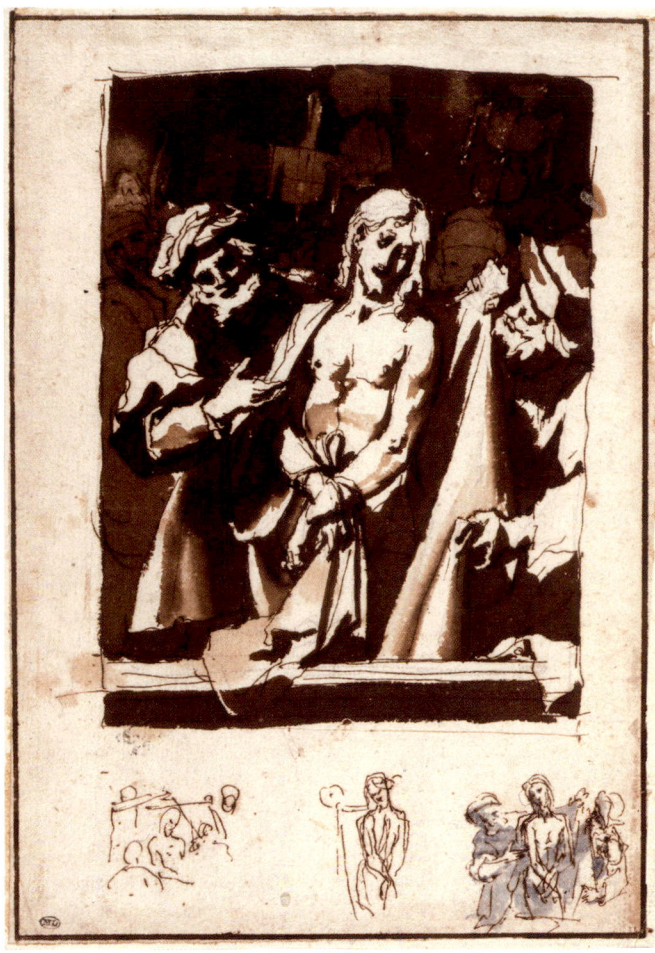

Fig. 191
Cigoli (Ludovico Cardi), *Study for the Ecce Homo*, Musée du Louvre, Paris, pen and wash, 25.2 x 17.5 cm.

Let us first consider Caravaggio's autograph note. According to this document, the master had already executed a *Crowning with Thorns* for Massimo Massimi. According to Lothar Sickel, this picture corresponds to the "large painting of the Crowning with Thorns of our Lord" inventoried among Massimi's possessions in his Roman palace on 25 June 1644.[10] Unfortunately, this *Crowning with Thorns* has not yet been identified with certainty, and I am among those who seriously doubt the authenticity of a painting with the same subject attributed to Caravaggio now at Palazzo Patrizi, Prato, which some scholars regard as the original commissioned by Massimi sometime before 1605.[11]

It is clear from Caravaggio's note that the painting he was promising to execute was meant to be the pendant of his previous *Crowning with Thorns*, which on two different occasions would be defined as "large," in Cigoli's 1607 note and in the 1644 Massimi inventory. That this second painting for Massimi was an *Ecce Homo* can be inferred solely from Bellori's testimony, although it must be admitted that this subject is particularly suited to accompany a *Crowning with Thorns*. However, since the dimensions of Cigoli's Pitti *Ecce Homo*, which was also conceived as a companion to Caravaggio's *Crowning*, are known, it is evident that they do not match those of Caravaggio's Genoa

10   See Sickel 2003, 247: "un quadro grande della Coronatione di spine di Nostro Signore con cornice messe a oro, con coperta di taffeta rosso." Cigoli's *Ecce Homo* seems to be mentioned nearby: "un quadro grande dentro vi è un Ecce Huomo con cornice messe a oro, e un taffettano rosso per coprire detto quadro." It must be said that Vannugli 2009, 378-81, remarks

that this last *Ecce Homo* cannot be the one executed by Cigoli, since the latter was in Florence at least since 1628 (see Ibidem, 371-2).

11   Gregori 1976 was the first to postulate that the Prato picture is an original.

picture, which proves to be perceptibly smaller. For this reason, the identification of Caravaggio's *Ecce Homo* for Massimi with the Genoa painting is problematic, albeit not impossible; among other possibilities, Caravaggio might have further renegotiated the commission and submitted a smaller canvas for acceptance.

On the other hand, the fact that Massimi engaged Cigoli to paint a second *Ecce Homo* two years after ordering the one by Caravaggio does not imply that Massimi had pitted the two painters against each other in competition and unbeknownst to one another. More likely, Massimi either never received or had already sold Caravaggio's painting when he decided to have it replaced with an *Ecce Homo* by Cigoli; in 1607, Caravaggio was in exile in Naples, busy with many commissions, and his work was feverishly coveted in Rome. In this regard, Antonio Vannugli has demonstrated that the Genoa *Ecce Homo* was sold to a Spaniard, Don Juan de Lezcano, who took it to Sicily, and thence to Naples, where it was inventoried on 5 October 1634, after his death.[12] Caravaggio's Lezcano *Ecce Homo*—if it was the same as Massimi's—certainly passed into the collection of the Spaniard viceroy in Naples, Don Garcia de Avellaneda y Haro, upon whose death (1657) the painting was most probably shipped to Spain.[13] No other subsequent document mentions the *Ecce Homo*. The likely shipment to Spain of Caravaggio's painting seems strongly to corroborate and hence legitimate Bellori's testimony, thereby suggesting that the Lezcano *Ecce Homo* and the Massimi one are the same painting.

Returning to Cigoli, I would like to consider a preparatory drawing (Louvre, Paris) in pen and wash for his 1607 *Ecce Homo* (Fig. 191). As Catherine Puglisi has remarked,[14] a small sketch of a *Crowning with Thorns* figures at the bottom left of the sheet, which might very well be a schematic reminder of Caravaggio's painting with the same subject for Massimo Massimi, in front of which Cigoli seems to have confronted the scale of the figures for its pendant, the *Ecce Homo*. More importantly, the detail of a low parapet in the main design on the Louvre sheet reminds one of its architectural analog in Caravaggio's *Ecce Homo*, which might indicate that Cigoli had also seen the Genoa painting before—if—Massimi sold it. In any case, despite its smaller size—the only element that prevents one from identifying it with the Massimi *Ecce Homo*—the Genoa painting fits well with Caravaggio's work and style around 1605.

As we have seen, Caravaggio promised to deliver the second Massimi painting by the beginning of August 1605; the contract is dated to the end of June of the same year. However, on 29 July 1605, Caravaggio attacked a Roman notary, Mariano Pasqualone de Accumulo, and was forced to leave Rome soon afterward.[15] He found refuge in Genoa with an eminent member of the Doria family, either Marcantonio or more probably Andrea.[16] According to Cardinal Francesco Maria del Monte, Marcantonio Doria wanted Caravaggio to paint a loggia in his palace for six thousand *scudi*, but the master refused the offer, as tempting as it must have been.[17] By the end of August, Caravaggio was

---

12 See Vannugli 1998, 7; and Vannugli 2009, 374-5. Caravaggio's painting is mentioned in the Lezcano inventory as follows: "Un ecce homo con Pilato que lo muestra al pueblo, y un sayon que le viste de detras la veste porpurea quadro grande original del Caravaggio y esta pintura es estimada en mas de 800 ducados" (Vannugli 2009, 463).

13 See Marini 2005, 497: "mas otro quadro de un Heccehomo de zinco palmos con marco de evano con un soldado y Pilatos que enseña al Pueblo es original de mano de Mi Cael Caravacho." Since the inventory was drawn up in Naples, where a *"palmo"* corresponded to ca. 26,36 cm., it is certain that the painting in question is the Genoa *Ecce Homo*.

14 Puglisi 1998, 231.

15 The main document related to this event was first published by Bertolotti 1881, 2: 73-4. See Macioce 2003, 173-4.

16 In a letter of August 6, 1605, first published by Venturi 1910, 281, Fabio Masetti, ambassador of Duke Cesare d'Este, relates to Count Giovan Battista Laderchi: "Sarà cosa impossibile l'haver i quadri per la cappella della Madonna di settembre, perché il Caravaggio è in contumacia della corte per alcune ferrite che egli diede ad un sustituto del Spada notar del vicario, et com'intendo si ritrova a Genova." See Macioce 2003, 172.

17 In a letter of 24 August 1605, first published by Venturi 1910, 281, Fabio Masetti relates to Count Giovan Battista Laderchi: "Et havendo inteso che il Caravaggio è comparso a Roma per la speranza della pace, son ricorso all'Illustrissimo del Monte che faccia comandargli l'ispeditione del quadro di Sua Altezza, che me l'ha con molta prontezza promesso, ancorché s'assicura poco di lui, dicendo che è un cervello stravagantissimo et che pur era stato ricercato dal principe

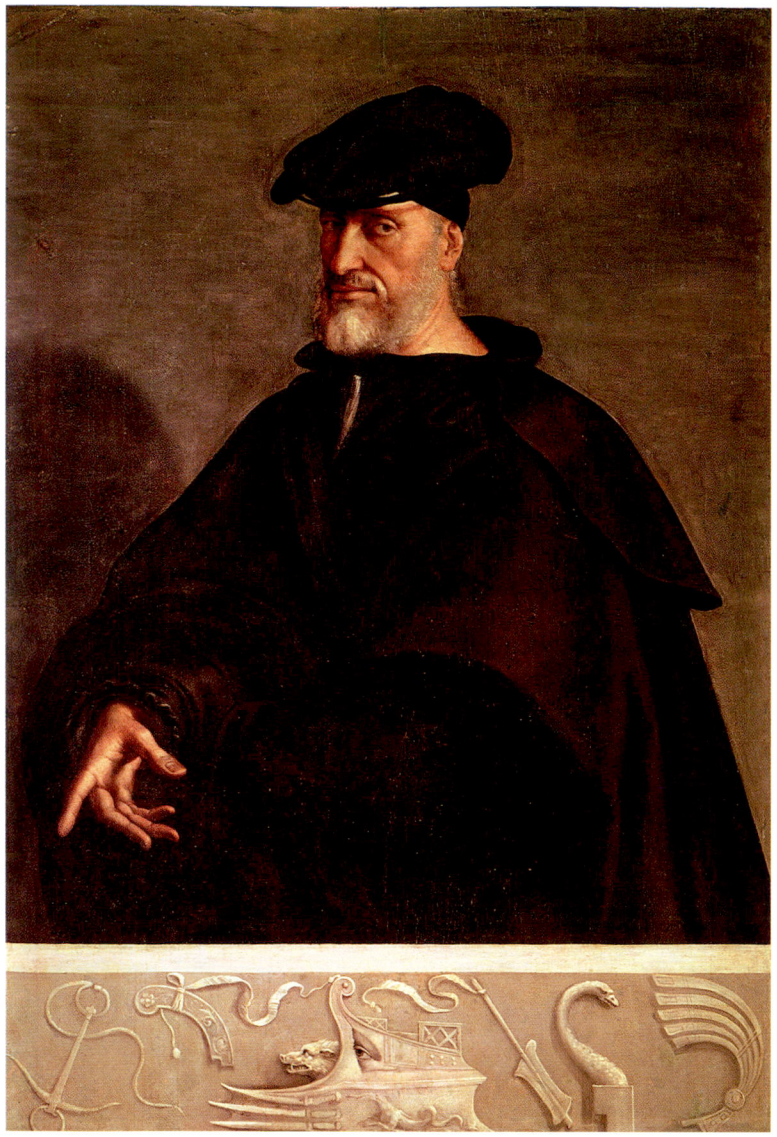

Fig. 192
Sebastiano del Piombo (Sebastiano Luciani), *Portrait of Andrea Doria*, Palazzo del Principe, Genoa, oil on panel, 153 x 107 cm.

back in Rome and ready to pursue his work. It is impossible to establish whether Caravaggio was able to deliver his *Ecce Homo* to Massimi before his forced departure to Genoa. But, as some scholars have stressed with reason, the figure of Pilate in Caravaggio's *Ecce Homo* conjures up the c.1526 *Portrait of Andrea Doria* by Sebastiano del Piombo, a painting that Caravaggio might have seen in Genoa (the painting is now in Palazzo del Principe, Genoa; Fig. 192).[18]

In Sebastiano's painting, the then admiral of the Genoese fleet is represented in half-figure, cloaked in a voluminous black mantle, sporting a black beret with cap, flinging his right arm outward while eloquently unfurling his hand toward a parapet adorned with antique naval trophies in bas-relief. His three-quarter face turned forward, Andrea gazes directly and implacably at the beholder. Not only is Caravaggio's Pilate clothed in a most similar way—which was certainly outdated at the beginning of the seventeenth century—but the grandiloquent attitude of Pilate's hands in a sense also duplicates, without copying, the grandiloquence of Andrea Doria's hand gesture. Notwithstanding these affinities, Caravaggio's Pilate is by no means a portrait of Andrea Doria.

Bearing in mind Cardi's testimony, Longhi remarked on the *Ecce Homo*'s lack of attraction and quasi-nonexistent influence on Roman seventeenth-century painting, explaining this phenomenon not only in light of the picture's early exportation, but also as a consequence of a change in taste:

Likely, this preference [for Cigoli's painting] was due to a detail that better suited the sophisticated and sumptuous taste of the upcoming era—that is, the accessory of Pilate's exotic costume, with his turban and embroidered robe; whereas Caravaggio, with his very personal formula, had startled and left everyone [disoriented] without straightforward clues by depicting [Pilate] as a portrait in pose and almost in the act of his profession: [that is,] as a criminal attorney pleading innocent or, more likely, as a painter with his large beret and black cloak.[19]

Doria a dipingergli una loggia, che volea dargli sei millia scudi, et non ha voluto accettare il partito, se bene havesse quasi promesso."

18   The first to suggest this fact was Marini 1974, 318. For the painting, see Hirst 1981, 105-6, and more recently Strinati and Lindemann 2008, 208, no. 46.

19   Longhi 1999-2000, 2:127 [1954]: "Ed è anche verosimile che a codesta preferenza potesse contribuire un particolare da venir meglio incontro al gusto fiorito e lussuoso dell'epoca saliente: intendo il pretesto del costume esotico nel Pilato in turbante e casacca damascata; mentre, nella sua formula personalissima, il Caravaggio aveva lasciato tutti interdetti e senza facile traccia avendolo, invece, svolto come ritratto

Once he had established that the painting had been executed earlier—not in Sicily during the years subsequent to Caravaggio's murder of Ranuccio Tomassoni, as he had originally thought, but in Rome when the painter was still at the apogee of his glory—Longhi was confronted with a chronological problem, namely the absurdly advanced age of the figure that he was sure represented Caravaggio in the *Ecce Homo*. To match the portrait to the painter's biography, Longhi came up with a subtle explanation that swiftly expanded into a gripping reading of the Genoa painting:

> For one thing, one would not easily understand why Caravaggio, planning to depict Pilate in the form of an aggressive and piquant portrait, and furthermore as a painter, would have chosen another model but himself. Nonetheless, if one compares [Pilate's] likeness to [Caravaggio's] effigy in the Accademia di San Luca, Rome, or to the rather ancient, and perhaps more accurate, portrait once in the Dell'Amore Collection, Rome, one will discover that the strong resemblance of the deep-set eye sockets, of the leather-thick eyelids, of the eyebrows pulled up as if out of constant horror, of the nose flattened at its base and nostrils impinged upon by two profound and sarcastic grooves, is almost irrefutable. It is true that, in the *Ecce Homo*, there is, too, the beard, precociously white, which Caravaggio, as far as is known, never wore. But who would rule out the possibility that here he wished to "overload" his features in advance, to make a caricature of himself projected onto the future, which he might have already sensed darkening, as if to say: "behold how I will be reduced soon"? (…) But there is more to add. In imagining the scene, Caravaggio contravened the traditional [iconographic] formula that showed Christ in the foreground, and behind, on either side, Pilate and the torturer, by bringing to the fore, next to the parapet, nothing but Pilate who, deploying his gesture askew, relegates Christ's figure to the second row, leaving the entire background to the torturer. Now, unless I am wrong, this is the distance and the ordinary emplacement of the artist with regard to the canvas while working; and even the gesture of Pilate's two hands is so similar to the "act of painting" that one would almost expect to see his left hand holding the canvas, while using the thumb of his right hand to stump the shades on Christ's depicted arm. Is it then too foolish to believe that Caravaggio, as usual, meant to be polemical by stating that, besides Pilate, only the painter is entitled to pronounce these words, "Ecce Homo," or, even better, to express them through the wholly blatant truth of his painting? The justification through which Pilate's words attempt to demonstrate Christ's innocence is, to Caravaggio, tantamount to the justification through which the painter demonstrates the truth in his paintings; I mean, the "realist" painter. Yet, over here, on the other side of the stage, there remains but us, the heedless audience, ready to condemn the truth in both faith and painting despite the claims of Pilate, and those of the realist painter…Along these lines, even if one does not intend to reach incontrovertible certainty, it does not seem inconceivable that the Genoa picture might be inflected with sadly autobiographical undertones, such as to enhance even more the true-to-life pathos of this sacred representation whose bouncer is Pilate-the-naturalist-painter. In sum, I do not see how any subject other than this, with its eminently emblematic and telling motto of "Ecce Homo," could have stimulated Caravaggio more vigorously to a demonstration in image. Due to the very necessity

'atteggiato' e, quasi, 'professionale'; o di avvocato criminale
qui plaide innocent o, più verosimilmente, di pittore in
berrettone a tesa rotonda e 'ferraiolo negro'."

of giving the greatest relevance to Christ and bringing him forward to the foreground, the shadows, which Caravaggio elsewhere had already made burst throughout the scene, here once again ebb away as they ordinarily do under rocks hit by overhanging light, so that Christ's torso comes out intact and pristine like an archaic sculpture through the mallet's work. However, one will better comprehend the refinement of means by which Caravaggio achieved sheer graphicness by mapping out, up close, the anxious fibrillations of his handling, and the vehemence of his *pentimenti* as he shifted over Christ's face and Pilate's hands repeatedly—of which one can still count the supplementary fingers from their previous emplacements—or by observing his wondrous mixing of blood, light, and matter amidst the [crown's] thorns where the victim's sweaty hair becomes entangled: briefly, [he showed] all the most celebrated exploits of Venetian painting. Here, though, [these feats are displayed] without the faintest indulgence and, on the contrary, exclusively obey the exemplary illusionism that is solely allowed to "realist" painting.[20]

Let us begin with the delicate question of Caravaggio's self-portrait as Pilate. As a general rule, and with very few exceptions, scholars have rejected Longhi's identification of the *Ecce Homo*'s dark figure with the Lombard master. I should note, though, that this rejection is very seldom spelled out with honesty and clarity, so that it is not easy to figure out the particular reasons that in each case have weighed against Longhi's opinion. I would hazard a guess: that scholars have become partly caught up with the anecdotal and biographical aspects of Longhi's identification. Comprehensibly enough, the idea of a prematurely aged, bearded Caravaggio might have appeared implausible, if not preposterous, when exclusively construed as an autobiographical self-reference. In this regard, I ought to point out that Longhi even afterward kept insisting on a biographical interpretation of

20 Ibidem, 2:127-9: "Intanto non s'intenderebbe facilmente perché il Caravaggio, escogitando di rappresentare Pilato in forma di ritratto aggressivo, pungente e, per giunta, in veste di pittore, dovesse scegliere altro modello da se medesimo. E chi poi venga a confrontarne l'aspetto con l'effigie dell'Accademia romana di San Luca o con quella, abbastanza antica, e forse più efficiente, che fu nella raccolta Dell'Amore a Roma, troverà che la somiglianza profonda delle orbite incassate, delle palpebre spesse come di cuoio, delle sopracciglia rialzate quasi per orrore fisso, del naso schiacciato alla radice e addentato alle nari dalle due rughe profonde e sarcastiche, è quasi incontrastabile. Nel dipinto dell'Ecce Homo, è vero, si aggiunge in più la barba precocemente incanutita che il Caravaggio, da quel che si sa, non portò mai; ma chi può escludere ch'egli non abbia qui voluto dare in anticipo un ritratto 'carico,' una caricatura di se medesimo proiettata nell'avvenire che già si presagiva fosco, come a dire: 'ecco come sarò ridotto in pochi anni?' (…) Ma v'è ancor altro da aggiungere. Il Caravaggio nell'immaginare la scena e, annullando lo schema tradizionale che mostrava il Cristo in primo termine e, alle sue spalle, sui due lati, il Pilato e il manigoldo, porta invece in primissimo piano, contro il davanzale, Pilato che, col suo gesto in tralice, respinge in secondo l'effigie del Cristo, il terzo piano restando all'aguzzino soltanto. Bene, questa—o m'inganno—è la distanza e la posizione normale dell'artista nei confronti della tela mentre la sta dipingendo; e persino l'azione delle due mani nel Pilato è così simile a quella del gesto 'pittorico' che, per poco, ci si attenderebbe di vedere una tavolozza retta dalla sinistra; mentre la destra sta fondendo col police l'ombra dipinta sul braccio di Cristo. Troppo imprudente credere che qui il Caravaggio intendesse, ancora una volta, polemizzare, affermando che, oltre a Pilato, soltanto il pittore ha il diritto di pronunciare le parole 'Ecce Homo,' o, meglio, di esprimerle con la verità tutta palese della sua pittura? La giustificazione di Cristo incolpevole che Pilato tenta con le sue parole è—per il Caravaggio—simile alla giustificazione della verità che il pittore dimostra nelle sue tele; il pittore 'realista,' s'intende. Così, al di qua della ribalta non restiamo che noi: la folla inconsulta, pronta a condannare la verità nella fede come nell'arte, non ostante le proteste di Pilato—e del pittore realista…Su questa via, anche ove non si voglia pretendere a una posizione di certezza apodittica, non pare incongruo che il quadro di Genova possa rivestirsi di qualche aspetto tristemente autobiografico, tale da rinforzare ancora la certezza patetica di questa sacra rappresentazione che ha per buttafuori Pilato-pittore naturalista. Non vedo, insomma, altro soggetto che più di questo, con la sua impresa strettamente emblematica e clamante dell'Ecce Homo, potesse stimolare il Caravaggio a una decisa dimostrazione in figura. Proprio per la necessità di massima evidenza nel Cristo spinto al proscenio, le ombre che altrove il Caravaggio aveva già saputo dirompere attraverso la scena, qui di nuovo si rimpiattano come sotto le pietre a lume alto, e il torso del Cristo ne sboccia intatto e verginale come, dal mallo, una scultura arcaica. Ma con che maturità di mezzi sia raggiunta questa palmare evidenza meglio s'intende quando l'occhio, avvicinandosi, scopra le fibre ansiose della 'manifattura,' la violenza dei 'pentimenti' che hanno spostato più volte la testa del Cristo e le mani del Pilato, ove ancora si contano le dita, in più, delle posizioni precedenti; o segua le mirabili mescolanze di sangue, luce e materia là dove fra le spine si aggrovigliano i capelli sudati del martire; tutti, insomma, i più celebri misteri della tavolozza veneta: ma senza più un solo compiacimento, anzi, posti a servizio esclusivo di quella illusione esemplare che è concessa soltanto al dipingere 'realistico'."

the Pilate-disguise. In his 1968 *Caravaggio*, he explained the oddity of Caravaggio's self-portrait as Pilate as a result of the master's distress at the numerous artistic defeats that he had endured during his last years in Rome. On this premise, it comes as little surprise that Cardi's doubtful anecdote about Massimi's refusal of the *Ecce Homo* and his preference for Cigoli's painting were to rub off on Longhi's reading of the Genoa picture: "that Caravaggio inserted in his masterpiece his own portrayal so fiercely 'overloaded' with black humor suggests that he had presaged the competition's [unfavorable] outcome as the work was in progress."[21] There is no doubt that, put this way, Longhi's suggestion sounds inconclusive and unconvincing. In this manner, the master's self-caricature solely depends on a matter of premonition.

Yet, in addition to its apparent absurdity, I think that Longhi's identification of Caravaggio with Pilate has constituted a truly unsolvable conundrum for scholars, an issue so ideologically intricate and repulsive that it has remained unacknowledged and unexplored. It is true, as Longhi contends, that Pilate repeatedly sought to defend Christ's innocence until he gave up and yielded to the crowd's ferocious will and thirst of martyrdom. In John's Gospel (19, 4-6), the only one to record the words "Ecce Homo," the Roman governor's good intentions transpire clearly:

> Once more Pilate went out and said to them [the Jews], "Look, I am bringing him out to you, so that you may know that I find no guilt in him." So Jesus came out, wearing the crown of thorns and the purple cloak. And he said to them, "Behold the man [Ecce Homo]!" When the chief priests and the guards saw him, they cried out, "Crucify him, crucify him!" Pilate said to them, "Take him yourselves and crucify him. I find no guilt in him."

However, Pilate's responsibility in Jesus' Passion was also universally recognized, and his subsequent gesture of washing his hands systematically stigmatized as an act of cowardly betrayal.[22] If one keeps in mind the negative connotations of Pilate's persona—also alluded to by the iconographic tradition—it becomes evident that the very thought of Caravaggio depicting himself as the legally ambiguous, if not morally responsible, Pilate might have seemed utterly aberrant to scholars. Hence, if one takes into account on the one hand the awkwardness of a Caravaggio who has grown prematurely old, and on the other the theoretical repugnance of associating Caravaggio with Pilate, one can easily understand why Longhi's identification of the master with the bearded figure in the *Ecce Homo* has been neither satisfactorily appraised nor thoroughly examined by scholars. That said, on a merely hypothetical level, it would not be surprising that Caravaggio, who dared represent himself in the form of a beheaded, bleeding, and deformed Goliath in his *c*.1606 *David* (Borghese Gallery, Rome), might also have wanted to challenge and shock viewers by transfiguring himself into Pilate.

Longhi's recognition of Caravaggio's features in the *Ecce Homo*'s dark figure is far from being nonsensical; thus, before emitting any rash verdict about the validity of his idea one must seriously think over its rejection or approval. In my opinion, Longhi was certainly right when he signaled the many, almost overwhelming similarities between the *Ecce Homo* Pilate and Caravaggio's portraits in the Accademia di San Luca and the Dell'Amore Collection. Since the effigy in these paintings is roughly identical to the woodcut portrayal of the master published in Bellori's 1672 *Vite*, I shall juxtapose this print and the detail of Pilate's figure from the painting in order to prove their resemblance (Figs.

21 Ibidem, 1:276: "Ma che il Caravaggio abbia immesso in quel capolavoro il proprio ritratto quasi ferocemente 'caricato' in umor nero, suggerisce ch'egli già nel corso del lavoro presagisse l'esito della gara."

22 For an interpretation of Pontius Pilate's figure over the centuries, see Bond 1998. For the iconography of Pontius Pilate in the Middle Ages, see Hourihane 2009. For the interpretation of Pilate's figure in Correggio's *Ecce Homo* as a possible portrait of the patron, see Periti 2005.

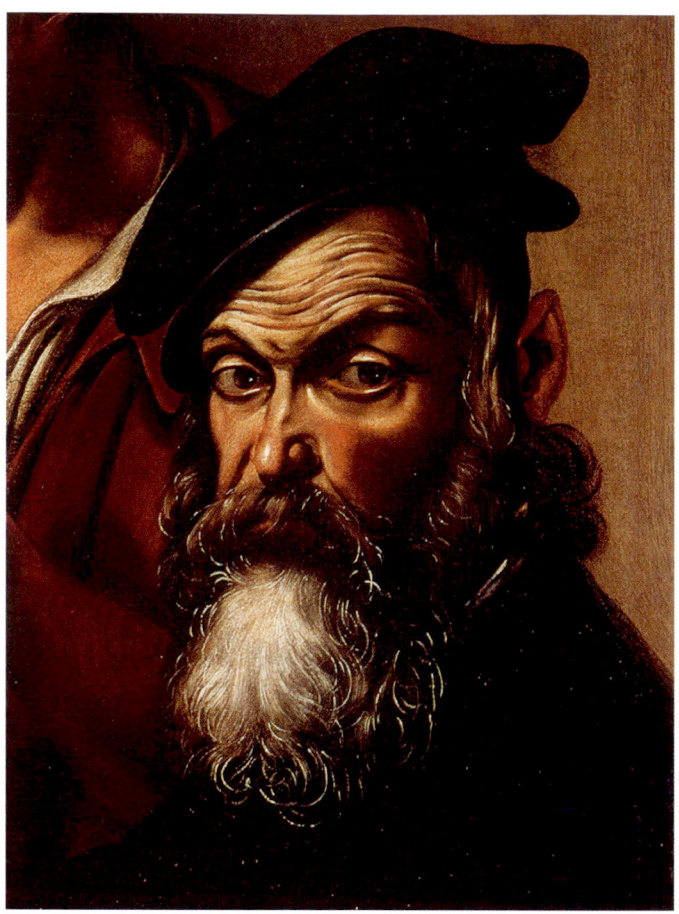

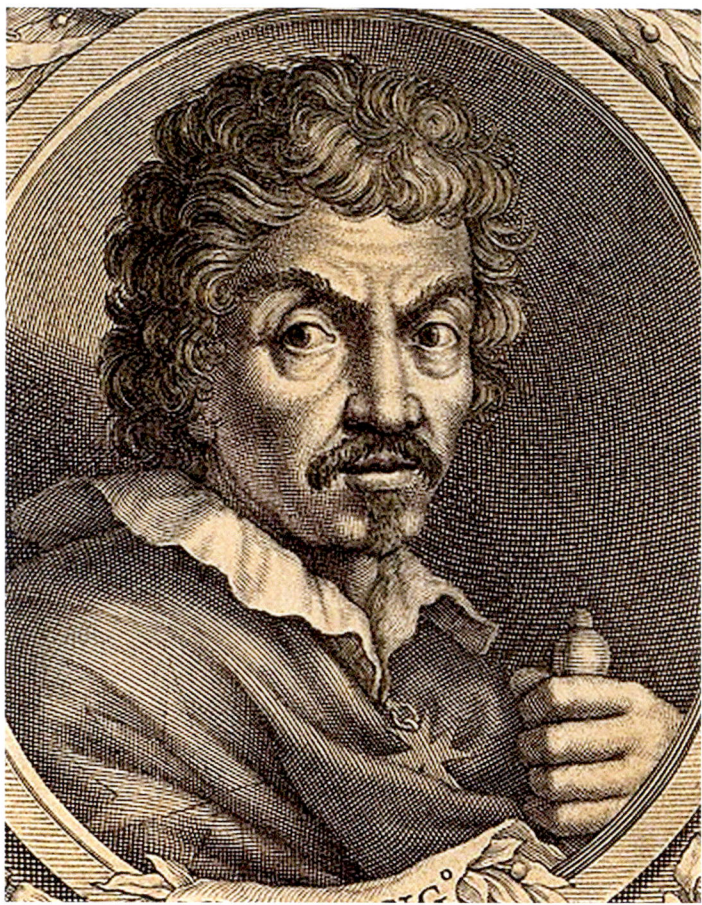

Fig. 193
Michelangelo Merisi da Caravaggio, *Ecce Homo*, Galleria di Palazzo
Rosso, Genoa, oil on canvas, 128 x 103 cm., detail.

Fig. 194
Portrait of Caravaggio from Giovan Pietro Bellori, *Le Vite*.

193, 194). In other words, I agree with Longhi's analysis of Caravaggio's physiognomy except for a
few elements: especially Pilate's nose, whose bridge and proportion diverge from those depicted in
the portraits of Caravaggio. Nonetheless, the Genoa picture presents an unfortunate abrasion on the
pictorial surface at the exact location of Pilate's nose, so that this point must remain in abeyance. It may
be objected that all these portraits of Caravaggio are posthumous, that they all rely on the master's
likeness drawn by the Roman painter Ottavio Leoni around 1615, after Caravaggio's death, and more
importantly that they are not immune to caricature, as Philip Sohm has rightly argued.[23] Therefore, it
is indispensable to compare Pilate's figure with Leoni's drawing (Fig. 195). Some features, assuredly,
still coincide, for instance the forehead's form and proportion, once one rids it of the wrinkles in the
painting, the arch-like curves of the eyebrows—much thicker in the drawing—and particularly the
structure of the eyelids, eye sockets and eyes. Incidentally, Pilate's eyes and eyebrows are comparable
with those of the *c.*1594 *Sick Bacchus* at the Borghese Gallery, Rome, unanimously considered an early
self-portrait of Caravaggio. As for Pilate's nose, it is problematic to judge its configuration, not least
because of the figure's almost grimacing expression.

Yet once one observes Leoni's portrait and Pilate's figure in the *Ecce Homo* side-by-side, one
has the inescapable impression that Pilate's physiognomy is an elongated, dried-out, and aged
version of Leoni's Caravaggio. Even if one ignores the beard and gray hair, disguises easy for a
painter to interpolate or expunge, it is obvious that Caravaggio, as Longhi observed, overloaded

23   See Sohm 2002.

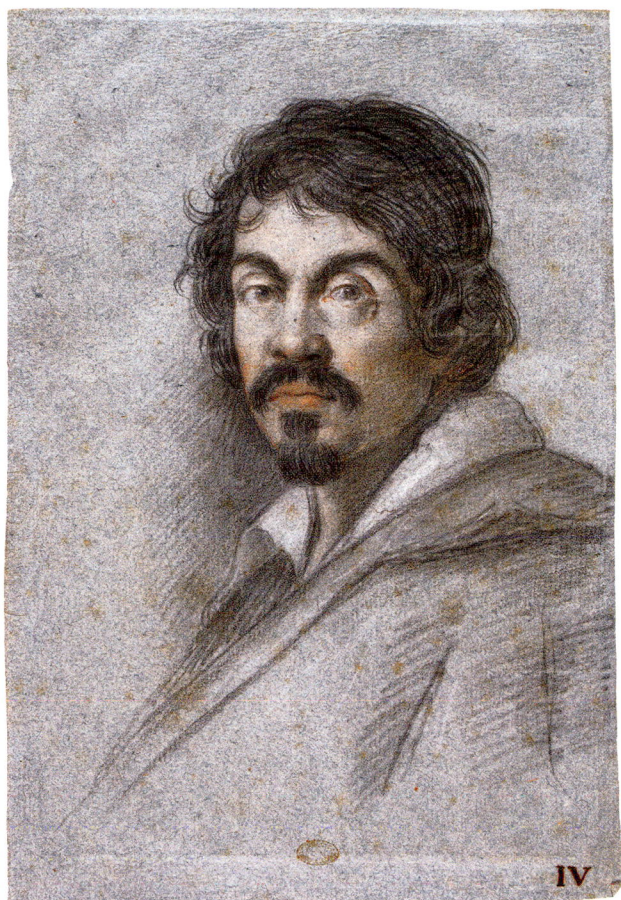

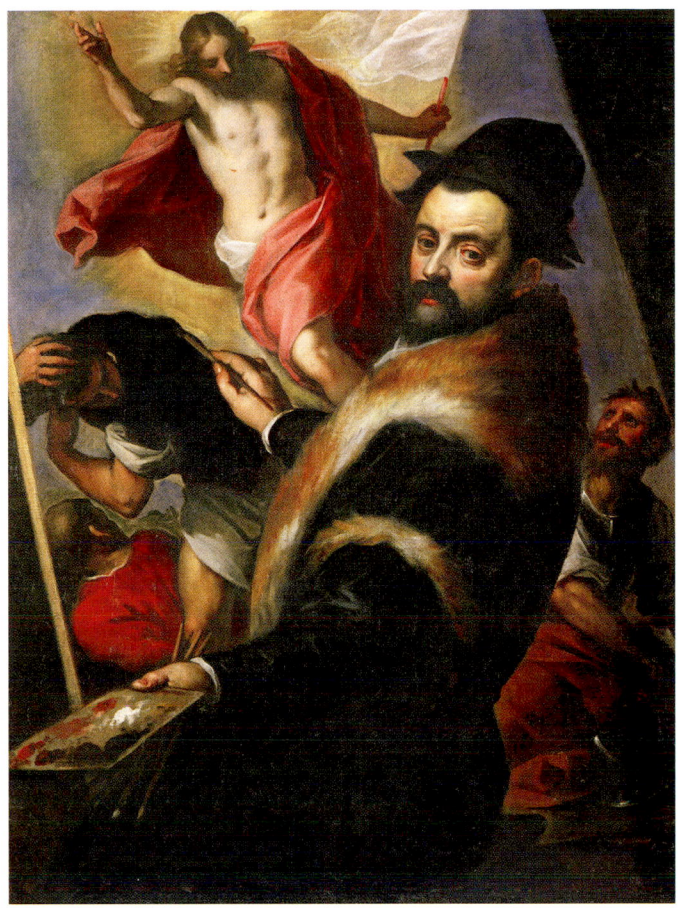

Fig. 195
Ottavio Leoni, *Portrait of Caravaggio*, Biblioteca Marucelliana, Florence, red and black chalk heightened with white on blue paper, 23.4 x 16.3 cm.

Fig. 196
Jacopo Palma il Giovane (Palma Giovane), *Self-Portrait*, Pinacoteca di Brera, Milan, oil on canvas, 126 x 96 cm.

his features, slightly lengthened his face, and refashioned his physiognomy into mild caricature and masquerade.

Corroborating this point leads me to ponder Longhi's description of Pilate's posture and attitude toward the figure of Christ in the *Ecce Homo,* which prefigures Michael Fried's concept of the painter's physical absorption into his work.[24] Is Pilate-the-painter here posing in a gesture mimicking the "act of painting"? Are his hands holding the canvas, or shading the contours of the depicted Christ's left arm with his bare thumb? Of course Longhi's phrases should not be taken too literally, but are they simply rhetorical ornaments in support of his exegesis? And is it likely that Pilate would be dressed like a painter in the *Ecce Homo*?

There is a striking precedent of a painter's self-representation and quasi-fusion into one of his paintings: Jacopo Palma il Giovane's *c.*1580 *Self-Portrait* now at the Brera, Milan (Fig. 196).[25] Leaning backward while swiveling forward to meet the viewer's eyes, Palma soars into the foreground clothed in a black cloak sumptuously lined with fur. Covering his head, a tall dark beret with uplifted brims parted at the extremities may qualify as a professional clothing. Thrusting his left arm forward, Palma exhibits his rectangular palette smeared with red, black, and white pigments, and a bundle of brushes. Wielding a brush in his right hand, he re-enforces the contours of a hunching figure represented on a canvas behind, which is placed askew and fills almost the

---

24   For Fried's interpretation of Caravaggio, see Fried 1997 and Fried 2010.

25   For the painting, see Ivanoff and Zampetti 1980, 542-3, no. 105; and Mason Rinaldi 1980, no. 80

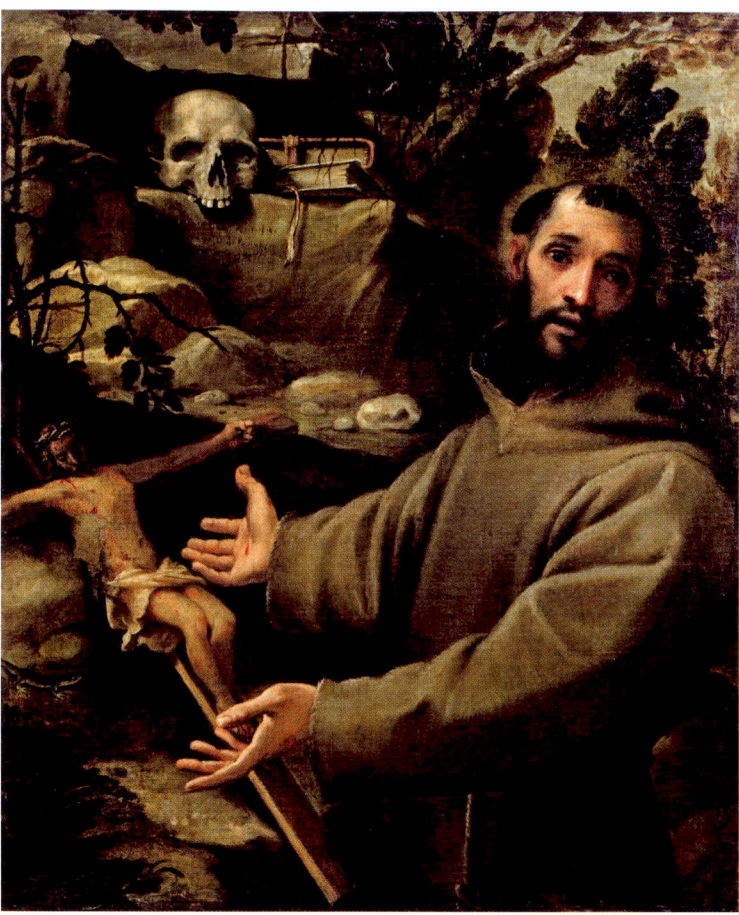

Fig. 197
Annibale Carracci, *Saint Francis Showing the Crucifix*, Gallerie dell'Accademia, Venice, oil on canvas, 96 x 79 cm.

entire background of the composition. The tip of the brush seems to blend into the painted figure and Palma's right index finger appears to touch the painting's surface by dint of an illusionistic trick. Were it not for the fictive canvas' border slanting along the painting's left margin, and for the reduced scale of the Resurrection figures behind the painter, one might perceive Palma as standing in the foreground of his biblical *istoria*, as if the author could truly merge into his own invention, abolishing the boundaries between two different degrees of fiction: that of self-representation and that of the *istoria*. It would not be difficult to imagine a palette and a bundle of brushes in the left hand of the Genoa *Ecce Homo*'s Pilate. Nonetheless, it is difficult to discern in the gesture of Pilate's right hand an equivalent of an actual "act of painting." I am not seeking by this to undermine Longhi's intuition, which I believe to be essentially sound, but to test and circumscribe its efficacy.

The gesture of Pilate's hands in the *Ecce Homo* is a codified one of rhetorical presentation and exhortation. Compare Annibale Carracci's 1585-86 *Saint Francis Adoring the Crucifix*, now in the Gallerie dell'Accademia, Venice (Fig. 197).[26] In the right foreground, the saint cocks his head toward the viewers, addressing them with his parted lips and inviting them to direct their gaze onto the crucifix laid across a rocky outcrop behind. Like Caravaggio's Pilate, he opens his hand and uncurls his fingers toward the object to be seen: "Behold the crucifix," or "Behold the man."

Even if there is no ambiguity in the significance of Pilate's gesture, I would nonetheless argue that there is a pictorial gap between his dark figure in the foreground and the group of Christ and the torturer behind. Consider the proportions of the figures in the *Ecce Homo*: although Pilate/ Caravaggio precedes Christ and the thug, his dimensions are slightly shorter than, or almost the same as, those of the actors he introduces for consideration, as if the Roman praetor truly dwelt before a two-figure, life-size canvas whose borders are invisible to the beholder. In a manner not dissimilar to that employed by Palma in his *Self-Portrait*, the divergence of scale in the *Ecce Homo*, albeit attenuated and reversed here, engenders the impression that Pilate is grafted onto the Gospel scene—which, technically speaking, is true, since his figure was executed at the end, and painted over that of the torturer and Christ. In other words, Caravaggio, through the ambivalent proportions and the twofold staggering of his figures, stages a double level of fiction: on the one hand, the sacred representation of the Ecce Homo; on the other, the intermediate sphere of both the episode's and the scene's "anchorman"—Longhi preferred the term "bouncer"—Pilate/Caravaggio. On the other side of the painting, the viewer/audience appears to be separated from, yet invited into, the scene through the composition's beguiling proximity; indeed, the episode takes place just beyond

26 See Posner 1971a, 2:15, no. 29.

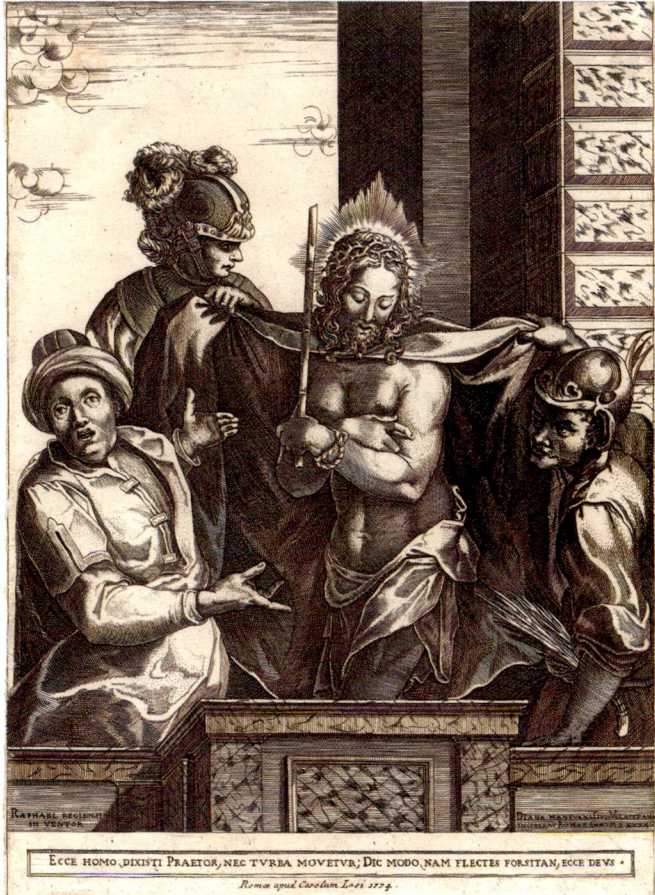

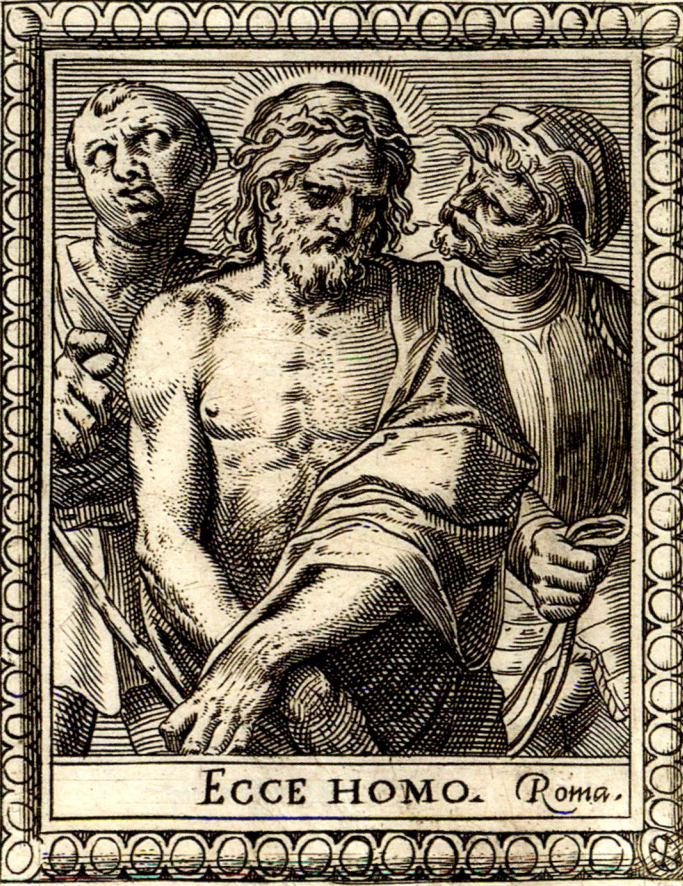

Fig. 198
Diana Scultori after Raffaellino da Reggio, *Ecce Homo*, engraving, 36.7 x 27 cm.

Fig. 199
Agostino Carracci, *Ecce Homo*, engraving, 8.7 x 7 cm.

a low and narrow parapet, a pictorial boundary easily climbed and thus easily overlooked. Unlike Palma's, however, Caravaggio's "fiction-within-a-fiction" is drastic and disturbing: by suppressing the canvas's borders and by disguising the author as an acting figure in the *istoria*, Caravaggio plunges the beholder into two diverse, yet indistinct, registers of perception; self-referentiality and narrative fuse together without solution of continuity. The alienation effect that this double factor entails is nevertheless amplified by the comedic and parodic connotations of both the clothing and the emphatic hand gesture of Pilate-the-painter.

I now pass to another point of Longhi's argument, the specificity of the Genoa painting in relation to the iconographic tradition. Rather than examining the social, religious, and ideological complexities of the Ecce Homo theme, I will select a few images that might be linked to Caravaggio's picture, firstly an engraving by Diana Scultori after Raffaellino da Reggio dating from the 1570s or 1580s (Fig. 198).[27] In this *Ecce Homo*, Christ is shown behind the protruding part of an elevated tribune as two soldiers remove his cloak in keeping with Pilate's exhortation to expose "the man" before the crowd. To the left, the Roman praetor, chubby, turbaned, and dressed in Oriental clothes, addresses the viewer while emphatically pointing his hands toward the Savior. The soldier to the left, donning a plumed helmet, shifts the mantle while intently locking his gaze on Christ, who stands below and steers his eyes downward. This soldier's attitude occurs in other prints with the same subject, and it evokes that of Caravaggio's torturer, whose action now can be interpreted: he

27 See Bellini 1991, 260-1, no. 60.

387

is removing the mantle in accordance with Pilate's cue "Ecce Homo," while insulting Jesus. The Latin inscription underneath Scultori's composition reads: "Praetor, you said, 'behold the man,' but did not move the crowd. Say now, 'behold God,' and perhaps you will convince them" ["Ecce Homo, dixisti praetor, nec turba movetur; Dic modo, nam flectes forsitan: Ecce Deus"].

In 1581, Agostino Carracci executed a small, lovely (technically speaking) engraving: a condensed *Ecce Homo* that Caravaggio is very likely to have known (Fig. 199).[28] Inside a rudimentary picture frame, Christ appears flanked by two thugs; the figure to the left mocks him by sticking his tongue out and making the obscene gesture of the *"fica"* (he puts his thumb between his index and middle fingers to mimic sexual intercourse). To the right, a soldier with a brutal face sporting a short beard yanks at Christ's mantle while turning to the left. His expression and the particular foreshortening of his head (tilted slightly forward as the nose vigorously veers sideward) conjure up those of Caravaggio's torturer.

These two works, in my view, suffice to ascertain a few facts. First of all, since the composition of the Ecce Homo iconographic theme varies dramatically from case to case, it is clear that artists had great latitude in visualizing the sacred episode in conformity with their goals. As Longhi pointed out, Caravaggio relied on what Erwin Panofsky in a 1956 essay consecrated to the Ecce Homo iconography called the "Milanese formula": a three-figure group formed by Christ in the middle and, on either side, Pilate and a torturer.[29] That said, it is also true that the emplacement of each figure in the "Milanese" variant of the Ecce Homo iconographic theme is far from being immutable, although Christ's centrality is very often preserved. Caravaggio unequivocally intended to distance Pilate from Christ by conceiving a zigzagging disposition of the figures so that the beholder's eyes wander from the right to the left and back to the right toward the background while discovering the *Ecce Homo*'s actors for the first time. If one isolates the three figures at the left of Scultori's engraving, thereby effacing the soldier to the right, a similar zigzag configuration will emerge into view straightaway. Secondly, in the Ecce Homo iconographic tradition the solemn "exposition," rich in pathos, of Christ's martyred body is both tempered and sharpened through the insertion of elements that pertain to the "comic" in the broadest sense of the term as understood in the early modern period—that is, a recourse to low-life, vile figures performing vulgarity and mockery, and a more or less pronounced allusion to Pilate's idiotic behavior. I should explain more fully what I mean by Pilate's "idiocy," which I might also define as "triviality" or "banality."

I shall seek evidence in two compositions, above all in Albrecht Dürer's 1509 *Ecce Homo* from the *Small Passion* (Fig. 200).[30] In this woodcut, I shall concentrate on the three figures within an arched opening beyond the tumultuous crowd. In this narrow recess, Christ is in the center, a rabid soldier to the right pulling at his mantle; to the left, Pilate leans down as if to uncover and behold the man whom he is presenting to the spectators. His contorted attitude, with his right arm bent above his head as if he was somehow burrowing his way toward Christ, is awkward to say the least. I do not find any other way of construing Pilate's contortionism here than as a visual pun on his solemn dictum "Ecce Homo," "behold the man." In other words, the strain of Pilate's body tends, in my opinion, to amplify rhetorically the importance and uniqueness of the praetor's revelation to the public, a revelation that, instead, turns out to be self-evident, even banal, since everyone can verify that what he is showing is "the man."

This idiotic, or perhaps involuntarily comedic, aspect of Pilate's sentence and act of exposition is emphasized in another print by Dürer: the 1512 *Pilate Washing His Hands* from the *Engraved Passion* (Fig. 201).[31] There, a turbaned Pilate, seated on a throne to the left, denies all responsibility

28 See DeGrazia 1979, 140, no. 42.

29 See Panofsky 1956.

30 See Hütt 1980, 2:1611; and Schoch et al. 2001, 2:316-7, no. 205.

31 See Hütt 1980, 2:1857; and Schoch et al. 2001, 1:140-1, no. 53.

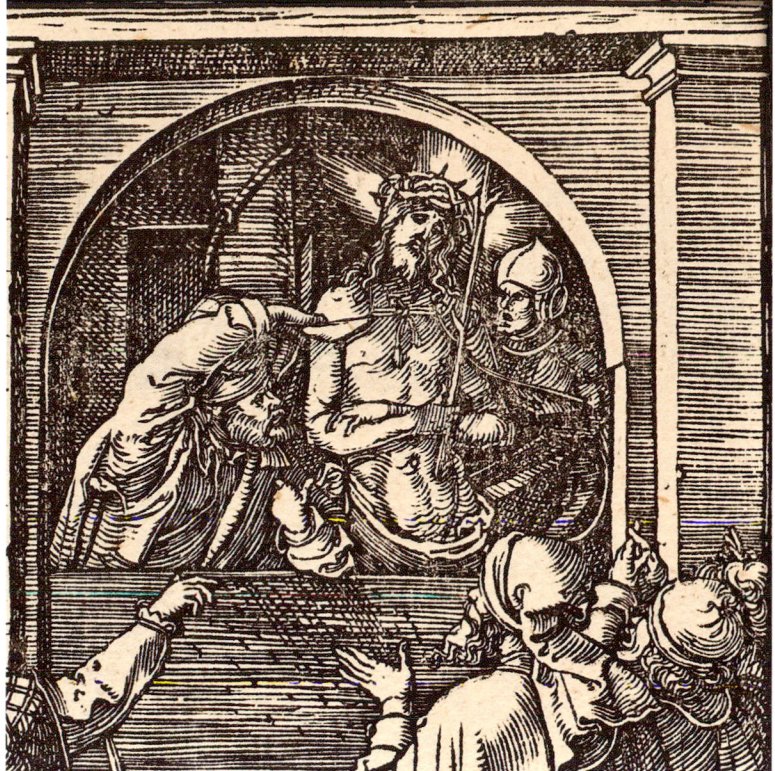

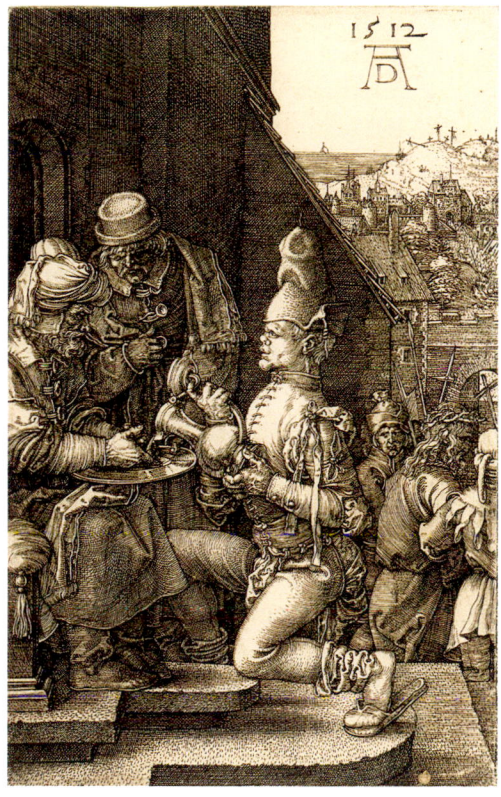

Fig. 200
Albrecht Dürer, *Ecce Homo*, woodcut, 12.8 x 9.7 cm., detail.

Fig. 201
Albrecht Dürer, *Pilate Washing His Hands*, engraving, 11.8 x 7.6 cm.

for Christ's martyrdom by washing his hands under a spout of water poured from a metal jug by a court buffoon. Curiously enough, Dürer spotlights the figure of this ugly-faced joker by accommodating him in the center of the print and by meticulously describing the ribbons and tassels of his garment. I do not suggest that Pilate is here likened to the buffoon—on the contrary, rare are the artists like Dürer who have managed to represent the seriousness and torment of the Roman praetor with such poignancy—but only that Pilate's persona as summoned by the iconographic tradition is endowed with comedic features and undertones. The gist of this figure's ridicule, in my view, resides in his profound "blindness," that is, in his inability to see God in the "man." On this misperception equally depends the captiousness of his pleading. As the inscription in Scultori's *Ecce Homo* suggests, Pilate disregarded Christ's claim to be God's offspring by presenting him merely as a man; had he known otherwise, he would have proclaimed "behold God."

As I suggested in the Introduction to Part Two, Pilate's attitude is a case—perhaps extreme—of comedic deception: a naïve misrecognition or misidentification that, paradoxically, turns into pure tragedy with the death of the misidentified character. Potentially, then, the Ecce Homo episode is an explosive compound of comedy and tragedy, a tragicomedy in its own right. In most cases, Pilate's "slip of the tongue" and unwilling naivety are not exploited by artists, who instead tend to underline Christ's pathos, strength, and resignation. This is not the case with Caravaggio; as Longhi so keenly perceived, the caricatural Pilate-the-painter, through his disguise and gesture, reactivates the comic register latent in the iconographic tradition, specifically in connection with the "Ecce Homo" dictum. Unlike Longhi, I do not think that Caravaggio, by representing himself as Pilate, aimed solely to indicate his artistry—his privilege as a "realist" painter—in modeling and recreating man's figure as if in flesh and blood. I see this as an optimistic and, in a sense, reassuring interpretation of the Genoa *Ecce Homo*.

I would argue instead that Caravaggio, by assuming the pose and misplaced verve of Pilate, intended to parody the role and scope of artistic creation with regard to sacred images. As Kathy Johnston-Keane has rightly argued,[32] Pilate's costume is not that of a contemporaneous painter, but of a mask: in my view, Caravaggio depicted himself here in the guise of the *dottore*, a stock character from the Italian *commedia dell'arte*. But before elucidating the reasons and repercussions of Pilate-the-painter's disguise as the *dottore,* and explaining how the use of this comedic character in Caravaggio's *Ecce Homo* intersects with the visual tradition of artistic self-representation, I must conclude the analysis of Longhi's 1954 essay on the Genoa picture.

At the end of the passage previously quoted, Longhi stressed the bodily purity of Caravaggio's Christ, which he deemed almost the work of an archaic mallet, perhaps the analog of a Greek *kouros*. In 1943, when he first encountered the *Ecce Homo* composition, Longhi had already equated Caravaggio's "austere and consummate" Christ with the achievement of a great Italian "primitive," the Sicilian quattrocento master Antonello da Messina. Needless to say, these comparisons should not be taken as historical statements, but as observations of an aesthetic nature. What Longhi meant to imply, in particular, was first and foremost the visual and chromatic graphicness of Christ's body, the way it detaches itself vividly from the network of shallow yet dense shadows that enfold it, and from the preeminently brown and black masses of color that surround it—even the purple cloak of the Gospel morphs here into a dim violet mantle in order to keep the interplay of tones low and make the bright hues reverberate with greater intensity. In this almost tetra-chromatic composition, the pictorial representation of Christ's body rivals the solidity and stereography of a relief sculpture, almost entirely carved out within the near-parallel plane of the Savior's rectangular torso, so purely enclosed by his bracketing arms. From this oblong, planar surface only Christ's hands jut out discreetly, the right one delicately holding the reed, the other uncurling in an indefinite, nervous motion. The effect of relief engendered by Caravaggio's rendering of Christ's body is remarkably enhanced by Pilate's pitch-black mantle, displayed as a chromatic foil, as if the two figures were not only interconnected through action—the gesture of "exposition"—but also opposed or complementary in brightness. Despite the anatomical simplicity of the Savior's figure that so appropriately translates his Stoic immobility, Caravaggio succeeded in registering the faintest hints of expression in Jesus' face: a touch of bright pigment above the left eyebrow engenders the impression of ephemeral movement, as if the Savior was caught in the middle of a dolorous rumination; and notice also how the transversal imbalance of shades upon Christ's fleshly lips might be assigned at first glance to the effect of a whisper.

If I dwell on these details, it is because the exegesis that I propose in the following pages might lead the reader to believe, wrongly, that Caravaggio ridiculed his capability of representing Christ's figure. This would only be a partial interpretation of my thesis; I, like Longhi, believe that the gesture of Pilate-the-painter in the Genoa *Ecce Homo* also conveys Caravaggio's pride in exposing, more graphically than others, the lifelike effigy of the Savior by means of a technique that both parallels and surpasses that of the great masters from Renaissance Venice. I refer not only to the mixture of blood, sweat, and wood in the crown of thorns commented upon by Longhi, but also to the feat of Christ's white loincloth abutting his living flesh. Yet, as usual with Caravaggio, this pride in and celebration of painting's mimetic force are not evidence against the master's well known "satirical" and dislocating spirit.

32   I refer to Kathy Keane-Johnston's lecture "Caravaggio's Theater: The Counter-Reformation, Early Italian Drama, and the Visual Arts," held on the occasion of the Mid-Atlantic Symposium at the Center for Advanced Study in the Visual Arts, National Gallery of Art, Washington DC, in April 2006. For Caravaggio and theater, see the unconvincing May 2000.

The Pictorial Macaronics of Pilate-the-**Dottore**

It is a particularly difficult task to outline the character, and detail the attributes of, the *commedia dell'arte* masks at the end of the sixteenth and the beginning of the seventeenth centuries.[33] What we define today as the *dottore*—the doctor—was named in multifarious ways at the time, each Italian or European city having slightly different denominations for a single mask. Nor were the roles of these comedic characters entirely established, so that some features merged into one another, thereby complicating their recognition by scholars. Probably one of the most famous *dottori* during Caravaggio's youth was the author and actor Lodovico de' Bianchi, known in the Florentine court as "el dottor Gratian," a Bolognese-speaking mask with a perverse proclivity to warp the noble Latin idiom and disfigure the Tuscan vernacular despite his being a "doctor in all the reasons," as he put it, that is, a doctor in all the disciplines.[34] De' Bianchi's is one of the best extant late sixteenth-century testimonies about the *dottore* mask.

From the outset, the *dottore* tended to qualify as a variant of a pre-existing mask: that of the pedant. Originally understood as a parody of a University officer, the "vicario," the *dottore* was sometimes associated with the figure of the lawyer, from whose mid sixteenth-century costume he took the black beret[35] and long black cloak often padded on the outside from the shoulders down to the armpits.[36] Preceding the dedicatory letter of de' Bianchi's 1587 *Le cento e quindici conclusioni*, there is a woodcut portraying *dottor Gratian*'s figure half-bust, wearing a black beret and mantle with white collar, sporting a mustache and a goatee (Fig. 202).[37]

In some cases, the *dottore* looks almost like another mask with whom he often collaborated: that of the elderly Pantaloon, the hopeless Venetian gallant.[38] In a woodcut dating from the second half of the sixteenth century representing a scene of the French

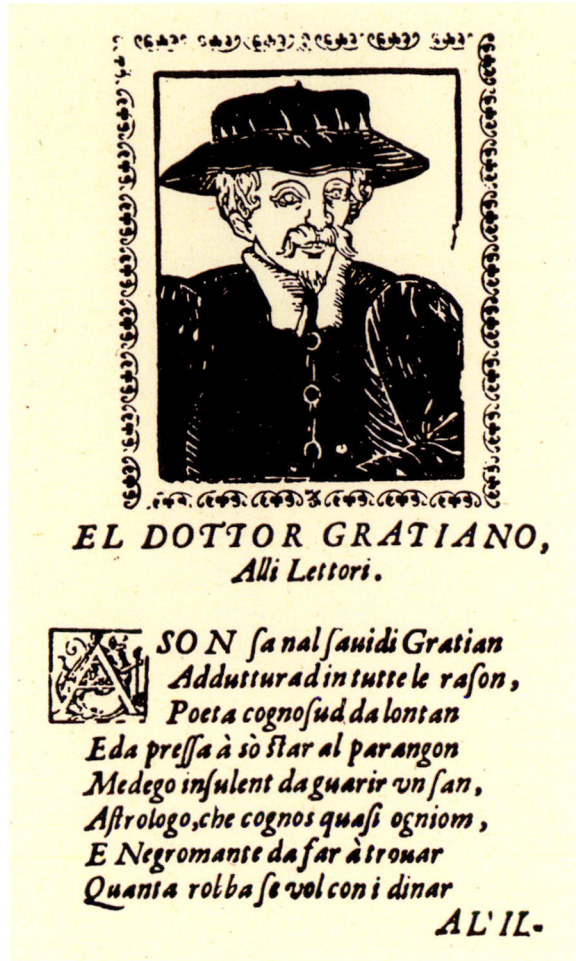

Fig. 202
Dottor Gratian, in Lodovico de' Bianchi, *Le cento e quindici conclusioni*, reproduced from Vito Pandolfi, *La Commedia dell'Arte*, 1957-1961.

33 One of the main visual sources for the early modern *commedia dell'arte* is the Recueil Frossard, National Museum, Stockholm. See McDowell 1942; Duchartre 1966; Beijer and Duchartre 1981; Molinari 1985; Katritzky 1988; Leik 1996; Katritzky 1997; Lawner 1998; Katritzky 2006. For the *commedia dell'arte* in general, see Taviani 1970; Mariti 1978; Richards and Richards 1990; Marotti and Romei 1991; Ferrone 1993; Castagno 1994; Rudlin 1994; Chiabò and Doglio 1996; Theile 1997; Henke 2002; Bossier 2004; and Testaverde 2007.

34 According to the 1699 testimony of Perrucci, 199, the *dottore*'s macaronics was already perceived as obsolete at his time: "Molti anni sono s'introdusse un modo di recitare da dottore che stravolgeva i vocaboli, v.g. 'teribil orinal' per 'tribunal'; 'Amerigo frega la groppa dell'asino' per dir 'l'America, l'Africa, l'Europa e l'Asia,' e così si cavava la risata dal nome storpio, che da' greci si chiama *paronomasia*."

35 That the black beret of scholars and lawyers was outdated is easy to confirm in Netherlandish seventeenth-century painting. See De Winkel 2006, esp. 37. De Winkel 2006, 278,

note 48, also quotes the 1631 statutes of Leyden University concerning the dress to be worn by candidates during the promotion ceremony. The candidate must be "gekleet met eenen swarten zijden Damasten tabbert met Fluwele op-slagen [dressed in a black silk-damask gown with velvet facings]."

36 A succinct description of the *dottore*'s costume is given by Rudlin 1994, 99-105; this mask wears a "black academic dress satirizing Bolognese scholars, long jacket with black coat over-reaching to his heels, black shoes, stockings and breeches, and a black skull-cap." See also Pandolfi 1957-1961, 2:9-32; Duchartre 1966, 196-207; Richards and Richards 1990, 127-8; 133.

37 See De' Bianchi.

38 It is noteworthy that in his 1699 *Dell'arte rappresentativa premeditata*, Perrucci, 194, assimilates the masks of Pantaloon and the *dottore*: "Or perché le parti de' vecchi sogliono essere per lo più ridicole per essere innamorati, e la vecchiaia quando cade in questo errore è derisibile; come anche per esser avari,

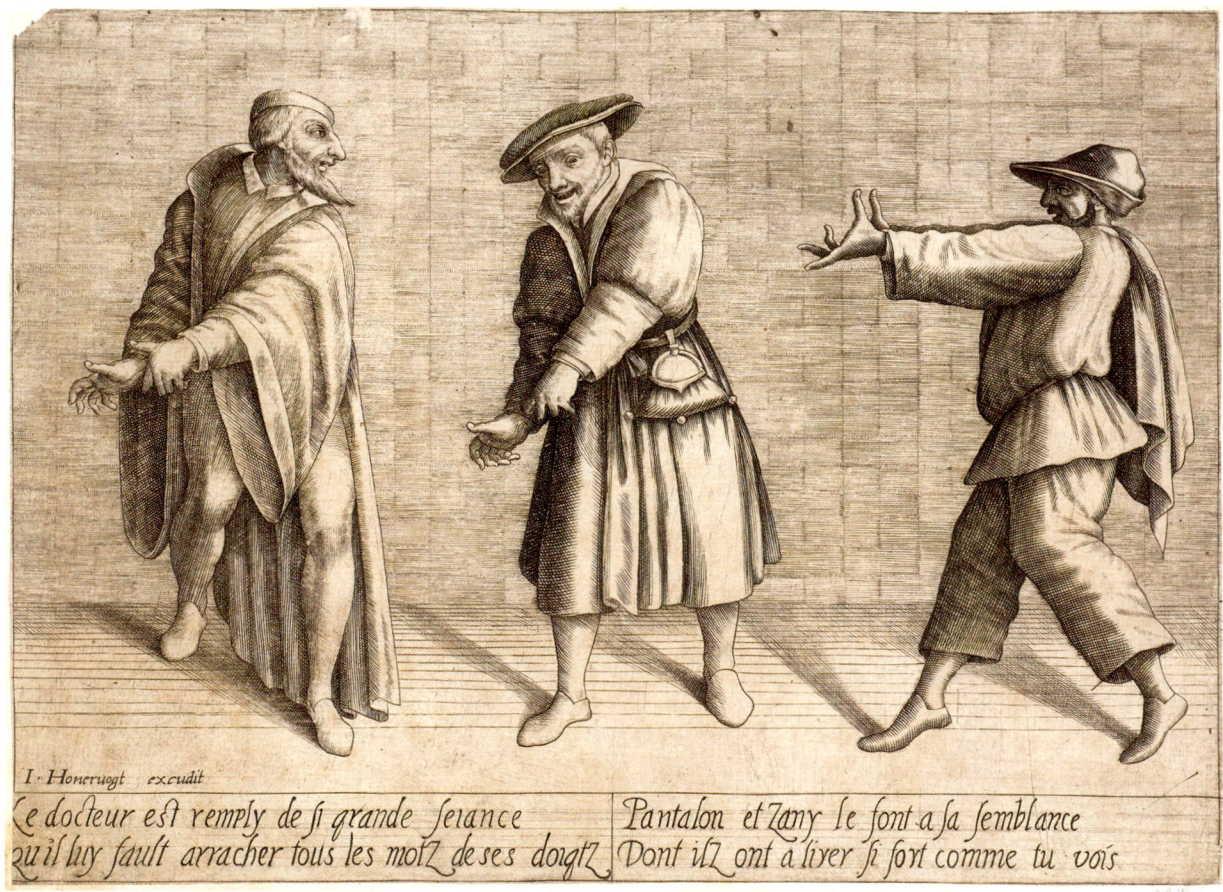

Fig. 203
Jacques Honervogt I, *The Dottore, Zani, and Pantaloon*, engraving, 19.3 x 27.2.

commedia dell'arte, the "Segnor Dotour" peers out from behind a curtain, wearing a flat hat, a cloak and a pointed gray beard, while a mask adheres to the upper part of his face.[39] Were it not for the shape of his hat, one could easily mistake him for "Segnor Pantalon."

The resemblance between the *dottore* and Pantaloon is apparent in an interesting engraving from the same period, executed by Jacques Honervogt I, in which the two masks figure alongside Zani, the irreverent, at times sly, at times foolish servant of *the commedia dell'arte* (Fig. 203). In this print, the three masks pose in rhetorical attitudes, as Pantaloon and Zani attempt to imitate the *dottore*'s hand gestures and attitudes. This is clearly stated by a French inscription present in one copy of the print.[40] In the center, the *dottore*, donning his traditional beret and a short robe, hilariously addresses the viewer while eloquently rotating the fingers of both hands. To the left, Pantaloon, wearing his Venetian toque and a long mantle with drooping large sleeves, performs a grandiloquent hand gesture learned from the *dottore*. To the right, Zani steps onto the stage in profile, with a short cloak, trousers, and pointed beret. He looks at the *dottore* as he flings both his hands toward him,

tenaci, sospetti e viziosi, quindi è ch'a' diversi linguaggi si sono attribuite le parti di padri: come al veneziano la parte di Pantalone, figurante un mercadante avaro, stitico e facile ad innamorarsi, e se gli dà anche la parte di consigliero, essendo quei saggi e venerandi padri di gran senno per le consulte; al bolognese se gli dà la parte del dottore detto Graziano, che sarà dotto ma cicalone, essendo da quella università uomini dottissimi, essendo verissimo l'attributo di quella nobilissima città: *Bononia docet.*"

39   See Leik 1996, 288-9, no. A 59.

40   For the print, see Weigert 1968, 225, no. 23. For the text, see Leik 1996, 299, no. A 72: "Le docteur est rempli de si grande séiance/ Qu'il luy fault arracher les motz de ses doigts/ Pantalon et Zany le font sa semblance/ Dont ils ont à [t]irer si fort, comme tu vois" ["the *dottore* is filled with such great propriety/That he must extract his words from his fingers./ Pantaloon and Zani enact his likeness,/Which, as you see, they must fiercely imitate"].

emulating the rhetorical gesture of presentation and exhortation that I have already defined as characteristic of Pilate-the-painter in the Genoa *Ecce Homo*. From the print and its valuable inscription one can determine two essential facts. First, the complex and sophisticated motions of the hands practiced by the three masks must have naturally inhered in the *dottore*'s theatrical persona: Pantaloon and Zani content themselves with rehearsing these gestures in a kind of parody-within-the-parody. One can imagine that, without uttering a single word, the *dottore* on stage ridiculously flaunted his alleged eloquence and knowledge by a rhetorical array of hand gestures, one that

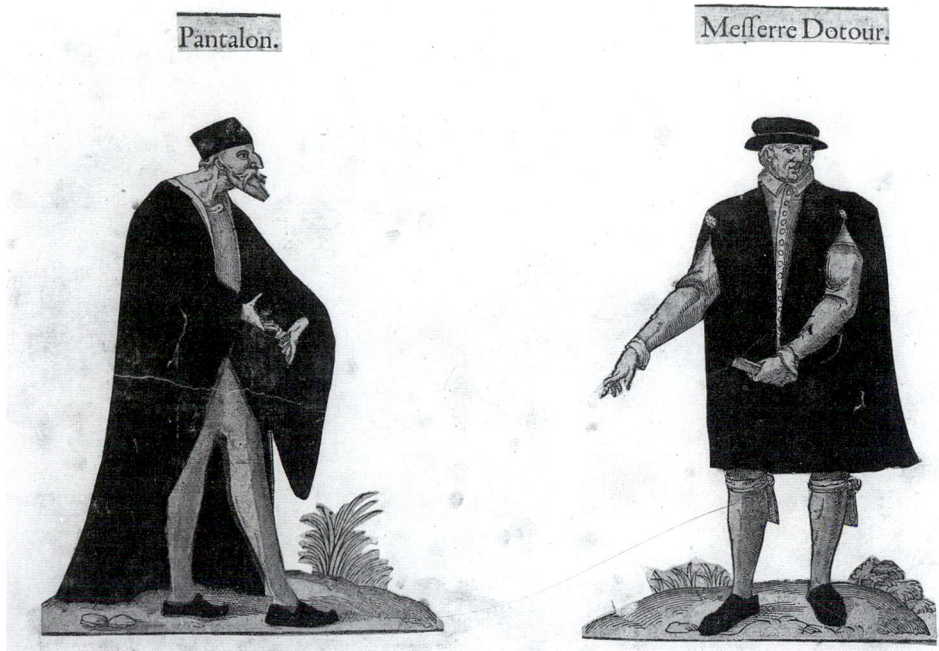

Fig. 204
The Dottore and Pantaloon, woodcut pasted on paper, from *Recueil Frossard,* National Museum, Stockholm.

was assuredly informed by the professional attitudes of the lawyer, the orator, and the savant.[41] Put otherwise, the *dottore*'s acting equally pertained to the art of pantomime. Secondly, the clothing of Pilate's figure in the Genoa *Ecce Homo* resembles Pantaloon's rather than the *dottore*'s, save for the beret.

The same observation applies to a mid sixteenth-century sheet from the Stockholm Frossard album, on which two separate figures, cut in wood, were pasted and colored at an unknown date:[42] to the left, Pantaloon, seemingly engaged in an oratorical speech, and to the right "Messerre Dotour," the *dottore* (Fig. 204). If one replaces Pantaloon's toque with the *dottore*'s beret, one obtains the exact equivalent of the costume worn by the *Ecce Homo* Pilate. Nevertheless, in some cases the *dottore* wears the costume of Pantaloon, as evidenced by an early seventeenth-century anonymous engraving that represents a scene from a French *commedia dell'arte* performance. In this piece, the central actor is explicitly named "Le Doctor Cornute," "the Cuckolded Doctor," and he bears the features, and wears the mantle, of a typical Pantaloon (Fig. 205).[43]

To corroborate my hypothesis further, I shall introduce three more images: first of all, the 1610 frontispiece to the *Fantastiche et ridicolose etimologie* by Aniello Soldano, a Neapolitan *dottore* figure (Fig. 206).[44] In this woodcut, the *dottore* is depicted as an elderly man, wearing the ordinary and by then out-of-fashion black beret and draped in a black mantle. The second image is a 1618 representation of "Dotor Grazian" from Giovan Battista Andreini's *La Campanaccia* ("Campanaz" in Bolognese dialect).[45] In this drawing, the *dottore*'s head is covered with an oversized black beret, and he dons a long black mantle with padded shoulders, also obsolete by that time. In an amazing

41 See in this regard Ceccarelli Pellegrino 1997 and her analysis of some of the gestures represented by masks in the Recueil Frossard.

42 See Leik 1996, 301, no. A77.

43 See Ibidem, 312-3, no. A88. The print's inscription reads, with regard to the *Dottore*: "Coquin, sache qu'en cette teste cornute/ L'on remarque un docteur parfaict/ Et que ces cornes, en effet,/ Ne me font point passer pour beste."

44 See Soldano.

45 This representation was executed by Dionisio Menaggio in 1618, and is now incorporated into the so-called *Feather Book* at the Life Sciences Library, McGill University, Montreal, fol. 103.

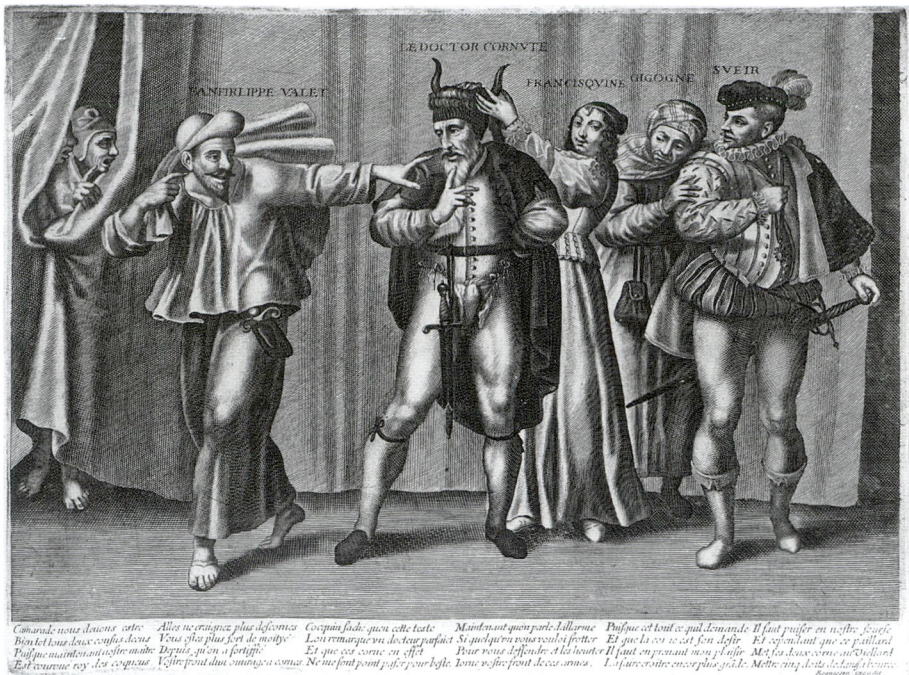

Fig. 205
Doctor Cornute, engraving, from *Recueil Frossard*, National Museum, Stockholm.

aquarelle executed at the end of the seventeenth century by Ludovico Ottavio Burnacini[46] (Österreichische Nationalbibliothek, Vienna), the *dottore* once again sports a black coat, whose wide sleeves drop emphatically in a manner similar to those of the Genoa Pilate (Fig. 207). Furthermore, the beret worn by Burnacini's *dottore* seems to be a caricatural, over-sized version of the one depicted in the *Ecce Homo*.

It is evident that the Pilate/Caravaggio in the Genoa *Ecce Homo*, because of his beret and rhetorical hand gesture, ranks as a *commedia dell'arte dottore*. On the other hand, Pilate's advanced age, pointed gray beard, and black mantle, although they can likewise refer to the Pantaloon figure, are not uncommon for a *dottore*. The eccentric makeover through which Caravaggio retouched his own features becomes more comprehensible in this new context of self-parody[47] as a *commedia dell'arte* mask. Nonetheless, it is important to underline the fact that, even if he adapted his own persona to the comic register, Caravaggio avoided morphing his dark Pilate completely into a ridiculous mask. The seriousness, even oratorical gravity of the figure's expression, lessens the effect of travesty relayed by the *dottore* costume, which no doubt impacted the seventeenth-century beholder with a vehemence that the modern spectator can only imagine.

In this connection, I must remark upon a strange detail: in spite of his hand gesture, the *Ecce Homo* Pilate is represented silent, rehearsing his role with the dedicated muteness of a mime, thereby delegating to the torturer in the background the mission to animate the scene with a suggestion of a soundtrack. This dusky thug, his head wrapped in a linen cloth, growls his menace to the Savior, or rather cackles it, as the bird feathers spurting out of the bandanna behind his neck seem to imply. By transferring the motif of allocution or elocution from Pilate to the torturer, and by partially ridiculing the thug's vileness, Caravaggio strove to balance the comic and the tragic elements implicit in the praetor's figure, mixing these opposites to the point of suspension, and even indistinctness, as if the exposition of the "man" were a serious, intimately convinced act of misrecognition: the unintentional banality of a stubbornly determined wit.

But how can the figure of the *dottore* be related to the Ecce Homo theme? Why did Caravaggio sense an analogy between a *commedia dell'arte* mask, the historical figure of Pilate, and his own identity as a painter? I believe that Caravaggio's contemporaries immediately understood some of these affinities, for they were used to seeing the *dottore* recite on stage. Against his own will, the *dottore* is in fact a windbag—often a naïve, and therefore not sanctimonious charlatan—a character so sure of his unlimited knowledge as to be unaware that his science boils down to blatant trivialities. The following extract is from de' Bianchi's 1587 *Le cento e quindici conclusioni*, a list of philosophical aphorisms concocted by Dottor Gratian's magnificent mind:

---

46 For Burnacini, see Biach-Schiffmann 1931; and Solf 1975.

47 An interesting interpretation of the concept of parody is in Hutcheon 2000.

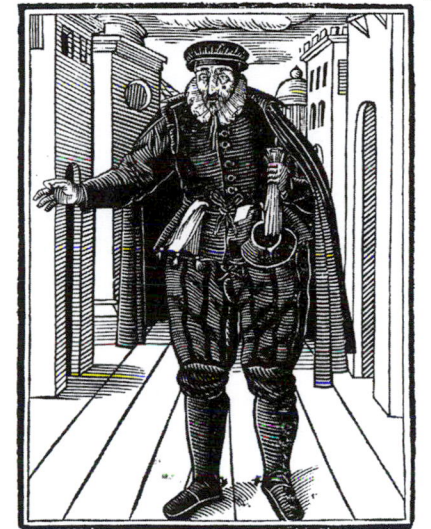

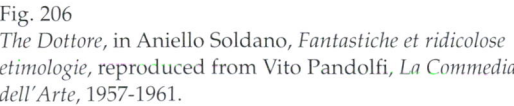

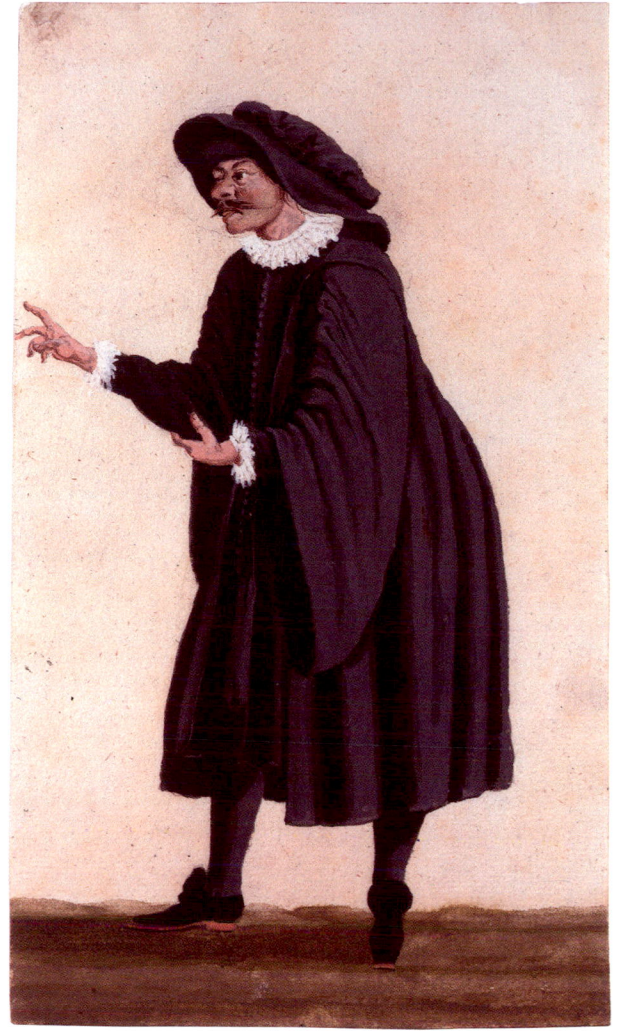

Fig. 206
The Dottore, in Aniello Soldano, *Fantastiche et ridicolose etimologie*, reproduced from Vito Pandolfi, *La Commedia dell'Arte*, 1957-1961.

Fig. 207
Ludovico Ottavio Burnacini, *Il Dottore*, Oesterreichische Nationalbibliothek, Vienna.

> The rose that is blossoming smells good;
> The man who walks is not dead;
> He who is always wrong is never right;
> The ship on the open sea has sailed off;
> He who does not want peace, should argue;
> He who does not want to go slow, walks fast;
> That which is square is not round;
> He who does not want to go first, should go second;
> A twisted man and a hunchback will never be straight;
> Today cannot be tomorrow;
> He who has committed a great crime
> Should take care not to end up with the hangman;
> He who is hungry has a good appetite…[48]

48 Pandolfi 1957-1961, 2:13-4: "La rosa ch'è fiorida sa da bon/ E l'uomo che camina non è mort,/ Un che sempre abbia stort, mai ha rason,/ La nave ch'è in alto mar è via dal port./ Chi non vol star in pas, faza costion, / E chi non vol andar

395

This extract is sufficient to illustrate the unmistakable tenor of the *dottore*'s wisdom and doctrine. Of course, what made his nonsensical speech irrepressibly funny was not the meaning of the sentences, but the profusion of grammatical errors, syntactical inconsistencies, and deformed words unceasingly flowing in the *dottore*'s mellow discourse, which was pronounced with a heavy Bolognese accent and illustrated with exaggerated rhetorical gestures. One of the *dottore*'s comic specialties resided in his preposterous use of the Latin language, which may be seen in this short passage from Adriano Banchieri's 1597 *Il Donativo di quatro asinissimi personaggi* ["The Donation of Four Very Asinine Personages"]. The translation I offer here is rather free, for obvious reasons:

> Ego am Doctor Gratianus from Francolin
> Sonus of latus Dominus Thomas
> He were a noble Mantuanus
> His eyes he wore upon his nosus.
> My mater was from Ferrara
> She was from an Oldus Familus
> Ego were made doctor in Bolognese…[49]

Only a brilliant performance could render the hilarity and the platitudinous idiocy of the *dottore*. In a sense, the *dottore* belongs to a quasi-autistic world, a cartoonish Mister Magoo blind to outside reality and satisfied with his self-explanatory banality, which he interprets as high-qualified knowledge.

From this prospect, Pilate's "Behold the man," or even better its Latin equivalent "Ecce Homo," along with the act of misidentification that the sentence so dramatically implies, seems to be a perfect script for a *dottore* character. Like "today is not tomorrow," and "he who is wrong is not right," the gesture through which Pilate pleads Christ's innocence is a potentially innocuous yet actually devastating truism. Extracted from its context, the assertion of the Savior's humanity is in and of itself ridiculous, since it claims to explain, but in fact avoids, the core of the juridical and theological issue at hand. The absurdity of Pilate's self-explanatory defense of Jesus-the-accused draws not only upon its legal inefficacy but especially upon the mystification it underlies: "the man" who is presented as just a "man" is "nothing" but the humanized God. On the whole, Pilate's banality is but one example of man's incapability to recognize the divine, a topic that, as I insist throughout this volume, constitutes one of Caravaggio's pictorial fixations.

In this light, Caravaggio turns Pilate's trivial exposition of God as a simple "man" into a tragicomic device[50] to thematize narrative blindness. Through the preposterous banality of Pilate's figure and gesture, beholders come to realize not Christ's hidden divinity—which, as I have already argued in Chapter 9, they commonly perceived as an axiom—but the facility and carelessness with which man misrecognizes God. To put it into slightly different terms, the eeriness of the association between Pilate and the *dottore* mask aims to jolt the viewers out of their routine approach to the Ecce Homo iconography, pushing them to focus not only on the injustice and cruelty of Christ's martyrdom, but also on the absurd mechanism through which the unjust verdict is reached—that is, by means of flat misidentification.

---

pian, camina fort,/ E quel ch'è fat a quadro non è tond,/ E chi non vol esser al prim sippa al segond. / Un stort e un gob non sarà mai drit, / e al dì d'ancua non pò esser doman/ Quel ch'arà fat qualche gran delit/ Ch'al guarda a non andar al boia in man./ Un affamad arà grand appetit…".

49 Ibidem, 2:293: "Dottor Gratianus sum Francolinensis/ Filius quondam d' msser Tomas,/ Nobilis civis fuit Mutinensis,/ Oculos habens dsovra dal nas:/ Martereq' mea

fuit Ferrariensis/ Appellabatur d' la casa Vecchias/ Ego in Bononia adoctoratus son…".

50 To my knowledge, there is no specific study on the concept of tragicomedy in seventeenth-century Italian art: in any case, nothing that compares to the excellent definition of "history as tragicomedy" in seventeenth-century Dutch painting as developed by Westermann 1997, 276-312.

As a result, the beholder's sudden awareness of Pilate's nonsensical misrecognition, caused as it is by the uncanny iconography of Pilate-the-*dottore*, provokes a twofold reaction. In the first place, it reinforces the impression of Christ's divinity as opposed to Pilate's misperception: the man represented in the painting is indeed God. Secondly, it makes one comprehend the limits of one's own perception: in a certain sense, there is no other way for man to perceive, and thus represent, divinity than in the form of humanity. Seeing God as "the" man is therefore tantamount to beholding "a" man, properly speaking. The banality of Pilate's dictum is also the banality of the beholder's seeing Christ. Only an act of faith allows one to see God in "the" man as he was habitually depicted. Most important here, however, is not the viewer's reaction to the Genoa painting, but the master's own interpretation of what I would term the banality of representing Christ. That Caravaggio was perfectly conscious about the theoretical stakes of his denoting Pilate as a *dottore* figure is demonstrated by his lending his own traits to the *Ecce Homo*'s praetor.

Before proceeding further along these lines, I shall consider another visual source for the Genoa picture: Niccolò della Casa's 1544 engraved *Portrait of Baccio Bandinelli* (Fig. 208).[51] In this print, the Florentine sculptor is represented from his knees up, standing before the viewer, sporting an overcoat or duster and a large beret. Affixed to his chest is a scallop shell imprinted with a cross, Bandinelli's insignia as a knight of the Spanish order of Santiago. His three-quarter face is proudly turned forward as he lays his eyes upon the viewer while furrowing his eyebrows in a sign of thoughtfulness and gravitas. In his right hand, Baccio seems to hold an ancient statuette, or a downscaled copy thereof, as his other hand, visibly out of proportion, points to the base of the artwork where the printer's name is engraved. I have no doubt that Caravaggio knew this portrait and decided to retouch his own features in a subtle allusion to Baccio. Not only do the orientations of Pilate's and the sculptor's faces and torsos mirror one another, but also Baccio's haircut, beard, and expression resurface in Pilate (Fig. 209). Observe also Baccio's left hand: if tilted and reversed, it entirely corresponds to Pilate's. Despite della Casa's clumsiness in designing his sitter's hands with regard to the statuette, it is evident that Baccio's left hand is directed toward the downscaled artwork, thereby linking the sculptor to his art: sculpture as its best, that is, in the form of an antique. As I have already said, Pilate's left hand is also meant to bind illusorily Pilate-the-painter to both Christ and the torturer behind, which can be interpreted as an independent pictorial work in its own right. Of course, the praetor's physiognomy does not match the sculptor's, it is fair to affirm that Pilate-the-painter-and-the-*dottore* is a self-parody of Caravaggio impersonating a figure of an artist like that of Baccio Bandinelli.

At this point, the question arises of how the mid-sixteenth-century Florentine sculptor, a notorious and envious rival of Michelangelo, relates to a *commedia dell'arte* mask. In what way does the artistic model incarnated by Baccio refer to the banality of the *dottore* figure? Caravaggio's disguise *à la* Bandinelli was probably not an uncommon practice among painters in Rome at that time. In one of his manuscript notes for the 1678 *Felsina pittrice*, Carlo Cesare Malvasia records:

> [Carlo] Cignani relates that he heard [Francesco] Albani saying that Annibale [Carracci] in Rome planned to make Giorgio Vasari's abjuration upon a chariot during a masquerade, and had talked about this with Cardinal Farnese who agreed on [the idea].[52]

---

51   For this engraving, its derivations, and the original self-portrait drawn by Bandinelli, see Franklin 2005, 274, no. 98; and Hegener 2008, 375-80, 447, 455-7. For Baccio Bandinelli, see also Heikamp 1966; Waldman 2004; Picchiarelli 2007; Greve 2008; and Gründler 2009.

52   Carracci, 34: "Dice il Cignani aver udito dire all'Albani che Annibale in Roma voleva in una mascherata far l'abiura di Giorgio Vasari sopra un carro, e l'avea conferito col cardinal Farnese che gl'aderiva."

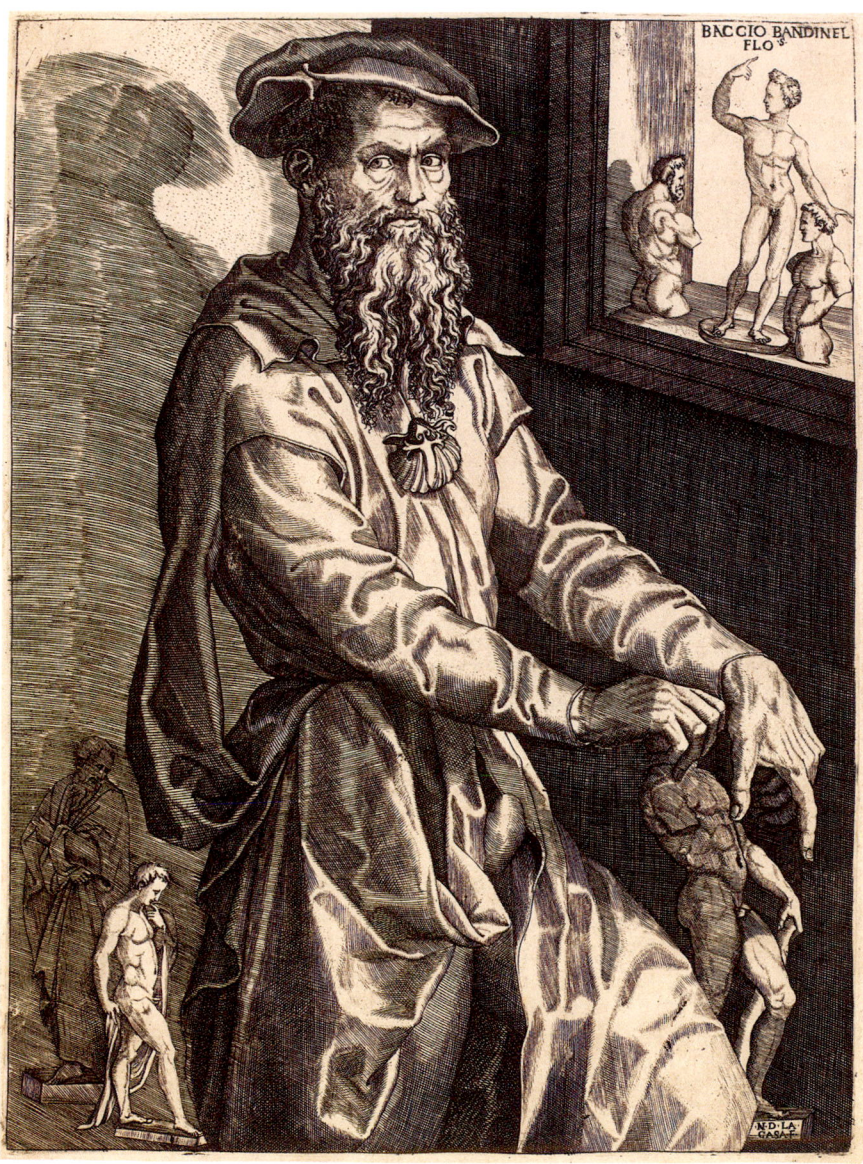

Fig. 208
Niccolò della Casa after Baccio Bandinelli, *Portrait of Baccio Bandinelli*, engraving, 29 x 21.8 cm.

Laconic as it is, Malvasia's information tells us a great deal about early seventeenth-century artists' parodic rituals and ideology in Rome. Annibale's contempt for Vasari's *Vite* is widely acknowledged. The painter's incendiary glosses on Vasari's anecdotes and tenets unmistakably betoken seething hostility. Since Malvasia mentions a chariot and a masquerade, I am inclined to believe that Annibale's project of ridiculing Vasari was to be fulfilled during carnival, that is, publicly in the streets of Rome. Although it is impossible to establish the date of these events—it is not even known whether the masquerade took place—Albani's oral testimony and the implication of Cardinal Odoardo Farnese point to a date around 1601-1605, a period in which Caravaggio also sojourned in Rome. From Malvasia's note it can be inferred that Annibale intended to disguise himself as Vasari, adjuring the biographer's "heretical" ideas in the matter of art from above a chariot in the course of a para-theatrical performance. Most likely Annibale's intention was to draft a speech in preparation for the masquerade, and to improvise on certain points as the parody unfolded. In order to counterfeit Vasari's persona, Annibale must have been familiar with portraits of the critic and artist, although I think that Annibale's impersonation of Vasari was limited to a costume travesty, with no integral makeover involved; a long beard and a few other outdated clothes from Vasari's time would have done the trick. The actual form of Annibale's disguise must of course remain a matter of speculation.

The way Caravaggio adjusted his physique in conformity with Bandinelli's portrait by della Casa might serve as a visual parallel to Annibale's planned personification of Vasari. The reasons for Annibale's polemic against, and parody of, Vasari are easily understood. But how is one to construe Caravaggio's allusion to Bandinelli? There are two aspects of Baccio's personality that Vasari, in his 1568 *Vite*, repeatedly mentions and that might help us to comprehend Caravaggio's opinion of the sculptor: Baccio's caustic tongue and his persistently thwarted attempts at surpassing the best masters of his time, first among them Michelangelo. These shortcomings crop up here and there very early on in Vasari's biography, following the young sculptor's collaboration with Andrea Sansovino in Loreto. After speaking ill of Andrea by declaring that his drawing technique was lacking, and after belittling all his own companions in the workshop, Baccio was compelled to bid farewell to Andrea and leave his work unfinished, as would happen many other times in his lifetime, but not before being duly reprimanded by Andrea:

> As a wise man, [Andrea] chastised Baccio tenderly, saying that works are done by hands, and not by tongues, and that good drawing does not rely on paper, but on the perfection of the artwork as achieved in stone, adding in the end that Baccio ought to speak of him with more respect in the future. But Baccio replied arrogantly and with many injurious words, and master Andrea could not take it any longer, and ran at him to beat him up.[53]

Unabashed, Baccio constantly claimed his superiority and stated that he was better even than Michelangelo, whom he viewed as his greatest rival, not only in drawing but also in sculpture and painting. When he obtained the prestigious commission to carve his gigantic *Hercules and Cacus*, he relentlessly boasted that it would surpass Michelangelo's *David*. As the Carrara marble in which Baccio was supposed to sculpt his work accidentally rolled down into the Arno and was lost, his detractors composed Latin and

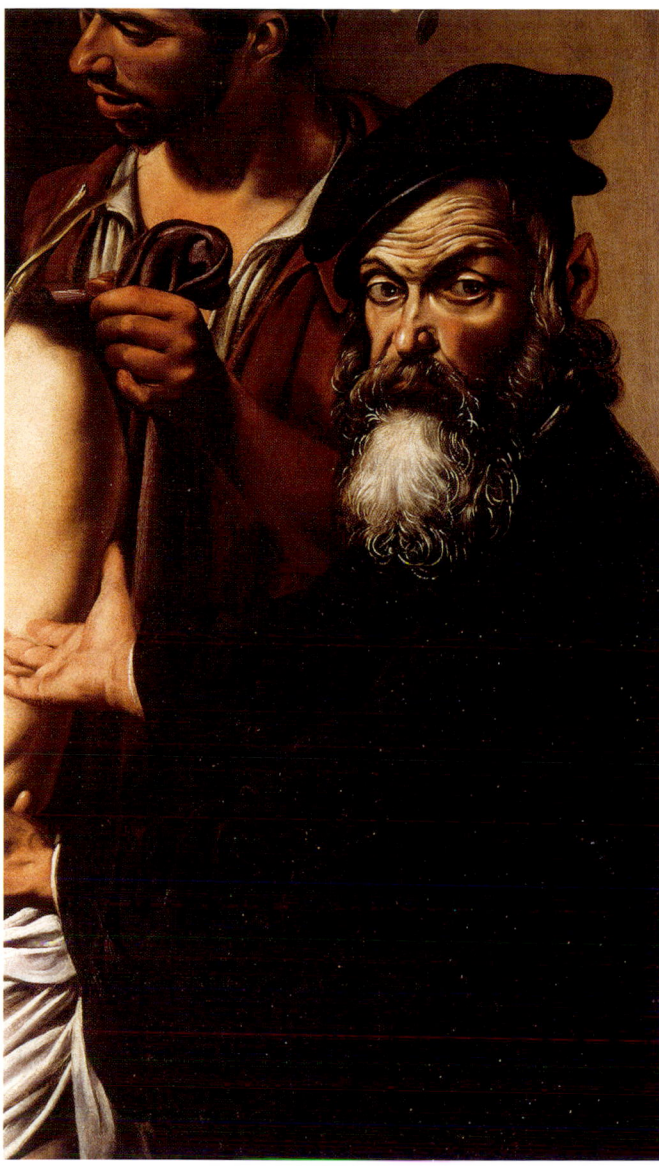

Fig. 209
Michelangelo Merisi da Caravaggio, *Ecce Homo*, Galleria di Palazzo Rosso, Genoa, oil on canvas, 128 x 103 cm., detail.

Tuscan verses to burlesque the sculptor because he "has an unstoppable tongue, and spoke ill of the other artists and Michelangelo."[54] (Analogously, in his 1649 *Vite*, Baglione relates that Caravaggio "came to speak ill of all the painters, past and present").[55] When Baccio's *Hercules and Cacus* was finally unveiled to the Florentines, the work was severely criticized and ridiculed. Impatient to know whether the sculptural group had met with the audience's approval, Baccio sent a "pedant" to spy on people's comments. Here is Vasari's account of this episode:

53   Vasari, 5:244: "Per la qual cosa venuto agli orecchi di maestro Andrea tutto quel che detto aveva Baccio di lui, egli come savio lo riprese amorevolmente, dicendo che l'opere si fanno con le mani, non con la lingua, e che 'l buon disegno non sta nelle carte, ma nella perfezzione dell'opera finita nel sasso, e nel fine ch'e' dovesse parlare di lui nell'avvenire con altro rispetto. Ma Baccio rispondendogli superbamente molte parole ingiuriose, non potette maestro Andrea più tollerare, e corsegli addosso per ammazzarlo."

54   Ibidem, 5:249: "Da questo caso del marmo invitati alcuni, feciono versi toscani e latini ingegnosamente mordendo Baccio, il quale, per esser loquacissimo e dir male degli altri artefici e di Michelagnolo, era odiato."

55   Baglione, 138. See Chapter 11.

As this pedant heard only criticism, he returned home sadly, and to Baccio's question he replied that all unanimously lambasted his giants [the *Hercules and Cacus* group] and that nobody liked them. "And what do you think about them?" asked Baccio. The pedant answered: "I say that they are good and I would like them to please you." And Baccio said: "I don't want you to like them. Go ahead and criticize them, too, since, as you may remember, I never speak good of anyone, and the same applies to me."[56]

Vasari stigmatized Baccio's pretentiousness and disclosed his artistic failures in countless other anecdotes. Baccio's sense of superiority manifested itself constantly in his criticism of other works and despite his boasts he rarely achieved a work that lived up to his claims; either because he was unable to complete them, or because his carving techniques failed him in the execution of his drawings, Baccio's sculptures never turned out as he intended. The most telling example of this disproportion between "telling" and "making" in Baccio's art is found in the comment of an unidentified lady about his statue of an *Eve*. There is no doubt that Vasari took great pleasure in recounting this anecdote:

> A noblewoman, who happened to be looking at these sculptures [Bandinelli's *Adam and Eve*], was requested to give her advice about the nudes. She replied: "I cannot judge those of men." She was then asked to give her opinion about the woman. She answered that she found two good features in Eve that were particularly commendable: she was white and firm. By pretending ingeniously to extol the artificer and his work, the lady covertly criticized and burlesqued them, commending the sculpture for those features of the female body that one should instead refer to the matter of marble, and that are true in the marble, but certainly do not apply to the artwork and its artifice, for these kinds of praises do not praise the artifice. Therefore, that keen lady showed that, in her opinion, nothing but the marble could be commended in the sculpture. [57]

I do not believe that any other appraisal could be more destructive of, and disrespectful to, Baccio's memory than the one enunciated by Vasari's lady—assuming she ever existed and was not an *alter ego* of the malignant biographer. The mere praise of the sculpture's firmness and whiteness nullifies the artwork's value at its core. If indeed sculpture—according to both Michelangelo and Vasari—purifies raw matter into an ideal form, the worst that could happen to a sculptor would be to extract matter out of matter, by producing marble out of marble. Between Baccio's verbal pretense to surpass Michelangelo and his manual inability to transform the marble into "idea," there is a wide chasm of artistic inefficacy and therefore much space for parody. From this point of view, Baccio's figure embodies the discrepancies between the artist's aspirations and their fulfillment in the final artwork. But how does this artistic insufficiency—the short circuit between the artist's

56   Ibidem, 5:254-5: "Desiderando lui sapere ciò che dell'opera sua si diceva, mandò in piazza un pedante, il quale teneva in casa, dicendo che non mancasse di riferirgli il vero di ciò che udiva dire. Il pedante non udendo altro che male, tornato malinconoso a casa, e domandato da Baccio, rispose che tutti per una voce biasimano i giganti e che e' non piacciono loro. 'E tu che ne di'?' disse Baccio. Rispose: 'Dicone bene e che e' mi piacciono per farvi piacere.' 'Non vo' ch'e' ti piacciano—disse Baccio—e di' pur male ancora tu, che come tu puoi ricordarti, io non dico mai bene di nessuno'."

57   Ibidem, 5:267: "Fu domandata una gentildonna, la quale s'era posta a guardare queste statue, da alcuni gentiluomini quello che le paresse di questi corpi ignudi. Rispose: 'degli uomini non posso dare giudizio.' Ed essendo pregata che della donna dicesse il parer suo, rispose che le pareva che quella Eva avesse due buone parti da essere commendata assai, perciò che ella è bianca e soda. Ingegnosamente mostrando di lodare, biasimò copertamente e morse l'artefice e l'artifizio suo, dando alla statua quelle lode proprie de' corpi femminili, le quali è necessario intendere della materia del marmo, e di lui son vere, ma dell'opera e dell'artifizio no, perciò che l'artifizio quelle lode non lodano. Mostrò addunque quella valente donna che altro non si poteva secondo lei lodare in quella statua se non il marmo."

idea and its concrete embodiment in the artwork—accord with the representation of Caravaggio as Pilate in the role of the *dottore*?

In the Introduction to Part Four, I showed that artistic invention in early seventeenth-century Rome was a matter of metaphysics. Through his enlightened intellect, the artist could bring light to the deep abysses of man's finitude and momentarily re-conquer God's vision. Significantly, he could witness the sacred *istoria* with his mind's eye and represent it in its pristine truth, as it transpired, albeit sometimes embellished with the accessories of righteous verisimilitude. By depicting himself as Pilate, Caravaggio appropriated the praetor's formula of the *Ecce Homo*, bending it to artistic purposes. With the artist's truest "act of painting"—that is, by showing, not by telling—he prompts the viewer to see his work, and more particularly Christ, the hero of his sacred *istoria*: "behold the man and how truly I have depicted him." Yet, unlike Pilate, Caravaggio-the-painter is deeply cognizant of his *istoria*'s meaning and implications; he knows that "the man" he has depicted is not just a man or, for that matter, a historical figure, but a deity. And indeed, as an excellent painter—Caravaggio considered himself as such, a "*valentuomo*"—he is perfectly entitled to represent God in the form of man, as theorists and painters insistently claimed at the time.

However, by disguising himself as a *dottore*, Caravaggio insinuates that the "act of painting" through which he, as a painter, comes to show God to beholders, however excellently it might be achieved, reduces itself to an irrefutable truism: the "man" who represents divinity cannot possibly be anything but a "represented man"—that is, mere representation. Moreover, Caravaggio's self-portrait and its insertion into the sacred *istoria* as a parodic "anchorman" disclose and accentuate the fictiveness of Christ's representation. Indeed, the beholder's direct involvement in the scene through the author's implicit invitation constitutes an obvious device of metafiction, and as such it clues the viewer into the artwork's self-referentiality. Nevertheless, the painter's presence in his own painting, inasmuch as it assumes the appearance of self-parody, dislodges, instead of upholding, the principle of authorship by revealing the intrinsic flaws of both the author and the creative process leading to the work's achievement: the gap between the artist's claims and his final product.

Paradoxically, like the *dottore*, the painter cannot go beyond Christ's humanity and its representation; for all his efforts, the divine remains inaccessible, or rather, can be accessed exclusively through fiction's encoding. Therein lies the original flaw, or sin, of a metaphysical conception of religious painting. For this reason, like Baccio's, the work of Pilate/Caravaggio eventually eschews any artist's most ambitious aspiration in representing Christ: unveiling divinity. The multi-layered facets of Caravaggio's disguise as Pilate-the-*dottore*-the-petulant-artist together configure a coherent artistic message: the impossible banality of representing Christ and the tragicomedy of being a Christian painter. It is probably no coincidence that Caravaggio, in ridiculing his and his fellows' dreams of pictorial excellence, resorted, among others, to Baccio's persona, the anti-Michelangelo by definition. As I have demonstrated in the previous chapter, Caravaggio's Vatican *Entombment* reads like the vibrant manifesto of the painter's challenge to, parity with, and superiority over Michelangelo. In the Genoa *Ecce Homo*, Caravaggio's association with Baccio both complements and contradicts that manifesto: the pretense of surpassing Michelangelo is virtually depicted as pretension. Given Caravaggio's deep-embedded feelings of identification with the other Michelangelo, the parody of his own artistic persona as staged in the Genoa picture may signal a dramatic break in self-esteem and artistic ambition on his part. All in all, Longhi was perhaps right to describe the *Ecce Homo* as a page of black autobiography in Caravaggio's painting.

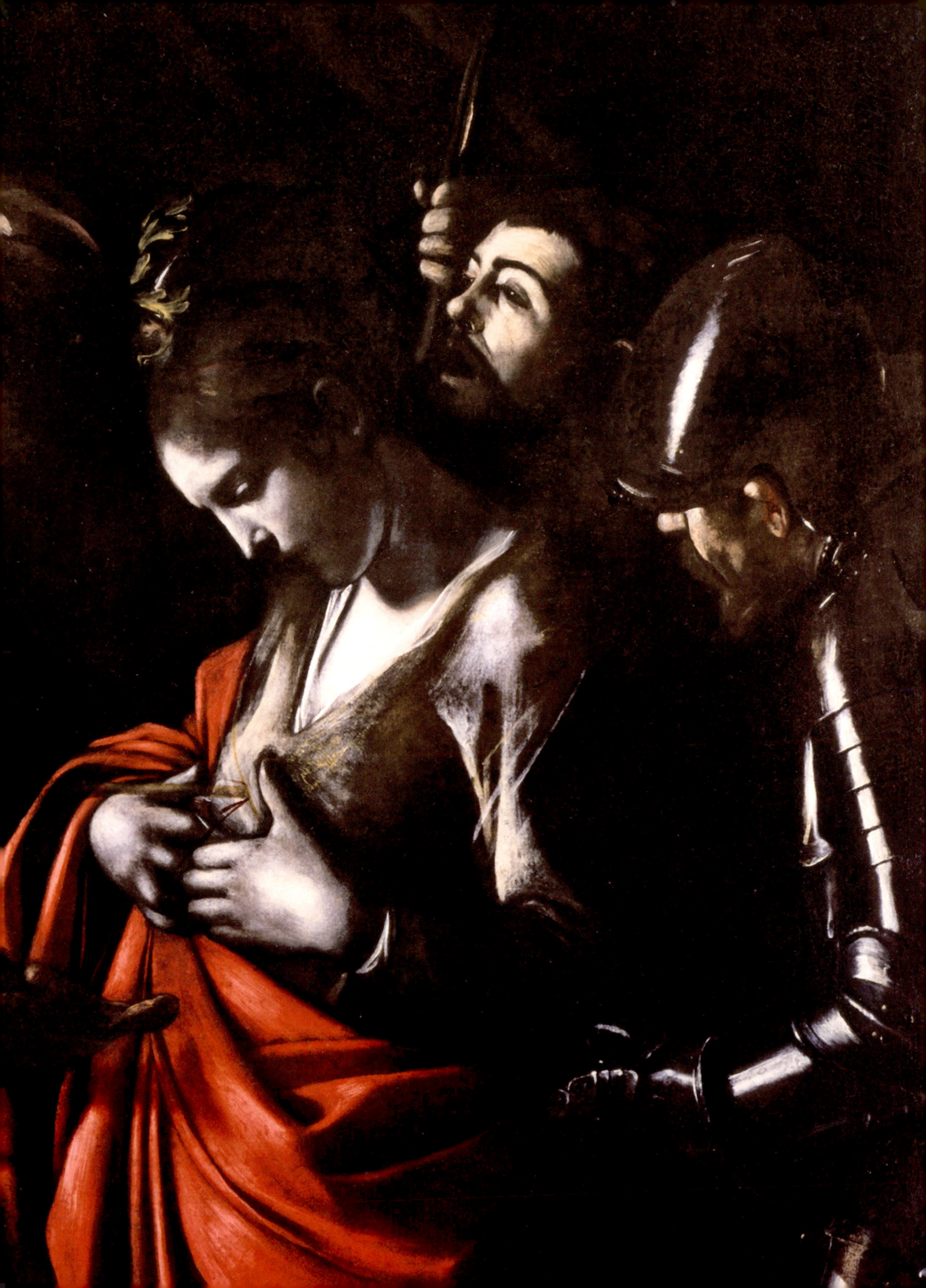

PART FIVE

The Work of Memory: Variations on Themes and Telescopic Parallels in Caravaggio's Late Pictorial Narratives

Artistic Memory and the Invention of the Istoria

In his 1590 *Idea del tempio della pittura*, Giovan Paolo Lomazzo describes the advantages for, and effects on, the artist of a paramount spiritual faculty that he names "discretion." In general, discretion is the mind's self-reflective capacity not only for evaluating and judging, but also for coordinating experience and knowledge in view of fulfilling determinate aims pre-established by discretion itself. In a sense, discretion is analogous to Zuccari's intellective *disegno*, although it is not confined to invention; it is a self-consciously glowing lantern that presides over any human intellectual and practical operation. As a faculty, though, discretion needs to be regularly and assiduously exercised, and only the most excellent artists are truly able to master it with appropriateness and success:

> Only through [discretion] are we able to know viscerally and clearly what we are doing, and from this cognition stem the purity of man's ingenuity and the steadiness of man's judgment, and eventually a true and reasonable method of operating. By exercising it, we come to understand how important the faculty of knowing ourselves is, and then how much authority and greatness art's perfection embodies, for the parts of the soul that God bestowed upon us are able to make resurface the beauty and profundity of the ideas funneled deep inside us by the supreme Idea. The more clearly the supreme Idea manifests itself to us, the more clearly and purely we enter its chambers, once they are relinquished by ignorance's pitch-black darkness.[1]

Discretion allows artists to avoid mistakes, to attain perfection, and achieve unconditional praise. To ensure the artwork's excellence, discretion step by step and persistently enlightens the processes of artistic invention, conception, and execution. Therefore, discretion is omnipresent and difficult both to improve and preserve. Among discretion's principal tasks there is an unexpected one: to set and keep alight in the artist's mind the memory of works produced by the most excellent artists of the past. Here is how Lomazzo explains discretion's mnemonic role:

---

1 Lomazzo, 1:254: "Imperoché per lei sola possiamo conoscere fin dalle viscere chiaramente ciò che facciamo e da questa cognizione ne risulta poi la purità dell'ingegno e la stabilità del giudicio e finalmente la vera e ragionevol via di operare. Nella qual essercitandoci, vegniamo ad intendere quanto importi la podestà che abbiamo di conoscere noi medesimi ed appresso quanta sia l'auttorità e grandezza che è nella perfezione dell'arte, potendosi dalle parti dell'animo, concesseci da Iddio, fare scaturire la bellezza e profondità delle idee colà pervenute per dritti canali da la suprema Idea, la quale tanto più chiaramente ci si rappresenta quanto noi più purgati e mondi penetriamo alle stanze sue, sgombre dalle tenebre oscure dell'ignoranza."

Moreover, discretion unceasingly represents to our memory art's commended and excellent works, from which we extract not only the way of imitating, but also of inventing the things and subjects of our paintings. This representation over and again ignites our desire both to operate and endow our works with the greatest excellence that all the artistry and the most intense effort of man's ingenuity can offer. In exactly the same manner soldiers, although they possess the principles of war's art, by reading the glorious deeds accomplished by Caesar, Scipio, and Hannibal, grow more eager both to combat and achieve illustrious exploits, just as did Alexander inspired by Achilles, and Caesar upon seeing Alexander's statue in Egypt.[2]

In Chapter 11 I showed to what degree Michelangelo's example stimulated Caravaggio to surpass both his predecessor's achievements and his own previous inventions in the Vatican *Entombment*. Emulation is a key concept in the theory and practice of early modern art, and its scope and effects are enormous. But this topic has been extensively addressed by scholars, and I have dwelt on its importance throughout this volume. I shall therefore examine another crucial, if often overlooked, component of Renaissance and seventeenth-century artistic invention: memory. More specifically, I will concern myself not only with the ways in which artists prey and elaborate upon patterns, schemas, and motifs from other masters' designs, but overall with the procedure whereby artists over time return to their own inventions and cash in on them through adjustments and deft re-employment. In accordance with the demanding principles of the early modern *istoria*, artists ought to adorn their works with harmonious variety, so that repetitiousness and compositional automatisms are ordinarily perceived in a bad light and therefore banished. In other words, artists must make sure that, within their own output, the abundance of their imagination and the multifariousness of their visual concepts constantly transpire. To put it more bluntly, artists are strongly discouraged from reusing their own ideas unabashedly and without restriction, and any patent contravention of this tacit norm is severely censured. In his 1678 *Felsina Pittrice*, Carlo Cesare Malvasia records the fierce criticism by Guido Reni's supporters of Francesco Albani, accused, among other things, of repeating himself clumsily and endlessly:

> In the matter of invention, on which he [Albani] insisted so much and of which he was overly proud, he did not turn out to be as abundant and inventive as he claimed, always returning to the same inventions and availing himself of the same concepts. For this reason, when he sent off his paintings, he sought to know if, and was afraid that, the same representation might already exist in that city. (…) His little Christs adoring the mysteries of the Passion, his Expulsions of Adam and Eve from Eden, his little Annunciates with the beautiful angel were so frequent, and so numerous were his sleeping Venuses, his bathing Dianas, his Galatheas in the sea, his Danaes lying in bed, his Dancing Cupids and similar inventions, that no one could boast to be the sole and legitimate owner of these compositions. Not only in many galleries in Italy, but also in a few cabinets in France, Holland, and England could one find two or three replicas by him of the same small composition, (…) so that not without reason, in passing through

2   Ibidem, 1:254-5: "Questa di più ci torna e rappresenta alla memoria l'opre lodate ed eccellenti dell'arte, onde veniamo non solamente a ritrarne il modo dell'imitare, ma anco dell'inventare le cose ed i soggetti delle nostre pitture, e con tal rappresentazione si accende maggiormente in noi il desiderio d'operare e di dare all'opere nostre quella maggiore eccellenza che possa darsi con tutta l'arte e co 'l maggior sforzo dell'ingegno umano, in quella guisa appunto che i soldati, ancor che abbino l'arte descritta della guerra, nondimeno, leggendo i gloriosi fatti che in essa hanno adoperato Cesare, Scipione ed Annibale, divengono più accesi e di combattere e di far imprese gloriose; come faceva Alessandro per Achille, e Cesare per la statua che vide di Alessandro in Egitto."

Bologna, the very erudite Monsieur de Piles said that, once one has seen a single work by Albani, one could declare to have seen all of them, since they were always the same.[3]

As Malvasia maliciously (or objectively) implies by producing first-hand testimony, memory on several occasions tricked the old Albani and wreaked havoc on his reputation. In a letter of 26 November 1658 to his former disciple Girolamo Bonini, Albani urged his younger colleague to tell him if "by any chance, [he] in Rome had come across one of his original Hermaphrodites and Lethean Cupids," as he had already begun two canvases with these subjects that might have been suitable for a Roman patron. Insistently, Albani asked Bonini "please, write, discover, inform me if you found these subjects replicated. I know that I have already varied that Diana from the one you saw in Venice." And to justify his compulsive propensity to self-replication, Albani reminded Bonini that he was eighty years old, and that Titian, to his knowledge, executed at least four *Magdalenes*, a not so subtle way of saying that even great masters are forced to repeat themselves.[4] Of course, Albani omitted the fact that, in Titian's case, the paintings originated as replicas deliberately commissioned as such by patrons. Be that as it may, Malvasia knew that Albani's statement was hardly tenable, not because he disapproved of replicas—far from it—but because, by resorting again and again to the same inventions, Albani had betrayed the barrenness of his pictorial imagination and laid himself bare to public mockery. In a sense, nothing was worse than being caught in the act of replicating oneself for lack of memory. To fully understand how foolish Albani's attitude was, one can turn to Michelangelo's counterexample. In his 1568 biography of the great master, Giorgio Vasari records:

> Michelangelo possessed a firm and vast memory. By seeing someone else's work but once he could store it in his memory and employ it in such a manner that almost no one was ever able to realize [what he had accomplished]. Nor did he ever execute any of his works as similar to another, for he remembered what he had already done. In his young age, as he was hanging out with his fellow painters, [the group] bet a dinner on who was better at making a figure wholly bereft of drawing, unskillful, and akin to the doodles that ignorant people trace to soil walls. And in this task, Michelangelo used his memory. He remembered that he had seen one of these scribbles on a wall, and reproduced it just as if he was standing in front of it, thereby outsmarting all the other painters: a difficult endeavor to pull off for a man so replete with drawing's [knowledge and practice], and used to [picking out] select things.[5]

3 Malvasia, 2:262-3: "Che nell'invenzione, in che tanto premea e di che troppo vantavasi, non riusciva quell'abbondante e copioso che si presumeva, tornando sempre a' stessi rappresentati e de' medesimi concetti valendosi; ché però ei stesso, mandando via quadri, non si assicurasse e temesse non vi fosse lo stesso pensiero in quella città. (…) esser que' suoi Cristini adoranti della Passione i misteri, quelle sue Cacciate de' primi parenti dal paradiso, quelle sue Nonziatine dal bell'angelo così frequenti, tante poi le Veneri addormentate, le Diane al bagno, le Galatee nel mare, le Danae nel letto, i Balli d'Amorini o simili, che più non vi era chi d'esserne possessor legitimo e singolare pregiar si potesse; in molte galerie d'Italia non solo, ma in qualche gabinetto ancora della Francia, dell'Inghilterra, dell'Olanda ed altrove, essersi ritrovate due e tre repliche d'un istesso quadretto; (…) onde non senza ragione, in passar per Bologna, lasciasse detto il dottissimo monsieur de Piles che, miratasi dell'Albani una sol'opra, tutte si potea dire aver veduto, essendo sempre le stesse."

4 Ibidem, 2:263: "onde, scrivendo sotto li 26 di novembre 1658 al suo diletto Bonini a Roma per certi quadri, detto

trovarsi duoi Ermafroditi ed Amori, lo pregava ad avvisarlo 'se abbia per sorte veduto per Roma qualche altro suo Ermafrodito originale ed Amori Letei, che di questi ne ha duoi principiati i quali si confano con le misure mandate delle cornici del Carrandini,' soggiongendo in fine: 'scrivete, scoprite, avvisatemi vi prego se i soggetti descritti si vedono duplicati; so di avere variata la Diana da quella che già vedesti in Venezia; datemi parte, perché li 80 anni che ho, ho dipinto molto, e Tiziano fece più di quattro Maddalene che so io, ed avvertite il vostro vecchio Albano.'

5 Vasari, 6:114-5: "È stato Michelagnolo di una tenace e profonda memoria, che nel vedere le cose altrui una sol volta l'ha ritenute sì fattamente e servitosene in una maniera che nessuno se n'è mai quasi accorto; né ha mai fatto cosa nessuna delle sue che riscontri l'una con l'altra, perché si ricordava di tutto quello che aveva fatto. Nella sua gioventù, sendo con gli amici sua pittori, giuocorno una cena a chi faceva una figura che non avessi niente di disegno, che fussi goffa, simile a que' fantocci che fanno coloro che non sanno ed imbrattano le mura. Qui si valse della memoria, perché ricordatosi aver

405

Vasari's insight into, and anecdote about, Michelangelo's memory have not yet attracted the attention they deserve. First of all, Vasari clearly states that Michelangelo, like all the other painters of his time, stole other artists' ideas for inspiration; they remained engraved in his memory and eventually redeployed upon elaboration with such mastery that no one could establish the degree and quality of his larceny. On the contrary, his re-appropriation of other masters' designs was so radical that Michelangelo could rightly claim that he had re-invented them.[6] Secondly, Michelangelo's memory was highly selective; it retained only the impression of works that might be thought of as canonical. In order to imitate a vandal's graffiti, he was compelled to block out the entire patrimony of images hoarded in his memory by concentrating on an insignificant doodle he had randomly discerned in the past. More important, even the execution of an artless figure is a matter of style. Without the scribble's template, Michelangelo would apparently have been unable to draw with propriety the artistically inconceivable: lines and contours "wholly bereft of drawing." This demonstrates how basic and indispensable the faculty of memory was for early modern artists. If they lacked the aptitude to select, cache, and conjure up through recollection the matrices of images necessary for invention, artists were either doomed to failure or subject to ridicule. Like Vasari and—implicitly—Malvasia, Lomazzo, too, regards artistic memory as a concrete implement and a moral encouragement toward creation; it is an all-pervasive phenomenon inherent in both the artist's imagination and practice, a habit that does not subside after the initial phase of indenture, but rather tends to—or should—relentlessly increase. Memory, in fact, constitutes an invaluable source of knowledge both on a theoretical and a practical level. In his life of the Carracci, Malvasia relates an interesting episode in this connection:

> As Agostino discoursed with various Roman gentlemen about the great knowledge of ancient sculptors, and especially about the unrivaled statue of Laocoön, getting carried away as usual in his enthusiasm, he was surprised that Annibale (who indeed disliked chatting) did not say anything, as if he did not know, or duly value, such an excellence. But at once, Annibale drew the statue from memory on a wall most precisely, thus demonstrating that he considered and appreciated it, and laughing, he said (…) "we painters should talk with our hands," thereby mocking Agostino, who boasted that he spoke elegantly and also composed poems.[7]

On the whole, scholars have insisted on the dichotomy between theory and practice that Malvasia's anecdote presupposes, but they have rarely touched on the pivotal role that memory—accurate memory—plays in this passage. And yet, Annibale's demonstration was valid and compelling only insofar as his memory did not fail him in evoking the exact diagram of the *Laocoön*. Memory indeed, if it does not substitute for discourse, at least provided Annibale with a condensed, mute argument: the drawing on the wall—an antithetical reminiscence of Michelangelo's artistic doodle?—in its precision proves that Annibale possessed a deep knowledge of the sculpture's proportions and configuration. Put otherwise, the drawing encapsulates the principles and rules of artistic perfection contained in the antique; its confident recollection guarantees the solidity of

visto in un muro una di queste gofferie, la fece come se l'avessi avuta dinanzi di tutto punto, e superò tutti que' pittori: cosa difficile in uno uomo tanto pieno di disegno, avvezzo a cose scelte, che ne potessi uscir netto."

6 For Michelangelo's elaboration of figures and motifs over time, see more recently Brothers 2008, 9-43.

7 Malvasia, 1:480: "Quando, discorrendo con molti signori Agostino in Roma del gran sapere de gli antichi statuari, ed in spezie della insuperabil statua del Laocoonte, e con tanta

energia, conforme il suo uso, vi si riscaldava, con istupore che Annibale (nemico delle ciarle) nulla dicesse, quasi che un tanto valore non conoscesse o almeno al pari del dovuto non stimasse, ed ei ben presto così giusta con un carbone la disegnò a mente sopra il muro, per dar a divedere s'ei l'aveva osservata e se la stimava, disse ridendo (scrisse il Mosini) 'noi altri dipintori abbiamo a parlar con le mani,' pungendo in tal guisa Agostino che di ben parlare e di comporre anche in poesia pregiavasi." This anecdote is first related by Agucchi, 153-4. See also Summercale 2000, 286, note 452.

Annibale's artistic knowledge and manual ability and, if one trusts Lomazzo's viewpoint, serves as a touchstone of excellence for Annibale's own inventions, past, present, and future. One cannot satisfactorily comprehend the substantiality and pervasiveness of memory in the creative processes of early modern artists without examining the pedagogic mechanisms through which the use of memory was taught from the very beginning of the artistic apprenticeship. Besides the innate talent of tracing the letters of the alphabet with sureness and elegance, Giovan Paolo Armenini in his 1586 *De' veri precetti della pittura* demands that the normally prepubescent apprentice also be able to handle deftly the drawing tools—pen, black chalk, sanguine and so forth. Although Armenini does not say anything in this regard, the young disciple is likewise supposed to reproduce the drawings furnished by his master. Once he becomes well acquainted with the technical aspects of drawing and, sometimes, of coloring, the would-be painter, according to Armenini, is required to copy the inventions of canonical, ancient or Renaissance, masters:

> The first and most general rule will always be to copy the most beautiful and masterfully crafted things that are closest to the good works of ancient sculptors, and forging one's own habit by continuously studying them, one must possess them so deeply as to be able actually to evoke one or more of these compositions as the occasion arises, and this familiarity must be such that the goodness of antiquity that one has studied marvelously comes to the fore not only in one's first sketches, but also in one's finished drawings and, accordingly, also in one's larger paintings, which I do not find very difficult to a certain point. In fact, by continuously working and continuously copying well-done things one is caused to make one's own works very well with certain rule, and this is certainly true since imitation is nothing but a diligent and judicious consideration that one applies in observing [the great masters' works] in order to become similar to other excellent artificers.[8]

Needless to say, if one excepts Rome, there were not many cities in early modern Italy in which first-rate antiques could be studied in overwhelming abundance. For this reason, Armenini recommends the usage of reduced wax or plaster casts, astonishingly cheap, as he puts it, easy for artists to carry about and hence fit to be proposed for further reproduction. Armenini himself had seen "studios and chambers, very well organized, filled with such material, as for instance in Milan, Genoa, Venice, Parma, Mantua, Florence, Bologna, Pesaro, Urbino, Ravenna, and other minor cities."[9] Because of Armenini's fondness for antiquity, he might be exaggerating the importance of ancient models in the apprentices' training, for it is evident from other early modern sources that prints were systematically copied and re-copied in early-modern workshops.[10] In any event, Armenini

8 Armenini, 76-7: "Ma della prima generalissima ed universal regola sarà di sempre ritrar le cose che sono più belle, più dotte e più alle buone opere de gli antichi scultori prossimane, e sopra di esse con lo studio continuo fattovi l'abito, ne sia possessor talmente ch'egli possa rapportar una o più composizioni ad ogni sua occasione in atto, e questo li sia famigliare in modo che quel buono dell'antico ch'egli avrà studiato gli apparisca mirabilmente, io dico così ne' primi schizzi, come ne' dissegni da lui finiti ed in conseguenza nelle pitture ancora grandi, il che io non lo trovo molto difficile infino a un certo segno. Conciosiacosaché il continuo fare e il continuo ritrarre le cose ben fatte è cagione che si facciano le sue per certa regola benissimo, ed è certo così, poiché l'imitazione non è altro che una diligente e giudiziosa considerazione che si usa per poter divenire, col mezzo delle osservazioni, simile a gli altri eccellenti."

9 Ibidem, 79: "Io ne ho veduto studi e camere piene di tal materia e formate benissimo, sì come in Milano, in Genova, in Venezia, in Parma, in Mantoa, in Firenze, in Bologna, in Pesaro, in Urbino, in Ravenna ed in altre minor città."

10 Malvasia, 1:63, compares prints with books and clearly states that artists' instruction is based on the knowledge and diffusion of prints: "Troppo grande è il beneficio che venne a sentirne la letteraria repubblica, né minore l'utile che ogni dì ne ricava la pittorica scuola, resa per essa, non meno che da gl'impressi libri da' stampati rami, di tutto ciò ch'a lei più s'appartiene pienamente informata ed istrutta. Ora, se mentre a favor de' pittori doppiamente in tal guisa gemono i torchi, con le intagliate carte assai più che co' gl'impressi volumi si consigliano essi e si reggono."

notes that even great painters, such as Perino del Vaga, used to diligently copy a select corpus of other masters' compositions:

> It is perhaps prudent (…) of everyone to always abide by a diversity of best things and be familiar with, and knowledgeable about, them so as to be able to vary others' figures in such a manner that they will appear as born out of one's own [mind], as I remember among other things was the case with many drawings that Perino [del Vaga] left after his death. (…) I saw [drawings] by his hand [reproducing] a great number of the works that Raphael, his former master, had painted, that were drawn in black chalk, as well as some *ignudi* from [Michelangelo's] Judgment. These drawings, as one could see, were modified by his soft style in such a manner that one would have said that they had sprung in, and been invented by, him rather than copied from others' [inventions]. And these were not the only ones, but there were also many sketches of prints, executed by both Italians and Germans, as well as a myriad of columns and bas-reliefs, statues and grotesques after the antique, alongside other things that are dispersed and concealed in Rome, but not unknown to me. In copying them, Perino changed now this and now that detail, and he added to, took away from, or enriched those that were broken or not truly effective. In sum, he transformed them with his beautiful style so much that it was most difficult for experts to determine from where he had derived them.[11]

It is curious that, among Perino's drawings of ancient sculpture, and works by Raphael and Michelangelo, there were also "sketches" of Italian and northern prints. One would expect that an accomplished artist such as Perino would not have availed himself of "German" inventions to the point of reproducing and storing them for further use, and it is certainly a pity that Armenini does not mention the names of these northern engravers. More importantly, the process of copying is clearly assimilated, in Perino's case, to a creative process: Raphael or Michelangelo, Marcantonio and Dürer, the Trajan Column and the bas-reliefs from the Arch of Constantine not only supplied Perino with a tremendous repertory of patterns, schemas, and motifs, but were also exploited as catalysts for immediate reinvention. By dint of elaboration, through additions, expunctions, and adornments, the select prototypes of antiquity and the Renaissance became unrecognizable, albeit intrinsically correct and legitimate because "well-founded."

One would be wrong to believe that Perino's drawings were intended to replace the work of memory. The very act of copying is the means by which artists penetrate the innermost structures of canonical artworks and impress their models upon their minds. The almost automatic practice of transcribing a print or a painting, a drawing or a sculpture allows artists to decode and encode, but especially to digest and incorporate those prototypes that, as Armenini phrases it, will resurface, transmuted, during the creative process and onward, until the final stage of the artwork's execution. The discretion—Lomazzo's term—in adjusting, transforming, and occulting

---

11 Armenini, 80-2: "Ma egli è forsi anco bene (…) tenersi (come è detto) sempre alle diverse cose migliori ed esser prattico e fondato di maniera su quelle che ridur possa le altrui figure che paiano esser nate da lui, sì come io bene mi tengo in mente fra i tanti li molti dissegni che ci rimase di Perino dopo la sua morte, (…) io vidi di sua man propria una gran parte dell'opere ch'avea dipinte Raffaello, già suo maestro, le quali erano dissegnate di lapis nero, ed alcuni ignudi del Giudizio, li quali dissegni si vedevano essere con tal arte ridotti alla sua dolce maniera che si potea dir più tosto quelli esser da lui nati e trovati che ritratti da altrui. E non era solamente questi ch'io dico, ma vi erano ancora di molti schizzi cavati da più dissegni di stampe, ch'erano invenzione d'italiani e di tedeschi, sì come ci era ancora un numero infinito di pilli, di partimenti, di statue, di grottesche pur cavate dalle antiche, con altre cose tali che sono sparse ed occulte per Roma e non ignote a noi; dove che esso, nel ritrarle, le veniva tuttavia mutando quando una cosa e quando un'altra, ed a quelle ch'erano rotte o non molto gagliarde gli aggiungeva, li levava e le aricchiva, ed insomma le riduceva in modo tale, con quella sua leggiadra maniera, ch'era cosa difficile da' ben prattichi a conoscere di dove egli cavate le avesse."

the traces of other masters' influence is the key element to achieving originality. As I have already remarked, the practice of copying, although it necessarily decreases over time as a result of the artist's maturity and richness of repertory, is never abandoned, or at least should be integrated into the everyday process of invention. In his *Felsina Pittrice*, Malvasia relates how drawing from life and remembering their own live models by duplicating them on paper was an integral part of Agostino and Annibale Carracci's daily training:

> In the evening, upon returning from drawing nudes at the Academy, before sitting at the table for dinner, they would retreat to their rooms and, evoking in their memory the exact posture they had previously drawn, strive to retain its recollection by representing it on a small sheet summarily, and it turned out to be even more intense and powerful than the original from life, as one can see in the few extant drawings among the numerous ones they threw on the fire.[12]

And in this regard, Armenini asserts:

> This study consists in continuously prodding and awakening one's mind [by making] diverse sketches on paper, which one must execute in different manners, now inventing something by oneself, now imitating and appropriating others' inventions, in different ways and media, and this in order for [these sketches] to be available for any necessity, besides the fact that in this way one obviously keeps one's memory alive and reminiscent of things once seen. [This is also to say] that this ordinary practice works wonders for the ability of the hand, which keeps itself most assured, agile, and prompt in any circumstance. [13]

The numerous methods through which artists resort to, and sift through, their own drawings in search of inspiration and new artistic solutions require further, more detailed study. I will only consider here the examples of Raphael and Michelangelo as interpreted by Armenini, since, for all their affinities, they contrast with one another, thereby constituting a twofold paradigm of artistic inventiveness:

> It is said that Raphael used another, very simple procedure. He displayed many drawings by his own hand among those that were more consonant with the subject matter at issue, of which he had already conceived a great part in his mind. And looking now at one and then at another, he kept drawing most swiftly, and in this manner he formed all his inventions, which seemed to occur because his mind, through this procedure, was assisted and enriched by the multitude of drawings.[14]

12   Malvasia, 1:468: "Ritornati la sera dall'Accademia del nudo, non vedeali la cena assettarsi a tavola prima che, ritiratisi in camera, repetendo nella memoria la stessa disegnata positura, non avessero forzato la retentiva a rappresentarla su picciol foglio in compendio, come qualcuna delle tante che subito abbrugiavano se ne vede, tanto più della vera ancora risaltata e terribile."

13   Armenini, 91: "Questo studio adunque si è che si tenti e che si svegli la mente tuttavia con diverse schizzi su le carte, i quali si dee fare per più vie, e quando una e quando un'altra cosa da sé formando, e quando con l'imitare l'altrui farle sue, con diverse maniere e modi di fare e con differenti materie ancora, e questo acciò che poi le siano tutti agevoli per ogni suo bisogno, oltre che ci è manifesto quanto così si tien viva

la memoria e delle cose vedute ricordevole, ed è più di tutto mirabile d'intorno alla prattica della mano, perché si mantien sicurissima, spedita e pronta in ogni sua occorrenza per questo così usitato costume."

14   Ibidem, 92: "Dicesi poi che Raffaelle teneva un altro stile assai facile, perciò che dispiegava molti dissegni di sua mano, de quelli che li pareva che fossero più prossimani a quella materia della quale egli già gran parte n'avea concetta nella idea, ed or nell'uno or nell'altro guardando e tuttavia velocemente dissegnando, così veniva a formar tutta la sua invenzione, il che pareva che nascesse per esser la mente, per tal maniera, aiutata e fatta ricca per la moltitudine di quelli." An interpretation of this passage is also offered by Nagel 2010, 23-4.

As scholars have already pointed out, Armenini's interpretation of Raphael's technique may rely on a passage of Ludovico Dolce's 1557 *Dialogo della pittura*:

> I shall also stress that, when the painter in his first sketches puts to the test the fantasies that the *istoria* arouses in his mind, he must not content himself with a single invention, but ought to create many inventions and then choose the most effectual by pondering all the things together and each one separately. Raphael himself used to do so, and he was so prolifically inventive that he visualized an *istoria* in four or six diverse ways, and all were graceful and did the trick well.[15]

The juxtaposition of these two passages by Armenini and Dolce demonstrates the originality of Armenini's take on Raphael's technique of invention. Although Raphael's inventiveness as expounded by Dolce constitutes the *sine qua non* of the method through which he, according to Armenini, collated, conflated, and elaborated upon previous designs, Armenini also records the material existence of a cache replete with preconceived templates suitable for occasional redeployment and rearrangement: the equivalent of Raphael's memory treasure couched on paper. Another crucial point in Armenini's argument concerns the adaptability of Raphael's templates; in fact, they can be reused in subject matters other than, but typologically consistent with, those that they originally represented or were intended to evoke. By this, he meant to suggest the partial indeterminateness and therefore malleability of Raphael's prototypes. By the same token, there is no doubt that Raphael tinkered with his own inventions just as he used to do with those of his canonical predecessors. Raphael's fertile imagination over the years yielded a remarkable patrimony of visual concepts that, through knowledge and experience, he eventually classified as worthy prototypes in their own right: a hoard of patterns, schemas, and motifs whose ingrained plasticity permitted a vast array of novel adaptations. Michelangelo's case differs noticeably from Raphael's. To elucidate Michelangelo's technique, Armenini relates an event that he himself had witnessed when he was a young man in Rome:

> One day, finding himself behind Saint Peter's, Michelangelo bumped into a young potter from Ferrara, whom he thanked for whatever terracotta work he had gotten him to bake, and offered his services for whatever the young man would require. Assured by the words of such a man, the youth brought him a sheet of paper and asked him to draw a standing Hercules on it. Michelangelo then took the sheet and retreated under a small roof nearby where there was a bench, upon which he rested his right foot, leaning his elbow high upon his knee, his hand supporting his face, and stayed there pensive for a while. Then, he began to draw [the Hercules] and finished it rapidly, beckoning the young man, who was a little farther away, to come, and thus he gave him the drawing, left, and headed for the curia. This drawing, to the extent of my knowledge at the time, seemed to me to be so well outlined, shaded, and achieved that it was superior to any work of miniature, and greatly astonished those who had seen him doing it in such a short time, whereas it would otherwise be judged as the labor of a month, and from this example one can infer with what ease Michelangelo must have produced his inventions.[16]

---

15 Dolce, 128: "Voglio ancora avertire che, quando il pittore va tentando ne' primi schizzi le fantasie che genera nella sua mente la istoria, non si dee contentar d'una sola, ma trovar più invenzioni, e poi fare iscelta di quella che meglio riesce, considerando tutte le cose insieme e ciascuna separatamente, come soleva il medesimo Rafaello, il quale fu tanto ricco d'invenzione che faceva sempre a quattro e sei modi, differenti l'uno dall'altro, una istoria, e tutti avevano grazia e stavano bene."

16 Armenini, 92-3: "Conciosiaché un dì, essendo egli dietro la chiesa di San Pietro, s'incontrò in un giovane ferrarese

As Armenini's anecdote on Michelangelo follows immediately after his passage on Raphael's technique of "collation" and "conflation," one may legitimately wonder in what way Michelangelo's drawing for the Ferrarese potter might be indicative of the master's method of invention. In his wandering through Rome, Michelangelo in fact does not carry any stock of drawings that might spark his imagination; yet, upon mere reflection, he comes up with a Hercules that, besides being accurately designed, is crisply and impeccably defined as if it had gone through the whole process of invention and production, thereby attaining a definitive configuration. Paradoxically, Michelangelo's mastery of drawing was so great that, at a certain moment in his career, he was able to dispense with drawing: that is, he could fast-forward the elaborate mental and practical circuitry through which artists were required to distill their ideas and reshape them into the actual artwork. Compared to Raphael's, Michelangelo's creative process could be successful only on one condition: that, in default of handy drawings, he should be able to "collate" and "conflate" the patterns and models that he had accumulated in his own memory. Michelangelo's high-speed computing of previous templates, which he kept operative through his resolute knowledge and long-lived experience, functioned as a deep-rooted habit, with instinctive and automatic certainty. It might even be assumed that Michelangelo would have despised Raphael's alleged technique of collating and conflating drawings as utterly unspiritual: as a rather sly shortcut in the divinely inspired unveiling of the artistic idea as processed by the artist's mind. At any rate, once again—and not coincidentally—Michelangelo's example supplies the best possible parallel to the technique of invention that Caravaggio seems to have followed during his final years.

That Caravaggio repeatedly copied other masters' inventions during his apprenticeship in Simone Peterzano's workshop is unquestionable. I do not know of any other kind of pedagogic training in painting practiced in early modern European studios. On the other hand, it is doubtful, and even highly unlikely, that, as Armenini prescribes, Caravaggio continued to put on paper his own inventions or copied those of others. Given the innumerable allusions to both canonical and unorthodox masters present in his work, it must be assumed that early on Caravaggio began to draw on his own memory, which must therefore have been as prodigious as Michelangelo's or Annibale Carracci's. If one considers the few traces of elaboration still detectable by X-ray or infrared in Caravaggio's pictures, one would be seriously tempted to compare his ease and assuredness in creating to those qualities of Michelangelo. Instead of couching his first inventions on paper, as Michelangelo did with his Hercules for the Ferrarese potter, Caravaggio deployed his ideas onto canvas, and it is arguable that, over time, he grew as prompt and confident as Michelangelo; in this respect, he was probably not an exception, since many other talented artists in the early modern period would have depended heavily on their own memory.

I want now to consider Caravaggio's complex usage of his own figurative repertory during his years of exile. As I have already mentioned in the introduction to Part Four, scholars have remarked on Caravaggio's frequent self-quotations at the end of his career, which they have mostly attributed to a dearth of available live models in Naples, Malta, and Sicily. I find this hypothesis unconvincing. Not only do we find in Caravaggio's late narratives figures whose physiognomies are definitely those of models, but it is also fair to postulate that, despite his vagrant life, he lacked

vasaro, il quale, ringraziato da Michel Angelo di non so che lavoro di terra, il quale gli avea fatto cuocere, li sogiunse di poi che a lui comandasse, ché volontieri lo servirebbe. Il giovene, così assicurato dalle parole di un uomo tale, li portò un foglio di carta e lo pregò che suso li dissegnasse un Ercole in piedi. Allora prese Michel Angelo quella carta e, tiratosi da parte sotto un picciol tetto che ivi era, dove era uno scanno da sedervi, sul quale postovi su il pié destro ed il gomito sul ginocchio alto, poggiatosi la mano al viso si stette pensoso un poco; dipoi si mise a dissegnar quello, il quale, finitolo in breve tempo, accennò al giovene, che ivi era poco da lunge, che egli venisse inanzi e così glielo porse e via si dipartì ed andossene verso palazzo. Il qual dissegno, per quanto io conosceva allora, mi parve così ben lineato, ombrato e finito che passava ogni uso di minio ed era uno stupor grande a quelli che ciò aveano veduto fare in così poco tempo, ché altri v'averebbe giudicato dentro la fatica di un mese, sì che si può fare da questo giudizio quanto egli doveva esser facile in far le sue invenzioni."

neither the money nor sufficient room to maintain his painting routine. Caravaggio used his own apartment in Rome as his workshop, a sparsely furnished space in which he ate and slept, kept his easel and canvases, and painted his models. He might have easily recreated the same working conditions in Naples, Malta, and Messina, if not in Syracuse. For this reason, I would argue that Caravaggio's re-employment of his own material at the time must be construed as both a normal tendency for older and more expert artists, and especially as an expansion on vital themes that he had formerly treated.

As some of these self-quotations are excerpted from their original narrative contexts and readapted to a new *istoria*, I propose to interpret these readaptations, for instance in the case of the Syracuse *Burial of Saint Lucy* or the Messina *Resurrection of Lazarus*, as telescopic parallels—that is, as pictorial devices through which Caravaggio invites the beholder not only to compare two diverse visual solutions of homologous narrative themes, but also to read the readjustments introduced by him in the light of, or via, their prototypes. In other words, paintings like *The Burial of Saint Lucy* and particularly *The Resurrection of Lazarus* subtly and almost surreptitiously carry enshrined within them aspects and reverberations of Caravaggio's earlier work, segments of his pictorial memory that critics, if not viewers, must link together in order to put into perspective and restore an artistic discourse.

Whereas in the fields of literature and cinema studies, the interplay of cross-references, variations, and oppositions of internal themes disclosed by writers or movie directors through self-quotation and self-elaboration—whether in the form of patterns, schemes or motifs used by them in patently analogous or, at times, even identical manners—has been long acknowledged as essential in reconstructing a literary or cinematic oeuvre as a whole in its diachronic and synchronic structure,[17] art historians have often, but fortunately not always, lagged behind, and seldom scouted for consistent clues of the internal memory's processes. In most cases, artists' reemployment of their previous inventions is regarded as signifying a stylistic, not a thematic, evolution. Because of its complexity, the internal inter-textuality of Caravaggio's work as it emerges in his final pictures does not solely concern "narrative" in the terms of the artistic debates that raged at the time.

I indeed contend that another primary theme of artistic reflection, only partially developed in his former production, comes to fruition and climaxes at the end of his career: that of the "meta-narrative." By tracing the parallel treatments of the "piercing act" in Caravaggio's *Incredulity of Saint Thomas* and his late *Martyrdom of Saint Ursula*, I shall investigate the pioneering ways in which Caravaggio endeavored both to transcend and reassess the physicality of the pictorial medium and its limits in interacting with beholders. Especially in the case of *The Martyrdom of Saint Ursula*, the re-emergence of Caravaggio's *alter ego* in the form in which the master had already depicted himself in the Dublin *Taking of Christ* reintroduces important artistic themes such as self-referentiality, authorial viewpoint, and artistic invention in a context that, very differently, thematizes, redefines and pushes to the extreme the "meta-narrative." By combining these different strands of reflection in his *Martyrdom of Saint Ursula*, Caravaggio not only produces one of the subtlest early modern artistic discourses on the *istoria*, its fallacies, and immense potentials, but also epitomizes his poetics of dislocation in its ultimate expression.

Nonetheless, in examining this and other works from Caravaggio's last years, one must constantly bear in mind that, by that time, the modalities through which the master had until then accustomed his public to enter, experience, and "read" his sacred narratives had dramatically changed on a technical level. The once characteristic compactness of his chiaroscuro layouts is often dismissed in favor of a *non-finito* technique, and his close-up narratives start to alternate with larger

---

17 A pioneering example of this methodology as applied to literature is set by Conte 1974. In the domain of cinema studies, see especially Gunning 2000 and his interpretation of Fritz Lang's films.

scale compositions in which the role of the human figure is not downgraded, but unmistakably reassessed in function of pure spatiality. In his 1672 *Vite*, Giovan Pietro Bellori had already pointed out the crucial shift that Caravaggio's brand new practice of the *non-finito* introduced into his pictorial narratives, starting with his 1608 *Beheading of Saint John the Baptiste* at Valletta:

> In this painting, Caravaggio infused all the power of his brush, and worked with such fierceness that he left the priming of the canvas as [the final picture's] half-tones, so that, besides [the knight's] cross, the Grand Master [of the Order of Malta] put around his neck a rich golden chain and presented him with two slaves, not to mention other manifestations of his own esteem and satisfaction with his work.[18]

I shall examine the furor of Caravaggio's late brushwork in the following chapter through the example of his *Denial of Saint Peter* (Metropolitan Museum, New York). For now, I make one final observation: the exceptional originality of Caravaggio's new inventions as conveyed through new techniques, diverse styles, and unusual formats, would not have been conceivable had the master remained in Rome. Doubtless the artistic periphery of Malta and Sicily constituted the most fecund terrain for Caravaggio's unorthodox Muse, a refuge in which he could finally unleash his untamed memory, enact a dialogue with his past achievements, and experiment further with pictorial narrative.

---

18 Bellori, 226: "In quest'opera il Caravaggio usò ogni potere del suo pennello, avendovi lavorato con tanta fierezza che lasciò in mezze tinte l'imprimitura della tela: sì che, oltre l'onore della croce, il Gran Maestro gli pose al collo una ricca collana d'oro e gli fece dono di due schiavi, con altre dimostrazioni della stima e compiacimento dell'operar suo."

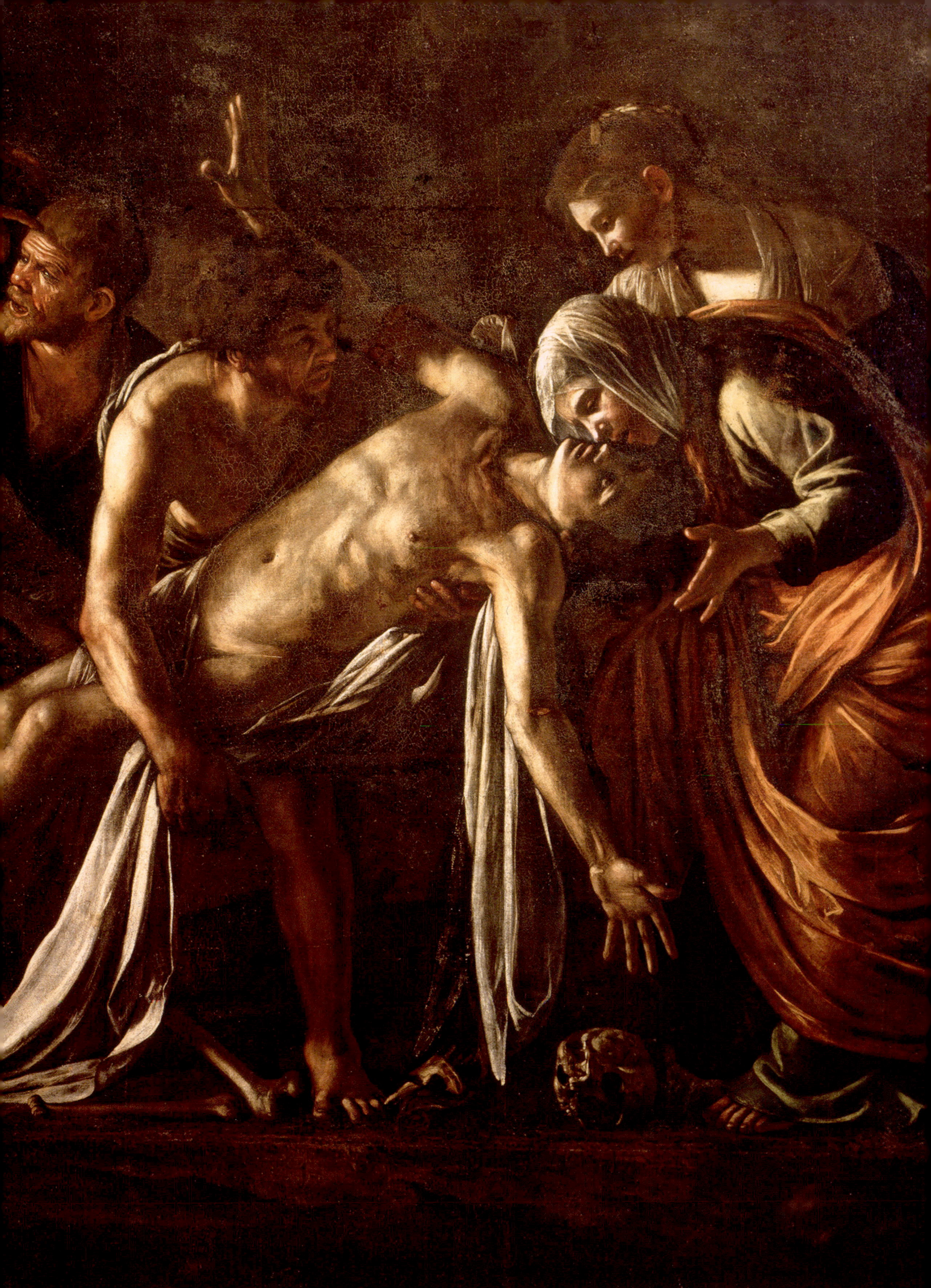

CHAPTER 13

Narratives of the *Non-Finito:* On Caravaggio's *Denial of Saint Peter, The Burial of Saint Lucy,* and *The Resurrection of Lazarus*

The Non-Finito *and Narrative*

Literally, *non-finito* means "unfinished," but in art history this term, often associated with Michelangelo's sculpture, has come to mean something slightly different.[1] *Non-finito* designates the specific quality of an artwork that, in some of its parts or in its entirety, has been purposefully left "unachieved" or "unpolished" by the artist so that beholders might easily detect the traces of its making. By extension, *non-finito* also characterizes the technique by which artists render the appearance of a pictorial or sculptural surface in a rough state that evokes an initial or intermediate phase of the working process. In this manner, the painter or sculptor discloses—unwillingly, as it were—the conceptive furor and wondrous artifice that announce, beget, and accompany the artwork's execution. Since the concept of *non-finito* refers to different techniques and usages, thereby incorporating manifold values, it is appropriate, before defining Caravaggio's *non-finito*, to establish what theoretical and practical implications the term might have carried at the beginning of the seventeenth century. To this end, I shall resort once again to Vasari, who offers many pertinent and complex insights into the *non-finito* and its various applications. In his 1568 *Vite*, Vasari opposes Luca della Robbia's bas-reliefs for Florence Cathedral's *cantoria*[2] to those for its pendant executed by Donatello around the same time[3] (started respectively in 1431 and 1433):

> [Donato] made his [work] with more judgment and deftness than Luca did, (…) for he executed it almost entirely as a draft without finish or polish, so that it might, and truly does, appear from a distance in a better view than Luca's work, which, though executed with good drawing and diligence, due to its polish and finish, becomes lost to sight in the distance, and cannot be discerned as effectively as Donato's work, drafted as it is. Artificers must take much care with this [factor], inasmuch as experience teaches us that all things placed at a distance—whether it be paintings, sculptures or other similar things—gain more effectiveness and vigor if they are beautifully drafted rather than finished. Besides the fact that distance

1 There is a vast bibliography devoted exclusively to Michelangelo's *non-finito*: De Benedetti 1951; Barocchi 1958; Sanpaolesi 1966; Brunius 1967; Colacicchi 1976; Maiorino 1983; Bockemühl 1986; and Gilbert 2003. For the *non-finito* in the work of other early modern artists, see Grassi 1948; Venturi 1954; Martinelli 1968 (Donatello); Ullmann 1978 (Leonardo); Gentili 1992 (Titian); Penny 1994; Hoff 2003; Gentili 2007 (Titian); Weigel 2006 (Tintoretto); Zikos 2008 (Vincenzo Danti).

2 For Luca Della Robbia's *cantoria*, see Gentilini 1992, 1:85-90.

3 For Donatello's *cantoria*, see Rosenauer 1993, 122-30, 148-52, no. 32.

determines this effect, it is equally apparent that one often, with a few strokes, is able to express one's concepts, as they suddenly surface through art's fury, whereas toil and excessive diligence sometimes drain vigor and knowledge from those who are unable to take their hands off the work that they are making. He who knows that the arts of drawing, not to mention painting alone, are similar to poetry, also knows that, just as poems dictated by poetic furor are true, good, and superior to those produced by chipping away, so too the works of men excellent in the arts of drawing prove to be better when they are done at once by force of furor rather than when they are conceived little by little, painfully, and with hardship. And he who from the outset bears in mind, as everyone should, what he plans to do, always heads to perfection resolutely and with great ease.[4]

There are two facets, optical and aesthetic, to Vasari's argument. The first more specifically concerns the notion of propriety and decorum; in order to be appreciated at its best, the artwork must be conducted in accordance with the physical conditions of exposure in which it is meant to be seen. In other words, artists are entitled to produce an artifact that, observed at close range, might appear crudely sketched, distorted or even shapeless as long as it becomes perfectly coherent, harmonious, and legible in its designated location. Vasari's second observation is more conceptually intricate, since it virtually undermines his tenacious belief in the artwork's ultimate perfection through drawing's constant intervention. Regardless of his "good drawing and diligence," Luca was unable to perfect his reliefs in an appropriate fashion, so that paradoxically his last, finishing touch should have corresponded to leaving his work unfinished. Put otherwise, Luca impeded his original design from entirely fulfilling its intended configuration in the artwork.

As Philip Sohm has pointed out, Vasari's praise of the *non-finito* might mislead scholars;[5] as Vasari himself boasts of his own furor and expeditiousness both in creating and executing, one would expect his paintings to be, if not dashed off, at least partially drafted, while in fact they tend to be exceedingly polished. That furor might have inspired Vasari's designs is highly likely, but this artistic fury hardly emerges in his finished paintings. Perhaps one can explain Vasari's take on the *non-finito* through a passage of his 1568 *Vite* in which he curiously extols Palma il Vecchio's spontaneity in conceiving and carrying out his *c.*1534 *Sea Storm* (Scuola Grande di San Marco, Venice).[6] This painting, now unfortunately in a poor state of conservation, fascinated Vasari because of Palma's terrific rendering of "the fury of the winds, the strength and prowess of the men, the motion of the waves, the thunderbolts and lightning in the sky, the water plowed by the oars, and the oars bent by the waves and the vigor of the rowers." In sum, Palma's *Sea Storm* excelled so much with regard to "drawing, invention, and color technique" that "it [seemed] that

---

4   Vasari, 3:51-2: "Se bene Donatello, che poi fece l'ornamento dell'altro organo che è dirimpetto a questo, fece il suo con molto più giudizio e pratica che non aveva fatto Luca, come si dirà al luogo suo, per avere egli quell'opera condotta quasi tutta in bozze e non finita pulitamente, acciò che apparisse di lontano assai meglio, come fa, che quella di Luca; la quale, se è fatta con buon disegno e diligenza, ella fa nondimeno con la sua pulitezza e finimento che l'occhio per la lontananza la perde e non la scorge bene come si fa quella di Donato, quasi solamente abbozzata. Alla quale cosa deono molto avere avvertenza gl'artefici, perciò che la sperienza fa conoscere che tutte le cose che vanno lontane—o siano pitture o siano sculture o qualsivoglia altra somigliante cosa—hanno più fierezza e maggior forza se sono una bella bozza che se sono finite; ed oltre che la lontananza fa questo effetto pare anco che nelle bozze molte volte, nascendo in un subito dal furore

dell'arte, si sprima il suo concetto in pochi colpi, e che per contrario lo stento e la troppa diligenza alcuna fiata toglia la forza ed il sapere a coloro che non sanno mai levare le mani dall'opera che fanno. E chi sa che l'arti del disegno, per non dir la pittura solamente, sono alla poesia simili, sa ancora che come le poesie dettate dal furore poetico sono le vere e buone e migliori che le stentate, così l'opere degli uomini eccellenti nell'arti del disegno sono migliori quando sono fatte a un tratto dalla forza di quel furore che quando si vanno ghiribizzando a poco a poco con istento e con fatica; e chi ha da principio, come si dee avere, nella idea quello che vuol fare, camina sempre risoluto alla perfezzione con molta agevolezza."

5   See Sohm 1991, 27-36.

6   For the painting, see Rylands 1992, 242-5, no. 99.

the picture [quaked], as if everything that [was] depicted there were true."[7] Vasari also identifies the cause of this successful feat in Palma's artistic mindset:

> In similar difficult things, many painters, as if moved by a certain furor upon their works' first drafting, happen to come up with some good and fierce stuff, which disappears upon [their] finishing, as does whatever good that furor has instilled in them. This occurs because in finishing, artists often consider the parts, and not the whole, of their works, so that, as their spirits abate, they lose their verve and fierceness. On the contrary, [Palma] always abided firmly by his intention and brought to perfection his concept, which was then—and will always be—commended enormously.[8]

As I have already mentioned, it is now difficult to appraise Palma's *Sea Storm* and to verify whether the fury of the elements it represents was rendered with an equivalent furor of the brushstroke. I prefer to think that Vasari was charmed more by the picture's naturalistic effects than by the spectacular touch of Palma's brush, which generally remains orderly and meticulous.[9] To put it more provocatively, Vasari commends Palma for his diligence in taming and therefore accurately transliterating his original furor: an oxymoron of sorts, if one takes into account that the painter's initial fury in visualizing and composing should contrast with, and even slow, his quest for accuracy. At any rate, it is evident that Vasari was prone to welcome the analogs in painting of Donatello's drafted bas-reliefs, as evidenced by his reading and celebration of Titian's late painting:[10]

> It is certainly true that his technique in making these last [works] differs greatly from the one that he used in his youth. His earlier [works], indeed, are executed with a certain fineness and incredible diligence, so that they can be appreciated up-close and from a distance, whereas his late works are made up of frank and grand brushstrokes, sketched out summarily, and blurred, so that they cannot be taken in up close, whereas from a distance they appear to be perfect. This style has led many who want to imitate him and show off their promptness to botch their pictures. And this happens because, although many believe that his paintings are executed with ease, this is false and they are wrong insofar as Titian clearly returned to his works by retouching them with colors so many times that his carefulness is patent. And this style is judicious, beautiful, and admirable since it makes the picture seem to be alive and done with art by concealing the toil.[11]

---

7 Vasari, 4:550-1: "Insomma quest'opera, per vero dire, è tale e sì bella per invenzione e per altro, che pare quasi impossibile che colore o pennello adoperati da mani anco eccellenti possino esprimere alcuna cosa più simile al vero o più naturale, attesoché in essa si vede la furia de' venti, la forza e destrezza degl'uomini, il moversi dell'onde, i lampi e ' baleni del cielo, l'acqua rotta dai remi e i remi piegati dall'onde e dalla forza de' vogadori. Che più? Io per me non mi ricordo aver veduto la più orrenda pittura di quella, essendo talmente condotta, e con tanta osservanza nel disegno, nell'invenzione e nel colorito, che pare che tremi la tavola, come tutto quello che vi è dipinto fusse vero."

8 Ibidem, 4:551: "In simili cose difficili a molti pittori vien fatto nel primo abbozzare l'opera, come guidati da un certo forore, qualche cosa di buono e qualche fierezza, che vien poi levata nel finire, e tolto via quel buono che vi aveva posto il furore; e questo avviene perché molte volte chi finisce considera le parti e non il tutto di quello che fa, e va, raffreddandosi gli spiriti, perdendo la vena della fierezza: là dove costui stette sempre saldo nel medesimo proposito e condusse a perfezzione il suo concetto, che gli fu allora e sarà sempre infinitamente lodato."

9 See in this regard Ridolfi, 122-3: "Fu Jacopo (…) di nobile idea e di buon disegno, assiduo e diligente come lo dimostrano le opere sue, le quali per lo più fanno mirabile effetto ove di vicino si godono, come che vedute le pitture in una certa distanza non ricercano tanta politezza, non discernendosi di lontano (come pur anche si osserva nel naturale) la minutezza de' capelli né le picciole rughe, ma solo alcuni principali lumi ed ombre che, tocche a quella simiglianza dall'industre pittore, le recano l'essere proprio e naturale, alle quali osservazioni essendo congiunto il buon disegno si forma quell'eccellente maniera."

10 Besides the bibliography mentioned in note 1 of this chapter, see the excellent remarks on Titian's late style in Sohm 2007, 92-8.

11 Vasari, 6:166: "Ma è ben vero che il modo di fare che tenne in queste ultime è assai diferente dal fare suo da giovane: con ciò sia che le prime son condotte con una certa

In a sense, Titian's accuracy in dissimulating his efforts through the apparent sketchiness of his paintings (his masterly "*sprezzatura*") is the brilliant solution to Vasari's theoretical conundrum; furor and spontaneity can finally fuse together with diligence and conceptive lucidity. However, the balance struck by Titian between sketchiness and finish is, in Vasari's eyes, almost exclusive to the old master. Accordingly Vasari does not hesitate to condemn Tintoretto's painting and its ostentatious facility and *non-finito*:

> In the matter of painting, [Tintoretto] was extravagant, inventive, swift, and resolute, and the most impressive brain ever engendered by painting, as one can see in all his works and inventions of fantastic narratives, which he did in a manner so different from the other painters' conventions. And yet, he surpassed his own extravagance with new and whimsical inventions and with the strange fantasies of his intellect, and he executed [these works] randomly and without design, as if to demonstrate that painting is but child's play. Sometimes he passed off his sketches for finished works, and they are dashed off so painfully that one sees the brushstrokes thrown down haphazardly and in a frenzy, without design or judgment.[12]

By examining Vasari's opinion on Titian's late *non-finito* and Tintoretto's picturesque brushwork, it is evident that Vasari does not disapprove of pictorial sketchiness as a deliberate strategy on the painter's part to show his inventive swiftness and technical virtuosity. What he truly dislikes is when artists avail themselves of this technique "without design"—that is, without obeying a pre-determined "plan of execution." In other words, art is never fortuitous even when it happens to appear so. Tintoretto's greatest sin is therefore his lack of finality, an element of his painting that seriously prejudices the notion of pictorial composition as construed by Vasari.

No scholar has so far attempted to evaluate Caravaggio's pictorial technique in connection with Vasari's principles of the *non-finito*. I should therefore underline the paradox embodied by Caravaggio's early practice of painting in relation to his vaunted refusal of drawing. Should one attempt to define the characteristics of Caravaggio's technique in his Roman works, especially those executed between 1595 and 1605, one would be forced to acknowledge that Vasari's definition of "diligence" would undoubtedly fill the bill. In stating this, I also need to explain the unpredictable ramifications of Caravaggio's pictorial accuracy and extreme finish with regard to the notion of naturalism. In conformity with Vasari's historical construction of art's evolution in Italy, naturalistic diligence pertains to the pictorial phase prior to the modern "style" of Leonardo, Raphael, and particularly Michelangelo, the masters of what we currently consider the high Renaissance.[13] To simplify a matter that requires much more scrutiny and distinction, Leonardo's *sfumato*, Raphael's "grace" and Michelangelo's "*terribilità*" constitute the means by which art has distanced itself from pedestrian, if marvelous, imitation. In Vasari's view, the almost calligraphic rendition of figures

---

finezza e diligenza incredibile, e da essere vedute da presso e da lontano, e queste ultime, condotte di colpi, tirate via di grosso e con macchie, di maniera che da presso non si possono vedere e di lontano appariscono perfette. E questo modo è stato cagione che molti, volendo in ciò immitare e mostrare di fare il pratico, hanno fatto di goffe pitture: e ciò addiviene perché, se bene a molti pare che elle siano fatte senza fatica, non è così il vero e s'ingannano, perché si conosce che sono rifatte, e che si è ritornato loro addosso con i colori tante volte che la fatica vi si vede. E questo modo sì fatto è giudizioso, bello e stupendo, perché fa parere vive le pitture e fatte con grande arte, nascondendo le fatiche."

diversi strumenti, ed oltre ciò piacevole in tutte le sue azzioni, ma nelle cose della pittura stravagante, capriccioso, presto e risoluto, ed il più terribile cervello che abbia avuto mai la pittura, come si può vedere in tutte le sue opere e ne' componimenti delle storie, fantastiche e fatte da lui diversamente e fuori dell'uso degl'altri pittori; anzi ha superata la stravaganza con le nuove e capricciose invenzioni e strani ghiribizzi del suo intelletto, che ha lavorato a caso e senza disegno, quasi mostrando che quest'arte è una baia. Ha costui alcuna volta lasciato le bozze per finite, tanto a fatica sgrossate che si veggiono i colpi de' pennegli fatti dal caso e dalla fierezza più tosto che dal disegno e dal giudizio."

12 Vasari, 5:468-9: "Jacopo Tintoretto, il quale si è dilettato di tutte le virtù e particolarmente di sonare di musica e

13 For Vasari's interpretation of the historical evolution of the arts, see Rubin 1995; and Sohm 2001, 86-114.

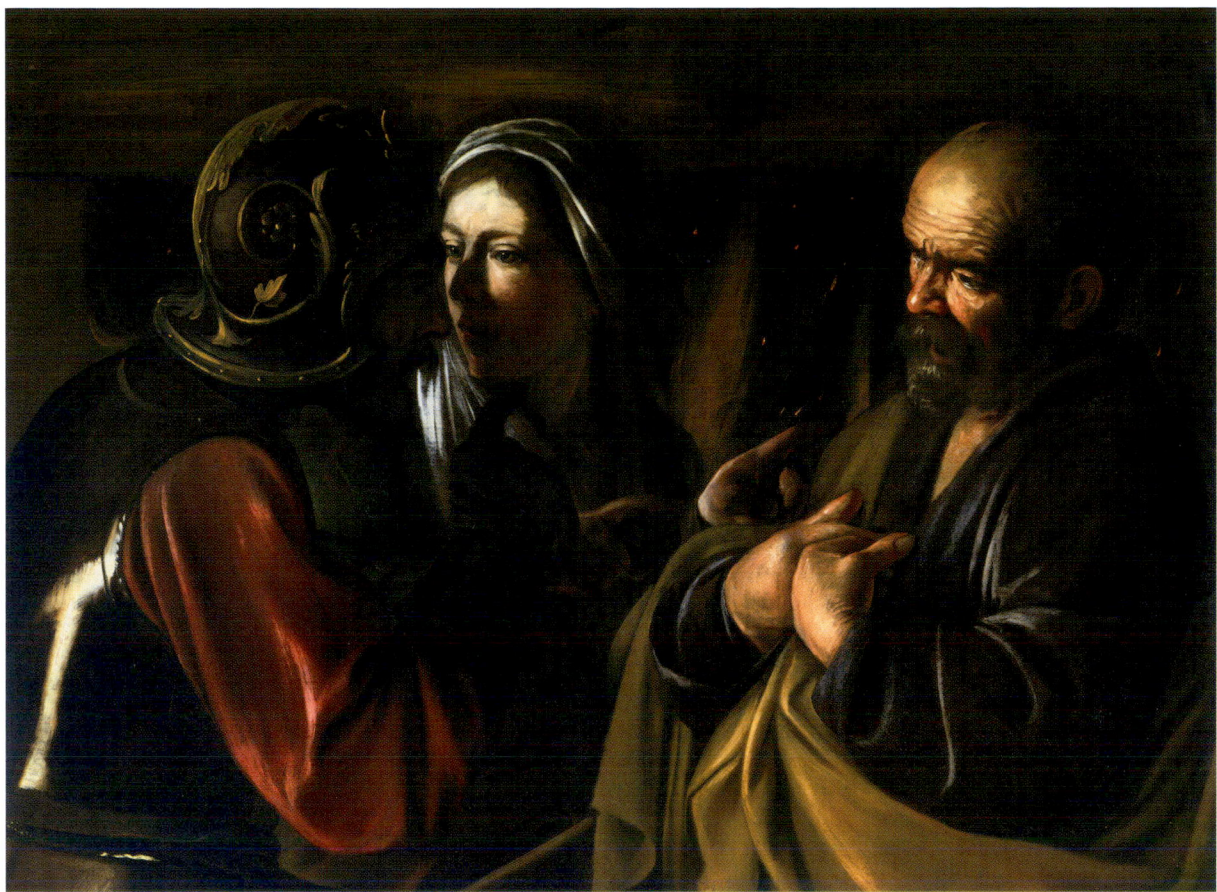

Fig. 210
Michelangelo Merisi da Caravaggio, *Denial of Saint Peter*, Metropolitan Museum of Art, New York, oil on canvas, 94 x 125.5 cm.

and objects as practiced by quattrocento painters lacked the transcendence and idealism necessary for art to proclaim its ultimate triumph and perfection.

In the light of these considerations, I assume that Vasari would have deemed "prehistoric," literally speaking, paintings such as Caravaggio's *Basket of Fruit*, *Bacchus* or *The Crucifixion of Saint Peter* on account of their thoroughness and polish; even worse, their technique of execution would have seemed to him almost alien to the Italian tradition. It would be superfluous to insist here on the fact that Caravaggio was aware of his initial neo-primitivism, which was all the more conceptually disruptive in that it allied itself with a Venetian color technique and disdained the practice of drawing. In fact, in Caravaggio's time, the virtuoso artworks of the old Titian and Tintoretto, rather than the "diligent" paintings of Giorgione and the young Titian, were ordinarily perceived as representative of Venetian painting. In a sense, then, the execution of a painting in a Venetian vein carried out with the tedious diligence of an early Netherlandish master encompassed a practical and theoretical contradiction: potentially, it was a work of color without furor.

On the other hand, it was artistic furor that Caravaggio claimed as the novel hallmark of his art when he renounced the canonical practice of drawing; working directly on the canvas was the young master's way of giving free rein to invention, to prevent "his creative spirits" from ebbing away by spoiling the vividness of his concepts. One might be tempted to see in Caravaggio's conceptually perilous and rebellious endeavor a trace of Palma's exploits as expounded by Vasari—the combination of furor and conceptive tenacity—but nothing could be more different. Palma's *Sea Storm* remains, in Vasari's opinion, the product of an abstract, and abstracting, concept: a paradigmatic representation, and not a literal reproduction, of Nature's multifarious turmoil.

419

Instead, by painting from life, Caravaggio conflated reproduction and representation in a manner that denied the artwork's indispensable ideality as required in his time. As I have already dealt with the inherent mismatches of norms and conventions implied by Caravaggio's naturalism or, from another angle, realism, I shall merely emphasize once again to what extreme degree Caravaggio's early practice of pictorial, mirror-like accuracy reshuffles and plays with the principles of painting and the *istoria* operative in the early modern period.

More importantly, I shall now argue that Caravaggio's later use of a sketch-like technique not only clashes with his widely-celebrated true-to-life mimetic diligence, but also dislodges the consistency of practices and rules on which the notion of the *non-finito* then relied. I shall begin by examining one of Caravaggio's final paintings, the 1609-1610 *Denial of Saint Peter* in the Metropolitan Museum of Art, New York (Fig. 210).[14] Although nothing is known of this compelling picture—no seventeenth-century biographer of Caravaggio mentions it—there is a very strong possibility that it is to be identified with a work listed on three different occasions as belonging to the Savelli family in Ariccia and later in Rome. The clearest of these testimonies, dated to 1650, reads: "a servant with a denying Saint Peter, and another half-figure, horizontal (…) by Caravaggio," valued at 250 *ducati*, a considerable price.[15] Even if the *Denial* presents some abrasions on its pictorial surface, its state of conservation is satisfactory, and therefore allows for closer analysis.

As with many other works executed at the end of his career, Caravaggio prepared his canvas with a substratum of bole, a reddish-brown clay, upon which he progressively yet resolutely sketched the bulk of his three half-figures through fluid layers of pigments, thus using the priming as the work's overall half-tone. At a preliminary stage of the execution—though some of the effects continue to operate in the finished work—these differently colored swaths, similar to translucent silhouettes, because of their thinness and liquidity might have seemed to linger over the picture's surface and only imperceptibly detached themselves from the dark priming beneath it. Although it is impossible to ascertain whether Caravaggio worked the canvas uniformly, or if he first concentrated on a particular portion of it, it is obvious that, by superimposing thicker strata of brighter tints in determinate areas, by veiling the dark portions of the priming left out in advance, or by simultaneously sparing some of the half-tone layers, the master proceeded to build and redefine the composition's entire structure.

I imagine that, in order to model Saint Peter's face (Fig. 211), Caravaggio drafted the contours and main lineaments of his head with an almost diaphanous dark tint. Then, he set out to highlight the apostle's nose, cheeks, eyelids and forehead, layer after layer in conformity with the desired effect, more and more thickly, so that these parts might jut out from the priming or half-tone stratum beneath more or less powerfully. To accentuate the chiaroscuro on the saint's face, Caravaggio darkened the underlying shades through veiling. Note the almost parallel strips of highlights over Peter's forehead, neatly emerging from the background, that imitate the pattern of a tree's knitted bark; the patch of beige pigment that slants from his left eye's lachrymal sac across his upper cheek; the filaments of white at the base of his eyes and the dabs of white pigment that dribble under his left pupil or blot the tip of his nose. From the dark mass of shadow wrapping the apostle's head Caravaggio created the large blotch of the figure's beard, combed by the brush with a few fibers of brighter pigment and reverberations of white highlights. More impressively, the narrow ellipse of Peter's mouth sinks into the canvas like an imploding black hole amid the nebula of his beard, or like a bottomless well, to use a metaphor current in Caravaggio's time—an optical effect of great

14 For the painting, see Marini 1973; Cinotti 1983, 548-9, no. 67; Hibbard 1983, 340-1, note 192; Christiansen 1985, 350, no. 100 [catalogue entry by Mina Gregori]; Bologna 1992, 444, 452; Pacelli 1994, 99-100; Puglisi 1998, 351; Cassani and Sapio 2005, 140-2, no. 17 [catalogue entry by Keith Christiansen]; Marini 2005, 521-3, no. 81; Varriano 2006, 117-8 [on the soldier's costume]; Schütze 2009, 284-5, no. 65; Von Rosen 2009, 128-33.

15 See Campori 1975, 172: "Un'ancella con San Pietro negante, et una altra meza figura per traverso, palmi 5 e 4 del Caravaggio, ducati 250."

dramatic impact, but also a pictorial feat in its own right.

If, for comparison, one turns to the servant's face, the divergence of the technique is immediately apparent to the viewer. Despite the evident abrasions in this specific portion of the canvas, it is evident that here Caravaggio applied fewer layers of liquid flesh-white as if simply drafting the woman's head, delicately bringing out the penumbra cast by the shadow upon her face's lower part, and blending the shades upon the cheek with pink pigment to contrast the brightness of her forehead and the zone around her eyes. Somewhat like Donatello in his *cantoria*, Caravaggio left his servant's figure summarily "drafted," and the thick ribs of her veil's white folds, especially atop her head, truly react to light like the initial outcrops of a sketchily carved relief. Different again is the treatment of the soldier's face, whose few highlights are tinged in red, and in which the pupil and eyelashes, colored with the same pigment as that of this figure's pointed beard, come to the fore only through a stronger graduation of dark tint by forming a hint of an eye.

Caravaggio constantly varied the density of the pictorial textures in his execution of the Metropolitan *Denial*, although these variations essentially subsist in a context dominated by vast tracts of translucent colors that impart coherence to the entire composition. This opalescence (to

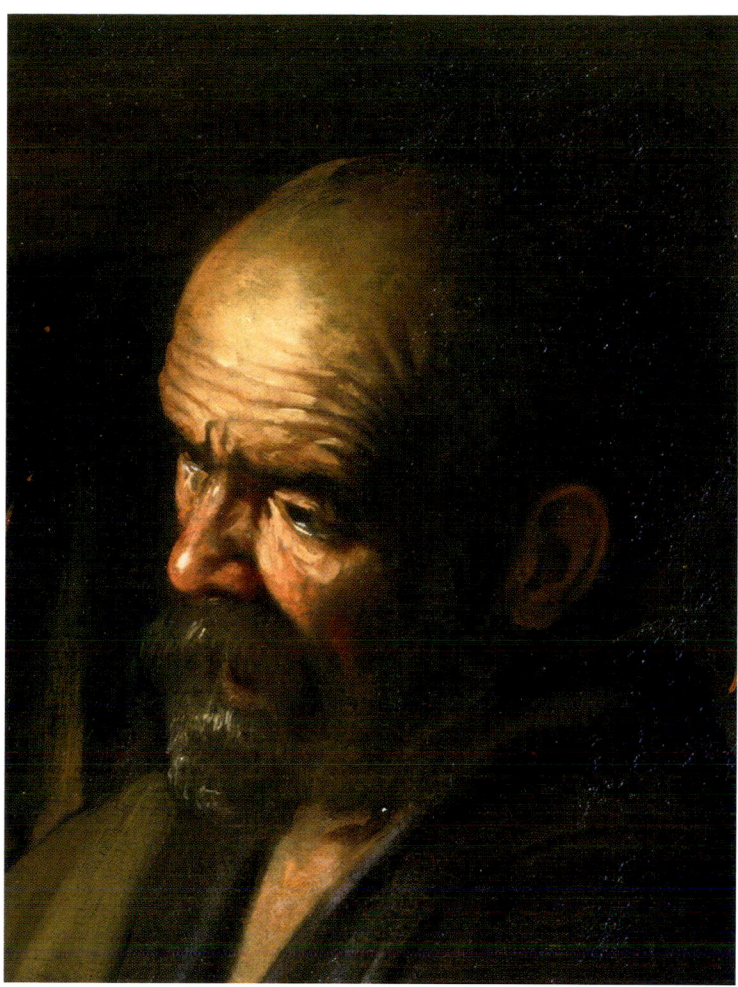

Fig. 211
Michelangelo Merisi da Caravaggio, *Denial of Saint Peter*, Metropolitan Museum of Art, New York, oil on canvas, 94 x 125.5 cm., detail.

use a term already employed in Chapter 9 with regard to the Brera *Supper at Emmaus*) not only animates the picture through the interplay and dialectic of light and darkness in a shallow space, but also constitutes the neutral ground onto which Caravaggio succeeded in grafting multiple, yet confined and select textural inflections: the sweeps of the brush upon the mantelpiece or in the chimney's fire; the thick bright stretches of the folds' peaks or the ribs of the woman's veil; the sprinkles of ruby that simulate the fire's incandescence; the smooth filaments of golden pigment on the back of the soldier's cuirass, and above all the huge, jagged splotch ("*macchia*") of Peter's face. The coexistence of diluted pictorial swaths and occasional protrusions of dense pigment doubtless denotes Caravaggio's pictorial technique as an equivalent of the *non-finito*. However, to my knowledge, the effect of "unfinishedness" obtained by Caravaggio here and in almost all of his late narratives does not compare to any other *non-finito* as practiced by previous masters.

In describing Peter's face, I have in mind the picturesque brushwork of, for example, Tintoretto or Jacopo Bassano. Perhaps, to be more precise, I should say that Caravaggio's rendition of Peter's face reminds me of Paolo Veronese's drawing practice, as seen in a drawing by Veronese now in the Louvre, Paris: the *c*.1550 *Temptation of Saint Anthony* executed in pen, ink, and wash, heightened with white on grey prepared paper (Fig. 212).[16] Though Veronese uses the pen to circumscribe his figures

16   See Cocke 1984, 107, no. 36.

and objects—Caravaggio's circumscriptions in the end result from the juxtaposition without overlapping of colored areas—it is evident that the way in which the Venetian master exploits the sheet's grey priming as a half-tone, by shading with brown wash and illuminating with lead white, is not dissimilar, given the different media, to that employed by Caravaggio in depicting Peter's face. If one isolates Saint Anthony's face in Veronese's drawing, one notices a few affinities with Caravaggio's apostle: the bold foreshortening of the saint's three-quarter face, the almost parallel hatchings of lead white on the forehead, which intensify Anthony's distress, and the use of the beard's mass to magnify the gesture of his mouth—Veronese's saint sticks out his tongue—corroborate the point. Veronese's artistry enhances the twisted mimicry of the devil's face; through a syncopated application of lead white, Veronese dramatizes the moral deformity and spite of his figure. I am not suggesting that Veronese's drawing inspired Caravaggio; but a comparison of these two masters' techniques demonstrates that, in representing his Saint Peter, Caravaggio availed himself of a working procedure close to that of a preparatory study by Veronese.

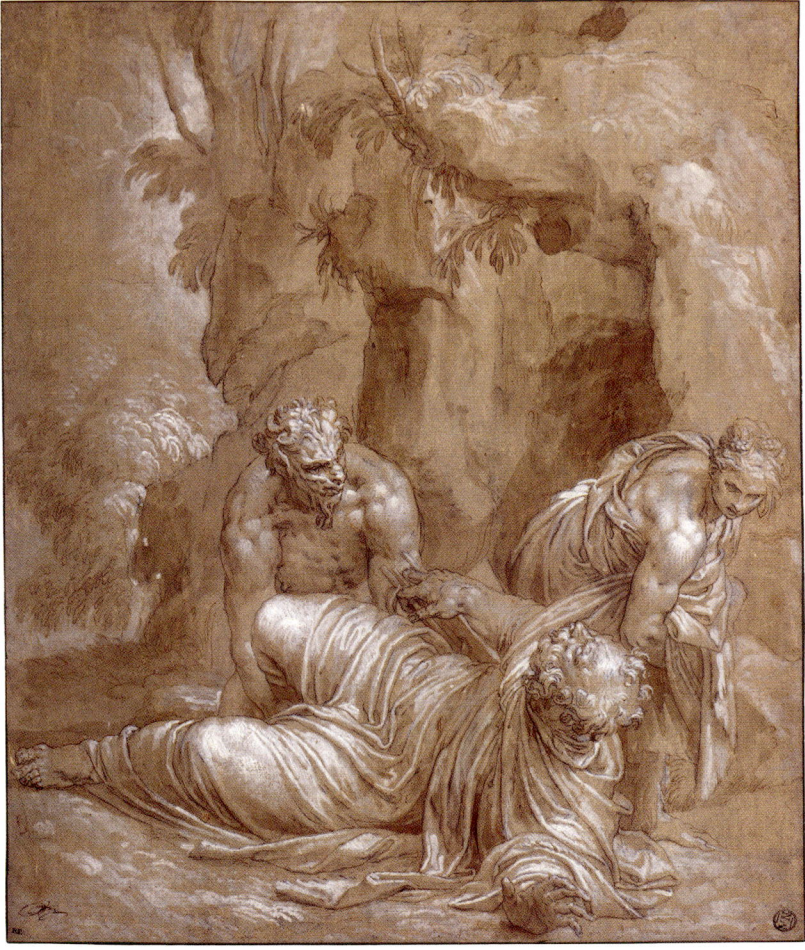

Fig. 212
Veronese (Paolo Caliari), *The Temptation of Saint Anthony*, Musée du Louvre, Paris, pen and ink and wash on grey prepared paper heightened with white, 41.4 x 35.6 cm.

More significantly, the apparent sketchiness of Saint Peter's face ranks as a technical exception in Caravaggio's *Denial*; in other words, the picture is neither integrally "made up of frank and grand brushstrokes, sketched out summarily and blurred," as is the case of Titian's late works, nor "dashed off" "haphazardly and in a frenzy," as Tintoretto used to do. Not only is Caravaggio's *non-finito* a truly original "mode of painting," but it also challenges the conventional concept of the *non-finito* through the eclecticism of its techniques. It is inappropriate to judge Caravaggio's *non-finito* as a mere stylistic hallmark, a signature declaring the prodigy of his pictorial handling. First and foremost, Caravaggio's practice of the *non-finito* is functional, and hence intended to act upon the beholder's perception and reading of the represented *istoria*.

As a general rule, the variety of pictorial techniques introduced by Caravaggio in his *Denial* aims successfully at generating distinct narrative foci. There is little doubt that in approaching the painting for the first time, viewers are intuitively led to center their attention on the figure of Saint Peter to the right; the audacious smear of his face is hard to miss. In a second move, the beholders' eyes will certainly fall upon the half-illuminated figure of the servant; however, more than one viewer is likely to overlook the soldier's presence at first glance. But the enhancement, diminution, and manipulation of narrative foci by no means represent a specificity of the late Caravaggio; the master had been experimenting with these devices for a very long time. So what, in this particular case, is the difference?

To put it in the simplest possible way, the *istoria*'s dramatic essence is now channeled more through the pictorial surface's technical handling—its facture—than through the figures' exalted and volumetric physicality. I do not claim that the human figure in Caravaggio's late narratives loses its preeminent role: attitudes, gestures, and expressions do not stop transmitting the "affects" of the *istoria*. Nonetheless, the dramatic language of the figural body is now subordinated to, sometimes even subdued by, the global arrangement of the painting's surface; the figure can serve as a vessel through which the pictorial matter expresses its dramatic force and unrestricted potentialities. As a result, the work's chiaroscuro and chromatic layout acquire an unprecedented independence by configuring a syntax of their own, which does not necessarily match, and occasionally even surmounts, the *istoria*'s cause-and-effect interconnectedness as enforced by the figures' disposition.

To illustrate the point, let us return to the Metropolitan *Denial*. Almost at the center of the composition Caravaggio placed a chain of three hands, a visual rhetorical device employed by the master in many of his pictures: the iron gloved claw of the soldier, and the two pointing hands of the servant (in the beginning, Caravaggio developed this threefold motif in a slightly different manner, by depicting the woman's left palm open and almost impinging upon Peter's figure). If one thinks of the capital role that these assemblages of hands play in some of Caravaggio's close-up narratives—for instance, in the Uffizi *Sacrifice of Isaac* or in the Sans-Souci *Incredulity of Saint Thomas*, which I shall examine in the following chapter—then one must admit that in the *Denial*, the chain of hands in a sense tends to vanish in front of the viewer amidst the opalescent half-tones of the painting. In fact, the iron glove is sensed much more by the viewer than described by the painter, and operates as a loose shadow partially occluding the maid's torso. The novel accessoriness of the pointing hands bears profoundly on the narrative's reading: in fact, the motif of Peter's accusation is here downplayed as an "accident," and thus visually dissociated from Peter's tormented figure. Much more than the gesture of the soldier's pointing glove, the disembodied depiction of his helmet adorned with acanthus foliage, his reflecting cuirass and his red sleeve hovering in the foreground, marked by the masterful Y of its folds' highlights and chromatically opposed to the ochre of Peter's mantle and the brownish whites of his face and hands, conjure up—by its material impalpability—an impression of blind menace closing in almost as if impersonally on the apostle.

In this connection, note that the enlightened portion of the servant's face, from which the glittering of the gaze so vividly emerges, is conceived as a foil to the soldier's vaporous figure; through the woman's look, the beholder becomes aware of the man's appearance, and not of Peter's distress. The theater of shadows deployed by Caravaggio at the left of his *Denial* not only inhibits the dramatic function of the figures' gestures and expressions, but also replaces it; indeed, Caravaggio endows the quasi-immaterial shadowiness of the soldier with the psychological charge of an advancing, indeterminate threat. In other words, the interplay of shadows and luminous swaths composing the soldier's appearance, by dissolving at first glance the physical consistency of his figure, provides individual parts of his armor not only with a life of their own, but also with an acting function—the helmet, cuirass, and red sleeve act as substitutes for the human body. The acting presence of these props is concretely relayed by the shifting chiaroscuro and impalpable materiality in the left part of the painting. It should now be clear how Caravaggio's *non-finito* also taps into the mechanisms of the *istoria*'s temporality. Peter's denial is described in the Gospels in slightly different versions; this is the account given by Mark (14, 66-72):

> While Peter was below in the courtyard, one of the high priest's maids came along. Seeing Peter warming himself, she looked intently at him and said, "You too were with the Nazarene, Jesus." But he denied it saying, "I neither know nor understand what you are talking about." So he went out into the outer court. The maid saw him and began again to say to the bystanders, "this man is one of them." Once again he denied

423

it. A little later the bystanders said to Peter once more, "Surely, you are one of them; for you too are a Galilean." He began to curse and swear, "I do not know this man about whom you are talking." And immediately a cock crowed a second time. Then Peter remembered the word that Jesus had said to him, "Before the cock crows twice you will deny me three times." He broke down and wept.

The intervention of a soldier in the Metropolitan *Denial* is certainly justified by Saint John's Gospel (18, 26), in which Mark's bystanders are identified as the "guards" of the high priest's gate. Since both the maid and the soldier are accusing Peter, Caravaggio seems to depict the outcome of the biblical episode: the apostle's eloquent ultimate denial through "cursing and swearing." In his 1644 *Chironomia, or The Art of Manuall Rhetorique*, John Bulwer writes: "by his hand referred unto him, an orator may show himself when he speaks anything concerning himself" (Fig. 213). To better explain the meaning of this gesture, illustrated in the book's plates with a hand cupped apparently upon the chest, Bulwer adds: "Caesar used this pathetical demonstration of himself when one accused Brutus unto him, and bade him beware of him. What, said he again, clapping his hand on his breast, think ye that Brutus will not tarry till this body dies?"[17] Because the episode of Peter's denial was rarely represented at Caravaggio's time or even earlier, I must rely on Bulwer's testimony in interpreting the Metropolitan picture. As Peter's mouth is blatantly open, one can infer that he is denying that he knows Jesus by pointing to his breast with the clamps of his hands: "I swear I do not know who this man is." Yet many scholars have construed Peter's hand gesture as the manifestation of his oncoming repentance:[18] Peter would then "beat and knock the hand upon the breast"—I quote once again from Bulwer, but this time from the first volume of his 1644 book, the *Chirologia, or The Naturall Language of the Hand*—in a "natural expression (…) used in sorrow, contrition, repentance, shame, and in reprehending ourselves, or when anything is irksome unto us because the breast is the cabin of the heart."[19] In the case of the repentance gesture, early modern iconography abounds in examples of penitent saints beating their breasts with their fists. But is Peter here pounding his chest with his hands in realization that he has just betrayed Christ?

Caravaggio does not seem to have represented Peter's fists clenched in contrition, but rather cupped in self-assertion. Depending on how one interprets Peter's hand gesture, the temporality of Caravaggio's *istoria* changes radically. In the case of self-assertion, there would be temporal coherence and hence simultaneousness, but in the second case, Peter's presumed act of contrition would bring about an obvious chronological discontinuity; it should then be regarded as a narrative prolepsis, a pictorial fast-forward toward the denial's aftermath. Even if I read Peter's hand gesture as self-assertive, I still believe that Caravaggio attempted to suggest the saint's repentance rather than his denial.

17   Bulwer, 44, XXIV.

18   See Cinotti 1983, 549: "Il gesto di Pietro è ambiguo: esso esprime contemporaneamente la discolpa ('io no') e il 'mea culpa' del traditore"; Mina Gregori in Christiansen 1985, 350: "Even the gesture of Saint Peter, who holds his hands to his chest as though expressing remorse after his denial of the servant's accusation, is analogous to Saint Ursula's gesture of humility and acceptance, as well as to that of the Virgin in the Annunciation of 1609-10 in the Musée des Beaux-Arts, Nancy." These three gestures, though, are extremely different. See also Puglisi 1998, 351: "Instead of showing Peter's tearful repentance, a favorite post-Tridentine subject painted by the Carracci and their pupils, the canvas illustrates the earlier point in the Gospel narrative when the apostle renounced the arrested Christ. (…) The saint's gesture apparently declares negation but its double-handed emphasis is self-accusatory at

the same time"; Marini 2005, 522: "Il gesto di Pietro (…) è (…) allo stesso tempo di negazione, auto-accusa e pentimento"; and Von Rosen 2009, 130: "Für wesentlich wahrscheinlicher ist in meinen Augen eine Lesart, die der noch heute in Neapel zu beobachtenden Verwerdung der Geste entspricht, und zwar im Sinne eines sprachgebundenen Abgrenzungsgestus, der etwa die Bemerkung 'so nicht mit mir,' oder 'ich bin nicht schuld' zum Ausdruck bringt, was mit dem—von Caravaggio ja dargestelltem—Stirnrunzeln der Person einhergeht. Dabei handelt es sich eher um lokalen 'Straßenjargon' als um eine kodifizierte rhetorische Gestensprache, was die schwierige Dechriffierbarkeit in einem Heiligenbild erklärt." Interestingly enough, Von Rosen also examines the ways in which the Pensionante del Saraceni and Giuseppe Vermiglio developed Caravaggio's take on the biblical episode of Peter's denial.

19   Bulwer, 89, LIII.

As I have already explained, Caravaggio's *Denial* can be approached in a two-pronged manner: by deciphering its figures' gestures and expressions, or through the materiality of its pictorial surface. Read in this second way, the gestural and expressive components of the *istoria* give way to the unevenness of its impasto, luminosity, and chiaroscuro; the painting's facture creates a competing taxonomy of perception and reading. By his eclectic handling of the brushwork, Caravaggio contrasts the almost impalpable shadows of Peter's accusers with the outburst of pictorial matter as rendered particularly in the saint's blotchy face, but also in the massive outgrowth of his cupped hands, vigorously projected beyond the picture's surface. The disruptive charge of the splotch forming his face, and to a lesser degree the vortices of his hands, by its visual impact, impose itself upon the viewer to the detriment of the figures' expression; in the raw form

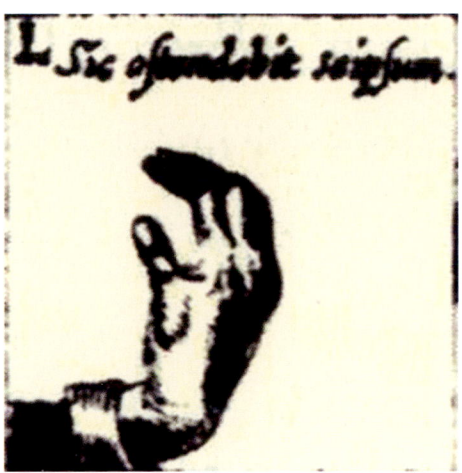

Fig. 213
Showing Yourself, in John Bulwer, *Chironomia*, reproduced from John Bulwer, *Chironomia*, 1974.

of a furor-driven draft, these explosions of pigments and brushwork embody an indeterminate, blind torment—that is, the physical and moral crumbling of Peter's figure. It is the indeterminacy and blindness of affect expressed through the vehement *non-finito* of Peter's face that allows viewers to sense and see the turbulence of repentance in his figure; although it is not literally represented, the bitterness of regret is alluded to through the brushwork's combusting fury.

If my interpretation is correct, I must conclude that in the Metropolitan *Denial* Caravaggio once again set up a major dislocation of the *istoria*'s temporality, but this time in a completely new way. Whereas Peter's figure plays out denial, the nearly distorted smear of his face transmits the ineffable throes of his subsequent ordeal, an ordeal synonymous to repentance in the viewer's eyes. It is not necessary to explain here how diversely Titian's artistic sketchiness or Tintoretto's fantastic *non-finito* operate in their pictures; since their procedures concern the entire surface of the painting, and are not selective as in Caravaggio's *Denial*, their narratives affect the viewer in a very different manner. On the other hand, as I shall show, Caravaggio's *non-finito* lends itself to diversified goals when applied on larger scales and formats, such as those of the Syracuse *Burial of Saint Lucy* and the Messina *Resurrection of Lazarus*. Despite the obvious disparities of effect determined by the vastness of their surfaces, these paintings, too, deploy the intrinsic energy of the pictorial matter, albeit more in their lighting and chiaroscuro than in their impasto.

Labor, Death, and a Lack of Transcendence

In his 1672 *Vite*, Giovan Pietro Bellori records in concise terms both Caravaggio's sojourn in Syracuse after fleeing from Malta and the painting that he executed there:

> Having arrived in Syracuse, he made the picture for the church of Saint Lucy outside the city, on the seafront: he depicted the dead saint with the bishop who blesses her, and there are two figures who dig into the ground with a spade in order to bury her.[20]

---

20   Bellori, 227: "Pervenuto in Siracusa fece il quadro per la chiesa di Santa Lucia che sta fuori alla marina: dipinse la santa morta col vescovo che la benedice; e vi sono due che scavano la terra con la pala per sepelirla."

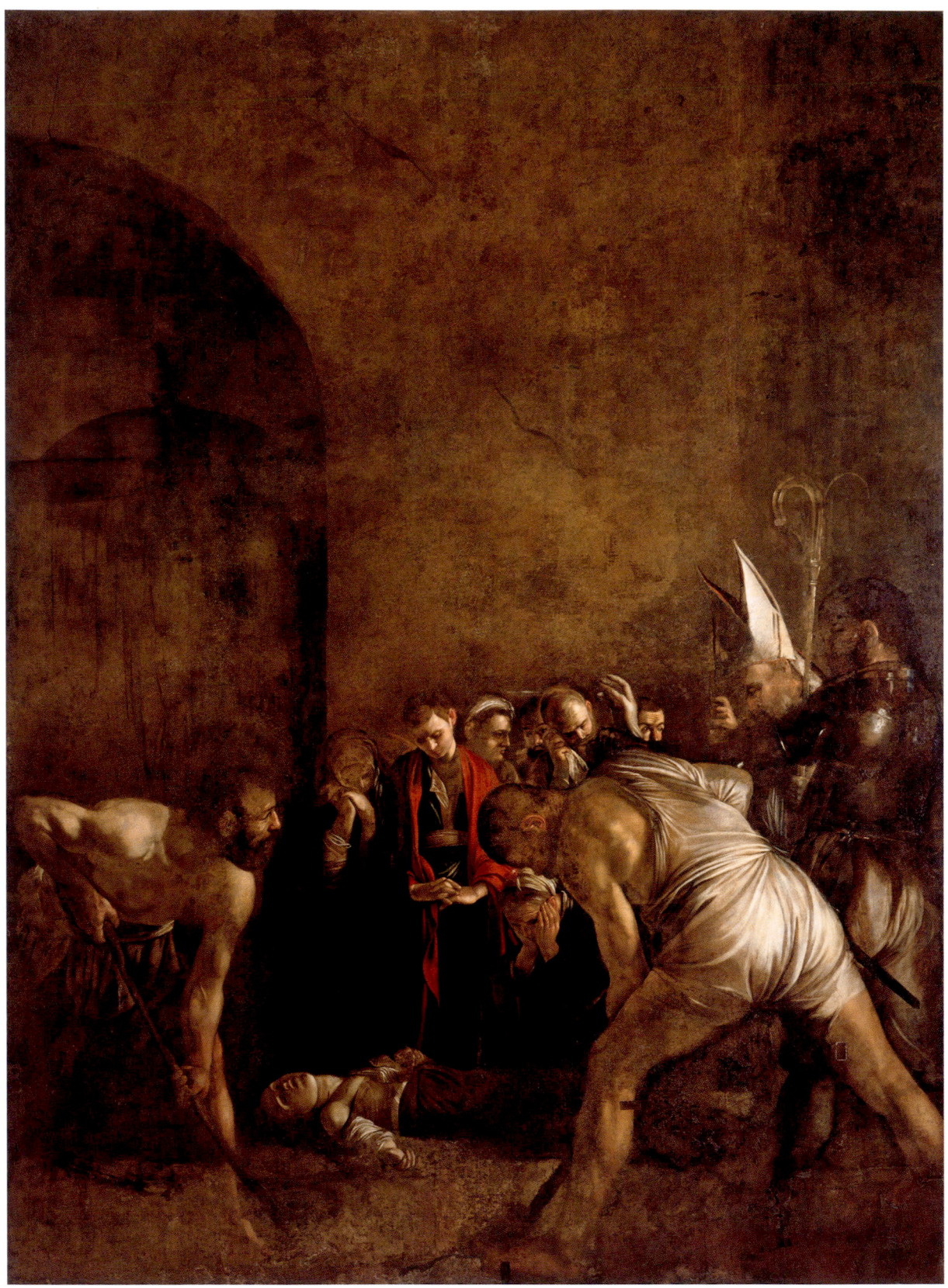

Fig. 214
Michelangelo Merisi da Caravaggio, *The Burial of Saint Lucy*, Museo Regionale di Palazzo Bellomo, Syracuse, oil on canvas, 408 x 300 cm.

Since Bellori never saw the painting, and was describing it either from the report of a local correspondent or from a copy, it would be inconsiderate to comment upon his emphatic mention of the two diggers at the end of the sentence, although, knowing Bellori's aesthetic tenets, this fact sounds somewhat suspect. A better informed Francesco Susinno, in his 1724 *Le vite de' pittori messinesi,* relates that, after escaping from his prison in Malta, Caravaggio was welcomed in Syracuse by Mario Minniti, his friend and probable former apprentice in Rome. According to Susinno, Minniti "entreated the senate of that city to engage Caravaggio in some job, so that he might enjoy his friend's company for some time and observe the degree of excellence that Michelangelo [Caravaggio] had attained, as the rumor that he was the best painter in Italy was widely spread."[21] Minniti's request to the senate of Syracuse was fulfilled forthwith:

> The authority of that institution did not disregard this opportunity and immediately commissioned Caravaggio to execute a large canvas of the Sicilian virgin and martyr Saint Lucy. One can admire it nowadays in the church of the reformed fathers of Saint Francis, outside the city walls, which is dedicated to that glorious saint. In this canvas, the master represented the saint's corpse lying upon the ground as the bishop and populace come to bury her, and two porters, the picture's main figures, on either side, work with their spades by digging a grave in which to place her. This large canvas met with such great success that it is commonly praised, and the deserved esteem of this painting is such that one can see many copies of it in Messina as well as in other cities of the kingdom.[22]

As documentary evidence suggests that Caravaggio left Malta at the beginning of October 1608 and was already in Messina on 6 December of the same year,[23] he must have conceived and executed the large *Burial of Saint Lucy,* now in the Museo Nazionale di Palazzo Bellomo, Syracuse (Fig. 214),[24] in less than two months, a short period of time that may account for some technical features of the painting. As Bellori and Susinno rightly state, Caravaggio's work was destined for the church of Santa Lucia extra moenia, a paramount place of devotion in early modern Syracuse since it was believed that the saint had been martyred there and buried in a catacomb underneath it.

Unfortunately, the *Burial* has suffered greatly and its damage is so extensive that it is now impossible to discern many details of the original composition, some of them crucial for the

21 Susinno, 110: "Ma di notte tempo, scalati i muri fuggì in Sicilia, e ricovratosi nella città di Siracusa, fu ivi accolto dall'amico suo e collega nello studio di pittura, Mario Minniti pittore siracusano, da cui ricevette tutta la compitezza che poté farle la civiltà di un tal galantuomo. Lo stesso supplicò quel senato della città acciò impiegasse il Caravaggio in qualche lavoro, e così potesse aver campo di godere per qualche tempo l'amico ed altresì osservarsi a qual grado di altezza erasi portato Michelagnolo, mentre se ne udiva grande il rumore e ch'egli fosse in Italia il primo dipintore."

22 Ibidem: "L'autorità di quel magistrato non pose in non cale l'occasione, ed insubito l'impiegò nella fattura di una gran tela della vergine e martire santa Lucia siciliana. Oggi giorno ammirasi nella chiesa de' padri riformati di San Francesco, dedicata alla stessa gloriosa santa, fuori le mura della medesima città. In questa gran tela il dipintore fece il cadavere della martire disteso in terra, mentre il vescovo con il popolo viene per sepellirlo e due facchini, figure principali dell'opera, una di una parte ed una dall'altra, con pale in azzione che fanno un fosso acciò in esso lo collochino. Riuscì di tal gradimento questa gran tela che comunemente vien celebrata, ed è tale di questa dipintura il meritato concetto che

in Messina ed altresì in tutte le città del regno se ne veggono molte copie."

23 Caravaggio's flight from Malta is mentioned in a document issued on 6 October 1608, and first published by Ashford 1935, 174, and Sammut 1949: see Macioce 2003, 246. On 6 December 1608, Giovan Battista de' Lazzari pledged to have built the main chapel in the church of the Crociferi, Messina, and to provide it with an altarpiece. On 10 June 1609, the fathers of the Crociferi acknowledged the receipt of Caravaggio's *Resurrection of Lazarus* for the altarpiece of the De' Lazzari Chapel. For these two documents, first published by Saccà 1907, 67-9, see Macioce 2003, 249-50, 251-2.

24 For the painting see Friedlaender 1969, 213; Moir 1982, 154; Cinotti 1983, 546-8, no. 66; Hibbard 1983, 235-40; Zuccari 1987; Bologna 1992, 338, 426-7; Pacelli 1994, 85-7; Barbera and Lapucci 1996; Zuccari 1996, 295-7; Puglisi 1998, 317-23; Longhi 1999-2000, 1:282 [1968]; Treffers 2002, 214-5; Barbera and Spagnolo 2005; Cassani and Sapio 2005, 122-4, no. 10 [catalogue entry by Gioacchino Barbera]; Marini 2005, 547-9, no. 96; Varriano 2006, 116; Schütze 2009, 280, no. 57; Ebert-Schiffer 2009, 226-9.

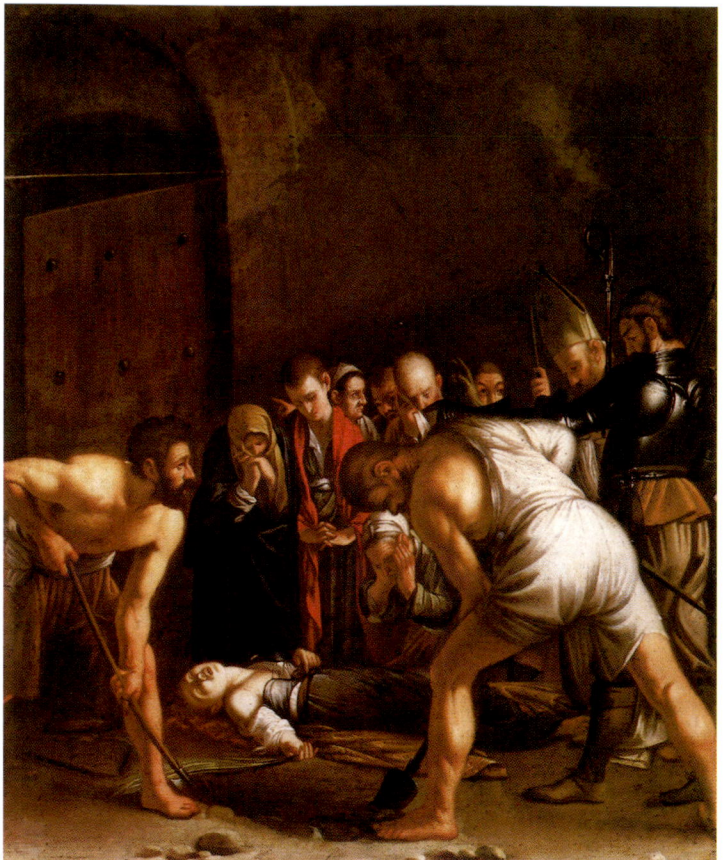

Fig. 215
Mario Minniti (attributed to) after Caravaggio, *The Burial of Saint Lucy*, private collection, Rome, oil on copper, 40.6 x 34 cm, reproduced from Maurizio Marini, *Caravaggio*, 2005.

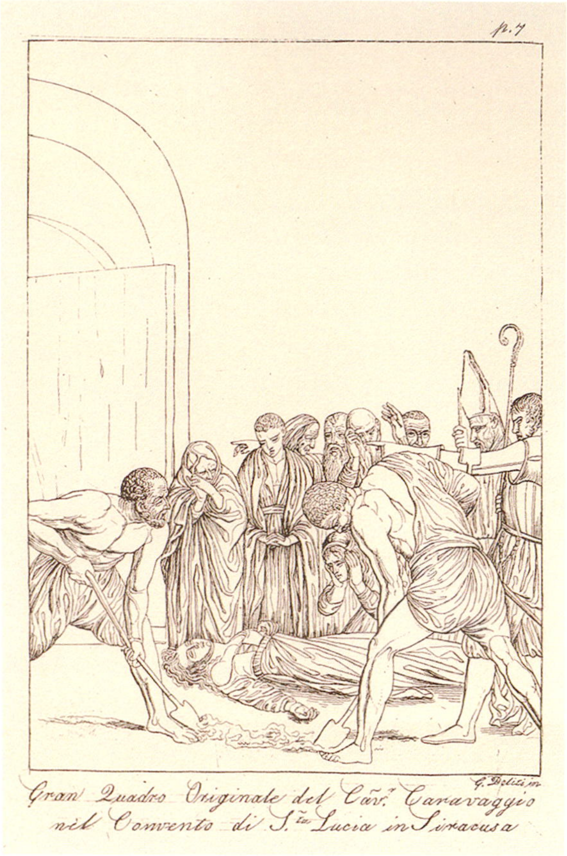

Fig. 216
Caravaggio's *The Burial of Saint Lucy*, reproduced from Giuseppe Politi, *Siracusa per i viaggiatori*, 1835.

comprehension of its narrative. However, one can fill in the painting's lacunae with the help of a copy attributed to Mario Minniti in a private collection, Rome (Fig. 215)[25] and with Giuseppe Politi's schematic reproduction of the already damaged picture published in his 1835 *Siracusa pei viaggiatori* (Fig. 216).[26] From these testimonies, it is clear that what now looks like an almost empty space occupying the canvas' upper half initially contained the depiction, to the left, of an arched gate opening onto a vaulted hallway through a massive, studded door, left ajar; to the right, viewers could spot a few cracks over the bare wall through the background's lingering shades. In the lower foreground, the figures of two diggers, represented in *contrapposto*—one frontally, the other with his back turned, both leaning in obvious symmetry—set out to dig the martyr's grave, beyond which, parallel to the picture's surface, Lucy's corpse lies supine, as her right hand, stretched toward the foreground, inertly wields a branch of palm, the humble trophy of her martyrdom.

Clustered around Lucy's cadaver, two women—one kneeling while pressing her hands against her cheeks out of desperation, the other standing with her head bent and supported by her clasped hands—along with a deacon clad in a red robe, silently mourn the young saint. Behind this group of figures, a man opens his mouth while pointing his right hand—which originally protruded from behind the deacon's shoulder—in the direction of the door, as if warning or informing the woman

25 This copy is mentioned for the first time by Maurizio Marini, who attributed it to Mario Minniti. See Marini 2005, 547. For Mario Minniti as a painter, see Frommel 1996 and, more recently, Barbera and Greco 2004.

26 See Politi 1835.

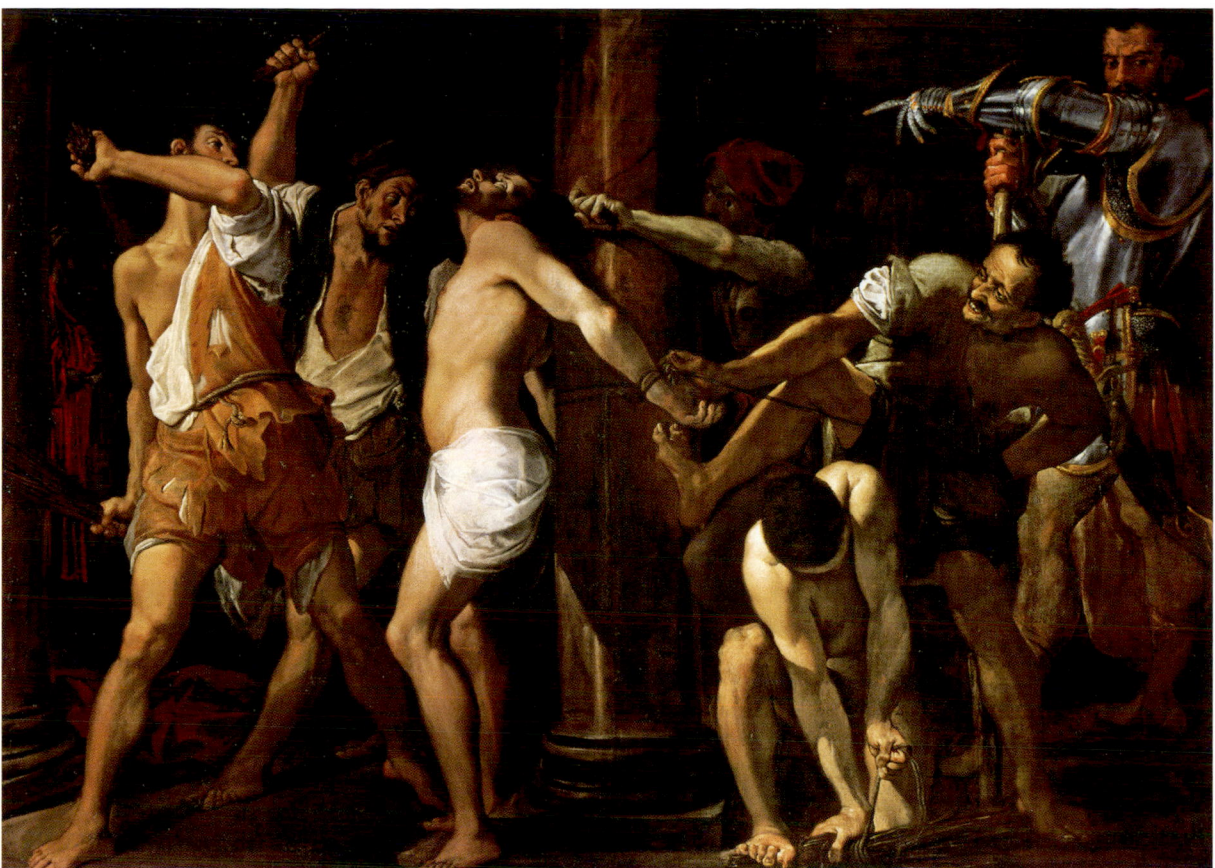

Fig. 217
Ludovico Carracci, *The Flagellation*, Musée de la Chartreuse, Douai, oil on canvas, 189 x 265 cm.

nearby. In front of this man, another male figure, holding a handkerchief, grieves the martyr's death. To the right, a soldier in a metallic cuirass and a bishop with a crosier and a towering miter seem to preside over the burial ceremony. Essential in this regard, the superimposed gesture of the soldier's and the bishop's hands figuring upon the bent shoulder of the digger at the right—a detail now regrettably lost—was given great relevance by Caravaggio. From a chromatic point of view, this crisscross of hands, placed at approximately forty-five degrees to one another, must have been utterly compelling: the soldier's iron dark glove pointed toward the digger at the left and the bright glove of the solemnly blessing bishop neatly stood out against the whiteness of the porter's shirt.

Since the digger to the left unequivocally fixes his eyes upon the pointing hand, it can be assumed that the soldier is ordering him to start digging.[27] If one trusts Minniti's copy of the *Burial*, the soldier was not looking at the digger, but rather staring at the grave area as if in concentration or, less probably, in meditation. The armed guard at the extreme right of Ludovico Carracci's *c.*1585 *Flagellation* (now at the Musée de la Chartreuse, Douai) plays a role analogous, albeit not identical, to Caravaggio's soldier in the Syracuse picture (Fig. 217).[28] But in Ludovico's *Flagellation*, the soldier looks outward as if inciting beholders to focus on the Savior's torture, which his gloved hand indicates, and therefore his figure is granted a meta-pictorial function extraneous, in this case,

27 Hibbard 1983, 237 is of the same opinion: "The man in armor holds out his left arm horizontally, in shadow, to direct the gravediggers."

28 For the painting see Emiliani 1993, 16-7, no. 7; and Brogi 2001, 1:119-22, no. 14.

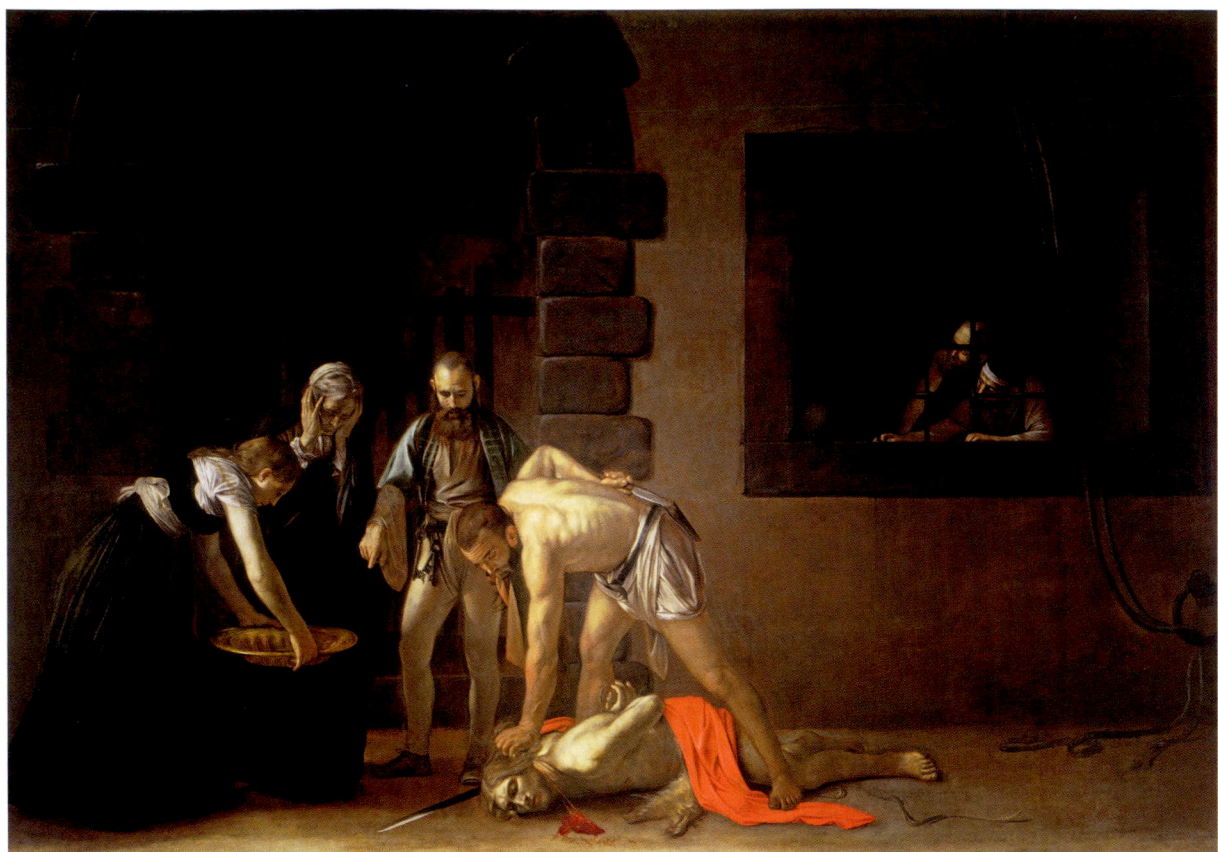

Fig. 218
Michelangelo Merisi da Caravaggio, *The Beheading of Saint John the Baptist*, Co-Cathedral of Saint John, Valletta, oil on canvas, 361 x 520 cm.

to Caravaggio's *Burial*. As Caravaggio undoubtedly did not plan to stay long in Syracuse—he must have thought of his sojourn there as a brief stopover and temporary refuge—it is predictable that, in accepting the commission for the *Burial*, he strove to maximize the process of execution as much as possible. Even if he was supplied with a spacious studio in which to work comfortably on such a large surface (the picture's height exceeds 4 meters), he most probably did not use live models, and drew largely on his memory. As many scholars have justly noted, Caravaggio's idea of erecting the truncated cone of his two diggers in the foreground—their hunched torsos and aligned heads outline this geometric pattern—as a proscenium to the saint's proper burial harks back to his 1608 *Beheading of Saint John the Baptist* for the co-cathedral of Saint John, Valletta (Fig. 218).[29]

In this painting, the correlated figures of Salome to the left and the executioner to the right bend toward one another, thus delineating the base of a dome. To my knowledge, it has never been pointed out that two woodcuts by Albrecht Altdorfer, both representing *The Beheading of Saint John the Baptist*, inspired Caravaggio for his Valletta painting, though it is possible that Caravaggio also had them in mind when painting his *Burial*. In the first print, commonly dated to 1512 despite the inscription "1517" at its top right, Altdorfer represented a group of three figures—Herodias to the left, the executioner to the right and Salome at the center—encircling John's beheaded corpse lying upon the ground in a position almost parallel to the woodcut's surface (Fig. 219).[30] To anchor the main episode to the foreground, Altdorfer designed a monumental ogive arch, whose thrust

29   The bibliography on this painting is vast. For a recent and informed outlook of Caravaggio's activity in Malta, see Sciberras and Stone 2006.

30   See Mielke 1988, 146, no. 69.

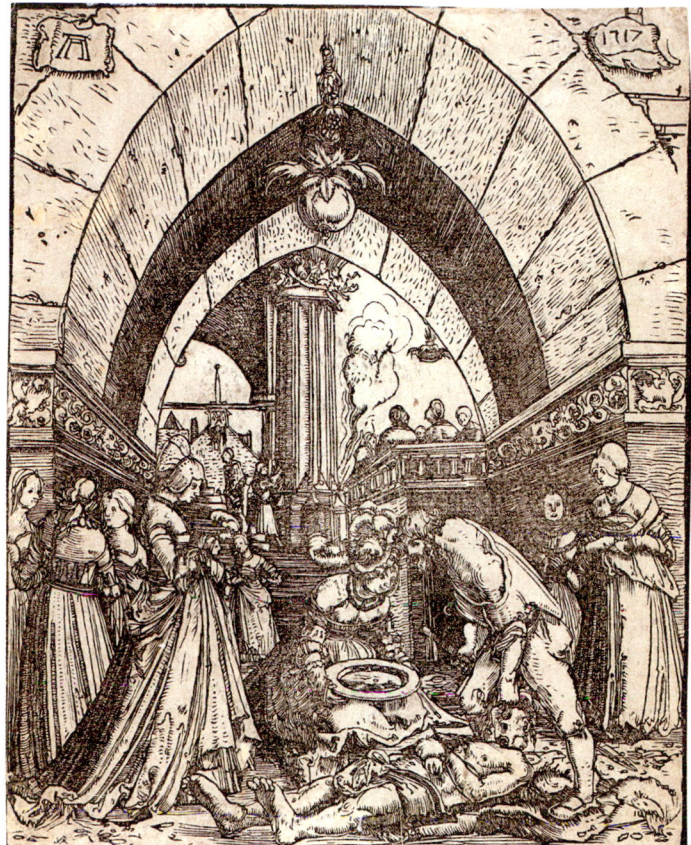

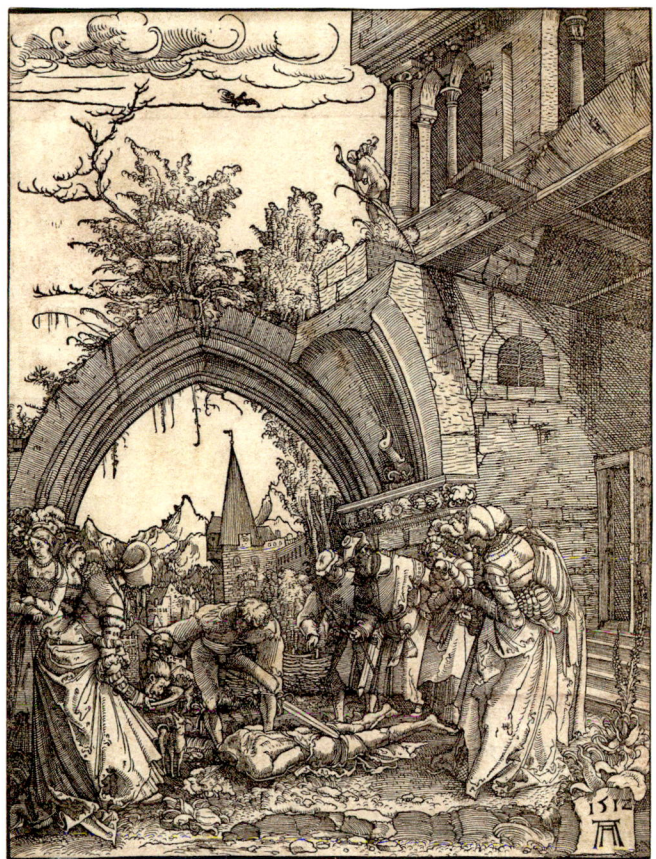

Fig. 219
Albrecht Altdorfer, *The Beheading of Saint John the Baptist*, woodcut, 20.5 x 15.7 cm.

Fig. 220
Albrecht Altdorfer, *The Beheading of Saint John the Baptist*, woodcut, 20 x 16 cm.

prolongs, albeit in different ways, the ascending curve of Herodias' silhouette and the spanned profile of the executioner's torso.

In Altdorfer's second woodcut, John's cadaver appears at a short distance from the foreground, lying on its belly and deprived of its head; bowed over John, and resting a sword upon his buttocks, the executioner reaches out toward Salome, who bends and sets out to receive John's head on a basin (Fig. 220).[31] With great ingenuity, Altdorfer placed a row of bystanders receding toward a ruined archway a little farther away, their bent bodies echoing the spanning motif of the ogive overhead. If one concentrates upon the central episode in this woodcut's lower register, one sees that, bracketed by the two women hunching in the foreground, Saint John's corpse forms a slightly diagonal axis inscribed within the truncated cone that all the bent onlookers comprise, including of course Salome.

As with other prototypes, Caravaggio here again synthesized and compacted Altdorfer's invention; in the Malta *Beheading of Saint John the Baptist*, four figures suffice to surround the martyr, placed horizontally upon the ground, but noticeably off-center with regard to the bystanders; through the common dome of their bodies, they link the almost decapitated saint to the quoined arch above. *The Beheading*'s monumental archway, along with the grilled window to the right, may derive from the architectural setting of an engraving by Johan Sadeler I after Maarten de Vos, *The Beheading of Saint John the Baptist*.[32] By disposing the two bent diggers in the foreground of the Syracuse *Burial*, by placing Lucy's horizontal body upon the ground as a visual link between

31 Ibidem, 146-7, no. 70.

32 See De Ramaix 1999, 197, no. 166.

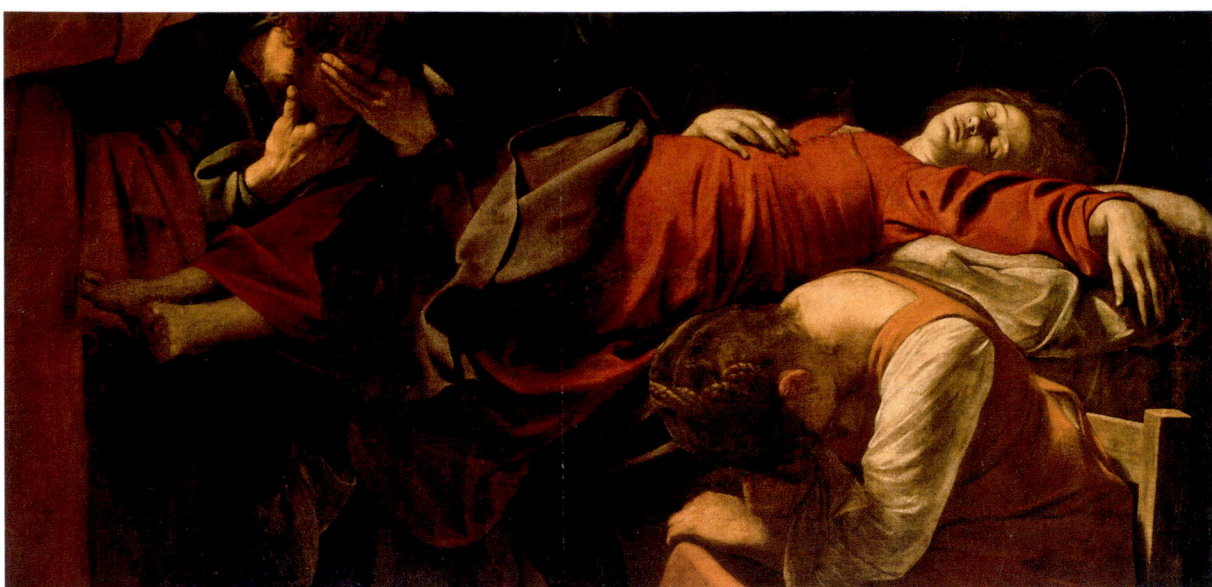

Fig. 221
Michelangelo Merisi da Caravaggio, *The Death of the Virgin*, Musée du Louvre, Paris, oil on canvas, 369 x 245 cm., detail.

those two laborers, and by opening a majestic archway to the left, Caravaggio not only retrieved his own previous material through self-elaboration, but also expanded upon Altdorfer's ideas as expressed in the two woodcuts of the *Beheading*. In the *Burial*, in fact, much more than in the Valletta picture, the opposition of scale between the huddled bystanders—so close to one another as to lose, with a few exceptions, their individuality—and the overhanging architecture becomes a vital matter of the narrative: the expressive means by which the theme of the hero's or heroine's death is depersonalized and, in a sense, dehumanized.[33]

That Caravaggio relied on compositional patterns and figures taken from his *Beheading of Saint John* is also clear from the kneeling old woman beside Lucy's corpse, who is the exact replica of the elderly lady standing to the left of the Valletta picture. More importantly, the figure of the martyred Lucy recalls, in reverse, the scandalous dead Mary that Caravaggio had depicted years before in his 1605-1606 *Death of the Virgin* (Louvre, Paris).[34] The damage suffered by the Syracuse painting inevitably conditions my reading of Lucy's figure. In my view, the saint's corpse in the *Burial* is not only a quotation from *The Death of the Virgin*—the even disposition of Mary's and the martyr's bodies, paralleling the painting's surface, with one arm stretched, the other hidden and a hand resting on their wombs, as well as the women's tilted heads lit from below, confirm this assumption—but originally Lucy must have looked like an "unfinished," or summarily sketched,

33 Longhi 1999-2000, 1:282: "Nel dipinto che fra quelli di Sicilia è il più antico, ma anche il più guasto (…), la 'Sepoltura di Santa Lucia' nella chiesa eponima siracusana, il Caravaggio ha il nuovo grande pensiero di diminuire nello spazio, rapidamente, la misura degli uomini sovrastati dalle mura gigantesche: un rapporto inedito nella tradizione italiana e già pronto per il Rembrandt incisore"; and Bologna 1992, 427: "Ma torniamo al *Seppellimento di santa Lucia*. S'è detto delle mura scortecciate; dell'interno di un rudere archeologico vuoto; dell'arcone cieco, di *allure* già rembrandtiana, dentro il quale—per come si riesce a intravedere da una vecchia copia— si schiudeva un'anta di porta sgangherata, non dissimile da quella che mena al cortile interno della *Decollazione* di Malta. Con queste scelte, il Caravaggio invertiva il rapporto fra figure e ambiente, scopriva anche il vuoto delle muraglie come

grandiose nature morte, e faceva altri passi avanti nel processo di trasformazione di 'questi stanzoni simili a vasti magazzini sgomberati' (riadopero le parole scritte ad altro proposito dal giovane Longhi) in 'vaso luminoso e in fondo come superficie coloristica'."

34 Longhi 1999-2000, 1:282: "Quanto ai primi piani, vi stanno la Santa a luce riversa come nella Vergine morta del 1606 o nella 'Maddalena' dipinta nella Campagna Romana"; Hibbard 1983, 237-8: "The pitiful saint with her throat cut so discreetly may owe something to Caravaggio's memory of the famous recovery of the body of St. Cecilia in Rome in 1599 and the commemorative statue by Stefano Maderno, produced in 1600, which is similar to Lucy in its simplicity."

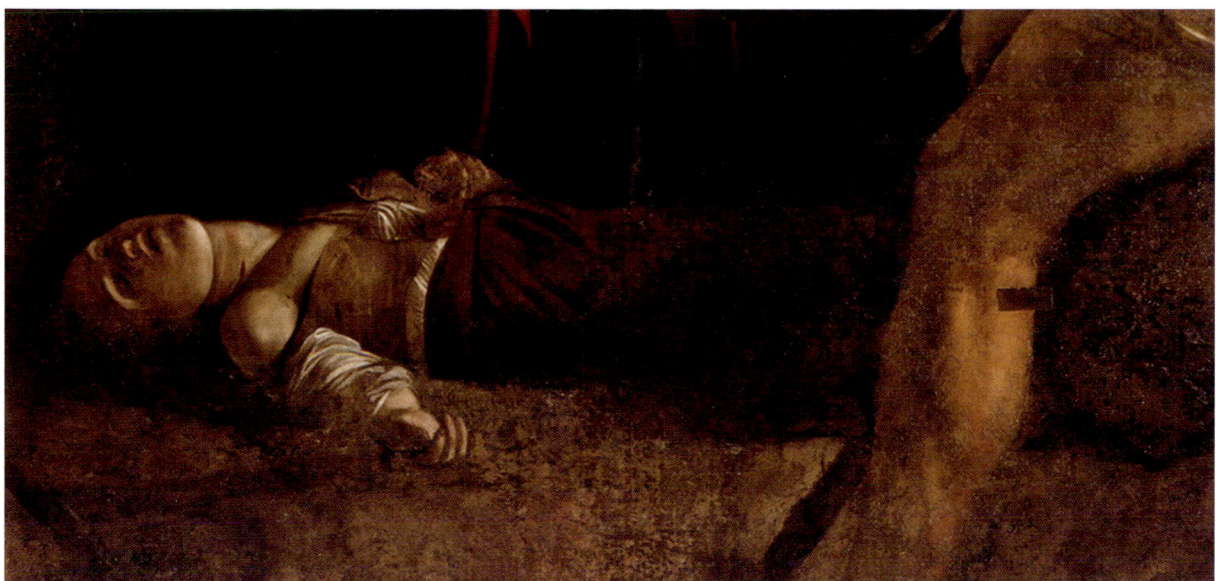

Fig. 222
Michelangelo Merisi da Caravaggio, *The Burial of Saint Lucy*, Museo di Palazzo Bellomo, Syracuse, oil on canvas, 408 x 300 cm., detail.

counterpart to the Louvre dead Madonna (Figs. 221, 222). As on other occasions at the end of his career, Caravaggio dug Lucy's figure out from the dark priming through thin and translucent layers of brushstrokes, as can be seen from the cursory traits of the martyr's face—the slit of her gasping mouth, the curl of her nose, the commas of her eyebrows, and her forehead that would sink into the dirt were it not for the cushion formed by her long reddish hair, now invisible but clearly discernable in Minniti's copy. The sketchiness and simplified silhouette of Lucy's corpse, along with her inert expression akin to a deep slumber, seem to have preoccupied Minniti, who obviously endowed the martyr's face with a fixed scream more suitable to a Christian martyr, and exalted her mortal pallor in opposition to the diggers' swarthiness, chromatic details completely absent from Caravaggio's painting.

If my reconstruction of the original chiaroscuro and color layout is correct, Caravaggio strongly opposed the almost systematic high-definition of the two diggers' corporeal volumes displayed as an opening frontispiece—nevertheless, the laborer's face to the right must also have been merely "sketched"—and Lucy's mannequin-like sketchiness. By making this observation, I do not imply that initially the saint was less visible or remarkable. I do however believe that Caravaggio deliberately avoided defining Lucy's individuality further; more than a figure, the martyr is represented as an indeterminate woman's body, a female corpse, and the impression of her sheer inanimate corporality must have been even greater when Caravaggio, in a first version of the painting now visible through X-rays, represented her head wholly detached from her neck.[35] In other words, Lucy's is not the physiognomic accuracy that makes the figure of Mary in the *Death of the Virgin* so poignant that Mancini could describe it as the portrait of a whore.

Another essential actor in the *Burial*, the now nearly effaced soldier, also stems from a previous work by Caravaggio, the 1599-1600 *Calling of Saint Matthew*. His placement at the right margin, and the orientation of his torso and downcast head recall those of the apostle accompanying Christ in the Contarelli picture. However, the soldier's lifted arm and pointing hand are borrowed from the figure of Christ in *The Calling*. Therefore, Caravaggio conflated in the *Burial*'s soldier the

35 For this point, and a discussion of its significance, see Zuccari 1997, 295-7.

reminiscences of the famous duo at the right of the Contarelli picture, the pointing and bursting-in Christ and Peter. As a result, the left digger's intent expression upon seeing the soldier's signal echoes the sudden attention and tension of Saint Matthew, or, even more, of the youth with his back turned in *The Calling*. These elements play—or originally played—a crucial role in the Syracuse *Burial*: the digger's reaction to the soldier's command in fact constitutes the painting's main action. From the outset, then, Caravaggio embedded in the composition's foreground a suspended action based on the cause-and-effect interrelation between a rhetorical gesture—the pointing hand—and the response to it.

That Caravaggio definitely had in mind the controversial narrative of his early *Calling* is buttressed by the fact that, a few months after depicting *The Burial*, the master represented a pointing Christ at the left of his *Resurrection of Lazarus*, a figure that not only evokes that of the Savior in the Contarelli picture, but also mirrors that of the soldier in the Syracuse painting. Whereas Christ's pointing gesture and its narrative ramifications in *The Calling* relay and support the theme of divine transcendence integral to the painting's subject, in *The Burial* the soldier's ceremonial command is supplied with an accessory and merely chronological function; along with the bishop's blessing glove it signals the climax of the woman's burial by introducing the final act of her entombment. Instead of translating the ineffability of God's irruption into a human event, the soldier's pointing hand emphasizes the mechanical action of digging, and hence underscores the motif of man's labor personified by the gigantic gravediggers that Caravaggio deliberately planted in the foreground, "the picture's main figures," or its protagonists, to paraphrase Susinno.

It is not that the sacred *istoria* does not permit the depiction of workers or acolytes in a prominent view; in an engraving by Johan Sadeler I after Pietro Candido (alias Pieter de Witte), *The Martyrdom of Saint Ursula*,[36] the figure of a bent soldier, his legs spread and his back turned as he slays one of the martyr's companions, appears in the foreground in a posture very similar to that of the digger at the right of *The Burial* (Figs. 223, 224). Nonetheless, the visual preeminence of these secondary figures does not interfere with, but strengthens, the centrality of the religious heroine; in Sadeler's print, for example, the soldier's sword represented in the shade not only stresses the idea of Ursula's martyrdom by interposing itself between the viewer and the saint, but also, acting as a dark foil, intensifies the martyr's luminosity. In Caravaggio's *Burial*, the manual act of digging neither relates to Lucy's martyrdom nor to her sanctity, nor necessarily highlights the saint's role in the painting. Although, as many scholars have noted, the *contrapposto* of the two diggers forms a breach through which the main episode can be watched, the presence of the red-clad deacon, vertically poised in contemplation and mute despair, catches the viewer's attention sooner than does Lucy's corpse. There is no doubt indeed that even originally this figure's crimson slashes vigorously jutted out amidst the picture's brownish hues and fluid penumbras; they guided the beholder toward the mourning crowd in the background and also, of course, to Lucy's cadaver upon the ground.

I do not hereby refute the centrality of Lucy's figure in *The Burial*, but rather argue that Caravaggio patently downplayed the saint's visual preeminence and, more relevantly, that he suppressed any allusion to divine transcendence by approaching the martyr's burial through the lens of the diggers' labor and by panning over the entire spectacle of the ceremony in a sort of "low-angle shot."[37] The depiction of a monumental archway at the upper left part of the canvas and of a large and empty space nearby conversely de-monumentalizes the figures of the crowd

---

36 Candido's 1588 *Martyrdom of Saint Ursula* is in the Michaelskirche, Munich. See Volk-Knüttel 2010, 138-40, no. G18.

37 In this regard, see the interesting remarks of Berenson 1953, 40-41: "Far more prominent than the rest are three figures on the fore-edge, more than twice the size of the others: one

brutally digging, one in armor, and a third bending over with a grand display of buttocks. Almost cynical in its incongruity is the reduction of the mourners to background figures and the gross importance given to the material fact. There was a beginning of this in Tintoretto, the merest beginning, and (by the way) the bending giant reminds me of one in Pordenone's fresco of the Magi in Treviso." Berenson alludes here to

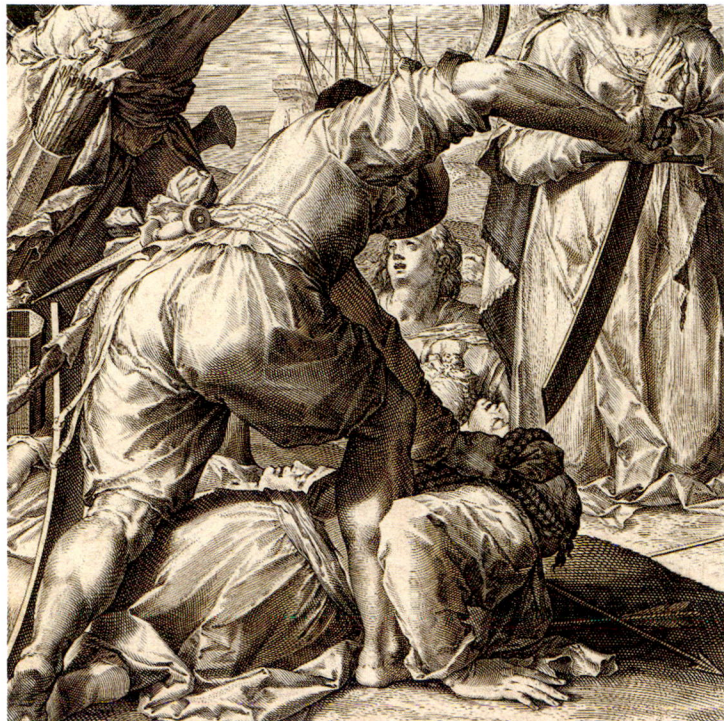

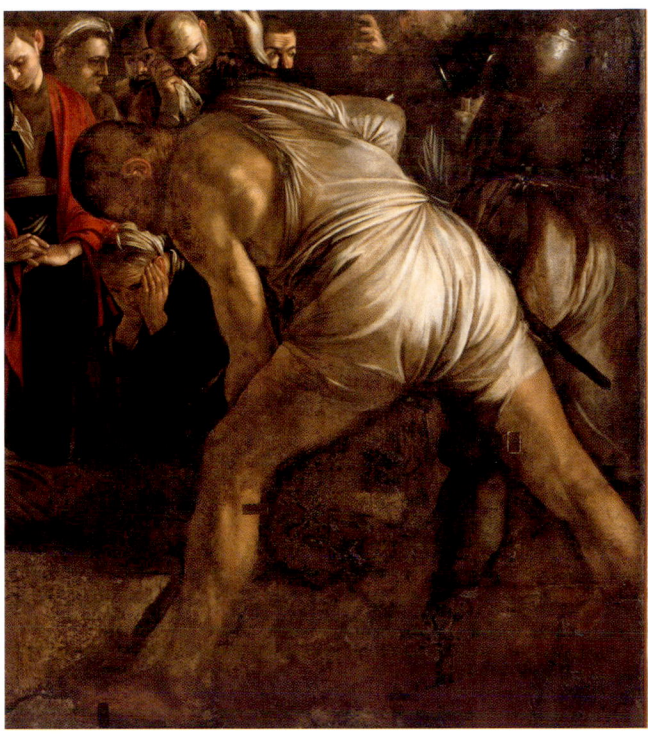

Fig. 223
Jan Sadeler I after Pietro Candido (Pieter de Witte), *The Martyrdom of Saint Ursula*, engraving, 43.2 x 27.4 cm., detail.

Fig. 224
Michelangelo Merisi da Caravaggio, *The Burial of Saint Lucy*, Museo di Palazzo Bellomo, Syracuse, oil on canvas, 408 x 300 cm., detail.

and the sacred body, an effect that Caravaggio could have avoided by placing the saint's corpse in the foreground, where instead he inserted the outsize masses of the diggers. (Many scholars, starting with Roberto Longhi, have repeatedly remarked upon *The Burial*'s leaps in perspective: the fact that, by manipulating his figures' proportions, Caravaggio illusorily wedged a supplementary stretch of space between, on the one hand, the diggers, the soldier, and bishop in the foreground and, on the other, the group of bystanders with Lucy's body at a certain distance).

One cannot justify *The Burial*'s lack of transcendence and descriptive materialism as a consequence of the short period of time allotted to Caravaggio in order to finish it. In reusing the narrative device of the pointing hand and eliminating its transcendent values, Caravaggio intentionally evolved his own narrative pattern toward an opposite effect: he reduced the suspenseful manifestation of a miracle as orchestrated in the Contarelli *Calling* to the matter-of-fact triteness of an act of labor in *The Burial* by simultaneously creating a kind of sequel to his *Death of the Virgin*. If indeed in the Louvre painting, by depicting the Virgin's swelling corpse surrounded by grieving apostles, he had already treated the theological mystery of Mary's *dormitio* as an ordinary funeral, thereby omitting any reference to the episode's divine significance, in *The Burial* Caravaggio goes even farther by grafting Lucy's sacred body onto the mechanical procedure of a manual labor, one in which the corpse's sacredness is eventually lost.

In this manner, Caravaggio not only dislocated the hero's or heroine's centrality as requested by the principles of the *istoria*, but also enlarged his subject-matter into one that encompasses a general pictorial theme: instead of representing Lucy's burial, the Syracuse painting ends up

Pordenone's 1520 *Adoration of the Magi* in the Cathedral od San Pietro, Treviso, and in particular to the male figure with

his back turned to the left. For the fresco, see Cohen C. 1996, 2:572-8, no. 32.

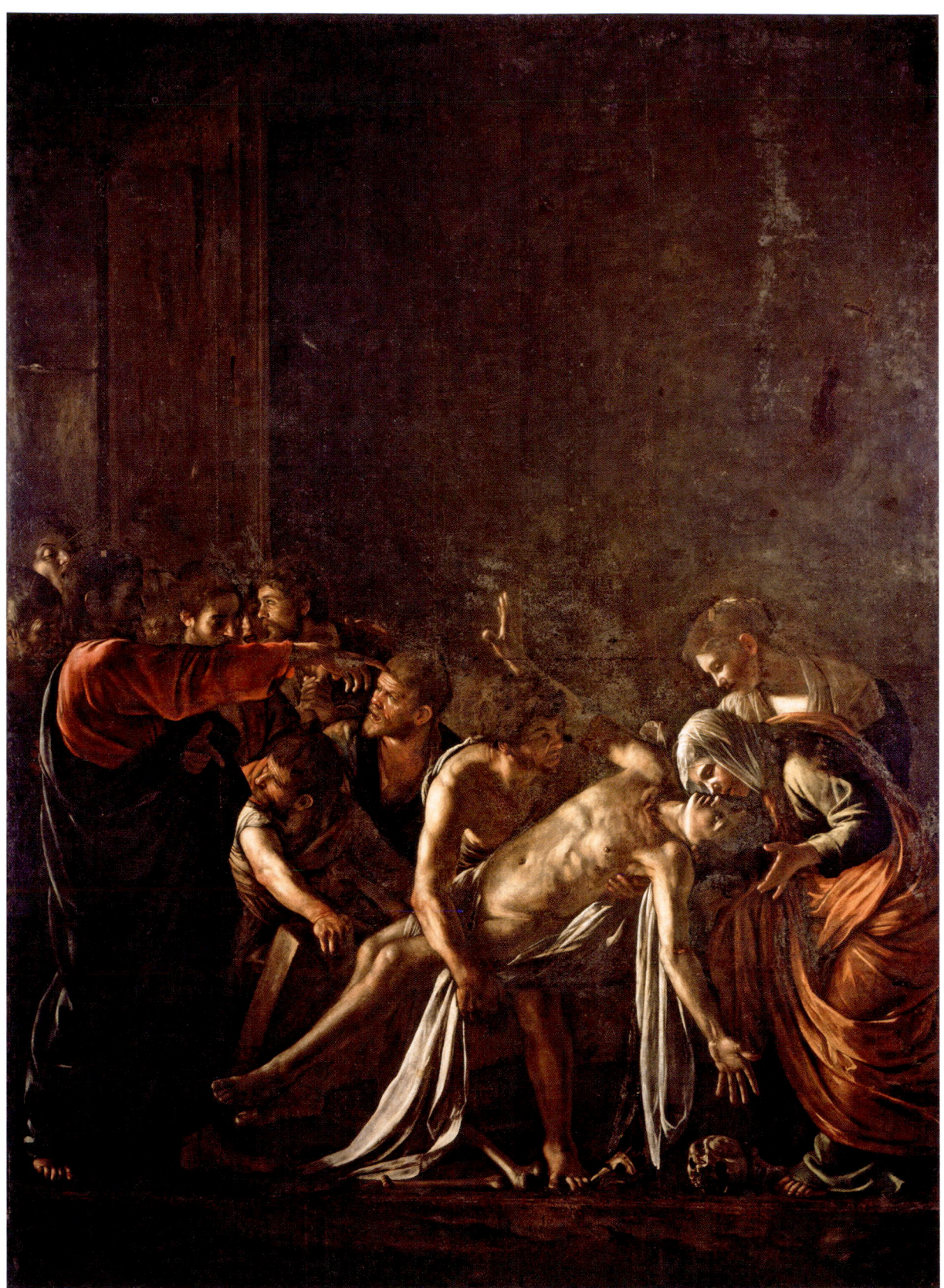

Fig. 225
Michelangelo Merisi da Caravaggio, *The Resurrection of Lazarus*, Museo Regionale, Messina, oil on canvas, 320 x 275 cm.

recording a woman's burial. In the end, *The Burial* is not even the contemporary chronicle of a virgin's entombment, a precedent in a sense to Gustave Courbet's *Enterrement à Ornans*; in this *Burial at Syracuse*, there is not even a wooden casket to shelter the girl, so that her body, lying upon the ground, already belongs to the ground in which she will finally lie. I cannot recall in the seventeenth century, or even before, any religious painting like this in which God's presence—even, for instance, in the diminutive form of a single sunray—is so radically absent.

Bending Temporality

Caravaggio's 1609 *Resurrection of Lazarus*, now in the Museo Regionale, Messina (Fig. 225), was certainly perceived by his author as a major work, and not only because of the high price that he was offered to paint it.[38] Although he never saw it, Bellori honored the picture with an interesting description not immune, as usual, to inaccuracies:

> In the church of the ministers of the sick, in the chapel of the Lazzari family, [Caravaggio depicted] the Resurrection of Lazarus who, held outside the sepulcher, opens his arms at the voice of Christ, who calls him and stretches his hand toward him. Martha cries, and the Magdalene is stunned, and there is a figure who places his hand over his nose to protect himself from the cadaver's stench. The painting is large, and the figures' background is a cave; the principal light is over the nude Lazarus and those who support him, and it is in high esteem because of its vigor in the matter of imitation.[39]

Susinno's description of the painting is far more detailed:

> As some rich Signori from the Lazzari family resolved to build a new chapel at the main altarpiece of the church of the Crociferi, they decided to engage this great artist [Caravaggio], with whom they settled for the price of 1000 *scudi*, to execute the painting. The painter conceived a Resurrection of Lazarus, an allusion to their family name. These Signori were highly satisfied as the artificer had vast latitude to achieve his invention felicitously (…). Setting out to work, he represented to the right the Savior with his back turned, along with his apostles, summoning the already departed spirit of the late Lazarus, who had been dead for four days, and in the center two porters who lift a great slab. Lazarus' corpse is shown supported by another porter and seems about to wake up. Around Lazarus' head, to the left, there are his sisters who, baffled, observe their brother awakening. In the sisters' faces Michelangelo [Caravaggio] represented the most beautiful ideas of beauty.[40]

38 Besides Bellori and Susinno, quoted in the text, *The Resurrection of Lazarus* is also mentioned in 1613 by Maruli, 427, and before 1654 by Samperi, 615 ("Michael Angelus Caravagius, pictor tota Italia praestantissimus, eo tempore quo Messanae versatus est, duo nobilissimi ingenii sui reliquit pignora, unum in templo Sancti Petri et Pauli pisanorum clericorum regularium ministrantium infirmis, hoc est Lazzari a Christo Domino in vitam revocati …"). For the painting, see Friedlaender 1969, 213-6; Spear 1965; Röttgen 1975; Marin 1977, 195-9; Moir 1982, 156; Cinotti 1983, 458-62, no. 30; Hibbard 1983, 240-5; Bologna 1992, 273-4, 338-9, 431-2; Lapucci 1994, 17-37; Spadaro 1995; Puglisi 1998, 323-7; Longhi 1999-2000, 1:282 [1968]; Cassani and Sapio 2005, 125-6, no. 11 [catalogue entry by Gioacchino Barbera]; Marini 2005, 549-51, no. 97; Schütze 2009, 281, no. 58; Ebert-Schifferer 2009, 231.

39 Bellori, 227: "E nella chiesa de' ministri de gl'infermi, nella cappella de' signori Lazzari, la Risurrezione di Lazzaro, il quale sostentato fuori del sepolcro, apre le braccia alla voce di Cristo che lo chiama e stende verso di lui la mano. Piange Marta e si maraviglia Madalena, e vi è uno che si pone la mano al naso per ripararsi dal fetore del cadavero. Il quadro è grande, e le figure hanno il campo d'una grotta, col maggior lume sopra l'ignudo di Lazzaro e di quelli che lo reggono, ed è sommamente in istima per la forza dell'imitazione."

40 Susinno, 110: "Dovendosi da certi signori ricchi di casa Lazzaro erger una nuova cappella nell'altare maggiore della chiesa de' padri crociferi, pensarono commettere la gran tela a questo virtuoso, con cui si aggiustarono pel prezzo di mille scudi. Il pittore ideossi la Resurrezione di Lazzaro, pensiero

According to Susinno, the central figure of the dead Lazarus was actually portrayed from life (or rather, from death) and his anecdote in this regard, though unreliable, merits quotation:

> One must know that before he set out to work on the painting for the Signori Lazzari, this foolish painter requested [his patrons] to see to it that he was supplied with a room in this hospital [that of the church of the Crociferi]. To fulfill his fanciful will and make him even more content, the best hall was given to him. (…) In order to depict the figure of Lazarus and, in accordance with his naturalistic bias, he had a cadaver unearthed, which already stank as it had been dead for a few days, and put it in the arms of porters, who could not stand the stench and wanted to quit that posture. But Caravaggio, moved by his usual wrath, gripped the dagger, attacked, and scared them, so that the miserable porters were forced to keep their poses, and they almost died like those poor men condemned by the impious Mezentius to die tethered to cadavers. By the same token, Caravaggio's studio in a sense could be defined as the butchery of that tyrant.[41]

Bellori's incorrect description of a figure in *The Resurrection* covering his nose because of Lazarus' stench, and Susinno's imaginary account of models compelled to support a stinking cadaver for days on end, are certainly indebted to Caravaggio's dark legend. In spite of these biographers' excesses and patent falsehoods, both Bellori and Susinno posit some considerations not only verifiable, but worth examining. It is wholly credible that Caravaggio was provided with a large chamber in which to locate the great canvas of *The Resurrection* (its height is over 3 meters) and to accommodate some models; the presence of incisions under the pictorial surface in the area where the figures of Lazarus and Martha are depicted tends to confirm that Caravaggio once again resorted to his ordinary method of posing sessions. Susinno's information about the location of Caravaggio's studio also has the ring of truth: the Crociferi fathers must have been personally involved in the commission of this important picture, and must have willingly lent the necessary space for its execution. In other words, even if it is unconceivable that Caravaggio could have had corpses unearthed in order to transform his studio into a mortuary, he might have caught more than a furtive glimpse of dead or severely sick bodies lying in the hospital; his coloristic rendition of Lazarus' cadaver was most probably obtained and enhanced through direct observation of deceased or suffering patients.

As Bellori states, the main luminous source spotlights Lazarus' body and, to a lesser degree, the group of figures who surround him, especially Martha who, her head wrapped in an almost transparent veil, leaning over her brother's face, checks that he has resumed breathing by leaning in close to his nose; at the same time, she gasps in astonishment. Immediately behind her, the Magdalene, whose profile is clearly replicated from that of her sister, attempts to observe the reactions of Lazarus' reawakening body. Supporting the dead, a porter, hunched over the cadaver's

allusivo al loro casato. N'ebbero i predetti signori molto gradimento, imperoché aveva l'artefice aperto campo da potervi felicemente condurre la sua ideata fantasia." Ibidem, 112: "Dato di mano all'opra, fece nella parte destra il Salvatore voltato di schiena, con gli apostoli, in atto di chiamare nel defonto e quattriduano Lazzaro lo spirito già partito, e nel mezo sonovi due facchini che alzano una gran lapide. Il cadavero di Lazzaro vedesi in braccio ad un altro facchino, e sembra come volesse svegliarsi. Da capo del Lazzaro nella parte sinistra vi sono le sorelle che istupidite osservano il fratello che si sveglia. Ne' visaggi delle sorelle Michele rappresentò le più belle idee della bellezza."

41   Ibidem, 112: "Dee dunque sapersi che prima che dasse

principio all'opera de' sudetti signori di Lazzaro, volle questo mentecatto pittore procurata una stanza per mezzo degli stessi nello spedale. Per secondare il suo capriccioso volere e per vieppiù contentarlo, ebbe il migliore salone. (…) e per condurre la principal figura del Lazzaro, e di gusto naturalesco, fe' dissepellire un cadavero già puzzolente di alcuni giorni, e poselo in braccio ai facchini, che non potendo resistere al fetore, volevano abbandonare quell'atto. Ma questi colla solita ira impugnato il suo pugnale, l'atterrì avventandosi su di loro, finché gli infelici proseguirono per forza l'azione, ed ebbero quasi a morire al pari di que' miseri condannati dall'empio Mezzentio a perire ligati co' cadaveri. Altresì la stanza pittoresca del Caravaggio poteva in qualche modo dirsi la carneficina dello stesso tiranno."

torso, is obviously upset upon sensing that Lazarus is returning to life: only his shoulder and right arm are illuminated by light streaming from the left. By this means, Caravaggio isolated the principal group at the center and to the right, an ensemble of figures that pivots around the oblique of Lazarus' splotched torso.

As Herwarth Röttgen correctly suggested, the pair of the porter and Lazarus' body recalls the figure of Menelaus supporting Patroklos in a frieze by Giulio Romano from the Sala di Troia (Ducal Palace, Mantua), a composition engraved by Diana Scultori and therefore accessible to Caravaggio (Fig. 226).[42] The motif of the porter supporting Lazarus' cadaver also recalls the Vatican *Entombment*, where Saint John keeps aloft Christ's bloodless body in a not dissimilar manner. In particular, the similarities between the two hands emerging from behind the dead figure's torso and reaching toward the chest are perhaps not without significance.

In the left portion of the Messina *Resurrection*, Caravaggio made Christ's figure soar in a ghostly, looming penumbra. Like the soldier's profile in the subsequent *Denial of*

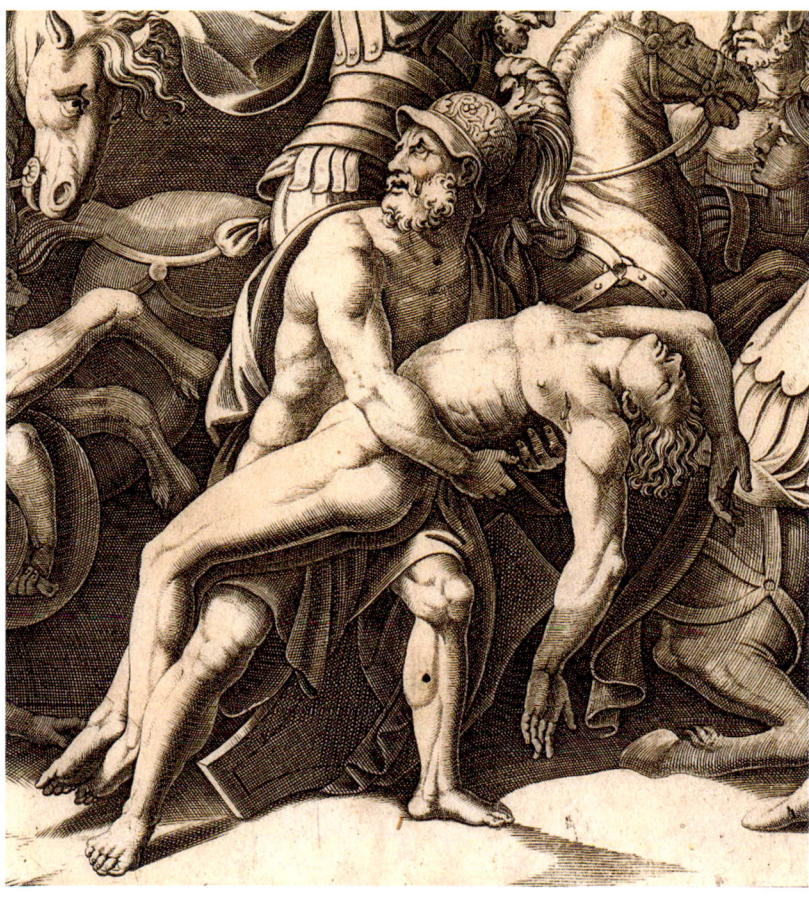

Fig. 226
Diana Scultori after Giulio Romano, *Menelaus Holding the Body of Patroclus*, engraving, 23.9 x 39.1 cm., detail.

Saint Peter, the Savior's face emerges from the canvas' priming through a graduation of dark tones: the more dense shades outline his profile and coagulate into the darkness of his pupil and eyebrow (Fig. 231). His open mouth is literally cut off from the adjoining hedge of the apostles' heads. Only the Savior's right ear-lobe is set ablaze by the light pouring into the cave from outside; this beam of glowing radiance splashes onto Christ's right shoulder, swerving down in majestic waves along the outermost folds of his blue mantle, puddling in froths of yellowish pigment while proceeding toward his right foot. By the same token, light ripples throughout the incandescent promontory of Christ's red tunic, its golden highlights whiplashing from the Savior's shoulder onward through thick parallel strokes of yellow, its swirls loosing momentum and intensity in crossing his stretched sleeve, and its wavering rim eventually catching an unexpected flare of radiance as if to indicate to the viewer Christ's pointing right hand, which hovers in brownish shadow. Caravaggio indeed bathed in light only a section of Jesus' wrist and tiny portions of his fanning fingers. Enfolded in bluish penumbra, the Savior's left hand discreetly cooperates in the miracle, as its index finger points to Lazarus' body.

It is astonishing that such complex and virtuoso brushwork—a symphony of reflections, reverberations, and colored shadows—is not intended to illuminate the figure of Christ, but to nuance the effects of his shadowy presence against the flow of light entering from the off-scene and dwelling upon the group of figures at the right. In fact, the glow from the outside diligently avoids

42   Röttgen 1975. For the print, see Bellini 1991, 184-6, no. 14.

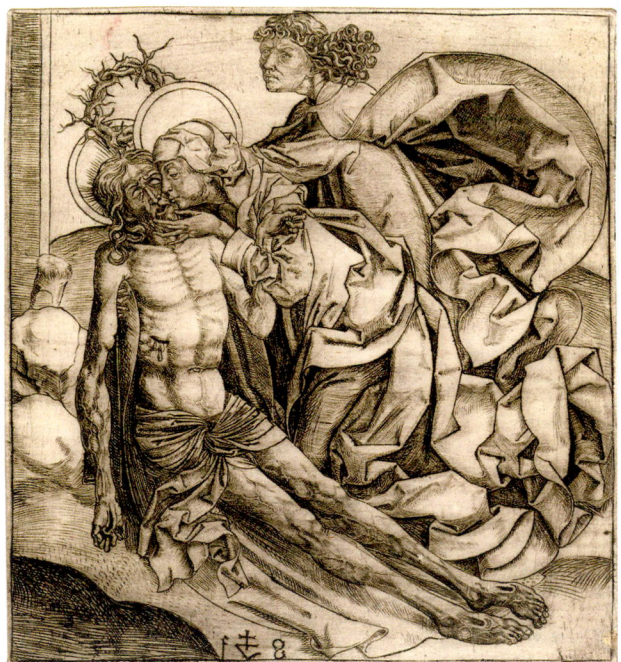

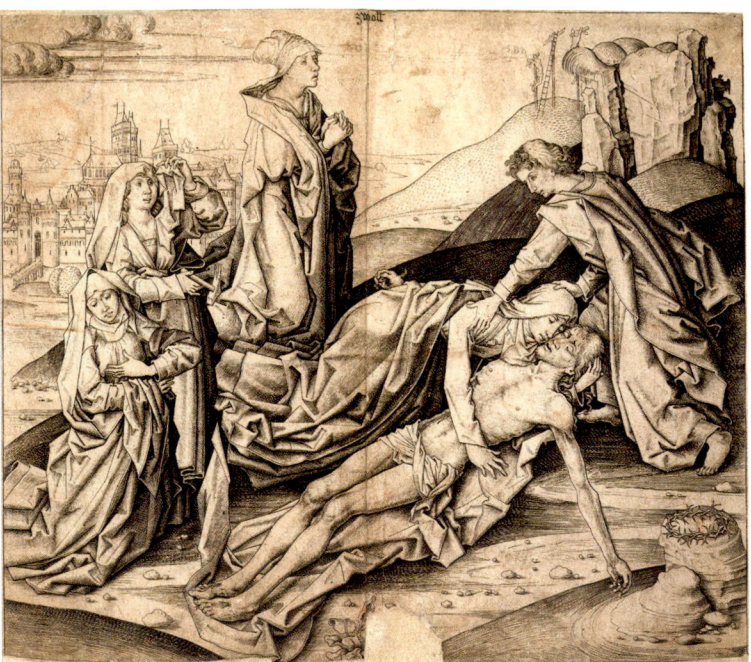

Fig. 227
Veit Stoss, *Lamentation*, woodcut, 13.7 x 12.8 cm.

Fig. 228
Master I A M of Zwolle, *Lamentation*, engraving, 26.3 x 30 cm.

interacting with Jesus' standing figure, whereas it strongly enlightens his disciples' heads, and even more the three-quarter oriented faces of the two porters behind him, lifting the slab from beneath which Lazarus' corpse has been freshly unearthed. In other words, the Savior's quasi-immateriality serves as a counterpoint to the action and motion of the external light, which courses along the diagonal tracks formed by the alignment of the two porters' and the two adjacent apostles' heads, and prolonged by the arms in traction of the porter raising the tomb slab. Paradoxically, the stream of light, after bypassing Christ's figure, manages finally to access the foreground, and its oblique course illusorily changes orientation, climbing up the counter-oblique of Lazarus' cadaver, punctuated in its ascent by the flexed bracket of the third porter's supporting arm and by the long diagonal of Lazarus' outflung arms.

Only the vertical block configured by the two standing and overlapping figures of Martha and the Magdalene breaks the zigzagging race of the outside light, resolving and ricocheting its impetus. Here again, at the canvas' right extremity, Caravaggio deployed the pyrotechnics of his masterful color technique and chiaroscuro, by placing the elliptical knot of Martha's garnet mantle twirling in endless motion, like the roll of a self-engulfing wave around its rippling green center. In this manner, Caravaggio funneled the outside light's stream rightward while retaining its momentum within the composition's boundaries: as if a loop, the lighting indeed seems to curve back toward Lazarus' body through the whirling circuitry of Martha's mantel.

If I have described the chiaroscuro configuration of the Messina *Resurrection* in such specific details, it is because I believe that in this picture, more than in others by Caravaggio, the incoming light acts as a narrative entity, employing the figures' disposition as a chain of transmission through which it unfolds and operates.[43] Before I go on to interpret the logic of the painting's lighting,

---

43   See in this regard Cinotti 1991, 167: "La luce, che fluisce in prevalenza da sinistra, riacquista un ruolo altamente drammatico, basata com'è su contrasti laceranti, rispetto alla Decollazione di Malta e alla Santa Lucia di Siracusa. La tecnica dell'abbozzo è usata come pittura compiuta, soprattutto nelle teste, ma in nessun punto balena così vividamente come nei volti accostati di Marta e di Lazzaro, di tragica essenzialità."

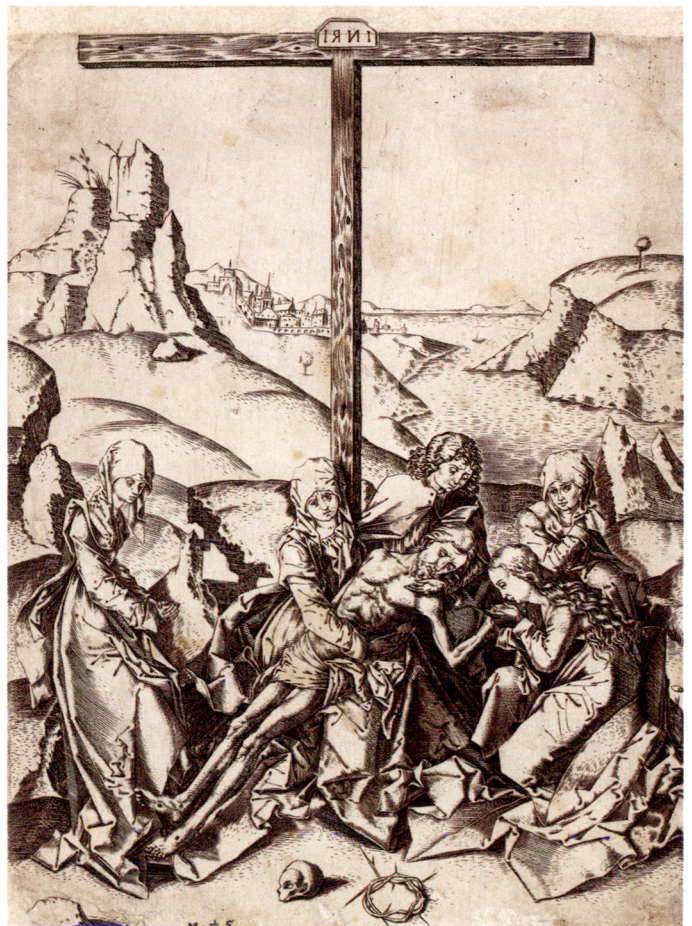

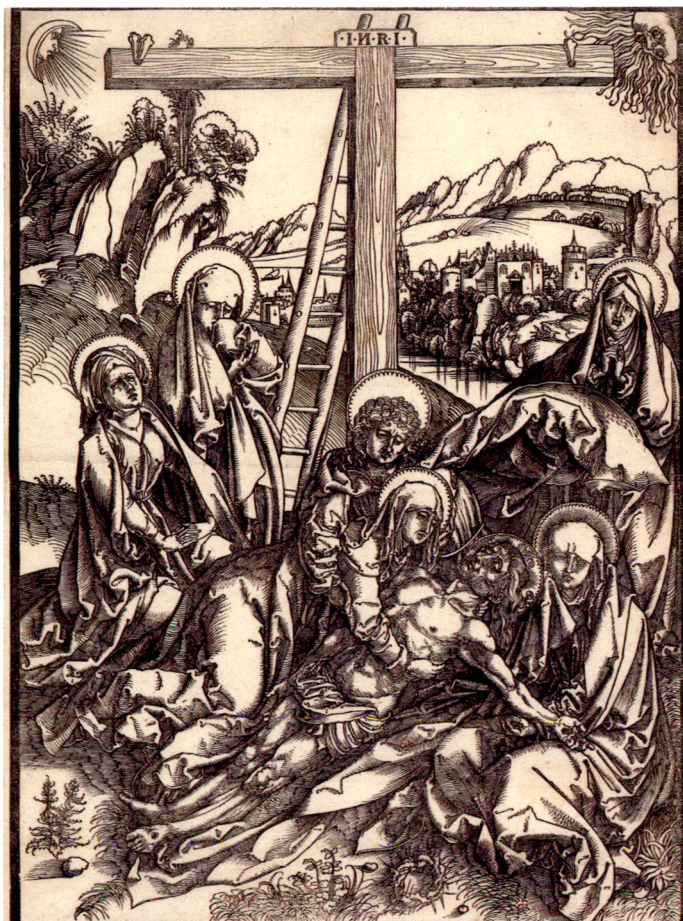

Fig. 229
Master BM, *Lamentation*, engraving, 22.5 x 16 cm.

Fig. 230
Albrecht Dürer (attributed to), *Lamentation*, woodcut, 39.5 x 28.8 cm.

whose performance as an invisible actor is also suggested in other ways by the painter, I ought to demonstrate the specificity of the narrative imagined by Caravaggio in the Messina picture.

Some scholars have correctly noted that Lazarus' outstretched arms evoke the symbol and mystery of the cross, which they have ordinarily construed as an allusion to the redeeming function of Christ's imminent Passion.[44] I think that this reasoning must be further developed by establishing that Caravaggio represented the Messina *Resurrection*'s central group as an analog of a Lamentation scene.[45] According to this iconographic schema, Lazarus's body replaces Christ's, whereas Martha's leaning figure and caressing face stand for those of the bereaved Virgin. I shall consider first an early sixteenth-century *Lamentation* by Veit Stoss[46] (Fig. 227). In this woodcut, the Virgin holds Christ's torso upright with her right hand, and with her left grazes his beard while bringing her profile toward his face to plant a kiss on his cheek. With artistry, Stoss depicts the

44   See Friedlaender 1969, 215: "The difference in Caravaggio's conception of the miracle from all previous examples (…) consists mainly in the position of Lazarus; the corpse is shown in an oblique position, stiff, with its arms outstretched; the only sign of life are the spread fingers of Lazarus' right hand, startlingly visible in the center of the painting above the heads of the group"; and Hibbard 1983, 243: "The unusual pose of Lazarus may be meant to foreshadow the crucifixion of the Christ who resurrects him, thereby encapsulating the Passion and the Resurrection in one miracle."

45   See in this regard Friedlaender 1969, 215: "The group of Lazarus and those around him bears a striking resemblance to the arrangement of the *Pietà* in Northern examples beginning with Roger van der Weyden (…). The diagonal body of Lazarus with one arm hanging down, his head thrown back and his legs crossed, is like that of Christ; and the sister who embraces Lazarus corresponds to the *Mater Dolorosa* of the *Pietà*. It is possible that Caravaggio saw some painting reflecting Roger's composition, perhaps even in Sicily."

46   See Hutchison 1980, 150, no. 2-II (67).

441

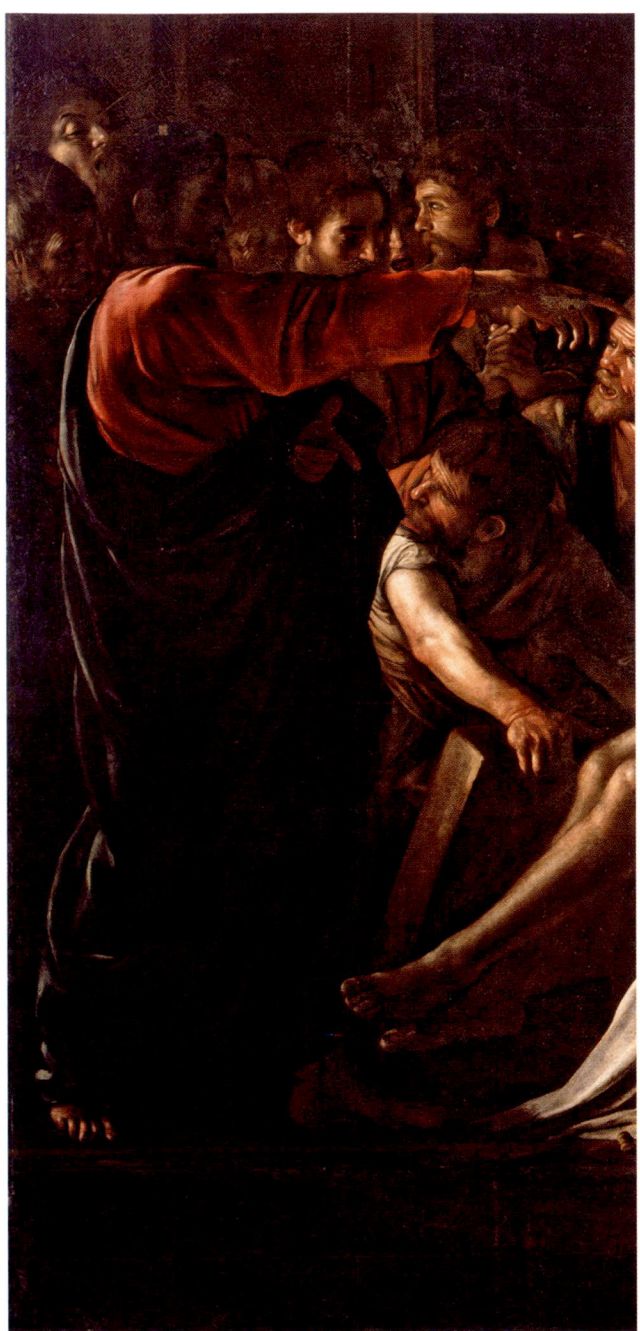

Fig. 231
Michelangelo Merisi da Caravaggio, *The Resurrection of Lazarus*,
Museo Regionale, Messina, oil on canvas, 320 x 275 cm., detail.

salience of Christ's thorax, the depth of his wounds, and especially, over his parallel legs, the web of his arteries and veins.

In a late fifteenth-century engraving by the Master I. A. M. of Zwolle, also a *Lamentation*,[47] Christ's rigid corpse stretches diagonally along the composition's lower foreground; beside him lies his Mother, who embraces his torso while caressing his face with hers (Fig. 228). It is noteworthy that Christ's obliqueness—an element that presents the canonicity of an iconographic attribute—is accentuated by the perpendicular of Christ's stretched left arm, a motif that is equally characteristic of Caravaggio's *Resurrection* of Lazarus.

In a *c*.1480-1500 *Lamentation* attributed to the Master BM,[48] bearing Martin Schongauer's monogram, one can see Christ's diagonal, stiff cadaver in a position particularly akin to Lazarus' in the Messina painting (Fig. 229). Like the other printers previously mentioned, the author of this engraving also stresses the meagerness and boniness of the Savior's body. Finally, in a *c*.1500 woodcut representing the *Lamentation* ascribed to Albrecht Dürer, Christ's corpse is once again depicted obliquely, his left arm flung out perpendicularly, resting on his shroud; he is mourned by the Virgin, who pulls his torso toward her in order to caress and kiss her Son's face (Fig. 230).[49] The affinities between these prints and the central group of Caravaggio's Messina *Resurrection* should be obvious.

In this painting, not only is Lazarus' body supplied with a stiffness and obliqueness typical of Christ's corpse in a northern *Lamentation*, but Martha's head is also fastened onto her brother's in the same fashion in which the Virgin's face typically adheres to her son's in that iconographic tradition. Martha's expression is visually ambiguous so that the viewer might also read it as an act of caressing and kissing. Because the shadowiness and quasi-transparency of Christ's standing figure beguile the beholder into focusing on the group at the right, one may also be tricked into interpreting the painting as a straightforward *Lamentation*, with Christ keeping his arms stretched as if he had just been taken down from the cross, and the Virgin

---

47 For the print, see Hutchison 1980, 201, no. 7 (94).

48 See Hutchison 1991, 350, no. 003.

49 Hütt 1980, 2:1732; and Schoch et al. 2001, 2:495-6, no. A5 (as attributed to Dürer or doubtful).

sobbing and caressing her dead Son; the porter, in this case, would be cast as Saint John or Nicodemus or Joseph of Arimathea.

Of course, this impression of trickery is deliberate on Caravaggio's part: the way in which he built Lazarus' body not only turns him into the *istoria*'s protagonist to the detriment of Jesus' figure, but also morphs him literally into a second Jesus. Supported by the trapeze of his drooping shroud— a technical wonder on account of its phantasmagoric whiteness and the impressive length and ease of its brushstrokes—Lazarus' body is beaten into life by a brushwork that operates as a hammer or a burin upon a metal plate; that is, it "embosses" the body's shades by bringing out flat patches of flesh, partially disconnected from the anatomy, or subtly gouges its surface, for example, at the base of Lazarus' neck and immediately above his chest, by creating irregular ridges of scarlet, a sign that blood is pumping back into the dead man's heart or the last vestige of his lost life. This pictorial technique certainly classifies as a virtuoso *non-finito*, and here Caravaggio truly seems to recreate the vibrancy of Donatello's bronze reliefs (though it is not known whether Caravaggio was acquainted with this sculptor's work).

The exceptional artistry displayed by Caravaggio in the

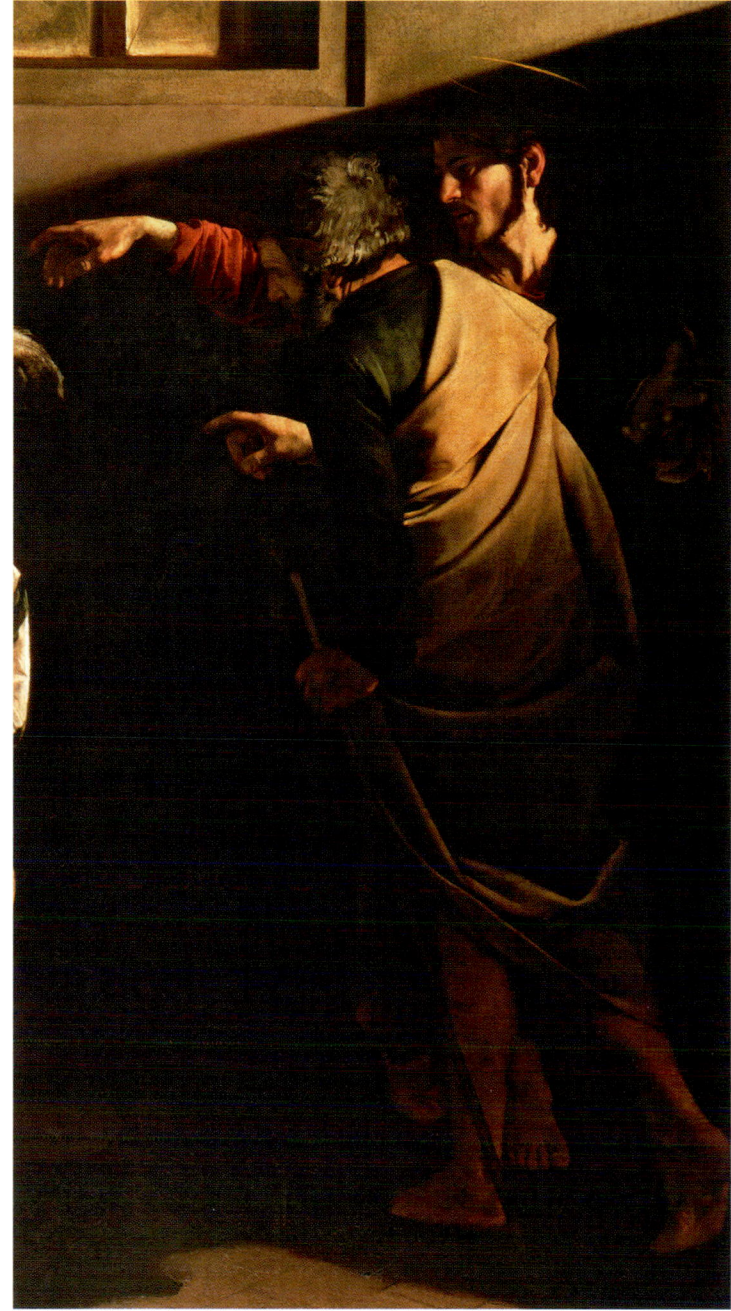

Fig. 232
Michelangelo Merisi da Caravaggio, *The Calling of Saint Matthew,* Contarelli Chapel, San Luigi dei Francesi, Rome, oil on canvas, 322 x 340 cm., detail.

blotchiness of Lazarus' body animates the pictorial surface in the eeriest manner: the bumps and clashes of the incoming light over the dead man's flesh give the impression of a spasmodic, internal motion, an impression that viewers can perceive either as a burst of life jerking up the cadaver or as the signs of death's ravages. In other words, the pictorial treatment of Lazarus' body embodies an inextricable dichotomy between life and death, and as such it also showcases the picture's main theme in a paradigmatic way.[50] Indeed, by making Christ attend an action that, in its visual

50 See Marin 1977, 198: "Les deux mains de Lazare ou le geste énonciatif 'originaire:' la main de profile pour moi est de face pour le Christ. La main de face pour moi est de profil pour le Christ; la première est celle de la vie revenue ou accueillie; l'autre est celle de la mort abandonée, lâchée. L'instantané de la représentation est l'instant neutre ou

443

configuration, exactly reproduces and duplicates his own death, Caravaggio bends the temporality of fiction and juxtaposes, as it were, the present of Christ's miracle and the future of his sacrifice: Lazarus' resurrection, unfolding as a lamentation, assumes the function of a premonitory vision.

In technical terms, Caravaggio disguises a narrative prolepsis—a flash forward—in the form of a simultaneous event inside the general action. Many scholars would regard Caravaggio's manipulation of temporality as a token of optimistic faith: Christ witnesses his own death in the framework of Lazarus' return to life; the divine power that now jolts the dead man to life will soon prove its infallibility by resurrecting the Savior himself. Yet the vision unspooling before Christ is also one of desolation and inevitability, a vision of sorrowful fate. In this prospect, the living Jesus is projected onto death and attends his Mother's lamentation over his dead body: a vision of sheer horror. Both interpretations are legitimate and, to a certain extent, they are not mutually exclusive; as I have already suggested, the Messina painting thematizes the dialectics of life and death as an ongoing, and hence suspended transition between the two, the one being conducive to the other, as the sub-textual prolepsis inserted by Caravaggio clearly expresses.

Yet in the *Resurrection of Lazarus* Caravaggio also accentuated the humanity and solitude of Christ to an unprecedented degree. The Savior in the Messina picture is the *alter ego*—a self-quotation of—the figure of Christ in the Contarelli *Calling of Saint Matthew* (Figs. 231, 232). Through his insertion, Caravaggio once again brings to the fore the theme of divine grace and its epiphany in human events. In Chapter 7, I established that Caravaggio dissociated the figure of Christ from the stream of light entering the scene from the right, and sought to explain this visual and narrative ambivalence as both a discourse on the limits of painting in representing divinity, and a reflection on grace's unpredictability. In *The Resurrection of Lazarus*, any ambiguity vanishes, and the figure of Christ, plunged in impalpable penumbra, is unequivocally disjoined from light's ominous stream so that, from the viewpoint of narration, the Savior is literally invisible: not a single actor in the painting acknowledges his persona, and some of them are instead turned leftward, pointing off scene, which accordingly is experienced by the viewer as an uncharted yet interacting space.

In the light of the pictorial action, the figures oriented to the left might well be commenting on the miracle with other bystanders, an anonymous crowd with a great variety of attitudes and expressions. As I have already argued, the pictorial materiality of light and its motion across the composition act as the picture's animating principle; it is the main vector of narrative action, and Caravaggio increased its momentum by contrasting its luminous flow with the darkness reigning in the vast upper half of the picture. The effect of light is concentrated on the frieze of figures in the canvas' lower section.

In the Messina picture Christ, although he virtually takes part in the *istoria* as an emblematic figure enacting his by now canonical pointing gesture, is segregated from the flow of narration that sweeps throughout the composition in the guise of an in-pouring light. Whatever causes Lazarus to extract himself from death is conjured up as a pictorial force that transcends Jesus' intervention by relegating him to the margins of light. In a sense, Christ and lighting play on two different registers of narrative technique, the former on the gestural level, the latter on the overall compositional level, and their disparities of scope become blatant through the Savior's visual isolation: even the rhetorical gesture of his pointing hand lessens its impact for, through another trick of illusion, it seems to target the forehead of the porter placed immediately behind it.

Visually deprived of his transcendental power—which operates not through but past him—Christ now faces his deadly fate as foreshadowed by an external providence: his Father's will, but

plutôt le neutre de l'instant: ni vie ni mort, l'impensable de la résurrection, le lieu inoccupable, le non-lieu du cogito de ma mort"; and Hibbard 1983, 243: "It is also possible, as Röttgen has argued, that the right hand, which catches the light, is deliberately raised in an antique gesture of acclamation, whereas the left arm leads our eyes down to the skull (we think again of Golgotha) as if to show that Lazarus is in a struggle, both physical and psychological, between death and life."

not his own. In Christ's separateness thus lie the tragic undertones of *The Resurrection of Lazarus*. More importantly, the Messina picture appears to be Caravaggio's ultimate variation on a theme that, a decade earlier, had brought him celebrity and recognition: that of the pointing Jesus as a figurative device to play out the irruption of the supernatural into the *istoria*'s narrative structure. Yet, this time, the original playfulness of the Contarelli *Calling of Saint Peter*, with its dislocations and misdirections, has yielded to the brooding profundity of an extreme meditation on life and death, one in which God's role remains as invisible as the space off scene from which it seems to emanate.

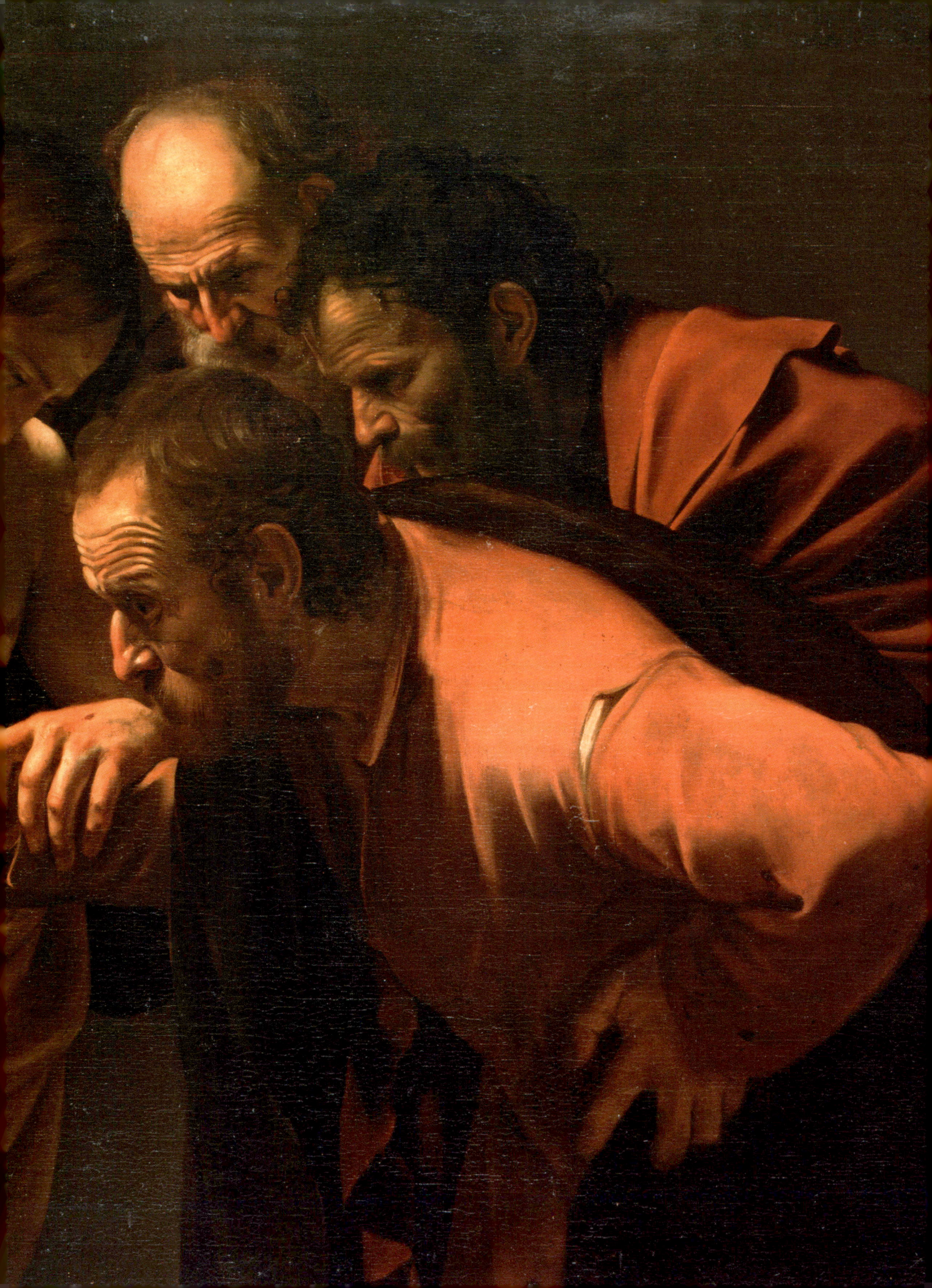

Piercing the Canvas: Painting and Meta-Narrative in Caravaggio's *The Incredulity of Saint Thomas* and *The Martyrdom of Saint Ursula*

The Threads of the Canvas

Painting "living flesh" is far from being merely a metaphor for a painter's astounding naturalism; in the early modern period—that is, in the context of an aesthetic and pictorial hierarchy in which the depiction of the human figure overwhelmingly prevailed—the representation of flesh also entails a technical process whereby the two-dimensional medium of a wall's surface or a canvas yields up its flatness and passive materiality, thereby rising to life as a result of the effects of relief and reality that the artist summons through his craftsmanship in representing the body. Depicting the flesh, therefore, is the ultimate frontier in both animating and abolishing the pictorial medium; by duplicating the flesh, the painter endows the human figure— the quintessential achievement of painting as an act of creation and invention—with the perfection of a renewed life. In Caravaggio's time, the quest for "living flesh" in painting also constituted an antidote to the contrived automatisms through which mannerist painters had represented human figures and their movement, and thus embodied the terms of the artistic challenge underpinning the late sixteenth-century reform of art in Italy.

In a letter of 18 April 1580 to his cousin Ludovico, Annibale Carracci voices his admiration for Correggio's frescoes in Parma Cathedral; although he had expected to be impressed, he remained literally dumbstruck "in seeing such a grand machine," its rigorous yet wondrous foreshortenings and its figures' colors, which were of "true flesh" [*vera carne*].[1] In his 1678 *Felsina Pittrice*, Malvasia compares Annibale's 1593 *San Giorgio Altarpiece* to Ludovico's 1595-1596 *The Pool of Bethesda* (both at the Pinacoteca Nazionale, Bologna); the two paintings were then on view almost side by side in San Giorgio in Poggiale, Bologna.[2] Despite his bias in favor of Ludovico, Malvasia extols Annibale's picture for its impasto, "so lively and of true flesh [*vera carne*]," the more so because the *San Giorgio Altarpiece*, executed with many layers of color and retouched, had remained "in all its freshness," whereas *The Pool of Bethesda*, executed *"alla prima"*—that is, leaving the painting's surface as it had materialized during the first steps of its execution—had its tints "absorbed by the canvas."[3] It is evident that, in this passage, Malvasia opposes the "corporality" of Annibale's painting,

---

1 Carracci, 150: "Non potei stare di non andare subito a vedere la gran cupola, che voi tante volte mi avete comendato, ed ancora io rimasi stupeffato, vedere una così gran machina, così ben intesa, ogni cosa così ben veduta di sotto in su con sì gran rigore, ma sempre con tanto giudizio e con tanta grazia, con un colorito ch'è di vera carne."

2 For Annibale's *Madonna and Child with Saints*, formerly in San Giorgio, Bologna, see Posner 1971a, 2:31, no. 72; For Ludovico's painting, see Brogi 2001, 1:173, no. 58.

3 Malvasia, 1:388: "Ché se bene più strepitosa è questa di Lodovico, più risoluta, più dotta, più grandiera, un misto del Primaticcio e del Tibaldi, di Paolo e del Tentoretto, e lasciando tutta la grazia alla Nonziata sudetta, la profondità del sapere nel gran composto, ne' ben intesi scorti, nel sicuro disegno ha affettato, così ricercando anche il suggetto, così dovendo alla grande istoria fattasi a tale effetto lasciare in elezione dal Torfanini, che ne fu il padrone e suo confidente, per isfogarsi, per isbizzarirsi, ad ogni modo quell'impasto così vivo e di vera carne, con che tanto teneramente la sua contigua colorito

447

◀ Plate XIX: Michelangelo Merisi da Caravaggio, *The Incredulity of Saint Thomas*, Schloß Sans-Souci, Potsdam, oil on canvas, 107 x 146 cm., detail.

obtained through superposition of pictorial strata and enhanced through the visible touches of his brushwork, to the accidental "flatness" of Ludovico's composition. In the latter, the linen canvas in a sense has re-appropriated its intrinsic bi-dimensionality by feeding on—or dissolving—the picture's "living flesh" as reproduced by the painter's mimetic ability.

In an excellent recent essay on the concepts of "skin" and "flesh" in Italian early modern art and theory, Daniela Bohde pointed out that the artwork's surface and its fictive, lively relief—referred to as its "flesh" [*carne*] in regard to the depiction of the human figure—tend to be perceived, if not as antagonistic notions, at least as dialectically interrelated factors.[4] Bohde made use of a considerable number of primary sources, and I will rely on some of her indications to clarify this question. In a crucial, but little-known passage of his 1582 *De' veri precetti della pittura*, Giovan Paolo Armenini indicates the paramount importance of the skin in the depiction of human bodies:

> And then comes the skin, which covers everything, and which Nature created soft and delicate, strewn with a beautiful and alluring variety of tints; as a covering, the skin renders the body's whole composition pleasant, graceful, and marvelous; [the execution of] this part is difficult by all means, but especially so in the representation of those nudes demanding much artifice, which therefore causes knowledgeable artists to insist ordinarily to an excess upon whatever lies underneath it, which they believe to be accomplished and, always keeping this in mind, they hardly tolerate [adding] the ultimate finish of the skin, as if they were displeased to employ [here] their knowledge, which they [instead] strive to express outside [in representing whatever lies underneath the skin] with such hardship.[5]

Armenini's remark proves to be less abstract than it appears at first glance. In simple terms, he exhorts artists not to waste too much energy in demonstrating their expertise in anatomy; as he puts it, only patrons of the highest rank would be able to appreciate this kind of anatomical knowledge. However, it is noteworthy that Armenini evokes the relationship between the outside and the inside of the artwork in grappling with the notion of skin as evoked through the human figure in art. To understand fully the implications of this passage, it is worth recalling that the technical term "skin" (*pelle,* or *cutis* in Latin) not only harks back to Leon Battista Alberti's 1435 *De Pictura*,[6] but was also used as a synonym of both the canvas or wall upon which artists worked, and the picture's upper layers. In his 1584 *Il Riposo*, Raffaello Borghini describes the preparation phase specific to the fresco technique:

> One must apply this mixture upon the wall with a large brush, spreading it with a

avea Annibale, massime che ricoprendola e ritoccandola è rimasta freschissima, ove quella di Lodovico, fatta alla prima, è alquanto dalla tela assorbita, ferma sulle prime e si guadagna l'affetto altrettanto quanto quella dell'emulo cugino lo stupore e la disperazione."

4   See Bohde 2007. See further Fend 2007a, for the concepts of "skin" and "flesh" in seventeenth-century France.

5   Armenini, 85: "Di poi vien la pelle, che cuopre ogni cosa, la quale la natura ha fatto molle e delicata, sparsa di belle e vaghe varietà de' colori, la qual coperta fa che tutto il componimento del corpo riesce piacevole, vago e maraviglioso; la qual parte è difficile in tutte le maniere, ma è molto più ne gl'ignudi di molto artificio, il che ne cagiona la troppo impressione che gli studiosi si sogliono pigliare delle parti di sotto, le quali essi trovano esser terminate e così, tenendo in mente tuttavia, fan che mal patiscono poi quest'ultimo compimento della

pelle, come che siano quasi constretti a dover mostrare quella intelligenza di loro così spiacevole, che con tanta fatica si sforzano voler esprimer fuori, dove che molti se ne levano poi finalmente, tardi accorgendosi quella dover essere maniera più conveniente ed atta per i sommi principi che per le private persone, alle quali essi più spesso servono e dove, con più riputazione e men fatica, fanno i fatti loro."

6   Alberti, 14-5: "Ancora ritorniamo alla superficie. Sia pure persuaso, quanto all'orlo sue linee e angoli non si mutano, tanto sarà medesima superficie. Abbiamo adunque mostro una qualità che mai si parte datorno dalla superficie. Abbiamo a dire dell'altra qualità quale sta quasi come buccia sopra il dosso della superficie. [Iterum ad superficiem redeamus. Docuimus quo pacto una per fimbriam qualitas superficiei inhaereat. Sequitur ut altera superficierum qualitas referatur, quae est, ut ita loquar, tamquam cutis per totum superficiei dorsum distenta]."

heated trowel in order to cover all the holes of the plaster layer, thereby making a uniform and smooth skin throughout the wall.[7]

And similarly, for easel paintings:

> One must put aside the canvas for many days until the applied colors are dry; then, one must consider it attentively, and emend what needs to be emended, giving it its ultimate skin of finest colors, diluted in little oil, so that they will always be beautiful and lively.[8]

On reading these passages, it becomes clear that skin, *pelle*, designates both the primary medium on which painters execute their creations—generally a linen canvas or wall—and, by transposition, the outward evenness of a painting's layer as it emerges either in the final steps of, or even during, the execution. As a general rule, therefore, the term "skin" conjures up the bi-dimensionality of the pictorial medium.

That said, one should take care not to interpret "skin" as the opposite of "flesh." In his 1568 life of Niccolò Tribolo, Giorgio Vasari records this sculptor's dissatisfaction with the quality of the marble on which he had set out to carve an *Assumption*; this fact frustrated him because he felt deprived of the pleasure that one takes in working good pieces of marble, for, once achieved, these surfaces "show a skin that truly seems to be made of flesh."[9] In other words, the artwork's skin attains its technical perfection when it acts as the plastic membrane of the flesh underneath it; through the sculpture's surface, the fictive three-dimensionality of the human figure comes to be fully perceived and exhibited. Armenini implies the same concept when he asserts that the body's underlying anatomy must not surge into view abruptly and without transition by usurping the skin's function of covering at the risk of exacerbating and denaturing the effect of relief. Accordingly, the skin both masks and intensifies the artifice of creating flesh by imparting the ultimate touch of verisimilitude to the illusion of corporality.

I began this chapter with a brief discussion of painting's "skin" and "flesh," not only to prove that, in Caravaggio's time, these terms were imbued with commonly accepted implications of a conceptual and practical nature, but also because the dialectics between the "interior" and the "exterior" of the pictorial representation lie at the core of two works by Caravaggio: his *c.*1602 *Incredulity of Saint Thomas* (Schloss Sans-Souci, Potsdam)[10] and his 1610 *Martyrdom of Saint Ursula* (Banca Intesa, Naples).[11]

7   Borghini, 1:145: "Il secondo modo è questo. Facciasi di stucco di marmo e di matton pesto sottilissimo un arricciato al muro, e si spiani bene, e si rada col taglio della cazzuola acciò rimanga ruvido; poi gli si dia sopra una mano di olio di linseme; poscia s'abbia in una pentola fatto bollire ed incorporare insieme pece greca, mastico e vernice grossa, e questa mistura con un pennel grosso si metta sopra il muro e si vada distendendo con una cazzuola infocata che riturerà tutti i buchi dell'arricciato e farà una pelle unita e liscia per lo muro, sopra cui, essendo secca, si darà la mestica e poi si dipignerà."

8   Ibidem, 1:184: "Il buon pittore (...) dee, posciaché ha calcato il cartone sopra il suo quadro, andarlo campeggiando co' colori, perciocché quello, in seccandosi, divien nero, e poi metter da canto il quadro per molti giorni, tantoché i colori dati siano secchi; poi lo rivegga diligentemente, e racconci quello che gli pare da racconciare, e gli dia l'ultima pelle di colori finissimi e temperati con poco olio, ché di tal maniera saranno sempre vaghi e vivi."

9   Vasari, 5:207: "E fatto il modello d'una Madonna che saglie

in cielo, e sotto i dodici apostoli in varie attitudini, che piacque, essendo bellissima, mise mano a lavorare; ma con poca sua sodisfazione, perché essendo il marmo che lavorava di quelli di Milano, saligno, smeriglioso e cattivo, gli pareva gettar via il tempo, senza una dilettazione al mondo di quelle che si hanno nel lavorare, i quali si lavorano con piacere, ed in ultimo condotti mostrano una pelle che par propriamente di carne."

10   Besides the ancient sources mentioning Caravaggio's *The Incredulity of Saint Thomas* that I quote in the text, see Scannelli, 198-9. For the painting see Friedlaender 1969, 161-2; Moir 1982, 110; Cinotti 1983, 489-91, no. 44; Hibbard 1983, 167-8; Calvesi 1990, 40; Bologna 1992, 320; Puglisi 1998, 216; Bal 1999, 27-39; Danesi Squarzina 2001, 278-80, no. D2; Krüger 2001, 259-61; Danesi Squarzina 2003, 1:397-9; Suthor 2003, 267-73; Koos 2005; Marini 2005, 460-1, no. 47; Most 2005, 160-5, 188-205; Koos 2007, 72-3, 77; Pichler 2007, 26-8; Schütze 2009, 263, no. 50; and Ebert-Schifferer 2009, 167-70.

11   For the painting, see *Caravaggio e caravaggeschi* 1963, 53, no. 50 [catalogue entry by Giuseppe Scavizzi]; Gregori 1975,

I am not the first to propose that Caravaggio played with the interconnected notions of "flesh" and "skin" in his work. Marianne Koos has devoted a thoughtful article to this topic, besides offering a detailed interpretation of the Potsdam *Incredulity of Saint Thomas* in another essay.[12] However, I disagree with Koos' approach and conclusions for a number of reasons. First of all, she argues that a dichotomy between "flesh" and "skin" permeates Caravaggio's production in general, especially on a technical level,[13] whereas I contend that the correlation between these notions is not specific to Caravaggio's pictures, and in any case his pictorial technique, because of its variety and complexity, does not lend itself to being construed with such broad criteria. This is not to claim that Caravaggio was reluctant to exploit the potential of the pictorial "skin" and "flesh"; on the contrary, he purposely thematized, and enlarged the scope of, their mutual dialectics in his pictures, but only occasionally, and in terms that likewise reassess the notion and validity of the *istoria*. My second objection is to Koos' interpretation of the "piercing act" of Thomas' finger in the Potsdam picture as a metaphor for the viewer's desire to merge physically with the depicted Christ, even to the point of profaning his figure's corporality in a sort of pictorial "sodomy," justifiable—in Koos' view—on mystical grounds.[14]

The fallacy of this interpretation does not reside in its anachronistic premises—there are obvious limits to the mysticism of the senses even as practiced at the time, and I firmly believe that visually insinuating the "penetration" of Christ's body would have constituted an intolerable cultural and religious shock for a seventeenth-century viewer—but on Koos' assumption that *The Incredulity of Saint Thomas* revolves around the theme of the viewer's longing for, and attraction to, the image: a theme that neither the picture nor its subject matter truly presupposes in these specific terms (as I shall explain later, Caravaggio seems also to suggest Thomas' hesitancy in inserting his finger into Jesus' side wound).

I would argue instead that Thomas' gesture in the Postdam picture invites the beholder to focus and reflect on the materiality of the canvas—that is, on the artwork's medium. However, this reflection on the "matter" of painting cannot be separated from the picture's narrative context,

44-8; Bologna 1980; Pacelli 1980; Whitfield and Martineau 1982, 131-3 no. 19 [catalogue entry by Mina Gregori]; Cinotti 1983, 474-6, no. 37; Hibbard 1983, 252-4; Calvesi 1990, 381-2; Bologna 1992, 263-80; Pacelli 1994, 100-17; Fried 1997, 54-6; Puglisi 1998, 354-5; Rossi F. 2000 [for the cuirass and helmets in the painting]; *L'Ultimo Caravaggio* 2004; Cassani and Sapio 2005, 144-6, no. 18 [catalogue entry by Ferdinando Bologna]; Marini 2005, 570-4, no. 110; Pacelli 2005; Schütze 2009, 285-6, no. 67; and Ebert-Schifferer 2009, 234.

12   The first essay is Koos 2007, the second, on Caravaggio's *The Incredulity of Saint Thomas*, is Koos 2005.

13   See Koos 2007.

14   See Koos 2005, 1145: "Und mehr: Caravaggio führt seinen Bildgegenstand so vor Augen, daß er eine Art des Begehrensverhältnisses etabliert. Das wird im Gemälde des 'Ungläubigen Thomas' wesentlich durch die Makellosigkeit der gleichwohl profanisierten Christusfigur bewirkt. So ist die Schönheit des jungen, hellhäutigen und spärlich bedekten Körpers Christi—nicht nur sein Oberkörper, sondern auch sein rechtes Bein bleibt unbedeckt—unübersehbar, eine Schönheit, die sich durch die Kombination mit den alten, derben manner in aller Deutlichkeit zu erkennen gibt. Der Betrachter dieses Bildes wird nicht nur in das vorgestellte Geschehen unmittelbar miteinbezogen, sondern gleichsam zum Begehrenden vor dem Gemälde. Damit operiert Caravaggio nicht nur im Sinne der mystischen Literatur, die Christus zum Objekt des Begehrens stilisierte (...). Vielmehr operiert Caravaggio auch im Sinne der Kunsttheorie Leonardos, der (...) von der angestrebten Verweltlichung eines heiligen Sujets zugunsten des Begehrens

seines Betrachters berichtet. Wie Leonardo schreibt, sei er von einem seiner Auftraggeber aufgefordert worden, die Zeichen der Heiligkeit einer dargestellten Figur abzunehmen, damit dieser das Bild ohne Vorbehalte küssen könne." A different interpretation of Leonardo's passage commented upon by Koos is in Nagel 2010, esp. 17-23. As she herself admits, Koos greatly depends on the "homoerotic" reading of *The Incredulity of Saint Thomas* proposed by Bal 1996, 117-28, and reasserted again by Bal 1999, esp. 37. A little later, Koos 2005, 1146-7, states: "Was Caravaggio somit über die Relation zwischen Christus und Thomas vor Augen stellt, ist ein Bild-Betrachter-Verhältnis, das nicht nur bei Begehren endet, sondern gar in einem Akt der Penetration kulminiert. (...) Christi ideal schöner Leib, der weibliche Qualitäten gewinnt, wird zur Metapher für das weiblich konnotierte Bild. Und in dieser Betrachtung des Verhältnisses von Christus und Thomas lost sich auch eine Frage, die bei Caravaggio immer wieder zum Thema wird: die des homosexuellen Begehrens."A similar reading is independently offered by Most 2005, 164: "The contrast between the elegance and delicacy of Jesus' wounded body and Thomas' crude violation of it is concentrated in the vulva-like form of Jesus' wound, the stiffly erect shape of Thomas' probing finger, and, in what is perhaps the single most disagreeable detail of all, his dirty, blackened thumbnail. We need not search for hidden psychoanalytic meaning for these unequivocally sexual overtones (...)." And a little farther, in comparing the Dublin *Taking of Christ* with *The Incredulity of Saint Thomas*, Most (Ibidem, 213-4) concludes: "The homoerotic and sadomasochistic implications that we may sense as a nuance of the *Doubting Thomas* seem here to achieve a particularly drastic expression."

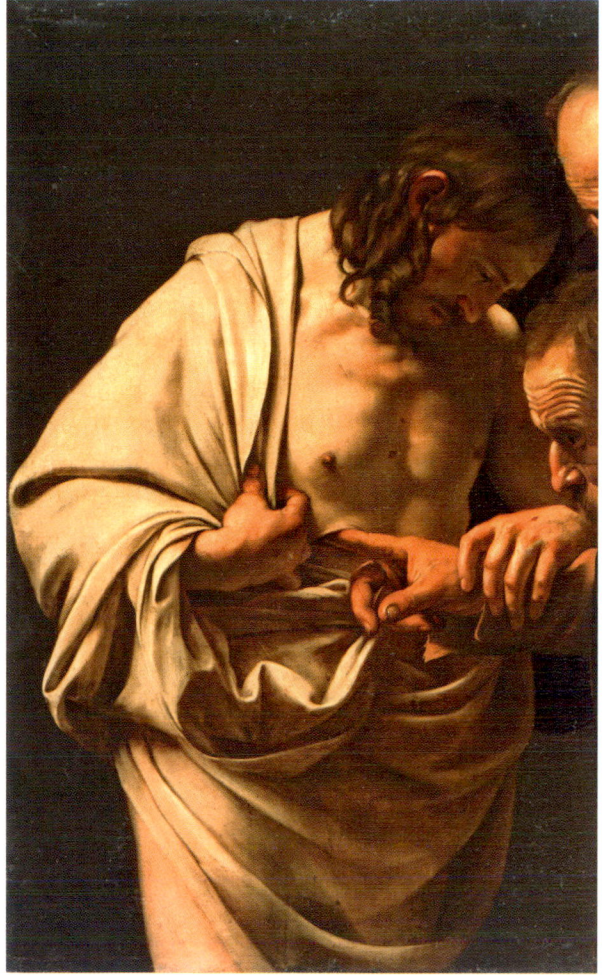

Fig. 233
Michelangelo Merisi da Caravaggio, *The Incredulity of Saint Thomas*, Schloß Sans-Souci, Potsdam, oil on canvas, 107 x 146 cm., detail.

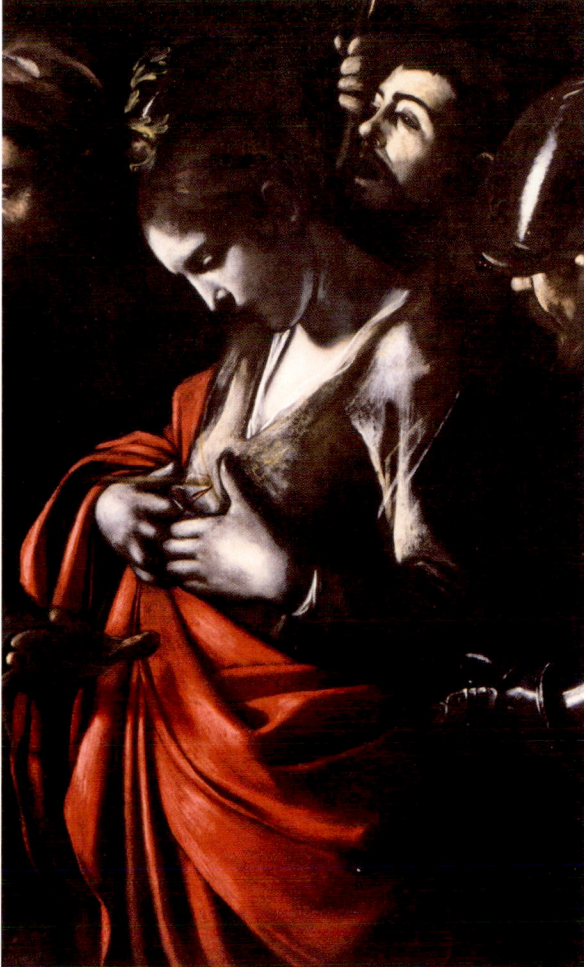

Fig. 234
Michelangelo Merisi da Caravaggio, *The Martyrdom of Saint Ursula*, Banca Intesa, Palazzo Zavalos, Naples, oil on canvas, 154 x 178 cm., detail.

which is instrumental in defining, deepening, and countering the meaning and repercussion of such reflection. Thomas' piercing act brings to the fore the inherent fictiveness of the *istoria* in view of both celebrating the artist's power of illusion and indicating the limits of painting as the vehicle of the "true" representation. Also, through the "piercing act" Caravaggio paradoxically unravels the latent potential of the medium of painting in broadening the impact, and inflecting the significance, of the pictorial narrative by revealing its fictive nature.

Aware of the picture's status as a painted surface, the viewer is now able to detach him- or herself emotionally from the representation and to consider the painting's separateness as a material artifact in relation, or opposition, to the represented action: a pictorial device able to transcend the purview of the depicted narrative, and as such an inductor of meta-narrative. In other words, meta-narrative designates the procedure by which a meta-pictorial device—the allusion to and evocation of the painting's medium and craft—is activated by the artist either in contrast to or in support of the *istoria* represented. In this case, the "meta-pictorial" is designed to interface with and complement the viewer's reception and interpretation of the pictorial narrative. In light of this definition, Ursula's gesture of signaling the spurting wound inflicted on her by her hopeless suitor as she frames the lethal arrow planted in her breast with the brackets of her thumbs and the socle of her entwined hands must also be regarded as an indicator of meta-narrative, and therefore be

451

compared to the piercing act depicted in *The Incredulity of Saint Thomas* (Figs. 233, 234). Ursula's profound consideration of her wound by locking her gaze hypnotically upon it mirrors Christ's alertness in directing Thomas' hand into his side wound by fixing his eyes upon it and inclining his head: telling evidence, in my view, that Ursula's action parallels Christ's, and deliberately elaborates upon its precedent's meaning. It may therefore reasonably be assumed that the Naples picture represents a deft variation on a theme previously treated by Caravaggio: an inter-textual elaboration on the master's part.

If many sources confirm that the notions of "skin" and "flesh" belong to the early modern terminology of art, to my knowledge the meta-narrative function of the pictorial medium, especially the linen canvas, has not been discussed at all by scholars, and hence requires supporting evidence. This can be provided by some relatively well-known poems from Giovan Battista Marino's *Galeria*, in which the motif of the canvas and, in part, of its threads, is clearly tackled in a meta-narrative light. Although Marino's *Galeria*, an anthology of ekphrastic compositions celebrating sometimes fictitious artworks by various painters and sculptors, was first published in 1619, some of its poems had been written many years earlier, and therefore might well reflect ideas and sensitivities specific not only to early seventeenth-century artists and amateurs, but also to Caravaggio himself. As I noted in Chapter 5, Marino and Caravaggio were in fact well acquainted.[15] In a sonnet on a *Narcissus* by Francesco Vanni, Marino writes:

> That Narcissus who, tired and thirsty, wallows
> In admiring his figure in the fountain, and
> Both target and arrow of Love's bow, is
> Beloved and lover, wounded and wounds,
> Enlivened by your divine brush, Vanni,
> Seems on the brink of proffering words,
> For you gave to his eyes that perfect and
> Free speech, which you denied to his tongue.
> Like a tiger in a mirror, Nature, astonished,
> Halts to admire herself intently in the linen
> In which her image is interwoven; thus,
> A single figure causes a twofold deceit
> By luring the boy and Nature: the
> Fountain the boy, and the picture Nature.[16]

Marino expresses in his poem a set of dualities that grandiosely culminate in the coda: Narcissus is both the subject of his own love and the object of others' love; his image reflected in the fountain entices him as much as his figure in the painting seduces the viewer. Although technically mute, the boy speaks through his eyes to the beholder's eyes; even Nature, the matrix from which the image derives, is deceived by the painter's artifice and stops to stare at his work, whereas it is the painter who is intended to stare at Nature in order to duplicate her appearance. More important, the threads of the linen canvas weave together an image that operates as the mirror-like surface of a fountain. In other terms, the theme of self-reflection inherent in the picture's subject and in Narcissus' self-absorbed action is transferred onto the painting's medium, as if the threads of the

---

15   See Chapter 5 for bibliography on Marino's *Galeria* and on the poet's relation with Caravaggio.

16   Marino c, 14: "Quel Narciso, che stanco ed assetato/ Su 'l fonte a vagheggiar se stesso alletta,/ E de l'arco d'Amor segno e saetta/ È ferito e ferisce, amante amato,/ Dal tuo divin pennel, Vanni, animato/ Par le parole ad or ad or prometta/ E la favella libera e perfetta/ Ch'a la lingua negasti, agli occhi hai dato./ Nel lino, onde l'imagine è contesta,/ Se stessa intenta e stupida Natura,/ Qual tigre in specchio, a rimirar s'arresta./ Tal che fa doppio inganno una figura,/ E delude e schernisce e quello e questa:/ L'un la fontana e l'altra la pittura."

canvas were so tightly and finely interwoven as to form a water surface or a looking glass capable of reflection. Marino's mention of the linen—that is, of painting's material, inert support—clues the reader in to the fictiveness of Vanni's composition, but at the same time accentuates the marvel of the painter's artifice by which artisanal matter becomes the mirror of an artistic concept. In a poem celebrating an *Ariadne* by Ludovico Carracci,[17] Marino makes the *istoria* physically interact with the materiality of the canvas:

> Sorrowful and sighing girl,
> And still tearless,
> You blame your Theseus,
> And cry without crying.
> Yet, I see your beautiful, sweet eyes
> Wet and laden with tears.
> Why then is your sad face not
> Soaked in beautiful tears?
> Oh great and sound trick of the wise painter!
> No, do not cry, for colors will suffer
> Damage from your flooding tears![18]

In this madrigal, Marino uses the picture's factuality to justify Ludovico's restraint in representing Ariadne's sadness more graphically: the painter avoided depicting tears that would express and magnify the subject's utter pathos not because he could not afford such a degree of mimesis, but only in order to prevent his artistic virtuosity from spoiling the work. Indeed, Ludovico's tears are real floods of water, and thus might smear and wash away the pigments of which the painting consists. In this case, by pointing to the artwork's materiality, Marino not only unveils Ludovico's wizardry in transforming colors into figures, but also allows the reader to approach the picture's narrative from the unusual angle of its technical components. By evoking the eerie image of a canvas effaced by water's erosion, Marino coaxes the reader into appreciating Ludovico's originality in suggesting, but not representing, Ariadne's excess of sorrow: tears remain suspended, but do not fall, from the girl's eyes. In the same vein, Marino imagines a canvas impregnated by the blood depicted on it by the artist. In singing the praise of a *Herodias with the Head of Saint John the Baptist* by Annibale Carracci,[19] the poet marvels:

> Oh dire tragedy,
> Cut off and exsanguine,
> The sacred head of the good Precursor
> Tinges the white threads with red blood!
> Only royal tables
> Are adorned with such meals.
> Believe me, impious woman, this spread
> Does not belong in a poor person's meal.[20]

17 It is not certain that the *Ariadne* by Ludovico Carracci celebrated by Marino is to be identified with a painting in the Museo Civico, Vercelli, a *Bacchus and Ariadne* whose authenticity has also been questioned. See Emiliani 1993, 68-70, no. 32 [catalogue entry by Gail Feigenbaum]; Brogi 2001, 1:242, no. A1, and 1:279-82, nos. P12, P17.

18 Ibidem, 29: "Del tuo Teseo ti lagni,/ Ma piangente non piagni./ Fanciulla addolorata e sospirosa,/ Non però lagrimosa./ E pur vegg'io que' begli occhi soavi/ Di perle umidi e gravi./ Perché dunque non bagni/ De le lagrime belle il mesto viso?/ Oh di saggio pittor ben sano aviso!/ Non pianger, no, ché da' cadenti umori/ Foran guasti i colori."

19 According to Pieri and Ruffino (in Marino c, CCXXIX), this painting is to be identified with a *Salome with the Head of Saint John the Baptist* by Ludovico (and not Annibale) Carracci mentioned in the 1623 inventory of Cardinal Ludovisi's paintings as a "Herodias with the head of Saint John the Baptist in a bassin and another figure nearby." The painting is now lost. See Brogi 2001, 1:296, no. P94.

20 Ibidem, 68: "Oh tragedia funesta/ Come tronca ed

Unlike Ariadne's tears that are forcefully contained to avoid damage to the picture, Saint John's blood is permitted to ooze and seep into the linen, so that the canvas's immaculate threads—that is, the canvas at its core—prove to be affected by the subject's dramatic tone: its direness. By alluding to the pictorial medium, Marino redoubles the effect of tragedy conveyed by Annibale's depiction, thereby insinuating that the image's horror has penetrated and absorbed even the picture's support. With strange wit, Marino counterpoises the tragic impact of the decapitated head with Herodias' hubris and her foolishness in serving John's head as a main course at a banquet. In a sonnet composed by Marino in honor of Alessandro Maganza's *Minerva Forbidding the Fates from Tearing their Yarn*,[21] the theme of the canvas' threads constitutes one of the key concepts of the entire ekphrasis:

> "Let the sacred studies pursue": behold,
> Minerva steps in to stop the fatal blow,
> Thus keeping her followers' memories alive,
> Although once cold, bones turn into ashes.
> Behold, imperious Death no longer holds
> Sway over the most beautiful arts, nor does
> The seething wrath of jealous Fates suffice
> To dig the grave of an illustrious mind.
> So, too, may the thread of the linen, on which
> You, Maganza, with your erudite and graceful
> Stylus engraved the spinners of human life,
> Never fall under their ruthless scissors.
> May the yarn of your immortality never
> Be torn by the cruel deities painted by you.[22]

Although the specific idea behind this allegory is not entirely clear, it seems that Marino distinguishes between the yarn of life and that of art, implying that only the former, but not the latter, is subjected to the Fates. Minerva can thus intervene and ensure that the artist's glory will continue to be "spun" endlessly. More intriguing, Marino opposes the canvas' fragility—its being made of linen threads—to the painter's virtuosity. With his stylus—a transparent metaphor for style—Maganza engraves his figures on the picture as on a marble or a metal surface. The image of the threads being incised—a kind of oxymoron referring to two types of craftsmanship, the painter's and the sculptor's—once again bears witness to the miraculous operation of art: the canvas' fabric voids its fragile transience through the painter's skill; his work transmutes the soft linen into the analog of bronze or stone. The mention of the picture's threads also incites the reader to perceive the Fates' inexorable industry as depicted by the artist in a new light, that is, as foiled and partially inefficient, for the horrid Parcae are unable to turn their scissors against the canvas and cut its threads, thereby making the picture's destruction their own. Moreover, the allegory ideated by Maganza assumes the value of a propitious pre-figuration: as Minerva prevents the Fates from tearing an artist's yarn, so too will the master's talent keep the yarn of his fame intact forever. Therefore, Marino's unveiling of the canvas' materiality is not limited to exalting the painter's masterful skills, but it

---

essangue/ Fa del buon Precursor la sacra testa/ I bianchi lini rosseggiar di sangue!/ Ahi pompose ne van di cibi tal/ Sol le mense reali./ Non è (credilo a me) donna nefanda,/ Da desco poverel simil vivanda."

21 This painting by Alessandro Maganza (Vicenza 1555-632) remains unidentified.

22 Ibidem, 37: "'Seguano i sacri studi.' Ecco Minerva,/ Che

s'interpone a la fatal percossa,/ E benché fredde inceneriscan l'ossa,/ Le memorie de' suoi vive conserva./ Ecco come non ha Morte proterva/ sovra l'arti più belle impero o possa,/ E come ingegno illustre a porre in fossa/ Non val d'invida Parca ira che ferva./ Così 'l fil di quel lino, in cui scolpite,/ Maganza, hai col tuo stil leggiadro e dotto/ Le Filatrici de l'umane vite,/ A la forbice rea non caggia sotto,/ Come da l'empie dee c'hai colorite/ Lo tuo stame immortal non fia mai rotto."

also interacts with the represented subject matter as its self-referential counterpoint by serving as a sounding board. In another sonnet, Marino gives a poignant eulogy of a *Spinning Clotho* by Giovanni Valesio:[23]

> Valesio, noble painter, faithful lover,
> You have depicted the living image
> Of your beautiful Clotho, upon whom
> Love bestowed the thread of your life.
> Thus, while she spins death's painful
> Yarn for your transfixed heart,
> You in her name trace an infinite thread
> Of immortal fame and eternal honor.
> From her, I believe, you took this power
> For, secluded in a fragile canvas, her
> Figure lives through your celestial colors.
> Your linen is interwoven with the same
> Threads with which she is wont to spin lives:
> Her spindle is not worthier than your brush.[24]

In my view, this is one of the most refined poems in Marino's *Galeria*. Heeding the long-lived poetic imagery of woman as source of death, the painter, Giovanni Valesio, depicts his beloved as one of the Fates, Clotho, spinning the yarn of his life and love. Yet, as Marino ingeniously puts it, the real Fate is not the woman, but the artist who, through the metaphorical threads of his lines and contours, delineates his beloved's image, offering glorious eternity to her in exchange for the deadly torments that she makes him endure. In Marino's eyes, Valesio's brush is not the only entity to spin the yarn of living representation; the very canvas on which the master performs his mimetic spinning, through its interwoven threads, acts as a principle of life. In fact, it animates Clotho's image by insufflating the vital breath of perfect mimesis into her figure, the heartless spinner of her lover's death. That the canvas' threads, by interlacing with one another, recompose the yarn continuously unspooled by Death and her female ministers, is not only a bold and felicitous metaphor; the reassembling of life's yarn into the canvas equally signals the vitality of painting's inanimate medium. By a metaphorical osmosis, life percolates from the canvas into the flesh of the figure represented on it, flowing back into the canvas, which thereby becomes animated. Even more important, the act of painting is redefined by Marino as the life-inducing work of a spinning brush: the "infinite" line of creation is indeed assimilated to an ever-unfolding thread. For Marino, figures and objects not only impregnate, mirror, enliven, flood, or tinge the canvas; sometimes they also pierce it. This is Marino's poem describing a *Deianira* by Paolo Guidotti:[25]

> Flee, shrewd Centaur,
> Predator of divine beauty,
> Go and enjoy your rich booty.
> Hercules! Let your bow shoot, though he already

---

23 This painting by Giovan Luigi Valesio (*c*.1560-1633) remains unidentified. See Negro and Pirondini 1994, 340.

24 Ibidem, 53: "La bella Cloto a cui de la tua vita/ Pose, Valesio, in man lo stame Amore,/ Fedele amante e nobile pittore,/ In imagine viva hai colorita./ Onde, mentr'ella di tormenti ordita/ Fila la morte al tuo trafitto core,/ Tu di gloria immortal, d'eterno onore/ Torci al bel nome suo linea infinita./

Da lei (cred'io) la qualità prendesti/ Poi ch'un sembiante in fragil tela chiuso/ Vive in virtù de' tuoi color celesti./ Son di quel filo istesso, ond'ella ha in uso/ D'innaspar vite, i lini tuoi contesti,/ Né vale il tuo pennel men del suo fuso."

25 This painting by Paolo Guidotti (Lucca 1560-Rome 1629) remains unidentified.

Passes the river with the bloodless girl.
I know that one would escape,
And the other dart his arrow,
But the archer does not dare pierce
The fragile canvas where his dear bride stays,
And the abductor does not want to flee,
Lest he deprive the picture of so beautiful a piece.[26]

In this madrigal, Marino pithily plays with the *istoria*'s temporal frame. The male antagonists, the Centaur and Hercules, both set out to fulfill their actions; the one prepares to escape from his adversary's assault by leaving the pictorial field, while the other is positioned to shoot an arrow and wound his rival. Yet neither of them is enabled to finish what they have started. To explain the unaccomplished state of their actions—or more generally painting's intrinsic stillness—Marino summons two material components of the picture, the canvas and the frame. All but oblivious to the painting's fragile medium, Hercules decides to spare his arrow, afraid that it would both pierce the canvas and the figure depicted on it, his beloved Deianira. Conscious of the escape provided by the picture's frame—the material border beyond which figurative life ceases to exist altogether—the Centaur balks at robbing the beautiful depiction of Deianira from the beholder's eyes. Once again, Marino evokes the pictorial medium in order to attune the reader to the specificities of the narrative; the canvas and the frame, by forming material boundaries or an unexpected refuge for the figures, in turn enhance the viewer's perception of the two rivals' suspended movements. One can vividly see Hercules pointing his bow and the Centaur rushing toward the picture's margins, as if one were about to shoot and the other to flee. In addition, the beholder is also made aware of the "below" and "beyond" of the painting's spatial field: the space of representation greatly dilates through the evocation of the picture's physicality, since the fiction seems to prolong itself into and outside the artwork. In Marino's opinion, the canvas can also be the realm of living flesh, or of its fictive double. In celebrating an *Angelica* by Giovanni Baglione,[27] Caravaggio's archenemy, the poet declares:

The virtue of your hand,
Baglione, has brought again
To life the ungrateful beauty.
No other brush than yours could be
more fitted to depict such a beautiful face.
Apollo admires her, and is unable to say
Which one is more beautiful, whether the one
In the flesh, on paper or on canvas,
Whether the true or the fictive,
Whether the one living, the written of, or the painted.[28]

The "beauty" evoked by Marino, depicted by Baglione, and admired by Apollo himself is Ludovico Ariosto's famous heroine Angelica. Through his representation, Baglione resuscitates not only

---

26 Ibidem, 45: "Fuggi, accorto centauro,/ Depredator de la beltà divina,/ Vanne lieto a goder l'alta rapina./ Scocca pur l'arco, Alcide! Ecco ei sen porta/ Di là dal rio la giovinetta smorta./ So che l'un fuggirebbe/ E l'altro ferirebbe,/ Ma 'l fragil lino ov'è la cara sposa/ L'arcer ferir non osa,/ Né vuol fuggire il ladro,/ Per non privar di sì bell'opra il quadro."

27 This *Angelica* by Giovanni Baglione (1571-1644) remains unidentified.

28 Ibidem, 55: "Virtù de la tua mano/ Ha tra noi suscitata,/ Baglion, la bella ingrata./ Né certo era a formar volto sì bello/ Uopo d'altro pennello./ L'ammira Apollo e non sa dir qual sia/ Di maggior leggiadria,/ In carne, in carte, in tela, o vera o finta,/ Viva, scritta o dipinta."

the woman, but also her literary counterpart in the *Orlando Furioso*. This fact allows Marino to triplicate Angelica's persona in a marvelous hall of shifting mirrors. At the end of the poem, the reader, like Apollo, is presented with eight different versions of the same female prototype: in the flesh, on paper, on canvas, true, fictive, living, written about, and painted. Of course, some of these variations of Angelica are identical, but I would like above all to underline the concept of the heroine's multiple avatars in Marino's madrigal. Apollo's indecision in ascertaining the most beautiful Angelica relies on the commonplace parallel between poetry and painting, and thus I will not dwell on this aspect of the poem. Rather, I will remark that the canvas—a medium like the paper on which Ariosto's poem is reproduced—possesses the ability to reproduce the flesh and life of Angelica. Just as Valesio gives life to his Clotho through the picture's threads, so too does Baglione endow Angelica with the new life of the pictorial flesh that he duplicates on the canvas. The array of Marino's poems on which I have commented demonstrates how vital the theme of the painting's materiality was at the beginning of the seventeenth century. There is no doubt that the evocation of the canvas' threads, but also of the frame, or of its pigments, fulfills a meta-narrative task; the linen, indeed, can be associated with a diversity of concepts, and the value and significance of these associations are deeply rooted in the fiction's subject and in the *istoria*'s particularities.

By fictively and metaphorically piercing the canvas, Caravaggio, like Marino later, not only activates the pictorial medium as an interconnected factor in the picture's perception and reading, but also charges it with metaphorical resonances that are "colored" by the narrative context in which this activation operates. Unfortunately Marino did not compose any poem to honor Caravaggio's achievement in *The Incredulity of Saint Thomas*—a painting that he must have seen in the Giustiniani Collection, Rome—but one may imagine that Caravaggio's depiction of Christ's pierced torso and his intimation of the canvas underneath it might have aroused in Marino a myriad of poetic concepts bearing on the "fleshiness" of the Savior's body and its reincarnation through the linen threads. It is now time to attempt an interpretation of Caravaggio's "piercing acts" as staged in the Potsdam and Naples pictures.

"An Haut und Fleisch"

According to Bernardo Bizoni, Marchese Vincenzo Giustiniani mentioned Caravaggio's *The Incredulity of Saint Thomas* (Fig. 235) as his property in August 1606, when, during a sojourn in Genoa, he recognized a copy after the painting in the collection of Orazio del Negro.[29] In the 1638 inventory of the Giustiniani Collection, the painting in fact appears with his black frame molded and decorated with golden arabesques.[30] Giovanni Baglione mistakenly relates that Ciriaco Mattei, the owner of the London *Supper at Emmaus* and the Dublin *Taking of Christ*, had commissioned the picture.[31] Giovan Pietro Bellori in his 1672 *Vite* correctly records that Caravaggio, at the behest of Marchese Giustiniani, represented "Saint Thomas putting his finger in the side wound of the Lord, who pulls [the apostle's] hand toward it as he unveils his chest by removing the shroud from his nipple."[32] Although he dates the painting to 1606-1607—that is, after Caravaggio's murder of Ranuccio Tomassoni—Joachim von Sandrart in his 1675 *Teutsche Academie* rightly implies that *The Incredulity of Saint Thomas* was executed for Marchese Giustiniani:

29 Bizoni, 200: "Il signor Orazio del Negro ha (…) una copia del San Tommaso del signor Vincenzo, del Caravaggio."

30 See more recently Danesi Squarzina 2003, 1:397-9.

31 Baglione, 137: "Anzi fé cadere al romore anche il signor Ciriaco Mattei, a cui il Caravaggio avea dipinto un San Giovanni Battista e quando Nostro Signore andò in Emmaus,

ed allora che san Tomasso toccò co 'l dito il costato del Salvadore, ed intaccò quel signore di molte centinaia di scudi."

32 Bellori, 222: "Seguitava egli nel favore del marchese Vincenzo Giustiniani, che l'impiegò in alcuni quadri, l'Incoronazione di spine e San Tomaso che pone il ditto nella piaga del costato del Signore, il quale gli accosta la mano e si svela il petto da un lenzuolo, discostandolo dalla poppa."

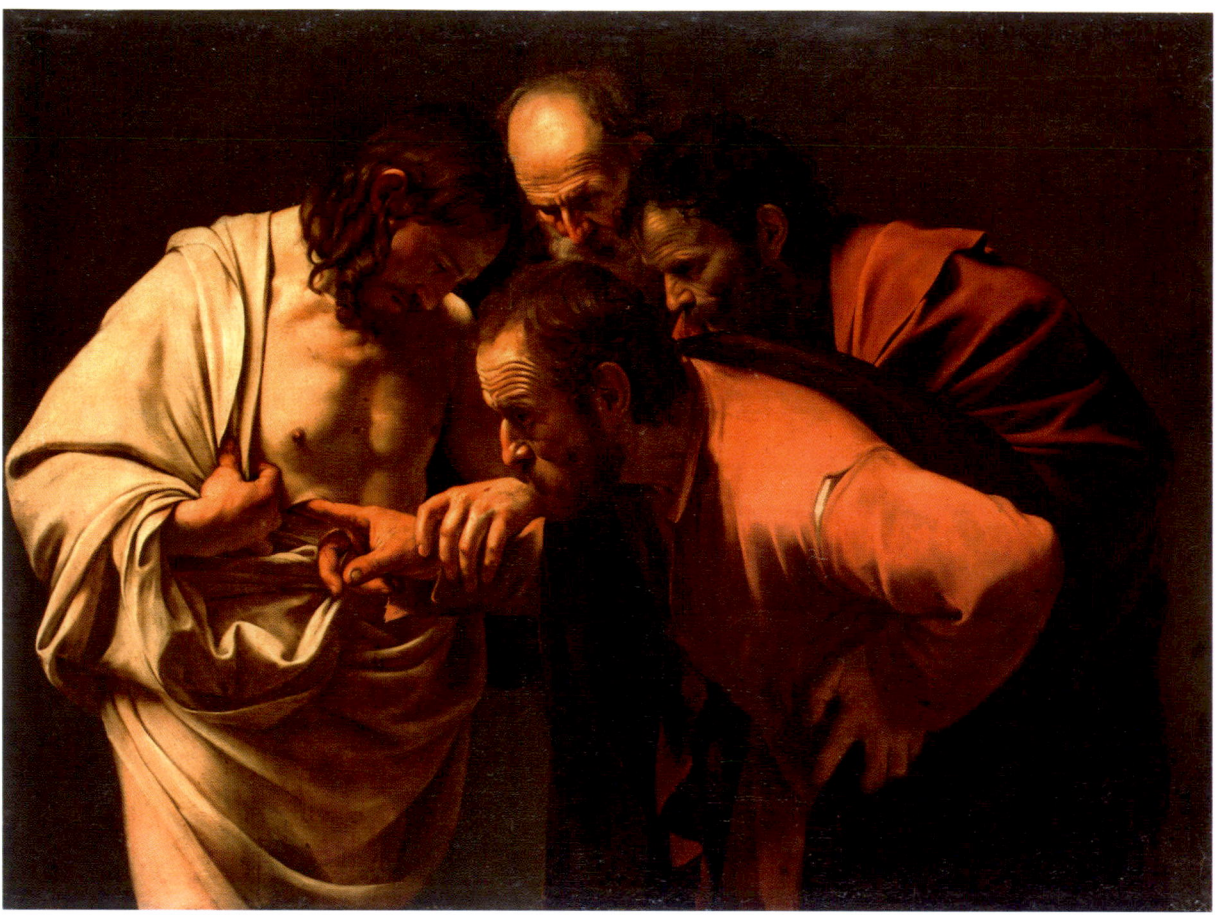

Fig. 235
Michelangelo Merisi da Caravaggio, *The Incredulity of Saint Thomas*, Schloß Sans-Souci, Potsdam, oil on canvas, 107 x 146 cm.

During the time in which he was forced to hide, he [Caravaggio] depicted in the [Giustiniani] Palace Christ introducing Thomas' finger into his sacred wound in the presence of other apostles. Through good painting and relief, he expressed such a bafflement and naturalness of skin and flesh [*an Haut und Fleisch*] in all the bystanders' faces that any other painting in comparison appears to be but colored paper.[33]

Surprisingly enough, Sandrart in the last sentence views Caravaggio's rendition of the human figure's appearance and stereography as essentially centered on the actors' faces, whereas he overlooks Christ's naked torso, which is a prodigy of pictorial "skin" and "flesh." It comes as no surprise that Sandrart explicitly conjures up the notions of "*Haut*" and "*Fleisch*" in connection with the Potsdam picture. In his 1673 *Pinacotheca, sive Romana pictura et sculptura*, Giovanni Michele Silos describes Caravaggio's painting in an intriguing Latin epigram:

Oh lucky man, who is allowed to touch
The sweet Lord's side split by the wound!
Yet, Thomas longs and dreads, burns and freezes:

---

33 Sandrart, 276: "In wärender Zeit nun, da er sich so verstecken musste, mahlte er in gedachten Palast, wie Christus des Thomas Finger in Gegenwart der andern Aposteln in seine heilige Wunden steckt. Da bildete er nun in aller Anwesenden Angesichtern durch gutes mahlen und rundiren eine solche Verwunderung und Natürlichkeit an Haut und Fleisch aus, daß meist alle andere Gemälde dabei nur als illuminirt Papier scheinen."

You can see desire and fear in his timid face.
In the end, [his finger] lands in the divine side,
Suckling dewy honey from his nectareous wound.
Oh Caravaggio, Thomas has once again deserved
To touch Christ's breast, right here, in this painted effigy.
But touch is sweeter now, as Thomas cannot part from his
Chest, and Jesus' sweet side refuses to cease its fervor.[34]

Although Silos' poem is quoted in some catalogue entries on Caravaggio's oeuvre, scholars have not yet examined it with due attention. To begin, Silos stresses the duality of feelings to which Thomas is subject; in the Petrarchan tradition, the poet makes the apostle "long and dread, burn and freeze"; his "desire and fear" tear him apart, manifesting themselves on his tormented face. Even allowing for poetic licence, Silos' reading of Thomas' attitude should be taken seriously; it is no coincidence that the apostle's head appears in the center of the composition, so that the viewer enters the scene through this figure's intense expression. His wide-open eye, almost bulging out of its socket, and the grooved relief of his puckered forehead, are usually construed as the sign of intense concentration: Thomas, at first glance, seems to stare at the object of his incredulity, Christ's side wound, with unwavering, almost obsessive attention.

Yet despite appearances, the apostle's gaze is not directed toward the Savior's side wound; his figure, in fact, is situated in the canvas' immediate foreground, mostly in front of, and not on the same plane as, Christ's body.[35] Even his right arm is not entirely aligned with the nearly planar surface of Jesus' torso. The noticeably out-of-proportion hands of both the Savior and Thomas, which are accommodated almost in the picture's center, seem to occupy an implausible intermediate space between Christ and the apostle, so that the "act of piercing" takes place through a slight warping of the pictorial space. Most beholders are unable to detect this essential detail upon first glimpsing the painting, and even on further consideration some art historians peremptorily deny its blatant existence. Some believe that the spatial misalignments between Jesus and Thomas stem from Caravaggio's method of pictorial montage, that is, from the superposition of one figure upon the other during the picture's execution. This consideration, simplistic in my opinion, is preposterous insofar as in assembling multiple figures into a single narrative, early modern artists are used to, and very often succeed in, rendering the coherence of the pictorial space through simple alignments; furthermore, Caravaggio's practical skills at this point of his career should be unquestionable.

What I am implying here is that Caravaggio intentionally imagined the reciprocal positions of Thomas' and Christ's figures as spatially misaligned, but illusorily aligned on a perceptual level. In other words, while processing the picture's action, beholders intuitively link together its main actors in a global cause-and-effect connection that is suggested by the gesture of the two hands pushing toward the Lord's side wound, but that is not justified by the figures' emplacement in the pictorial space. The viewer's eye therefore corrects the visual perception by coordinating what is not truly related in the picture: the beholder automatically reroutes Thomas' gaze toward Jesus' side.

34   Silos, 92, CLXV: "O fortunam, scissum cui vulnere dulci/ Concessum Domini tangere posse latus!/ At cupit et trepidat Thomas; simul ardet et alget:/ Ore verecundo vota metumque vides./ Involat at tandem divinum in pectus, et illo/ vulnere nectareo roscida mella bibit./ Tangere nunc iterum, Caravagi, haec pectora Thomas/ promeruit: nempe hac pictus in effigie./ Dulcius hic tangit, nam avelli a pectore nescit,/ Atque hoc dulce latus defervisse nequit."

35   See, for example, Varriano 2006, 14, reaction to Hockney's

consideration: "In nearly all instances, the lack of psychological focus or unity is the result of Caravaggio's having elected to paint a classic profile instead of turning the head into the picture and toward the narrative, as would seem more natural. Hockney is not the first to suggest that Caravaggio tended to paint his models individually, 'collaging' them together into multifigure compositions afterward." Need I remind the reader that, in *The Incredulity of Saint Thomas*, the problem does not reside in the apostle's profile, but in his figure's position with regard to that of Christ?

Silos was most probably not aware of the painting's spatial oddities, yet his interpretation of Thomas' expression as both eagerness and fear helps us better elucidate the dynamics of the pictorial narrative as conceived by Caravaggio. Not daring to approach further and have to touch a dead man, Thomas freezes at a certain distance from the Savior, hunching his torso while gripping his hip as if to prevent himself from recoiling: his left hand, bathed in penumbra, inscribed within a slightly elongated circumference, literally claws at his dark mantle in fearful, relentless awareness. Not daring to watch his finger as it enters Christ's resurrected body, his gaze strays forward; he expects at any moment to feel what he is unable to see, actually feels the contact of the Savior's body in wonder, and is utterly disconcerted; in a sense, Thomas sees through his finger, and the almost hyperbolic peeling of his eye conveys the marvel and unsettlement of the vision of the wound as it looms in his mind's eye.

Thomas' temporary blindness to Christ's body—his refusal to see what he is touching—sheds new light on Jesus' conventional gesture, largely relayed by the early modern iconographic tradition, of guiding the apostle's hand toward his side wound; this time, guidance is even more necessary not only to boost the apostle's uncertain courage, but especially to allow him to center the target. The disjunction of the interrelated concepts of seeing and touching as conjured up by Thomas' figure relies on the Gospel of Saint John (20, 24-25):

> Thomas, called Didymus, one of the Twelve, was not with them when Jesus came. So the other disciples said to him, "We have seen the Lord." But he said to them: "Unless I see the mark of the nails in his hand and put my finger into the nail marks and put my hand into his side, I will not believe." Now a week later his disciples were again inside and Thomas was with them. Jesus came, although the doors were locked, and stood in their midst and said, "Peace be with you." Then he said to Thomas, "Put your finger here and see my hands, and bring your hand and put it into my side, and do not be unbelieving, but believe." Thomas answered and said to him, "My Lord and my God!" Jesus said to him, "Have you come to believe because you have seen me? Blessed are those who have not seen and have believed."

Even if, after convincing Thomas of his reincarnation, Jesus simply picks up on the apostle's necessity of seeing in order to believe, scripture registers Thomas' scruples as related to touch, too; it is not enough for him to see, he also needs to pierce Jesus' hand and side wounds respectively with his finger and hand. The Savior's invitation to "put [his] finger [there] and see" ties together the two perceptual spheres of seeing and touching into a hybrid notion: seeing through touching, and vice versa. In the iconographic tradition before Caravaggio, artists seldom fail to depict Thomas' figure as both seeing Christ's face and touching his side wound.

This slight disconnection between sight and touch is also characteristic of Albrecht Dürer's c.1509 woodcut of *The Incredulity of Saint Thomas* from the *Small Passion* (Fig. 236), an image that scholars rightly deem a source of inspiration for Caravaggio's Potsdam picture.[36] In the print, Christ soars in the middle, completely naked except for a loincloth, his torso poised frontally and flanked by his zigzagging arms, which are oriented in diverse directions. With his left hand, he performs the canonical blessing, thereby exhibiting his nail mark; with his right hand, he grabs Thomas' wrist and pushes the apostle's right hand into his side wound. While sensing Jesus' flesh closing in around his fingers, Thomas, his profile immersed in darkness, stares at the Savior's face; seeing and touching, albeit associated, do not converge toward the same target.

---

36   See Hütt 1980, 2:1625; and Schoch et al. 2001, 2:338-9, no. 219. For the relation between Dürer's print and the Potsdam picture, see Friedlaender 1969, 162-3.

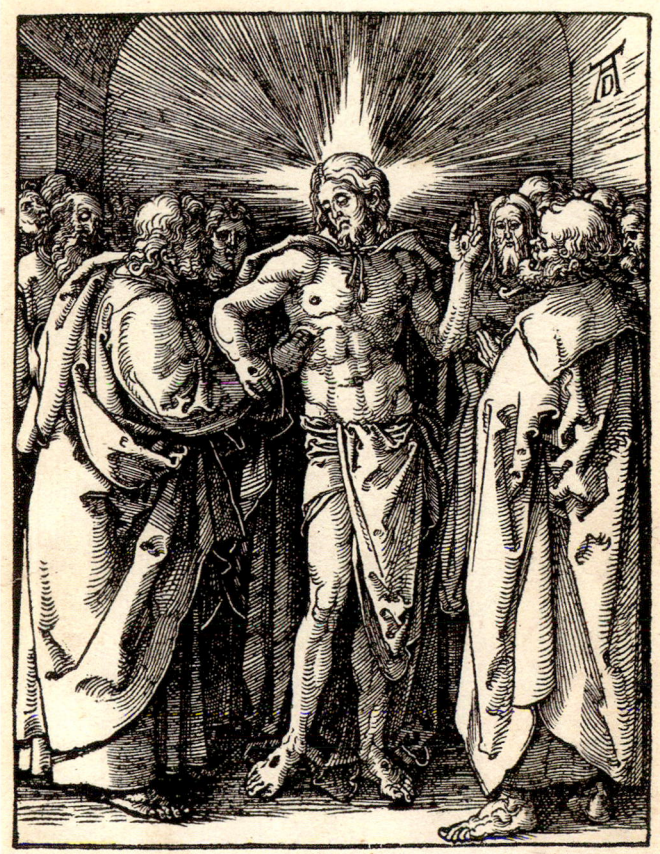

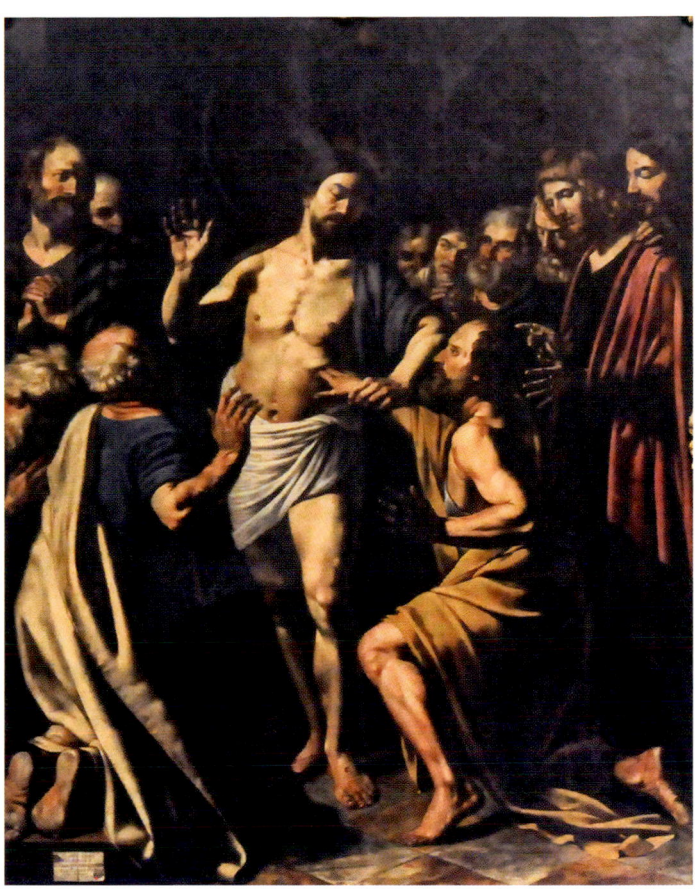

Fig. 236
Albrecht Dürer, *The Incredulity of Saint Thomas*, woodcut, 12.7 x 9.7 cm.

Fig. 237
Louis Finson, *The Incredulity of Saint Thomas*, Saint-Sauveur Cathedral, Aix-en-Provence, oil on canvas, 260 x 201 cm.

In this regard, it is noteworthy that Louis Finson, a Flemish follower of Caravaggio, resorted to Dürer's example in painting his *c.*1613 *Incredulity of Saint Thomas* for Saint-Sauveur Cathedral, Aix-en-Provence[37] (Fig. 237). In this picture, Thomas kneels in front of, and at a certain distance from, Christ; aware of these two figures' spatial misalignment, Finson made the apostle's arm recede toward Jesus' side wound, and turned his face toward the Savior's in mutual dialogue. Like Dürer, Finson thus disassociates Thomas' touch of the side wound from his seeing Christ, thereby emending Caravaggio's boldness in temporarily "blinding" the apostle by shifting him toward the foreground and steering his gaze forward.

Less frequently, early modern artists represented the apostle's gaze fixed upon the side wound, as is the case of Andrea del Verrocchio's famous bronze group of *The Incredulity of Saint Thomas* for Orsanmichele, Florence, completed in 1483 (Fig. 238).[38] Scholars commonly disregard this sculpture as a possible source of inspiration for Caravaggio—although it is not inconceivable that the painter halted in Florence on his way to Rome from northern Italy around 1592-1594—and yet some details of the Potsdam painting present astonishing affinities with Verrocchio's masterpiece. First of all, when seen from the right and below, the right hand of the Orsanmichele Christ, as a result of the foreshortening, takes on a form very similar to that of Jesus' right hand in Caravaggio's painting: not only do both hands accomplish an identical action by pulling aside the drapery that

37 See Bodart 1970, 89-94, no. 6.

38 For this sculptural group, see Dolcini 1992; Butterfield 1997, 64-80; Covi 2005, 71-88; and the many essays published in Beck et al., 1996. For the theme of seeing and touching as developed in Verrocchio's sculpture in Orsanmichele, see Kohl 2005, 226-33.

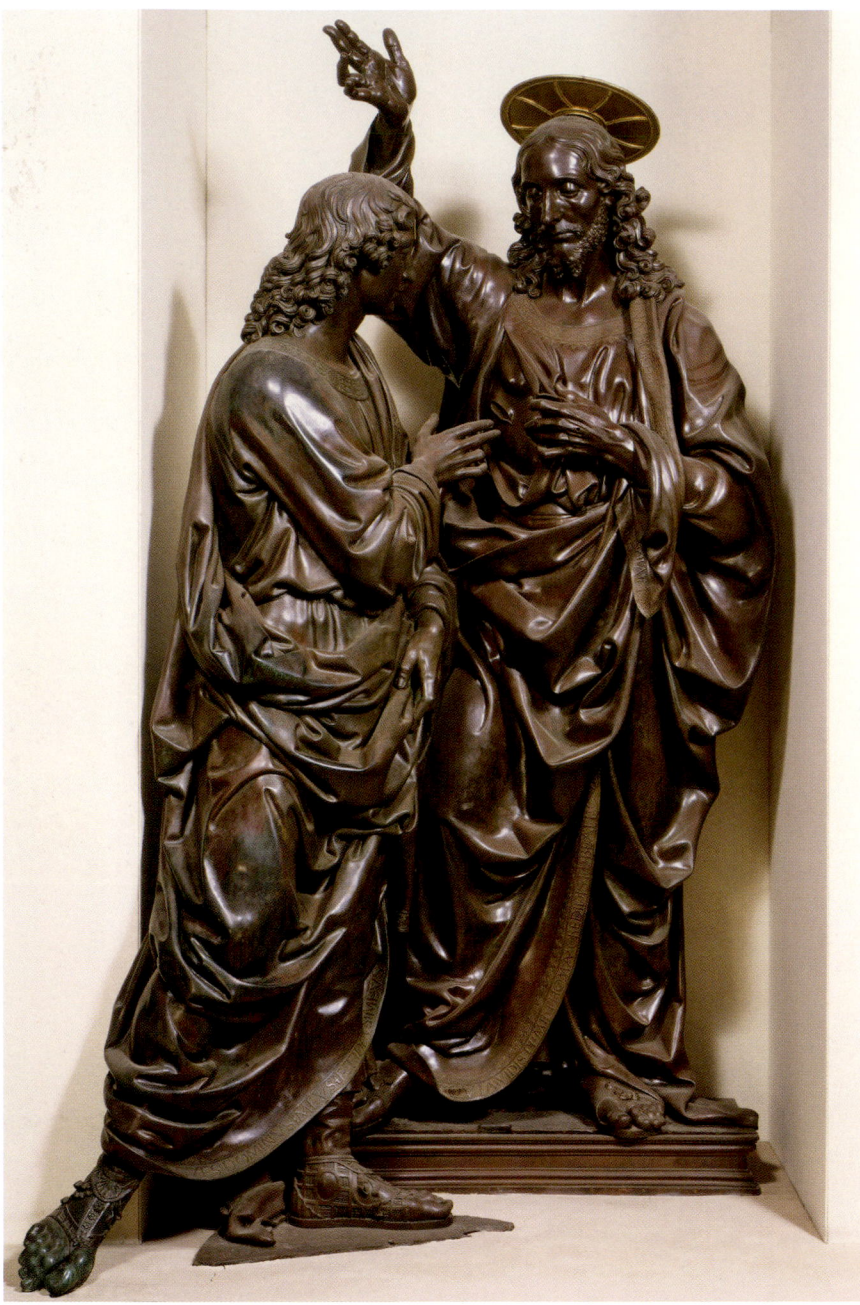

Fig. 238
Andrea del Verrocchio, *The Incredulity of Saint Thomas*, Orsanmichele, Florence, bronze with some gilding, 230 cm. (Christ's statue).

covers the side wound, but also, in both cases, the uppermost parts of the fingers disappear from view so that only the knuckles slightly protrude and press toward the chest (Figs. 239, 240). Moreover, in both cases, the thumb detaches itself from the hand's bulk in holding the drapery.

By the same token, Christ's side wound in the sculpture curls up at its edges and gapes as if in acceptance, yet without the intervention, of Thomas' touch, a motif that Caravaggio might have adjusted to his redefinition of the episode's temporality by causing the apostle's finger to pry open the wound in a mechanistic, not metaphorical, manner. I have always been intrigued by the complex fashion in which Caravaggio wraps the mantle around Christ's torso; although it is quite possible that, from a different viewpoint, the folds of this drapery would "make sense," from the beholder's standpoint it is problematic to understand how the Savior's shroud is knotted around his hips and stays in place. More interestingly, Caravaggio took great pleasure and care in designing the mantle's fall from Jesus' right hand and its subsequent rise toward his torso; although the outermost contour of this makeshift sleeve traces an elegant ellipse, its inner folds wave up and down outlining curved ridges that hollow out pools of shade.

Of course, this series of re-entrances serve as a prelude to Thomas' act of piercing in the Potsdam picture, but for this very reason, they possess a sculptural character that similarly recalls the example of Verrocchio's Orsanmichele group. Indeed, if one considers the way in which the right rim of the ripped tunic contours the bare portion of the Savior's chest in the sculpture, and the way in which the mantle encircles his torso by cascading around it as its tubular folds shape curvy ridges and elliptical crevices, it is easy to discern strong similarities with Caravaggio's treatment of Jesus' shroud in *The Incredulity of Saint Thomas*. The flatness and verticality of the shroud's folds descending along the Savior's chest, and the deep projection toward the foreground of his makeshift sleeve, corroborate this observation. And even the curly lock of Christ's hair that spirals down along his face brings to mind the flowing curls of Jesus' mane in Verrocchio's sculpture.

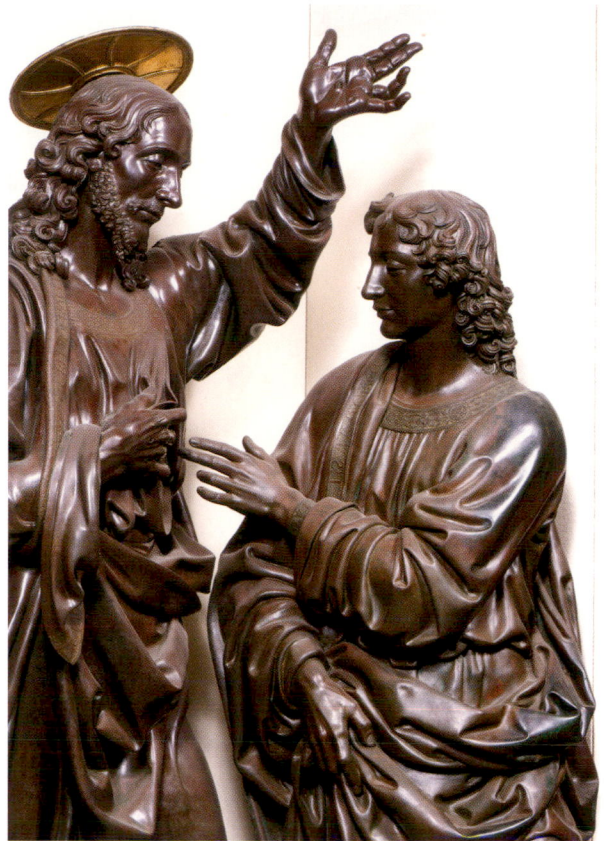

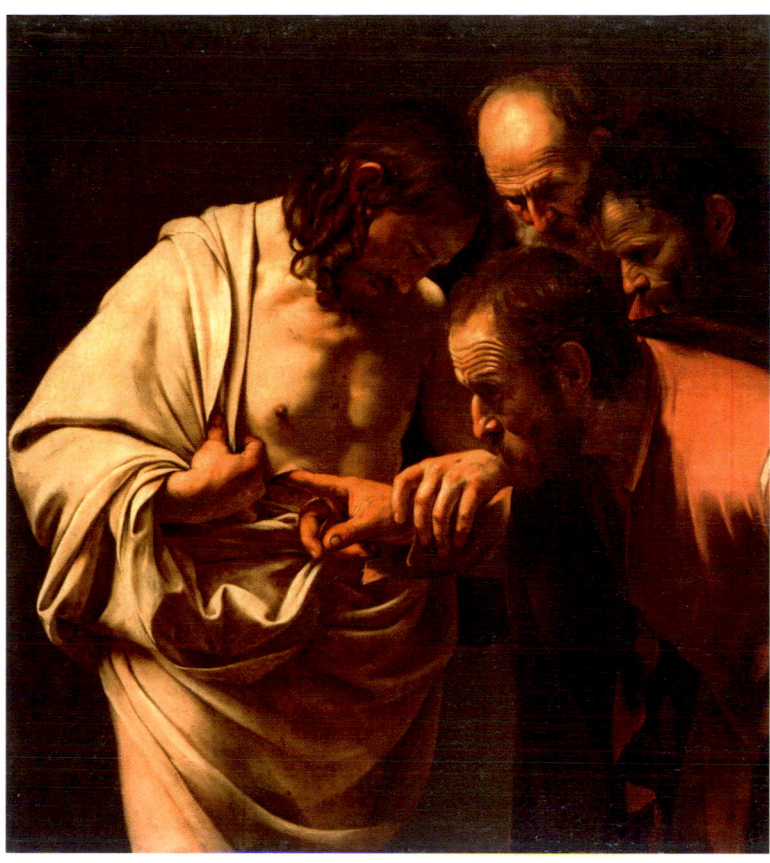

Fig. 239
Andrea del Verrocchio, *The Incredulity of Saint Thomas*,
Orsanmichele, Florence, bronze with some gilding, 230 cm.
(Christ's statue), detail reversed.

Fig. 240
Michelangelo Merisi da Caravaggio, *The Incredulity of Saint Thomas*, Schloß
Sans-Souci, Potsdam, oil on canvas, 107 x 146 cm., detail.

However, I am less interested in demonstrating Verrocchio's influence on Caravaggio, whether plausible or not, than in pointing out the exceptionality of Caravaggio's visual solutions in representing *The Incredulity of Saint Thomas*—that is, his distancing from the main stream of this theme's iconography—and the clear sculptural aspects, though limited to single spots, of his pictorial technique. These aspects confirm the importance of unusual relief effects in a composition in which Caravaggio simultaneously alludes to the skin and flesh of painting. On the other hand, I cannot leave behind Verrocchio's group without mentioning that some tendencies to hyperbolic effects as revealed in the Potsdam picture—for instance, in the depiction of the hands—are also characteristic of the Orsanmichele *Incredulity of Saint Thomas*—for example, the vigorous relief of the draperies' folds or the nervous rendering of veins and arteries in the figures' hands. But whereas these effects are necessary in a sculpture that must be seen out in the open, at a distance and mostly from below, they are out of place in an easel painting, and therefore must here fulfill a function other than a purely optical one.

More than in any other picture, in *The Incredulity of Saint Thomas* Caravaggio exalted the smoothness of the pictorial surface. I do not believe that any photographic reproduction could render the suffused brightness of the painting, the rosy luminosity that consistently irradiates from the canvas and results from a deft combination of fleshy tones and colors: the orange of Thomas' tunic, the carnelian of the adjacent apostle's, the amber of Christ's shroud and torso, the brownish-ochre of the disciples' heads, and the reddish opalescence of the Savior's shaded profile. From a chromatic point of view, the Potsdam picture is the realm of living flesh and its tonal harmonies.

Caravaggio obviously strove to stress the uniformity, or quasi-compactness, of the painting's

463

composition. As Lionello Venturi ingeniously put it, *The Incredulity of Saint Thomas* is a "compositional portent," "a tangle of bodies tending toward the same spiritual motive and bent to an architectural synthesis."[39] In fact, Caravaggio fused the half-figures of his four actors into a unique pictorial organism, a diamond-like prism of bodies that presents itself as a single, three-dimensional architectural structure to the viewer. To the right, Christ's two arms, almost symmetrically folded, bracket the vertical volume of his body, placed slightly askew, thereby configuring the lozenge pattern to which the whole composition is attuned. To the left, the reiterated motif of the two apostles' leaning torsos and protruding elbows delineates a large bracket echoing that of Christ's bent right arm. In the upper center of the canvas, the heads of the four figures respond to one another, profile against profile, with the exception of the older apostle's face in the background, all of them nonetheless delimiting a diamond through their spatial interrelations. There is no escape for the viewer; the rhombus of entangled bodies devised by Caravaggio, a centripetal composition in its purity, ensconces almost at its center the main action, a machinery of two hands—the piston of Thomas' pointing finger set into motion by Jesus' propelling wrench—on which the viewer is forced to dwell, and at which point the figures' concentrated gazes inexorably and unanimously appear to aim.

Because of its specific configuration, the Potsdam picture not only redoubles or even multiplies the intensity of the beholder's gaze, it also assimilates the figures' gaze to the viewer's and vice versa, so that Thomas' piercing act becomes the equivalent of an image-within-the-image, the epicenter of an action that figures and spectators equally attend with expectation and marvel. As Koos has suggested, contemporary viewers might have associated Christ's gesture of pulling his shroud aside with the act by which collectors at the time used to remove curtains from their most precious paintings in order to display them.[40] In this light, the essential theme of Caravaggio's *The Incredulity of Saint Thomas* pivots around the staging of a miraculous piercing: that of a pictorial body. However, the fact that this pictorial body is none other than the divine body—Christ's body—by definition modifies the scope of the optical and representational experiment carried out by Caravaggio. His is not merely an attempt to persuade the viewer that, through art's artifice, the human figure can be so fully and materially recreated as to endure and resist penetration just like any other three-dimensional object. In the Potsdam picture, Caravaggio more specifically displays and questions the artist's capacity to depict the incarnated divinity in its sensorial and material truth: to transform painting into the true embodiment of a deity that manifests itself on both a physical and a transcendental level. As I have explained in Part Three, Caravaggio is not averse to challenging and reassessing the concept of truth in religious painting as interpreted by the Counter-Reformation's art theorists.

Among the Christian painter's main finalities is that of reproducing the sacred event with such precision and graphicness as to induce the viewer into seeing, perceiving, and feeling the divinity and its operations as true to life and faithful to scripture. Layer after layer, one pictorial skin after the other, Caravaggio stretched and rounded the flesh of the Savior's torso, which he patterned into a slightly receding, delicately chiseled bas-relief, achieving its smoothness as an indispensable prerequisite to slit its surface and convey the impression of an elastic aperture, as if both the Savior's epidermis and the linen canvas could be split open and probed by Thomas' finger at the same time.[41] That all of this is not only about seeing is confirmed by Thomas' attitude: through his

39 Venturi 1963, 28: "La Incredulità di San Tommaso che purtroppo ci è giunta solo in copia è un portento compositivo, un groviglio di corpi teso verso il medesimo motivo spirituale, un piegare i corpi ad una sintesi architettonica."

40 Koos 2005, 1146: "Darüber hinaus gilt es jedoch zu beachten, wie Caravaggio diese Aktfigur im einzelnen

ausformt. Christi Körper is explizit wie ein Bild inszeniert: so erinnert das über Eck geführte helle Leinen-Leichentuch, mit dem Christus umwunden ist, an einen Vorhang, hinter dem ein Bild enthüllt wird."

41 See Suthor 2003, 277: "Bei Caravaggio könnte dieser Leinenstoff, der zum weißen Grabtuch ein verhaltenes Echo

temporary blindness to Christ's body, he visually insinuates the depth and prodigy of his sensation in touching—perhaps, the softness and dewiness of the Savior's flesh, which, like an ever-warm honeycomb, might be filled with nectar in accordance with Silos' poetic metaphors.

The intensity of the apostle's feeling of the sacred body can also be evinced by the temporal framework chosen by Caravaggio in this episode; as Silos pointed out, the dwelling of Thomas' finger inside the wound is indefinitely frozen and prolonged into the future by the picture's fictiveness. Even Christ's figure seems to be preeminently equated with the portion of his naked torso allotted to Thomas' curiosity, for his face, sunk into penumbra, loses much of its visual relevance, and one would hardly notice at first glance that the Savior is emitting the Gospel words "do not be unbelieving, but believe." Unless, feeling Thomas' finger inside his wound, he is instead voicing his physical discomfort. Structurally speaking, *The Incredulity of Saint Thomas* states the centrality of Christ's body, and not of his figure, by enhancing the haptic effects of his "living flesh," and yet, even if viewers can apprehend the sensation of Thomas' endless touch, the tactility of the Savior's body in the end can only be envisioned in visual terms. Even at its best, painting remains the primary domain of the optical, and not of the haptic; the effect of relief, of the pictorial flesh, is built into, but also hampered by, the canvas' surface and bi-dimensionality. More drastically, by representing Thomas' finger as piercing Christ's side wound, Caravaggio beguiles the viewer into crossing the limits of painting's medium, into penetrating the image through his or her own imagination.

But what lies beyond the bodily membrane transfixed by Thomas's finger? Should one expect to find an actual body there, or just the threads of the canvas? Here and there, Caravaggio prepares the eye to encounter the canvas: on Thomas' shoulder, the tunic rips and offers to view a patch of linen; in some spots on the borders of the apostle's literally threadbare mantle, one can see a few loose threads dangling as if from an un-stretched canvas. Whatever lies beyond the open wound, whether the canvas or Christ's transcendental body, constitutes another ineffable and invisible boundary, and it is up to the beholders whether they wish to believe in the transcendental presence of divinity through an act of faith and imagination, or to realize that, even in such a gripping rendition of the flesh as Caravaggio's, the sacred image at its core is the product of fiction, and hence unable truly to contain the divine.[42]

To state this tremendous alternative visually is the paramount goal of Caravaggio's allusion to the canvas in the Potsdam picture, and his use of it as a meta-narrative device. It may seem a paradox that, through his optical naturalism—or realism, as I defined it in Chapter 2—Caravaggio manages both to render the impression of living flesh (*vera carne*) better than any other master at the time, and crudely to disclose the irreducible fictive nature of his endeavor. Even as the viewer is invited to touch Jesus' body through Thomas' intermediary, Caravaggio indicates that the Savior's flesh also corresponds to the superficial skin of his pictorial fiction. If in the London *Supper at*

aufbaut, über die narrative Illustration hinaus auch—im Sinne eines 'metapikturalen Diskurses'—als Repräsentation der Leinwand die verdeckte Grundlage des Bildes selbst bezeichnen. Die geschlossene Oberfläche der Repräsentation selbst wird quasi mit einer Wunde ausgestattet—im Sinne einer Auslassung in der Textur des Bildes, auf die sich der Blick fixiert, da es hier nichts zu (be-)greifen gibt." Like Koos later, Suthor insists on the mystical function of this allusion to the canvas' medium: "die Einschreibung eines Zeichen der Abwesenheit, die sich als Wunde in die Repräsentation einschreibt."

42 From a very different perspective, Koos 2005, 1151, observes: "Bei aller taktilen Präsenz des gegenständlich Dargestellten beschränk Caravaggio die Rezeption seiner Kunst auf das Visuelle: Inwiefern—so stellt sich aber letzendlich

die Frage—entspricht Caravaggio damit nicht doch auch der religiösen Bilddirektive, vom Sinnlichen auf ein theologisch Höheres, Imaginäres hinauszuweisen? Diese Frage muß negativ beantwortet werden, denn Caravaggio verweigert in seiner Kunst jedes Signum der Transzendenz." See also Koos 2007, 73: "Christi Schieben von Thomas' Finger tief in die enthüllte Wunde, Thomas' angestrengtes Prüfen ohne Zeichen der Erkenntnis erzeugen den Eindruck, dass sich tastend hinter der äußeren Grenze keine inkarnierte Substanz erfahren ließe, geschweige die Transzendenz. Was dieser Gestus hingegen tatsächlich enthüllt, ist die Oberfläche des Körpers Christi, die Haut, die Caravaggio mit streifendem Licht und starken Schatten drastisch hervorhebt. Christi Körper scheint—in diesen gerahmten Partien—nicht so sehr aus Fleisch und Blut gebildet, denn aus Haut über Knochen, gleich einer über den Keilrahmen gespannte Leinwand eines Gemäldes."

Emmaus it was the visibility of Christ that Caravaggio put to the test, in *The Incredulity of Saint Thomas* it is instead the Savior's tactility that he sets out to investigate. In both cases, it is the possibility for painting to duplicate the divine presence—whether in visual or haptic terms—that is explored and seriously doubted. In *The Martyrdom of Saint Ursula*, if the depiction of the tyrant's arrow piercing the martyr's breast reopens the question of painting's fictiveness and materiality, Caravaggio abandons the problem of truth in the sacred image, focusing instead upon the multiple mechanisms through which the pictorial medium is capable of transcending the technical limits of the *istoria*.

Dissolving the Flesh

The origin and provenance of Caravaggio's *The Martyrdom of Saint Ursula* (Fig. 241) are exceptionally well documented. In a letter of 11 May 1610 to Prince Marcantonio Doria in Genoa, Lanfranco Massa, the nobleman's procurator and agent in Naples, writes:

> I planned to ship the picture of Saint Ursula to you this week, but to ensure that it was perfectly dry before I sent it, I exposed it to the sun yesterday, which rather than drying it caused the varnish to resurface, for Caravaggio spreads it very thick. I want to return to Caravaggio to have his advice as to how to prevent any damage. Signor *** has seen it and was stunned, as were all those who have seen it. (…) Your Lordship should think about another subject to propose to Car[avaggio], for I know he is your friend…[43]

About two weeks later, on 27 August, Massa sent Caravaggio's painting to Prince Doria by sea, packing it with great care into a box or crate.[44] From then on, *The Martyrdom of Saint Ursula* had remained in the possession of the Doria family, first in Genoa, then in Southern Italy, until it was sold to the Banca Commerciale Italiana in Naples in 1973. Although it is not known why Caravaggio was requested to depict the death of Saint Ursula, it has been observed that one of Prince Doria's stepdaughters, Livia Grimaldi, had taken her vows in Naples and lived there at the monastery of the Trinità delle Monache under the name of Sister Orsola. It is nonetheless certain that the picture was never meant to serve the private devotion of this nun, as it immediately went to embellish the picture gallery of Marcantonio Doria, who, as noted in Chapter 12, may have hosted Caravaggio during his short stay in Genoa in 1605, when the prince sought unsuccessfully to take the master into his service.

It is thus safe to assume that Caravaggio was given much latitude in representing a subject that was uncommon at the time, and apparently never treated before in close-up with half-figures. The excellent technical reports of the painting's restoration carried out in 2004 detail the extensive damage suffered by *The Martyrdom of Saint Ursula*, attributing them in part to Massa's crazy idea of exposing the canvas to the sun, and in part to the numerous aggressive cleanings and retouchings to which the picture had been subjected over the past centuries.[45]

There is no seventeenth-century description of the Naples painting, and so to clarify the extreme complexity of Caravaggio's invention and the various incongruities of its narrative layout, I shall

---

43 This document was first published by Pacelli 1980 and Bologna 1980. See Macioce 2003, 262: "Pensavo mandarle il quadro di Sant'Orzola questa settimana, però, per assicurarmi di mandarlo ben asciutato, lo posi ieri al sole, che più presto ha fatto revenir la vernice che asciutatolo per darcela il Caravaggio assai grossa. Voglio di nuovo esser da detto Caravaggio per pigliar parere come si ha da fare perché non

si guasti. Il signor Dam.o l'ha visto et ha stupito, come tutti l'altri che l'hanno visto. (…)Vostra Signoria prepari poi un altro soggetto per Car[avaggio] che ò esser amico suo (…)."

44 See Ibidem, 263.

45 See the excellent reports in *L'Ultimo Caravaggio* 2004, 91-111.

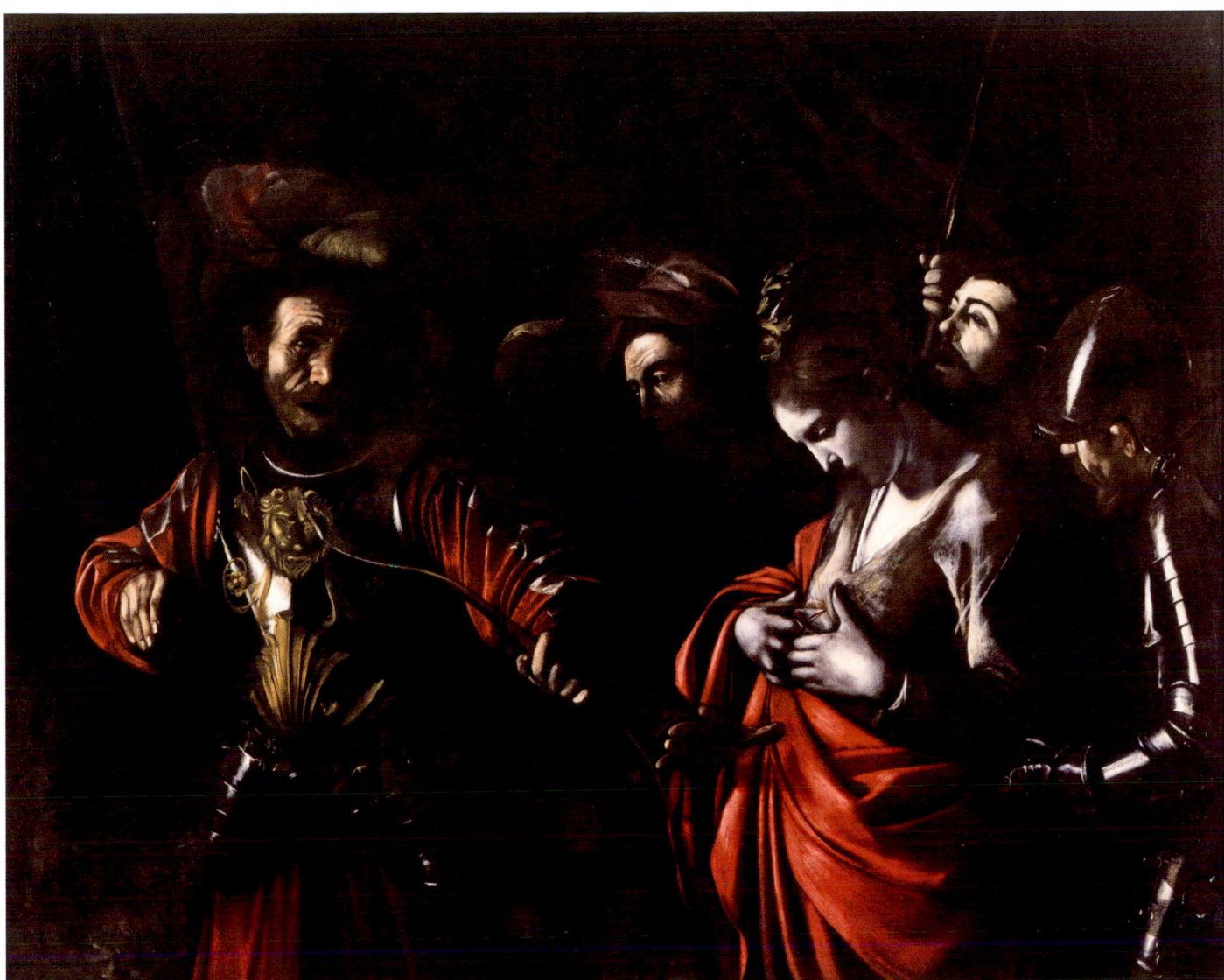

Fig. 241
Michelangelo Merisi da Caravaggio, *The Martyrdom of Saint Ursula*, Banca Intesa, Palazzo Zavalos, Naples, oil on canvas, 154 x 178 cm.

give a preliminary description. To the left, his torso and thighs placed almost frontally, the King of the Huns seems to step out of a tent now barely visible in the background—one can spot its opening behind the tyrant, and its heavy folds on the right upper tier of the composition. The King has just shot his arrow at Ursula's breast; hovering in mid-air, his right hand—which previously clutched the bow's string and held the dart—begins to uncurl, although he seems unable to complete this movement, horrified or startled by the dire consequence of his own action. His left arm, outstretched, reaches toward the foreground as his left hand solidly grasps the bow. From his attitude, one must infer that he has just shot Ursula point-blank, inexplicably close to her breast, a technically unlikely exploit.[46] More intriguingly, the position of the tyrant's arms, hands and rotating torso may give the impression at first glance that he prepares to aim the bow at the viewer after wounding Ursula, even if, turned leftward, his gaze remains fixed upon the martyr's face.

46 Von Rosen 2009, 61, makes a similar observation: "der Hünnenfürst im Neapolitaner Gemälde mit dem Martyrium der hl. Ursula (…) [steht] zu nah, als daß er mit seinem unmittelbar zuvor abgeschossenen Pfeil die direct neben ihm stehende Heilige hätte verletzen können…"

467

To the right, the beautiful Ursula, clad in a crimson mantle, her face in profile, observes the arrow that pierced her breast and, entwining her hands in an act of sorrow and desolation, uses them as a frame to circumscribe her deadly wound. Ursula's gesture fulfills multiple tasks: it draws the beholder's attention toward the piercing arrow that is curiously deprived of optical and material consistency, an almost translucent wooden shaft, intersected by a mysterious elliptical brushwork of the same color—the trace of a veil now lost?—and applied directly upon Ursula's hand and mantle. The jet of spurting blood around the wound is equally imperceptible, especially when compared to that which pours profusely from the decapitated tyrant in Caravaggio's *c*.1599 *Judith Beheading Holofernes*. Moreover, by indicating the arrow's position through the eloquent gesture of Ursula's hands, Caravaggio suggests that the martyr's eyes are locked exclusively upon her wound; she sees herself bleed to death as if waiting for the last drop of blood to leave her body; hers therefore is a meditation not upon death, but upon life surrendering to death, or more specifically upon the process of dying. And in fact, to depict the progressive voiding of the saint's spirit, Caravaggio distinguished the tint of Ursula's skin from those of the male actors around her; with thin, almost transparent layers of white lead, the master not only conjures up the woman's quasi-mortal pallor, but also insinuates that her body is fading away, as if re-absorbed by the picture's dark ground and by the canvas from which her figure ever so unstably and tenuously continues to emerge.

Even if, from a chromatic point of view, Ursula remains the composition's main focus, and even if the King's incredulous gaze invites the beholder to look at the martyr and her wound, Caravaggio inserted anecdotal, and partially incongruent, digressions into his sacred *istoria* through the attitudes of the two figures in the background. Between the tyrant and Ursula, one can in fact discern the profile of a man with nondescript headgear, whose eyes, turned to the left, literally stare into space, for there is no one that he might address on that side. (The silhouette of the acanthus-like metallic decoration on the back of a helmet near this figure belongs to a previous version of the composition; it was covered by Caravaggio, but has re-emerged as a result of the damage to the canvas. Equally, the vestige of a similar helmet above Ursula's head harks back to a former stage of the painting's execution). Still more disconcerting, this soldier, leaning on his lance, interposes his right hand between the King and the saint as if to protect Ursula from the blow, but in an untimely and incoherent fashion. Is he trying to prevent the tyrant from shooting a second time? And if so, why is his gaze averted from the main scene in the foreground?

Embedded above Ursula's neck, the upward-tilted profile of a bearded man sneaks into view: his mouth wide open, he expresses curiosity as he attempts to catch a glimpse of…who knows what? His gaze, oriented up and leftward, considers neither the faltering Ursula nearby nor the tyrant in the left foreground. It has rightly been noted that Caravaggio portrayed himself in this figure, and it is evident that this head is a reminiscence of the author's self-portrait as a lantern-bearer in the Dublin *The Taking of Christ*, discussed in Chapter 10 (Figs. 242, 243).

The armored figure relegated to the right margin of the canvas is a dark, ghostly apparition; Caravaggio swiftly sketched his nose, left cheek, and ear, concealing any other physiognomic element of his face, and admirably highlighted the blackness of his helmet and armor with flash-like refractions of white lead. Although it is difficult to make out the posture and role of the metallic glove worn by this figure, it can be said that the soldier either supports the collapsing Ursula with his left hand, or is on the point of doing so. As for his function, his presence in the painting's immediate foreground across from the figure of the slightly receding tyrant at the left enlarges the scope of the spatial field by opening the image toward the viewer and away from the pitch-black backdrop. I underline the specificity of the pictorial space and its vigorous projection beyond the painting's surface because I believe that it is highly instrumental in the beholder's perception of the image.

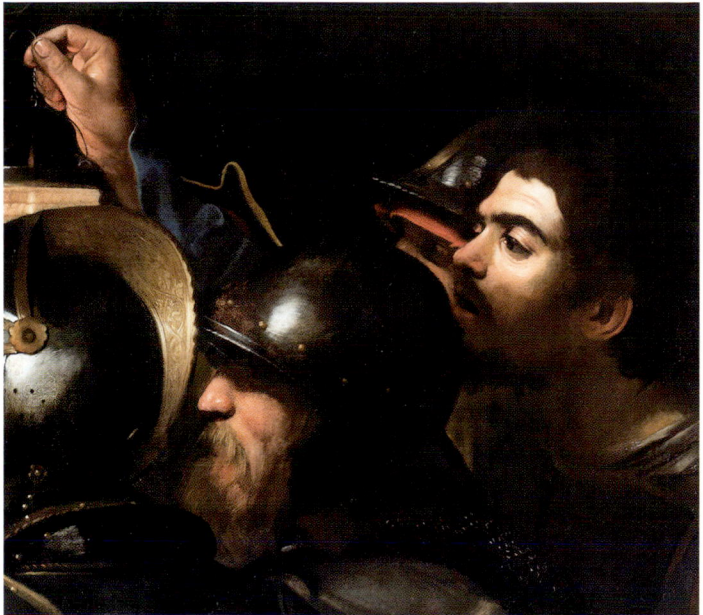

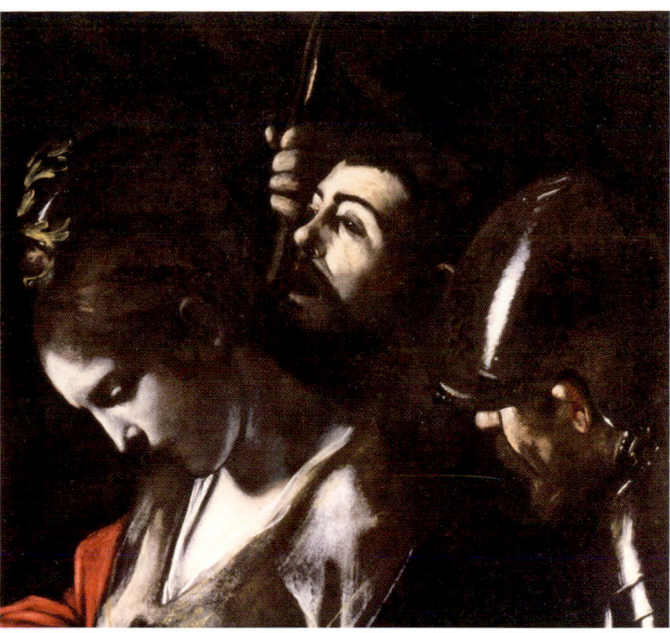

Fig. 242
Michelangelo Merisi da Caravaggio, *The Taking of Christ*, National Gallery of Ireland, Dublin, oil on canvas, 133.5 x 169.5 cm., detail.

Fig. 243
Michelangelo Merisi da Caravaggio, *The Martyrdom of Saint Ursula*, Banca Intesa, Palazzo Zavalos, Naples, oil on canvas, 154 x 178 cm., detail.

The narrative inconsistencies of *The Martyrdom of Saint Ursula* are numerous and disparate enough to be dismissed as fortuitous. I enumerate them in order to proceed to an articulate analysis of their function and meaning. In the first place, because of the King's attitude, the act of shooting is disjoined from its direct referent; in other words, the cause-and-effect interconnectedness of the painting's principal action—its heroic action—is deliberately blurred. Thus the act of shooting and the act of piercing might well be unrelated as far as their visual correlation goes; both had already taken place, but their chronological sequence and narrative verisimilitude are obscured by the divergences with which Caravaggio renders the temporal aspects of these actions. On the one hand, the tyrant has *just* shot his arrow; on the other, Ursula is *already* losing her force and life as a consequence of the dart planted in her breast. Moreover, neither the King's torso nor his arms are directed toward the woman; were it not for his insistent gaze on the saint, it would be uneasy to reconstruct the shooting sequence. This is almost to say that Ursula is entirely abstracted from the action and indifferent to the King's assault; if she posed as a separate figure on another canvas, her profundity and self-absorption would suffice for a compelling devotional icon.

Secondly, the background soldier's open hand—one of those pictorial bravados in which Caravaggio excelled, and which former restorers of the picture tried to erase perhaps because of its intrinsic oddity—is clearly cut off from the figure to which it relates. In a sense, one can reasonably state that the painter needed this hand there, at that spot, even at the cost of narrative inconsistency. However, Caravaggio did not wish, nor could he afford, to give more relevance to this soldier's face; he evidently did not want to redirect the viewer's attention toward this secondary actor. Hence he depicted him almost in profile, his gaze straying away from Ursula's martyrdom.

Last but not least, by inserting his own portrait into the Naples painting and disguising himself as a witness of the martyr's death, Caravaggio once again introduced the theme of self-referentiality into his *istoria*. And yet, in this case, so different from his *The Taking of Christ*, he suppressed the painter's lantern—the symbol of art's inventiveness—and his *alter ego* provocatively ignores what occurs in the composition. The master wanders amidst his figures, but veers his gaze toward an indeterminate target; his view or vision belongs only to himself (Figs. 243, 244). What Caravaggio

469

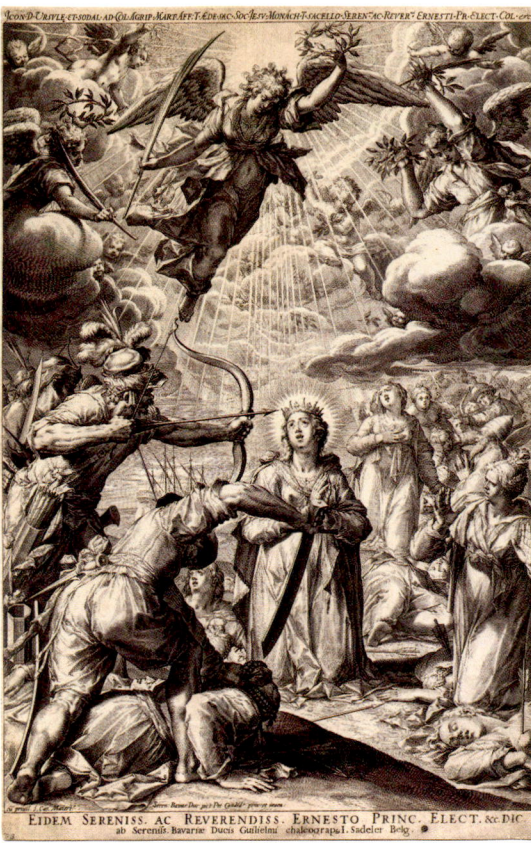
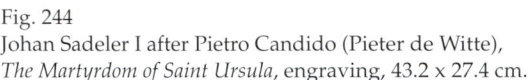

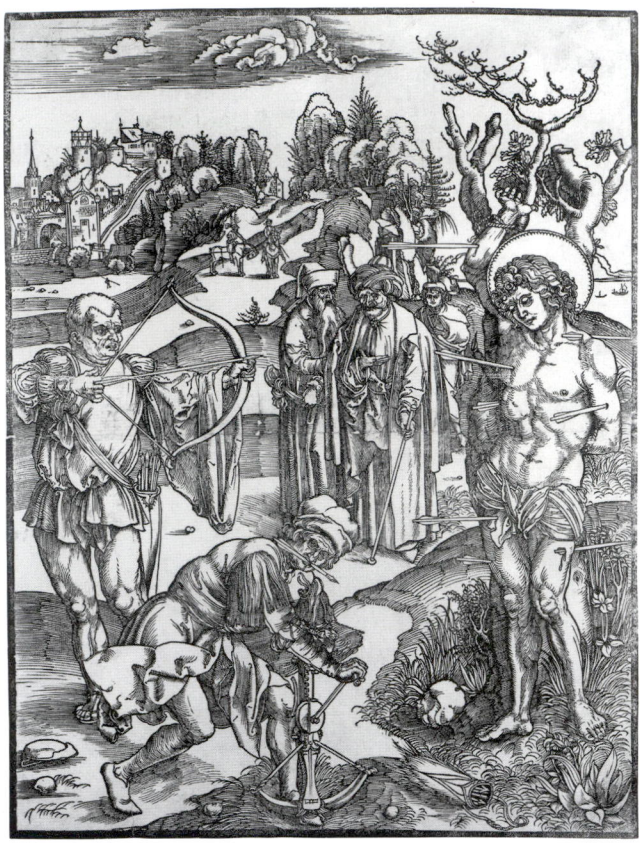

Fig. 244
Johan Sadeler I after Pietro Candido (Pieter de Witte),
The Martyrdom of Saint Ursula, engraving, 43.2 x 27.4 cm.

Fig. 245
Albrecht Dürer, *The Martyrdom of Saint Sebastian*, woodcut,
39.3 x 28.7 cm.

represents in *The Martyrdom of Saint Ursula* exceeds any traditional tenet or parameter of evaluation specific to the early modern *istoria*, and therefore defies any univocal hermeneutics. In this puzzling masterpiece, Caravaggio indeed dismantles the format and structure of the pictorial narrative as construed at his time, remolding it into a malleable receptor of artistic motifs and topics that he develops in multiple directions, sometimes in reciprocal interconnection, but not systematically. With the Naples picture, Caravaggio in my view proposes a brand new definition of the *istoria*, one informed by an inherent openness and structural polyvalence. Not that Caravaggio annihilates here pictorial narration altogether: there still exists an action in *The Martyrdom of Saint Ursula*. But the master now feels free to rig and occasionally sacrifice the exterior consistency of the *istoria*—its verisimilitude as an optical, aesthetic, and propositional artifact—to the necessities of an inner reflection and vision in which the *istoria* acts predominantly as a pre-text. Thus, the account—the raw material or "text" to be represented—becomes an armature shielding extra-narrative pictorial tropes at its core.

Not surprisingly, one of the themes on which Caravaggio expands in the Naples painting is that of meta-narrative: the evocation of shooting—the tyrant's bow turned to the foreground—and piercing—the arrow inside the woman and the pouring forth of her blood in return—directs the beholders' attention respectively to their own space, beyond the pictorial surface, and to the painting's medium, the canvas "perforated" and "bleeding." In other words, the interior and exterior of the picture are simultaneously engaged in a dialogue with the representation on the picture.

The subject matter, the story of Ursula's death, like its iconographic equivalent, the martyrdom

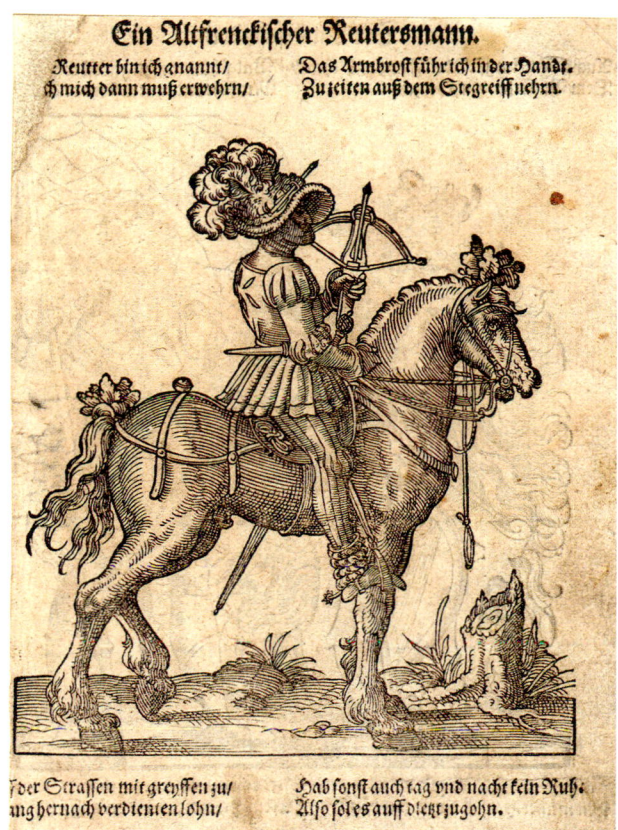

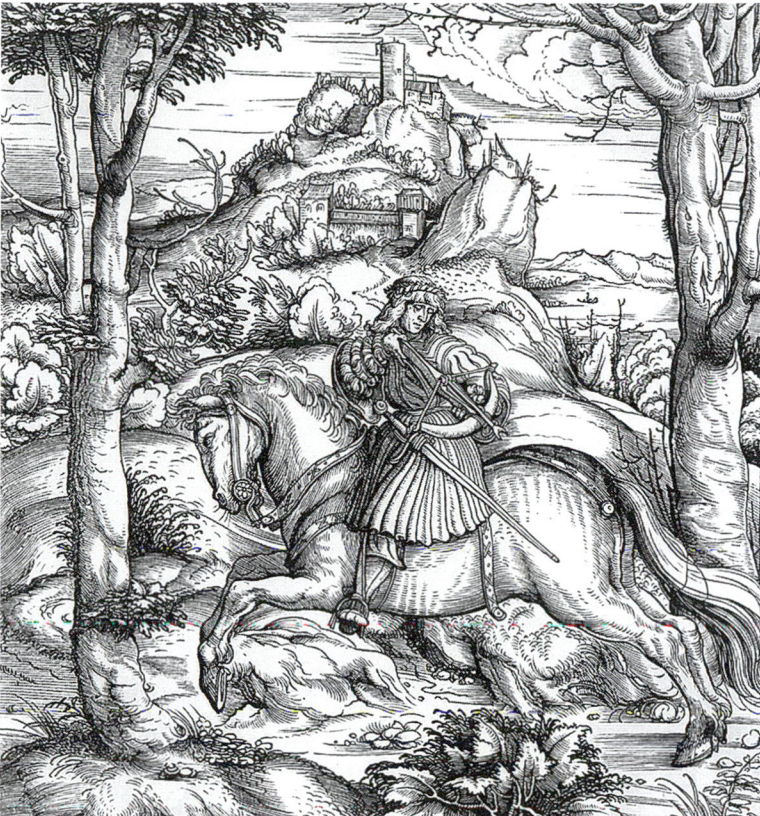

Fig. 246
Jost Amman, *A Rider with a Crossbow*, woodcut, 12 x 10.7 cm.

Fig. 247
Hans Burgkmair, *The White King Shooting with His Crossbow*, woodcut, 22 x 19.5 cm.

of Saint Sebastian, easily lends itself to triggering meta-narrative effects. In the previous chapter, I commented briefly on an engraving by Johan Sadeler I after Pietro Candido's *Martyrdom of Saint Ursula* (Fig. 244).[47] In this print, to the left, the King of the Huns bends his bow while seemingly targeting Ursula on a farther plane: the tyrant's fury resulting from the virgin's decline to marry him translates into the ample strain of his outstretched arms and into the shadow that darkens his profile: his is sheer rage in quest of revenge.

The idea of representing a torturer in the act of shooting, of course, had many precedents. In Albrecht Dürer's *c*.1500 woodcut of *The Martyrdom of Saint Sebastian* (Fig. 245), an archer aims his strained bow toward the young martyr, wounded by numerous arrows, who casts his gaze downward as if in acceptance of his torment and in contemplation.[48] In spite of the arrow motif recurrent in these images, one cannot necessarily talk of meta-narrative effects in such instances, insofar as the arrow is not oriented toward the foreground or the off-scene, and the artist does not emphasize the centrality of the piercing act—in both *The Incredulity of Saint Thomas* and *The Martyrdom of Saint Ursula* visual emphasis is instead laid on this very act, albeit to diverse degrees. Dürer's woodcut certainly provokes a mild effect of meta-narrative through the foreground figure who charges his crossbow by holding the bolt between his teeth: it is no coincidence that, busying himself with his weapon, the crossbowman stares at the viewer menacingly. Contemporary beholders might well have perceived this personage as likely to aim his crossbow at them. Nonetheless, images in which

47   See De Ramaix 2001, 169, no. 347.

48   For the print, see Hütt 1980, 2:1682; and Schoch et al. 2001, 2:497-8, no. A6 (as attributed to Dürer or doubtful).

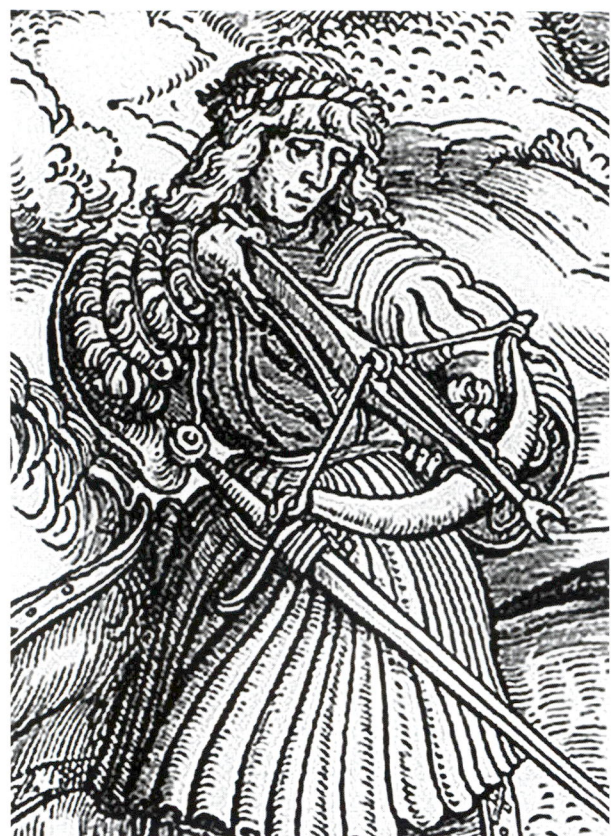

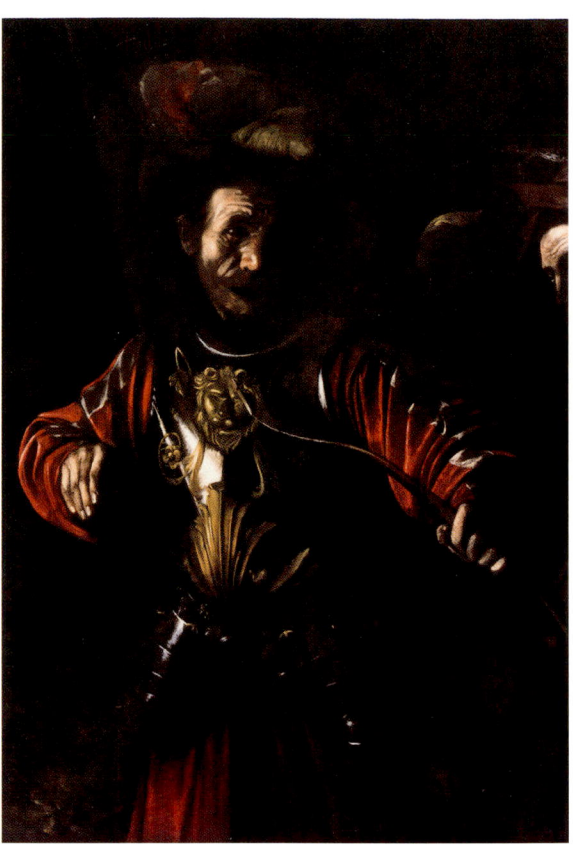

Fig. 248
Hans Burgkmair, *The White King Shooting with His Crossbow*, woodcut, 22 x 19.5 cm., detail.

Fig. 249
 Michelangelo Merisi da Caravaggio, *The Martyrdom of Saint Ursula*, Banca Intesa, Palazzo Zavalos, Naples, oil on canvas, 154 x 178 cm., detail.

the crossbow is oriented toward the composition's off-scene or squarely toward the viewer, though rare, are not exceptional, especially in early modern northern Europe.

A beautiful woodcut by Jost Amman, *A Rider with a Crossbow*,[49] in a sense initiates this iconographic tradition: even if the figure does not brace himself for shooting—far from it—his crossbow's bolt points upward toward the print's upper margin (Fig. 246). The knight's headgear with its waving brim and bush of feathers at its top presents the decorative exuberance of the mottled turban—now almost effaced—crowning Caravaggio's King of the Huns.

An early sixteenth-century woodcut by Hans Burgkmair, *The White King Shooting with His Crossbow* (Fig. 247),[50] constitutes a further instance of the shooting's meta-narrative function: firm on his horse's back, the man prepares to shoot while turning to the right. In an attitude not dissimilar to the tyrant's in the Naples picture—one might even say that Caravaggio's figure performs the action immediately subsequent to that of Burgkmair's crossbowman—the white king stretches his left arm while lifting his right hand toward his chest (Figs. 248, 249). Whatever his target might be, it remains beyond the viewer's visual field, opposite the galloping steed, a device that greatly projects the fictive space beyond the print's margins.

In a 1579 engraving attributed to Cherubino Alberti after Lelio Orsi[51] (Fig. 250), a hunter—a

49   For the print, see Peters 1985, 595, no. 5.73 (369); and Seelig et al. 2003, 149, no. 147.39.

50   For the print, see Falk 1980, 112, no. 80 (224).

51   The print derives from a drawing by Orsi in the Royal Library, Windsor Castle, associated with a façade project for the Casa Orsi (*c*.1575). See Romani 1984, 76-7; Monducci and Pirondini 1987, 208-11, nos. 177-81, esp. 181; and King 2006. For the attribution of the print to Cherubino Alberti, which I believe to be certain, see Parshall and Takahatake 2007.

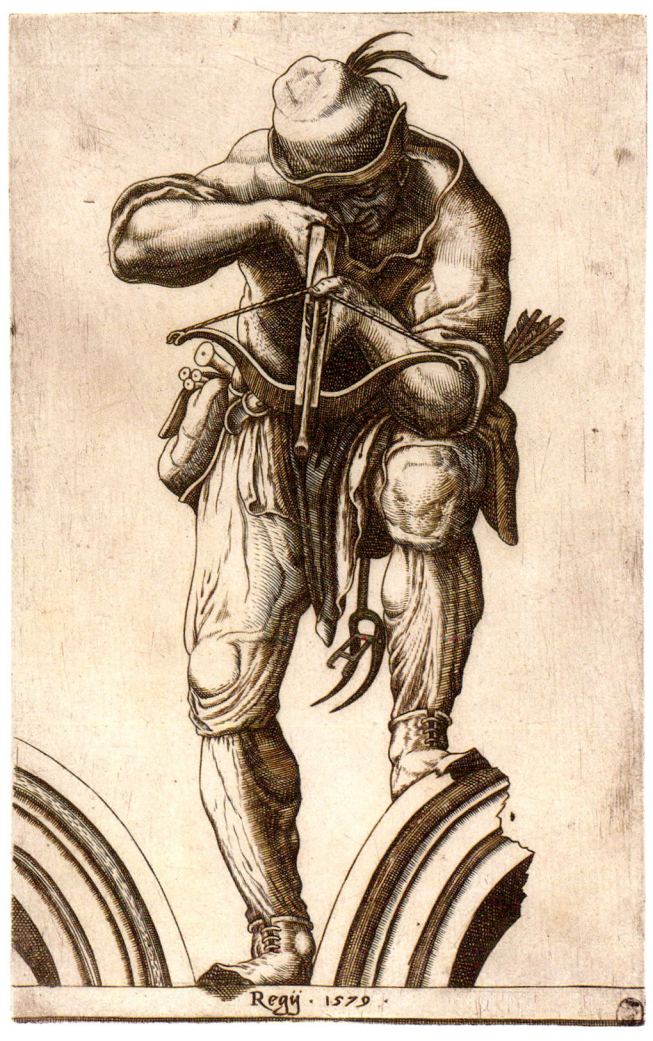

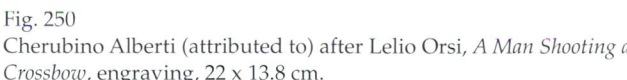

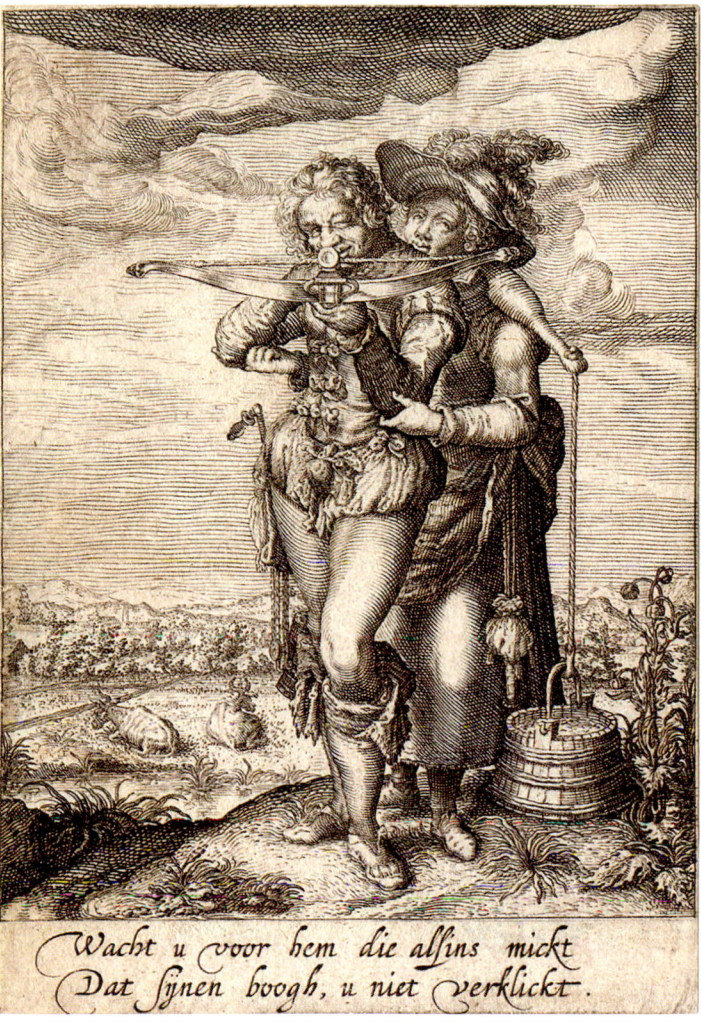

Fig. 250
Cherubino Alberti (attributed to) after Lelio Orsi, *A Man Shooting a Crossbow*, engraving, 22 x 13.8 cm.

Fig. 251
Jacques de Gheyn II (after), *Crossbowman with a Milkmaid*, engraving, 11.8 x 8 cm.

figure in a spandrel—stands between two arches, resting his right foot upon one of them as he hunches toward the ground and aims his crossbow at an invisible target that originally must have been the visitor to Orsi's house. Transposed into a print, the hunter's figure seems about to shoot at the beholder's feet. In both Orsi's depiction and Alberti's engraving, the illusory effect of the represented action—the fact that the hunter's bolt is destined to pierce a space that is the viewer's—cannot be denied.

Around 1610, the same year in which Caravaggio executed his *Martyrdom of Saint Ursula*, an unknown master engraved a design by Jacques de Gheyn II, *Crossbowman with a Milkmaid* (Fig. 251).[52] I would like to consider here two irrefutable elements of this composition, firstly its meta-narrative function. By aiming at the viewer, the crossbowman not only threatens to rip open the paper on which his figure is printed, but also to pierce the beholder's eyes. This point is wittily stressed by the print's Dutch caption: "Wacht u voor hem die alsins mickt/ Dat sijnen boogh u niet

52   See Kok et al. 2000, 237, no. 156. The print is tentatively ascribed to Andreas Stock. De Gheyn's drawing is now at the Fogg Art Museum, Harvard University.

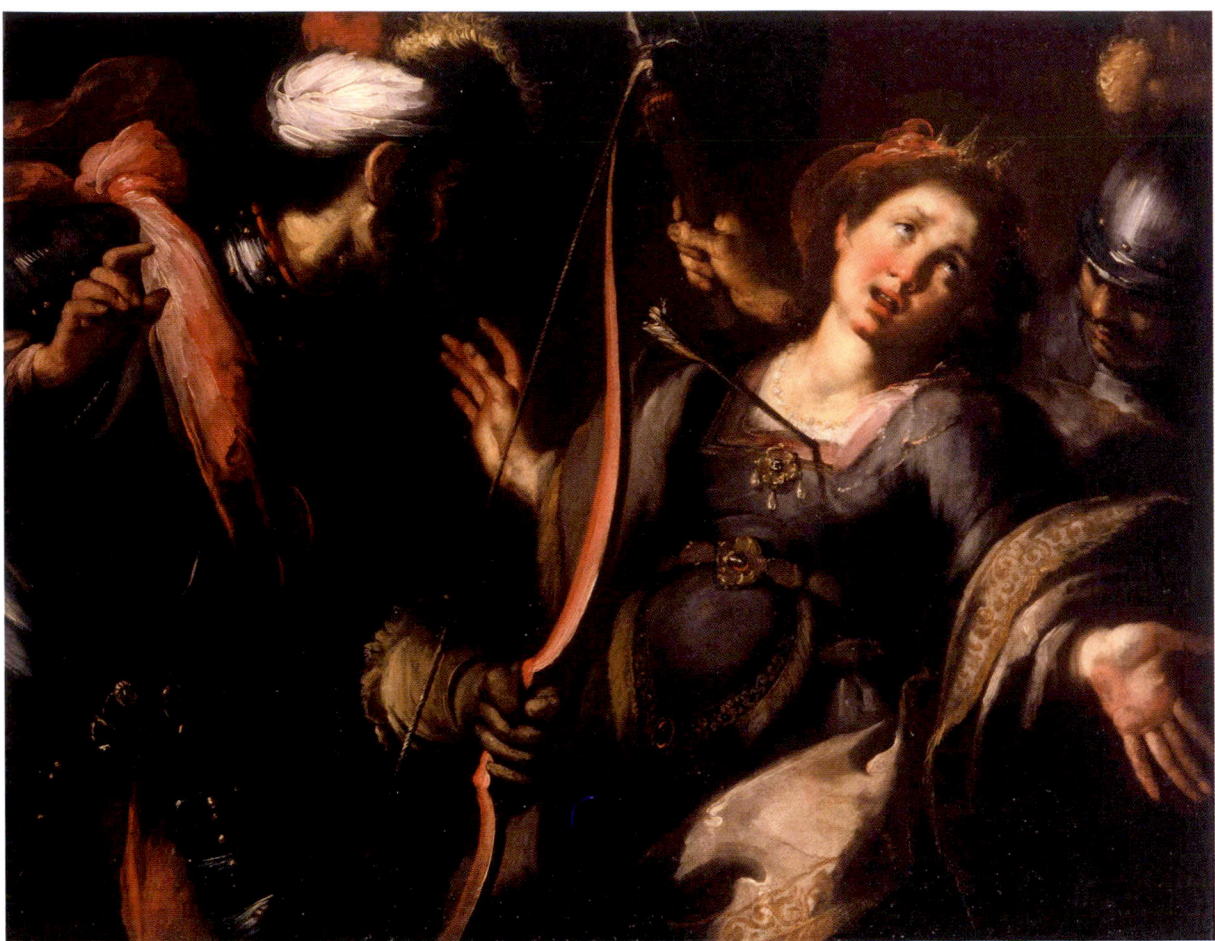

Fig. 252
Bernardo Strozzi, *The Martyrdom of Saint Ursula*, Koelliker Collection, Milan, oil on canvas, 104 x 130 cm.

verklickt" [Beware of him who aims in all directions/ Lest his crossbow track you].[53] Secondly, as can be surmised from the milkmaid's essential role in supporting her partner's elbows and therefore in directing and guiding the shooting, de Gheyn's print also presents half-comedic and half-lyric features; the woman—the arrow shooter in the Petrarchan tradition—perfects her shooting by usurping the man's skills, as well as appropriating his plumed hat. Because the lover has evidently become a weapon in his beloved's hands, the beholder knows that the crossbowman, the likely victim of the woman's metaphoric arrows, has already fallen under the milkmaid's spell. For this reason, the viewer—usually a man—has no choice: lest he too become the victim of the woman's assault performed with her lover's assistance, he must recoil and allow the crossbowman and the milkmaid to pursue their love ritual.

This iconography of the crossbowman is by no means extraneous to the theme of Caravaggio's *The Martyrdom of Saint Ursula*. In defiance of verisimilitude, Caravaggio depicted a crossbow bolt rather than an arrow as the object that pierces the martyr's breast, a detail remarked upon by the picture's restorers in 2004.[54] That Caravaggio's use of a bolt, instead of an arrow, might have

53   For the interpretation of this couplet, see Rosenberg J. 1954; and Luijten et al. 1993, 610-1, no. 282. In my opinion, both these authors have misinterpreted the Dutch verses, and more specifically the verb "verklicken." In Verdan's

Middelnederlandisch Handwoordenboek, it is clearly stated that "verclicken" (ancient spelling) can signify, among other things, "opsporen." That is, "to track" or even "to hunt down."

been problematic is confirmed by Bernardo Strozzi's *c.*1615 *Martyrdom of Saint Ursula* (Koelliker Collection, Milan, Fig. 252).[55] In this painting, in which scholars unanimously recognize the influence of Caravaggio's prototype, since Strozzi, a Genoese painter, was well acquainted with the art collection of Prince Doria in Genoa, Ursula falls backward as an arrow with a feathered tail pierces her breast. In the left foreground, the King of the Huns appears to have just released the deadly shaft, looking at Ursula attentively. Like many other painters fascinated by Caravaggio's originality, Strozzi seeks to make sense of the master's invention by adapting it to a more traditional schema of the *istoria*.

The visual sources that I have just examined will allow me to hone my exegesis of Caravaggio's Naples picture. The acts of shooting and piercing staged by the master in the painting may well hark back to the tradition of lyric poetry; in the end, what Caravaggio represents in *The Martyrdom of Saint Ursula* is the tragic conclusion of a non-mutual love. If, traditionally, it is the woman who metaphorically wounds the man by piercing his heart with the arrows of her eyes, inflicting a metaphorical death on the unfortunate lover, in the Naples picture it is the man who, rejected, literally wounds the woman by piercing her breast with a real arrow. The lyric components of the shooting/piercing theme—its interplay of metaphors pivoting around the conceptual dialectics of life and death—is pushed to extreme, tragic consequences by reversing the roles of the lover and the beloved, and by changing the metaphors of deadly love into their actual referents: life and death are truly at stake in the Naples picture.

Looked at in this light, the tyrant's open mouth and intense gaze—his deep bafflement—may express the suitor's horror in seeing the physical annihilation of the object of his love, the dying Ursula. On the other hand, Ursula's focus on her bleeding wound, a plausible expression of the beloved's detachment, visually evokes the woman's insensitivity to man's gaze, another lyric motif that I have examined in Chapter 6. One may perhaps imagine how Marino would have reacted to Caravaggio's exquisite conflation of lyric poetry and tragedy: the tyrant sensing himself dying in horror at his love's death; the martyr feeling herself rising to new life through her sacrifice in the profession of the faith; the man lost in the ultimate contemplation of his beloved, as the woman contemplates and senses her own mortal finitude with unwavering attention.

This exegesis of the picture implies an inversion of the inversions already accomplished by Caravaggio in his construction of the narrative action; despite his murderous act, it is still the man who spiritually dies with his beloved's death; in spite of her martyrdom, it is still the woman who triumphs over her suitor by earning the eternity of holiness. I stress the lyric and the tragic in *The Martyrdom of Saint Ursula* to underline the extent to which Caravaggio developed a theme that had remained dormant in his work since the end of the sixteenth century. If in the two versions of *The Fortune Teller* and in *The Cardsharps*, lyric fused with comedy, in the Naples picture the comedic element has completely vanished, to be replaced by the sacred and the tragic. One might infer from these observations that the playfulness of the young Caravaggio has turned into dark meditation in the later Caravaggio, but, while not entirely inaccurate, this statement proves to be rather unsatisfactory. There is, indeed, a different type of playfulness in the Naples picture, one introduced through the meta-narrative effects of the shooting and piercing act. Rather than in the picture's content, the tragic undertones of Caravaggio's invention resonate in his masterful yet deliberately unfulfilled unveiling of the painting's fictiveness.

To recapitulate the salient points of the shooting act in *The Martyrdom of Saint Ursula*, let us consider first of all the ambivalence of the tyrant's posture. Although his bow is oriented almost

54 See *L'Ultimo Caravaggio* 2004, 102: "la freccia che colpisce sant'Orsola non manca della parte finale, ma è corta perché di balestra."

55 See Gavazza et al. 1995, 120, no. 12.

frontally—that is, toward the viewer's visual space—his arrow, or more properly, bolt, is planted laterally, and quivers inside the saint's breast in a position parallel to the pictorial surface. Caravaggio's ambiguity in evoking the direction of the bow and the trajectory of the dart is intensified by the prodigious insertion of the background soldier's right hand, which not only intrudes toward the beholder's visual field, but also accomplishes a twofold mission. In fact, the hand may well distance the tyrant's bow from Ursula, or instead steer the King's arm away in another direction, toward the foreground. Of course, it is difficult to judge the reasons for such ambiguities, especially as Caravaggio himself highlighted the importance of the bow's and hand's misdirection by disregarding the narrative inconsistencies that these factors brought into the composition. I would argue that, unlike de Gheyn in his *Crossbowman and Milkmaid*, Caravaggio did not intend to underscore the efficiency of the meta-narrative effects induced by the shooting act, but instead contented himself with indicating the potential of this pictorial device; the tyrant's bow could be, but is not, directed toward the viewer; his arrow could, but does not materially, pierce the pictorial surface. In other words, Caravaggio alludes to, but simultaneously mitigates, the illusory charge of the painting.

This tendency becomes even more evident in the way in which he depicted the motifs of the piercing arrow or bolt and the spurting blood. I return to Caravaggio's *The Incredulity of Saint Thomas* and its representation of the apostle's piercing finger. In this picture, through the compactness and smoothness of his impasto, Caravaggio had succeeded in rendering the impression of both the Savior's skin and flesh, whose opticality and tactility are inflected toward the ends that I have previously elucidated. In the Naples picture, however, Caravaggio intentionally renounces rendering the relief and appearance of the "living flesh"; he builds up Ursula's half-figure as a pictorial form rather than as a pictorial body.

Caravaggio here dismisses the mimetic value of painting: that is, he entirely abandons a hallmark that had characterized most of his career. The most corporeal aspect of Ursula's figure resides in the majestic crimson mantle in which her body is enfolded; it is undeniable that this drapery possesses and demarcates real volume, thereby anchoring the saint's evanescent presence to the pictorial space. Equally endowed with vigorous stereography, Ursula's entwined hands anxiously move and stand out; yet they do so not through a contrasted chiaroscuro or a solid impasto, but through a skillful degradation of the pigment's density; fluid layers of lead white vary the surfaces' luminosity and, in opposition with the retouched shadows, contribute to the hands' three-dimensional appearance. These effects of relief thus result from a condensed *sfumato* technique that exploits tonal variations, so that the impression of volume is predominantly optical, and much less tactile.

But, if one examines Ursula's torso—according to the restorers' report, this is one of the best-preserved sections of the picture—one would have trouble telling apart the "flesh" underneath the chemise from the chemise itself; what seems to be the contour of the martyr's breast might well be a fold of her chemise, whose highlights in the sleeve area are executed with the same white lead used for her hands, chest, and face. More intriguing is the pictorial etherealness of the bolt and blood already mentioned; both are sketched as a sort of visual reminder, as pictorial signs rather than duplicates of real referents; more importantly, both are reduced to the rudimentary status of brushwork marks.

As a consequence, Caravaggio's *non-finito* in the Naples picture discloses the fictiveness of painting as a technical encoding and not as a reproductive mirror of reality: in this way, the canvas is redefined as a mere space of fiction, the realm of the pictorial imagery, and a vector of meanings that evokes, but does not reproduce, natural vision. Of course, Caravaggio is not the first artist to reveal the fictiveness of painting. But in his case, his approach to the canvas as a preeminently rhetorical device of representation dissolves the fruitful and complex ambivalence of his initial

manipulations of painting's opticality, so characteristic of an immense
part of his production. Thus he no
longer plays with the canvas-mirror
to dissimulate or amplify the fictiveness of his inventions. If Ursula's
bolt is meant to pierce the canvas,
if the canvas is meant to bleed, all
of this occurs in the direct mode of
fiction, so that the joyous interplay
between representation and reality
that had nourished the early modern aesthetics of mimesis and would
still feed Marino's ekphrastic poems,
ceases to be truly operative. Painting is not reproduction, and is much
more than representation as construed in the neo-Aristotelian terms
of the *istoria*; painting is vision, and
on this count it reformulates its own
principles of action, verisimilitude,
and congruousness in conformity
with its own finalities.

I cannot emphasize strongly
enough the artistic breakthrough
constituted by *The Martyrdom of
Saint Ursula*. It comes as no surprise
that the painting is so profoundly a
work of memory, a sedimentation of
recent and less recent motifs ideated
by Caravaggio throughout his

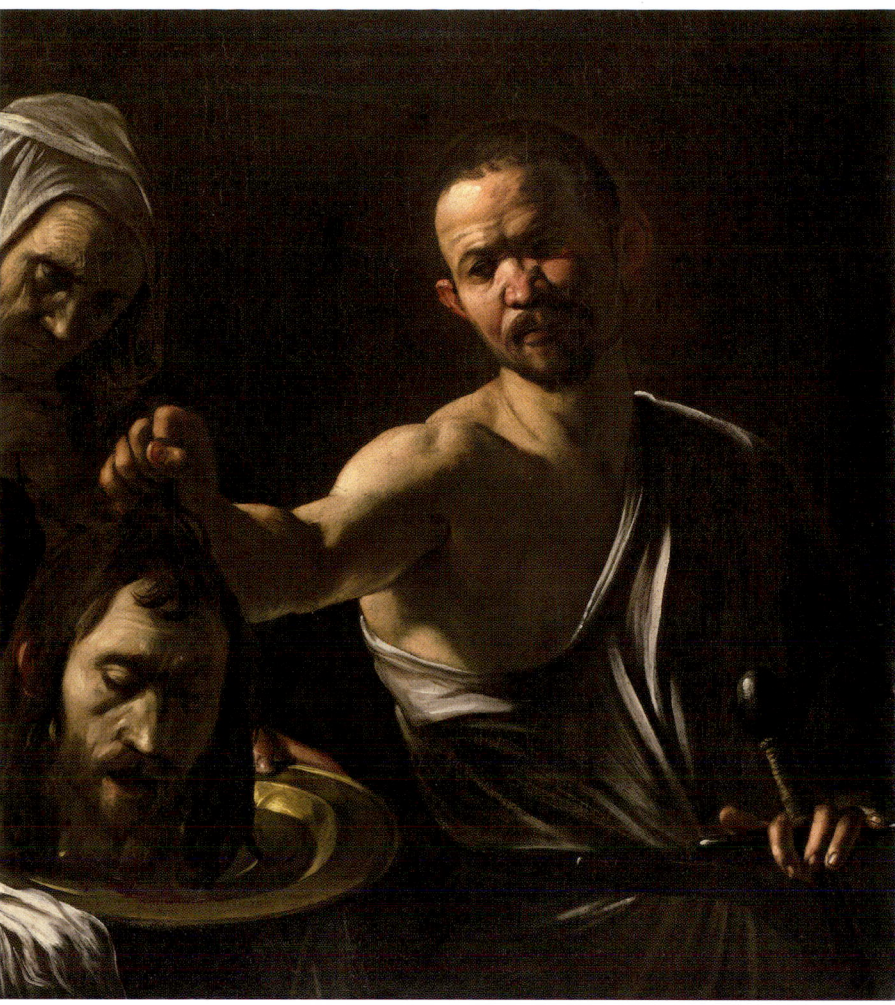

Fig. 253
Michelangelo Merisi da Caravaggio, *Salome Receiving the Head of Saint John the Baptist*,
National Gallery, London, oil on canvas, 91.5 x 106.7 cm., detail.

career. The physiognomy and attitude of the Naples tyrant calls to mind those of the torturer on
the left in the Capodimonte *Flagellation,* and especially of the executioner holding Saint John's head
in the London *Salome* (Fig. 253). Ursula's profile is almost identical to that of the Magdalene's in
the Messina *Resurrection of Lazarus* (Figs. 254, 255).[56] By employing these artistic templates stored in
his pictorial memory, Caravaggio did not merely intend to save time in order to finish the painting
swiftly. As I have argued in the Introduction to Part Five, he is elaborating upon themes of reflection
that were specifically his and that had underlain his artistic output from the beginning in a more
or less blatant way. Therefore, the recourse to stylistic templates confirms Caravaggio's insistence
on painting's fictiveness as the domain of artistic vision: the vision of an artist able to construct his
artistic identity and forge his own lexicon—to which the figures belong—and language.

That the Naples picture should also be interpreted as a fictional space of artistic memory and
vision is compellingly corroborated by the presence in it of Caravaggio's *alter ego*, a recollection
of an earlier work, *The Taking of Christ*. To understand exactly the role of this self-quotation, it is

56   See in this regard the rather curious remarks of Bologna
1992, 273-4: "La somiglianza della sant'Orsola con la donna
del Lazzaro è anzi tale (non meno nei tratti fisionomici che
nella posa, nel taglio e nella fattura specifica), da indurre a

riconoscere in entrambe la stessa modella: ricorrenza non rara
nelle opere del maestro e da Longhi osservata più volte in
quelle tarde."

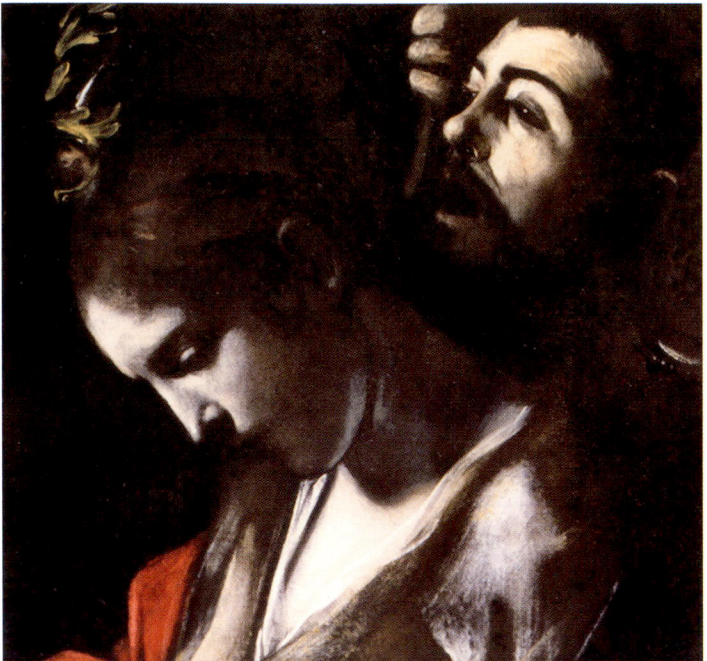

Fig. 254
Michelangelo Merisi da Caravaggio, *The Martyrdom of Saint Ursula*, Banca Intesa, Palazzo Zavalos, Naples, oil on canvas, 154 x 178 cm., detail.

Fig. 255
Michelangelo Merisi da Caravaggio, *The Resurrection of Lazarus*, Museo Regionale, Messina, oil on canvas, 320 x 275 cm., detail.

necessary to examine the Dublin picture once again. Holding the lantern of invention and artistic knowledge, Caravaggio there entered the scene as if to illuminate his own *istoria* (see Chapter 10). I do not believe that, in *The Martyrdom of Saint Ursula*, the absence of the lantern is particularly meaningful, at least not inasmuch as the metaphor of artistic creation now becomes less explicit.

What I think matters above all in the Naples picture is the fact that Caravaggio, through his pictorial avatar and unlike his counterpart in the Dublin picture, does not seem to suggest the limits of the *istoria* in visualizing the religious truth; the master, indeed, is not represented here as frustratingly unable to catch a glimpse of the principal action, but as quite indifferent to witnessing it. In fact, he segregates himself from his own *istoria* on purpose, in an attitude that, as I have already explained in Chapter 10, mimics the process of artistic creation through which the artist envisages and achieves his own invention. But this time, his quest for a pictorial vision directs Caravaggio's gaze off scene, in a direction inaccessible to the viewer's eyes, thereby insinuating that the field of artistic creation bypasses the picture's confines, transcends its frame and margins and, as he shows through the evocation of the shooting and piercing acts, involves the material canvas itself and the viewer's space.

In my opinion, this concept is the most ingenious and eloquent manifesto of Caravaggio's poetics of dislocation, his unconventional statement that the canvas, along with the image materialized in it, is just a layover in the painter's artistic itinerary, a trajectory that takes place in the artist's mind and memory and that, regardless of creation's fictitiousness, occasionally assumes material form and substance in the artwork through the technical implements of pigments and brushes. From this point of view, Ursula's pictorial evanescence—her lingering between life and death, between form and relief, and between color and mono-chromatism—might well be a quintessential metaphor for the art of painting and its prodigy, the relentless process of extracting from the dark of the background figures and objects, and therefore events and thoughts. The *istoria*, as Caravaggio's pictorial itinerary demonstrates, remains the most valid and significant means by which a painter is enabled to channel his own questioning and artistic wandering, but on one condition: by admitting that its validity as a source of meaning and its potential for originality go far beyond the propositional and didactic purposes with which Caravaggio's contemporaries had encumbered its definition and functionality.

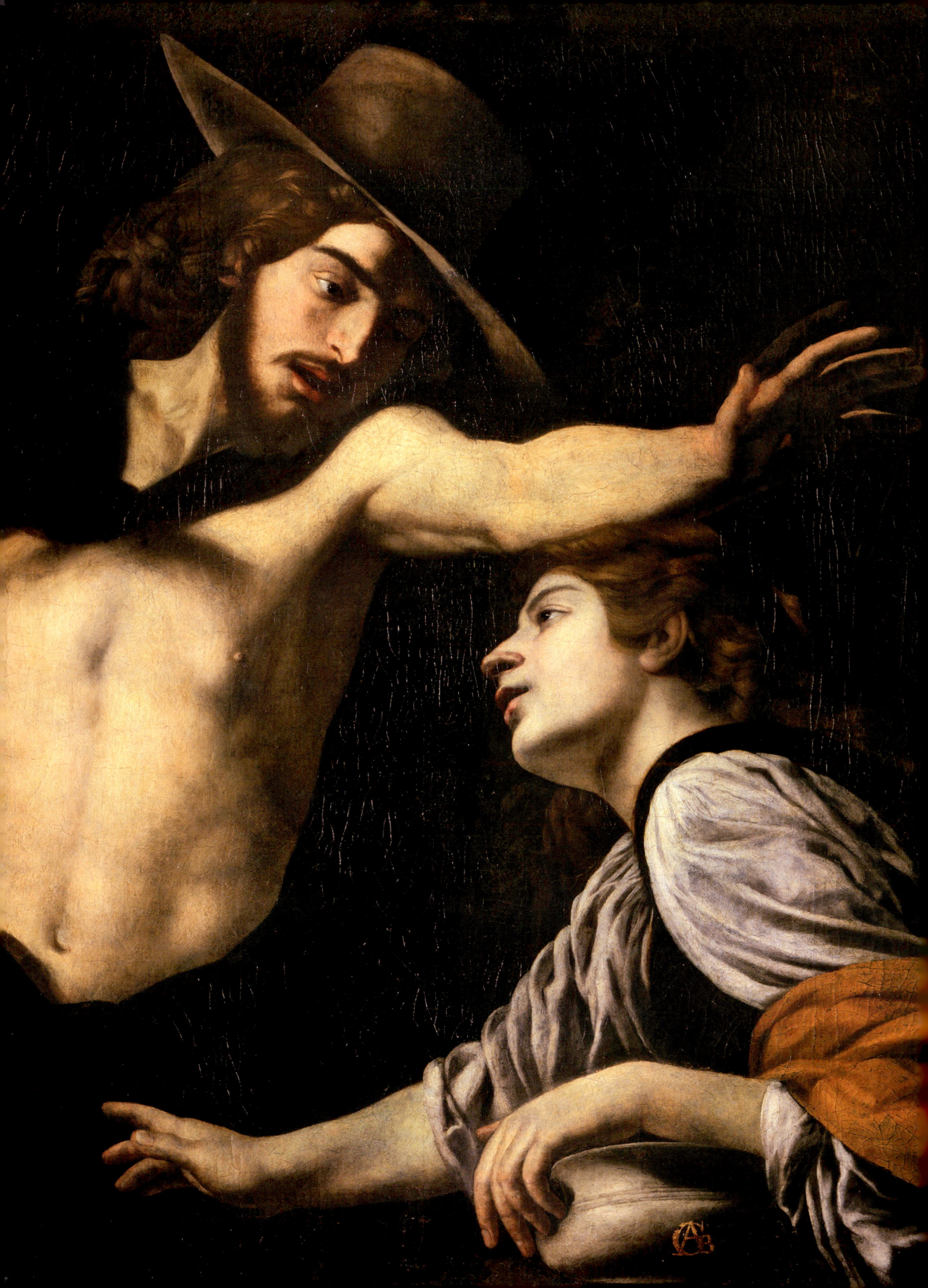

PART SIX

Reaction to Change: The Afterlife of Caravaggio's Poetics of Dislocation

The Black Tide of Caravaggio's Painting

In the seventeenth century, both on a moral and an artistic level, painters' adherence to Caravaggio's poetics was sometimes likened to a sort of pollution: a disease, or even a stigma, if not impossible to remove, at least difficult to redeem. Caravaggio's infection morphed its unfortunate victims into avatars of the master, subject to his extravagances and destined to relive his misfortunes. In the Introduction to Part One, I quoted Giovan Pietro Bellori's judgment on Bartolomeo Manfredi, whom he qualifies not only as Caravaggio's *alter ego*, but also as the extension of his master's eyes. In the same vein, Giovanni Baglione in his 1642 *Vite* concludes his recollection of Manfredi's work in lugubrious fashion:

> If the Mantuan Bartolomeo Manfredi had paired his good color technique with good drawing (*"disegno"*), he would have made wonderful things, and perhaps this would have occurred, had he lived. But he died young, replete with that bad disease (*"mal cattivo"*) that until the very end of his life kept consuming him.[1]

Manfredi's "bad disease" was most probably syphilis, which in Italy was then called the "ugly disease" (*"mal brutto"*), the "French sickness" or the "Neapolitan sickness." Of course, Manfredi is not the only follower of Caravaggio whose premature death truncated any hope of future artistic redemption. Here is how Baglione sketches the portrait of Giovanni Serodine,[2] another "imitator of Caravaggio," as he puts it:

> Serodine would have done much, but he was one of those who despise art's good principles; these minds remain always deceived by themselves and buried in ignorance; when they want to compose an *istoria*, they represent neither a beginning nor an end, which are not to be found [in their paintings]. And this is what happened to Giovanni Serodine. Perhaps he would have mended his ways had he lived to maturity, but he died in my home town, Rome, during the life of the most felicitous Urban VIII.[3]

1   Baglione, 159: "Se Bartolomeo Manfredi mantovano avesse accompagnato il buon colorito con il buon disegno, averia operato mirabili cose, e forse ciò sarebbe succeduto, se fusse campato. Ma egli morì in età giovanile, pieno di mal cattivo che infino all'estremo della vita l'andò consumando."

2   For Serodine, see *Serodine* 1987.

3   Baglione, 312: "Il Serodine averebbe fatto assai, ma era un di quelli che dispregiava i buoni ordini dell'arte, e questi ingegni restano da loro stessi ingannati e nell'ignoranza immersi, e quando vogliono condurre un'istoria non ne sanno uscire, e non vi si ritrova né principio né fine, e così avvenne a questo Giovanni Serodine. Ma forse si sarebbe ravveduto se in fino all'età perfetta fusse campato, ma in questa mia patria romana, mentre il felicissimo Urbano se ne vive, egli se ne giunse alla morte."

481

◄ Plate XX: Battistello (Giovan Battista) Caracciolo, *Noli Me Tangere*, Museo Civico, Prato, oil on canvas, 109 x 130.5 cm., detail.

Even richer in pathos is Baglione's description of Valentin de Boulogne's death:

> It was summer's hot season, and Valentin was heading to some place with his companions for pleasure. As usual, he had consumed much tobacco and drunk too much wine with his friends, and he was burning so much that he could not tolerate the heat he was feeling. As he was returning home at night, he came across the fountain of the Babbuino and, vexed by the great fire that had increased as he walked, he threw himself in the cold water, and expecting to be refreshed, he met his death instead. Indeed, the cold further accentuated the heat, and caused a fever so malignant that within a few days fatal Death extinguished him through its freezing grip. Thus, one must not be carried away easily by one's senses, which mostly brings one to a precipice, so that one loses in a moment what one has acquired in the course of many years. Were it not for Cavaliere Cassiano dal Pozzo's piety and courtesy, Valentin would not have received a burial; but because of his magnanimity, dal Pozzo provided for everything, and showed in the most honorable way how much he cherishes the virtue of drawing ("*disegno*"). Then, with these honors, Valentin ended the deeds of his own virtue.[4]

There is a slight contradiction in Baglione's obituary of Valentin. The inclination toward "the virtue of drawing" that had caused dal Pozzo to pay for Valentin's obsequies presupposes that the deceased master fully possessed this quality, but Baglione in a previous passage denies this fact:

> If Valentin had applied himself more to drawing ("*disegno*"), he would have painted much better, and if he had lived, he would have consecrated more time to it for the sake of his honor. But for some excesses (youth's most frequent and miserable mistakes), at the apex of his career he lost the fruits of both his work and life.[5]

In a sense, Baglione considers Valentin's case with true compassion, whereas he becomes ruthless in describing the personality of Orazio Gentileschi,[6] Caravaggio's accomplice in a few misdeeds:

> If Orazio had been of a more sociable temperament, he would have greatly profited from his artistic virtue, but he was more inclined to be bestial than human. He did not care if a subject was eminent or otherwise, for he abided by his own opinion and offended everyone with his satirical tongue. We must trust God's benignity to forgive all of his faults, for it is conceivable that, as the Lord bestowed upon him the gift of artistic virtue, he might also manifest himself [to him] through the grace of salvation.[7]

---

4   Ibidem, 338: "Era nella stagione calda della state e Valentino, andato co' suoi compagni a diporto in un luogo ed avendo preso gran tabacco (sì come era suo costume) e con quelli soverchiamente bevendo vino, s'infiammò di modo che non poteva vivere del grand'ardore che egli sentiva. Ritornando a casa di notte, ritrovossi fra via alla fonte del Babbuino e, traportato dal grave incendio che col moto ogni ora cresceva, gettossi dentro a quell'acqua fredda e, pensando d'acquistarvi ristoro, vi trovò la morte. Il freddo maggiormente riconcentrò il calore e gli accese una febre sì maligna che in pochi dì fu estinto dal gelo della micidiale Morte. Però non dobbiamo così agevolmente lasciarsi traportar dal senso, che per lo più ci precipita e ci fa perdere in un punto quello che appena per tratto di molti anni acquistato abbiamo. Se non era per la pietà e la cortesia del signor cavaliere Cassiano dal Pozzo, non v'era da dargli sepoltura, ma egli con la sua magnanimità supplì al tutto e mostrò onoratissimamente quanto è amatore di questa virtù del disegno, e con questi onori terminò Valentino gli atti della sua virtù."

5   Ibidem, 337-8: "Se Valentino avesse più atteso al disegno, averebbe assai meglio operato, e se fusse vissuto, per suo maggiore onore forse v'averia impiegato il tempo e le forze; ma per disordini (errori frequentissimi e miserabili della gioventù) nel fiore dell'operare mancò de' frutti dell'utile e della vita."

6   For Orazio Gentileschi, see Bissell 1981.

7   Baglione, 360: "Se Orazio Gentileschi fusso stato di umore più pratticabile, averebbe fatto assai buon profitto nella virtù, ma più nel bestiale che nell'umano egli dava, e di qualsivoglia soggetto, per eminente ch'egli fusse, conto non faceva; era di sua opinione e con la sua satirica lingua chiascheduno offendeva, e dalla benignità di Dio abbiamo da sperare il perdono d'ogni suo fallo: ché agevol cosa è che, dove il Signore è concorso col dono della virtù, anche si sia manifestato con la grazia della salute."

Spurred by lust and insatiability, controlled by their own senses, personifying mockers and sinners, and even worse, all these unaccomplished painters waste their talents in reproducing nature pedantically: this is how Baglione, in differing degrees, characterizes whoever might have been touched by Caravaggio's disgrace. Caravaggio's followers, in other words, continue the black tide released by their master's poisoning depravity. Caravaggio's dark legend—constructed with impeccable coherence by seventeenth-century artists and art theorists, as Philip Sohm and David M. Stone have demonstrated[8]—rubs off on his disciples and friends, and cannot be contained. Besides knowing almost nothing about *disegno*, the minds of Caravaggio's followers are so confused in some cases that their eccentricity translates directly into their works. In commenting briefly upon Carlo Saraceni's achievements and individuality, Bellori notes:

> In his compositions, Carlo used to introduce eunuchs and shaved heads without beards. Nor did he imitate his master solely in his paintings, but also in other things, and since Caravaggio owned a black dog called Barbone that was trained to do tricks, he also got a similar one and called him Barbone, which he took with him to do tricks when meeting with friends.[9]

Bellori's remark on Saraceni's bald and beardless figures insinuates that his painting lacks virility, and is therefore deeply anti-heroic. Saraceni's art,[10] by the same token, marks an obvious decline even with regard to Caravaggio's production; whereas the master's degeneracy reflected itself in his choice of plebeian characters, his follower's eeriness is echoed by the oddity of his "eunuchs." Bellori also inserts a satirical coda in his evocation of Saraceni: his black dog's name, *Barbone*, means, among other things, "hirsute" or "endowed with a long beard" in Italian, so that the painter's preferences linger between opposites, his figures being "hairless," but his pet definitely "bearded." Needless to say, the two *Barbones*, Caravaggio's and Saraceni's, share the same blackness. Despite the obvious condemnation of Caravaggio's model as inflected by the master himself or interpreted by his followers, neither Baglione nor Bellori mention that, for at least two decades, the influence of Caravaggio not only impacted upon the art of those who explicitly sought to imitate him, but was also the object of reflection, contamination, and elaboration by many who did not adhere to the Caravaggesque movement. In his 1678 *Felsina Pittrice*, Carlo Cesare Malvasia evokes Alessandro Tiarini's predilection for Caravaggio:[11]

> He [Tiarini] also liked Caravaggio's work owing to a certain purity, truth, and vigor of his colors, and was surprised at how much these features stimulated and enraptured him, although he could not find any decorum, majesty or erudition in [his paintings]. He had his son make a copy after the copy of Saint Thomas touching the Lord's side that belonged to the Legnani, and kept it with him for a long time, saying that he greatly profited from it, for, in observing it, he felt he rid himself of that dullness of colors to which he was prone in the beginning.[12]

8   See Sohm 2002; Stone 2002; and Stone 2006.

9   Bellori, 234-5: "Soleva Carlo nelli suoi componimenti introdurre eunuchi e teste rase senza barbe, né solo imitava il maestro nel dipingere, ma ancora nell'altre cose, e perché il Caravaggio aveva un cane nero chiamato Barbone ammaestrato a far giuochi, anch'egli ne trovò uno simile e gli pose nome Barbone, conducendolo seco a far giuochi nelle conversazioni."

10   For Saraceni, see Ottani Cavina 1968.

11   For Caravaggio and his reception in Bologna, see Perini 1995; and Perini 2002a. For Tiarini, see Pirondini et al. 2000.

12   Malvasia, 2:107-8: "Gli piacquero anco le cose del Caravaggio per una certa purità, verità e forza del colorito, maravigliandosi come tanto si sentisse da esse svegliare e rapire, quando nulla poi di decoro, di maestà e d'erudizione vi trovava. Volle che il figlio da una copia di quel San Tomaso che tocca il costato al Signore, posseduta da' signori Legnani, una ne ricavasse che gran tempo presso di sé ritenne, asserendo cavarne gran beneficio per sentire dall'osservarla rimoversi da quel colorire languido nel quale sul principio cadea."

Another Bolognese painter, Lorenzo Garbieri,[13] a disciple of Ludovico Carracci, also happened to admire Caravaggio's *Incredulity of Saint Thomas*, which he only knew through a copy, probably the same mentioned in the previous passage. In his manuscript notes, Malvasia writes:

> Since he [Garbieri] was infatuated with Caravaggio's fierceness of color, and found it congenial, as he had seen his famous painting [of the *Incredulity of Saint Thomas*] through an exquisite copy sent to Bologna, he praised his color technique and vigor greatly, but also felt he needed to critique his drawing ("*disegno*"), and should not be satisfied until he added a certain grace to Caravaggio's good naturalness. [He in fact believed] that Our Lord's act of seizing Thomas' hand and bringing it into his side wound was a gross invention. Thus, he set out to make a painting in this vein and carried it out in such a manner that it was appreciated as much as Caravaggio's, and some liked it even better: the Carracci.[14]

From Malvasia's text, it is not clear whether Garbieri emended Caravaggio's invention through some modifications, or if he executed a different *Incredulity of Saint Thomas* inspired by that of Caravaggio. In his *Felsina Pittrice*, Malvasia mentions only Garbieri's copy of Caravaggio's composition. Like Garbieri, another Bolognese painter, Leonello Spada,[15] succumbed to Caravaggio's spell when studying a copy of his *Incredulity of Saint Thomas*. In this case, though, Leonello decided to go to Rome and meet the master in person, at his own risk:

> The vivacity of his [Spada's] spirit rather than real knowledge drove him to compose poems, especially satiric and burlesque ones, in which he succeeded much better than average. This is why he was willfully welcomed and favored by Caravaggio, who said that he had finally met a man to his taste, perhaps because Leonello, subservient to his every wish, tried to satisfy him in everything—up to the point of stripping naked and posing as his model—or because the bizarreness of Leonello, whose mores were not dissimilar from his, fit well with Caravaggio's fantastic temperament. I know as a fact, at any rate, that Michelangelo [Caravaggio] did not turn out to be what Leonello had expected, since—as he used to say—he was too inconsiderate and reckless in painting as well as in his behavior and life; [in his opinion], he was rather ungraceful in his contours, completely ignoble in his inventions, and excelled only in vividly expressing whatever aspect of nature he saw before him; [furthermore], he lacked the exclusive taste and the sublimity of ideas that Leonello acknowledged and confessed were to be found in his master, Ludovico, and even more in the painter who would become his inspiration, Guido. Consequently, Leonello attempted several times to leave and quit him, but always in vain, especially when Caravaggio took him to Naples and forced him to pose as his model for four days, locking him up in his studio and passing him food through a small window, out of fear that he would escape. Caravaggio had done the same in Rome when he portrayed Leonello as the boy with his back turned in his painting of Christ calling Saint Matthew to the apostolate. Then, eager to have a change of air and visit another country, and encouraged by Caravaggio's promises to help him

---

13 For Lorenzo Garbieri, see Negro and Pirondini 1994, 175-9.

14 Malvasia a, 92: "E perché era invaghito della fierezza e gl'andava a genio il colorire del Caravaggio, avendogli veduto il famoso quadro di quel valentuomo per via di una squisita copia che venne a Bologna, come lodò in estremo il colorito e la forza, così ebbe animo di riprendere il disegno e di non soddisfare di una certa grazia che desiderava aggionta a quel buon naturale, come che l'atto di prendere Nostro Signore la mano di Tomaso ed accostarla al costato fosse rozza invenzione; ché perciò si pose a farne uno su quel gusto e lo tirò in maniera che piacque quanto quello del Caravaggio, e vi fu chi assai più lo lodò: i Carrazzi. Io poi lo vidi nello studio del Basenghi."

15 For Spada, see Pirondini et al. 2002.

in his career and share a part of his revenue with him, Leonello had little choice but to follow [the master] to Malta. But just as their talents were judged equal there, so too did their arrogance and insolence seem to be even; if Michelangelo [Caravaggio], after being graciously knighted, dared argue with an officer of justice and treat him with such outrage that he deserved having his face monstrously disfigured by many scars, Leonello became so close to these people and engaged in so many controversies with them that, should Commendatore Zambeccari not have excused and protected him, he might have lost his life, especially because, falling in love with a beautiful black slave, who was also crazy about him, Leonello sought to snatch her from a knight and flee.[16]

It is well known that Malvasia's account of Leonello's relation with Caravaggio is mostly invented and substantially false. Less well known is the fact that Malvasia's main source for Leonello's misadventures was most probably Guercino, the great painter of the Bolognese school who knew Caravaggio as well as Leonello did: that is, not at all. From other passages of Malvasia's manuscript notes, it is evident that Guercino gleaned information about Caravaggio—some of it fairly reliable—during his sojourn in Rome (1621-1623).[17] Whatever pushed Guercino to accept the story of Caravaggio imprisoning one of his models and to identify the victim with Leonello, can only be a matter of speculation. Guercino was extremely attuned to Caravaggio's painting, so that his "gossip" about the master's tortures does not seem to rest upon personal hostility.[18] What he related to Malvasia must have been rumors that were circulating in Rome even a decade after Caravaggio's death, which testify not only to the master's persisting popularity, but also to the extent to which his dark legend had grown in the meantime. Caravaggio's blackness sullies his color technique even in retrospect—Leonello was heard to say that the master "shaded his pictures by cleaning his brushes upon his shoes' soles"[19]—and in turn "blackens" even his followers' sexual taste—Leonello's fatal attraction for a female Moor.

16 Malvasia, 2:105-6: "Erasi egli reso molto pratico delle favole e delle storie, e dal proprio spirito vivace più tosto che per real fondamento tratto a comporre in poesia, massime giocosa e satirica, portavasi più che mediocremente bene. Queste fur le cagioni per le quali sì volentieri fu accolto ed accarezzato dal Caravaggio, ch'ebbe a dire aver pur finalmente trovato un uomo secondo il cuor suo, non so se perché, buttandosegli sotto Leonello, non altro procurò che di compiacerlo in tutto, sino a farsi nudo e servirgli di modello, o se perché, poco a lui dissimile di costumi, colle sue bizzarrie anch'egli incontrasse nel suo umore fantastico. So che per lo contrario non riuscì Michelangelo a Leonello quello che figurato si era, precipitoso troppo (soleva egli dire) e sregolato nel dipingere non meno che nel procedere e nel vivere; grazioso poco ne' contorni, ignobile affatto nelle invenzioni, non in altro prevalendo che in una viva espressione di ciò che naturalmente si vedea davanti, senza quella sceltezza delle parti e sublimità d'idee che conobbe e confessò poi dopo trovarsi nel maestro Ludovico, ma più nell'emulo Guido. Tentò perciò di scostarsene più volte e di licenziarsi, ma sempre in darno, massime allora che, condottolo seco a Napoli l'Amerigi, lo tenne sotto ben quattro giorni a servirsene di modello per un San Giovanni, riserandolo per di fuori entro la stanza e porgendogli per un finestrino il vitto, per timore che non gli fuggisse; sì come avea fatto in Roma quando nel suo San Matteo chiamato da Cristo all'apostolato, per colui che ivi sta volto in ischiena il ritrasse. Non poté dunque non passare con esso lui a Malta, indottovi dalla curiosità di mutar aria e veder altro paese, ed animatovi dalle promesse d'aiutarlo nella professione e participargli il guadagno. Ma come pari colà fu giudicato dell'uno e dell'altro il valore, così uguale parve l'ardire e l'insolenza, perché se Michelangelo osò, fatto cavaliere di grazia, di piccare con uno di giustizia e fargli tale affronto che meritò poi di portarne con

più tagli mostruosamente segnata la faccia, si addimesticò tanto con que' signori Leonello e fece loro tante partite che, se scusato non era e protetto dal comendatore Zambeccari, portava pericolo della vita, massime allora che, incapricciatosi di bella schiava mora, che di lui pure andava pazza, tentò rubarla ad un cavaliere e fuggirsene."

17 Besides the information on Leonello Spada and Caravaggio, quoted in the next note, see Malvasia a, 388: "Si disgustò il Caravaggio col ... perché, amalatosi, lo mandò all'ospitale e gli lo raccomandò all'ospitaliero promettendogli di fare il suo ritratto, il che, sanato, fece, essendo poi questo esposto per le rogazioni, fu venduto né conosciuto di chi fosse; ne stupì l'istesso...e lo lodò; fece subito sapere il Caravaggio esser lui; allora vollero il maestro e gl'altri retrattarne la lode (...) ma non ferono in tempo. Barbieri. Fece il Caravaggio mentre stava nella stanza del...una caraffa naturalissima con dentro fiori; portò il caso che la vedesse presso il Cardinal del Monte il Caravaggio che l'accertò esser di sua mano, non del... come gl'era falsamente da lui stato supposto e gl'avrebbe fatto vedere quando gle la fece altri più belli. Barbieri."

18 Malvasia, 2:265, in transcribing the life of Guercino written by the master's brother, Paolo Antonio Barbieri, and other members of his family, relates under the year 1622: "[Guercino] ebbe stretta amicizia con Michelangelo da Caravaggio, con Leonello Spada e con tutti gli altri pittori di quel tempo, essendo molto stimato per la sua virtù e rara modestia." Albeit false, the information relayed by Guercino's relatives seem to imply that the painter looked at Caravaggio's paintings with interest.

19 Malvasia a, 265: "Per avere ocasione d'imparare dal Caravaggio gli faceva modello e l'osservava, ma poi diceva

Even if one ignores the falsity of Leonello's alleged experience with Caravaggio, one cannot overlook the artistic implications of Leonello's fascination with the "dark master," a phenomenon that is easily evinced by Leonello's paintings from the 1610s. It has been proven that Leonello was invited to Malta in 1609, where he arrived long after Caravaggio had left.[20] If, on his way from Bologna to Valletta that year, Leonello halted in Naples, he might have seen Caravaggio there, but this is unlikely. Nevertheless, it is undeniable that when Leonello returned to Bologna in 1611, he was painting in a distinctly Caravaggesque manner; by then, he must have been most familiar with Caravaggio's pictures not only in Malta, but probably also in Rome and Naples.

Regardless of Leonello's actual contacts with Caravaggio's art, it is much more interesting in my view to dwell on Malvasia's interpretation of Leonello's subsequent adjuration of Caravaggio's influence, as well as of his repentance and redemption obtained by resorting to the examples of both his former master, Ludovico Carracci, and his famous compatriot, Guido Reni. Predictably enough, Malvasia opposes Caravaggio's painting to that of the Carracci and Guido, who, to paraphrase Leonello, were well-pondered, graceful in their contours, noble in their inventions, select in their choices, and sublime in their ideas.

And yet there is an aspect of Caravaggio's painting in which his Bolognese rivals did not excel, and which his Bolognese imitators wished to appropriate: his naturalness and power of color.[21] Malvasia is perfectly aware of this conundrum, and in fact he adroitly suggests that both Guido and Guercino, albeit in divergent ways, endeavored not only to imitate Caravaggio's lifelikeness and vigor of color, but also—and in particular—to perfect them. At the beginning of his life of Guercino,[22] Malvasia asserts:

> He [Guercino] had a style which was the complete opposite of Guido's; if the latter was perhaps excessively enamored of gracefulness, Guercino was drawn to fierceness and, taking up Caravaggio's force of color and naturalness, embellished them through many corrections and added more grace to them. His tints were overloaded [*una caricatura*: literally, a caricature] so as to exceed nature, whereas the masters of the past had deemed it not a little task to achieve just this [that is, naturalness], so that if they attenuated their colors lest they be discordant, Guercino on the contrary enjoyed reinforcing them to an extreme of discordance, although he moderated his audacity with such judgment that he made his excess likable.[23]

In other words, Guercino is a revised and improved-upon Caravaggio: he manages to subjugate Caravaggio's naturalness to a practice of coloring based upon an aesthetics of concord and discord, and therefore much more rhetorical in character than optically inspired. Malvasia's paramount exegesis of Guercino's chromatic style would reward further consideration. Suffice it here to highlight the fact that, according to Malvasia, Guercino takes away the final glory left to Caravaggio: a color technique so compelling as to reproduce, and enact the effect of, real vision. Malvasia's account of Guido's revenge upon Caravaggio's lifelikeness is certainly more complex,

---

non aver potuto imparare cosa alcuna perché era un fare bizzarro che niente più, e che sfumava nettandosi i pennelli alle suole delle scarpe. Barbieri."

20 See Pirondini et al. 2002, 29-41.

21 For the interpretation of Caravaggio's color technique in the seventeenth century, see Bell 1993.

22 For the influence of Caravaggio on Guercino, see more recently Cropper 2008.

23 Malvasia, 2:359-60: "Ebbe egli un fare a quello di Guido contrario ed opposto, ché dove questi della vaghezza troppo forse fu vago, della fierezza mostrossi egli seguace e, ripigliando dal Caravaggio sudetto il colorire forte e la naturalezza, l'abbellì con molta correzione, v'aggiunse più grazia. Fu il suo tingere una caricatura che oltrepassò il naturale, quando ai passati maestri giunger solo a quel segno non parve pur poco, onde quanto tennero essi mortificati i colori perché non discordassero, si dilettò egli di rinforzarli perché esorbitassero, così moderandone però con giudizio l'ardire che ne rese anche gradito l'eccesso."

and assumes the character of a "foundational myth."[24] Once again, everything revolves around a painting by Caravaggio, an as yet unidentified *Ecce Homo*, but this time Malvasia includes in the picture, besides Guido, Ludovico and Annibale Carracci:

> As one of these paintings [by Caravaggio] happened to be in Bologna, at the house of the Lambertini family, it is impossible to record the great pleasure felt by Ludovico, who could [finally] verify through the work itself if the merit of this painter corresponded to his renown as it was spread everywhere. Ludovico remained astonished, as he was unable to discern in it nothing but a great contrast of light and shadow, an excessive attachment to nature, without decorum, with little grace, and even lesser intelligence. But he was even more puzzled at his fame: a Fame so blind in supporting and exalting what was the evident ruin of good drawing ("*disegno*"). Annibale, who was then present, said: what is all this marveling? Do you believe that this is a new effect of newness? I tell you that, whoever might come up with an unheard-of and entirely fabricated style, will always encounter the same destiny and meet with praises not inferior. And he added: I would certainly know another way of making a big splash, and even of defeating and mortifying everyone. I would oppose an extreme tenderness to his fierceness of color. If he uses a falling light in a closed space, I would employ a frontal light in an open space. As he conceals the difficulties of art amidst the shadows of night, I would like to uncover the subtlest inventions of knowledge in the broad light of midday. If he throws down [on the canvas] whatever he sees in nature, without seizing the good and the best, I would choose the most perfect parts, more adjusted, endowing the figures with the nobility and harmony missing in the original. Guido, among others of his disciples, attended this speech, and his master's voice sounded to him like that of the oracle at Delphi, from which he could derive a certain and secure enlightenment in achieving the excellence he had long been chasing. He set out to apply these principles, refined this practice with much study, and could pride himself on being the first and fortunate inventor of this new style.[25]

Malvasia's evocation of this episode is equally false, and nothing but a fine piece of rhetoric, a figure of verisimilitude through which the author elucidates and dramatizes Guido's formulation of a new pictorial style. Rhetorically speaking, the emergence of Guido's originality through the criticism

---

24 On this anecdote and the way in which it should be interpreted, see the excellent Perini 1990.

25 Malvasia, 2:10: "Uno dunque di questi, capitando a Bologna in casa de' signori Lambertini, è impossibil il ridire quanto gusto ne sentisse Lodovico, per potere sull'opra medesima conoscere se il merito di questo soggetto fosse uguale al nome che così vantaggioso di lui per tutto correa. Rimase stordito quando altro non seppe rintralciarne che un gran contrasto di lumi e d'ombre, che un'ubbidienza troppo fedele al naturale, senza decoro, con poca grazia, minor intelligenza, ma più attonito della fortuna così cieca in favorire ed esaltare una ruina manifesta del buon disegno; quando: 'che tante maraviglie?' disse Annibale ivi presente, 'parvi egli questo un nuovo effetto della novità? Io vi dico che tutti quei che con non più veduta e da essi loro inventata maniera usciran fuore, incontreranno sempre la stessa sorte e non minore la loda.' 'Saprei ben io,' soggions'egli, 'un altro modo per far gran colpo, anzi da vincere e mortificare costui; a quel colorito fiero vorrei contrapporne uno affatto tenero; prende egli un lume serrato e cadente, ed io lo vorrei aperto ed in faccia; cuopre quegli le difficoltà dell'arte fra l'ombre della notte, ed io a un chiaro lume di mezzo giorno vorrei scoprire i più dotti ed eruditi ricerchi; quanto ved'egli nella natura, senza isfiorarne il buono e 'l meglio, tanto mette giù, ed io vorrei scegliere il più perfetto delle parti, un più aggiustato, dando alle figure quella nobiltà ed armonia di che manca l'originale. Stava fra gli altri scolari presente Guido a questo discorso, e parvegli la voce del maestro quella dell'oracolo delfico da che traesse un certo e sicuro lume al da lui tanto tempo ricercato vantaggio. Se ne pose alla pratica, la raffinò col gran studio ed ebbe il vanto di essere il primo e fortunato introduttore di questa nuova maniera." For Caravaggio's painting in the Lambertini Collection, see Malvasia's manuscript note in Malvasia a, 101: "Avea [Lorenzo Garbieri] un Ecce Homo coppiato dal Caravaggio, quadro originale ch'avevano i Lambertini, tre mezze figure: Cristo, Pilato ed un armato (…)." Perhaps, this *Ecce Homo* is the painting that, executed by Garbieri for Cardinal Giustiniani, passed in Rome for an original by Caravaggio. See Malvasia, 2:298: "come a dire l'Ecce Homo famoso che si diede a credere colà [in Rome], con felice riuscita, di mano del Caravaggio, ed anche oggi per tale si tiene, ricavando uno di que' ladroni dalla testa, in questo genere bellissima, del Righettone speciale, e l'altro da un basso rilievo." Garbieri's painting is lost. See Negro and Pirondini 1994, 179.

and annihilation of Caravaggio's newness—"do you believe that this is a new effect of newness?," interjects Annibale—responds to Caravaggio's assault on Guido as narrated by Malvasia himself (see Chapter 10) in connection with Guido's *Crucifixion of Saint Peter*. In attacking the young painter, Caravaggio accused him of stealing his stylistic newness. Evidently Malvasia seals the question by asserting that Guido was the real and "fortunate inventor" of a new style, an originality on which he had been working since his youth. In Malvasia's words, Guido's style configures itself as antithetical to Caravaggio's: tenderness against fierceness; frontal lighting against zenithal lighting; open space against closed space; selection against indiscriminate reproduction; nobility and harmony against baseness and disharmony; and idea against nature.[26]

Surprisingly enough, to fulfill his own originality Guido had to turn Caravaggio upside down, his painting thus becoming an anti-paradigm of perfection. More importantly, Guido's new style is described by Malvasia as the completion of Annibale's project. Were it not for his deep depression and premature death, Annibale might have completed the enterprise of developing his own newness. Between the lines, a strong contradiction underlies Malvasia's interpretation of painting's evolution in the beginning of the seventeenth century. In Bellori's *Vite*, the true renovator and re-inventor of art was indeed Annibale. For reasons too long to illustrate here, Malvasia, who was perfectly acquainted with Bellori's work, was unable to give Annibale this honor; as Annibale's artistic apogee had occurred in Rome, and not in Bologna, Malvasia divides the trophy of artistic perfection between painters whose work was profoundly related to his city, Guercino, Domenichino, Francesco Albani and, in particular, Guido. Both Bellori and Malvasia, albeit through different procedures and strategies, tried to belittle the artistic novelty and groundbreaking change embodied by Caravaggio's painting in early seventeenth-century Rome, a merit that they nevertheless could not entirely erase.

As has become clear, from Mancini to Baglione and from Bellori to Malvasia, seventeenth-century art theorists and artists unanimously acknowledged the emergence of a profound and disruptive change in the ideal and practice of painting in Italy around 1600. Following in the footsteps of Giorgio Vasari and, before him, of Pliny the Elder, Bellori and Malvasia among others adopted a physiological paradigm, derived in the main from Aristotle's physics and Aristotelian historiography, which assimilated the evolution of art to the ascending and descending parabola of organic development. In their opinion, after the senescence of artistic creativity subsequent to the peak of the High Renaissance, artists, especially the Carracci and their disciples, restored art and brought it to new perfection. Modern scholars have unanimously accepted the idea that a paramount artistic breakthrough took place at the end of the sixteenth century. Unlike Bellori and Malvasia, they include Caravaggio's name in the reformers' list with reason: his "realism," albeit doomed to extinction within two decades after expanding into a multifarious movement, and condemned as an aberration by seventeenth-century theorists, not only contributed to artistic change, but—more realistically—marked a real caesura in art history.

Just after the end of the Second World War, Denis Mahon sparked off a debate on how exactly artistic change around 1600 should be defined, particularly in connection with the Carracci's painting.[27] Arguing that previous scholarship had misinterpreted sources by downgrading the Carracci's reform to mere eclecticism and academic classicism, Mahon highlighted the newness and importance especially of Annibale's painting, which according to him foreshadows the

---

26 Malvasia, 2:81, describes Guido's lighting and chiaroscuro even at the end of his career in terms antithetical to Caravaggio's procedure: "Non volle (…) usar l'ombre terribili e forzate, come cadenti d'alto e da finestra socchiusa, cagionate da lume di sole o di torchio acceso, artifiziose troppo ad ogni modo, violent[e] ed affettate, che non vediamo naturalmente e per l'ordinario salvo che in caso di rappresentare una notte, un incendio e simili."

27 See Mahon 1971, published originally in 1947, esp. 195-229. At the beginning of the 1950s, Mahon was greatly engaged in analyzing Caravaggio's works and refining their chronology. See among others Mahon 1951a; Mahon 1951b; Mahon 1952a; Mahon 1952b; and Mahon 1953a.

more mature Baroque of Pietro da Cortona. Though highly innovative and provocative, Mahon's interpretation relies on the formal distinctions introduced by Heinrich Wölfflin in *Renaissance and Baroque*, and thereby tends to detect and analyze change in exclusively stylistic terms. Not surprisingly, the most authoritative reactions to Mahon's exegesis (from Charles Dempsey[28] to Sydney J. Freedberg[29]) aimed to reconsider the Carracci's originality also from a formal viewpoint. If these scholars focused on the Carracci's reform to explain the artistic change that occurred in Italian art around 1600, this was because they took for granted Caravaggio's essential role and pervasive influence in this process. Since Bellori and Malvasia, historical perspective has thus been completely overturned.

The attention with which scholars studied and construed the notion of artistic change around 1600 dramatically decreased by the end of the 1980s. From this crucial debate contemporary scholarship of seventeenth-century art has inherited a more dynamic model for interpreting the artistic evolution of that period, one that elucidates the subtle interrelations between the Carracci's reform of art and Caravaggio's "realism." As a consequence, more pressing and inescapable questions remain unsolved. One of these questions seems to me as essential as it is widely neglected or blandly tackled by art historians: how is one to explain the implosion and defeat of the Caravaggesque movement around 1630? If Caravaggio's revolution is not a matter of pure style, as I have demonstrated throughout this volume, does it suffice to chalk up the extinction of the Caravaggesque movement to the simple emergence of a new pictorial taste that pushed Caravaggio's followers to brighten their colors, abandon their half-figures, and repress their proclivities for low-life representations? In other words, what are the real factors that counteracted and eventually blocked the formidable thrust of Caravaggio's vanguard in the two decades after the master's death? This question cannot be answered without taking into account the different ways in which Caravaggio's subversive models of pictorial narratives were interpreted, developed and, in turn, dismantled by his followers.

As I have shown especially in Part Three, to explain Caravaggio's "realism" scholars have more recently related it either to the religious context of early seventeenth-century Rome—in which case, Caravaggio's style is the translation of his pauperism and radical devotion—or to scientific progress as incarnated by Galileo's experimental methodology and refutation of neo-Aristotelian physics,[30] according to which the photographic quality of Caravaggio's painting betrays and channels the master's empirical attitude toward nature. In both instances, scholars have invested social or cultural circumstances with the prodigious power of mechanically generating artistic expression. Even in so simplified a manner, it is easy to recognize two hermeneutic models behind these interpretations, one informed by the principle of the *Zeitgeist* and the *Kunstwollen*, and the other inspired by the tenets of the sociology of art. When it comes to evaluating Caravaggio's newness, the limits of these approaches above all reside in the reflexive, implicitly passive role that scholars tend to ascribe to the painter and his works. Imbued with the spirit of his time, and imprinted by the mold of the actual circumstances bearing upon him, Caravaggio merely becomes a translator of external trends, ceasing to be a personal interpreter and creator of his own culture and art.

Renouncing the abstract framing of these hermeneutics, I embrace a distinct epistemological model in order to explain the radical change represented by Caravaggio's painting and the multiple reactions that this change inexorably determined; I take the view that artists are prompted by, and react to, but do not obey, historical, social or cultural pressures. In my opinion, there is no immediately identifiable one-to-one cause-and-effect relationship between art and history, since

---

28 See Dempsey 2000, originally published in 1977; and further Dempsey 2006.

29 See Freedberg 1983. For an overview of the art criticism with regard to the Carracci's reform, see Keazor 2007, 79-96.

30 See for instance Bardon 1978; Bologna 1992; and Panzera 1994. Cropper 2009 is a fine essay on the interrelation between Galileo's ideas and art.

artworks do not necessarily parallel or mirror the laws of history as formulated by scholars in a symmetrical and univocal network of meanings. As a corollary, I do not deem artistic innovation as systematically geared to impose itself on society and culture. There may be shifts, caesuras, and even leaps between art and history. The paintings of Caravaggio and his followers are a case in point.

In this volume, I have consistently argued that to understand Caravaggio's disruptive originality, it is necessary to scrutinize his techniques of pictorial narration. After analysis of many of his narratives, I have concluded that his unusual method of painting after life and the coherence with which Caravaggio enhances the optical functionalities of the *istoria*—the quintessence of his realism—are the substantial tools, but not the main purpose, of his pictorial newness. Caravaggio, in particular at the apex of his pictorial career around 1600 until his flight from Rome in 1606, used his portentous aptitude for lifelike mimesis as a compelling device of bewilderment in counterpoint to his procedure of narrative dislocations. Through dislocation, Caravaggio discarded the then statutory functions of the image, thereby manipulating the mechanisms of perception and reading to which viewers were accustomed in assessing pictorial narratives.

The means by which Caravaggio dislocated the principles and conventions of the *istoria* of his time are manifold: by adjusting schemes or patterns traditionally associated with one specific genre to genres where they did not belong (dislocations of genre); by endowing pictorial characters with attributes and attitudes that make their identification problematic (dislocations of character); by misleading viewers in the recognition and reconstruction of visual plots (dislocations of narrative legibility and intelligibility); by dissolving the coherence of pictorial synchrony, and disconnecting the actions of his actors (dislocations of temporality); or by introducing doubles of the author who, engaged in the depicted action, engender a narrative viewpoint dissimilar from that afforded to the beholder (dislocations of authorship): in some of these last cases, the authorial principle is even questioned, submitted to parody, and hence desacralized. Historically speaking, some of these narrative dislocations will find their equivalents in the kindred field of literature only centuries later.

Caravaggio's innovations in the field of pictorial narrative unveiled two unsettling truths with regard to the *istoria*, one concerning the relationship between form and content, and another regarding indeterminacy. On the one hand, the techniques through which painters capture the beholder's gaze by eliciting an emotional and intellectual response can be independent from, and are not contingent upon, the represented subject matter: the perfect accord of form with content on which the early modern aesthetics solidly relied becomes all at once obsolete. On the other, new typologies of pictorial "affects"—which might be opportunely called states of mind or situations of indefinite consciousness—by transcending the requirements of legibility and intelligibility consubstantial with the concept of the *istoria*, can considerably enlarge the appeal and significance of pictorial narratives; if deftly employed, obscurity and indeterminacy, instead of discouraging, awakens the viewer's curiosity by challenging his or her habit-based capacity to decipher characters and situations. As a corollary, it can be said that through obscurity and indeterminacy painters can surmount the technical limits that the pictorial medium—the bi-dimensional canvas—ineluctably carries with it. Meaning can therefore lurk in narrative ambivalences of any sort.

If it is certain that a meaningful rupture marks the emergence of Caravaggio's painting, it is even more critical to understand why the drive of such an unprecedented artistic change, despite its two-decade-long impact, subsided and eventually vanished. Not only did the Caravaggesque movement fail to acquire social and cultural consensus—unlike the Carracci's reform—but it also expired at the hands of his own representatives. In Part Six, I intend to investigate how some of Caravaggio's followers interpreted the artistic change and originality introduced by the master himself, and to what extent they were aware of the artistic and cultural implications engendered by his innovations. Many of the painters we associate with Caravaggio's painting never met with the master in person; between the movement's founder and his acolytes there is not only discontinuity and a real hiatus of direct knowledge, but also enough room for novel reflection and independent interpretation. In the following chapters, I intend to demonstrate that the innovations introduced by Caravaggio with regard to pictorial narrative did not go unnoticed by his followers, several of whom correctly sensed and seized their intrinsic disruptive charge. These painters reacted to Caravaggio's artistic newness in completely different ways.

Some preferred diligently to avoid the pitfalls of Caravaggio's narrative dislocations; therefore, they endeavored to apply the principles of the canonical *istoria* to the comedic themes inherited from Caravaggio, although they also often indulged in multiplying the gags and intrigues of the pictorial comedy in pyrotechnics of narrative bravura. Aware of the rhetorical effect obtained in disclosing the fictive nature of their compositions, they equally underscored the meta-pictorial components of both their comedies and narratives. As a general rule, they grew most sensitive to the model set by the Carracci's painting over time, with which they frequently happened to interact. To this group of painters belong artists like Simon Vouet and Gerrit van Honthorst. Other members of the Caravaggesque movement tried to exploit Caravaggio's innovations in a somewhat mechanical, though brilliant, fashion. They experimented with narrative dislocations, and sometimes pushed to its extremes the master's lesson. Among these artists I would place Cecco del Caravaggio, Battistello Caracciolo and, to a certain extent, Jusepe de Ribera.

A third, and by far the most interesting, group of Caravaggio's followers elaborates upon two of the most problematic aspects of the master's poetics of dislocation: the potential independence of painting's compositional structure from the subject matter, and the narrative indeterminacy and suspense generated by the representation of inner states of mind and absorption. Some of the solutions they adopted are both subversive and highly innovative. Yet for reasons that cannot be discussed in this study, these painters deliberately refrained from pursuing further their experimentations in the field of pictorial narrative. In a certain sense, they are unwittingly responsible for the inner exhaustion of the movement itself. Bartolomeo Manfredi, Valentin de Boulogne, Hendrik ter Brugghen and, on a very different score, the young Velázquez belong to this category.

By examining Cecco del Caravaggio's *Resurrection of Christ*, Diego Velázquez's *Supper at Emmaus* along with his two versions of *La Mulata*, and Valentin de Boulogne's *Merry Company with Fortune Teller*, I hope to demonstrate that Caravaggio's newness triggered an artistic chain reaction the extinction of which was determined by inner factors as much as by external ones. Like an earthquake, change in art not only dislodges the order and balance of pre-existing artistic conditions, but also opens up previously uncharted faults whose entity, extension, and significance can be evaluated only in the course of time.

Change in art puts artists in situations of virtual *aporia*: at their own expense, they have latitude to explore new avenues or recoil from unknown ventures. Change boosts artistic freedom but also brings about incalculable risks. Heeding Caravaggio's unorthodox paradigms of pictorial narration could, for painters, have meant the possibility of earning renown for originality, but also that of hitting a wall of public incomprehension and social disregard. In my opinion, the insurmountable *aporia* that the most lucid and acute followers of Caravaggio were forced to face was the sheer possibility of eclipsing narrative—I intentionally use a term inspired by Paul Ricœur's "*éclipse du récit*":[31] that is, the *aporia* of reinstating and reconfiguring the essence, scope, functionalities, and finalities of pictorial narration on wholly new grounds. In a sense, by dismantling the principles of Aristotle's concepts of mimesis and narration, Caravaggio, like Galileo in the domain of physics and astronomy, accomplished a real revolution. Yet, at the beginning of the seventeenth century, the conditions were not mature enough to redesign the *istoria* in terms that far exceeded and even overturned those of Alberti.

31   See Ricœur 1983, 171-216.

More generally, the great artistic change of around 1600, in which both the Carracci and Caravaggio played a fundamental part, produced a tremendous reaction and counter-reaction; on the one hand, Caravaggio's followers tried to stretch the limits of pictorial narration and, despite occasional success, resolved, or were compelled, to stop their experimentations; on the other, the Carracci's disciples, and in particular Nicolas Poussin as their symbolic heir, widened and over-defined the principles of Alberti's *istoria* through subtler rules and more cogent strictures, a process that would culminate in the foundation and activities of the French *Académie de Peinture et Sculpture* from 1648 onward. Caravaggio's art has finally been recognized for its enormous complexity, visual impact, originality, and prodigious facture, yet the reemergence of Caravaggio's crucial role in early modern art history has occurred only after a three-century-long eclipse of his fortune.

Plate XXI: Diego Velázquez, *The Supper at Emmaus*, Metropolitan Museum of Art, New York, ▶
oil on canvas, 123.2 x 132.7 cm., detail.

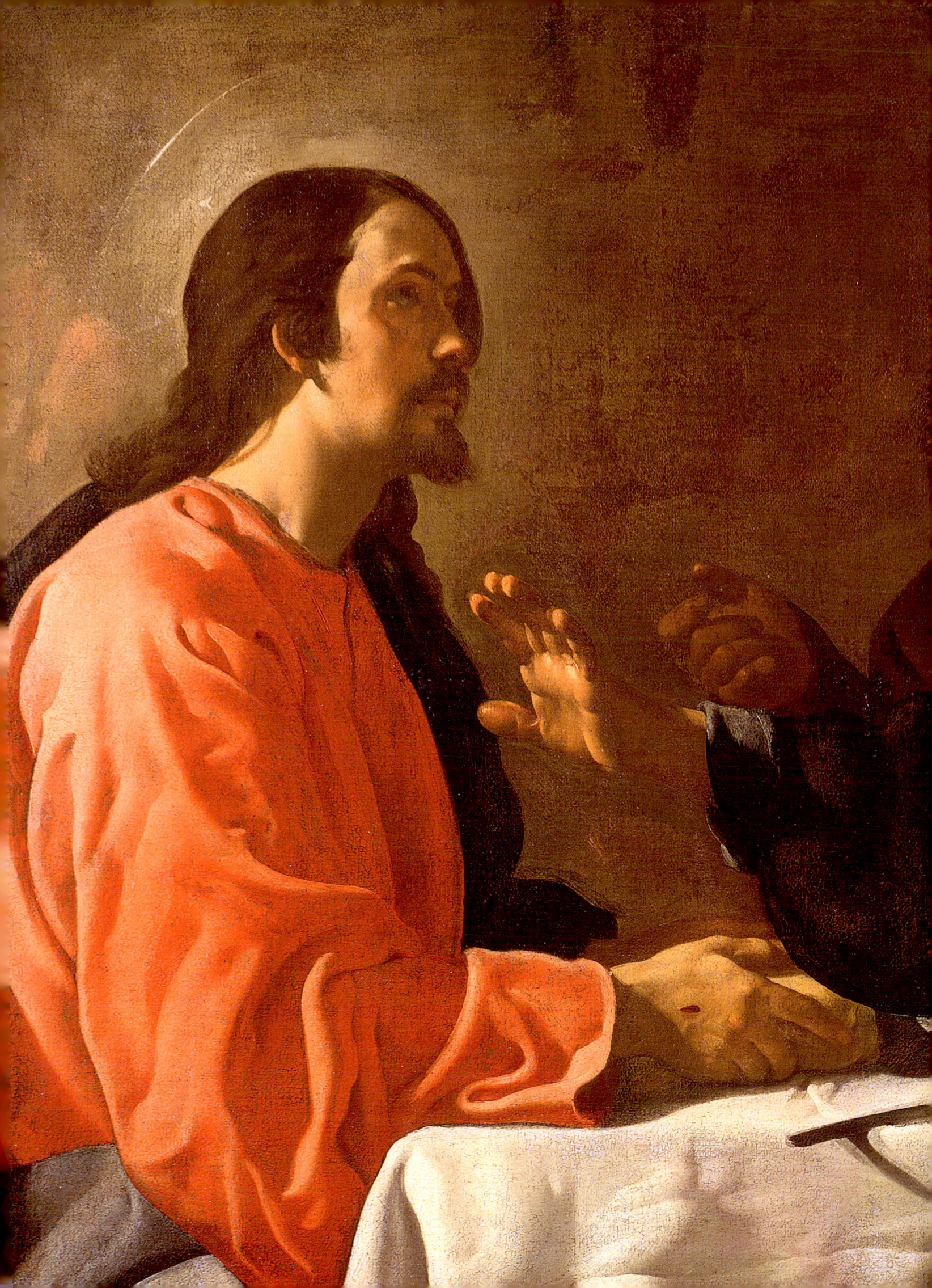

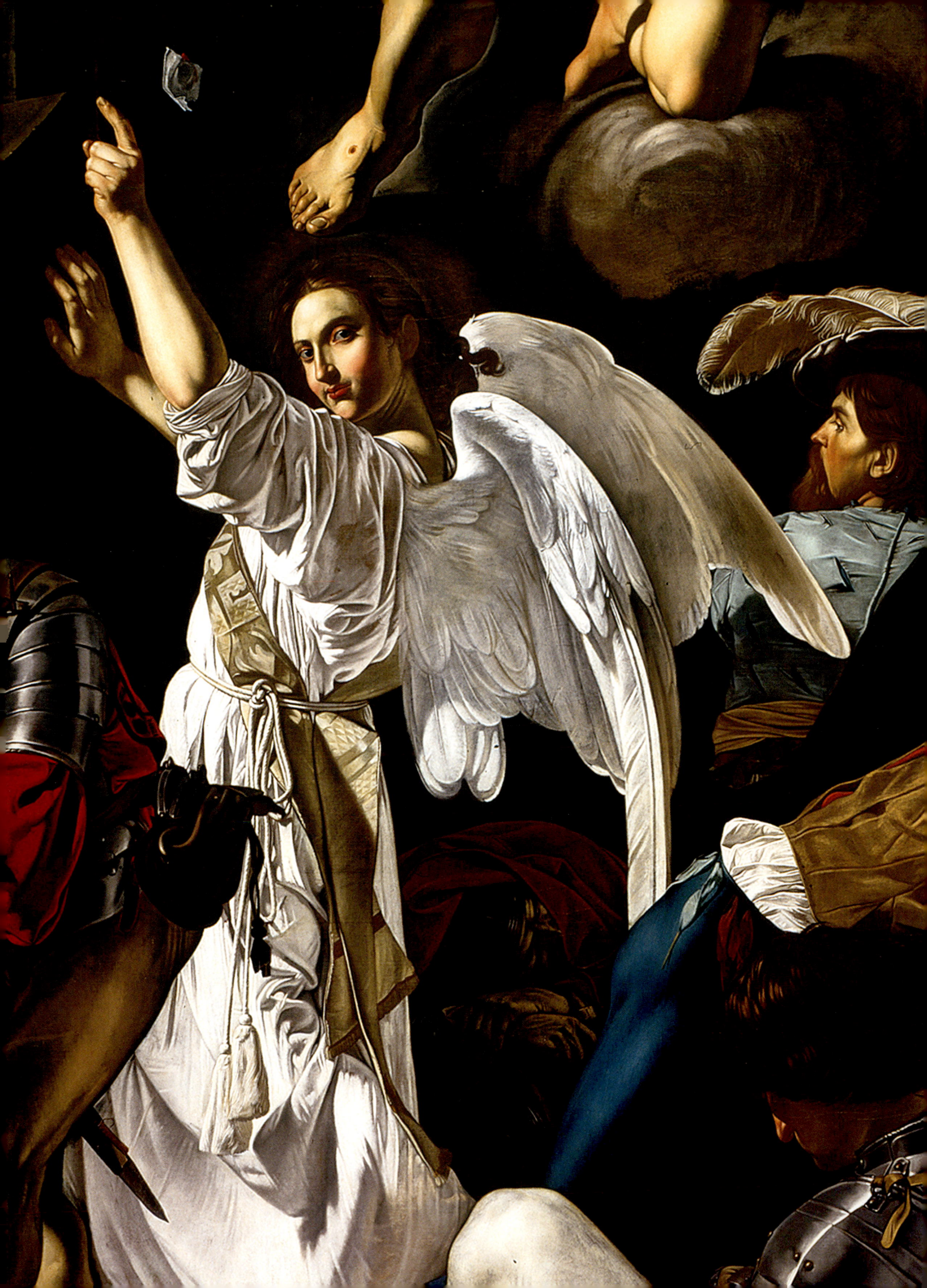

CHAPTER 15

Blind and Deaf Actions: Cecco del Caravaggio's Chicago *Resurrection*

Inaudible Pictures

On a cartouche in Giovanni Bellini's famous *Pietà* at the Brera, Milan, there is an elegiac couplet in the style of Propertius which reads: "HAEC FERE QVVM GEMITVS TURGENTIA LUMINA PROMANT/ BELLINI POTERAT FLERE IOANNIS OPVS."[1] This inscription is often translated loosely into English so that many scholars have construed it as an evocation of the painting's quasi-animistic powers: Bellini's *Pietà* might literally be able to "shed tears." I propose a slightly different interpretation: "if these eyes swelling with tears uttered groans, the work of Giovanni Bellini could weep." Rhetorically speaking, this sentence is a paradox: Bellini's mourning figures, of which the welling tears are a synecdoche, cannot utter any sound, although the Virgin's lips mimic a murmur as John gasps as if groaning. However visually poignant, Bellini's lamentation lacks voice. That is, it lacks those acoustic effects that would perfect the impression of weeping. Implicit in the painting's inscription is the idea that the only limit to Bellini's excellence in the field of the devotional image resides in the intrinsic inability of painting as a medium to speak or, more pertinently, to produce sounds. Otherwise, the adequacy of Bellini's figures to the religious drama proves completely achieved: the short elegy indirectly states that Mary and John truly and convincingly enact their sorrow around Christ's dead body.

The tenor of the inscription also implies a typical *paragone* between poetry and painting; just as Bellini's *Pietà* remains a silent poem, so too a poetic account of the lamentation will always be a blind picture, in spite of its *enargeia* or graphicness. However, there is another, less conventional edge to the comparison between visual and verbal arts as posited by the elegiac couplet. Through the ambivalence of its syntax, its author, most probably a Venetian humanist, envisions the possibility that Bellini's weeping figures actually utter groans. Thus, mute as it is, Bellini's painting might arouse acoustic associations in the beholder's mind; the representation of parted lips or an open mouth in this context invites the viewer to fill in the blanks of the image, and to reconstruct its groans. Bellini's artistry endows the picture with synesthetic powers, inexorably restrained by the medium's specificity, yet latently operative. It is important to stress this point for at least two reasons. First of all, art historians have largely avoided examining the complex devices through which early modern painters tend to evoke acoustic effects, whether amorphous sounds, interjections or fragments of speech.[2] The efficacy of these devices relies on mnemonic functions and visual codifications specific to early modern culture, whether in Italy or elsewhere in western Europe. Secondly, art historians have not sufficiently analyzed the mechanisms of causality or interconnectedness inherent in the early modern *istoria*, and how they bear on the cognitive process through which

---

1 I discuss this inscription in the epilogue to Pericolo 2002. See also Belting 1985, esp. 28-32; and Goffen 1989, 71-2.

2 I have examined these issues in relation to Philippe de Champaigne (Pericolo 2002), and Antonello da Messina (Pericolo 2009a).

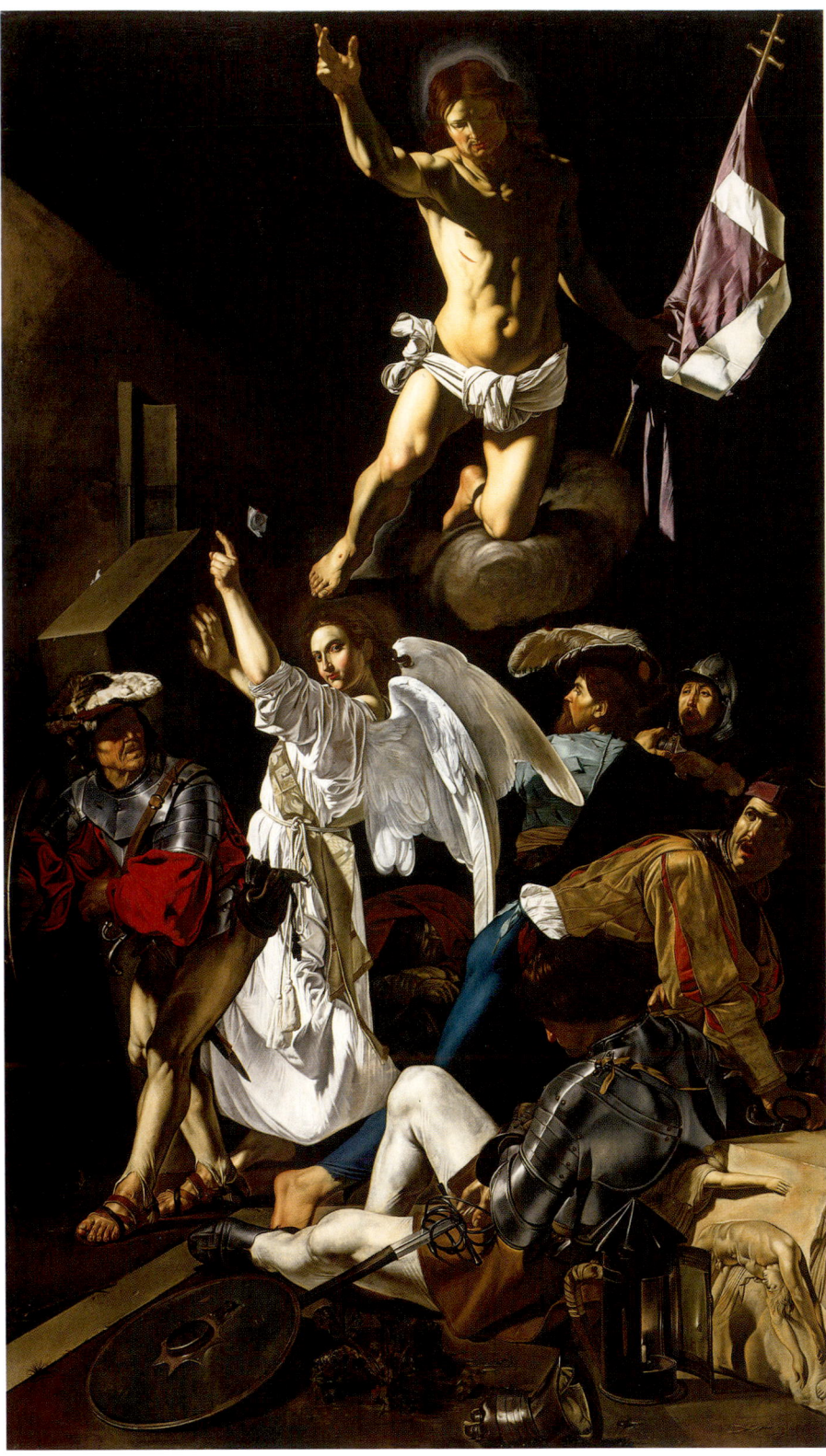

Fig. 256
Cecco del Caravaggio (Francesco Boneri), *The Resurrection*, Art Institute, Chicago,
oil on canvas, 339 x 199.5 cm.

beholders perceive, experience, and reconfigure narration. Not only do painters coordinate action in order to single out cause-and-effect sequences within the narrative, but they also evoke the acoustic through the visual, stringing them together into coherent, synesthetic interrelations. In some minor cases, they also disconnect the visual from the acoustic, thereby creating narrative disjunctions. Needless to say, art theorists, especially from the second half of the sixteenth century onward, almost systematically condemn inconsistency in the composition of the *istoria*.

These incongruities between the visual and the acoustic, and between the various cause-and-effect sequences built into the narrative, are the main interest of this chapter. Throughout this volume, I have shown that such disparities—or dislocations, as I like to call them—constitute an essential element of Caravaggio's painting. As noted in the Introduction to Part Six, some followers of Caravaggio also experimented with these pictorial innovations, adjusting them to new contexts and stretching their potentialities to a point of "no return," a point at which the story's intelligibility and verisimilitude are intrinsically compromised. Cecco del Caravaggio's Chicago *Resurrection* offers a telling example of this tendency (Fig. 256). In this picture, mentioned in Chapter 9, the network of visual and acoustic effects that underlie the structure of the narrative is drastically dismantled and dislodged. Blindness and deafness are not mere metaphors: in Cecco's *Resurrection*, characters mostly act as if unaware of each other's presence, their actions set in motion by an initiating event—a supernatural lighting preceded by an earthquake—whose tremendous blaze and roar they are either unable to trace back or do not acknowledge. Therefore, their actions might be defined as blind or deaf.

I return now to Bellini's Brera *Pietà*. To my knowledge, Bellini is probably among the first painters to disassociate the visual from the acoustic in a way that prefigures Cecco's enterprise.[3] In Bellini's *Transfiguration* (*c*.1460) at the Museo Correr, Venice (Fig. 257),[4] a dazzling white-clad Christ soars at the top of Mount Tabor, flanked by Moses and Elijah; below, Peter and John seem to extract themselves from a deep lethargy while James, still slumbering, lies ignorant of the miracle. On first analysis, Bellini takes up the bipartite structure of a then traditional Transfiguration, the steep incline of the mountain accommodating three figures in its lower and higher registers respectively. However, Bellini differentiates the attitudes of the three apostles, by representing, as it were, three phases of the story's unfolding: the placid sleep of James, the confused awakening of John, and Peter's reaction to the voice coming from above: "This is my beloved Son, with whom I am well pleased; listen to him" (Matthew, 17, 5).

Bellini's *Transfiguration*, like many other representations of the same subject, does not precisely obey the text of the Gospels, which offer noticeably divergent versions of the same event. In any case, all the depictions of this biblical episode are symbolic insofar as they decompose then rearrange the chronological layout of the written narrative into distinct, paradigmatic visual configurations. What is particular to Bellini's Correr picture is the

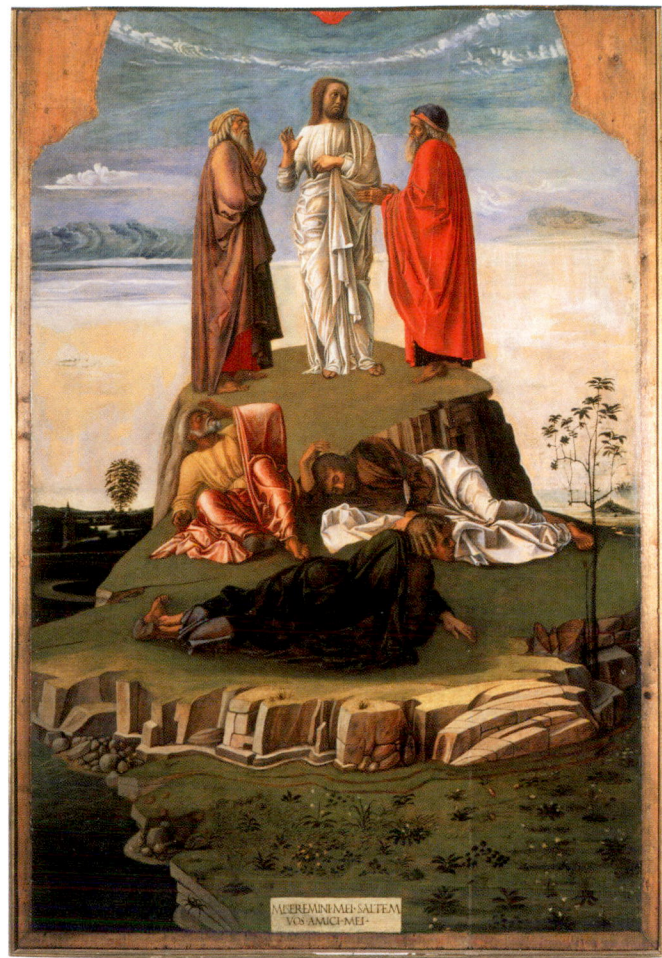

Fig. 257
Giovanni Bellini, *The Transfiguration*, Museo Correr, Venice, tempera on panel, 133 x 90.3 cm.

apostles' apparent extraneousness to the divine epiphany behind and above them. While Peter explores the heavens to identify the origin of God's voice, John, half-awake, steers his gaze away from both the majestic Christ above and the sky; his face oriented off scene, he sinks in a sort of dreamily contemplation, as though he were either incapable of tracing the divine sound's source or were entirely unaware of it. As for James' attitude, it is evident that the miracle in both its visual and acoustic form does not concern him at all: the apostle is blind to Christ's apotheosis and deaf to God's imperious voice.

The disjunction between the visual and the acoustic operating here—although in a very inchoate manner—is boldly developed by Bellini in his later *Transfiguration* for the funerary chapel of Archdeacon Alberto Fioccardo in Vicenza Cathedral, now at the Museo di Capodimonte, Naples (Fig. 258).[5] The apostles respond in different ways to the voice that interrupts their temporary coma. Of Christ's disciples, only Peter seems to vaguely understand that the mysterious sound originates in heaven. Disoriented, James rivets his gaze onto an indefinite spot as John, barely conscious,

3   It is also true that, as I suggest in my comments on the Brera painting, Bellini was devoted to evoking acoustic effects not only in opposition to, but also in synchrony with, the visual. A telling example of this is offered by his *Saint Francis in the Wilderness* at the Frick Collection, New York. As Anderson 1997, 158-9, has compellingly suggested, Saint Francis is represented in the painting in the act of singing.

4   For the painting, see Goffen 1989, 14-9.

5   See Ibidem, 138-40.

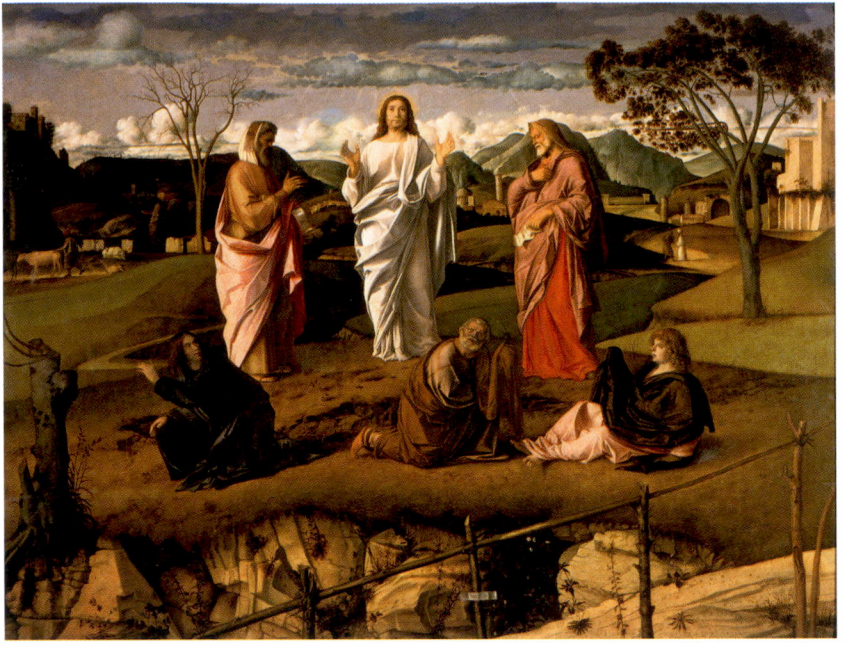

Fig. 258
Giovanni Bellini, *The Transfiguration*, Museo di Capodimonte, Naples, oil on canvas,
115 x 151 cm.

recovers his senses slowly. None of them looks at Christ's transfigured persona, his epiphany being invisible to them. The invisibility evoked by Bellini in his two *Transfigurations* is not justified by the Gospels' account. In the three versions of the episode,[6] the apostles indeed hear the divine voice and witness Jesus' radiant transformation. Only Luke records that "Peter and his companions had been overcome by sleep," specifying nevertheless that, "becoming fully awake, they saw [Christ's] glory and the two men standing with him" (Luke, 9, 32). Subsequently, after hearing God's voice, Peter turns to Jesus and finds him alone, Moses and Elijah fading out of sight. Counter to the text of scripture, Peter, John, and James in Bellini's two *Transfigurations* are no longer the witnesses of Christ's apotheosis: this role now is transferred to the viewer, whose knowledge of the event seemingly exceeds that of the apostles.

As in other circumstances, Bellini restores the effect of marvel associated with the episode of recognition—Aristotle's *anagnorisis*—by inducing in the beholder an emotional detachment from the fiction's figures. Fully informed of the miracle and, in a certain sense, omniscient, the viewer however realizes the chasm between the epiphany evoked in the painting and the apostles' reaction to it. This gap between two levels of the narrative, running parallel to each other though partially disconnected, engenders a powerful effect of disorientation: beholders are both clued in to the limits of their vision and alerted to a frequency of action inaccessible to them, a frequency in which the visible shifts into the invisible, and the mute into the audible. Technically speaking, this process of estrangement qualifies as the opposite of dramatic irony: the viewer's interaction with the narrative involves a reversal from presumed knowledge to uncertainty or indeterminacy.

Circumstantial evidence seems to prove that Bellini might have adopted a similar device of estrangement and narrative disjunction in another religious theme, the Resurrection. At an indeterminate date, but most probably in the first decade of the sixteenth century, the Venetian engraver Girolamo Mocetto[7] executed a print (Fig. 259) whose design has sometimes been related to a lost painting by Giovanni Bellini, the *c*.1483 *Resurrection* altarpiece for the funerary chapel of Gaspare Trissino in Vicenza Cathedral.[8] Although it is impossible to confirm or refute this hypothesis, Mocetto is known to have scavenged selectively from compositions by Bellini; in a sense, he produced collages based on Bellini's ideas and motifs. Mocetto's *Baptism of Christ*, for instance, basically recalls Bellini's painting of the same subject for the Garzadori Chapel in Santa Corona, Vicenza. Similarly, Mocetto's *The Virgin in Glory with Eight Saints* roughly reproduces in reverse a picture by Bellini and his workshop originally destined for San Pietro Martire, Murano.[9] In this case, the differences between the original and the engraving are reduced to a minimum,

---

6   The third one, not specified in the text, is Mark, 9, 2-8.

7   For Mocetto as a printer, see Levenson et al. 1973, 382-5. For the print, see Zucker 1984, 45, no. 003.

8   See Goffen 1989, 260, 290.

9   See Goffen 1989, 163-6. For the print, see Zucker 1984, 46, no. 005.

with the exception of the Virgin's attitude: in Bellini's painting, Mary is standing, whereas Mocetto apparently represented her kneeling. It is fair to assume that Mocetto's *Resurrection* echoes elements initially present in one or more compositions by Bellini. In this regard, the posture of the soldier in the print's left foreground recalls that of Saint Peter in the Correr *Resurrection*. Their right arm leaning against the ground or a rock, the soldier and the apostle lift their left arm while curiously looking upward. Moreover, the narrative situation in which they figure presents clear affinities: both seem to scan the sky in search of the cause that has just abruptly put an end to their sleep.

Matthew is the only evangelist to mention the soldiers' bafflement at Christ's apotheosis. According to his text, a "great earthquake" accompanied the angel's irruption into Jesus' tomb: the divine messenger "descended from the heaven, approached, rolled back the stone, and sat upon it." Matthew also reports that the angel's "appearance was like lightning and his clothing was white as snow." He goes on: "the guards were shaken with fear of him and became like dead men" (Matthew, 28, 2-4). As a general rule, no representation of the Resurrection adheres to the letter of the Gospel, which incidentally would have been very complicated to depict. In fact, scripture does not specifically describe Christ's Resurrection, but almost unanimously focus on the angel's, or the two angels', encounter with the three women who had gone to the sepulcher to anoint

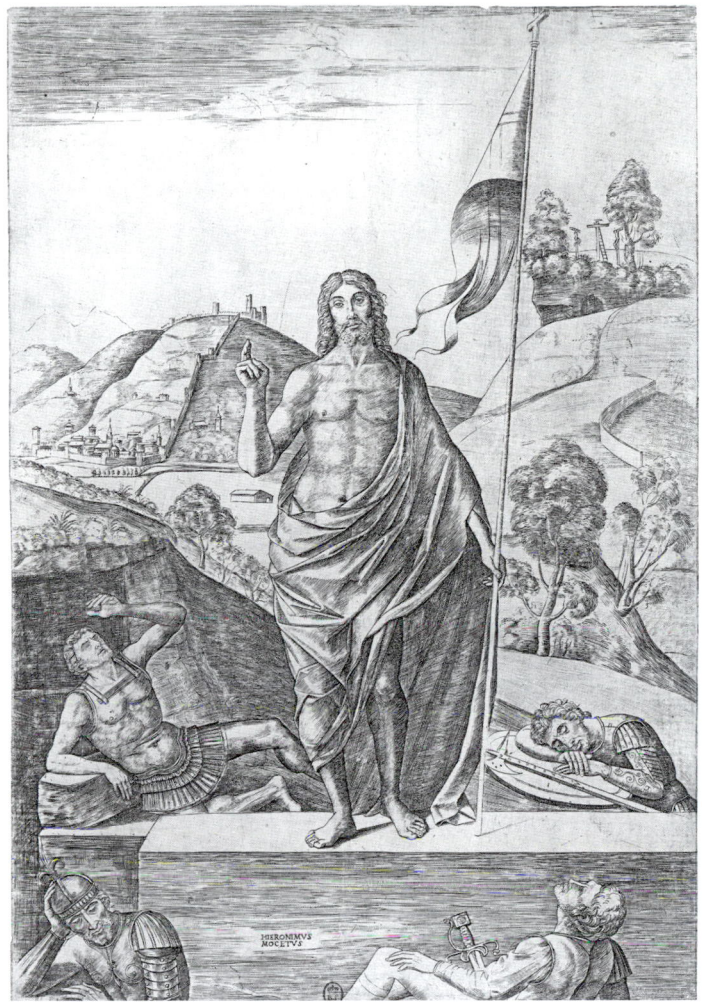

Fig. 259
Girolamo Mocetto, *The Resurrection*, engraving, 44.7 x 30 cm.

Jesus' body. Considering the intricate iconography of the Resurrection, it is impossible to ascertain what exactly the soldier in Mocetto's print looks for in the sky. It might be a rumble, a glowing angel, a triumphant Christ or an unidentified object or sound. What is certain is that the guard does not acknowledge Christ's majestic presence in the foreground; blind to the resurrected man, he appears incapable of recognizing the miracle's origin. Even worse, a second guard at the right continues to sleep, indifferent to the divine epiphany, and a third, leaning on his folded right arm, is barely able to keep his eyes open, let alone acknowledge the miracle. Like his counterpart on the left at Christ's feet, a fourth soldier, entrenched in the right foreground, directs his gaze alertly toward the print's upper margin, the figure of the resurrected Savior being equally transparent to him. The boldness of Mocetto's composition, at first glance, might have originated in Bellini: Bellini's, in any case, seems to be the disconnection between the glorious Christ in the foreground and the temporarily blind or deaf soldiers at the sepulcher's feet. It seems clear that Bellini inspired Mocetto's engraving, but, in the iconographic tradition of the Resurrection, Cristofano Robetta[10] goes even farther than Bellini by disjoining the visual from the acoustic in much bolder terms

10   For Robetta as a printer, see Levenson et al. 1973, 289-93.
For the print, see Zucker 1984, 545, no. 018.

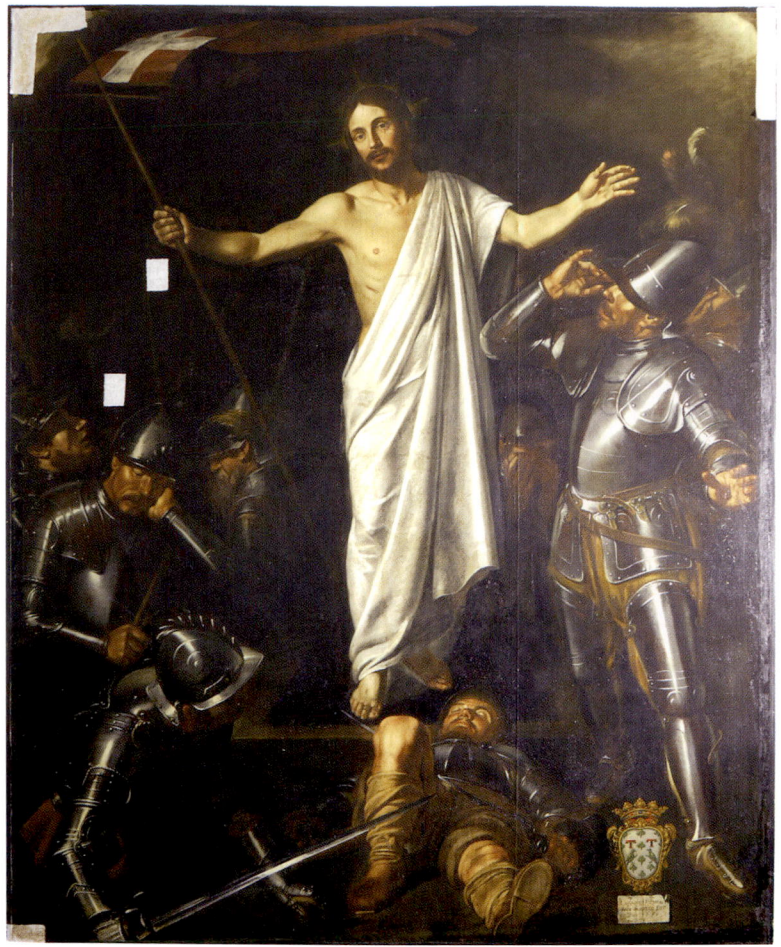

Fig. 260
Louis Finson, *The Resurrection*, Saint-Jean-de-Malte, Aix-en-Provence, oil on canvas, 218 x 168 cm. (before restoration).

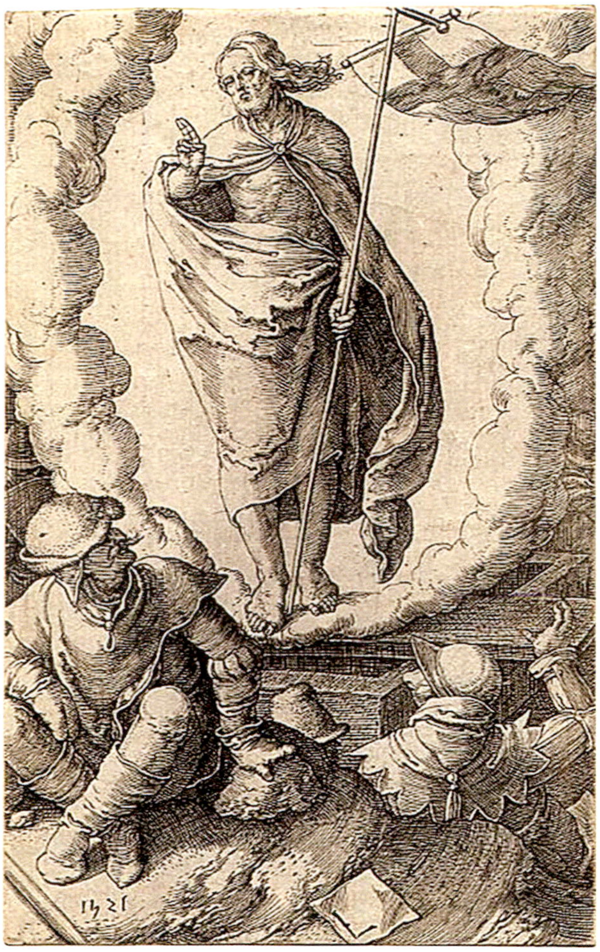

Fig. 261
Lucas van Leyden, *The Resurrection*, engraving, 11.5 x 7.4 cm.

as evidenced by a print he produced at about the same time as Mocetto. I shall return shortly to Robetta's outstanding composition.

Cecco's audacious visualization of the Resurrection is not totally unprecedented. It is important to keep this in mind in order to comprehend why Cecco's Chicago picture was rejected, then resold, after the patron had already paid for it. Exceptionally, numerous documents permit us to reconstruct the painting's commissioning. In September 1619, Piero Guicciardini, an agent of the Medici Grand Duke in Rome, engaged Cecco to depict a large *Resurrection*. By June 1620, the painting, destined for the Guicciardini Chapel in Santa Felicita, Florence, was ready to join the other two altarpieces soon to be placed there: an *Adoration of the Shepherds* by Gerrit Honthorst (at the Uffizi, Florence, almost entirely destroyed in 1993) and a *Crucifixion* by Spadarino, now lost.[11] As it turned out, Cecco's picture never went to its original destination. By October 1620, Guicciardini had already decided to rid himself of the picture; most likely, he sold it to Cardinal Scipione Borghese for 160 *scudi*, losing 40 *scudi* in the transaction. A year later, Guicciardini engaged Antonio Tempesta to replace Cecco's painting. There is no doubt that, as he himself put it, Guicciardini had not been "satisfied" with Cecco's work. To avoid any confusion, it must be said that Guicciardini in decorating his family

11   For the Chicago *Resurrection*, see Spear 1971, 82-4; Corti 1989, 125-33; Marini 1993, 175, note 38; Longhi 1999-2000, 1:22 [1943]; and esp. Papi 2001, 132-5, no 16. For the Guicciardini Chapel in Santa Felicita and Honthorst's almost entirely destroyed *Adoration of the Shepherds*, see Judson and Ekkart 1999, 61-3, no. 22; and Papi 2003 b. For Spadarino, see Papi 2003 a.

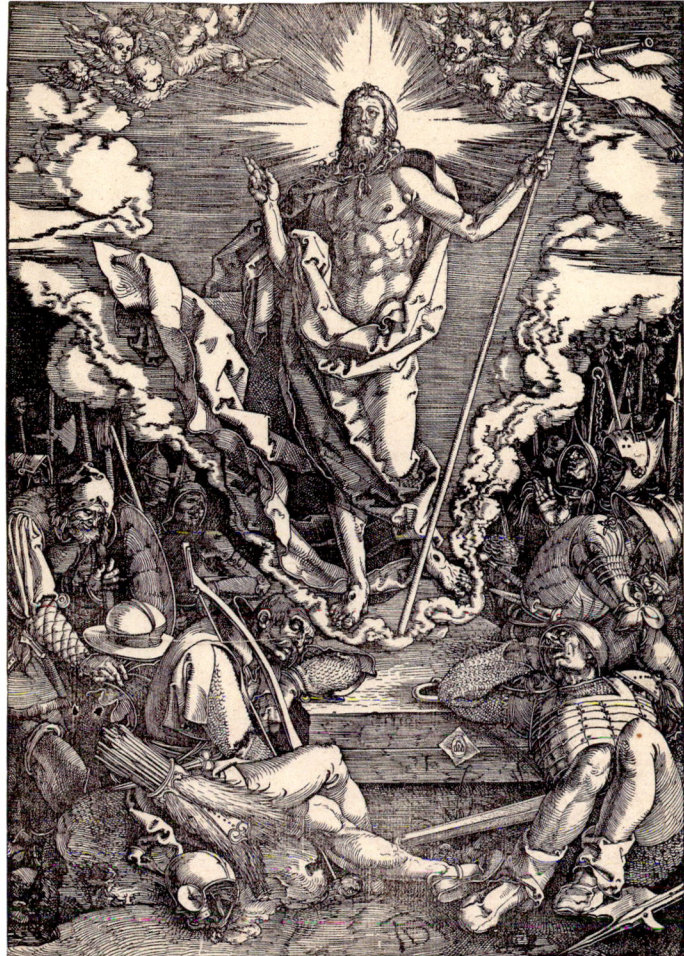

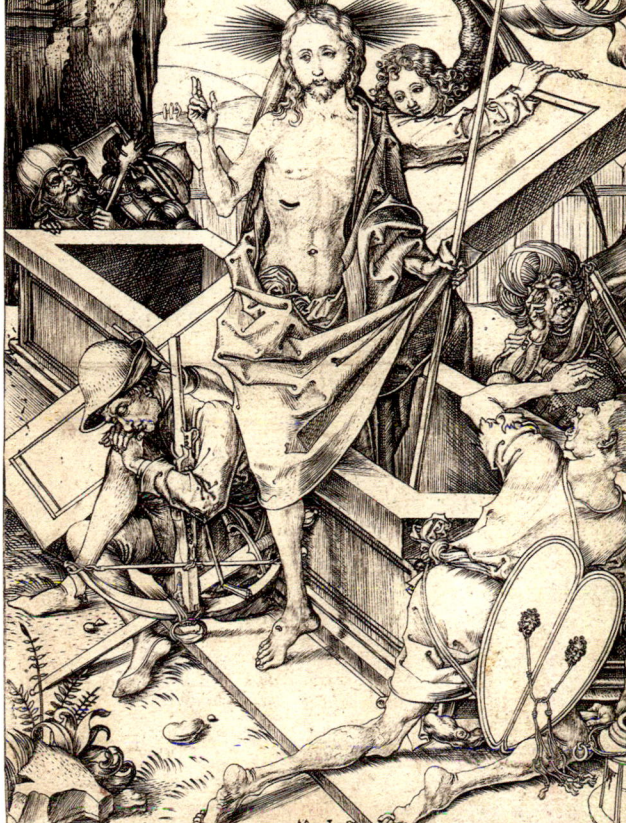

Fig. 262
Albrecht Dürer, *The Resurrection*, woodcut, 38.9 x 27.6 cm.

Fig. 263
Martin Schongauer, *The Resurrection*, engraving, 16.3 x 11.6 cm.

chapel in Santa Felicita deliberately called in painters from the circle of Caravaggio's emulators: Honthorst and Spadarino, of course, but also Cecco who had been the master's apprentice and "boy" for a very long time. In other words, Guicciardini's rejection was not dictated by ideological prejudice. He knew the reputation of Caravaggio and his followers and arguably expected to obtain paintings that were not exactly canonical. Yet he was repulsed by Cecco's composition, and this is irrefutable evidence that he found something very disturbing in it.

Guicciardini must have known about Caravaggio's eccentric *Resurrection* in Sant'Anna dei Lombardi, Naples, executed in 1609, just a few months before the painter's death;[12] nevertheless, he did not hesitate to commission from Cecco, the master's closest follower, a painting of the same subject. Conversely, Cecco must have felt challenged to compete with Caravaggio in his first public commission: until then, it seems that Cecco had only made paintings for private galleries. Surprisingly enough, Cecco did not by any means imitate Caravaggio's *Resurrection*: with sheer audacity, he imagined a sophisticatedly original composition, something never seen before and which would remain unparalleled. Any comparison between Caravaggio and Cecco's paintings is almost impossible: the Naples *Resurrection* was destroyed in 1798, and no copy of it has survived. Yet it can be easily established that the two pictures radically differ from one another. In his 1674

12   For the painting, see Cinotti 1983, 572, no. 112; Bologna 1992, 97-107; and Marini 2005, 582-3.

Le finezze de' pennelli italiani, Luigi Scaramuccia relates that Caravaggio represented "Christ not as is usually done, lithe and triumphant aloft, but [he depicted him] with his fierce coloring as he sets a foot on the ground outside the sepulcher, the other [foot] inside." Scaramuccia defines Caravaggio's invention as "extravagant" and "bizarre," arguing that the painting, despite its obvious novelty, deserves censure for its lack of decorum.[13] Bernardo de Dominici, in his 1742 *Vite de' pittori, scultori e architetti napoletani* inveighs against Caravaggio's *Resurrection*, noting that "Our Lord exits the tomb as if scared: a vile idea, and indecent with relation to the person represented."[14] More interestingly, in his 1763 *Voyage d'Italie* Charles-Nicolas Cochin, who does not know the author's name, marvels at his "singular imagination" in depicting Christ "not in the air, but walking among the guards," thereby "akin to a convict who flees from his guards." Cochin also touches upon Christ's complexion, specific in his view to "an emaciated man who has suffered."[15]

In 1951, Roberto Longhi suggested that Louis Finson's 1610 *Resurrection* in Saint-Jean-de-Malte, Aix-en-Provence, must have been inspired by Caravaggio's Naples picture (Fig. 260).[16] Unfortunately, this suggestion is entirely unsubstantiated, for Finson's *Resurrection* does not match the description of Caravaggio's painting as evoked by Scaramuccia, de Dominici, and Cochin. More importantly, Finson, a Flemish painter, resorted to the northern Renaissance tradition, especially but not exclusively to Albrecht Dürer[17] and Lucas van Leyden,[18] in imagining his Christ miraculously stepping over the empty tomb, his arms outflung as if preparing for ascension (Figs. 261, 262). The boldly foreshortened soldier asleep in the foreground also recalls Dürer's example. That said, Caravaggio's painting might in a sense have inspired Finson, who places Christ very close to the guards, moving amidst them toward the viewer. The Aix-en-Provence *Resurrection* was most likely executed in Naples, prior to Finson's arrival in Provence. Therefore, it can be inferred that the composition still resonates with echoes from Caravaggio's then very recent picture. In whatever way he might have modified and elaborated upon the original, Finson could not bring himself to depict Jesus' disquiet and unsettlement while re-awakening to life among soldiers. Furthermore, Finson determined not to follow Caravaggio in representing the resurrected Christ as he leaps out of the tomb, one foot in and the other outside. Yet Caravaggio's "bizarre" invention was not really unprecedented. For instance, in a print by Martin Schongauer Jesus strides to the light as his left leg remains in the tomb (Fig. 263).[19] It would come as no surprise if, once again, Caravaggio derived his "extravagant" idea from the early northern tradition as popularized by prints. In this way, he ensured the originality of his picture, thereby short-circuiting the beholder's expectations. If this

13 Scaramuccia 75-6: "Ed una di queste si fu una tavola d'altare situata nella chiesa di Sant'Anna dei Lombardi, ov'è la Ressurezzione di Cristo, come altresì un'altra nel tempio della Misericordia sopra l'altar maggiore, nella cui per appunto vi espresse le Sette Opere della Misericordia con modo pittoresco ed in tutto bizzarro, e doppo ciò aver veduto si tragittarono di bel nuovo nella sodetta chiesa di Sant'Anna a rimirar più curiosamente l'altra, e quando osservarono il Cristo non come d'ordinario far si suole, agile e trionfante per l'aria, ma, con quella sua fierissima maniera di colorire, con un piede dentro e l'altro fuori del sepolcro posando in terra, restarono per simile stravaganza con qualche apprensione, tanto che richiese Girupeno al Genio suo maestro se potea immaginarsi per che ciò avesse fatto il Caravagio. A che rispose il Genio: Quantunque questo pittore abbi dato in tal bizzarria e che per essa ne sia stato gradito, piacendo ad ogn'uno la novità dell'invenzioni, non resta però ch'ei non ne possa venirne (da coloro che sanno) alquanto biasimato, essendo uscito assai da quel decoro che si conviene alla persona di Cristo Signor Nostro."

14 De Dominici, II, 2:275: "[Caravaggio] fece per la chiesa di Sant'Anna della nazione lombarda tre quadri per una cappella, con figurare in quello dell'altare la resurrezzione del Signore, che quasi con ispavento esce dal suo sepolcro: idea bassa ed indecente al rappresentato."

15 Cochin, 1:171-2: "Dans la troisième chapelle, à gauche, on voit un tableau représentant la Résurrection de Jésus-Christ. C'est une imagination singulière, le Christ n'est point en l'air et passe en marchant au travers des gardes: ce qui donne une idée basse et le fait ressembler à un coupable qui s'échappe de ses gardes. D'ailleurs le caractère de la nature est d'un homme maigre et qui a souffert. La composition du côté de l'agencement pittoresque est fort belle et la manière en est ferme et ressentie avec goût. Il est fort noirci. On ignore le nom de l'auteur. Ce morceau est beau."

16 Longhi 1999-2000, 1:100. For Finson's painting, see Bodart 1970, 72-4, no. 1.

17 See Hütt 1980, 2:1546; and Schoch et al. 2001, 2:211-2, no. 165.

18 See Kok et al. 1996, 71-7, esp. 76.

19 See Bernhard 1980, 69; and Béguerie 1991, 392, no. G95.

is true, this can also explain why Cecco in his *Resurrection* resorted to narrative motifs generally to be found in the quattrocento pictorial tradition. I shall return to this point soon.

To have an idea of what Jesus' expression might have looked like in the Naples *Resurrection*, it is necessary to consider Battistello Caracciolo's *c.*1615 *Liberation of Saint Peter* (Fig. 264).[20] This picture, well documented, is still located at the Pio Monte della Misericordia, Naples, close to Caravaggio's 1606-1607 *Seven Acts of Mercy*. Battistello was deeply influenced by Caravaggio, whom he must have known during the master's first and second sojourns in Naples. In the *Liberation of Saint Peter*, the old apostle creeps through the dark dungeon, a radiant angel escorting him and pointing to the exit. Perhaps distrusting his divine rescuer, Peter stares intently and exhales deeply, as if panting, afraid of awakening the sleeping guards around him. Battistello stages the flight episode with consummate ability: he places Peter and the angel in a clearing, surrounded by silent soldiers, some admirably back-lit, two others revealed by the raking light slanting across the foreground. Intuitively beholders imagine the scene's muteness, and through and with Peter they look around to detect the slightest motion from the guards. Battistello manages through visual devices—

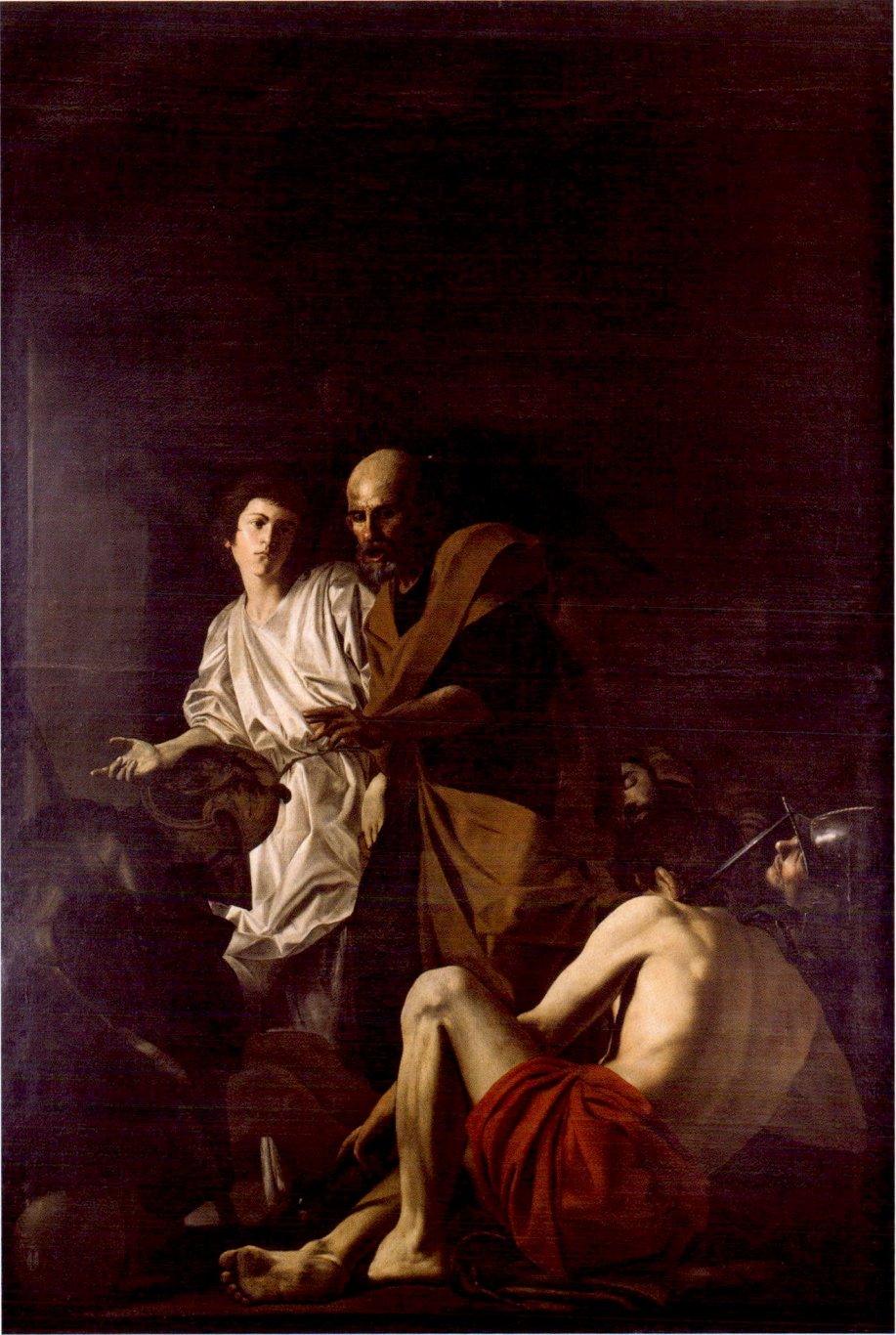

Fig. 264
Battistello (Giovan Battista) Caracciolo, *The Liberation of Saint Peter*, Pio Monte della Misericordia, Naples, oil on canvas, 310 x 207 cm.

mostly lighting, expression, and attitude—to give an impression of profound silence. At the same time, he engenders a mighty effect of suspense by emphasizing Peter's fearful face. In fact, the apostle's anti-heroic expression contradicts the viewer's anticipation: conditioned by centuries of iconographic habit, beholders are no longer sure whether Peter will soon be safe, entrusted as he is to the angel's watchful care. In and of itself, this unusual detail complicates the story's outcome,

20 See Causa S. 2000, 182-3, no. A33.

21 See Causa Picone 1993, 82; and Causa S. 2000, 155, no.

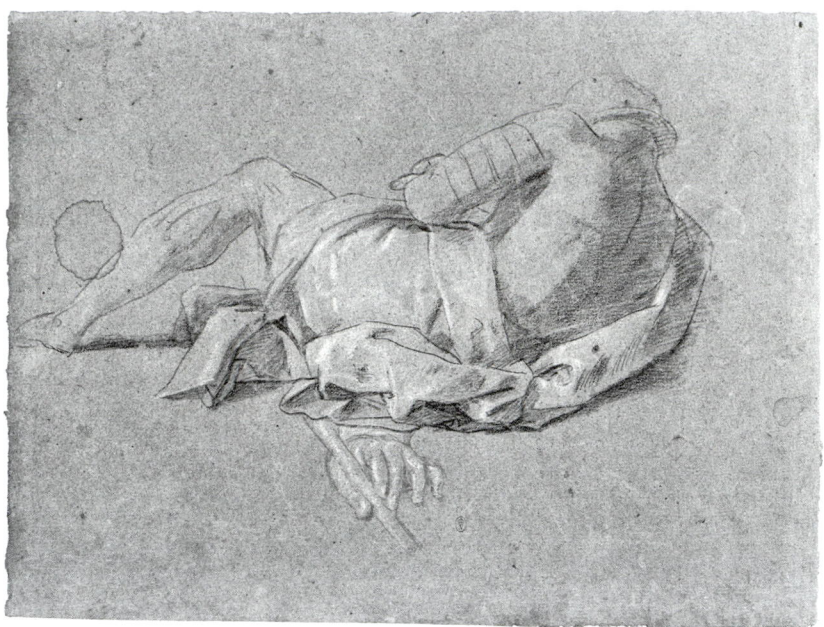

Fig. 265
Battistello (Giovan Battista) Caracciolo, *Study of a Soldier*, Musée du Louvre, Paris, black chalk and red chalk heightened with white on blue paper, 21.4 x 28.2 cm.

by interfering with the mechanisms of expectation and reconfiguration typical of early modern spectatorship. It is also noteworthy that Battistello was not pilloried on account of Peter's timorous expression. To borrow Cochin's description of Caravaggio's *Resurrection*, Battistello's Peter resembles a convict who escapes from his guards, his action likewise qualifying as utterly vile and indecent according to seventeenth- and eighteenth-century notion of decorum. Battistello's picture helps us visualize Christ's attitude in Caravaggio's lost *Resurrection*: his body still bearing the signs of the tortures he had endured during the Passion, a vulnerable Jesus abandons his tomb cautiously, maybe fearing to disrupt the guards' siesta and, ultimately, to fall again into their custody. In the Naples *Resurrection*, we undoubtedly lost one of Caravaggio's most subversive paintings.

Returning to Battistello, three studies of sleeping soldiers, none of them directly used in the *Liberation of Saint Peter*, attest to the painter's accuracy in preparing the composition. One of these drawings, executed with chalk, sanguine, and highlighted with lead white on blue paper, now in the Louvre, Paris (Fig. 265),[21] shows a soldier lying down, seen from behind, the outmost contours of his body zigzagging in quiet symmetry; the detail of a hand holding a rod appears underneath. This study somehow relates to the figure of the guard, bare torso and legs, ensconced in the right foreground of the *Liberation of Saint Peter* (Fig. 266). It has already been noted that, not unexpectedly, the figure in the Louvre drawing prefigures that of the slumbering soldier in the foreground of Cecco's *Resurrection* (Fig. 267). No other follower of Caravaggio evokes Cecco's art more closely than Battistello himself. Both Battistello and Cecco tend to imbricate and intertwine bodies together and to create syncopated rhythms by making the canvas' margins encroach upon, and press against, the figures; they also like collapsing the distance between the painting's upper and lower tiers. Most importantly, Battistello and Cecco, albeit diversely, play with the backdrops' shallowness; they expand or contract the pictorial depth by interlocking surfaces and body parts without verisimilitude.

In Battistello's c.1620 *Noli Me Tangere* at the Museo Civico, Prato (Fig. 268),[22] the work's horizontal format, as well as its half-figures and close-up view, suggests that Battistello relied on *Chist as a Gardener Appearing to the Magdalene* engraved by Lucas van Leyden (Fig. 269).[23] There Jesus, dressed in a tunic and sporting a gardener's hat, brushes Mary Magdalene's forehead with two fingers—an apocryphal account popular in the sixteenth and seventeenth centuries relates this event.[24] Kneeling before the Savior, the woman lifts the lid of the ointment vase, her head tipping forward, her gaze lowered out of modesty or in contemplation. Reverting to the more orthodox

G50. Another drawing by Battistello of a sleeping soldier, at the Statens Museum for Kunst, Copenhagen, related to the same theme, has been recently exhibited by Spinosa 2009, 2:56, no. 3.8.

22   See Causa S. 2000, 189, no. A60.

23   See Kok et al. 1996, 95, no. 77.

24   See Malgouyres 2000.

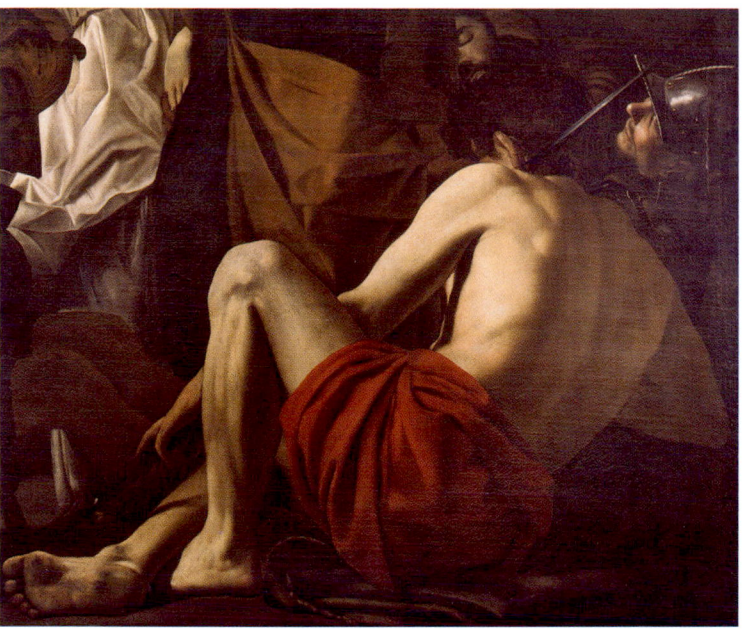

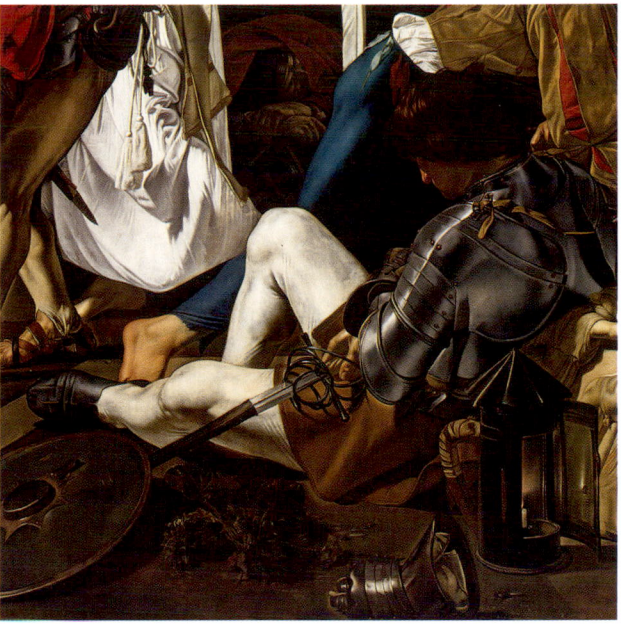

Fig. 266
Battistello (Giovan Battista) Caracciolo, *The Liberation of Saint Peter*, Pio Monte della Misericordia, Naples, oil on canvas, 310 x 207 cm., detail.

Fig. 267
Cecco del Caravaggio (Francesco Boneri), *The Resurrection*, Art Institute, Chicago, oil on canvas, 339 x 199.5 cm., detail.

version of this scene, Battistello represents the Magdalene's attempt to grasp the resurrected Christ, who in turn keeps the woman at bay with the words "Do not touch me." A priori, the subject of the *Noli Me Tangere* might lend itself to exalting the opposition between the human and the divine in terms of visibility and tactility: Mary Magdalene groping for untimely touch is nonetheless able to see momentarily the resurrected Christ. As a general rule, though, artists exempt themselves from problematizing the relationship between sight and touch in regard to this subject. Notably, this does not apply to Battistello.

Kneeling in front of the Savior while laying the ointment vase on an invisible support, the Magdalene dooms herself never to touch the resurrected Christ. Indeed, her head tilted upward and her lips parted as if whispering Christ's name—John's Gospel (20,16) states that she calls him "master" at that very moment—she is patently unable to see the divine apparition. On the other hand, watching her while ordering her not to touch him, Jesus seeks to stop her, but in a contradictory manner. Instead of eschewing contact, his protruding left arm and partially lit palm—where the nail wound is still visible—reach toward the Magdalene. The beautiful *pentimento* still discernible on the canvas betrays Battistello's hesitation in assessing the hand's position. Curiously enough, the arm's strong thrust is spatially dislocated, and the halting palm does not align itself with the Magdalene's head. Therefore, not only would the Savior fail to stop the woman, but his gesture is also useless because of the Magdalene's ephemeral blindness.

Battistello's interplay of the visible, the haptic, and the audible depends on a collage-like structure of the image. Whereas the Magdalene is seen in an angular view from below, it is difficult to pin down Jesus' location in relation to the viewer: his spotlit torso recedes toward the background while his face is disproportionately large by comparison with his out-jutting arm that supposedly pierces forward. Evidently Battistello did not care about perspective when it came to bending his figures in accordance with his pictorial goals. By warping space and proportions, Battistello aimed at a twofold objective: enhancing the eeriness of the miracle and, more important, dramatizing the disconnections between the visible, the tactile, and the acoustic in the precise context of the human-divine interrelations. In Chapter 9, I showed how Caravaggio achieved similar effects in his

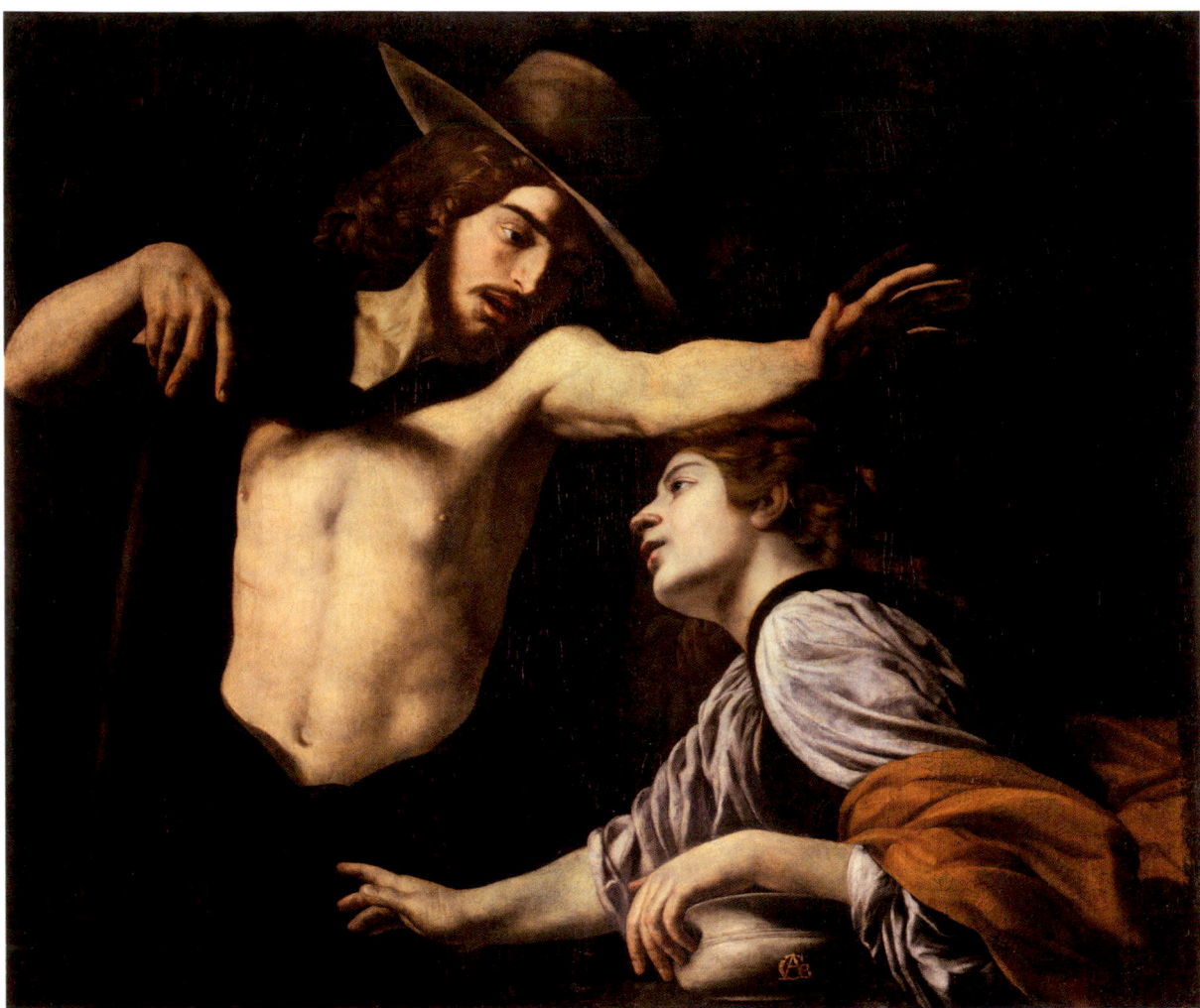

Fig. 268
Battistello (Giovan Battista) Caracciolo, *Noli Me Tangere*, Museo Civico, Prato, oil on canvas, 109 x 130.5 cm.

Supper at Emmaus at the National Gallery, London, and I discussed the significance of the apostle's arm hovering on the right that, despite its length, runs short of touching the Savior. In light of Caravaggio's novel solutions in this regard, it is fair to argue that Cecco and Battistello went well beyond the master's audacity.

In the *Noli Me Tangere*, the incommunicability between the divine and the human reaches its climax. If Mary Magdalene is both blind to Jesus' epiphany and unable to verify his corporal presence, the beholder is lured into believing that Christ himself lacks corporality by failing to visually intercept Mary's contact. Circumscribed by the two figures' innermost contours, a rough diamond of black emptiness indicates the distance separating the human and the divine. With ingenuity Battistello links Jesus to the Magdalene through the intersecting dialogue they perform on the canvas; the sounds of the woman's invocation and the man's command cross the painting's surface and restore the communication. Thus the acoustic dimension of Battistello's painting is reinforced in direct proportion to the narrative disjunctions I have just exposed. At will, beholders can imagine the Magdalene guided by Jesus' voice to sense his presence and Jesus suddenly reacting to the woman's whisper and groping out of fear of being touched. Without these acoustic effects, the picture would be instantly deprived of a vital element, one integral to its dramatic intensity and finality.

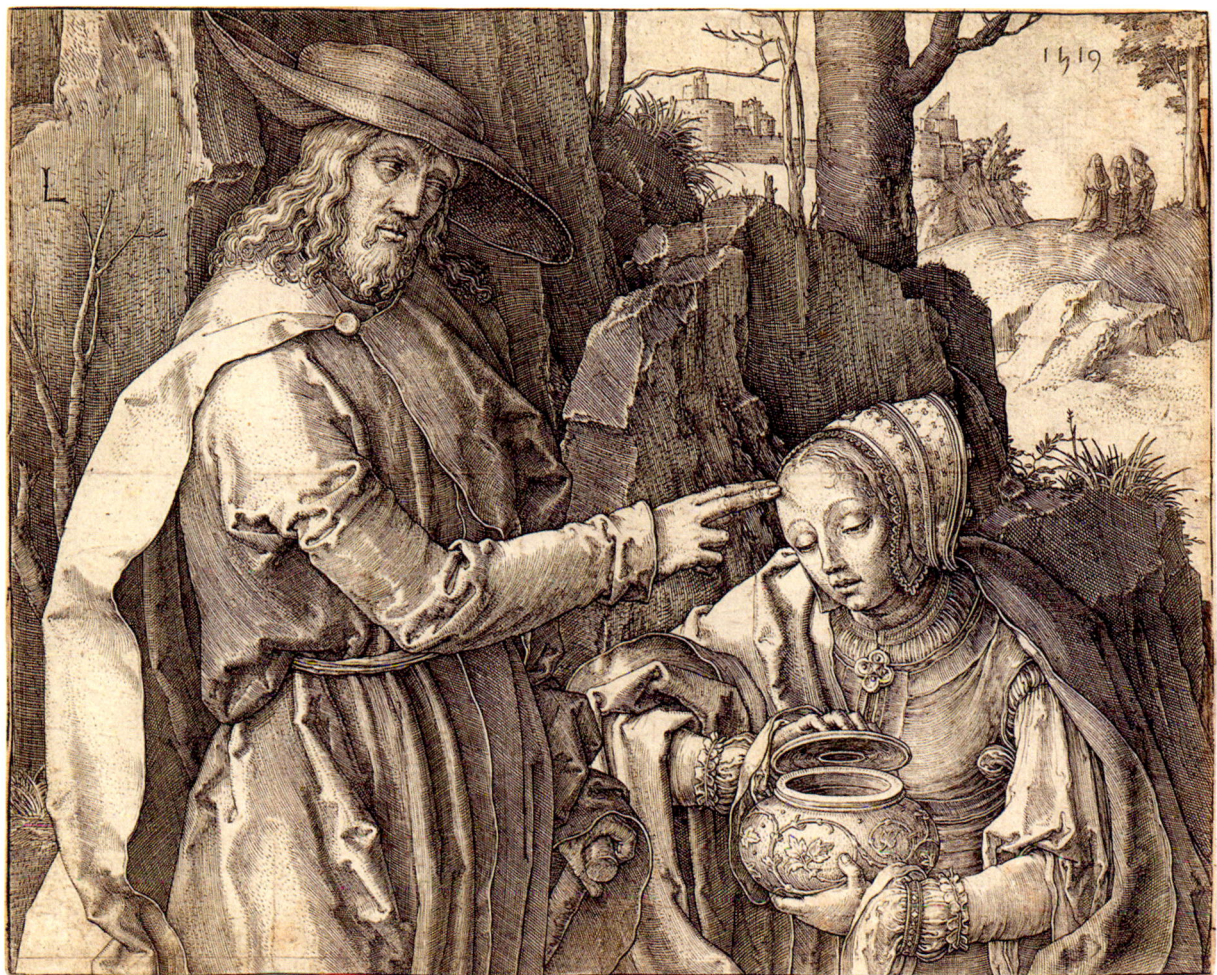

Fig. 269
Lucas van Leyden, *Christ as a Gardener Appearing to Mary Magdalene*, engraving, 13.2 x 16.8 cm.

The subtle miscommunications orchestrated by Battistello in his *Noli Me Tangere* become pervasive disconnectedness in Cecco's *Resurrection*. The painting's gigantic scale accentuates the separateness of each figure by paradoxically binding them together in what appears a single space and narrative. About two thirds of the way up the picture, Cecco grafted the central figure of an out-of-scale resurrected Christ onto the composition's lower register; there, Jesus' bare foot impinges on, but does not touch, the angel's head: a device already found in Battistello's Prato picture, which I shall discuss later. In turn, by raising his hand, the equally out-of-scale angel trespasses on the upper register. Together the divine messenger and Christ form an oblique axis that serves as the structural and visual pivot of the action. The angel's eloquent gesture of raising the hand, tied to the curvilinear silhouettes of his wings through his left arm, determines an elliptical motif counterbalanced, but also intensified, by the spanning contour of the soldier's bent figure to the right, whose curvilinear outline is in turn reiterated by the dangling body represented on a fragmented relief underneath: the section of an ancient *Death of the Niobids*, of which a well preserved first-century example can be seen at the Hermitage, Saint Petersburg.[25] Its depiction of a dead man falling to the ground represents a witty counterpoint to the motif of Christ's ascending body characteristic of a Resurrection.

25   See Papi 2001, 133.

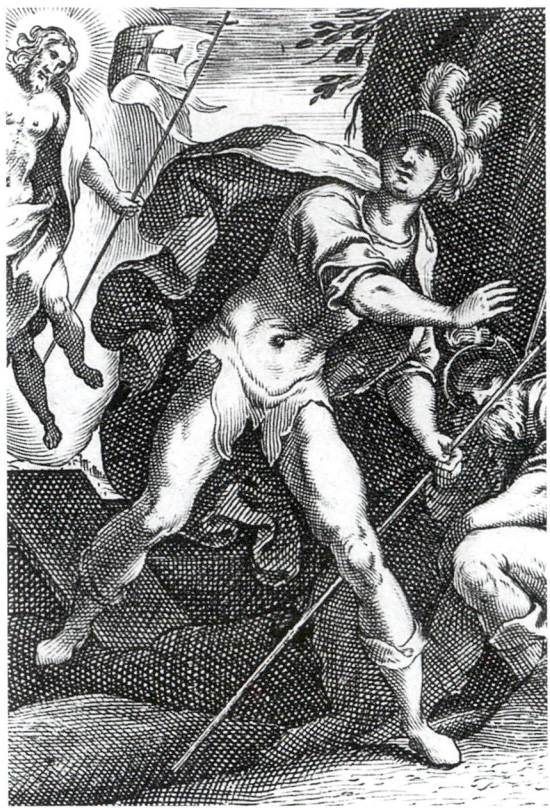

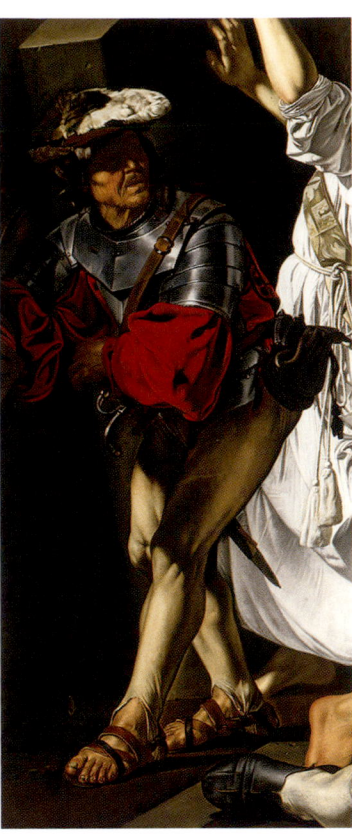

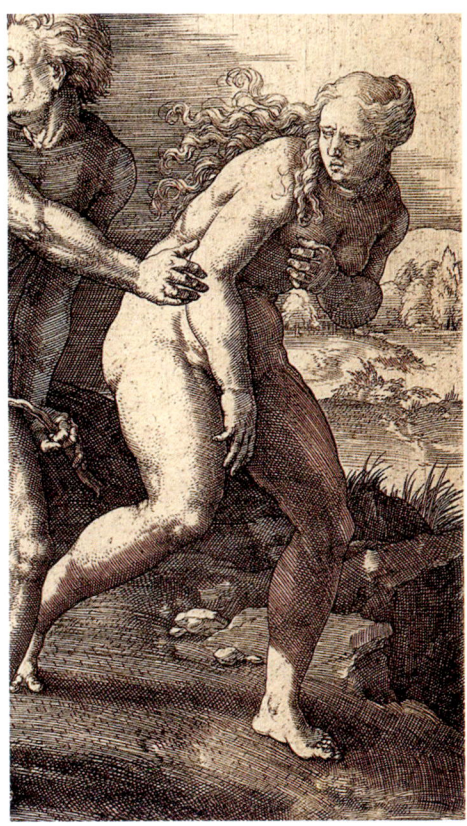

Fig. 270
Luca Ciamberlano after Raffaello Sciaminossi,
The Resurrection, engraving, 9.9 x 15.3 cm., detail.

Fig. 271
Cecco del Caravaggio (Francesco
Boneri), *The Resurrection*, Art
Institute, Chicago, oil on canvas,
339 x 199.5 cm., detail.

Fig. 272
Lucas van Leyden, *Adam and Eve Chased from
Paradise*, engraving,
16.4 x 11.5 cm, detail.

Both the angel and the bent guard are visually related to two other figures, the man asleep in the foreground, and the old soldier to the left. Farther on, at the right, a guard, seen from behind, tries to hobble his companion by holding his right shoulder and left wrist. Structurally, Cecco conceived a wondrous clockwork of action and attitudes: an irresistible wave of figures sweeping the lower register from the left to the right, the slumbering soldier breaking and slowing its motion. At the top, canonically, a blessing Christ crowns the composition and triumphs over the viewer. Yet, upon closer observation, one comes to the conclusion that these figures do not belong together; they certainly dovetail with, and overlap, each other, but their actions transcend the network of visual interconnections on which pictorial verisimilitude rested at the time.

To begin with, the posture of the legs of the arching soldier in the right foreground implies that he has just run from the left in order to unsheathe his sword. His impetus is not dissimilar from that of fleeing figures frequently present in the iconography of the Resurrection. The fugitive soldier in the right foreground of Luca Ciamberlano's engraved *Resurrection* (Fig. 270)[26] might be compared to Cecco's guard. Of course, their actions have different meanings: the one, frightened, dashes away from Christ while the other, irritated, tries to assault whatever threatens him. Both nonetheless turn their eyes upward, facing the beholder. Ciamberlano's puppet-like figure acts almost mechanically, his gaze betraying conventional fear and puzzlement. By contrast, Cecco's guard is truly responding to an aggression, his mouth open as if to scream or menace. More importantly, the source of his belligerency is undetectable. He might be the only figure in the

26   For the print, see Buffa 1983, 48. See also Bellini and Leach
1983, 72, no. 14 (31).

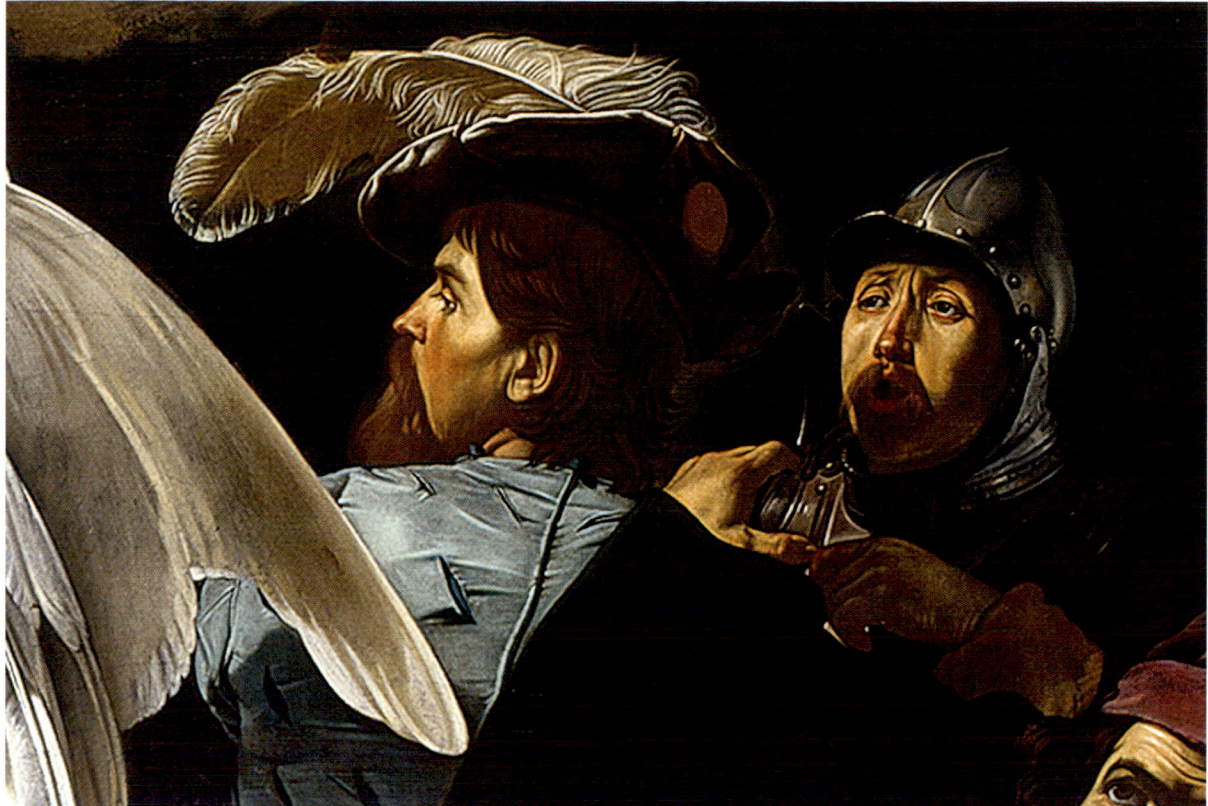

Fig. 273
Cecco del Caravaggio (Francesco Boneri), *The Resurrection*, Art Institute, Chicago,
oil on canvas, 339 x 199.5 cm., detail.

picture aware of Christ's epiphany above, and in this case he seemingly rushes to combat the miraculous fugitive. But he more probably cannot pinpoint the origin of the rumble or blaze that has unexpectedly awakened him. I am inclined to interpret his gaze as directed not to Christ, but to the upper off-scene. The narrative context corroborates this interpretation.

Nearby an old soldier skulks away with circumspection, ready to grab his sword should he be attacked. Hunched forward as he gazes backward, this guard looks rather like the parody of an Eve just chased from Eden, as represented by Lucas van Leyden in a 1529 engraving (Figs. 271, 272).[27] It is also possible that Cecco had in mind one of the woodcuts of Hans Holbein's 1538 *The Dance of Death* series: *Death and the Count*.[28] The orientation of the old guard's head and the cautiousness of his motion clearly express his blindness to both the angel just behind him and Christ above. Whatever caught him off guard, thunder or lightning, has momentarily vanished, and in the meantime he leaves the sepulcher as if anticipating ambush by an invisible or inaudible presence. If one takes a glimpse at the right background, where the "bravo" with the feathered beret and the helmeted guard cluster together, it becomes clear that neither of these figures understand where the menace comes from. Turned leftward, the "bravo" glances to the sepulcher's entrance, his beret's feather hindering him from discovering Christ above. The other guard's gaze, illuminated by a breach of light, expresses clueless confusion and awe (Fig. 273). Everywhere around the angel and beneath Christ, soldiers are fighting the invisible and the inaudible, separately and with uncoordinated reactions.

27 See Kok et al. 1996, 35, no. 4.

28 See Müller 1997, 283, no. 105.32.

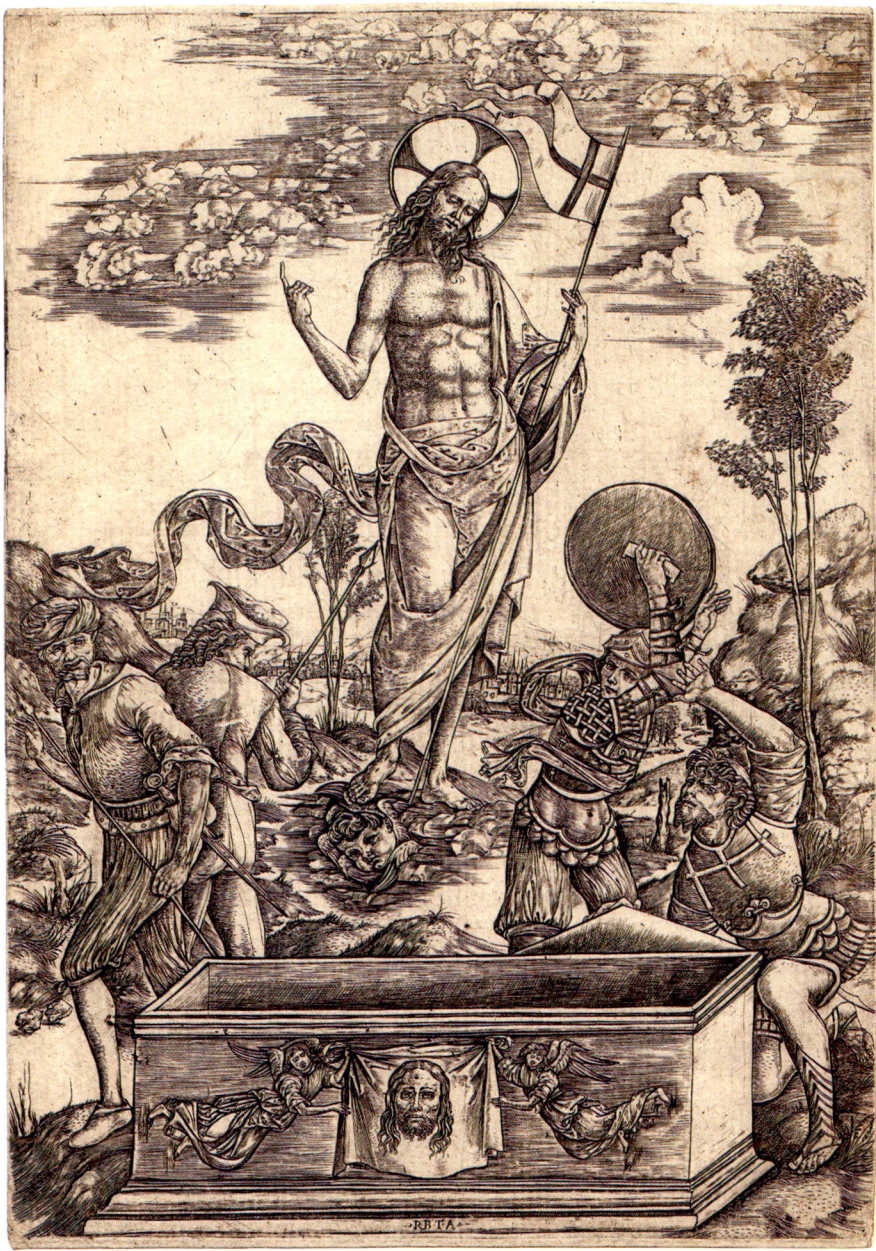

Fig. 274
Cristofano Robetta, *The Resurrection*, engraving, 29.9 x 21.6 cm.

Cecco's tragicomic melee is not entirely unparalleled: Cristofano Robetta tried out similar motifs in his early sixteenth-century engraved *Resurrection* (Fig. 274). To the left, a couple of guards, side-by-side and similar to Siamese twins, symmetrically rotate their torsos and faces in opposite directions, their gazes scrutinizing the empty sarcophagus and the ground respectively. To the right, a soldier in armor hoists his arms while lifting the shield in a desperate attempt to protect himself from an undetectable danger. His straying gaze and twisted posture equally bespeak his alienation. Close to the tomb, at the right, another soldier, crouched, uses his lifted arm as a screen against an invisible radiance streaming from above. At the center of the composition, a resurrected Christ levitates triumphantly, transparent to the men underneath yet plainly visible to the viewer. The eccentricity of this composition might have attracted Cecco and given him the opportunity to display his originality through skillful, brand-new variants of the soldiers' estranged attitudes. However, neither Robetta nor Mocetto, nor even Bellini, could have imagined anything as sacrilegious as Cecco's *Resurrection*. The extreme point of disruption in the Chicago painting lies in the visual disconnection between the radiant angel and the blessing Christ above.

There is no doubt that, because of his chromatic relevance and central position, the angel usurps the centrality of Christ's role in the *Resurrection*. Even more disconcerting, despite his proximity to the blessing Jesus, the angel's uplifted arm and finger point in a direction inexplicably divergent from the divine apparition above; they are oriented toward the dawn light filtering into the sepulcher through the pitch black air of the dying night. The strangeness of this narrative situation is increased by the angel's awareness of the beholder outside the canvas: not only does he neglect Christ's presence, but he also invites the viewer to look for the resurrected deity where he evidently is not. With explicit impertinence, the light inundates the angel's figure and magnifies his snow-white glow, whereas Jesus' body is eroded by the surrounding darkness. Last but not least, Cecco makes the angel's pointing arm and Christ's blessing arm rhyme together across the distance.

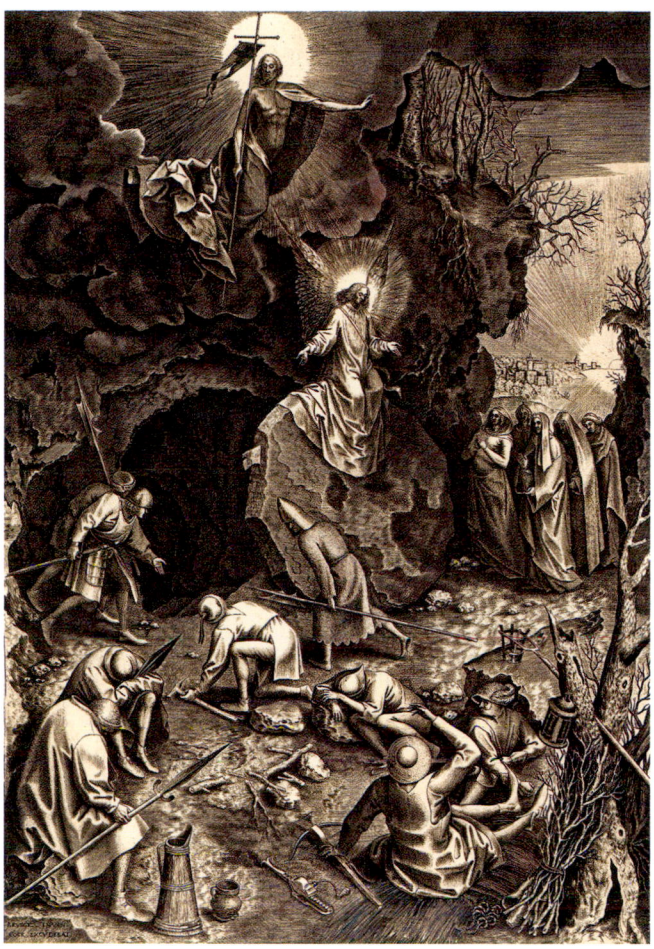

Fig. 275
Philips Galle after Pieter Brueghel the Elder, *The Resurrection*, engraving, 45.1 x 33 cm.

Yet it is the angel's gesture that visually predominates over Christ's, a detail at odds with the narrative theme and the religious importance of the Resurrection.

Cecco's composition is not the only visual source to show the angel intervening in the episode without acknowledging Christ's persona. And yet, in order to grasp the unprecedented scope of Cecco's invention, it is important to closely examine some of these other *Resurrections*. An extraordinary print by Philips Galle after Pieter Brueghel the Elder (Fig. 275)[29] shows the angel perched atop a hexagonal rock; he speaks to the holy women entering the scene from the right, revealing to them that the sepulcher is empty. Above him, but invisible to all the figures in the engraving, Jesus climbs to heaven. In this case the angel's unawareness of Christ's epiphany is accounted for by his narrative function: addressing the women, he introduces a sequence of the Resurrection subsequent to the sepulcher's supernatural opening. In a more complex manner, a print by Johan Sadeler I after Maarten de Vos represents two angels (Fig. 276):[30] the first, sitting on the tomb's rim, witnesses Christ's apotheosis with wonder. A second, placed at the sepulcher's entrance, observes the soldiers' uproar as he points to the sky. Far away, three silhouettes mark the holy women's arrival. By gazing outward and overlooking Christ, the second angel seemingly alludes to an upcoming episode of the story; he therefore serves as a narrative prolepsis. Nonetheless, the narrative indeterminacy of this angel's posture is disorienting, and somehow constitutes a precedent to Cecco's invention. Cecco transforms this ambivalence into pure enigma.

In 1596, Hendrick Goltzius designed and engraved a compelling *Resurrection* (Fig. 277).[31] In the foreground, a landsknecht leans on his halberd as if stealing a brief nap; half-asleep, he caresses the sheath of his sword ready to riposte if necessary. This important figure contrasts with the guards to the right, shrieking with fear and withdrawing. (In Cecco's picture, the soldier asleep in the foreground fulfills a similar dramatic role in contrast to his companions' turbulence. Leaning upon an ancient bas-relief, he lies in deep lethargy, one hand still wearing a metal glove, the other, bare, holding his sword hilt. In the immediate foreground, a second metal glove and a round shield appear randomly scattered around the soldier, along with a lantern: these elements of a military still life, through their inertness, accentuate the tournament of interacting bodies in the lower register, and around

29   For the print, see Dolders 1987, 138, no. 044; and Sellink and Leesberg 2001, 2:59, no. 172.

30   For the print, see Schuchman and De Hoop Scheffer 1996, 1:99, no. 433; and De Ramaix 1999, 236, no. 194.

31   See Strauss 1977, 2:612, no. 333.

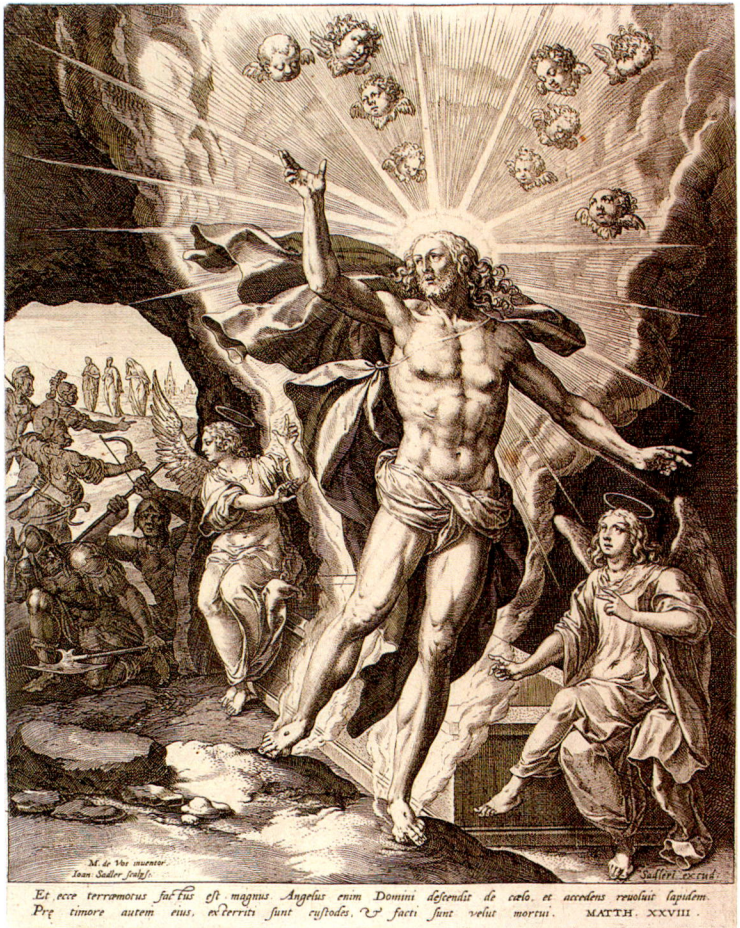

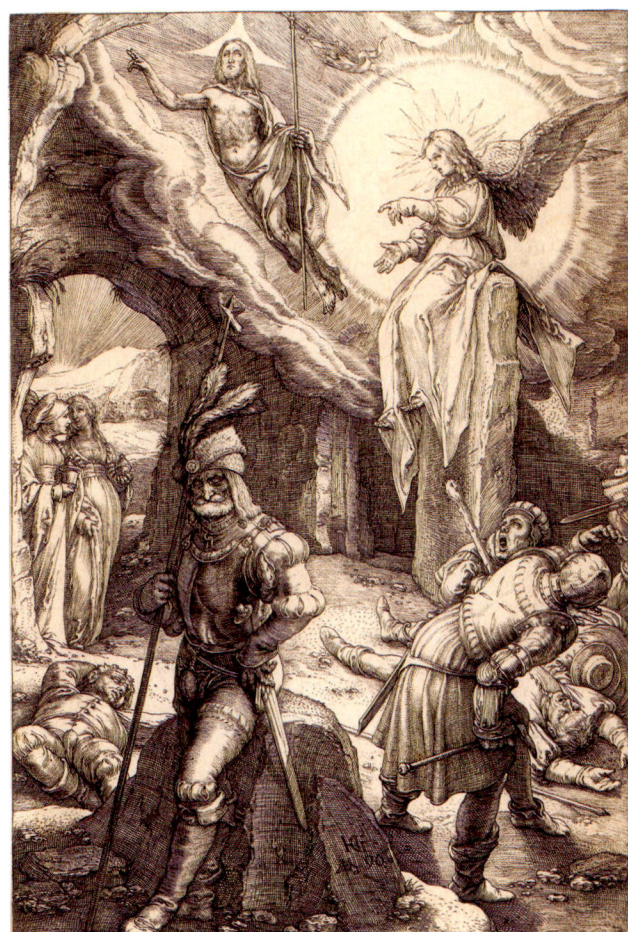

Fig. 276
Johan Sadeler I after Maarten de Vos, *The Resurrection*, engraving, 25 x 19.7 cm.

Fig. 277
Hendrick Goltzius, *The Resurrection*, engraving, 19.7 x 13 cm.

the angel). In Goltzius's engraving, in the middle ground, an angel sits on top of a rock, awaiting the women's arrival. Farther on, toward the upper margin, Christ flies away incognito. Although the narrative coherence in Goltzius' print is stretched beyond verisimilitude, the angel's task remains clear. Once again he is a transitional figure connecting two episodes, the miracle of the Resurrection and its discovery by the women. The angel's function is still more obvious in Santi di Tito's *c*.1574 *Resurrection* in Santa Croce, Florence,[32] of which a preparatory drawing (Art Institute, Chicago) also survives (Fig. 278). In this composition, Christ's feet are visually superimposed on the wings of the angel sitting at a distance. Evidently the divine messenger does not mind Jesus' presence: he points to the empty sepulcher while informing the three holy women about the epiphany. As I have just demonstrated, the figure of the angel may be disjoined from both the soldiers' attitude around him and Christ rising heavenward. However, this disconnectedness encompasses a chronological transition between two related episodes of the story: the opening of the tomb and the holy women's discovery of the epiphany. This factor does not apply to Cecco's *Resurrection*.

In the painting, the angel's conniving gaze assimilates the beholder to the holy women approaching the sepulcher;[33] his gesture definitely clarifies that the Savior has left the tomb and

32 An interesting discussion of Bronzino's *Resurrection* in Santissima Annunziata, Florence, as opposed to Santi di Tito's *Resurrection* in Santa Croce, within the context of Counter-Reformation painting, is in Lingo 2008, 145-7. For a survey of Santi di Tito's career and production, see Collareta in *Seicento Fiorentino* 1986, 3:161-3.

33 A similar empathetic identification of the viewer with a figure of the sacred *istoria* relating to the representation but absent from it is postulated by Pardo 2006 in connection with Savoldo's *Magdalene*.

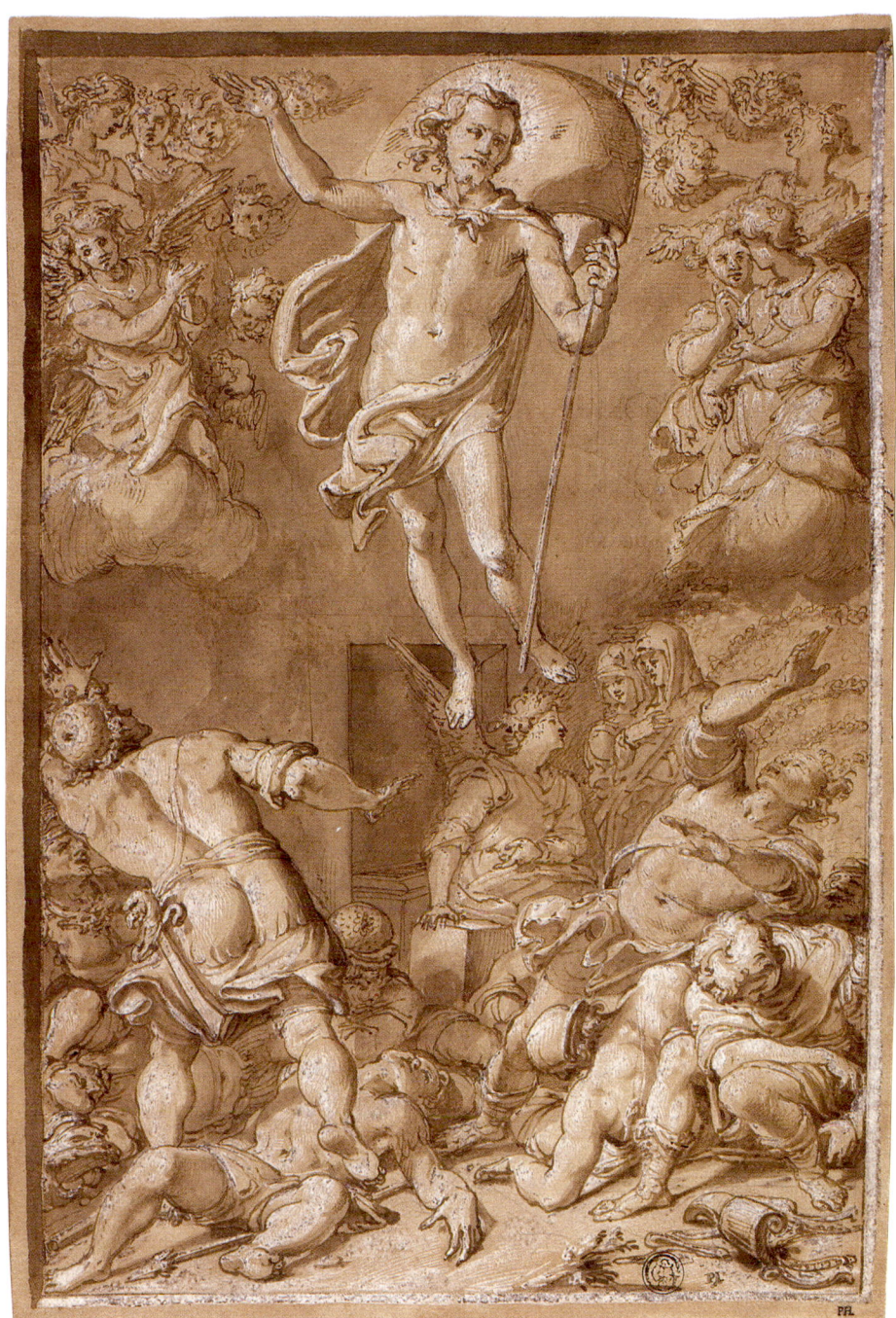

Fig. 278
Santi di Tito, *The Resurrection*, Art Institute, Chicago, pen and brown ink, brush and brown wash, heightened with white over traces of black chalk, 31.9 x 21.7 cm.

ascended to his Father. Yet even as he refers to an action in the recent past, the angel keeps pushing the once obstructing rock as if to remove it, even though the traces of the broken white wax seal upon the sepulcher's wall, which can be seen directly behind the angel's pointing finger, confirms that the place of the burial has already been unlocked. In other words, Cecco telescopes two moments of the story into a single action. To comprehend fully to what extent Cecco obscured the narrative structure and temporality of the Chicago painting, I quote from Federico Borromeo's *Della pittura sacra*:

513

In connection with the Resurrection, one must remark upon an error committed by many painters who represent the resurrecting Christ, and depict the soldiers around him filled with terror. It did not occur in this manner because the Savior was resuscitated without the soldiers being aware of it. But then, after some time, the soldiers became frightened and awoke because of the roar stirred by the angel, who shifted the rock of the sepulcher. It is also an error in this episode to depict the resurrecting Savior as the sepulcher opens, for glorious bodies do not need these sorts of openings, scripture also saying that it was the angel who removed the rock. Thus, when one represents the soldiers frightened, one should also show the angel shifting the rock or sitting atop it.[34]

It is particularly difficult to reconstitute the exact order of events leading up to the holy women's discovery of the empty tomb as reported by the Gospel. Disliking the idea that Christ's ethereal body might have needed to unlock the sepulcher in order to exit it like a common man, Borromeo sustains that the removal of the rock and the luminous and roaring epiphany of the angel followed the Savior's resurrection. Even if one dismisses the ambivalence of the angel's gesture in Cecco's painting and accepts the possibility that the rock's removal and the soldiers' panic occurred after Christ had left the sepulcher, the raw visual juxtaposition of the Savior and the angel greatly contributes to blurring the chronological unfolding of the Resurrection. As a consequence, viewers also lose their ability to reconfigure the episode with any coherence. To be sure, the Resurrection theme usually tolerates this sort of visual license and fluctuating temporality. Nevertheless, Cecco intentionally exploits the traditional incongruities of the iconography in order to alienate the divine not from the human, but from the divine itself. In fact, the angel and Christ incarnate two aspects of the divinity operating independently and without coordination, although they abut each other within the pictorial field.

The tiny interstice separating the two figures in the composition entails an abyssal failure of communication. The angel's centrality and misleading gesture do not allow viewers to construe his action as subordinate to Christ's resurrection. In the few cases I have touched upon, artists use space not only to distance the angel from Christ, but also to stagger temporality; through these figures' spatial intervals, beholders are intuitively invited to read the Resurrection story in two or more phases. In Cecco's *Resurrection*, the coexistence on a single plane of the angel and Christ tends to annul any temporal distinction: their two actions must be perceived as synchronous. Hence, within the fictive space, two divinities are visually in conflict with one another. Where is the real Christ? Is he already invisible and pure light, as the angel's pointing gesture indicates? Or is he still visible, wrapped in darkness yet glorious above the soldiers' tumult? In at least two instances, *The Calling of Saint Matthew* and *The Resurrection of Lazarus*, Caravaggio had disassociated the flow of light, conceived as a symbol of divinity and its action, from the figure of Christ. Here Cecco seems to push his master's experimentations to their extreme consequences.

By accentuating the duality between the divine light and the figure of Christ, Cecco provocatively asserts that pictorially speaking either representation of the divinity is valid, for both are purely conventional. I believe that the unsolved visual dichotomy and lack of coordination between the angel and Christ was the main reason why Piero Guicciardini refused Cecco's *Resurrection*. Initially an ingenious conceit, the two figures' disjunction and coalescence on Cecco's canvas audaciously and immediately reveals and brings to the fore the charge of subversion that ordinarily lurks

---

34 Borromeo, 83: "E intorno a questa Resurrezione, è da notarsi un fallo di molti pittori che fanno Cristo risorgente e attorno esprimono i soldati pieni di spavento. Non fu così imperoché resuscitò il Salvatore senza avvedersene i soldati. Ma indi poi a qualche spazio di tempo, per lo strepito che fece l'angelo, il qual angelo rivolse la pietra del monumento, essi si spaventarono e si destarono. Ed è eziandio errore in questo misterio il dipingere il Salvatore che resusciti aprendosi il monumento, poiché i corpi gloriosi non ne hanno bisogno di queste aperture, e anche perché l'istoria sacra dice che l'angelo rivolse la pietra. Però quando si esprime lo spavento dei soldati si dovrebbe esprimere l'angelo che rivolge la pietra, overo che si sieda sopra di essa."

in Caravaggio's similar inventions. The blind and deaf actions played out by the soldiers in the lower register inexorably exasperate the impression of invisibility and trans-audibility of Christ's presence. If around 1460 Giovanni Bellini started experimenting with acoustic effects to evoke the impression of divine transcendence; if Caravaggio at the beginning of the seventeenth century developed narrative inconsistencies to unveil the fictiveness of religious images; then Battistello, and especially Cecco, discovered the endless possibilities of dislocating the visible, the audible, and the tactile in the field of the *istoria*. Their pictorial experiments, however, were destined to clash with the dominant taste of their times, eminently attuned to congruity and verisimilitude. Guicciardini's rejection of Cecco's *Resurrection* is only one of the many episodes in which patrons and art theorists were blind and deaf to the artistic innovations inaugurated and advertised by Caravaggio and his followers.

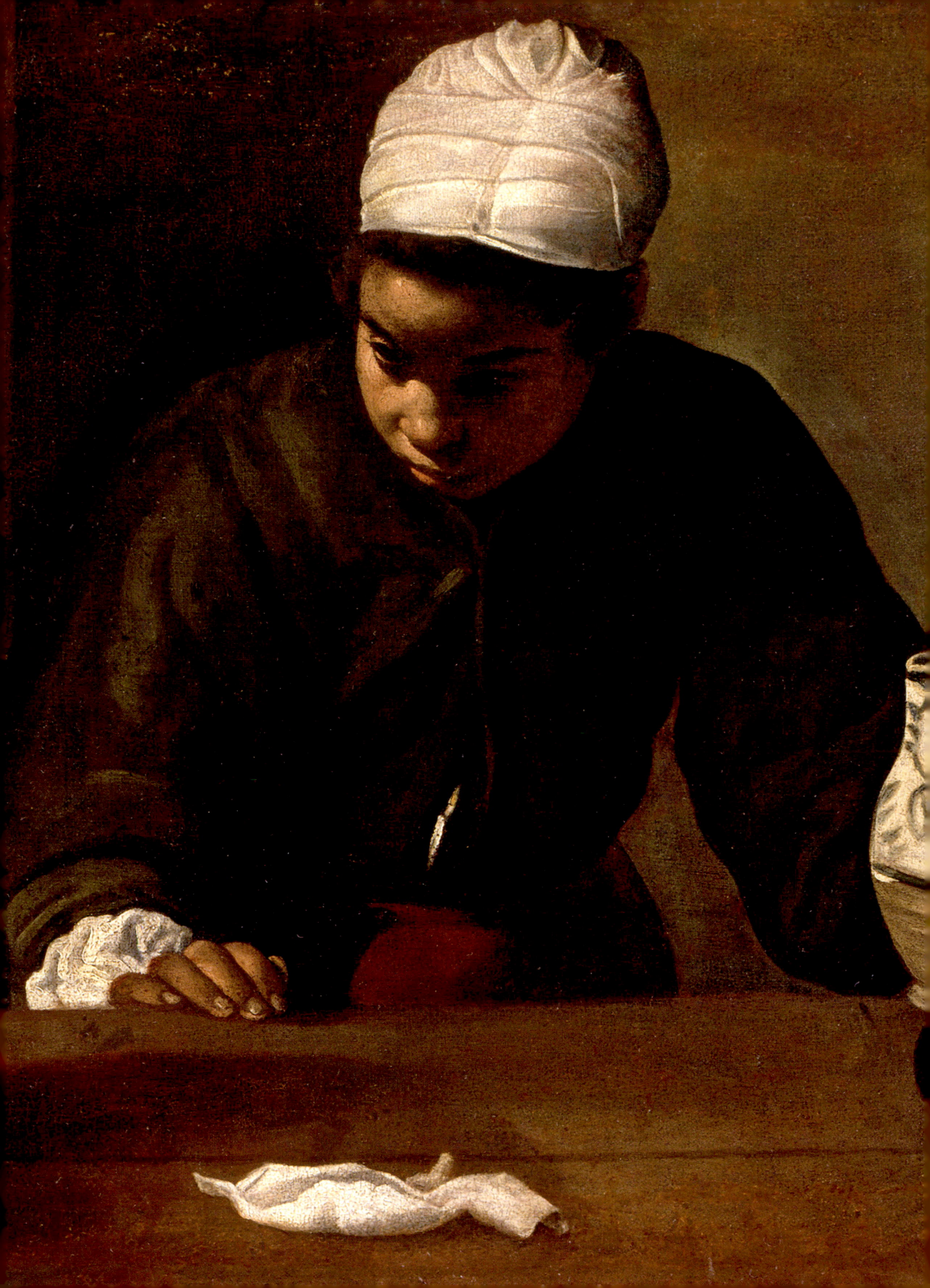

CHAPTER 16

The Antichrist of Spanish Painting: Diego Velázquez' *Supper at Emmaus* and the Two Versions of *La Mulata*

Caravaggio's Legacy and Velázquez

It is very risky to define the young Diego Velázquez as a follower of Caravaggio, since it cannot be proved by any means that the Spaniard truly saw works by the Italian master before his first sojourn in Italy from 1629 through 1631. On the contrary, it is apparent that no original painting by Caravaggio was available to Velázquez in Seville. Because of the scarcity of conclusive evidence even with regard to copies of Caravaggio's paintings in Sevillian collections, most scholars have been forced to recognize that the Italian's influence upon the Spaniard is a matter of self-evidence: their relationship is somehow apparent from a comparison between their pictures.[1] Yet it is possible to ascertain that the young Velázquez at the outset of his career explicitly acknowledged Caravaggio's artistic leadership as an inspirational source for his art; if the early sources do not mention this important fact, or only with extreme discretion, it is most likely due to censorship. Almost immediately after his arrival in Madrid in 1622-1623, Velázquez's work seduced the Spanish court and particularly the King, Philip IV. Compared to the careers of his senior colleagues, Velázquez's rise was dazzling. Of course, his success aroused jealousy, and consequently many painters must have sought to belittle his prodigious talent. The Achilles' heel of Velázquez's art paradoxically resided in his wondrous "naturalism," so akin to, and thereby as vulnerable as, Caravaggio's.

A prominent painter at the Spanish court, Vincencio Carducho,[2] led the main attack against Velázquez and his naturalism. Without ever naming his real target—understandably, given the King's support of Velázquez—Carducho in his 1633 *Diálogos de la pintura* inveighs against imitation unaccompanied by knowledge and science, using Caravaggio as a case in point. Pretending to extol Caravaggio's painting, Carducho wonders:

> Who has ever painted and managed to do as well as this monster of ingenuity and naturalness did almost without precepts, without doctrine or study, but only through the force of his genius and keeping before him nature (*y con el natural delante*), which he exclusively imitated in a wondrous manner?

1 For this point, see Harris 1982, 54; and López-Rey 1996, 1:29-33. A different point of view is expressed by Brown J. 1986, 12-3: "Lacking much in the way of external evidence to connect Velázquez and Caravaggio, we must look at the pictures themselves, and there, it must be admitted, we see little that is shared by the two artists except the use of dramatic light effects. (...) Next to the rough-hewn, earthy figures of Velázquez, those of Caravaggio seem almost smooth and idealized. And next to the affecting, dramatic intensity of Caravaggio's compositions, those of Velázquez are almost cool and detached. The common ground between these two great artists is too small to have accommodated them both." I agree entirely with Umberger 1993, who demonstrates that the association of Velázquez with Caravaggio is implicit in Carducho's attacks on the Italian master. In my opinion, to properly judge the influence of Caravaggio's painting on Velázquez, especially on a technical level, one must consider the possibility that Velázquez studied works by the young Jusepe de Ribera: a possibility that must be taken into serious consideration now that we can reconstruct the early production of the young Ribera. On Caravaggio's influence on Spanish "naturalism," see Benedetti 2005. There has been no real attempt to define the concept of the *istoria* in Velázquez's art, although an exhibition has been devoted to Velázquez's sacred story: see Portús 2007.

2 For Carducho and Caravaggio, see Gauna 1998. For Carducho as an art theorist, see Waźbiński 1990; and Albero Muñoz 2006. See also Volk 1977.

517

◀ Plate XXIII: Diego Velázquez, *La Mulata*, National Gallery of Ireland, Dublin, oil on canvas, 55 x 118 cm.

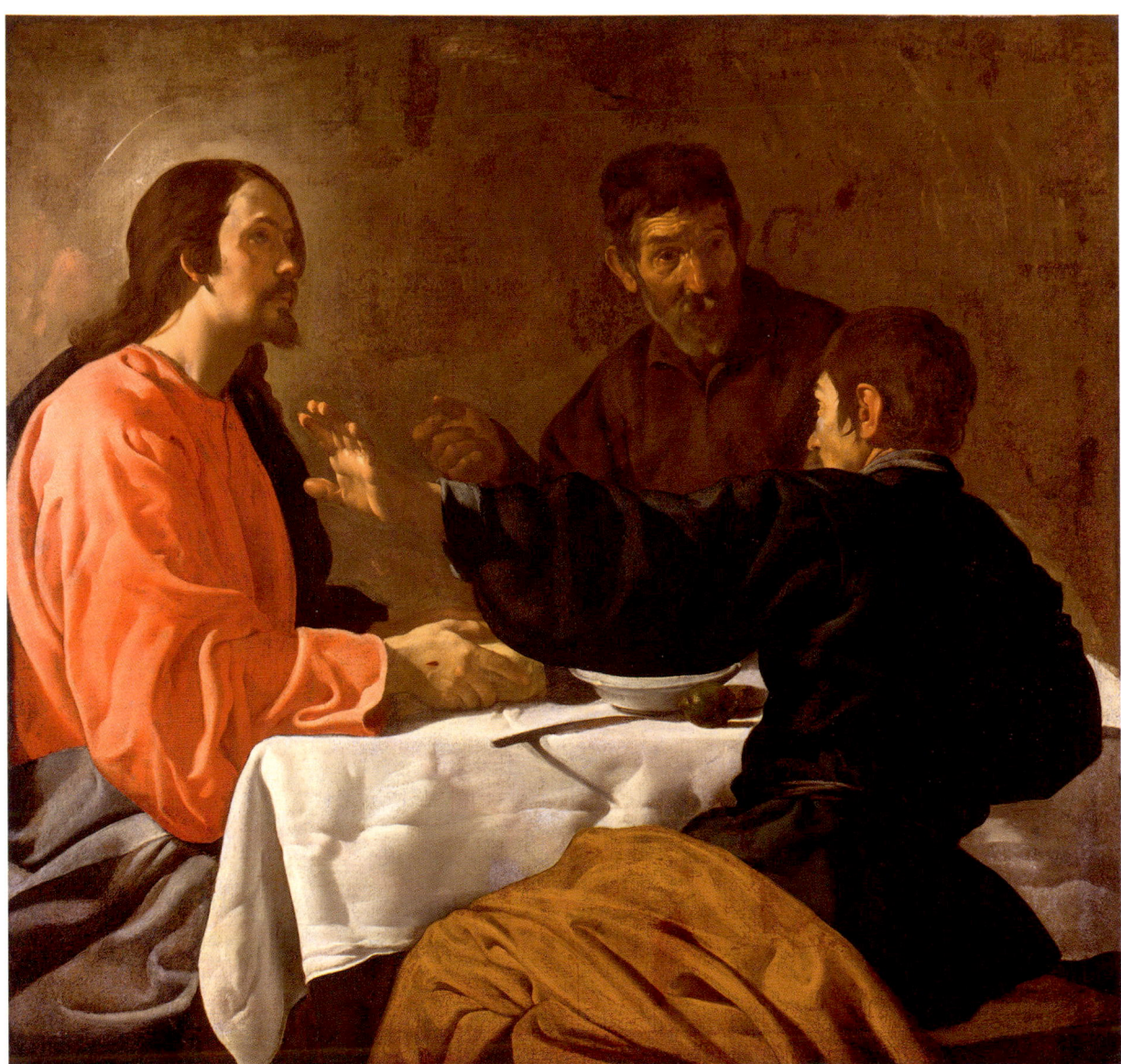

Fig. 279
Diego Velázquez, *The Supper at Emmaus*, Metropolitan Museum of Art, New York, oil on canvas, 123.2 x 132.7 cm.

However, Carducho objects that many had likened Caravaggio to the Antichrist, and punning on the master's name, Michelangelo, had referred to him as an

> Anti-Michelangelo, who with his affected and exterior imitation, admirable manner and liveliness, was able to persuade numerous sorts of people that his was good painting, and his manner and doctrine true, so that they turned their backs to the true way of becoming eternal and being knowledgeable about art with reason and truth.[3]

3 Carducho, 270-1: "En nuestros tiempos se levantó en Roma Michael Angelo de Carabaggio, en el Pontificado del Papa Clemente VIII, con nuevo plato, con tal modo y salsa guisado, con tanto sabor, apetito y gusto que pienso se ha llevado el de todos con tanta golosina y licencia, que temo en ellos alguna apoplexia en la verdadera doctrina: porque le siguen glotonicamente el mayor golpe de los pintores, no reparando si el calor de su natural (que es su ingenio) es tan poderoso, o tiene la actividad que el del otro, para poder digerir simple tan recio, ignoto e incompatible modo como es el obrar sin las preparaciones para tal accion? Quien pintó jamas y llegó a hazer tan bien como este monstruo de ingenio y natural casi hizo sin preceptos, sin doctrina, sin estudio, mas solo con la fuerza de su genio y con el natural delante, a quien simplemente imitava con tanta admiracion? Oi dezir a un zeloso de nuestra profesion que la venida deste hombre al mundo seria presagio de ruina y fin de la pintura, y que asi como al fin deste mundo visible el Antecristo con falsos y portentosos milagros y prodigiosas acciones se llevará tras de si a la perdicion tan gran numero de gentes, movidas de

518

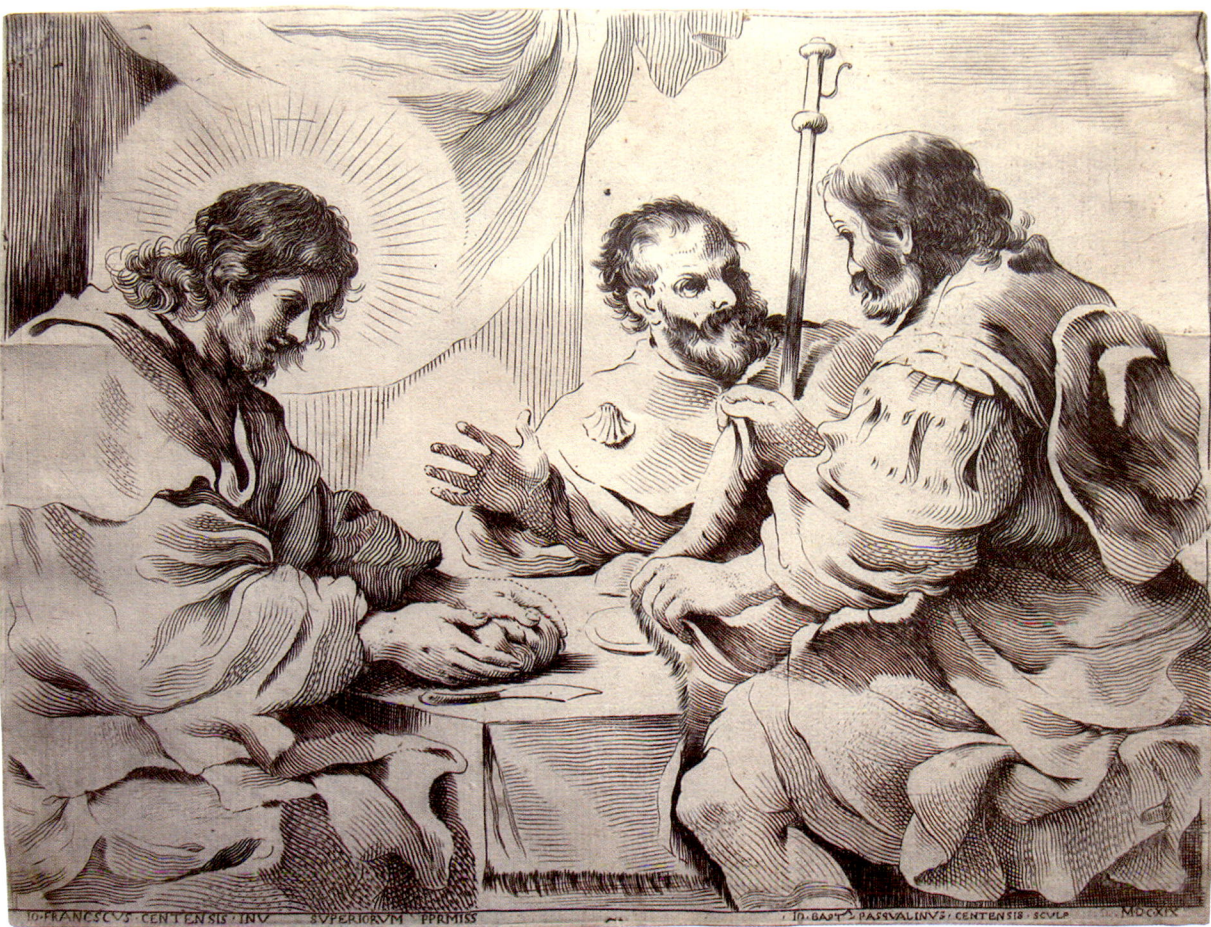

Fig. 280
Giovan Battista Pasqualini after Guercino (Giovan Francesco Barbieri), *The Supper at Emmaus*, engraving, 18.3 x 24.2 cm.

I would not hesitate to include Velázquez among those painters who, according to Carducho, following in Caravaggio's footsteps, had renounced doctrine and truth to embrace the false idol of "affected and exterior imitation." It is no coincidence that Francisco Pacheco,[4] Velázquez's master and father-in-law, in his 1644 *Arte de la Pintura* recommended the very method that Carducho vilified in his 1633 treatise:

> But I abide by nature in everything, and if you could keep it before you (*tenerlo* [*el natural*] *delante*) constantly and at any time, not only [in representing] heads, nudes, feet, and hands, but also drapes and silks, it would be the best thing. That is what Michelangelo da Caravaggio did so felicitously, as shown by his Crucifixion of Saint Peter, albeit a copy (…). And in the case of my son-in-law who pursues this course, one can also see how he differs from all the rest because he always keeps nature before him.[5]

ver sus obras al parecer tan admirables (aunque ellas en si engañosas, falsas y sin verdad ni permanencia), diziendo ser el verdadero Cristo, asi este AnteMichael Angelo con su afectada y exterior imitacion, admirable modo y viveza, ha podido persuadir a tan gran numero de todo genero de gente que aquella es la buena pintura, y su modo y doctrina verdadera, que han buelto las espaldas al verdadero modo de eternizarse y de saber con evidencia y verdad desta materia."

4   For Pacheco and his ideas on art, see Fallay D'Este 2001; Augé 2003; Bassegoda i Hugas 2004a; and Augé 2004.

5   Pacheco, 443: "Pero yo me atengo al natural para todo; y si pudiese tenerlo delante siempre y en todo tiempo, no sólo para las cabezas, desnudos, manos y pies, sino también para los paños y sedas y todo lo demás, sería lo mejor. Así lo hacía Micael Angelo Caravacho; ya se ve en el Crucificamiento de San Pedro (con ser copias) con cuanta felicidad; así lo hace Jusepe de Ribera, pues sus figuras y cabezas entre todas las grandes pinturas que tiene el Duque de Alcalá parecen vivas y lo demás, aunque sea junto a Guido Boloñés; y mi yerno, que sigue este camino, también se ve la diferencia que hace a los demás, por tener siempre delante el natural."

In another passage, Pacheco defends the pictorial genre of still life (*bodegón*),[6] declaring that it is "worthy of esteem" if practiced like Velázquez, "rising in this field so as to yield to no one", and hitting "upon the true imitation of nature."[7] In light of these testimonies, it is fair to surmise that, on the one hand, the parallel between Caravaggio and Velázquez was transparent to artists in Seville in the 1620s and at the Spanish court in the 1630s, and that on the other, inasmuch as it laid itself bare to criticism, this assimilation between the two masters was either discreetly alluded to or left deliberately unmentioned. And indeed, only a later source, Antonio Palomino,[8] who nonetheless was well informed about Velázquez's ideas, relates in his 1724 *Museo Pictorico* that the Spanish master "admired Caravaggio for his extraordinary and subtle talent," adding that "he was called a second Caravaggio because he imitated nature so successfully and with such great propriety, keeping it before his eyes in all things and at all times."[9]

There is no doubt that the young Velázquez—most likely through copies—tried to imitate Caravaggio's technique and poetics, and it can be reasonably assumed that he meditated on the specificity of his narratives. An examination of Velázquez's *Supper at Emmaus* in the Metropolitan Museum, New York (Fig. 279),[10] executed in 1628-1629, will also serve as an introduction to my analysis of the two versions of *La Mulata*. The New York picture is perhaps the last work in which Velázquez clearly elaborated upon a visual concept first developed by Caravaggio in his 1601 London *Supper at Emmaus*. On a preliminary basis, the two paintings differ in so many details as to render it unlikely that the one exerted a direct influence, if any, on the other. Stylistically, Velázquez had already relinquished the more tenebrous palette and fierce color technique of his Sevillian years when he depicted his own version of the *Supper at Emmaus*. Although here he still relishes chiaroscuro contrasts, his palette has sensibly brightened, and the influence of Titian's saturated blue, red, and ochre hues is unquestionable. Yet on account of its tight framing of the episode, its narrative oddities, and its plebeian actors, the New York painting is surely indebted to Caravaggio's art.

It is true, nevertheless, that the influence of Caravaggio's *Supper at Emmaus* might have been filtered through Guercino's own interpretation of the London prototype. Around 1619, Guercino in fact executed a *Supper at Emmaus,* now lost but reproduced in a 1619 engraving by Giovan Battista Pasqualini (Fig. 280).[11] According to Carlo Cesare Malvasia's manuscript notes for his 1678 *Felsina Pittrice*, Guercino, like his Bolognese colleagues Alessandro Tiarini, Leonello Spada, and especially Lorenzo Garbieri, particularly valued Caravaggio's *The Incredulity of Saint Thomas*, known to them through excellent copies then available in Bologna. In commenting on Garbieri's fascination with the picture and his determination to improve upon Caravaggio's original, Malvasia relates that "Barbieri [Guercino] executed another one [another *Incredulity of Saint Thomas*], superbly beautiful, in the possession of Cardinal Ginetti, who owns its pendant, the Taking of Our Lord in the Garden." Both these paintings, now respectively in the National Gallery (London) and the Fitzwilliam Museum (Cambridge), were completed in 1621, and both unequivocally evoke Caravaggio's pictures of the same subject.[12] Guercino's 1619 *Supper at Emmaus* also reflects the painter's interest

6   For the concept of bodegón, see Wind B. 1987.

7   Pacheco, 519: "(...) Claro está que sí, si son pintados como mi yerno los pinta alzándose con esta parte sin dexar lugar a otro, y merecen estimación grandisima." For the artistic culture of Velázquez's Seville, see Morales 1999; and Méndez Rodríguez 2005. For Velázquez in Seville, see more recently Clarke 1996.

8   For Palomino, see Olmos 1956; Tello and Sanz Sanz 1979; Úbeda de los Cobos 2001; Bassegoda i Hugas 2004b.

9   Palomino, 3:209: "Compitió Velázquez con Caravaggio en la valentía del pintar; y fué igual con Pacheco en lo especulativo. A aquél estimó por lo exquisito, y por la agudeza de su ingenio; y a éste eligió por maestro, por el conocimiento de sus estudios, que le constituían digno de su elección. (...) Diéronle el nombre de Segundo Caravaggio, por contrahecer en sus obras a el natural felizmente, y con tanta propiedad, teniéndole delante para todo, y en todo tiempo."

10   For the painting, see Brown J. 1986, 56; Domínguez Ortiz et al. 1989, 84-7, no. 6; López-Rey 1996, 2:100, no. 42.

11   See Bagni 1988, 19, no. 16.

12   For the paintings, see Salerno 1988, 153-4, nos. 73-74; and Stone 1991a, 94-5, nos. 72-73. For a preparatory study for the *Incredulity of Saint Thomas*, see Stone 1991b, 23-5, no. 10.

in Caravaggio, constituting one of his first experiments with the master's compositional schemas and narrative formulas.

Because of Guercino's growing success in Rome (where Guercino lived between 1621 and 1623), it is perfectly conceivable that Velázquez studied his paintings from prints and easily recognized Caravaggio's imprint in his compositions. Pasqualini also engraved the designs of the two pendants mentioned by Malvasia as soon as they were painted, in 1621.[13] In Guercino's *Supper at Emmaus*, the figure of Christ is removed from the central position he occupied in Caravaggio's London picture. Sitting at the left, his leaning face almost in profile, the Savior fixes his eyes upon the loaf

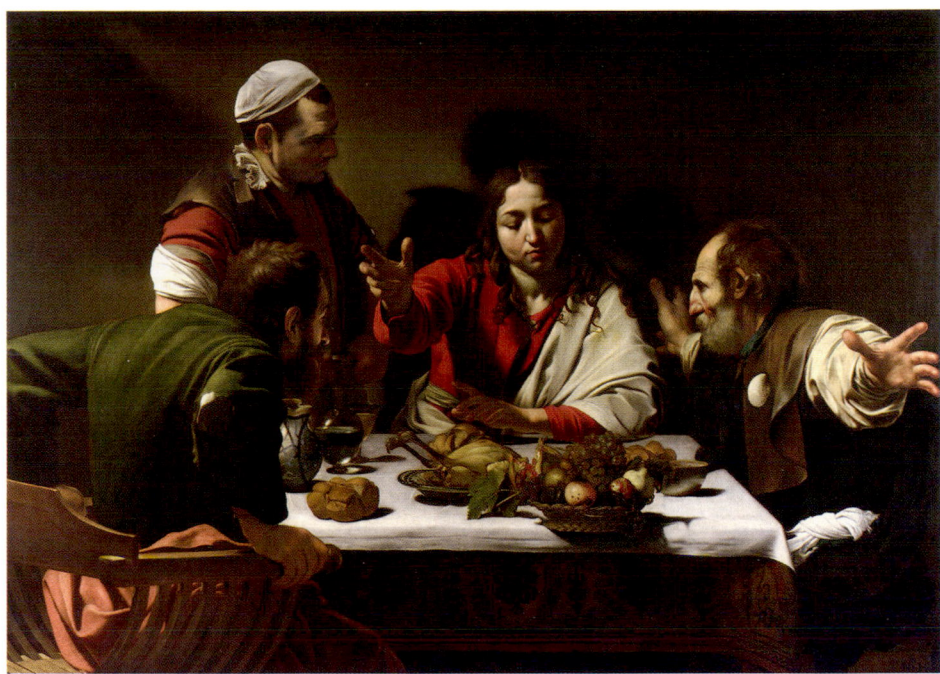

Fig. 281
Michelangelo Merisi da Caravaggio, *The Supper at Emmaus*, National Gallery, London, oil on canvas, 141 x 196.2 cm.

of bread he is breaking while murmuring the ritual blessing. An immense aureole—its brightness must have represented a powerful feat of lighting in the original painting—frames Christ's head, indicating that the apotheosis is taking place; the sign of the wound on the Savior's right hand—a detail faithfully reiterated by Velázquez—confirms that Jesus has already resumed his real physiognomy and identity. Despite the splendor of this transfiguration, the two apostles, relegated to the right of the composition, are obviously unaware of Christ's theophany, as they look at one another as if puzzled and disoriented. In the right foreground, Guercino accommodated the massive figure of a disciple, his pilgrim's hat dangling upon his back, his face almost entirely concealed in an arduous foreshortening that is undoubtedly inspired by that of Caravaggio's apostle at the left of the London *Supper at Emmaus* (Fig. 281).

More difficult to understand, Guercino's figure lifts the border of the tablecloth, either disconcertedly or as if he were about to stand up. His companion across the table keeps his pilgrim's cane nearby as he opens his hand in wonder. A heavy curtain hangs over Christ's figure, covering a section of the wall behind, which in a sense creates a partition between the two halves of the composition. In this kind of diptych, the apostle's open hand, its palm evocatively shaded by the stream of light pouring from Christ's brilliance, acts as a bridge between the two sub-scenes of the episode. Analogous to the groping right hand of the apostle with his arms outspread in the London *Supper at Emmaus*, the open hand of Guercino's disciple pierces the space of the divine as if unwillingly, yet is not meant to suggest a contact with Christ's isolated figure. Although it is impossible to establish the sequence of events as conjured up in Guercino's picture, I would venture to suggest that the two disciples' dialogue refers to the moment subsequent to Christ's simultaneous disappearance and unveiling: instead of betraying their surprise upon recognizing Christ, the two elderly men in fact seem to bespeak their incredulity and bafflement in the aftermath of the miracle.

13   Bagni 1988, 29-30, nos. 31, 33.

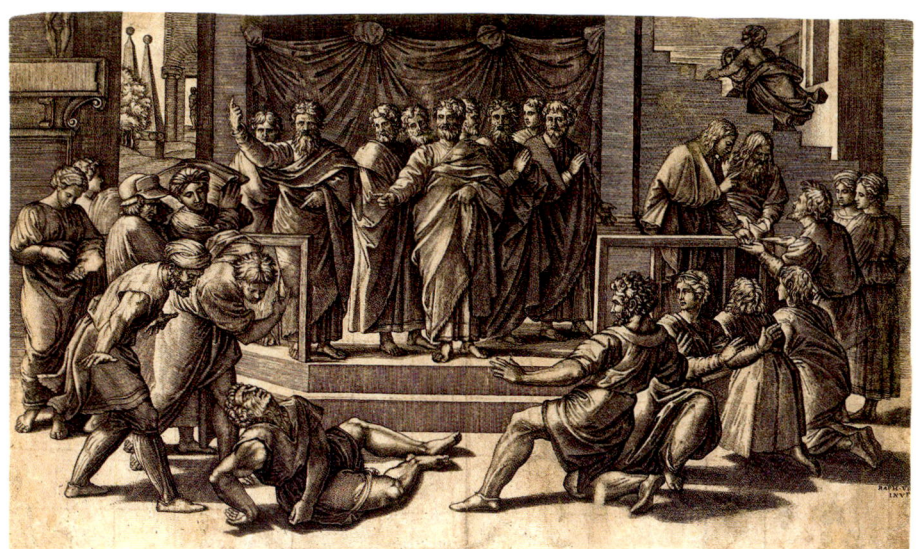

Fig. 282
Agostino Veneziano (Agostino Musi) after Raphael (Raffaello Santi), *The Death of Ananias*,
engraving, 26.6 x 35.1 cm.

If this is correct, Guercino dissolved the diverse inconsistencies determined by Caravaggio's a-synchronies, thereby setting up a dual temporality: to the left, the pre-sequel of Christ breaking the bread, and to the right the sequel of the apostles in wonder processing the epiphany and questioning its authenticity by exchanging gazes. Regardless of the episode's temporality, it is evident that Guercino separates the scene into two groups that hardly interact with one another on a dramatic level, just as in Velázquez's *Supper at Emmaus*, so that a connection between Guercino's and Velázquez's pictures seems undeniable.

Although Velázquez modified Guercino's disposition of the figures by shifting higher the apostle behind the table, thereby renouncing the prototype's stasis with its frieze-like configuration, he kept the face of the disciple in the foreground almost entirely hidden: a plausible homage not only to Guercino, but also to Caravaggio himself. That Velázquez here might have taken the apostle in the left foreground from Caravaggio's London painting is corroborated by some affinities. Besides their heads in *profil perdu*, the outermost bent arms of the two figures echo each other. As if to acknowledge Caravaggio's affinity with Renaissance sources, Velázquez combined the apostle's attitude in the London picture to that of a well-known model by Raphael: the nonplussed figure in the right foreground of *The Death of Ananias* (Fig. 282), a composition engraved by Agostino Veneziano,[14] and therefore available to Velázquez. The oblique thrust of his leg, thigh, and torso, the lifted arm and the head in profile constitute sufficient evidence of borrowing (Figs. 283, 284). But the interrelations between Caravaggio's painting and Velázquez's go well beyond formal re-elaborations, and concern structural elements of the composition.

In Chapter 9, I examined the London *Supper at Emmaus*, and underlined that, as far as action goes, serious disconnections of timing and space underlie the plot's visual unfolding. Caravaggio did not coordinate the figures' attitudes and expressions in order to suggest an Aristotelian unity of time and action. Rather, through narrative disjunctions, he blurred the perception and reading of the biblical story, so that Jesus' presence in the painting might even be doubted, and the possibility of his miraculous disappearance visually insinuated. In a shrewd act of clarification, Velázquez in the New York picture unhitched whatever refrained Caravaggio from visualizing Christ's invisibility: here any ambivalence is left out. If the rectangular table still accomplishes its structural task of a horizontal pivot, this time it does not channel the gaze toward the central figure of Christ. In his place, by contrast, Velázquez, like Guercino before him, inserted a slightly off-center apostle, his marveling gaze turned to his companion who, in response, stretches his arm as if to indicate that the divine pilgrim—that is, the disguised Christ whom they did not recognize during the supper—has vanished from sight.

14   For the print, see Oberhuber 1978, 1:60, no. 42 (47); and
Bernini Pezzini et al. 1985, 132.

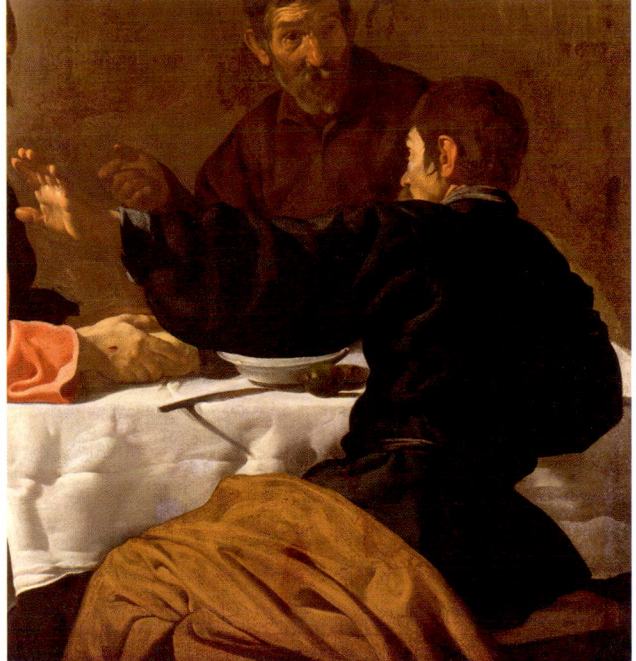
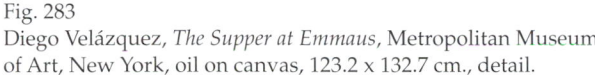

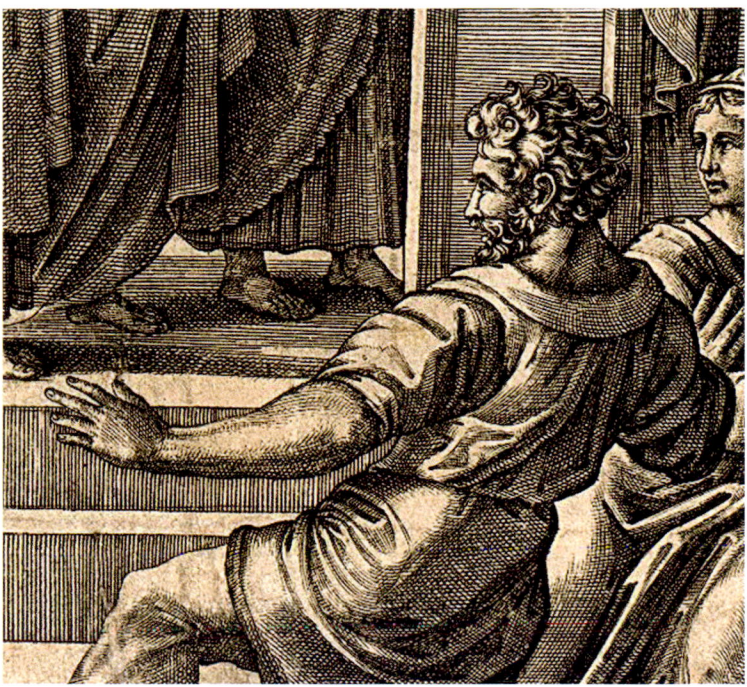

Fig. 283
Diego Velázquez, *The Supper at Emmaus*, Metropolitan Museum of Art, New York, oil on canvas, 123.2 x 132.7 cm., detail.

Fig. 284
Agostino Veneziano (Agostino Musi) after Raphael (Raffaello Santi), *The Death of Ananias*, engraving, 26.6 x 35.1 cm., detail.

Swiveling his left arm outward, toward the beholder's visual space, Velázquez's apostle seems to wave in the direction in which the masked Savior disappeared, as if saying: "he was right here, now he is gone." Through their disorderly reactions, the two apostles abandon the decorous attitudes of their counterparts in Guercino's *Supper at Emmaus*, and re-don the rusticity of Velázquez's *bodegón* actors: they re-appropriate their comic, low-life, characters. In opposition to the viewer, both apostles are unable to see the out-of-scale Christ on the left, his eyes indifferent to the surrounding haze and majestically fixed upon heaven, his wounded hand cutting the loaf of bread in a rehearsal of the last supper.

Like Guercino, Velázquez here represents a sort of two-tempi sequel to Caravaggio's London picture. Jesus has already blessed the Eucharistic bread, and the apostles react to his sudden disappearance. But if Guercino sought to dissimulate the disruptions of temporality specific to his visualization of the scene, Velázquez did not hesitate, through the animated dialogue between his two apostles/peasants, to exhibit the temporal fractures of his invention. Not that temporality seriously matters to Velázquez, who as always seems much more interested in pushing to the extremes the opposition between the genre components of his narratives, pitting tragedy against comedy, the sacred against the profane, the humble against the noble, man against divinity, stillness against motion.

Accordingly, it is no surprise that Velázquez liked Guercino's idea of a bipartite composition, which he undeniably accentuated even on a chromatic level: at the left, where the divine permanence reigns, are bright colors; at the right, where the rustic apostles perform their act of comedic blindness, earthly tints prevail. Unlike Caravaggio, Velázquez does not lay out the composition as a machine of optical and tactile surprises. Nor is he primarily concerned with the religious significance of the Eucharistic meal he represents. The drooping sleeve of the apostle's jacket here partially conceals the food on the table, whereas Caravaggio, through the spread of courses exhibited in his London *Supper at Emmaus*, uncannily misdirects the viewer's gaze in search of the sacred bread.

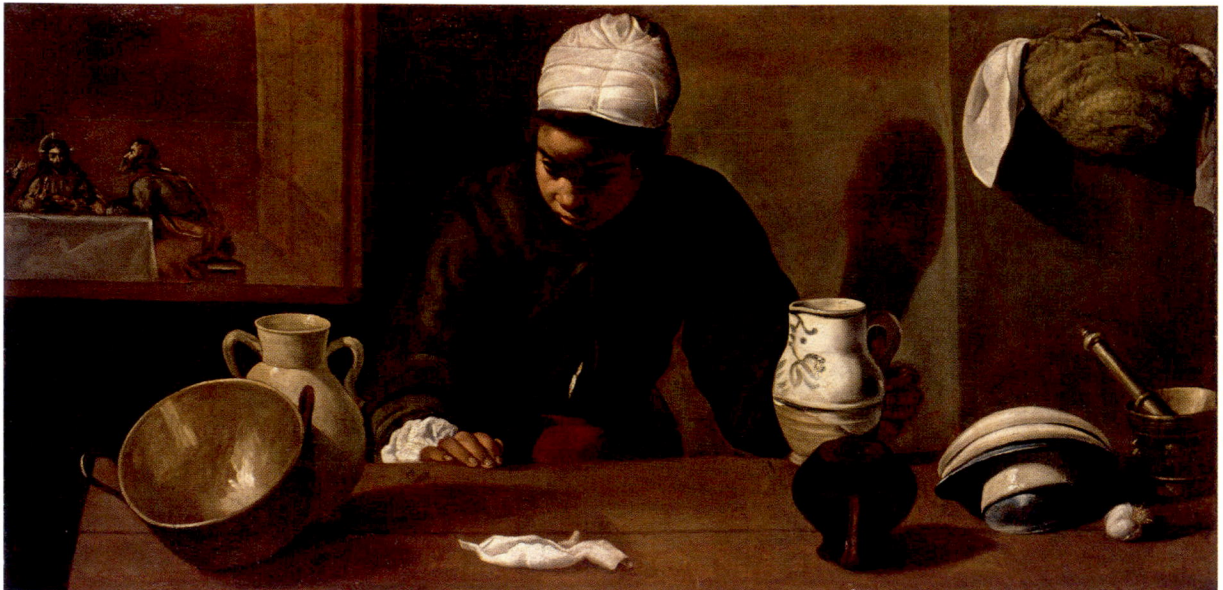

Fig. 285
Diego Velázquez, *La Mulata*, National Gallery of Ireland, Dublin, oil on canvas, 55 x 118 cm.

More to the point, Velázquez shared with Caravaggio an irresistible urge to juggle with, or even jettison, the principles of the *istoria*. By yoking together two different acts in the same picture—Christ's reenactment of the Eucharistic sacrament and the apostles' perplexed discussion—and by mounting their conflicting interrelation as the core of the pictorial subject, he likewise reveals the artifice of the sacred *istoria* as well as the intrinsic arduousness of its claim to represent a transcendental truth through the conventions of optical and rhetorical verisimilitude. As a graphic trope of this difficulty, the apostle's hand in the foreground, albeit swathed in radiance, strays away from the very divinity whose disappearance it vainly evokes. Steering away not only from Jesus' figure but also from the pictorial field, this hand not only fails to incorporate the divine into the human, thus binding one episode to another in a coherent narrative action, but also seals the picture's fictiveness by entering the beholder's spatial field and mixing the inner and outer spaces of the representation. This detail is significant. In Caravaggio's *Supper at Emmaus*, the hand of the apostle to the right blindly reaches for a divinity that, though in his proximity, escapes being touched. By revolving the scene approximately 90 degrees in accordance with Guercino's intuition, Velázquez accentuates the scope of this incommunicability. Visually, the open hand of Velázquez's apostle thematizes what Caravaggio has only implied. By transforming the hand into a sign of separation and disconnectedness, Velázquez also configures the story not only as a fiction, but as a meta-fiction: the place where two levels of fiction, the sacred and the comedic, are spliced together yet showcased with suture for the sake of demonstration.

The collage-like quality of this and other early works by Velázquez may derive from technical inexperience or—as some scholars believe—from a compositional procedure in which every figure is conceived independently, then juxtaposed or linked to the others. Even in this case, though, the technique of montage reflects a notion of composition and of the *istoria* that does not recoil from, but rather tends toward, visual and narrative disconnections. In this regard, it is not surprising that Carducho, in disparaging Caravaggio's—and indirectly Velázquez's—obsessive imitation of nature, compares the works of such painters with the performances of an actor clueless about the subject he enacts:

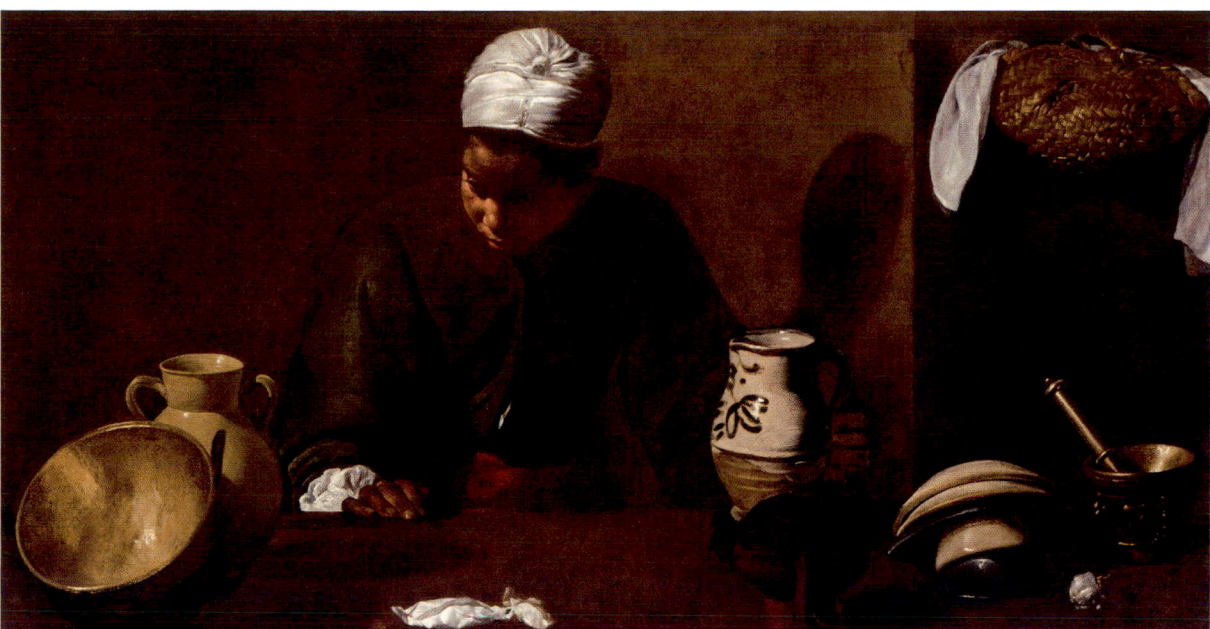

Fig. 286
Diego Velázquez, *La Mulata*, Art Institute, Chicago, oil on canvas, 55.5 x 104 cm.

It can happen that a performer recites a theological or philosophical discourse in Latin, or in another foreign language, and as he does not understand it, nor even its subject, he disfigures it with the awkwardness of his diction, and with actions mistimed or inappropriate because, if it ought to be short, he makes it long or conversely, distancing the syllables out of place in spite of the grammar and rhetoric, so that one comprehends neither the language nor the subject, and it does not pan out as it should, although the populace, as ignorant as the performer, grows enthralled, admiring its loquacity and verbosity, deeming the actions as congruous and the movements as eloquent as if they were to attend the wisest orator and theological preacher, or a great philosopher and rhetorician.[15]

By paraphrasing the canonical assimilation of painting to rhetoric, Carducho satirizes those painters who, when dealing with religious subjects, reproduce them without grasping their significance. Out of ignorance, they represent "mistimed" and incongruous actions, cherished by the populace, but incomprehensible to the learned. It is probably fortuitous that Carducho's satire can apply to Velázquez's mistiming and incongruousness in the *Supper at Emmaus*—or for that matter, to others of his early pictures. However, to an artist like Carducho, trained as a painter of the *istoria* and imbued with its principles, Velázquez's New York painting must have appeared as a botched narrative, resulting from intellectual carelessness and a dearth of doctrine and science. Carducho's criticism also sheds light on the troubles endured by a court artist when experimenting with the *istoria* as Velázquez dared to do. More important for my purposes, the New York picture can be interpreted as the final stage of a reflection that Velázquez conducted upon the biblical theme of the *Supper at*

15 Carducho, 193-4: "Tal vez sucede que el representante decora un discorso teologo o filosofico en lengua latina, o en alguna otra estrangera, que por no entenderla, ni la materia de que trata, le echa a perder con el desaire de la pronunciacion, y con las acciones hechas sin tiempo, ni proposito, porque la diccion que avia de ser breve, la haze larga y por el contrario, apartando silabas fuera de su lugar sin gramatica ni retorica ninguna; de tal suerte que ya ni la lengua ni la materia se entiende, ni es que la que ha de ser, si bien el vulgo que ignora lo mismo que el que lo representa, se dexa llevar y se admira de verle tan loquaz y verboso, tan propio en las acciones y tan airoso en los movimientos que le parece es lo mismo oirle a el que a un orador muy docto y predicador teologo, o un gran filosofo y retorico."

Emmaus, and which was inaugurated by the two versions of *La Mulata*. The subject of at least one of these paintings is again the *Supper at Emmaus*, or rather the depiction of its backstage activity.

Backstage at the Supper at Emmaus

Were it not for the partial image of the supper at Emmaus in the background of the Dublin *La Mulata* (Fig. 285), no scholar would ever have thought to relate this biblical episode to the kitchen scene that Velázquez depicted twice at an early phase of his career, around 1618. In the second version, now in the Art Institute, Chicago (Fig. 286), there is indeed no trace of a religious story, which has raised several questions not only about the authenticity of this picture, regarded for a long time as a copy after the Dublin composition, but also about its genre and subject.[16] In addition, it must be recalled that the Dublin *Mulata* also showed a gloomy, neutral backdrop until it was cleaned in 1933, when the scene of the Emmaus supper unexpectedly resurfaced.

Ever since, the *Mulata* has been linked to another early painting by Velázquez, the *Kitchen Scene with Christ in the House of Martha and Mary* (National Gallery, London),[17] whose format—albeit slightly dissimilar—and overall concept—a sort of dilated *bodegón* with the insertion of a sacred subject in the background—may suggest that Velázquez conceived of these paintings as pendants. Although the compositions surely present themselves as analogs, I will not discuss their relation here, but rather concentrate on the two versions of *La Mulata*, which are relevant to the problem of pictorial narration.

First, however, I must briefly refute Tanya J. Tiffany's most recent interpretation of *La Mulata* as a devotional painting celebrating the conversion to Christianity of African slaves living in Velázquez's Seville.[18] Tiffany likens the composition of the Dublin *Mulata* to images of devotion inspired by Jesuit theologians and widely circulating at the time throughout Catholic Europe, picking out the example of the prints illustrating Jerónimo Nadal's 1595 *Adnotationes et meditationes in Evangelia*, especially the apparatus of "painting-within-the-painting" images that accompany its depictions of Evangelical episodes. But these engravings do not constitute the equivalent of Velázquez's insertion of a Supper at Emmaus into a kitchen scene. Indeed, in Nadal's treatise, the small roundels with scenes from the Gospel create, in relation to a major depiction of an episode from Christ's life, a network of exclusively sacred images that help the reader and beholder—along with the inscriptions below—to imagine vividly and situate exactly an event of the life of Christ within its original context, bringing to the fore the theological meaning foreshadowed in those passages of scripture. Typologically and structurally, Velázquez's *La Mulata* classifies as a *bodegón*, not as a sacred story, and therefore the presence of a biblical episode in it cannot be judged against the tradition of Jesuit imagery.

Furthermore, the usage of roundels in Nadal's *Adnotationes*—and by the same token the depiction of the martyrdom of Saint Sebastian within a window frame in Francisco Pacheco's *Saint Sebastian Attended by Saint Irene*[19]—accomplishes functions of visual prolepsis, and sometimes analepsis, that do not apply to Velázquez's Dublin painting. There, the episode of the servant is depicted as synchronous to the supper sketched in the left background.

---

16   There is no doubt, in my opinion, that the Chicago *Mulata* is also an original by Velázquez. For the two versions of this composition, see Harris 1982, 44-6; Brown J. 1986, 21; Bryson 1990, 154-5; López-Rey 1996, 2:42-4, nos. 17-18; Boyd and Esler 2004, 53-9; Carr et al. 2006, 126-7, no. 5-6; and Tiffany 2008.

17   For the painting, see Harris 1982, 44-6; Brown J. 1986, 16-21; López-Rey 1996, 2:22, no. 7; Boyd and Esler 2004; Tiffany 2005; and Carr et al. 2006, 122-4, no. 4.

18   See Tiffany 2008. A similar interpretive tendency is to be observed in Boyd and Esler 2004.

19   For Pacheco and Nadal, see Moffitt 1990. For the painting, once at San Sebastián, Alcalà de Guadaira, see Barbadillo 1963, 104.

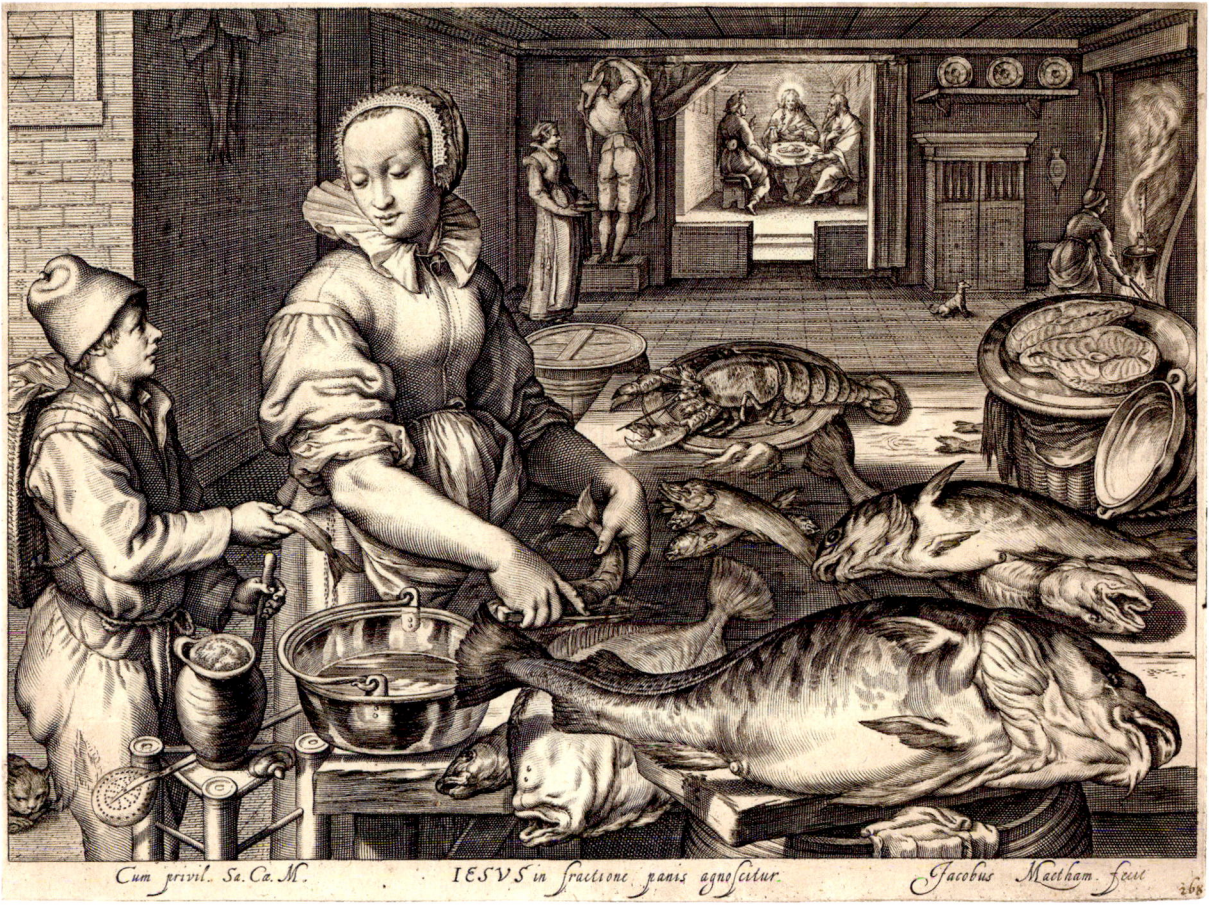

Fig. 287
Jacob Matham after Pieter Aertsen, *Kitchen Scene with the Supper at Emmaus*, engraving, 24.2 x 32.3 cm.

Finally, if Velázquez's original intention was to extol the religious enlightenment of a Sevillian slave, one would expect him to render the message in an unambiguous and crystalline fashion. Propaganda—or epideictic rhetoric as a means of persuasion—demands that contents be perfectly transparent to recipients, whether beholders or readers. And yet one of the salient features in Velázquez's Dublin *Mulata* is its intrinsic elusiveness; viewers may not agree on what exactly the servant in the picture is doing. For Tiffany, it is clear that the servant is visited by God's grace, to the point that she interprets the light on the girl's face as related to, and originating in, the scene of the supper at Emmaus behind. However distractedly one observes the painting, one would immediately verify that the source of lighting is located not in the background, but in the foreground.

It has been rightly observed that a *c.*1600 engraving by Jacob Matham after Pieter Aertsen,[20] a *Kitchen Scene with Christ at the Supper at Emmaus* (Fig. 287), sparked Velázquez's invention. There, a bonneted female cook attentively scans a fish that a boy offers for sale. In front of her, a kitchen table is laden with many kinds of fish, the most prominent of which, displayed with pride in the foreground, competes in dimension with the female protagonist nearby. The similarity of her attitude with that of the innkeeper in Titian's Louvre *Supper at Emmaus* (before 1530) is striking. Undoubtedly Aertsen knew this painting or a copy of it, and wittily metamorphosed Titian's figure—who looks at a loaf of bread on the table with curious attention—into a female cook

20   See Strauss 1980, 150, no. 165 (171); and Widerkehr 2007, 2:41, no. 161.

527

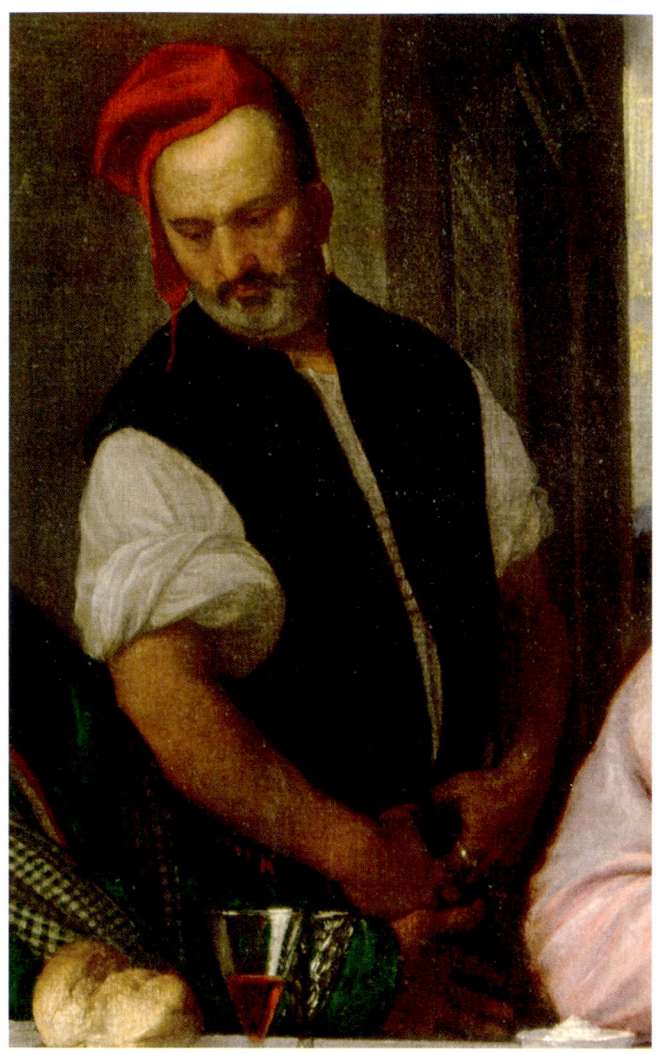

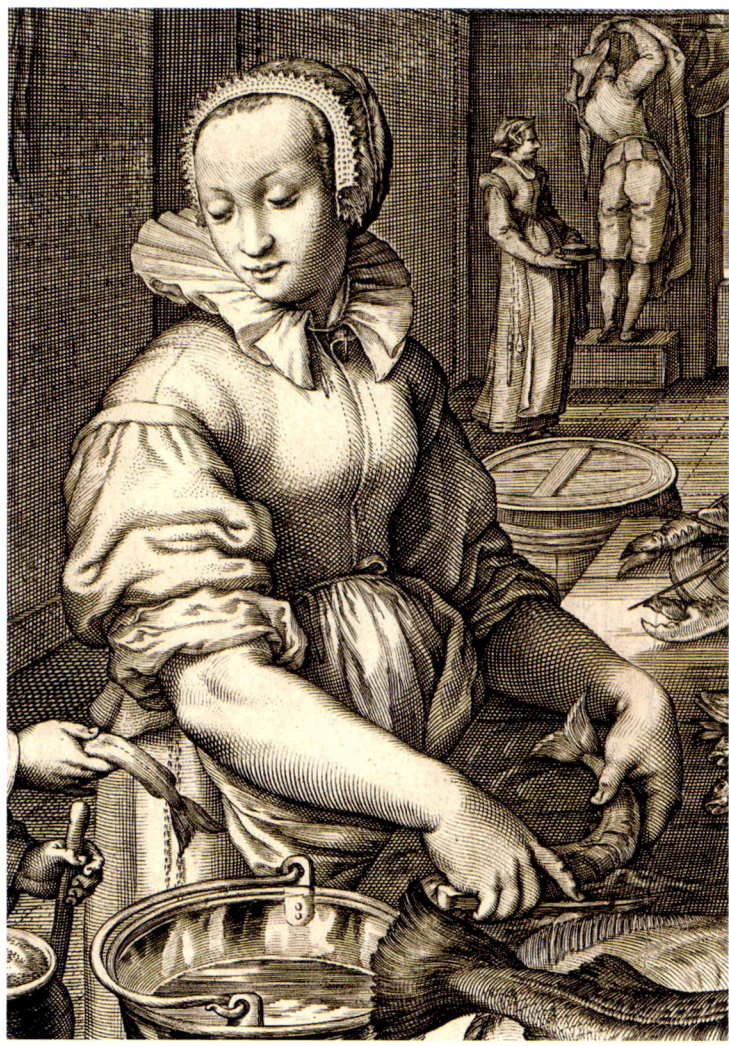

Fig. 288
Titian (Tiziano Vecellio), *The Supper at Emmaus*, Musée du Louvre, Paris, oil on canvas, 169 x 244 cm., detail.

Fig. 289
Jacob Matham after Pieter Aertsen, *Kitchen Scene with the Supper at Emmaus*, engraving, 24.2 x 32.3 cm., detail.

gauging the fish's quality with a diligent gaze (Figs. 288, 289). In other words, Aertsen detected the comedic undertone of this secondary feature in Titian's painting, and made of the cook's female counterpart the main character of his genre scene. Emphasis must be placed on this factor. As comic figures, the equivalents of Titian's innkeeper frequently play the role of clueless spectators in many other representations of the *Supper at Emmaus*. Thus the innkeeper's metamorphosis into a female cook also encompasses a definitive change of pictorial mode: from comedy to a genre not yet patented, one in which labor is paradoxically treated as a sort of central anecdote. Velázquez evolved Aertsen's basic idea of manipulating modes and genres in quite another direction.

To return to Matham's engraving, beyond the overloaded table in the foreground an intermediary space opens up, where a maid stokes the fire under a cauldron as a man with a hat, perched upon a stool, removes a curtain to usher a servant into the dining room. Beyond the kitchen, the scene of Jesus' disappearance is about to occur. The episode evoked here is substantially the same as the one in the background of the Dublin *Mulata*, except for the fact that Velázquez shifted it to the picture's left margin, diminished it to the side, and made it visible through a window, not as an adjacent space. Moreover, Velázquez downplayed the print's perspectival effect by suppressing its transitional space. In this way, the mulatto servant directly interacts with the sacred episode in the background. The ambivalence of the window, which also resembles the frame of a picture, renders the connection between the main figure and the religious scene doubtful. Is whatever transpires through the opening indeed a miracle? Or is this the trimmed surface of another painting, a picture-within-the-picture?

This pictorial ambiguity is deliberate; it modifies the viewer's perception of the narrative in its unity and diachronic unfolding. Depending on the beholder's preference, the miracle might intervene as the servant turns her head sideways—in this case, two actions run parallel or interweave into each other. Or else the mulatto girl might halt momentarily for unspecified motives during her duty—in this case, on the contrary, a single action is summoned, one without apparent referent. From whichever perspective one analyzes *La Mulata*, it is clear that its narrative lends itself to a multi-pronged approach. To grasp the specificity of the image and its author's intention, it is necessary to study the scene within the purview of its alternative readings. Yet it is even more important to define the status of the servant who gives the Dublin and Chicago paintings their Spanish title. Where does she come from? How did she end up being the focus of such a condensed, yet elaborate composition? One thing is certain: the "*mulata*" began her iconographic career as a humble walk-on.

Like the clueless spectator, an absentminded walk-on very often features in early modern representations not only of the *Supper at Emmaus*, but

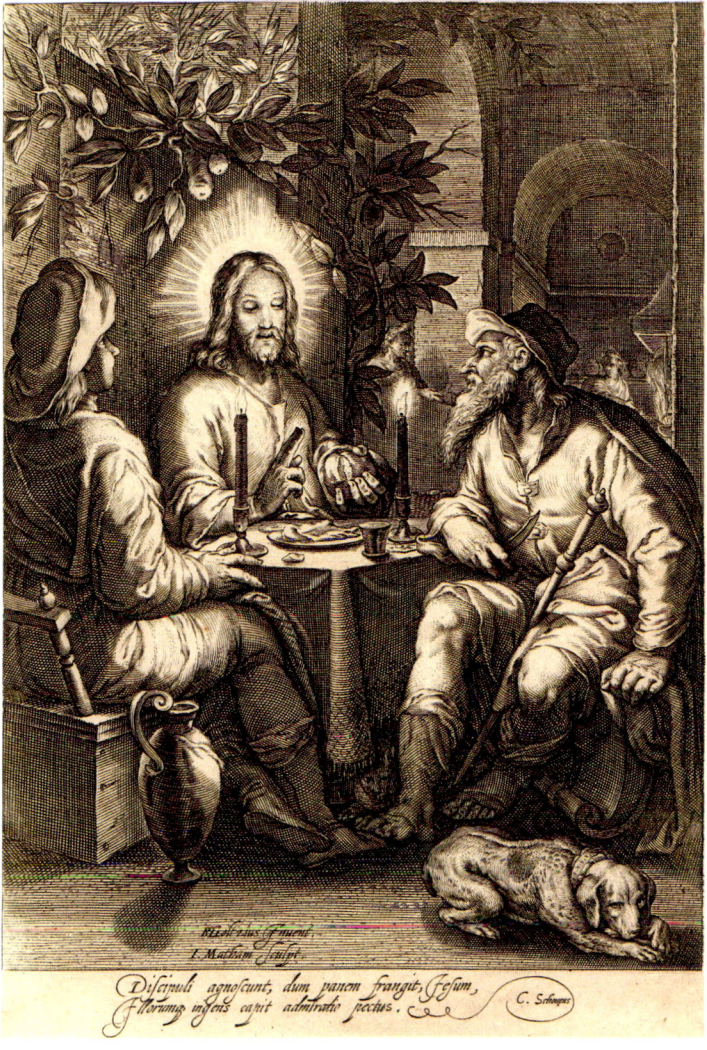

Fig. 290
Jacob Matham after Sebastian Vrancx, *The Supper at Emmaus*, engraving, 40.5 x 54.5 cm.

also of other biblical stories. In Chapter 9, I traced the origin of this character, and explained its function. Its inattention and detachment from the miracle at the heart of the narrative tends to be perceived both as a comic digression and as an allusion to the divine transcendence of the human senses. However, there is a further aspect of this figure that deserves closer analysis with respect to *La Mulata*. On occasion, the walk-on turns into a visual pretext through which artists represent everyday labor, its mechanical processes and, to a certain extent, its repetitiousness.

Let us look first of all at a 1606 engraving by Jacob Matham after Sebastian Vrancx (Fig. 290).[21] In the high-vaulted recess of this *Supper at Emmaus*, a cook, heedless of Christ's imminent disappearance in the foreground, seems to stir the content of a cauldron hanging over the fire. Curiously enough, his face veers away from the stove, so that it is unclear if his action responds to the cue of a secondary figure outside the kitchen, or if he has simply lost concentration. Despite its vague rendition, this detail helps us understand the accomplishment of Velázquez in *La Mulata*. Like Aertsen, he reversed the beholder's standpoint by lodging the kitchen scene in the foreground, therefore

21 See Strauss 1980, 92, no. 102 (158) [as after Hendrick Goltzius]; and Widerkehr and Leeflang 2007, 1:99, no. 46. The print is dated 1606.

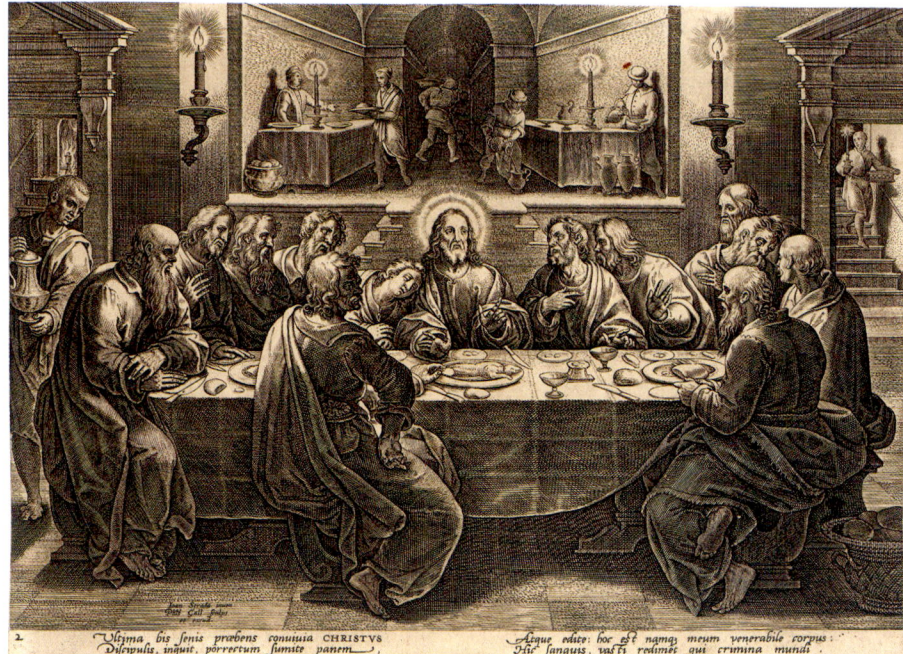

Fig. 291
Philips Galle after Johannes Stradanus, *Last Supper*, engraving, 19.3 x 26.4 cm.

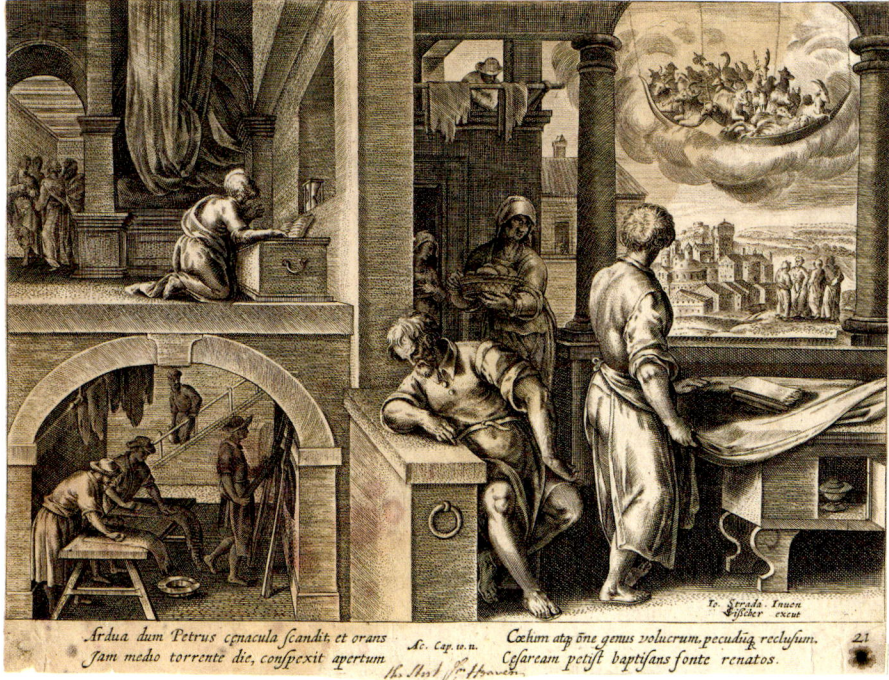

Fig. 292
Philips Galle after Johannes Stradanus, *The Vision of Saint Peter*, engraving, 20.4 x 26.7 cm.

relegating the miracle to the periphery. In other words, he moved the action in the *Supper at Emmaus* from backstage to the proscenium. Yet, unlike Aertsen, he did not sever the dramatic ties between the foreground and the background through the extraction of an independent anecdote from the primary script.

In the Dublin *Mulata*, Velázquez intentionally maintained a dialogue, however tenuous and indefinite, between the servant and the Eucharistic supper beyond the window. In other words, the two episodes, in the foreground and at a distance, may or may not dovetail with each other as the complementary elements of a single action. Accordingly, the girl's attitude may bespeak either a mechanical gesture, or express a reaction to the miracle behind. By contrast, Aertsen deploys two distinct narratives, each related to a separate pictorial mode, religious and comedic. Notwithstanding the striking novelty of his composition, Aertsen thus continues to propagate the iconographic tradition: the sacred plays out on a different frequency from the comic.

Even when the depiction of mindless walk-ons is given more salience, the space assigned to them is visually, even concretely, restrained. In Johannes Stradanus' *Last Supper* engraved by Philips Galle around 1580 (Fig. 291),[22] the sphere of physical labor is strictly cordoned off: downstairs, in the foreground, the institution of the Eucharist takes place; upstairs, backstage, the wine is poured into jugs; the food is prepared, dispatched or brought in. Almost faceless, indistinguishable, cooks and servants loom there in ignorance of the Eucharistic ritual. Similarly, a young boy with a basket and a candle is about to enter the scene; a door framing a staircase once again fences him out of the proscenium. Only a waiter, to the left, in the dark, is allowed into the

22   See Dolders 1987, 134, no. 040:2; and Sellink and Leesberg 2001, 2:88, no. 207.

530

sacred scene; he seems pensive, though it is unclear for what reason. Velázquez may well have fallen under the spell of this print, with its various rooms opening into one another. In any case, much later he used the device of a staircase framed within a door to introduce the Queen of Spain's "aposentador," Don José Nieto Velázquez, in *Las Meninas*.

In *The Vision of Saint Peter* (Fig. 292), another print by Galle after Stradanus (1582),[23] the sheet is divided into three different zones; at the left, above, Peter prays as he has the vision of a sky teeming with all kinds of earthly animals; to the right, a male servant sets the table for lunch while a woman carries in a basket with food; both are apparently unaware of the miracle in the heavens, as is a third figure, sitting in the foreground, staring down into space. Downstairs—and this is what deserves our attention—a

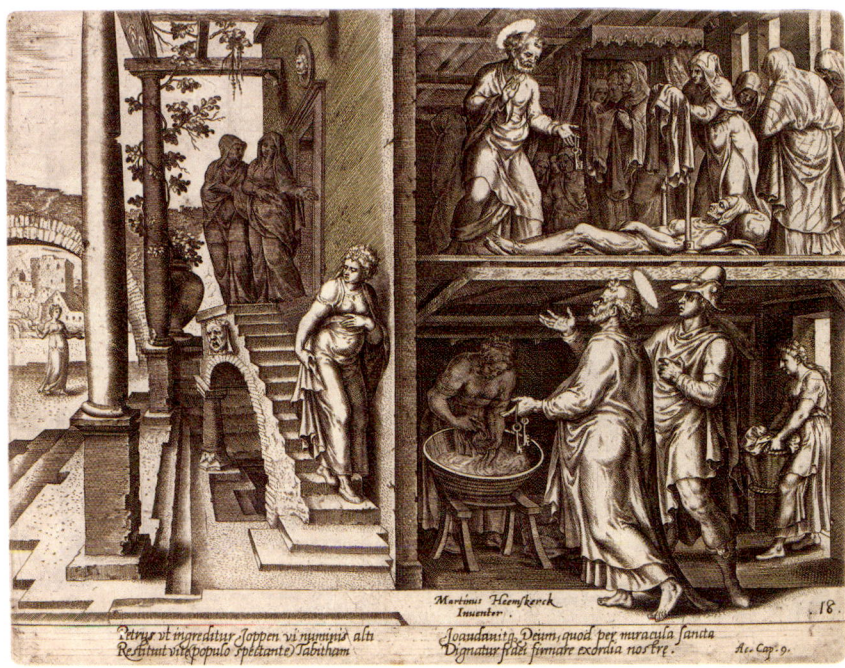

Fig. 293
Philips Galle after Maarten van Heemskerck, *The Resurrection of Tabitha*, engraving, 21.3 x 27.5 cm.

group of workers intently tan and hang hides. The principal subject, Peter's prayer and vision, occupies only a third of the available space—the upper left corner of the composition—whereas the anecdotal episode of the table's dressing is spotlighted in the right foreground. More importantly, the beautiful aperture onto the tanner's workshop is conceived as the entrance to an autonomous stage, and thereby its figures do not fulfill any role in the narrative.

The workers' subordinate world seldom impinges upon the religious sphere, and never actively. In *Saint Peter Resurrecting Tabitha* (Fig. 293), a 1575 engraving by Galle after Maarten van Heemskerck, the space likewise splits into three sections, with the aim of representing different moments of the same story.[24] Upstairs, Peter enacts the miracle of resuscitating Tabitha; in the right lower stage, Peter reappears a few minutes earlier, prompted into Tabitha's house. Here, Heemskerck also depicted a lively laundry scene: one woman hunched over a basin wrings a piece of fabric with amazing concentration, while another carries in a basket loaded with drapes. Though contiguous, the figures of Peter and the laundresses do not interface with each other; the industrious walk-ons remain extraneous to the miracle beside and above.

I can think of only one instance in which a distracted walk-on serves as a foil for the main figure, albeit with no straightforward interaction: an engraving by Giulio Bonasone representing *The Virgin Washing the Feet of the Infant Christ* (Fig. 294). This print is clearly an adaptation of a homonymous design by Giulio Romano, which Bonasone himself had also engraved.[25] In Giulio Romano's composition, the Virgin seemingly rubs the infant's left foot; with haste, Saint Anne brings a dry towel to her daughter as an angel carrying a jug addresses her. To the left, behind Anne, a servant dries a towel upon a fire, close to the fireplace. Stretching both arms forward, she suddenly turns her face backward without a discernable motive.

23 See Dolders 1987, 167, no. 049.5; and Sellink and Leesberg 2001, 2:87-8, no. 205.

24 For the print, see Dolders 1987, 162, no. 048:16.

25 For the two prints, see Massari 1983, 96, no. 124.

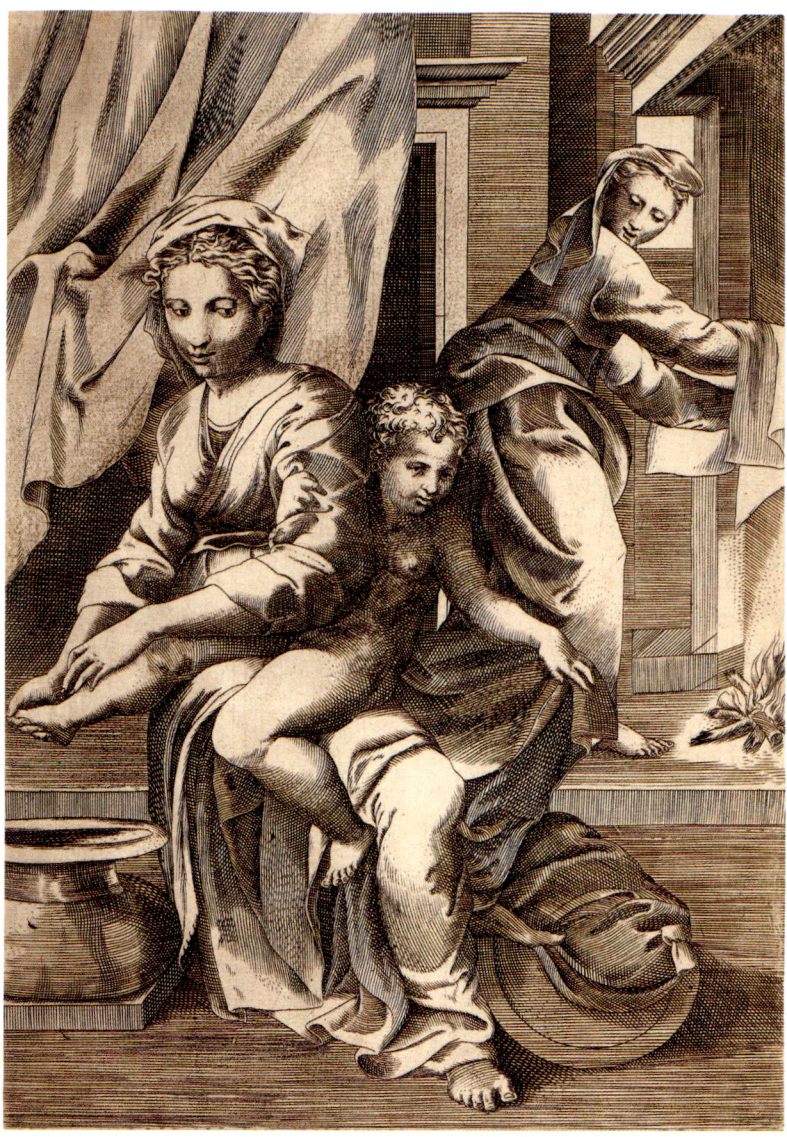

Fig. 294
Giulio Bonasone, *The Virgin Washing the Feet of the Infant Christ*, engraving,
24.7 x 17.5 cm.

In the second print, Bonasone removed the angel and Anne, thereby increasing the intimacy of the domestic scene. Washing Jesus' foot, the Virgin turns her gaze to the child as if to check on him. To the right, closer than in the previous print, a servant leans her body forward while holding a towel upon the fire with both arms flung out. Again, she incomprehensibly directs her gaze backward. Although Bonasone's adaptation of Giulio Romano's drawing is limited to retouching and cutting-off, its visual effect is compelling. By positioning the infant at the intersection of two oblique torsos and downcast gazes—of which the Virgin's is perhaps intentional, and the servant's random—Bonasone subsumes the anecdotal within the religious.

However secondary and unrelated, the maid's figure participates, almost against her will, in the action, not only by orienting the beholder's gaze back to the infant, but especially by engendering the strange yet false impression that her thought dwells on the sacred scene. If, for the sake of experiment, one moves the servant down to the foreground, replacing her in the background with the Virgin and Child reduced to fit into a picture frame, the result does not differ much from what Velázquez represented in *La Mulata* (Fig. 295). In the end, all this might well boil down to a simple inversion of visual relevance, and overall of perspective.[26] But switching roles in seventeenth-century European painting was an audacious and perilous enterprise: the painter risked lasting damage to his reputation, or even being labeled the Antichrist.

It can be argued that, despite her prominent position in the painting, Velázquez's "mulata" remains a modest walk-on, an essentially comic figure in accordance with seventeenth-century aesthetics: she induces laughter, raises a smile or, at best, distracts the viewer. She can by no means perform a noble role, and therefore resembles her peers in many genre scenes. A similar figure appears in Jacopo Bassano's *Parable of Dives and Lazarus*, engraved by Johan Sadeler I (Fig. 296).[27] Almost at the center of the composition, behind a table yet in the foreground, a turbaned female cook lets her gaze distractedly wander from her work of plucking the chickens in front of her (Fig. 297). Although Bassano does not show what might have drawn the woman's curiosity—is she intrigued by the woman nearby, or is it a physiological gesture of distraction?—he certainly employs her as a directional sign: in other words, she guides the viewer amidst the labyrinth of figures and objects close by or further back. She is eminently a functional digression. Should

26   A concept more recently stressed in Knox 2009, 67-8.   27   De Ramaix 1999, 205, no. 171.

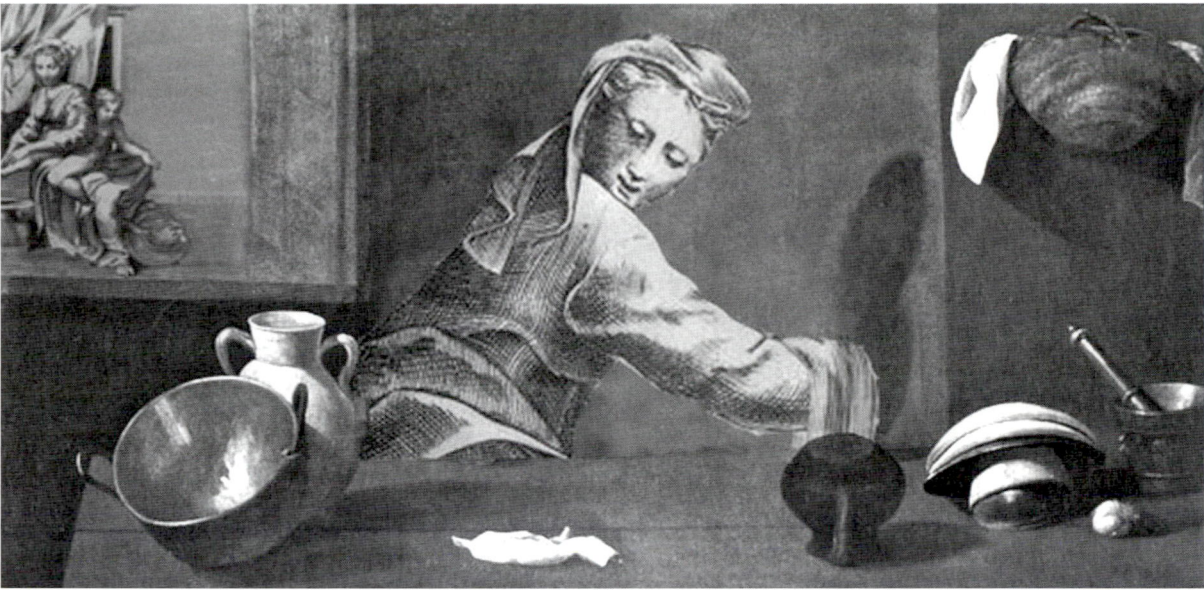

Fig. 295
Photocomposition of Diego Velázquez's *La Mulata*, National Gallery of Art, Dublin, and Giulio Bonasone's *The Virgin Washing the Feet of the Infant Christ*.

Velázquez's servant be judged by the same token? Does she act purely as an animation of the superb *bodegón* in the foreground? And if so, does the summary depiction of the *Supper at Emmaus* in the background of the Dublin painting serve as a pretext for depicting a parsimonious Sevillian kitchen? Perhaps, though this would be a very reductive explanation, as Velázquez conceived of this image as an ongoing action, so that even the disposition of the utensils on the table conveys a specific notion of time and expectancy.

First of all, it is clear that supper is over: a head of garlic, to the side, is the only food to be seen on the table. Nearby, glazed bowls, plates, and a jug lie upside down to dry, whereas a brass pot, leaning against a jar, tilts forward, showing its sparkling inside, reflecting a glow as the light orbits along its rim. In front of the servant, a wrinkled cloth lies solitary and motionless. Albeit at rest, all these kitchen implements latently verge on motion; they pose precariously, ready to lose balance. Just as the esparto basket hangs suspended from the wall, a rag dangling out of it unsteadily, so too does the pestle recline in suspension within the mortar. Of course, some of these motifs recur in other kitchen scenes. In Matham's print after Aertsen, a pot akin to Velázquez's, and similarly tipped, appears across the table. In the foreground, to the left, a jug balances majestically atop a tripod, a skimmer slanting at its base (Figs. 298, 299, 300, 301). Despite these affinities, Velázquez clearly arranged this set of objects to compose motion, and to tell a story. Not only do they suggest a certain temporality: in their paratactic isolation and tense stillness, they encapsulate movement. They are devices of narrative suspense. Moreover, by pointing to the mulatto maid, they accomplish the task that, in early modern art theory, is specific to the secondary characters: strengthening the protagonist's visibility. Velázquez thus turned these everyday catering wares into second leads in action.

But what action? In his *Supper at Emmaus*, Velázquez staged the theme of the problematic coexistence of man and God in a pictorial narrative. Is he demonstrating, in his earlier *Mulata*, how uncoordinated these two dimensions can be? Is he contrasting the maid's mechanical indifference with the deity's transcendence in the background? In this case, *La Mulata* could be viewed as another, more radical, example of meta-fiction. To opt for this reading, though, would be to miss the point, for the divine is here demoted to a visual accessory. Indeed, all the suspense and tension

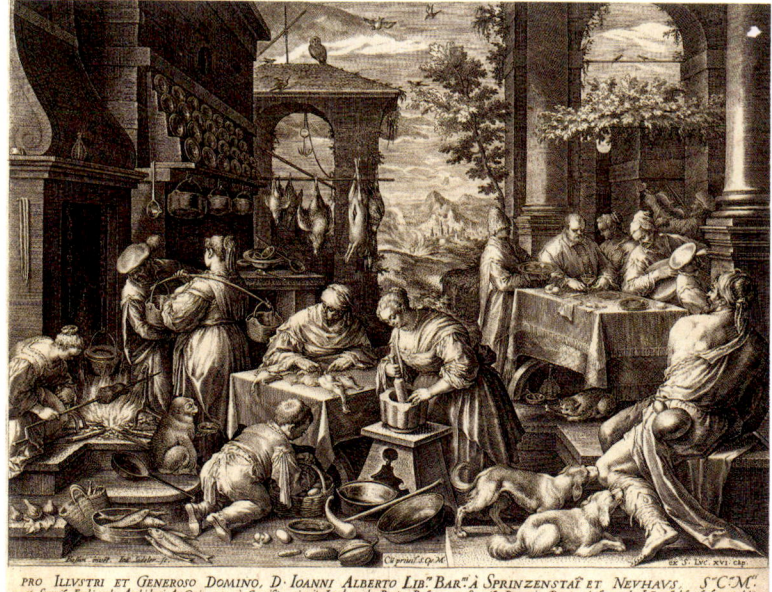

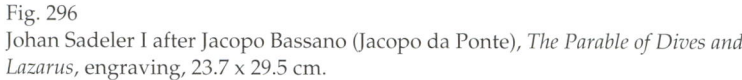

Fig. 296
Johan Sadeler I after Jacopo Bassano (Jacopo da Ponte), *The Parable of Dives and Lazarus*, engraving, 23.7 x 29.5 cm.

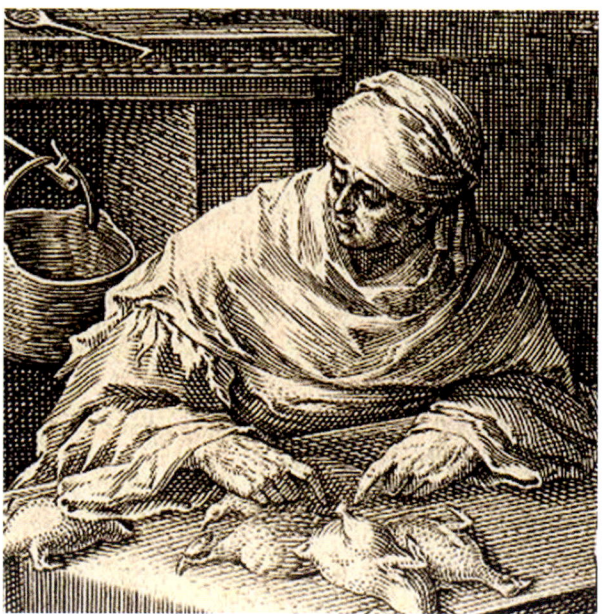

Fig. 297
Johan Sadeler I after Jacopo Bassano (Jacopo da Ponte), *The Parable of Dives and Lazarus*, engraving, 23.7 x 29.5 cm., detail.

conveyed through the still life in the foreground converge toward the servant; the living *bodegón* frames and heralds her action. She is the focal point of the story, and as such she represents the key to grasping Velázquez's intention. To complicate matters, Velázquez provided her attitude with a nuance of prophetic furor. Her sudden motion—she is caught almost off-guard in the middle of a manual activity—and her mysterious expression—oscillating between concentration and dreaminess—endows the mulatto girl with a kind of monumentality, intensified by the powerful shadow cast by her body upon the wall. In the same way, Michelangelo's Sibyls and Prophets on the vault of the Sistine Chapel swing sideways unexpectedly, inexplicably, responding to an inner stimulus. See for instance Joel's posture:[28] his arms outstretched in rolling out a scroll, his shoulder arched, he strives toward the light as his shadow projects upon the niche, counterbalancing his mighty thrust. I do not imply that Velázquez took up Michelangelo's figure in imagining his maid's gesture (Figs. 302, 303). Rather, I contend that he availed himself of a visual schema that suits a prophetic or allegorical figure as well as a comic one. As a consequence, the viewer may perceive the "*mulata*'s" action in the Dublin painting as interconnected with the religious scene: she too might have an inkling of the miracle behind her.

Let us look more closely at her. It is possible that, grabbing the jug, she is about to put it somewhere under the table. Or conversely, she has just set the jug down, and is bracing herself to return to the dining room. Or else, during her duty, she hears something that awakens her curiosity. Perhaps, in the middle of an errand, she is daydreaming. Any of these possibilities is admissible, and others could undoubtedly come to mind. However, all of these actions do have a common denominator: they all relate to man's mechanical or physiological states. In and of themselves, they do not build up action as required of the *istoria*. Even worse, their indeterminacy and ambivalence fool the viewer in his or her attempt to read and comprehend the image exhaustively. And here lies the gist of Velázquez's poetics as expressed in *La Mulata*. Albeit a "dead imitation," the image

28   The prophet Joel was reproduced in the early 1570s by the engraver Giorgio Ghisi. See Boorsch et al. 1985, 151, no. 44.

534

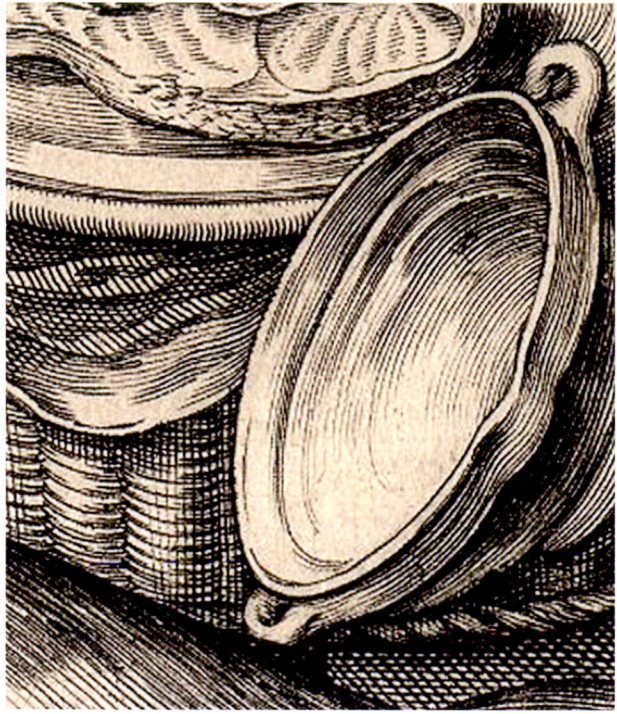

Fig. 298
Jacob Matham after Pieter Aertsen, *Kitchen Scene with the Supper at Emmaus*, engraving, 24.2 x 32.3 cm., detail.

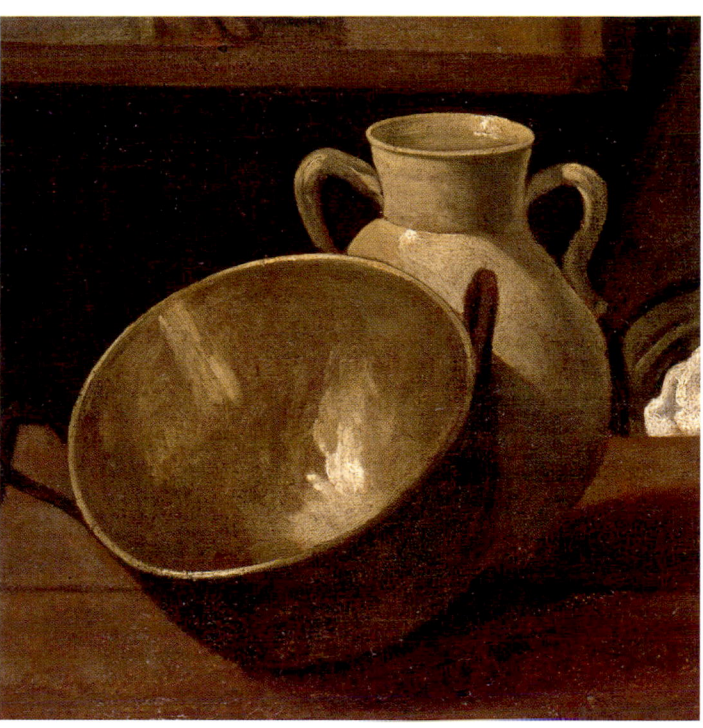

Fig. 299
Diego Velázquez, *La Mulata*, National Gallery of Ireland, Dublin, oil on canvas, 55 x 118 cm., detail.

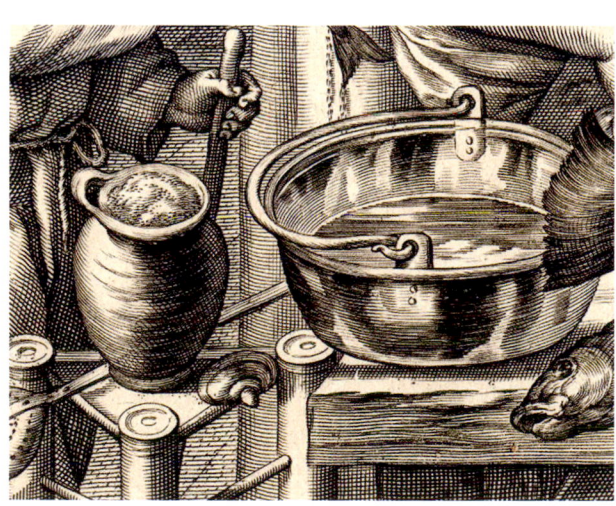

Fig. 300
Jacob Matham after Pieter Aertsen, *Kitchen Scene with the Supper at Emmaus*, engraving, 24.2 x 32.3 cm., detail.

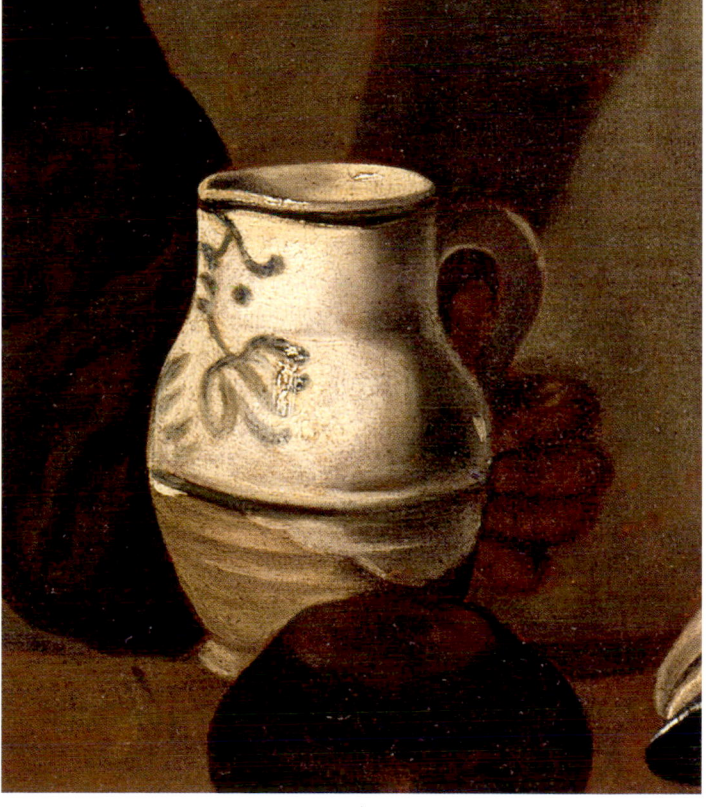

Fig. 301
Diego Velázquez, *La Mulata*, National Gallery of Ireland, Dublin, oil on canvas, 55 x 118 cm., detail.

535

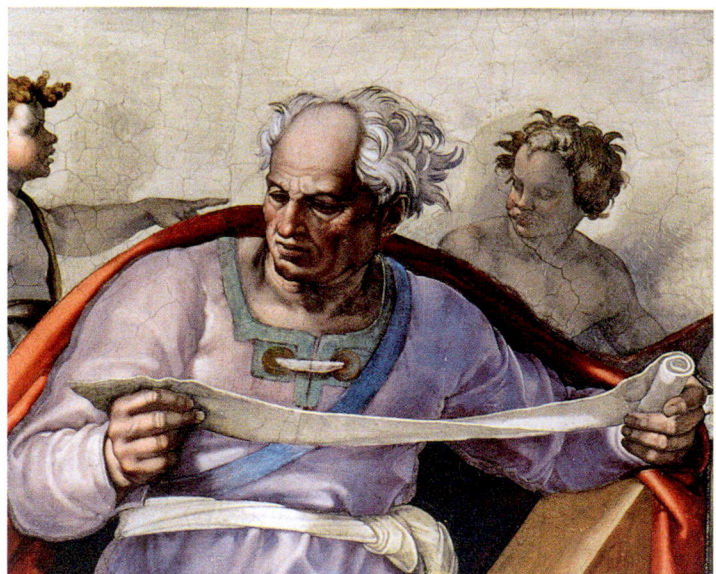

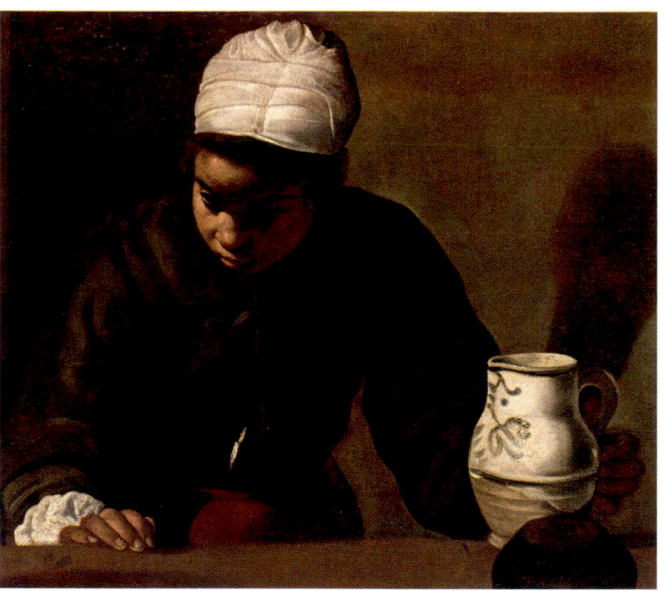

Fig. 302
Michelangelo Buonarroti, *The Prophet Joel*, Sistine Chapel,
Vatican Palace, fresco, detail reversed.

Fig. 303
Diego Velázquez, *La Mulata*, National Gallery of Ireland,
Dublin, oil on canvas, 55 x 118 cm., detail.

through its suspense, ambiguity, and multi-valence functions as a powerful vector of attention: a compound of virtual motion to be endlessly enacted and reenacted by the beholder.

Whether one construes the Dublin *Mulata* as the depiction of a humble maid's prophetic insight into the divine, as a parody staging the incommunicability of man and God, or just as an amusing genre scene, what matters is that narrative action becomes a kind of *tabula rasa* onto which the beholder can project his or her reading, a half-written script to be developed in whatever genre or mode one wishes: religious, comic, allegorical, and so forth. The viewer is involved with narrative as a complementary author. There is no doubt that paintings like the Dublin *Mulata* bid farewell to the principles of legibility and intelligibility with which action was globally identified in the late Renaissance and in the seventeenth century.

Yet Velázquez goes beyond the issue of action altogether by dismantling the very concept of character in his Chicago version of *La Mulata* (Fig. 287). It is unlikely that we will ever know if this picture, so enticing in spite of its poor state, was left unfinished by Velázquez, or if he deliberately erased the view of the supper at Emmaus in the background. In any event, by eliminating this meaningful detail, the viewer's attention focuses strictly on the servant and her action. Here, more than in the Dublin version, the "*mulata*" radically exceeds comprehension. Simultaneously, she is a low character, a comic walk-on, an abstracted prophetess, and a daydreamer. Nothing informs the viewer of her deepest identity, much less her action.

In the second half of the sixteenth century, painters and art theorists had sought in Aristotle's *Poetics* a compass to map out narrative into a well-defined system of hermeneutical notions, religious dogmas, and social principles, in which action and its enactment depends on a rigid classification of characters. The *istoria* is the realm of heroes and gods; genre scenes, barely tolerated because they lack heroic action, were the dwelling of servants and peasants. The maid in the Chicago painting—a "*mulata*," and hence a doubly marginal figure—transcends characterization. Ignorant of what she is and what she does, the viewer is both disoriented and fascinated by her. Velázquez's "*mulata*" has momentarily lost the identity of her role, the definition of her character. If Caravaggio's *Conversion of Saint Paul* prefigures the end of narrative according to Bellori, Velázquez's *Mulata* could be said to symbolize the end of character. To pursue his pictorial experimentation, Velázquez was nevertheless compelled to abandon the taverns and kitchens of his native Seville, and to approach his ineffable walk-on characters through the eyes of, and within the stage of, the Spanish court. In one way or another, however, the triumph of the *istoria*, introduced to Spain by Carducho, discredited and buried Caravaggio's lesson. Albeit through concessions, Velázquez figured out a way to pursue Caravaggio's innovations in painting.

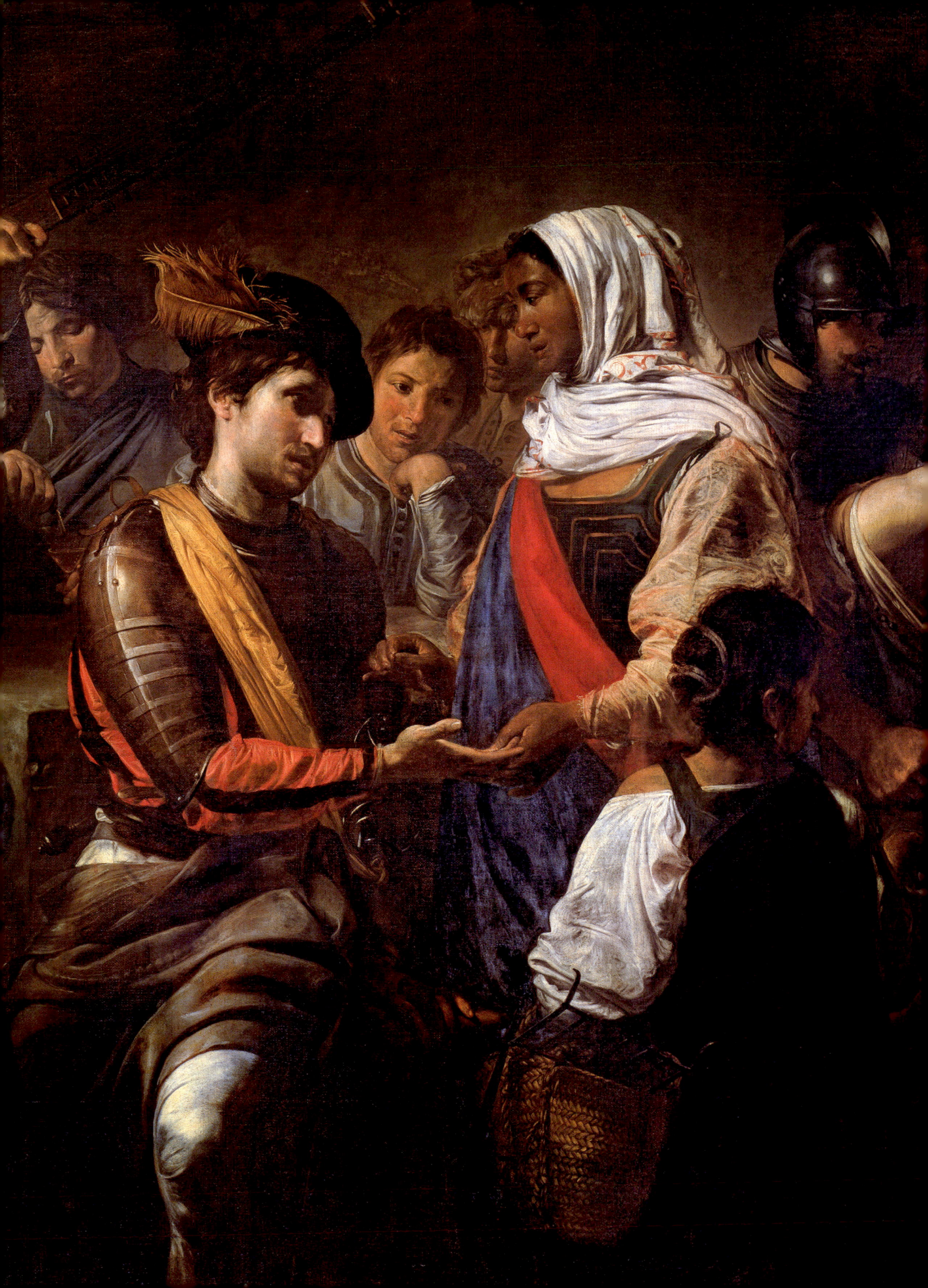

CHAPTER 17

Without a Plot:
Valentin de Boulogne's Liechtenstein *Merry Company with Fortune Teller*

A World of Brawlers, Fortune Tellers, and Music Players

It is a pity that so little is known about one of the most brilliant, talented, and independent followers of Caravaggio, the Frenchman Valentin de Boulogne.[1] When they exist, documents do not offer a great deal of information, and even Valentin's date of birth, 1591, reported in the now lost record of his baptism in the church of Saint-Denis, Coulommiers, has been questioned by scholars on reasonable grounds. In fact, upon Valentin's death in 1632, his servant, a certain Carlo, testified that the master was thirty-eight, which would thus place his birth in 1594.[2] It is impossible to establish when Valentin arrived in Rome. If executed around 1615-1616, as Jean-Pierre Cuzin and Arnauld Brejon de Lavergnée have proposed,[3] his first known paintings of impeccable pictorial quality—the Chatsworth *Concert with Three Musicians* and the Dresden *The Cardsharps* (Fig. 67)—would indicate that at that time Valentin had been living in Rome for a few years; only this would explain both the young master's obvious acquaintance with the painting of Cecco del Caravaggio and Bartolomeo Manfredi, and his already masterful interpretation of these artists' style and technique. Counter to many of Caravaggio's followers—from Simon Vouet to Nicolas Régnier, from Gerrit van Honthorst to Hendrik ter Brugghen—Valentin remained faithful to the stylistic language and pronounced chiaroscuro of the Caravaggesque movement until his premature death, a fact worth stressing because it constitutes a blatant exception.

To my knowledge, no first-rank painter in Rome at the beginning of the 1630s was still practicing the dark palette of Caravaggio, who by then had fallen completely from favor, whereas many, seduced by the neo-Venetian vogue that had emerged in the mid 1620s,[4] were attempting to apply the color technique of Titian's early work to a paradigm of the *istoria* inspired by Annibale Carracci and his disciples. In a sense, Valentin was the lucid survivor of a pictorial current doomed to extinction, and on this account an analysis of his oeuvre allows us to understand, at least in part, the reasons why Caravaggio's lesson lost its appeal entirely as a credible alternative to the classicism that was then reasserting itself and which would dominate for the next one hundred and fifty years. In my view, Valentin's *Merry Company with Fortune Teller*, now at the Liechtenstein Gallery, Vienna (Fig. 304),[5] tellingly and complexly epitomizes the dissolution and collapse of the pictorial models offered by Caravaggio's comedic narratives as developed by his followers after the master's death in 1610. Fortunately enough, the Liechtenstein picture's origin and date are

---

1 It is shocking that, besides Mojana 1989, there is no monograph devoted to the artist. Only a few essays have been devoted to the French master: Brejon de Lavergnée and Cuzin 1973, 122-78; Cuzin 1975; *Manfredi* 1987, 119-22; and Brejon de Lavergnée 1991.

2 See Mojana 1989, 4.

3 See Brejon de Lavergnée and Cuzin 1973, 126-8.

4 Among these painters, one must single out Nicolas Poussin and Pietro da Cortona. See for instance Blunt 1967, 1:54-99; Briganti 1982, 65-6; and Merz 1991, 140-64.

5 For the painting, see Brejon de Lavergnée and Cuzin 1973, 176-8, no. 54; and Mojana 1989, 178, no. 64.

539

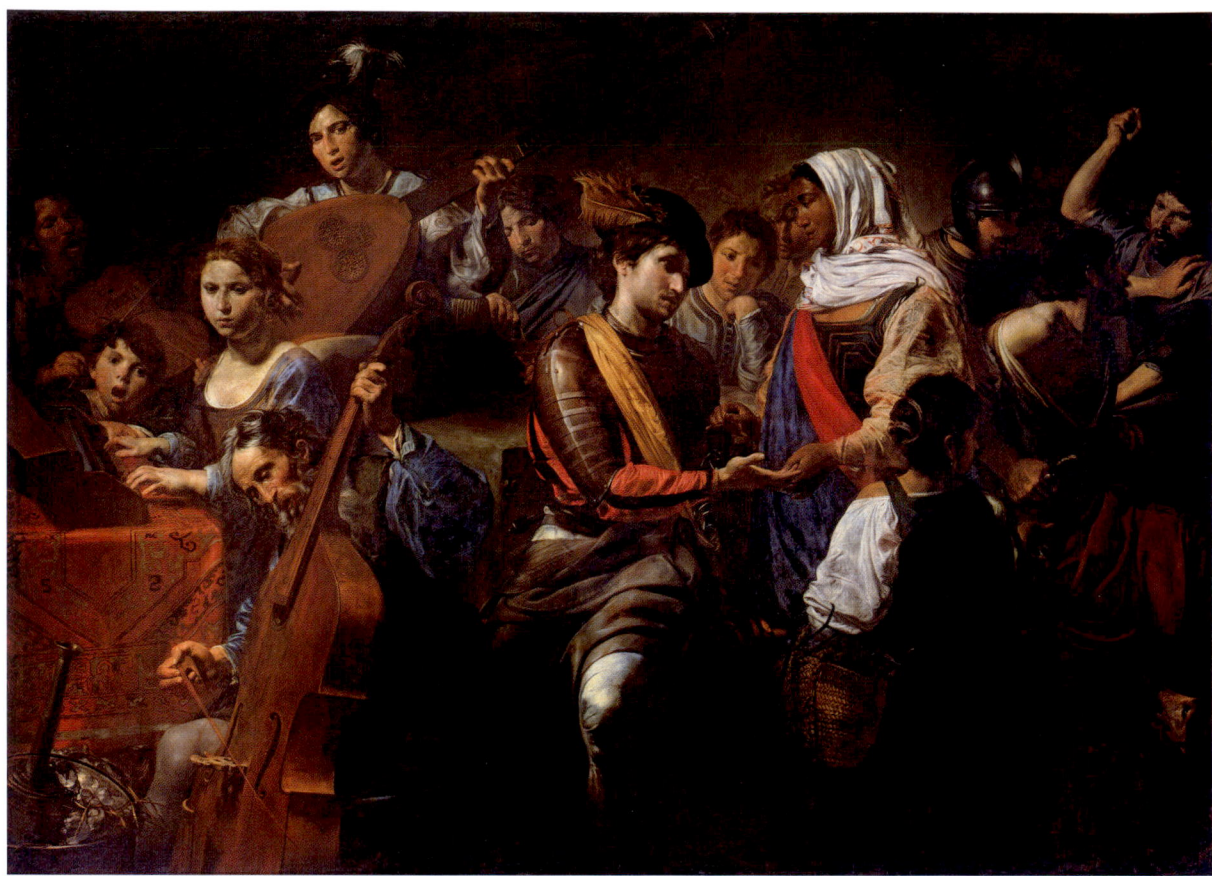

Fig. 304
Valentin de Boulogne, *Merry Company with Fortune Teller*, Liechtenstein Museum, Vienna, oil on canvas, 190 x 265 cm.

excellently documented. On 30 July 1631, Valentin was subpoenaed and heard as a witness in the trial of Fabrizio Valguarnera, a Sicilian nobleman accused of "laundering" stolen diamonds, which he sold to purchase, and traded for, paintings. This is Valentin's testimony:

> A few months ago, Don Fabrizio approached me in the street several times; I did not know him at all, [but] he knew (I don't know how, though someone might have told him) that I was a painter. He told me that he wanted me to make a large painting with many figures, in which a gypsy, soldiers, and other women playing musical instruments would appear. Because I did not feel like working on it, I stalled, [but] eventually, the following Lent, he showed up at my house, and begged me again to make this painting, and I decided to make it and asked for a hundred *scudi*, which he thought was too much, and in the end we settled for eighty *scudi*. Then, I prepared the canvas and started working on it, which I finished and gave to him at Pentecost, as he urged me to finish it every day, for he wanted to leave and was only waiting for the painting. And so, I finished and gave it to him as I said, and I delivered it in my house where he came with four porters and took it away along with another picture, a Judgment of Solomon that I had retouched for six *scudi*, and he paid the rest of the eighty *scudi* for the painting I made for him, as he had already given me some money as a down payment, and this is my entire business with the said Don Fabrizio.[6]

6 Costello 1950, 278-9: "Alcuni mesi sono più volte per strada m'incontrò detto don Fabrizio, del quale io non havevo cognoscenza alcuna et non so come mi cognoscesse per pittore, se ben puol essere gli fossi monstrato da qualche

In the light of this testimony, Marina Mojana, following in the footsteps of Cuzin and Brejon de Lavergnée, defined the Liechtenstein picture as an "artificial" work executed "without enthusiasm," "a sample collection of themes recurrent in Valentin's repertoire," whose structure is therefore "archaic," its composition being "bereft of originality." The painting," Mojana concludes, "casts all the actors from Valentin's theater as it happens in the end of the play, when the interpreters come on stage to bid farewell to the public."[7] While I cannot agree with her definition of the composition as "archaic," there is some truth in Mojana's assessment of the picture; despite its "pictorial refinement," Valentin's last known work feels indeed like an assemblage of motifs, and its narrative disconnections are all too manifest to be denied. But I do not believe that *Merry Company with Fortune Teller* is the product of a fatigued and subservient Muse, insofar as its "artificiality"— that is, its staging of actors that, compositionally interdependent, are nevertheless disconnected in separate groups without a unitary plot to keep them together—is not an isolated phenomenon in Valentin's work.

I intend to demonstrate that the painting's structural inconsistencies represent the apogee of an artistic evolution initiated much earlier and to a certain degree transcending Valentin's individuality as a painter. With Cuzin and Brejon de Lavergnée,[8] I believe that the Liechtenstein picture is one of the twelve paintings displayed in the parish of Santa Maria di Costantinopoli, Rome, on the Tuesday after Pentecost 1631, most likely at the instigation of Fabrizio Valguarnera. If this is correct, Joachim von Sandrart, who had his *Death of Seneca* exhibited on the same occasion,[9] is most probably describing Valentin's Liechtenstein painting in his 1675 *Teutsche Akademie*, although there *Merry Company with Fortune Teller* is erroneously interpreted as an *Allegory of the Five Senses*, and its description barely matches the picture's content. I quote Sandrart's text, regardless of its notorious confusions, because it records both the public's admiration for the master's virtuosity and the criticism aroused by his painting in 1631:

> The seventh [picture] was executed by a Frenchman, Valentin from Coulommiers ["*Colombie*"], and represented the Five Senses in a room at a table in the form of a friendly party. Some eat and drink, others play chess, checkers, and cards; some examine coins, enjoy the smell of flowers, blow on flutes, and strum lutes. Finally, some beat one another and argue. It was painted in an excellent manner. However, the picture was much more commended for its facture and color technique than for its invention and drawing.[10]

d'uno, dicendomi che voleva ch'io gli facessi un quadro grande con gente dove intervenissero una zingara, soldati et altre donne che sonassero instrumenti, et perché io non mi sentivo da lavorare, differii di farlo e finalmente questa quaresima prossima venne un giorno a casa mia, et mi pregò di nuovo ch'io gli facessi questo quadro, et havendo resoluto di farglilo, gli domandai cento scudi, et lui parendogli troppo la domanda, finalmente restassemo d'accordo per ottanta scudi, et così mesi in ordine la tela, e lo cominciai a lavorare, quale gli diedi fenito per pasqua rosata, solecitandomi lui giorna[l]mente che lo perfettionasse, perché voleva andar via, né aspettava altro che questo, et così per il tempo sudetto gli lo diedi fenito, gli lo consignai in casa dove venne con quattro facchini et se lo portò via, assieme con un altro quadro ch'era il Giuditio di Salomone, quale io gl'havevo ritoccato per prezzo di sei scudi, et mi diede il compimento delli 80 scudi, prezzo del quadro che gli lavorai, havendomi prima dato altri denari a detto conto, et questo è quanto io ho havuto da negoziare con detto don Fabrizio."

7   Brejon de Lavergnée and Cuzin 1973, 178: "Ma il Valentin dipinge qui una delle sue tele estreme, forse addirittura l'ultima. Si direbbe che, presentando la morte vicina, egli

voglia riunire qui, in un'estrema galleria, i personaggi dei suoi quadri; o piuttosto, gli attori del suo proprio teatro"; Mojana 1989, 178: "Eseguita su commissione con scarso entusiasmo, come confermano le parole dello stesso artista, la tela è un campionario di temi ricorrenti nel repertorio del Valentin e ancora molto manfrediana nella concezione. Risulta quindi un lavoro artificioso, privo di originalità compositiva (...). La *Riunione con indovina*, notevole per qualità pittorica, è tuttavia arcaica nella composizione e priva di autentica unità compositiva. Il dipinto mette in scena tutti gli attori del teatro del Valentin, come avviene alla fine della rappresentazione, quando gli interpreti escono alla ribalta tutti insieme per salutare il pubblico."

8   See Brejon de Lavergnée and Cuzin 1973, 176-8.

9   See Klemm 1986, 63-7, no. 11.

10   Sandrart, 28-9: "Das siebente war durch Valentin von Colombie, einen Franzosen, gebildet und präsentierte die fünf Sinne in einem Zimmer bey der Tafel in Form einer freundlichen Conversation: etliche aßen un tranken, andere spielten im Schach, Damm und Karten, wiederum andere besahen die Münzen, genoßen den Geruch der Blumen, pfiffen auf Flöten, schlugen die Lauten. Letzlich waren auch etliche,

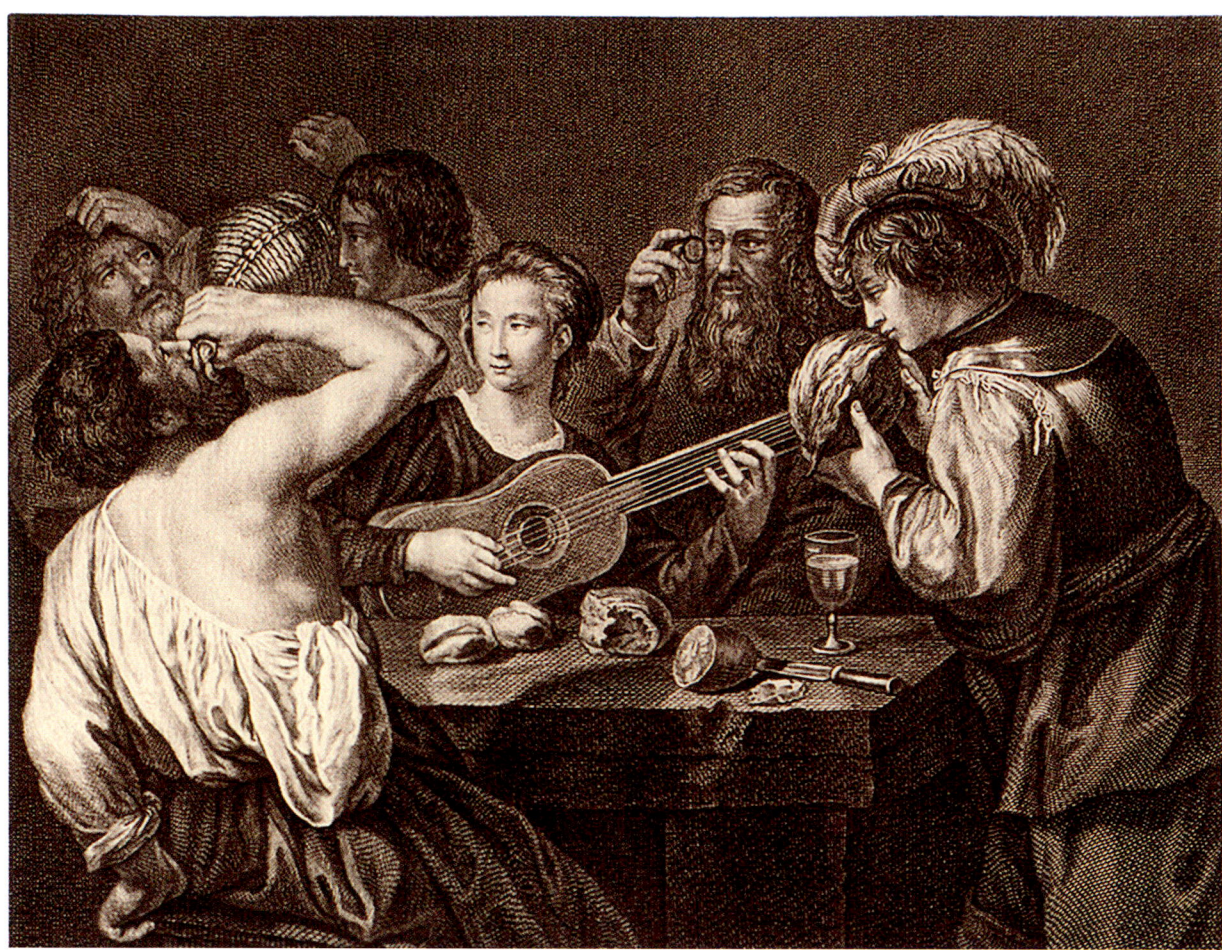

Fig. 305
Valentin de Boulogne (after?), *Allegory of the Five Senses*, reproduced from *La Galerie du Palais-Royal*, 1786-1806.

No extant painting by Valentin fits Sandrart's description, and Jane Costello's 1950 proposal to identify the picture with an *Allegory of the Five Senses*—now lost, but reproduced in an engraving from the 1786-1806 *La Galerie du Palais-Royal* (Fig. 305)—cannot be accepted. This painting, once in the Duke of Orleans' Gallery in Paris with an attribution to Valentin, depicts a group of seven figures:[11] a man drinking, another smelling a flower, an old man examining a coin, a woman playing a lute, and two men fighting: at first glance, it is true, a fair match to Sandrart's text. Yet, much as I would like to justify Sandrart's exaggerations as the result of describing Valentin's picture nearly forty years after he had seen it, I cannot bring myself to believe that the impressive number of figures and situations evoked by the German is the fruit of his imagination, especially if one takes into account Valentin's description of his painting for Valguarnera in his 1631 deposition.

In other words, Sandrart must have seen a painting in which Valentin had indeed represented a plethora of actors and a multiplicity of actions, a compositional exploit meant to impress the public by its inventive variety. The Duke of Orleans' *Allegory of the Five Senses*, whether by Valentin or not, does not correspond to these standards. Since Sandrart described Caravaggio's *Martyrdom of Saint Matthew* in San Luigi dei Francesi, Rome—a picture with which he was undoubtedly well

die sich mit einander schlugen und rauften. Es war alles fürtrefflich gemahlet. Dieses Stuck wurde aber mehr wegen des Wolmahlens und Colorirens als wegen der Invention und Zeichnung gerühmet."

11   See Mojana 1989, 242, no. 151.

acquainted—as *Christ Driving the Merchants out of the Temple*, his confusion in relating and evoking the subject of the Liechtenstein picture is not astonishing by any token. Most probably he conflated his recollection of an *Allegory of the Five Senses* by Valentin with that of *Merry Company with Fortune Teller*; a similar conflation occurs in Sandrart's description of Caravaggio's *Calling of Saint Matthew* (see Chapter 6), in which he evokes the figures of card players that do not figure there, but rather in Caravaggio's *The Cardsharps* and in Hans Holbein's *Death and the Gambler*. Moreover, as Cuzin and Brejon de Lavergnée have pointed out, the fact that Valentin's painting was shown on the Tuesday after Pentecost would account for the pressure exerted by Valguarnera on the master to have the work delivered by that deadline. Furthermore, Sandrart's misreading of Valentin's picture might equally betray the conceptual impasse of the German painter in determining the picture's subject: that it was a *"freundliche Conversation"* was clear, but the mutual correlations of the numerous figures represented in it was a matter of vagueness. Interpreting the subject's disparateness as the consequence of an allegorical message—allegory by definition permits a certain amount of license in combining diverse sorts of actions—was perhaps Sandrart's way of coping with the oddity of Valentin's concept.

If the Liechtenstein picture was indeed put on view in 1631, Sandrart's remark on the painting's lack of invention and drawing becomes even more significant, for a number of reasons. One of the most valuable paintings exhibited at that time, Nicolas Poussin's *The Plague of Ashdod*[12]— also commissioned by Valguarnera—was celebrated by the public in unequivocal terms, at least according to Sandrart: the picture was "no less masterful than rich in [the representation of the] affects," and therefore "was subsequently appraised, purchased, and paid for with 1000 crowns."[13] It is noteworthy that Valguarnera had commissioned Poussin's *The Plague of Ashdod* and *The Realm of Flora* long before he had contacted Valentin for a painting;[14] the Sicilian's request for a genre scene with multiple figures was probably aimed at obtaining a work that could be opposed to, and compared with, the *istoria* and the mythological allegory by Poussin that he already owned. This fact becomes even more plausible if one recalls that in 1629, when Valentin unveiled his *The Martyrdom of Saints Processus and Martinianus*[15] for Saint Peter's, the painting was immediately contrasted with its quasi-pendant, Poussin's 1627-1628 *The Martyrdom of Saint Erasmus*. Both pictures are now at the Pinacoteca Vaticana, Rome.[16] It comes as no surprise that the main source of this artistic debate is Sandrart himself, who had just arrived in Rome when Valentin finished his picture. Sandrart's remarks on these two paintings are of great importance, since his testimony confirms how the appraisal of these works underlay an aesthetic cleavage and conceptual opposition specific to Rome's artistic climate in the late 1620s:

> He [Valentin] was also charged with executing an altarpiece for Saint Peter's in Rome, in which he depicted soldiers stretching [the bodies of] two holy martyrs on the rack with the nearby ruffians beating them, besides other actions: a painting so well drawn and colored, and crafted with such relief, that it is not inferior to any other work, as all the critics and knowledgeable painters at the time stated.[17]

12 See Rosenberg and Pratt 1994, 200-2, no. 43.

13 Sandrart, 29: "Ware nicht minder künstlich als affectuos: massen es nachgehends zu Rom für 1000 Cronen geschätzet, angenommen und bezahlt worden."

14 For the painting, see Rosenberg and Pratt 1994, 203-5, no. 44.

15 See Mojana 1989, 152-4, no. 50.

16 See Rosenberg and Pratt 1994, 172-4, no. 26.

17 Sandrart, 256: "Es ist ihme aber auch sonsten in Rom ein Altarblatt su S. Peter angedinget worden, worinnen enthalten, wie zween heilige Märtyrer an der Folter durch die Soldaten angespannet und von denen umstehenden Böswichten gebrügelt werden, welches dann mit andern Umständen dermaßen wol gezeichnet, coloriret, ausrundiret und gemahlet ist, daß es keinem andern Kunstblatt zu weichen Ursach hat, wie solches alle unpartheyische und verständige Künstlere zu jederzeit ausgesprochen haben."

And on Poussin's *The Martyrdom of Saint Erasmus*:

> Along with Valentin, whom I have previously mentioned, he [Poussin] also painted a canvas for Saint Peter's, in which executioners reel Saint Erasmus's bowels out of his abdomen. As the already recorded painting by Valentin was celebrated, and everyone was eager to see it, a great debate arose, insofar as many ranked this painting higher than Poussin's, and others vice versa. However, the critics and connoisseurs considered them both highly commendable, and established that neither was to yield to, or be more praised than, the other. Indeed, whereas Poussin had excelled in invention, and in the representation of [man's] passions and affects, Valentin had done better in rendering true naturalness, in the vigor and greatness of his color technique, and in the harmony of his colors. Hence, both painters have operated masterfully and neither surpassed, or was surpassed by, the other. But Poussin, blessed with a long life, was able to keep his preeminence and improve himself through the example of the most glorious Roman school.[18]

It might sound strange that in 1629 or 1631 Poussin's painting was judged against Valentin's, and yet Sandrart's testimony is wholly reliable in this regard. Not surprisingly, the German painter had been so absorbed in the artistic debates raging during his long-past sojourn in Rome that, in presenting Poussin's artistic personality, he once again contrasted it with Valentin's:

> Because his genius led him to painting not images with life-size figures in closed spaces, like Valentin, but in open air and fields, he [Poussin] endeavored to represent above all the famous stories and poetic myths of the ancient world, and therefore to depict the affects and motions necessary to them in pictures two or three "*Spannen*" tall.[19]

No doubt Sandrart perceived Poussin's and Valentin's modes of painting not only as dialectically interrelated, but also in terms that evoke—especially in the case of Valentin—the criticism then addressed against Caravaggio's art and "artistic path," as Francesco Albani would define it (see the Introduction to Part One). On the one hand, Poussin is the unrivaled master of the *istoria*, and in this respect he prevails in whatever pictorial devices contribute to a legible and intelligible rendition of human action: "*Affekten*," "*Passionen*," and "*Bewegungen*" (movement). Heeding the principles of the early modern *istoria*, Poussin particularly cares for, and reigns sovereign in, "*Invention*" and "*Zeichnung*" (drawing). To deploy his pictorial narratives coherently and fluently, and to accommodate a convenient number of actors, Poussin diminishes the scale of his figures, which he thereby cannot contrive in a single room, so he arranges them instead in ampler architectures or open spaces. Although Sandrart is sensitive to Valentin's art—he was trained in Honthorst's workshop—for him Valentin's painting is the realm of color and true nature, but not

18 Sandrart, 257: "Neben vorgemeldtem Valentin mahlte er auch eine Tafel in S. Peters Kirchen von dem heiligen Erasmo, wie ihme durch die Henkersknechte seine Därme aus dem Leib gehaspelt werden, welches dann eben damals, als Valentins schon gemeldtes Kunststück erhoben worden, herfür kommen, worüber, weil jederman solches zu sehen begierig gewesen, nachgehends ein großer Disputat entstanden, sintemalen ihrer viel dieses jenem, andere aber jenes diesem vorziehen wollen, die Kunstverständige und unpartheyische aber beyde hochschätzbar gehalten, und daß keines dem andern zu weichen oder sich vor dem andern zu erheben Ursach hätte, geurtheilet; dann wo Pousin in denen Passionen, Affecten und der Invention vorgezogen worden,

da hat Valentin in der wahren Natürlichkeit, Stärke, Erhebung des Colorits, Harmonia der Farben es bevor gethan, daß also beede den Meister gespielet und keener dem andern vor oder nach gegangen. Allein daß Pousin durch Glückseligkeit seines langen Lebens den Vortheil erhalten und sich allezeit auf der weitberühmten Römischen Kunstschul bäßern können."

19 Ibidem: "Weil sein Genius ihn nicht zu den Lebens-großen Bildern in verschloßenen Orten, wie Valentin, sondern mehr in die offene Luft oder das weite Feld zu mahlen, angetrieben, aus allen der alter Welt ruhmwürdigen Historien, Poetereyen und darzu nothwendige Affecten und Bewegungen durch 2 oder 3 Spannenhohe Bilder vorzustellen sich bemühet."

that of drawing and invention. Admittedly, Valentin remains a double of Caravaggio, whereas Poussin, as Sandrart himself declares, is both a new Raphael and a new young Titian: an original combination of pictorial methods with which Valentin is unable to compete. In 1629 and 1631 Poussin incarnated newness, while Valentin simply represented the extreme refinement of the then criticized style inaugurated by Caravaggio, an unorthodox and anti-canonical master of the past.

Valentin would surely have been aware of this situation. He was protected and appreciated by powerful patrons in Rome—chief among them Cardinal Francesco Barberini, Pope Urban VIII's favorite nephew—but in view of the newest artistic trends, he could not even remotely claim that his art qualified as truly avant-garde. When prompted by Valguarnera to execute a painting with gypsies, soldiers, and innumerable women, he certainly knew that his hallmark remained these inn scenes with their low-life actors, a pictorial genre as avidly sought-after as it was disdained for its hierarchical "baseness." Nonetheless, Valguarnera's commission entailed an unprecedented challenge for Valentin: that of creating a genre scene with a multiplicity of figures as requested of an *istoria*. In other words, he was granted the opportunity to compete with Poussin's multi-figure compositions, but on his own terrain. Perhaps he truly failed in this enterprise, though this is open to question. But he did not fail simply for lack of enthusiasm.

Indeed, how is one to explain his lack of enthusiasm? Did it depend on an awareness of his artistic limits? Was he fed up with a genre that had brought about his controversial yet solid fortune? In a sense, both the "disconnectedness" and formal elegance of the Liechtenstein painting share a pictorial boldness that cannot be confused with artistic fatigue and masterful ease respectively, all the more so in that *Merry Company with Fortune Teller* is a magnificent piece of painting; a triptych of tavern situations, or transversal slices of low-life themes articulated in three tempi: to the left, a concert; to the right, a brawl; at the center, a fortune telling.

This tripartite structure is punctuated by deft parallelisms: to the left and right, the figures are coordinated through open triangulations, determining a zigzagging itinerary of perception and reading for the viewer; at the center, the soldier and the gypsy triangulate with the melancholic boy behind them at the table, configuring a closed triangular group, and thereby anchoring the beholder's gaze onto the central scene. Albeit similar, the lateral, zigzagging trajectories of reading predisposed by Valentin operate in opposite ways and fulfill divergent goals. Whereas the episode of the concert to the left proceeds from the upper middle ground toward the foreground, that of the fight recedes from the middle ground toward the background: two narrative foci with antithetical focalizations, the former sharply defined, the latter blurry or in a transitional phase of fading out. As a result, the composition appears slightly unbalanced, overcrowded on the left, moderately breathing on the right, which mitigates the impression of figural claustrophobia that the Liechtenstein picture might convey.

By means of these features, Valentin invites viewers to wander across the canvas, passing from one episode to the other, propelling their gaze from the left foreground to the right background. This disposition of figures indicates that Valentin adopted different strategies in outlining perceptual and reading paths through which the beholder might not only access the picture, but also bind its figures and actions together. Nonetheless, the three episodes of the composition do not interact with one another, neither on a diachronic level nor with respect to a general plot. There is no unity of action whatsoever in *Merry Company with Fortune Teller*: the narrative armature is present, but empty. The figures and episodes do not blend together into a flow of narration. On the contrary, numerous actors in the Liechtenstein picture recite their own soliloquies. But to what degree is this orientation unusual for Valentin?

I propose to follow the development of these three separate themes—the concert, the fortune telling, and the fight—not only in Valentin's work, but also in some of the paintings of his colleagues

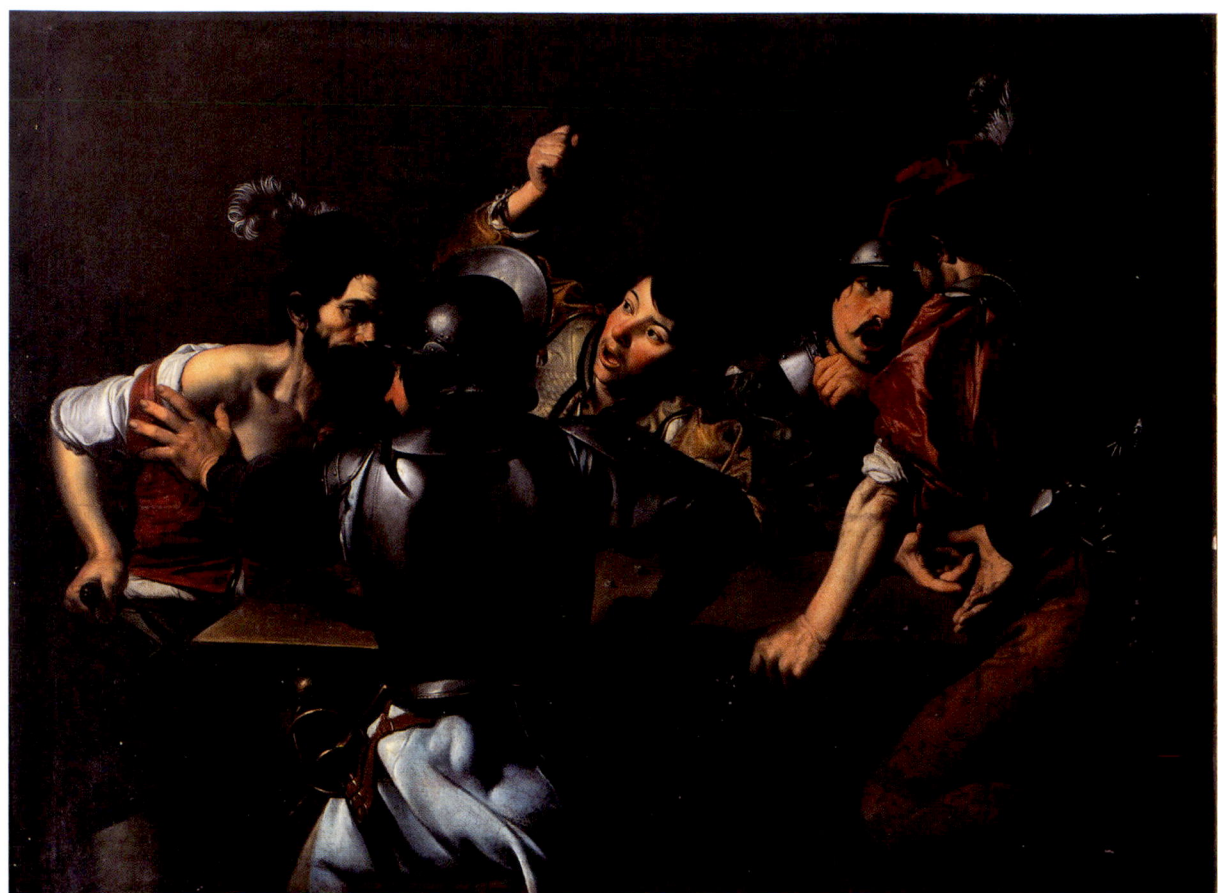

Fig. 306
Valentin de Boulogne (after), *Soldiers Playing Dice and Morra*, Musée des Beaux-Arts et d'Archéologie, Besançon, oil on canvas, 133 x 236 cm.

and contemporaries in Rome. In this way, I shall be able to answer the two crucial questions at the core of this chapter: in what measure does the Liechtenstein painting embody the wearing-out and dissolution of comedic schemas inherited from Caravaggio? What sort of narrative—and, if any, with what originality—is envisioned by Valentin during his brief career? I will start with the theme of the brawl, to which Valentin consecrated an entire composition, now lost, but reproduced in many copies and two engravings.

An early copy, now at the Musée des Beaux-Arts et Archéologie, Besançon, is unanimously considered to be of decent quality (Fig. 306).[20] In his *Soldiers Playing Dice and Morra*, Valentin represents five figures around a table. To the left, a trio of soldiers, interconnected in a triangular diagram, engage in a fight, probably as a result of a suspected swindle or a disagreement over the score; his back turned, the figure with the metallic cuirass and helmet presses his right hand against the table while seeking to block his companion, wearing a feathered beret, who in turn grabs the hilt of his sword threateningly, responding to the assault of the young man nearby, who yells at him as he sets out to beat him with his fist. To the right, two soldiers zealously play *morra* (a popular game similar to rock-paper-scissors, in which two players open their fists while proffering any number between two and ten; the winner is the one whose number equals or surpasses the total score determined by the uncurled fingers of both contestants); Valentin portrays the two soldiers in the very act of guessing the number and opening their fists. One of the players, sporting a plumed beret, leans over the table while resting his knee on a chair; his opponent, equipped with a

20   See Mojana 1989, 235, no. 139.

helmet, is open-mouthed and stares directly at his adversary. Taken together, the five figures build a symmetrical and animated compound, a sort of arrow whose tip corresponds to the figure at the left, the one seated at the table's end.

Two substantial factors of *Soldiers Playing Dice and Morra* should be noted. First, although they clearly compose two separate groups, Valentin succeeded in tying together the brawlers and the players through a felicitous synchronization; at first glance, the beholder might indeed believe that the two soldiers at the right—the ones absorbed in the *morra* game—also participate in the brawl. Second, the salient characteristic of the subject treated by Valentin resides in its bringing together two different, though homologous, pictorial themes: the soldiers' gaming and fighting. In other words, Valentin here expands upon a comedic theme through ingenious duplication; by representing both the *morra* and the dice games, the master manages to join together and conjure up two distinct aspects of the gaming, the playing itself and the inevitable, picturesque brawl that occasionally ensues in this iconographic tradition. In this manner, Valentin is also able to introduce a certain impression of diachroneity into his picture, the fight to the left being an iconographical sequel of the gaming to the right.

In *Merry Company with Fortune Teller*, the three figures of the Besançon brawlers reappear, reenacting their original script: one seizing the sword; the second lifting his right arm and preparing to beat his adversary with his fist; and the third, a soldier with a metal helmet, pushing away the aggressor of his companion. In configuring this group, Valentin took up and preserved almost intact the attitude of the figure with his raised fist in *Soldiers Playing Dice and Morra*, but instead wedged the helmeted man from this previous composition between the two brawlers, presenting him in profile and not with his back turned: a typical case of variation upon an already employed formula, which in this case results in the equivalent of a self-quotation. The most formulaic part of the Liechtenstein picture, the episode of the brawl, occupies a minor space in the composition despite the fact that, from a narrative viewpoint, the action it represents is among the most coherently marshaled of the painting. A completely different discourse applies to the central scene of fortune telling, a theme that enjoyed a huge success among the followers of Caravaggio and that Valentin had already painted at least twice before. Needless to say, Caravaggio's two versions of *The Fortune Teller* (see Chapter 4) had given rise to this iconography, but Bartolomeo Manfredi's interpretation of this theme undoubtedly exerted a greater influence on Valentin.

Dated to *c*.1615, Manfredi's *Fortune Teller*, now in the Detroit Institute of Arts, Detroit (Fig. 307) is a masterpiece in its own right.[21] Like Caravaggio, Manfredi depicted a gorgeous gypsy revealing the future to a youth, but he suppressed the lyrical undertones specific to his predecessor's prototypes, and delegated the comedic function—the robbery—to two supplementary figures represented in the background: an older gypsy to the left and a thief with a plumed hat—perhaps a self-portrait—to the right. Manfredi's elaboration upon Caravaggio's examples proves to be particularly innovative. Bound to one another through the undulating chain of his right and her left arms—the three hands converging midway between the two figures, and fashioned into an elegant helicoid—the gypsy and the boy no longer direct furtive glances at one another. Observing his palm's lines as the woman's divinatory finger grazes his hand, the youth seems exclusively preoccupied by the verdict of the chiromancy, the untold future whose anxious expectation is expressed through his concentrated gaze. Entirely immersed in her foretelling vision, the gypsy stares into space in profound concentration, and her parted lips emit an oracle inaudible to the viewer. Taking advantage of the couple's absorption, the older gypsy extracts the money wrapped in a handkerchief from the youth's pocket, whereas the thief snatches the hen ensconced in the

---

21   For the painting, see *Manfredi* 1987, 78, no. 11; and Hartje
2004, 333-5, no. A20.

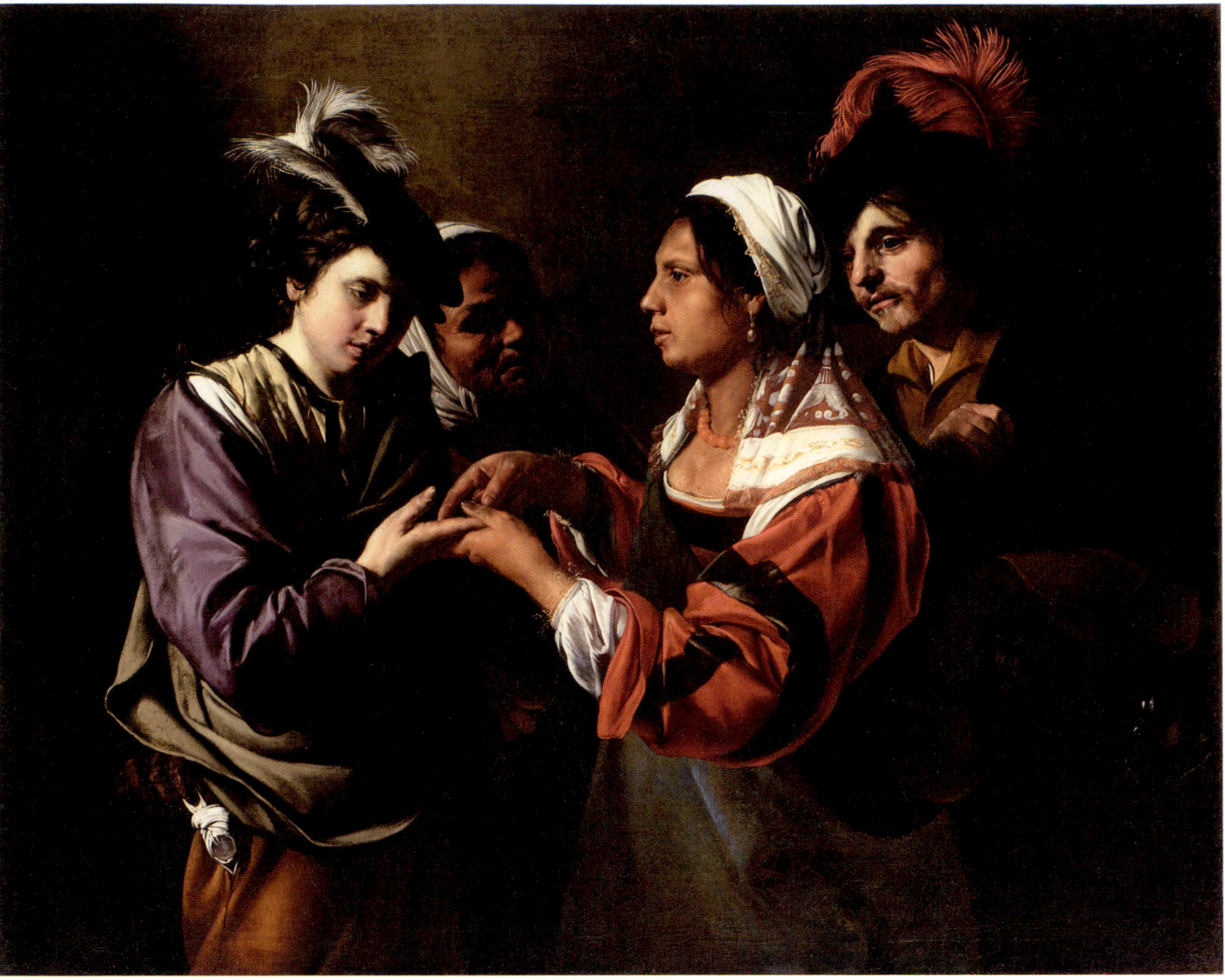

Fig. 307
Bartolomeo Manfredi, *The Fortune Teller*, The Detroit Institute of Arts, Detroit, oil on canvas, 120.9 x 152.4 cm.

fortune-teller's satchel. In other words, both the gypsy and the boy are the naïve victims of professional swindlers.

Manfredi rids his *Fortune Teller* of the inherent ambivalences of Caravaggio's two precedents—action here does not lend itself to multiple interpretation or indeterminacy. The opposition he sets up between the young man and woman in the foreground and the cheats behind them imparts to the comedic plot—a twofold scam that doubles the one imagined by Caravaggio in his two paintings—an atmosphere of tense uncertainty and narrative vibrancy that far transcends the scope of the pictorial comedy. Manfredi's amplification of the comic effects latent in Caravaggio's two versions of the *Fortune Teller*, while simultaneously inflecting his own comedic plot with greater clarity and intelligibility, is part of a tendency that can be discerned in paintings of the same subject by other followers of Caravaggio.

In Valentin's *Fortune Teller* at the Toledo Museum of Art, Toledo (Fig. 308),[22] the divination theme is expanded into a multi-figure inn scene. As in other paintings by Valentin, the table—in this

22　See Mojana 1989, 60, no. 4. See also Von Rosen 2009, 138.

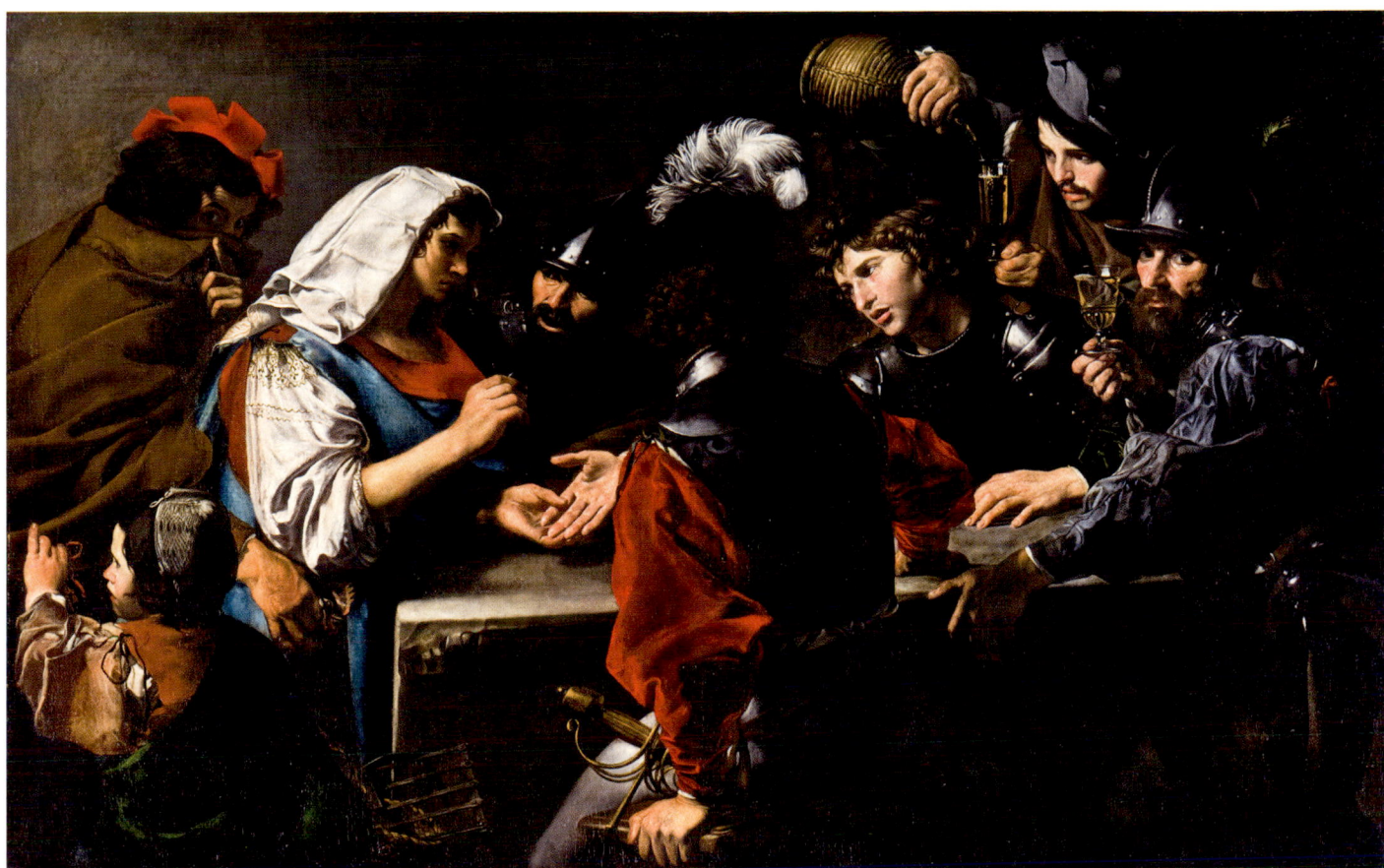

Fig. 308
Valentin de Boulogne, *The Fortune Teller*, Museum of Art, Toledo, oil on canvas, 149.5 x 238.5 cm.

case, its analog, an ancient sarcophagus adorned with a barely visible chipped molding—serves as a compositional pivot around which the pictorial action unfolds and is articulated. The central group of the gypsy and the youth is now relegated to the middle ground, one figure at a certain distance from the other—the boy is forced to hunch over the table and stretch his hand to reach the woman—and visually cut off from one another through the insertion of a soldier with his back turned, clutching the border of his chair's seat with his left hand and resting his right hand on the sarcophagus-table as if reacting to the chiromancy occurring in front of him.

The addition of this figure at the center of the composition allows Valentin to shape the scene into a diptych, leaving the canvas' left portion to an episode of double swindle, and devoting the right section to the evocation of a drinking party. To the left a thief, his mantle masking part of his face, regards the viewer and enjoins silence with his index finger, while his right hand ferrets into the gypsy's satchel and pulls out a hen. Unbeknownst to him, a little girl—some critics describe her as a dwarf or midget—removes the pouch of money from the thief's pocket, a canonical instance of a comedic double twist in which the deceiver becomes the deceived and the robber the robbed. The three figures of the gypsy, the thief, and the girl once again form an open triangulation, a zigzagging disposition characteristic of Valentin. To the right, the boy is flanked by two figures: a helmeted soldier sitting at the table's end, lifting a glass goblet likely filled with wine and glancing at the beholder, and a waiter pouring wine and fixing his gaze onto the fortune-teller. Almost opposite the figure with his back turned, another actor, a helmeted soldier, his mouth wide open, is either enthralled at the divination or, less likely, catches a glimpse of the thief's maneuvering behind the gypsy.

Despite the obvious visual caesura constituted by the turned back of the soldier at the center—a visual interference that conceals a segment of the action and thereby increases the viewer's curiosity—and notwithstanding the picture's accentuated dual articulation, Valentin succeeds in implementing a unitary plot through calculated synchronies and orchestrated figural attitudes: with the exception of the soldier looking outward and the two thieves—these three actors are deliberately segregated at the painting's margins—all the figures seem to turn, or be oriented, toward the fortune-teller. Interestingly enough, by downplaying the comic trick—the robbery—to a secondary, albeit reiterated, episode, Valentin reinstates and reinforces the lyrical component present in Caravaggio's two versions of *The Fortune Teller*. In fact, the gypsy has started neither to read the hand's lines nor to pronounce her oracle, so that visual emphasis is laid on the intense gaze that she exchanges with the youth, a gaze accentuated by the distance separating the two figures and, paradoxically, by the narrative interpolation determined by the soldier's back at the center.

Valentin accentuates the thrill and suspense brought about by the gypsy and the boy's encounter through the bystanders' attitudes of wonder (the open-mouthed, helmeted soldier), enthrallment (the waiter pouring the wine), and feverish, yet inexplicable expectation (the clutched hands of the warrior looking outward and of the turned soldier who, in addition, rests his other hand on the sarcophagus as if ready to stand). On the level of verisimilitude, it is perhaps difficult to understand why a simple fortune telling might be fraught with such anticipation.

Of course, the act of chiromancy concerns the unveiling of the future and, more crucially, the exchange of gazes between the gypsy and the youth may announce amorous attraction, as suggested in my examination of Caravaggio's two versions of *The Fortune Teller*. And yet I am convinced that the key to comprehending Valentin's *Merry Company with Fortune Teller* resides not in its half-divinatory, half-lyrical, and accessorily comedic plot, but above all in the mounting expectancy with which the master endows the scene, as if he strove to make the viewer sense that something—the revelation of the future, a nascent passion or a double robbery—is about to happen. This device of enhancing the beholder's attention is most likely designed to assimilate the narrative of this inn scene to that of an *istoria*: that is, to provide the genre episode with the climactic suspense of a heroic action, thereby insinuating the impression of a flux of events that exceeds the scope of the plot actually represented.

To this end, Valentin inserts into the composition the figures of two "monitors" in accordance with Alberti's precepts on the *istoria*: to the left, the thief who addresses the beholder by shushing him or her; to the right, the helmeted soldier who beckons the audience with his straightforward gaze to watch the scene and, in particular, the boy on his side. Of course, these "monitors" are meant to disclose the picture's fictiveness, and therefore to induce meta-pictorial effects: the viewer is alerted that what occurs in the painting is a matter of pictorial fiction. Yet there is more to these figures than their roles as vectors of meta-painting.[23]

As I have already suggested, the figures greatly collaborate in fostering expectancy: the thief in drawing attention to the robbery and the fortune-teller, and the soldier in coaxing the viewer's gaze into dwelling upon the boy. If I insist on the concept of narrative expectation, it is because I believe that Valentin intended to improve upon Caravaggio's comedic formulas in a twofold manner: besides expanding the plots typical of pictorial comedy through grafts of correlated themes, the French master attempts to clarify and ennoble the contents of the comedic plot. It is no coincidence that the purely burlesque episode of the double swindle becomes secondary in *Fortune Teller*.

By sifting out the comic from the comedic, and by intensifying the impression of climactic momentum conveyed by the picture's action, Valentin seeks to create a novel typology of comedy provided with the narrative mechanisms of the *istoria*. If this is indeed the master's purpose, then

---

23 For the concept of meta-painting in the seventeenth century, see Stoichita 1999.

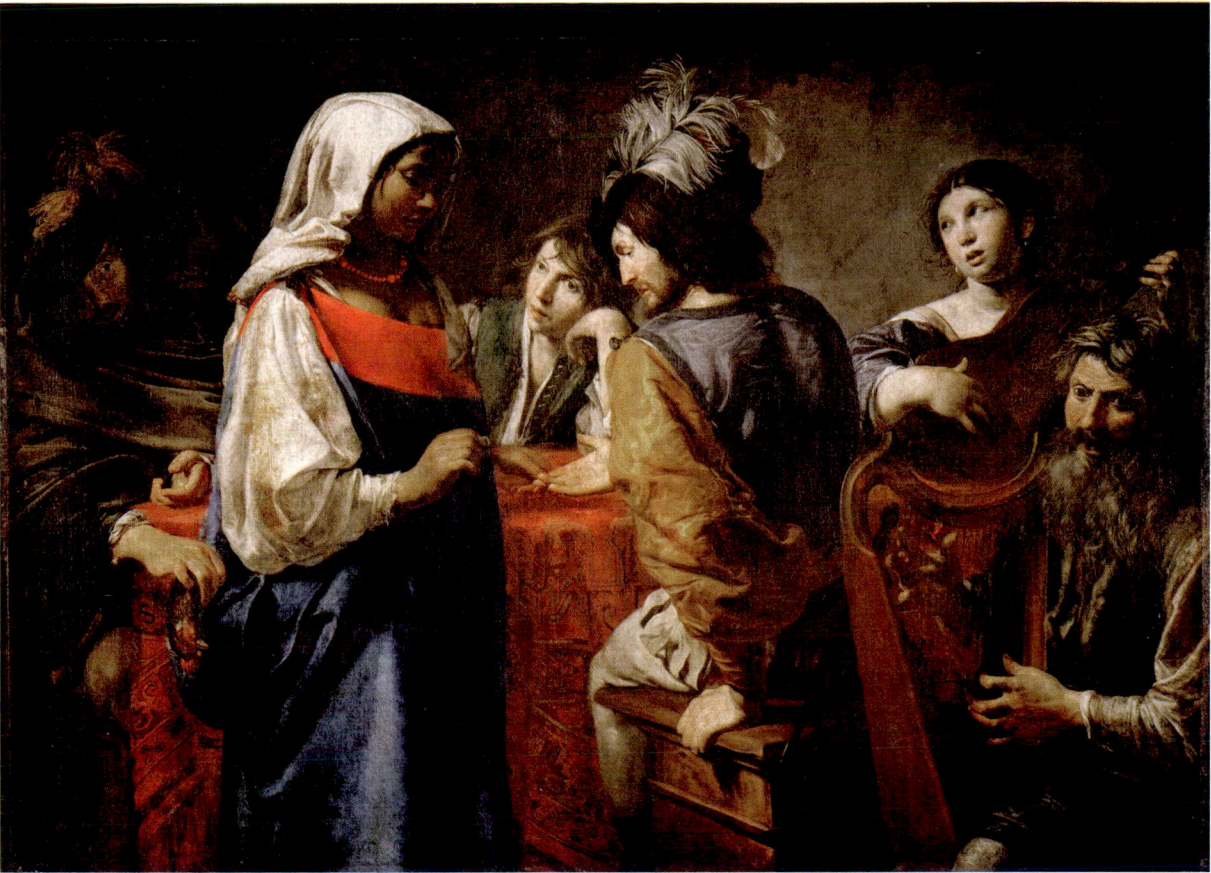

Fig. 309
Valentin de Boulogne, *The Fortune Teller*, Musée du Louvre, Paris, oil on canvas, 125 x 175 cm.

the Toledo picture certainly succeeds. However, I believe that, as an experiment, the painting also betrays the limits of the experimentation. With his composition Valentin proves that painters of tavern scenes are not fated to repeat their stock tricks in perpetuating the iconographic tradition; through wise modifications, genre scenes can truly suggest more than swindling, brawling, and gaming. But at the same time, to galvanize this genre's narrative and greatly stir the viewer's attention, it is necessary that verisimilitude be reduced or compromised, and intelligibility occasionally disregarded. Indeed, creating climactic expectation dictates that the painter handle, and cash in on, the obscure and the mysterious. Even if Valentin was willing to accept the inconsistencies stemming from such pictorial license, tavern scenes offered a limited repertoire of narrative situations that could consistently sustain the comparison with the breadth of action of which the *istoria* was capable. The subsequent evolution of Valentin's painting indicates that he was not satisfied with the solution he had concocted in the Toledo picture.

Around a decade later, Valentin painted another version of *Fortune Teller*, now at the Louvre, in which he radically modified his previous pictorial formulas (Fig. 309).[24] Dated to *c*.1628, the Paris picture once again depicts a gypsy poised to read the hand of a man who, his back turned and his face in profile, clenches the border of his chair's seat while fixing his gaze on his open palm. Represented at the center and in the foreground, these two figures attract the viewer's attention immediately. In the background, his elbow leaning upon a table covered with an oriental carpet, a boy supports his face with his hand while staring into space: from his expression, it is clear

24   See Mojana 1989, 146, no. 47.

that, uninterested in the chiromancy, he is daydreaming. By framing the boy's bust-length figure between the gypsy and the man standing on the other side of the table, Valentin leads the viewer to focus on the youth's distractedness and emotional detachment. His lips parted, the boy either sings along with the musicians to the right or talks to himself, a poignant and unusual depiction. At the table's end and behind the gypsy, a thief lurks in penumbra, his torso draped in a mantle, his face partially concealed by the brim of his hat. With extreme circumspection, waiting for the gypsy to initiate her divination, he dexterously pulls a hen out of the woman's satchel; as the reader can easily verify, this sort of thievery, very common in this iconographic tradition, becomes utterly perfunctory here. To the right, in the foreground, an elderly man strums a small harp; behind him, a woman plays a guitar: both are represented with their mouths open, and hence in the act of singing.

Unlike the Toledo *Fortune Teller*, the Paris painting ceases to propose a unitary narrative: the couple enshrined at the center of the composition is no longer at the center of the other actors' attention; the act of fortune telling indeed goes largely unacknowledged by these bystanders. On the contrary, each figure and group possess their own force of attraction in an exclusive fashion: the gypsy and the man, the daydreaming boy, the thief, the guitar player and the elderly musician act independently from one another, and on this count constitute distinct narrative foci defined not according to their specific function in the overall action, which does not exist, but to the figural disposition set up by the painter.

The most likely candidate for the role of protagonist in the Paris picture would be the daydreaming boy, since the actions of the gypsy, whose three-quarter face is noticeably shaded, and the man, the impact of whose attitude is deliberately weakened by his turned back and the profile view of his head, are partly eclipsed by the youth's visual salience. The fortune telling in the foreground acts as a foil to introduce the boy's reverie. From a narrative perspective, this figure's expression is among the most elusive and impenetrable to interpretation that one can imagine in a painting. As I have already suggested with regard to Velázquez's *mulata*, the daydreaming attitude—for want of a more scientific term—corresponds to a blank in the pictorial script that the viewer can fill in many, though not infinite, ways. Because of his narrative blankness, the boy continuously and inexorably solicits the beholder's curious scrutiny: lack of information is among the most powerful motors of curiosity. In other words, the blurriness of the boy's expression—the very fact that no one can put exact words, thoughts or impressions in his mind—serves as a catalyst for attention, while it simultaneously renders the narrative content, and its reconstitution on the beholder's part, if not useless, at least secondary.

A similar observation can be made in connection with the two musicians to the right. However engrossed in their singing and playing, the old man with his apparently but deceptively direct gaze at the viewer, and the girl with her indifference to the beholder, are difficult to decode. Has the young musician tilted her head because something has caught her eye? Is she purely immersed in the music? Are she or her elderly companion following the threads of their own thoughts? Is the old man attempting to address the beholder? Compared to these evasive, intriguing characters, the gypsy, the man and the thief in the Paris *Fortune Teller* risk being downgraded to "staffage," all too recognizable and therefore anodyne epithets of a tavern scene. If my interpretation is correct, it can be assumed that Valentin regarded his inn scenes with their low life not as sites of narrative action, but as spaces of reverie mixed with, or undistinguishable from, introspection, their actors thus incarnating tropes of indefinite moods and atmospheres.

That this assumption is a viable exegesis of the way Valentin meant to evolve his late genre scenes can be evinced by one of his most compelling pictures, the *Concert with Eight Figures* also in the Louvre (Fig. 310).[25] In this picture there are no swindlers, no gypsies, no brawlers, no players,

25 See Brejon de Lavergnée and Cuzin 1973, 152-4, no. 46;
and Mojana 1989, 148, no. 48.

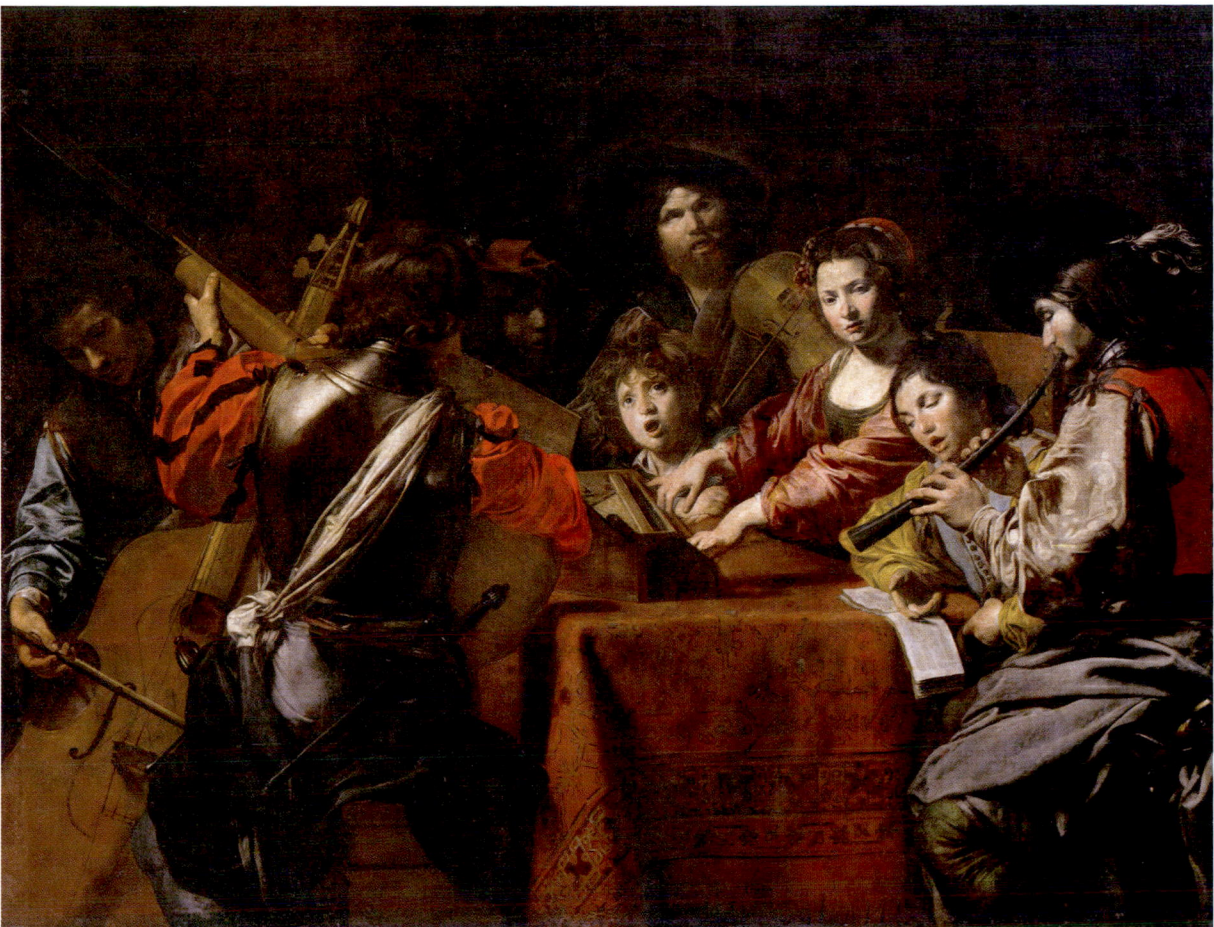

Fig. 310
Valentin de Boulogne, *Concert with Eight Figures*, Musée du Louvre, Paris, 175 x 216 cm.

and no thieves. All the figures are hermetically sealed in their musical activities so that viewers cannot guess anything of their inner characters with one possible exception, the beautiful spinet player who, at once and unexpectedly, seems to turn her gaze outward as if in concern or weighing a delicate question. The entire composition revolves around this engaging figure and her puzzling gaze and expression. And yet, from a narrative viewpoint, she does not qualify as the picture's heroine, not because she lacks the visual relevance necessary for the role, but because the action in which she is involved and which governs the whole image is nothing but a mechanic assemblage of interconnected activities, an action devoid of a significant epicenter. Nothing is taking place here but a musical performance without the climax of an *istoria*.

Owing to the ordinariness of the situation represented in it, Valentin's *Concert* succeeds in summoning the indefinable—but not the ineffable—of human nature through its figures' attitudes and expressions, pictorial gestures lingering at the threshold of labor's absorption, spiritual introspection or, in other cases, sheer distractedness. The impenetrability of its music players as proper actors—that is, as figures enacting a remarkable or exceptional action—is what makes Valentin's *Concert* such a piece of great visual mysteriousness: an allegory of man's elusiveness, or perhaps just a pictorial feat by which Valentin manages to visualize action without definable or transcendental meaning. Bearing this in mind, one can also understand how Valentin's Paris *Fortune Teller* appears unresolved in comparison with *Concert with Eight Figures*, a contemporary

26   See Mojana 1989, 100, no. 24.

work. In the Paris *Fortune Teller* absorbed figures coexist with stock actors of the pictorial comedy—thieves and fortune-tellers—rehearsing their somewhat trite gags, as if the master hesitated at the crossroads of potentially irreconcilable or difficult-to-combine pictorial solutions. And yet the concert scene has not always been the realm of human elusiveness in Valentin's art.

At the beginning of his career, the painter had likewise aspired to make the concert theme adhere to some of the principles ruling the *istoria*. In his *c.*1622 *Concert with Bas-Relief*, now in the Louvre (Fig. 311),[26] Valentin represented a group of musicians singing and playing their instruments in a tavern, around an ancient bas-relief once again transformed into a table. To the right, a knight sits at the end of the table, one leg over the other to hold in place the lute that he plays as he stares at the viewer with nonchalant intensity—an oxymoron that seems nonetheless appropriate to describe the attitude of this figure. Next to him, a woman strums her guitar as she sings and looks outward. Aware, like her partner, of the beholder's presence, the female musician's gaze and expression are more tense and more alert than her companion's to the right, although for no apparent reason. At the center and behind the table, a child sings without passion and almost apathetically, resting his face on his hand and staring into space, his thoughts and emotions adrift. To the left, a violinist, sitting on a stool and resting his left leg on a chair, strikes his violin's strings with his bow as he takes a glimpse at a score whose pages are turned by a singer nearby, close to the child, who attempts to read its text more clearly. Counter to the other musicians, these two figures do not direct their eyes toward the viewer's space, and are deeply absorbed in the music. Crouching in the foreground, a soldier wearing a cuirass and a yellow scarf pours wine from a bottle into a narrow-necked jar. He is also entirely occupied with his work and therefore ignores the beholder's gaze. Finally, in the background and behind the woman and child, a man drinks eagerly from a bottle.

To construe the painting correctly, the bas-relief figuring in it should be studied with care; it is an antique once in the Farnese Collection, Rome, now in the Louvre, representing *The Wedding of Thetis and Peleus*, as Harold Wethey justly observed.[27] A favorite prop of Valentin's, this bas-relief is partially evoked in his *Denial of Saint Peter* (Fondazione Roberto Longhi, Florence).[28] As Annick Lemoine has pointed out, the depiction of this antique might well be a ludicrous parody of ancient art's nobility and grandiloquence:[29] not surprisingly, lying atop it, a dish with a pie and, not far away, a knife—select elements of a low-life meal—might seem unabashedly to mock the elegance of the marble artwork. I do not deny that Valentin, through the insertion of this antique into his tavern scene, intended to burlesque the paradigm of aesthetic perfection and theoretical loftiness incarnated by antiquity. However, I believe that Valentin's intention is subtler than this: the ancient bas-relief can legitimately be construed as the model of a canonical *istoria*. Viewed in this light, the Farnese antique embodies the principles of a pictorial narration opposed to the comedic one depicted by Valentin. The bas-relief in Valentin's picture represents a "poetic myth" ("*Poeterey*," to borrow Sandrart's definition of Poussin's subjects) slipped into a tavern scene, but the reason for this figurative and hierarchical misalliance is not exclusively parodic; as a graft, the antique proposes an artistic *paragone* between sculpture and painting, between the normative *istoria* and Valentin's unorthodox pictorial comedy. Valentin intended to contrast for argument's sake the concept and treatment of his low-life *istoria* with those of the then paradigmatic *istoria*.

Valentin was not averse to experimenting with pictorial comedy by endowing his inn scenes with the temporal devices and dramatic structures of the *istoria*. But is this the case with *Concert with Bas-Relief*? If, on the one hand, it is evident that Valentin took great care in organizing the figures in the pictorial space through his characteristic triangulations, partial alignments, and interpenetrations of planes devised in a frieze-like manner, it is true, on the other hand, that once

27 Wethey 1964, 157. See also Sénéchal 1996, 32.

28 See Mojana 1989, 62, no. 5.

29 See Lemoine 2007, 56.

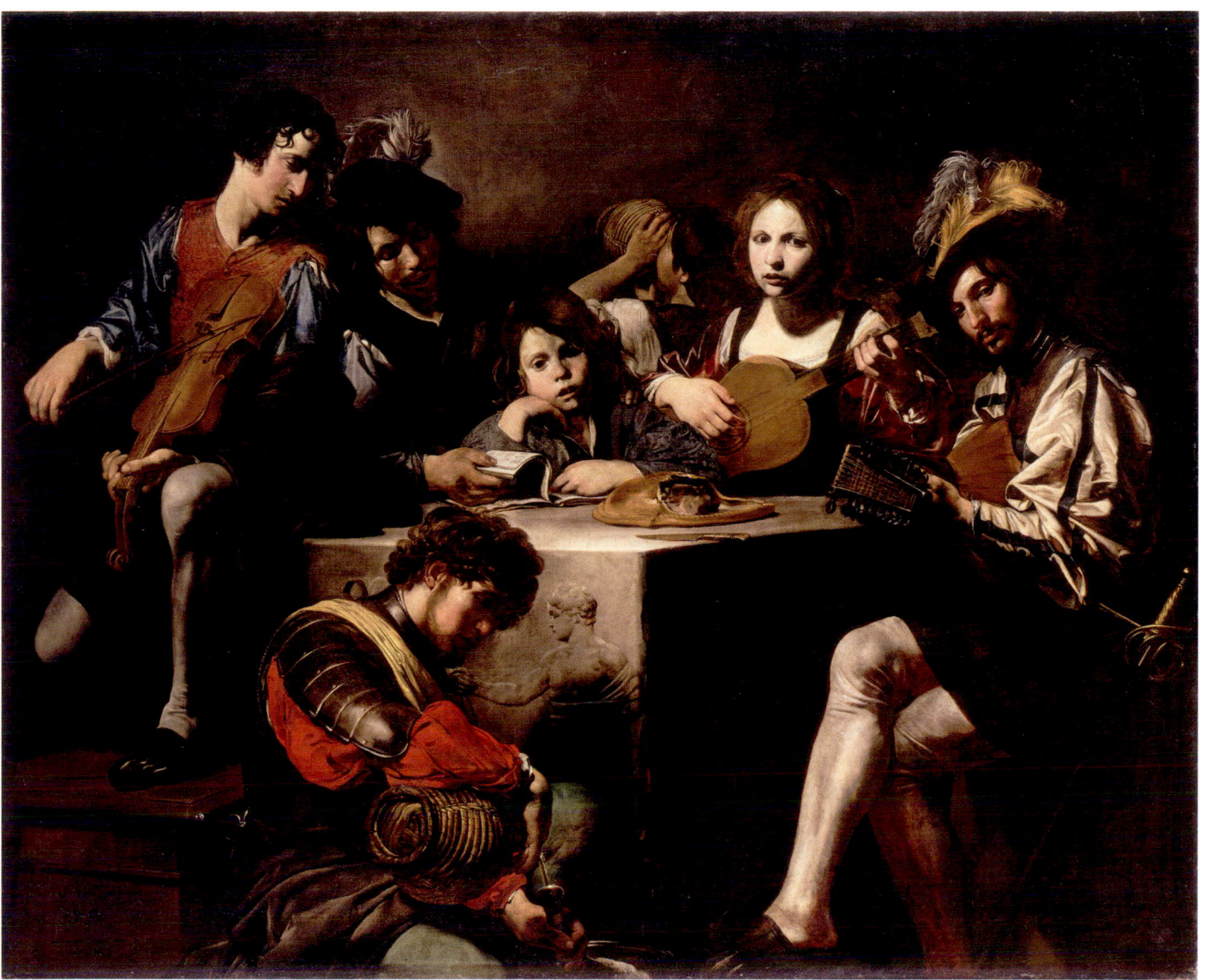

Fig. 311
Valentin de Boulogne, *Concert with Bas-Relief*, Musée du Louvre, Paris, oil on canvas, 173 x 214 cm.

again he neglected the unity of action requested of an *istoria*; despite the figures' interconnectedness to one another through disposition, Valentin's actors are mostly conceived to be observed one by one and independently. I would contend that, whereas Valentin's compositions are structurally polynomial, they paradoxically tend to be seriously "monadic" when it comes to the figures' "affects," "passions," and "movements" that are instrumental in granting narrative fluency and coherence to the image (I refer once again to Sandrart's definitions of "*Affekten*," "*Passionen*," and "*Bewegungen*"). Valentin's "monadism" is substantially contingent upon the master's propensity toward representing indefinite states of minds, insofar as these figures of innerness cannot be coordinated with one another in a cause-and-effect dynamic of narration. If then, in his *Concert with Bas-Relief*, Valentin truly aimed to compete with the noble paradigm of the *istoria*, it must be admitted that his model of composing a comedic action is as original as it is unsuitable for narrative as interpreted at his time.

I now return to *Merry Company with Fortune Teller*. That Valentin heavily relied on his artistic memory in executing this painting becomes clear upon analyzing the group of the fortune-teller at

555

the center of the painting, and that of the musicians to the left. The idea of representing the gypsy and the man in the foreground, face to face, their figures bridged by a distracted boy on the other side of the table, harks back to the Paris *Fortune Teller*. By the same token, the figure of the gypsy's little girl, her face in *profil perdu*, and turning her back to the viewer, is obviously copied from the Toledo *Fortune Teller*. Also, the spinet player in the Liechtenstein picture has her counterpart in the female musicians of both *Concert with Bas-Relief* and *Concert with Eight Figures*. *Merry Company with Fortune Teller* is indeed an anthology of Valentin's former themes and ideas. As others have argued, it is possible that the short period of time allotted to Valentin to achieve his picture accounts for the high density of self-quotations present in it. But what matters most, in my view, is the fact that Valentin was undoubtedly able not only to vary his own formulas—which he partially did in the painting—but also to create connections between the figures and link the different episodes together at least in a perfunctory manner. Yet he decided to do otherwise, and deliberately resorted to a mere juxtaposition of distinct comedic themes: the music playing, the fortune telling, and the brawl.

Some details of the composition are compellingly evocative: the exchange of gazes between the gypsy and the man in the foreground; the earnest concentration of the youth behind them; the elegance with which the gypsy's little girl invites the viewer to look at the fight to the right, and the dog that in turn fixes its eyes on her while panting. Similarly, the profound absorption of the old man playing the viol and warming himself at the brazier, and the blind violinist's elation in playing his violin must be deemed admirable and impressive new inflections of the tavern scenes' iconographic tradition. On the whole, though, Valentin intentionally exposes his inability to revive a worn-out repertoire.

Nicolas Régnier's *Card Players with Fortune Teller* at the Szépmüvészeti Mùzeum, Budapest (Fig. 312),[30] dated to *c*.1622-1623, responds to the same pictorial solicitations that lie at the core of Valentin's *Merry Company with Fortune Teller*: to compose an original multi-figure pictorial comedy informed by Caravaggio's precedents. By planting the corner of the sarcophagus-table in the foreground and roughly at the composition's center, Régnier brings to the fore the theme of card playing, which, in this case, is unequivocally a *primera*. At the left of the table, the sumptuous figure of a courtesan clad in a red robe straightaway engages the viewer with her direct gaze; her right hand posing in an ostentatious and somewhat gratuitous gesture points to the high score of her cards (fives of each suit). Behind her, a soldier with armor and a plumed helmet squints at her cards while extracting a six of spades, perhaps from his belt, to beat her score, a situation clearly inspired by Caravaggio's *The Cardsharps*. And yet if one considers this portion of the scene carefully, one would discover that the soldier cannot be a participant in the game; the three other figures around the table with the woman are the four and unique contestants of this *primera*.

This is not the only incongruousness of the painting: to the right, in the foreground, a young man, donning a beret with a pompous yellow feather, turns his intrigued gaze off scene, allowing the courtesan behind him to glance at his cards. Accordingly, the woman signals the score to her accomplice, whose identity remains obscure. If this is the young man clad in a black mantle who stands in the background, he is too captivated by the fortune telling on the right to catch the woman's cue. By the same token, the youth absorbed in his cards near the courtesan—another reminiscence of Caravaggio's *The Cardsharps*—is completely abstracted from the interplay of gazes and motions around him. Like Valentin, Régnier depicts figures that interact only in appearance, while in reality they pose separately and are mostly detached from one another. But unlike Valentin, Régnier camouflages the disconnectedness and dramatic eeriness of his plot with exceptional bravura; because of their intensity or vivacity, the figures' gestures and expressions hold the viewer's

30   See Lemoine 2007, 233-4, no. 30.

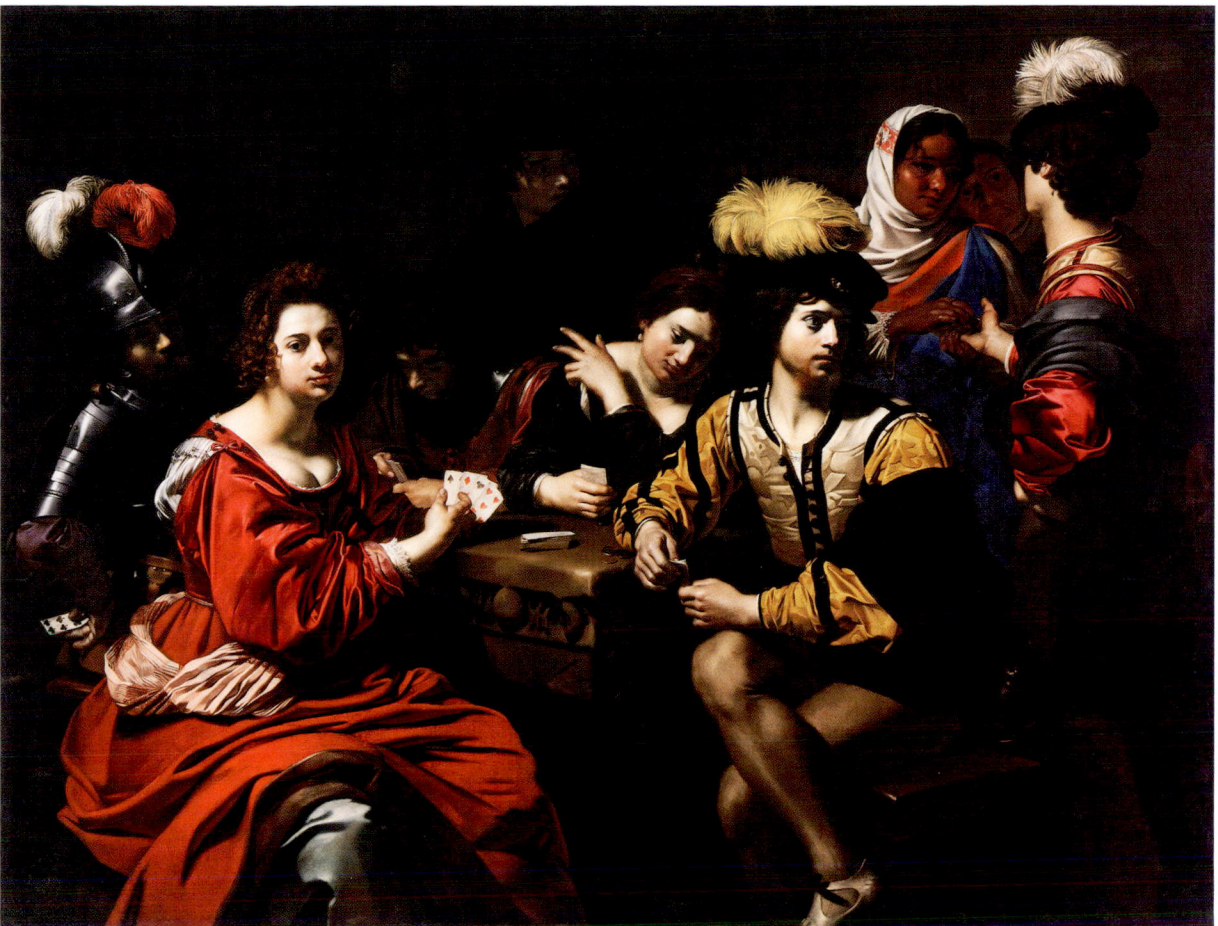

Fig. 312
Nicolas Régnier, *Card Players with Fortune Teller*, Szépmüvészeti Mùzeum, Budapest, oil on canvas, 174 x 228 cm.

attention and give the false impression that a trick—or better, a complex swindle—is occurring in the composition, that a unitary action binds together all the actors around the table. Even the overrated group of the fortune-teller, the youth and the older gypsy fishing in the youth's pocket loses a little of its cliché through its insertion into the spirited animation of the scene.

In his *Merry Company with Fortune Teller*, Valentin instead not only renounces unifying the parallel plots of his composition, but also stops pretending to unify them. He deliberately reassembles his actors in a pictorial container as a "sample collection" of his previous inventions in the domain of pictorial comedy. By laying bare the fictitiousness of his operation, Valentin does not exalt his inventiveness and the abundance of his imagination. Rather, he declares that the tavern scene as a pictorial formula has reached maximum saturation, unable either to expand into narratives as visually sophisticated as those of the *istoria*, or even to exploit the suspenseful and evocative indeterminacy caused by its actors' emotional "opacity." Because of its atomization of gestures and attitudes and its extensive recourse to commonplace narrative situations, the Liechtenstein painting is a courageous, honest, and even provocative manifesto, the *ne plus ultra* of pictorial comedy as inaugurated by Caravaggio and developed by his followers, and therefore a bold declaration of creative exhaustion without nuances or pretensions, justifications or hesitations.

With *Merry Company with Fortune Teller*, Valentin becomes fully aware that the thematic and iconic repertory of comedic figures and virtual gags inherited from Caravaggio has ceased to produce pictorial newness. To reform Caravaggio's comic tradition, or elaborate on its vast potential, it was necessary to think outside the box of the genre, that is, outside its consecrated formulas, schemas, and even stock characters, just as Velázquez had done in his early paintings, from the two versions of *La Mulata* to *The Water Seller of Seville*. But Valentin was not ready to cross that Rubicon, and probably would never have crossed it, even if, as Sandrart remarked of Poussin, he had been "blessed with a longer life."

EPILOGUE

The End of Narrative? Afterthoughts on the Definition and Function of the *Istoria* in an Age of Subjectivity

"Ruin" and "destruction": if, in the early modern period, art is viewed as evolving in cycles, up and down the curves of a parabola, now coming to life, now growing and thriving, now securing perfection only to decline through natural obsolescence, but then again providentially recovering its force and drive, geared to climb back toward its ever-coveted but not always attainable apogee, one must confess that Caravaggio constituted an anomaly, insofar as, according to seventeenth-century artists and theorists, he almost put an end to the evolution of art by precipitating it from its long-sought and freshly obtained recovery through the Carracci reform into premature decay and self-annihilation. Destruction, much more than ruin, is the key word that embodies the exceptionality of Caravaggio's painting; in the prospect of history, had Caravaggio's paradigm prevailed, art might have died out altogether. Like the Goths, Huns, and other barbarians that determined the collapse of ancient art as practiced throughout the Roman Empire in the wake of their invasions, Caravaggio and his cohort of followers might have determined a second dark age of art. This is an exaggeration of course, but the terms "ruin" and "destruction" that qualify Caravaggio's artistic deeds and misdeeds are not mine, but those of Vincencio Carducho, Francesco Albani, Giovanni Baglione and, last but not least, Nicolas Poussin. Yet Caravaggio's historical role in reforming the arts after the so-called Mannerist decline is duly acknowledged, even by some of his detractors. In his 1672 *Vite*, Giovan Pietro Bellori gauged the merits of Caravaggio's painting in the course of art's recent evolution as follows:

> Undoubtedly, he did good to painting as he appeared at a time when the natural was not much in use, figures were executed routinely and artificially, and painters satisfied a taste for gracefulness rather than a sentiment of truth. Whereas Caravaggio, removing any veneer and vanity from color, invigorated tints by restoring their blood and flesh, thus reminding painters of imitation.[1]

As I have already pointed out in the Introduction to Part Six, Caravaggio's reform often boils down, in the eyes of seventeenth-century painters, to his color technique. According to Bellori, Caravaggio's use of colors was nothing but a reminder to artists that it was time to restore the old principles of pictorial mimesis—that is, bodies resembling actual bodies with real flesh and blood.

---

1 Bellori, 229: "Giovò senza dubbio il Caravaggio alla pittura, venuto in tempo che, non essendo molto in uso il naturale, si fingevano le figure di pratica e di maniera, e sodisfacevasi più al senso della vaghezza che della verità. Laonde costui, togliendo ogni belletto e vanità al colore, rinvigorì le tinte e restituì ad esse il sangue e l'incarnazione, ricordando a' pittori l'imitazione."

But apart from this contribution, Caravaggio deliberately trampled on art's quintessential ideality, misleading numerous unfortunate minds in the process:

> Infatuated with his style, many embraced it willingly, for without further study or hardship it made easy for them to copy nature upon the example of vulgar bodies devoid of beauty. Since Caravaggio had subdued art's majesty in this manner, everyone felt relieved from rules, which brought about a contempt for beautiful things as the authority of antiquity and Raphael was entirely dismissed; due to the ease of employing live models and depicting a head from life, they applied themselves to half-figures, which were in little use before, abandoning the practice of the *istoria* specific to painters.[2]

Caravaggio not only ignored the majestic foundations of art as exemplified by antiquity and Raphael, but he also reduced painting to a trivial exercise of reproduction: heads and bodies unsuitable for, and wholly independent of, pictorial narratives, which are instead the unique rationale for, and solid touchstone of, painting. In Bellori's opinion, Caravaggio's reform of art represented both an efficient antidote and a nefarious poison:

> Just as some herbs produce both beneficial medicines and most pernicious toxins, so too was Caravaggio very harmful—though he did good in part—by turning upside down any ornament and good habit of painting. It is true that painters, straying away from nature's imitation, needed someone to lead them back onto a good path. But as at times, to avoid an extreme, one stumbles into another, painters, in dodging artificiality, deviated from art altogether by overly heeding nature, and remained caught up in error and darkness until Annibale Carracci came to enlighten their minds and return beauty to imitation.[3]

It is noteworthy that Bellori intentionally twists the course of history in order to appoint Annibale Carracci as the sole reformer and savior of painting at the beginning of the seventeenth century. In reality, when Annibale was already near the end of his career, Caravaggio's reform had barely begun. The ominous tide of "error and darkness" triggered by Caravaggio's painting immediately followed Annibale's death and stretched until the beginning of the 1630s. The Carracci restoration coexisted, dialogued with, and opposed Caravaggio's "new wave": the identity of the classicist movement spawn by the Carracci's lesson configured itself against the newness of Caravaggio's painting and the poetics of his followers. As a looming shadow or as an in-built principle of negation, Caravaggio's painting lurks in the theoretical and practical tenets of seventeenth-century classicism and academism. However, despite his aversion to Caravaggio, Bellori does not define his painting as "destructive"; it is "harmful" and ruinous, but never such a radical thing as a vector of destruction.

2 Ibidem, 230: "Molti nondimeno, invaghiti della sua maniera, l'abbracciavano volentieri, poiché senza altro studio e fatica si facilitavano la via al copiare il naturale, seguitando li corpi vulgari e senza bellezza. Così sottoposta dal Caravaggio la maestà dell'arte, ciascuno si prese licenza, e ne seguì il dispregio delle cose belle, tolta ogni autorità all'antico ed a Rafaelle, dove per la comodità de' modelli e di condurre una testa dal naturale, lasciando costoro l'uso dell'istorie che sono proprie de' pittori, si diedero alle mezze figure che avanti erano poco in uso."

3 Ibidem, 231: "Sì come adunque alcune erbe producono medicamenti salutiferi e veleni perniciosissimi, così il Caravaggio, se bene giovò in parte, fu nondimeno molto dannoso e mise sottosopra ogni ornamento e buon costume della pittura. E veramente li pittori, sviati dalla naturale imitazione, avevano bisogno di uno che li rimettesse nel buon sentiero; ma come facilmente, per fuggire uno estremo, s'incorre nell'altro, così nell'allontanarsi dalla maniera, per seguitar troppo il naturale, si scostarono affatto dall'arte, restando ne gli errori e nelle tenebre, finché Annibale Carracci venne ad illuminare le menti ed a restituire la bellezza all'imitazione."

To my knowledge, besides Carducho, only Poussin went so far as to condemn Caravaggio's painting as the source of art's extermination, at least in accordance with André Félibien's testimony. In his 1679 *Entretiens*, Félibien records:

> Monsieur Poussin (…) could not stand anything in Caravaggio and said that he was born to destroy painting. But his bias against Caravaggio is not surprising. For if Poussin sought nobility in his subjects, Caravaggio was carried away by the truth of nature, as he saw it. Therefore, they were quite the opposite of one another.[4]

As Louis Marin correctly argued in his 1977 *Détruire la peinture*—a title obviously inspired by Félibien's paraphrase of Poussin's insight into Caravaggio's art—the opposition between Caravaggio and Poussin is not only antithetical, but in some respects also dialectical. Although he incarnates the apocalypse of art, Caravaggio also proves to be the best painter in the domain of pictorial mimesis, as admitted by Poussin's most fervent champion, Félibien himself: "if one considers what pertains to the art of painting in particular, (…) one will see that Michelangelo da Caravaggio possessed it all." And more explicitly:

> Observing the portrait of the Grand Master of Malta by Caravaggio in the King's Cabinet, you will avow that nothing more beautiful can be done because, as he had to accomplish nothing but a portrait, he imitated nature so perfectly that nothing more can be desired.[5]

As mesmerizing as it might have seemed, the voluntary and apparent preeminence of the optical as frequently sponsored by Caravaggio in his pictorial narratives was persistently construed by his contemporaries as mere reproduction, bereft of all the rhetorical infrastructures that made painting an intellectual and spiritual profession—a liberal art in and of itself. As long as Caravaggio limited himself to portraiture—the "reproductive" genre by definition—his technique betokened perfection. Nevertheless, portraiture is not painting. According to the principles posited by Leon Battista Alberti in his 1435 *De Pictura*, a standing figure flanked by a page—a summary description of Caravaggio's *Portrait of Alof de Wignacourt* at the Louvre—would have been defined as a "colossus,"[6] the conceptual antithesis of the *istoria*. But the *istoria* is painting by definition, therefore a half-figure—not a half-colossus, but a colossus truncated into magnified chunks of its body—cannot be the foundation of a pictorial narrative. In the theoretical system of early modern aesthetics, there is no painting worthy of the name without action, because the depiction of a human action, as both Alberti in the fifteenth century and Poussin in the seventeenth century claimed, is what designates painting. When Poussin accused Caravaggio of "destroying" painting, he was clearly alluding not to the technique of painting—a craft in which Caravaggio excelled—but to the practice and concept of the *istoria*. In other words, Caravaggio was born to destroy pictorial narrative. Did Caravaggio truly mean to instigate the end of the *istoria*? And, for that matter, is it

---

4 Félibien a, II, 3:205: "Monsieur Poussin, lui repartis-je, ne pouvait rien souffrir du Caravage, et disait qu'il était venu au monde pour détruire la peinture. Mais il ne faut pas s'étonner de l'aversion qu'il avait pour lui. Car si le Poussin cherchait la noblesse dans ses sujets, le Caravage se laissait emporter à la vérité du naturel tel qu'il le voyait. Ainsi, ils étaient bien opposés l'un à l'autre."

5 Ibidem: "Cependant, si l'on considère en particulier ce qui depend de l'art de peindre, et ce qui regarde le jugement et l'esprit du peintre, on verra que pour ce qui est de l'art, Michel-Ange de Caravage l'avait tout entier: j'entends l'art d'imiter ce qu'il avait devant les yeux. En voyant le portrait qu'il a fait du Grand Maître de Malte qui est dans le Cabinet du Roi, vous avouerez qu'on ne peut jamais rien faire de plus beau, parce que comme il n'avait à faire qu'un portrait, il a imité si parfaitement la Nature qu'il n'a rien laissé à désirer."

6 Alberti, 60-1: "Grandissima opera del pittore non uno collosso, ma istoria. Maggiore loda d'ingegno rende l'istoria che qual sia collosso. [Amplissimum pictoris opus non colossus sed historia. Maior enim est ingenii laus in historia quam in colosso]."

possible for narrative to be completely exterminated? I begin with the second question because, to a great extent, it encompasses all the issues I have been examining in this volume.

Narrative is an indispensable part of human nature. As rational beings immersed in a flux of time and space, men and women perceive, interpret, and meditate on their world through diverse categories of narratives. Whether fictive or argumentative, historical, philosophical, juridical or mathematical—in a sense, even an equation partakes of a narrative-like logic—narratives in substance are powerful and complex structures of interpretation. There is no narrative without hermeneutics, and the insistence of early modern theorists and artists in fostering and enforcing their notion of the *istoria* as the ultimate cause of painting indicates that they were all well aware of this essential fact: only by incorporating into the practice of painting the interpretive functions and modalities of narrative would they be able to prove the intellectual nobility of their profession. But—and here come both the culprit and the conundrum—the early modern model of narrative had been conceived for arts other than painting and sculpture, and informed by oral and verbal techniques—rhetorical tools—in which the image is a trope, and its inflections are rhetoric's "figures" of speech (the pun is intentional). By transliterating the principles of the Aristotelian *"mythos"*—the account or subject matter susceptible to elaboration—into the rules of the *istoria*, Alberti not only revolutionized the theory and practice of the visual arts, but also forced painting into an armature whose deficiencies, limits, and contradictions would progressively, and at times frenetically, resurface. Narrating in images is much more than what Alberti originally imagined: structurally, pictorial narrative largely exceeds the definition of the *istoria*.

Personally, I do not believe that we as scholars can comprehend exhaustively how images narrate. By this, I do not mean that pictorial narration is still an object of study to be pursued and clarified from its foundations—which is partly true—but only that the forms of narration in which the image plays an essential role happen to evolve so rapidly that we are barely able to keep abreast of their novelties and the profound implications of these changes. In the domain of film-making—to mention an example immediately understandable to all—a movie such as James Cameron's 2009 *Avatar* has recently introduced new structural technologies of which we can hardly foresee all the future applications, effects, and consequences. It is no coincidence that these technological advances in particular concern the image and its reception by the spectator; not only the sophisticated rendering of cinematic stereoscopy, in which the seams between the virtual and the actual are deftly masked by diminishing, among others, the causes of strobing, blurring, ghosting, and background flatness in the three-dimensional image, but especially the prodigious enhancement of the digital counterparts' acting capability and expressivity, achieved through novel technologies of motion-capture animation, profoundly modify both the configuration and the perception of the filmed narrative. I underline this point for one simple reason: without its technological props, the plot of *Avatar* turns out to be simple, even hackneyed. As Poussin put it four centuries ago, originality does not reside in the narrative's subject matter, but in its rendition: it is not only a matter of what one narrates, but also of how one visualizes and structures the story to be narrated.

Of what does the novelty of Caravaggio's paintings consist? For his adversaries and detractors, it depended solely on his style, particularly on his technique of color and naturalistic rendering: the "photographic" quality of his pictures, carried out at the cost of exacerbating the contrasts of light and shadow. For me, though, Caravaggio's originality resides greatly, but not exclusively, on his techniques of narration. In a sense, Poussin was absolutely right when he declared that Caravaggio was born to destroy painting—that is, to destroy the notion and practice of the *istoria*. But there are several kinds of destruction; and as much as I am driven to apply the term of "iconoclasm" to Caravaggio's painting, it would be erroneous to assimilate his poetics of dislocation to an iconoclastic design: Caravaggio did not intend to destroy the *istoria*. Rather, he meant to shake it up, and refashion it into a new pictorial technology by dislocating its functions and applications.

Caravaggio thus created new types of narrative by reassessing and overhauling the tenets on which the early modern concept of the *istoria* was based.

One of Caravaggio's most significant achievements in painting concerns the disclosure and intensification of what I propose to term the "subjectivity" of pictorial narrative. I do not use this term in the sense in which Alois Riegl construed it in many of his art theoretical essays. For Riegl, the search of subjectivity is the propulsive force that drives artistic development from antiquity through modernity, and he believed that the emergence of the Baroque style constitutes a key moment in the groundbreaking of a subjective art. As I will demonstrate soon, my interpretation of subjectivity is not at all the same as that of Riegl.[7]

As stated in Arthur Burda's and Max Dvořák's foreword to both the 1908 and the 1923 editions of Riegl's *Die Entstehung der Barockkunst in Rom* [The Emergence of Baroque Art in Rome], this volume offers to the reader the notes that Riegl made for the courses in the history of early modern Italian art at Vienna University, which he gave between 1894 and 1902. In editing these notes, Burda and Dvořák tried to impart some structural coherence to Riegl's thoughts on Baroque art. Despite the editors' efforts, Riegl's text tends to be laconic and occasionally cryptic, and therefore calls out for exegesis. On a preliminary basis, Riegl's definition of the Baroque style mostly focuses on two correlated topics: Michelangelo's and Correggio's roles as forerunners of the new style and sensitivity, and the importance of late sixteenth- and early seventeenth-century architecture in forging a novel language of forms embodying artistic change. Only at the end of the volume does Riegl explore the emergence of the new style in painting, by swiftly evoking the figures of Federico Barocci and Federico Zuccari, and then devoting more space to the Carracci and his followers. Caravaggio's "*Naturalismus*" occupies the last section of *Die Entstehung der Barockkunst*, in total six pages. Here is Riegl's description of the naturalistic movement inaugurated by Caravaggio:

> Naturalism. As the name implies, [these painters] wanted to paint nature as it is: that is, as they saw or believed to see it. By this, they obviously meant through optical vision, which nonetheless—as is always the case with Italians—entails essentially corporeal elements ["*körperliche Elemente*"], and is thus always more or less subjective ["*subjektives*"]. Then, for the first time, there is the acknowledgment of a conscious subjectivism, and hence of the optical ["*Einbekenntnis des bewußten Subjektivismus, und zwar des optischen*"]: this is why they are colorists and see things as colored phenomena, and not simply as bodies ["*Körper*"]. This goes hand in hand with a patent contempt for all the other pictorial styles, past and present. Naturalism is the only law; it burns all its bridges. They believe they were able to extract themselves altogether from the historical evolution of painting in Italy, which distinguishes them from the Bolognese. The Carracci still honored the great masters of the sixteenth century, and detested the Mannerists. But their ambition is to combine Raphael's drawing with Titian's color. Naturalists are indifferent to either. They do not busy themselves with traditional canons of beauty, which cannot be separated from a tactile delimitation of parts ["*tastbare Begrenzung der Teile*"]. They take their figures in the street and depict them as they appear, without caring for the canons fabricated by Raphael and others.[8]

7 For Riegl's theory of art and cultural profile, see Kemp W. 1990; Iversen 1991; Iversen 1993; Wolfgang Kemp in Riegl 1999; Rampley 2003; Huemer and Vasold 2005; Fend 2005; Scarrocchia 2006; Rampley 2007; Fend 2007b; and *Alois Riegl* 2008. For Riegl's influence and the Vienna School, see Wood 2003.

8 Riegl 1923, 186: "Der Naturalismus. Wie schon der Name besagt, wollen sie die Natur malen, wie sie ist, d.h. so, wie sie dieselbe sahen oder zu sehen glaubten. Natürlich meinten sie darunter das optische Sehen, das aber bei ihnen, wie bei allen Italienern, immer noch wesentlich körperliche Elemente mitenthielt, das immer ein mehr oder minder subjektives ist. Also zum erstenmal das offene Einbekenntnis des bewußten Subjektivismus, und zwar des optischen: daher sind sie Koloristen und sehen die Dinge als farbige Erscheinungen, nicht bloß als Körper. Hand in Hand damit geht die offene Verachtung aller übrigen Malweisen, aller vergangenen sowohl als aller gleichzeitigen. Der Naturalismus ist das

At the core of Riegl's opposition between the optical ("*das optische*") and the tactile ("*das tastbare*"), which he pairs respectively with the subjective and the objective, there is the assumption that man's perception interacts with reality in a twofold manner: by isolating single objects in a close-up view ("*Nahbild*") or by seizing the whole in a distant view ("*Fernbild*"). Not only does each form of perception, close and distant, correspond to diverse kinds of knowledge, but the predominance of the one over the other in the course of human history also serves as a parameter of artistic evolution: ancient art is preeminently objective and tactile, modern art subjective and optical. During the Renaissance, an artistic balance was struck between these two components: perspective indeed holds together the single objects of representation by creating a common binding structure.

But Renaissance art, for Riegl, is still the realm of will and exteriority: it expresses man's attempt to dominate reality, to tame it in accordance with his own purposes. For this reason, Alberti's *istoria*, with its emphasis on human action and its structural over-determination, perfectly incarnates the spirit of the Renaissance in Italy. But Riegl's predilection rather inclines toward seventeenth-century northern art, which he considers as the paradigmatic expression of modern inwardness ("*Empfindung*"): man's capability to fuse within, and embrace, the world as a unity and living entity. Riegl's views on Dutch art of the Golden Age as delineated in his 1902 *Holländische Gruppenporträt* [The Group Portraiture of Holland] largely confirm this point. In this essay, Riegl envisions the intrinsic character of the northern man and art as a highly moral one, as the triumph of a collective spirit at odds with Italian individualism. As is the case with many other art interpreters of his time, Riegl's hermeneutical system draws upon a grid of conceptual opposites posited as universal categories—the optical and the tactile, the subjective and the objective, inwardness and will, and so forth. In evaluating Caravaggio's art, Riegl therefore observes the symptoms of an increased subjectivity that manifests itself through a stubborn refusal of whatever might inhibit the pictorial rendition of things as they "appear," that is, as "colored phenomena." It is not surprising that Riegl describes the goals of naturalism in terms that mirror the tenets of French Impressionism:

> Afterward, they [naturalist painters] elaborated their own rendering of color, which best fit their brutally naturalistic conception. They came close to the Venetians, but then emancipated themselves from them because they needed shadows, thereby creating oppositions of light and shadow in a manner never to be found in Italian painting. Finally, they often did not care for composition. (...) Caravaggio executed paintings whose structure is wholly asymmetrical (the Vatican *Entombment*). That this might be possible in an Italian painter is certainly noteworthy![9]

One might therefore expect Riegl to consider the art of Caravaggio and his followers as the culmination of Baroque subjectivity along with Dutch painting, but nothing is farther from he truth:

einzig Richtige. Er bricht alle Brücken hinter sich ab. Sie glaubten von der historischen Entwicklung der Malerei in Italien ganz absehen zu können. Das scheidet sie von den Bolognesen. Die Carracci verehren noch immer die großen Cinquecentisten, sie hassen nur die Manieristen. Aber ihr Ehrgeiz ist, die Linienführung Raffaels mit der Farbe Tizians zu vereinen. Den Naturalisten ist das eine wie das andere gleichgültig. Sie bekümmern sich nicht um die herkömmlichen Schönheitstypen, die von der tastbaren Begrenzung der Teile unzertrennbar sind: die Figuren nehmen sie von der Straße und malen dieselben, wie sie eben aussehen, ohne sich um die von Raffael und anderen geschaffenen Schönheitstypen zu kümmern."

9 Ibidem, 187: "Aber in der Folge bilden sie auch eine eigene Farbengebung aus, die für ihre schroffe naturalistische Auffassung am entsprechendsten scheint. Sie stehen den Venezianern nahe, dann aber emanzipieren sie sich von ihnen, weil sie Schatten brauchen, und bilden nun die Gegensätze von Licht und Schatten in einer Weise aus, wie sie in der italienischen Malerei nicht ihresgleichen findet. Endlich kümmern sie sich oft nicht um den Aufbau der Komposition. Freilich gerade darin konnten sie die große Vergangenheit nicht leugnen. Aber von Caravaggio gibt es Bilder, die ganz unsymmetrisch aufgebaut sind (Grablegung im Vatikan). Daß es überhaupt bei einem Italiener möglich war, ist schon zu verzeichnen!"

Instead of associating them to northern painters, these oppositions of light and shadow distance the ones from the others. The background is dark, without any reflection, and the figures spring forth from the background with metallic sharpness, through tactile demarcation, just as the single elements are modeled by detaching themselves from the dark. This is why they are called "tenebrists." Relatively few among them can be defined as real naturalists, but they influenced the entire subsequent painting of the seventeenth century.[10]

Not surprisingly, Riegl dislikes many aspects of Italian naturalism and, in particular, of Caravaggio's painting. From the outset, he notes that the optical subjectivity of these painters and their master eminently exerts itself upon the body, whose close-up framing and view—the principle of the "*Nahbild*"—necessarily heightens the tactility of their artworks. By remarking that Caravaggio, as an Italian, inexorably indulges in the corporeal, Riegl suggests that naturalism's opticality and subjectivity was doomed to failure in its southern form. And indeed, Riegl reduces Caravaggio's merits to his technical innovations. In a sense, Caravaggio practices an optical "subjectivity" that is exclusively of surface since it is not rooted in the inwardness characteristic of northern artists. It is therefore understandable that Riegl, exactly like Bellori, admires the color technique of the early Caravaggio, assimilating it not only to that of Giorgione, but especially of Correggio: the master who, foreshadowing a new era of subjectivity, nevertheless remains a sheer product of the Italian Renaissance and, consequently, of Italianism. And in fact, as soon as Caravaggio abandons his original Venetian imprint, he evolves a naturalistic style that, in Riegl's opinion, proves to be unnatural, exaggerated, and unpleasant. But this is not all:

> Apart from his peculiar lighting, often accentuated to the point of estrangement, there is something concerning expression. If, early on, Caravaggio picked up figures from life, from the circle of merely meaningless occupations, just as they presented themselves to him, now he starts to be selective. He deliberately seeks specific types, as far removed as possible from any general canon of beauty. But his search of individuality is much less successful than that of Netherlandish painters: he was too Italian for this endeavor. Accordingly, we often remark upon his vulgarity without being able to come to terms with it through art's incentive of the genuinely characteristic. We, northern men, do not conceal vulgarity when it appears to us as a necessity of nature: the painter must possess the strength to show it as it is. In addition, Caravaggio obeys the expectations of his time in depicting an accentuated pathos. This pathos is ever authentic, always gripping, and frequently touching, but it often repels us as it comes with an estranging lighting and wild physiognomies.[11]

10 Ibidem: "Die Gegensätze von Licht und Schatten nähern sie aber nicht den Nordländern, sondern entfernen sie von ihnen. Der Grund ist dunkel, ohne alle Reflexe, und die Figuren springen in metallischer Schärfe, in taktischer Begrenzung aus dem Grund heraus, und ebenso sind die einzelnen Teile aus dem Dunkel heraus modelliert. Daher heißen die die Tenebrosen. Es sind ihrer verhältnismäßig nicht viele, die man als reine Naturalisten bezeichnen kann; beeinflußt aber haben sie die ganze folgende Malerei des 17. Jahrhunderts."

11 Ibidem, 190-1: "Zu dieser eigentümlichen, oft bis zur Unheimlichkeit gesteigerten Beleuchtung kommt noch ein weiteres, den Ausdruck Betreffendes: hat er früher Figuren aus Leben, aus dem Kreise gegenständlich unbedeutender Beschäftigungen genommen, so, wie sie sich eben darboten,

so beginnt er jetzt zu wählen. Er sucht absichtlich nach charakteristischen Gestalten, die von einem allgemeinen Schönheitstypus möglichst weit entfernt waren. Das Individualisieren gelingt ihm dabei weit weniger wie die Niederländern: dazu war er eben zu sehr Italiener. Daher bemerken wir oft das Gemeine daran, ohne durch das künstlerische Moment des echt Charakteristischen versöhnt zu werden. Wir Nordländer verbergen das Gemeine nicht, wenn es uns als eine Naturnotwendigkeit erscheint: der Maler muß also die Kraft haben, es so erscheinen zu lassen. Ferner folgt er den Anforderungen der Zeit durch Darstellung eines gesteigerten Pathos. Dieses Pathos ist niemals unecht, immer packend, häufig ergreifend, aber oft wirkt es in Verbindung mit der unheimlichen Beleuchtung und den wilden Gesichtstypen abstoßend."

If Riegl's disproval of Caravaggio's most contrasted chiaroscuro betrays an aesthetic idiosyncrasy that by no means connotes as epistemic and is hence arbitrary, his statement about Caravaggio's lack of the "genuinely characteristic" ("*das echt Charakteristische*") most likely relates to his conviction that northern artists successfully manage to render the specific mood or atmosphere of a scene, so that all the represented figures naturally adapt to, and merge into, it. In other words, an inn or genre scene requires its necessary dose of vulgarity, whereas Caravaggio's anti-types of noble figures do not conform to the gravity of the religious narratives in which they happen to appear.

Although I recognize the intelligence and importance of Riegl's hermeneutics, I have a profound antipathy for an epistemological system based on conceptual dichotomies. Riegl's exegesis of Caravaggio's painting seems to me to be a missed opportunity and, worse, a radical miscomprehension due to epistemological prejudice. It is evident that Riegl did not give much thought to Caravaggio's work, and it is no coincidence that his succinct description and analysis of the master's life and oeuvre are interwoven everywhere with criticisms directly stemming from Baglione's and Bellori's biographies. More important, by laying considerable emphasis on Caravaggio's naturalism as the new technique of the "optical" and the "subjective," Riegl, not unlike the master's detractors in the seventeenth century, refuses to deal with the "content" of his work. But is Caravaggio's originality truly limited to his portentous ability for reproduction? Is his mimesis real, pure reproduction? And if so, is this its only significance? To answer these questions, I must borrow Riegl's term of "subjectivity," which has constantly stimulated my reflection on the characteristics of seventeenth-century art.

I should perhaps remind the reader what the *istoria* is in Counter-Reformation art theory, and thus in Caravaggio's time. Not only prelates such as Johannes Molanus, Gabriele Paleotti, and Federico Borromeo, but also artists like Giovan Paolo Lomazzo and Giovan Battista Armenini unanimously underscore the validity of pictorial sacred narratives as visual propositions through which beholders can be taught essential truths: the dogmas of the Catholic Church, the principles of Christian ethics, and the order of the created world as instantiated by God himself. As a backlash against Calvin's iconoclasm and Luther's distrust of images, Counter-Reformation art theorists not only validate the status of the painted sacred story as the equivalent of scripture, but also believe that the *istoria*, if perfectly legible and intelligible, becomes a perfect tool of pedagogy and persuasion on account of its directness as a medium based upon, and destined to, the organ of vision—besides encouraging emotional and intellectual involvement, sight abolishes the barrier between fiction and reality, engendering a hybrid perceptual continuum in which the viewer's actuality is subsumed into painting's fictiveness.

Through religious narratives, beholders are illusorily transported into the sacred event, and watch it as if they were actually witnessing it. Theorists' interest in verisimilitude acquires a distinct valence in this specific context: to ensure that the transition between actuality and fictiveness unfolds smoothly, images must mimic the causality of the outside world. In addition to lending rhetorical ornaments to action, verisimilitude buttresses the paramount analogy between the real and the fictive. As visual propositions, pictorial narratives must thus perform as indexes of external objectivity. By the same token, even miracles—the irruptions of the divine and the supernatural into nature's order—ought to be objectified and hence identified as such visually. Because of their pedagogic function, Counter-Reformation images are required to be predictable: truth, by definition, is atemporal, and its pictorial unveiling a matter of reminiscence. As epistemological analogs, pictorial narratives are moreover supposed to show the truth unambiguously.

These theoretical strictures not only greatly narrow the possibility for painters to venture an original take on the *istoria*, but overall invalidate the very mechanisms through which any narrative operates, that is, by withholding and releasing information at will. Already in Aristotle's *Poetics*, the beginning of a story is determined by a "catastrophe," the reversal of a pre-existing order.

Through its vicissitudes, the story calls upon the reader, spectator or beholder to discover how the disrupted order is to be transfigured and re-installed; the story distills suspenseful information over time, more or less progressively, until it reaches its very end. The emotional effects of the new order's discovery are powerful, and result in a drastic "purification," or catharsis, of the audience. In this light, it is evident that sacred narratives, insofar as they are designed to disclose information forthwith, tend to depict "catastrophes" whose outcomes are both largely anticipated and visually assumed. Of course, painters can deepen the devotional and contemplative undertones of the sacred narrative, collapse temporality in view of signaling providence's grand design, or modify the story's format stylistically and formally. Yet, as a general rule, because the painted religious narrative is requested to be propositional, it necessarily eschews the suspense of the unknown that instead nourishes and supports the beholder's absorption in an ongoing action. If executed in accordance with Counter-Reformation aesthetic norms, the sacred *istoria* will demonstrate its truth, affect or involve the beholder, but will not un-resolve the visual plot—that is, suspend it on the brink of the unknown—by reassessing or jeopardizing its denouement.

But what if, by means of whatever pictorial device, the beholder is, say, led to question Christ's unflinching determination to pursue his own death by accepting Judas' kiss, or to second-guess Thomas' willingness to put his finger into the Savior's wound? What if the viewer momentarily loses his or her certainty of seeing the divine, because a mighty steed obstructs his or her vision of the miracle, or because the Savior does not seem to be at the time and place where he is allegedly represented? Paradoxically, Caravaggio's "opticality" presents us with segments and sequels of actions as if they were truly prolongations of our visual field only to plunge us into hermeneutical blindness and causal incoherence, into temporal short-circuits and visual double-entendres. Indeed, the fictive universe he interweaves for us on the canvas contains innumerable perceptual traps, but candidly, we step into them persuaded that his fiction somehow conforms to the logic of our reality. Is this candidness or naivety? Neither, merely any beholder's instinctive reaction to Caravaggio's work as nimbly calculated by the painter himself.

All the dislocations I have noted throughout this volume are technical innovations through which Caravaggio repudiates the *istoria*'s objectivity. As regards Caravaggio's use of pictorial space, it has been repeatedly observed that there is no true perspective in Caravaggio's work; the space is shallow, and figures loosely oscillate in the shallowness of their chiaroscuro. For many, this is a matter of inexperience or a consequence of Caravaggio's montage techniques. However, nothing is easier than to adjust a few figures to a barred and exiguous depth by anchoring them to one another in spatial coordination. But even at the zenith of his craftsmanship Caravaggio renounces squeezing his figures, half-figures, and parts of bodies into a strictly pre-defined perspective: out of proportion, a hand might fail to touch a shoulder that appears to be within its reach, or a sight might be directed to a torso that, abnormally and inexplicably, recedes beyond its scope. In my view, space for Caravaggio is not an objective construction, and certainly not the section of Alberti's visual pyramid in which figures and objects are arranged commensurately to a determinate whole. For Caravaggio space is instead a fictive and hence subjective variant. By distorting the spatial coordinates, Caravaggio re-appropriates space as a variable that he manipulates as he pleases. In his narratives, space is thus a mere function of fiction. In the same vein, time and duration impose their own measure in Caravaggio's painting: a female saint, bloodless and whitening away, might be staring at a wound freshly inflicted upon her breast. Or, to touch succinctly upon Caravaggio's lighting, an apostle, invested by a stream of radiance, might not cast a shadow upon an adjacent young man. What I am arguing here is that space, time, lighting, and the other basic components of the early modern *istoria* might become independent variants in Caravaggio's narrative, as if acting absolutely and on their own behalf. But fictively uncoordinated absolutes generate a network of relativity that inherently denies the image's pretended objectivity, channeled in Caravaggio's case

567

through the accuracy of his optical effects and the graphicness of his tactile renditions. Caravaggio ensconces the seeds of subjectivity at the core of his narratives' structures.

This subjectivity must be understood in a twofold manner. On the one hand, the painter rigs the apparatus of causal interconnections that regulate the diverse elements of the *istoria* by making them accord primarily with his own finalities: his authorial viewpoint. As a creator, Caravaggio is the master of his fictions' time and space, lighting and figural disposition, which together amounts to a vision escaping the logic of reality, its immediate and designated referent. In this way, the artwork integrates the subjectivity of his author's vision in the most explicit terms: that is, as a distortive factor of mimetic and narrative objectivity. On the other hand, by dislocating the causal interconnectedness of his narratives on one or more levels, Caravaggio induces bewilderment in the beholder. Unable to reconfigure the plot in its coherence and at first glance compelling objectivity, the viewer resorts to a multiple array of interpretations; the artwork becomes a domain of semantic openness, and therefore stirs and solicits the external intervention of its recipient in order to achieve its message. This procedure does not qualify as pedagogy; instead of instilling the certitude of propositions, Caravaggio's narratives elicit exegetical indeterminacy and conjectural responses. By means of this structural openness, beholders are thus invited to co-author the narrative by improvising portions of a mental script: conjectures destined to fill in the story's blanks. In this manner, one may legitimately wonder whether an open-mouthed apostle is asserting his innocence or repenting of his cowardice; likewise, to take an example from Diego Velázquez, one may doubt whether a mulatto servant is feeling the impulse of conversion, merely daydreaming or rearranging her kitchen utensils.

In evoking the notion of bewilderment in connection with the image's manipulated legibility and intelligibility, I also designate the effects of surprise and suspense that Caravaggio's narratives arouse. There is a deliberate gap between the optical and tactile "objectivity" deployed in some of Caravaggio's paintings (I am intentionally emending Riegl here) and the inconsistencies of the visual plot's causal interrelations. By acknowledging and then surmounting this gap, the viewer not only incorporates the image's fictiveness, but also progresses through an itinerary of perceptual and intellectual marveling. The painting's superficial objectivity as a mirror of the outside world doubles into the painter's subjective vision as the domain of fiction by revealing its intrinsic dislocations. Through these numerous and varied pictorial disjunctions, Caravaggio jolts his viewer out of a passive seeing and reading into self-estrangement; new layers of facts and possibilities unexpectedly come to the fore, amplifying the image's impact and prefiguring new prospects of interpretation. Accordingly, the story's familiar outcome becomes problematic, or at least the represented action is contemplated in a perspective that suppresses the filter of expectations through which viewers would have approached the sacred plot in precognition. In this sense, Caravaggio's narratives inaugurate a poetics of relativity that not only contravenes the absolutist foundations of the early modern *istoria,* but more significantly legitimates the usage of pictorial technologies censored by contemporary artists and theorists, among others the warping of space, time, and lighting through and against which Caravaggio tests the value and meaning of his religious stories.

Herein lies the gist of these final considerations: the principle of relativism planted by the master into the living structure of the Counter-Reformation *istoria* is by no means innocent or sheer bravado. Indeed, it dismantles not only the image's propositional coherence, but also the entire hermeneutics upon which the Catholic Church as the main religious, political, cultural, and social agency of Caravaggio's Rome had constructed its identity. Not that Caravaggio was a public agitator or a political protester of his time. But the ways in which he subtly and intelligently blurs the distinction between high and low, heroic and anti-heroic, noble and ignoble—to mention but a few examples—dramatically relativize the notions of self and social identity current in this period. Are gypsies despicable outcasts or neo-Petrarchan prototypes of beauty and seduction? Will cardsharps systematically yield to their treacherous compulsions, or can anything discourage them from following the fatal instincts preordained to their characters?

Caravaggio's most unconventional meditations concern the sacred much more than the secular, as proven above all by his pictorial renditions of Christ in both his human and divine nature. In some cases, Caravaggio dissociates divinity from the Savior's figure, as if Jesus the man were enacting scripture not as the agent of God, but as his vehicle. Remember Christ's repulsion at Judas' embrace as depicted by Caravaggio, the Savior's desperation and horror in trying to accept his imminent Passion, or his eradication from the dramatic plot while resurrecting Lazarus, as Caravaggio makes him foresee his own death and mourned cadaver. By highlighting the "humanity" of Christ, Caravaggio inflects his narratives with uncanny implications; because he temporarily rids Jesus of his providential outlook, he manages to unravel the pristine intensity and ambit of this sacred hero's pathos.

As a divine personification, Caravaggio's Christ exceeds the confines of representation, and therefore dwells between the visible and the invisible, presence and absence, contingence and transcendence. The *istoria* seems unable to contain the depiction of the divine. In this regard, I emphasize the originality and rebelliousness of Caravaggio's enterprise: whereas the Catholic Church had demonstrated the validity of representing, not reproducing, divinity, Caravaggio questions this very principle by erasing or dissimulating God's pictorial acts. By insinuating Christ's invisibility, for instance, Caravaggio uncovers the purely iconographic nature of the Savior's figure, an iconic sign that cannot epitomize its referent lest divinity be reduced to a visual commonplace— that is, to a conventional, fully-known entity. Paradoxically, representing the divine does not necessarily increase the viewer's knowledge of it; representation in fact reifies transcendence, and therefore proves to be a synecdoche: a part for a whole that nevertheless defies definition and circumscription. However, unleashing divinity's disruptive charge within the religious *istoria* involves dislodging the lexicon and syntax of early modern representation, a relativization of its epistemological functionalities.

Where is God in Caravaggio's Cerasi *Conversion of Saint Paul*? How does divine grace operate in the picture? By removing the signs of divinity, save for a few perfunctory sunrays in the painting's right corner, Caravaggio obscures the *raison d'être* of the sacred narrative. To put it more crudely, Caravaggio destroys the *istoria* of Paul's conversion by sinking the viewer into hermeneutical blindness: God may or may not be acting inside the apostle's heart; the image is opaque to transcendence. But the representation of a sacred event without the certainty of knowledge is tantamount to an *istoria* without action, which is how Bellori defined the Cerasi *Conversion of Saint Paul*: he intuitively understood the pictorially blasphemous gesture behind Caravaggio's painting—the master's peremptory denial of pictorial transcendence. And yet relativizing the "signs" of divinity is not an expression of atheism; in Caravaggio's case, it is rather a profound act of dissatisfaction with a system of knowledge relying on indisputable axioms such as those endorsed by the Catholic Church. By obscuring God's presence, Caravaggio indicates not only the limits of man's perception and intellect in comprehending divinity, but also the inadequacy of a theological hermeneutics in which God's act and significance can be clarified through dogma and the divine's representation turned into aesthetic maxims. Paul's blindness in Caravaggio's Cerasi picture is the beholder's blindness, and the nature of the grace he receives is as obscure as the action staged in the painting: a grace without visual or verbal content because technically un-inscribable into a proposition or a figure. Not surprisingly, the most pertinent procedure with which to transliterate grace into an image is by concealing it.

Caravaggio's conflicting relation to faith and the Church's use of religious images also transpires in his parody and denigration of pictorial authorship. No longer the receptor of divine truth and the witness of true biblical events, Caravaggio as a Christian painter denounces the hopeless relativity of the authorial viewpoint. Even as he, through his alter ego in the picture, declares his miraculous ability to render the figure of Christ as flesh and blood, he unveils the folly of representing the humanized divinity by burlesquing the pictorial act of "showing" the Savior. Wandering in his own work, Caravaggio's fictive counterpart is, by the same token, hampered from glimpsing Christ's arrest, the very scene visualized and represented by the authorial eye that the author's avatar in the painting is supposed to personify.

A consideration of Albrecht Dürer's 1500 *Self-Portrait* and the pithy assimilation of his own figure to Christ's,[12] or of Michelangelo's self-portrayal as a new Nicodemus carrying the Savior's dead body, reveals immediately how scandalous and unsettling Caravaggio's self-parody as Pilate introducing "the man"—Jesus—turns out to be. That Caravaggio even perceived himself as the impious Goliath and consequently depicted his mutilated head as the trophy of David's divine virtue does not eclipse the fact that some of his contemporaries had saluted him as a quasi-divine painter. Whether an angel or a demon, as Baglione disguised him in one of his pictures,[13] Caravaggio's self-identity as an artificer—the visionary creator of images—constantly contradicts the artistic and moral principles that early modern painters so obsessively strove to assert. It is fair to affirm that nothing resists Caravaggio's reassessment of both authorship and authority, artistic principles that once again become relative variants in Caravaggio's reflection.

Undoubtedly Riegl was right in stating that Caravaggio and his followers aimed to extirpate themselves from the course of history. By ostentatiously disregarding the canons and canonical formulas of all his predecessors—but in words much more than through facts—Caravaggio proposed himself both as the unique paradigm of painting and the antithesis of any historical style, the inventor of a new style with no affiliation. But the newness of a style cannot be established absolutely or hermetically preserved forever: Caravaggio must have soon grown aware that, despite his best intentions, his art was subject to interpretation, emulation, and elaboration, thereby entering the realm of history and rivalry. But a historicized style loses its absoluteness, hence Caravaggio's style is a contradictory notion. As self-authoritative, it does not obey any former authority, but simultaneously, as the paradigm of a new authorial mode of painting, engages in competition with other styles, past and present. In a sense, Caravaggio's response to this quandary is expressed through self-parody and ironic displacement of pictorial authorship; even at the height of its technical potentiality, his extreme naturalism, which is the distinctive trademark of his artistic novelty, is expressed by Caravaggio as incapable of moving beyond its own limits—to transform lifelikeness into life, Christ into real presence, and fictive vision into a truly absolute and authorial event. For this reason, Caravaggio's style and pictorial authority qualify as artistic variables: the perfect objectivity of painting as formulated in the early modern period cannot be fulfilled by them.

In stressing the scope of relativism in Caravaggio's work, I argue that specific elements of subjectivity innervate the master's poetics of dislocation. But to what degree is this subjectivity also a substantial feature of Caravaggio's age? Is it possible to postulate the existence of such an epochal phenomenon as an age of subjectivity? Unless I follow in Riegl's footsteps and isolate segments of universal evolution in art history, I must resign myself to the idea that the material gleaned and analyzed in this volume does not enable me to speak of an age of subjectivity. That term is intended as a provocation, a challenge both to myself and to future scholarship.

On a preliminary basis, the seventeenth century in art is overwhelmingly normative; never before had artists and theorists attempted to define artistic creation with such exhaustiveness, or

---

12 See Koerner 1993.

13 I refer to Baglione's 1602 *Triumph of Divine Love over Earthly Love* in the Galleria Nazionale d'Arte Antica, Palazzo Barberini, Rome. See Möller 1991, 103-4, no. 17; Röttgen 1993; Smith 'O Neil 2002, 27-30, 204-5, no. 24; and Vodret 2002.

even obsession. The artwork's conception, elaboration, execution, reception, and significance are minutely submitted to scrutiny throughout the entire century, while more and more sophisticated norms and rules in the matter of art are produced and enunciated. No other century has sought so hard to objectify art, to intrude into and prise open its innermost anatomy and mechanisms. In this light, one might qualify the seventeenth century as an "age of objectivity." Yet in my opinion there is something vigorously perverse in seventeenth-century art's tendency toward objectification and regulation: its inherent attraction to license and trespass, and the vastness of its visual experimentation. How do Velázquez and Rembrandt, Guido Reni and Vermeer fit within this age of "objectivity"? How do they coexist with the stricter rules that keen artists like Domenichino and Poussin seek to apply to painting? The essence of my argument is that the acknowledgment and exploitation of the *istoria*'s own logic as an autonomous space of fiction, and therefore of fictive relativism as showcased by Caravaggio's painting, seems to have set an example that, amidst innumerable contradictions and oppositions, will disrupt the early modern concept of the image, thus inspiring the works of the most ingenious representatives of seventeenth-century art. At its core, Caravaggio's poetics of dislocation therefore adumbrates the greatest novelties of painting to come. Without being a universal aesthetic category, subjectivity as I have defined it here may be an efficient hermeneutical instrument through which to interpret the incommensurable achievements of seventeenth-century art, a "vast and delicate"[14] age of creativity and artistic pioneering.

14   This is a quotation from Paul Verlaine's description of the Middle Ages in *Sagesse*, Part I, X: "C'est vers le Moyen-Âge énorme et délicat/ Qu'il faudrait que mon cœur en panne naviguât/ Loin de nos jours d'esprit charnel et de chair triste."

LIST OF ILLUSTRATIONS

Illustrations

1. Louis Marin, Diagram of Caravaggio's *Resurrection of Lazarus*, reproduced from Louis Marin, *Détruire la peinture*, 1977.

2. Michelangelo Merisi da Caravaggio, *The Resurrection of Lazarus*, Museo Regionale, Messina, oil on canvas, 320 x 275 cm., detail. © Luciano Pedicini.

3. Michelangelo Merisi da Caravaggio, *The Penitent Magdalene*, Galleria Doria-Pamphilj, Rome, oil on canvas, 123 x 98.3 cm. © Alinari/ Art Resource, NY.

4. Parmigianino (Francesco Mazzola), *Saint Thaïs*, etching, 13 x 11.2 cm. © The Trustees of the British Museum.

5. Raphael (Raffaello Santi), *Nude Figure Study for the Left Foreground Group in the Disputa*, Städelsches Institut, Frankfurt, pen and ink over black chalk and stylus underdrawing, 28 x 41.6 cm. © U. Edelmann/Städel Museum/Artothek.

6. Reconstruction Diagram of the X-Rays of Caravaggio's *The Martyrdom of Saint Matthew*, detail, reproduced from Leonello Venturi, *Caravaggio*, 1963.

7. Anonymous engraver after Raphael (Raffaello Santi), *The Battle of Ostia*, engraving, 37.9 x 52.4 cm., detail. © The Trustees of the British Museum.

8. Francesco Albani, *The Annunciation*, San Bartolomeo di Porta Ravegnana, Bologna, oil on canvas, 365 x 295 cm.© Soprintendenza ai Beni Artistici e Culturali delle Province di Bologna e Parma.

9. Ludovico Carracci, *The Annunciation*, San Pietro Cathedral, Bologna, fresco. © Soprintendenza ai Beni Artistici e Culturali delle Province di Bologna e Parma.

10. Correggio (Antonio Allegri), *Noli Me Tangere*, Museo del Prado, Madrid, oil on canvas, 130 x 103 cm. © Erich Lessing/ Art Resource, NY.

11. Annibale Carracci, *The Baptism of Christ*, Santi Gregorio e Siro, Bologna, oil on canvas, 383 x 225 cm. © Soprintendenza ai Beni Artistici e Culturali delle Province di Bologna e Parma.

12. Annibale Carracci, *Study of a Boy Taking Off His Shirt*, Musée du Louvre, Paris, red chalk, 35.9 x 22.1 cm. © Réunion des Musées Nationaux/ Art Resource, NY.

13. Michelangelo Merisi da Caravaggio, *The Death of the Virgin*, Musée du Louvre, Paris, oil on canvas, 369 x 245 cm. © Réunion des Musées Nationaux/ Art Resource, NY.

14. Michelangelo Merisi da Caravaggio, *The Flagellation*, Musée des Beaux-Arts, Rouen, oil on canvas, 134.5 x 174.5 cm. © Réunion des Musées Nationaux/ Art Resource, NY.

15. Battista Franco, *The Flagellation*, engraving, 42 x 54.7 cm. © The Trustees of the British Museum.

16. Giulio Clovio after Michelangelo Buonarroti, *The Flagellation*, Royal Library, Windsor Castle, red chalk and stylus on white paper, 23.5 x 23.6 cm. © The Royal Collection/ 2010 Her Majesty Queen Elizabeth II.

17. Lucas Cranach, *The Flagellation*, woodcut, 24.5 x 17.1 cm., detail. © The Trustees of the British Museum.

18. Michelangelo Merisi da Caravaggio, *The Flagellation*, Museo di Capodimonte, Naples, oil on canvas, 266 x 213 cm. © Scala/ Ministero per i Beni e le Attività Culturali/ Art Resource, NY.

19. Michelangelo Buonarroti, *Christ at the Column*, British Museum, London, black chalk on white paper, 27.5 x 14.3 cm. © The Trustees of the British Museum.

20. Michelangelo Merisi da Caravaggio, *Saint John the Baptist*, Pinacoteca Capitolina, Rome, oil on canvas, 129 x 95 cm. © Erich Lessing/ Art Resource, NY.

21. Michelangelo Buonarroti, *Study for an Ignudo*, Teylers Museum, Haarlem, red chalk, 27.9 x 21.4 cm. © Teylers Museum, Haarlem, The Netherlands.
22. Ludovico Carracci, *Nude Figure of a Sleeping Boy*, Ashmolean Museum, Oxford, red chalk, 23.7 x 22.3 cm. © Ashmolean Museum.
23. Annibale Carracci, *Study of a Foreshortened Head*, Galleria degli Uffizi, Florence, red chalk, 12.2 x 85 cm. © Soprintendenza Speciale per il Polo Museale Fiorentino.
24. Correggio (Antonio Allegri), *Nude Man with Supporting Putto*, Musée du Louvre, Paris, red chalk, 16.9 x 14.8 cm. © Réunion des Musées Nationaux/ Art Resource, NY.
25. Agostino Veneziano (Agostino Musi) after Raphael (Raffaello Santi), *The Israelites Gathering the Manna in the Desert*, engraving, 27.8 x 40.8 cm. © The Trustees of the British Museum.
26. Titian (Tiziano Vecelli), *The Annunciation*, Museo di Capodimonte, Naples, oil on canvas, 280 x 193.5 cm. © Scala/ Ministero per i Beni e le Attività Culturali/ Art Resource, NY.
27. Michelangelo Merisi da Caravaggio, *The Annunciation*, Musée des Beaux-Arts, Nancy, oil on canvas, 285 x 205 cm. © Scala/ Art Resource, NY.
28. Albrecht Altdorfer, *The Annunciation*, woodcut, 12.1 x 9.4 cm. © The Trustees of the British Museum.
29. Moretto da Brescia (Alessandro Bonvicino), *The Virgin Adoring the Child*, Sant'Alessandro in Colonna, Bergamo, 129 x 92 cm. © Don Giovanni Carzaniga, Sant'Alessandro in Colonna.
30. Jan Saenredam after Abraham Bloemaert, *Adam and Eve Mourning the Death of Abel*, engraving, 25.6 x 19.1 cm. © The Trustees of the British Museum.
31. Jan Saenredam after Abraham Bloemaert, *Adam and Eve Mourning the Death of Abel*, engraving, 25.6 x 19.1 cm., detail. © The Trustees of the British Museum.
32. Michelangelo Merisi da Caravaggio, *The Annunciation*, Musée des Beaux-Arts, Nancy, oil on canvas, 285 x 205 cm., detail. © Scala/ Art Resource, NY.
33. Charles Le Brun, *The Family of Darius at the Feet of Alexander* or *The Tent of Darius*, Châteaux de Versailles et Trianon, Versailles, oil on canvas, 298 x 453 cm. © Réunion des Musées Nationaux/ Art Resource, NY.
34. Nicolas Poussin, *The Israelites Gathering the Manna in the Desert*, Musée du Louvre, Paris, oil on canvas, 149 x 200 cm. © Réunion des Musées Nationaux/ Art Resource, NY.
35. Michelangelo Merisi da Caravaggio, *Judith Beheading Holofernes*, Galleria Nazionale d'Arte Antica, Palazzo Barberini, Rome, oil on canvas, 145 x 195 cm. © Luciano Pedicini.
36. Anonymous engraver after Giulio Romano, *Judith Beheading Holofernes*, engraving, 15.5 x 21.8 cm. © Albertina, Vienna.
37. Master LPH, *Judith Beheading Holofernes*, engraving, 14.2 cm. (diameter). © Kunstsammlungen der Fürsten zu Waldburg-Wolfegg.
38. Rosso Fiorentino (Giovan Battista di Jacopo), *Judith and Her Servant*, Los Angeles County Museum, Los Angeles, red chalk on gray buff paper, 23.2 x 19.69 cm.© 2009 Museum Associates/ LACMA/ Art Resource, NY.
39. Michelangelo Buonarroti, *Study of the Head of the Cumaean Sybil*, Biblioteca Reale, Turin, black chalk, 23 x 31.5 cm.© Biblioteca Reale, Torino.
40. Master I E, *Saint Dorothy*, engraving, 10.8 x 8.1. © Réunion des Musées Nationaux/ Art Resource, NY.
41. Hendrick Goltzius, *Apollo*, engraving, 26. 4 x 34.9 cm. © The Trustees of the British Museum.
42. Marco Dente, *Laocoön*, engraving, 47.2 x 32.4 cm. © The Trustees of the British Museum.
43. Ludovico Carracci, *Medea Rejuvenating Aeson*, Palazzo Fava, Bologna, fresco, detail. © Soprintendenza per i Beni Artistici e Culturali delle Province di Bologna e Parma.

44. Bartolomeo Passerotti, *Head of a Laughing Old Woman in Profile*, Galleria Estense, Modena, ink and pen, 47 x 36 cm. © Soprintendenza per i Beni Storici, Artistici ed Etnoantropologici di Modena e Reggio Emilia.

45. Michelangelo Buonarroti, *Head of an Ideal Female Beauty*, British Museum, London, black chalk, 28.7 x 23.5 cm. © The Trustees of the British Museum.

46. Michelangelo Merisi da Caravaggio, *The Fortune Teller*, Pinacoteca Capitolina, Rome, oil on canvas, 115 x 150 cm. © Erich Lessing/ Art Resource, NY.

47. Michelangelo Merisi da Caravaggio, *The Fortune Teller*, Musée du Louvre, Paris, oil on canvas, 99 x 131 cm. © Réunion des Musées Nationaux/ Art Resource, NY.

48. Wenzel von Olmutz after the Master of the Housebook, *The Lovers*, engraving, 16.8 x 10.8 cm. © The Trustees of the British Museum.

49. Lucas van Leyden, *Young Man with a Skull*, engraving, 18.4 x 14.5 cm. © The Trustees of the British Museum.

50. Jan Saenredam after Hendrick Goltzius, *Allegory of Vanity*, engraving, 22.9 x 17.3 cm. © The Trustees of the British Museum.

51. Jan Saenredam after Hendrick Goltzius, *Allegory of Vanity*, engraving, 22.9 x 17.3 cm., detail. © The Trustees of the British Museum.

52. Michelangelo Merisi da Caravaggio, *The Fortune Teller*, Musée du Louvre, Paris, oil on canvas, 99 x 131 cm., detail. © Réunion des Musées Nationaux/ Art Resource, NY.

53. Albrecht Dürer, *The Promenade*, engraving, 19.5 x 12.3 cm. © National Gallery of Art, Washington DC.

54. Simon Frisius (attributed to) after Lucas van Leyden, *The Betrothal*, etching, 16.7 x 13 cm. © The Trustees of the British Museum.

55. Simon Frisius (attributed to) after Lucas van Leyden, *The Betrothal*, etching, 16.7 x 13 cm., detail. © The Trustees of the British Museum.

56. Michelangelo Merisi da Caravaggio, *The Fortune Teller*, Pinacoteca Capitolina, Rome, oil on canvas, 115 x 150 cm., detail. © Erich Lessing/ Art Resource, NY.

57. Israel van Meckenem, *Old Woman and Young Man*, engraving, 14.6 x 11.4 cm. © The Trustees of the British Museum.

58. Israel van Meckenem, *Old Man and Young Woman*, engraving, 14.5 x 11.2 cm. © The Trustees of the British Museum.

59. Lucas van Leyden, *Tavern Scene* or *The Prodigal Son*, woodcut, 67 x 48.5 cm. © Bibliothèque Nationale de France.

60. Urs Graf, *Young Woman with an Old Man and a Youth*, engraving, 32.5 x 22.7 cm.© The Trustees of the British Museum.

61. Urs Graf, *Young Woman with an Old Man and a Youth*, engraving, 32.5 x 22.7 cm., detail. © The Trustees of the British Museum.

62. Michelangelo Merisi da Caravaggio, *The Fortune Teller*, Pinacoteca Capitolina, Rome, oil on canvas, 115 x 150 cm., detail. © Erich Lessing/ Art Resource, NY.

63. Quentin Massys, *Ill-Matched Lovers*, National Gallery of Art, Washington DC, oil on panel, 43.2 x 63 cm. © National Gallery of Art, Washington DC.

64. Master b x g, *The Lovers*, engraving, 15.5 x 13.7 cm. © Réunion des Musées Nationaux/ Art Resource, NY.

65. Michelangelo Merisi da Caravaggio, *The Cardsharps*, Kimbell Museum of Art, Fort Worth, oil on canvas, 91.5 x 128.2 cm. © Kimbell Art Museum, Fort Worth, Texas/ Art Resource, NY.

66. Valentin de Boulogne, *The Cardsharps*, Gemäldegalerie Alte Meister, Dresden, oil on canvas, 94.5 x 137 cm. © Bildarchiv Preussischer Kulturbesitz/ Art Resource, NY.

67. Anton Woensam of Worms, *Two Soldiers Playing Cards*, engraving, 12.4 x 8.5 cm., detail. © Albertina Vienna.

68. Titian (Tiziano Vecelli), *The Bravo*, Kunsthistorisches Museum, Vienna, oil on canvas, 75 x 67 cm. © Erich Lessing/ Art Resource, NY.

69. Anton Van Dyck after Giorgione (or Titian), *The Bravo*, British Museum, London, pen and brown ink, 20 x 15.8 cm. © The Trustees of the British Museum.

70. Giacomo Piccini after Titian (Tiziano Vecelli), *Allegory of Venice-Justice*, 30 x 36 cm. © The Trustees of the British Museum.

71. Anton Maria Zanetti after Titian (Tiziano Vecelli), *Allegory of Venice-Justice*, 23.9 x 28.6 cm. © Museo Correr, Venezia.

72. Alessandro Leopardi (after Antonio Lombardo?), *Bronze Pedestal*, Piazza San Marco, Venice, detail. © Paola Modesti.

73. The Housebook Master, *The Card Players*, engraving, 13.2 x 12 cm. © Rijksmuseum Amsterdam.

74. Master b x g, *The Card Players*, engraving, 8.9 cm. (diameter). © Staatliche Graphische Sammlung München.

75. Israel van Meckenem, *The Card Players*, engraving, 15.9 x 10.9 cm. © The Trustees of the British Museum.

76. *The Card Players*, reproduced from Johan de Brune's 1624 *Emblemata of zinne-werck*. © National Gallery of Art Library, Washington DC.

77. Johan Sadeler I, *Blessing Christ*, engraving, 9.5 x 6.5 cm. © The Trustees of the British Museum.

78. Hendrick Goltzius, The *Magdalene in the Desert*, engraving, 29 x 19.7 cm. © The Trustees of the British Museum.

79. Israel van Meckenem, *Saint Lawrence*, engraving, 12.3 x 7 cm. © Albertina Vienna.

80. Michelangelo Merisi da Caravaggio, *Conversion of Mary Magdalene*, Detroit Institute of Arts, Detroit, oil on canvas, 97.7 x 132.7 cm. © Detroit Institute of Arts/ The Bridgeman Art Library.

81. Titian (Tiziano Vecelli), *Woman at Her Toilet*, Musée du Louvre, Paris, oil on panel, 93 x 76 cm. © Réunion des Musées Nationaux/ Art Resource, NY.

82. Albrecht Altdorfer, *Allegory of Vanity*, engraving, 9.9 x 7.6 cm. © Ashmolean Museum.

83. Erhard Altdorfer, *Allegory of Vanity*, engraving, 8.8 x 5 cm. © The Trustees of the British Museum.

84. Hans Brosamer, *The Prostitute and the Fool*, woodcut, 27.5 x 20 cm. © Albertina Vienna.

85. *Aversum Caeteris*, reproduced from Camillo Camilli, *Imprese illustri*, 1586. © National Gallery of Art Library, Washington DC.

86. Hendrick Goltzius, *Allegory of Sight*, Museum Boijmans-van Beuningen, Rotterdam, pen, brown ink and wash with white heightening on pink paper, 16 x 12.4 cm. © Museum Bojimans Van Beuningen, Rotterdam/ Studio Buitenhof.

87. *Receptum Exhibet*, reproduced from Scipione Bargagli, *Dell'imprese*. 1594. © National Gallery of Art Library, Washington DC.

88. *Ut Valeo*, reproduced from Battista Pittoni, *Imprese*, 1562. © National Gallery of Art Library, Washington DC.

89. Bernardino Luini, *Martha and Mary Magdalene*, San Diego Museum of Art, San Diego, oil on panel, 63.7 x 82.5 cm. © San Diego Museum of Art/ The Bridgeman Art Library.

90. Michelangelo Merisi da Caravaggio, *The Calling of Saint Matthew*, Contarelli Chapel, San Luigi dei Francesi, Rome, oil on canvas, 322 x 340 cm. © Scala/ Art Resource, NY.

91. Cavalier d'Arpino (Giuseppe Cesari), *The Calling of Saint Matthew*, Albertina, Vienna, black and red chalk, 22.3 x 26.4 cm. © Albertina Vienna.

92. Cavalier d'Arpino (Giuseppe Cesari), *Study for the Figure of Saint Matthew*, Holkham Hall, Lord Leicester's Collection, black and red chalk. © Holkham Estate Enterprises.

93. Hans Holbein, *Death and the Gambler*, woodcut, 6.4 x 4.9 cm., reproduced from *Les Images de la mort*, Lyons, 1547. © Courtesy of the Richard C. Kessler Reformation Collection, Pitts Theology Library, Candler School of Theology, Emory University.

94. Michelangelo Merisi da Caravaggio, *The Calling of Saint Matthew*, Contarelli Chapel, San Luigi dei Francesi, Rome, oil on canvas, 322 x 340 cm., detail. © Scala/ Art Resource, NY.

95. Hans Holbein, *Death and the Gambler*, woodcut, 6.4 x 4.9 cm., detail, reproduced from *Les Images de la mort*, Lyons, 1547. © Courtesy of the Richard C. Kessler Reformation Collection, Pitts Theology Library, Candler School of Theology, Emory University.

96. Michelangelo Merisi da Caravaggio, *The Calling of Saint Matthew*, Contarelli Chapel, San Luigi dei Francesi, Rome, oil on canvas, 322 x 340 cm., detail. © Scala/ Art Resource, NY.

97. Michelangelo Buonarroti, *The Creation of Adam*, Sistine Chapel, Vatican Palace, Rome, fresco, detail. © Erich Lessing/ Art Resource, NY.

98. Michelangelo Merisi da Caravaggio, *The Calling of Saint Matthew*, Contarelli Chapel, San Luigi dei Francesi, Rome, oil on canvas, 322 x 340 cm., detail. © Scala/ Art Resource, NY.

99. Ludovico Carracci, *The Calling of Saint Matthew*, Pinacoteca Nazionale, Bologna, oil on canvas, 449 x 265 cm. © Pinacoteca Nazionale, Bologna.

100. Bartolomeo Manfredi, *Tavern Scene*, Trafalgar Galleries, London, oil on canvas, 120 x 190 cm. © Trafalgar Galleries, London.

101. Giovanni Martinelli, *Death Comes to the Banquet*, New Orleans Museum of Art, New Orleans, oil on canvas, 120.7 x 174 cm. © New Orleans Museum of Art, New Orleans.

102. Nicolas Tournier, *Drinking Party with Lute Player*, Musée du Berry, Bourges, oil on canvas, 120 x 60 cm. © Musées de la ville de Bourges, France.

103. Bernardo Strozzi, *The Calling of Saint Matthew*, Worcester Art Museum, Worcester, oil on canvas, 139 x 188.5 cm. © Worcester Art Museum, Massachussetts, USA/ The Bridgeman Library.

104. Jan van Bijlert, *The Calling of Saint Matthew*, Museum Catharijneconvent, Utrecht, oil on canvas, 144 x 199.5 cm. © Museum Catharijneconvent, Utrecht.

105. Matthias Stomer, *The Calling of Saint Matthew*, Fine Arts Museum, San Francisco, oil on canvas, 174.9 x 224 cm. © Fine Arts Museum, San Francisco.

106. Hendrick ter Brugghen, *The Calling of Saint Matthew*, Musée des Beaux-Arts, Le Havre, oil on canvas, 152 x 195 cm. © Réunion des Musées Nationaux / Art Resource, NY.

107. Hendrick ter Brugghen, *The Calling of Saint Matthew*, Centraal Museum, Utrecht, oil on canvas, 102.3 x 136.9 cm. © Centraal Museum, Utrecht/ Ernst Moritz.

108. Michelangelo Merisi da Caravaggio, *Conversion of Saint Paul*, Odescalchi Collection, Rome, oil on panel, 237 x 189 cm. © Principessa Nicoletta Odescalchi/ Photo Pasquale Rizzi.

109. Titian (Tiziano Vecelli), *Head of a Frightened Horse*, location unknown, black chalk on gray paper heightened with white, 20.9 x 20.7 cm, reproduced from Harold Wethey, *Titian and His Drawings*, 1987.

110. Michelangelo Merisi da Caravaggio, *Conversion of Saint Paul*, Odescalchi Collection, Rome, oil on panel, 237 x 189 cm., detail. © Principessa Nicoletta Odescalchi/ Pasquale Rizzi.

111. Michelangelo Buonarroti, *Conversion of Saint Paul*, Pauline Chapel, Vatican Palace, Rome, fresco, 620 x 670 cm., detail. © The Bridgeman Art Library.

112. Raphael (Raffaello Santi), *The Expulsion of Heliodorus from the Temple*, Stanza d'Eliodoro, Vatican Palace, Rome, fresco, 750 cm., detail. © Scala/ Art Resource, NY.

113. Raphael (Raffaello Santi), *Cartoon for the Figure of Moses in The Burning Bush*, Museo di Capodimonte, Naples, black chalk with white highlights, 140 x 138 cm. © Alinari/ Art Resource, NY.

114. Raphael (Raffaello Santi), *Study of Three Male Nudes*, Devonshire Collection, Chatsworth, black chalk, 23.4 x 36.5 cm. © Devonshire Collection, Chatsworth. Reproduced by permission of Chatsworth Settlement Trustees.

115. Michelangelo Merisi da Caravaggio, *Conversion of Saint Paul*, Odescalchi Collection, Rome, oil on panel, 237 x 189 cm., detail. © Principessa Nicoletta Odescalchi / Photo Pasquale Rizzi.

116. Niklas Stoer, *Eusterwon, King of the Upper Germans*, from Burchard Waldis, *Ursprung und Herkümen der zwoelff ersten alten Koenig und Fürstem Deutscher Nation…* (Nuremberg, 1543), woodcut, 27.7 x 15.3 cm. © Germanisches Nationalmuseum, Nüremberg.

117. Michelangelo Merisi da Caravaggio, *Conversion of Saint Paul*, Cerasi Chapel, Santa Maria del Popolo, Rome, oil on canvas, 230 x 175 cm. © Scala / Art Resource.

118. Cherubino Alberti after Taddeo Zuccari, *Conversion of Saint Paul*, engraving, 46.5 x 34 cm. © The Trustees of the British Museum.

119. Workshop of Pieter van Aelst after Raphael (Raffaello Santi), *Conversion of Saint Paul*, Musei Vaticani, Rome, wool, silk and gilt-metal-wrapped thread, 484 x 540 cm. © Scala / Art Resource, NY.

120. Albrecht Dürer, *The Large Horse*, engraving, 16.7 x 11.9 cm. © The Trustees of the British Museum.

121. Michelangelo Merisi da Caravaggio, *The Supper at Emmaus*, National Gallery, London, oil on canvas, 141 x 196.2 cm. © National Gallery, London / Art Resource NY.

122. Titian (Tiziano Vecelli), *The Supper at Emmaus*, Musée du Louvre, Paris, oil on canvas, 169 x 244 cm. © Réunion des Musées Nationaux / Art Resource, NY.

123. Pietro Monaco after Giovanni Bellini, *The Supper at Emmaus*, etching and engraving, 36.3 x 50.5 cm. © The Trustees of the National Gallery.

124. Veronese (Paolo Caliari), *The Supper at Emmaus*, Musée du Louvre, Paris, oil on canvas, 242 x 416 cm. © Réunion des Musées Nationaux / Art Resource, NY.

125. Veronese (Paolo Caliari), *The Supper at Emmaus*, Devonshire Collection, Chatsworth, pen, ink and wash on green prepared paper heightened with white, 42.1 x 57.5 cm. © Devonshire Collection, Chatsworth. Reproduced by permission of Chatsworth Settlement Trustees.

126. Michelangelo Merisi da Caravaggio, *The Supper at Emmaus*, National Gallery, London, oil on canvas, 141 x 196.2 cm., detail. © National Gallery, London / Art Resource.

127. Leonardo da Vinci (attributed to), *Head of Christ*, Pinacoteca di Brera, Milan, black and red chalk, tempera on light green paper, 40 x 32 cm. © Scala / Art Resource, NY.

128. Master of the Pala Sforza (attributed to), *Head of a Female Figure*, British Museum, London, metal point on green-brown prepared paper heightened with white, 24 x 15.8 cm. © The Trustees of the British Museum.

129. Leonardo da Vinci (after), *Head of an Old Man in Profile (Study for Saint Simon in the Last Supper)*, Royal Library, Windsor Castle, red chalk on red prepared paper, 19 x 15.2 cm. © The Royal Collection / 2010 Her Majesty Queen Elizabeth II.

130. Michelangelo Merisi da Caravaggio, *The Supper at Emmaus*, National Gallery, London, oil on canvas, 141 x 196.2 cm., detail. © National Gallery, London / Art Resource.

131. Moretto da Brescia (Alessandro Bonvicino), *The Last Supper*, Pinacoteca Tosio e Martinengo, Brescia, oil on canvas, 147 x 305 cm. © Per concessione dei Civici Musei d'Arte e Storia di Brescia.

132. Marcantonio Raimondi after Raphael (Raffaello Santi), *Resurrected Christ*, engraving, 20.8 x 13.6 cm. © The Trustees of the British Museum.

133. Cecco del Caravaggio (Francesco Boneri), *The Resurrection*, Art Institute, Chicago, oil on canvas, 339 x 199.5 cm., detail. © The Art Institute, Chicago.

134. Bartolomeo Cavarozzi, *The Supper at Emmaus*, The J. Paul Getty Museum, Los Angeles, oil on canvas, 139.7 x 194.3 cm. © The J. Paul Getty Museum, Los Angeles.

135. Michelangelo Merisi da Caravaggio, *The Supper at Emmaus*, Pinacoteca di Brera, Milan, oil on canvas, 141 x 175 cm. © Erich Lessing/ Art Resource, NY.

136. Johan Sadeler I after Pietro Candido (Pieter de Witte), *The Supper at Emmaus*, engraving, 20 x 15.3 cm. © Kunstsammlungen der Fürsten zu Waldburg-Wolfegg.

137. Aegidius Sadeler II after Pietro Candido (Pieter de Witte), *The Supper at Emmaus*, engraving, 24 x 18 cm. © Bibliothèque Nationale de France.

138. Michelangelo Merisi da Caravaggio, *The Supper at Emmaus*, Pinacoteca di Brera, Milan, oil on canvas, 141 x 175 cm., detail. © Erich Lessing/ Art Resource, NY.

139. Aegidius Sadeler II after Pietro Candido (Pieter de Witte), *The Supper at Emmaus*, engraving, 24 x 18 cm., detail. © Bibliothèque Nationale de France.

140. Guido Reni, *The Crucifixion of Saint Peter*, Pinacoteca Vaticana, Rome, oil on canvas, 305 x 175 cm. © Scala/ Art Resource, NY.

141. Michelangelo Merisi da Caravaggio, *The Taking of Christ*, National Gallery of Ireland, Dublin, oil on canvas, 133.5 x 169.5 cm. © Courtesy of the National Gallery of Ireland and the Jesuit Community.

142. Albrecht Dürer, *The Taking of Christ*, woodcut, 12.7 x 9.7 cm. © The Trustees of the British Museum.

143. Master AG (Anton Gerbel of Pforzheim?), *The Taking of Christ*, engraving, 14.5 x 10.8 cm. © Albertina Vienna.

144. Master AG (Anton Gerbel of Pforzheim?), *The Taking of Christ*, engraving, 14.5 x 10.8 cm., detail. © Albertina Vienna.

145. Martin Schongauer, *The Taking of Christ*, engraving, 16.4 x 11.6 cm. © The Trustees of the British Museum.

146. Michelangelo Merisi da Caravaggio, *The Taking of Christ*, National Gallery of Ireland, Dublin, oil on canvas, 133.5 x 169.5 cm. © Courtesy of the National Gallery of Ireland and the Jesuit Community.

147. Albrecht Dürer, *The Taking of Christ*, woodcut, 12.7 x 9.7 cm., detail. © The Trustees of the British Museum.

148. Master AG (Anton Gerbel of Pforzheim?), *The Taking of Christ*, engraving, 14.5 x 10.8 cm., detail. © Albertina Vienna.

149. Martin Schongauer, *The Taking of Christ*, engraving, 16.4 x 11.6 cm., detail reversed. © The Trustees of the British Museum.

150. Lucas van Leyden, *The Embrace*, etching and engraving, 10.5 x 7.4 cm. © The Trustees of the British Museum.

151. Ludovico Carracci (after), *The Taking of Christ*, Princeton University Art Museum, Princeton, oil on canvas, 80 x 97 cm. © Princeton University Art Museum.

152. Jacob Cornelisz van Oostsanen, *The Taking of Christ*, engraving, 23.2 cm. (diameter). © The Trustees of the British Museum.

153. Urs Graf, *The Agony in the Garden and The Taking of Christ*, engraving, 21.6 x 15.7 cm. © The Trustees of the British Museum.

154. Ludovico Carracci (after), *The Taking of Christ*, Princeton University Art Museum, Princeton, oil on canvas, 80 x 97 cm., detail. © Princeton University Art Museum.

155. Jacob Cornelisz van Oostsanen, *The Taking of Christ*, engraving, 23.2 cm. (diameter), detail. © The Trustees of the British Museum.

156. Urs Graf, *The Agony in the Garden and The Taking of Christ*, engraving, 21.6 x 15.7 cm., detail. © The Trustees of the British Museum.

157. Ludwig Krug, *The Embrace*, engraving, 11 x 7.8 cm., detail. © Albertina Vienna.

158. Hans Schäufelein, *Pyramus and Thisbe*, woodcut, 22.9 x 15.5 cm. © The Trustees of the British Museum.

159. Guido Reni, *The Agony in the Garden*, Musée du Louvre, Paris, oil on copper, 67 x 43 cm. © Réunion des Musées Nationaux/ Art Resource, NY.

160. Hans Sebald Beham, *The Taking of Christ*, woodcut, 12.5 x 8.5 cm. © The Trustees of the British Museum.

161. Albrecht Dürer, *Last Supper*, woodcut, 39.5 x 28.4 cm., detail. © The Trustees of the British Museum.

162. Valentin de Boulogne, *Last Supper*, Galleria Nazionale d'Arte Antica, Palazzo Barberini, Rome, oil on canvas, 139 x 230 cm., detail. © Scala/ Art Resource, NY.

163. Cavalier d'Arpino (Giuseppe Cesari) and workshop, *The Taking of Christ*, Accademia di San Luca, Rome, oil on canvas, 100 x 70 cm. © Scala/ Art Resource, NY.

164. Annibale Carracci, *The Annunciation*, Royal Library, Windsor Castle, brown ink on paper, 11.5 x 18.8 cm. © The Royal Library/ 2010 Her Majesty Queen Elizabeth II.

165. Tintoretto (Jacopo Robusti), *The Annunciation*, Scuola Grande di San Rocco, Venice, oil on canvas, 422 x 545 cm. © Cameraphoto Arte, Venice/ Art Resource, NY.

166. Michelangelo Merisi da Caravaggio, *The Entombment*, Pinacoteca Vaticana, Rome, oil on canvas, 300 x 203 cm. © Scala/ Art Resource, NY.

167. Hans Baldung Grien, *Lamentation*, woodcut, 22.5 x 15.2 cm. © University of Michigan Museum of Art.

168. Albrecht Dürer, *Lamentation*, engraving, 11.5 x 7.1 cm. © The Trustees of the British Museum.

169. Lucas Cranach the Elder, *Lamentation*, woodcut, 24.5 x 17.1 cm. © The Trustees of the British Museum.

170. Aegidius Sadeler II after Tintoretto (Jacopo Robusti), *The Deposition*, engraving, 31.7 x 39 cm. © The Trustees of the British Museum.

171. Battista Franco, *The Deposition*, engraving, 22.3 x 15.8 cm. © The Trustees of the British Museum.

172. Michelangelo Buonarroti, *Lamentation (Pietà for Vittoria Colonna)*, Isabella Stewart Gardner Museum, Boston, black chalk, 29.4 x 18.1 cm. © Isabella Stewart Gardner Museum.

173. Giulio Bonasone after Michelangelo Buonarroti, *Lamentation*, engraving, 36 x 20.6 cm. © The Trustees of the British Museum.

174. Agostino Carracci after Michelangelo Buonarroti, *Lamentation*, engraving, 41.1 x 28.7 cm. © Bibliothèque Nationale de France.

175. Michelangelo Buonarroti, *Pietà*, Saint Peter's, Rome, marble, 175 cm. © Scala/ Art Resource, NY.

176. Agostino Carracci after Michelangelo Buonarroti, *Pietà*, engraving, 44.9 x 30.4 cm. © Erich Lessing/ Art Resource, NY.

177. Hendrick Goltzius, *Pietà*, engraving, 17.5 x 12.6 cm. © The Trustees of the British Museum.

178. Michelangelo Merisi da Caravaggio, *The Entombment*, Pinacoteca Vaticana, Rome, oil on canvas, 300 x 203 cm., detail. © Scala/ Art Resource, NY.

179. Michelangelo Buonarroti, *Pietà*, Saint Peter's, Rome, marble, 175 cm., detail. © Scala/ Art Resource, NY.

180. Michelangelo Buonarroti, *Pietà*, Museo dell'Opera del Duomo, Florence, marble, 226 cm. © Scala/ Art Resource, NY.

181. Cherubino Alberti after Michelangelo Buonarroti, *Pietà*, engraving, 44.5 x 30.1 cm. © The Trustees of the British Museum.

182. Jacopino del Conte (attributed to), *Portrait of Michelangelo*, Metropolitan Museum of Art, New York, oil on panel, 88.3 x 64.1 cm. © The Metropolitan Museum of Art/ Art Resource, NY.

183. Daniele da Volterra, *Head of an Apostle with the Likeness of Michelangelo*, Teylers Museum, Haarlem, black chalk on lead point heightened with white on paper, 29.5 x 21.8 cm. © Teylers Museum Haarlem, The Netherlands.

184. Daniele da Volterra, *Portrait of Michelangelo,* Musei Capitolini, Rome, bronze, 30 cm (head). © Vanni/ Art Resource, NY.

185. Leone Leoni, *Portrait of Michelangelo*, British Museum, London, pink wax on black slate, 43 cm. (diameter) © The Trustees of the British Museum/ Art Resource, NY.

186. Michelangelo Merisi da Caravaggio, *The Entombment*, Pinacoteca Vaticana, Rome, oil on canvas, 300 x 203 cm., detail. © Scala/ Art Resource, NY.

187. Michelangelo Buonarroti, *Pietà*, reproduced from Jack Wasserman, *Michelangelo's Florence Pietà*, 2003.

188. Michelangelo Buonarroti, *Pietà*, reproduced from Jack Wasserman, *Michelangelo's Florence Pietà*, 2003.

189. Michelangelo Merisi da Caravaggio, *Ecce Homo*, Galleria di Palazzo Rosso, Genoa, oil on canvas, 128 x 103 cm. © Scala/ Art Resource.

190. Cigoli (Ludovico Cardi), *Ecce Homo*, Palazzo Pitti, Florence, oil on panel, 175 x 135.5 cm. © Scala/ Art Resource.

191. Cigoli (Ludovico Cardi), *Study for the Ecce Homo*, Musée du Louvre, Paris, pen and wash, 25.2 x 17.5 cm. © Réunion des Musées Nationaux/ Art Resource, NY.

192. Sebastiano del Piombo (Sebastiano Luciani), *Portrait of Andrea Doria*, Palazzo del Principe, Genoa, oil on panel, 153 x 107 cm. © Giraudon/ The Bridgeman Art Library.

193. Michelangelo Merisi da Caravaggio, *Ecce Homo*, Galleria di Palazzo Rosso, Genoa, oil on canvas, 128 x 103 cm., detail. © Scala/ Art Resource.

194. Portrait of Caravaggio from Giovan Pietro Bellori, *Le Vite*, 1672. © The Getty Research Institute, Los Angeles.

195. Ottavio Leoni, *Portrait of Caravaggio*, Biblioteca Marucelliana, Florence, red and black chalk heightened with white on blue paper, 23.4 x 16.3 cm. © Scala/ Art Resource.

196. Jacopo Palma il Giovane (Palma Giovane), *Self-Portrait*, Pinacoteca di Brera, Milan, oil on canvas, 126 x 96 cm. © Erich Lessing/ Art Resource, NY.

197. Annibale Carracci, *Saint Francis Showing the Crucifix*, Gallerie dell'Accademia, Venice, oil on canvas, 96 x 79 cm. © Cameraphoto Arte, Venice/ The Bridgeman Art Library.

198. Diana Scultori after Raffaellino da Reggio, *Ecce Homo*, engraving, 36.7 x 27 cm. © The Trustees of the British Museum.

199. Agostino Carracci, *Ecce Homo*, engraving, 8.7 x 7 cm. © The Trustees of the British Museum.

200. Albrecht Dürer, *Ecce Homo*, woodcut, 12.8 x 9.7 cm., detail. © Courtesy of the Fannie Wetmore Print Collection, Connecticut College, New London.

201. Albrecht Dürer, *Pilate Washing His Hands*, engraving, 11.8 x 7.6 cm. © The Trustees of the British Museum.

202. *Dottor Gratian*, in Lodovico de' Bianchi, *Le cento e quindici conclusioni*, reproduced from Vito Pandolfi, *La Commedia dell'Arte*, 1957-1961.

203. Jacques Honervogt I, *The Dottore, Zani, and Pantaloon*, engraving, 19.3 x 27.2 cm. © Nationalmuseum, Stockholm.

204. *The Dottore and Pantaloon*, woodcut pasted on paper, from *Recueil Frossard*, Nationalmuseum, Stockholm. © Nationalmuseum, Stockholm.

205. *Doctor Cornute*, engraving, from *Recueil Frossard*, Nationalmuseum, Stockholm © Nationalmuseum, Stockholm.

206. *The Dottore*, in Aniello Soldano, *Fantastiche et ridicolose etimologie*, reproduced from Vito Pandolfi, *La Commedia dell'Arte*, 1957-1961.

207. Ludovico Ottavio Burnacini, *Il Dottore*, Oesterreichische Nationalbibliothek, Vienna. © Österreichische Nationalbibliothek/ Vienna, Picture Archive, Cod. Min. 29, fol. 71,2.

208. Niccolò della Casa after Baccio Bandinelli, *Portrait of Baccio Bandinelli*, engraving, 29 x 21.8 cm. © The Trustees of the British Museum.

209. Michelangelo Merisi da Caravaggio, *Ecce Homo*, Galleria di Palazzo Rosso, Genoa, oil on canvas, 128 x 103 cm., detail. © Scala/ Art Resource.

210. Michelangelo Merisi da Caravaggio, *Denial of Saint Peter*, Metropolitan Museum of Art, New York, oil on canvas, 94 x 125.5 cm. © The Metropolitan Museum of Art/ Art Resource, NY.

211. Michelangelo Merisi da Caravaggio, *Denial of Saint Peter*, Metropolitan Museum of Art, New York, oil on canvas, 94 x 125.5 cm., detail. © The Metropolitan Museum of Art/ Art Resource, NY.

212. Veronese (Paolo Caliari), *The Temptation of Saint Anthony*, Musée du Louvre, Paris, pen and ink and wash on grey prepared paper heightened with white, 41.4 x 35.6 cm. © Réunion des Musées Nationaux/ Art Resource, NY.

213. *Showing Yourself*, in John Bulwer, *Chironomia*, reproduced from John Bulwer, *Chironomia*, 1974.

214. Michelangelo Merisi da Caravaggio, *The Burial of Saint Lucy*, Museo di Palazzo Bellomo, Syracuse, oil on canvas, 408 x 300 cm. © Luciano Pedicini.

215. Mario Minniti (attributed to) after Caravaggio, *The Burial of Saint Lucy*, private collection, Rome, oil on copper, 40.6 x 34 cm, reproduced from Maurizio Marini, *Caravaggio*, 2005.

216. Caravaggio's *The Burial of Saint Lucy*, reproduced from Giuseppe Politi, *Siracusa per i viaggiatori*, 1835. © National Gallery of Art Library, Washington DC.

217. Ludovico Carracci, *The Flagellation*, Musée de la Chartreuse, Douai, oil on canvas, 189 x 265 cm. © Erich Lessing/ Art Resource, NY.

218. Michelangelo Merisi da Caravaggio, *The Beheading of Saint John the Baptist*, Co-Cathedral of Saint John, Valletta, oil on canvas, 361 x 520 cm. © Scala/ Art Resource, NY.

219. Albrecht Altdorfer, *The Beheading of Saint John the Baptist*, woodcut, 20.5 x 15.7 cm. © Albertina Vienna.

220. Albrecht Altdorfer, *The Beheading of Saint John the Baptist*, woodcut, 20 x 16 cm. © The Trustees of the British Museum.

221. Michelangelo Merisi da Caravaggio, *The Death of the Virgin*, Musée du Louvre, Paris, oil on canvas, 369 x 245 cm., detail. © Réunion des Musées Nationaux/ Art Resource, NY.

222. Michelangelo Merisi da Caravaggio, *The Burial of Saint Lucy*, Museo di Palazzo Bellomo, Syracuse, oil on canvas, 408 x 300 cm., detail. © Luciano Pedicini.

223. Jan Sadeler I after Pietro Candido (Pieter de Witte), *The Martyrdom of Saint Ursula*, engraving, 43.2 x 27.4 cm., detail. © The Trustees of the British Museum.

224. Michelangelo Merisi da Caravaggio, *The Burial of Saint Lucy*, Museo di Palazzo Bellomo, Syracuse, oil on canvas, 408 x 300 cm., detail. © Luciano Pedicini.

225. Michelangelo Merisi da Caravaggio, *The Resurrection of Lazarus*, Museo Regionale, Messina, oil on canvas, 320 x 275 cm. © Luciano Pedicini.

226. Diana Scultori after Giulio Romano, *Menelaus Holding the Body of Patroclus*, engraving, 23.9 x 39.1 cm., detail. © The Trustees of the British Museum.

227. Veit Stoss, *Lamentation*, woodcut, 13.7 x 12.8 cm. © The Trustees of the British Museum.

228. Master I A M of Zwolle, *Lamentation*, engraving, 26.3 x 30 cm.© The Trustees of the British Museum.

229. Master BM, *Lamentation*, engraving, 22.5 x 16 cm. © The Trustees of the British Museum.

230. Albrecht Dürer (attributed to), *Lamentation*, woodcut, 39.5 x 28.8 cm. © The Trustees of the British Museum.

231. Michelangelo Merisi da Caravaggio, *The Resurrection of Lazarus*, Museo Regionale, Messina, oil on canvas, 320 x 275 cm., detail. © Luciano Pedicini.

232. Michelangelo Merisi da Caravaggio, *The Calling of Saint Matthew*, Contarelli Chapel, San Luigi dei Francesi, Rome, oil on canvas, 322 x 340 cm., detail. © Scala/ Art Resource, NY.

233. Michelangelo Merisi da Caravaggio, *The Incredulity of Saint Thomas*, Schloß Sans-Souci, Potsdam, oil on canvas, 107 x 146 cm., detail. © Bildarchiv Preussischer Kulturbesitz/ Art Resource, NY.

234. Michelangelo Merisi da Caravaggio, *The Martyrdom of Saint Ursula*, Banca Intesa, Palazzo Zavalos, Naples, oil on canvas, 154 x 178 cm., detail. © Luciano Pedicini.

235. Michelangelo Merisi da Caravaggio, *The Incredulity of Saint Thomas*, Schloß Sans-Souci, Potsdam, oil on canvas, 107 x 146 cm. © Bildarchiv Preussischer Kulturbesitz/ Art Resource, NY.

236. Albrecht Dürer, *The Incredulity of Saint Thomas*, woodcut, 12.7 x 9.7 cm. © The Trustees of the British Museum.

237. Louis Finson, *The Incredulity of Saint Thomas*, Saint-Sauveur Cathedral, Aix-en-Provence, oil on canvas, 260 x 201 cm. © Cathédrale Saint-Sauveur, Aix-en-Provence/ Yannick Blaise.

238. Andrea del Verrocchio, *The Incredulity of Saint Thomas*, Orsanmichele, Florence, bronze with some gilding, 230 cm. (Christ's statue). © Scala/ Ministero per i Beni e le Attività Culturali/ Art Resource, NY.

239. Andrea del Verrocchio, *The Incredulity of Saint Thomas*, Orsanmichele, Florence, bronze with some gilding, 230 cm. (Christ's statue), detail reversed. © Scala/ Ministero per i Beni e le Attività Culturali/ Art Resource, NY.

240. Michelangelo Merisi da Caravaggio, *The Incredulity of Saint Thomas*, Schloß Sans-Souci, Potsdam, oil on canvas, 107 x 146 cm., detail. © Bildarchiv Preussischer Kulturbesitz/ Art Resource, NY.

241. Michelangelo Merisi da Caravaggio, *The Martyrdom of Saint Ursula*, Banca Intesa, Palazzo Zavalos, Naples, oil on canvas, 154 x 178 cm. © Luciano Pedicini.

242. Michelangelo Merisi da Caravaggio, *The Taking of Christ*, National Gallery of Ireland, Dublin, oil on canvas, 133.5 x 169.5 cm., detail. © National Gallery of Ireland, Dublin.

243. Michelangelo Merisi da Caravaggio, *The Martyrdom of Saint Ursula*, Banca Intesa, Palazzo Zavalos, Naples, oil on canvas, 154 x 178 cm., detail. © Luciano Pedicini.

244. Johan Sadeler I after Pietro Candido (Pieter de Witte), *The Martyrdom of Saint Ursula*, engraving, 43.2 x 27.4 cm. © The Trustees of the British Museum.

245. Albrecht Dürer, *The Martyrdom of Saint Sebastian*, woodcut, 39.3 x 28.7 cm. © Bildarchiv Preussischer Kulturbesitz / Art Resource, NY.

246. Jost Amman, *A Rider with a Crossbow*, woodcut, 12 x 10.7 cm.© The Trustees of the British Museum.

247. Hans Burgkmair, *The White King Shooting with His Crossbow*, woodcut, 22 x 19.5 cm. © Österreichische Nationalbibliothek, Vienna.

248. Hans Burgkmair, *The White King Shooting with His Crossbow*, woodcut, 22 x 19.5 cm., detail. © Österreichische Nationalbibliothek, Vienna.

249. Michelangelo Merisi da Caravaggio, *The Martyrdom of Saint Ursula*, Banca Intesa, Palazzo Zavalos, Naples, oil on canvas, 154 x 178 cm., detail. © Luciano Pedicini.

250. Cherubino Alberti (attributed to) after Lelio Orsi, *A Man Shooting a Crossbow*, engraving, 22 x 13.8 cm. © National Gallery of Art, Washington DC.

251. Jacques de Gheyn II (after), *Crossbowman with a Milkmaid*, engraving, 11.8 x 8 cm. © The Trustees of the British Museum.

252. Bernardo Strozzi, *The Martyrdom of Saint Ursula*, Koelliker Collection, Milan, oil on canvas, 104 x 130 cm. © Manusardi Art Studio Milano.

253. Michelangelo Merisi da Caravaggio, *Salome Receiving the Head of Saint John the Baptist*, National Gallery, London, oil on canvas, 91.5 x 106.7 cm., detail. © National Gallery, London/ Art Resource, NY.

254. Michelangelo Merisi da Caravaggio, *The Martyrdom of Saint Ursula*, Banca Intesa, Palazzo Zavalos, Naples, oil on canvas, 154 x 178 cm., detail. © Luciano Pedicini.

255. Michelangelo Merisi da Caravaggio, *The Resurrection of Lazarus*, Museo Regionale, Messina, oil on canvas, 320 x 275 cm., detail. © Luciano Pedicini.

256. Cecco del Caravaggio (Francesco Boneri), *The Resurrection*, Art Institute, Chicago, oil on canvas, 339 x 199.5 cm. © The Art Institute, Chicago.

257. Giovanni Bellini, *The Transfiguration*, Museo Correr, Venice, tempera on panel, 133 x 90.3 cm. © Cameraphoto Arte, Venice/ Art Resource, NY.

258. Giovanni Bellini, *The Transfiguration*, Museo di Capodimonte, Naples, oil on canvas, 115 x 151 cm. © Scala/ Ministero per i Beni e le Attività Culturali/ Art Resource, NY.

259. Girolamo Mocetto, *The Resurrection*, engraving, 44.7 x 30 cm. © Bibliothèque Nationale de France.

260. Louis Finson, *The Resurrection*, Saint-Jean-de-Malte, Aix-en-Provence, oil on canvas, 218 x 168 cm. (before restoration). © CICRP/Kévin Amiel.

261. Lucas van Leyden, *The Resurrection*, engraving, 11.5 x 7.4 cm. © The Trustees of the British Museum.

262. Albrecht Dürer, *The Resurrection*, woodcut, 38.9 x 27.6 cm. © The Trustees of the British Museum.

263. Martin Schongauer, *The Resurrection*, engraving, 16.3 x 11.6 cm. © The Trustees of the British Museum.

264. Battistello (Giovan Battista) Caracciolo, *The Liberation of Saint Peter*, Pio Monte della Misericordia, Naples, oil on canvas, 310 x 207 cm. © Luciano Pedicini.

265. Battistello (Giovan Battista) Caracciolo, *Study of a Soldier*, Musée du Louvre, Paris, black chalk and red chalk heightened with white on blue paper, 21.4 x 28.2 cm. © Réunion des Musées Nationaux/ Art Resource, NY.

266. Battistello (Giovan Battista) Caracciolo, *The Liberation of Saint Peter*, Pio Monte della Misericordia, Naples, oil on canvas, 310 x 207 cm., detail. © Luciano Pedicini.

267. Cecco del Caravaggio (Francesco Boneri), *The Resurrection*, Art Institute, Chicago, oil on canvas, 339 x 199.5 cm., detail. © The Art Institute, Chicago.

268. Battistello (Giovan Battista) Caracciolo, *Noli Me Tangere*, Museo Civico, Prato, oil on canvas, 109 x 130.5 cm. © Scala/ Art Resource, NY.

269. Lucas van Leyden, *Christ as a Gardener Appearing to Mary Magdalene*, engraving, 13.2 x 16.8 cm. © The Trustees of the British Museum.

270. Luca Ciamberlano after Raffaello Sciaminossi, *The Resurrection*, engraving, 9.9 x 15.3 cm., detail. © Albertina Vienna.

271. Cecco del Caravaggio (Francesco Boneri), *The Resurrection*, Art Institute, Chicago, oil on canvas, 339 x 199.5 cm., detail. © The Art Institute, Chicago

272. Lucas van Leyden, *Adam and Eve Chased from Paradise*, engraving, 16.4 x 11.5 cm, detail. © The Trustees of the British Museum.

273. Cecco del Caravaggio (Francesco Boneri), *The Resurrection*, Art Institute, Chicago, oil on canvas, 339 x 199.5 cm., detail. © The Art Institute, Chicago

274. Cristofano Robetta, *The Resurrection*, engraving, 29.9 x 21.6 cm. © The Trustees of the British Museum.

275. Philips Galle after Pieter Brueghel the Elder, *The Resurrection*, engraving, 45.1 x 33 cm. © The Trustees of the British Museum.

276. Johan Sadeler I after Maarten de Vos, *The Resurrection*, engraving, 25 x 19.7 cm. © Kunstsammlungen der Fürsten zu Waldburg-Wolfegg.

277. Hendrick Goltzius, *The Resurrection*, engraving, 19.7 x 13 cm. © The Trustees of the British Museum.

278. Santi di Tito, *The Resurrection*, Art Institute, Chicago, pen and brown ink, brush and brown wash, heightened with white over traces of black chalk, 31.9 x 21.7 cm. © The Art Institute, Chicago.

279. Diego Velázquez, *The Supper at Emmaus*, Metropolitan Museum of Art, New York, oil on canvas, 123.2 x 132.7 cm. © The Metropolitan Museum of Art/ Art Resource, NY.

280. Giovan Battista Pasqualini after Guercino (Giovan Francesco Barbieri), *The Supper at Emmaus*, engraving, 18.3 x 24.2 cm. © David M. Stone.

281. Michelangelo Merisi da Caravaggio, *The Supper at Emmaus*, National Gallery, London, oil on canvas, 141 x 196.2 cm. © National Gallery, London/ Art Resource NY.

282. Agostino Veneziano (Agostino Musi) after Raphael (Raffaello Santi), *The Death of Ananias*, engraving, 26.6 x 35.1 cm. © The Trustees of the British Museum.

283. Diego Velázquez, *The Supper at Emmaus*, Metropolitan Museum of Art, New York, oil on canvas, 123.2 x 132.7 cm., detail. © The Metropolitan Museum of Art/ Art Resource, NY.

284. Agostino Veneziano (Agostino Musi) after Raphael (Raffaello Santi), *The Death of Ananias*, engraving, 26.6 x 35.1 cm., detail. © The Trustees of the British Museum.

285. Diego Velázquez, *La Mulata*, National Gallery of Ireland, Dublin, oil on canvas, 55 x 118 cm. © Courtesy of the National Gallery of Ireland.

286. Diego Velázquez, *La Mulata*, Art Institute, Chicago, oil on canvas, 55.5 x 104 cm. © The Art Institute, Chicago.

287. Jacob Matham after Pieter Aertsen, *Kitchen Scene with the Supper at Emmaus*, engraving, 24.2 x 32.3 cm. © The Trustees of the British Museum.

288. Titian (Tiziano Vecelli), *The Supper at Emmaus*, Musée du Louvre, Paris, oil on canvas, 169 x 244 cm., detail. © Réunion des Musées Nationaux/ Art Resource, NY.

289. Jacob Matham after Pieter Aertsen, *Kitchen Scene with the Supper at Emmaus*, engraving, 24.2 x 32.3 cm., detail. © The Trustees of the British Museum.

290. Jacob Matham after Sebastian Vrancx, *The Supper at Emmaus*, engraving, 40.5 x 54.5 cm. © The Trustees of the British Museum.

291. Philips Galle after Johannes Stradanus, *Last Supper*, engraving, 19.3 x 26.4 cm. © The Trustees of the British Museum.

292. Philips Galle after Johannes Stradanus, *The Vision of Saint Peter*, engraving, 20.4 x 26.7 cm. © The Trustees of the British Museum.

293. Philips Galle after Maarten van Heemskerck, *The Resurrection of Tabitha*, engraving, 21.3 x 27.5 cm. © The Trustees of the British Museum.

294. Giulio Bonasone, *The Virgin Washing the Feet of the Infant Christ*, engraving, 24.7 x 17.5 cm. © The Trustees of the British Museum.

295. Photocomposition of Diego Velázquez's *La Mulata*, National Gallery of Art, Dublin, and Giulio Bonasone's *The Virgin Washing the Feet of the Infant Christ*. © Jasmine Lin.

296. Johan Sadeler I after Jacopo Bassano (Jacopo da Ponte), *The Parable of Dives and Lazarus*, engraving, 23.7 x 29.5 cm. © The Trustees of the British Museum.

297. Johan Sadeler I after Jacopo Bassano (Jacopo da Ponte), *The Parable of Dives and Lazarus*, engraving, 23.7 x 29.5 cm., detail. © The Trustees of the British Museum.

298. Jacob Matham after Pieter Aertsen, *Kitchen Scene with the Supper at Emmaus*, engraving, 24.2 x 32.3 cm., detail. © The Trustees of the British Museum.

299. Diego Velázquez, *La Mulata*, National Gallery of Ireland, Dublin, oil on canvas, 55 x 118 cm., detail. © Courtesy of the National Gallery of Ireland.

300. Jacob Matham after Pieter Aertsen, *Kitchen Scene with the Supper at Emmaus*, engraving, 24.2 x 32.3 cm., detail. © The Trustees of the British Museum.

301. Diego Velázquez, *La Mulata*, National Gallery of Ireland, Dublin, oil on canvas, 55 x 118 cm., detail. © Courtesy of the National Gallery of Ireland.

302. Michelangelo Buonarroti, *The Prophet Joel*, Sistine Chapel, Vatican Palace, fresco, detail reversed. © Erich Lessing/ Art Resource, NY.

303. Diego Velázquez, *La Mulata*, National Gallery of Ireland, Dublin, oil on canvas, 55 x 118 cm., detail. © Courtesy of the National Gallery of Ireland.

304. Valentin de Boulogne, *Merry Company with Fortune Teller*, Liechtenstein Museum, Vienna, oil on canvas, 190 x 265 cm. © Liechtenstein Museum Vienna.

305. Valentin de Boulogne (after?), *Allegory of the Five Senses*, reproduced from *La Galerie du Palais-Royal*, 1786-1806. © National Gallery of Art Library, Washington DC.

306. Valentin de Boulogne (after), *Soldiers Playing Dice and Morra*, Musée des Beaux-Arts et d'Archéologie, Besançon, oil on canvas, 133 x 236 cm. © Musée des Beaux-Arts et d'Archéologie, Besançon/ Jean-Louis Dousson.

307. Bartolomeo Manfredi, *The Fortune Teller*, The Detroit Institute of Arts, Detroit, oil on canvas, 120.9 x 152.4 cm. © The Detroit Institute of Arts/ The Bridgeman Library.

308. Valentin de Boulogne, *The Fortune Teller*, Museum of Art, Toledo, oil on canvas, 149.5 x 238.5 cm. © The Toledo Museum of Art.

309. Valentin de Boulogne, *The Fortune Teller*, Musée du Louvre, Paris, oil on canvas, 125 x 175 cm. © Réunion des Musées Nationaux/ Art Resource, NY.

310. Valentin de Boulogne, *Concert with Eight Figures*, Musée du Louvre, Paris, 175 x 216 cm. © Réunion des Musées Nationaux/ Art Resource, NY.

311. Valentin de Boulogne, *Concert with Bas-Relief*, Musée du Louvre, Paris, oil on canvas, 173 x 214 cm. © Réunion des Musées Nationaux/ Art Resource, NY.

312. Nicolas Régnier, *Card Players with Fortune Teller*, Szépmüvészeti Mùzeum, Budapest, oil on canvas, 174 x 228 cm. © Szépmüvészeti Mùzeum, Budapest.

PLATES

Plate I: Michelangelo Merisi da Caravaggio, *The Penitent Magdalene*, Galleria Doria-Pamphilij, Rome, oil on canvas, 123 x 98.3 cm., detail. © Alinari/ Art Resource, NY.

Plate II: Michelangelo Merisi da Caravaggio, *The Flagellation*, Museo di Capodimonte, Naples, oil on canvas, 266 x 213 cm., detail. © Scala/ Ministero per i Beni e le Attività Culturali/ Art Resource, NY.

Plate III: Michelangelo Merisi da Caravaggio, *The Annunciation*, Musée des Beaux-Arts, Nancy, oil on canvas, 285 x 205 cm., detail. © Scala/ Art Resource, NY.

Plate IV: Michelangelo Merisi da Caravaggio, *Judith Beheading Holofernes*, Galleria Nazionale d'Arte Antica, Palazzo Barberini, Rome, oil on canvas, 145 x 195 cm., detail. © Luciano Pedicini.

Plate V: Michelangelo Merisi da Caravaggio, *The Cardsharps*, Kimbell Museum of Art, Fort Worth, oil on canvas, 91.5 x 128.2 cm., detail. © Kimbell Art Museum, Fort Worth, Texas/ Art Resource, NY.

Plate VI: Michelangelo Merisi da Caravaggio, *The Fortune Teller*, Musée du Louvre, Paris, oil on canvas, 99 x 131 cm., detail. © Réunion des Musées Nationaux/ Art Resource, NY.

Plate VII: Michelangelo Merisi da Caravaggio, *The Cardsharps*, Kimbell Museum of Art, Fort Worth, oil on canvas, 91.5 x 128.2 cm., detail. © Kimbell Art Museum, Fort Worth, Texas/ Art Resource, NY.

Plate VIII: Michelangelo Merisi da Caravaggio, *Conversion of Mary Magdalene*, Detroit Institute of Arts, Detroit, oil on canvas, 97.7 x 132.7 cm., detail. © Detroit Institute of Art/ The Bridgeman Art Library.

Plate IX: Michelangelo Merisi da Caravaggio, *The Conversion of Saint Paul*, Odescalchi Collection, Rome, oil on panel, 237 x 189 cm., detail. © Principessa Nicoletta Odescalchi/ Photo Pasquale Rizzi.

Plate X: Michelangelo Merisi da Caravaggio, *The Calling of Saint Matthew*, Contarelli Chapel, San Luigi dei Francesi, Rome, oil on canvas, 322 x 340 cm., detail. © Scala/ Art Resource, NY.

Plate XI: Michelangelo Merisi da Caravaggio, *The Conversion of Saint Paul*, Cerasi Chapel, Santa Maria del Popolo, Rome, oil on canvas, 230 x 175 cm., detail. © Scala/ Art Resource.

Plate XII: Michelangelo Merisi da Caravaggio, *The Supper at Emmaus*, Pinacoteca di Brera, Milan, oil on canvas, 141 x 175 cm., detail. © Erich Lessing/ Art Resource, NY.

Plate XIII: Michelangelo Merisi da Caravaggio, *The Taking of Christ*, National Gallery of Ireland, Dublin, oil on canvas, 133.5 x 169.5 cm., detail. © Courtesy of the National Gallery of Ireland and the Jesuit Community.

Plate XIV: Michelangelo Merisi da Caravaggio, *The Taking of Christ*, National Gallery of Ireland, Dublin, oil on canvas, 133.5 x 169.5 cm., detail. © Courtesy of the National Gallery of Ireland and the Jesuit Community.

Plate XV: Michelangelo Merisi da Caravaggio, *The Entombment*, Pinacoteca Vaticana, Rome, oil on canvas, 300 x 203 cm., detail. © Scala/ Art Resource, NY.

Plate XVI: Michelangelo Merisi da Caravaggio, *Ecce Homo*, Galleria di Palazzo Rosso, Genoa, oil on canvas, 128 x 103 cm., detail. © Scala/ Art Resource.

Plate XVII: Michelangelo Merisi da Caravaggio, *The Martyrdom of Saint Ursula*, Banca Intesa, Palazzo Zavalos, Naples, oil on canvas, 154 x 178 cm., detail. © Luciano Pedicini.

Plate XVIII: Michelangelo Merisi da Caravaggio, *The Resurrection of Lazarus*, Museo Regionale, Messina, oil on canvas, 320 x 275 cm., detail. © Luciano Pedicini.

Plate XIX: Michelangelo Merisi da Caravaggio, *The Incredulity of Saint Thomas*, Schloß Sans-Souci, Potsdam, oil on canvas, 107 x 146 cm., detail. © Bildarchiv Preussischer Kulturbesitz/ Art Resource, NY.

Plate XX: Battistello (Giovan Battista) Caracciolo, *Noli Me Tangere*, Museo Civico, Prato, oil on canvas, 109 x 130.5 cm., detail. © Scala/ Art Resource, NY.

Plate XXI: Diego Velázquez, *The Supper at Emmaus*, Metropolitan Museum of Art, New York, oil on canvas, 123.2 x 132.7 cm., detail. © The Metropolitan Museum of Art/ Art Resource, NY.

Plate XXII: Cecco del Caravaggio (Francesco Boneri), *The Resurrection*, Art Institute, Chicago, oil on canvas, 339 x 199.5 cm., detail. © The Art Institute, Chicago.

Plate XXIII: Diego Velázquez, *La Mulata*, National Gallery of Ireland, Dublin, oil on canvas, 55 x 118 cm. © Courtesy of the National Gallery of Ireland.

Plate XXIV: Valentin de Boulogne, *Merry Company with Fortune Teller*, Liechtenstein Museum, Vienna, oil on canvas, 190 x 265 cm., detail. © Liechtenstein Museum Vienna.

BIBLIOGRAPHY

Sources

Agucchi: Giovan Battista Agucchi, *Trattato della pittura*, in Ricardo de Mambro Santos, *Arcadie del vero: Arte e teoria nella Roma del Seicento* (Rome: Apeiron, 2001): 139-64.

Alberti: Leon Battista Alberti, *Opere volgari. Volume Terzo: Trattati d'arte…*, ed. Cecil Grayson (Bari: Laterza, 1973).

Alberti R.: Romano Alberti, *Trattato della nobiltà della pittura* (Rome: F. Zanetti, 1585).

Alberti and Zuccari: Romano Alberti, *Origine et progresso dell'Accademia del dissegno…*(Pavia: Pietro Bartoli, 1604).

Ariosto: Ludovico Ariosto, *Opere minori*, ed. Cesare Segre (Milan and Naples: Ricciardi, 1954).

Armenini: Giovan Battista Armenini, *De' veri precetti della pittura*, ed. Marina Gorreri (Turin: Einaudi, 1988).

Baglione: Giovanni Baglione, *Le vite de' pittori, scultori et architetti dal pontificato di Gregorio XIII del 1572 in fino a' tempi di papa Urbano Ottavo del 1642* (Rome: Andrea Fei, 1642).

Baldinucci: Filippo Baldinucci, *Notizie dei professori del disegno da Cimabue in qua…* (Florence: V. Batelli e Compagni, 1846).

Bargagli: Scipione Bargagli, *Dell'Imprese* (Venice: Francesco de' Franceschi Senese, 1594).

Baronio: Cesare Baronio, *Martyrologium romanum ad novam kalendarii rationem et Ecclesiasticae historiae restitutum* (Antwerp: J. Moretus, 1613).

Bellori: Giovan Pietro Bellori, *Le vite de' pittori, scultori e architetti moderni*, ed. Evelina Borea (Turin: Einaudi, 1976).

Bellori a: Giovan Pietro Bellori, *Nota delli musei, librerie, galerie, et ornamenti di statue e pitture ne' palazzi, nelle case, e ne' giardini di Roma* (Rome: Biagio Deversin & Felice Cesaretti, 1664).

Bembo: Pietro Bembo, *Prose e Rime*, ed. Carlo Dionisotti (Turin: UTET, 1960).

Berni: Francesco Berni, *Poesie e Prose*, ed. Ezio Chiorboli (Geneva and Florence: Olschki, 1934).

Bizoni: Bernardo Bizoni, *Relazione in forma di diario del viaggio che corse per diverse province di Europa il signor Vincenzo Giustiniano marchese di Bassano l'anno 1606,* ed. Anna Banti (Milan: Rizzoli, 1942).

Bocchi A.: Achille Bocchi, *Symbolicarum quaestionum de universo genere, quas serio ludebat, libri quinque* (Bologna: Apud Societatem Typographiae Bononiensis, 1574).

Bocchi F.: Francesco Bocchi, *Opera di M. Francesco Bocchi sopra l'imagine miracolosa della Santissima Annunziata di Fiorenza…*(Florence: s.n., 1592).

Borghini: Raffaello Borghini, *Il Riposo* (Reggio: Pietro Fiaccadori, 1986).

Borromeo: Federico Borromeo, *Della pittura sacra libri due,* ed. Barbara Agosti (Pisa: Scuola Normale Superiore, 1994).

Borromeo a: Federico Borromeo, *Sacred Painting—Museum*, eds. Kenneth S. Rothwell and Pamela M. Jones (Cambridge: Harvard University Press, 2010).

Boschini: Marco Boschini, *La Carta del navegar pittoresco: Edizione critica con la "Breve Instruzione" premessa alle "Ricche Minere della Pittura Veneziana,"* ed. Anna Pallucchini (Venezia: Istituto per la collaborazione culturale, 1966).

Bulwer: John Bulwer, *Chirologia or the Natural Language of the Hand* (London: Thomas Harper, 1644).

Camilli: Camillo Camilli, *Imprese illustri di diversi coi discorsi di Camillo Camilli et con le figure intagliate in rame di Girolamo Porro, Padovano*, (Venice: Appresso Francesco Ziletti, 1586).

Cardano: Girolamo Cardano, *Opera Omnia*, (Lyons: J.-A. Huguetan et M.-A. Ravaud 1663).

Cardi: Giovan Battista Cardi, *Vita di Lodovico Cardi, Cigoli*, ed. Guido Battelli (Florence: Barbera, 1913).

Carducho: Vicente Carducho, *Diálogos de la pintura, su defensa, origen, esencia, definición, modos y diferencias*, ed. Francisco Calvo Serraller (Madrid: Turner, 1977).

Carracci: Giovanna Perini, ed., *Gli scritti dei Carracci: Ludovico, Annibale, Agostino, Antonio, Giovanni Antonio* (Bologna : Nuova Alpha, 1990).

Castelvetro: Lodovico Castelvetro, *Poetica d'Aristotele vulgarizzata e sposta*, ed. Werther Romani (Rome and Bari: Laterza, 1978-1979).

Castiglione: Ghino Ghinassi, ed., *La seconda redazione del 'Cortegiano' di Baldassare Castiglione* (Florence: Sansoni, 1968).

Celano: Carlo Celano, *Delle Notitie del bello, dell'antico e del curioso della città di Napoli…*(Naples: Stamperia Floriana, 1856-60).

Celio: Gaspare Celio, *Memoria delli nomi dell'artefici delle pitture che sono in alcune chiese, facciate e palazzi di Roma* (Naples: Scipione Bonino, 1638).

Cellini: Piero Calamandrei, *Scritti e inediti celliniani*, ed. Carlo Cordié (Florence: La Nuova Italia, 1971).

Chantelou: Paul Fréart de Chantelou, *Journal du voyage du cavalier Bernin en France*, ed. Milovan Stanić (Paris: Macula-L'Insulaire, 2001).

Cochin: Charles-Nicolas Cochin, *Voyage d'Italie*, ed. Christian Michel (Rome: École Française de Rome, 1991).

Comanini: Gregorio Comanini, *Il Figino, overo Del fine della pittura* (Mantua: Francesco Osanna, 1591).

Condivi: Ascanio Condivi, *Vita di Michelagnolo Buonarroto*, ed. Giovanni Nencioni (Florence: Spes, 1998).

Conférences: Jacqueline Lichtenstein and Christian Michel, eds., *Les Conférences au temps d'Henri Testelin: 1648-1681* (Paris: École nationale supérieure des Beaux-Arts, 2006).

Correggio: Niccolò da Correggio, *Opere: Cefalo-Psiche-Silva-Rime*, ed. Antonia Tissoni Benvenuti (Bari: Laterza, 1969).

Dall'Aquila a: Serafino de' Ciminelli Dall'Aquila, *Le Rime*, ed. Mario Menghini (Bologna: Romagnoli-Dall'Acqua, 1894).

Dall'Aquila b: Barbara Bauer Formiconi, ed., *Die* Strambotti *des Serafino Dall'Aquila: Studien und Texte zur italienischen Spiel- und Scherzdichtung des ausgehenden 15. Jahrhunderts* (Munich: Fink, 1967).

De' Bianchi: Lodovico de' Bianchi, *Le cento e quindici conclusioni in ottava rima del plusquamperfetto Dottor Gratiano Partesana da Francolin…*(s.l., 1587).

De Dominici: Bernardo de Dominici, *Vite de' pittori, scultori ed architetti napoletani* (Naples: Ricciardi, 1742).

Dezallier d'Argenville: Antoine-Joseph Dezallier d'Argenville, *Abrégé de la vie des plus fameux peintres…* (Paris: De Bure l'aîné, 1745-1752).

Dio Chrysostom: Dio Chrysostom, *Discourses*, trans. J. W. Cohoon (London: Loeb Classical Library, 1932-51).

Dolce: Mark W. Roskill, ed., *Dolce's* Aretino *and Venetian Art Theory of the Cinquecento* (Toronto: University of Toronto Press, 2000).

Félibien a: André Félibien, *Entretiens sur les vies et sur les ouvrages des plus excellents peintres anciens et modernes* (Paris: Pierre Le Petit, 1666-1688).

Félibien b: André Félibien, *Recueil de descriptions de peintures et d'autres ouvrages faits pour le roi* (Paris: Veuve de Sébastien Mabre-Cramoisy, 1689).

Gaurico: Pomponio Gaurico, *De Sculptura*, ed. Paolo Cutolo (Naples: Edizioni Scientifiche Italiane, 1999).

Ghini: Costantino Ghini, *Dell'imagini sacre dialoghi* (Siena: Luca Bonetti, 1595).

Gilio: Giovanni Andrea Gilio, *Degli errori e degli abusi de' pittori circa l'istorie*, in Paola Barocchi, ed., *Scritti d'Arte del Cinquecento: IV Pittura* (Turin: Einaudi, 1978) 1: 834-62.

Giustiniani: Vincenzo Giustiniani, *Discorsi sulle arti e sui mestieri*, ed. Anna Banti (Florence: Sansoni, 1981).

Holtzwart: Mathias Holtzwart, *Emblematum Tirocinia*, eds. Peter von Düffel and Klaus Schmidt (Stuttgart: Philipp Reclam Jun., 1968).

John of Damascus a: *Translatio latina Ioannis Damasceni (De orthodoxa fide 1.III, c. 1-8) saeculo XII in Hungaria confecta*, ed. Remigius L. Szegeti (Budapest: Kr. M. Pázmány Péter Tudományegyetemi Görög Fiológiai Intézet, 1940).

John of Damascus b: John of Damascus, *Opera omnia quaequidem extant, maxima parte hactenus non visa*, trans. Francesco Zino (Basel: ex officina Henricpetrina, 1575).

Leonardo: Leonardo da Vinci, *Trattato della pittura*, ed. Gaetano Milanesi (Rome: Unione Cooperativa Editrice, 1890).

Lomazzo: Gian Paolo Lomazzo, *Scritti sulle arti*, ed. Roberto Paolo Ciardi (Florence: Marchi & Bertoli, 1973).

Maggi: Vincenzo Maggi and Bartolomeo Lombardi, *In Aristotelis librum de poetica communes explanationes* (Venice: Officina Erasmiana Vincentii Valgrisii, 1550).

Malvasia: Carlo Cesare Malvasia, *Felsina Pittrice: Vite de' pittori bolognesi…* (Bologna: Erede di D. Barbieri, 1678).

Malvasia a: Lea Marzocchi, ed., *Scritti originali del conte Carlo Cesare Malvasia spettanti alla sua Felsina Pittrice* (Bologna: Accademia Clementina, s. d.).

Mancini: Giulio Mancini, *Considerazioni sulla pittura*, eds. Adriana Marucchi and Luigi Salerno (Rome: Accademia Nazionale dei Lincei, 1956-1957).

Manilli: Giacomo Manilli, *Villa Borghese fuori di Porta Pinciana* (Rome: Grignani, 1650).

Maranta: Bartolomeo Maranta, *Discorso…nel quale si difende il quadro della cappella del Sig. Cosmo Pinelli, fatto per Tiziano…*, in Paola Barocchi, ed., *Scritti d'Arte del Cinquecento: IV Pittura* (Turin: Einaudi, 1978) 1: 863-900.

Marino a: Giovanni Pozzi, *Tutte le opere di Giambattista Marino: L'Adone* (Milan: Mondadori, 1976).

Marino b: Giovan Battista Marino, *Amori*, ed. Alessandro Martini (Milan: Rizzoli, 1982).

Marino c: Giambattista Marino, *La Galeria*, eds. Marzio Pieri and Alessandra Ruffino (Trento: La Finestra, 2005).

Marino d: Giambattista Marino, *Lettere*, ed. Marziano Guglielminetti (Turin: Einaudi, 1966).

Maruli: Silvestro Maruli, *Historia sagra intitolata Mare oceano di tutte le religioni del mondo…* (Messina, P. Brea, 1613).

Moerman: Jan Moerman, *De cleyn werelt…* (Amsterdam: Dirck Pietersz, 1608).

Molanus: Johannes Molanus, *De historia sanctarum imaginum et picturarum pro vero earum usu contra abusus libri IIII* (Antwerp: Apud Gasparem Bellerum, 1617).

Murtola: Gaspare Murtola, *Rime… cioé sonetti* (Venice: R. Meglietti, 1604).

Nikephoros: Jacques-Paul Migne, ed., *Patrologiae cursus completes: Patres graeci. 100. S.P.N. Nicephori, archiepiscopi Constantinopolitani, opera quae reperiri potuerunt omnia* (Paris: J.P. Migne, 1860).

Nivelon: Claude Nivelon, *Vie de Charles Le Brun et description détaillée de ses ouvrages: Introduction et édition critique,* ed. Lorenzo Pericolo (Geneva: Droz, 2004).

Pacheco: Francisco Pacheco, *El arte de la pintura*, ed. Bonaventura Bassegoda i Hugas (Madrid: Cátedra, 1990).

Paleotti: Gabriele Paleotti, *Discorso intorno alle imagini sacre e profane* (Bologna: A. Benacci, 1582).

Palomino: Antonio Palomino, *El Museo pictórico y escala óptica*, ed. Juan A. Ceán y Bermúdez (Madrid: Aguilar, 1988).

Passeri: Giambattista Passeri, *Vite de' pittori, scultori ed architetti che hanno lavorato in Roma…* (Rome: Natale Barbiellini, 1772).

Perrucci: Andrea Perrucci, *Dell'arte rappresentativa premeditata ed all'improvviso*, ed. Anton Giulio Bragaglia (Florence: Sansoni, 1961).

Petrarca: Francesco Petrarca, *Canzoniere*, ed. Mario Santagata (Milan: Mondadori, 2004).

Pino: Paolo Pino, *Dialogo di pittura*, ed. Susanna Falabella (Rome: Lithos, 2000).

Pittoni: Battista Pittoni, *Imprese di diversi prencipi, duchi, signori e d'altri personaggi et uomini letterati et illustri* (Venice: s.n., 1562).

Poussin: Nicolas Poussin, *Lettres et propos sur l'art*, ed. Anthony Blunt (Paris: Hermann, 1989).

Ridolfi: *Le maraviglie dell'arte, overo Le vite degli illustri pittori veneti e dello Stato*, ed. Detlev Freiherrn von Hadeln (Berlin: G. Grote, 1914).

Ruscelli: Girolamo Ruscelli and Vincenzo Ruscelli, *Le imprese illustri* (Venice: Francesco de' Franceschi Senese, 1584).

Samperi: Placido Samperi, *Messana S. P. Q. R. regumque decreto, nobilis exemplaris et regni Siciliae caput duodecim titulis, illustrata…* (Messina: P. Grillo, 1742).

Sandrart: Joachim von Sandrart, *Academie der Bau-, Bild- und Mahlerey-Künste…*, ed. A.R. Peltzer (Munich: G. Hirth, 1925).

Sansovino: Francesco Sansovino, *Venetia città nobilissima et singolare descritta in XIIII libri* (Venice: Sansovino, 1981).

Scannelli: Francesco Scannelli, *Il microcosmo della pittura* (Cesena: Per il Neri, 1657).

Scaramuccia: Luigi Pellegrini Scaramuccia, *Le finezze de' pennelli italiani…* (Pavia: G.A. Magri, 1674).

Sextus Empiricus: Sextus Empiricus, *Outlines of Pyrrhonism,* trans. R.G. Bury, (Cambridge: Harvard University Press, 1933).

Silos: Giovanni Michele Silos, *Pinacotheca sive Romana pictura et sculptura libri duo* (Rome: Filippo Maria Mancini, 1673).

Soldano: Aniello Soldano, *Fantastiche et ridicolose etimologie recitate in commedia…*(Bologna: Vittorio Brancacci, 1610).

Susinno: Francesco Susinno, *Le vite de' pittori messinesi*, ed. Valentino Martinelli (Florence: Le Monnier, 1960).

Symeon of Thessalonika: Jacques-Paul Migne, ed., *Patrologiae Cursus Completus: Patres Graeci. 155: Symeonis Thessalonicensis Archiepiscopi Opera omnia* (Turnhout: Brepols, 1979).

Syropoulos: Vitalien Laurent, ed., *Les Mémoires du Grand ecclésiarque de l'Église de Constantinople, Sylvestre Syropoulos sur le concile de Florence (1438-1439)* (Paris: Centre National de la Recherche Scientifique, 1971).

Tasso a: Torquato Tasso, *Aminta e Rime*, ed. Francesco Flora (Milan: Ricciardi, 1976).

Tasso b: Torquato Tasso, *Il Gonzaga secondo overo del giuoco: Dialogo* (Venice: Bernardo Giunti, 1582).

Tasso c: Torquato Tasso, *Scritti sull'arte poetica*, ed. Ettore Mazzali (Turin: Einaudi, 1977).

Tebaldeo: Antonio Tebaldeo, *Rime della vulgata*, ed. Tania Basile (Modena: Panini, 1992).

Testa: Elizabeth Cropper, *The Ideal of Painting: Pietro Testa's Düsseldorf Notebook* (Princeton: Princeton University Press, 1984).

Van Mander: Carel van Mander, *Het Schilder-Boeck…*(Haarlem: Paschier van Wesbach, 1604).

Vasari: Giorgio Vasari, *Le vite de' più eccellenti pittori, scultori e architettori*, eds. Rosanna Bettarini and Paola Barocchi (Florence: Sansoni; Florence: Spes, 1966-1987).

Zuccari: Federico Zuccari, *L'idea de' pittori, scultori et architetti* (Turin: Agostino Disserolio, 1607).

Books, Articles, Essays, Exhibition Catalogs

Acidini Luchinat 1998: Cristina Acidini Luchinat, *Taddeo e Federico Zuccari: Fratelli pittori del Cinquecento* (Rome: Jandi Sapi, 1998).

Acidini Luchinat 2001: Cristina Acidini Luchinat, "Federico Zuccari a Venezia," in Mario Piantoni and Laura De Rossi, eds., *Per l'arte: Da Venezia all'Europa* (Monfalcone and Gorizia: Edizioni della Laguna, 2001) 1: 235-40.

Adriani 1940: Gert Adriani, *Anton Van Dyck: Italienisches Skizzenbuch* (Vienna: Schroll, 1940).

Agosti 1992: Barbara Agosti, "Federico Borromeo, le antichità cristiane e i primitivi," *Annali della Scuola Normale Superiore di Pisa* 22 (1992): 481-93.

Agosti 1996: Barbara Agosti, *Collezionismo e archeologia cristiana nel Seicento: Federico Borromeo e il Medioevo artistico tra Roma e Milano* (Milan: Jaca Books, 1996).

Agosti 1997: Barbara Agosti, "La Pinacoteca Ambrosiana: Aperture e chiusure," *Prospettiva* 87/88 (1997): 175-81.

Aikema 1990: Bernard Aikema, *Pietro della Vecchia and the Heritage of the Renaissance Venice* (Florence: Istituto universitario olandese di storia dell'arte, 1990).

Albero Muñoz 2006: Maria del Mar Albero Muñoz, "La expressión de las pasiones y la fisiognomía en la literatura artística española del s. XVII: Dos ejemplos, Carducho y Pacheco," in Maria de los Reyes Hernández Soccorro, ed., *XVI Congreso Nacional de Historia del Arte: la multiculturalidad en las artes y en la arquitectura* (Las Palmas: Anroart Ediciones, 2006): 267-74.

Allrath and Gymnich 2006: Gaby Allrath and Marion Gymnich, eds., *Narrative Strategies in Television Series* (Basingstoke: Palgrave Macmillan, 2006).

Alois Riegl **2008**: *Alois Riegl (1858-1905), un secolo dopo: Convegno internazionale organizzato d'intesa con l'Istituto Archeologico Germanico, l'Istituto Storico Austriaco, la Scuola Normale Superiore di Pisa, l'Istituto Italiano per gli Studi Filosofici* (Rome: Bardi, 2008).

Alpers 1976: Svetlana Alpers, "Describe or Narrate? A Problem in Realistic Representation," *New Literary History* 8 (1976): 15-41.

Alpers 1983: Svetlana Alpers, *The Art of Describing: Dutch Art in the Seventeenth Century* (Chicago: University of Chicago Press, 1983).

Altman 2008: Rick Altman, *A Theory of Narrative* (New York: Columbia University Press, 2008).

Ambrosini 2009: Alberto Ambrosini, *Immaginazione visiva e conoscenza: Teoria della visione e pratica figurative nei trattati di Leon Battista Alberti, Lorenzo Ghiberti, Leonardo da Vinci* (Pisa: Plus Pisa University Press, 2009).

Ames Lewis 1986: Francis Ames Lewis, *The Draftsman Raphael* (New Haven: Yale University Press, 1986).

Anderson 1997: Jaynie Anderson, *Giorgione: Painter of "Poetic Brevity," Including a Catalogue Raisonné* (New York: Flammarion, 1997).

Andrews 1995: Lew Andrews, *Story and Space in Renaissance Art: The Rebirth of Continuous Narrative* (Cambridge: Cambridge University Press, 1995).

Arkin 1997: Moshe Arkin, "One of the Marys...: An Interdisciplinary Analysis of Michelangelo's Florentine *Pietà*," *Art Bulletin* 79 (1997): 493-517.

Ashford 1935: Faith Ashford, "Caravaggio's Stay in Malta," *Burlington Magazine* 67 (1935): 168-74.

Askew 1990: Pamela Askew, *Caravaggio's Death of the Virgin* (Princeton: Princeton University Press, 1990).

Askew 1996: Pamela Askew, "Caravaggio: Outward Action, Inward Vision," in Stefania Macioce, ed., *Michelangelo Merisi da Caravaggio: La vita e le opere attraverso i documenti. Atti del Convegno Internazionale di Studi...*(Rome: Logart Press, 1996): 248-69.

Auerbach 2003: Erich Auerbach, *Mimesis: The Representation of Reality in Western Literature*, trans. William R. Trask (Princeton: Princeton University Press, 2003).

Augé 2003: Jean-Louis Augé, "Francisco Pacheco et 'La vraie imitation de la Nature'," in Pascal-François Bertrand and Stéphanie Trouvé, eds., *Nicolas Tournier et la peinture caravagesque en Italie, en France et en Espagne: Colloque international…*(Toulouse: CNRS, 2003): 201-05.

Augé 2004: Jean-Louis Augé, "Diego Velázquez y Francisco Pacheco: El aprendizaje de un genio de la pintura, 1611-1616," in Alfredo J. Morales, *Symposium Internacional Velázquez: Actas* (Seville: Junta de Andalucia, Consejería de Cultura, 2004): 39-46.

Azzolini 2005: Monica Azzolini, "In Praise of Art: Text and Context of Leonardo's *Paragone* and its Critique of the Arts and Sciences," *Renaissance Studies* 19 (2005): 487-510.

Bagni 1988: Prisco Bagni, *Il Guercino e i suoi incisori* (Rome: Ugo Bozzi Editore, 1988).

Bailey 1999: Gauvin A. Bailey, "*Le style jésuite n'existe pas*: Jesuit Corporate Culture and the Visual Arts," in John W. O' Malley, Gauvin A. Bailey, Steven J. Harris and T. Frank Kennedy, eds., *The Jesuits: Cultures, Sciences and the Arts 1540-1773* (Toronto: Toronto University Press, 1999): 38-89.

Bailey 2003: Gauvin A. Bailey, *Between Renaissance and Baroque: Jesuit Art in Rome, 1565-1610* (Toronto: University of Toronto Press, 2003).

Bal 1996: Mieke Bal, *Double Exposures: The Subject of Cultural Analysis* (New York: Routledge, 1996).

Bal 1997: Mieke Bal, *Narratology: Introduction to the Theory of Narrative* (Toronto: University of Toronto Press, 1997).

Bal 1999: Mieke Bal, *Quoting Caravaggio: Contemporary Art, Preposterous History* (Chicago: University of Chicago Press, 1999).

Balestreri 2005: Isabella Balestreri, *Le fabbriche del cardinale: Federico Borromeo (1595-1631), l'arcivescovado e l'Ambrosiana* (Benevento: Hevelius, 2005).

Barash 1987: Moshe Barash, *Giotto and the Language of Gesture* (Cambridge: Cambridge University Press, 1987).

Barbadillo 1963: Manuel Barbadillo, *Pacheco, su tierra y su tiempo* (Jerez: Editorial Jerez Industrial, 1963).

Barber 2002: Charles Barber, *Figure and Likeness: On the Limits of Representation in Byzantine Iconoclasm* (Princeton: Princeton University Press, 2002).

Barbera and Greco 2004: Gioacchino Barbera and Vera Greco, *Mario Minniti: L'Eredità di Caravaggio a Siracusa*, exh. cat. (Naples: Electa, 2004).

Barbera and Lapucci 1996: Gioacchino Barbera and Roberta Lapucci, eds., *'Il Seppellimento di Santa Lucia' del Caravaggio: Indagini radiografiche e riflettografiche* (Syracuse: Galleria Regionale di Palazzo Bellomo, 1996).

Barbera and Spagnolo 2005: Gioacchino Barbera and Donatella Spagnolo, "From the *Burial of Saint Lucy* to the *Scenes of the Passion*: Caravaggio in Syracuse and Messina," in Silvia Cassani and Maria Sapio, eds., *Caravaggio: The Final Years*, exh. cat. (Milan: Electa, 2005): 80-87.

Barbiellini Amidei 1989: Rosanna Barbiellini Amidei, "Della committenza Massimo," in *Caravaggio: Nuove riflessioni* (Rome: Palombi Editore, 1989): 47-69.

Barbieri 2000: Giuseppe Barbieri, "*Tumultuare historia videatur*: Una precisazione per Leon Battista Alberti critico d'arte," in Valerio Terraroli, Franca Varallo and Laura De Fanti, eds., *L'arte nella storia: Contributi di critica e storia dell'arte per Gianni Carlo Sciolla* (Milan: Skira, 2000): 51-56.

Bardon 1978: Françoise Bardon, *Caravage ou l'expérience de la matière* (Paris: Presses Universitaires de France, 1978).

Barner 2003: Wilfried Barner, "Le *Laocoon* de Lessing: Déduction et induction," in Élisabeth Décultot, Jacques Le Rider and François Queyrel, eds., *Le Laocoon: Histoire et reception* (Paris: Presses Universitaires de France, 2003): 131-44.

Barnes 1998: Bernadine Barnes, *Michelangelo's* Last Judgment: *The Renaissance Response* (Berkeley: University of California Press, 1998).

Barnes 2010: Bernadine Barnes, *Michelangelo in Print: Reproductions as Response in the Sixteenth Century* (Aldershot: Ashgate, 2010)

Barocchi 1958: Paola Barocchi, "Finito e non-finito nella critica vasariana," *Arte Antica e Moderna* 3 (1958): 221-35.

Barocchi 1962: Paola Barocchi, ed., *Giorgio Vasari: La Vita di Michelangelo nelle redazioni del 1550 e 1568* (Milan and Naples: Ricciardi, 1962).

Baroni 1947: Costantino Baroni, *Introduzione al Barocco* (Milan: Vita e Pensiero, 1947).

Barroero 1997: Liliana Barroero, "L'*Isacco* di Caravaggio nella Pinacoteca Capitolina," *Bollettino dei musei comunali di Roma* 11 (1997): 37-41.

Barthes et al. 1977: Roland Barthes, Wolfgang Kayser, Wayne C. Booth and Philippe Hamon, *Poétique du récit* (Paris: Éditions du Seuil, 1977).

Barzman 1991: Karen-edis Barzman, "Perception, Knowledge, and the Theory of *Disegno* in Sixteenth-Century Florence," in Larry Feinberg, ed., *From Studio to Studiolo: Florentine Draftsmanship under the First Medici Grand Dukes* (Seattle: University of Washington Press, 1991): 37-48.

Bassani and Bellini 1994: Riccardo Bassani and Fiora Bellini, *Caravaggio assassino: La carriera di un 'valenthuomo' fazioso nella Roma della Controriforma* (Rome: Donzelli, 1994).

Bassegoda i Hugas 2004a: Bonaventura Bassegoda i Hugas, "Las tareas intelectuales del pintor Francisco Pacheco," in Alfredo J. Morales, ed., *Symposium Internacional Velázquez: Actas* (Seville: Junta de Andalucia, Consejería de Cultura, 2004): 39-46.

Bassegoda i Hugas 2004b: Bonaventura Bassegoda i Hugas, "Antonio Palomino y la memoria histórica de los artistas en España," in Fernando Checa Cremades, ed., *Arte barroco e ideal clásico: Aspectos del arte cortesano en la segunda mitad del siglo XVII* (Rome: Sociedad Estatal para la Acción Cultural Exterior, 2004): 89-113.

Bätschmann 1990: Oskar Bätschmann, *Nicolas Poussin: Dialectics of Painting*, transl. Marko Daniel (London: Reaktion Books, 1990).

Bätschmann 1997: Oskar Bätschmann, "Leon Battista Alberti über *inventum* und *inventio*," in Gerhart Schröder and Barbara Cassin, eds., *Anamorphosen der Rhetorik: Die Wahrheitsspiele der Renaissance* (Munich: Fink, 1997): 231-48.

Bätschmann 1998: Oskar Bätschmann, "Perspektive, Proportion und *Inventio* bei Leon Battista Alberti," in Rocco Sinisgalli, ed., *La prospettiva: Fondamenti teoretici ed esperienze figurative dall'antichità al mondo moderno* (Fiesole: Cadmo, 1998): 94-102.

Bätschmann 2002: Oskar Bätschmann, "Kunstgenuß statt Bilderkult: Wirkung und Rezeption des Gemäldes nach Leon Battista Alberti," in Peter Blickle and André Holenstein, eds., *Macht und Ohnmacht der Bilder: Reformatorischer Bildersturm im Kontext der europäischen Geschichte* (Munich: Oldenbourg, 2002): 359-75.

Battaglia 1961-2002: Salvatore Battaglia, *Grande Dizionario della Lingua Italiana* (Turin: UTET, 1961-2002).

Baxandall 1964: Michael Baxandall, "Bartholomaeus Facius on Painting: A Fifteenth-Century Manuscript of the *De Viris Illustribus*," *Journal of the Warburg and Courtauld Institutes* 27 (1964): 90-107.

Baxandall 1971: Michael Baxandall, *Giotto and the Orators: Humanist Observers of Paintings in Italy and the Discovery of the Pictorial Composition (1350-1450)* (Oxford: Oxford University Press, 1971).

Beck et al. 1996: Herbert Beck, Maraike Bückling and Edgar Lein, eds., *Die Christus-Thomas-Gruppe von Andrea del Verrocchio* (Frankfurt: Henrich, 1996).

Begni Redona 1988: Pier Virgilio Begni Redona, *Alessandro Bonvicini, il Moretto da Brescia* (Brescia: Banca San Paolo: 1988).

Béguerie 1991: Pantxika Béguerie, ed., *Le Beau Martin: Gravures et dessins de Martin Schongauer (vers 1450-1491)*, exh. cat. (Colmar: Musée d'Unterlinden, 1991).

Beijer and Duchartre 1981: Agne Beijer and Pierre-Louis Duchartre, *Le Recueil Frossard* (Paris: Librairie Théâtrale, 1981).

Bell 1993: Janis C. Bell, "Some Seventeenth-Century Appraisals of Caravaggio's Coloring," *Artibus et historiae* 27 (1993): 103-29.

Bell 1995: Janis C. Bell, "Light and Color in Caravaggio's *Supper at Emmaus*," *Artibus et Historiae*, 31 (1995): 139-70.

Bellini 1991: Paolo Bellini, *L'opera incisa di Adamo e Diana Scultori* (Vicenza: Neri Pozza Editore, 1991).

Bellini and Leach 1983: Paolo Bellini and Mark Carter Leach, *The Illustrated Bartsch. 44. Italian Masters of the Seventeeth Century* (New York: Abaris Books, 1983).

Bellosi 1998: Luciano Bellosi, *Duccio: La Maestà* (Milan: Electa, 1998).

Belting 1985: Hans Belting, *Giovanni Bellini, Pietà: Ikone und Bilderzählung in der venezianischen Malerei* (Munich: Fischer, 1985).

Belting 1990: Hans Belting, *Bild und Kult: Eine Geschichte des Bildes vor dem Zeitalter der Kunst* (Munich: Beck, 1990).

Benati 2005: Daniele Benati, "Per Guido Reni 'incamminato,' tra i Carracci e Caravaggio," *Nuovi Studi* 9-10 (2005): 231-47.

Benati and DeGrazia 1999: Daniele Benati and Diane DeGrazia, *The Drawings of Annibale Carracci*, exh. catalogue (Washington DC: National Gallery of Art, 1999).

Benati and Paolucci 2008: Daniele Benati and Antonio Paolucci, *I Bari della Collezione Mahon*, (Milan: Silvana Editoriale, 2008).

Benati and Riccomini 2006: Daniele Benati and Eugenio Riccomini, *Annibale Carracci*, exh. cat. (Milan, Electa, 2006).

Benedetti 1993a: Sergio Benedetti, "Caravaggio's *Taking of Christ*: A Masterpiece Rediscovered," *Burlington Magazine* 135 (1993): 731-41.

Benedetti 1993b: Sergio Benedetti, *Caravaggio: The Master Revealed*, exh. cat. (Dublin: The National Gallery of Ireland, 1993).

Benedetti 1995: Sergio Benedetti, "Caravaggio's *Taking of Christ*," Burlington Magazine 137 (1995): 37-8.

Benedetti 2005: Sergio Benedetti, "Alcune osservazioni sugli influssi italiani agli inizi della pittura naturalistica in Spagna," in Luigi Spezzaferro, ed., *Caravaggio e l'Europa: Il movimento caravaggesco internazionale da Caravaggio a Mattia Preti*, exh. cat. (Milan: Skira, 2005): 65-74.

Berenson 1916: Bernard Berenson, *Venetian Painting in America: The Fifteenth Century* (London: F.F. Shearman, 1916).

Berenson 1953: Bernard Berenson, *Caravaggio: His Incongruity and His Fame* (New York: The Macmillan Company, 1953).

Bernardini 2001: Maria Grazia Bernardini, ed., *Caravaggio, Carracci, Maderno: La Cappella Cerasi in Santa Maria del Popolo a Roma* (Cinisello Balsamo: Silvana, 2001).

Bernhard 1978: Marianne Bernhard, *Hans Baldung Grien: Handzeichnungen—Druckgraphik* (Munich: Südwest-Verlag, 1978).

Bernhard 1980: Marianne Bernhard, *Martin Schongauer und sein Kreis—Durchgraphik—Handzeichnungen* (Munich: Südwest Verlag, 1980).

Bernini Pezzini et al. 1985: Grazia Bernini Pezzini, Stefania Massari and Simonetta Prosperi Valenti Rodinò, *Raphael Invenit: Stampe da Raffaello nelle collezioni dell'Istituto Nazionale per la Grafica* (Rome: Quasar, 1985).

Berra 2005: Giacomo Berra, *Il giovane Caravaggio in Lombardia: Ricerche documentarie sui Merisi, gli Aratori e i marchesi di Caravaggio* (Florence: Fondazione Longhi, 2005).

Berra 2007: Giacomo Berra, "Il *Fruttaiolo* del Caravaggio, ovvero il giovane dio Vertunno con cesta di frutta," *Paragone Arte* 73 (2007): 3-54.

Bersani and Dutoit 1998: Leo Bersani and Ulysse Dutoit, *Caravaggio's Secrets* (Cambridge: MIT Press, 1998).

Bertolotti 1881: Antonino Bertolotti, *Artisti lombardi a Roma nei secoli XV, XVI, e XVII: Studi e ricerche negli archivi romani* (Milan: Hoepli, 1881).

Beyer et al. 2006: Vera Beyer, Jutta Voorhoeve and Anselm Haverkamp, eds., *Das Bild ist der König: Repräsentation nach Louis Marin* (Munich: Fink, 2006).

Biach-Schiffmann 1931: Flora Biach-Schiffman, *Giovanni und Ludovico Burnacini: Theater und Feste am Wiener Hofe* (Vienna: Krystall, 1931).

Bialostocki 1985: Jan Bialostocki, "Review of Svetlana Alpers' *The Art of Describing: Dutch Art in the Seventeenth Century*," *Art Bulletin* 67 (1985): 520-26.

Bianchi 2008: Ilaria Bianchi, *La politica delle immagini nell'età della Controriforma: Gabriele Paleotti teorico e committente* (Bologna: Editrice Compositori, 2008).

Binaghi 1975: Maria Teresa Binaghi, "L'immagine sacra in Luini e il circolo di Santa Marta," in *Sacro e profano nella pittura di Bernardino Luini*, exh. cat. (Milan: Silvana, 1975): 51-76.

Biscottini 2004: Paolo Biscottini, *Caravaggio: Cattura di Cristo*, exh. cat. (Milan: Fondazione Sant'Ambrogio, 2004).

Biscottini 2005: Paolo Biscottini, ed., *Carlo e Federico: La luce dei Borromeo nella Milano spagnola*, exh. cat. (Milan: Museo Diocesano, 2005).

Bissell 1981: Ward R. Bissel, *Orazio Gentileschi and the Poetic Tradition in Caravaggesque Painting* (University Park: Pennsylvania State University Press, 1981).

Blake McHam 2006: Sarah Blake McHam, "La bottega dei Lombardo alla cappella di Sant'Antonio e la teoria di Pomponio Gaurico," in Andrea Guerra, Manuela M. Morresi and Richard Schofield, eds., *I Lombardo: Architettura e scultura a Venezia tra '400 e '500* (Venice: Marsilio, 2006): 225-39.

Blunt 1967: Anthony Blunt, *Nicolas Poussin* (New York: Pantheon Books, 1967).

Boccardo 1988: Piero Boccardo, "Le rotte mediterranee del collezionismo genovese," *Bollettino dei Musei Civici Genovesi* 28-30 (1988): 99-116.

Bockemühl 1986: Michael Bockemühl, "Vom unvollendeten zum offenen Kunstwerk: Zur Diskussion des non-finito in der Plastik von Michelangelo," in Michael Hesse and Max Imdahl, eds., *Studien zu Renaissance und Barock Manfred Wundraum zum 60. Geburtstag: Eine Festschrift* (Frankfurt: Lang, 1986): 111-33.

Bodart 1970: Didier Bodart, *Louis Finson: Bruges, avant 1580- Amsterdam, 1617* (Bruxelles: Académie Royale de Belgique, 1970).

Bodmer 1939: Heinrich Bodmer, *Lodovico Carracci* (Burg b.M.: A. Hopfer, 1939).

Bohde 2007: Daniela Bohde, "*Le tinte delle carni*: Zur Begrifflichkeit für Haut und Fleisch in italienischen Kunsttraktaten des 15. bis 17. Jahrhunderts," in Daniela Bohde and Mechthild Fend, eds., *Weder Haut noch Fleisch: Das Inkarnat in der Kunstgeschichte* (Berlin: Mann, 2007): 41-63.

Bohn 2004: Babette Bohn, *Ludovico Carracci and the Art of Drawing* (London: Harvey Miller, 2004).

Bologna 1980: Ferdinando Bologna, "Caravaggio, 1610: La 'Sant'Orsola confitta dal Tiranno' per Marcantonio Doria," Prospettiva 23 (1980): 30-44.

Bologna 1992: Ferdinando Bologna, *L'incredulità del Caravaggio e l'esperienza delle 'cose naturali'* (Turin: Bollati Boringhieri, 1992).

Bolzoni 2002: Lina Bolzoni, "Qualche appunto su Federico Borromeo e la cultura fra Cinque e Seicento," in Santo Burgio and Luisa Ceriotti, eds., *Federico Borromeo uomo di cultura e di spiritualità: Atti delle giornate di studio...* (Milan: Biblioteca Ambrosiana, 2002).

Bolzoni 2008: Lina Bolzoni, *Poesia e ritratto nel Rinascimento* (Rome: Laterza, 2008).

Bond 1998: Helen K. Bond, *Pontius Pilate in History and Interpretation* (Cambridge: Cambridge University Press, 1998).

Bonnefoy 1988: Yves Bonnefoy, "Time and the Timeless in Quattrocento Painting," in Norman Bryson, ed., *Calligram: Essays in New Art History from France* (Cambridge: Cambridge University Press, 1988): 8-26.

Boorsch 1982: Suzanne Boorsch, *The Illustrated Bartsch 29: Italian Masters of the Sixteenth Century* (New York: Abaris Books, 1982).

Boorsch and Spike 1985: Suzanne Boorsch and John Spike, eds., *The Illustrated Bartsch 28: Italian Masters of the Sixteenth Century* (New York: Abaris, 1985).

Boorsch and Spike 1986: Suzanne Boorsch and John Spike, eds., *The Illustrated Bartsch 31: Italian Artists of the Sixteenth Century* (New York: Abaris, 1986).

Boorsch et al. 1985: Suzanne Boorsch, Michal Lewis and R.E. Lewis, *The Engravings of Giorgio Ghisi*, exh. cat. (New York, The Metropolitan Museum of Art, 1985).

Booth 1961: Wayne C. Booth, *The Rhetoric of Fiction* (Chicago: University of Chicago Press, 1961).

Bora 1987: Giulio Bora, "Per un catalogo dei disegni dei leonardeschi lombardi: Indicazioni e problemi di metodo," *Raccolta Vinciana* 22 (1987): 139-82.

Bora 2002: Giulio Bora, "Da Peterzano a Caravaggio: Un'ipotesi sulla pratica disegnativa," *Paragone Arte* 41-42 (2002): 3-20.

Bora et al. 1988: Giulio Bora et al., eds., *The Legacy of Leonardo: Painters in Lombardy 1490-1530* (Milan: Skira, 1988).

Bordignon Favero 1994: Elia Bordignon Favero, *Giovanni Battista Volpato: Critico e pittore* (Treviso: De Longhi, 1994).

Borea 1990: Evelina Borea, "Vasari e le stampe," *Prospettiva* 57-60 (1990): 18-38.

Borea 1992: Evelina Borea, "Giovan Pietro Bellori e la commodità delle stampe," *Documentary Culture* (1992): 263-85.

Borea 1993: Evelina Borea, "Le stampe dai primitivi e l'avvento della storiografia artistica illustrata," *Prospettiva* 69 (1993): 28-40; 70 (1993): 50-74.

Borea 2000: Evelina Borea, "Bellori 1645: Una lettera a Francesco Albani e la biografia di Caravaggio," *Prospettiva* 100 (2000): 57-69.

Borea and Gasparri 2000: Evelina Borea and Carlo Gasparri, eds., *L'idea del Bello: Viaggio per Roma nel Seicento con Giovan Pietro Bellori*, exh. cat. (Rome: De Luca, 2000).

Bossier 2004: Philiep Bossier, *'Ambasciatore della risa:' La commedia dell'arte nel secondo Cinquecento (1545-1590)* (Florence: Cesati, 2004).

Bottacin 2002: Francesca Bottacin, "Giochi di carte, inganni e cortigiane: Caravaggio e gli olandesi," *Critica d'Arte* 65 (2002): 70-79.

Bousquet 1953: Jacques Bousquet, "Documents inédits sur Caravage: La date des tableaux de la chapelle Saint-Matthieu à Saint-Louis-des-Français," *Revue de l'Art* 3 (1953): 103-05.

Boyd and Esler 2004: Jane Boyd and Philip E. Esler, *Visuality and Biblical Text: Interpreting Velázquez' 'Christ with Martha and Mary' as a Test Case* (Florence: Olschki, 2004).

Branigan 1992: Edward Branigan, *Narrative Comprehension and Film* (London: Routledge, 1992).

Brejon de Lavergnée 1991: Arnauld Brejon de Lavergnée, "Valentin portraitiste," *Revue de l'Art* 94 (1991): 66-8.

Brejon de Lavergnée and Cuzin 1973: Arnauld Brejon de Lavergnée and Jean-Pierre Cuzin, *I Caravaggeschi francesi*, exh. cat. (Rome: De Luca, 1973).

Brinkmann 2007: Bodo Brinkmann, ed., *Hexenlust und Sündenfall: Die seltsamen Phantasien des Hans Baldung Grien*, exh. cat. (Petersberg: Imhof, 2007).

Briganti 1982: Giuliano Briganti, *Pietro da Cortona o della pittura barocca* (Florence: Sansoni, 1982).

Brogi 2001: Alessandro Brogi, *Ludovico Carracci (1555-1619)* (Ozzano Emilia: Tipoarte, 2001).

Brothers 2008: Cammy Brothers, *Michelangelo, Drawing, and the Invention of Architecture* (New Haven: Yale University Press, 2008).

Brown 1981: David Allan Brown, *The Young Correggio and His Leonardesques Sources* (New York: Garland, 1981).

Brown 1992: David Allan Brown, "Il Cenacolo di Leonardo: La prima eco a Venezia," in Giovanna Nepi Sciré et al., eds., *Leonardo & Venezia*, exh. cat. (Milan: Bompiani, 1992): 85-96.

Brown 2001: David Allan Brown, "Quando *L'Ultima Cena* era nuova," in Pietro C. Marani, ed., *Il Genio e le Passioni* (Milan: Skira; and Florence: Artificio, 2001): 263-6.

Brown 2008: David Allan Brown, "Giorgione's *Man in Armor*," in Sylvia Ferino-Pagden, ed., *Giorgione Entmythisiert* (Turnhout: Brepols, 2008): 143-54.

Brown C. 1990: Clifford M. Brown, "The Picture Gallery of Gerolamo Garimberto Offered to the Duke of Bavaria," *Journal of the History of Collections* 2 (1990): 199-203.

Brown J. 1986: Jonathan Brown, *Velázquez: Painter and Courtier* (New Haven: Yale University Press, 1986).

Brunius 1967: Teddy Brunius, "Michelangelo's Non Finito," in Rudolf Zeitler, ed., *Contributions to the History and Theory of Art* (Uppsala: Almqvist & Wiksell, 1967): 29-67.

Bruyn 1985: J. Bruyn, "Review of Svetlana Alpers' *The Art of Describing: Dutch Art in the Seventeenth Century*," *Oud-Holland* 99 (1985): 155-60.

Bryson 1990: Norman Bryson, *Looking at the Overlooked: Four Essays on Still Life and Painting* (Cambridge: Harvard University Press, 1990).

Buffa 1982: Sebastian Buffa, *The Illustrated Bartsch. 34. Italian Artists of the Sixteenth Century* (New York: Abaris Books, 1982).

Buffa 1983: Sebastian Buffa, *The Illustrated Bartsch. 38. Italian Artists of the Sixteenth Century* (New York: Abaris Books, 1983).

Burgard 1998: Peter J. Burgard, "The Art of Dissimulation: Caravaggio's *Calling of St. Matthew*," *Pantheon* 56 (1998): 95-102.

Burke and Cherry 1997: Marcus B. Burke and Peter Cherry, *Collections of paintings in Madrid, 1601-1755* (Los Angeles: Provenance Index of the Getty Information Institute, 1997).

Bury 1985: Michael Bury, "The Taste for Prints in Italy to *c*.1600," *Print Quarterly* 1 (1985): 12-26.

Bury 2003: Michael Bury, "Giulio Mancini and the Organization of a Print Collection in Early Seventeenth-Century Italy," in Christopher Baker, Caroline Elam and Genevieve Warwick, eds., *Collecting Prints and Drawings in Europe, c. 1500-1750* (Aldershot: Ashgate, 2003): 79-84.

Butterfield 1997: Andrew Butterfield, *The Sculptures of Andrea del Verrocchio* (New Haven: Yale University Press, 1997).

Buzzi and Ferro 2005: Franco Buzzi and Roberta Ferro, eds., *Federico Borromeo fondatore della Biblioteca Ambrosiana: Atti delle giornate di studio…* (Rome: Bulzoni, 2005).

Buzzoni 1985: Andrea Buzzoni, ed., *Torquato Tasso tra letteratura, musica, teatro ed arti figurative*, exh. cat. (Bologna: Nuova Alfa 1985).

Calvesi 1990: Maurizio Calvesi, *Le realtà del Caravaggio* (Turin: Einaudi, 1990).

Campbell 2002: Stephen J. Campbell, "*Fare una cosa morta parer viva*: Michelangelo, Rosso, and the (Un)Divinity of Art," *Art Bulletin* 84 (2002): 596-620.

Campbell 2004: Stephen J. Campbell, "Counter-Reformation Polemic and Mannerist Counter-Aesthetics: Bronzino's *Martyrdom of St. Lawrence* in San Lorenzo," *RES* 46 (2004): 99-119.

Campbell 2005: Stephen J. Campbell, "Eros in the Flesh: Petrarchan Desire, the Embodied Eros and Male Beauty in Italian Art 1500-1540," *Journal of Medieval and Early Modern Studies* 35 (2005): 629-62.

Campi 1997: Emidio Campi, "Kruzifixus und Pietà Michelangelos für Vittoria Colonna: Der Versuch einer theologischen Interpretation," in Sylvia Ferino Pagden, ed., *Vittoria Colonna: Dichterin und Muse Michelangelos*, exh. cat. (Milan: Skira, 1997): 405-12.

Campori 1975: Giuseppe Campori, *Raccolta di cataloghi ed inventarii inediti di quadri, statue, disegni, bronzi, dorerie, smalti, medaglie, avori, ecc., dal secolo XV al secolo XIX* (Sala Bolognese: A. Forni, 1975).

Canova and Spiazzi 1997: Giordana Mariani Canova and Annamaria Spiazzi, "Il tema di Emmaus nella pittura veneziana e veneta," in Giordana Mariani Canova, Annamaria Spiazzi and Crispino Valenziano, eds., *Incontrarsi a Emmaus*, exh. cat. (Padua: Diocesi di Padova, 1997): 117-43.

Cappelletti 1993: Francesca Cappelletti, "The Documentary Evidence of the Early History of Caravaggio's *Taking of Christ*," *Burlington Magazine* 135 (1993): 742-46.

Cappelletti 2009: Francesca Cappelletti, *Caravaggio: Un ritratto somigliante* (Milan: Electa, 2009).

Cappelletti and Testa 1990a: Francesca Cappelletti and Laura Testa, "Ricerche documentarie sul 'San Giovanni Battista' dei Musei Capitolini e sul 'San Giovanni Battista' della Galleria Doria Pamphilj," in Giampaolo Correale, ed., *Identificazione di un Caravaggio: Nuove tecnologie per una rilettura del 'San Giovanni Battista'* (Venice: Marsilio, 1990): 75-84.

Cappelletti and Testa 1990b: Francesca Cappelletti and Laura Testa, "I quadri di Caravaggio nella collezione Mattei: I nuovi documenti e i riscontri con le fonti," *Storia dell'Arte* 69 (1990): 234-44.

Cappelletti and Testa 1994: Francesca Cappelletti and Laura Testa, *Il trattenimento di virtuosi: Le collezioni seicentesche di quadri nei Palazzi Mattei di Roma* (Rome: Argos, 1994).

Capretti 2009: Elena Capretti, "Federico Zuccari: L'uomo, l'artista, il teorico, il polemista," in Cristina Acidini Luchinat, ed., *Innocente e calunniato: Federico Zuccari (1539/40-1609) e le vendette d'artista* (Florence: Giunti, 2009): 80-83.

Caputo 2008: Vincenzo Caputo, "Gli 'abusi' dei pittori e la 'norma' dei trattatisti: Giovanni Andrea Gilio e Gabriele Paleotti," *Studi Rinascimentali* 6 (2008): 99-110

***Caravaggio e caravaggeschi* 1963**: *Caravaggio e caravaggeschi*, exh. cat. (Naples: Macchiaroli, 1963).

Cardinali et al. 2005: Marco Cardinali, Maria Beatrice De Ruggeri and Claudio Falcucci, "Le incisioni nel processo compositivo di Caravaggio: Dall'illuminazione del soggetto alla rappresentazione delle ombre," *Ricerche di Storia dell'Arte* 87 (2005): 50-62.

Caretta 2008: Paola Caretta, "Disegni Lombardo-veneti in relazione a Caravaggio," in Margherita Fratarcangeli, ed., *Intorno a Caravaggio: Dalla formazione alla fortuna* (Rome: Campisano Editore, 2008): 13-24.

Careri 2005: Giovanni Careri, *Gestes d'amour et de guerre: La Jérusalem delivrée, images et affects (XVIe-XVIIIe siècles)* (Paris: École des Hautes Études en Sciences Sociales, 2005).

Carr et al. 2006: Dawson Carr, ed., *Velázquez*, exh. cat. (London: National Gallery, 2006).

Carr D. et al. 2006: Diane Carr, David Buckingham, Andrew Burn and Gareth Schot, *Computer Games: Text, Narrative and Play* (Cambridge: Polity, 2006).

Carroll 1987: Eugene A. Carroll, *Rosso Fiorentino: Drawings, Prints, and Decorative Arts*, exh. cat. (Washington DC: National Gallery of Art, 1987).

Cassani and Sapio 2005: Silvia Cassani and Maria Sapio, eds., *Caravaggio: The Final Years*, exh. cat. (Milan: Electa, 2005).

Castagno 1994: Paul C. Castagno, *The Early Commedia dell'Arte (1550-1621): The Mannerist Context* (New York: Lang, 1994).

Causa 1992: Raffaello Causa, "La pittura del Seicento a Napoli dal naturalismo al barocco," in *Storia di Napoli* (Naples: Società Editrice Storia di Napoli, 1992).

Causa S. 2000: Stefano Causa, *Battistello Caracciolo: L'opera completa* (Naples, Electa, 2000).

Causa Picone 1993: Marina Causa Picone, "Giunte a Battistello: Appunti per una storia critica di Battistello disegnatore," *Paragone Arte* 44 (1993): 24-87.

Ceccarelli Pellegrino 1997: Alba Ceccarelli Pellegrino, "Gravures et légendes du *Recueil Frossard*: Essai d'analyse sémiologique," in Elio Moselle, ed., *La Commedia dell'arte tra Cinque e Seicento in Francia e in Europa: Atti del Convegno Internazionale di Studio, Verona-Vicenza, 19-21 ottobre 1995* (Fasano: Schena Editore, 1997): 129-57.

Chastel and Klein 1969: André Chastel and Robert Klein, eds., *De Sculptura (1504)...* (Geneva: Droz, 1969).

Chiabò and Doglio 1996: Maria Chiabò and Federico Doglio, eds., *Origini della commedia improvisa o dell'arte* (Rome: Torre d'Orfeo, 1996).

Chiappini di Sorio 1975: Ileana Chiappini di Sorio, *Cristoforo Roncalli detto il Pomarancio* (Bergamo: Bolis, 1975).

Choné 1992: Paulette Choné, ed., *Jacques Callot: 1592-1635*, exh. cat. (Paris: Réunion des Musées Nationaux, 1992).

Christiansen 1985: Keith Christiansen, ed., *The Age of Caravaggio*, exh. cat. (Milan: Electa, 1985).

Christiansen 1986: Keith Christiansen, "Caravaggio e *L'Esempio davanti del naturale*," *Art Bulletin* 68 (1986): 421-45.

Christiansen 1996: Keith Christiansen, "Thoughts on the Lombard Training of Caravaggio," in Mina Gregori, ed., *Come dipingeva il Caravaggio: Atti della giornata di studio* (Milan: Electa, 1996): 7-28.

Cieri Via 2007: Paola Cieri Via, "Riflessioni ecphrastiche nel 'De pictura' di Leon Battista Alberti," in Arturo Calzona, Francesco Paolo Fiore and Alberto Tenenti, eds., *Leon Battista Alberti teorico delle arti e gli impegni civili del 'De re aedificatoria'* (Florence: Olschki, 2007) 1: 275-85.

Cinotti 1983: *Michelangelo Merisi detto il Caravaggio: Tutte le opere*, in Gian Alberto dell'Acqua, ed., *I pittori bergamaschi dal XIII al XVIII secolo*, (Bergamo: Bolis, 1983).

Cinotti 1987: Mia Cinotti, "Caravaggio, gli enigmi: l'*Ecce Homo* Massimi," in Maurizio Calvesi, ed., *L'ultimo Caravaggio e la cultura artistica a Napoli e a Malta* (Syracuse: Ediprint, 1987): 43-58.

Cinotti 1991: Mia Cinotti, *Caravaggio: La vita e l'opera* (Bergamo: Bolis, 1991).

Cirillo Archer 1995: Madeline Cirillo Archer, *The Illustrated Bartsch. 28 Commentary: Italian Masters of the Sixteenth Century* (New York: Abaris, 1995).

Clarke 1996: Michael Clarke, ed., *Velázquez in Seville*, exh. cat. (Edinburgh: National Gallery of Scotland, 1996).

Cleri 1997: Bonita Cleri, ed., *Federico Zuccari: Le idee, gli scritti. Atti del Convegno di Sant'Angelo in Vado* (Milan: Electa, 1997).

Cocke 1984: Richard Cocke, *Veronese's Drawings* (London: Sotheby's, 1984).

Cohen C. 1996: Charles E. Cohen, *The Art of Giovanni Antonio da Pordenone: Between Dialect and Language* (New York: Cambridge University Press, 1996).

Cohen E. 2009: Elizabeth Cohen, "The Early Accademia di San Luca and Artists in Rome: A Historian's Observations," in Peter M. Lukehart, *The Accademia Seminars: The Accademia di San Luca in Rome, c.1590-1635* (Washington DC: National Gallery of Art, 2009): 325-45.

Colacicchi 1976: Giovanni Colacicchi, "Il Non Finito ed alcuni aspetti della pittura michelangiolesca," in *Tavola rotonda su Michelangelo* (Florence: Centro Internazionale del Libro, 1976): 52-62.

Colantuono 2006: Anthony Colantuono, "Caravaggio's Literary Culture," in Genevieve Warwick, ed., *Caravaggio: Realism, Rebellion, Reception* (Newark: University of Delaware Press, 2006): 57-68.

Cole 2001: Michael Cole, "The *Figura Sforzata*: Modelling, Power, and the Mannerist Body," *Art History* 24 (2001): 520-51.

Cole 2002: Michael W. Cole, *Cellini and The Principles of Sculpture* (Cambridge: Cambridge University Press, 2002).

Cole 2008: Michael Cole, "Giambologna and the Sculpture with No Name," *Oxford Art Journal* 31 (2008): 337-60.

Collareta 1988: Marco Collareta, "*Le arti sorelle*: Teoria e pratica del *paragone*," Giuliano Briganti, ed., *La pittura in Italia: Il Cinquecento* (Milan: Electa) 2: 569-80.

Collareta 2007: Marco Collareta, "Aspetti del 'paragone' al tempo di Tullio Lombardo," in Matteo Ceriana, ed., *Tullio Lombardo scultore e architetto nella Venezia del Cinquecento* (Verona: Cierre Edizioni, 2007): 183-85.

Colli 1994: Maddalena Colli, "Simone Peterzano e la Certosa di Garegnano," in *Certosa in nuova luce: Quattro itinerari inediti di arte, storia e architettura nella Certosa di Garegnano* (Milan: Cooperativa G. Donati, 1994): 81-97.

Conte 1974: Gian Biagio Conte, *Memoria dei poeti e sistema letterario: Catullo, Virgilio, Ovidio, Lucano* (Turin: Einaudi, 1974).

Contini 1991: Roberto Contini, *Il Cigoli* (Soncino: Edizioni del Soncino, 1991).

Coppa 1970: Simonetta Coppa, "Federico Borromeo teorico d'arte: Annotazioni in margine al *De pictura sacra* ed al *Musaeum*," *Arte Lombarda* 15 (1970): 65-70.

Corrain 2002: Lucia Corrain, "Cristo nell'orto di Caravaggio: Un esempio di narrazione prodromica," in Caterina Volpi, ed., *Caravaggio nel IV Centenario della Cappella Contarelli…*(s.l.: CAM, 2002): 221-32.

Correale 1990: Giampaolo Correale, ed., *Identificazione di un Caravaggio: Nuove tecnologie per una rilettura del 'San Giovanni Battista'* (Venice: Marsilio, 1990).

Corsato 1997: C. Corsato, "Emmaus nei Padri della Chiesa," in Giordana Mariani Canova, Annamaria Spiazzi and Crispino Valenziano, eds., *Incontrarsi a Emmaus*, exh. cat. (Padua: Diocesi di Padova, 1997): 27-35.

Corti 1989: Gino Corti, "Il 'Registro de' mandati' dell'ambasciatore ducale Piero Guicciardini e la committenza artistica fiorentina a Roma nel secondo decennio del Seicento," *Paragone Arte* 40 (1989): 108-46.

Cosmo 1999: Giulia Cosmo, "Guido Reni tra Masaccio e Caravaggio: Debiti e tributi," *Art e Dossier* 143 (1999): 35-38.

Costa Restagno 2004: Josepha Costa Restagno, *Ottavio Costa (1554-1639), le sue case e i suoi quadri: Ricerche di archivio* (Bordighera-Albenga: Istituto Internazionale di Studi Liguri, 2004).

Costello 1950: Jane Costello, "The Twelve Pictures 'Ordered by Velasquez' and the Trial of Valguarnera," *Journal of the Warburg and Courtauld Institutes* 13 (1950): 237-84.

Coutts 1987: Howard Coutts, "A Print and Two Drawings from the Circle of Zelotti," *Print Quarterly* 4 (1987): 47-50.

Covi 2005: Dario A. Covi, *Andrea del Verrocchio: Life and Work* (Florence: Olschki, 2005).

Cranston 2000: Jodi Cranston, *The Poetics of Portraiture in the Italian Renaissance* (New York: Cambridge University Press, 2000).

Cropper 1976: Elizabeth Cropper, "On Beautiful Women, Parmigianino, Petrarchismo and the Vernacular Style," *Art Bulletin* 58 (1976): 374-94.

Cropper 1986: Elizabeth Cropper, "The Beauty of Woman: Problems in the Rhetoric of Renaissance Portraiture," in Margaret W. Ferguson, Maureen Quilligan, and Nancy Vickers, eds., *Rewriting the Renaissance: The Discourses of Sexual Difference in Early Modern Europe* (Chicago: University of Chicago Press, 1986).

Cropper 1991: Elizabeth Cropper, "The Petrifying Art: Marino's Poetry and Caravaggio," *The Metropolitan Museum Journal* 26 (1991): 193-212.

Cropper 1995: Elizabeth Cropper, "The Place of Beauty in the High Renaissance and its Displacement in the History of Art," in Alvin Vos, ed., *Place and Displacement in the Renaissance* (Binghamton: Medieval and Renaissance Texts and Studies,1995): 159-205.

Cropper 2004: Elizabeth Cropper, "Pontormo and Bronzino in Philadelphia: A Double Portrait," Carl B. Strehlke, ed., *Pontormo, Bronzino and the Medici: The Transformation of the Renaissance Portrait in Florence*, exh. cat. (Philadelphia: Philadelphia Museum of Art, 2004): 11-14.

Cropper 2005: Elizabeth Cropper, *The Domenichino Affair: Novelty, Imitation, and Theft in Seventeenth-Century Rome* (New Haven: Yale University Press, 2005).

Cropper 2006: Elizabeth Cropper, "Caravaggio and the Matter of Lyric," in Genevieve Warwick, ed., *Caravaggio: Realism, Rebellion, Reception* (Newark: University of Delaware Press, 2006): 47-56.

Cropper 2008: Elizabeth Cropper, "I disegni del Guercino nel Gabinetto Disegni e Stampe degli Uffizi," in Nicholas Turner, ed., *Guercino: la scuola, la maniera, i disegni agli Uffizi*, exh. cat. (Florence: Olschki, 2008): 11-17.

Cropper 2009: Elizabeth Cropper, "Galileo Galilei e Artemisia Gentileschi tra storia delle idee e microstorie," in Lucia Tomasi Tongiorgi and Alessandro Tosi, eds., *Il cannocchiale e il pennello: Nuova scienza e nuova arte nell'età di Galileo*, exh. cat. (Florence: Giunti, 2009): 195-213.

Cummings 1974: Frederick Cummings, "Detroit's *Conversion of the Magdalene* (the Alzaga Caravaggio). I. Introduction. 3. The Meaning of Caravaggio's *Conversion of the Magdalene*," *Burlington Magazine* 116 (1974): 563-4, 572-8.

Curzietti 2004: Jacopo Curzietti, "Un interrogativo sulla *Presa di Cristo* di Caravaggio," in *Studi sul barocco romano: Scritti in onore di Maurizio Fagiolo dell'Arco* (Milan: Skira, 2004): 29-34

Cuzin 1975: Jean-Pierre Cuzin, "Problèmes du caravagisme: Pour Valentin," *Revue de l'Art* 28 (1975): 53-61.

Cuzin 1977: Jean-Pierre Cuzin, *La Diseuse de bonne aventure de Caravage* (Paris: Musées nationaux, 1977).

Czobor 1955: Ágnes Czobor, "Autoritratti del giovane Caravaggio," *Acta historiae artium Academiae Scientiarum Hungaricae* 2 (1955): 301-10.

DaCosta Kaufmann 2009: Thomas DaCosta Kaufmann, *Arcimboldo: Visual Jokes, Natural History, and Still-Life Painting* (Chicago: The University of Chicago Press, 2009).

Dagron 1991: Gilbert Dagron, "Holy Images and Likeness," *Dumbarton Oaks Papers* 45 (1991): 23-33.

Damisch 1987: Hubert Damisch, *L'origine de la perspective* (Paris: Flammarion, 1987).

Danesi Squarzina 1996: Silvia Danesi Squarzina, "Caravaggio e i Giustiniani," in Stefania Macioce, ed., *Michelangelo Merisi da Caravaggio: La vita e le opere attraverso i documenti* (Rome: Logart Press, 1996): 94-122.

Danesi Squarzina 2000: Silvia Danesi Squarzina, "Caravaggio e il teatro della crudeltà," in Claudio Strinati and Rossella Vodret, eds., *Caravaggio: La luce nella pittura lombarda*, exh. cat. (Milan: Electa, 2000): 89-101.

Danesi Squarzina 2001: Silvia Danesi Squarzina, ed., *Caravaggio e i Giustiniani: Toccar con mano una collezione del Seicento*, exh. cat. (Milan: Electa, 2001).

Danesi Squarzina 2003: Silvia Danesi Squarzina, *La Collezione Giustiniani* (Milan: Einaudi, 2003).

Daniele 2001: Umberto Daniele, "Da Pomponio Gaurico a Pierantonio degli Abbati: Sul 'terzo metodo' della prospettiva padovano," in Mario Piantoni and Laura De Rossi, eds., *Per l'arte: Da Venezia all'Europa* (Monfalcone: Edizioni della Laguna, 2001) 1: 149-52.

Da Pozzo 1995: Giovanni da Pozzo, ed., *La ragione e l'arte: Torquato Tasso e la Repubblica Veneta*, exh. cat. (Venice: Cardo, 1995).

Davis C. 2009: Charles Davis, "Michelangelo, 'Figura Serpentinata,' 'Bellezza del corpo,' 'Potentissima Virtù Immaginativa'," in Christian Hecht, ed., *Beständig im Wandel: Innovationen, Verwandlungen, Konkretisierung* (Berlin: Matthes & Seitz, 2009): 145-63.

Davis M. 2007: Margaret D. Davis, "Giovan Pietro Bellori: From Glyptic Interpretation to Pictorial Invention," in Wolfgang Augustyn and Eckhard Leuschner, eds., *Kunst und Humanismus: Festschrift für Gosbert Schüßler zum 60. Geburtstag* (Passau: Klinger, 2007): 515-29.

De Benedetti 1951: Michele De Benedetti, "Il cosidetto 'non finito' di Michelangelo e la sua ultima Pietà," *Emporium* 57 (1951): 99-108.

De Benedictis and Roani 2005: Christina De Benedictis and Roberta Roani, *Riflessioni sulle 'Regole per comprare, collocare e conservare pitture' di Giulio Mancini* (Florence: Edifir Edizioni, 2005).

DeGrazia 1979: Diane DeGrazia Bohlin, *Prints and Related Drawings by the Carracci Family: A Catalogue Raisonné* (Washington DC: National Gallery of Art, 1979).

De Hoop Scheffer 1980: Dieuwke de Hoop Scheffer, *Hollstein's Dutch and Flemish Etchings, Engravings and Woodcuts, ca. 1450-1700: 21. Aegidius Sadeler-Raphael Sadeler II* (Amsterdam: M. Hertzberger, 1980).

De Jongh 1984: Eddy de Jongh, "Review of Svetlana Alpers' *The Art of Describing: Dutch Art in the Seventeenth Century*," *Simiolus* 14 (1984): 51-9.

Dell'Acqua and Cinotti 1971: Gian Alberto Dell'Acqua and Mia Cinotti, *Il Caravaggio e le sue grandi opere da San Luigi dei Francesi* (Milan: Rizzoli, 1971).

Della Pergola 1955: Paola Della Pergola, *Galleria Borghese: I dipinti* (Rome: Istituto Poligrafico dello Stato, 1955).

De Marco 1982: Nicholas De Marco, "Caravaggio's *Calling of Saint Matthew,*" *Iris: Notes on the History of Art* (1982): 5-7.

Dempsey 1986: Charles Dempsey, "The Carracci *Postille* to Vasari's Lives,"*Art Bulletin* 68 (1986): 72-6.

Dempsey 1990: Charles Dempsey, "*Dormition* with a Difference," *Times Literary Supplement* (7-18 December 1990), 1322.

Dempsey 2000: Charles Dempsey, *Annibale Carracci and the Beginnings of Baroque Style: Second Edition with New Introduction and Select Bibliography* (Fiesole: Cadmo, 2000).

Dempsey 2006: Charles Dempsey, "Caravaggio and the Two Naturalistic Styles: Specular versus Macular," in Genevieve Warwick, ed., *Caravaggio: Realism, Rebellion, Reception* (Newark: University of Delaware Press, 2006): 91-100.

Dempsey 2009: Charles Dempsey, "*Disegno* and Logos, *Paragone* and Academy," in Peter M. Lukehart, ed., *The Academia Seminars: The Accademia di San Luca in Rome, c. 1590-1635* (Washington DC: National Gallery of Art, 2009): 43-53.

Dempsey 2010: Charles Dempsey, "Review of Stuart Lingo, *Federico Barocci: Allure and Devotion in Late Renaissance Painting,*" *Art Bulletin* 92 (2010): 251-56.

De Ramaix 1997: Isabelle de Ramaix, *The Illustrated Bartsch. 72, Part 1: Aegidius Sadeler II* (New York: Abaris, 1997).

De Ramaix 1999: Isabelle de Ramaix, *The Illustrated Bartsch. 70, Part 1: Johan Sadeler I* (New York: Abaris, 1999).

De Ramaix 2001: Isabelle de Ramaix, *The Illustrated Bartsch. 70, Part 2: Johan Sadeler I* (New York: Abaris, 2001).

Deshman 1997: Robert Deshman, "Another Look at the Disappearing Christ: Corporeal and Spiritual Vision in Early Medieval Images," Art Bulletin 79 (1997): 518-46.

De Tolnay 1953: Charles de Tolnay, "Michelangelo's *Pietà*: Composition for Vittoria Colonna," *Record of the Princeton University Art Museum* 12 (1953): 44-62.

De Tolnay 1969: Charles De Tolnay, *Michelangelo* (Princeton: Princeton University Press, 1969).

De Tolnay 1975-1980: Charles De Tolnay, *Corpus dei disegni di Michelangelo* (Novara: Istituto Geografico De Agostini, 1975-1980).

De Winkel 2006: Marieke de Winkel, *Fashion and Fancy: Dress and Meaning in Rembrandt's Paintings* (Amsterdam: Amsterdam University Press, 2006).

Di Giampaolo 2000: Mario Di Giampaolo, "Simone Peterzano: Qualche aggiunta al corpus dei disegni," in Valerio Terraroli and Franca Varallo, eds., *L'arte nella storia: Contributi di critica e storia dell'arte per Gianni Carlo Sciolla* (Milan: Skira, 2000): 353-4.

Di Giampaolo and Muzzi 1990: Mario Di Giampaolo and Andrea Muzzi, *Le Corrège: Les dessins* (Turin: Umberto Allemandi, 1990).

Di Stefano 2000: Elisabetta Di Stefano, *L'altro sapere: Bello, arte, imagine in Leon Battista Alberti* (Palermo: Centro Internazionale Studi di Estetica, 2000).

Di Stefano 2007: Elisabetta Di Stefano, "Leon Battista Alberti e l'idea della bellezza," in Arturo Calzona, Francesco Paolo Fiore and Alberto Tenenti, eds., *Leon Battista Alberti teorico delle arti e gli impegni civili del 'De re aedificatoria'* (Florence: Olschki, 2007) 1: 33-45.

Di Vito 2007: Mauro di Vito, "*Foglie stravolte e luccicanti*: Il *verbascum* nel Caravaggio," *Paragone Arte* 73 (2007): 69-89.

Dixon 1983: John W. Dixon, "Michelangelo's *Last Judgment*: Drama of Judgment or Drama of Redemption," *Iconography* 9 (1983): 67-82.

Dolcini 1992: Loretta Dolcini, ed., *Il maestro di Leonardo: Il restauro dell'Incredulità di San Tommaso di Andrea del Verrocchio* (Cinisello Balsamo: Silvana, 1992).

Dolders 1987: Arno Dolders, *The Illustrated Bartsch. 56. Netherlandish Artists: Philips Galle* (New York: Abaris Book, 1987).

Domínguez Ortiz et al. 1989: Antonio Domínguez Ortiz, Alfonso E. Pérez Sánchez and Julián Gallego, *Velázquez*, exh. cat. (New York: Metropolitan Museum of Art, 1989).

Duchartre 1966: Pierre-Louis Duchartre: *The Italian Comedy, the Improvisation Scenarios, Lives, Attributes, Portraits, and Masks of the Illustrious Characters of the Commedia dell'arte*, trans. Randolph T. Weaver (New York: Dover, 1966).

Duro 1997: Paul Duro, *The Academy and the Limits of Painting in Seventeenth-Century France* (New York: Cambridge University Press, 1997).

Ebert-Schifferer 2009: Sybille Ebert-Schifferer, *Caravaggio: Sehen—Staunen—Glauben: Der Maler und sein Werk* (Munich: C.H. Beck, 2009).

Eco 1979: Umberto Eco, *Lector in fabula: La cooperazione interpretativa nei testi narrativi* (Milan: Bompiani, 1979).

Emiliani 1993: Andrea Emiliani, ed., *Ludovico Carracci*, exh. cat. (Bologna: Nuova Alfa Editoriale, 1993).

Emiliani and Venturi 1997: Andrea Emiliani and Gianni Venturi, eds., *Tasso, Tiziano e i pittori del parlar disgiunto: Un laboratorio tra le arti sorelle*, exh. cat. (Venice: Marsilio, 1997).

Emison 2004: Patricia A. Emison, *Creating the 'Divine' Artist: From Dante to Michelangelo* (Leiden: Brill, 2004).

Eymard 1975: Julien Eymard, *Le Thème du miroir dans la poésie française (1540-1815)* (unpublished doctoral dissertation: University of Lille, 1975).

Fagiolo Dell'Arco 1996: Maurizio Fagiolo Dell'Arco, "La vera *Galeria* del Cavalier Marino: l'apparato in morte (1625) nell'Accademia degli Humoristi," *Strenna Romanista* (1996): 293-303.

Faietti 1993: Marzia Faietti, "Da Costanza a Zwolle: Grafica renana del Quattrocento nella Pinacoteca Nazionale di Bologna," in Béatrice Hernad, *Pinacoteca Nazionale di Bologna, Gabinetto dei Disegni e delle Stampe. Catalogo Generale delle Incisioni. VIII: Inventario degli Incisori Tedeschi e Fiamminghi del secolo XV* (Bologna: Arts & Co., 1993): 19-37.

Falk 1980: Tilman Falk, *The Illustrated Bartsch. 11. Sixteenth-Century German Artists: Hans Burgkmair the Elder, Hans Schäufelein, Lucas Cranach the Elder* (New York: Abaris Books, 1980).

Fallay D'Este 2001: Laurianne Fallay D'Este, *L'Art de la peinture: Peinture et théorie à Séville au temps de Francisco Pacheco (1564-1644)* (Paris: Champion, 2001).

Farago 1992: Claire Farago, *Leonardo da Vinci's 'Paragone:' A Critical Interpretation with a New Edition of the Text in the 'Codex Urbinas'* (Leiden: Brill, 1992).

Featherstone 2006: Rupert Featherstone, "The 'Resurrection' of *The Calling of Saints Peter and Andrew*," in *Come lavorava Caravaggio*, exh. cat. (Rome: Viviani Editore, 2006): 36-48.

Fehl 2002: Philipp Fehl, "Michelangelo's Tomb in Rome: Observations on the *Pietà* in Florence and the Rondanini *Pietà*," *Artibus et Historiae* 45 (2002): 9-27.

Feigenbaum 1989: Gail Feigenbaum, "*The Kiss of Judas* by Lodovico Carracci," *Record of the Art Museum Princeton University* 48 (1989): 3-18.

Feigenbaum 1993: Gail Feigenbaum, "La pratica nell'Accademia dei Carracci," *Accademia Clementina: Atti e Memorie* 32 (1993): 169-200.

Feigenbaum 1997: Gail Feigenbaum, "Gamblers, Cheats and Fortune-Tellers," in Philip Conisbee, ed., *Georges de La Tour and His World*, exh. cat. (Washington DC: National Gallery of Art, 1997): 150-81.

Fend 2005: Mechthild Fend, "Körpersehen: Über das Haptische bei Alois Riegl," in Andreas Meyer and Alexandre Métraux, eds., *Kunstmaschinen: Spielräume des Sehens zwischen Wissenschaft und Ästhetik* (Frankfurt: Fischer, 2005): 166-202.

Fend 2007a: Mechthild Fend, "Die Substanz der Oberfläche: Haut und Fleisch in der französischen Kunsttheorie des 17. bis 19. Jahrhunderts," in Daniela Bohde and Mechthild Fend, eds., *Weder Haut noch Fleisch: Das Inkarnat in der Kunstgeschichte* (Berlin: Mann, 2007): 87-104.

Fend 2007b: Mechthild Fend, "Sehen und Tasten: Zur Raumwahrnehmung bei Alois Riegl und in der Sinnesphysiologie des 19. Jahrhunderts," in Barbara Lange, ed., *Visualisierte Körperkonzepte: Strategien in der Kunst der Moderne* (Berlin: Reimer, 2007): 15-38.

Fend and Koos 2004: Mechthild Fend and Marianne Koos, eds., *Männlichkeit im Blick: Visuelle Inszenierungen in der Kunst seit der Frühen Neuzeit* (Cologne: Böhlau, 2004).

Ferino-Pagden 1990: Sylvia Ferino-Pagden, in *Titian Prince of Painters*, exh. cat. (Venice: Marsilio, 1990).

Ferino-Pagden 2007: Sylvia Ferino-Pagden, *Late Titian and the Sensuality of Painting*, exh. cat. (Venice: Marsilio, 2007).

Ferrari 2006: Simone Ferrari, *Jacopo de' Barbari: Un protagonista del Rinascimento tra Venezia e Dürer* (Milan: Mondadori, 2006).

Ferrone 1993: Siro Ferrone, *Attori mercanti corsari: La commedia dell'arte in Europa tra Cinque e Seicento* (Turin: Einaudi, 1993).

Finaldi 1998: Gabriele Finaldi, ed., *Caravaggio: The Flagellation of Christ, a Loan from the Musée des Beaux-Arts Rouen at the National Gallery* (London: National Gallery, 1998).

Finaldi 2000: Gabriele Finaldi, ed., *The Image of Christ*, exh. cat. (London: National Gallery, 2000).

Finney 1997: Paul C. Finney, *The Invisible God: The Earliest Christians on Art* (Oxford: Oxford University Press, 1997).

Fiocco 1928: Giuseppe Fiocco, *Paolo Veronese: 1528-1588* (Bologna: Apollo, 1928).

Fiorio 1974: Maria Teresa Fiorio, "Note su alcuni disegni inediti di Simone Peterzano," *Arte Lombarda* 19 (1974): 87-100.

Fiorio 1989: Maria Teresa Fiorio, "Simone Peterzano nella Milano borromaica," *Osservatorio delle Arti* 3 (1989): 59-63.

Fiorio 2000: Maria Teresa Fiorio, *Giovanni Antonio Boltraffio: Un pittore milanese nel lume di Leonardo* (Milan: Janda Sapi, 2000).

Fiorio 2003: Maria Teresa Fiorio, "Simone Peterzano: Il ciclo pittorico nel presbiterio," in Carlo Capponi, ed., *La Certosa di Garegnano in Milano* (Cinisello Balsamo: Silvana Editoriale, 2003): 80-9.

Firpo and Mongini 2008: Massimo Firpo and Guido Mongini, eds., *Ludovico Castelvetro: Letterati e grammatici nella crisi religiosa del Cinquecento…* (Florence: Olschki, 2008).

Forcellino 2002: Antonio Forcellino, *Michelangelo Buonarroti: Storia di una passione eretica* (Turin: Einaudi, 2002).

Fornari Schianchi 2008: Lucia Fornari Schianchi, ed., *Correggio*, exh. cat. (Milan: Skira, 2008).

Fornari Schianchi and Ferino-Pagden 2003: Lucia Fornari Schianchi and Sylvia Ferino-Pagden, *Parmigianino e il manierismo europeo*, exh. cat. (Cinisello Balsamo: Silvana, 2003).

Forster and Locher 1999: Kurt W. Forster and Hubert Locher, eds., *Theorie der Praxis: Leon Battista Alberti als Humanist und Theoretiker der bildenden Künste* (Berlin: Akademie, 1999).

Fortini Brown 1988: Patricia Fortini Brown, *Venetian Narrative Painting in the Age of Carpaccio* (New Haven: Yale University Press, 1988).

Francastel 1938: Pierre Francastel, "Le réalisme de Caravage," *Gazette des Beaux-Arts* 140 (1938): 45-62.

Franits 1997: Wayne Franits, ed., *Looking at Seventeenth-Century Dutch Art: Realism Reconsidered* (Cambridge: Cambridge University Press, 1997).

Franklin 1994: David Franklin, *Rosso in Italy: The Italian Career of Rosso Fiorentino* (New Haven: Yale University Press, 1994).

Franklin 2003: David Franklin, ed., *The Art of Parmigianino*, exh. cat. (Ottawa: National Gallery of Art, 2003).

Franklin 2005: David Franklin, ed., *Leonardo da Vinci, Michelangelo, and the Renaissance in Florence*, exh. cat. (Ottawa: National Gallery of Art, 2005).

Freedberg S. 1983: Sydney J. Freedberg, *Circa 1600: A Revolution of Style in Italian Painting* (Cambridge: Harvard University Press, 1983).

Freedberg D. 1989: David Freedberg, *The Power of Images: Studies in the History and Theory of Response* (Chicago: Chicago University Press, 1989).

Freedman 1985: Luba Freedman, "Bartolomeo Maranta on a Painting by Titian," *The Hebrew University Studies in Literature and the Arts* 13 (1985): 175-201

Frey 1923-1930: Karl Frey, *Der literariche Nachlass Giorgio Vasaris* (Munich: Müller, 1923-1930).

Fried 1997: Michael Fried, "Thoughts on Caravaggio," *Critical Inquiry* 24 (1997): 13-56.

Fried 2010: Michael Fried, *The Moment of Caravaggio* (Princeton: Princeton University Press, 2010).

Friedlaender 1945: Walter Friedlaender, "The *Crucifixion of St. Peter*: Caravaggio and Reni," *Journal of the Warburg and Courtauld Institutes* 8 (1945): 152-60.

Friedlaender 1969: Walter Friedlaender, *Caravaggio Studies* (New York: Schocken Books, 1969).

Frommel 1971: Christoph L. Frommel, "Caravaggios Frühwerk und der Kardinal Francesco Maria Del Monte," *Storia dell'Arte* 9-10 (1971): 5-52.

Frommel 1996: Christoph L. Frommel, "Caravaggio, Minniti e il cardinal Francesco Maria del Monte," in Stefania Macioce, ed., *Michelangelo Merisi da Caravaggio: La vita e le opere attraverso i documenti* (Rome: Logart Press, 1996): 18-41.

Fulco 1979: Giorgio Fulco, "Il sogno di una Galleria: Nuovi documenti sul Marino collezionista," *Antologia di Belle Arti* 3 (1979): 84-99.

Fulco 1980: Giorgio Fulco, "*Ammirate l'altissimo pittore*: Caravaggio nelle rime inedite di Marzio Milesi," *Ricerche di Storia dell'Arte* 10 (1980): 65-90.

Fulco 2001: Giorgio Fulco, *La maravigliosa passione: Studi sul barocco tra letteratura ed arte* (Rome: Salerno, 2001).

Fumaroli 1982: Marc Fumaroli, "Muta Eloquentia: La représentation de l'éloquence dans l'œuvre de Nicolas Poussin," *Bulletin de la Société de l'Histoire de l'Art Français* (1982): 29-48.

Fumaroli 1988: Marc Fumaroli, "La *Galeria* de Marino et la Galerie Farnèse: Épigrammes et œuvres d'art profanes vers 1600," in André Chastel, ed., *Les Carrache et les décors profanes: Actes du Colloque organisé par l'École française de Rome (Rome, 2-4 octobre 1986)* (Rome: De Boccard, 1988).

Gabrielli 2009: Francesca Maria Gabrielli, "God, Gender, and Friendship: A Reading of Michelangelo's *Pietà* and Vittoria Colonna's Sonnet 87," in Lindsay Eufusia, Elena Bellina and Paola Ugolini, eds., *About Face: Depicting the Self in the Written and Visual Arts* (Newcastle upon Tyne: Cambridge Scholars Publishing, 2009): 57-70.

Gage 2008: Frances Gage, "Exercise for Mind and Body: Giulio Mancini, Collecting, and the Beholding of Landscape Painting in the Seventeenth Century," *Renaissance Quarterly* 61 (2008): 1167-207.

Gage 2009: Frances Gage, "Giulio Mancini and Artist-Amateur Relations in Seventeenth-Century Roman Academies," in Peter M. Lukehart, ed., *The Accademia Seminars: The Accademia di San Luca in Rome, c. 1590-1635* (Washington DC: National Gallery of Art, 2009): 247-87.

Gallo 1996: Marco Gallo, "Il *Sacrificio di Isacco* di Caravaggio agli Uffizi come meccanica visiva della *satisfactio*," in Stefania Macioce, ed., *Michelangelo Merisi da Caravaggio: La vita e le opere attraverso i documenti* (Rome: Logart Press, 1996): 331-60.

Gareffi 2009: Andrea Gareffi, "Il disegno di Federico Zuccari," in Marina Formica, ed., *Roma e la campagna romana nel Grand Tour: Atti del convegno interdisciplinare* (Bari: Laterza, 2009): 105-26.

Garrard 1988: Mary D. Garrard, *Artemisia Gentileschi: The Image of the Female Hero in Italian Baroque Art* (Princeton: Princeton University Press, 1988).

Gash 1998: John Gash, "Review of Mina Gregori, ed., *Come dipingeva il Caravaggio: Atti della giornata di studi* (Milan: Electa, 1996)," *Burlington Magazine* 140 (1998): 41-2.

Gaskell 1984: Ivan Gaskell, "Review of Svetlana Alpers' *The Art of Describing: Dutch Art in the Seventeenth Century*," *Oxford Art Journal* 7 (1984): 57-60.

Gaudreault 1999: André Gaudreault, *Du littéraire au filmique* (Paris: Armand Colin, 1999).

Gauna 1998: Chiara Gauna, "Giudizi e polemiche intorno a Caravaggio e Tiziano nei trattati d'arte spagnoli del XVII secolo: Carducho, Pacheco e la tradizione artistica italiana," *Ricerche di Storia dell'Arte* 64 (1998): 57-78.

Gavazza et al. 1995: Ezia Gavazza, Giovanna Nepi Sciré and Giovanna Rotondi Terminiello, eds., *Bernardo Strozzi: Genova 1581/82—Venezia 1644*, exh. cat. (Milan: Electa, 1995).

Gazier 1891: Auguste Gazier, "La critique d'art au XVIIe siècle: Lettres inédites relatives à Philippe et Jean-Baptiste de Champaigne," *L'Art: Revue bi-mensuelle illustrée* 51 (1891): 113-20.

Geimer 2003: Peter Geimer, "Times of Perception: Lessing, Manet, Londe," in Antoinette Roesler-Friedenthal and Johannes Nathan, eds., *The Enduring Instant: Time and Spectator in the Visual Arts* (Berlin: Gebr. Mann Verlag, 2003): 93-9.

Geisberg 1924: Max Geisberg, *Der Meister E.S.* (Leipzig: von Klinkhardt, 1924).

Genette 2007: Gérard Genette, *Discours du récit* (Paris: Éditions du Seuil, 2007).

Gentili 1992: Augusto Gentili, "Tiziano e il non finito," *Venezia Cinquecento* 2 (1992): 93-127.

Gentili 2007: Augusto Gentili, "Problemi dell'ultimo Tiziano: Finito e non finito tra variazioni e perdite di senso," in Lionello Puppi, ed., *Tiziano: L'ultimo atto*, exh. cat. (Milan: Skira, 2007): 135-43.

Gentilini 1992: Giancarlo Gentilini, *I Della Robbia: La scultura invetriata nel Rinascimento* (Florence: Cantini, 1992).

Germer 1997: Stefan Germer, *Kunst—Macht—Diskurs: Die intellektuelle Karriere des André Félibien im Frankreich von Louis XIV* (Munich: Fink, 1997).

Ghirardi 1990: Angela Ghirardi, *Bartolomeo Passerotti* (Rimini: Luisè Editori, 1990).

Gilbert 1995: Creighton E. Gilbert, *Caravaggio and His Two Cardinals* (University Park: Pennsylvania State Press, 1995).

Gilbert 2003: Creighton E. Gilbert, "What is expressed in Michelangelo's Non-Finito," *Artibus et Historiae* 24 (2003): 57-64.

Glynne 1984: Jonathan Glynne, "Review of Svetlana Alpers, *The Art of Describing: Dutch Art in the Seventeenth Century*," *Art History* 7 (1984): 247-52.

Goffen 1989: Rona Goffen, *Giovanni Bellini* (New Haven: Yale University Press, 1989).

Goffen 1997: Rona Goffen, *Titian's Women* (New Haven: Yale University Press, 1997).

Goldstein 1971: Carl Goldstein, "Attitudes towards Caravaggio in Seventeenth-Century France," *The Art Quarterly* 34 (1971): 345-55.

Goldstein 1988: Carl Goldstein, *Visual Fact over Verbal Fiction: A Study of the Carracci and the Criticism, Theory, and Practice of Art in Renaissance and Baroque Italy* (Cambridge: Cambridge University Press, 1988).

Goodman 1983a: Elise Goodman Soellner, "Poetic Interpretations of the Lady at Her Toilette Theme in Sixteenth-Century Painting," *The Sixteenth-Century Journal* 14 (1983): 426-42.

Goodman 1983b: Elise Goodman Soellner, "Nicolas Lancret's *Le Miroir Ardent*: An Emblematic Image of Love," *Simiolus* 13 (1983): 218-24.

Gould 1976: Cecil Gould, *The Paintings of Correggio* (Ithaca: Cornell University Press, 1976).

Graeve 1958: Mary Anne Graeve, "The Stone of Unction in Caravaggio's Painting for the *Chiesa Nuova*," *Art Bulletin* 40 (1958): 223-37.

Grafton 2003: Anthony Grafton, "*Historia* and *Istoria*: Alberti's Terminology in context," in John Jeffries Martin, ed., *The Renaissance: Italy and Abroad* (London: Routledge, 2003): 199-223.

Grassi 1948: Luigi Grassi, "Osservazioni sul 'non finito' nella storia del disegno," in *Atti del primo Convegno internazionale per le arti figurative* (Florence: Edizioni U, 1948): 34-6.

Grayson 1993: Cecil Grayson, "Leon Battista Alberti and the Beginnings of the Italian Grammar," in George Holnes, ed., *Art and Politics in Renaissance Italy: British Academy Lectures* (Oxford: Oxford University Press, 1993): 91-112.

Greaves and Johnson 1974: James L. Greaves and Meryl Johnson, "Detroit's *Conversion of the Magdalen* (the Alzaga Caravaggio). 2. New Findings on Caravaggio's Technique in the Detroit *Magdalen*," Burlington Magazine 116 (1974): 564-72.

Greenstein 1992: Jack M. Greenstein, *Mantegna and Painting as Historical Narrative* (Chicago: University of Chicago Press, 1992).

Gregori 1975: Mina Gregori, "Significato delle mostre caravaggesche dal 1951 a oggi," in Mia Cinotti, ed., *Novità sul Caravaggio: Saggi e contributi* (Milan: Amilcare Pizzi, 1975): 27-60.

Gregori 1976: Mina Gregori, "Addendum to Caravaggio: The Cecconi *Crowning with Thorns* Reconsidered," *Burlington Magazine* 118 (1976): 671-80.

Gregori 1991: Mina Gregori, ed., *Michelangelo Merisi da Caravaggio: Come nascono i capolavori*, exh. cat. (Milan: Electa, 1991).

Gregori 1992: Mina Gregori, "Sul venetismo di Simone Peterzano," *Arte Documento* 6 (1992): 263-9.

Greve 2008: David Greve, *Status und Statue: Studien zum Leben und Werk des Florentiner Bildhauers Baccio Bandinelli* (Berlin: Frank & Timme, 2008).

Gronau 1930: Georg Gronau, *Klassiker der Kunst in Gesamtausgaben: Giovanni Bellini …* (New York: E. Weyhe, 1930).

Grosshans 1980: Rainald Grosshans, *Maerten van Heemskerck: Die Gemälde* (Berlin: Horst Boettcher, 1980).

Grossman 1984: Sheldon Grossman, ed., *Caravaggio: The Deposition from the Vatican Collections*, exh. cat. (Washington DC: National Gallery of Art, 1984).

Gründler 2009: Hana Gründler, ed., *Das Leben des Baccio Bandinelli: Giorgio Vasari* (Berlin: Wagenbach, 2009).

Guardiani 1988: Francesco Guardiani, "L'idea dell'immagine nella *Galeria* di Giovan Battista Marino," in Antonio Franceschetti, ed., *Letteratura italiana ed arti figurative…*(Florence: Olschki, 1988): 647-54.

Guarino 1999: Sergio Guarino, "The Fortune Teller," in Maria Elisa Tittoni, Patrizia Masini and Sergio Guarino, eds., *Caravaggio's 'St. John' and Masterpieces from the Capitoline Museum*, exh.cat. (Hartford: Wadsworth Atheneum, 1999): 34-49.

Gunning 2000: Tom Gunning, *The Films of Fritz Lang: Allegories of Vision and Modernity* (London: British Film Institute, 2000).

Hall 1976: Marcia B. Hall, "Michelangelo's *Last Judgment*: Resurrection of the Body and Predestination," *Art Bulletin* 58 (1976): 85-92.

Hall 2005: Marcia B. Hall, ed., *Michelangelo's Last Judgment* (Cambridge: Cambridge University Press, 2005).

Halliwell 2002: Stephen Halliwell, *The Aesthetics of Mimesis: Ancient Texts and Modern Problems* (Princeton: Princeton University Press, 2002).

Harris 1982: Enriqueta Harris, *Velázquez* (Ithaca: Cornell University Press, 1982).

Hartje 2004: Nicole Hartje, *Bartolomeo Manfredi (1582-1622): Ein Nachfolger Caravaggios und seine Europäische Wirkung. Monographie und Werkverzeichnis* (Weimar: VDG, 2004).

Hartlaub 1951: Gustav Friedrich Hartlaub, *Zauber des Spiegels: Geschichte und Bedeutung des Spiegels in der Kunst* (Munich: Piper, 1951).

Hass 1988: Angela Hass, "Caravaggio's *Calling of Saint Matthew* Reconsidered," *Journal of the Warburg and Courtauld Institutes* 51 (1988): 245-50.

Hecht 1997: Christian Hecht, *Katholische Bildertheologie im Zeitalter von Gegenreformation und Barock: Studien zu den Traktaten von Johannes Molanus, Gabriele Paleotti und anderen Authoren* (Berlin: Mann, 1997).

Hegener 2008: Nicole Hegener, *DIVI IACOBI EQUES: Selbstdarstellung im Werk des Florentiner Bildhauers Baccio Bandinelli* (Munich and Berlin: Deutscher Kunstverlag, 2008).

Heikamp 1966: Detlef Heikamp, "In margine alla vita di Baccio Bandinelli del Vasari," *Paragone Arte* 17 (1966): 52-62.

Heimbürger 1998: Mina Heimbürger, "Caravaggio e Dürer," *Paragone Arte* 49 (1998): 19-48.

Hémery 2001: Axel Hémery, ed., *Nicolas Tournier 1590-1639: Un peintre caravagesque*, exh. cat. (Paris: Somogy, 2001).

Henke 2002: Robert Henke, *Performance and Literature in the* Commedia dell'Arte (Cambridge: Cambridge University Press, 2002).

Hermann Fiore 1982: Kristina Hermann Fiore, "Disegno and Giudizio: Allegorical Drawings by Federico Zuccaro and Cherubino Alberti," *Master Drawings* 20 (1982): 247-56.

Hermann Fiore 1995: Kristina Hermann Fiore, "Caravaggio's *Taking of Christ* and Dürer's Woodcut of 1509," *Burlington Magazine* 137 (1995): 24-7.

Hermann Fiore 2000: Kristina Hermann Fiore, "Caravaggio e la quadreria del Cavalier d'Arpino," in Claudio Strinati and Rossella Vodret, eds., *Caravaggio: La luce nella pittura lombarda*, exh. cat. (Milan: Electa, 2000): 57-76.

Hess D. 1994: Daniel Hess, *Meister um das "mittelalterliche Hausbuch": Studien zur Hausbuchmeisterfrage* (Mainz: P. von Zabern, 1994).

Hess J. 1951: Jacob Hess, "The Chronology of the Contarelli Chapel," Burlington Magazine 93 (1951): 186-201.

Hibbard 1983: Howard Hibbard, *Caravaggio* (New York: Harper & Row, 1983).

Hinks 1953: Roger P. Hinks, *Michelangelo Merisi da Caravaggio: His Life—His Legacy—His Works* (London: Faber and Faber, 1953).

Hinz B. 1974: Berthold Hinz, "Studien zur Geschichte des Ehepaarbildnisses," *Marburger Jahrbuch für Kunstwissenschaft* 19 (1974): 139-218.

Hinz P. 1973: Paulus Hinz, *Deus Homo: Das Christusbild von seine Ursprüngen bis zur Gegenwart* (Berlin: Evangelische Verlaganstalt, 1973).

Hirdt 1998: Willi Hirdt, "Caravaggio's *Wahrsagende Zigeunerin*: Versuch einer Deutung," in Birgit Tappert and Willi Jung, eds., *Willi Hirdt: Lesen und Sehen. Aufsätze zu Literatur und Malerei in Italien und Frankreich. Festschrift zum 60. Geburtstag* (Tübingen: Stauffenburg, 1998): 75-111.

Hirst 1981: Michael Hirst, *Sebastiano del Piombo* (Oxford: Clarendon Press, 1981).

Hochmann 1988: Michel Hochmann, "Les annotations marginales de Federico Zuccaro à un exemplaire des *Vies* de Vasari: La réaction anti-vasarienne à la fin du XVIᵉ siècle," *Revue de l'Art* 80 (1988): 64-71.

Hockney 2006: David Hockney, *Secret Knowledge: Rediscovering the Lost Techniques of the Old Masters* (New York: Viking Studio, 2006).

Hoff 2003: Michael Hoff, "Epiphanie im non-finito: Nichtvollendung als Strategie der Frömmigkeit und Auslöser von Sinnzuschreibung in der Kunst der Florentiner Renaissance," in Friedrich Weltzien and Amrei Volkmann, eds., *Modelle künstlerischer Produktion: Architektur, Kunst, Literatur, Philosophie, Tanz* (Berlin: Reimer, 2003): 39-56.

Hollstein 1955: F.W.H. Hollstein, *Dutch and Flemish Etchings, Engravings, and Woodcuts ca. 1450-1700 XII: Masters and Monogrammists of the 15ᵗʰ Century* (Amsterdam: Hertzberger, 1955).

Hollstein 1956: F.W.H. Hollstein, *Dutch and Flemish Etchings, Engravings, and Woodcuts ca. 1450-1700 XIII: Monogrammists of the 16ᵗʰ and 17ᵗʰ Century* (Amsterdam: Hertzberger, 1956).

Hollstein 1957: F.W.H. Hollstein, *German Engravings, Etchings and Woodcuts ca. 1400-1700. IV: Breischlag-Brosamer* (Amsterdam: Hertzberger, 1957).

Hourihane 2009: Colum Hourihane, *Pontius Pilate, Anti-Semitism, and the Passion in Medieval Art* (Princeton: Princeton University Press, 2009).

Huemer and Vasold 2005: Christian Huemer and Georg Vasold, "Alles Seiende ist schön: Alois Riegl und die Grundlegung der modernen Kunstwissenschaft," *Parnassus* 25 (2005): 112-5.

Humfrey 1992: Peter Humfrey, "I rapporti fra Leonardo e la pittura veneta nella storiografia," in Giovanna Nepi Sciré et al., eds., *Leonardo & Venezia*, exh. cat. (Milan: Bompiani, 1992): 37-43.

Huisman et al. 2006: Rosemary Huisman, Julian Murphet, Anne Dunn and Helen Fulton, *Narrative and Media* (Cambridge: Cambridge University Press, 2006).

Hutcheon 2000: Linda Hutcheon, *A Theory of Parody: The Teachings of Twentieth-Century Art Forms* (Urbana and Chicago: University of Illinois Press, 2000).

Hutchison 1972: Jane C. Hutchison, *The Master of the Housebook* (New York: Collectors Editions, 1972).

Hutchison 1980: Jane C. Hutchison, *The Illustrated Bartsch. 8. Early German Masters* (New York: Abaris Books, 1980).

Hutchison 1991: Jane C. Hutchison, *The Illustrated Bartsch. 9 Commentary, Part 2: Early German Artists* (New York: Abaris, 1991).

Hutchison 1996: Jane C. Hutchison, *The Illustrated Bartsch. 8 Commentary, Part 1: Early German Artists. Martin Schongauer, Ludwig Schongauer, and Copyists* (New York: Abaris, 1996).

Hutchison and Koreny 1981: Jane C. Hutchison and Fritz Koreny, *The Illustrated Bartsch: 9. Early German Artists. Israhel van Meckenem, Wenzel von Olmütz and Monogrammists* (New York: Abaris Books, 1981).

Hütt 1980: Wolfgang Hütt, *Albrecht Dürer 1471 bis 1528: Das gesamte graphische Werk—Druckgraphik* (Herrsching: Manfred Pawlak, 1980).

Huys Janssen 1998: Paul Huys Janssen, *Jan van Bijlert, 1597/98-1671: Catalogue raisonné* (Amsterdam: John Benjamin, 1998).

615

Ilchman 2009: Frederick Ilchman, ed., *Titian, Tintoretto, Veronese: Rivals in Renaissance Venice*, exh. cat. (Boston: Museum of Fine Arts, 2009).

Imdahl 1985: Max Imdahl, "Caritas und Gnade: Zur ikonischen Zeitstruktur in Poussins *Mannalese*," in Fritz Nies and Karlheinz Stierle, eds., *Französische Klassik: Theorie, Literatur, Malerei* (Munich: Fink, 1985): 137-66.

Iser 1993: Wolfgang Iser, *The Fictive and the Imaginary: Charting Literary Anthropology* (Baltimore: Johns Hopkins University Press, 1993).

Ivanoff and Zampetti 1980: Nicola Ivanoff and Pietro Zampetti, *Giacomo Negretti detto Palma il Giovane* (Bergamo: Bolis, 1980).

Iversen 1991: Margaret Iversen, "Alois Riegl and the Aesthetics of Disintegration," in Peter Ganz and Martin Gosebruch, eds., *Kunst und Kunsttheorie 1400-1900* (Wiesbaden: Harrassowitz, 1991): 439-51.

Iversen 1993: Margaret Iversen, *Alois Riegl: Art History and Theory* (Cambridge: MIT Press, 1993).

Jacobowitz and Stepanek 1983: Ellen S. Jacobowitz and Stephanie L. Stepanek, *The Prints of Lucas van Leyden and his Contemporaries*, exh. cat. (Washington DC: National Gallery of Art, 1983).

Jahn 1975: Johannes Jahn, *1472-1553 Lucas Cranach d. Ä.: Das gesamte graphische Werk* (Herrsching: Manfred Pawlak, 1975).

Jakobson 1990: Roman Jakobson, *Language in Literature* (Cambridge: Harvard University Press, 1990).

Jauss 1982: Hans Robert Jauss, *Toward an Aesthetic of Reception*, trans. Timothy Bahti (Minneapolis: University of Minnesota Press, 1982).

Joannides 2001: Paul Joannides, *Titian to 1518: The Assumption of Genius* (New Haven: Yale University Press, 2001).

Joannides 2003: Paul Joannides, *Musée du Louvre-Musée d'Orsay, Département des Arts Graphiques: Inventaire général des dessins italiens. VI. Michel-Ange, élèves et copistes* (Paris: Réunion des Musées Nationaux, 2003).

Joffroy 1959: Berne Joffroy, *Le Dossier Caravaggio* (Paris: Éditions de Minuit, 1959).

Jollet 2002: Étienne Jollet, "La cause de l'œuvre: de la causalité en histoire de l'art," *Revue de l'Art* 136 (2002): 73-8.

Jones 1993: Pamela M. Jones, *Federico Borromeo and the Ambrosiana: Art Patronage and Reform in Seventeenth-Century Milan* (Cambridge: Cambridge University Press, 1993).

Jones 2008: Pamela M. Jones, *Altarpieces and their Viewers in the Churches of Rome from Caravaggio to Guido Reni* (Aldershot: Ashgate, 2008).

Judson and Ekkart 1999: J. Richard Judson and Rudolph E.O. Ekkart, *Gerrit van Honthorst 1592-1656* (Doornspijk: Davaco, 1999).

Katritzky 1988: M.A. Katritzky, "A Renaissance *Commedia dell'Arte* Performance: Towards a Definitive Sequence of Sieur Frossard's Woodcuts?," *Nationalmuseum Bulletin* 12 (1988): 37-53.

Katritzky 1997: M.A. Katritzky, "Harlequin in Renaissance pictures," *Renaissance Studies* 11 (1997): 381-419.

Katritzky 2006: M. A. Katritzky, *The Art of* Commedia: *Study in the* Commedia dell'Arte, *1560-1620, with Special Reference to the Visual Records* (Amsterdam and New York: Rodopi, 2006).

Keazor 2007: Henry Keazor, *'Il vero modo': Die Malereireform der Carracci* (Berlin: Mann, 2007).

Kemp 1974: Martin Kemp, "*Disegno*: Beiträge zur Geschichte des Begriffs zwischen 1547 und 1607," *Marburger Jahrbuch für Kunstwissenschaft* 19 (1974): 219-40.

Kemp 1989: Martin Kemp, *Leonardo on Painting: An Anthology of Writings by Leonardo da Vinci with a Selection of Documents Relating to His Career as an Artist* (New Haven: Yale University Press, 1989).

Kemp 1990: Martin Kemp, *The Science of Art: Optical Themes in Western Art from Brunelleschi to Seurat* (New Haven: Yale University Press, 1990).

Kemp W. 1990: Wolfgang Kemp, "Alois Riegl (1858-1905)," in Heinrich Dilly, ed., *Altmeister moderner Kunstgeschichte* (Berlin: Reimer, 1990): 37-60.

Kessler and Wolf 1996: Herbert L. Kessler and Gerhard Wolf, eds., *The Holy Face and the Paradox of Representation...*(Bologna: Nuova Alpha, 1996).

Keyes 1980: George S. Keyes, *Hollstein's Dutch and Flemish Etchings, Engravings and Woodcuts ca. 1450-1700. Volume XXIII. Jan Saenredam to Roelandt Savery* (Amsterdam: M. Hertzberger, 1980).

King 2006: Catherine King, "An Etching and Lelio Orsi's House," *Print Quarterly* 23 (2006): 176-82.

Klemm 1986: Christian Klemm, *Joachim von Sandrart: Kunst, Werke und Lebenslauf* (Berlin: Deutscher Verlag für Kunstwissenschaft, 1986).

Klibansky et al. 1964: Raymond Klibansky, Erwin Panofsky and Fritz Saxl, *Saturn and Melancholy: Studies in the History of Natural Philosophy, Religion and Art* (London: Nelson, 1964).

Kliemann 2001: Julian Kliemann, *Il Bersaglio dell'arte:* La Caccia di Diana *di Domenichino nella Galleria Borghese* (Rome: Artemide Edizioni, 2001).

Kliemann 2007: Julian Kliemann, "L'*Amore al fonte* di Cecco del Caravaggio e l'ultimo quadro del Merisi: Omaggio al maestro o pittura ambigua?," in Sybille Ebert-Schifferer, Julian Kliemann, Valeska von Rosen and Lothar Sickel, eds., *Caravaggio e il suo ambiente: Ricerche e interpretazioni* (Cinisello Balsamo: Silvana, 2007): 181-216.

Kloek 2002: Wouter Kloek, "Two Northern Examples for Caravaggio," in Anton W.A. Boschloo and Edward Grasman, eds., *Aux quatre vents: Festschrift für Bert W. Meijer* (Florence: Centro Di, 2002): 287-92.

Knab et al. 1983: Eckhart Knab, Erwin Mitsch and Konrad Oberhuber, *Raffaello: I Disegni* (Florence: Nardini, 1983).

Knox 2009: Giles Knox, *The Late Paintings of Velázquez: Theorizing Painterly Performance* (Aldershot: Ashgate, 2009).

Koch 1978: Robert A. Koch, *The Illustrated Bartsch. 15. Early German Masters: Barthel Beham, Hans Sebald Beham* (New York: Abaris Books, 1978).

Koch 1980: Robert A. Koch, *The Illustrated Bartsch. 16: Early German Masters. Jacob Bink, Georg Pencz, Heinrich Aldegrever* (New York: Abaris, 1980).

Koerner 1993: Joseph L. Koerner, *The Moment of Self-Portraiture in German Renaissance Art* (Chicago: University of Chicago Press, 2003).

Kohl 2005: Jeanette Kohl, "Schleier, Hülle, Schwelle: Verrocchios Bildstrategien," in Johannes Endres, Barbara Wittmann and Gerhard Wolf, eds., *Ikonologie des Zwischenraums: Der Schleier als Medium und Metapher* (Paderborn : Fink, 2005): 213-42.

Kok 1985: Jan Piet Filedt Kok, ed., *Livelier than Life. The Master of the Amsterdam Cabinet or the Housebook Master ca. 1470-1500*, exh. cat. (Amsterdam: Reijksprentenkabinett, 1985).

Kok et al. 1996: Jan Piet Filedt Kok, Bart Cornelis and Anneloes Smits, *The New Hollstein Dutch and Flemish Etchings, Engravings and Woodcuts. 1450-1700: Lucas van Leyden* (Rotterdam: Sound & Vision, 1996).

Kok et al. 2000: Jan Piet Filedt Kok, Marjolein Leesberg and Ger Luijten, *The New Hollstein Dutch and Flemish Etchings, Engravings and Woodcuts. 1450-1700: The De Gheyn Family, Part 1* (Rotterdam: Sound & Vision, 2000)

König 2001: Eberhard König, "Vincenzo Giustiniani und Michelangelo da Caravaggio: Über den Stellenwert von Bildung und Natur im Urteil über die Malerei," in Hannah Baader, Ulrike Müller Hofstede, Kristine Patz and Nicola Suthor, eds., *Ars et scriptura: Festschrift für Rudolf Preimesberger zum 65. Geburtstag* (Berlin: Mann, 2001): 199-213.

Koos 2005: Marianne Koos, "Kunst und Berührung: Materialität versus Imagination in Caravaggios Gemälde des *Ungläubigen Thomas*," in Johann Anselm Steiger, ed., *Passion, Affekt und Leidenschaft in der frühen Neuzeit* (Wiesbaden: Harrassowitz, 2005): 2: 1135-51.

Koos 2007: Marianne Koos, "Haut als mediale Metapher in der Malerei von Caravaggio," in Daniela Bohde and Mechthild Fend, eds., *Weder Haut noch Fleisch: Das Inkarnat in der Kunstgeschichte* (Berlin: Gebr. Mann, 2007): 65-85.

Koreny 1974: Fritz Koreny, ed., *Spielkarte: Ihre Kunst und Geschichte in Mitteleuropa*, exh. cat. (Vienna: Albertina, 1974).

Koreny 1986: Fritz Koreny, *Hollstein's German Engravings, Etchings and Woodcuts. 1400-1700. Volume XXIV. Israel van Meckenem* (Amsterdam: M. Hertzberger, 1986).

Kretschmer 1988: Hildegard Kretschmer, "Zu Caravaggios Berufung des Matthäus in der Cappella Contarelli," *Pantheon* 45 (1988): 63-6.

Kristof 1989: Jane Kristof, "Michelangelo as Nicodemus," *Sixteenth-Century Journal* 20 (1989): 163-82.

Krohn 2002: Wolfgang Krohn, "Technik, Kunst und Wissenschaft: Die Idee einer konstruktiven Naturwissenschaft des Schönen bei Leon Battista Alberti," in Frank Fehrenbach, ed., *Leonardo da Vinci: Natur im Übergang* (Munich: Fink, 2002): 37-56.

Kroschewki 2002: Nevranka Koschewki, *Über das almähliche Verfertigen der Bilder: Neue Aspekte zu Caravaggio* (Munich: Scaneg, 2002).

Krüger 1999: Klaus Krüger, "Innerer Blick und ästhetisches Geheimnis: Caravaggios *Magdalena*," in Joseph Imorde, Fritz Neumeyer and Tristan Weddigen, eds., *Barocke Inszenierung* (Emsdetten: Imorde, 1999): 32-49.

Krüger 2001: Klaus Krüger, *Das Bild als Schleier des Unsichtbaren: Ästhetische Illusion in der Kunst der frühen Neuzeit* (Munich: Fink, 2001).

Krüger P. 2002: Peter Krüger, "*Istoria* und *virtus* bei Alberti und in der Malerei der frühen Renaissance," in Joachim Poeschke and Thomas Weigel, eds., *Tugenden und Affekte in der Philosophie, Literatur und Kunst der Renaissance* (Münster: Rhema, 2002): 195-219.

Laclotte 1993: Michel Laclotte, ed., *Le Siècle de Titien: L'âge d'or de la peinture à Venise*, exh. cat. (Paris: Réunion des musées nationaux, 1993).

Lagny 1998: Anne Lagny, "Les frontières de la peinture et de la poésie: Le *Laokoon* de Lessing," in Anne Sauvagnargues, ed., *Art et philosophie* (Fontenay-aux-Roses: ENS Éditions, 1998): 27-44.

Lampe 1961: G.W.H. Lampe, ed., *A Patristic Greek Lexicon* (Oxford: Oxford University Press, 1961).

Landrus 1998: Matthew H. Landrus, *Caravaggism in the Work of Guido Reni: A Study of Guido Reni's Appropriation, from 1601 through 1615, of Stylistic Techniques Associated with Caravaggio* (unpublished M.A. dissertation, University of Louisville).

Langdon 1998: Helen Langdon, *Caravaggio: A Life* (London, Chatto & Windus, 1998).

Langdon 2001: Helen Langdon, "Cardsharps, Gypsies and Street Vendors," in Beverley L. Brown, ed., *The Genius of Rome*, exh. cat. (London: Thames and Hudson, 2001): 42-65.

Lapucci 1994: Roberta Lapucci, *Come dipingeva il Caravaggio: le opere messinesi* (Messina: Museo Regionale di Messina, 1994).

Lavin 1993: Irving Lavin, "Caravaggio's *Calling of St. Matthew*: The Identity of the Protagonist," in Lavin, *Past-Present: Essays on Historicism in Art from Donatello to Picasso* (Berkeley: University of California Press, 1993): 85-99.

Lavin 2000: Irving Lavin, *Caravaggio e La Tour: La luce occulta di Dio* (Rome: Donzelli, 2000).

Lavin 2001: Irving Lavin, "Caravaggio Revolutionary or the Impossibility of Seeing," in Klaus Bergdolt and Giorgio Bonsanti, eds., *Opere e giorni: Studi su mille anni di arte europea dedicati a Max Seidel* (Venice: Marsilio, 2001): 625-44.

Lawner 1998: Lynne Lawner, *Harlequin on the Moon: Commedia dell'Arte and the Visual Arts* (New York: Abrams, 1998).

Lechner 2006: Sonja Lechner, *Nuda Veritas—Caravaggio als Aktmaler: Rezeption und Revision von Aktdarstellungen der römischen Reifezeit* (Munich: Scaneg, 2006).

Lee 1967: Rensselaer W. Lee, *Ut Pictura Poesis: The Humanistic Theory of Painting* (New York: Norton, 1967).

Lemoine 2007: Annick Lemoine, *Nicolas Régnier (alias Niccolò Renieri) ca. 1588-1667: Peintre, collectionneur et marchand d'art* (Paris, Arthéna, 2007).

Leik 1996: Angelika Leik, *Frühe Darstellungen der Commedia dell'Arte: Eine Theaterform als Bildmotiv* (Neuried: Ars Una, 1996).

Levenson et al. 1973: Jay Levenson, Konrad Oberhuber and Jacquelyn L. Sheehan, *Early Italian Engravings from the National Gallery of Art*, exh. cat. (Washington DC: National Gallery of Art, 1973).

Lichtenstein 1993: Jacqueline Lichtenstein, *The Eloquence of Color: Rhetoric and Painting in the French Classical Age*, trans. Emily McVarish (Berkeley: University of California Press, 1993).

Liebert 1977: Robert S. Liebert, "Michelangelo's Mutilation of the Florence *Pietà*: A Psychoanalytic Inquiry," *Art Bulletin* 59 (1977): 47-54.

Lingo 2008: Stuart Lingo, *Federico Barocci: Allure and Devotion in Late Renaissance Italy* (New Haven: Yale University Press, 2008).

Loire 2006: Stéphane Loire, *École italienne, XVIIe siècle: Musée National du Louvre. 2. Florence, Gênes, Lombardie, Naples, Rome et Venise* (Paris, Réunion des Musées Nationaux, 2006).

Longhi 1999-2000: Roberto Longhi, *Studi caravaggeschi* (Florence: Sansoni 1999-2000).

López-Rey 1996: José López-Rey, *Velázquez. 1. Painter of Painters. 2. Catalogue Raisonné—Werkverzeichnis* (Cologne: Taschen, 1996).

Los Leoni **1994**: *Los Leoni (1509-1608): Escultores del Renacimiento italiano al servicio de la corte de España* (Madrid, Museo del Prado, 1994).

Lubbock 2006: Jules Lubbock, *Storytelling in Christian Art from Giotto to Donatello* (New Haven: Yale University Press, 2006).

Luijten et al. 1993: Ger Luijten, Ariane van Suchtelen, Reinier Baarsen, Wouter Kloek and Marijn Schapelhouman, eds., *Dawn of the Golden Age: Northern Netherlandish Art 1580-1620*, exh. cat. (Amsterdam: Rijksmuseum, 1993).

L'Ultimo Caravaggio **2004**: *L'Ultimo Caravaggio: Il Martirio di Sant'Orsola restaurato, Collezione Banca Intesa*, exh. cat. (Milan: Electa, 2004).

Maccherini 1997: Michele Maccherini, "Caravaggio nel carteggio familiare di Giulio Mancini," *Prospettiva* 86 (1997): 71-92.

Maccherini 1999: Michele Maccherini, "Novità su Bartolomeo Manfredi nel carteggio familiare di Giulio Mancini: lo 'Sdegno di Marte' e i quadri di Cosimo II granduca di Toscana," *Prospettiva* 93/94 (1999): 131-41.

Maccherini 2002: Michele Maccherini, "Novità sulle Considerazioni di Giulio Mancini," in Caterina Volpi, ed., *Caravaggio nel IV Centenario della Cappella Contarelli…*(s.l.: CAM, 2002): 123-28.

Maccherini 2004: Michele Maccherini, "Ritratto di Giulio Mancini," in Olivier Bonfait and Anna Coliva, eds., *Bernini dai Borghese ai Barberini: La cultura a Roma intorno agli anni venti* (Rome: De Luca, 2004): 47-57.

Macioce 1994: Stefania Macioce, "Caravaggio a Malta e i suoi referenti: Notizie d'archivio," *Storia dell'Arte* 81 (1994): 207-28.

Macioce 2003: Stefania Macioce, *Michelangelo Merisi da Caravaggio: Fonti e Documenti 1532-1724* (Rome: Bozzi, 2003).

Macioce 2007: Stefania Macioce, "Ut Pictura Rhetorica: Affetti, devozione e retorica nei dipinti di Caravaggio," *Storia dell'Arte* 116-117 (2007): 67-100.

Maguire 1996: Henry Maguire, *The Icons of their Bodies: Saints and their Images in Byzantium* (Princeton: Princeton University Press, 1996).

Mahon 1951a: Denis Mahon, "Egregius in Urbe Pictor: Caravaggio Revised," *Burlington Magazine* 93 (1951): 223-34.

Mahon 1951b: Denis Mahon, "Caravaggio's Chronology Again," *Burlington Magazine* 93 (1951): 286-92.

Mahon 1952a: Denis Mahon, "Addenda to Caravaggio," *Burlington Magazine* 94 (1952): 3-23.

Mahon 1952b: Denis Mahon, "An Addition to Caravaggio's Early Period," *Paragone Arte*, 3 (1952): 20-31.

Mahon 1953a: Denis Mahon, "Contrasts in Art Historical Method: Two Recent Approaches to Caravaggio," *Burlington Magazine* 85 (1953): 212-20.

Mahon 1953b: Denis Mahon, "Die Dokumente über die Contarelli-Kapelle und ihr Verhältnis zur Chronologie Caravaggios," *Zeitschrift für Kunstwissenschaft* 7 (1953): 183-208.

Mahon 1971: Denis Mahon, *Studies in Seicento Art and Theory* (Westport: Greenwood Press, 1971).

Mahon and Christiansen 1988: Denis Mahon and Keith Christiansen, "Fresh Light on Caravaggio's Earliest Period: His 'Cardsharps' Recovered," *Burlington Magazine* 130 (1988): 11-27.

Maiorino 1983: Giancarlo Maiorino, "In Search of True Form: Michelangelo's Power of Expression and the Aesthetic Lure of the Non-Finito," *Rivista di Studi Italiani* 1 (1983): 51-81.

Maiorino 2001: Giancarlo Maiorino, ed., *The Figino, or On the Purpose of Painting: Art Theory in the Late Renaissance* (Toronto: University of Toronto Press: 2001).

Malgouyres 2000: Philippe Malgouyres, "Maraîchage et dévotion: Le *Noli Me Tangere* de Nicolas Mignard à la cathédrale de Cavaillon," *Bulletin de la Société de l'Histoire de l'Art Français* (2000): 51-62.

Manfredi **1987**: *Dopo Caravaggio: Bartolomeo Manfredi e la manfrediana methodus*, exh. cat. (Milan: Mondadori, 1987).

Mango 1986: Cyril Mango, *Sources and Documents: The Art of the Byzantine Empire, 312-1453* (Toronto: University of Toronto Press, 1986).

Marani 1992: Pietro C. Marani, "Leonardo a Venezia e nel Veneto," in Giovanna Nepi Sciré et al., eds., *Leonardo & Venezia*, exh. cat. (Milan: Bompiani, 1992).

Marani 2001: Pietro C. Marani, ed., *Il Genio e le Passioni* (Milan: Skira; and Florence: Artificio, 2001).

Marghetich 1988: Tiziano Marghetich, "Per una rilettura critica del Musaeum di Federico Borromeo," *Arte Lombarda* 84/85 (1988): 102-18.

Marin 1977: Louis Marin, *Détruire la peinture* (Paris: Galilée, 1977).

Marin 1986: Louis Marin, "In Praise of Appearance," *October* 37 (1986): 99-112.

Marin 1988: Louis Marin, "Towards a Theory of Reading in the Visual Arts: Poussin's *The Arcadian Shepherds*," in Norman Bryson, ed., *Calligram: Essays in New Art History from France* (Cambridge: Cambridge University Press, 1988): 63-90.

Marin 1989: Louis Marin, *Opacité de la peinture: Essais sur la représentation au Quattrocento* (Paris: Usher, 1989).

Marin 1994: Louis Marin, *De la représentation*, eds. Daniel Arasse, Alain Cantillon, Giovanni Careri, Danièle Cohn, Pierre-Antoine Fabre and Françoise Marin (Paris: Gallimard Le Seuil, 1994).

Marini 1973: Maurizio Marini, "Caravaggio 1607: *La Negazione di Pietro*," *Napoli Nobilissima* 12 (1973): 189-94.

Marini 1974: Maurizio Marini, *Io Michelangelo da Caravaggio* (Rome: Studio B di Bestetti e Bozzi, 1974).

Marini 1981a: Maurizio Marini, "Del Signor Giovanni Battista Crescentij, Pittore," *J. Paul Getty Museum Journal* 9 (1981): 127-31.

Marini 1981b: Maurizio Marini, "Caravaggio e il naturalismo internazionale," in Federico Zeri, ed., *Storia dell'arte italiana*, VI, parte II: *Dal Medioevo al Novecento*, vol. II: *Dal Cinquecento all'Ottocento*, I, *Cinquecento e Seicento* (Turin: Einaudi, 1981): 347-445.

Marini 1983: Maurizio Marini, "Equivoci del caravaggismo," *Artibus et Historiae* 8 (1983): 119-54.

Marini 2005: Maurizio Marini, *Caravaggio: Michelangelo Merisi da Caravaggio "pictor praestantissimus"…* (Rome: Newton Compton, 2005).

Marini and Corradini 1993: Maurizio Marini and Sandro Corradini, "*Inventarium omnium et singulorum bonorum mobilium* di Michelangelo da Caravaggio pittore," *Artibus et Historiae* 28 (1993): 161-76.

Mariti 1978: Luciano Mariti, *Commedia ridicolosa: Comici di professione, dilettanti, editoria teatrale nel Seicento* (Rome: Bulzoni, 1978).

Marotti and Romei 1991: Ferruccio Marotti and Giovanna Romei, *La Commedia dell'Arte e la società barocca: La professione del teatro* (Rome: Bulzoni, 1991).

Marmer 1984: Nancy Marmer, "Review of Svetlana Alpers' *The Art of Describing: Dutch Art in the Seventeenth Century*," *Art in America* 72 (1984): 23-7.

Marrow and Shestack 1981: James H. Marrow and Alan Shestack, eds., *Hans Baldung Grien: Prints & Drawings*, exh. cat. (Washington DC: National Gallery of Art, 1981).

Martin 1985: Gregory Martin, "Review of Svetlana Alpers' *The Art of Describing: Dutch Art in the Seventeenth Century*," *Apollo* 121 (1985): 66.

Martinelli 1958: Valentino Martinelli, "Il non-finito di Donatello," in *Donatello e il suo tempo: Atti del VIII Convegno Internazionale di Studi sul Rinascimento* (Florence: Istituto Nazionale di Studi sul Rinascimento, 1968): 179-94.

Mason Rinaldi 1980: Stefania Mason Rinaldi, *Palma il Giovane 1548-1628: Disegni e dipinti*, exh. cat. (Milan: Electa, 1980).

Massari 1983: Stefania Massari, *Giulio Bonasone* (Rome: Quasar, 1983).

Maurer 1995: Emil Maurer, "*Figura serpentinata*: Von der Renaisssance zur *maniera*," in Hildegard Kuester, ed., *Das 16. Jahrhundert: Europäische Renaissance* (Regensburg: Pustet, 1995): 77-98.

Maurer 2001: Emil Maurer, *Manierismus: Figura serpentinata und andere Figurenideale, Studien, Essays, Berichte* (Munich, Fink, 2001).

May 2000: Suzanne E. May, "The Artifice of Depicting Reality: Caravaggio and the Theatrical Spotlight," *Rutgers Art Review* 18 (2000): 27-49.

McClain 1985: Jeoraldean McClain, "Time in the Visual Arts: Lessing and Modern Criticism," *The Journal of Aesthetics and Art Criticism* 44 (1985): 41-58.

McDonald 2004: Mark P. McDonald, ed., *The Print Collection of Ferdinand Columbus (1488-1539): A Renaissance Collector in Seville* (London: The British Museum Press, 2004).

McDonald 2006: Mark P. McDonald, "A Genealogy for the Count Duke of Olivares," *Print Quarterly* 23 (2006): 359-82.

McDowell 1942: John H. McDowell, "Some Pictorial Aspects of Early 'Commedia dell'Arte' Acting," *Studies in Philology* 39 (1942): 47-64.

McGregor and Langmuir 2000: Neil McGregor and Erika Langmuir, *Seeing Salvation: Images of Christ in Art*, exh. cat. (New Haven: Yale University Press, 2000).

Meadow 1992: Mark A. Meadow, "The Observant Pedestrian and Albrecht Dürer's *Promenade*," *Art History* 15 (1992): 196-222.

Melion 1991: Walter S. Melion, *Shaping the Netherlandish Canon: Karel van Mander's Schilder-Boek* (Chicago: University of Chicago Press, 1991).

Méndez Rodríguez 2005: Luis Méndez Rodríguez, *Velázquez y la cultura sevillana* (Seville: Universidad de Sevilla, 2005).

Merlini and Storti 2008: Valeria Merlini and Daniela Storti, eds., *Caravaggio a Milano: La Conversione di Saulo* (Milan: Skira, 2008).

Merz 1991: Jörg Martin Merz, *Pietro da Cortona: Der Aufstieg zum führenden Maler im barocken Rom* (Tübingen: Wasmuth, 1991).

Mielke 1988: Hans Mielke, *Albrecht Altdorfer: Zeichnungen. Denkfarbenmalerei. Druckgraphik*, exh. cat. (Berlin: Reiner, 1988).

Mielke et al. 1998: Ursula Mielke, Holm Bevers and Christiane Wiebel, *The New Hollstein. German Engravings, Etchings and Woodcuts 1400-1700: Heinrich Aldegrever* (Rotterdam: Sound & Vision, 1998).

Milicua and Cuyàs 2005: José Milicua and María Margarita Cuyàs, eds., *Caravaggio y la pintura realista europea*, exh. cat. (Barcelona: Museu Nacional d'Art de Catalunya, 2005).

Miller 2000: Robert S. Miller, "Simone Peterzano in Milan: Contracts for Frescoes in San Maurizio and San Francesco Grande," *Paragone Arte* 50 (1999): 89-108.

Miller 2002: Robert S. Miller "Birth and Death Dates of Simone Peterzano," *Paragone Arte* 53 (2002): 157-8.

Mirollo 1963: James V. Mirollo, *The Poet of the Marvelous: Giambattista Marino* (New York: Columbia University Press, 1963).

Missirini 1823: Melchior Missirini, *Memoria per servire alla storia della romana Accademia di San Luca fino alla morte di Antonio Canova* (Rome: Stamperia De Romanis, 1823).

Mitchell 1984: W.J.T. Mitchell, "The Politics of Genre: Space and Time in Lessing's *Laocoön*," *Representations* 6 (1984): 98-115.

Moffitt 1990: John F. Moffitt, "Francisco Pacheco and Jerome Nadal: New Light on the Flemish Sources of the Spanish Picture-within-the-Picture," *Art Bulletin* 72 (1990): 631-8.

Moffitt 2002: John F. Moffitt, "Caravaggio and the Gypsies," *Paragone Arte* 41-42 (2002): 129-56.

Moffitt 2004: John F. Moffitt, *Caravaggio in Context: Learned Naturalism and Renaissance Humanism* (Jefferson: McFarland, 2004).

Moffitt 2005: John F. Moffitt, "Sluter's *Pleurants* and Timanthes' *Tristitia Velata*: Evolution of, and Sources for, a Humanist Topos of Mourning," *Artibus et Historiae* 51 (2005): 73-84.

Moir 1976: Alfred Moir, *Caravaggio and His Copyists* (New York: New York University Press, 1976).

Moir 1982: Alfred Moir, *Caravaggio* (New York: Abrams, 1982).

Moir 1987: Alfred Moir, "Le sviste di Caravaggio," in Maurizio Calvesi, ed., *L'ultimo Caravaggio e la cultura artistica a Napoli e a Malta* (Syracuse: Ediprint, 1987): 139-45.

Mojana 1989: Marina Mojana, *Valentin de Boulogne* (Milan: Eikonos, 1989).

Molinari 1985: Cesare Molinari, *La commedia dell'arte* (Milan: Mondadori, 1985).

Möller 1991: Renate Möller, *Der römische Maler Giovanni Baglione: Leben und Werk unter besonderer Berücksichtigung seiner stilgeschichtlichen Stellung zwischen Manierismus und Barock* (Munich: Tuduv, 1991).

Monducci and Pirondini 1987: Elio Monducci and Massimo Pirondini, eds., *Lelio Orsi*, exh. cat. (Cinisello Balsamo: Amilcare Pizzi, 1987).

Moralejo Ortega 2001: Macarena Moralejo Ortega, "Teoría artística y academicismo en Federico Zuccari," *Academia* 92-93 (2001): 81-102.

Morales 1999: Alfredo J. Morales, ed., *Velázquez y Sevilla* (Seville: Junta de Andalucía, 1999).

Morassi 1947: Antonio Morassi, "Il Caravaggio di Casa Balbi," *Emporium* 105 (1947): 95-102.

Morello and Wolf 2000: Giovanni Morello and Gerhard Wolf, eds., *Il Volto di Cristo*, exh. cat. (Milan: Electa, 2000).

Morrall 2002: Andrew Morrall, "Soldiers and Gypsies: Outsiders and Their Families in Early Sixteenth-Century German Art," in Pia Cuneo, ed., *Artful Armies, Beautiful Battles: Art and Warfare in Early Modern Europe*, (Leiden: Brill, 2002): 159-80.

Mortari 1995: Luisa Mortari, *Bernardo Strozzi* (Rome: De Luca, 1995).

Most 2005: Glenn W. Most, *Doubting Thomas* (Cambridge: Harvard University Press, 2005).

Moxey 1980: Keith P.F. Moxey, "Master E.S. and the Folly of Love," *Simiolus* 11 (1980): 125-48.

Moxey 1985a: Keith P.F. Moxey, "Chivalry and the Housebook Master (Master of the Amsterdam Cabinet)," in J.P.Filedt Kok, ed., *Livelier than Life. The Master of the Amsterdam Cabinet or the Housebook Master ca. 1470-1500*, exh. cat. (Amsterdam : Rijksprentenkabinet/Rijksmuseum, 1985): 65-78.

Moxey 1985b: Keith P.F. Moxey, "The Criticism of Avarice in Sixteenth-Century Netherlandish Painting," in Görel Cavalli-Björkman, ed., *Netherlandish Mannerism: Papers Given at a Symposium in Nationalmuseum, Stockholm, September 21-22, 1984* (Stockholm: Nationalmuseum Stockholm, 1985): 21-34.

Mozzarelli 2004: Cesare Mozzarelli, ed., *Federico Borromeo principe e mecenate: Atti delle giornate di studio…* (Milan: Biblioteca Ambrosiana, 2004).

Mühlmann 1981: Heiner Mühlmann, *Ästhetische Theorie der Renaissance: Leon Battista Alberti* (Bonn: Habelt, 1983).

Müller 1997: Christian Müller, *Hans Holbein d.J.: Die Druckgraphik im Kupferstichkabinett Basel* (Basle: Schwabe & Co., 1997).

Nagel 1996: Alexander Nagel, "Observations on Michelangelo's Late *Pietà* Drawings and Sculptures," *Zeitschrift für Kunstgeschichte* 59 (1996): 548-72.

Nagel 1997: Alexander Nagel, "Gifts for Michelangelo and Vittoria Colonna," *Art Bulletin* 79 (1997): 647-68.

Nagel 2000: Alexander Nagel, *Michelangelo and the Reform of Art* (Cambridge: Cambridge University Press, 2000).

Nagel 2004: Alexander Nagel, "Fashion and the Now-Time of Renaissance Art," *RES* 46 (2004): 33-52.

Nagel 2010: Alexander Nagel, "Structural Indeterminacy in Early Sixteenth-Century Italian Painting," in Alexander Nagel and Lorenzo Pericolo, eds., *Subject as Aporia in Early Modern Art* (Aldershot: Ashgate, 2010): 17-42.

Nagel and Pericolo 2010: Alexander Nagel and Lorenzo Pericolo, eds., *Subject as Aporia in Early Modern Art* (Aldershot: Ashgate, 2010).

Nagel and Wood 2010: Alexander Nagel and Christopher S. Wood, *Anachronic Renaissance* (New York: Zone Books, 2010).

Negro and Pirondini 1994: Emilio Negro and Massimo Pirondini, eds., *La scuola dei Carracci: Dall'Accademia alla bottega di Ludovico* (Modena: Artioli, 1994).

Nicolson 1979: Benedict Nicolson, *The International Caravaggesque Movement: List of Pictures by Caravaggio and His Followers throughout Europe from 1590 to 1650* (Oxford: Phaidon, 1979).

Niebaum 2007: Jens Niebaum, "Die spätantike Rotunden an Alt-St.-Peter in Rom: Mit Anmerkungen zur Erweiterungsprojekt Nikolaus' V. für die Peterskirche und zur Aufstellung von Michelangelos römischer *Pietà*," *Marburger Jahrbuch für Kunstwissenschaft* 34 (2007): 101-61.

Nova 1994: Alessandro Nova, *Girolamo Romanino* (Turin: Allemandi, 1994).

Nova 2003: Alessandro Nova, "Paragone-Debatte und gemalte Theorie in der Zeit Cellinis," in Alessandro Nova and Anna Schreurs, eds., *Benvenuto Cellini: Kunst und Kunsttheorie im 16. Jahrhundert* (Cologne: Böhlau, 2003): 183-202.

Oberhuber 1978: Konrad Oberhuber, ed., *The Illustrated Bartsch: The Works of Marcantonio Raimondi and His School* (New York: Abaris, 1978).

Olds et al. 1976: Clifton C. Olds, Ralph G. Williams and William R. Levin, eds., *Images of Love and Death in Late Medieval and Renaissance Art*, exh. cat. (Ann Arbor: University of Michigan Museum of Art, 1976).

Olmos 1956: Emilio Aparicio Olmos, "Palomino, el pintor teólogo," *Archivo de Arte Valenciano* 27 (1956): 67-78.

Olson 2002: Todd P. Olson, "Pitiful Relics: Caravaggio's *Martyrdom of St. Matthew*," *Representations* 77 (2002): 107-42.

Olson 2006: Todd P. Olson, "The Street Has Its Masters: Caravaggio and the Socially Marginal," in Genevieve Warwick, ed., *Caravaggio: Realism, Rebellion, Reception* (Newark: University of Delaware Press, 2006): 69-81.

Ore 1953: Øystein Ore, *Cardano: The Gambling Scholar* (Princeton: Princeton University Press, 1953).

Ostrow 2007: Steven F. Ostrow, "Bernini e il paragone," in Tomaso Montanari, ed., *Bernini pittore*, exh. cat. (Cinisello Balsamo: Silvana, 2007): 223-33.

Ottani Cavina 1968: Anna Ottani Cavina, *Carlo Saraceni* (Milan: Spagnol, 1968).

Ottino della Chiesa 1956: Angela Ottino della Chiesa, *Bernardino Luini* (Novara: Istituto Geografico De Agostini, 1956).

Pacelli 1977: Vincenzo Pacelli, "New Documents Concerning Caravaggio in Naples," *Burlington Magazine* 119 (1977): 819-29.

Pacelli 1980: Vincenzo Pacelli, "Caravaggio, 1610: La 'Sant'Orsola confitta dal Tiranno' per Marcantonio Doria," *Prospettiva* 23 (1980): 24-30.

Pacelli 1994: Vincenzo Pacelli, *L'ultimo Caravaggio: Dalla Maddalena a mezza figura ai due san Giovanni (1606 - 1610)* (Todi: Ediart, 1994).

Pacelli 2005: Vincenzo Pacelli, "*Il Martirio di Sant'Orsola* di Caravaggio : Riconsiderazioni sulle copie e su inediti tra Napoli e Genova nella prima metà del '600," *Studi di Storia dell'Arte* 16 (2005): 159-80.

Pagano 2004: Denise Maria Pagano, ed., *La Flagellazione di Caravaggio: Il restauro* (Milan: Electa, 2004).

Pagano 2005: Denise Maria Pagano, ed., *Caravaggio a Napoli dalle Opere di Misericordia alla Sant'Orsola trafitta: Tecnica e restauro* (Milan: Electa, 2005).

Pagliara 1980: P.N. Pagliara, "Monterotondo," in Federico Zeri, ed., *Storia dell'arte italiana*, pt. 3, *Situazioni, monumenti, indagini*, vol. 1, *Inchieste su centri minori* (Turin: Einaudi, 1980), 8, 1, 258-60.

Pallucchini 1970: Anna Pallucchini, "L'edizione critica del 'De Sculptura' del Gaurico," *Arte Veneta* 23 (1970): 262-3.

Pallucchini 1971: Anna Pallucchini, "Per una situazione storica di Giovan Pietro Bellori," *Storia dell'Arte* 12 (1971): 285-95.

Pallucchini and Rossi 1982: Rodolfo Pallucchini and Paola Rossi, *Tintoretto: Le opere sacre e profane* (Milan: Electa, 1982).

Panazza 1965: Gaetano Panazza, ed., *Mostra di Girolamo Romanino*, exh. cat. (Brescia: Comitato della mostra di Girolamo Romanino, 1965).

Pandolfi 1957-1961: Vito Pandolfi, ed., *La Commedia dell'arte: Storia e testo* (Florence: Sansoni, 1957-1961).

Panofsky 1924-1925: Erwin Panofsky, "Die Perspektive als Symbolische Form," in Fritz Saxl, ed., *Vorträge der Bibliothek Warburg* 5 (Leipzig: Teubner, 1924-5 [1927]): 258-330.

Panofsky 1955: Erwin Panofsky, *The Life and Art of Albrecht Dürer* (Princeton: Princeton University Press, 1955).

Panofsky 1956: Erwin Panofsky, "Jean Hey's *Ecce Homo*: Speculations about Its Author, Its Donor and Its Iconography," *Bulletin des Musées Royaux des Beaux-Arts, Bruxelles* 5 (1956): 95-132.

Panofsky 1969: Erwin Panofsky, *Problems in Titian: Mostly Iconographic* (New York: New York University Press, 1969).

Panza 1994: Pierluigi Panza, *Leon Battista Alberti: Filosofia e teoria dell'arte* (Milan: Guerini Studio, 1994).

Panzera 1994: Anna Maria Panzera, *Caravaggio e Giordano Bruno fra nuova arte e nuova scienza: La bellezza dell'artefice* (Rome: Palombi, 1994).

Papa 2001: Rodolfo Papa, "La *Deposizione* di Caravaggio: L'artista come testimone," *Art e dossier* 16 (2001): 34-40.

Papi 1996: Gianni Papi, "Riflessioni sul percorso caravaggesco di Bartolomeo Cavarozzi," *Paragone Arte* 47 (1996): 85-96.

Papi 1997: Gianni Papi, "Il Maestro dell'Incredulità di San Tommaso," *Arte Cristiana* (1997): 121-30.

Papi 2001: Gianni Papi, *Cecco del Caravaggio* (Soncino: Edizioni del Soncino, 2001).

Papi 2003a: Gianni Papi, *Spadarino* (Soncino: Edizioni del Soncino, 2003).

Papi 2003b: Gianni Papi, "La cappella Guicciardini in Santa Felicita: la difficile trasferta fiorentina della 'schola' del Caravaggio," in Antonio Natali, ed., *Gherardo delle Notti, lacerti lirici: L'Adorazione dei pastori di Gherardo delle Notti risanata dopo l'attentato* (Milan: Silvana Editore, 2003): 41-65.

Pardo 2006: Mary Pardo, "The Subject of Savoldo's *Magdalene*," in Michael W. Cole, ed., *Sixteenth-Century Italian Art* (Oxford : Blackwell, 2006) : 441-84.

Pariset 1948: François-Georges Pariset, *Georges De La Tour* (Paris: Laurens, 1948).

Parshall 1974: Peter Parshall, *Lucas van Leyden and the Rise of Pictorial Narrative* (unpublished doctoral dissertation: University of Chicago, 1974).

Parshall 2001: Peter Parshall, "Hans Holbein's *Pictures of Death*," in Mark Roskill and John O. Hand, eds., *Hans Holbein: Paintings, Prints, and Reception* (Washington DC, National Gallery of Art, 2001): 83-94.

Parshall and Takahatake 2007: Peter Parshall and Naoko Takahatake, "Cherubino Alberti, Lelio Orsi and Cornelis Cort," *Print Quarterly* 24 (2007): 430-1.

Passarelli 2007: Maria Antonietta Passarelli, "Leon Battista Alberti grammatico e teorico d'arte," in Arturo Calzona, Francesco Paolo Fiore and Alberto Tenenti, eds., *Leon Battista Alberti teorico delle arti e gli impegni civili del 'De re aedificatoria'* (Florence: Olschki, 2007) 1:225-33.

Payne 2007: Alina Payne, "Alberti and the Origins of the 'Paragone' between Architecture and the Figural Arts," in Arturo Calzona, Francesco Paolo Fiore and Alberto Tenenti, eds., *Leon Battista Alberti teorico delle arti e gli impegni civili del De re aedificatoria* (Florence: Olschki, 2007): 347-68.

Pedrocchi 2000: Anna Maria Pedrocchi, *Le stanze del tesoriere: La quadreria Patrizi. Cultura senese nella storia del collezionismo romano del Seicento* (Milan: Alcon, 2000).

Penny 1994: Nicholas Penny, "Non-Finito in Italian Fifteenth-Century Bronze Sculpture," *Antologia di Belle Arti* 48-51 (1994): 11-15.

Pepper 1971: Stephen Pepper, "Caravaggio and Guido Reni: Contrasts in Attitude," *The Art Quarterly* 34 (1971): 325-44.

Pepper 1988: Stephen Pepper, *Guido Reni: L'opera completa* (Novara: Istituto Geografico De Agostini, 1988).

Pericolo 1998: Lorenzo Pericolo, "Le clavi delle calighe: Qualche riflessione su Rubens, Peiresc et l'archeologia del quadro," *Artes* 6 (1998): 82-96.

Pericolo 2001a: Lorenzo Pericolo, "Le roi et le favori: Essai d'interprétation des *Reines de Perse* par Charles Le Brun," *Annali della Scuola Normale Superiore di Pisa. Classe di Lettere e Filosofia* 6 (2001): 125-48.

Pericolo 2001b: Lorenzo Pericolo, "Le fantasiette di Nicolas Poussin per Giovan Battista Marino," *Critica d'arte* 12 (2001): 35-45.

Pericolo 2002: Lorenzo Pericolo, *"Philippe, homme sage et vertueux": Essai sur l'art et l'œuvre de Philippe de Champaigne (1602-1674)* (Tournai: La Renaissance du Livre, 2002).

Pericolo 2003: Lorenzo Pericolo, "Smoderato piacer termina in doglia. Sul *Trionfo d'Ovidio* della Galleria Corsini a Roma attribuito a Nicolas Poussin. Prima parte," *Annali dell'Università di Ferrara. Sezione Lettere* 4 (2003): 263-92.

Pericolo 2005: Lorenzo Pericolo, " Smoderato piacer termina in doglia. Sul *Trionfo d'Ovidio* della Galleria Corsini a Roma attribuito a Nicolas Poussin. Seconda parte," *Annali dell'Università di Ferrara. Sezione Storia* 2 (2005): 209-49.

Pericolo 2007: Lorenzo Pericolo, "Visualizing Appearance and Disappearance: On Caravaggio's London *Supper at Emmaus*," *Art Bulletin* 89 (2007): 519-39.

Pericolo 2008: Lorenzo Pericolo, "Caravaggio's *The Cardsharps* and Marino's "Gioco di Primera": A Case of Intertextuality?," *Memoirs of the American Academy in Rome* 53 (2008): 129-51.

Pericolo 2009a: Lorenzo Pericolo, "The Invisible Presence: Close-Up, Cut-In, and Off-Scene in Antonello da Messina's Palermo *Annunciate*," *Representations* 107 (2009): 1-29.

Pericolo 2009b: Lorenzo Pericolo, "Love in the Mirror: A Comparative Reading of Titian's *Woman at Her Toilet* and Caravaggio's *Conversion of Mary Magdalene*," *Villa I Tatti Studies* 12 (2009): 149-79.

Pericolo 2010: Lorenzo Pericolo, "Nude in Motion: Rembrandt's *Danae* and the Indeterminacy of the Subject," in Alexander Nagel and Lorenzo Pericolo, eds., *Subject in Aporia in Early Modern Art* (Aldershot: Ashgate, 2010): 195-216.

Perini 1990: Giovanna Perini, "Biographical Anecdotes and Historical Truth: An Example from Malvasia's 'Life of Guido Reni'," *Studi Secenteschi* 31 (1990): 149-60.

Perini 1991: Giovanna Perini, "Review of Carl Goldstein, *Visual Fact over Verbal Fiction: A Study of the Carracci and the Criticism, Theory and Practice of Art in Renaissance and Baroque Italy*," *Burlington Magazine* 133 (1991): 203-4.

Perini 1995: Giovanna Perini, "Caravaggio a Bologna," in Francesco Abbate and Fiorella Sricchia Santoro, eds., *Napoli e l'Europa: Ricerche di storia dell'arte in onore di Ferdinando Bologna* (Catanzaro: Meridiana Libri, 1995): 199-203.

Perini 1997: Giovanna Perini, "L'ultima *Annunciazione* di Ludovico," in Roberta Terra, ed., *La cattedrale di San Pietro in Bologna* (Cinisello Balsamo: Silvana, 1997): 86-101.

Perini 2002a: Giovanna Perini, Caravaggio e i Carracci: Appunti su un intreccio di percorsi," in Caterina Volpi, ed., *Caravaggio nel IV Centenario della Cappella Contarelli*…(s.l.: CAM, 2002): 303-12.

Perini 2002b: Giovanna Perini, "*Belloriana methodus*: A Scholar's *Bildungsgeschichte* in Seventeenth-Century Rome," in Janis C. Bell and Thomas Willette, eds., *Art History in the Age of Bellori: Scholarship and Cultural Politics in Seventeenth-Century Rome* (Cambridge: Cambridge University Press, 2002): 55-74.

Periti 2005: Giancarla Periti, "Correggio, Prati e l'*Ecce Homo*: Nuovi intrecci intorno a problemi di devozione nella Parma rinascimentale," in Giancarla Periti, ed., *Emilia e Marche nel Rinascimento: L'identità visiva della periferia* (Azzano San Paolo: Bolis, 2005).

Pestilli 2000: Livio Pestilli, "Michelangelo's *Pietà*: Lombard Critics and Plinian Sources," *Source* 19 (2000): 21-30.

Peters 1985: Jane C. Peters, *The Illustrated Bartsch. 20 (Part 2) German Masters of the Sixteenth Century: Jost Amman, Woodcuts, Continued* (New York: Abaris Books, 1985).

Pfatteicher 1987: Philip H. Pfatteicher, "Caravaggio's Conception of Time in his Two Versions of *The Supper at Emmaus*," *Source* 7 (1987): 9-13.

Picchiarelli 2007: Veruska Picchiarelli, "Baccio Bandinelli e Giorgio Vasari: Modelli comportamentali a confronto nella seconda edizione delle *Vite*," in Antonino Caleca, ed., *Arezzo e Vasari: Vite e Postille* (Foligno: Cartei & Bianchi, 2007): 97-137.

Pichler 2007: Wolfram Pichler, "Il dubbio e il doppio: Le evidenze in Caravaggio," in Sybille Ebert-Schifferer, Julian Kliemann, Valeska von Rosen and Lothar Sickel, eds., *Caravaggio e il suo ambiente: Ricerche e interpretazioni* (Rome: Silvana, 2007): 9-33.

Pierce 1953: Stella M. Pierce, "Costume in Caravaggio's Painting," *Magazine of Art* 46 (1953): 147-54.

Pierguidi 2006: Stefano Pierguidi, "Federico Zuccari: Tra reazione antivasariana e ossequio al culto di Michelangelo," *Schede umanistiche* 20 (2006): 165-77.

Pignatti and Pedrocco 1995: Terisio Pignatti and Francesco Pedrocco, *Veronese* (Milan: Electa, 1995).

Pirondini et al. 2000: Massimo Pirondini, Emilio Negro, Nicosetta Roio and Elio Monducci, *Alessandro Tiarini (1577-1668)* (Reggio Emilia, Merigo Art Books, 2000).

Pirondini et al. 2002: Massimo Pirondini, Emilio Negro, Nicosetta Roio and Elio Monducci, *Leonello Spada (1576-1622)* (Reggio Emilia: Merigo Art Books, 2002).

Poeschke 1985: Joachim Poeschke, "Zum Begriff der *concinnitas* bei Leon Battista Alberti," in Frank Büttner and Christian Lenz, eds., *Intuition und Darstellung: Erich Hubala zum 24. März 1985* (Munich: Nymphenburger, 1985): 45-50.

Polichetti 2001: Maria Luisa Polichetti, ed., *Ianua Coeli: Disegni di Cristoforo Roncalli e Cesare Maccari per la cupola della basilica di Loreto* (Rome: Artemide, 2001).

Politi 1835: Giuseppe Politi, *Siracusa pei viaggiatori ovvero descrizione storica, artistica, topografica delle attuali antichità di Ortigia, Acradina, Tica, Napoli, ed Epipoli che componevano l'antica Siracusa* (Syracuse: Pulejo, 1835).

Popham 1957: A.E. Popham, *Correggio's Drawings* (London: The British Academy and Oxford University Press, 1957).

Popp 2007: Jessica Popp, *Sprechende Bilder–Verstummte Betrachter: Zur Historienmalerei Domenichinos (1581-1641)* (Cologne: Böhlau, 2007).

Portús 2007: Javier Portús, ed., *Velázquez's Fables: Mythology and Sacred History in the Golden Age*, exh. cat. (Madrid: Museo del Prado, 2007).

Posèq 1998: Avigdor W.G. Posèq, *Caravaggio and the Antique* (London: Avon Books, 1998).

Posner 1971a: Donald Posner, *Annibale Carracci: A Study in the Reform of Italian Painting around 1590* (London: Phaidon, 1971).

Posner 1971b: Donald Posner, "Caravaggio's Homo-Erotic Early Works," *The Art Quarterly* 34 (1971): 301-24.

Pozzi 1993: Giovanni Pozzi, *Sull'orlo del visibile parlare* (Milan: Adelphi, 1993).

Pozzi and Mattioda 2006: Mario Pozzi and Enrico Mattioda, *Giorgio Vasari: Storico e critico* (Florence: Olschki, 2006).

Prater 1985: Andreas Prater, "Wo ist Matthäus: Beobachtungen zu Caravaggios Anfängen als Monumentalmaler in der Contarelli-Kapelle," *Pantheon* 43 (1985): 70-4.

Prater 1992: Andreas Prater, *Licht und Farbe bei Caravaggio: Studien zur Ästhetik und Ikonologie des Helldunkels* (Stuttgart: Steiner, 1992).

Prater 1995: Andreas Prater, "Matthäus und kein Ende? Eine Entgegnung," *Pantheon* 53 (1995): 53-61.

Preimesberger 2001: Rudolf Preimesberger, "Paragone-Motive und theoretische Konzepte in Vincenzo Giustinianis *Discorso sopra la scultura*," in Silvia Danesi Squarzina, ed., *Caravaggio in Preußen: Die Sammlung Giustiniani und die Berliner Gemäldegalerie*, exh. cat. (Milan: Electa, 2001): 50-6.

Preimesberger 2007: Rudolf Preimesberger, "Un doppio diletto nell'imitazione? Qualche riflessione sulla *Cattura di Cristo* di Caravaggio," in Sybille Ebert-Schifferer, Julian Kliemann, Valeska von Rosen and Lothar Sickel, eds., *Caravaggio e il suo ambiente: Ricerche e interpretazioni* (Rome: Silvana Editore, 2007): 87-97.

Prodi 1967: Paolo Prodi, *Il cardinale Gabriele Paleotti (1522-1597)* (Rome: Edizioni di Storia e Letteratura, 1967).

Previtali 1989: Giovanni Previtali, *La fortuna dei primitivi: Dal Vasari ai neoclassici* (Turin: Einaudi, 1989).

Puglisi 1998: Catherine Puglisi, *Caravaggio* (London: Phaidon, 1998).

Puglisi 1999: Catherine Puglisi, *Francesco Albani* (New Haven: Yale University Press, 1999).

Pupillo 1996: Marco Pupillo, "I Crescenzi, Francesco Contarelli e Michelangelo da Caravaggio," in Stefania Macioce, ed., *Michelangelo Merisi da Caravaggio: La vita e le opere attraverso i documenti* (Rome: Logart Press, 1996): 148-66.

Pupillo Ferrari-Bravo 1972: Anna Maria Pupillo Ferrari-Bravo, "*Il Figino ovvero del Fine della Pittura di Gregorio Comanini*," *Storia dell'Arte* 13 (1972): 57-66.

Puttfarken 1991: Thomas Puttfarken, "The Dispute about *Disegno* and *Colorito* in Venice: Paolo Pino, Lodovico Dolce and Titian," in Peter Ganz, ed., *Kunst und Kunsttheorie 1400-1900* (Wiesbaden: Harrassowitz, 1991): 75-99.

Puttfarken 1998: Thomas Puttfarken, "Caravaggio's Story of St. Matthew: A Challenge to the Conventions of Painting," *Art History* 21 (1998): 163-81.

Puttfarken 2000: Thomas Puttfarken, *The Discovery of Pictorial Composition: Theories of Visual Order in Painting 1400-1800* (New Haven: Yale University Press, 2000).

Quint 1986: Arlene Quint, *Cardinal Federico Borromeo as a Patron and Critic of the Arts and his Musaeum* (New York: Garland, 1986).

Raabe 1996: Rainald Raabe, *Der imaginierte Betrachter: Studien zur Caravaggio's römischem Werk* (Hildesheim: Georg Olms Verlag, 1996).

Ragionieri 2008: Pina Ragionieri, ed., *Il Volto di Michelangelo*, exh. cat. (Florence: Mandragora, 2008).

Rampley 2003: Matthew Rampley, "Zwischen nomologischer und hermeneutischer Kunstwissenschaft: Alois Riegl und das Problem des Kunstwollens," *Kritische Berichte* 31 (2003): 5-19.

Rampley 2007: Matthew Rampley, "Alois Riegl (1858-1905)," in Ulrich Pfisterer, ed., *Klassiker der Kunstgeschichte* (Munich: Beck, 2007) 1: 152-62.

Reineke 2003: Brigitte Reineke, *Eros und Tod: Zur Bildlichkeit von Feminität in den halbfigurigen Judith-Darstellungen des 16. Jahrhunderts* (Weimar: VDG, 2003).

Reznicek 1961: Emil K.J. Reznicek, *Die Zeichnungen von Hendrik Goltzius: Mit einem beschreibenden Katalog* (Utrecht: Haentjens Dekker & Gumbert, 1961).

Rhein 2008: Gudrun Rhein, *Der Dialog über Malerei: Lodovico Dolces Traktat und die Kunsttheorie des 16. Jahrhunderts* (Cologne: Böhlau, 2008).

Richards and Richards 1990: Kenneth Richards and Laura Richards, *The Commedia dell'Arte: A Documentary History* (Oxford: Blackwell, 1990).

Ricœur 1983: Paul Ricœur, *Temps et récit: 1. L'intrigue et le récit historique* (Paris: Seuil, 1983).

Riegl 1923: Alois Riegl, *Die Entstehung der Barockkunst in Rom*, eds. Arthur Burda and Max Dvorák (Vienna: Kunstverlag Anton Schroll, 1923).

Riegl 1999: Alois Riegl, *The Group Portraiture of Holland*, trans. Evelyn M. Kain and David Britt (Los Angeles: Getty Research Center, 1999).

Ringbom 1965: Sixten Ringbom, *Icon to Narrative: The Rise of the Dramatic Close-Up in Fifteenth-Century Devotional Painting* (Aisbo: Aisbo Academi, 1965).

Ringbom 1966: Sixten Ringbom, "Nuptial Symbolism in Some Fifteenth-Century Reflections of Roman Sepulchral Portraiture," *Temenos: Studies in Comparative Religion* 2 (1966): 68-97.

Robertson 2008: Clare Robertson, *The Invention of Annibale Carracci* (Cinisello Balsamo: Silvana Editoriale, 2008).

Roethlisberger 1993: Marcel G. Roethlisberger, *Abraham Bloemaert and his Sons: Paintings and Prints* (Doornspijk: Davaco, 1993).

Rogers 1992: Mary Rogers, "Decorum in Lodovico Dolce and Titian's *Poesie*," in Francis Ames-Lewis and Anka Bednarek, eds., *Decorum in Renaissance Narrative Art: Papers Delivered at the Annual Conference of Art Historians…* (London: University of London Press, 1992): 111-20.

Roggenkamp 1996: Bernd Roggenkamp, *Die Töchter des "Disegno:" Zur Kanonisierung der drei bildenden Künste durch Giorgio Vasari* (Münster: Lit, 1996).

Romani 1984: Vittoria Romani, *Lelio Orsi* (Modena: Aedes Muratoriana, 1984).

Romani 2004: Vittoria Romani, ed., *Daniele da Volterra, amico di Michelangelo*, exh. cat. (Florence: Mandragora, 2004).

Roncaccia 2006: Alberto Roncaccia, *Il metodo critico di Ludovico Castelvetro* (Rome: Bulzoni, 2006).

Rosand 1997: David Rosand, *Painting in Sixteenth-Century Venice: Titian, Veronese, Tintoretto* (Cambridge: Cambridge University Press, 1997).

Rosand 2001: David Rosand, *Myths of Venice: The Figuration of a State,* (Chapel Hill: University of North Carolina Press, 2001).

Rosand and Muraro 1976: David Rosand and Michelangelo Muraro, *Titian and the Venetian Woodcut,* exh. cat. (Washington DC: International Exhibitions Foundation, 1976).

Rosenauer 1993: Artur Rosenauer, *Donatello* (Milan: Electa, 1993).

Rosenberg 1966: Pierre Rosenberg, *Rouen, Musée des Beaux-Arts: Tableaux français du XVII siècle et italiens des XVII et XVIII siècles* (Paris: Éditions des Musées Nationaux, 1966).

Rosenberg 1973: Pierre Rosenberg, *La 'Mort de Germanicus' de Poussin du Musée de Minneapolis* (Paris: Éditions des Musées Nationaux, 1973).

Rosenberg and Pratt 1994: Pierre Rosenberg and Louis-Antoine Pratt, eds., *Nicolas Poussin: 1594 – 1665*, exh. cat. (Paris: Réunion des Musées Nationaux, 1994).

Rosenberg J. 1954: Jakob Rosenberg, "A Drawing by Jacques de Gheyn," *Art Quarterly* 17 (1954): 166-71.

Rossi F. 2000: Francesco Rossi, "Caravaggio e le armi: Immagine descrittiva," in Claudio Strinati and Rossella Vodret, eds., *Caravaggio: La luce nella pittura lombarda*, exh. cat. (Milan: Electa, 2000): 77-88.

Rossi S. 1996: Sergio Rossi, "Peccato e redenzione negli autoritratti del Caravaggio," in Stefania Macioce, ed., *Michelangelo Merisi da Caravaggio: La vita e le opere attraverso i documenti* (Rome: Logart Press, 1996): 316-30.

Röttgen 1964: Herwarth Röttgen, "Giuseppe Cesari, die Contarelli-Kapelle und Caravaggio," *Zeitschrift für Kunstgeschichte* 27 (1964): 201-27.

Röttgen 1965: Herwarth Röttgen, "Die Stellung der Contarelli Kapelle in Caravaggios Werk," *Zeitschrift für Kunstgeschichte* 28 (1965): 47-68.

Röttgen 1969: "Caravaggio-Probleme," *Münchner Jahrbuch der bildenden Kunst* 20 (1969): 143-70.

Röttgen 1974: Herwarth Röttgen, *Il Caravaggio: Ricerche e interpretazioni*, (Rome: Bulzoni, 1974).

Röttgen 1975: Herwarth Röttgen, "La *Resurrezione di Lazzaro* del Caravaggio," in Mia Cinotti, ed., *Novità sul Caravaggio: Saggi e contributi* (Milan: Amilcare Pizzi, 1975): 61-74.

Röttgen 1991: Herwarth Röttgen, "Da ist Matthäus," *Pantheon* 49 (1991), 97-9.

Röttgen 1993: Herwarth Röttgen, "Quel diavolo è Caravaggio: Giovanni Baglione e la sua denuncia satirica dell'Amore terreno," *Storia dell'Arte* 79 (1993): 326-40.

Röttgen 2002: Herwarth Röttgen, *Il Cavalier Giuseppe Cesari d'Arpino: Un grande pittore nello splendore della fama e nell'incostanza della fortuna* (Rome: Bozzi, 2002).

Rowlands 1977: John K. Rowlands, *Hollstein's German Engravings, Etchings and Woodcuts. Volume XI. Urs Graf* (Amsterdam: Hertzberger, 1977).

Rubin 1995: Patricia L. Rubin, *Giorgio Vasari: Art and History* (New Haven: Yale University Press, 1995).

Rudlin 1994: John Rudlin, *Commedia dell'Arte: An Actor's Handbook* (London: Routledge, 1994).

Rudolph and Ostrow 2001: Conrad Rudolph and Steven F. Ostrow, "Isaac Laughing: Caravaggio, Non-traditional Imagery and Traditional Identification," *Art History* 24 (2001): 646-81.

Rudrauf 1955-1956: Lucien Rudrauf, *Le Repas d'Emmaüs: Étude d'un thème plastique et de ses variations en peinture et sculpture* (Paris: Nouvelles Éditions Latines, 1955-1956).

Ruggeri 1984: Ugo Ruggeri, *Domenico Carpinoni*, in *I pittori bergamaschi dal XIII al XIX secolo: Il Seicento* (Bergamo: Bolis, 1984): 2:205-89.

Ryan 2003: Marie Laure Ryan, *Narrative as Virtual Reality: Immersion and Interactivity in Literature and Electronic Media* (Baltimore: Johns Hopkins University Press, 2003).

Rylands 1992: Philip Rylands, *Palma Vecchio* (Cambridge: Cambridge University Press, 1992).

Saccà 1906-1907: Virgilio Saccà, "Michelangelo da Caravaggio pittore: Studi e ricerche," *Archivio Storico Messinese* 7 (1906): 40-69; 8 (1907): 41-79.

Salerno 1950: Luigi Salerno, "Sul trattato di Giulio Mancini," *Commentari* 2 (1950): 26-39.

Salerno 1974: Luigi Salerno, "Detroit's *Conversion of the Magdalen* (the Alzaga Caravaggio). 5. The Art-Historical Implications of the Detroit *Magdalen*," *Burlington Magazine* 116 (1974): 587-93.

Salerno 1988: Luigi Salerno, *I dipinti del Guercino* (Rome: Ugo Bozzi Editore, 1988).

Salerno et al. 1966: Luigi Salerno, Duncan T. Kinkead, and William H. Wilson, "Poesia e simboli nel Caravaggio," *Palatino* 10 (1966): 106-17.

Salvarani 1994: Renata Salvarani, "La lezione albertiana nella trattatistica artistica della riforma cattolica: Note in margine alle esperienze normative di Carlo Borromeo, Antonio Possevino e Gabriele Paleotti," *Civiltà Mantovana* 29 (1994): 85-91.

Sammut 1949: Edward Sammut, *Caravaggio in Malta* (Malta: Progress Press, 1949).

Sanpaolesi 1966: Piero Sanpaolesi, "Il 'non finito' di Michelangelo in scultura e architettura," in *Atti del Convegno di Studi Michelangioleschi* (Rome: Edizioni dell'Ateneo, 1966): 228-40.

Santore 1997: Cathy Santore, "The Tools of Venus," *Renaissance Studies* 11 (1997): 179-207.

Sapir 2005-2006: Itay Sapir, "The Destruction of Painting: An Art History for Art that Resists History," *Leitmotiv* 5 (2005-2006): 67-76.

Scarrocchia 2006: Sandro Scarrocchia, *Oltre la storia dell'arte: Alois Riegl, vita e opere di un protagonista della cultura viennese* (Milan: Martinotti, 2006).

Scavizzi 1992: Giuseppe Scavizzi, *The Controversy on Images from Calvin to Baronius* (New York: Lang, 1992).

Schäpers 1997: Petra Schäpers, *Die junge Frau bei der Toilette: Ein Bildthema im venezianischen Cinquecento* (Frankfurt am Main: Lang, 1997).

Schapiro 1943: Meyer Schapiro, "The Image of the Disappearing Christ: The Ascension in English Art around the Year 1000," *Gazette des Beaux-Arts* 23 (1943): 133-52.

Schapiro 1979: Meyer Schapiro, *Selected Papers: Late Antiquity, Early Christian and Medieval Art* (New York: G. Brazillier, 1979).

Schleier 1969: Erich Schleier, "Emilio Savonanzi: Inediti del periodo romano," *Antichità Viva* 8 (1969): 3-15.

Schmitt 1993: Stefan Schmitt, *Diogenes: Studien zu seiner Ikonographie in der niederländischen Emblematik und Malerei des 16. und 17. Jahrhunderts* (Hildesheim: Olms, 1993).

Schneider 1988: Norbert Schneider, "Review of Svetlana Alpers, *The Art of Describing: Dutch Art in the Seventeenth Century*," *Kritische Berichte* 16 (1988): 107-10.

Schoch et al. 2001: Rainer Schoch, Matthias Mende and Anna Scherbaum, eds., *Albrecht Dürer: Das druckgraphische Werk* (Munich and New York: Prestel, 2001).

Schrader 2005: Monika Schrader: *Laokoon—"Eine volkommene Regel der Kunst": Ästhetische Theorien der Heuristik in der zweiten Hälfte des 18. Jahrhunderts, Winckelmann, (Mendelssohn), Lessing, Herder, Schiller, Goethe* (Hildesheim: Olms, 2005).

Schröter 1995: Elisabeth Schröter, "Caravaggio und die Gemäldesammlung der Familie Mattei: Addenda und Corrigenda zu den jüngsten Forschungen und Funden," *Pantheon* 53 (1995): 62-87.

Schuchman and De Hoop Scheffer 1996: Christiaan Schuchman and D. De Hoop Scheffer, *Hollstein's Dutch and Flemish Etchings, Engravings and Woodcuts 1450-1700. XLIV. Maarten De Vos* (Rotterdam: Sound & Vision, 1996).

Schuttwolf 1998: Allmuth Schuttwolf, ed., *Jahreszeiten der Gefühle: Das Gothaer Liebespaar und die Minne im Spätmittelalter*, exh. cat. (Ostfildern bei Stuttgart: G. Hatje, 1998).

Schütze I. 2000: Irene Schütze, "Zeigefinger—Fingerzeige: Konzepte der Geste in der Debatte um Caravaggios *Berufung des Matthäus*," in Margreth Egidi and Oliver Schneider, eds., *Gestik: Figuren des Körpers in Text und Bild* (Tübingen: Narr, 2000): 185-99.

Schütze 2009: Sebastian Schütze, *Caravaggio: The Complete Works* (Cologne: Taschen, 2009).

Schwedes 2000: Kerstin Schwedes, "Michelangelos *Römische Pietà*," in Michael Rohlmann and Andreas Thielemann, eds., *Michelangelo: Neue Beiträge* (Munich: Deutscher Kunstverlag, 2000): 93-112.

Sciberras and Stone 2006: Keith Sciberras and David M. Stone, *Caravaggio: Art, Knighthood, and Malta* (Valletta: Midsea Books, 2006).

Sciolla 2000: Gianni Carlo Sciolla, "Grazia, prestezza, terribilità: Definizione e ricezione della pittura in Paolo Pino e Lodovico Dolce," in *Omaggio secondo all'arte veneta nel ricordo di Rodolfo Pallucchini* (Monfalcone: Edizioni della Laguna, 2000): 92-5.

Scorrano 2005: Luigi Scorrano, "Gabriele Paleotti e il 'catechismo' dei pittori, 'teologi mutoli'," *Studi Rinascimentali* 3 (2005): 113-27.

Scribner 1977: Charles Scribner III, "*In Alia Effigie*: Caravaggio's London *Supper at Emmaus*," *Art Bulletin* 59 (1977): 375-82.

Seelig et al. 2003: Gero Seelig, Giulia Bartrum and Marjolein Leesberg, *The New Hollstein. German Engravings, Etchings and Woodcuts 1400-1700: Jost Amman. Book Illustrations, Part VI* (Rotterdam: Sound & Vision, 2003).

Seicento Fiorentino **1986**: *Il Seicento fiorentino: Arte a Firenze da Ferdinando I a Cosimo III*, exh. cat. (Florence: Cantini, 1986).

Seidel 1993: Linda Seidel, *Jan van Eyck's* Arnolfini Portrait: *Stories of an Icon* (Cambridge: Cambridge University Press, 1993).

Sellink and Leesberg 2001: Manfred Sellink and Marjolein Leesberg, *The New Hollstein: Dutch and Flemish Etchings, Engravings and Woodcuts 1450-1700. Philips Galle* (Rotterdam: Sound & Vision, 2001).

Sénéchal 1996: Philippe Sénéchal, "Fortune de quelques antiques Farnèse auprès des peintres à Rome au début du XVIIᵉ siècle," in Olivier Bonfait, Christoph Luitpold Frommel, Michel Hochmann and Sebastian Schütze, eds., *Poussin et Rome: Actes du colloque à l'Académie de France à Rome et à la Bibliotheca Hertziana, 16-18 novembre 1994* (Paris: Réunion des Musées Nationaux, 1996): 31-45.

Serodine 1987: *Serodine: L'opera completa* (Milan : Electa, 1987).

Serres 2003: Karen Serres, "L'utilisation du modèle vivant dans la peinture caravagesque à Rome," in Pascal-François Bertrand and Stéphanie Trouvé, eds., *Nicolas Tournier et la peinture caravagesque en Italie, en France et en Espagne...* (Toulouse: Framespa-CNRS France méridionale et Espagne, 2003): 77-90.

Settis 1978: Salvatore Settis, *La 'Tempesta' interpretata: Giorgione, i committenti, il soggetto* (Turin: Einaudi, 1978).

Shearman 1972: John Shearman, *Raphael's Cartoons in the Collection of Her Majesty the Queen and the Tapestries for the Sistine Chapel* (London: Phaidon, 1972).

Shearman 1992: John Shearman, *Only Connect...Art and the Spectator in the Italian Renaissance* (Princeton: Princeton University Press, 1992).

Shrimplin Evangelidis 1989: Valerie Shrimplin Evangelidis, "Michelangelo and Nicodemism," *Art Bulletin* 71 (1989): 693-4.

Sickel 2001: Lothar Sickel, "Remarks on the Patronage of Caravaggio's *Entombment of Christ*," *Burlington Magazine* 143 (2001): 426-9.

Sickel 2003: Lothar Sickel, *Caravaggios Rom: Annäherungen an ein dissonantes Milieu* (Emsdetten: Imorde, 2003).

Silver 1974: Larry A. Silver, "The *Ill-Matched Pair* by Quinten Massys," *Studies in the History of Art* 6 (1974): 105-23.

Silver 1984: Larry A. Silver, *The Paintings of Quinten Massys with Catalogue Raisonné* (Montclair: Allanheld & Schram, 1984).

Silver 1998: Larry A. Silver, "Middle Class Morality: Love and Marriage in the Art of Lucas van Leyden," in Lucinda S. Dixon, ed., *In Detail: New Studies of Northern Renaissance Art in Honor of Walter S. Gibson* (Turnhout: Brepols, 1998): 97-111.

Silver 2000: Larry A. Silver, "Caravaggism's Missing Link, or What Ter Brugghen Brought Home from Rome," *Pantheon* 58 (2000): 187-91.

Simonato 2009: Lucia Simonato, "Esperienze visive e storiche in Sandrart," in Sybille Ebert-Schifferer and Cecilia Mazzetti in Pietralata, eds., *Joachim von Sandrart: Ein europäischer Künstler und Theoretiker zwischen Italien und Deutschland* (Munich: Hirmer, 2009): 211-31.

Slatkes and Franits 2007: Leonard J. Slatkes and Wayne Franits, *The Paintings of Hendrick Ter Brugghen, 1588-1629: Catalogue Raisonné* (Amsterdam: John Benjamins, 2007).

Smick-McIntire 1996a: Rebekah J. Smick-McIntire, *Image and the Rhetorics of Feminine Compassion: Art Critical and Poetic Reception of Michelangelo's Vatican Pietà in the Sixteenth and Seventeenth Centuries* (unpublished doctoral dissertation, University of Toronto, 1996).

Smick-McIntire 1996b: Rebekah J. Smick-McIntire, "Evoking Michelangelo's Vatican *Pietà*: Transformations in the Topos of Living Stone," in Amy Golahny, ed., *The Eye of the Poet: Studies in the Reciprocity of the Visual and Literary Arts from the Renaissance to the Present* (Lewisburg: Bucknell University Press, 1996): 23-52.

Smith 1992: Elise L. Smith, *The Paintings of Lucas van Leyden: A New Appraisal, with Catalogue Raisonné* (Columbia: University of Missouri Press, 1992).

Smith O'Neil 2002: Maryvelma Smith O'Neil, *Giovanni Baglione: Artistic Reputation in Baroque Rome* (Cambridge: Cambridge University Press, 2002).

Snow-Smith 1978: Joanne Snow-Smith, "The *Salvator Mundi* of Leonardo da Vinci," *Arte Lombarda* 50 (1978): 69-81.

Snow-Smith 1982: Joanne Snow-Smith, *The Salvator Mundi of Leonardo da Vinci*, exh. cat. (Seattle: Henry Art Gallery, University of Washington, 1982).

Sohm 1985: Philip Sohm, "Affectation and 'Sprezzatura' in Sixteenth- and Early Seventeenth-century Italian Painting, Prosody and Music," in Hermann Fillitz and Martina Pippal, eds., *Akten des 25. Kongresses für Kunstgeschichte* (Vienna: Böhlau, 1985): 23-40.

Sohm 1991: Philip Sohm, *Pittoresco: Marco Boschini, His Critics, and Their Critiques of Painterly Brushwork in Seventeenth- and Eighteenth-Century Italy* (Cambridge: Cambridge University Press, 1991).

Sohm 2001: Philip Sohm, *Style in the Art Theory of Early Modern Italy* (Cambridge: Cambridge University Press, 2001).

Sohm 2002: Philip Sohm, "Caravaggio's Deaths," *Art Bulletin* 84 (2002): 449-68.

Sohm 2007: Philip Sohm, *The Artist Grows Old: The Aging of Art and Artists in Italy, 1500-1800* (New Haven: Yale University Press, 2007).

Solf 1975: Sabine Solf, *Festdekoration und Groteske: Der Wiener Bühnenbildner Lodovico Ottavio Burnacini; Inszenierung barocker Kunstvorstellung* (Baden-Baden: Koerner, 1975).

Solimene 1952: Giuseppe Solimene, *Un umanista venosino (Bartolomeo Maranta) giudica Tiziano* (Naples: Società Aspetti Letterari, 1952).

Spadaro 1995: Alvise Spadaro, *La 'Resurrezione di Lazzaro' e la famiglia di Giovanni Battista Lazzari Patrizio di Castelnuovo, Signore del Castello di Alfano, committente messinese di Caravaggio* (s.l.: Centro di Ricerca Economica e Scientifica, 1995).

Sparti 2002: Donatella Sparti, "La formazione di Giovan Pietro Bellori, la nascita delle *Vite* e il loro scopo," *Studi di Storia dell'arte* 13 (2002): 177-248.

Sparti 2008: Donatella L. Sparti, "Novità su Giulio Mancini: Medicina, arte e presunta *connoisseurship*," *Mitteilungen des Kunsthistorischen Institutes in Florenz* 52 (2008): 53-72.

Spear 1965: Richard E. Spear, "The *Raising of Lazarus*: Caravaggio and the Sixteenth-Century Tradition," *Gazette des Beaux-Arts* 65 (1965): 65-70.

Spear 1971: Richard E. Spear, *Caravaggio and His Followers*, exh. cat. (Cleveland: Cleveland Museum of Art, 1971).

Spear 1982: Richard E. Spear, *Domenichino* (New Haven: Yale University Press, 1982).

Spear 1987: Richard E. Spear, "Leonardo, Raphael and Caravaggio," in Helmut Hagger and Susan Scott Mushower, eds., *Light on the Eternal City* (University Park: Pennsylvania State University Press, 1987) 2: 59-90.

Spear 1997: Richard E. Spear, *The 'Divine' Guido: Religion, Sex, Money, and Art in the World of Guido Reni* (New Haven: Yale University Press, 1997).

Spear 2002: Richard E. Spear, *From Caravaggio to Artemisia: Essays on Painting in Seventeenth-Century Italy and France* (London: Pindar, 2002).

Spezzaferro 1974: Luigi Spezzaferro, "Detroit's *Conversion of the Magdalen* (the Alzaga Caravaggio). 4. The Documentary Findings: Ottavio Costa as a Patron of Caravaggio," *Burlington Magazine* 116 (1974): 579-86.

Spezzaferro 1985: Luigi Spezzaferro, "Un imprenditore del primo Seicento: Giovanni Battista Crescenzi," *Ricerche di Storia dell'Arte* 26 (1985): 50-73.

Spezzaferro 2001: Luigi Spezzaferro, "La Cappella Cerasi e il Caravaggio," in Maria Grazia Bernardini, ed., *Caravaggio, Carracci, Maderno: La Cappella Cerasi in Santa Maria del Popolo a Roma* (Cinisello Balsamo: Silvana, 2001): 9-34.

Spike 2001: John T. Spike, *Caravaggio* (New York: Abbeville Press, 2001).

Spinosa 2009: Nicola Spinosa, *Ritorno al barocco: Da Caravaggio a Vanvitelli*, exh. cat. (Naples: Electa, 2009).

Squizzato 2004: Alessandra Squizzato, "Michelangelo negli scritti d'arte di Giovan Paolo Lomazzo," in Alessandro Rovetta, ed., *Tracce di letteratura artistica in Lombardia* (Bari: Edizioni di Pagina, 2004): 61-96.

Stechow 1964: Wolfgang Stechow, "Joseph of Arimathea or Nicodemus?," in Wolfgang Lotz and Lise Lotte Möller, eds., *Studien zur toskanischen Kunst: Festschrift für Ludwig Heinrich Heidenreich* (Munich: Prestel, 1964): 289-302.

Stechow 1967: Wolfgang Stechow, "Emmaus," in *Reallexikon zur deutschen Kunstgeschichte* (Stuttgart: A. Druckenmüller. 1967): 5:228-42.

Steinberg 1959: Leo Steinberg, "Some Observations on the Cerasi Chapel," *Art Bulletin* 41 (1959): 183-90.

Steinberg 1975: Leo Steinberg, "The *Last Judgment* as Merciful Heresy," *Art in America* 63 (1975): 48-63.

Steinberg 1988: Leo Steinberg, "Michelangelo's Florentine *Pietà*," *Art Bulletin* 71 (1988): 480-505.

Steinberg 2001: Leo Steinberg, *Leonardo's Incessant Supper* (New York: Zone Books, 2001).

Steinberg 2006: Leo Steinberg, "Michelangelo's Florentine *Pietà*: The Missing Leg," in Michael W. Cole, ed., *Sixteenth-Century Italian Art* (Oxford: Blackwell, 2006): 196-219.

Stewart 1979: Alison G. Stewart, *Unequal Lovers: A Study of Unequal Couples in Northern Art* (New York: Abaris, 1979).

Stoichita 1999: Viktor I. Stoichita, *L'instauration du tableau: Métapeinture à l'aube des temps modernes* (Geneva: Droz, 1999).

Stoichita 2004: Viktor I. Stoichita, "Beautiful Helen and Her Double in the *Galleria* by Cavalier Marino," *RES* 46 (2004): 120-33.

Stone 1991a: David M. Stone, *Guercino* (Florence: Cantini, 1991).

Stone 1991b: David M. Stone, *Guercino: Master Drawings*, exh. cat. (Bologna: Nuova Alfa Editoriale, 1991).

Stone 2002: David M. Stone, "*In Figura Diaboli*: Self and Myth in Caravaggio's *David and Goliath*," in Pamela J. Jones and Thomas Worcester, eds., *From Rome to Eternity* (Leiden: Brill, 2002): 19-43.

Stone 2006: David M. Stone, "Self and Myth in Caravaggio's *David and Goliath*," in Genevieve Warwick, ed., *Caravaggio: Realism, Rebellion, Reception* (Newark: University of Delaware Press, 2006): 36-46.

Strauss 1977: Walter L. Strauss, *Hendrik Goltzius 1558-1617: The Complete Engravings and Woodcuts* (New York: Abaris, 1977).

Strauss 1980: Walter L. Strauss, *The Illustrated Bartsch.4. Netherlandish Artists. Matham, Saenredam, Muller* (New York: Abaris, 1980).

Strauss 1981: Walter L. Strauss, *The Illustrated Bartsch. 13. Sixteenth-Century Artists* (New York: Abaris Books, 1981).

Strauss 1984: Walter L. Strauss, *The Illustrated Bartsch. 13 (Commentary) German Masters of the Sixteenth Century: Erhard Schoen, Niklas Stoer* (New York: Abaris Books, 1984).

Strinati and Lindemann 2008: Claudio Strinati and Bernd Wolfgang Lindemann, eds., *Sebastiano del Piombo 1485-1547*, exh. cat. (Milan: Motta, 2008).

Strinati and Vodret 1995: Claudio Strinati and Rossella Vodret, eds., *Caravaggio e la collezione Mattei*, exh. cat. (Milan: Electa, 1995).

Strinati and Vodret 2000: Claudio Strinati and Rossella Vodret, eds., *Caravaggio: La luce nella pittura lombarda*, exh. cat. (Milan: Electa, 2000).

Stumpel 1984: Jeroem Stumpel, "Review of Svetlana Alpers, *The Art of Describing: Dutch Art in the Seventeenth Century*," *Burlington Magazine* 126 (1984): 580-1.

Stumpfhaus 2007: Bernhard Stumpfhaus, *Modus—Affekt—Allegorie bei Nicolas Poussin: Emotionen in der Malerei des 17. Jahrhunderts* (Berlin: Reimer, 2007).

Summers 1972: David Summers, "Maniera and Movement: *The Figura Serpentinata*," *Art Quarterly* 35 (1972): 265-301.

Summers 1981: David Summers, *Michelangelo and the Language of Art* (Princeton: Princeton University Press, 1981).

Summerscale 2000: Anne Summerscale, *Malvasia's Life of the Carracci: Commentary and Translation* (University Park: The Pennsylvania State University Press, 2000).

Suthor 2003: Nicola Suthor, "Bad Touch?: Zum Körpereinsatz in Michelangelo/Pontormos *Noli me tangere* und Caravaggios *Ungläubigem Thomas*," in Valeska von Rosen, Klaus Krüger, and Rudolf Preimesberger, eds., *Der stumme Diskurs der Bilder: Reflexionsformen des Ästhetischen in der Kunst der Frühen Neuzeit* (Munich: Deutscher Kunstverlag, 2003): 261-81.

Talbot 1981: Charles W. Talbot, "Baldung and the Female Nude," in James H. Marrow and Alan Shestack, eds., *Hans Baldung Grien: Prints and Drawings*, exh. cat. (New Haven: Yale University Press, 1981): 19-37.

Taviani 1970: Ferdinando Taviani, *La commedia dell'arte e la società barocca* (Rome: Bulzoni, 1970).

Tello and Sanz Sanz 1979: Francisco José León Tello and María Merced V. Sanz Sanz, *La teoría española en la pintura en el siglo XVIII: El tratado de Palomino* (Valencia: Nácher, 1979).

Terpening 1997: Ronnie H. Terpening, *Lodovico Dolce, Renaissance Man of Letters* (Toronto: University of Toronto Press, 1997).

Terzaghi 2007: Maria Cristina Terzaghi, *Caravaggio, Annibale Carracci, Guido Reni tra le ricevute del Banco Herrera & Costa* (Rome: L'Erma di Bretschneider, 2007).

Testaverde 2007: Anna Maria Testaverde, ed., *I canovacci della commedia dell'arte* (Einaudi: Turin, 2007).

Teyssèdre 1957: Bernard Teyssèdre, *Roger de Piles et les débats sur le coloris au siècle de Louis XIV* (Paris: La Bibliothèque des Arts, 1957).

Theile 1997: Wolfgang Theile, ed., *Commedia dell'Arte: Geschichte—Theorie—Praxis* (Wiesbaden: Harrassowitz, 1997).

Thomas B. 2001: Ben Thomas, "*The Lantern of Painting*: Michelangelo, Daniele da Volterra and the *Paragone*," *Apollo* 154 (2001): 46-53.

Thomas T. 1985: Troy Thomas, "Expressive Aspects of Caravaggio's First *Inspiration of Saint Matthew*," *Art Bulletin* 67 (1985): 636-52.

Thuillier 1967: Jacques Thuillier, "Temps et tableau: La théorie des 'péripéties' dans la peinture française du XVIIe siècle," in *Stil und Überlieferung in der Kunst des Abendlandes: Akten des 21. Internationalen Kongresses für Kunstgeschichte in Bonn 1964* (Berlin: Mann, 1967): 191-206.

Thürlemann 1990: Felix Thürlemann, *Vom Bild zum Raum: Beiträge zu einer semiotischen Kunstwissenschaft* (Cologne: Dumont, 1990).

Tiffany 2005: Tanya J. Tiffany, "Visualizing Devotion in Early Modern Seville: Velázquez's *Christ in the House of Martha and Mary*," *Sixteenth Century Journal* 36 (2005): 436-9.

Tiffany 2008: Tanya J. Tiffany, "Light, Darkness, and African Salvation: Velázquez's *Supper at Emmaus*," *Art History* 31 (2008): 33-56.

Tittoni Monti 1989: Maria Elisa Tittoni Monti, "*La Buona Ventura* del Caravaggio: Note e precisazioni in margine al restauro," *Quaderni di Palazzo Venezia* 6 (1989): 179-84.

Toesca 1961: Ilaria Toesca, "Observations on Caravaggio's *Repentant Magdalen*," *Journal of the Warburg and Courtauld Institutes* 24 (1961) 114-5.

Tomasi Velli 2007: Silvia Tomasi Velli, *Le immagini e il tempo: Narrazione visiva, storia e allegoria tra Cinque e Seicento* (Pisa: Edizioni della Normale, 2007).

Treffers 1989: Bert Treffers, "Dogma, esegesi e pittura: Caravaggio nella Cappella Contarelli in San Luigi dei Francesi," *Storia dell'arte* 67 (1989): 241-55.

Treffers 1996: Bert Treffers, "Immagine e predicazione nel Caravaggio," in Stefania Macioce, ed., *Michelangelo Merisi da Caravaggio: La vita e le opere attraverso i documenti* (Rome: Logart Press, 1996): 270-88.

Treffers 2002: Bert Treffers, *Caravaggio: Die Bekehrung des Künstlers* (Amsterdam : Castrum Peregrini, 2002).

Úbeda de los Cobos 2001: Andrés Úbeda de los Cobos, *Pensamiento artístico español del siglo XVIII: De Antonio Palomino a Francisco Goya* (Madrid: Museo Nacional del Prado, 2001).

Ullmann 1978: E. Ullmann, "O Leonardo, warum plagst du dich so sehr!: Zur Frage des non-finito im Werke Leonardos da Vinci," *Acta Historiae Artium Academiae Scientiarum Hungaricae* 24 (1978): 185-8.

Umberger 1993: Emily Umberger, "Velázquez and Naturalism I: Interpreting *Los Borrachos*," *RES* 24 (1993): 21-43.

Unglaub 2006: Jonathan Unglaub, *Poussin and the Poetics of Painting: Pictorial Narrative and the Legacy of Tasso* (Cambridge: Cambridge University Press, 2006).

Uppenkamp 2004: Bettina Uppenkamp, *Judith und Holofernes in der italienischen Malerei des Barock* (Berlin: Reimer, 2004).

Valsecchi 1978: Marco Valsecchi, "Contributo per Simone Peterzano," *Arte Veneta* 32 (1978): 285-7.

Vannugli 1998: Antonio Vannugli, "Orazio Borgianni, Juan de Lezcano and a *Martyrdom of St Lawrence* at Roncesvalles," *Burlington Magazine* 140 (1998): 5-15.

Vannugli 1999: Antonio Vannugli, "Caravaggio: L'ultima traccia della *Crocefissione di San Pietro* Sannesio, " *Bollettino d'Arte* 84 (1999): 103-6.

Vannugli 2009: Antonio Vannugli, *La collezione del segretario Juan de Lezcano: Borgianni, Caravaggio, Reni e altri nella quadreria di un funzionario spagnolo nell'Italia del primo Seicento* (Rome: Accademia Nazionale dei Lincei, 2009).

Varotto 2006: Donatella Varotto, "Il 'De Sculptura' di Pomponio Gaurico: Una testimonianza sulla fortuna critica dell'arte di Donatello a Padova," *Storia dell'Arte*, 13/14 (2006): 77-102.

Varriano 1986: John Varriano, "Caravaggio and the Decorative Arts in the two *Suppers at Emmaus*," *Art Bulletin* 68 (1986): 218-24.

Varriano 1999a: John Varriano, "Caravaggio and Violence," *Storia dell'Arte* 97 (1999): 317-32.

Varriano 1999b: John Varriano, "Caravaggio and Religion," in Franco Mormando, ed., *Saints & Sinners: Caravaggio & the Baroque Image*, exh. cat. (Chicago: University of Chicago Press, 1999): 191-207.

Varriano 2006: John Varriano, *Caravaggio: The Art of Realism* (University Park: Pennsylvania State University Press, 2006).

Veldman and Luijten 1994: I.M. Veldman and G. Luijten, eds., *The New Hollstein Dutch and Flemish Etchings, Engravings and Woodcuts: 1450-1700: Maarten van Heemskerk* (Amsterdam: Koninklijke van Poll, 1994).

Veltman 1984: Kim H. Veltman, "Review of Svetlana Alpers' *The Art of Describing: Dutch Art in the Seventeenth Century*," *Kunstchronik* 37 (1984): 262-7.

Venturi 1910: Lionello Venturi, "Studi su Michelangelo da Caravaggio," *L'Arte* 13 (1910): 191-201; 268-84.

Venturi 1912: Lionello Venturi, "Opere inedite di Michelangelo da Caravaggio," *Bollettino d'Arte* 6 (1912): 1-8.

Venturi 1952: Lionello Venturi, "Studi radiografici sul Caravaggio," *Memorie dell'Accademia Nazionale dei Lincei, Classe di Scienze Morali, Storiche e Filologiche* 8 (1952): 37-46.

Venturi 1954: Lionello Venturi, "Il 'non finito' di Leonardo," *Raccolta Vinciana* 17 (1954): 17-20.

Venturi 1963: Lionello Venturi, *Il Caravaggio* (Novara: Istituto Geografico De Agostini, 1963).

Verheyen 1966: Egon Verheyen, "Tizians Eitelkeit des Irdischen *Prudentia et Vanitas*," *Pantheon* 24 (1966): 88-99.

Vlam 1977: Grace A.H. Vlam, "The Calling of Saint Matthew in Sixteenth-Century Flemish Painting," *Art Bulletin* 59 (1977): 561-70.

Vloberg 1946: Maurice Vloberg, *L'Eucharistie dans l'art* (Grenoble: B. Arthaud, 1946).

Vodret 2002: Rossella Vodret, "Giovanni Baglione: Nuovi elementi per le due versioni dell'*Amor sacro e Amor profano*," in Caterina Volpi, ed., *Caravaggio nel IV Centenario della Cappella Contarelli…* (s.l.: CAM, 2002): 291-302.

Vodret 2006: Rossella Vodret, ed., *Il Caravaggio Odescalchi: Le due versioni della Conversione di San Paolo a confronto* (Milan: Skira, 2006).

Volk 1977: Mary Crawford Volk, *Vicencio Carducho and Seventeenth-Century Castilian Painting* (unpublished doctoral dissertation, Yale University, 1977).

Volk Knüttel 2010: Brigitte Volk Knüttel, *Peter Candid (um 1548-1628): Gemälde—Zeichnungen—Druckgraphik* (Berlin: Deutscher Verlag für Kunstwissenschaft, 2010).

Von Einem 1940: Herbert von Einem, "Bemerkungen zur Florentiner *Pietà* Michelangelos," *Jahrbuch der Preußischen Kunstsammlungen* 61 (1940): 77-99.

Von Einem 1956: Herbert von Einem, *Michelangelo: Die Pietà im Dom zu Florenz* (Stuttgart: Reclam, 1956).

Von Rosen 2007: Valeska von Rosen, "Ambiguità intenzionale: L'*Ignudo* nella Pinacoteca Capitolina e altre raffigurazioni del San Giovanni Battista di Caravaggio e dei Caravaggisti," in Sybille Ebert-Schifferer, Julian Kliemann, Valeska von Rosen and Lothar Sickel, eds., *Caravaggio e il suo ambiente: Ricerche e interpretazioni* (Cinisello Balsamo: Silvana, 2007): 59-86.

Von Rosen 2009: Valeska von Rosen, *Caravaggio und die Grenzen des Darstellbaren: Ambiguität, Ironie und Performativität in der Malerei um 1600* (Berlin: Akademie, 2009).

Vos 1978: Rik Vos, *Lucas van Leyden* (Bentveld: Landshoff; and Maarssen: G. Schwartz, 1978).

Waldman 2004: Louis A. Waldman, *Baccio Bandinelli and Art at the Medici Court: A Corpus of Early Modern Sources* (Philadelphia: American Philosophical Society, 2004).

Wallace 1992: William E. Wallace, "Michelangelo's Rome *Pietà*: Altarpiece or Grave Memorial?," in Steven Bule, Alan Phipps Darr and Fiorella Superbi Gioffredi, eds., *Verrocchio and Late Quattrocento Italian Sculpture* (Florence: Le Lettere, 1992): 243-55.

Wallace 2000: William E. Wallace, "Michelangelo, Tiberio Calcagni, and the Florentine *Pietà*," *Artibus et Historiae* 42 (2000): 81-99.

Wallestein 2010: Sven-Olov Wallenstein, "Space, Time, and the Arts: Rewriting the *Laocoön*," *Journal of Aesthetics and Culture* 2 (2010): 1-13.

Warma 1990: Susanne J. Warma, "Christ, First Fruits, and the Resurrection: Observations on the Fruit Basket in Caravaggio's London *Supper at Emmaus*," *Zeitschrift für Kunstgeschichte*, 53 (1990): 583-6.

Warncke 2005: Carten-Peter Warncke, "Starke Frauen—starke Gefühle: Zur Darstellung weiblicher Leidenschaft in der bildenden Kunst des Barock," in Johann Anselm Steiger, ed., *Passion, Affekt und Leidenschaft in der Frühen Neuzeit* (Wiesbaden: Harrassowitz, 2005): 1:11-38.

Wasserman 2001: Jack Wasserman, "Michelangelo's *Pietà* in Florence: Transformation of Place and Intent," in Margaret Haines, ed., *Santa Maria del Fiore: The Cathedral and Its Sculpture* (Fiesole: Cadmo, 2001): 289-98.

Wasserman 2003: Jack Wasserman, *Michelangelo's Florence* Pietà (Princeton: Princeton University Press, 2003).

Watson 1993: Elizabeth S.Watson, *Achille Bocchi and the Emblem Book as Symbolic Form* (Cambridge: Harvard University Press, 1993).

Waźbiński 1990: Zygmunt Waźbiński: "Los diálogos de la pintura de Vicente Carducho, el manifiesto del academismo español y su origen," *Archivo Español de Arte* 63 (1990): 435-47.

Waźbiński 1994: Zygmunt Waźbiński, *Il cardinale Francesco Maria del Monte 1549-1626* (Florence: Olschki, 1994).

Weigel 2006: Thomas Weigel, "Tintoretto und das Non-finito," in Joachim Poeschke and Thomas Weigel, eds., *Die Virtus des Künstlers in der italienischen Renaissance* (Münster: Rhema, 2006): 231-49.

Weigert 1968: Roger-Armand Weigert, *Bibliothèque Nationale, Département des Estampes: Inventaire du fonds français. Graveurs du XVIIe siècle. Tome cinquième: Gilibert-Jousse* (Paris: Bibliothèque Nationale, 1968).

Weisz 1984: Jean S. Weisz, *Pittura e Misericordia: The Oratory of S. Giovanni Decollato in Rome* (Ann Arbor: UMI, 1984).

Weller 1998: Dennis P. Weller, ed., *Sinners & Saints, Darkness and Light: Caravaggio and His Dutch and Flemish Followers*, exh. cat. (Raleigh: North Carolina Museum of Art, 1998).

Wescher 1938: Paul Wescher, "Ein *Ungleiches Liebespaar* von Hans von Kulmbach," *Pantheon* 22 (1938): 376-9.

Westermann 1997: Mariët Westermann, *The Amusements of Jan Steen: Comic Painting in the Seventeenth Century* (Zwolle: Waanders, 1997).

Wethey 1964: Harold E. Wethey, "Orazio Borgianni in Italy and Spain," *Burlington Magazine* 106 (1964): 147-59.

Wethey 1969-1975: Harold E. Wethey, *The Paintings of Titian* (London: Phaidon, 1969-1975).

Wethey 1987: Harold E. Wethey, *Titian and His Drawings: With Reference to Giorgione and Some Close Contemporaries* (Princeton: Princeton University Press, 1987).

White 1967: John White, "*Paragone*: Aspects of the Relationship Between Sculpture and Painting," in Charles S. Singleton, ed., *Art, Science, and History in the Renaissance* (Baltimore: The Johns Hopkins Press, 1967): 43-108.

White 1987: John White, *The Birth and Rebirth of Pictorial Space* (Cambridge: Harvard University Press, 1987).

Whitfield 2007: Clovis Whitfield, "Caravaggio's *Shepherd Corydon*," *Paragone Arte* 73 (2007): 55-68.

Whitfield and Martineau 1982: Clovis Whitfield and Jane Martineau, eds., *Painting in Naples 1606-1705: From Caravaggio to Giordano*, exh. cat. (London: Weidenfeld & Nicolson, 1982).

Widerkehr 2007: Leda Widerkehr, ed., *The New Hollstein: Dutch and Flemish Etchings, Engravings and Woodcuts 1450-1700. Jacob Matham* (Rotterdam: Sound & Vision, 2007).

Wiemers 1986: Michael Wiemers, "Caravaggios 'Amore Vincitore' im Urteil eines Romfahrers um 1650," *Pantheon* 44, (1986): 59-61.

Williamson 1907: Georges Charles Williamson, *Bernardino Luini* (London: Bell, 1907).

Wind B. 1974: Barry Wind, "Pitture Ridicole: Some Late Cinquecento Comic Genre Painting," *Storia dell'Arte* 20 (1974): 25-35.

Wind B. 1987: Barry Wind, *Velázquez's Bodegones: A Study in Seventeenth-Century Spanish Genre Painting* (Fairfax: George Mason University Press, 1987).

Wind B. 1989: Barry Wind, "A Note on Card Symbolism in Caravaggio and his Followers," *Paragone Arte* 40 (1989): 15-8.

Wind E. 1969: Edgar Wind, *Giorgione's Tempesta with Comments on Giorgione's Poetic Allegories* (Oxford: Clarendon Press, 1969).

Winner 1968: Matthias Winner, "Federskizzen von Benvenuto Cellini," *Zeitschrift für Kunstgeschichte* 31 (1968): 293-304.

Winner 1989: Matthias Winner, "Annibale Carracci's Self-Portraits and the *Paragone* Debate," in Irving Lavin, ed., *Acts of the XXVIth International Congress of the History of Art* (University Park: Pennsylvania State University Press, 1989) 2: 509-15.

Winternitz 1970: Emanuel Winternitz, "The Role of Music in Leonardo's *Paragone*," in Maurice Natanson, ed., *Phenomenology and Social Reality: Essays in Memory of Alfred Schutz* (The Hague: M. Nijhoff, 1970): 270-96.

Winzinger 1963: Franz Winzinger, *Albrecht Altdorfer Graphik: Holzschnitte-Kupferstiche-Radierungen* (Munich: Piper, 1963).

Wittkower 1973: Rudolph Wittkower, *Art and Architecture in Italy, 1600 to 1750* (London: Penguin, 1973).

Wolf et al. 2004: Gerhard Wolf, Colette Dufour Bozzo and Anna Rosa Calderoni Masetti, eds., *Mandylion: Intorno al Sacro Volto, da Bisanzio a Genova*, exh. cat. (Milan: Skira, 2004).

Wood 2003: Christopher S. Wood, ed., *Vienna School Reader: Politics and Art Historical Method in the 1930s* (New York: Zone Books, 2003).

Wolters 1987: Wolfgang Wolters, *Storia e politica nei dipinti di Palazzo Ducale: Aspetti dell'autocelebrazione della Repubblica di Venezia nel Cinquecento* (Venice: Arsenale, 1987).

Yamey 1989: Basil S. Yamey, *Art and Accounting* (New Haven: Yale University Press, 1989).

Zacchi 1985: Alessandro Zacchi, "La figura dell'artefice cristiano nel *Discorso intorno alle imagini sacre e profane* di Gabriele Paleotti," *Il Carrobbio* 11 (1985): 339-47.

Zerner 1979: Henri Zerner, *The Illustrated Bartsch. 32. Italian Artists of the Sixteenth Century: School of Fontainebleau* (New York: Abaris Books, 1979).

Zikos 2008: Dimitrios Zikos, "Limina incerta: Filosofia e tecnica del 'non finito' nell'opera di Vincenzo Danti," in Charles Davis and Beatrice Paolozzi Strozzi, eds., *I grandi bronzi del Battistero: L'arte di Vincenzo Danti*, exh. cat. (Florence: Giunti, 2008): 273-97.

Zitzlsperger 2002: Philipp Zitzlsperger, *Gianlorenzo Bernini: Die Papst- und Herrscherporträts: Zum Verhältnis von Bildnis und Macht* (Munich: Hirmer Verlag, 2002).

Zöllner 2007: Frank Zöllner, *Leonardo da Vinci 1452-1519: The Complete Paintings and Drawings* (Cologne: Taschen, 2007).

Zorzi 1988: Ludovico Zorzi, *Carpaccio e la rappresentazione di Sant'Orsola: Ricerche sulla visualità dello spettacolo nel Quattrocento* (Turin: Einaudi, 1988).

Zuccari 1983: Alessandro Zuccari, "La 'Cappella della Pietà' alla Chiesa Nuova e i committenti del Caravaggio," *Storia dell'Arte* 47-49 (1983): 53-6.

Zuccari 1987: Alessandro Zuccari, "La pala di Siracusa e il tema della sepoltura in Caravaggio," in Maurizio Calvesi, ed., *L'ultimo Caravaggio e la cultura artistica a Napoli e a Malta* (Syracuse: Ediprint, 1987):147-73.

Zuccari 1996: Alessandro Zuccari, "Storia e tradizione nell'iconografia religiosa del Caravaggio," in Stefania Macioce, ed., *Michelangelo Merisi da Caravaggio: La vita e le opere attraverso i documenti* (Rome: Logart Press, 1996): 289-308.

Zucker 1984: Mark J. Zucker, *The Illustrated Bartsch. 25 (Commentary): Early Italian Masters* (New York: Abaris Books, 1984).

INDEX

Names, Works, and Concepts Contained in this Volume

accessory (*parergon*): 25, 38, 40, 64, 91, 206, 208, 216, 226, 232, 259-60, 334-5, 533

acoustic, acoustic effects: 244, 495-7, 499, 505-6, 515

Aertsen, Pieter (1507/1508-1575):
    Kitchen Scene with Christ at the Supper of Emmaus: 527-30, 533

Agostino Veneziano (Musi, Agostino; *c*.1490-after1536):
    Death of Ananias: 522
    Israelites Gathering the Manna in the Desert: 68

Albani, Francesco (1578-1660): 4, 15-21, 26-7, 346, 397-8, 404-5, 488, 544, 559
    Annunciation (San Bartolomeo): 29-33
    Borghese Cycle: 15

Alberti, Cherubino (1553-1615):
    Conversion of Saint Paul: 258
    Man Shooting with a Crossbow: 472-3
    Pietà: 364

Alberti, Leon Battista (1404-1472): 3-5, 7, 10-1, 17, 35-6, 38-41, 44-5, 49-50, 57, 64-5, 67-70, 73, 85-6, 89-91, 93-4, 99, 105, 200, 257, 344, 346, 346, 448, 491-2, 550, 561-2, 564, 567

Alberti, Romano (active 1585-1604): 329

Aldegrever, Heinrich (1502-*c*.1561):
    Titus Manlius Torquatus Attending His Son's Decapitation: 254

Allegri, Antonio: see Correggio

Alpers, Svetlana: 4-5, 7-8, 257, 262

Altdorfer, Albrecht (*c*.1480-1538):
    Allegory of Vanity: 181
    Annunciation: 81-2
    Beheading of Saint John the Baptist (inscribed 1512): 430-1
    Beheading of Saint John the Baptist (inscribed 1517): 431-2

Altdorfer Erhard (*c*.1485-1561/1562):
    Allegory of Vanity: 181

ambiguity, ambivalence: 36, 49, 71, 73-4, 93, 122, 141-2, 151-3, 171, 175, 181, 208, 211, 219, 222, 224-5, 237, 265, 273, 278, 284, 288, 294, 316, 444, 475-6, 490, 495, 511, 514, 522, 529, 536, 534, 548

Amman, Jost (1539-1591):
    Rider with Crossbow: 472

Ames-Lewis, Francis: 24

amphiboly, amphibology: 74-5, 84-5, 221

anachronism: 220, 224, 254, 260, 340, 344

anagnorisis: 268, 278, 498

analepsis: 101, 526

Andreini, Giovan Battista: 393

Andrews, Lew: 70

Antonello da Messina (*c*.1430-1479): 376, 390

Apelles: 44, 187-8, 250

Ariosto, Ludovico: 185, 197, 456-7

Aristotle: 17, 36, 44, 70, 77-9, 94-6, 126, 130, 208, 230, 330, 332, 340, 370, 488, 491, 498, 536, 566

Armenini, Giovan Battista (1530-1609): 97-103, 106, 305-6, 309, 407-11, 448-9

author, authorship: 11, 96-100, 103, 108, 297-8, 306-9, 336-7, 339-41, 386-7, 401, 412, 490, 536, 568-70

Avellaneda y Haro, Garcia de: 379

Ayrolo, Agostino: 247

Baglione, Giovanni (*c*.1566-1643): 4, 18-9, 50, 63, 93, 212, 214, 246-7, 343, 347-8, 399, 481-3, 488, 559, 566, 570
    Angelica: 456-7

Baldung Grien, Hans (1484/1485-1545):
    Death Seizing a Woman: 181
    Lamentation: 348-9

Banchieri, Adriano: 396

Bandinelli, Baccio (1488-1560): 309, 397-401
    Eve: 400
    Hercules and Cacus: 399-400
    Pietà (Santissima Annunziata): 365
    Self-Portrait: 397-8

Bandini, Francesco: 364-5

Barberini, Francesco: 545

Barberini, Maffeo: see Urban VIII

Barbieri, Giovan Francesco: see Guercino

Bargagli, Scipione: 191, 193

Barocci, Federico (1528-1612): 64

Baroque: 489, 563-4

Bassano, Jacopo (Da Ponte, Jacopo; *c*.1510-1592): 104-8
    Parable of Dives and Lazarus: 532-3

Baxandall, Michael: 38

Béatrizet, Nicolas (1507/1515-*c*.1565)
    Pietà for Vittoria Colonna (after Michelangelo): 352

Beham, Hans Sebald (1500-1550)
    Taking of Christ: 323
Bellarmino, Roberto: 194
Bellini, Giovanni (1431/1436-1516): 265, 274-5, 282-3,
          294, 510, 515
    Baptism of Christ (Santa Corona): 498
    Circumcision: 275
    Deposition (Florence): 275
    Resurrection (Vicenza Cathedral): 498-9
    Supper at Emmaus: 271-3
    Transfiguration (Naples): 497-8
    Transfiguration (Venice): 497
    Virgin in Glory with Eight Saints: 498
Bellori, Giovan Pietro: 4, 18-22, 26-7, 29, 49, 58, 64, 93,
          108, 138-41, 151, 158, 161, 164, 208, 215-6,
          219, 226, 246, 257, 259-63, 270, 284, 289, 291,
          304, 315-6, 322, 325-7, 344, 346, 377-9, 383,
          413, 425, 427, 437-8, 457, 481, 483, 488-9, 536,
          559-60, 565-6, 569
Benati, Daniele: 339
Berni, Francesco: 169
Bijlert, Jan van (*c*.1597-1671)
    Calling of Saint Matthew: 232-3, 235
Bizoni, Bernardo: 457
blindness, narrative blindness: 171, 209, 230-1, 243-4,
          251-5, 258, 262-3, 268, 273, 284, 306, 308, 337,
          389, 396, 460, 465, 496, 505, 509, 523, 567, 569
Bloemaert, Abraham (1566-1651)
    Adam and Eve Mourning the Slain Abel: 83-4
Bocchi, Achille: 193
Bodmer, Heinrich: 225
bodegón: 520, 523, 526, 533-4
Bohde, Daniela: 448
Boltraffio, Giovanni Antonio (1466/1467-1516): 276
Bonasone, Giulio (*c*.1510-after 1576)
    Pietà for Vittoria Colonna (after Michelangelo): 352-4
    Virgin Washing the Feet of the Infant Christ: 531-3
Boneri, Francesco: see Cecco del Caravaggio
Bonini, Girolamo (active *c*.1660-1680): 406
Bonvicino, Alessandro: see Moretto da Brescia
Booth, Wayne C.: 94
Borghese, Scipione: 15, 18, 270, 311-2, 500
Borghini, Raffaello: 448-9
Borromeo, Federico: 63, 202-5, 208-9, 239, 245-6, 272,
          288, 307, 340-1, 513-4, 566
Brejon de Lavergnée, Arnauld: 539, 541, 543
Brosamer, Hans (*c*.1500-1552)
    Prostitute and the Fool: 181
Brueghel, Pieter the Elder (*c*.1525-1569)
    Resurrection: 511
Bulwer, John: 424
Buonarroti, Lionardo: 365
Buonarroti, Michelangelo (1475-1564): 15, 29, 42, 64, 84,
          249, 252, 397, 401, 404-6, 408-11, 415, 418, 427,
          518, 563, 570
    Christ at the Column: 55-6

Conversion of Saint Paul: 250-1, 258
Creation of Eve: 57
Creation of Man: 223, 227, 232
Flagellation: 53
Hercules: 410-1
Ideal Head of Woman: 123
Joel: 534
Last Judgment: 44-6, 57, 285
Moses: 360
Pietà (Florence): 309, 346, 362-73
Pietà (Saint Peter's): 346, 354-61
Pietà (Vittoria Colonna): 352-4
Study of an Ignudo (Teylers Museum): 59-62
Study of the Head of the Sybil of Cumae: 111-2, 122
Burgard, Peter J.: 221-5, 240
Burgkmair, Hans (1473-1531)
    White King Shooting with his Crossbow: 472
Burda, Arthur: 563
Burnacini, Ludovico Ottavio (1636-1707):
    Dottore: 394
Byzantine art theory: 36-8, 48, 200-1

Caliari, Paolo: see Veronese
Calcagni, Tiberio (1532-1565): 364
Callot Jacques (1592-1635):
    Fall of Simon Magus
Calvaert, Denys (*c*.1540-1619): 41
Cameron, James: 562
Camilli, Camillo: 186, 192-3
Candido, Pietro (De Witte, Pieter; 1548-1628)
    Martyrdom of Saint Ursula: 434, 471
    Supper at Emmaus (Aegidius Sadeler): 292-3
    Supper at Emmaus (Johan Sadeler): 292-3
Caracciolo, Giovan Battista (Battistello; 1578-1635): 491,
          515
    Liberation of Saint Peter: 503-4
    Noli Me Tangere: 504-7
    Study of a Soldier (Louvre): 504
Caravaggio (Merisi, Michelangelo da; 1571-1610)
    Annunciation: 81-5
    Bacchus: 419
    Basket of Fruit: 419
    Beheading of Saint John the Baptist: 430-2
    Boy Carrying a Basket of Fruit: 171
    Burial of Saint Lucy: 412, 425-37,
    Calling of Saint Matthew: 4, 208-9, 211-41, 243-4, 433-
          5, 444-5, 484, 514, 543
    Calling of Saints Peter and Andrew: 232
    Cardsharps: 123, 130-2, 157-75, 212, 217, 219, 232, 475,
          543, 556
    Conversion of Mary Magdalene: 124, 132, 177-97
    Conversion of Saint Paul (Odescalchi Collection):
          243-7, 249-55
    Conversion of Saint Paul (Cerasi Chapel): 208-9, 225,
          243-7, 257-63, 536, 569
    Crowning with Thorns (for Massimo Massimi): 377-9

Crucifixion of Saint Peter (Cerasi Chapel): 225, 246, 257, 311-3, 419, 488, 519
Crucifixion of Saint Peter (lost): 246-7
David and Goliath (Borghese Gallery): 315, 328, 383, 570
Death of the Virgin: 49-52, 432-3, 435
Denial of Saint Peter: 413, 420-5, 439
Ecce Homo: 308, 313-5, 375-401
Entombment: 309, 343-73, 401, 404, 439
Flagellation (Naples): 55-7, 477
Flagellation (Rouen): 53
Fortune Teller (Paris): 123, 130, 132, 135-55, 475
Fortune Teller (Rome): 123, 130, 132, 135, 155, 160-1, 475
Incredulity of Saint Thomas: 412, 423, 449-50, 452, 457-66, 471, 476, 484, 520
Judith Beheading Holofernes: 7, 109-19, 122, 468
Lute Player (New York, Saint Petersburg): 171
Madonna dei Pellegrini: 49, 63
Martyrdom of Saint Matthew: 25-6, 211, 213-5, 218, 239, 249, 315-6, 542
Martyrdom of Saint Ursula: 412, 466-79
Medusa: 8, 157
Palafrenieri Madonna: 291, 294, 328
Portrait of Alof de Wignacourt: 561
Portrait of Giovan Battista Marino: 157
Repentant Magdalene: 20-1
Resurrection 501-4
Resurrection of Lazarus: 8-10, 412, 425, 434, 437-45, 477
Sacrifice of Isaac: 423
Saint John the Baptist: 58-60
Salome Receiving the Head of Saint John the Baptist: 477
Seven Acts of Mercy: 503
Sick Bacchus: 384
Supper at Emmaus (London): 208-9, 232, 265-89, 315, 344, 457, 465-6, 506, 520-4
Supper at Emmaus (Milan): 290-5, 421
Taking of Christ: 308-9, 311-41, 348, 412, 457, 468-9, 477-8
Carducho, Vicencio (*c.*1576-1638): 18, 346, 517-9, 524-5, 537, 559, 561
Cardi, Giovan Battista: 377, 380, 383
Cardi, Ludovico: see Cigoli
Caretta, Paola: 53, 111
carne (flesh): 48-9, 447-9, 465
Carracci, Agostino (1557-1602)
Ecce Homo: 388
Pietà for Vittoria Colonna (after Michelangelo): 352-4
Pietà (after Michelangelo's sculpture in Saint Peter's): 355
Carracci, Annibale (1560-1609): 25, 31, 58, 65, 322, 348, 361, 397-8, 406-7, 409, 411, 487-8, 539
Annunciation (Windsor Castle): 337-40
Assumption of the Virgin (Cerasi Chapel): 225, 246, 257

Baptism of Christ: 41-3
Boy Taking his Shirt Off (drawing): 42-3
Herodias with the Head of Saint John the Baptist: 453-4
Saint Francis Presenting the Crucifix: 386
San Giorgio Altarpiece: 447-8
Study of a Foreshortened Head (Uffizi): 60-1
Carracci, Ludovico (1555-1619): 211, 484, 486-7
Annunciation (Bologna Cathedral): 31-2
Ariadne: 453
Conversion of Saint Matthew: 225-7
Flagellation: 429
Medea Rejuvenating Aeson: 116
Pool of Bethesda: 447-8
Study of a Sleeping Boy (Ashmolean Museum): 60
Taking of Christ: 320-2, 327
Castelvetro, Lodovico: 95-6, 126-30, 132, 208
causality, cause-and-effect relation: 4, 8-10, 104-5, 117-8, 208, 227, 236, 239, 254, 272, 344, 364, 423, 434, 495-6
Cavalier d'Arpino (Cesari, Giuseppe; 1568-1640): 65, 311-2, 335, 348
Calling of Saint Matthew (drawing): 213-4
Prophets (San Luigi dei Francesi): 212
Saint Matthew Resurrecting the Daughter of the Ethiopian King Egyppus: 212
Study for the figure of Saint Matthew: 214
Taking of Christ (Accademia di San Luca, Borghese Gallery): 327
Cavarozzi, Bartolomeo (1590-1625)
Supper at Emmaus: 286-7
Cavedone, Giacomo (1577-1660): 347
Cecco del Caravaggio (Boneri, Francesco; *c.*1589-active 1620): 13, 62, 229, 506
Resurrection: 285-6, 491, 496-7, 500-1, 503-4, 507-15
Cerasi, Tiberio: 246-7
Cesari, Giuseppe: see Cavalier d'Arpino
Champaigne, Jean-Baptiste (1631-1681): 269-70, 273
Chantelou, Paul Fréart de: 88-9
character, (main, secondary) characters: 63, 68, 94-7, 99, 261, 278, 282-3, 388-90, 490, 523, 529, 533, 536-7, 569
chiaroscuro: 10, 25, 58, 61, 91, 95, 106-8, 208, 221-2, 224, 236, 238-9, 243, 281, 291, 293-5, 313, 335, 412, 420, 423, 425, 433, 440, 476, 520, 539, 566-7
Ciamberlano, Luca (born *c.*1570)
Resurrection: 508
Cignani, Carlo (1628-1719): 397
Cigoli (Cardi, Ludovico; 1559-1613)
Ecce Homo (Florence): 377-80, 383
Ecce Homo (drawing): 379
close-up, narrative close-up: 4, 27, 53, 62, 64, 91, 105, 122, 147, 150, 184, 228, 275, 278, 280, 282, 316, 322, 341, 412, 466, 504, 565
Clovio, Giulio (1498-1578):
Flagellation: 53
Cochin, Charles-Nicolas: 502, 504

Colonna, Vittoria: 352

color, color technique: 6, 19-20, 25, 32, 35, 37, 39-40, 57-8, 81, 95, 97-8, 107, 138-9, 159, 216, 219, 250, 270, 295, 302-3, 312-3, 330-3, 335, 361, 407, 416-7, 419-22, 433, 439-40, 447, 449, 481, 483-7, 489, 502, 539, 541, 544, 559, 562-5

Comanini, Gregorio: 121-3, 126, 131

comedy, comic, comedic: 11, 29, 63, 70, 94, 96, 121-32, 137, 140-1, 148, 151, 153-5, 161, 163-4, 219, 231, 238, 387-91, 474-5, 491, 523-4, 528, 539, 546-50, 554-7

commedia dell'arte: 130, 140, 145, 390-7

Condivi, Ascanio: 352-3, 363-4, 368, 371

Contarelli, Matteo (Cointrel, Matthieu): 212-3

Contarini, Pietro: 167

Correggio (Allegri, Antonio; *c.*1489-1534): 15, 58, 64, 216, 447, 563, 565
  Lamentation: 20
  Noli Me Tangere: 31-2
  Saint John Escaping: 325
  Study of a Figure (Louvre): 61

Cortona, Pietro da (Berrettini, Pietro; 1596-1669): 489

Costa, Ottavio: 289-90

Counter-Reformation: 11, 21, 48-9, 65, 78, 199-209, 222, 239, 244, 254, 267, 270, 288, 306-7, 337, 340, 464, 566-8

Cranach, Lucas the Elder (1472-1553)
  Flagellation: 53
  Lamentation: 350

Crescenzi, Pietro Paolo: 212

Cropper, Elizabeth: 157, 159-60, 175

Cummings, Frederick: 177-8, 194-5, 197

Cuzin, Jean-Pierre: 539, 541, 543

Da Correggio, Niccolò: 187

Dal Pozzo, Cassiano: 482

Daniele da Volterra (Ricciarelli, Daniele; *c.*1509-1566)
  Assumption of the Virgin: 366
  Portrait of Michelangelo (Teylers Museum): 366-7
  Portrait of Michelangelo (bust): 367

Death of the Niobids (ancient bas-relief): 507

De' Bianchi, Lodovico: 391, 394

De Brune, Johan: 170

decorum, propriety: 27, 29, 39, 41, 46-8, 50-2, 60, 70, 109, 121, 125, 127-8, 205, 214, 246, 270, 284, 259, 344, 416, 483, 487, 502, 504

De Dominici, Bernardo: 502

De Ferrari, Orazio (1605-1657)
  Almsgiving of Saint Charles Borromeo: 220

Del Conte, Jacopino (1510-1598)
  Portrait of Michelangelo: 365-6

Della Carda, Ottaviano: 184

Della Casa, Niccolò (active 1543-1547)
  Portrait of Baccio Bandinelli: 397-8

Della Robbia, Luca (1399/1400-1482)
  Cantoria: 415-6

Del Monte, Francesco Maria: 13, 158, 195, 212, 379

Del Negro, Orazio: 457

Del Vaga, Perino (1501-1547): 408

Democritus: 301-3, 308

Dempsey, Charles: 65, 489

Dente, Marco: see Marco da Ravenna

De Piles, Roger: 405

D'Este, Cesare: 289

De Vos, Maarten (1532-1603)
  Beheading of Saint John the Baptist: 431
  Resurrection: 511
  Saint Peter Resurrecting Tabitha: 532

De Witte, Pieter: see Candido, Pietro

Dio Chrysostom: 250

Diogenes Laërtius: 328

discretion: 403-4, 408

disegno, design, drawing: 297-8, 302, 304-5, 308-9, 329-35, 340, 399, 405-11, 415-6, 418-9, 481-4, 487, 541, 543-5

D'Oggiono, Marco (1467-1524)
  Salvator Mundi: 277

Dolce, Lodovico: 42, 44-5, 58, 68, 70-1, 89, 410

Domenichino (Zampieri, Domenico; 1581-1641): 22, 29, 41, 488, 571
  Communion of Saint Jerome: 259-60
  Hunt of Diana: 78

Donatello (Bardi, Donato di Niccolò di Betto; *c.*1386-1466): 443
  Cantoria: 415-7, 421

Doria, Andrea: 379

Doria, Marcantonio: 379, 466, 475

drawing: see *disegno*

duration: 4, 5, 7, 105, 108-9, 116, 278, 282, 288, 567

Dürer, Albrecht (1471-1528): 104, 356, 408
  Deposition (*Engraved Passion*): 349
  Ecce Homo (*Small Passion*): 388
  Incredulity of Saint Thomas (*Small Passion*): 460-1
  Lamentation (*Engraved Passion*): 348-9
  Lamentation (attributed to): 442
  Large Horse: 260-1
  Last Supper (*Small Passion*): 325
  Martyrdom of Saint Sebastian: 471
  Pilate Washing His Hands: 388-9
  Promenade: 145-6, 152
  Resurrection: 502
  Self-Portrait (Munich): 570
  Taking of Christ (*Engraved Passion*): 320
  Taking of Christ (*Small Passion*): 316-9

Dvórak, Max: 563

emphasis: 74, 84, 99

enargeia: 7, 38, 74, 84, 495

Enríquez de Cabrera, Juan Alfonso: 247

Eupompos: 138

eurythmy, symmetry: 4, 39-41, 43, 55, 57-8, 60, 85, 99, 105, 112, 121, 151, 298, 300 *expression*: 5, 13, 16, 20-2, 27, 31-2, 39-41, 44, 50, 73, 76-7, 84, 87, 91, 95, 99-100, 123, 125, 137, 142, 152, 215, 222, 253-5, 259, 265, 267, 282, 290, 336, 344, 522, 553-4, 556

Farinati, Orazio (1599-after 1616)
    Crossing of the Red Sea: 249-50
Farinati, Paolo (1524-1606):
    Crossing of the Red Sea: 249-50
Farnese, Odoardo: 397-8
Fazio, Bartolomeo: 184
Feigenbaum, Gail: 226-7, 320
Félibien, André: 87, 561
Ferdinand I de' Medici: 157
Ferrari, Gaudenzio (*c*.1470-1546): 300
figura sforzata, serpentinata: 46, 60, 105, 113, 369-72
Finson, Louis (*c*.1580-1617)
    Incredulity of Saint Thomas: 461
    Resurrection: 502
flashback: see *analepsis*
flashforeward: see *prolepsis*
flesh: see *carne*
focus, narrative focus: 5, 64, 67, 81, 96-9, 105-6, 284
Franco, Battista (*c*.1510-1561)
    Deposition: 351
    Flagellation: 53
Freedberg, Sydney J.: 489
Friedlaender, Walter: 141, 149, 260
Fried, Michael: 385
Frisius, Simon (Vries, Simon Wynhoutsz; *c*.1580-1629)
    Betrothal: 146-7

Galilei, Galileo: 489, 491
Galle, Philips (1537-1612)
    Last Supper: 530-1
    Resurrection: 511
    Saint Peter Resurrecting Tabitha: 531
    Vision of Saint Peter: 531
Garbieri, Lorenzo (1580/1581-1654): 484, 520
Garimberto, Gerolamo: 325
Gaurico, Pomponio: 7, 74-5, 84, 221
Genette, Gérard: 5
Gentileschi, Orazio (1563-1639): 482
Gheyn, Jacques II de (1565-1629)
    Crossbowman with Milkmaid: 473-4
Ghiberti, Lorenzo (*c*.1381-1455): 70
Gilio, Giovanni Andrea: 45-8, 50, 53, 55
Ginetti, Marzio: 520
Giorgione (Barbarelli, Giorgio; 1477-1510): 26, 58, 138-9, 164-8, 214, 216, 219, 302-4, 419, 565
    Christ Carrying the Cross: 275
    La Vecchia: 294
Giulio Romano (Pippi, Giulio; *c*.1499-1546)
    Menelaus Supporting Patroklos: 439
    Virgin Washing the Feet of the Infant Christ: 531
Giustiniani, Vincenzo: 13, 27, 216, 218, 457-8

Glykon: 138
Gobbo da Milano (Solari, Cristoforo; *c*.1468-1524): 359, 368
Goodman, Elise: 182-3
Goltzius, Hendrick (1558-1617):
    Allegory of Vanity: 144-5
    Allegory of Sight: 191
    Apollo: 114
    Pietà: 355-7
    Repentant Magdalene: 172
    Resurrection: 511-2
Graf, Urs (*c*.1485-1527)
    Agony in the Garden and Taking of Christ: 320
    Venal Lovers: 149
Guercino (Barbieri, Giovan Francesco; 1591-1666): 485-6, 488
    Incredulity of Saint Thomas: 520
    Supper at Emmaus: 520-4
    Taking of Christ: 520
Guicciardini, Piero: 500-1, 514-5
Guidotti, Paolo (*c*.1560-1629)
    Deianira: 455-6

Haecht, Willem van (1593-1637): 184
Hartje, Nicole: 229
Heemskerck, Maarten van (1498-1574):
    Portrait of Pieter Bicker Gerritsz: 220
    Saint Peter Resurrecting Tabitha: 531
Heraklitos: 206
Hermann Fiore, Kristina: 316, 320, 328
Hibbard, Howard: 122, 271
Holbein, Hans (1497/1498-1543)
    Ambassadors: 9
    Death and the Count: 509
    Death and the Gambler: 216-7, 219, 543
Holtzwart, Mathias: 329
Homer: 67, 96, 301-2, 308
Honervogt, Jacques I: 392
Honthorst, Gerrit van (1590-1656): 491, 539, 544
    Adoration of the Shepherds: 500-1

imitation, mimesis: 5, 17, 20, 27, 36, 38-9, 44, 49, 64, 90, 94-6, 98, 126, 128-9, 131-2, 178, 209, 216, 259-60, 301, 308, 343-4, 346, 356, 361, 407, 418, 453, 455, 477, 490-1, 559, 561, 566
instantaneity: 7, 9-10, 79, 89
invention: 16, 22, 25-6, 30-1, 41-4, 64, 67-8, 72, 97, 100-6, 108, 178, 201, 295, 297, 299-304, 309, 313, 315, 332-3, 335-6, 340, 348, 360, 372, 401, 403-13, 447, 478, 484, 486-7, 502, 541, 543-5
irony, dramatic irony: 62, 241, 272, 287, 498

John of Damascus: 266-7, 284
Johnston-Keane, Kathy: 390
Joyce, James: 288

Koos, Marianne: 450, 464
Krug, Ludwig (1490-1532)
    Embrace: 320-1

Lavin, Irving: 271
Le Brun, Charles (1619-1690): 6, 90, 98
    Tent of Darius: 86-7
Lemoine, Annick: 554
Leo X (Medici, Giovanni de'): 26, 258
Leonardo da Vinci (1452-1519): 71-3, 80, 112, 187-8, 371-2
    Last Supper: 276
    Study for the Head of Christ: 276-7
    Study for the Head of Simon: 277-8
    Virgin of the Rocks: 73
Leoni, Leone (c.1509-1590)
    Portrait of Michelangelo (medal): 367
Leoni, Ottavio (1578-1630)
    Portrait of Caravaggio: 384
Leopardi, Alessandro (1450-c.1523): 167
Lezcano, Juan de: 379
litotes: 84, 253-4, 262
Lomazzo, Giovan Paolo (1538-1600): 78, 97, 99, 116, 123-5, 130-1, 142-3, 300-4, 307-9, 337, 356-7, 368-72, 403, 406-8, 566
Lombardo, Antonio (c.1458-c.1516): 167
Longhi, Roberto: 177, 196-7, 276, 375-7, 380-90, 401, 435, 502
Loyola, Ignacio de: 308
Lucas van Leyden (c.1494-1533)
    Adam and Eve Driven out of Paradise: 509
    Betrothal: 146-7
    Christ Appearing to the Magdalene as a Gardener: 504
    Embrace: 319, 321-2
    Resurrection: 502
    Tavern Scene (Prodigal Son): 148-50
    Young Man with a Skull (Allegory of Vanity): 144
Luciani, Sebastiano: see Sebastiano del Piombo
Luini, Bernardino (c.1480-c.1532)
    Martha and Mary Magdalene: 195
lyric, lyrical: 11, 121, 124, 131, 140-1, 144, 147, 152-5, 157-9, 169-75, 179-86, 189-93, 196-7, 474-5, 547, 550
Lysippus: 187

Maderno, Carlo (c.1556-1629): 246
Maganza, Alessandro (1556-after 1630)
    Minerva Forbidding the Fates from Tearing their Yarn: 454-5
Mahon, Denis: 488-9
Malvasia, Carlo Cesare: 22, 29, 31, 41, 43, 62, 93, 225, 311-3, 347, 397-8, 404-6, 409, 447, 483-9, 520
Mancini, Giulio: 4, 8, 21-3, 26-7, 44, 50, 67, 78-80, 93, 136-8, 140, 152, 246-7, 289, 433, 488
Manfredi, Bartolomeo (c.1582-1622): 19, 211, 238-9, 481, 491, 539

Fortune Teller: 547-8
    Tavern Scene with Musicians and Drinkers: 227-31
Mannerism: 302, 313, 346, 447, 559, 563
Mantegna, Andrea (c.1431-1506): 104, 182, 275, 322
Maranta, Bartolomeo: 75-8, 80-1, 83
Marco da Ravenna (Dente, Marco; c.1486-1527)
    Laocoön: 114
Marin, Louis: 5-10, 13, 561
Marini, Maurizio: 247, 328, 346
Marino, Giovan Battista: 157, 159-61, 168-9, 173-5, 452-7, 475, 477
Martinelli, Giovanni (1600/1604-1659)
    Death Comes to the Banquet: 229
Masaccio (Tommaso di ser Giovanni; 1401-1428): 70
Masetti, Fabio: 289
Massa, Lanfranco: 466
Massys, Quentin (1466-1530): 220
    Ill-Matched Pair: 149-50
Master AG (active c.1475-1490)
    Taking of Christ: 317-8
Master I A M of Zwolle (active c.1470-1495)
    Lamentation: 442
Master b x g (active c.1470-1490)
    Lovers: 154
    Two Card Players: 170
Master BM (active late fifteenth century)
    Lamentation: 442
Master ES (active c.1450-1467)
    Crucifixion: 322-3
Master I E (active fifteenth century)
    Saint Dorothy: 113-4
Master LPH
    Judith Beheading Holofernes: 111
Master of the Housebook (Housebook Master; active c.1470-1500): 145-6, 152, 154
    Card Players: 170
    Lovers: 143-4
    Old Man and Young Woman: 148
    Young Man and Old Woman: 147
Master of the Pala Sforza (active c.1490-c.1500)
    Study of a Head: 276
Matham, Jacob (1571-1631)
    Kitchen Scene with Christ at the Supper at Emmaus: 527-30, 533
    Supper at Emmaus: 529
Mattei, Ciriaco: 265, 270, 315, 325, 457
Mazzola, Francesco: see Parmigianino
Meckenem, Israel van (c.1440-1503): 142
    Card Players: 170
    Old Man and Young Woman: 148
    Saint Lawrence: 172-3
    Young Man and Old Woman: 147
Meleager (sarcophagus of): 40, 344, 346
Melissenus, Gregory: 36, 38
memory: 11, 22, 26, 43, 72, 80, 86, 100-1, 103, 132, 178, 265, 287, 291, 303, 403-13, 477-8, 555

Merisi, Michelangelo: see Caravaggio
meta-narrative: 11, 412, 451-7, 465, 470-2, 475-6
meta-pictorial: 99, 429, 451, 491, 550
Milesi, Marzio: 214-5, 240
mimesis: see *imitation*
Minniti, Mario (1557-1640): 427
    Burial of Saint Lucy: 428-9, 433
Mocetto, Girolamo (*c*.1470-after 1531)
    Baptism of Christ: 498
    Resurrection: 498-9
    Virgin in Glory with Eight Saints: 498
Moerman, Jan: 328
Mojana, Marina: 541
Molanus, Johannes: 244-5, 340, 566
Monaco, Pietro (1700-after 1775)
    Supper at Emmaus: 271
morbidezza: 58
Moretto da Brescia (Bonvicino, Alessandro; 1498-1554): 265
    Madonna Adoring the Infant Christ: 82-3
    Supper at Emmaus: 283
Motta, Raffaellino: see Raffaellino da Reggio
Moxey, Keith: 220
Murtola, Gaspare: 139-40
Musi, Agostino: see Agostino Veneziano

Nadal, Jerónimo: 526
Nagel, Alexander: 353
narrative voice: 94, 96, 308, 337
narrator: 94-99, 308
naturalism: 38, 50, 201, 225, 322, 335, 356, 418, 420, 447, 465, 517, 563-6, 570
Nikephoros of Constantinople: 37, 39, 47-8
Nivelon, Claude: 87
Nocret, Jean (1615-1672): 273
non-finito: 412-3, 415-8, 420, 422, 425, 443, 476
novelty, originality: 58, 81, 85, 101, 106, 126, 128, 132, 178, 203-5, 227, 240, 301, 309, 313, 316, 320-4, 326-7, 340-1, 349, 351, 356, 360, 409-10, 413, 453, 479, 487-92, 502, 562, 566, 569-70

objectivity: 288, 566-8, 570-1
obscurity: 93, 206-8, 223, 226-7, 232, 235-6, 239, 243-4, 294, 490
Olmutz, Wenzel von (active 1481-1497)
    Lovers: 143-4
optics, optical: 5, 32, 36, 43-4, 48-9, 58, 64-5, 70, 73, 89-91, 201-3, 216, 238-9, 241, 243, 278, 280-1, 288, 333, 416, 420, 463-5, 468, 470, 476-7, 486, 490, 523-4, 561, 563-8
originality: see *novelty*
Orsi, Lelio (1508/1511-1587)
    Man Shooting with a Crossbow: 472-3
Ostsaanen, Jacob Cornelisz von (before 1470-1533)
    Taking of Christ: 320

Pacheco, Francisco (1564-*c*.1644): 519-20
    Saint Sebastian Attended by Saint Irene: 526
Paleotti, Gabriele: 79, 200-9, 239, 245, 266-7, 288, 307, 309, 340, 566
Palomino, Antonio: 520
Palma, Jacopo: see Palma Vecchio; Palma Giovane
Palma Giovane (*c*.1548-1628)
    Self-Portrait: 385-7
Palma Vecchio (*c*.1479-1528): 177, 303
    Sea Storm: 416-7, 419
Panofsky, Erwin: 100
paragone: 173, 182, 189, 309, 346, 360-1, 495, 554
parergon: see *accessory*
Parmigianino (Mazzola, Francesco; 1503-1540)
    Saint Thais: 21
parody, self-parody: 123, 147, 280, 297, 304, 309, 339-40, 390-1, 393-4, 397-8, 400-1, 490, 509, 536, 554, 569-70
Pasqualini, Giovan Battista (born 1585)
    Supper at Emmaus: 520-24
Pasqualone de Accumulo, Mariano: 379
Passerotti, Bartolomeo (1529-1592): 41
    Study of a Laughing Old Woman in Profile: 122-3
Passignano, Domenico (Cresti, Domenico; 1559-1638): 377
pelle, skin: 448-50
Peterzano, Simone (*c*.1540-*c*.1596): 108, 142, 303, 411
Petrarch (Petrarca, Francesco): 140, 182-4, 197
Phidias: 67, 138
Philip IV (King of Spain): 517
Piccini, Giacomo (*c*.1617-*c*.1669): 167
Pino, Paolo (active 1534-1565): 299-300
Pippi, Giulio: see Giulio Romano
Pittoni, Battista: 193
Plato: 301-2, 308, 329-30
Pordenone (Giovanni Antonio da; 1483/1484-1539): 303
Plutarch: 165
Polyclitus: 187
Politi, Giuseppe
    Burial of Saint Lucy: 428
Pomarancio (Roncalli, Cristoforo; *c*.1567-1629): 348
Poussin, Nicolas (1594-1665): 5-10, 29, 88-91, 98, 259-60, 492, 545, 554, 558-9, 561-2, 571
    Death of Germanicus: 52
    Et in Arcadia Ego: 8
    Israelites Gathering the Manna in the Desert: 6, 88-90
    Martyrdom of Saint Erasmus: 543-4
    Plague of Ashdod: 543
    Realm of Flora: 543
Prater, Andreas: 219-21
prolepsis: 83, 101, 270, 283, 323, 424, 444, 511, 526
propriety: see *decorum*
Proust, Marcel: 5
Puglisi, Catherine: 379

Quintilian: 206, 208

Raffaellino da Reggio (Motta, Raffaellino; 1550-1578)
   Ecce Homo: 387-9
Raimondi, Marcantonio (1470/1482-1527/1534)
   Resurrected Christ: 285-6
Raphael (Raffaello Santi; 1483-1520): 15, 17, 24-6, 31, 42,
      89, 104, 107, 138, 249, 257, 300, 348, 408-11,
      418, 545, 560, 563
   Battle of Ostia: 25
   Burning Bush (cartoon): 251-3
   Conversion of Saul: 258-60
   Death of Ananias: 522
   Disputa (study for): 24-5
   Expulsion of Heliodorus from the Temple: 251
   Israelites Gathering the Manna in the Desert: 68-9
   Jacob's Ladder: 340-1
   Resurrected Christ: 285-6
   Study of Three Nude Men: 252
realism: 49, 51, 58, 62-5, 68, 117, 152, 201, 209, 238, 420,
      465, 488-90
Régnier, Nicolas (*c*.1590-1667)
   Card Players with Fortune Teller: 556-7
Rembrandt Harmensz van Rijn (1606-1669): 62, 571
Reni, Guido (1575-1642): 18, 29, 311-3, 404, 484, 486-8,
      571
   Agony in the Garden: 323
   Crucifixion: 323
   Crucifixion of Saint Peter: 312-3
reproduction: 5-6, 13, 22, 36, 38, 48, 50, 62, 65, 419-20, 477,
      488
rhetoric, rhetorical: 3, 29, 38-9, 44, 64, 67, 70, 74, 89, 91,
      155, 201, 203-5, 208, 253, 351, 385-6, 392-4,
      396, 423, 434, 476, 486-7, 491, 524-5
Ribera, Jusepe de (1591-1652): 491
Ricoeur, Louis: 103-4, 491
Ricciarelli, Daniele: see Daniele da Volterra
Ridolfi, Carlo: 165-6
Riegl, Alois: 563-6
Ringbom, Sixten: 275
Robetta. Cristofano (1462-*c*.1535)
   Resurrection: 499-500, 510
Robusti, Jacopo: see Tintoretto
Romanino (Romani, Girolamo; *c*.1484-after 1562)
   Flagellation: 55
Rosso Fiorentino (Giovan Battista di Jacopo; 1494-1540)
   Judith and Her Servant: 111
Röttgen, Herwarth: 220-1
Ruscelli, Vincenzo: 194

Sadeler, Aegidius II (*c*.1570-1629)
   Deposition of Christ: 351
   Supper at Emmaus: 292-3
Sadeler, Johan I (1550-1600)
   Beheading of Saint John the Baptist: 431
   Blessing Christ: 172
   Martyrdom of Saint Ursula: 434, 471
   Parable of Dives and Lazarus: 532-3

   Resurrection: 511
   Supper at Emmaus: 292
Saenredam, Jan (1565-1607)
   Adam and Eve Mourning the Slain Abel: 83-4
   Allegory of Youth: 144
Sandrart, Joachim von (1606-1688): 19, 216-9, 221, 229,
      457-8, 541-5, 554-5, 558
   Death of Seneca: 541
Sannesio, Francesco: 247
Sannesio, Giacomo: 246-7
Sansovino, Andrea (*c*.1460-1529): 388-9
Saraceni, Carlo (*c*.1579-1620): 483
Scannelli, Francesco: 20-2, 27, 29, 93, 216
Scaramuccia, Luigi: 502
Schäufelein, Hans (*c*.1482-1539/1540)
   Crucifixion: 323
   Lamentation: 349-50
   Pyramus and Thisbe: 323
Schongauer, Martin (*c*.1430-1491): 113
   Resurrection: 502
   Taking of Christ: 318-9
Sciaminossi, Raffaello (1572-1622)
   Resurrection: 508
Scribner, Charles: 271
Scultori, Diana (*c*.1535-1587)
   Ecce Homo: 387-9
   Menelaus Supporting Patroklos: 439
Sebastiano del Piombo (Luciani, Sebastiano; *c*.1485-
      1547)
   Flagellation: 46-8, 53, 55
   Portrait of Andrea Doria: 380
Serodine, Giovanni (*c*.1600-1630): 481
Sextus Empiricus: 250
Sickel, Lothar: 13
Silos, Giovanni Michele: 458-60, 465
Silver, Larry: 150, 220
skin: see *pelle*
Sohm, Philip: 384, 416, 483
Solari, Cristoforo: see Gobbo da Milano
Soldano, Aniello: 393
space, pictorial space: 5-6, 32, 35, 44, 70-1, 73, 81, 90-1, 162,
      221, 225, 239, 262, 278-81, 288, 294, 421, 428,
      434-5, 444-5, 552, 567-8
Spada, Leonello (1576-1622): 484-6, 520
Spadarino (Galli, Giovanni Antonio; 1585-1651/1653)
   Crucifixion: 500
Spezzaferro, Luigi: 247
Sprezzatura: 45, 121, 418
Stella, Jacques (1596-1657): 88
still life: 15, 21, 26-7
Stimmer, Tobias (1539-1584): 329
Stoer, Niklas (died 1562/1563)
   Eusterwon, King of the Germans: 254
Stomer, Matthias (*c*.1600-after 1650): 211, 239
   Calling of Saint Matthew: 234-5
Stone, David M.: 483

Stoss, Veit (1445/1450-1533)
    Lamentation: 441-2
Stradanus, Johannes (Van der Straet, Jan; 1523-1605)
    Last Supper: 530-1
    Vision of Saint Peter: 531
Strozzi, Bernardo (1581-1644): 211, 235, 239
    Calling of Saint Matthew: 231-2
    Calling of Saints Peter and Andrew: 232
    Martyrdom of Saint Ursula: 475
subject matter: 39, 41, 48, 68, 80-1, 93-4, 100, 103, 108-9,
        116, 127, 129-30, 132, 255, 260, 268, 289, 306,
        313, 324, 337, 341, 410, 455, 490-1, 562
subjectivity: 103, 265, 288, 563-6, 568, 570-1
Susinno, Francesco: 427, 434, 437-8
Symeon of Thessalonika: 36, 38, 48
symmetry: see *eurythmy*
Syropoulos, Sylvester: 36

Tasso, Torquato: 17, 117-8, 131-2, 191, 197
Tebaldeo, Antonio: 186-9
Tempesta, Antonio (1555-1630)
    Resurrection: 500
temporality, narrative time: 6-10, 55, 69-91, 93, 101, 103-5,
        115-6, 209, 240, 291, 344, 423-5, 444, 462, 490,
        513-4, 522-3, 533, 567
Ter Brugghen, Hendrick (1588-1629): 211, 239, 491, 539
    Calling of Saint Matthew (Le Havre): 235-7
    Calling of Saint Matthew (Utrecht): 237-8
Tiarini, Alessandro (1577-1668): 483, 520
Tiffany, Tanya J.: 526-7
Timanthes: 84, 253
Tintoretto (Robusti, Jacopo; 1519-1594): 106-8, 418-9,
        421-2
    Annunciation (Scuola Grande di San Rocco): 338-40
    Crucifixion (Scuola Grande di San Rocco): 104
    Deposition of Christ: 351
    Massacre of the Innocents: 105
Titian (Vecelli, Tiziano; *c*.1488-1576): 15, 25-6, 64, 71,
        104-8, 139, 216, 219, 249, 265, 300, 302-3, 348,
        405, 417-9, 422, 425, 520, 539, 545
    Allegory of Venice as Justice: 167-8, 171, 173, 175
    Annunciation (Naples): 75-81, 83
    Bravo: 165-6, 317
    Christ Carrying the Cross: 275
    Crossing of the Red Sea: 249
    Deposition (Louvre): 361
    Study of Horses: 250
    Supper at Emmaus: 269-70, 273, 275, 281-3, 527-8
    Woman at Her Toilet: 124, 177-91, 195-7
Tito, Santi di (1536-1602)
    Resurrection (Santa Croce): 512
    Resurrection (drawing): 512
Tomasi Velli, Silvia: 78
Tomassoni, Ranuccio: 13, 289, 381
Tournier, Nicolas (1590-*c*.1660)
    Drinking Party with Lute Player: 229-30

Tribolo, Niccolò (1500-1550): 449
truth, pictorial truth: 19-21, 27, 29, 37, 46-9, 58, 65, 96, 102,
        118, 199-205, 208-9, 216, 239, 306-9, 336-7,
        339-41, 381, 401, 464, 466, 478, 566

Urban VIII (Barberini, Maffeo): 545

Valentin de Boulogne (1591/1594-1632): 19, 482
    Allegory of the Five Senses: 541-2
    Cardsharps: 163, 539
    Concert with Bas-Relief: 554-6
    Concert with Eight Figures: 552-4, 556
    Concert with Three Musicians: 539
    Denial of Saint Peter: 554
    Fortune Teller (Louvre): 551-2
    Fortune Teller (Toledo): 548-50
    Last Supper: 325
    Martyrdom of Saints Processus and Martinianus: 543-4
    Merry Company with Fortune Teller: 491, 539-47
    Soldiers Playing Dice and Morra: 546-7
Valesio, Giovanni (1583-1650)
    Spinning Clotho: 455, 457
Valguarnera, Fabrizio: 540-3, 545
Van der Aelst, Pieter
    Conversion of Saul: 258
Van Dyck, Anton (1599-1641)
    Bravo (sketch): 165-6
Van Eyck, Jan (*c*.1390-1441): 184
Vanni, Francesco (1563-1610)
    Fall of Simon Magus: 78-9
    Narcissus: 452-3
Vannugli, Antonio: 379
variety: 40-1, 44-5, 67, 69, 81, 89, 91, 95, 100, 121, 226,
        404, 448
Vasari, Giorgio (1511-1574): 25-6, 44-7, 167, 175, 295,
        299-300, 302-3, 358-65, 368, 371-2, 397-400,
        405-6, 415-9, 449, 488
Vecelli, Tiziano: see Titian
Velázquez, Diego (1599-1660): 5, 571
    *Kitchen Scene with Christ in the House of Martha and
        Mary*: 526
    Meninas: 531
    Mulata (Chicago): 491, 526, 536-7
    Mulata (Dublin): 491, 526-36
    Supper at Emmaus: 491, 520-6
verisimilitude: 203-5, 208, 225, 238-9, 243, 245-6, 251, 260,
        269-70, 282, 285, 295, 336, 340, 344, 401, 449,
        551, 566
Vermeer, Jan (1632-1675): 5, 571
Veronese (Caliari, Paolo; 1528-1588): 104, 106, 108, 265,
        282-3, 303
    Mystic Marriage of Saint Catherine (Venice): 104
    Supper at Emmaus (Chatsworth): 275, 279
    Supper at Emmaus (Louvre) 273-4
    Temptation of Saint Anthony: 421-2
Verrocchio, Andrea del (1435-1488)

Incredulity of Saint Thomas: 461-3
Vico, Enea (1523-1567): 367
Volpato, Giovan Battista (1633-1706): 104-9, 115, 294
Vouet, Simon (1590-1649): 491, 539
Vrancx, Sebastian (1573-1647)
    Supper at Emmaus: 529-30

Warburg, Aby: 12
Wedding of Thetis and Peleus (ancient bas-relief): 554
Wethey, Harold: 554
Wittkower, Rudolph: 141, 152, 155
Woensam of Worms, Anton (before 1500-1541)
    Two Soldiers Playing Cards: 163-4

Wölfflin, Heinrich: 489

Zamboni, Orazio: 29, 31, 88
Zampieri, Domenico: see Domenichino
Zanetti, Anton Maria (1680-1757): 167
Zeuxis: 26, 44
Zuccari, Federico (*c*.1541-1609): 65, 104, 214, 216, 219,
    257, 304-6, 309, 328-36, 340-1, 348, 373, 403,
    563
Zuccari, Taddeo (1529-1566)
    Conversion of Saint Paul: 257-8, 260